Primitive Data Types

Type	Size	Values
Integer		
byte	1 byte	-128 to 127
short	2 bytes	-32,768 to 32,767
int	4 bytes	-2,147,483,648 to 2,147,483,647
long	8 bytes	-9,223,372,036,854,775,808 to 9,223,372,036,854,775,807
Real		
float	4 bytes	-3.402824×10^{38} to 3.402824×10^{38}
double	8 bytes	$-1.79769313486232 \times 10^{308}$ to $1.79769313486232 \times 10^{308}$
Character (Unicode)		
char	2 bytes	All Unicode values between 0 and 65,535
Boolean		
boolean	1 bit	true, false

Data Structures and Abstractions with Java™

Second Edition

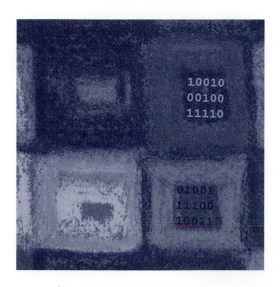

Frank M. Carrano
University of Rhode Island

PEARSON

Prentice Hall

Upper Saddle River, NJ 07458

Library of Congress Cataloging-in-Publication Data on File

Vice President and Editorial Director, ECS: *Marcia J. Horton*
Executive Editor: *Tracy Dunkelberger*
Associate Editor: *Carole Snyder*
Editorial Assistant: *Christianna Lee*
Executive Managing Editor: *Vince O'Brien*
Managing Editor: *Camille Trentacoste*
Production Editor: *Rose Kernan*
Director of Creative Services: *Paul Belfanti*
Creative Director: *Juan Lopez*
Art Director and Cover Manager: *Maureen Eide*
Cover Design and Interior Illustrations: *Liann Dunn*
Copy Editor: *Rebecca Pepper*
Managing Editor, AV Management and Production: *Patricia Burns*
Art Editor: *Xiaohong Zhu*
Director, Image Resource Center: *Melinda Reo*
Manager, Rights and Permissions: *Zina Arabia*
Manager, Visual Research: *Beth Brenzel*
Manager, Cover Visual Research and Permissions: *Karen Sanatar*
Manufacturing Manager, ESM: *Alexis Heydt-Long*
Manufacturing Buyer: *Lisa McDowell*
Executive Marketing Manager: *Robin O'Brien*
Marketing Assistant: *Mack Patterson*

© 2007 Pearson Education, Inc.
Pearson Prentice Hall
Pearson Education, Inc.
Upper Saddle River, NJ 07458

Printed in the United States of America

10 9 8 7 6 5 4 3 2 1

ISBN 0-13-237045-X

Pearson Education Ltd., *London*
Pearson Education Australia Pty. Ltd., *Sydney*
Pearson Education Singapore, Pte. Ltd.
Pearson Education North Asia Ltd., *Hong Kong*
Pearson Education Canada, Inc., *Toronto*
Pearson Educación de Mexico, S.A. de C.V.
Pearson Education—Japan, *Tokyo*
Pearson Education Malaysia, Pte. Ltd.
Pearson Education, Inc., *Upper Saddle River, New Jersey*

To Walt, Alan, and Toni

Preface

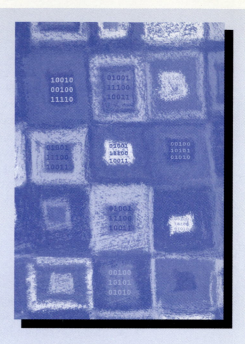

Welcome to the second edition of *Data Structures and Abstractions with Java*, a book for an introductory course in data structures, typically known as CS-2.

Approach

This book was created specifically with objects and Java in mind. Its approach makes learning easier by focusing the reader's attention on one issue at a time, by providing flexibility in the order in which you can cover topics, and by clearly distinguishing between the specification and implementation of abstract data types, or ADTs. To accomplish these goals, the material is divided into short, numbered segments that are organized into 31 relatively short chapters. Each segment covers a single idea. Individual chapters deal with either the specification and use of an ADT or its implementations. You can choose to cover the specification of an ADT followed by its various implementations, or you can treat the specification and use of several ADTs before you consider any implementation issues. The book's organization makes it easy for you to choose the topic order that you prefer.

New to This Edition

- New features of Java 5, including generic data types, the Scanner class, enumerations, for-each loops, the interface Iterable, and boxing and unboxing, are covered and used throughout.

- Assertions within code are enforced using the assert statement.

- The linked implementation of the ADT list is covered in two chapters instead of one. The result provides an example of how to approach the implementation of a class by first focusing on core methods.

- The introduction to iterators occupies one chapter instead of two. The new interface `Iterable` is covered, and the nonstandard iterator of the first edition is no longer included.
- Hashing is covered in two chapters instead of one long chapter.
- The implementations of various ADTs, notably the linked implementation of the list and the binary search tree, have been improved.
- Important Java code is identified as a listing.
- Exercises, projects, and self-test questions have been supplemented and improved.
- Appendix B on exceptions has been revised to include the `finally` clause.
- Appendix C on file I/O has been revised to reflect aspects of Java 5.

Features

- 31 relatively short chapters can be covered in several sequences.
- Individual but consecutive chapters separate the specification and implementation of ADTs.
- Short, bite-sized segments focus attention on one issue at a time.
- Many examples illustrate new concepts.
- Highlighted notes emphasize key material and provide supplementary comments.
- Programming tips give additional programming advice.
- Numerous figures make the presentation visual and accessible.
- Questions throughout the book—and their answers—elaborate on the material presented.
- Initial chapters cover Java classes, inheritance, polymorphism, and class design.
- Java code includes `javadoc` comments.
- Appendices review Java basics, exceptions, files, and documentation.
- The website at `prenhall.com/carrano` provides the Java code that appears in the book, as well as any updates or corrections.
- Supplements for instructors include PowerPoint slides, laboratory materials, complete source code, and answers to selected exercises and programming projects.

A Note to Students

After looking over this preface, you should read the Introduction. There you will quickly see what this book is about and what you need to know about Java before you begin. Appendices A through D review Java and serve as a primer on some new features of Java 5, exceptions, files, and `javadoc` comments. Note that inside the front and back covers you will find Java's reserved words, its primitive data types, the precedence of its operators, and a list of Unicode characters.

The topics that we cover in this book are fundamental to your future study of computer science. Even if you do not study all of these topics now, you are likely to encounter them later. We hope that you will enjoy reading the book now, and that it will serve as a useful reference for your future courses.

Throughout each chapter, you will find questions that should help you to understand the material. The answers to these questions are in Appendix E at the back of the book. Unfortunately, we cannot give you answers to the exercises and programming projects that appear at the end of each chapter, even if you are not enrolled in a class. Only instructors who adopt the book can receive selected answers from the publisher. For help with these exercises and projects, you will have to contact your instructor.

All of the Java code that appears in this book is available for download from the website at `prenhall.com/carrano`.

An Overview

Readers of this book should have completed a programming course, preferably in Java. Appendix A covers the essentials of Java that we assume readers will know. You can use this appendix as a review or as the basis for making the transition to Java from another programming language. You can also consult this appendix to learn about some of the new features of Java 5 that we use in this book.

The book itself begins with the Introduction, which sets the stage for the data organizations that we will study. Chapter 1 thoroughly reviews classes and methods in Java. We follow this review with a discussion of composition, inheritance, and polymorphism in Chapter 2. This chapter also introduces generic data types, a new feature of Java that is important to our discussion. Chapter 3 presents object-oriented design, discusses Java interfaces, and provides an introduction to such design tools as the CRC card and the Unified Modeling Language.

Chapters 4 through 7 introduce the list as an abstract data type. By dividing the material across several chapters, we clearly separate the specification, use, and implementation of the list. For example, Chapter 4 specifies the list and provides several examples of its use. Chapter 5 covers implementations that use arrays and vectors, while Chapters 6 and 7 discuss implementations that use chains of linked nodes.

In a similar fashion, we separate specification from implementation throughout the book when we discuss various other ADTs. You can choose to cover the chapters that specify and use the ADTs and then later cover the chapters that implement them. Or you can cover the chapters as they appear, implementing each ADT right after studying its specification and use. A dependency chart appears later in this preface to help you plan your path through the book.

Chapters 6 and 7 do more than simply implement the list. They show how to approach the implementation of a class. Chapter 6 begins the linked implementation of the ADT list by focusing on core methods. When defining a class, it is often useful to implement and test these core methods first and to leave definitions of the other methods for later. The next chapter completes the linked implementation of the list and explores some variations of that approach.

Chapter 8 discusses iterators in the context of a list. It considers and implements Java's iterator interfaces `Iterator` and `ListIterator`. This chapter also introduces the interface `Iterable`.

Chapters 9 and 10 introduce the complexity of algorithms and recursion, two topics that we integrate into future chapters. For example, Chapters 11 and 12 discuss various sorting techniques and their relative complexities. We consider both iterative and recursive versions of these algorithms.

The next two chapters, 13 and 14, return to the notion of a list. Chapter 13 discusses the sorted list, looking at two possible implementations and their efficiencies. Chapter 14 shows how to use the list as a base class for the sorted list and discusses the general design of a base class.

Chapter 15 introduces mutable objects, immutable objects, and cloning. If a client can maintain a reference to the data within an ADT, it can change that data without using the class's public methods, if the data is mutable. We consider steps that you can take to prevent the client from doing so.

Chapter 16 examines strategies for searching an array or chain in the context of a list or sorted list. This discussion is a good basis for Chapter 17, which covers the specification and use of the ADT dictionary. Chapter 18 presents implementations of the dictionary that are linked or that use arrays. Chapter 19 introduces hashing, and Chapter 20 uses it as a dictionary implementation.

Chapter 21 discusses stacks, giving examples of their use and examining the relationship between stacks and recursion. Chapter 22 implements the stack using an array, a vector, and a chain.

Chapter 23 presents queues, deques, and priority queues, and Chapter 24 considers their implementations. It is in this chapter that we discuss circularly linked and doubly linked chains.

Chapter 25 discusses trees and their possible uses. Included among the several examples of trees is an introduction to the binary search tree and the heap. Chapter 26 considers implementations of the binary tree and the general tree, and Chapter 27 focuses on the implementation of the binary search tree. Chapter 28 shows how to use an array to implement the heap. Chapter 29 introduces balanced search trees. Included in this chapter are the AVL, 2-3, 2-4, and red-black trees, as well as B-trees.

Chapters 30 and 31 discuss graphs, looking at several applications and two implementations.

Appendices A through D provide supplemental coverage of Java. As we mentioned earlier, Appendix A reviews Java up to but not including classes. This appendix also presents some new features of Java 5, including the Scanner class, enumerations, boxing and unboxing, and the for-each loop. Appendix B covers exception handling, and Appendix C discusses files. Appendix D considers programming style and comments. It introduces javadoc comments and defines the tags that we use in this book.

Appendix E contains the answers to the questions that appear throughout each chapter.

Instructor Resources

We have prepared several supplements for instructors. Included are PowerPoint slides, laboratory materials, answers to selected exercises and programming projects, and a complete version of the Java code that appears in this book. While the book often leaves aspects of an implementation for readers to complete, the instructor's version of the code is complete. Note that the code as it appears in the book is available on the website at prenhall.com/carrano. This website also contains additional resources and any updates or corrections to the book.

To obtain a copy of the supplements, instructors should contact their Prentice Hall sales representative. For the name and e-mail address of your sales representative, please visit the website prenhall.com/replocator or call Prentice Hall Faculty Services at 1-800-526-0485. Additional information on this book and other Prentice Hall products can be found on Prentice Hall's home page at prenhall.com.

Contact Us

Your comments, suggestions, and corrections are always welcome. Please e-mail them to

carrano@acm.org

Acknowledgments

Thank you to the following reviewers for carefully reading the manuscript and making candid comments and suggestions that greatly improved the work:

Harold Anderson—*Marist College*
Razvan Andonie—*Central Washington University*
Tom Blough—*Rensselaer Polytechnic Institute*
Chris Brooks—*University of San Francisco*
Adrienne Decker—*University at Buffalo, SUNY*

Henry Etlinger—*Rochester Institute of Technology*
Derek Harter—*Texas A&M University*
Timothy Henry—*University of Rhode Island*
Robert Holloway—*University of Wisconsin, Madison*
Charles Hoot—*Oklahoma City University*
Teresa Leyk—*Texas A&M University*
Robert McGlinn—*Southern Illinois University, Carbondale*
Edward Medvid—*Marymount University*
Charles Metzler—*City College of San Francisco*
Daniel Zeng—*University of Arizona*

Thank you once again to the reviewers of the first edition:

David Boyd—*Valdosta State University*
Dennis Brylow—*Purdue University*
Michael Croswell—*Industry trainer/consultant*
Matthew Dickerson—*Middlebury College*
Robert Holloway—*University of Wisconsin, Madison*
John Motil—*California State University, Northridge*
Bina Ramamurthy—*University at Buffalo, SUNY*
David Surma—*Valparaiso University*

Special thanks go to my copy editor, Rebecca Pepper, who not only corrected my grammar but also ensured that my explanations are clear and correct. Charles Hoot was an invaluable resource providing additional exercises and projects and preparing some of the supplements for instructors. And thanks to Lianne Dunn, who designed the cover and drew all of the figures in the first edition of the book, and to Steve Armstrong, who prepared the PowerPoint slides.

Thank you to all of the people at Prentice Hall who contributed to the development and production of this book and its supplements. In particular, I thank my editor, Tracy Dunkelberger, as well as Carole Snyder, Christianna Lee, Camille Trentacoste, Vince O'Brien, Xiaohong Zhu, Mike Giacobbe, and John Lovell. Their efforts are greatly appreciated. And special thanks to my production editor, Rose Kernan, who made all of our work tangible.

For their contributions to both editions of this book, I especially thank my collaborator, Walt Savitch, and my former editors, Alan Apt and Toni Holm. Many others also helped with the first edition. They are Steve Armstrong, James Blanding, Charles Hoot, Brian Jepson, Patrick Lindner, Patty Roy, Ben Schomp, Heather Scott, Chirag Thakkar, Nate Walker, and Xiaohong Zhu.

Other wonderful people have contributed in various ways. They are Doug McCreadie, Ted Emmott, Lorraine Berube, Marge White, Tom Manning, Jeff Barbeau, Joan Peckham, James Kowalski, Ed Lamagna, Victor Fay-Wolfe, Gérard Baudet, Tim Henry, Lisa DiPippo, Jean-Yves Hervé, James Heltshe, and Bala Ravikumar.

Thank you, everyone, for your expertise and good cheer.

FRANK M. CARRANO

Chapter and Appendix Dependencies

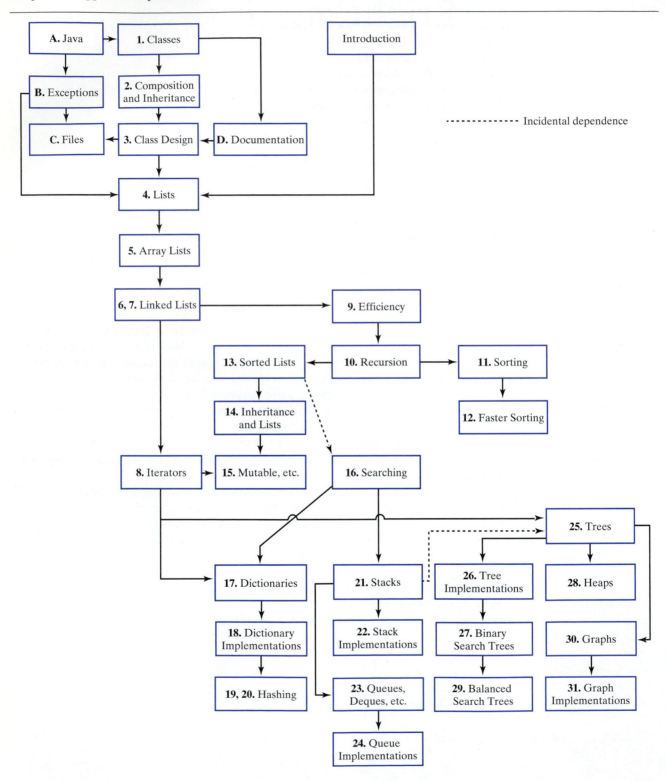

Brief Contents

Contents

Chapter 14   Inheritance and Lists 377

Chapter 15   Mutable, Immutable, and Cloneable Objects 391

Chapter 16   Searching 417

Chapter 17   Dictionaries 439

Introduction

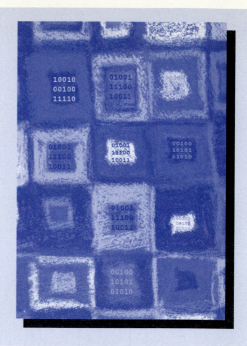

Look around and you will see ways that people organize things. When you stopped at the store this morning, you went to the back of a line to wait for the cashier. The line organized people chronologically. The first person in the line was the first to be served and to leave the line. Eventually, you reached the front of the line and left the store with a bag containing your purchases. The items in the bag were in no particular order, and some of them were the same.

At your desk, you see your to-do list. Each entry in the list has a position that might or might not be important to you. You may have written them either as you thought of them, in their order of importance, or in alphabetical order. You decide the order; the list simply provides places for your entries.

Do you see a stack of books or a pile of papers on your desk? It's easy to look at or remove the top item of the stack or to add a new item to the top of the stack. The items in a stack also are organized chronologically, with the item added most recently on top and the item added first on the bottom.

Your dictionary is an alphabetical list of words and their definitions. You search for a word and get its definition. If your dictionary is printed, the alphabetical organization helps you to locate a word quickly. If your dictionary is computerized, its alphabetical organization is hidden, but it still speeds the search.

Speaking of your computer, you have organized your files into folders, or directories. Each folder contains several other folders or files. This type of organization is hierarchical. If you drew a picture of it, you would get something like a family tree or a chart of a company's internal departments. These data organizations are similar and are called trees.

Finally, notice the road map that you are using to plan your weekend trip. The diagram of roads and towns shows you how to get from one place to another. Often, several ways are possible. One way might be shorter, another faster. The road map has an organization known as a graph.

1

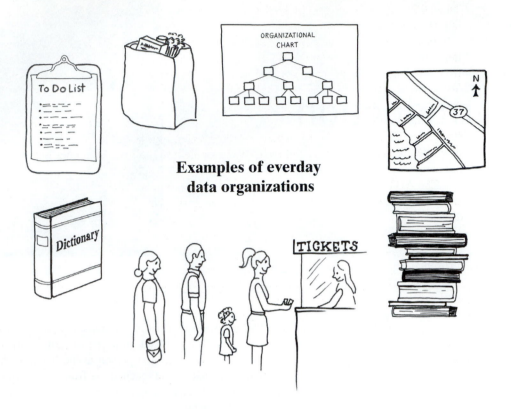

**Examples of everday
data organizations**

Computer programs also need to organize their data. They do so in ways that parallel the examples we just cited. That is, programs can use a list, a stack, a dictionary, and so on. These ways of organizing data are represented by abstract data types. An **abstract data type**, or **ADT**, is a specification that describes a data set and the operations on that data. Each ADT specifies what data is stored and what the operations on the data do. Since an ADT does not indicate how to store the data or how to implement the operations, we can talk about ADTs independently of any programming language. In contrast, a **data structure** is an implementation of an ADT within a programming language.

A **collection** is a general term for an ADT that contains a group of objects. Some collections allow duplicate items, some do not. Some collections arrange their contents in a certain order, while others do not. A **container** is a class that implements a collection. Some people use the terms "container" and "collection" interchangeably.

We might create an ADT **bag** consisting of an unordered collection that allows duplicates. It is like a grocery bag, a lunch bag, or a bag of potato chips. Suppose you remove one chip from a bag of chips. You don't know when the chip was placed into the bag. You don't know whether the bag contains another chip shaped exactly like the one you just removed. But you don't really care. If you did, you wouldn't store your chips in a bag!

A bag does not order its contents, but sometimes you do want to order things. ADTs can order their items in a variety of ways. The ADT **list**, for example, simply numbers its items. A list, then, has a first item, a second item, and so on. Although you can add an item to the end of a list, you can also insert an item at the beginning of the list or between existing items. Doing so renumbers the items after the new item. Additionally, you can remove an item at a particular position within a list.

Thus, the position of an item in the list does not necessarily indicate when it was added. Notice that the list does not decide where an item is placed; you make this decision.

In contrast, the ADTs **stack** and **queue** order their items chronologically. When you remove an item from a stack, you remove the one that was added most recently. When you remove an item from a queue, you remove the one that was added the earliest. Thus, a stack is like a pile of books. You can remove the top book or add another book to the top of the pile. A queue is like a line of people. People leave a line from its front and join it at its end.

Some ADTs maintain their entries in sorted order, if the items can be compared. For instance, strings can be organized in alphabetical order. When you add an item to the ADT **sorted list**, for example, the ADT determines where to place the item in the list. You do not indicate a position for the item, as you would with the ADT list.

The ADT **dictionary** contains pairs of items, much as a language dictionary contains a word and its definition. In this example, the word serves as a **key** that is used to locate the entries. Some dictionaries sort their entries and some do not.

The ADT **tree** organizes its entries according to some hierarchy. For example, in a family tree, people are associated with their children and their parents. The ADT **binary search tree** has a combined hierarchical and sorted organization that makes locating a particular entry easier.

The ADT **graph** is a generalization of the ADT tree that focuses on the relationship among its entries instead of any hierarchical organization. For example, a road map is a graph that shows the existing roads and distances between towns.

This book shows you how to use and implement these data organizations. Before we begin, you need to know Java. Appendix A reviews the basic statements in Java. Chapter 1 discusses the basic construction of classes and methods. You can choose to glance at this material, read it carefully, or come back to it as necessary. Chapters 2 and 3 also focus on Java, but some or all of the material might be new to you. Chapter 2 covers techniques, including composition and inheritance, for creating new classes from existing classes. Chapter 3 discusses how to design classes, specify methods, and write Java interfaces. Using interfaces and writing comments to specify methods are essential to our presentation of ADTs.

CHAPTER

1

Java Classes

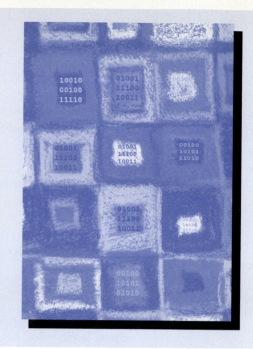

CONTENTS

PREREQUISITES

OBJECTIVES

After studying this chapter, you should be able to

- Create an object of a class
- Call a method given its header
- Describe the effect of a given invocation of a method
- Write a method definition

- Write a class definition
- Describe, define, and use constructors
- Describe the use of the access modifiers `public` and `private`
- Describe the use of static methods and data fields
- Add methods to an enumeration
- Create and use packages

This chapter reviews the use and creation of Java classes, methods, and packages. Even if you are familiar with this material, you should at least skim it to learn our terminology.

Objects and Classes

1.1   An **object** is a program construct that contains data and can perform certain actions. Like the objects in the world around us, the objects in a Java program interact with one another to accomplish a particular task. Thus, **object-oriented programming**, or **OOP**, views a program as a sort of world consisting of objects that interact with one another by means of actions. For example, in a program that simulates automobiles, each automobile is an object.

The actions that an automobile object can take might be moving forward, moving backward, accelerating, and so on. These actions are defined by **methods**. When you ask an object to perform an action, you **invoke**, or **call**, a method.

Objects of the same kind are said to have the same **type** and are in the same **class**. A class specifies the kind of data the objects of that class have. A class also specifies what actions the objects can take and how they accomplish those actions. When you define a class in Java, the class is like a plan or a blueprint for constructing specific objects. For example, Figure 1-1 describes a class called `Automobile` and shows three `Automobile` objects. The class is a general description of what an automobile is and what it can do.

Each **instance**, or object, of the class `Automobile` is a particular automobile. You can name each object that you create, or **instantiate**. In Figure 1-1, the names are `bobsCar`, `suesCar`, and `jakesTruck`. In a Java program, `bobsCar`, `suesCar`, and `jakesTruck` would be variables of type `Automobile`. So among other things, a class is a data type.

The definition of the `Automobile` class says that an `Automobile` object has data such as its model, its year, and how much fuel is in its tank. The class definition contains no actual data—no string and no numbers. The individual objects have the data, and the class simply specifies what kind of data they have.

The `Automobile` class also defines methods such as `goForward` and `goBackward`. In a program that uses the class `Automobile`, the only actions an `Automobile` object can take are defined by those methods. All objects of a given class have exactly the same methods. The implementations of the methods indicate how the actions are performed and are included in the class definition. The objects themselves actually perform the method's actions, however.

The objects in a single class can have different characteristics. Even though these objects have the same types of data and the same methods, the individual objects can differ in the values of their data.

Note: An **object** is a program construct that contains data and performs actions. The objects in a Java program interact, and this interaction forms the solution to a given problem. The actions performed by objects are defined by **methods**.

Note: A **class** is a type or kind of object. All objects in the same class have the same kinds of data and the same methods. A class definition is a general description of what that object is and what it can do.

Figure 1-1   An outline of a class and three of its instances

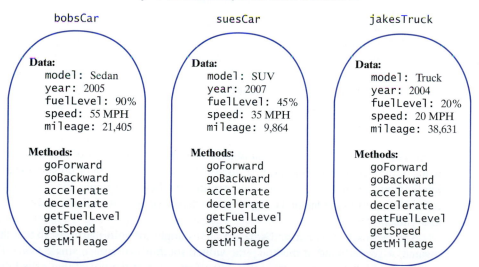

The Class Automobile

Class Name: Automobile

Data:
    model_____
    year_____
    fuelLevel_____
    speed_____
    mileage_____

Methods (actions):
    goForward
    goBackward
    accelerate
    decelerate
    getFuelLevel
    getSpeed
    getMileage

Objects (Instantiations) of the Class Automobile

bobsCar

Data:
    model: Sedan
    year: 2005
    fuelLevel: 90%
    speed: 55 MPH
    mileage: 21,405

Methods:
    goForward
    goBackward
    accelerate
    decelerate
    getFuelLevel
    getSpeed
    getMileage

suesCar

Data:
    model: SUV
    year: 2007
    fuelLevel: 45%
    speed: 35 MPH
    mileage: 9,864

Methods:
    goForward
    goBackward
    accelerate
    decelerate
    getFuelLevel
    getSpeed
    getMileage

jakesTruck

Data:
    model: Truck
    year: 2004
    fuelLevel: 20%
    speed: 20 MPH
    mileage: 38,631

Methods:
    goForward
    goBackward
    accelerate
    decelerate
    getFuelLevel
    getSpeed
    getMileage

 Note: You can view a class in several different ways when programming. When you instantiate an object of a class, you view the class as a data type. When you implement a class, you can view it as a plan or a blueprint for constructing objects—that is, as a definition of the objects' data and actions. At other times, you can think of a class as a collection of objects that have the same type.

Using the Methods in a Java Class

1.2   Let's assume that someone has written a Java class called `Name` to represent a person's name. We will describe how to use this class and, in doing so, we will show you how to use a class's methods. A program component that uses a class is called a **client** of the class. We will reserve the term "user" to mean a person who uses a program.

To declare a variable of data type `Name`, you would write, for example,

```
Name joe;
```

At this point, the variable `joe` contains nothing in particular; it is uninitialized. To create a specific object of data type `Name`—that is, to create an instance of `Name`—called `joe`, you write

```
joe = new Name();
```

The `new` operator creates an instance of `Name` by invoking a special method within the class, known as a **constructor**. The memory address of the new object is assigned to `joe`, as Figure 1-2 illustrates. We will show you how to define constructors a bit later, in Segment 1.17. Note that you can combine the previous two Java statements into one:

```
Name joe = new Name();
```

Figure 1-2   A variable that references an object

joe   Object of type `Name`

1.3   Suppose that a person's name has only two parts: a first name and a last name. The data associated with the object `joe` then consists of two strings that represent the first and last names. Since you want to be able to **set**—that is, initialize or change—a person's name, the `Name` class should have methods that give you this capability. To set `joe`'s first and last names, you can use two methods from the class `Name`—`setFirst` and `setLast`—as follows:

```
joe.setFirst("Joseph");
joe.setLast("Brown");
```

A method is usually invoked by an object, such as `joe`, of the class that defines it. You write the name of the **calling object** (`joe`) first, followed by a dot, the name of the method to be invoked, and finally a set of parentheses that contain **arguments**. In this example, the arguments are strings that represent inputs to the methods. The methods set the object's data fields to the specific values given as arguments.

The methods `setFirst` and `setLast` are examples of **void methods**, in that they do not return a value. A second kind of method—the **valued method**—returns a single value. For example, the method `getFirst` returns a string that is the first name of the object that called the method. Similarly, the method `getLast` returns the last name.

You can invoke a valued method anywhere that you can use a value of the type returned by the method. For example, `getFirst` returns a value of type `String`, and so you can use a method invocation such as `joe.getFirst()` anywhere that it is legal to use a value of type `String`. Such places could be in an assignment statement, like

```
String hisName = joe.getFirst();
```

or within a `println` statement, like

```
System.out.println("Joe's first name is " + joe.getFirst());
```

Notice that the methods `getFirst` and `getLast` have no arguments in their parentheses. Any method—valued or void—can require zero or more arguments.

Note: **Valued methods** return a single value; **void methods** do not return a value. For example, the valued method `getFirst` returns the string that represents the first name. The void method `setFirst` sets the first name to a given string but does not return a value. For now, you will distinguish valued methods and void methods by the description of what they do. Later, in Segments 1.7 through 1.9, you will see that their Java definitions distinguish one kind of method from another.

Question 1   Write Java statements that create an object of type `Name` to represent your name.

Question 2   Write a Java statement that uses the object you created in Question 1 to display your name in the form *last name, comma, first name*.

Question 3   Which methods of the class `Automobile`, as given in Figure 1-1, are most likely valued methods, and which are most likely void methods?

References and Aliases

1.4   Java has eight primitive data types: `byte`, `short`, `int`, `long`, `float`, `double`, `char`, and `boolean`. A variable of a primitive type actually contains the primitive value. All other data types are **reference**, or **class, types**. The `String` variable `greeting` in

```
String greeting = "Hello";
```

is a variable of a reference type or, more simply, a **reference variable**. A reference variable contains the address in memory of an actual object. This address is called a **reference**. It is not important here to know that `greeting` contains a reference to the string `"Hello"` instead of the actual string. In such cases, it is easier to talk about the string `greeting`, when in fact this is not an accurate description of that variable. This book makes the distinction between an object and a reference to an object when it is important to do so.

Now suppose that you write

```
Name jamie = new Name();
jamie.setFirst("Jamie");
jamie.setLast("Jones");
Name friend = jamie;
```

The two variables `jamie` and `friend` reference the same instance of `Name`, as Figure 1-3 shows. We say that `jamie` and `friend` are **aliases**, because they are two different names for the same object. You can use `jamie` and `friend` interchangeably when referencing the object.

For example, if you use the variable `jamie` to change Jamie Jones's last name, you can use the variable `friend` to access it. Thus, the statements

```
jamie.setLast("Smith");
System.out.println(friend.getLast());
```

Figure 1-3   Aliases of an object

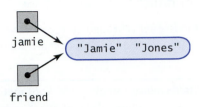

display *Smith*. Also note that the boolean expression `jamie == friend` is true, since both variables contain the same address.

Defining a Java Class

1.5   We now show you how to write the Java class `Name` that represents a person's name. You store a class definition in a file whose name is the name of the class followed by `.java`. Thus, the class `Name` should be in the file `Name.java`. Typically, you store only one class per file.

The data in a `Name` object consists of the person's first and last names as strings. The methods in the class will enable you to set and look at these strings. The class has the following form:

```
public class Name
{
   private String first; // first name
   private String last;  // last name

   < Definitions of methods are here >
   . . .
} // end Name
```

The word `public` simply means that there are no restrictions on where the class is used. That is, the class `Name` is available for use in any other Java class. The two strings `first` and `last` are called the class's **data fields** or **instance variables** or **data members**. Each object of this class will have these two data fields inside of it. The word `private` that precedes the declaration of each data field means that only the methods within the class can refer to the data fields by their names `first` and `last`. No other class will be able to do this. The words `public` and `private` are examples of an **access modifier** or **visibility modifier**, which specifies where a class, data field, or method can be used. A third access modifier, `protected`, is possible, as you will see in the next chapter.

Note: **Access (visibility) modifiers**
The words `public` and `private` are examples of access modifiers that specify where a class, method, or data field can be used. Any class can use a public method, but a private method can be used only by the class that defines it. Chapter 2 discusses the access modifier `protected`, and the section "Packages" of this chapter shows when you can omit the access modifier.

1.6   Since the data fields are private, how will a class that uses the class `Name` be able to change or look at their values? You can define methods in a class that look at or change the values of its data fields.

You declare such methods to be public, so that anyone can use them. A method that enables you to look at the value of a data field is called an **accessor method** or **query method**. A method that changes the value of a data field is called a **mutator method**. Java programmers typically begin the names of accessor methods with get and the names of mutator methods with set. Because of this convention, accessor methods are sometimes called **get methods** or **getters**, and mutator methods are called **set methods** or **setters**. For example, the class Name will have methods that include getFirst, getLast, setFirst, and setLast.

You may think that accessor methods and mutator methods defeat the purpose of making data fields private. On the contrary, they give the class control over its data fields. For example, a mutator method can check that any change to a data field is appropriate and warn you if there is a problem. The class would be unable to make this check if its data fields were public, since anyone could alter the fields.

Note: An **accessor (query) method** enables you to look at the value of a data field. A **mutator method** changes the value of a data field. Typically, you begin the names of accessor methods with get and the names of mutator methods with set.

Programming Tip: You should make each data field in a class private by beginning its declaration with the access modifier private. You cannot make any direct reference to a private data field's name outside of the class definition. The programmer who uses the class is forced to manipulate the data fields only via methods in the class. The class then can control how a programmer accesses or changes the data fields. Within any of the class's method definitions, however, you can use the name of the data field in any way you wish. In particular, you can directly change the value of the data field.

Question 4   Is the method setFirst an accessor method or a mutator method?

Question 5   Should a typical accessor method be valued or void?

Question 6   Should a typical mutator method be valued or void?

Question 7   What is a disadvantage of making a data field in a class public?

Method Definitions

1.7   The definition of a method has the following general form:

access-modifier   use-modifier   return-type   method-name(parameter-list)
{
   method-body
}

The **use modifier** is optional and in most cases is omitted. When used, it can be either abstract, final, or static. Briefly, an abstract method has no definition and must be overridden in a derived class. A final method cannot be overridden in a derived class. A static method is shared by all instances of the class. You will encounter these use modifiers later in either this chapter or the next chapter.

Next comes the **return type**, which for a valued method is the data type of the value that the method returns. For a void method, the return type is `void`. You then write the name of the method and a pair of parentheses that contain an optional list of **formal parameters** and their data types. The formal parameters, or simply **parameters**, specify values or objects that are inputs to the method.

So far, we have described the first line of the method definition, which is called the method's **header** or **declaration**. After the header is the method's **body**—which is simply a sequence of Java statements—enclosed in curly braces.

1.8   As an example of a valued method, here is the definition of the method `getFirst`:

```
public String getFirst()  ◄── Header
{
   return first;          } Body
} // end getFirst
```

This method returns the string in the data field `first`. The return type of this method is, therefore, `String`. A valued method must always execute a `return` statement as its last action. The data type of the value returned must match the data type declared as the return type in the method's header. Notice that this particular method does not have formal parameters.

1.9   Now let's look at an example of a void method. The void method `setFirst` sets the data field `first` to a string that represents a first name. The method definition is as follows:

```
public void setFirst(String firstName)
{
   first = firstName;
} // end setFirst
```

This method does not return a value, so its return type is `void`. The method has one formal parameter, `firstName`, that has the data type `String`. It represents the string that the method should assign to the data field `first`. The declaration of a formal parameter always consists of a data type and a parameter name. If you have more than one formal parameter, you separate their declarations with commas.

1.10   **The object this**. Notice that the bodies of the previous two method definitions refer to the data field `first` by name. This is perfectly legal. Exactly whose data field is involved here? Remember that each object of this class contains a data field `first`. The data field `first` that belongs to the object invoking the method is the one involved. Java has a name for this invoking object when you want to refer to it within the body of a method definition. It is simply `this`. For example, in the method `setFirst` you could write the statement

```
first = firstName;
```

as

```
this.first = firstName;
```

Some programmers use `this` in this way either for clarity or when they want to give the parameter the same name as the data field. For example, you could name `setFirst`'s parameter `first` instead of `firstName`. Clearly, the statement

```
first = first;
```

in the method's body would not work correctly, so instead you would write

```
this.first = first;
```

We typically will not use `this` for these reasons. Another situation, however, will occur where the use of `this` is essential, as you will see in Segment 1.26.

Note: Members
Both the data fields and the methods of an object are sometimes called **members** of the object, because they belong to the object.

Note: Naming classes and methods
The normal convention when naming classes and methods is to start all class names with an uppercase letter and to start all method names with a lowercase letter. Use a noun or descriptive phrase to name a class. Use a verb or action phrase to name a method.

Note: Local variables
A variable declared within a method definition is called a **local variable**. The value of a local variable is not available outside of the method definition. If two methods each have a local variable of the same name, the variables are different, even though they have the same name.

1.11   Methods should be self-contained units. You should design methods separately from the incidental details of other methods of the class and separately from any program that uses the class. One incidental detail is the name of the formal parameters. Fortunately, formal parameters behave like local variables, and so their meanings are confined to their respective method definitions. Thus, you can choose the formal parameter names without any concern that they will be the same as some other identifier used in some other method. For team programming projects, one programmer can write a method definition while another programmer writes another part of the program that uses that method. The two programmers need not agree on the names they use for formal parameters or local variables. They can choose their identifier names completely independently, without any concern that some, all, or none of their identifiers might be the same.

Arguments and Parameters

1.12   Earlier you saw that an object of a class usually invokes the methods defined within that class. For example, you saw that the statements

```
Name joe = new Name();
joe.setFirst("Joseph");
joe.setLast("Brown");
```

set the first and last names for the object `joe`. The strings `"Joseph"` and `"Brown"` are the arguments. These arguments must correspond to the formal parameters of the method definition. In the case of `setFirst`, for example, the formal parameter is the string `firstName`. The argument is the string `"Joseph"`. The argument is plugged in for the corresponding formal parameter. Thus, in the body of the method, `firstName` represents the string `"Joseph"` and behaves like a local variable.

A method invocation must provide exactly as many arguments as there are formal parameters in the corresponding method definition. In addition, the arguments in the invocation must correspond to the formal parameters in the method's definition with respect to both the order in which they occur and their data types. In some cases, however, Java will perform an automatic type conversion when the data types do not match.

Java does have a notation for formal parameters that allows a variable number of arguments. Since we really do not need this feature, we will not cover it.

Programming Tip: The arguments in the invocation of a method must correspond to the formal parameters in the method's definition with respect to number, order, and data type.

Note: **Use of the terms "parameter" and "argument"**
The use of the terms "formal parameter" and "argument" in this book is consistent with common usage, but some people use the terms "parameter" and "argument" interchangeably. Some people use the term "parameter" for both what we call (formal) parameters and what we call arguments. Other people use the term "argument" for both what we call (formal) parameters and what we call arguments.

Passing Arguments

1.13   When a formal parameter has a primitive type, such as `int` or `char`, the parameter is initialized to the value of the corresponding argument in the method invocation. The argument in a method invocation can be a literal constant—like 2 or 'A'—or it can be a variable or any expression that yields a value of the appropriate type. Note that the method cannot change the value of an argument that has a primitive data type. Such an argument serves as an input value only. This mechanism is known as the **call-by-value** parameter mechanism.

For example, suppose that the class `Name` provided for a middle initial by defining another data field and the method `setMiddleInitial`. Thus, the class might appear as follows:

```java
public class Name
{
   private String first;
   private char   initial;
   private String last;
   . . .

   public void setMiddleInitial(char middleInitial)
   {
      initial = middleInitial;
   } // end setMiddleInitial
   . . .
```

A client of this class could contain the following statements:

```java
char joesMI = 'T';
Name joe = new Name();
. . .
joe.setMiddleInitial(joesMI);
. . .
```

Figure 1-4 shows the argument joesMI, the parameter middleInitial, and the data field initial as the method setMiddleInitial executes. (Although the data field has an initial value, it is not relevant, so the figure shows it as a question mark.)

If a method changes the value of its parameter, the corresponding argument will be unaffected. So if, for example, setMiddleInitial contained the statements

```
initial = middleInitial;
middleInitial = 'X'
```

the value of middleInitial in Figure 1-4c would be *X*, but the rest of the figure would not change. In particular, the value of joesMI would not change.

Figure 1-4   The effect of executing the method setMiddleInitial on its argument joesMI, its parameter middleInitial, and the data field initial

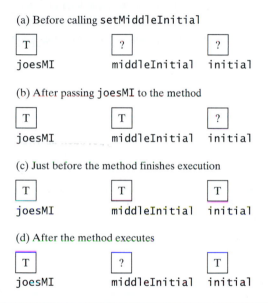

1.14   When a formal parameter has a class type, the corresponding argument in the method invocation must be an object of that class type. The formal parameter is initialized to the memory address of that object.[1] Thus, the formal parameter will serve as an alternative name for the object. This implies that the method can change the data in the object, if the class has mutator methods. The method, however, cannot replace an object that is an argument with another object.

For example, if you adopt a child, you might give that child your last name. Suppose that you add the following method giveLastNameTo to the class Name that makes this change of name:

```
public void giveLastNameTo(Name child)
{
   child.setLast(last);
} // end giveLastNameTo
```

Notice that the formal parameter of this method has the type Name.

---

1. The parameter mechanism for parameters of a class type is similar to **call-by-reference** parameter passing. If you are familiar with this terminology, be aware that parameters of a class type in Java behave a bit differently from call-by-reference parameters in other languages.

Now if Jamie Jones adopts Jane Doe, the following statements would change Jane's last name to Jones:

```
public static void main(String[] args)²
{
    Name jamie = new Name();
    jamie.setFirst("Jamie");
    jamie.setLast("Jones");

    Name jane = new Name();
    jane.setFirst("Jane");
    jane.setLast("Doe");

    jamie.giveLastNameTo(jane);
    . . .
} // end main
```

Figure 1-5 shows the argument jane and the parameter child as the method giveLastNameTo executes.

Figure 1-5   The method giveLastNameTo modifies the object passed to it as an argument

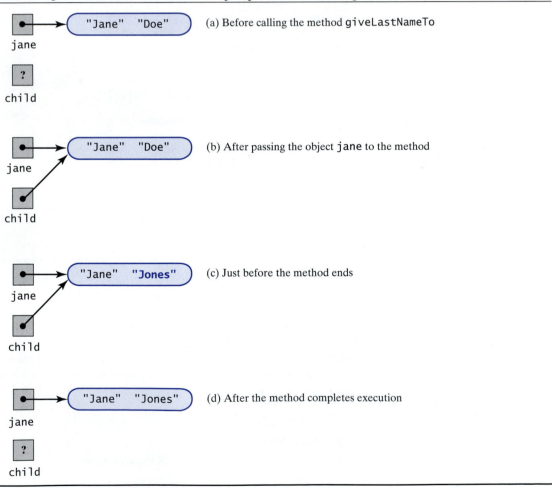

(a) Before calling the method giveLastNameTo

(b) After passing the object jane to the method

(c) Just before the method ends

(d) After the method completes execution

---

2. If you are not familiar with main methods and application programs, consult the beginning of Appendix A.

1.15   What happens if you change the method definition to allocate a new name, as follows?

```
public void giveLastNameTo2(Name child)
{
   String firstName = child.getFirst();
   child = new Name();
   child.setFirst(firstName);
   child.setLast(last);
} // end giveLastNameTo2
```

With this change, the invoking statement

```
jamie.giveLastNameTo2(jane);
```

has no effect on `jane`, as Figure 1-6 illustrates. The parameter `child` behaves like a local variable, so its value is not available outside of the method definition.

Figure 1-6   A method cannot replace an object passed to it as an argument

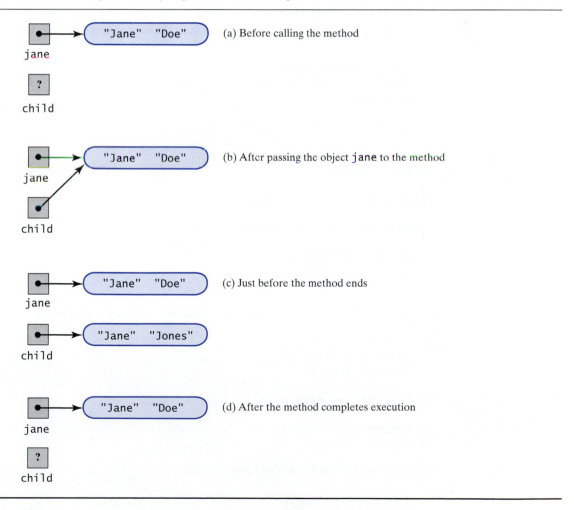

Question 8   Consider a method definition that begins with the statement

```
public void process(int number, Name aName)
```

If `jamie` is defined as in Segment 1.14 and you invoke this method with the statement

```
someObject.process(5, jamie);
```

what values are given to the parameters within the definition of the method?

Question 9   In Question 8, can the method `process` change the data fields in `jamie`?

Question 10   In Question 8, can the method `process` assign a new object to `jamie`?

A Definition of the Class **Name**

1.16   A complete definition for the class `Name` appears in Listing 1-1. We typically place data field declarations at the beginning of the class, but some people place them last. Although Java allows you to intermix method definitions and data field declarations, we prefer that you do not.

The sections that follow examine some other details of this class definition.

Listing 1-1   The class Name

```java
public class Name
{
  private String first; // first name
  private String last;  // last name

  public Name()
  {
  } // end default constructor

  public Name(String firstName, String lastName)
  {
    first = firstName;
    last = lastName;
  } // end constructor

  public void setName(String firstName, String lastName)
  {
    setFirst(firstName);
    setLast(lastName);
  } // end setName

  public String getName()
  {
    return toString();
  } // end getName

  public void setFirst(String firstName)
  {
    first = firstName;
  } // end setFirst
```

```java
  public String getFirst()
  {
    return first;
  } // end getFirst

  public void setLast(String lastName)
  {
    last = lastName;
  } // end setLast

  public String getLast()
  {
    return last;
  } // end getLast

  public void giveLastNameTo(Name aName)
  {
    aName.setLast(last);
  } // end giveLastNameTo

  public String toString()
  {
    return first + " " + last;
  } // end toString
} // end Name
```

Constructors

1.17   Segment 1.2 mentioned that you create an object by using the `new` operator to invoke a special method called a constructor. A **constructor** allocates memory for the object and initializes the data fields. The method definition of a constructor has certain special properties. A constructor

- Has the same name as the class
- Has no return type, not even `void`
- Has any number of formal parameters, including no parameters

A class can have several constructors that differ in the number or type of parameters.

A constructor without parameters is called the **default constructor**. A class can have only one default constructor. The definition of the default constructor for `Name` is

```java
  public Name()
  {
  } // end default constructor
```

This particular default constructor has an empty body, but it need not be empty. It could explicitly initialize the data fields `first` and `last` to values other than the ones Java assigns by default.

For example, we could have defined the constructor as follows:

```java
  public Name()
  {
    first = "";
    last = "";
  } // end default constructor
```

Here we initialize the fields `first` and `last` to an empty string. If the constructor had an empty body, it would initialize these fields to `null` by default.

Programming Tip: In the absence of any explicit initialization within a constructor, data fields are set to default values: Reference types are `null`, primitive numeric types are zero, and boolean types are false. If a class depends on a data field's initial value, its constructor should set these values explicitly. Standard default values have been known to change.

Programming Tip: If a data field references an object, and it invokes a method, initialize it to something other than `null`. Failure to do so can result in an execution-time error.

1.18   If you do not define any constructors for a class, Java will automatically provide a default constructor—that is, a constructor with no parameters. If you define a constructor that has parameters but you do not define a default constructor—one without parameters—Java will not provide a default constructor for you. Because classes are often reused again and again, and because eventually you might want to create a new object without specifying parameters, your classes typically should include a default constructor.

Programming Tip: Once you start defining constructors, Java will not define any other constructors for you. Most of the classes you define should include a default constructor.

1.19   The class `Name` contains a second constructor, one that initializes the data fields to values given as arguments when the client invokes the constructor:

```
public Name(String firstName, String lastName)
{
   first = firstName;
   last = lastName;
} // end constructor
```

This constructor has two parameters, `firstName` and `lastName`. You invoke it with a statement such as

```
Name jill = new Name("Jill", "Jones");
```

that passes first and last names as arguments.

1.20   After creating the object `jill`, you can change the values of its data fields by using the class's set (mutator) methods. You saw that this step was in fact necessary for the object `joe` in Segment 1.2, since `joe` was created by the default constructor and had default values—probably `null`—as its first and last names.

Let's see what would happen in the case of `jill` if you tried to use the constructor to change the values of `jill`'s data fields. After you created the object, the variable `jill` contained the memory address of that object, as Figure 1-7a illustrates. If you now write the statement

```
jill = new Name("Jill", "Smith");
```

a new object is created, and `jill` contains its memory address. The original object is lost, because no program variable has its address, as shown in Figure 1-7b.

What happens to a memory location when the variables in your program no longer reference it? Periodically, the Java run-time environment **deallocates** such memory locations by returning them to the operating system so that they can be used again. In effect, the memory is recycled. This process is called **automatic garbage collection**.

Note: Memory leak

If the Java run-time environment did not track and recycle memory that a program no longer references, a program could use all the memory available to it and subsequently fail. If you use another programming language—C++, for example—you would be responsible for returning unneeded memory to the operating system for reuse. A program that failed to return such memory would have what is known as a **memory leak**. Java programs do not have this problem.

Note: Classes without mutator methods

After you create an object of a class that has no set methods, you cannot change the values of its data fields. If they require change, you must use the constructor to create a new object. Chapter 15 discusses these classes further.

Figure 1-7   An object (a) after its initial creation; (b) after its reference is lost

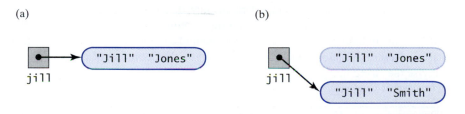

Question 11   What is a default constructor?

Question 12   How do you invoke a constructor?

Question 13   What happens if you do not define constructors for a class?

Question 14   What happens if you do not define a default constructor but you do define a constructor that has parameters?

Question 15   What happens when an object no longer has a variable that references it?

The Method `toString`

1.21   The method `toString` in the class `Name` returns a string that is the person's full name. You can use this method, for example, to display the name that the object `jill` represents by writing

```
System.out.println(jill.toString());
```

What is remarkable about `toString` is that Java will invoke it automatically when you write

```
System.out.println(jill);
```

For this reason, providing a class with a method `toString` is a good idea in general. If you fail to do so, Java will provide its own `toString` method, which produces a string that will have little meaning to you. The next chapter provides more detail about the `toString` method.

Methods That Call Other Methods

1.22   Notice the method `setName` in the class definition for `Name`. Although `setName` could use assignment statements to initialize `first` and `last`, it instead invokes the methods `setFirst` and `setLast`. Since these methods are members of the class, `setName` can invoke them without preceding the name with an object variable and a dot. If you prefer, you can use `this`, and write the invocation as

```
this.setFirst(firstName);
```

When the logic of a method's definition is complex, you should divide the logic into smaller pieces and implement each piece as a separate method. Your method can then invoke these other methods. Such helping methods, however, might be inappropriate for a client to use. If so, declare them as private instead of public so that only your class can invoke them.

Programming Tip: If a helping method is not appropriate for public use, declare it as private.

1.23   The method `getName` in the class `Name` also invokes another of `Name`'s methods, namely `toString`. Here, we want both `getName` and `toString` to return the same string. Rather than writing the same statements in both methods, we have one method call the other. This ensures that both methods will always return the same values. If you later revise the definition of `toString`, you will automatically revise the string that `getName` returns.

Programming Tip: If you want two methods to have the same behavior, one of them should call the other.

1.24   Although it generally is a good idea for methods to call other methods to avoid repeating code, you need to be careful if you call public methods from the body of a constructor. For example, it is tempting to have the constructor mentioned in Segment 1.19 call `setName`. But another class derived from your class could change the effect of `setName` and hence of your constructor. One solution is to define a private method that both the constructor and `setName` call. Another approach is given in Segment 2.23 of the next chapter.

1.25   **Using `this` to invoke a constructor.** You can use the reserved word `this` to call a constructor from within the body of another constructor. For example, the class `Name` has two constructors. The default constructor, as given in Segment 1.16, has an empty body. Segment 1.17 suggested that it is a good idea to have the default constructor initialize the class's data fields explicitly, so we rewrote it, as follows:

```
public Name()
{
  first = "";
  last = "";
} // end default constructor
```

We could accomplish the same thing by revising the default constructor so that it initializes `first` and `last` by calling the second constructor, as follows:

```
public Name()
{
   this("", "");
} // end default constructor
```

The statement

```
this("", "");
```

calls the constructor that has two parameters. In this way, the initialization occurs in one place.

Programming Tip: Link the definitions of several constructors by using `this` to invoke one of them. Any use of `this` must be first in the body of the constructor's definition.

Question 16   A third constructor for the class `Name` could have the following header:

```
public Name(Name aName)
```

This constructor creates a `Name` object whose data fields match those of the object `aName`. Implement this new constructor by invoking one of the existing constructors.

Methods That Return an Instance of Their Class

1.26   The method `setName` in the class `Name` is a void method that sets both the first and last names of a `Name` object. We might use this method as follows:

```
Name jill = new Name();
jill.setName("Jill", "Greene");
```

Here, `setName` sets the first and last names of the invoking object `jill`.

Instead of defining `setName` as a void method, we could have it return a reference to the revised instance of `Name`, as follows:

```
public Name setName(String firstName, String lastName)
{
   setFirst(firstName);
   setLast(lastName);

   return this;
} // end setName
```

Here `this` represents the invoking object, whose first and last names were just set.

We can call this definition of `setName` just as we called its void version, or we could invoke it as follows:

```
Name jill = new Name();
Name myFriend = jill.setName("Jill", "Greene");
```

As before, `setName` sets the first and last names of the invoking object `jill`. But then it returns a reference to the invoking object. Here we used an assignment statement to retain this reference as an alias for jill. However, the invocation of setName could appear as an argument to another method.

Methods that return an instance of their class are not unusual within the classes of the Java Class Library.

Static Fields and Methods

1.27 **Static fields.** Sometimes you need a data field that does not belong to any one object. For example, a class could track how many invocations of the class's methods are made by all objects of the class. Such a data field is called a **static field**, **static variable**, or **class variable**. You declare a static field by adding the reserved word static. For example, the declaration

```
private static int numberOfInvocations = 0;
```

defines one copy of numberOfInvocations that every object of the class can access. Objects can use a static field to communicate with each other or to perform some joint action. In this example, each method increments numberOfInvocations. Such static fields normally should be private to ensure that access occurs only through appropriate accessor and mutator methods.

The definition of a named constant provides another example of a static field. The statement

```
public static final double YARDS_PER_METER = 1.0936;
```

defines a static field YARDS_PER_METER. The class has one copy of YARDS_PER_METER, rather than each object of the class having its own copy, as Figure 1-8 illustrates. Since YARDS_PER_METER is also declared as final, its value cannot change, so we can safely make it public. But static fields in general can change value if you omit the modifier final.

Note: Static does not mean constant
A static field is shared by all objects of its class, but its value can change. If you want a field's value to remain constant, you must declare it as final. Although they often appear together, the modifiers static and final are not related. Thus, a field can be static, final, or both static and final.

Figure 1-8   A static field YARDS_PER_METER versus a nonstatic field value

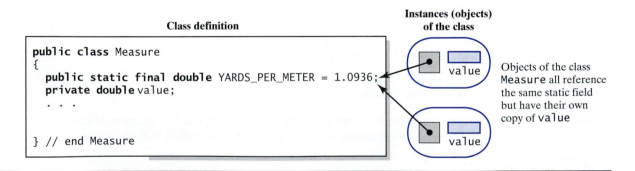

1.28 **Static methods.** Sometimes you need a method that does not belong to an object of any kind. For example, you might need a method to compute the maximum of two integers or a method to compute the square root of a number. These methods have no obvious object to which they should

belong. In these cases, you can define the method as static by adding the reserved word `static` to the header of the method.

A **static method** or **class method** is still a member of a class. However, you use the class name instead of an object name to invoke the method. For example, Java's predefined class `Math` contains several standard mathematical methods, such as `max` and `sqrt`. All of these methods are static, so you do not need—and in fact have no real use for—an object of the class `Math`. You call these methods by using the class name in place of a calling object. Thus, you write statements such as

```java
int maximum = Math.max(2, 3);
double root = Math.sqrt(4.2);
```

The definition of a static method cannot reference any data field in its class that is not static. It can, however, reference its class's static fields. Likewise, it cannot invoke a nonstatic method of the class, unless it creates a local object of the class and uses it to invoke the nonstatic method. However, a static method can call other static methods within its class. Since every application program's `main` method is static, these restrictions apply to `main` methods.

Programming Tip: **Every class can have a `main` method**

You can include a test of a class as a `main` method in the class's definition. Anytime you suspect something is wrong, you can easily test the class definition. Since you—and others—can see what tests you performed, flaws in your testing will become apparent. If you use the class as a program, the `main` method is invoked. When you use the class to create objects in another class or program, the `main` method is ignored.

Note: **Constructors cannot be static**

A constructor creates an object of its class, so it makes no sense to disassociate a constructor from such objects.

Question 17   What happens if you do not declare a constant data field as static?

Overloading Methods

1.29   Several methods within the same class can have the same name, as long as the methods do not have identical parameters. Java is able to distinguish among these methods since their parameters differ in number or data type. We say that these methods are **overloaded**.

For example, the class `Name` has the method `setName` whose header is

```java
public void setName(String firstName, String lastName)
```

Imagine that we want another method that gives a `Name` object the same name as another `Name` object. The header for this method could be, for example,

```java
public void setName(Name otherName)
```

The two versions of `setName` are not exactly the same, as they have different numbers of parameters. We could then overload `setName` with a third method whose header is

```java
public void setName(String firstName, Name otherName)
```

Imagine that this method sets the first name to the string `firstName` and the last name to `other-Name`'s last name. Although two of the three versions of `setName` have two parameters each, the data types of the parameters are not exactly the same. The data types of the first parameter in each method match, but the data types of the second parameters do not.

Simply changing the names of the parameters is not enough to overload a method. The parameter names are not relevant. When two methods have the same name and the same number of parameters, at least one pair of corresponding parameters must differ in data type. Also, changing only the return type is insufficient. The compiler cannot distinguish between two methods that differ only in their return types.

Finally, note that by defining more than one constructor for a class, you are actually overloading them. Thus, their parameters must differ in either number or data type.

Note: **Overloading a method definition**
A method in a class overloads another method in the same class when both methods have the same name but differ in the number or types of parameters.

Note: **The signature of a method**
A method's **signature** consists of its name and parameters. Thus, overloaded methods have the same name but different signatures.

Question 18 If a method overloads another method, can the two methods have different return types?

Enumeration as a Class

Appendix A introduces enumerations. As Segments A.53 and A.55 mention, the compiler creates a class when it encounters an enumeration. This section expands that discussion. Although you should consider using enumerations in your programs, they are not central to the presentation in the rest of the book.

1.30   When you define an enumeration, the class created has methods such as `toString`, `equals`, `ordinal`, and `valueOf`. For example, let's define a simple enumeration for the suits of playing cards, as follows:

```
enum Suit {CLUBS, DIAMONDS, HEARTS, SPADES}
```

We then can use these methods in the following ways:

- `Suit.CLUBS.toString()` returns the string *CLUBS*. That is, `toString` returns the name of its invoking object.
- `System.out.println(Suit.CLUBS)` calls `toString` implicitly, and so it displays *CLUBS*.
- `s.equals(Suit.DIAMONDS)` tests whether `s`, an instance of `Suit`, equals `DIAMONDS`.
- `Suit.HEARTS.ordinal()` returns 2, the ordinal position of `HEARTS` in the enumeration.
- `Suit.valueOf("HEARTS")` returns `Suit.HEARTS`.

1.31   You can define additional methods—including constructors—for any enumeration. By defining a private data field, you can assign values to each of the objects in the enumeration. Adding a get method will provide a way for the client to access these values. Listing 1-2 contains a new definition for the enumeration `Suit` that shows how these ideas are realized.

Listing 1-2   The enumeration `Suit`

```
/** An enumeration of card suits. */
enum Suit
{
   CLUBS("black"), DIAMONDS("red"), HEARTS("red"), SPADES("black");

   private final String color;

   private Suit(String suitColor)
   {
      color = suitColor;
   } // end constructor

   public String getColor()
   {
      return color;
   } // end getColor
} // end Suit
```

We have chosen strings as the values for the enumerated objects. Notation such as `CLUBS("black")` invokes the constructor that we have provided and sets the value of `CLUBS`'s private data field `color` to the string *black*. Note that `color`'s value cannot change, since it is declared as final. Also observe that the constructor is private, so it is not available to the client. It is called only within the definition of `Suit`. The method `getColor` provides public access to the value of `color`.

Note: Constructors within enumerations must be private.

1.32   The class in Listing 1-3 provides a simple demonstration of the enumeration `Suit` that appears in the previous segment. We use a for-each loop, described in Segment A.62 of Appendix A. In addition to the methods that we defined in `Suit`, the enumeration also has the methods `equals`, `ordinal`, and `valueOf` described in Segment 1.30 of this chapter and Segment A.55 of Appendix A.

Listing 1-3   A class that demonstrates the enumeration `Suit` given in Listing 1-2
                of Segment 1.31

```
/** A demonstration of the enumeration Suit. */
public class SuitDemo
{
   private enum Suit
   {
      . . .  < See Listing 1-2 >
   } // end Suit
```

```java
public static void main(String[] args)
{
  for (Suit nextSuit : Suit.values())
  {
    System.out.println(nextSuit + " are " + nextSuit.getColor() +
                       " and have an ordinal value of " +
                       nextSuit.ordinal());
  } // end for
} // end main
} // end SuitDemo
```

OUTPUT

CLUBS are black and have an ordinal value of 0
DIAMONDS are red and have an ordinal value of 1
HEARTS are red and have an ordinal value of 2
SPADES are black and have an ordinal value of 3

Note: Enumerations can have an access modifier such as `public` or `private`. If you omit the access modifier, the enumeration is private. You can define a public enumeration within its own file, just as you would define any other public class.

1.33   **Example.** Segment A.53 in Appendix A defined an enumeration for the letter grades A, B, C, D, and F. Here we expand that definition to include plus and minus grades as well as the quality-point values associated with each grade. As in the previous definition of Suit, we provide private data fields and a private constructor to represent and initialize the string representation and numeric value for each grade. We also provide accessor methods for the data fields and override the method `toString`.

Listing 1-4 shows our new definition of the enumeration `LetterGrade`. We have made it public and will store it in the file `LetterGrade.java`.

Listing 1-4   The enumeration `LetterGrade`

```java
public enum LetterGrade
{
  A("A", 4.0), A_MINUS("A-", 3.7), B_PLUS("B+", 3.3), B("B", 3.0),
  B_MINUS("B-", 2.7), C_PLUS("C+", 2.3), C("C", 2.0), C_MINUS("C-", 1.7),
  D_PLUS("D+", 1.3), D("D", 1.0), F("F", 0.0);

  private final String grade;
  private final double points;

  private LetterGrade(String letterGrade, double qualityPoints)
  {
    grade = letterGrade;
    points = qualityPoints;
  } // end constructor
```

```java
public String getGrade()
{
    return grade;
} // end getGrade

public double getQualityPoints()
{
    return points;
} // end getQualityPoints

public String toString()
{
    return getGrade();
} // end toString
} // end LetterGrade
```

If we define

```java
LetterGrade myGrade = LetterGrade.B_PLUS;
```

then

- `myGrade.toString()` returns the string *B+*.
- `System.out.println(myGrade)` displays *B+*, since it calls `toString` implicitly.
- `myGrade.getGrade()` returns the string *B+*.
- `myGrade.getQualityPoints()` returns 3.3.

If we had not overriden the method `toString` with our own definition, `myGrade.toString()` would return the string *B_PLUS*.

Like the enumeration `Suit` given in Segment 1.31, `LetterGrade` has the methods `equals`, `ordinal`, and `valueOf`.

Question 19 If `myGrade` is an instance of `LetterGrade` and is assigned the value `Letter-Grade.B_PLUS`, what is returned by each of the following expressions?

a. `myGrade.ordinal()`
b. `myGrade.equals(LetterGrade.A_MINUS)`
c. `LetterGrade.valueOf("A_MINUS")`

Question 20 What does the following statement display?

```java
System.out.println(LetterGrade.valueOf("A_MINUS"));
```

Packages

1.34   Using several related classes is more convenient if you group them together within a Java **package**. To identify a class as part of a particular package, you begin the file that contains the class with a statement like

```java
package myStuff;
```

You then place all of the files within one directory or folder and give it the same name as the package.
To use a package in your program, you begin the program with a statement such as

```java
import myStuff.*;
```

The asterisk makes all public classes within the package available to the program. You could, however, replace the asterisk with the name of a particular class in the package that you want to use. You probably have already used packages provided by Java, such as the package `java.util`.

Why did we just say "public classes"? What other kind of class is there? You can use an access modifier to control access to a class just as you can to control access to a data field or method. A public class—whether it is within a package or not—is available to any other class. If you omit the class's access modifier entirely, the class is available only to other classes within the same package. This kind of class is said to have **package access**. Similarly, if you omit the access modifier on data fields or methods, they are available by name inside the definition of any class within the same package but not outside of the package. You can use package access in situations where you have a package of cooperating classes that act as a single encapsulated unit. If you control the package directory, you control who is allowed to access the package.

The Java Class Library

1.35   Java comes with a collection of many classes that you can use in your programs. For example, Segment 1.28 mentioned the class `Math`, which contains several standard mathematical methods such as `sqrt`. This collection is known as the **Java Class Library**, and sometimes as the **Java Application Programming Interface**, or **API**. The classes in this library are organized into several standard packages. For example, the class `Math` is a part of the package `java.lang`. Note that no `import` statement is needed when you use a class from this particular package.

From time to time, we will mention classes within the Java Class Library that are like or relevant to the classes that we will define. You should become familiar with the documentation provided for the Java Class Library at `java.sun.com/j2se/1.5/docs/api/`.

CHAPTER SUMMARY

- An object is a program component that contains data and can perform certain actions. When the program is run, the objects interact with one another to accomplish a particular task. The actions performed by objects are defined by the methods in a class.

- A class is a type or kind of object. A class definition is a general description of what an object is and what it can do. All objects in the same class have the same kinds of data and the same methods.

- An access modifier, such as `public` or `private`, specifies where you can use a class, method, or data field.

- A private data field is not accessible by name outside of the class definition. Within any of the class's method definitions, you can use the data field name in any way you wish. In particular, you can directly change the value of the data field. However, outside of the class definition, you cannot make any direct reference to the data field name. The programmer who uses the class is forced to manipulate the data fields only via methods in the class. The class then can control how a programmer accesses or changes its data fields.

- A public method that returns the data in a private data field is called an accessor method. A public method that changes the data in a private data field is called a mutator method.

- Valued methods return a single value; void methods do not return any value.

- A method invocation must provide exactly the same number of arguments as there are formal parameters in the corresponding method definition. In addition, the arguments in the invocation must correspond to the method's formal parameters in its definition with respect to the order in which they occur and their data types. In some cases, however, Java will perform an automatic type conversion when the data types do not match.

- When a formal parameter has a primitive type such as `int`, the parameter is initialized to the value of the corresponding argument in the method invocation. When a formal parameter has a class type, the corresponding argument in the method invocation must be an object of that class type. The formal parameter is initialized to the memory address of that object.

- A valued method must always execute a `return` statement as its last action. The data type of the value returned must match the data type declared as the return type in the method's header.

- A variable declared within a method definition is called a local variable. The value of a local variable is not available outside of the method definition. If two methods each have a local variable of the same name, the variables are different, even though they have the same name. Java does not give an initial value to a local variable, regardless of its data type.

- A constructor allocates memory for an object and initializes its data fields. A constructor has the same name as the class, has no return type, not even `void`, and has any number of formal parameters, including zero parameters.

- A class can have several constructors, but their parameters must differ in number or type.

- A constructor without parameters is called the default constructor. A class can have only one default constructor. If you do not define any constructors for a class, Java automatically provides a default constructor. If you define a constructor but not a default constructor, Java will not provide one for you.

- When the logic of a method's definition is complex, you should divide the logic into smaller pieces and implement each piece as a separate method. Your method can then invoke these other methods. If such helping methods are inappropriate for a client to use, declare them as private instead of public so that only your class can invoke them.

- You can use the reserved word `this` to call a constructor from within the body of another constructor. In this way, initialization occurs in one place. When used within a method definition, `this` represents the object that invokes the method.

- Every class can have a `main` method. If you use the class as a program, the method `main` is invoked. When you use the class to create objects in another class or program, `main` is ignored.

- A static field or static method is associated with the class and not the individual objects of the class.

- A method in a class overloads another method in the same class when both methods have the same name but differ in the number or types of parameters. A method's signature consists of its name and parameters. Thus, overloaded methods have the same name but different signatures.

- Since an enumeration is really a class, you can add data fields, a constructor, and methods to its definition.

- A package is a group of related classes that you place into a single directory or folder. Classes within a package can access by name any field or method within any other class in the package, if the field or method has no access modifier or is not private.

PROGRAMMING TIPS

- All data fields in a class should be private.

- You cannot make any direct reference to a private data field's name outside of the class definition.

- Provide public methods to look at or change the data fields in an object.

- When you invoke a method, the arguments must correspond to the method's formal parameters in its definition with respect to number, order, and data type.

- In the absence of any explicit initialization within a constructor, data fields are set to default values: Reference types are `null`, primitive numeric types are zero, and boolean types are false.

- If a data field contains an object, and it invokes a method, initialize it to something other than `null`. Failure to do so can result in an execution-time error.

- Once you start defining constructors, Java will not define any other constructors for you. Most of the classes you define should include a default constructor.

- If a helping method is not appropriate for public use, declare it as private.

- If you want two methods to have the same behavior, one of them should call the other.

- Link the definitions of several constructors by using `this` to invoke one of them. Any use of `this` must be first in the body of the constructor's definition.

- Include a test of a class as a `main` method in the class's definition. Anytime you suspect something is wrong, you can easily test the class definition.

EXERCISES

(Several exercises involve the class `Name`, as given in Listing 1-1 of Segment 1.16.)

1. What is the difference between how a method handles a parameter of a primitive type and a parameter of a reference (class) type?

2. If you remove the default constructor from the class `Name`, what happens if you write the statement

   ```
   Name me = new Name();
   ```

3. If you remove all constructors from the class `Name`, what happens if you write the statement

   ```
   Name me = new Name();
   ```

4. Consider a class called `Person` that has two data fields, one for the person's name and one for the person's age. Write two constructors for this class. The implementation of one constructor should invoke the other.

5. List the accessor methods and the mutator methods for the class `Name`.

6. Suppose that `jack` and `jill` are two distinct objects of the class `Name`.

   a. Write Java statements that create a variable `friend` as an alias of `jack`.
   b. What is the value of the boolean expression `friend == jack`? Why?
   c. What happens to the last names of `jack` and `jill` after the following statements execute? Explain your answer.

   ```
   jill.giveLastNameTo(friend);
   jack.giveLastNameTo(jill);
   ```

7. Implement the following methods for the class `Name`:

   ```
   /** Task: Changes the last name to the last name of aName. */
   public void changeLastNameTo(Name aName)

   /** Task: Changes the last name to the string newLastName. */
   public void changeLastNameTo(String newLastName)
   ```

8. Segment 1.13 proposed the addition of a middle initial to the names represented by the class `Name`. Describe the changes that you would make to `Name` to accommodate a middle initial.

9. a. Suppose that we add one static accessor method to the class `Name`. Would this make sense? Explain.
   b. Repeat Part *a*, but add a static mutator method instead of an accessor method.
   c. Give an example of a static method that is not an accessor method or a mutator method, but that could be added to `Name`.

10. Write a static method `readName` suitable for a client of the class `Name` that returns a `Name` object. This object should have a first and last name that `readName` reads as strings from the keyboard.

11. Consider the following class `Test`:

```
public class Test
{
   public static final int w = 1;
   public static int x = 2;
   public final int y = 3;
   public int z = 4;

   public void showAllOne()
   {
      System.out.println("w is " + w);
      System.out.println("x is " + x);
      System.out.println("y is " + y);
      System.out.println("z is " + z);
   } // end showAllOne

   public static void showAllTwo()
   {
      System.out.println("w is " + w);
      System.out.println("x is " + x);
      System.out.println("y is " + y);
```

```
            System.out.println("z is " + z);
   } // end showAllTwo
} // end Test
```

a. Which lines in the class as defined will cause compile-time errors?

b. Suppose that you comment out the erroneous lines that you identified in Part *a*. Which of the following lines of code within a client of Test will cause compile-time errors?

```
Test tester = new Test();
tester.w += 3;
tester.x += 3;
tester.y += 3;
tester.z += 3;
tester.showAllOne();
tester.showAllTwo();
Test.w += 3;
Test.x += 3;
Test.y += 3;
Test.z += 3;
Test.showAllOne();
Test.showAllTwo();
```

12. Given the enumeration LetterGrade, as defined in Segment 1.33, what is the output of the following statements?

```
LetterGrade jacksGrade = LetterGrade.A;
LetterGrade jillsGrade = LetterGrade.B_PLUS;
LetterGrade johnsGrade = LetterGrade.C_MINUS;
LetterGrade fredsGrade = LetterGrade.B_PLUS;
LetterGrade charliesGrade = jillsGrade;

System.out.println(jacksGrade);
System.out.println(jillsGrade.toString());
System.out.println(johnsGrade.ordinal());
System.out.println(jillsGrade == fredsGrade);
System.out.println(jillsGrade == charliesGrade);
System.out.println(jillsGrade.equals(fredsGrade));
System.out.println(jillsGrade.equals(charliesGrade));
System.out.println(LetterGrade.valueOf("B_PLUS"));
System.out.println(LetterGrade.valueOf("B").getQualityPoints());
```

PROJECTS

1. Define a class called Counter. An object of this class is used to count things, so it records a count that is a nonnegative whole number. Include methods to set the counter to a given integer, to increase the count by 1, and to decrease the count by 1. Be sure that no method allows the value of the counter to become negative. Also include a method that returns the current count value as an integer, a method toString that returns the current count value as a string suitable for display on the screen, and a method that tests whether the current count value is zero.

   Write a program to test your class definition.

2. Write a class called `Person` that has two data fields, one for the person's name and one for the person's age. Include set and get methods for each of these data fields. Also include methods to test whether

- Two `Person` objects are equal—that is, have the same name and age
- One person is older than another

Finally, include a `toString` method that returns a string consisting of a person's name and age.

   Write a test program that demonstrates each method.

3. Write a Java enumeration `Rank` that represents the rank of a playing card. The ranks should be `ACE`, `TWO`, `THREE`, `FOUR`, `FIVE`, `SIX`, `SEVEN`, `EIGHT`, `NINE`, `TEN`, `JACK`, `QUEEN`, and `KING`. Define a private data field to hold a boolean value that is true if the card is a face card (Jack, Queen, or King). Include a constructor that initializes this field and an accessor method that returns its value. Also, define a method `toString`.

   Write a test program that demonstrates the enumeration.

4. Define a class `GenericCoin` that represents a coin with no value or name. The coin should have a heads side and a tails side and should be able to tell you which side is up. You should be able to "toss" the coin so that it lands randomly either heads up or tails up.

   a. Write a program that tosses two coins 50 times each. Record and report how many times each coin lands heads up. Also report which coin landed heads up most often.

   b. Write a program that plays a simple coin-toss game. You ask the user to guess whether the coin will be heads or tails. Then you toss the coin, tell the user the results, announce whether the user's guess was correct, and tabulate the results. The user can continue playing the game for as long as desired. When the user quits, display a summary of the game, including the number of coin tosses, the number of heads, the number of tails, the number of correct guesses, and the percentage of guesses that were correct. If desired, use graphics to illustrate the result of each coin toss.

5. Many games depend on the roll of two dice. Define a class `Die` that represents one n-sided die. The default value for n is 6. You should be able to roll the die and discover the value of its upper face. Use random numbers to simulate the roll of the die. If desired, use graphics to display this face.

6. The largest positive integer of type `int` is 2,147,483,647. Another integer type, `long`, represents integers up to 9,223,372,036,854,775,807. Imagine that you want to represent even larger integers.

   Design and implement a class `Huge` of very large nonnegative integers. The largest integer should contain at least 30 digits. Provide operations for the class that

- Set the value of a nonnegative integer (provide both set methods and constructors)
- Return the value of a nonnegative integer as a string
- Read a large nonnegative integer (skip leading zeros, but remember that zero is a valid number)
- Write a large nonnegative integer (do not write leading zeros, but if the integer is zero, write a single zero)
- Add two nonnegative integers to produce the sum as a third integer
- Multiply two nonnegative integers to produce the product as a third integer

You should handle overflow when reading, adding, or multiplying integers. An integer is too large if it exceeds MAX_SIZE digits, where MAX_SIZE is a named constant that you define.

Write a test program that demonstrates each method.

7. Write a Java class CalendarDate that represents a calendar date consisting of a month, day, and year. You can use three integers to represent a date. For example, July 4, 1776, is month 7, day 4, and year 1776. Include reasonable constructors, set and get methods, and a toString method. In addition, provide methods that

- Decide whether two dates are equal
- Get the day of the week for the current date
- Decide whether the current year is a leap year
- Advance the current date by one day

A year is a leap year if it is divisible by 4 but not by 100. If the year is divisible by 100, it is a leap year only if it is also divisible by 400.

To discover the day of the week, you can use the following algorithm. First, define the following integers:

- M represents the month. M is 1 for March, 2 for April, and so on. M is 11 for January and 12 for February, but for these two months, subtract 1 from the year before proceeding.
- D represents the day of the month (1 through 31).
- C is the first two digits of the year (after any adjustment for January and February).
- Y is the last two digits of the year (after any adjustment for January and February).

Now compute

$$F = (26 M - 2)/10 + D + Y + Y/4 + C/4 - 2 C$$

All divisions are integer divisions in the sense that you discard any remainders. Now let

$$W = F \text{ (modulo 7)}$$

That is, you divide F by 7 and retain only the remainder. Then, if the remainder is negative, you add 7 to get W. W now represents the day of the week: 0 is Sunday, 1 is Monday, and so on.

Write a test program that demonstrates each method in your class.

8. Write a Java class Time that represents the time of day in hours and minutes on a 24-hour clock. Include constructors, set and get methods, a method that advances the time by a given number of minutes, and a toString method. Provide another method, similar to toString, that returns the current time in 12-hour notation. For example, toString might return the string "13:05", while the other method returns the string "1:05pm". Optionally, you can write a method that displays the time on a digital or analog clock face.

9. Write a Java class `GeometricSequence` that represents a geometric sequence of numbers that are generated one at a time. The sequence has the following form:

$$a, a\,r, a\,r^2, a\,r^3, a\,r^4, a\,r^5,\ldots$$

The class should have four private data fields, as follows:

- The first term, a, in the sequence
- The ratio r between successive terms in the sequence
- The value of the current term in the sequence
- The value of the exponent for the current term in the sequence

Include a reasonable constructor, an accessor for each data field, and a method `toString`. In addition, provide a mutator method for each of the following tasks:

- Replace the current term in the sequence with the next term
- Replace the current term in the sequence with the previous term (if there is one)
- Reset the current term in the sequence to the initial term in the sequence

Write a program that tests your class definition.

10. A **magic square** is a square two-dimensional array of positive integers such that the sum of each row, column, and diagonal is the same constant. For example,

16	3	2	13
5	10	11	8
9	6	7	12
4	15	14	1

is a magic square because the sum of the integers in each row is 34, the sum of the integers in each column is 34, and the sum of the integers in each of the two diagonals $(16 + 10 + 7 + 1$ and $4 + 6 + 11 + 13)$ is 34. The size of this magic square array is 4 because it has 4 rows and 4 columns.

Write a Java class `Square` to represent an n-by-n square array of integers. Include methods that set or return the square's size n, read integers into the square, display the square, and decide whether the square is a magic square.

Write a test program that demonstrates each method.

11. Write a Java class `LinearMeasure` that represents a linear measurement in either yards, feet, inches, meters, centimeters, or millimeters. Use an enumeration to represent these units of measure.

Define a constructor that has two parameters. One parameter represents the value of the measurement, and the other is a string that names the unit of measure. The case of the letters in this string should be irrelevant.

Define methods that convert any measurement to any given unit. These methods should change the invoking object and return a reference to it. For example, statements such as

```
LinearMeasure length = new LinearMeasure(8.5, "yards");
System.out.println(length + " = " + length.toMeters());
System.out.println(length + " is in meters.");
System.out.println("Converting " + length.toMeters() +
                    " to meters leaves it unchanged.");
```

should produce the following output:

8.5 yards = 7.7724 METERS
7.7724 METERS is in meters.
Converting 7.7724 METERS to meters leaves it unchanged.

2

Creating Classes from Other Classes

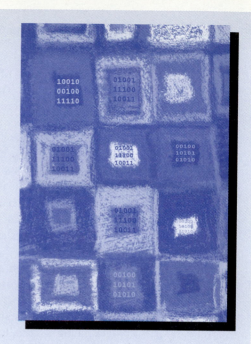

PREREQUISITES

OBJECTIVES

After studying this chapter, you should be able to

- Use an instance of an existing class in the definition of a new class
- Use generic types
- Use inheritance to derive a new class from an existing class
- Override and overload method definitions
- Describe the purpose and methods of the class `Object`
- Describe the purpose of an abstract class
- State which overridden method an object invokes

A major advantage of object-oriented programming is the ability to use existing classes when defining new classes. That is, you use classes that you or someone else has written to create new classes, rather than reinventing everything yourself. We begin this chapter with two ways to accomplish this feat.

In the first way, you simply declare an instance of an existing class as a data field of your new class. In fact, you have done this already if you have ever defined a class that had a string as a data field. Since your class is composed of objects, this technique is called composition.

The second way is to use inheritance, whereby your new class inherits properties and behaviors from an existing class, augmenting or modifying them as desired. This technique is more complicated than composition, so we will devote more time to it. As important as inheritance is in Java, you should not ignore composition as a valid and desirable technique in many situations.

Both composition and inheritance define a relationship between two classes. These relationships are often called, respectively, *has a* and *is a* relationships. You will see why when we discuss them in this chapter.

Polymorphism is another key feature of object-oriented programming. In fact, object-oriented programming is usually described in terms of its main features: encapsulation, inheritance, and polymorphism. Used in conjunction with inheritance, polymorphism enables different objects that call methods having the same name to act appropriately.

Composition

2.1   Chapter 1 introduced you to the class Name to represent a person's name. It defined constructors, accessor methods, and mutator methods that involved the person's first and last names. The data fields in Name are instances of the class String. A class uses **composition** when it has a data field that is an instance of another class. And since the class Name has an instance of the class String as a data field, the relationship between Name and String is called a ***has a*** relationship.

Let's create another class that uses composition. Consider a class of students, each of whom has a name and an identification number. Thus, the class Student contains two objects as data fields: an instance of the class Name and an instance of the class String:

```
private Name    fullName;
private String id;
```

Figure 2-1 shows an object of type Student and its data fields. Notice that the Name object has two String objects as its data fields. It is important to realize that these data fields actually contain references to objects, not the objects themselves.

For methods, we give the class Student constructors, accessors, mutators, and toString. Recall that toString is invoked when you use System.out.println to display an object, so it is a handy method to include in your class definitions.

Note: **Composition (*has a*)**
A class uses composition when it has objects as data fields. The class's implementation has no special access to such objects and must behave as a client would. That is, the class must use an object's methods to manipulate the object's data. Since the class "has a," or contains, an instance (object) of another class, the classes are said to have a *has a* relationship.

Figure 2-1   A Student object is composed of other objects

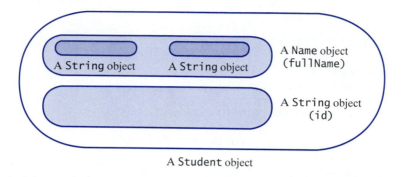

A Student object

2.2   Look at the definition of the class Student in Listing 2-1, and then we will make a few more observations.

Listing 2-1   The class Student

```java
public class Student
{
   private Name    fullName;
   private String id;        // identification number

   public Student()
   {
      fullName = new Name();
      id = "";
   } // end default constructor

   public Student(Name studentName, String studentId)
   {
      fullName = studentName;
      id = studentId;
   } // end constructor

   public void setStudent(Name studentName, String studentId)
   {
      setName(studentName); // or fullName = studentName;
      setId(studentId);     // or id = studentId;
   } // end setStudent

   public void setName(Name studentName)
   {
      fullName = studentName;
   } // end setName

   public Name getName()
   {
      return fullName;
   } // end getName
```

```
    public void setId(String studentId)
    {
        id = studentId;
    } // end setId

    public String getId()
    {
        return id;
    } // end getId

    public String toString()
    {
        return id + " " + fullName.toString();
    } // end toString
} // end Student
```

The method `setStudent` is useful when we create a student object by using the default constructor or if we want to change both the name and identification number that we gave to a student object earlier. Notice that the method invokes the other set methods from this class to initialize the data fields. For example, to set the field `fullName` to the parameter `studentName`, `setStudent` uses the statement

```
    setName(studentName);
```

We could also write this statement as

```
    this.setName(studentName);
```

where `this` refers to the instance of `Student` that invokes the method `setStudent`. Or we could write the assignment statement

```
    fullName = studentName;
```

Implementing methods in terms of other methods is usually desirable. It might not be desirable when implementing constructors, however, as you will see later in this chapter.

Suppose that we want `toString` to return a string composed of the student's identification number and name. It must use methods in the class `Name` to access the name as a string. For example, `toString` could return the desired string by using either

```
    return id + " " + fullName.getFirst() + " " + fullName.getLast();
```

or, more simply,

```
    return id + " " + fullName.toString();
```

The data field `fullName` references a `Name` object whose private fields are not accessible by name in the implementation of the class `StudentName`. We can access them indirectly via the accessor methods `getFirst` and `getLast` or by invoking `Name`'s `toString` method.

Question 1   What data fields would you use in the definition of a class `Address` to represent a student's address?

Question 2   Add a data field to the class `Student` to represent a student's address. What new methods should you define?

Question 3   What existing methods need to be changed in the class Student as a result of the added field that Question 2 described?

Question 4   What is another implementation for the default constructor that uses this, as described in Segment 1.25?

Generic Types

2.3   If the data fields of your class can be objects of any class type, you can use a **generic type** when declaring them. To establish a generic type when you define a class, you follow the class name with an identifier enclosed in angle brackets:

```
public class MyClass<T>
```

The identifier T—which can be any identifier but usually is a single capital letter—represents the data type within the class definition. When you use the class, you supply an actual data type to replace T.

For example, to create an instance of MyClass by invoking its default constructor, you could write a statement such as

```
MyClass<String> item = new MyClass<String>();
```

Now, whenever T appears as a data type in the definition of MyClass, String will be used. A generic type must be a reference type, not a primitive type.

2.4   **Example.** Let's create a class to represent pairs of objects of the same type. The class OrderedPair, given in Listing 2-2 assumes that we care about the order in which the objects appear in the pair, and enables us to change that order.

The notation <T> follows the name of the class in the first line of its definition. Within the definition, T represents the data type of the two private data fields, the two parameters of the method setPair, and the local variable temp within the method changeOrder.

Listing 2-2   The class OrderedPair

```
public class OrderedPair<T>
{
   private T first, second;

   public OrderedPair()
   {
   } // end default constructor

   public void setPair(T firstItem, T secondItem)
   {
      first = firstItem;
      second = secondItem;
   } // end setPair

   public void changeOrder()
   {
      T temp = first;
      first = second;
      second = temp;
   } // end changeOrder
```

```
    public String toString()
    {
        return "(" + first + ", " + second + ")";
    } // end toString
} // end OrderedPair
```

___

2.5   You can use the class `OrderedPair` to create a pair of `String` objects, a pair of `Name` objects, and so on. For example, the statements

```
OrderedPair<String> fruit = new OrderedPair<String>();
fruit.setPair("apples", "oranges");
System.out.println(fruit);
fruit.changeOrder();
System.out.println(fruit);

Name tweedleDee = new Name("Tweedle", "Dee");
Name tweedleDum = new Name("Tweedle", "Dum");
OrderedPair<Name> couple = new OrderedPair<Name>();
couple.setPair(tweedleDee, tweedleDum);
System.out.println(couple);
couple.changeOrder();
System.out.println(couple);
```

produce the following output:

(apples, oranges)
(oranges, apples)
(Tweedle Dee, Tweedle Dum)
(Tweedle Dum, Tweedle Dee)

Question 5   What method must a class such as `String` or `Name` define so that `Ordered-Pair`'s method `toString` works correctly?

2.6   You can define more than one generic type within a class definition by writing their identifiers, separated by commas, within the angle brackets after the class's name. In the previous example, the objects in a pair have the same data type. If you want to use two different data types, you can specify two generic types, as in the class `Pair` shown in Listing 2-3.

Listing 2-3   The class `Pair`

___

```
public class Pair<S, T>
{
    private S first;
    private T second;

    public Pair(S firstItem, T secondItem)
    {
        first = firstItem;
        second = secondItem;
    } // end constructor
```

```
   public String toString()
   {
     return "(" + first + ", " + second + ")";
   } // end toString
} // end Pair
```

You can use this class to pair a name and a telephone number, for example, by writing the following statements:

```
Name joe = new Name("Joe", "Java");
String joePhone = "(401) 555-1234";
Pair<Name, String> joeEntry = new Pair<Name, String>(joe, joePhone);
System.out.println(joeEntry);
```

The output displayed is

(Joe Java, (401) 555-1234)

Question 6   Can you use the class OrderedPair, as defined in Segment 2.4, to pair two objects having different data types? Why or why not?

Question 7   Can you use the class Pair, as defined in the previous segment, to pair two objects having the same data type? Why or why not?

Question 8   Using any of the classes defined previously in this chapter, write statements that pair two students as lab partners.

Question 9   Using any of the classes defined previously in this chapter, write statements that pair a student and the name of the student's dean.

Adapters

2.7   Suppose that you have a class, but the names of its methods do not suit your application. Or maybe you want to simplify some methods or eliminate others. You can use composition to write a new class that has an instance of your existing class as a data field and defines the methods that you want. Such a new class is called an **adapter class**.

For example, suppose that instead of using objects of the class Name to name people, we want to use simple nicknames. We could use strings for nicknames, but like Name, the class String has more methods than we need. The class NickName in Listing 2-4 has an instance of the class Name as a data field, a default constructor, and set and get methods. Arbitrarily, we use the first-name field of the class Name to store the nickname.

Listing 2-4   The class NickName

```
public class NickName
{
  private Name nick;

  public NickName()
  {
    nick = new Name();
  } // end default constructor
```

```
    public void setNickName(String nickName)
    {
       nick.setFirst(nickName);
    } // end setNickName

    public String getNickName()
    {
       return nick.getFirst();
    } // end getNickName
} // end NickName
```

Notice how this class uses the methods of the class Name to implement its methods. A NickName object now has only NickName's methods, and not the methods of Name.

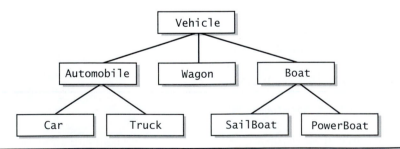

Question 10   Write statements that define bob as an instance of NickName to represent the nickname *Bob*. Then, using bob, write a statement that displays *Bob*.

Inheritance

2.8   **Inheritance** is a major aspect of object-oriented programming that enables you to organize classes. The name comes from the notion of inherited traits like eye color, hair color, and so forth, but it is perhaps clearer to think of inheritance as a classification system. Inheritance allows you to define a general class and then later to define more specialized classes that add to or revise the details of the older, more general class definition. This saves work, because the specialized class inherits all the properties of the general class and you need only program the new or revised features.

For example, you might define a class for vehicles and then define more specific classes for particular types of vehicles, such as automobiles, wagons, and boats. Similarly, the class of automobiles includes the classes of cars and trucks. Figure 2-2 illustrates this hierarchy of classes. The Vehicle class is the **base class** for the **derived classes**, such as Automobile. The Automobile class is the base class for the derived classes Car and Truck. Another term for base class is **superclass**, and another term for derived class is **subclass**.

Figure 2-2   A hierarchy of classes

As you move up in the diagram, the classes are more inclusive. A car is an automobile and therefore is also a vehicle. However, a vehicle is not necessarily a car. A sailboat is a boat and is also a vehicle, but a vehicle is not necessarily a sailboat.

2.9   Java and other programming languages use inheritance to organize classes in this hierarchical way. A programmer can then use an existing class to write a new one that has more features. For example, the class of vehicles has certain properties—like miles traveled—that its data fields record. The class also has certain behaviors—like going forward—that its methods define. The classes `Automobile`, `Wagon`, and `Boat` have these properties and behaviors as well. Everything that is true of all `Vehicle` objects, such as the ability to go forward, is described only once and inherited by the classes `Automobile`, `Wagon`, and `Boat`. The derived classes then add to or revise the properties and behaviors that they inherit. Without inheritance, descriptions of behaviors like going forward would have to be repeated for each of the derived classes `Automobile`, `Wagon`, `Boat`, `Car`, `Truck`, and so on.

Note: **Inheritance**

Inheritance is a way of organizing classes so that common properties and behaviors can be defined only once for all the classes involved. Using inheritance, you can define a general class and then later define more specialized classes that add to or revise the details of the older, more general class definition.

Since the `Automobile` class is derived from the `Vehicle` class, it inherits all the data fields and public methods of that class. The `Automobile` class would have additional fields for such things as the amount of fuel in the fuel tank, and it would also have some added methods. Such fields and methods are not in the `Vehicle` class, because they do not apply to all vehicles. For example, wagons have no fuel tank.

Inheritance gives an instance of a derived class all the behaviors of the base class. For example, an automobile will be able to do everything that a vehicle can do; after all, an automobile *is a* vehicle. In fact, inheritance is known as an *is a* relationship between classes. Since the derived class and the base class share properties, you should use inheritance only when it makes sense to think of an instance of the derived class as also being an instance of the base class.

Note: **An *is a* relationship**

With inheritance, an instance of a derived class is also an instance of the base class. Thus, you should use inheritance only when this *is a* relationship between classes is meaningful.

Question 11   Some vehicles have wheels and some do not. Revise Figure 2-2 to organize vehicles according to whether they have wheels.

2.10   **Example.** Let's construct an example of inheritance within Java. Suppose we are designing a program that maintains records about students, including those in grade school, high school, and college. We can organize the records for the various kinds of students by using a natural hierarchy that begins with students. College students are then one subclass of students. College students divide into two smaller subclasses: undergraduate students and graduate students. These subclasses might further subdivide into still smaller subclasses. Figure 2-3 diagrams this hierarchical arrangement.

A common way to describe derived classes is in terms of family relationships. For example, the class of students is said to be an **ancestor** of the class of undergraduate students. Conversely, the class of undergraduate students is a **descendant** of the class of students.

Although our program may not need any class corresponding to students in general, thinking in terms of such classes can be useful. For example, all students have names, and the methods of

Figure 2-3   A hierarchy of student classes

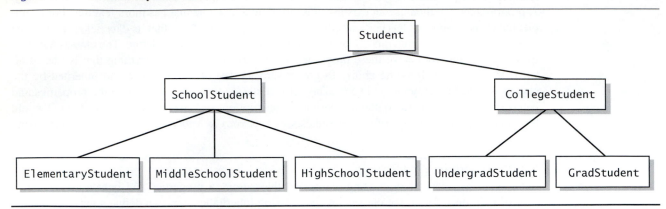

initializing, changing, and displaying a name will be the same for all students. In Java, we can define a class that includes data fields for the properties that belong to all subclasses of students. The class likewise will have methods for the behaviors of all students, including methods that manipulate the class's data fields. In fact, we have already defined such a class—Student—in Segment 2.2.

2.11   Now consider a class for college students. A college student is a student, so we use inheritance to derive the class CollegeStudent from the class Student. Here, Student is the existing base class and CollegeStudent is the new derived class. The derived class inherits—and therefore has—all the data fields and methods of the base class. In addition, the derived class defines whatever data fields and methods we wish to add.

To indicate that CollegeStudent is a derived class of Student, we write the phrase extends Student on the first line of the class definition. Thus, the class definition of CollegeStudent begins

public class CollegeStudent **extends** Student

When we create a derived class, we define only the added data fields and the added methods. For example, the class CollegeStudent has all the data fields and methods of the class Student, but we do not mention them in the definition of CollegeStudent. In particular, every object of the class CollegeStudent has a data field called fullName, but we do not declare the data field fullName in the definition of the class CollegeStudent. The data field is there, however. But because fullName is a private data field of the class Student, we cannot reference fullName directly by name within CollegeStudent. We can, however, access and change this data field by using Student's methods, since the class CollegeStudent inherits all of the public methods in the base class Student.

For example, if cs is an instance of CollegeStudent, we can write

cs.setName(**new** Name("Warren", "Peace"));

even though setName is a method of the base class Student. Since we have used inheritance to construct CollegeStudent from the class Student, every college student *is a* student. That is, a CollegeStudent object "knows" how to perform Student behaviors.

2.12   A derived class, like CollegeStudent, can also add some data fields and/or methods to those it inherits from its base class. For example, CollegeStudent adds the data field year and the methods setYear and getYear. We can set the graduation year of the object cs by writing

cs.setYear(2010);

Suppose that we also add a data field that represents the degree sought and the methods to access and change it. We could also add fields for an address and grades, but to keep it simple, we will not. Let's look at the class as given in Listing 2-5 and focus on the constructors first.

Listing 2-5   The class `CollegeStudent`

```
public class CollegeStudent extends Student
{
  private int    year;    // year of graduation
  private String degree;  // degree sought

  public CollegeStudent()
  {
    super();       // must be first
    year = 0;
    degree = "";
  } // end default constructor

  public CollegeStudent(Name studentName, String studentId,
                        int graduationYear, String degreeSought)
  {
    super(studentName, studentId); // must be first
    year = graduationYear;
    degree = degreeSought;
  } // end constructor

  public void setStudent(Name studentName, String studentId,
                         int graduationYear, String degreeSought)
  {
    setName(studentName); // NOT fullName = studentName;
    setId(studentId);     // NOT id = studentId;
// or setStudent(studentName, studentId); (see Segment 2.21)

    year = graduationYear;
    degree = degreeSought;
  } // end setStudent

  < The methods setYear, getYear, setDegree, and getDegree go here. >
  . . .

  public String toString()
  {
    return super.toString() + ", " + degree + ", " + year;
  } // end toString
} // end CollegeStudent
```

Invoking Constructors from Within Constructors

2.13   **Calling the base class's constructor.** Constructors typically initialize a class's data fields. In a derived class, how can the constructor initialize data fields inherited from the base class? One way is to call the base class's constructor. The derived class's constructor can use the reserved word super as a name for the constructor of the base class, also known as the superclass.

Notice that the default constructor in the class CollegeStudent begins with the statement

```
super();
```

This statement invokes the default constructor of the base class. Our new default constructor must invoke the base class's default constructor to properly initialize the data fields that are inherited from the base class. Actually, if you do not invoke super, Java will do it for you. In this book, we will always invoke super explicitly, to make the action a bit clearer. Note that the call to super must occur first in the constructor. You can use super to invoke a constructor only from within another constructor.

In like fashion, the second constructor invokes a corresponding constructor in the base class by executing the statement

```
super(studentName, studentId);
```

If you omit this statement, Java will invoke the default constructor, which is not what you want.

Programming Tip: **Calling the constructor of the base class**
You can use super within the definition of a constructor of a derived class to call a constructor of the base class explicitly. When you do, super always must be the first action taken in the constructor definition. You cannot use the name of the constructor instead of super. If you omit super, each constructor of a derived class automatically calls the default constructor of the base class. Sometimes this action is what you want, but sometimes it is not.

Note: **Constructors are not inherited**
A constructor of a class C creates an object whose type is C. It wouldn't make sense for this class to have a constructor named anything other than C. But that is what would happen if a class like CollegeStudent inherited Student's constructors: CollegeStudent would have a constructor named Student.

Even though CollegeStudent does not inherit Student's constructors, its constructors do call Student's constructors, as you have just seen.

2.14   **Reprise: Using this to invoke a constructor.** As you saw in Segment 1.25, you use the reserved word this much as we used super here, except that it calls a constructor of the same class instead of a constructor of the base class. For example, consider the following definition of a constructor that we might add to the class CollegeStudent in Segment 2.12:

```
public CollegeStudent(Name studentName, String studentId)
{
  this(studentName, studentId, 0, "");
} // end constructor
```

The one statement in the body of this constructor definition is a call to the constructor whose definition begins

```
public CollegeStudent(Name studentName, String studentId,
                      int graduationYear, String degreeSought)
```

As with `super`, any use of `this` must be the first action in a constructor definition. Thus, a constructor definition cannot contain both a call using `super` and a call using `this`. What if you want both a call with `super` and a call with `this`? In that case, you would use `this` to call a constructor that has `super` as its first action.

Private Fields and Methods of the Base Class

2.15   **Accessing inherited data fields.** The class `CollegeStudent` has a `setStudent` method with four parameters, `studentName`, `studentId`, `graduationYear`, and `degreeSought`. To initialize the inherited data fields `fullName` and `id`, the method invokes the inherited methods `setName` and `setId`:

```
setName(studentName); // NOT fullName = studentName
setId(studentId);     // NOT id = studentId
```

Recall that `fullName` and `id` are private data fields defined in the base class `Student`. Only a method in the class `Student` can access `fullName` and `id` directly by name from within its definition. Although the class `CollegeStudent` inherits these data fields, none of its methods can access them by name. Thus, `setStudent` cannot use an assignment statement such as

```
id = studentId; // ILLEGAL in setStudent
```

to initialize the data field `id`. Instead it must use some public mutator method such as `setId`.

Programming Tip: A data field that is private in a base class is not accessible by name within the definition of a method for any other class, including a derived class. Even so, a derived class inherits the data fields of its base class.

The fact that you cannot access a private data field of a base class from within the definition of a method of a derived class seems wrong to people. To do otherwise, however, would make the access modifier `private` pointless: Anytime you wanted to access a private data field, you could simply create a derived class and access it in a method of that class. Thus, all private data fields would be accessible to anybody who was willing to put in a little extra effort.

2.16   **Private methods of the base class.** A derived class cannot invoke a base class's private methods directly. This should not be a problem, since you should use private methods only as helpers within the class in which they are defined. That is, a class's private methods do not define behaviors. Thus, we say that a derived class does not inherit the private methods of its base class. If you want to use a base class's method in a derived class, you should make the method either protected or public. We discuss protected methods in the next segment.

Suppose that base class B has a public method m that calls a private method p. A class D derived from B inherits the public method m, but not p. Even so, when a client of D invokes m, m calls p. Thus, a private method in a base class still exists and is available for use, but a derived class cannot call it directly by name.

Programming Tip: A derived class does not inherit and cannot invoke by name a private method of the base class.

Protected Access

2.17   You know that you control access to a class's data fields and methods by using an access modifier like `public` or `private`. As you saw in Chapter 1, you can omit the access modifier entirely when the class is within a package and you want the class to be available only to other classes in the package. You also have one other choice for controlling access: You can use the access modifier `protected` for methods and data fields.

A method or data field that is modified by `protected` can be accessed by name only within

- Its own class definition `C`
- Any class derived from `C`
- Any class within the same package as `C`

That is, if a method is marked `protected` in class `C`, you can invoke it from within any method definition in a class derived from class `C`. However, with classes that are not derived from `C` or that are not in the same package as `C`, a protected method behaves as if it were private.

You should continue to declare all data fields as private. If you want a derived class to have access to a data field in the base class, define protected accessor or mutator methods within the base class.

Note that package access is more restricted than protected access and gives more control to the programmer defining the classes. If you control the package directory, you control who is allowed package access.

Figure 2-4 illustrates the various kinds of access modifiers.

Figure 2-4   Public, private, protected, and package access of the data fields and methods of class `C`

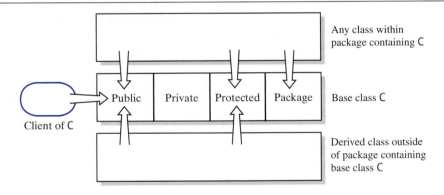

Overriding and Overloading Methods

2.18   The set and get methods of the class `CollegeStudent` are straightforward, so we will not bother to look at them. However, we have provided the class with a method `toString`. Why did we do this, when our new class inherits a `toString` method from its base class `Student`? Clearly, the string that the base class's `toString` method returns can include the student's name and identification number, but it cannot include the year and degree that are associated with the derived class. Thus, we need to write a new method `toString`.

But why not have the new method invoke the inherited method? We can do this, but we'll need to distinguish between the method that we are defining for `CollegeStudent` and the method inherited from `Student`. As you can see from the class definition in Segment 2.12, the new method `toString` contains the statement

```
return super.toString() + ", " + degree + ", " + year;
```

Since `Student` is the superclass, we write

```
super.toString()
```

to indicate that we are invoking the superclass's `toString`. If we omitted `super`, our new version of `toString` would invoke itself. Here we are using `super` as if it were an object. In contrast, we used `super` with parentheses as if it were a method within the constructor definitions.

If you glance back at Segment 2.2, you will see that `Student`'s `toString` method appears as follows:

```
public String toString()
{
   return id + " " + fullName.toString();
} // end toString
```

This method calls the `toString` method defined in the class `Name`, since the object `fullName` is an instance of the class `Name`.

2.19   **Overriding a method.** In the previous segment, you saw that the class `CollegeStudent` defines a method `toString` and also inherits a method `toString` from its base class `Student`. Both of these methods have no parameters. The class, then, has two methods with the same name, the same parameters, and the same return type.

When a derived class defines a method with the same name, the same number and types of parameters, and the same return type as a method in the base class, the definition in the derived class is said to **override** the definition in the base class. Objects of the derived class that invoke the method will use the definition in the derived class. For example, if `cs` is an instance of the class `CollegeStudent`,

```
cs.toString()
```

uses the definition of the method `toString` in the class `CollegeStudent`, not the definition of `toString` in the class `Student`, as Figure 2-5 illustrates. As you've already seen, however, the definition of `toString` in the derived class can invoke the definition of `toString` in the base class by using `super`.

Figure 2-5   The method `toString` in `CollegeStudent` overrides the method `toString` in `Student`

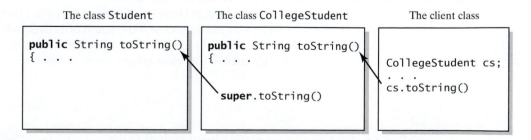

Note: Overriding a method definition

A method in a derived class overrides a method in the base class when both methods have the same name, the same number and types of parameters, and the same return type. Since a method's signature is its name and parameters, a method in a derived class overrides a method in the base class when both methods have the same signature and return type.

Note: Overriding and access

An overriding method in a derived class can have either public, protected, or package access according to the access of the overridden method in the base class, as follows:

Access of the overridden method in the base class	Access of the overriding method in the derived class
public	public
protected	protected or public
package	package, protected, or public

A private method in a base class cannot be overridden by a method in a derived class.

Programming Tip: You can use super in a derived class to call an overridden method of the base class.

Question 12   Question 10 asked you to create an instance of NickName to represent the nickname *Bob*. If that object is named bob, do the following statements produce the same output? Explain.

```
System.out.println(bob.getNickName());
System.out.println(bob);
```

2.20   **Covariant return types (Optional).** A class cannot define two methods that have different return types but the same signatures—that is, the same name and parameters. However, if the two methods are in different classes, and one class is a subclass of the other, this can be possible. In particular, when a method in a derived class overrides a method in the base class, their signatures are the same. But the return type of the method in the derived class can be a subclass of the return type of the method in the base class. Such return types are said to be **covariant**.

For example, Segment 2.12 derived the class CollegeStudent from the class Student defined in Segment 2.2. Now imagine a class School that maintains a collection of Student objects. (Subsequent chapters will give you the tools to actually do this.) The class has a method getStudent that returns a student given his or her ID number. The class might appear as follows:

```
public class School
{
    . . .

    public Student getStudent(String studentId)
```

```
    {
      . . .
    } // end getStudent
} // end School
```

Now, consider a class `College` that has a collection of college students. We can derive `College` from `School` and override the method `getStudent`, as follows:

```
public class College extends School
{
    . . .

    public CollegeStudent getStudent(String studentId)
    {
      . . .
    } // end getStudent
} // end College
```

The method `getStudent` has the same signature as `getStudent` in `School`, but the return types of the two methods differ. In fact, the return types are covariant—and therefore legal—because `CollegeStudent` is a subclass of `Student`.

2.21   **Reprise: Overloading a method.** Segment 1.29 of Chapter 1 discussed overloaded methods within the same class. Such methods have the same name but different signatures. Java is able to distinguish between these methods since their parameters are not identical.

Suppose that a derived class has a method with the same name as a method in its base class, but the methods' parameters differ in number or data type. The derived class would have both methods—the one it defines and the one it inherits from the base class. The method in the derived class overloads the method in the base class.

For example, the base class `Student` and the derived class `CollegeStudent` each have a method named `setStudent`. The methods are not exactly the same, however, as they have a different number of parameters. In `Student`, the method's header is

```
public void setStudent(Name studentName, String studentId)
```

whereas in `CollegeStudent` it is

```
public void setStudent(Name studentName, String studentId,
                       int graduationYear, String degreeSought)
```

An instance of the class `Student` can invoke only `Student`'s version of the method, but an instance of `CollegeStudent` can invoke either method. Again, Java can distinguish between the two methods because they have different parameters.

Within the class `CollegeStudent`, the implementation of `setStudent` can invoke `Student`'s `setStudent` to initialize the fields `fullName` and `id` by including the statement

```
setStudent(studentName, studentId);
```

instead of making calls to the methods `setName` and `setId`, as we did in Segment 2.15. Since the two versions of `setStudent` have different parameter lists, we do not need to preface the call with `super` to distinguish the two methods. However, we are free to do so by writing

```
super.setStudent(studentName, studentId);
```

Note: **Overloading a method definition**
A method in a class overloads another method in either the same class or its base class when both methods have the same name but differ in the number or types of parameters. Thus, overloaded methods have the same name but different signatures.

Although the terms "overloading" and "overriding" are easy to confuse, you should distinguish between the concepts, as they both are important.

2.22   **Multiple use of super.** As we have already noted, within the definition of a method of a derived class, you can call an overridden method of the base class by prefacing the method name with super and a dot. However, if the base class is itself derived from some other superclass, you cannot repeat the use of super to invoke a method from that superclass.

For example, suppose that the class UndergradStudent is derived from the class CollegeStudent, which is derived from the class Student. You might think that you can invoke a method of the class Student within the definition of the class Undergraduate, by using super.super, as in

```
super.super.toString(); // ILLEGAL!
```

As the comment indicates, this repeated use of super is not allowed in Java.

Programming Tip: **super**
Although a method in a derived class can invoke an overridden method defined in the base class by using super, the method cannot invoke an overridden method that is defined in the base class's base class. That is, the construct super.super is illegal.

Question 13   Are the two definitions of the constructors for the class Student (Segment 2.2) an example of overloading or overriding? Why?

Question 14   If you add the method

```
public void setStudent(Name studentName, String studentId)
```

to the class CollegeStudent and let it give some default values to the fields year and degree, are you overloading or overriding setStudent? Why?

2.23   **The final modifier.** Suppose that a constructor calls a public method m. For simplicity, imagine that this method is in the same class C as the constructor, as follows:

```
public class C
{
  . . .
  public C()
  {
    m();
    . . .
  } // end default constructor

  public void m()
  {
```

```
       . . .
    } // end m
       . . .
```

Now imagine that we derive a new class from C and we override the method m. If we invoke the constructor of our new class, it will call the base class's constructor, which will call our overridden version of the method m. This method might use data fields that the constructor has not yet initialized, causing an error. Even if no error occurs, we will, in effect, have altered the behavior of the base class's constructor.

To specify that a method definition cannot be overridden with a new definition in a derived class, you make it a **final method** by adding the final modifier to the method header. For example, you can write

```
public final void m()
{
   . . .
}
```

Note that private methods are automatically final methods, since you cannot override them in a derived class.

 Programming Tip: If a constructor invokes a method in its class, declare that method to be final so that no subclass can override the method and hence change the behavior of the constructor.

Constructors cannot be final. Since a derived class does not inherit, and therefore cannot override, a constructor in the base case, final constructors are unnecessary.

You can declare an entire class as a **final class**, in which case you cannot use it as base class to derive any other class from it. Java's String class is an example of a final class.

 Programming Tip: String cannot be the base class for any other class because it is a final class.

 Programming Tip: When you design a class, consider the classes derived from it, either now or in the future. They might need access to your class's data fields. If your class does not have public accessor or mutator methods, provide protected versions of such methods. Keep the data fields private.

Multiple Inheritance

2.24   Some programming languages allow one class to be derived from two different base classes. That is, you can derive class C from classes A and B. This feature, known as **multiple inheritance**, is not allowed in Java. In Java, a derived class can have only one base class. You can, however, derive class B from class A and then derive class C from class B, since this is not multiple inheritance.

A derived class can implement any number of interfaces—which we describe in Chapter 3—in addition to extending any one base class. This capability gives Java an approximation to multiple inheritance without the complications that arise with multiple base classes.

Type Compatibility and Base Classes

2.25   **Object types of a derived class.** Previously, you saw the class `CollegeStudent`, which was derived from the class `Student`. In the real world, every college student is also a student. This relationship holds in Java as well. Every object of the class `CollegeStudent` is also an object of the class `Student`. Thus, if we have a method that has a formal parameter of type `Student`, the argument in an invocation of this method can be an object of type `CollegeStudent`.

Specifically, suppose that the method in question is in some class and begins as follows:

public void someMethod(Student scholar)

Within the body of `someMethod`, the object `scholar` can invoke public methods that are defined in the class `Student`. For example, the definition of `someMethod` could contain the expression `scholar.getId()`. That is, `scholar` has `Student` behaviors.

Now consider an object `joe` of `CollegeStudent`. Since the class `CollegeStudent` inherits all the public methods of the class `Student`, `joe` can invoke those inherited methods. That is, `joe` can behave like an object of `Student`. (It happens that `joe` can do more, since it is an object of `CollegeStudent`, but that is not relevant right now.) Therefore, `joe` can be the argument of `someMethod`. That is, for some object `o`, we can write

o.someMethod(joe);

No automatic type casting[1] has occurred here. As an object of the class `CollegeStudent`, `joe` is also of type `Student`. The object `joe` need not be, and is not, type-cast to an object of the class `Student`.

We can take this idea further. Suppose that we derive the class `UndergradStudent` from the class `CollegeStudent`. In the real world, every undergraduate is a college student, and every college student is also a student. Once again, this relationship holds for our Java classes. Every object of the class `UndergradStudent` is also an object of the class `CollegeStudent` and so is also an object of the class `Student`. Thus, if we have a method whose formal parameter is of type `Student`, the argument in an invocation of this method can be an object of type `UndergradStudent`. Thus, an object can actually have several types as a result of inheritance.

Note: An object of a derived class has more than one data type. Everything that works for objects of an ancestor class also works for objects of any descendant class.

2.26   Because an object of a derived class also has the types of all of its ancestor classes, you can assign an object of a class to a variable of any ancestor type, but not the other way around. For example, since the class `UndergradStudent` is derived from the class `CollegeStudent`, which is derived from the class `Student`, the following are legal:

```
Student amy = new CollegeStudent();
Student brad = new UndergradStudent();
CollegeStudent jess = new UndergradStudent();
```

However, the following statements are all illegal:

```
CollegeStudent cs = new Student();          // ILLEGAL!
UndergradStudent ug = new Student();         // ILLEGAL!
UndergradStudent ug2 = new CollegeStudent(); // ILLEGAL!
```

---

1. Segment A.21 of Appendix A reviews type casts.

This makes perfectly good sense. For example, a college student is a student, but a student is not necessarily a college student. Some programmers find the phrase "is a" to be useful in deciding what types an object can have and what assignments to variables are legal.

Note: Because an object of a derived class is also an object of the base class, do not use inheritance when an *is a* relationship does not exist between your proposed class and an existing class. Even if you want class C to have some of the methods of class B, use composition if these classes do not have an *is a* relationship.

Question 15   If `HighSchoolStudent` is a derived class of `Student`, can you assign an object of `HighSchoolStudent` to a variable of type `Student`? Why or why not?

Question 16   Can you assign an object of `Student` to a variable of type `HighSchoolStudent`? Why or why not?

The Class `Object`

2.27   As you have already seen, if you have a class A and you derive class B from it, and then you derive class C from B, an object of class C is of type C, type B, and type A. This works for any chain of derived classes no matter how long the chain is.

Java has a class—named `Object`—that is at the beginning of every chain of derived classes. This class is an ancestor of every other class, even those that you define yourself. Every object of every class is of type `Object`, as well as being of the type of its class and also of the types of all the other ancestor classes. If you do not derive your class from some other class, Java acts as if you had derived it from the class `Object`.

Note: Every class is a descendant class of the class `Object`.

The class `Object` contains certain methods, among which are `toString`, `equals`, and `clone`. Every class inherits these methods, either from `Object` directly or from some other ancestor class that ultimately inherited the methods from the class `Object`.

The inherited methods `toString`, `equals`, and `clone`, however, will almost never work correctly in the classes you define. Typically, you need to override the inherited method definitions with new, more appropriate definitions. Thus, whenever you define the method `toString` in a class, for example, you are actually overriding `Object`'s method `toString`.

2.28   **The `toString` method.** The method `toString` takes no arguments and is supposed to return all the data in an object as a `String`. However, you will not automatically get a nice string representation of the data. The inherited version of `toString` returns a value based upon the invoking object's memory address. You need to override the definition of `toString` to cause it to produce an appropriate string for the data in the class being defined. You might want to look again at the `toString` methods in Segments 2.2 and 2.12.

2.29   **The `equals` method.** Consider the following objects of the class `Name` that we defined in Chapter 1:

```
Name joyce1 = new Name("Joyce", "Jones");
```

```
Name joyce2 = new Name("Joyce", "Jones");
Name derek = new Name("Derek", "Dodd");
```

Now `joyce1` and `joyce2` are two distinct objects that contain the same name. Typically, we would consider these objects to be equal, but in fact `joyce1.equals(joyce2)` is false. Since `Name` does not define its own `equals` method, it uses the one it inherits from `Object`. `Object`'s `equals` method compares the addresses of the objects `joyce1` and `joyce2`. Because we have two distinct objects, these addresses are not equal. However, `joyce1.equals(joyce1)` is true, since we are comparing an object with itself. This comparison is an **identity**. Notice that identity and equality are different concepts.

The method `equals` has the following definition in the class `Object`:

```
public boolean equals(Object other)
{
  return (this == other);
} // end equals
```

Thus, the expression `x.equals(y)` is `true` if `x` and `y` reference the same object. We must override `equals` in the class `Name` if we want it to behave more appropriately.

As you will recall, `Name` has two data fields, `first` and `last`, that are instances of `String`. We could decide that two `Name` objects are equal if they have equal first names and equal last names. The following method, when added to the class `Name`, detects whether two `Name` objects are equal by comparing their data fields:

```
public boolean equals(Object other)
{
  boolean result;

  if ((other == null) || (getClass() != other.getClass()))
    result = false;
  else
  {
    Name otherName = (Name)other;
    result = first.equals(otherName.first) &&
             last.equals(otherName.last);
  } // end if

  return result;
} // end equals
```

To ensure that the argument passed to the method `equals` is an object of the same class as the object that invokes the method, you can use the method `getClass`. This method is in the class `Object` and returns an object of type `Class`. So if

```
getClass() != other.getClass()
```

is true, we are comparing two objects of different classes. Thus, `equals` should return false. The method also returns false if `other` is `null`.

Otherwise, the method compares the data fields of the two objects. Notice that we first must cast the type of the parameter `other` from `Object` to `Name` so that we can access `Name`'s data fields. To compare two strings, we use `String`'s `equals` method. The class `String` defines its own version of `equals` that overrides the `equals` method inherited from `Object`.

Note: **Short-circuit evaluation**
The method `equals` just given contains the expression

```
(other == null) || (getClass() != other.getClass())
```

When two boolean expressions are joined by either `||` or `&&`, the second expression is not evaluated if the value of the first expression implies the value of the entire expression. Here, the operator is `||`, so if the first expression is true, the entire expression is true. Thus, Java ignores the second expression in this case. So, if `other` is `null`, `other.getClass()` does not execute. If it did execute, a `NullPointerException` would occur. Therefore, writing `other == null` as the first operand of `||` is essential. Segment A.44 of Appendix A provides another example of short-circuit evaluation.

Question 17 If `sue` and `susan` are two instances of the class `Name`, what `if` statement can decide whether they represent the same name?

Question 18   Consider the class `OrderedPair`, as given in Segment 2.4. Suppose that we did not use generic types, but instead omitted `<T>` and declared the data types of the private fields, method parameters, and local variable to be `Object` instead of `T`. What would the effect of these changes be on the use of the class?

2.30   **The `clone` method.** Another method inherited from the class `Object` is the method `clone`. This method takes no arguments and returns a copy of the calling object. The returned object is supposed to have data identical to that of the calling object, but it is a different object (an identical twin or a "clone"). As with other methods inherited from the class `Object`, we need to override the method `clone` before it can behave properly in our class. However, in the case of the method `clone`, there are other things we must do as well. A discussion of the method `clone` appears in Chapter 15.

Abstract Classes and Methods

2.31   The class `Student` defined in Segment 2.2 is a base class for other classes such as `CollegeStudent`. We really do not need to create objects of type `Student`, although it is certainly legal to do so. We might, however, want to prevent a client from creating objects of type `Student`. To do so, we can declare the class to be an **abstract class** by including the reserved word `abstract` in the header of the class definition, as follows:

```
public abstract class Student
{
    . . .
```

Note: An abstract class will be the base class of another class. Thus, an abstract class is sometimes called an **abstract base class**.

Often when programmers define an abstract class, they declare one or more methods that have no body. The intention in doing so is to require that every derived class implement such methods in an appropriate way for that class. For example, we might want every derived class of `Student` to implement a method `display`. We certainly cannot write such a method for a future class that is not yet defined, but we can require one. To do so, we declare `display` as an **abstract method** by including the reserved word `abstract` in the header of the method, as follows:

```
public abstract void display();
```

Note that the method header is followed by a semicolon; the method has no body.

Note: An abstract method declaration within an abstract class consists of the method's header followed by a semicolon. The header must include the reserved word `abstract`. An abstract method cannot be private, static, or final.

2.32   If a class has at least one abstract method, Java requires that you declare the class itself as abstract. This makes sense, for otherwise you could create an object of an incomplete class. In our example, the object would have a method `display` without an implementation.

What if the derived class of an abstract class does not implement all of the abstract methods? Java will treat the derived class as abstract and prevent you from creating an object of its type. For example, if the class `CollegeStudent`, which is derived from `Student`, did not implement `display`, `CollegeStudent` would have to be abstract.

Programming Tip: A class with at least one abstract method must be declared as an abstract class. Thus, abstract methods can appear only within an abstract class.

Even after we've made the class `Student` abstract by adding the abstract method `display`, not all of its methods are abstract. All the method definitions, except for the method `display`, are exactly the same as in our original definition. They are full definitions that do not use the reserved word `abstract`. When it makes sense to implement a method in an abstract class, you should do so. In this way, you include as much detail as possible in the abstract class, detail that need not be repeated in derived classes.

Note: Constructors cannot be abstract
Since a class cannot override a constructor in its base class, if the constructor were abstract, it could not be implemented. Thus, constructors are never abstract.

2.33   **Example.** Let's add another method to the class `Student`, one that invokes the abstract method `display`. Before you complain about invoking a method that has no body, remember that `Student` is an abstract class. When we finally derive a class from `Student` that is not abstract, `display` will be implemented.

The method we have in mind serves mainly as an example, rather than doing anything useful. It simply skips the specified number of lines before displaying an object:

```
/** Task: Displays the object after skipping
 *        numberOfLines lines. */
public void displayAt(int numberOfLines)
{
   for (int count = 0; count < numberOfLines; count++)
      System.out.println();
```

```
        display();
    } // end displayAt
```

The method `displayAt` invokes the abstract method `display`. Here the abstract method serves as a placeholder for a method that will be defined in a future derived class. If `display` were not abstract, we would have to give it a body that really would be useless, since every derived class would override it.

Question 19   Suppose that you change the name of the previous method `displayAt` to `display`. Does the resulting method overload or override the method `display`? Why?

Polymorphism

2.34   The term "polymorphism" comes from a Greek word meaning "many forms." Polymorphism as a concept is actually common in English. For example, the English instruction "Play your favorite sport" means different things to different people. To one person it means to play baseball. To another person it means to play soccer. In Java, **polymorphism** allows the same program instruction to mean different things in different contexts. In particular, one method name, used as an instruction, can cause different actions depending on the kind of object performing the action.

Originally, overloading a method name was considered polymorphism. However, the modern usage of the term refers to an object determining at execution time which action of a method it will use for a method name that is overridden either directly or indirectly.

Note: Polymorphism
One method name in an instruction can cause different actions according to the kinds of objects that invoke the method.

2.35   **Example.** For example, a method named `display` can display the data in an object. But the data it displays and how much it displays depend on the kind of object invoking the method. Let's add the method `display` to the class `Student` of Segment 2.2 and assume that neither the method nor the class is abstract. Thus, `display` has an implementation within the class `Student`. Now add to the class the method `displayAt` as it appears in Segment 2.33.

If the only class around were `Student`, these changes would not be exciting. But we derived the class `UndergradStudent` from the class `CollegeStudent`, which we derived from the class `Student`. The class `UndergradStudent` inherits the method `displayAt` from the class `Student`. In addition, `UndergradStudent` overrides the method `display` defined in `Student` by providing its own implementation. So what? you might be wondering.

Well, look at the poor compiler's job when it encounters the following Java statements (we are ignoring the constructor's arguments):

```
UndergradStudent ug = new UndergradStudent(. . .);
ug.displayAt(2);
```

The method `displayAt` was defined in the class `Student`, but it calls the method `display` that is defined in the class `UndergradStudent`, as Figure 2-6 illustrates. The code for `displayAt` could have been compiled with the class `Student` *before* the class `UndergradStudent` was even written.

In other words, this compiled code could use a definition of the method `display` that was not even written at the time that `displayAt` was compiled. How can that be?

When the code for `displayAt` is compiled, the call to `display` produces an annotation that says, "use the appropriate definition of `display`." Then, when we invoke `ug.displayAt(2)`, the compiled code for `displayAt` reaches this annotation and replaces it with an invocation of the version of `display` that goes with ug. Because in this case ug is of type `UndergradStudent`, the version of `display` that is used will be the definition in the class `UndergradStudent`.

Figure 2-6   The method `displayAt` calls the correct version of `display`

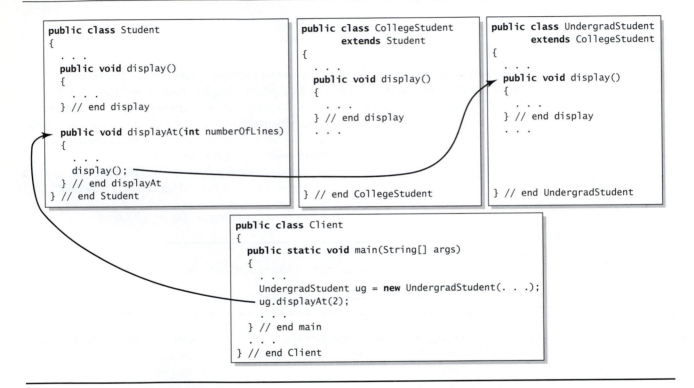

2.36   The decision as to which method definition to use depends on the invoking object's place in the inheritance chain, not on the type of the variable naming the object. For example, consider the following code:

```
UndergradStudent ug = new UndergradStudent(. . .);
Student s = ug;
s.displayAt(2);
```

As we noted in Segment 2.26, assigning an object of the class `UndergradStudent` to a variable of type `Student` is perfectly legal. Here, the variable s is just another name for the object that ug references, as Figure 2-7 illustrates. That is, s and ug are aliases. But the object still remembers that it was created as an `UndergradStudent`. In this case, `s.displayAt(2)` ultimately will use the definition of `display` given in `UndergradStudent`, not the definition of `display` given in `Student`.

A variable's **static type** is the type that appears in its declaration. For example, the static type of the variable s is `Student`. The static type is fixed and determined when the code is compiled. The type of object that a variable references at a point in time during execution is called its **dynamic type**. A variable's dynamic type can change as execution progresses. When the assignment s = ug executes in the previous code, the dynamic type of s is UndergradStudent. A variable of a reference type is called a **polymorphic variable**, since its dynamic type can differ from its static type and change during execution.

For our example, Java decides which definition of display to use by seeing which constructor created the object. That is, Java uses the dynamic type of the variable s to make this determination.

Figure 2-7   The variable s is another name for an undergraduate object

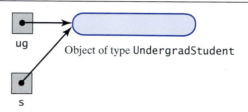

ug

Object of type UndergradStudent

s

Note: Java uses an object's type, not its name, to see which method to invoke.

This way of handling a call to a method that might be overridden later is called **dynamic binding** or **late binding**, because the *meaning* of the method invocation is not bound to the *location* of the method invocation until you run the program. If Java did not use dynamic binding when you ran the preceding code, you would not see the data for an undergraduate student. Instead you would see only what the method display of the class Student provided.

Note: **Dynamic binding**
Dynamic binding is the process that enables different objects to use different method actions for the same method name.

2.37   Java is so good at figuring out which definition of a method to use that even a type cast will not fool it. Recall that you use a type cast to change the type of a value to some other type. The meaning of s.displayAt(2) in the previous segment will always be appropriate for an UndergradStudent, even if we use a type cast to change the type of ug to the type Student, as in the following statements:

```
UndergradStudent ug = new UndergradStudent(. . .);
Student s = (Student) ug;
s.displayAt(2);
```

Despite the type cast, s.displayAt(2) will use the definition of display given in UndergradStudent, not the definition of display given in Student. An object's type, not its name, is the determining factor in choosing the correct method to invoke.

To see that dynamic binding really is a big deal, consider the following code:

```
UndergradStudent ug = new UndergradStudent(. . .);
```

```
Student s = ug;
s.displayAt(2);
GradStudent g = new GradStudent(. . .);
s = g;
s.displayAt(2);
```

The two lines shown in color are identical, yet each one invokes a different version of display. The first line displays an UndergradStudent and the second displays a GradStudent, as Figure 2-8 illustrates. An object remembers what method definitions it had when the new operator created it. You can place the object in a variable of a different (but ancestor) class type, but that has no effect on which method definition the object uses for an overridden method.

Let's pursue this process a bit more to see that it is even more dramatic than it may appear at first glance. Note that objects of the classes UndergradStudent and GradStudent inherit the method displayAt from the class Student and do not override it. Thus, the text of the method definition is even the same for objects of the classes UndergradStudent and GradStudent. It is the method display, invoked in the definition of displayAt, that is overridden.

Note: Objects know how they are supposed to act
When an object calls either an overridden method or a method that calls an overridden method, the action of that method is the one defined in the class whose constructor created the object. The choice of action is not affected by the static type of the variable naming the object. A variable of any ancestor class can reference an object of a descendant class, but the object always remembers which method actions to use for every method name, because Java uses dynamic binding.

Figure 2-8   An object, not its name, determines its behavior

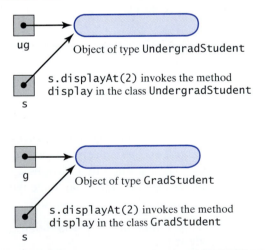

2.38   **Type checking and dynamic binding.** You need to be aware of how dynamic binding interacts with Java's type checking. For example, if UndergradStudent is a derived class of the class Student, we can assign an object of type UndergradStudent to a variable of type Student, as in

```
Student s = new UndergradStudent();
```

But that is not the end of the story.

Although we can assign an object of type UndergradStudent to a variable s of type Student, s cannot invoke a method that is only in the class UndergradStudent. However, if the method is overridden in the definition of the class UndergradStudent, the version of the method defined in UndergradStudent will be used. In other words, the variable determines what method names can be used, but the object determines which definition of the method name will be used. If we want to use a method name that was first introduced in the class UndergradStudent with the object named by the variable s of type Student, we must use a type cast.

2.39   **Example.** For example, recall that Student is not abstract and implements the method display. Also remember that UndergradStudent is a derived class of Student. The following statements are legal:

```
Student s = new UndergradStudent(. . .);
s.setName(new Name("Jamie", "Jones"));
s.display();
```

The definition of display given in the class UndergradStudent is used. *Remember, the object, not the variable, determines which definition of a method will be used.*

On the other hand, the following is illegal:

```
s.setDegree("B.A."); // ILLEGAL
```

because setDegree is not the name of a method in the class Student. *Remember, the variable determines which method names can be used.*

The variable s is of type Student, but it references an object of type UndergradStudent. That object can still invoke the method setDegree, but the compiler does not know this. To make the invocation legal, we need a type cast, such as the following:

```
UndergradStudent ug = (UndergradStudent)s;
ug.setDegree("B.A."); // LEGAL
```

You may think this is all just a silly exercise, because you would never assign an object of type UndergradStudent to a variable of type Student. Not so. You might not often make such an assignment directly, but you frequently will do so unwittingly. Recall that we can have an argument of type UndergradStudent for a method parameter of type Student and that a formal parameter behaves like a local variable that is assigned the value of its corresponding argument. In this case an object of type UndergradStudent (the argument in the method invocation) is assigned to a variable of type Student (the formal parameter in the method definition).

2.40   **Example.** Since each of the classes Student and Name has an appropriate version of the method toString, we can display an object of this class as follows:

```
Name joe = new Name("Joe", "Student");
Student s = new Student(joe, "5555");
System.out.println(s.toString());
```

But thanks to dynamic binding, we do not even need to write toString in our invocation of System.out.println. The method invocation System.out.println(s) will work just as well and will produce exactly the same output. Let's see why.

The object System.out invokes the method println. One definition of the method println has a single parameter of type Object. The definition is equivalent to the following:

```
public void println(Object theObject)
{
  System.out.println(theObject.toString());
} // end println
```

The method `println` invoked inside the braces is a different, overloaded definition of the method `println` that has a parameter of type `String`, not `Object`.

These definitions of `println` existed before the class `Student` was defined. Yet the invocation

```
System.out.println(s);
```

with an object `s` of type `Student`—and hence also of type `Object`—uses `Student`'s `toString`, not `Object`'s `toString`. Dynamic binding is what makes this work.

Question 20 Is a method `display` with no parameters that is defined explicitly in each of the classes `Student`, `CollegeStudent`, and `UndergradStudent` an example of overloading or overriding? Why?

Question 21 Is overloading a method name an example of polymorphism?

Question 22 In the following code, will the two invocations of `displayAt` produce the same output?

```
Student s = new UndergradStudent(. . .);
s.displayAt(2);
s = new GradStudent(. . .);
s.displayAt(2);
```

CHAPTER SUMMARY

- When you use composition to define a class, you use objects of one or more existing classes as data fields. The new class's implementation must behave like any other client of the existing classes. That is, the class must use an object's methods to manipulate the object's data.

- Composition defines a *has a* relationship between two classes.

- You can use one or more generic types within a class definition to represent the actual data types that are specified when someone creates objects of the class.

- Inheritance groups classes that have properties and behaviors in common. The common properties and behaviors are defined only once for all the classes. Thus, you can define a general class—the base class—and later define more-specialized classes—the derived classes—simply by adding to or revising the details of the older, more general class definition.

- Use inheritance only when you have an *is a* relationship between two classes.

- A method in a derived class overrides a method in the base class when both methods have the same name, the same return type, and the same number and types of parameters. That is, the methods have the same signatures and return types.

- A method in a class overloads a method in either the same class or its base class when both methods have the same name but differ in the number or types of parameters. That is, the methods have the same name but different signatures.

- All actions of objects of an ancestor class can be performed by objects of any descendant class.

- A protected method can be accessed by name within its own class, a derived class, or a class within its class's package. Other classes cannot invoke it; the protected method behaves as if it were private.

- Every class is a descendant of the class `Object`.

- An abstract class has no instances and serves only as a base class. Any class that omits the definition of one or more of its methods must be declared abstract.

- A constructor cannot be abstract, final, or static.

- Polymorphism is the concept whereby an object determines at execution time which action of a method it will use for an overridden method name. Dynamic binding is the process that implements polymorphism.

- When an object invokes an overridden method (or a method that calls an overridden method), the action of that method is the one defined in the class whose constructor created the object. This action is not determined by the static type of the variable naming the object. A variable of any ancestor class can reference an object of a descendant class, but the object always remembers which method actions to use for every method name, because Java uses dynamic binding.

- The variable that names an object determines which method names an object can invoke. The object, not its name, determines which definition of a method it will use.

PROGRAMMING TIPS

- You can use **super** within the definition of a constructor of a derived class to call a constructor of the base class explicitly. When you do, **super** must always be the first action taken in the constructor definition. You cannot use the name of the constructor instead of **super**. If you omit **super**, each constructor of a derived class automatically calls the default constructor of the base class.

- A data field or method that is private in a base class is not accessible by name in the definition of a method for any other class, including a derived class.

- You can use **super** in a derived class to call an overridden method of the base class.

- A method in a derived class cannot invoke an overridden method that is defined in the base class's base class. That is, the construct **super.super** is illegal.

- If a constructor invokes a method in its class, declare that method to be final so that no subclass can override the method and hence change the behavior of the constructor.

- **String** cannot be the base class for any other class because it is a final class.

- When you design a class, consider the classes derived from it, either now or in the future. They might need access to your class's data fields. If your class does not have public accessor or mutator methods, provide protected versions of such methods.

- A class with at least one abstract method must be declared an abstract class.

EXERCISES

1. Given the class `Student` defined in Segment 2.2, write Java statements that create a `Student` object for Jill Jones. Do this in two ways, using a different constructor each time. Jill's ID number is 8001.

2. If joe is an object of the class Student, as defined in Segment 2.2, is it legal to write joe.getFirst() to get joe's first name? Why or why not?

3. Consider the class Student defined in Segment 2.2.

    a. Add a constructor that has three String parameters representing the student's first name, last name, and identification number.

    b. Add a method getFirst that returns a student's first name.

4. Consider the class NickName as defined in Segment 2.7. Why is composition a more appropriate way to reuse the class Name than inheritance?

5. Suppose that we have the class Pair defined as follows:

```java
public class Pair<S, T>
{
  private S myFirst;
  private T mySecond;

  public Pair(S first, T second)
  {
    myFirst = first;
    mySecond = second;
  } // end constructor

  public S getFirst()
  {
    return myFirst;
  } // end getFirst

  public T getSecond()
  {
    return mySecond;
  } // end getSecond

  public void setFirst(S first)
  {
    myFirst = first;
  } // end setFirst

  public void setSecond(T second)
  {
    mySecond = second;
  } // end setSecond

  public String toString()
  {
    return "(" + myFirst + ", " + mySecond + ")";
  } // end toString
} // end Pair
```

Now suppose that we have an application that will create a pair. The first item in the pair will always be an Integer object. It will be set when the item is created and then never changed. The second item in the pair can change. Write an adapter class for this situation.

6. Show how the class `Name` could be created as an adapter class using `Pair`, as defined in the previous exercise.

7. Revise the hierarchy in Figure 2-2 to include categories of land, sea, air, and space vehicles.

8. Consider the class `CollegeStudent` as defined in Segment 2.12. The method `toString` contains the invocation `super.toString()`. What string does this invocation return?

9. The class `CollegeStudent` has the method `setStudent`. Does this method overload or override the `setStudent` method in the class `Student`? Explain.

10. The class `CollegeStudent` has no definitions for methods that set or get the student's name. Why?

11. Can you omit the call to `super` in the default constructor of the class `CollegeStudent`? Can you omit it in the second constructor? Give reasons for your answers.

12. Suppose that `joe` is an object of the class `CollegeStudent`. Write Java statements that display joe's name. Repeat this in two other distinct ways.

13. You could revise the constructor in the class `Student` as follows:

```
public Student(Name studentName, String studentId)
{
   setStudent(studentName, studentId);
} // end constructor
```

The derived class `CollegeStudent` could override `setStudent`, thereby affecting this constructor. How can you prevent any derived class of `Student` from overriding `setStudent`?

14. Given the class `Student` and its derived class `CollegeStudent`, which of the following statements are legal and which are not?

a. `Student bob = new Student();`
b. `Student bob = new CollegeStudent();`
c. `CollegeStudent bob = new Student();`
d. `CollegeStudent bob = new CollegeStudent();`

15. Assuming that you have added an `equals` method to the class `Name`, as described in Segment 2.29, write an `equals` method for the class `Student` and one for the class `CollegeStudent`.

16. An abstract class has the implementation of some methods but not others. A method without an implementation—that is, without a body—is abstract.

a. What is the purpose of an abstract method?
b. What is the purpose of an abstract class?

17. Consider the following Java statements:

```
jillJones = new Name("Jill", "Jones");
joeCool = new Name("Joseph", "Cool");
Student jill = new Student(jillJones, "2222");
```

```
CollegeStudent joe = new CollegeStudent(joeCool, "33", 2012,
                                         "B.S.");
```

a. Can joe be the argument of a method whose parameter's type is Student? Why or why not?

b. Can jill be the argument of a method whose parameter's type is CollegeStudent? Why or why not?

c. Is jill.getYear() legal? Why or why not?

d. Is joe.getId() legal? Why or why not?

18. Suppose that the class Student is defined as in Segment 2.2, and we derive the class CollegeStudent from it. Let's add to Student the method displayAt, as it appears in Segment 2.33. The method displayAt calls display, which we also implement in both Student and CollegeStudent. Assume that jill and joe are defined as in Exercise 17, and that none of the classes or methods are abstract. Which version of the method display will displayAt invoke when each of the following statements executes?

a. jill.displayAt(2);

b. joe.displayAt(2);

c. Student s = joe;
s.displayAt(2);

d. Student s = (Student)joe;
s.displayAt(2);

19. Consider the following Java statements:

```
public static Student s1 = new GraduateStudent(...);

public static void main(String args[])
{
   Student ug = new UndergradutateStudent(...);
   GraduateStudent grad = new GraduateStudent(...);
   winner(ug);
}

public static void winner(Student pupil)
{
   System.out.println("And the winner is ");
   pupil.displayAt(1);
}
```

a. What are the static and dynamic types for each variable when the code is executed?

b. If we change the call winner(ug) to winner(s1), what are the resulting static and dynamic types for pupil?

20. Consider the following Java statements

```
Student s1 = new GraduateStudent(...);
GraduateStudent s2 = new GraduateStudent(...);
```

a. Which methods can s1 call?

b. Which methods can s2 call?

21. Imagine two classes, A and B.

Class A has a private data field theData and the following methods:

```
public void w();
public void x();
protected void y();
private void z();
```

Class B extends class A and has the following methods:

```
public void x();
protected void r();
private void s();
```

Suppose that the client declares instances of these classes as follows:

```
A inA = new A();
B inB = new B();
```

a. Which of the objects inA and inB can the client use to directly access the field theData?

b. Which of these objects can the client use to invoke the method w?

c. Which of these objects can the client use to invoke the method y?

d. Which of these objects can the client use to invoke the method r?

e. Which of these objects can the client use to invoke the method z?

f. Which method definitions can invoke the method y?

g. Which method definitions can invoke the method r?

h. Which method definitions can invoke the method z?

i. Which version of the method x does inB.x() invoke?

j. Which methods are available to the implementation of the class B?

k. Which methods are available to clients of B?

PROJECTS

1. Implement the class Die, as described in Project 5 of Chapter 1. Then implement a class TwoDice that represents two six-sided dice. You should be able to roll the dice and find the sum of their face values. You should also be able to detect various special cases, such as a pair of ones (snake eyes) or a pair of sixes (boxcars).

2. Design and implement a class to play a game that uses dice. Use the class TwoDice that Project 1 describes.

   You can use the following simple game or choose one of your own. Players take turns in rolling the dice. For each player, maintain a cumulative sum of the face values of the rolled dice. Double the value of any matching pair of dice. The first player to reach a certain number, such as 50 or 100, wins.

3. Define the class Address to represent a person's mailing address. Include data fields for at least the street address, city, and state. Provide reasonable constructors and set and get methods. Next add an Address field to the class Student, as defined in Segment 2.2. Add methods to Student that access or modify the address. Revise any existing methods of Student to accommodate this new field.

4. Define the class `Transcript` to record a student's grades for a semester. Begin by creating other classes such as `Course` and `Grade`. A `Course` object could contain the title, number of credits, and grade for a course. A `Grade` object could contain a letter grade and the quality points that the grade represents. The class `Transcript` then contains an instance of `Course` for each course taken by a student in one semester.

   Now add an instance of `Transcript` as a data field of the class `Student`. Add appropriate methods to `Student` that deal with the transcript.

5. Textile designers often use computers to create new patterns. Design and implement a class `SquarePattern` that represents a pattern for a fabric square of a given dimension. Methods in the class should enable you to create objects that have different patterns. Use this class in another class `Fabric` that represents a piece of fabric whose pattern is composed of various squares. Your classes should be able to display the patterns on the screen.

6. Define a class `PlayingCard` that represents a playing card with a given rank and suit. Use the enumeration `Rank` from Project 3 of Chapter 1 along with the enumeration `Suit` from Segment 1.30 of Chapter 1. Override the methods `toString` and `equals` so that they behave correctly for the new class. The class should have just one constructor that has two parameters (one each for rank and suit). Since the playing card should not change once it has been created, do not provide any mutator methods. Define other accessor methods as needed.

   Write a program that creates different playing cards and adequately demonstrates the methods of `PlayingCard`.

7. The class `Name` given in Segment 1.16 of Chapter 1 represents a person's first and last names. Derive the class `ProperName` from `Name`, adding data fields for a middle initial and a title such as Ms., Mrs., Mr., or Dr. Provide reasonable constructors and set and get methods for the new fields. Override the `toString` method so that it behaves correctly for the new class.

   Explain why inheritance is appropriate in the definition of `ProperName` but is not a reasonable choice for the definition of the class `NickName` that Segment 2.7 describes.

8. Project 1 of Chapter 1 describes the class `Counter` that records a nonnegative integer count. Given this class, define a class `GraphicCounter` by using either composition or inheritance. You should be able to display a `GraphicCounter` object on the screen, as Figure 2-9 illustrates. Provide the class with reasonable methods.

   Use the class to create an application or applet that behaves like a timer. You set the timer to an initial value in seconds and, at a signal, it counts down to zero. You should see the timer's value change as it counts.

Figure 2-9   A graphic counter for Project 8

9. Project 4 of Chapter 1 asked you to define a class GenericCoin. Each GenericCoin object can be tossed so that it randomly lands either heads up or tails up. Derive a class Coin from GenericCoin that adds a monetary value and a name as data fields. Provide your class with appropriate methods.

Write a program that tests your class and shows that your new coins inherit the behaviors of a GenericCoin object. In particular, your new coins can be tossed.

Now write a program that creates ten of each kind of coin (for example, ten pennies, ten nickels, and so on).Toss each coin once and form two groups, one for heads and one for tails. Compute the monetary value of the coins in each group.

10. Design and implement the classes Student, CollegeStudent, UndergradStudent, and GradStudent according to the hierarchy shown in Figure 2-3. Although you can use aspects of these classes that you saw in this chapter, make the classes Student and CollegeStudent abstract classes.

The classes UndergradStudent and GradStudent should each ensure that the degree field of CollegeStudent is set to a legal value. For example, you could restrict an undergraduate student to B.A. and B.S. degree programs and a graduate student to M.S. and Ph.D. programs. Consider using an enumeration for this aspect.

11. Project 1 of Chapter 1 describes the class Counter that records a nonnegative integer count. Given this class, define a class RolloverCounter using inheritance. The new class will need private data fields for a minimum and maximum value. When the count reaches the maximum value, an increase will roll the counter over to the minimum value. Similarly, when the counter is at the minimum value, a decrease will roll the counter over to the maximum value.

Provide two constructors for the class RolloverCounter. The first constructor has two parameters and sets the minimum and maximum values to the values of its arguments. The second constructor has one parameter, which it uses to set the maximum value, and sets the minimum to zero.

In addition to the methods that Counter has, the RolloverCounter should have a method that returns true if the last increase or decrease resulted in a rollover. If RolloverCounter overrides any methods of Counter, consider calling the original Counter method.

Write a program that adequately demonstrates the methods of the class RolloverCounter.

3

Designing Classes

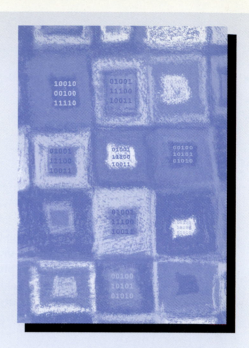

CONTENTS

PREREQUISITES

OBJECTIVES

After studying this chapter, you should be able to

- Describe encapsulation, information hiding, and data abstraction

- Write specifications for methods that include preconditions and postconditions
- Write a Java interface for a class
- Choose appropriate classes and methods during the design of a program, including classes that might be written already

Object-oriented programming embodies three design concepts: encapsulation, inheritance, and polymorphism. We have already discussed inheritance and polymorphism. Now, building on our earlier discussion of classes, this chapter introduces encapsulation as a way to hide the details of an implementation during the design of a class. It then goes on to emphasize the importance of specifying how a method should behave before you implement it and of expressing your specifications as comments in your program.

We introduce Java interfaces as a way to separate the declarations of a class's behavior from its implementation. Finally, we present, at an elementary level, some techniques for identifying the classes necessary for a particular solution.

Encapsulation

3.1   What is the most useful description of an automobile, if you want to learn to drive one? It clearly is not a description of how its engine goes through a cycle of taking in air and gasoline, igniting the gasoline/air mixture, and expelling exhaust. Such details are unnecessary when you want to learn to drive. In fact, such details can get in your way. If you want to learn to drive an automobile, the most useful description of an automobile has such features as the following:

- If you press your foot on the accelerator pedal, the automobile will move faster.
- If you press your foot on the brake pedal, the automobile will slow down and eventually stop.
- If you turn the steering wheel to the right, the automobile will turn to the right.
- If you turn the steering wheel to the left, the automobile will turn to the left.

Just as you need not tell somebody who wants to drive a car how the engine works, you need not tell somebody who uses a piece of software all the fine details of its Java implementation. Likewise, suppose that you create a software component for another programmer to use in a program. You should describe the component in a way that tells the other programmer how to use it but that spares the programmer all the details of how you wrote the software.

3.2   **Encapsulation** is one of the design principles of object-oriented programming. The word "encapsulation" sounds as though it means putting things into a capsule, and that image is indeed correct. Encapsulation hides the fine detail of what is inside the "capsule." For this reason, encapsulation is often called **information hiding**. But not everything should be hidden. In an automobile, certain things are visible—like the pedals and steering wheel—and others are hidden under the hood. In other words, the automobile is encapsulated so that the details are hidden, and only the controls needed to drive the automobile are visible, as Figure 3-1 shows. Similarly, you should encapsulate your Java code so that details are hidden and only the necessary controls are visible.

Encapsulation encloses data and methods within a class and hides the implementation details that are not necessary for using the class. If a class is well designed, its use does not require an understanding of its implementation. A programmer can use the class's methods without knowing the details of how they are coded. The programmer must know only how to provide a method with appropriate arguments, leaving the method to perform the right action. Stated simply, the programmer need not worry about the internal details of the class definition. The programmer who uses encapsulated software to write more software has a simpler task. As a result, software is produced more quickly and with fewer errors.

Note: **Encapsulation** is a design principle of object-oriented programming that encloses data and methods within a class, thereby hiding the details of a class's implementation. A programmer receives only enough information to be able to use the class. A well-designed class can be used as though the body of every method was hidden from view.

Figure 3-1   An automobile's controls are visible to the driver, but its inner workings are hidden

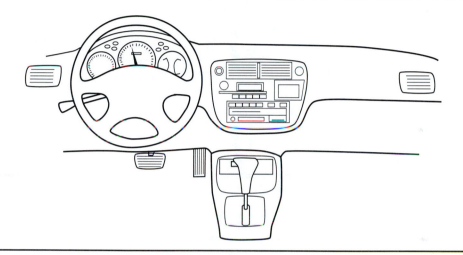

3.3   **Abstraction** is a process that asks you to focus on *what* instead of *how*. When you design a class, you practice **data abstraction**. You focus on what you want to do with or to the data without worrying about how you will accomplish these tasks and how you will represent the data. Abstraction asks you to focus on what data and operations are important. When you abstract something, you identify the central ideas. For example, an abstract of a book is a brief description of the book, as opposed to the entire book.

When designing a class, you should not think about any method's implementation. That is, you should not worry about *how* the class's methods will accomplish their goals. This separation of specification from implementation allows you to concentrate on fewer details, thereby making your task easier and less error-prone. Detailed, well-planned specifications facilitate an implementation that is more likely to be successful.

Note: The process of **abstraction** asks you to focus on *what* instead of *how*.

3.4   When done correctly, encapsulation divides a class definition into two parts, which we will call the **client interface** and the **implementation**. The client interface describes everything a programmer needs to know to use the class. It consists of the headers for the public methods of the class, the comments that tell a programmer how to use these public methods, and any publicly defined constants of the class. The client interface part of the class definition should be all you need to know to use the class in your program.

The implementation consists of all data fields and the definitions of all methods, including those that are public, private, and protected. Although you need the implementation to run a client (a program that uses the class), you should not need to know anything about the implementation to write the client. Figure 3-2 illustrates an encapsulated implementation of a class and the client interface. Although the implementation is hidden from the client, the interface is visible and provides a well-regulated means for the client to communicate with the implementation.

Figure 3-2   An interface provides well-regulated communication between a hidden implementation and a client

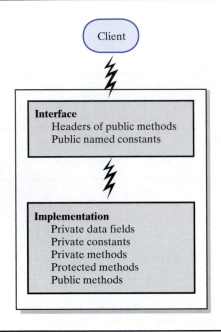

The client interface and implementation are not separated in the definition of a Java class. They are mixed together. You can, however, create a separate **Java interface** as a companion to your class. A Java interface contains the headers for a class's public methods and can define public named constants. A later section of this chapter describes how to write and use a Java interface. We will write a number of Java interfaces in the rest of the book.

Question 1   How does a client interface differ from a class implementation?

Question 2   Think of an example, other than an automobile, that illustrates encapsulation. What part of your example corresponds to a client interface and what part to an implementation?

Specifying Methods

3.5   Separating the purpose of a class and its methods from their implementations is vital to a successful software project. You should specify what each class and method does without concern for its implementation. Writing descriptions enables you to capture your ideas initially and to develop them so that they are clear enough to implement. Your written descriptions should reach the point where they are useful as comments in your program. You need to go beyond a view that sees comments as something you add after you write the program to satisfy an instructor or boss.

Let's focus on comments that you write for a class's methods. Although organizations tend to have their own style for comments, the developers of Java have specified a commenting style that you should follow. If you include comments written in this style in your program, you can run a utility program called `javadoc` to produce documents that describe your classes. This documentation tells people what they need to know to use your class but omits all the implementation details, including the bodies of all method definitions.

The program `javadoc` extracts the header for your class, the headers for all public methods, and comments that are written in a certain form. Each such comment must appear immediately before a public class definition or the header of a public method and must begin with `/**` and end with `*/`. Certain **tags** that begin with the symbol @ appear within the comments to identify various aspects of the method. For example, you use `@param` to identify a parameter, `@return` to identify a return value, and `@throws` to indicate an exception that the method throws. You will see some examples of these tags within the comments in this chapter. Appendix D provides the details for writing comments acceptable to `javadoc`.

Rather than talk further about the rules for `javadoc` here, we want to discuss some important aspects of specifying a method. First, you need to write a concise statement of the method's purpose or task. Beginning this statement with a verb will help you to avoid many extra words that you really do not need.

In thinking about a method's purpose, you should consider its input parameters, if any, and describe them. You also need to describe the method's results. Does it return a value, does it cause some action, or does it affect the state of an argument? In writing such descriptions, you should keep in mind the following ideas.

3.6   A **precondition** is a statement of the conditions that must be true before a method begins execution. The method should not be used, and cannot be expected to perform correctly, unless the precondition is satisfied. A precondition can be related to the description of a method's parameters. For example, a method that computes the square root of x can have $x \geq 0$ as a precondition.

A **postcondition** is a statement of what is true after a method completes its execution, assuming that the precondition was met. For a valued method, the postcondition will describe the value returned by the method. For a void method, the postcondition will describe actions taken and any changes to the calling object. In general, the postcondition describes all the effects produced by a method invocation.

Thinking in terms of a postcondition can help you to clarify a method's purpose. Notice that going from precondition to postcondition leaves out the *how*—that is, we separate the method's specification from its implementation.

 Programming Tip: A method that cannot satisfy its postcondition, even though its precondition is met, can throw an exception. (See Appendix B for a discussion of exceptions.)

3.7   **Responsibility.** A precondition implies responsibility for guaranteeing that certain conditions are met. If the client is responsible for meeting the conditions before calling the method, the method need not check the conditions. On the other hand, if the method is responsible for enforcing the conditions, the client does not check them. A clear statement of who must check a given set of conditions increases the probability that someone will do so and avoids duplication of effort.

For example, you could specify the square root method that we mentioned in the previous segment by writing the following comments before its header:

```
/** Task: Computes the square root of a number.
 *   @param x   a real number >= 0
```

```
 *  @return the square root of x
 */
```

In this case, the method assumes that the client will provide a nonnegative number as an argument.

On the other hand, the method could assume responsibility for checking the argument. In that case, its comments could read as follows:

```
/** Task: Computes the square root of a number.
 *  @param x  a real number
 *  @return the square root of x if x >= 0
 *  @throws ArithmeticException if x < 0
 */
```

Although we've integrated the precondition and postcondition into the previous comments, we could instead identify them separately, as we did for the task.

Programming Tip: Specify each public method fully in comments placed before the method's header. State whether a method or its client is responsible for ensuring that the necessary conditions are met for the successful execution of the method. In this way, checking is done but not duplicated. During debugging, however, a method should check that its precondition has been met.

3.8   When you use inheritance and polymorphism to override a method in a base class, the method in the derived class could be inconsistent with the method in the base class. Preconditions and post-conditions will help you to avoid this problem. A postcondition must apply to all versions of a method throughout the subclasses. An overriding method can add to a postcondition—that is, it can do more—but it should not do less. However, an overriding method cannot augment its precondition. In other words, it cannot require more than a version of the method in a base class requires.

Question 3   Assume that the class Square has a data field side and the method setSide to set the value of side. What header and comments can you write for this method? Keep in mind a precondition and postcondition as you do this.

Assertions

3.9   An **assertion** is a statement of truth about some aspect of your program's logic. You can think of it as a boolean expression that is true, or that at least should be true, at a certain point. Preconditions and postconditions, for example, are assertions made about conditions at the beginning and end of a method. If one of these assertions is false, something is wrong with your program.

You can state assertions as comments within your code. For example, if at some point in a method's definition, you know that the variable sum should be positive, you could write the following comment:

```
// Assertion: sum > 0
```

Such comments point out aspects of the logic that might not be clear. Additionally, they provide places for you to check the accuracy of your code during debugging.

Question 4   Suppose that you have an array of positive integers. The following statements find the largest integer in the array. What assertion can you write as a comment after the if statement in the following loop?

```
int max = 0;
for (int index = 0; index < array.length; index++)
```

```
  {
    if (array[index] > max)
      max = array[index];
    // Assertion:
  } // end for
```

3.10   **The `assert` statement.** Java enables you to do more than simply write a comment to make an assertion. You can enforce the assertion by using an `assert` statement, such as

> **`assert`** `sum > 0;`

If the boolean expression that follows the reserved word `assert` is true, the statement does nothing. If it is false, an **assertion error** occurs and program execution terminates. An error message such as the following is displayed:

> Exception in thread "main" java.lang.AssertionError

You can clarify this error message by adding a second expression to the `assert` statement. The second expression must represent a value, since its representation as a string is displayed within the error message. For example, the statement

> **`assert`** `sum > 0 : sum;`

adds the value of `sum` to the error message in case `sum` ≤ 0. For example, the error message might be

> Exception in thread "main" java.lang.AssertionError: –5

By default, `assert` statements are disabled at execution time. Thus, you can leave `assert` statements in your program after you have finished it without wasting execution time. When you run a program, you must enable the `assert` statements if you want them to execute. Exactly how you enable them depends on your programming environment.[1]

Note: Assertions within a program identify aspects of your logic that must be true. In Java, you can use an `assert` statement to make an assertion. It has the following form:

> **`assert`** *boolean_expression* : *valued_expression*;

The value of the optional second expression appears in the error message that occurs if the first expression is false.

Programming Tip: Using the `assert` statement is a simple but effective way to find errors in your program's logic. After serving this purpose, assertions left in your program document its logic for those who want to revise or expand its capability. Remember, Java ignores `assert` statements unless the user of your program specifies otherwise.

Programming Tip: Use an `assert` statement to enforce that a method's precondition has been met.

---

1. If you use the J2SE Development Kit (JDK) from Sun Microsystems, the command `java -ea MyProgram` executes `MyProgram` with assertions enabled. Further details about enabling assertions when using the JDK are available at `java.sun.com/j2se/1.5/docs/guide/language/assert.html`.

> **Programming Tip:** An `assert` statement is not a substitute for an `if` statement. You should use `assert` statements as a programming aid, not as part of a program's logic.

Java Interfaces

3.11   Earlier in this chapter, we spoke in general terms about the client interface, which tells you all you need to know to use a particular class in your program. Although a Java class intermixes its interface with its implementation, you can write a separate interface.

A **Java interface** is a program component that declares a number of public methods. An interface should include comments that specify the methods, in order to provide a programmer with the necessary information to implement them. Some interfaces describe all the public methods in a class, while others specify only certain methods. An interface also can define public named constants.

When you write a class that defines the methods declared in an interface, we say that the class **implements** the interface. A class that implements an interface must define a body for every method that the interface specifies. The interface, however, might not declare every method defined in the class.

You can write your own interfaces, and you can use those that are in the Java Class Library. When you write a Java interface, you place it in its own file. That is, the interface and the class that implements it are in two separate files.

Writing an Interface

3.12   A Java interface begins like a class definition, except that you use the word `interface` instead of `class`. That is, an interface begins with the statement

public interface *interface-name*

rather than

public class *class-name*

The interface can contain any number of public method headers, each followed by a semicolon. An interface does not declare the constructors for a class. Note that methods within an interface are public by default, so you can omit `public` from their headers. The interface can also define any number of public named constants.

3.13   **Example.** Imagine objects such as circles, squares, or plots of land that have both a perimeter and an area. Suppose that we want the classes of these objects to have get methods that return these quantities. If various programmers implemented these classes, they likely would not name or specify these get methods in the same way. To ensure that these classes define our methods in a uniform way, we write the following interface:

```
/** An interface for methods that return
 *  the perimeter and area of an object.
 */
public interface Measurable
{
   /** Task: Gets the perimeter.
    *  @return the perimeter */
   public double getPerimeter();
```

```
    /** Task: Gets the area.
     *  @return the area */
    public double getArea();
} // end Measurable
```

This interface provides a programmer with a handy summary of the methods' specifications. The programmer should be able to use these methods without looking at the class that implements them.

You store an interface definition in a file with the same name as the interface, followed by .java. For example, the previous interface is in the file Measurable.java.

Note: A Java interface is a good place to provide comments that specify each method's purpose, parameters, precondition, and postcondition. In this way, you can specify a class in one file and implement it in another.

Note: An interface can declare data fields, but they must be public. By convention, a class's data fields are private, so any data fields in an interface should represent named constants. Thus, they should be public, final, and static.

Note: Methods declared within an interface cannot be final. However, such methods can be declared as final within a class that implements the interface.

3.14   **Example.** Recall the class Name that we presented in Segment 1.16 of Chapter 1. The following statements define a Java interface for this class. We have included comments for only the first two methods, to save space:

```
/** An interface for a class of names. */
public interface NameInterface
{
  /** Task: Sets the first and last names.
   *  @param firstName  a string that is the desired first name
   *  @param lastName   a string that is the desired last name */
  public void setName(String firstName, String lastName);

  /** Task: Gets the full name.
   *  @return a string containing the first and last names */
  public String getName();

  public void setFirst(String firstName);
  public String getFirst();

  public void setLast(String lastName);
  public String getLast();

  public void giveLastNameTo(NameInterface aName);

  public String toString();
} // end NameInterface
```

This interface provides specifications of the desired methods for an entire class. You could use it when implementing a class such as `Name`. Additionally, you should be able to write a client for the class just by looking at the interface.

Notice that the parameter of the method `giveLastNameTo` has `NameInterface` as its data type instead of `Name`, as it did in Chapter 1. We will talk about interfaces as data types beginning with Segment 3.17. For now, simply be aware that an interface should not restrict the name of the class or classes that might implement it.

Programming Tip: **Naming an interface**

Interface names, particularly those that are standard in Java, often end in "able," such as `Measurable`. That ending does not always provide a good name, so endings such as "er" or "Interface" are also used. Just as Java's exception names end in "Exception," we will usually end our interface names with "Interface."

Implementing an Interface

3.15   Any class that implements an interface must state this at the beginning of its definition by using an `implements` clause. For example, if a class `C` implemented the interface `Measurable`, it would begin as follows:

```
public class C implements Measurable
```

The class then must provide a definition for each method declared in the interface. In this example, the class `C` must implement at least the methods `getPerimeter` and `getArea`.

If we wrote a class `Name` that implemented `NameInterface`, as given in the previous segment, the class would begin as follows:

```
public class Name implements NameInterface
```

The rest of the class could look just like the one defined in Chapter 1, except that the method `giveLastNameTo` would have a parameter whose data type was `NameInterface` instead of `Name`, to match its declaration in the interface.

Figure 3-3 illustrates the three files that contain `NameInterface`, `Name`, and their client.

Figure 3-3   The files for an interface, a class that implements the interface, and the client

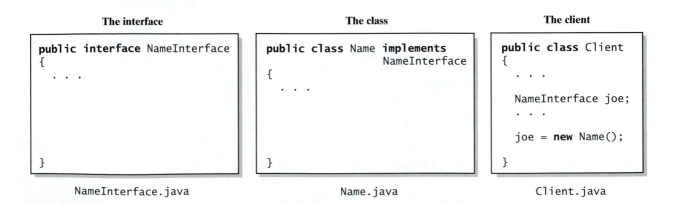

Note: Writing an interface is a way for a class designer to specify methods for another programmer. Implementing an interface is a way for a programmer to guarantee that a class has defined certain methods.

Note: Several classes can implement the same interface, perhaps in different ways. For example, many classes can implement the interface `Measurable` and provide their own version of the methods `getPerimeter` and `getArea`.

3.16 **Multiple interfaces.** A class can implement more than one interface. If it does, you simply list all the interface names, separated by commas. If the class is derived from another class, the `implements` clause always follows the `extends` clause. Thus, you could write

public class C **extends** B **implements** Measurable, AnotherInterface

To remember this order, note that the reserved words `extends` and `implements` appear alphabetically in the heading of the class.

A class that implements several interfaces must define each method declared in the interfaces. If the same method header appears in more than one interface that a class implements, the class defines only one corresponding method.

As Segment 2.24 mentioned, you cannot derive a class from more than one base class. This restriction avoids the possibility of inheriting conflicting implementations. But a Java interface contains method specifications, not implementations. A class can implement these specifications regardless of whether they appear in one interface or are spread among several interfaces. By allowing a class to implement any number of interfaces, Java approximates multiple base classes without the complications they cause.

Question 5   Write a Java interface for the class `Student` given in Segment 2.2 of Chapter 2.

Question 6   What revision(s) should you make to the class `Student` so that it implements the interface you wrote for the previous question?

An Interface as a Data Type

3.17 You can use a Java interface as you would a data type when you declare a variable, a data field, or a method's parameter. For example, the method `giveLastNameTo` in Segment 3.14 has a parameter whose type is `NameInterface`:

public void giveLastNameTo(NameInterface aName);

Any argument that you pass to this method must be an object of a class that implements `NameInterface`.

Why didn't we declare aName's type to be `Name`, as we did in Chapter 1? We want the interface to be independent of any class that implements it, since more than one class can implement an interface. By using `NameInterface` as the parameter's type, you ensure that the method's argument will be able to invoke all of the methods declared in `NameInterface`. In general, you can be sure that a method's parameter can invoke particular methods, namely those declared in an interface, if its data type is the interface. Additionally, the parameter can invoke only those methods.

What if a class C does not begin with the phrase `implements NameInterface`, yet still implements the methods in the interface? You could not pass an instance of C to `giveLastNameTo`.

> **Note:** By using an interface as a variable's type, you indicate that the variable can invoke a certain set of methods and only those methods.

3.18   A variable declaration such as

        `NameInterface myName;`

makes `myName` a reference variable. Now `myName` can reference any object of any class that implements `NameInterface`. So if you have

        `myName = new Name("Coco", "Puffs");`

then `myName.getFirst()` returns a reference to the string `"Coco"`. If the class `AnotherName` also implements `NameInterface`, and you later write

        `myName = new AnotherName("April", "MacIntosh");`

then `myName.getFirst()` returns a reference to the string `"April"`.

Chapter 2 introduced polymorphic variables when discussing inheritance. In that discussion, you saw that you could write

        `A item = new B();`

if the class `B` is derived from the class `A`. The variable `item` is polymorphic, since its dynamic type can differ from its static type. Here you see that the variable `myName` also is polymorphic. Thus, polymorphic variables can occur as a result of using either inheritance or interfaces.

Question 7   What revision(s) should you make to both the interface you wrote for Question 5 and the class `Student` that implements it to make use of `NameInterface`?

Generic Types Within an Interface

3.19   Segment 2.4 of Chapter 2 introduced a class to represent pairs of objects of the same type. Since each pair can be of any class type, we used a generic type in the definition of the class. In particular, the method `setPair` has parameters of a generic type.

Imagine an interface `Pairable` that declares this method. We use a notation for the generic type that is analogous to the notation we used for a class, as follows:

```
public interface Pairable<S>
{
   public void setPair(S firstItem, S secondItem);
} // end Pairable
```

A class that implements this interface could begin with the statement

```
public class OrderedPair<T> implements Pairable<T>
```

The rest of the class could be as given in Segment 2.4. In this example, the data type that we pass to the interface in the `implements` clause is the generic type `T` declared for the class. In general, one could pass the name of an actual class to the interface that appears in an `implements` clause. You will see an example of this situation in Segment 3.22.

Note that the definition of the interface `Pairable` could have used `T` instead of `S` for its generic type, even though we use `T` for the same purpose when defining the class that implements the interface.

The Interface Comparable

3.20   Recall from Appendix A the method `compareTo` for the class `String`. This method returns an integer as a result of comparing two strings. If `s` and `t` are strings, `s.compareTo(t)` is

- Negative if `s` comes before `t`
- Zero if `s` and `t` are equal
- Positive if `s` comes after `t`

Other classes can have their own `compareTo` method that behaves in an analogous way. All such classes implement the interface `Comparable`, which is in the Java Class Library in the package `java.lang`.

Note: The method `compareTo` compares two objects and returns a signed integer that indicates the result of the comparison. For example, if `x` and `y` are two instances of the same class that implements the interface `Comparable`, `x.compareTo(y)` returns

- A negative integer if `x` is less than `y`
- Zero if `x` equals `y`
- A positive integer if `x` is greater than `y`

If `x` and `y` have different types, `x.compareTo(y)` throws the exception `ClassCastException`.

Note: Enumerations have a `compareTo` method. The order in which the enumerated objects appear in the enumeration determines the result of a comparison. For example, if we have

```
enum Coin {PENNY, NICKEL, DIME, QUARTER}
```

and `myCoin` is an instance of `Coin`, `myCoin.compareTo(Coin.DIME)` decides whether `myCoin` is before, after, or equal to `Coin.DIME`. In particular, if `myCoin` has the value `Coin.PENNY`, the result of the comparison with `Coin.DIME` is a negative integer.

3.21   The interface `Comparable` is shown in Listing 3-1. The `T` in this interface designates a generic type. Here, `T` represents the class that implements this interface. Thus, an object of the class `T`, by invoking `compareTo`, is compared to an object of the class `T`.

Listing 3-1   The interface `java.lang.Comparable`

```
package java.lang;
public interface Comparable<T>
{
    public int compareTo(T other);
} // end Comparable
```

3.22   Let's create the class `Circle`, giving it the methods `equals`, `compareTo`, and the methods in the interface `Measurable`. The class implements two interfaces, so we begin it as follows:

```
public class Circle implements Comparable<Circle>, Measurable
{
   private double radius;

   < Definitions of constructors and methods are here >
   . . .
```

The name of the class appears in brackets after the interface name `Comparable`. Thus, `Circle` corresponds to `T` in the interface and is therefore the data type of `compareTo`'s parameter.

The method `compareTo` has the following implementation within the class:

```
public int compareTo(Circle other)
{
   int result;
   if (this.equals(other))
      result = 0;
   else if (radius < other.radius)
      result = -1;
   else
      result = 1;

   return result;
} // compareTo
```

This version of `compareTo` assumes that `Circle` has its own `equals` method. While `compareTo` need not invoke `equals`, these two methods usually should return consistent results. That is, if `object1.equals(object2)` is true, `object1.compareTo(object2)` should return zero.

3.23 Although the previous version of `compareTo` returns either –1 or +1 for unequal objects, the specification of `compareTo` does not insist on these values. Only the sign of the result must be correct. Thus, when the comparison involves integers, a simple subtraction often produces a suitable return value. For example, if the data field `radius` in the class `Circle` were an integer instead of a real value, `compareTo` could have had the following simple definition:

```
// assumes radius is an integer
public int compareTo(Circle other)
{
   return radius - other.radius;
} // compareTo
```

3.24 You might wonder why `compareTo` does not belong to the class `Object`. The reason is that not all classes should have a `compareTo` method. Classes of objects without a natural ordering are possible and not at all unusual. For example, consider a class of mailing addresses. Deciding whether two addresses are equal should be simple, but what does it mean for one address to be less than another?

Note: Not all classes should implement the interface `Comparable`.

Question 8 Implement the method `equals` for the previously described class `Circle`. Use the `equals` method given in Segment 2.29 for the class `Name` as a guide.

Question 9 Revise the class `Name` given in Segment 1.16 of Chapter 1 so that it implements the interface `Comparable`.

Extending an Interface

3.25   Once you have an interface, you can derive another interface from it by using inheritance. In fact, you can derive an interface from several interfaces, even though you cannot derive a class from several classes.

When an interface extends another interface, it has all the methods of the inherited interface. Thus, you can create an interface that consists of the methods in an existing interface plus some new methods. For example, consider classes of pets and the following interface:

```java
public interface Nameable
{
   public void setName(String petName);
   public String getName();
} // end Nameable
```

We can extend Nameable to create the interface Callable:

```java
public interface Callable extends Nameable
{
   public void come(String petName);
} // end Callable
```

A class that implements Callable must implement the methods come, setName, and getName.

3.26   You also can combine several interfaces into a new interface and add even more methods if you like. For example, suppose that in addition to the previous two interfaces, we define the following interfaces:

```java
public interface Capable
{
   public void hear();
   public void respond();
} // end Capable

public interface Trainable extends Callable, Capable
{
   public void sit();
   public void speak();
   public void lieDown();
} // end Trainable
```

A class that implements Trainable must implement the methods setName, getName, come, hear, and respond, as well as the methods sit, speak, and lieDown.

Note: A Java interface can be derived from several interfaces, even though you cannot derive a class from several classes.

Question 10   Imagine a class Pet that contains the method setName, yet does not implement the interface Nameable of Segment 3.25. Could you pass an instance of Pet as the argument of the method with the following header?

```java
public void enterShow(Nameable petName)
```

Interfaces Versus Abstract Classes

3.27   The purpose of an interface is similar to that of an abstract base class. However, an interface is not a base class. In fact, it is not a class of any kind. When should you use an interface and when should you use an abstract class? Use an abstract base class if you want to provide a method definition or declare a private data field that your classes will have in common. Otherwise, use an interface. Remember that a class can implement several interfaces but can extend only one abstract class.

   Let's look at two examples. One uses an interface and the other an abstract class.

3.28   **Example: An interface.** Imagine classes for various geometric forms like circles, spheres, and cylinders. Each of these forms has a radius. We could define the following interface that our classes would implement:

```java
public interface Circular
{
   public void setRadius(double newRadius);
   public double getRadius();
} // end Circular
```

This interface recognizes that a radius will exist, and so declares both set and get methods for it. However, it cannot declare a field for the radius. The class that implements the interface will do that.

   A class `Circle` that implements this interface could appear as follows:

```java
public class Circle implements Circular
{
   private double radius;

   public void setRadius(double newRadius)
   {
      radius = newRadius;
   } // end setRadius

   public double getRadius()
   {
      return radius;
   } // end getRadius

   public double getArea()
   {
      return Math.PI * radius * radius;
   } // end getArea
} // end Circle
```

The class defines a private data field `radius`, and implements the methods `setRadius` and `getRadius` that the interface `Circular` declares. An interface cannot contain a data field like `radius`, since it is private.

3.29   **Example: An abstract class.** Instead of using an interface in the implementation of a class like `Circle`, let's define an abstract class:

```java
public abstract class CircularBase
{
   private double radius;

   public void setRadius(double newRadius)
   {
```

```
    radius = newRadius;
  } // end setRadius

  public double getRadius()
  {
    return radius;
  } // end getRadius

  public abstract double getArea();
} // end CircularBase
```

This class declares the data field `radius` that descendant classes will inherit. Since the data field `radius` is private, the class `CircularBase` must implement set and get methods so that its descendant classes can access it. If `CircularBase` simply declared `setRadius` and `getRadius` as abstract—omitting their implementations—a descendant class would be unable to implement them because it would be unable to access `radius`.

If the definition of `CircularBase` stopped here, it would not need to be abstract, but it still would be a useful base class. However, this class also declares the abstract method `getArea`, which its descendant classes must implement in their own way.

The following class is derived from the base class `CircularBase`. It implements the abstract method `getArea`, invoking the inherited method `getRadius` to access the inherited data field `radius`. `Circle` cannot reference the data field `radius` by name.

```
  public class Circle extends CircularBase
  {
    public double getArea()
    {
      double radius = getRadius();
      return Math.PI * radius * radius;
    } // end getArea
  } // end Circle
```

In this method, `radius` is simply a local variable.

 Programming Tip: If you want to define a method or declare a private data field that your classes will have in common, use an abstract base class. Otherwise, use an interface.

Named Constants

An interface can contain named constants, that is, public data fields that you initialize and declare as final. If you want to implement several classes that share a common set of named constants, you can define the constants in an interface that the classes implement. You also could define your constants in a separate class instead of an interface. We will look at both ways in this section. Whichever way you choose, you have only one set of constants to keep current.

Imagine several classes that must convert measurements to the metric system. We can define conversion factors as constants that these classes can share. Let's place the constants in an interface.

3.30   **An interface of constants.** The following interface defines three named constants:

```
  public interface ConstantsInterface
  {
    public static final double INCHES_PER_CENTIMETER = 0.39370079;
    public static final double FEET_PER_METER = 3.2808399;
```

```
   public static final double MILES_PER_KILOMETER = 0.62137119;
} // end ConstantsInterface
```

Any interface can define constants in addition to declaring methods, but this interface contains only constants.

To use these constants in a class, you write an `implements` clause in the class definition. The constants then will be available by name throughout the class. For example, consider the following simple class:

```
public class Demo implements ConstantsInterface
{
   public static void main(String[] args)
   {
      System.out.println(FEET_PER_METER);
      System.out.println(ConstantsInterface.MILES_PER_KILOMETER);
   } // end main
} // end Demo
```

Qualifying the constants with the name of the interface is optional. However, if the same named constant is defined in more than one interface that a class implements, the class must qualify the constant with the name of the interface.

3.31   **A class of constants.** Instead of defining constants in an interface, you can define them in a class just for that purpose:

```
public class Constants
{
   private Constants()
   {
   } // end private default constructor

   public static final double INCHES_PER_CENTIMETER = 0.39370079;
   public static final double FEET_PER_METER = 3.2808399;
   public static final double MILES_PER_KILOMETER = 0.62137119;
} // end Constants
```

Notice the private constructor. Since we provide a constructor, Java will not. And since our constructor is private, a client cannot create instances of the class.

Using this class is simple, as the following example shows:

```
public class Demo
{
   public static void main(String[] args)
   {
      System.out.println(Constants.FEET_PER_METER);
      System.out.println(Constants.MILES_PER_KILOMETER);
   } // end main
} // end Demo
```

Since the constants are static, you must precede their names with the name of the class and a period. This can be an advantage, as readers of your program will see immediately the source of the constant. If doing so becomes an annoyance, you can always define a local copy of the constant, such as

```
final double FEET_PER_METER = Constants.FEET_PER_METER;
```

and use it instead.

3.32   **Should you define constants in an interface or in a class?** Programmers seem to disagree about the answer to this question. Even the Java Class Library contains examples of both techniques. Generally, constant definitions are an implementation detail that should appear within a class. Interfaces declare methods and so are in the realm of specification, not implementation. Reserving interfaces solely for methods is a reasonable guideline.

Choosing Classes

We have talked about specifying classes and implementing classes, but up to now, we have described the class to specify or implement. If you must design an application from scratch, how will you choose the classes you need? In this section, we introduce you to some techniques that software designers use in choosing and designing classes. Although we will mention these techniques in subsequent chapters from time to time, our intent is simply to expose you to these ideas. Future courses will cover ways to select and design classes in more depth.

3.33   Imagine that we are designing a registration system for your school. Where should we begin? A useful way to start would be to look at the system from a functional point of view, as follows:

- **Who or what will use the system?** A human user or a software component that interacts with the system is called an **actor**. So a first step is to list the possible actors. For a registration system, two of the actors could be a student and the registrar.
- **What can each actor do with the system?** A **scenario** is a description of the interaction between an actor and the system. For example, a student can add a course. This basic scenario has variations that give rise to other scenarios. For instance, what happens when the student attempts to add a course that is closed? Our second step, therefore, is to identify scenarios. One way to do this is to complete the question that begins "What happens when...".
- **Which scenarios involve common goals?** For example, the two scenarios we just described are related to the common goal of adding a course. A collection of such related scenarios is called a **use case**. Our third step, then, is to identify the use cases.

You can get an overall picture of the use cases involved in a system you are designing by drawing a **use case diagram**. Figure 3-4 is a use case diagram for our simple registration system.

Figure 3-4   A use case diagram for a registration system

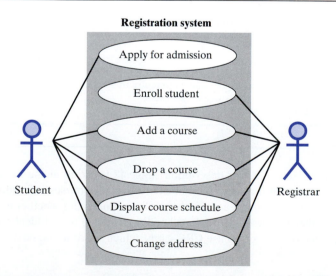

Each actor—the student and the registrar—appears as a stick figure. The box represents the registration system, and the ovals within the box are the use cases. A line joins an actor and a use case if an interaction exists between the two.

Some use cases in this example involve one actor, and some involve both. For example, only the student applies for admission, and only the registrar enrolls a student. However, both the student and the registrar can add a course to a student's schedule.

Note: Use cases depict a system from the actors' points of view. They do not necessarily suggest classes within the system.

Identifying Classes

3.34   Although drawing a use case diagram is a step in the right direction, it does not identify the classes that are needed for your system. Several techniques are possible, and you will probably need to use more than one.

One simple technique is to describe the system and then identify the nouns and verbs in the description. The nouns can suggest classes, and the verbs can suggest appropriate methods within the classes. Given the imprecision of natural language, this technique is not foolproof, but it can be useful.

For example, we could write a sequence of steps to describe each use case in Figure 3-4. Figure 3-5 gives a description of the use case for adding a course from the point of view of a student. Notice the alternative actions taken in Steps 2a and 4a when the system does not recognize the student or when a requested course is closed.

Figure 3-5   A description of a use case for adding a course

```
System:    Registration
Use case:  Add a course
Actor:     Student
Steps:
    1. Student enters identifying data.
    2. System confirms eligibility to register.
       a. If ineligible to register, ask student to enter identification data again.
    3. Student chooses a particular section of a course from a list of course offerings.
    4. System confirms availability of the course.
       a. If course is closed, allow student to return to Step 3 or quit.
    5. System adds course to student's schedule.
    6. System displays student's revised schedule of courses.
```

What classes does this description suggest? Looking at the nouns, we could decide to have classes to represent a student, a course, a list of all courses offered, and a student's schedule of courses. The verbs suggest actions that include confirming whether a student is eligible to register, seeing whether a course is closed, and adding a course to a student's schedule. One way to assign these actions to classes is to use CRC cards, which we describe next.

CRC Cards

3.35   A simple technique for exploring the purpose of a class uses index cards. Each card represents one class. You begin by choosing a descriptive name for a class and writing it at the top of a card. You then list the actions that represent the class's **responsibilities**. You do this for each class in the system. Finally, you indicate the interactions, or **collaborations**, among the classes. That is, you write on each class's card the names of other classes that have some sort of interaction with the class. Because of their content, these cards are called **class-responsibility-collaboration**, or **CRC**, **cards**.

For example, Figure 3-6 shows a CRC card for the class CourseSchedule that represents the courses in which a student has enrolled. Notice that the small size of each card forces you to write brief notes. The number of responsibilities must be small, which suggests that you think at a high level and consider small classes. The size of the cards also lets you arrange them on a table and move them around easily while you search for collaborations.

    Question 11   Write a CRC card for the class Student given in Segment 2.2 of Chapter 2.

Figure 3-6   A class-responsibility-collaboration (CRC) card

```
┌─────────────────────────────────────────────┐
│              CourseSchedule                   │
├─────────────────────────────────────────────┤
│  Responsibilities                             │
│       Add a course                            │
│       Remove a course                         │
│       Check for time conflict                 │
│       List course schedule                    │
│                                               │
│  Collaborations                               │
│       Course                                  │
│       Student                                 │
│                                               │
└─────────────────────────────────────────────┘
```

3.36   The use case diagram in Figure 3-4 is part of a larger notation known as the **Unified Modeling Language**, or **UML**. Designers use the UML to illustrate a software system's necessary classes and their relationships. The UML gives people an overall view of a complex system more effectively than either a natural language or a programming language can. English, for example, can be ambiguous, and Java code provides too much detail. Providing a clear picture of the interactions among classes is one of the strengths of the UML.

Besides the use case diagram, the UML provides a **class diagram** that places each class description in a box analogous to a CRC card. The box contains a class's name, its **attributes** (data fields), and **operations** (methods). For example, Figure 3-7 shows a box for the class CourseSchedule. Typically, you omit from the box such common operations as constructors, get methods, and set methods.

As your design progresses, you can provide more detail when you describe a class. You can indicate the visibility of a field or method by preceding its name with + for public, - for private, and

Figure 3-7   A class representation that can be a part of a class diagram

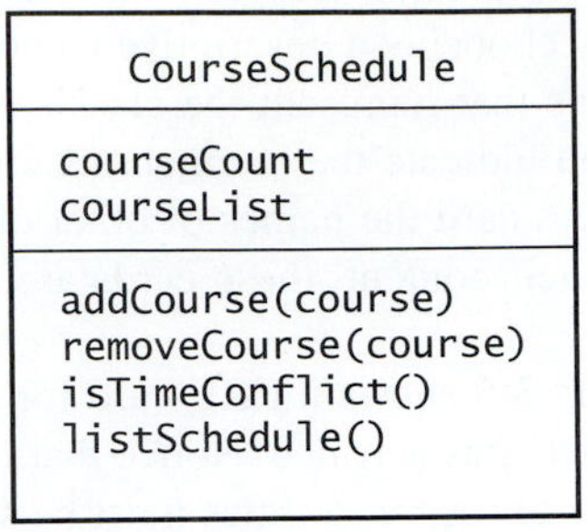

```
┌─────────────────────────────┐
│       CourseSchedule        │
├─────────────────────────────┤
│  courseCount                │
│  courseList                 │
├─────────────────────────────┤
│  addCourse(course)          │
│  removeCourse(course)       │
│  isTimeConflict()           │
│  listSchedule()             │
└─────────────────────────────┘
```

for protected. You also can write the data type of a field, parameter, or return value after a colon that follows the particular item. Thus, in Figure 3-7 you can write the data fields as

```
-courseCount: integer
-courseList: List
```

and the methods as

```
+addCourse(course: Course): void
+removeCourse(course: Course): void
+isTimeConflict(): boolean
+listSchedule(): void
```

You represent an interface in UML much as you represent a class, but you precede its name with <<interface>>. Figure 3-8 shows the notation for the interface Measurable that appears in Segment 3.13.

Question 12   How would the class Name, given in Segment 1.16 of Chapter 1, appear in a class diagram of the UML?

Figure 3-8   UML notation for the interface Measurable

```
┌─────────────────────────────┐
│         <<interface>>       │
│          Measurable         │
├─────────────────────────────┤
│                             │
├─────────────────────────────┤
│  +getPerimeter(): double    │
│                             │
│  +getArea(): double         │
└─────────────────────────────┘
```

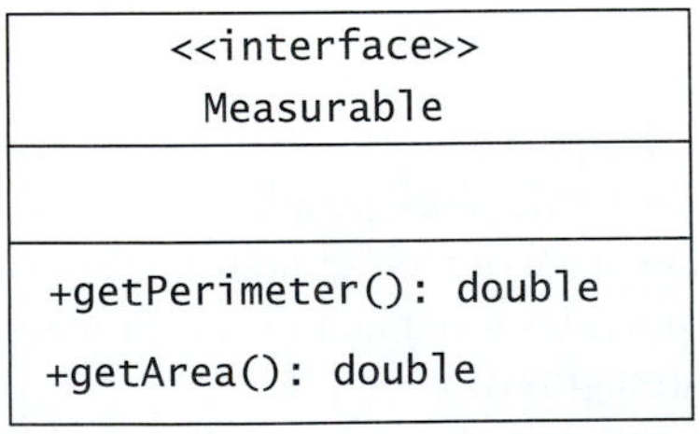

3.37   In a class diagram, lines join the class boxes to show the relationships among the classes, including any inheritance hierarchy. For example, the class diagram in Figure 3-9 shows that the classes UndergradStudent and GradStudent are each derived from the class Student. An arrow with a hollow head points to the base class. Within the UML, the base class Student is said to be a **generalization** of UndergradStudent and GradStudent. If a class implements an interface, you draw an arrow having a dotted shaft and hollow head from the class to the interface.

Figure 3-9   A class diagram showing the base class Student and two derived classes

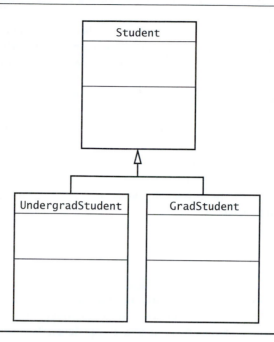

An **association** is a line that represents a relationship between instances of two classes. Basically, an association represents what a CRC card calls a collaboration. For example, relationships exist among the classes Student, CourseSchedule, and Course. Figure 3-10 shows how the UML pictures these relationships. The association (line) between the classes CourseSchedule and Course, for example, indicates a relationship between objects of the class CourseSchedule and objects of the class Course. This association has an arrow pointing toward Course. The arrow indicates responsibilities. Thus, a CourseSchedule object should be able to tell us the courses it contains, but a Course object need not be able to tell us to which schedules it belongs. The UML calls this aspect of the notation the **navigability**.

Figure 3-10   Part of a UML class diagram with associations

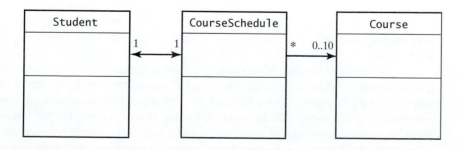

This particular arrow is said to be **unidirectional**, since it points in one direction. An association with arrowheads on both ends is called **bidirectional**. For example, a Student object can find

its course schedule, and a `CourseSchedule` object can discover the student to which it belongs. You can assume that the navigability of an association without arrowheads is unspecified at the present stage of the design.

At the ends of each association are numbers. At the end of the line beginning at `Course-Schedule` and extending to `Course`, you see the notation 0..10. This notation indicates that each `CourseSchedule` object is associated with between zero and ten courses. If you follow the line in the other direction, you encounter an asterisk. It has the same meaning as the notation 0..infinity. Each `Course` object can be associated with many, many course schedules—or with none at all. The figure also indicates a relationship between one `Student` object and one `CourseSchedule` object. This notation on the ends of an association is called the association's **cardinality** or **multiplicity**.

Question 13   Combine Figures 3-9 and 3-10 into one class diagram. Then add a class `AllCourses` that represents all courses offered this semester. What new association(s) do you need to add?

Reusing Classes

3.38   When you first start to write programs, you can easily get the impression that each program is designed and written from scratch. On the contrary, most software is created by combining already existing components with new components. This approach saves time and money. In addition, the existing components have been used many times and so are better tested and more reliable.

For example, a highway simulation program might include a new highway object to model a new highway design, but it would probably model automobiles by using an automobile class that had already been designed for some other program. As you identify the classes that you need for your project, you should see whether any of the classes exist already. Can you use them as is, or would they serve as a good base class for a new class?

3.39   As you design new classes, you should take steps to ensure that they are easily reusable in the future. You must specify exactly how objects of that class interact with other objects. This is the principle of encapsulation that we discussed in the first section of this chapter. But encapsulation is not the only principle you must follow. You must also design your class so that the objects are general and not tailored too much for one particular program. For example, if your program requires that all simulated automobiles move only forward, you should still include a reverse in your automobile class. Some other simulation may require automobiles to back up.

Admittedly, you cannot foresee all the future uses of your class. But you can and should avoid dependencies that will restrict its use later. Chapter 14 describes the design of a class with its future use in mind.

Using the principles that this chapter discusses to design a reusable class with an interface that has comments suitable for `javadoc` takes work. Hacking together a solution to your specific problem would take less time. But the payback for your effort will come later on, when you or another programmer needs to reuse an interface or a class. If you planned for the future when you wrote those components, every use of them will be faster and easier. Actual software developers use these principles to save time over the long term, because saving time saves them money. You should use them, too.

CHAPTER SUMMARY

- Encapsulation is a design principle of object-oriented programming that encloses data and methods into a class, thereby hiding the details of a class's implementation. Only enough information to allow a programmer to use the class is given. The programmer should be able to use a well-designed class as if the body of every method was hidden from view.

- The utility program `javadoc` extracts the header for your class, the headers for all public methods, and comments that are written in a certain form. It produces HTML documents that describe your classes, telling people what they need to know to use them. The documentation omits all the implementation details.

- Abstraction is a process that asks you to focus on *what* instead of *how*.

- A precondition is a statement of the conditions that must be true before a method begins execution. A postcondition is a statement of what is true after a method completes its execution.

- An assertion is a statement of truth about some aspect of your program's logic. You can use an `assert` statement during debugging to enforce an assertion.

- A Java interface can contain any number of public method headers, each followed by a semicolon. An interface can also define any number of public named constants.

- A class that implements an interface has an `implements` clause at the start of the class definition. The class must implement all the methods declared in the interface.

- A Java class can implement any number of interfaces. This feature gives Java an approximation to multiple inheritance, a concept that Java does not support.

- By using an interface as a variable's type, you indicate that the variable can invoke a certain set of methods and only those methods.

- An interface can use generic data types. The interface `Comparable` in the Java Class Library is one such class. It declares the method `compareTo`, which compares two objects and returns a negative integer, zero, or a positive integer, according to whether the comparison is less than, equal to, or greater than.

- You can derive another interface from one or more interfaces by using inheritance.

- You can define named constants within interfaces and classes. Generally, constant definitions are an implementation detail that should appear within a class. Reserving interfaces solely for methods is a reasonable guideline.

- Use cases depict a system from the point of view of one or more actors. Use cases do not necessarily suggest classes within the system.

- A class-responsibility-collaboration (CRC) card lists a class's name, actions, and other classes that collaborate with it.

- A class diagram depicts the relationships among classes and, for each class, lists its name, data fields, and methods. The notation used is a part of the Unified Modeling Language (UML).

PROGRAMMING TIPS

- Specify each public method fully in comments placed before the method's header. State whether a method or its client is responsible for ensuring that the necessary conditions are met for the successful execution of the method. In this way, checking is done but not duplicated. However, during debugging, a method should check that its precondition has been met.

- A method that cannot satisfy its postcondition, even though its precondition is met, can throw an exception.

- Using the `assert` statement is a simple but effective way to find errors in your program's logic. After serving this purpose, assertions left in your program document its logic for those who want to revise or expand its capability. Remember that Java ignores `assert` statements unless the user of your program specifies otherwise.

- Use an `assert` statement to enforce that a method's precondition has been met.

- An `assert` statement is not a substitute for an `if` statement. You should use `assert` statements as a programming aid, not as part of a program's logic.

- Interface names, particularly those that are standard in Java, often end in "able," such as `Comparable`. That ending does not always provide a good name, so endings such as "er" or "Interface" are also used. Just as Java's exception names end in "Exception," we will usually end our interface names with "Interface."

- If you want to define a method or declare a private data field that your classes will have in common, use an abstract base class. Otherwise, use an interface.

EXERCISES

1. Consider the interface `NameInterface` defined in Segment 3.14. We provided comments for only two of the methods. Write comments in `javadoc` style for each of the other methods.

2. Consider the interface `Circular` and the class `Circle`, as given in Segment 3.28.

   a. Is the client or the method `setRadius` responsible for ensuring that the circle's radius is positive?
   b. Write a precondition and a postcondition for the method `setRadius`.
   c. Write comments for the method `setRadius` in a style suitable for `javadoc`.
   d. Revise the method `setRadius` and its precondition and postcondition to change the responsibility mentioned in your answer to Part *a*.

3. Imagine a class `Square` that implements the interface `Comparable`. Implement the method `compareTo` so that squares are compared according to their sides.

4. Revise the class `Circle`, as given in Segment 3.29, so that it implements the interface `Comparable`. Implement the method `compareTo` so that circles are compared according to their radii.

5. Consider the class `Counter`, as described in Project 1 of Chapter 1.

   a. Create an interface for the class. Include comments, suitable for `javadoc`, that specify the methods of the class.
   b. Write `assert` statements that could be added to the implementations of the methods of the class.

6. Write a Java interface for the class `CollegeStudent` given in Segment 2.12 of Chapter 2.

7. What revision(s) should you make to the class `CollegeStudent` so that it implements the interface that you wrote for the previous exercise?

8. Revise the classes `Student` and `CollegeStudent` so that each class implements the interface `Comparable` and, therefore, implements the method `compareTo`.

9. Suppose you want to design a class that is given numbers one at a time. The class computes the smallest, second smallest, and average of the numbers that have been seen so far.

   a. Create an interface for the class. Include comments, suitable for `javadoc`, that specify the methods of the class.

   b. Write `assert` statements that could be added to the implementations of the methods of the class.

10. Suppose you want to design software for a restaurant. Give use cases for placing an order and settling the bill. Identify a list of possible classes. Pick two of these classes, and write CRC cards for them.

PROJECTS

1. Consider a class `Fraction` of fractions. Each fraction is signed and has a numerator and a denominator that are integers. Your class should be able to add, subtract, multiply, and divide two fractions. These methods should have a fraction as a parameter and should return the result of the operation as a fraction.

   The class should also be able to find the reciprocal of a fraction, compare two fractions, decide whether two fractions are equal, and convert a fraction to a string. Your class should handle denominators that are zero.

   Fractions should always occur in lowest terms, and the class should be responsible for this requirement. For example, if the user tries to create a fraction such as 4/8, the class should set the fraction to 1/2. Likewise, the results of all arithmetic operations should be in lowest terms. Note that a fraction can be improper—that is, have a numerator that is larger than its denominator. Such a fraction, however, should be in lowest terms.

   Design, but do not implement, the class `Fraction`. Begin by writing a CRC card for this class. Then write a Java interface that declares each public method. Include `javadoc`-style comments to specify each method.

2. Write a Java class `Fraction` that implements both the interface you designed in Project 1 and the `Comparable` interface. Begin with reasonable constructors. Design and implement useful private methods, and include comments that specify them.

   To reduce a fraction such as 4/8 to lowest terms, you need to divide both the numerator and the denominator by their greatest common denominator. The greatest common denominator of 4 and 8 is 4, so when you divide the numerator and denominator of 4/8 by 4, you get the fraction 1/2. The following recursive algorithm finds the greatest common denominator of two positive integers:

```
Algorithm gcd(integerOne, integerTwo)
if (integerOne % integerTwo == 0)
    result = integerTwo
else
    result = gcd(integerTwo, integerOne % integerTwo)
return result
```

It will be easier to determine the correct sign of a fraction if you force the fraction's denominator to be positive. However, your implementation must handle negative denominators that the client might provide.

Write a program that adequately demonstrates your class.

3. A mixed number contains both an integer portion and a fractional portion. Design a class MixedNumber of mixed numbers that uses the class Fraction that you designed in Project 1. Provide operations for MixedNumber that are analogous to those of Fraction. That is, provide operations to set, retrieve, add, subtract, multiply, and divide mixed numbers. The fractional portion of any mixed number should be in lowest terms and have a numerator that is strictly less than its denominator.

Write a Java interface, including javadoc comments, for this class.

4. Implement the class MixedNumber that you designed in Project 3. Use the operations in Fraction whenever possible. For example, to add two mixed numbers, convert them to fractions, add the fractions by using Fraction's add operation, and then convert the resulting fraction to mixed form. Use analogous techniques for the other arithmetic operations.

Handling the sign of a mixed number can be a messy problem if you are not careful. Mathematically, it makes sense for the sign of the integer part to match the sign of the fraction. But if you have a negative fraction, for example, the toString method for the mixed number could give you the string "-5 -1/2", instead of "-5 1/2", which is what you would normally expect. Here is a possible solution that will greatly simplify computations.

Represent the sign of a mixed number as a character data field. Once this sign is set, make the integer and fractional parts positive. When a mixed number is created, if the given integer part is not zero, take the sign of the integer part as the sign of the mixed number and ignore the signs of the fraction's numerator and denominator. However, if the given integer part is zero, take the sign of the given fraction as the sign of the mixed number.

5. Consider two identical pails. One pail hangs from a hook on the ceiling and contains a blue liquid. The other pail is empty and rests on the floor directly below the first pail. Suddenly a small hole develops in the bottom of the full pail. Blue liquid streams from the full pail and falls into the empty pail on the floor, as Figure 3-11 illustrates. Liquid continues to fall until the upper pail is empty. Notice that the outlines of the pails are black; only the liquid is blue.

Design classes for a program that illustrates this action. When the program begins execution, it should display both pails in their original condition before the leak occurs. Decide whether the leak will occur spontaneously or at a user signal, such as pressing the Return key or clicking the mouse. If the latter, you could have the user position the cursor on the pail bottom to indicate where the leak will occur.

Write CRC cards and Java interfaces that include comments in javadoc style.

Figure 3-11   A leaking pail (Project 5)

6. Implement your design for the leaking pail, as described in Project 5.

7. An odometer records a car's mileage. It contains a number of wheels that turn as the car travels. Each wheel shows a digit from 0 to 9. The rightmost wheel turns the fastest and increases by 1 for every mile traveled. Once a wheel reaches 9, it rolls over to 0 on the next mile and increases by 1 the value on the wheel to its left.

    You can generalize the behavior of such wheels by giving them symbols other than the digits from 0 to 9. Examples of such wheel counters include

   - A binary odometer whose wheels each show either 0 or 1
   - A desktop date display with three wheels, one each for year, month, and day
   - A dice roll display whose wheels each show the spots for a single die

   Write a Java interface for a general wheel counter that has up to four wheels. Also, write a Java interface for any class that represents a wheel. Include comments in `javadoc` style.

8. Implement your design for a general wheel counter, as described in the previous project. Write a program to compute the probability that the sum of the values shown on four dice will be greater than 12. (Divide the number of configurations of the dice where the sum is greater than 12 by the total number of possible configurations of the dice.) Use an instance of the wheel counter to get all the possible configurations of four six-sided dice. For example, if the wheels start at [1, 1, 1, 1], the wheel counter will advance, as follows: [1, 1, 1, 2], [1, 1, 1, 3], [1, 1, 1, 4], [1, 1, 1, 5], [1, 1, 1, 6], [1, 1, 2, 1], and so on.

9. Using your design and implementation of a general wheel counter, as described in Projects 7 and 8, write a class to represent a desktop date display with four wheels, one each for the day of the week, the month, the day, and the year. Note that the name and number of the day increment at the same rate, but rollover at different points. They are not part of the same wheel counter.

4

Lists

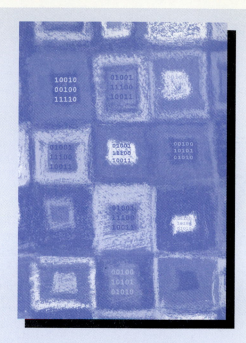

CONTENTS

PREREQUISITES

OBJECTIVES

After studying this chapter, you should be able to

- Describe the concept of an abstract data type (ADT)
- Describe the ADT list
- Use the ADT list in a Java program

This chapter builds on the concepts of encapsulation and data abstraction that were presented in the previous chapter, and it develops the notion of an abstract data type, or ADT. As an example of an abstract data type, we specify and use the ADT list. In doing so we will provide a Java interface for our list. Knowing just this interface, you will be able to use a list in a Java program. You do not need to know how the entries in the list are represented or how the list operations are implemented. Indeed, your program will not depend on these specifics. As you will see, this important program feature is what data abstraction is all about.

Specifications for the ADT List

4.1   A list provides a way to organize data. We can have to-do lists, gift lists, address lists, grocery lists, even lists of lists. These lists provide a useful way for us to organize our lives, as illustrated in Figure 4-1. Each list has a first item, a last item, and usually items in between. That is, the items in a list have a position: first, second, and so on. An item's position might be important to you, or it might not. When adding an item to your list, you might always add it at the end, or you might insert it between two other items already in the list.

Figure 4-1   A to-do list

Everyday lists such as to-do lists, gift lists, address lists, and grocery lists have entries that are strings. What can you do to such lists?

- Typically, you **add** a new entry **at the end** of the list.
- Actually, you can **add** a new entry **anywhere**: at the beginning, the end, or in between items.
- You can cross out an entry—that is, **remove** it.
- You can **remove all** entries.
- You can **replace** an entry.
- You can **look at** any entry.

- You can find out whether the list **contains** a particular entry.
- You can **count** the number of entries in the list.
- You can see whether the list is **empty** or **full**.
- You can **display** all of the entries in the list.

4.2   When you work with a list, you determine where an entry is or should be. You probably are not conscious of its exact position: Is it tenth? Fourteenth? However, when your program uses a list, a convenient way to identify a particular entry is by the entry's position within the list. It could be first, that is, at position 1, or second (position 2), and so on. This convention allows you to describe, or specify, the operations on a list more precisely.

At this point, you should *not* be thinking about how to represent a list in your program or how to implement its operations. Don't think about arrays, for example. You first need to clearly know what the list operations do: Focus on *what* the operations do, not on *how* they do them. That is, you need a detailed set of specifications before you can use a list in a program. In fact, you should specify the list operations before you even decide on a programming language.

At this point, the list is an abstract data type. An **abstract data type**, or **ADT**, represents a collection of data having the same type and the operations on that data. An ADT only describes its data and specifies its operations. It does not indicate how to store the data or how to implement the operations. Thus, we can discuss ADTs independently of a programming language. In contrast, a **data structure** is an implementation of an ADT within a programming language.

Note: Since an abstract data type, or ADT, describes a data organization independently of a programming language, it can be implemented in any programming language.

4.3   To specify the ADT list, we describe its data and specify the operations on that data. Unlike common lists whose entries are strings, the ADT list is more general and has entries that are objects of the same type. The following is a specification of the ADT list:

ABSTRACT DATA TYPE LIST

DATA

- A collection of objects in a specific order and having the same data type
- The number of objects in the collection

OPERATIONS

`add(newEntry)`

Task: Adds `newEntry` to the end of the list.
Input: `newEntry` is an object.
Output: None.

`add(newPosition, newEntry)`

Task: Adds `newEntry` at position `newPosition` within the list. Position 1 indicates the first entry in the list.
Input: `newPosition` is an integer, `newEntry` is an object.
Output: None.

remove(givenPosition)

Task: Removes from the list the entry at position givenPosition.
Input: givenPosition is an integer.
Output: None.

clear()

Task: Removes all entries from the list.
Input: None.
Output: None.

replace(givenPosition, newEntry)

Task: Replaces the entry at position givenPosition with newEntry.
Input: givenPosition is an integer, newEntry is an object.
Output: None.

getEntry(givenPosition)

Task: Retrieves the entry at position givenPosition in the list.
Input: givenPosition is an integer.
Output: Returns the entry at position givenPosition.

contains(anEntry)

Task: Sees whether the list contains anEntry.
Input: anEntry is an object.
Output: Returns true if anEntry is in the list, or false if not.

getLength()

Task: Gets the number of entries currently in the list.
Input: None.
Output: Returns the number of entries currently in the list.

isEmpty()

Task: Sees whether the list is empty.
Input: None.
Output: Returns true if the list is empty, or false if not.

isFull()

Task: Sees whether the list is full.
Input: None.
Output: Returns true if the list is full, or false if not.

display()

Task: Displays all entries that are in the list in the order in which they occur, one per line.
Input: None.
Output: None.

We have only begun to specify the behaviors of these list operations, as the specifications just given leave some details to the imagination. Some examples will help us to better understand these operations so that we can improve the specifications. We'll need precise specifications before we implement the operations.

Programming Tip: After designing a draft of an ADT, confirm your understanding of the operations and their design by writing some pseudocode that uses the ADT.

4.4 **Example.** When you first declare a new list, it is empty and its length is zero. If you add three objects—a, b, and c—one at a time and in the order given, to the end of the list, the list will appear as

    a
    b
    c

The object a is first, at position 1, b is at position 2, and c is last at position 3.[1] To save space here, we will sometimes write a list's contents on one line. For example, we might write

    a b c

to represent this list.

The following pseudocode represents the previous three additions to the specific list myList:

    myList.add(a)
    myList.add(b)
    myList.add(c)

At this point, myList is not empty, so myList.isEmpty() is false. Since the list contains three entries, myList.getLength() is 3. Notice that adding entries to the end of a list does not change the positions of entries already in the list. Figure 4-2 illustrates these add operations as well as the operations that we describe next.

Figure 4-2   The effect of ADT list operations on an initially empty list

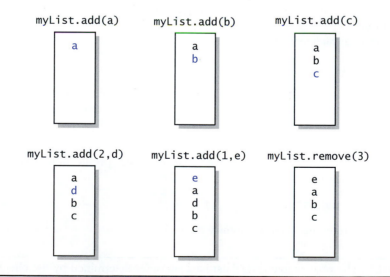

---

1. Some people number the entries in a list beginning with 0 instead of 1.

4.5　Now suppose that we add entries at various positions within the list. For example,

```
myList.add(2, d)
```

places d second—that is, at position 2—within the list. Doing so, however, moves b to position 3 and c to position 4, so that the list now contains

```
a d b c
```

If we add e to the beginning of the list by writing

```
myList.add(1, e)
```

the current entries in the list move to the next higher position. The list then contains

```
e a d b c
```

Look at Figure 4-2 again to see the effect of these operations.

4.6　We can get the second entry in this list by writing

```
entry2 = myList.getEntry(2)
```

Remember that we are writing pseudocode here and ignoring details such as semicolons.
　　What happens when we remove an entry? For example,

```
myList.remove(3)
```

removes the third entry—d in the previous example—from the list. The list then contains

```
e a b c
```

Notice that entries after the one that was removed move to the next lower position within the list. Figure 4-2 illustrates this change to the list.

　　What if an application requires us to remove an entry from a list but retain the entry for another purpose? Our specification of remove would force us to first use getEntry to obtain the entry and then use remove to remove it from the list. We could refine the specification of remove to return the object removed from the list. To use this revised version of remove, we would write a pseudocode statement such as

```
oldEntry3 = myList.remove(3)
```

This change makes remove more versatile, as the client could either save or ignore the returned entry.
　　We can replace the third entry b of our list with f by writing

```
myList.replace(3, f)
```

No other entries move or change. We could refine the specification of replace to return the object that was replaced. So if we wrote

```
ref = myList.replace(3, f)
```

ref would reference the former entry b.

Note:　The objects in an ADT list have an order determined by the client of the list. To add, remove, or retrieve an entry, you must specify the entry's position within the list. The first entry in the list is at position 1.

Refining the Specifications

4.7   The previous specifications ignore at least three difficulties that might arise during the use of the ADT list:

- The operations add, remove, replace, and getEntry are well behaved when the given position is valid for the current list. What happens when one of these operations receives an invalid position number?
- The methods remove, replace, and getEntry are not meaningful for empty lists. What happens when an empty list invokes one of these operations?
- A list could become full, depending on the list's implementation. What happens when the client tries to add an entry to a full list?

You as the class designer need to make decisions about how to handle unusual conditions and include these decisions in your specifications. The documentation for the ADT list should reflect both these decisions and the detail that the previous examples demonstrate.

4.8   In general, you can address unusual situations in several ways. Your method could

- Assume that the invalid situations will not occur. This assumption is not as naive as it might sound. A method could state as an assumption—that is, a precondition—restrictions to which a client must adhere. It is then up to the client to enforce the precondition by checking that the precondition is satisfied before invoking the method. Notice that the client can use other methods of the ADT list such as isEmpty and getLength to help with this task. As long as the client obeys the restriction, the invalid situation will not occur.
- Ignore the invalid situations. A method could simply do nothing when given invalid data. Doing absolutely nothing, however, leaves the client without knowledge of what happened.
- Guess at the client's intention. For example, if a client tries to remove the sixth entry from a three-entry list, the remove method could remove the last entry instead. Like the previous option, this choice can cause problems for the client.
- Return a value that signals a problem. For example, if a client tries to retrieve an entry at a non-existent position in the list, the getEntry method could return null. The value returned must be something that cannot be in the list.
- Return a boolean value that indicates the success or failure of an operation.
- Throw an exception.

As Appendix B shows, throwing an exception is often a desirable way for a Java method to react to unusual events that occur during its execution. The method can simply report a problem without deciding what to do about it. The exception enables each client to do what is needed in its own particular situation. However, the method invocation in the client must appear within a try block. For simplicity, we adopt the philosophy that methods should throw exceptions only in truly exceptional circumstances, when no other reasonable solution exists. Future chapters will include some examples of handling exceptions.

4.9   After you have identified all unusual circumstances, you should specify how your methods will behave under each of these circumstances. For example, it would be reasonable for the add method to throw an exception if it tries to add an entry at an invalid position. However, it might be just as reasonable for the method to return false in these situations.

The documentation you write for your ADT should describe these specifications. As your specifications become more detailed, they increasingly should reflect your choice of programming language. Ultimately, you can write a Java interface for the class that will implement the ADT. (The previous chapter described how to write an interface.)

Note: A first draft of an ADT's specifications often overlooks or ignores situations that you really need to consider. You might intentionally make these omissions to simplify this first draft. Once you have written the major portions of the specifications, you can concentrate on the details that make the specifications complete.

4.10   The Java interface in Listing 4-1 contains the methods for an ADT list and detailed comments that describe their behaviors. Recall that a class interface does not include data fields, constructors, private methods, or protected methods.

   The items in the list will be objects of the same class. For example, we could have a list of strings. To accommodate entries of any class type, the list methods use a generic type for each entry. Once the actual data type is chosen within a client, all entries must have that type. The compiler will enforce this restriction for us.

   For lists of primitive types, you can place instances of an appropriate wrapper class in your list. For example, instead of instances of the primitive type `int`, you could use instances of the wrapper class `Integer`. (Appendix A discusses wrapper classes.)

   As you examine the interface, notice the decisions that were made to address the unusual situations discussed in Segment 4.7. In particular, each of the methods add, `remove`, `replace`, and `getEntry` returns a value. Since our programming language is Java, notice that `remove` and `getEntry` each return a reference to an entry, not the entry itself.

Listing 4-1   The interface `ListInterface`

```
/** An interface for the ADT list.
 *  Entries in the list have positions that begin with 1.
 */
public interface ListInterface<T>
{
   /** Task: Adds a new entry to the end of the list.
    *        Entries currently in the list are unaffected.
    *        The list's size is increased by 1.
    *  @param newEntry  the object to be added as a new entry
    *  @return true if the addition is successful, or false if the list
    *          is full */
   public boolean add(T newEntry);

   /** Task: Adds a new entry at a specified position within the list.
    *        Entries originally at and above the specified position
    *        are at the next higher position within the list.
    *        The list's size is increased by 1.
    *  @param newPosition  an integer that specifies the desired
    *                      position of the new entry
    *  @param newEntry     the object to be added as a new entry
    *  @return true if the addition is successful, or
    *          false if either the list is full, newPosition < 1, or
    *          newPosition > getLength()+1 */
   public boolean add(int newPosition, T newEntry);

   /** Task: Removes the entry at a given position from the list.
    *        Entries originally at positions higher than the given
    *        position are at the next lower position within the list,
    *        and the list's size is decreased by 1.
```

```
 *     @param givenPosition  an integer that indicates the position of
 *                               the entry to be removed
 *     @return a reference to the removed entry or null, if either
 *             the list was empty, givenPosition < 1, or
 *             givenPosition > getLength() */
   public T remove(int givenPosition);

   /** Task: Removes all entries from the list. */
   public void clear();

   /** Task: Replaces the entry at a given position in the list.
 *     @param givenPosition  an integer that indicates the position of the
 *                               entry to be replaced
 *     @param newEntry  the object that will replace the entry at the
 *                               position givenPosition
 *     @return true if the replacement occurs, or false if either the
 *             list is empty, givenPosition < 1, or
 *             givenPosition > getLength() */
   public boolean replace(int givenPosition, T newEntry);

   /** Task: Retrieves the entry at a given position in the list.
 *     @param givenPosition  an integer that indicates the position of
 *                               the desired entry
 *     @return a reference to the indicated entry or null, if either
 *             the list is empty, givenPosition < 1, or
 *             givenPosition > getLength() */
   public T getEntry(int givenPosition);

   /** Task: Sees whether the list contains a given entry.
 *     @param anEntry  the object that is the desired entry
 *     @return true if the list contains anEntry, or false if not */
   public boolean contains(T anEntry);

   /** Task: Gets the length of the list.
 *     @return the integer number of entries currently in the list */
   public int getLength();

   /** Task: Sees whether the list is empty.
 *     @return true if the list is empty, or false if not */
   public boolean isEmpty();

   /** Task: Sees whether the list is full.
 *     @return true if the list is full, or false if not */
   public boolean isFull();

   /** Task: Displays all entries that are in the list, one per line,
 *             in the order in which they occur in the list. */
   public void display();
} // end ListInterface
```

Question 1   Write pseudocode statements that add some objects to a list, as follows. First add c, then a, then b, and then d, such that the order of the objects in the list will be a, b, c, d.

Question 2   Write pseudocode statements that exchange the third and seventh entries in a list of ten objects.

Note: The entries in a list of *n* entries are numbered from 1 to *n*. Although you cannot add a new entry at position 0, you can add one at position *n* + 1.

4.11   After specifying an ADT and writing a Java interface for its operations, you should write some Java statements that use the ADT. In this way, you check both the suitability and your understanding of the specifications. It is better to revise the design or documentation of the ADT now instead of after you have written its implementation. An added benefit of doing this task carefully is that you can use these same Java statements later to test your implementation.

Programming Tip: **Write a test program before you implement a class**

Writing Java statements that test a class's methods will help you to fully understand the specifications for the methods. Obviously, you must understand a method before you can implement it correctly. If you are also the class designer, your use of the class might help you see desirable changes to your design or its documentation. You will save time if you make these revisions before you have implemented the class. Since you must write a program that tests your implementation sometime, why not get additional benefits from the task by writing it now instead of later?

The following section looks at several examples that use a list. These examples can be part of a program that tests your implementation.

Using the ADT List

Imagine that we hire a programmer to implement the ADT list in Java, given the interface and specifications that we have developed so far. If we assume that these specifications are clear enough for the programmer to complete the implementation, we can use the ADT's operations in a program without knowing the details of the implementation. That is, we do not need to know *how* the programmer implemented the list to be able to use it. We only need to know *what* the ADT list does.

Figure 4-3   A list of numbers that identify runners in the order in which they finished a race

This section assumes that we have an implementation for the list and demonstrates how we can use a list in our program.

4.12 **Example.** Imagine that we are organizing a local road race. Our job is to note the order in which the runners finish the race. Since each runner wears a distinct identifying number, we can add each runner's number to the end of a list as the runners cross the finish line. Figure 4-3 illustrates such a list.

The Java program in Listing 4-2 shows how we can perform this task by using the ADT list. It assumes that the class `AList` implements the Java interface `ListInterface` that you saw in the previous section. Since `ListInterface` assumes that the items in the list are objects, we will treat each runner's identifying number as a string.

Listing 4-2   A client of a class that implements `ListInterface`

```java
public class ListClient
{
  public static void main(String[] args)
  {
    testList();
  } // end main

  public static void testList()
  {
    ListInterface<String> runnerList = new AList<String>();
//  runnerList has only methods in ListInterface

    runnerList.add("16"); // winner
    runnerList.add(" 4"); // second place
    runnerList.add("33"); // third place
    runnerList.add("27"); // fourth place
    runnerList.display();
  } // end testList
} // end ListClient
```

OUTPUT
```
16
 4
33
27
```

Notice that the data type of `runnerList` is `ListInterface<String>`. This declaration obliges `runnerList` to call only methods in the interface and to add only strings to the list. If the data type was `AList<String>` instead, `runnerList` would be able to call any public methods in `AList` even if they were not declared in `ListInterface`.

 Question 3   In the previous example, what changes to `testList` are necessary to represent the runner's numbers as `Integer` objects instead of strings? Use Java's auto-boxing feature, as described in Segment A.98 of Appendix A.

4.13 **Example.** The previous example uses the list method `display` to display the items in the list. We might want our output in a different form, however. The following method is an example of how a client could display the items in a list without using the method `display`. Notice the use of the list methods `getLength` and `getEntry`.

```
public static void displayList(ListInterface<String> list)
{
  int numberOfEntries = list.getLength();
  System.out.println("The list contains " + numberOfEntries +
                     " entries, as follows:");

  for (int position = 1; position <= numberOfEntries; position++)
    System.out.println(list.getEntry(position) +
                       " is entry " + position);

  System.out.println();
} // end displayList
```

Assuming the list runnerList from the example in Segment 4.12, the expression display-List(runnerList) produces the following output:

The list contains 4 entries, as follows:

16 is entry 1
 4 is entry 2
33 is entry 3
27 is entry 4

The data type of displayList's input parameter list is ListInterface<String>. Thus, the argument of the method must be an object that satisfies both of the following conditions:

- The object's class must implement ListInterface.
- The object must be instantiated as a list of strings.

Although the method works for any implementation of the ADT list, it works only for lists of strings. You could remove the latter restriction by revising the header of the method as follows:

```
public static <T> void displayList(ListInterface<T> list)
```

Now the list passed to the method can contain objects of any one class.

4.14   **Example.** A professor wants an alphabetical list of the names of the students who arrive for class today. As each student enters the room, the professor adds the student's name to a list. It is up to the professor to place each name into its correct position in the list so that the names will be in alphabetical order. The ADT list does *not* choose the order of its entries.

The following Java statements place the names Amy, Ellen, Bob, Drew, Aaron, and Carol in an alphabetical list. The comment at the end of each statement shows the list after the statement executes.

```
// make an alphabetical list of names as students enter a room
ListInterface<String> alphaList = new AList<String>();

alphaList.add(1, "Amy");    // Amy
alphaList.add(2, "Ellen");  // Amy Ellen
alphaList.add(2, "Bob");    // Amy Bob Ellen
alphaList.add(3, "Drew");   // Amy Bob Drew Ellen
alphaList.add(1, "Aaron");  // Aaron Amy Bob Drew Ellen
alphaList.add(4, "Carol");  // Aaron Amy Bob Carol Drew Ellen
```

After initially adding Amy to the beginning of the list and Ellen to the end of the list (at position 2), the professor inserts

- Bob between Amy and Ellen at position 2
- Drew between Bob and Ellen at position 3
- Aaron before Amy at position 1
- Carol between Bob and Drew at position 4

This technique of inserting each name into a collection of alphabetized names is called an **insertion sort.** We will discuss this and other ways of ordering items in a later chapter.

If we now remove the entry at position 4—Carol—by writing

```
alphaList.remove(4);
```

Drew and Ellen will then be at positions 4 and 5, respectively. Thus, alphaList.getEntry(4) would return a reference to Drew.

Finally, suppose that we want to replace a name in this list. We cannot replace a name with just any name and expect that the list will remain in alphabetical order. Replacing Bob with Ben by writing

```
alphaList.replace(3, "Ben");
```

would maintain alphabetical order, but replacing Bob with Nancy would not. The list's alphabetical order resulted from our original decisions about where to add names to the list. The order did not come about automatically as a result of list operations. That is, the client, not the list, maintained the order. We could, however, design an ADT that maintains its data in alphabetical order. You will see an example of such an ADT in Chapter 13.

Question 4   Suppose that alphaList contains a list of the four names Amy, Ellen, Bob, and Drew as strings. Write Java statements that swap Ellen and Bob and that then swap Ellen and Drew so that the list will be in alphabetical order.

4.15   **Example.** Let's look at a list of objects that are not strings. Suppose that we have the class Name from Chapter 1 that represents a person's first and last names. The following statements indicate how we could make a list of the names Amy Smith, Tina Drexel, and Robert Jones:

```
// make a list of names as you think of them
ListInterface<Name> nameList = new AList<Name>();
Name amy = new Name("Amy", "Smith");
nameList.add(amy);
nameList.add(new Name("Tina", "Drexel"));
nameList.add(new Name("Robert", "Jones"));
```

Now let's retrieve the name that is second in the list, Tina Drexel:

```
Name secondName = nameList.getEntry(2);
```

The definition of getEntry declares its return type as T, the generic type of the entries in the list. This type for nameList is Name, so getEntry returns a Name object.

Question 5   Suppose that the return type of getEntry was Object instead of a generic type. Would this change affect how you use the method? In particular, would the statement in the previous example that retrieved the second name in nameList be correct? Why?

4.16   **Example.** Let's talk a bit more about the previous example. The variable secondName is a reference to the second object in the list. Using this reference, we can modify the object. For example, we could change its last name by writing

```
secondName.setLast("Doe");
```

If the class `Name` did not have set methods like `setLast`, we would be unable to modify the objects in this list. For instance, if we had a list of strings, we would not be able to alter one of the strings in this way. The class `String` has no set methods, so once we create a `String` object, we cannot alter it. We could, however, replace an entire object in the list—regardless of its type—by using the ADT list operation `replace`.

A class, such as `Name`, that has set methods is a class of **mutable objects**. A class, such as `String`, without set methods is a class of **immutable objects**. Chapter 15 talks about such classes in more detail.

Using a List Is Like Using a Vending Machine

4.17   Imagine that you are in front of a vending machine, as Figure 4-4 depicts; or better yet, take a break and go buy something from one!

Figure 4-4   A vending machine

When you look at the front of a vending machine, you see its interface. By inserting coins and pressing buttons, you are able to make a purchase. Here are some observations that we can make about the vending machine:

- You can perform only the specific tasks that the machine's interface presents to you.
- You must understand these tasks—that is, you must know what to do to buy a soda.
- You cannot access the inside of the machine, because a locked shell encapsulates it.
- You can use the machine even though you do not know what happens inside.
- If someone replaced the machine's inner mechanism with an improved version, leaving the interface unchanged, you could still use the machine in the same way.

You, as the user of a vending machine, are like the client of the ADT list that you saw earlier in this chapter. The observations that we just made about the user of a vending machine are similar to the following observations about a list's client:

- The client can perform only the operations specific to the ADT list. These operations often are declared within a Java interface.
- The client must adhere to the specifications of the operations that the ADT list provides. That is, the author of the client must understand how to use these operations.
- The client cannot access the data within the list without using an ADT operation. The principle of encapsulation hides the data representation within the ADT.
- The client can use the list, even though it cannot access the list's entries directly—that is, even though the programmer does not know how the data is stored.
- If someone changed the implementation of the list's operations, the client could still use the list in the same way, as long as the interface did not change.

4.18 In the examples of the previous section, each list is an instance of a class that implements the ADT list. That is, each list is an object whose behaviors are the operations of the ADT list. You can think of each such object as being like the vending machine we just described. Each object encapsulates the list's data and operations, just as the vending machine encapsulates its product (soda cans) and delivery system.

Some ADT operations have inputs analogous to the coins you insert into a vending machine. Some ADT operations have outputs analogous to the change, soda cans, messages, and warning lights that a vending machine provides.

Now imagine that you are the designer of the front, or interface, of the vending machine. What can the machine do, and what should a person do to use the machine? Will it help you or hinder you to think about how the soda cans will be stored and transported within the machine? We maintain that you should ignore these aspects and focus solely on how someone will use the machine—that is, on your design of the interface. Ignoring extraneous details makes your task easier and increases the quality of your design.

Recall that abstraction as a design principle asks you to focus on *what* instead of *how*. When you design an ADT, and ultimately a class, you use data abstraction to focus on what you want to do with or to the data without worrying about how you will accomplish these tasks. We practiced data abstraction at the beginning of this chapter when we designed the ADT list. We referred to each entry in our list by its position within the list. As we chose the methods that a list would have, we did not consider how we would represent the list. Instead, we focused on what each method should do.

Ultimately, we wrote a Java interface that specified the methods in detail. We were then able to write a client that used the list, again without knowledge of its implementation. If someone wrote the implementation for us, our program would presumably run correctly. If someone else gave us a better implementation, we could use it without changing our already-written client. This feature of the client is a major advantage of abstraction.

Java Class Library: The Interface List

4.19   The standard package `java.util` contains an interface `List` for an ADT list that is similar to the list that our interface describes. One difference between a list in the Java Class Library and our ADT list is the numbering of a list's entries. A list in the Java Class Library uses the same numbering scheme as a Java array: The first entry is at position, or index, 0. In contrast, we begin our list at position 1.

The interface `List` also declares more methods than our interface does. You'll see a few of those additional methods in Chapter 8. However, it does not specify a method to display a list.

The following method headers from the interface `List` are for a selection of methods that are similar to the ones you have seen in this chapter. We have used blue to indicate where they differ from our methods. Once again, `T` is the generic type of the entries in the list.

```
public boolean add(T newEntry)
public void add(int index, T newEntry)
public T remove(int index)
public void clear()
public T set(int index, T anEntry)  // like replace
public T get(int index)             // like getEntry
public boolean contains(Object anEntry)
public int size()                   // like getLength
public boolean isEmpty()
```

The second add method is a void method. It throws an exception if `index` is out of range, instead of returning the boolean value false, as our add method does. The methods `remove` and `get` also throw an exception if `index` is out of range. Our analogous methods return `null` instead. The method `set` is like our `replace` method, but it returns a reference to the entry that was replaced in the list instead of returning a boolean value. It also throws an exception if `index` is out of range. The data type of `contains`' parameter is `Object` instead of a generic type. In practice, this difference has little consequence. Lastly, the method `get` is like our `getEntry`, and `size` is like our `getLength`.

You can learn more about the interface `List` at `java.sun.com/j2se/1.5/docs/api/`.

CHAPTER SUMMARY

- An abstract data type, or ADT, represents both data and a set of operations on the data. An ADT provides a way to design a new data type independently of the choice of programming language.

- A list is an ADT whose data consists of ordered entries. Each entry is identified by its position within the list.

- A client manipulates or accesses a list's entries by using only the operations defined for the ADT list. The manifestation of the ADT in a programming language encapsulates the data and operations. As a result, the particular data representations and method implementations are hidden from the client.

- When you use data abstraction to design an ADT, you focus on what you want to do with or to the data without worrying about how you will accomplish these tasks. That is, you ignore the details of how you represent data and how you manipulate it.

<table>
<tr><td>PROGRAMMING TIPS</td><td>

● After designing a draft of an ADT, confirm your understanding of the operations and their design by writing some pseudocode that uses the ADT.

● After specifying an ADT and writing a Java interface for its operations, write some Java statements that use the ADT. In this way, you check both the suitability and your understanding of the specifications. An added benefit of doing this task carefully is that later you can use these same Java statements to test your implementation.

</td></tr>
</table>

EXERCISES

1. If myList is an empty list of strings, what does it contain after the following statements execute?

```java
myList.add("A");
myList.add("B");
myList.add("C");
myList.add("D");
myList.add(1, "one");
myList.add(1, "two");
myList.add(1, "three");
myList.add(1, "four");
```

2. If myList is an empty list of strings, what does it contain after the following statements execute?

```java
myList.add("alpha");
myList.add(1, "beta");
myList.add("gamma");
myList.add(2, "delta");
myList.add(4, "alpha");
myList.remove(2);
myList.remove(2);
myList.replace(3, "delta");
```

3. Suppose that you want an operation for the ADT list that returns the position of a given object in the list. The header of the method could be as follows:

   public int getPosition(T anObject)

   Write comments that specify this method.

4. Suppose that you want an operation for the ADT list that removes the first occurrence of a given object from the list. The header of the method could be as follows:

   public boolean remove(T anObject)

   Write comments that specify this method.

5. Suppose that you want an operation for the ADT list that moves the first item in the list to the end of the list. The header of the method could be as follows:

   public void moveToEnd()

   Write comments that specify this method.

6. Write Java statements at the client level that return the position of a given object in the list myList. Assume that the object is in the list.

7. Suppose that the ADT list did not have a method replace. Write Java statements at the client level that replace an object in the list nameList. The object's position in the list is givenPosition and the replacement object is newObject.

8. Suppose that the ADT list did not have a method contains. Suppose further that nameList is a list of Name objects, where Name is as defined in Chapter 1. Write Java statements at the client level that see whether the Name object myName is in the list nameList.

9. Suppose that you have a list that is created by the following statement:

    ```
    ListInterface<Student> studentList = new AList<Student>();
    ```

    Imagine that someone has added to the list several instances of the class Student that Chapter 2 defined in Segment 2.2.

    a. Write Java statements that display the last names of the students in the list in the same order in which the students appear in the list. Do not alter the list.
    b. Write Java statements that interchange the first and last students in the list.

10. Suppose that you have a list that is created by the following statement:

    ```
    ListInterface<Double> quizScores = new AList<Double>();
    ```

    Imagine that someone has added to this list the quiz scores received by a student throughout a course. The professor would like to know the average of these quiz scores, ignoring the lowest score.

    a. Write Java statements at the client level that will find and remove the lowest score in the list.
    b. Write Java statements at the client level that will compute the average of the scores remaining in the list.

11. Consider a class Coin that represents a coin. The class has methods such as getValue, toss, and isHeads. The method getValue returns the value, or denomination, of a coin. The method toss simulates a coin toss in which the coin lands either heads up or tails up. The method isHeads returns true if a coin is heads up.

    Suppose that coinList is an ADT list of coins that have randomly selected denominations. Toss each of these coins. If the result of a coin toss is heads, move the coin to a second list called headsList; if it is tails, leave the coin in the original list. When you are finished tossing coins, compute the total value of the coins that came up heads. Assume that the list headsList has been created for you and is empty initially.

1. A **shoe** of playing cards contains some number of standard decks of cards. Cards in the shoe can be shuffled together and dealt one at a time. The number of cards in the shoe can also be calculated.

After a hand is complete, you should be able to return all cards to the shoe and shuffle them. Some card games require that the discard pile be returned to the shoe when the shoe becomes empty. Then the cards in the shoe can be shuffled. In this case, not all cards are in the shoe; some are held by the players.

Design an ADT for a shoe assuming that you have the class `PlayingCard`, which was described in Project 6 of Chapter 2. You do not need an ADT deck since a deck is a shoe whose number of decks is 1.

Specify each ADT operation by stating its purpose, by describing its parameters, and by writing preconditions, postconditions, and a pseudocode version of its header. Then write a Java interface for the ADT that includes `javadoc`-style comments.

2. The introduction to this book spoke of a bag as a way to organize data. A grocery bag, for example, contains items in no particular order. Some of them might be duplicate items. The ADT bag, like the grocery bag, is perhaps the simplest of data organizations. It holds objects but does not arrange or organize them further.

Design an ADT bag. Many operations are analogous to those of the ADT list, but the entries do not have positions. In addition to these basic operations, include the following:

- A union operation that combines the contents of two bags into a third bag
- An intersection operation that creates a bag of those items that occur in both of two bags
- A difference operation that creates a bag of the items that would be left in one bag after removing those that also occur in another bag

Note that the intersection or difference of two bags might contain duplicate items. For example, if object *x* occurs five times in one bag and twice in another, the intersection of these bags contains *x* twice. The difference of these bags contains *x* three times.

Specify each ADT operation by stating its purpose, by describing its parameters, and by writing preconditions, postconditions, and a pseudocode version of its header. Then write a Java interface for the ADT bag that includes `javadoc`-style comments.

3. You might have a piggy bank or some other receptacle to hold your spare coins. The piggy bank holds the coins but gives them no other organization. And certainly the bank can contain duplicate coins. The piggy bank is like the ADT bag that you designed in Project 2, but it is simpler. It has only three operations: You can add a coin to the bank, remove one (you shake the bank, so you have no control over what coin falls out), or see whether the bank is empty.

Design the ADT piggy bank, assuming that you have the ADT bag from Project 2 and the class `Coin` from Exercise 11. Specify each ADT operation by stating its purpose, by describing its parameters, and by writing preconditions, postconditions, and a pseudocode version of its header. Then write a Java interface for the ADT bag that includes `javadoc`-style comments.

4. Project 2 describes the ADT bag. A **set** is a special bag that does not allow duplicates. Specify each operation for the ADT set by stating its purpose, by describing its parameters, and by writing preconditions, postconditions, and a pseudocode version of its header. Then write a Java interface for the ADT set that includes `javadoc`-style comments.

5. Santa Claus allegedly keeps lists of those who are naughty and those who are nice. On the naughty list are the names of those who will get coal in their stockings. On the nice list are those who will receive gifts. Each object in this list contains a name (an instance of `Name`, as defined in Chapter 1) and a list of that person's gifts (an instance of an ADT list).

   Design an ADT for the objects in the nice list. Specify each ADT operation by stating its purpose, by describing its parameters, and by writing preconditions, postconditions, and a pseudocode version of its header. Then write a Java interface for the ADT that includes `javadoc`-style comments.

6. A **ring** is a collection of items that has a reference to a current item. A cycle operation moves the reference to the next item in the collection. When the reference reaches the last item, the next occurrence of the cycle operation will move the reference back to the first item. A ring also has operations to get the current item, add an item, and remove an item. The details of where an item is added and which one is removed are up to you.

   Design an ADT that represents any ring. Specify each ADT operation by stating its purpose, by describing its parameters, and by writing preconditions, postconditions, and a pseudocode version of its header. Then write a Java interface for the ADT that includes `javadoc`-style comments.

7. A bid for installing an air conditioner consists of the name of the company, a description of the unit, the performance of the unit, the cost of the unit, and the cost of installation.

   Design an ADT that represents any bid. Then design another ADT to represent a collection of bids. The second ADT should include methods to search for bids based on price and performance. Also note that a single company could make multiple bids, each with a different unit.

   Specify each ADT operation by stating its purpose, by describing its parameters, and by writing preconditions, postconditions, and a pseudocode version of its header. Then write a Java interface for the ADTs that includes `javadoc`-style comments.

8. A recipe contains a title, a list of ingredients, and a list of directions. An entry in the list of ingredients contains an amount, a unit, and a description. For example, an object that represents *2 cups of flour* could be an entry in this list. An entry in the list of directions is a string.

   Design an ADT that represents any entry in a list of ingredients, assuming that you have the class `MixedNumber`, which was described in Project 3 of Chapter 3. Then design another ADT to represent any recipe. Specify each ADT operation by stating its purpose, by describing its parameters, and by writing preconditions, postconditions, and a pseudocode version of its header. Then write a Java interface for the ADT that includes `javadoc`-style comments.

5

List Implementations That Use Arrays

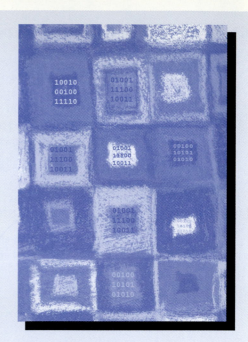

PREREQUISITES

OBJECTIVES

After studying this chapter, you should be able to

- Implement the ADT list by using a fixed-size array, an array that you expand dynamically, or an instance of **Vector**
- Discuss the advantages and disadvantages of the three implementations presented

You have seen several examples of how to use the ADT list in a program. This chapter presents three different ways that you can implement a list in Java. Each of these ways involves an array. You will see a completely different approach in the next chapter.

We begin by using an ordinary Java array to represent the entries in a list. With this implementation, your list could become full, just as a handwritten list can fill a page. We then offer two other implementations that do not suffer from this problem. When you use all of the space in an array, Java enables you to move the data to a larger array. The effect is to have an array that apparently expands to meet your needs. Alternately, you can use an instance of the Java class Vector to represent the list entries. The result is like using an array that can expand, since the underlying implementation of Vector uses such an array. But this list implementation is simpler to write than one that uses an array, because Vector does the work for you.

Using a Fixed–Size Array to Implement the ADT List

We begin by using an analogy to describe how a fixed-size array could represent a list. In doing so, we show how the add and remove methods would work. Subsequently, we present a corresponding Java implementation for the list.

An Analogy

5.1   Imagine a classroom—call it room A—containing 40 desks in fixed positions. If a course is restricted to 30 students, 10 desks are idle and wasted. If we lift the enrollment restriction, we can accommodate only 10 more students, even if 20 more want to take the course.

An array is like this classroom, and each desk is like one array location. Suppose that we number the 40 desks in the room sequentially, beginning with zero, as Figure 5-1 illustrates. Although desks are arranged in rows in typical classrooms, we will ignore this detail and treat the desks as a one-dimensional array.

Figure 5-1   A classroom that contains desks in fixed positions

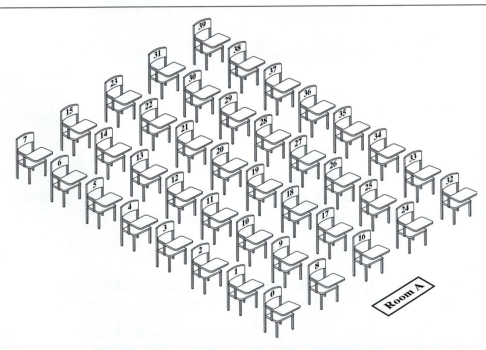

Suppose that the first student who arrives at the classroom sits at desk 0; the second student sits at desk 1, and so on. Eventually, 30 students occupy the desks numbered 0 through 29. They are organized by arrival time. The instructor knows immediately who arrived first (that person is at desk 0) and who arrived last (that person is at desk 29). Additionally, the instructor could ask for the name of the student seated at any particular desk, just as a programmer can access any array element directly. Thus, the instructor could ask for each student's name in order of arrival by polling desks 0 through 29, or in reverse order by polling desks 29 through 0. This action is called a **traversal**, or **iteration**, of the data. When you use an array to organize data in this manner, the implementation is said to be **array based**.

Instead of arranging the students in room A by arrival time, suppose that we arrange them alphabetically by name. Doing so requires a **sorting algorithm**, such as the ones that Chapters 11 and 12 will discuss. That is, the ADT list does not choose the order of its entries; the client must do so.

5.2   **Adding a new student.** Imagine that we have already arranged the students in room A alphabetically by name. Suppose that a new student wants to join the students already in the room. Recall that the 30 occupied desks are numbered sequentially from 0 to 29. Since 40 desks are in the room, the desk numbered 30 is available. When the students were arranged by arrival time, we would simply have assigned the new student to desk 30. Since the students are now arranged alphabetically by name, we must do more work.

Suppose that the new student belongs between the two students who occupy desks 10 and 11. That is, the new student's name is alphabetically between the names of the two students who occupy desks 10 and 11. Since the desks' positions are fixed, the new student must occupy desk 11. Before the new student can be seated, the student currently at desk 11 needs to move to desk 12, as Figure 5-2 illustrates. This requirement, however, causes a chain reaction: The student currently at desk 12 needs to move to desk 13, and so on. That is, each student seated in desks 11 through 29 must move to the next higher-numbered desk. If only one student moves at a time, the student in desk 29 must move to desk 30 before the student in desk 28 can move to desk 29, and so on. As you can see, adding a new student requires moving several other students. However, we do not disturb the students seated in the desks that are before the new student's desk—desks 0 through 10 in our example.

Figure 5-2   Seating a new student between two existing students: At least one other student must move

Question 1   In the previous example, under what circumstance could you add a new student alphabetically by name without moving any other student?

5.3   **Removing a student.** Now imagine that the student in desk 5 of room A drops the course. The desk stays in its fixed location within the room. If we still want students to sit in consecutively numbered desks, several students will need to move. In fact, each student in desks 6 through 30 must move to the next lower-numbered desk, beginning with the student in desk 6. That is, if only one student moves at a time, the student in desk 6 must move to desk 5 before the student in desk 7 moves to desk 6, and so on.

Question 2   What is an advantage of moving students as just described so that the vacated desk does not remain vacant?

Question 3   What is an advantage of leaving the vacated desk vacant?

The Java Implementation

5.4   The Java array-based implementation for the ADT list incorporates some of the ideas that our classroom example illustrates. The implementation is a class ALi st[1] that implements the interface ListInterface that you saw in Chapter 4. Each public method within the class corresponds to an ADT list operation. The private data fields are

- An array of objects
- An integer that counts the number of entries in the list
- An integer constant that defines the size of the array, which is the maximum length of the list

The Java definitions for these items appear as follows:

```
private T[] list;   // array of list entries
private int length; // current number of entries in list
private static final int MAX_SIZE = 50; // max length of list
```

T represents the data type of the entries in the list. It will be defined as a generic type within the class.

5.5   The class ALi st has the form shown in Listing 5-1. Notice the overall organization of the class, the private data, and the constructors. We use the class Object when allocating the array, but must cast it to an array whose entries have the generic type T. Also, notice the simple implementations of the methods clear, getLength, isEmpty, isFull, and display. We will provide implementations for the other methods shortly.

Listing 5-1   The class ALi st

```
public class AList<T> implements ListInterface<T>
{
   private T[] list;   // array of list entries
   private int length; // current number of entries in list

   private static final int MAX_SIZE = 50; // max length of list
```

---

1. Ordinarily we would name this class ArrayList. But as you will see at the end of this chapter, Java already provides a class with that name. Although we certainly could have named our class ArrayList as well, we chose a different name to avoid confusion.

```java
public AList()
{
   this(MAX_SIZE); // call next constructor
} // end default constructor

public AList(int maxSize)
{
   length = 0;
   list = (T[]) new Object[maxSize]; // necessary cast to generic type
} // end constructor

public boolean add(T newEntry)
{ < Implementation deferred >
} // end add

public boolean add(int newPosition, T newEntry)
{ < Implementation deferred >
} // end add

public T remove(int givenPosition)
{ < Implementation deferred >
} // end remove

public void clear()
{
   length = 0;
   < But see Question 4. >
} // end clear

public boolean replace(int givenPosition, T newEntry)
{ < Implementation deferred >
} // end replace

public T getEntry(int givenPosition)
{ < Implementation deferred >
} // end getEntry

public boolean contains(T anEntry)
{ < Implementation deferred >
} // end contains

public int getLength()
{
   return length;
} // end getLength

public boolean isEmpty()
{
   return length == 0; // or getLength() == 0
} // end isEmpty

public boolean isFull()
{
   return length == list.length;
} // end isFull
```

```
public void display()
{
   for (int index = 0; index < length; index++)
      System.out.println(list[index]);
} // end display
```

< This class will define two private methods that will be discussed later. >
```
} // end AList
```

Question 4   The method `clear` sets `length` to zero. Although the list methods will correctly behave as though the list is empty, the objects that were in the list will remain allocated. Suggest at least two ways to deallocate these objects.

5.6   **The first add method.** Now consider the implementations that we deferred. Adding a new entry to the end of the list is easy; we simply add the entry to the array immediately after its last occupied location. Of course, since we are using a fixed-size array, adding a new entry is possible only if the array has available space. If the array is full, our implementation returns false. Thus, the first add method has the following implementation:

```
public boolean add(T newEntry)
{
   boolean isSuccessful = true;

   if (!isFull())
   {
      // Assertion: Length of list < length of array
      assert length < list.length;

      // position of new entry will be after last entry in list,
      // that is, at position length+1; corresponding array index is
      // 1 less than this position, so index is length
      list[length] = newEntry;
      length++;
   }
   else
      isSuccessful = false;

   return isSuccessful;
} // end add
```

During the testing of this method, we can enable the assert statement to check that `isFull` executes correctly.

5.7   **The second add method.** Adding a new entry at an arbitrary position within the list is like adding a student to room A in our example in Segment 5.2. Although that example positions students alphabetically by their names, remember that the list's client—not the list itself—determines the desired position of each entry. Thus, if that position is before the end of the list, we need to shift existing entries to vacate the desired location so that it can accommodate the new entry. If the addition is to the end of the list, no such shift is necessary. In either case, space must be available in the array to accommodate a new entry.

The following implementation of add uses a private method `makeRoom` to handle the details of moving data within the array. Remember that we can add to the list at positions that range from 1 to the length of the list plus 1. According to the method's specifications given in Segment 4.10 of Chapter 4, we must return false if the list is full or the given position is invalid.

```java
public boolean add(int newPosition, T newEntry)
{
   boolean isSuccessful = true;

   if (!isFull() && (newPosition >= 1) && (newPosition <= length + 1))
   {
      makeRoom(newPosition);
      list[newPosition - 1] = newEntry;
      length++;
   }
   else
      isSuccessful = false;

   return isSuccessful;
} // end add
```

Now we must implement the private method makeRoom. Typically, the method shifts list entries toward the end of the array, beginning with the last entry, as Figure 5-3 illustrates. However, if newPosition is length + 1, the addition is at the end of the list, so no shift is necessary. In this case, makeRoom does nothing, since its for statement exits immediately.

```java
/** Task: Makes room for a new entry at newPosition.
 *  Precondition: 1 <= newPosition <= length+1;
 *                length is list's length before addition. */
private void makeRoom(int newPosition)
{
   assert (newPosition >= 1) && (newPosition <= length + 1);

   int newIndex = newPosition - 1;
   int lastIndex = length - 1;

   // move each entry to next higher index, starting at end of
   // list and continuing until the entry at newIndex is moved
   for (int index = lastIndex; index >= newIndex; index--)
      list[index + 1] = list[index];
} // end makeRoom
```

Notice that the add method enforces the precondition of makeRoom. While testing makeRoom, however, we can enable the assertion to be sure.

Figure 5-3   Making room to insert Carla as the third entry in an array

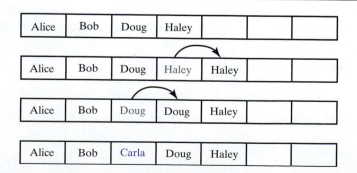

Note: For simplicity, our figures and discussion portray arrays as if they actually contained objects. In reality, Java arrays contain references to objects, as Figure 5-4 illustrates.

Figure 5-4   An array of objects contains references to those objects

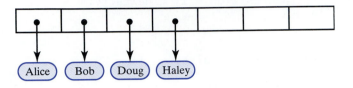

Question 5   You could implement the first add method, which adds an entry to the end of the list, by invoking the second add method, as follows:

```java
public boolean add(T newEntry)
{
    return add(length + 1, newEntry);
} // end add
```

Discuss the pros and cons of this revised approach.

Question 6   Suppose that myList is a list that contains the five entries a b c d e.

a. What does myList contain after executing myList.add(5, w)?
b. Starting with the original five entries, what does myList contain after executing myList.add(6, w)?
c. Which of the operations in Parts *a* and *b* of this question require elements in the array to shift?

Question 7   If myList is a list of five entries, each of the following statements adds a new entry to the end of the list:

```java
myList.add(newEntry);
myList.add(6, newEntry);
```

Which way requires fewer operations?

5.8   **The method remove.** Removing a list entry at an arbitrary position is like a student leaving room A in our example in Segment 5.3. We need to shift existing entries to avoid a gap in the array, except when removing the list's last entry. The following implementation uses a private method removeGap to handle the details of moving data within the array. Like the method add, remove is responsible for checking the validity of the given position.

```java
public T remove(int givenPosition)
{
    T result = null; // return value

    if ((givenPosition >= 1) && (givenPosition <= length))
    {
        assert !isEmpty();
        result = list[givenPosition - 1]; // get entry to be removed
```

```
      // move subsequent entries toward entry to be removed,
      // unless it is last in list
      if (givenPosition < length)
        removeGap(givenPosition);

      length--;
    } // end if

    return result; // return reference to removed entry, or
                   // null if either list is empty or givenPosition
                   // is invalid
} // end remove
```

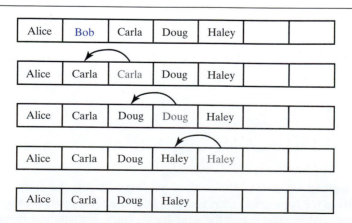

Question 8   Since the method remove does not explicitly check for an empty list, why is the assertion given in the method true?

Question 9   When a list is empty, why does remove return null?

The following private method removeGap shifts list entries within the array, as Figure 5-5 illustrates. Beginning with the entry after the one to be removed and continuing until the end of the list, removeGap moves each entry to its next lower position.

```
/** Task: Shifts entries that are beyond the entry to be removed
 *        to the next lower position.
 *  Precondition: 1 <= givenPosition < length;
 *                length is list's length before removal. */
private void removeGap(int givenPosition)
{
  assert (givenPosition >= 1) && (givenPosition < length);

  int removedIndex = givenPosition - 1;
  int lastIndex = length - 1;

  for (int index = removedIndex; index < lastIndex; index++)
    list[index] = list[index + 1];
} // end removeGap
```

Figure 5-5   Removing Bob by shifting array entries

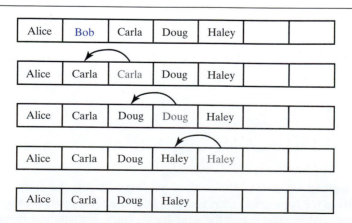

Note that no shift is necessary if the deletion is at the end of the list. In that case, the last entry in the list is at position `length`, since the first entry is at position 1. If `givenPosition` equals `length`, the `for` statement in `removeGap` will exit immediately. Although this case is not an error, we can skip it, as the method's precondition indicates. Note how the `remove` method enforces this precondition. You can enable the `assert` statement to verify this enforcement.

This precondition of `removeGap` implies that the method should not be called if a list is empty. In fact, `remove` ensures that requirement is followed.

Question 10   Figure 5-5 shows Haley shifted toward the beginning of the array. Actually, the reference to Haley is copied, not moved, to its new location. Should we assign `null` to Haley's original location?

5.9   **The methods replace and getEntry.** Replacing a list entry and retrieving a list entry are two straightforward operations when an array is used to represent the entries. You simply replace or retrieve the object that is in the indicated array location. Like earlier methods, `replace` and `getEntry` are responsible for validating the given position. Like `remove`, these methods do not need an explicit test for an empty list to behave correctly. The `assert` statement is available to verify this claim during testing.

The following methods implement these two operations:

```java
public boolean replace(int givenPosition, T newEntry)
{
   boolean isSuccessful = true;

   if ((givenPosition >= 1) && (givenPosition <= length))
   {
      assert !isEmpty();
      list[givenPosition - 1] = newEntry;
   }
   else
      isSuccessful = false;

   return isSuccessful;
} // end replace

public T getEntry(int givenPosition)
{
   T result = null; // result to return

   if ((givenPosition >= 1) && (givenPosition <= length))
   {
      assert !isEmpty();
      result = list[givenPosition - 1];
   } // end if

   return result;
} // end getEntry
```

Question 11   What is an advantage of using an array to organize data? What is a disadvantage?

5.10   **The method contains.** The method `getEntry` locates the entry at a given position by going directly to the appropriate array element. In contrast, the method `contains` is given an entry, not its position, and so must search the array for the entry. Beginning at index zero, the method examines each array element until it either locates the desired entry or reaches the end of the list without success. In the following implementation, we use a local boolean variable to terminate the loop when we find the desired entry:

```java
public boolean contains(T anEntry)
{
  boolean found = false;

  for (int index = 0; !found && (index < length); index++)
  {
    if (anEntry.equals(list[index]))
      found = true;
  } // end for

  return found;
} // end contains
```

This way of looking for a particular entry in an array is called a **sequential search**. Chapter 16 discusses this technique further and presents another algorithm that is generally faster.

5.11 **Testing the implementation.** Testing our class can begin well before we have completed its implementation. Imagine that the incomplete class appears as it does in Listing 5-1 of Segment 5.5. To avoid syntax errors, add a `return` statement to each method that returns a value. Since the methods are incomplete at this point, return a dummy value. For example, methods that return a boolean value could return true. Methods that return an object could return `null`.

After you define the constructors, implement the method `display` and one or both of the `add` methods. Now write a `main` method to test what you have completed at this point. As you define more methods, test them by adding statements to `main`. As Chapter 1 noted, you can include your method `main` in the definition of `AList` for future use and reference.

Note: Using a fixed-size array to implement the ADT list limits the size of the list. Some lists naturally have a finite size, so this implementation is both appropriate and useful. For other lists, one of the other implementations given in this chapter and in Chapters 6 and 7 would be more fitting.

5.12 **Serialization.** Before we continue, we want to make a small change to our implementation so that clients can save a list in a file with little effort. Appendix C introduces a process called **object serialization** that represents an object as a sequence of bytes that are written to a file. This process is possible for any instances of a class that implements the interface `Serializable`. This interface—which is in the package `java.io` of the Java Class Library—is empty, so you have no additional methods to implement. Adding only the words `implements java.io.Serializable` to the class's definition is enough.

For example, we could begin the class `AList` as follows:

```java
public class AList<T> implements ListInterface<T>,
                                 java.io.Serializable
{
  . . .
```

The `Serializable` interface tells the compiler that instances of `AList` can be **serialized**, that is, can be written to a file using object serialization.

If the list `myList` is an instance of `AList`, you serialize it by using the method `writeObject` from the class `ObjectOutputStream`. To reconstruct an object, you use the method `readObject` from the class `ObjectInputStream`. Any objects that are in `myList` must also belong to a class that implements `Serializable`. Such objects are serialized when `myList` is serialized. Appendix C provides an example of serialization and more information about writing and reading files.

 Programming Tip: A class that represents a collection of objects should implement the interface `Serializable`. By simply adding `java.io.Serializable` to the list of interfaces that a class implements, you can provide clients of that class with an easy way to place instances of the class in a file.

Using Array Expansion to Implement the ADT List

5.13   An array, of course, has a fixed size. You choose this size when the array is created. Segment 5.5 of the previous section used a fixed-size array to represent the entries in a list. When the array, and hence the list, becomes full, the method `isFull` returns true and subsequent calls to the add methods return false.

The fixed-size array in the previous implementation of the ADT list is like our classroom. If the room contains 40 desks but only 30 students, we waste 10 desks. If 40 students register for the course, the room is full and cannot accommodate anyone else. Likewise, if we do not use all of the locations in an array, we waste memory. If we need more, we are out of luck. For example, the implementation in the previous section denies a request to add to a list that already contains a maximum number of entries.

Some applications can use a list that has a limited length. For example, the length of a list of airline passengers or a list of ticket holders to a movie should not exceed a known maximum. For other applications, however, the length of a list can grow without bound. We will now show you how a list can be as long as you want but still use an array to represent its entries.

Expanding an Array

5.14   One way to accommodate additional students is to use a larger room. Imagine that you are seated at your desk waiting for class to start. The professor arrives and announces that the class must move to a larger room. Suppose that the students leave one room and move to another without changing desk numbers. That is, a student at desk *n* in the old room will occupy desk *n* in the new room.

In a similar manner, when an array becomes full, you can move its contents to a larger array. This process is called the **dynamic expansion** of an array. Figure 5-6 shows two arrays: an original array of five consecutive memory locations and another array—twice the size of the original array—that is in another part of the computer's memory. If you copy the data from the original smaller array to the first five locations in the new larger array, the result will be like expanding the original array. The only glitch in this scheme is the name of the new array: You want it to be the same as the name of the old array. This is possible, as you will see momentarily.

Figure 5-6   The dynamic expansion of an array copies the array's contents to a larger second array

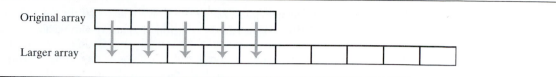

5.15   Let's work with a simple array of integers:

```
int[] myArray = new int[INITIAL_SIZE];
```

where INITIAL_SIZE is an integer constant. At this point, myArray references the array in Figure 5-7a. Next, we'll save the reference to this array by writing

```
int[] oldArray = myArray; // save reference to myArray
```

Both oldArray and myArray contain the same value, namely the address of the array. That is, old-Array and myArray each reference the array, as Figure 5-7b illustrates. For example, oldArray[0] and myArray[0] reference the same location: the first location of the array.

Now we'll allocate a new, larger array, but we'll let only myArray reference it:

```
myArray = new int[2 * oldArray.length]; // double size of array
```

Figure 5-7c illustrates the two arrays.

Finally, we'll copy the data from the original array (oldArray) to the new array (myArray):

```
for (int index = 0; index < oldArray.length; index++)
    myArray[index] = oldArray[index];
```

Figure 5-7   (a) An array; (b) the same array with two references; (c) the original array variable now references a new, larger array

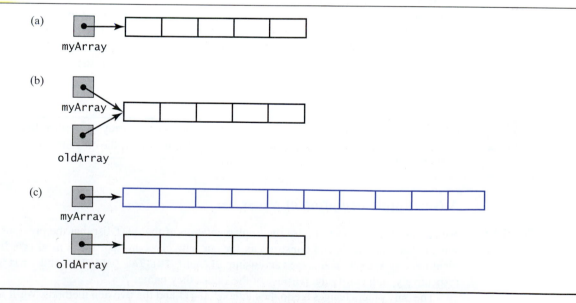

Note: Copying arrays

The class System in the package java.lang of the Java Class Library has the following static method arraycopy that quickly copies all or a portion of an array of objects:

```
/** Task: Copies the count objects in fromArray beginning at the
           index fromIndex to toArray starting at toIndex. */
public static void arraycopy(Object fromArray, int fromIndex,
                             Object toArray, int toIndex, int count)
```

For example, if the arrays a and b contain objects of the same type, and b is at least as large as a, the statement

```
System.arraycopy(a, 0, b, 0, a.length);
```

copies all of a to b.

If fromArray and toArray reference the same array, arraycopy behaves as if the relevant elements are copied to a temporary array and then copied back to the desired position within the original array.

Note that the method name is arraycopy, not arrayCopy.

5.16   Expanding the size of an array is not as attractive as it might first seem. Each time you expand an array, you must copy its contents. If you were to expand an array by one element each time you needed additional space in the array, the process would be expensive. For example, if a 50-element array represented a full list of 50 entries, adding an entry to the list would require that you copy the array to a 51-element array. Adding another entry would require that you copy the 51-element array to a 52-element array, and so on. Each addition would cause the array to be copied. If you added 50 entries to the original 50-entry list, you would copy the array 50 times.

However, expanding the array by *m* elements spreads the copying cost over *m* additions instead of just one. Doubling the size of an array each time it becomes full is a typical approach. For example, when you add an entry to a full list of 50 entries, you copy the 50-element array to a 100-element array before completing the addition. The next 49 additions then can be made quickly without copying the array. Thus, you will have added 50 entries to the original list but will have copied the array only once.

Note: During dynamic array expansion, the elements of an array are copied to a larger array. You should expand the array sufficiently to reduce the impact of the cost of copying.

A New Implementation of a List

5.17   We can use these ideas to revise the implementation of the ADT list that the previous section presented. The data fields and constructors for our new class are like those in AList. Instead of the identifiers MAX_SIZE and maxSize, using DEFAULT_INITIAL_CAPACITY and initialCapacity, respectively, will clarify the purpose of the values they name.

The only other changes are to the method isFull and the two add methods. We'll revise isFull to always return false. Since we will expand the array when it becomes full, the list is never full.

Instead of ignoring an addition when the array is full, each of the revised add methods doubles the array by calling a new private method doubleArray. To detect when the array is full, we define another private method isArrayFull, whose implementation is the same as the method isFull in the class AList. (See Segment 5.5.) For example, the first add method would appear as follows:

```
public boolean add(T newEntry)
{
  if (isArrayFull())
    doubleArray();

  // add new entry after last current entry
  list[length] = newEntry;
  length++;

  return true;
} // end add
```

You would make similar changes to the second add method.

Question 12 Revise the second add method, which adds an entry at a given position within the list, so that it uses dynamic array expansion.

5.18   The private method doubleArray incorporates our recent discussion of expanding an array, and appears as follows:

```
/** Task: Doubles the size of the array of list entries. */
private void doubleArray()
{
  T[] oldList = list; // save reference to array of list entries
  int oldSize = oldList.length; // save old max size of array

  list = (T[]) new Object[2 * oldSize]; // double size of array

  // copy entries from old array to new, bigger array
  for (int index = 0; index < oldSize; index++)
    list[index] = oldList[index];
} // end doubleArray
```

This completes the revised implementation. We will call the new class ExpandableArrayList.

Question 13 What call to System.arraycopy can replace the for loop in the method doubleArray?

5.19   If the method isFull always returns false, why bother implementing it? The short answer is that isFull is in ListInterface, so any class that implements ListInterface must define it. If ExpandableArrayList did not implement isFull, we would have to declare the class as abstract. Thus, we would not be able to create an instance of ExpandableArrayList. Should we omit isFull from ListInterface? If we do, our array-based implementation AList can still define isFull. That is, a class that implements an interface can contain methods that are not specified in the interface. However, let's see what happens if we do omit isFull from ListInterface.

Suppose that AList implements isFull, but ExpandableArrayList does not. If the client uses isFull, changing from one implementation of the ADT list (AList) to another

(ExpandableArrayList) would not be as simple as it should be. We would need to modify the client so that it did not use isFull. In addition, any instance of ListInterface, such as myList in the statement

        ListInterface myList = **new** AList();

would be unable to invoke isFull, even though AList implements it.

Programming Tip: A class implementing a single interface that declares the operations of an ADT should define the methods declared in the interface as its only public methods. The class can also define private methods and protected methods.

Java Class Library: The Classes **ArrayList** and **Vector**

5.20   The Java Class Library has two classes—ArrayList and Vector—that use dynamic array expansion, as we described in the preceding section. As such, they are similar to our class Expandable-ArrayList in that their instances never get full. Both classes are in the package java.util, and both implement the interface List, which is in the same package. Both classes are defined in terms of a generic type.

Recall from Chapter 4 that compared to our ListInterface, List

- Begins numbering a list's entries at 0 instead of 1
- Specifies more methods
- Specifies that methods throw an exception if passed an illegal position
- Has some different method names and return values
- Does not specify a method to display a list

ArrayList and Vector implement other interfaces besides List. Although both classes implement the same interfaces, Vector contains a few more methods than ArrayList. We will ignore these extra methods, as they mostly are redundant.

5.21   Each of the classes ArrayList and Vector has several constructors. Here is a description of some of them:

public ArrayList()
Creates an empty list with an initial capacity of 10. The list increases its capacity as needed by an unspecified amount.

public ArrayList(**int** initialCapacity)
Creates an empty list with the specified initial capacity. The list increases its capacity as needed by an unspecified amount.

public Vector()
Creates an empty **vector**, or arraylike container, with an initial capacity of 10. When the vector needs to increase its capacity, the capacity doubles.

public Vector(**int** initialCapacity)
Creates an empty vector with the specified initial capacity. When the vector needs to increase its capacity, the capacity doubles.

You can learn more about ArrayList and Vector at java.sun.com/j2se/1.5/docs/api/.

5.22   If you like the interface List, you can use either ArrayList or Vector as its implementation. For example, you could write the following statement to define a list of strings:

```
List<String> myList = new ArrayList<String>();
```

Now myList has only the methods declared in the interface List.

Our ListInterface is somewhat simpler than Java's List. It has fewer methods, which do not throw an exception when given an illegal position. We can retain the simplicity of our interface and still make use of an existing class by using either ArrayList or Vector in an implementation of ListInterface. We will show you how in the next segment. Although we will use Vector, you can use ArrayList just as easily.

Using a Vector to Implement the ADT List

5.23   One way to let a list grow as needed is to use dynamic array expansion, as we did in the implementation of ExpandableArrayList. Another way uses an instance of Java's Vector class to represent the list's entries. The class Vector provides the capabilities of an array that expands dynamically, but it hides the details of the process. If we store our list entries in an instance of Vector, we can use Vector's methods to manipulate our list entries. Figure 5-8 shows a client interacting with a list by using the methods in ListInterface. The implementations of these methods in turn interact with Vector's methods to produce the desired effects on the list.

Figure 5-8   A client uses the methods given in ListInterface, but the implementation of the list uses Vector methods to perform its operations

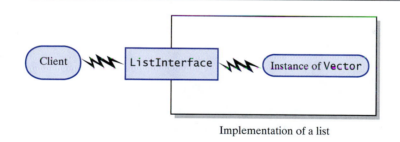

Implementation of a list

5.24   **Beginning the class.** We begin our new class as follows:

```
import java.util.Vector;

public class VectorList<T> implements ListInterface<T>
{
    private Vector<T> list; // entries in list
    . . .
```

We must provide the import statement, since the code that follows uses the class Vector from the package java.util. Sometimes programmers will replace Vector in this statement with an asterisk to make all classes in the package java.util available to their programs.

The data field list is now an instance of Vector instead of an array, as it was earlier in this chapter. Since Vector is defined in terms of a generic type, you provide a data type when declaring a vector. However, within our class `VectorList`, the data type of the list's objects is still unknown, so we use the generic type T in the declaration of the field `list`.

Since a vector keeps track of the number of entries it contains, a data field `length` is not required. Any time we want to know the number of entries in the vector, and hence the list, we can write `list.size()`.

5.25   **The constructors.** The constructors for our class create an instance of `Vector` by invoking `Vector`'s constructors. Our default constructor simply invokes `Vector`'s default constructor with the generic type T:

```
public VectorList()
{
   list = new Vector<T>();
} // end default constructor
```

`Vector`'s default constructor creates a vector that can hold ten entries. This vector will double in size after it becomes full.

Our second constructor enables the client to specify the initial capacity of the list. It invokes a corresponding constructor of `Vector`:

```
public VectorList(int initialSize)
{
   list = new Vector<T>(initialSize);
} // end constructor
```

Here, `Vector`'s constructor creates a vector that can hold `initialSize` entries. This vector also will double in size after it becomes full.

If we wanted a different initial capacity for our default list, we could define the default constructor, as follows, instead of as given previously:

```
public VectorList()
{
   this(INITIAL_CAPACITY);
} // end default constructor
```

This version of the default constructor calls `VectorList`'s second constructor, passing it a constant `INITIAL_CAPACITY`, which the class must define.

5.26   **The add methods.** To add to the end of a list, you use `Vector`'s add method. This method adds a given object to the end of a vector. If necessary, the vector increases its capacity to accommodate the new entry. Thus, our add method does not test whether the vector is full:

```
public boolean add(T newEntry)
{
   return list.add(newEntry);
} // end add
```

To add an entry at a given position in the list, we use another of `Vector`'s add methods. This method throws an exception if `newPosition` is illegal, but we simply want to return false in this case. By checking the validity of `newPosition`, we can avoid the exception. Remember that `Vector` numbers its entries beginning with 0 instead of 1.

```
public boolean add(int newPosition, T newEntry)
{
   boolean isSuccessful = true;
```

```
      if ((newPosition >= 1) && (newPosition <= list.size() + 1))
        list.add(newPosition - 1, newEntry);
      else
        isSuccessful = false;

      return isSuccessful;
  } // end add
```

5.27 **The method replace.** The method replace has an implementation similar to the one you just saw. It uses the statement

```
    list.set(givenPosition - 1, newEntry);
```

to replace a designated entry in the list.

```
      public boolean replace(int givenPosition, T newEntry)
      {
        boolean isSuccessful = true;

        if ((givenPosition >= 1) && (givenPosition <= list.size()))
        {
          assert !isEmpty();
          list.set(givenPosition - 1, newEntry);
        }
        else
          isSuccessful = false;

        return isSuccessful;
      } // end replace
```

5.28 **The method remove.** Our method remove uses Vector's method remove, which returns the object it removes from the vector. Like add, Vector's remove throws an exception when given an illegal position. Our method, however, will return null in this case. Thus, our remove method has the following implementation:

```
      public T remove(int givenPosition)
      {
        T result = null; // return value

        if ((givenPosition >= 1) && (givenPosition <= list.size()))
        {
          assert !isEmpty();
          result = list.remove(givenPosition - 1);
        } // end if

        return result;
      } // end remove
```

5.29 **The method getEntry.** The method getEntry has a similar implementation. It uses the expression

```
    list.get(givenPosition - 1);
```

to retrieve a particular entry from the list.

```
public T getEntry(int givenPosition)
{
  T result = null; // return value

  if ((givenPosition >= 1) && (givenPosition <= list.size()))
  {
    assert !isEmpty();
    result = list.get(givenPosition - 1);
  } // end if

  return result;
} // end getEntry
```

5.30   **Remaining methods.** The method `clear` uses the statement

```
list.clear();
```

to remove all entries from the vector and hence from the list. Likewise, the implementations of the methods `contains`, `getLength`, `isEmpty`, and `display` are simple and left as exercises. As in the previous section, the method `isFull` always returns false.

5.31   The methods in our class `VectorList` function similarly to methods in Java's class `Vector`, but their specifications differ. In implementing `ListInterface`, `VectorList` simply invokes methods of the class `Vector`. `VectorList` is an example of an adapter class, which we described in Segment 2.7 of Chapter 2.

Writing `VectorList` is certainly easier than writing either of the other two array-based implementations that this chapter describes. However, since the methods of `VectorList` invoke the methods of `Vector`, they typically require more execution time than those of `AList` and `ExpandableArrayList`.

 Note: Implementations of the ADT list that use either dynamic array expansion or an instance of `Vector` let the list grow as needed.

The Pros and Cons of Using an Array to Implement the ADT List

5.32   This chapter discussed three implementations of the ADT list. Since Java's class `Vector` uses an array in its implementation, all of this chapter's implementations are based on an array.

An array is simple to use and enables you to access any element immediately, if you know its index. Thus, the list's retrieval operation `getEntry` is easy to write and quick to execute. Adding to the end of a list, and hence to the array, is equally easy and fast.

On the other hand, using a fixed-size array limits the size of a list, which is usually a disadvantage. Using either dynamic array expansion or a vector enables you to increase the array's size but requires copying data.

Regardless of whether the size of the array is fixed or dynamic, adding or removing entries that are between other entries requires shifting elements in the array. This data movement degrades the time efficiency of these operations, particularly when the list is long and the position of the addition or removal is near the beginning of the list. The implementation in the next chapter avoids this particular disadvantage but has disadvantages of its own.

You should realize that the elements that we shift in the array are references, and so do not occupy much space nor take much time to move. Some languages other than Java store the data itself within the array. In that case, moving large, complex objects can be quite time-consuming.

Note: When you use an array or vector to implement the ADT list,

- Retrieving the entry at a given position is fast
- Adding an entry at the end of a list is fast
- Adding or removing an entry that is between other entries requires shifting elements in the array
- Increasing the size of the array or vector requires copying elements

---

CHAPTER SUMMARY

- The three implementations of the ADT list in this chapter use an array to store the items in a list.

- Using an array results in relatively simple implementations of the list.

- An array provides direct access to any of its elements, so a method such as `getEntry` has a simple, efficient implementation.

- Using a fixed-size array can result in a full list. Using either dynamic array expansion or an instance of `Vector` avoids this drawback.

- Adding an entry to or removing an entry from an array-based list typically requires that other entries shift by one position within the array.

- Object serialization enables you to write objects to a file. Such objects must belong to a class that implements the interface `java.io.Serializable`.

- Expanding the size of an array requires copying the contents of the array to a larger array. The method `arraycopy` in the class `java.lang.System` quickly copies the elements from one array to another.

- Using an instance of `java.util.Vector` has the same advantages and disadvantages as using dynamic array expansion but results in an implementation that is much easier to write.

PROGRAMMING TIPS

- A class that represents a collection of objects should implement the interface `Serializable`. By simply adding `java.io.Serializable` to the list of interfaces that a class implements, you can provide clients of that class with an easy way to place instances of the class in a file.

- A class implementing a single interface that declares the operations of an ADT should define the methods declared in the interface as its only public methods. The class can also define private methods and protected methods.

EXERCISES

1. Add a constructor to each of the classes `AList`, `ExpandableArrayList`, and `VectorList` that creates a list from a given array of objects.

2. Suppose that you want an operation for the ADT list that returns the position of a given object in the list. The header of the method could be as follows:

   public int getPosition(T anObject)

   where T is the generic type of the objects in the list. Write an implemention of this method for each of the three classes described in this chapter.

3. Suppose that you want an operation for the ADT list that removes the first occurrence of a given object from the list. The header of the method could be as follows:

   public boolean remove(T anObject)

   where T is the generic type of the objects in the list. The method returns true if the list contained anObject and that object was removed. Write an implementation of this method for each of the three classes described in this chapter.

4. Suppose that you want an operation for the ADT list that moves the first item in the list to the end of the list. The header of the method could be as follows:

   public void moveToEnd()

   Write an implemention of this method for each of the three classes described in this chapter.

5. Exercise 7 in the previous chapter asked you to write statements at the client level that replace an object in a given list. Write a method at the client level that performs such a replacement. How does your method compare with the method replace of the ADT list?

6. Implement a method replace for the ADT list that returns the replaced object. Do this for each of the three classes described in this chapter.

7. Suppose that a list contains Comparable objects. Implement the following methods for each of the three classes described in this chapter.

   a. The method getMin that returns the smallest object in the list
   b. The method removeMin that removes and returns the smallest object in the list

8. Implement an equals method for the ADT list that returns true when the entries in one list equal the entries in a second list. In particular, add this method to the classes AList and VectorList.

9. Implement the methods contains, getLength, isEmpty, and display in the class VectorList.

10. The class ExpandableArrayList has an array that can grow in size as objects are added to the list. Consider a similar class whose array also can shrink in size as objects are removed from the list. Accomplishing this task will require two new private methods.
    The first new method checks whether we should reduce the size of the array:

    private boolean isTooBig()

    This method returns true if the number of elements in the list is less than half the size of the array and the size of the array is greater than 20.
    The second new method creates a new array that is three quarters the size of the current array and then copies the objects in the list to the new array:

    private void reduceArray()

    Implement each of these two methods for our new class. Then use these methods in the definition of the method remove.

11. Consider the two private methods described in the previous question.

    a. The method `isTooBig` requires the size of array to be greater than 20. What problem could occur if this requirement is dropped?

    b. The method `reduceArray` is not analogous to the method `doubleArray` in that it does not reduce the size of the array by one half. What problem could occur if the size of the array is reduced by half instead of three quarters?

PROJECTS

1. Complete the implementation of the class `ExpandableArrayList`.

2. Complete the implementation of the class `VectorList`.

3. Write a class that implements the interface `ListInterface` by using an instance of the class `java.util.ArrayList`. Compare your new class with the class `VectorList`.

4. Implement the interface `ListInterface` by using an array in which you ignore the first array location. Thus, you store the list's i^{th} entry in the array location at index i.

5. Implement as the class `Bag` the ADT bag that Project 2 of Chapter 4 describes. Represent the bag as an array that you expand dynamically as necessary. Then write a program that adequately demonstrates the methods of the class `Bag`.

6. Using the class `Bag` described in the previous project, implement a class `PiggyBank` as described in Project 3 of Chapter 4. Then write a program that adequately demonstrates `PiggyBank`.

7. Repeat Project 5, but instead use an instance of `java.util.Vector` to represent the bag.

8. Project 4 of Chapter 4 describes the ADT set. Implement this ADT by using

    a. An array that you expand dynamically as necessary

    b. An instance of `java.util.Vector`

    c. An instance of `Bag`

    Then write a program that adequately demonstrates your implementations.

9. Implement as the class `Shoe` the ADT shoe that Project 1 of Chapter 4 described. *Hint*: To shuffle the shoe, use two private lists of cards, a source list and a shuffled list. Put all the available cards into the source list. Initially, this will be every card. Later, only those cards not held by a player will be available. Use the class `java.util.Random` to repeatedly generate a random position in the source list, remove the card at that position, and put it at the end of the shuffled list.

    Write a program that adequately demonstrates the operation of the class `Shoe`.

10. Implement the ADT for the objects in Santa's nice list that Project 5 of Chapter 4 describes. Then create some instances of your class and place them on the nice list.

11. Implement the ADT bid that Project 7 of Chapter 4 describes.

12. Implement the ADT recipe that Project 8 of Chapter 4 describes.

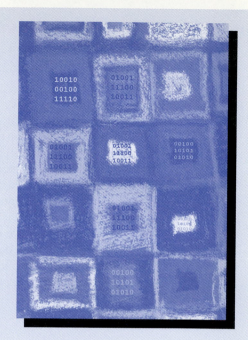

CHAPTER

6

A List Implementation That Links Data

PREREQUISITES

OBJECTIVES

After studying this chapter, you should be able to

- Describe a linked organization of data
- Implement the **add** methods of the ADT list by using a linked chain of nodes
- Test a partially complete implementation of a class

Using an array to implement the ADT list has both advantages and disadvantages, as you saw in Chapter 5. An array can either have a fixed size or be moved to a larger array when it becomes full. A fixed-size array can lead to a full list. Although dynamic array expansion can provide as much space as the list needs, you must move data each time you expand the array. In addition, any array requires you to move data either to make room for a new entry or to close up a gap after a deletion.

This chapter introduces a data organization that uses memory only as needed for a new entry and returns the unneeded memory to the system after an entry is removed. By linking data, this new organization avoids moving data when adding or removing list entries. These features make this way of implementing a list an important alternative to array-based approaches.

In this chapter, we will begin to describe a linked implementation of the list and focus on some core methods. When defining a class, it is often useful to implement and test these core methods first and to leave definitions of the other methods for later. That is the technique we shall use here. The next chapter completes the linked implementation of the list and explores some variations of that approach.

Linked Data

6.1   In Chapter 5, we used the analogy of a classroom to describe how data is stored in an array. Here we use a classroom to show you another way to organize data.

Imagine an empty classroom—room L—that is assigned to a course. All available desks are in the hallway. Any student who registers for the course receives a desk, takes it into the room, and sits at it. Assume that the room can accommodate all of the desks in the hall.

Each desk in the hallway has a number stamped on its back. This number—called an **address**—never changes and is not considered when desks are given to students. Thus, the room will eventually contain desks whose addresses are not sequential.

Now imagine that Jill is among 30 students who are seated in room L at exactly 30 desks. Taped to each desktop is a piece of paper. As Jill entered the room, we wrote on her paper the desk number (address) of another desk in the room. For example, the paper on Jill's desk might contain the number 20. If her desk is desk 15, we say that desk 15 **references** desk 20 and that desks 15 and 20 are **linked**. Since the desks are linked to one another, we say that they form a **chain** of desks.

Figure 6-1 shows a chain of five desks. No desk references the first desk in the chain, but the instructor knows its desk number, 22. Notice that the last desk in the chain does not reference another desk; the piece of paper on this desk is blank.

6.2   The chain of desks provides an order for the desks. Suppose that first in the chain is the student who arrived most recently. Written on this student's desk is the desk number of the student who arrived just before. With one exception, everyone's desk references the desk of the student who arrived just before. The exception is the person who arrived first. That person sits at the last desk, which does not reference another desk.

The instructor knows the address of the first desk in the chain and so can ask questions of the student at that first desk. Then, by looking at the address, or desk number, that is written on the paper on the first desk, the instructor can locate the second desk in the chain and can question its occupant. Continuing in this way, the instructor can visit every desk in the order in which they appear in the chain. Ultimately, the instructor reaches the desk that references no other desk. The only way the instructor can locate the student in this last desk is to begin at the first desk. The instructor can traverse this chain in only one order. In Chapter 5, however, the instructor in room A was able to ask questions of any student in any order.

Figure 6-1   A chain of five desks

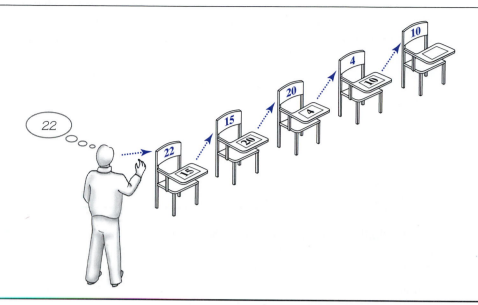

Forming a Chain by Adding to Its Beginning

6.3   How did we form the chain of desks in the first place? Let's return to the time when room L was empty and all available desks were in the hallway.

Suppose that Matt arrives first. He gets a desk from the hallway and enters the room. The instructor notes Matt's desk number (address), and we leave the paper on his desk blank to indicate that no other student has arrived. The room appears as in Figure 6-2.

Figure 6-2   One desk in the room

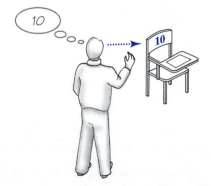

6.4   When the second student arrives, we write Matt's desk number on the new desk's paper and give the instructor the number of the new (second) desk to remember. Let's assume that the instructor can remember only one desk number at a time. The room appears as in Figure 6-3.

Figure 6-3   Two linked desks, with the newest desk first

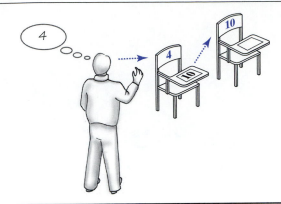

6.5   When the third student arrives, we write the instructor's memorized desk number, which is that of the second desk, on the new desk's paper and then tell the instructor to remember the number of the new (third) desk. The room appears as in Figure 6-4.

6.6   After all the students have arrived, the instructor knows only the desk number of the student who arrived most recently. On that student's desk is the desk number of the student who arrived just previously. In general, written on each student's desk is the number of the desk that belongs to the previous student who arrived. Since Matt was the first student to arrive, the paper on his desk is still blank. In Figures 6-1 through 6-4, Matt is the person at desk 10.

Figure 6-4   Three linked desks, with the newest desk first

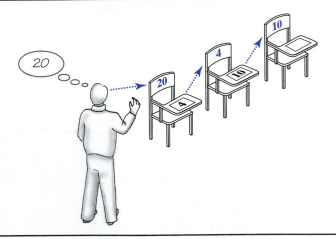

Question 1   The instructor knows the address of only one desk.

a.   Where in the chain is that desk: first, last, or somewhere else?

b.   Who is sitting at that desk: the student who arrived first, the student who arrived last, or someone else?

Question 2   Where in the chain of desks is a new desk added: at the beginning, at the end, or somewhere else?

6.7   The following pseudocode details the steps taken to form a chain of desks by adding new desks to the beginning of the chain:

```
// Process the first student
newDesk represents the new student's desk
New student sits at newDesk
Instructor memorizes address of newDesk

// Process the remaining students
while (students arrive)
{
    newDesk represents the new student's desk
    New student sits at newDesk
    Write the instructor's memorized address on newDesk
    Instructor memorizes address of newDesk
}
```

Notice that the chain of desks organizes the students in reverse order of their arrival times. When done, the instructor knows the address of the first desk in the chain; seated at this desk is the last student to arrive.

Forming a Chain by Adding to Its End

6.8   Suppose that we want to organize the chain in a different way, so that the first student to arrive will be first in the chain and the last student to arrive will be last. Once again, suppose that Matt is the first student to arrive. He is accommodated as in the previous example. That is, his desk number (address) is given to the instructor and the paper on his desk is left blank. So far, the situation is the same as the one shown in Figure 6-2.

When the second student arrives, we write the number of the second desk on the paper that is on Matt's desk and leave the new desk's paper blank. (Recall that in the previous chain Matt's paper remained blank the entire time.) Note that the instructor remembers only the address of Matt's desk, since he was the first student to arrive. Figure 6-5 shows the chain at this point.

Figure 6-5   Two linked desks, with the newest desk last

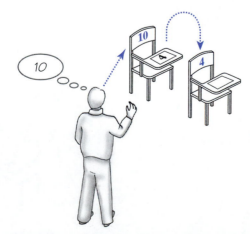

When the third student arrives, we must write the number of the third desk on the paper that is on the second desk. The instructor no longer knows the address of the second desk, but we can get it by looking at the paper on the first desk. As we did previously, we leave the new desk's paper blank. Figure 6-6 shows what the chain looks like now.

Figure 6-6   Three linked desks, with the newest desk last

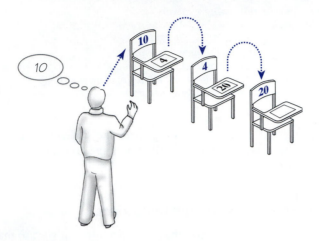

6.9   For each new student, we must write the number of the new desk on the paper that is on the last desk in the chain. To locate the last desk, we begin by asking the instructor for the address of the first desk. Next, we look at the paper on the first desk and get the address of the second desk, then look at the paper on the second desk and get the address of the third desk, and so on until we find the address of the last desk. That is, we must traverse the chain of desks each time we link a new desk to the end of the chain of desks. After all of the students have arrived, the instructor still remembers Matt's desk number, since he was the first student to arrive. Figure 6-7 shows the room after five students have arrived.

Figure 6-7   Five linked desks, with the newest desk last

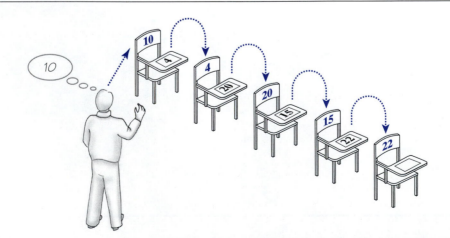

Written on the paper that is on Matt's desk—which is first in the chain—is the desk number for the second student to arrive. That is, his desk references the desk of the second student to arrive. The second desk references the desk of the third student to arrive. Except for the last desk, each desk references the desk that belongs to the student who arrived next. The paper on the last student's desk is blank.

Question 3   The instructor remembers the address of only one desk.

a.   Where in the chain is that desk: first, last, or somewhere else?
b.   Who is sitting at that desk: the student who arrived first, the student who arrived last, or someone else?

Question 4   Where in the chain of desks is a new desk added: at the beginning, at the end, or somewhere else?

6.10   The following pseudocode details the steps taken to form a chain of desks by adding new desks to the end of the chain:

```
// Process the first student
newDesk represents the new student's desk
New student sits at newDesk
Instructor memorizes address of newDesk

// Process the remaining students
while (students arrive)
{
    newDesk represents the new student's desk
    New student sits at newDesk
    Traverse the chain to locate its last desk
    Write the address of newDesk on this last desk
}
```

This chain of desks organizes the students in order of their arrival times. When done, the instructor knows the address of the first desk in the chain; seated at this desk is the first student to arrive.

You can see that we did more work this time. Each time we added a new desk to the end of the chain, we traversed the entire chain to locate the last desk. It is much easier to add a desk to the beginning of the chain than to its end.

Question 5   What is an advantage of using a linked organization of data? What is a disadvantage?

Forming a Chain by Adding at Various Positions

6.11   Organizing students chronologically by their arrival times required us to add each new student to the beginning or end of the chain of desks. No student or desk currently in the room had to move.

Suppose that we instead want to organize the students alphabetically by their names. We can examine the details of the necessary algorithm by considering room L after a few students enter the room and are organized alphabetically. Assume that the students' desks are linked, that the instructor knows the address of the first desk in the chain, and that this desk is occupied by the student whose name is alphabetically earliest.

6.12   **Adding at a particular position in a chain.** Imagine that a new student wants to join the students in room L. The student gets any available desk from the hallway. We must link this new desk to the desks currently in the room so that the new student is in the correct position within the current arrangement of students. This link can be made without moving any current student in the room. To simplify our discussion, when we mention an address *on* a desk, we mean the address that is written on the paper that is on the desk—in other words, the address of the next desk in the chain. In contrast, a desk's address is the fixed address that is stamped on the back of each desk.

The details of how to insert a new desk into the chain depend on where in the chain the desk belongs. Consider the following cases:

- Case 1: The new desk belongs before all current desks.
- Case 2: The new desk belongs between two current desks.
- Case 3: The new desk belongs after all current desks.

As you will see, the last case is really not a special case.

6.13   **Case 1.** Figure 6-8 depicts Case 1 before we add the new desk to the beginning of the chain. In this figure,

- newDesk represents the new student's desk
- firstDesk represents the first desk in the chain

Figure 6-8   A chain of desks just prior to adding a new desk to the beginning of the chain

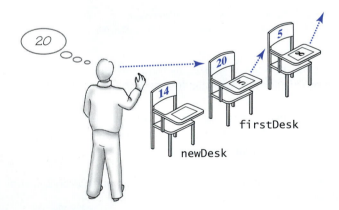

Recall that the instructor, or **head** of the chain, knows the address of the first desk. Two steps are necessary in this case:

1. Place the address of firstDesk on newDesk. (newDesk now references firstDesk.)
2. Give the address of newDesk to the instructor (head).

Figure 6-9 illustrates the result of these steps. Notice that this case is like the situations depicted in Figures 6-3 and 6-4 that added desks to the beginning of a chain.

Figure 6-9   The addition of a new desk to the beginning of a chain of desks

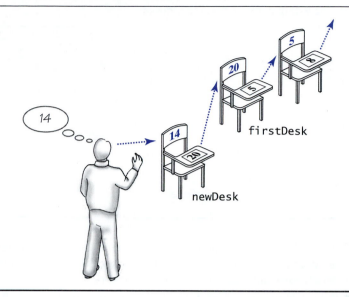

6.14   **Case 2.** Figure 6-10 shows Case 2 before we add the new desk between two desks currently in the chain, where

- newDesk represents the new student's desk
- deskBefore represents the desk that will be before newDesk in the final arrangement
- deskAfter represents the desk currently after deskBefore; its address is on deskBefore

Figure 6-10   Two consecutive desks within a chain of desks just prior to adding a new desk between them

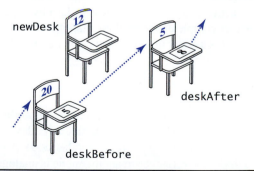

The following steps are necessary to place the new desk between the two consecutive desks desk-Before and deskAfter:

1. Copy the address on deskBefore (that is, deskAfter's address) and place it on newDesk.
2. Place the address of newDesk on deskBefore.

Figure 6-11 illustrates the result of these steps.

Figure 6-11   The addition of a new desk between two other desks

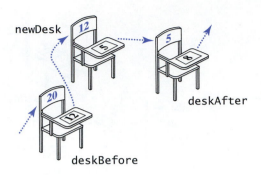

6.15   **Case 3.** When the new desk belongs after all current desks, the situation is like Case 2, except that deskAfter does not exist. Remember that the paper on the desk of the last student is blank. That desk is deskBefore and does not reference any other.

In this situation, Step 1 of Case 2 copies blank from deskBefore to newDesk. This step, together with the other step of Case 2, is exactly what needs to happen so that newDesk is last in the arrangement of desks. Thus, we can handle Case 3 in the same way that we handle Case 2.

Question 6   If a chain of desks organizes students alphabetically by name, how can you find the student whose name is alphabetically first? Alphabetically last?

A Linked Implementation of the ADT List

The previous section described how you can organize data without physically moving it when adding entries. This section expresses these ideas in Java by beginning the implementation of the ADT list. The next chapter completes the implementation.

Recall that a list is a collection of objects that are organized by their positions in the collection.

The Private Class Node

6.16   We begin by defining the Java equivalent of a desk, the **node**. Nodes are objects that you typically link together to form a data structure. Our particular nodes have two data fields each: one to reference an entry in the list and one to reference another node. An entry in the list is analogous to a person who sits at a desk. The reference to another node is analogous to the desk address written on the paper that is on each desk.

The class that represents these nodes can have the following form:

```java
class Node
{
   private T    data; // entry in list
   private Node next; // link to next node
   < Constructors >
   . . .
```

> *< Accessor and mutator methods:* getData, setData, getNextNode, setNextNode *>*
> . . .
> } // end Node

6.17 Let's focus on the data fields. The field data contains a reference to one of the objects in the list. Sometimes we will call this field the **data portion** of the node. The data type of data is represented here by T. Soon, you will see that T is a generic type that the class of lists will declare.

 The field next contains a reference to another node. Notice that its data type is Node, which is the class that we are currently defining! Such a circular definition might surprise you, but it is perfectly legal in Java. It also enables one node to reference another node, just as one desk referenced another desk in the first section of this chapter. Notice that a desk did not reference a student in another desk. Likewise, a node does not reference a list entry in another node but rather references the entire other node. Sometimes we will call the field next the **link portion** of the node. Figure 6-12 illustrates two nodes that are linked and contain references to objects in the list.

Figure 6-12   Two linked nodes that each reference object data

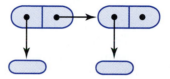

6.18 The rest of the definition of the class Node is uneventful. Constructors to initialize the node are useful, and since the data fields are private, methods to access and alter their contents are necessary. But are they really? If we intend Node to be for public use, like our other classes, such methods are necessary; however, Node is an implementation detail of the ADT list that should be hidden from the list's client. One way to hide Node from the world is to define it within a package that also contains the class that implements the list. Another way—the way we will use here—is to define Node within the class that implements the list. Such a class is called an **inner class**, and we declare it to be private. The data fields of an inner class are accessible directly by the enclosing class without the need for accessor and mutator methods. Thus, we can simplify the definition of Node greatly:

```
private class Node
{
   private T    data; // entry in list
   private Node next; // link to next node

   private Node(T dataPortion)
   {
      data = dataPortion;
      next = null;
   } // end constructor

   private Node(T dataPortion, Node nextNode)
   {
      data = dataPortion;
      next = nextNode;
   } // end constructor
} // end Node
```

We did not include a default constructor because we will not need one.

Because Node will be an inner class, the generic type T will be the same as the generic type declared by the enclosing class. Thus, we do not write <T> after Node. If, however, Node was not an inner class but instead had package access or public access, you would write Node<T>. In that case, Node would also require set and get methods for its data fields. The next chapter talks about such situations.

Note: **Terminology**

A **nested class** is defined entirely within another class definition. Nested classes can be static, although we will not encounter any in this book. An **inner class** is a nested class that is not static.

A class that contains a nested class is the nested class's **outer class**, or **enclosing class**. A **top level class** is one that is not nested.

The Data Fields and Constructor

6.19   This implementation of the ADT list uses a chain of linked nodes to represent the list's entries. In the example in the first section of this chapter, the instructor remembered the address of the first desk in a chain of desks. Similarly, our implementation must "remember" the address of the first node in the chain of nodes. We use a data field called the **head reference** to record a reference to this first node. Listing 6-1 contains an outline of the class LList[1] that implements the ADT list and contains the class Node as an inner class. Recall that Chapter 4 introduced the interface List-Interface. It and the classes that implement it define a generic type for the objects in the list. The identifier T that we use for this generic type must match the one that we use in the class Node.

Listing 6-1   An outline of the class LList

```
public class LList<T> implements ListInterface<T>
{
   private Node firstNode; // reference to first node
   private int  length;    // number of entries in list

   public LList()
   {
      clear();
   } // end default constructor

   public final void clear()
   {
      firstNode = null;
      length = 0;
   } // end clear
```

---

1. We named this class LList instead of LinkedList to avoid confusion with Java's class LinkedList in the package java.util. You will see Java's LinkedList at the end of Chapter 7.

```
< Implementations of the public methods add, remove, replace, getEntry, contains,
  getLength, isEmpty, isFull, and display go here. >
  . . .

// ---------------private!----------------------------
   /** Task: Returns a reference to the node at a given position.
    *  Precondition: List is not empty; 1 <= givenPosition <= length. */
   private Node getNodeAt(int givenPosition)
   {
      < Implementation deferred >
   } // end getNodeAt

   private class Node // private inner class
   {
      < See Segment 6.18. >
   } // end Node
} // end LList
```

The data field firstNode is the head reference of the chain of nodes. Just like the instructor who knew the address of the first desk in the chain of desks, firstNode references the first node in the chain of nodes. Another data field, length, records the number of entries in the current list. This number is also the number of nodes in the chain. The default constructor simply initializes these data fields by calling clear. So initially, a list is empty, firstNode is null, and length is 0.

As we mentioned in Chapter 2, when a constructor calls another public method such as clear, that method should be final so that no subclass can override it, thereby changing the effect of the constructor. Adding final to clear's header is an implementation detail that is not reflected in ListInterface. Recall from Chapter 3 that an interface cannot declare a method to be final.

Choosing a Core Group of Methods to Implement

6.20   Implementing and testing a core group of methods often is advantageous when you write a class. By leaving the definitions of the other methods for later, you can focus your attention and simplify your task. But what methods should be part of this core group?

When dealing with a collection of objects, as we do in this book, you cannot test most methods until you have created the collection. Thus, adding objects to a collection is a fundamental operation. If the method add does not work correctly, testing other methods such as remove would be pointless. Such is the case with a list, so its add methods are part of the core group of methods that we implement first.

To be able to tell whether add works correctly, we need a method that allows us to see the list. The method display serves this purpose, and so it is in our core group. The constructor is also fundamental, and since it calls the method clear, both are in the core group. Similarly, any methods that add might call are part of the core group as well.

Note: Methods such as add and remove that can alter the underlying structure of a collection are likely to have the most involved implementations among the methods in the implementing class. In general, you should define such methods before the others. But since we can't test remove before add is correct, we will delay implementing it until after add is completed and thoroughly tested.

Programming Tip: When defining a class, implement and test a core group of methods. Begin with methods that add to a collection of objects and/or have involved implementations.

Adding to the End of the List

6.21   We will now implement the core public methods of the class LList, beginning with the first add method. This method adds a new entry to the end of the list. Recall from Segment 6.10 the steps that we took when the instructor added a new desk to the end of the chain. Initially, when the first student arrived, we had the following steps:

> newDesk *represents the new student's desk*
> *New student sits at* newDesk
> *Instructor memorizes address of* newDesk

Here are the analogous steps that add must take to add the first entry to an initially empty list. Note that a new desk is analogous to a new node and the instructor is analogous to firstNode.

> newNode *references a new instance of* Node
> *Place data in* newNode
> firstNode = *address of* newNode

In Java, these steps appear as follows, where newEntry references the entry to be added to the list:

```
Node newNode = new Node(newEntry);
firstNode = newNode;
```

Figure 6-13 illustrates these two steps. Part *a* of this figure shows the empty list and the node created by the first statement. Part *b* shows the result of the second statement. Notice that in Part *b*, both firstNode and newNode reference the same node. After the insertion of the new node is complete, only firstNode should reference it. We could set newNode to null, but as you will see shortly, newNode is a local variable of the method add. As such, newNode will not exist after add ends its execution. The same is true of the parameter newEntry, which behaves like a local variable.

Figure 6-13   (a) An empty list and a new node; (b) after adding a new node to a list that was empty

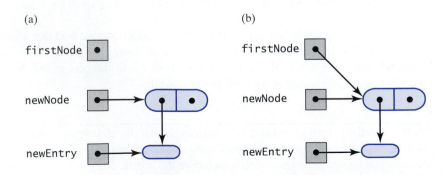

6.22   Now, to add a desk to the end of the chain, we took the following steps:

> newDesk *represents the new student's desk*
> *New student sits at* newDesk
> *Traverse the chain to locate its last desk*
> *Write the address of* newDesk *on this last desk*

The analogous steps that add must take to add a new entry to the end of a list are

> newNode *references a new instance of* Node
> *Place data in* newNode
> *Locate the last node in the chain*
> *Place the address of* newNode *in this last node*

That is, we make the last node in the chain reference the new node.
In Java, these steps appear as follows:

```
Node newNode = new Node(newEntry);
Node lastNode = getNodeAt(length); // get reference to last node
lastNode.next = newNode; // make last node reference new node
```

The method getNodeAt is a private method of the class LList that locates the node at a given position within the chain and returns a reference to it. The method's specifications are given in Listing 6-1 of Segment 6.19. Notice that lastNode is an instance of Node, so lastNode.next is that node's field next.

Figure 6-14 illustrates this addition to the end of a chain of nodes. To simplify the figure, we have omitted the actual entries in the list. These entries are objects that the nodes reference.

Figure 6-14   A chain of nodes (a) prior to adding a node at the end; (b) after locating its last node; (c) after adding a node at the end

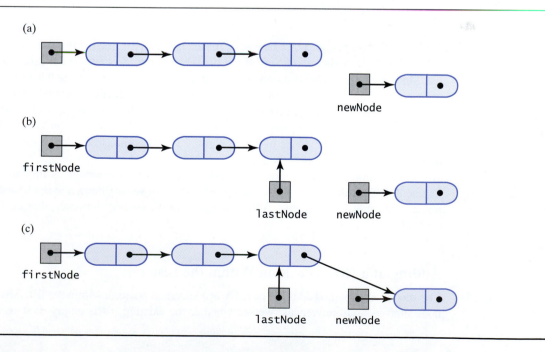

This implementation does not retain a reference to the last node, so we do not bother to update lastNode. In fact, as in Figure 6-13, we are left with external references into the chain of nodes that we do not want. However, since the reference variables lastNode and newNode will be local to the method add, they will not exist for long. If they did persist, we would set these variables to null after the addition was complete.

Question 7   Adding an entry to an empty list could be thought of as adding an entry to the end of a list that is empty. Can you use the statements in Segment 6.22 instead of

```
Node newNode = new Node(newEntry);
firstNode = newNode;
```

which we developed in Segment 6.21 to add an entry to an empty list? Why or why not?

6.23   **The Java method.** Assuming that we have the private method getNodeAt, we can complete the method add based on the previous thoughts:

```
public boolean add(T newEntry)
{
   Node newNode = new Node(newEntry);

   if (isEmpty())
      firstNode = newNode;
   else                                  // add to end of nonempty list
   {
      Node lastNode = getNodeAt(length);
      lastNode.next = newNode; // make last node reference new node
   } // end if

   length++;
   return true;
} // end add
```

This method first creates a new node for the new entry. If the list is empty, it adds the new node by making firstNode reference it. If the list is not empty, however, we must locate the end of the list. Since we have a reference only to the first node, we must traverse the list until we locate the last node and obtain a reference to it. We will define a private method getNodeAt to accomplish this task. Since the data field length contains the size of the list, and since we identify list entries by their positions within the list beginning with 1, the last node is at position length. We need to pass this value to getNodeAt. Once getNodeAt gives us a reference to the last node, we can set the last node's link to reference the new node.

The method getNodeAt does the messy work; we will examine its implementation later, in Segment 6.30. In the meantime, knowing only what getNodeAt does, and not how it does it, we can implement other methods that call getNodeAt. We do assume, however, that getNodeAt executes correctly.

Adding at a Given Position Within the List

6.24   The second add method adds a new entry at a specified position within the list. After creating a new node that newNode references, we see whether the existing list is empty. If it is, we add the new node to the list by writing firstNode = newNode, as we did in the first add method. If the list is not empty, we must consider two cases:

- Case 1: Adding the entry to the beginning of the list
- Case 2: Adding the entry at a position other than the beginning of the list

6.25   **Case 1.** In the context of desks in a room, the necessary steps for the first case are

> newDesk *represents the new student's desk*
> *New student sits at* newDesk
> *Place the address of the first desk on* newDesk *(the instructor knows the address of the first desk)*
> *Give the address of* newDesk *to the instructor*

As a result of these steps, the new desk references the current first desk in the chain and becomes the new first desk.

Here are the analogous steps that add must take to add to the beginning of a list:

> newNode *references a new instance of* Node
> *Place data in* newNode
> *Set* newNode's *link to* firstNode
> *Set* firstNode *to* newNode

That is, we make the new node reference the first node in the chain, making it the new first node. Figure 6-15 illustrates these steps, and the following Java statements implement them:

```
Node newNode = new Node(newEntry);
newNode.next = firstNode;
firstNode = newNode;
```

Figure 6-15   A chain of nodes (a) just prior to adding a node at the beginning; (b) just after adding a node at the beginning

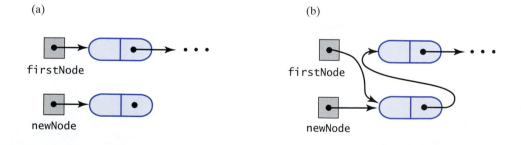

(a)   (b)

firstNode   firstNode

newNode   newNode

Adding a node to an empty chain, as Figure 6-13 depicts, is actually the same as adding a node to the beginning of a chain.

Question 8   The code that we developed in Segment 6.21 to add a node to an empty chain is

```
Node newNode = new Node(newEntry);
firstNode = newNode;
```

The code that we just developed to add to the beginning of a chain is

```
Node newNode = new Node(newEntry);
newNode.next = firstNode;
firstNode = newNode;
```

Why do these statements work correctly when the chain is empty?

6.26   **Case 2.** In the second case, we add an entry to the list at a position other than the beginning. The necessary steps for the second case in the context of desks in a room are

> newDesk *references the new student's desk*
> deskBefore *represents the desk that will be before the new desk*
> deskAfter *represents the desk after* deskBefore*; its address is on* deskBefore
> *Place the address of* deskAfter *on* newDesk
> *Place the address of* newDesk *on* deskBefore

Here, the analogous steps that add must take are

> newNode *references the new node*
> nodeBefore *references the node that will be before the new node*
> *Set* nodeAfter *to* nodeBefore*'s link*
> *Set* newNode*'s link to* nodeAfter
> *Set* nodeBefore*'s link to* newNode

The following Java statements implement these steps:

```
Node newNode = new Node(newEntry);
Node nodeBefore = getNodeAt(newPosition - 1);
Node nodeAfter = nodeBefore.next;
newNode.next = nodeAfter;
nodeBefore.next = newNode;
```

Figure 6-16   A chain of nodes (a) just prior to adding a node between two adjacent nodes; (b) just after adding a node between two adjacent nodes

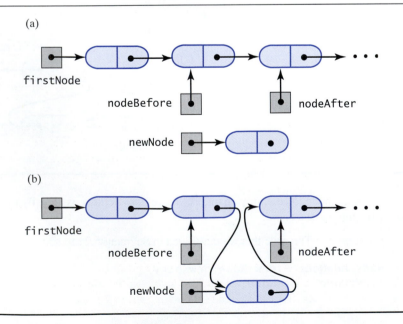

Figure 6-16a shows the chain after the first three statements execute, and Figure 6-16b shows it after the node has been added.

6.27   **The Java method.** The following implementation of the add method summarizes these ideas:

```java
public boolean add(int newPosition, T newEntry)
{
  boolean isSuccessful = true;

  if ((newPosition >= 1) && (newPosition <= length+1))
  {
    Node newNode = new Node(newEntry);

    if (isEmpty() || (newPosition == 1)) // case 1
    {
      newNode.next = firstNode;
      firstNode = newNode;
    }
    else                                   // case 2: list is not empty
    {                                      // and newPosition > 1
      Node nodeBefore = getNodeAt(newPosition - 1);
      Node nodeAfter = nodeBefore.next;
      newNode.next = nodeAfter;
      nodeBefore.next = newNode;
    } // end if

    length++;
  }
  else
    isSuccessful = false;

  return isSuccessful;
} // end add
```

Question 9   Consider the first `else` clause of the previous method add.

a. What `assert` statement could you add to this clause?
b. What call to `getNodeAt` could replace the value assigned to `nodeAfter`?
c. Should we make the change suggested in Part *b*? Why?

Question 10   The second `if` statement of the previous method add tests for an empty list. Is this test necessary?

6.28   **An out-of-memory error.** One of the list implementations given in Chapter 5 used a fixed-size array to represent the list entries. You saw that the array—and therefore the list—could become full. With a linked implementation, the list cannot become full. Anytime you add a new entry, you create a new node for that entry. It is possible, however, for your program to use all of your computer's memory. If this occurs, your request for a new node will cause the error `OutOfMemoryError`. You could interpret this condition as a full list; however, an `OutOfMemoryError` is fatal, and the client will not have the opportunity to react to it.

Note: **Allocating memory**
When you use the `new` operator, you create, or **instantiate**, an object. At that time, the Java run-time environment **allocates**, or assigns, memory to the object. When you create a node for a linked chain, we sometimes say that you have allocated the node.

The Private Method getNodeAt

6.29   To complete our implementation of the add methods, we need to implement the method getNodeAt, which returns a reference to the node at a given position within the list. Since the method returns a reference to a node, the method is an implementation detail that we would not want a client to use. Thus, getNodeAt should be a private method. Recall the specifications for this method:

```
/** Task: Returns a reference to the node at a given position.
 *  Precondition: List is not empty; 1 <= givenPosition <= length. */
private Node getNodeAt(int givenPosition)
```

Segments 6.2 and 6.9 discussed how we locate a particular desk within a chain of desks by beginning at the head of the chain and traversing it from one desk to another. The technique is the same here. The data field firstNode contains a reference to the first node in the chain. That node contains a reference to the second node in the chain, the second node contains a reference to the third node, and so on.

We can use a temporary variable currentNode to reference the nodes one at a time, as we traverse the chain from the first node to the desired node. Initially, we set currentNode to first-Node so that it references the first node in the chain. If we are seeking the first node, we are done. Otherwise, we move to the next node by executing

```
currentNode = currentNode.next;
```

If we are seeking the second node, we are done. Otherwise, we move to the next node by executing

```
currentNode = currentNode.next;
```

once again. We continue in this manner until we locate the node at the desired position within the list.

6.30   The implementation for getNodeAt follows:

```
/** Task: Returns a reference to the node at a given position.
 *  Precondition: List is not empty; 1 <= givenPosition <= length. */
private Node getNodeAt(int givenPosition)
{
   assert !isEmpty() &&
          (1 <= givenPosition) && (givenPosition <= length);
   Node currentNode = firstNode;

   // traverse the list to locate the desired node
   for (int counter = 1; counter < givenPosition; counter++)
      currentNode = currentNode.next;

   assert currentNode != null;
   return currentNode;
} // end getNodeAt
```

Within the for loop, currentNode should never become null if the method's precondition is met. Thus, currentNode.next never executes if currentNode is null. Notice that the previous add methods enforce this method's precondition. You can enable the assert statements during the testing of getNodeAt to verify these claims.

Programming Tip: If ref is a reference to a node in a chain, be sure that ref is not null before you use it to access ref.data or ref.next.

Question 11   How do the add methods given in Segments 6.23 and 6.27 enforce the precondition of getNodeAt?

Question 12   How does getNodeAt's precondition prevent currentNode from becoming null?

Assertions and the Method isEmpty

6.31   The implementation of the method isEmpty could simply test that the length of the list is zero, as it did in the array-based implementations that you saw in Chapter 5. However, we have another criterion that we could use here. When a list is empty, the reference firstNode is null. If our implementation is correct, either criterion is fine, but what happens during development when some part of our class might contain an error in logic? We can use assert statements involving the second criterion to help us catch an error, as in the following version of isEmpty:

```java
public boolean isEmpty()
{
  boolean result;

  if (length == 0)
  {
    assert firstNode == null;
    result = true;
  }
  else
  {
    assert firstNode != null;
    result = false;
  } // end if

  return result;
} // end isEmpty
```

6.32   **Example.** Let's look at an example of how the previous implementation of isEmpty can help us find an error in logic. Consider the definition of the first add method given in Segment 6.23. If we had been concerned that we might forget to increment the data field length, we might have written length++ as the method's first action instead of as one of its last. This change would have caused an error. If the list was empty when the method was called, length would have been given the value 1 and isEmpty would have been invoked. Since firstNode would have been null, the second assertion within isEmpty would have produced an error message like the following one, assuming that we had enabled assertions:

Exception in thread "main" java.lang.AssertionError
    at LList.isEmpty(LList.java:165)
    at LList.add(LList.java:34)
    at Driver.testList(driver.java:14)
    at Driver.main(driver.java:5);

This message indicates that the method add called isEmpty, which produced the assertion error. We could clarify this message by adding to the assert statements in isEmpty. For example, if the second assert statement is

```
assert firstNode != null : "length not 0 but firstNode is null";
```

the previous error message would begin as follows:

Exception in thread "main" java.lang.AssertionError: length not 0 but firstNode is null

If we ran our program without enabling assertions, isEmpty would simply test length. Since length would not be zero, isEmpty would return false, so add's else clause would execute. When add invoked getNodeAt(1), null would be returned—since firstNode would be null—and assigned to lastNode. As a result, the reference lastNode.next would cause an exception and would produce an error message such as

Exception in thread "main" java.lang.NullPointerException
    at LList$Node.access$102(LList.java:222)
    at LList.add(LList.java:34)
    at Driver.testList(driver.java:14)
    at Driver.main(driver.java:5);

This message is not as clear as the previous one, so more effort is needed to discover the problem.

Question 13 Suppose that the implementation of the method isEmpty contained the following single statement:

```
return (length == 0) && (firstNode == null);
```

If we make the error in the method add that is described in the previous segment, what happens when add is called and the list is empty? Assume that assertions are enabled.

The Method display

6.33   By implementing the method display, we will be able to test the previous methods that we have written before we complete the rest of LList. The method needs a local variable to reference each node in the chain. For example, currentNode could reference the node whose data we want to display. That data is currentNode.data.

Initially, we want currentNode to reference the first node in the chain, so we set it to first-Node. To make currentNode reference the next node, we would execute the statement

```
currentNode = currentNode.next;
```

Thus, we can write a loop that iterates until currentNode becomes null.

The following method display uses these ideas:

```
public void display()
{
  Node currentNode = firstNode;
  while (currentNode != null)
  {
    System.out.println(currentNode.data);
    currentNode = currentNode.next;
  } // end while
} // end display
```

Question 14 In the previous implementation of display, suppose that you replace

```
while (currentNode != null)
```

with

```
for (int counter = 0; counter < length; counter++)
```

a. What is an advantage of this change?
b. What is an advantage of the original version of display?

Question 15 Compare the work required to display a list using the previous method display with that required using the following version of the method:

```
public void display()
{
  for (int position = 1; position <= length; position++)
  {
    Node currentNode = getNodeAt(position);
    System.out.println(currentNode.data);
  } // end for
} // end display
```

Testing the Incomplete Implementation

6.34   Earlier, we realized that the add methods are fundamental to our class, so they are part of the core group of methods that we implement and test first. The method display lets us see whether add works correctly, so it too is in our core group. The constructor is also fundamental, and so is the method clear, since the constructor calls it. Similarly, since add calls isEmpty and getNodeAt, they are among the core methods that we implement and test first.

Now that we have implemented a core group of methods, we can test them. But what about the other methods in ListInterface? Since LList implements ListInterface, Java's syntax checker will look for definitions of each method declared in this interface. The next chapter will complete the rest of the implementation of LList. Should we wait until then to begin testing? Absolutely not! Testing methods as you write them makes finding logical errors easier.

We still have the problem of the syntax checker. Instead of writing a complete implementation of each method in ListInterface, we can write an incomplete definition called a **stub**. The stub needs only to keep the syntax checker happy.

For example, a stub for the method remove could appear as follows:

```
public T remove(int givenPosition)
{
  return null;
} // end remove
```

Since remove ultimately will return the removed entry, its stub must contain a return statement. If you plan to call a stub within your test program, the stub should report that it was invoked by executing a print statement.

Programming Tip: Do not wait until you complete the implementation of an ADT before testing it. By writing stubs, which are incomplete definitions of required methods, you can begin testing early.

6.35   Let's choose the add method that adds to the end of the list for our first tests. Listing 6-2 contains an example of a main method that we could use for this purpose. Notice how the descriptive output makes it easier to see whether our implementation is correct.

Listing 6-2   A main method that tests part of the implementation of the ADT list

```java
public static void main(String[] args)
{
    ListInterface<String> myList = new LList();
    System.out.println("List should be empty; isEmpty returns " +
                        myList.isEmpty());

    System.out.println("\nTesting add to end:");
    System.out.println("Add 15: returns " + myList.add("15"));
    System.out.println("\nList should not be empty; isEmpty() returns " +
                        myList.isEmpty() + "\n");

    System.out.println("Add 25: returns " + myList.add("25"));
    System.out.println("Add 35: returns " + myList.add("35"));
    System.out.println("Add 45: returns " + myList.add("45"));
    System.out.println("\nList should not be empty; isEmpty() returns " +
                        myList.isEmpty());

    System.out.println("\nList should contain\n15 25 35 45 ");
    System.out.println("\nTesting display():");
    myList.display();

    System.out.println("\nTesting clear():");
    myList.clear();

    System.out.println("List should be empty; isEmpty returns " +
                        myList.isEmpty());

    System.out.println("\nTesting display():");
    myList.display();
} // end main
```

OUTPUT

List should be empty; isEmpty returns true

Testing add to end:
Add 15: returns true

List should not be empty; isEmpty() returns false
Add 25: returns true
Add 35: returns true
Add 45: returns true

List should not be empty; isEmpty() returns false

List should contain
15 25 35 45

Testing display():
15
25
35
45

Testing clear():
List should be empty; isEmpty returns true

Testing display():

CHAPTER SUMMARY

- You can form a chain of linked data by using objects called nodes. Each node has two parts. One part contains a reference to a data object, and a second part references the next node in the chain. The last node, however, references no other node and contains **null**. A head reference external to the chain references the first node.

- You can add a node anywhere within a chain of linked nodes by changing at most two references.

- Adding a node to the beginning of a chain of linked nodes is a special case; adding a node to the end is not.

- Locating a particular node in a chain of linked nodes requires a traversal of the chain. Beginning at the first node, you move from node to node sequentially until you reach the desired node.

- Displaying a list requires traversing the entire chain of nodes.

PROGRAMMING TIPS

- If **ref** is a reference to a node in a chain, be sure that **ref** is not **null** before you use it to access **ref.data** or **ref.next**.

- When defining a class, implement and test a core group of methods. Begin with methods that add to a collection of objects and/or have involved implementations.

- Do not wait until you complete the implementation of an ADT before testing it. By writing stubs, which are incomplete definitions of required methods, you can begin testing early.

EXERCISES

1. Add a constructor to the class `LList` that creates a list from a given array of objects. Consider at least two different ways to implement such a constructor. Which way does the least amount of work?

2. Consider the definition of the add method that appears in Segment 6.27 and adds an element to a list at a given position. Interchange the two statements that execute in case 1, as follows:

```
if (isEmpty() || (newPosition == 1)) // case 1
{
   firstNode = newNode;
   newNode.next = firstNode;
}
```

a. What is displayed by the following statements in a client of the modified `LList`?

```
ListInterface<String> myList = new LList();
myList.add(1, "30");
myList.add(2, "40");
myList.add(3, "50");

myList.add(1, "10");
myList.add(5, "60");
myList.add(2, "20");

int numberOfEntries = myList.getLength();
for (int position = 1; position <= numberOfEntries; position++)
    System.out.print(myList.getEntry(position) + " ");
```

b. What methods, if any, in `LList` could be affected by the change to the method add when they execute? Why?

3. Suppose that you want an operation for the ADT list that adds an array of items to the end of the list. The header of the method could be as follows:

```
public void addAll(T[] items)
```

Write an implementation of this method for the class `LList`.

4. Suppose that you want an operation for the ADT list that returns the position of a given object in the list. The header of the method could be as follows:

```
public int getPosition(T anObject)
```

Write an implementation of this method for the class `LList`.

5. Implement an `equals` method for the class `LList` that returns true when the entries in one list equal the entries in a second list.

6. Suppose that a list contains `Comparable` objects. Implement a method that returns a new list of items that are less than some given item. The header of the method could be as follows:

```
public LList<T> getAllLessThan(Comparable<T> anObject)
```

Write an implementation of this method for the class `LList`. Make sure that your method does not affect the state of the original list.

7. In a **doubly linked chain,** each node can reference the previous node as well as the next node. Figure 6-17 shows a doubly linked chain that has both a head reference and a tail reference. Write a class to represent a node in a doubly linked chain. Write the class as an inner class of a class that implements the ADT list. You can omit set and get methods.

Figure 6-17   A doubly linked chain for Exercises 7, 8, 9

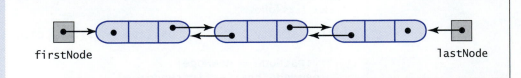

firstNode   lastNode

8. Repeat Exercise 7, but instead write the class within a package that contains an implementation of the ADT list. Set and get methods will be necessary.

9. List the steps necessary to add a node to the doubly linked chain shown in Figure 6-17 when the new node is

   a. First in the chain
   b. Last in the chain
   c. Between existing nodes in the chain

PROJECTS

1. Write a program that thoroughly tests the add and display methods of the class LList.

2. Project 2 of Chapter 4 describes the ADT bag. Begin an implementation of the bag by representing it as a chain of linked nodes. Implement at least the following operations:
   - Add an item
   - Get the number of items in the bag
   - See whether the bag is empty
   - Get the union of two bags

   Thoroughly test these operations. You will be able to complete this implementation after studying the next chapter.

3. Project 4 of Chapter 4 describes the ADT set. Begin an implementation of this ADT by representing it as a chain of linked nodes. Include at least the operations listed in Project 2 of this chapter. Thoroughly test these operations. You will be able to complete this implementation after studying the next chapter.

4. Implement and test the core operations of the ADT list when a doubly linked chain, as shown in Figure 6-17, represents the entries in the list. Use the inner class of nodes that Exercise 7 defines.

5. Repeat the previous project, but define set and get methods in the inner class of nodes.

Completing the Linked Implementation of a List

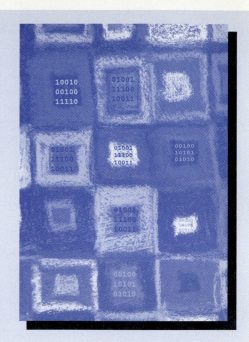

OBJECTIVES

After studying this chapter, you should be able to

- Implement the ADT list by using a linked organization of data
- Modify a linked implementation of the list by adding set and get methods to the class **Node**
- Add a tail reference to a linked implementation of the list
- Discuss the advantages and disadvantages of a linked implementation of the list

The previous chapter began an implementation of the ADT list that uses a chain of linked nodes to store the list's entries. You saw that the new implementation uses memory only as needed for a new entry. This chapter completes the implementation. It will show that removing an entry from a list returns the associated memory to the system. The chapter also presents variations of the implementation. The class Node can have set and get methods, and we can add a reference to the last node in the chain.

Removing an Item from a Linked Chain

7.1   Chapter 6 used the analogy of a classroom to describe how to form a linked chain of data. Available desks are in the hallway outside of the classroom. Each desk has a number (address) stamped on its back and a blank piece of paper taped to its desktop. As students enter the room, they take a desk from the hall. The number of another desk already in the room can be written on the new desk's piece of paper. The new desk's number can be written on another desk's paper. In this way, the desks are linked to one another, forming a chain of desks. As you saw in Figure 6-1, no desk references the first desk in the chain, but the instructor knows its address. The last desk does not reference another desk; its paper is blank.

7.2   Students who leave our classroom—room L—return their desks to the hall. Such desks can be reassigned to other students who enter either room L or other rooms that share this hallway. Suppose that you are a student in room L but you want to drop the course. If you simply move your desk to the hallway, you will not actually remove yourself from the chain of desks in the room: Either another desk or the instructor will still reference your desk. We need to disconnect your desk from the chain.The details of how we do this depend on where your desk is in the chain. Here are the possible cases:

- Case 1: The desk to be removed is first in the chain of desks.
- Case 2: The desk to be removed is between two current desks.
- Case 3: The desk to be removed is last in the chain of desks.

Like the case in Segment 6.15, in which we add a desk at the end of a chain, the last case is not really a special case.

7.3   **Case 1.** Figure 7-1 illustrates Case 1 before we remove the first desk from the chain. The following steps are necessary to remove the first desk:

1. Locate the first desk by asking the instructor for its address.
2. Give the address that is written on the first desk to the instructor. This is the address of the second desk in the chain.
3. Return the first desk to the hallway.

Figure 7-2 shows the chain after the first two steps take place. Notice that the first desk is no longer a part of the chain. Technically, it still references the second desk. But if this desk is ever used again, a new address will be written on its paper.

7.4   **Case 2.** Figure 7-3 shows Case 2 before we remove a desk that is between two current desks, where

- deskToRemove is the desk to be removed
- deskBefore is the desk before the one to be removed
- deskAfter is the desk after the one to be removed

Figure 7-1   A chain of desks just prior to removing its first desk

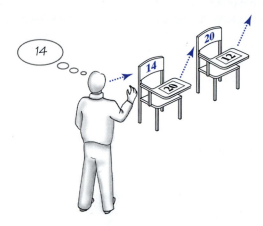

Figure 7-2   A chain of desks just after removing its first desk

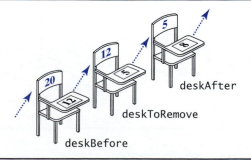

Figure 7-3   A chain of desks just prior to removing a desk between two other desks

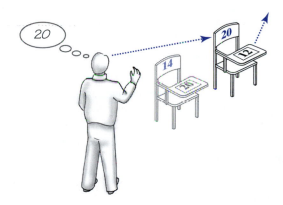

Note that the address on deskBefore is the address of deskToRemove and the address on deskToRemove is that of the next desk, deskAfter. We'll assume that we can get the address of deskBefore, and from it get the other addresses.

The following steps are necessary to remove deskToRemove:

1. Copy the address on deskToRemove to deskBefore. (deskBefore now references deskAfter, which is the desk currently after deskToRemove.)
2. Return deskToRemove to the hallway.

Figure 7-4 shows the chain after the first of these steps takes place.

Figure 7-4   A chain of desks just after removing a desk between two other desks

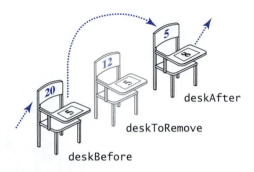

7.5   **Case 3.** Finally, when the desk to be removed is last in the chain of desks, we can proceed as for Case 2. Remember that the paper on the last desk in the chain is blank because that desk does not reference any other desk. Therefore, Step 1 of Case 2 would copy a blank from the last desk to deskBefore, as Figure 7-5 illustrates. This action is exactly what needs to happen so that deskBefore is last in the chain of desks.

Figure 7-5   Before and after removing the last desk from a chain

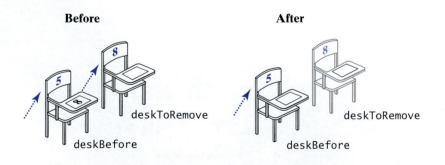

?   Question 1   What steps are necessary to remove the third desk in a chain of five desks?

Question 2   What steps are necessary to remove the first desk in a chain of five desks?

Completing the Linked Implementation of the ADT List

In the previous chapter, we began a linked implementation of the ADT list. Our class LList repre-sents the list as a chain of nodes. Each node is an instance of an inner class Node and references one item in the list. Recall that LList has two data fields: firstNode is a reference to the first node in the chain, and length is the number of nodes. We then implemented and tested a core group of methods. In this core group are two versions of the method add that add a new entry to a list. In defining these methods, we implemented the method isEmpty and a private method getNodeAt, which returns a reference to the node at a given position in the chain. Also in the core group are a constructor and the methods clear and display. We now will complete the implementation of LList.

The Method remove

7.6   The remove method removes the entry at a specified position within a nonempty list. We must con-sider two cases:

● Case 1: Removing the entry at the beginning of the list
● Case 2: Removing an entry at a position other than the beginning of the list

7.7   **Case 1.** Segment 7.3 discussed the first case in the context of desks in a room. The necessary steps then were

Locate the first desk by asking the instructor for its address.
Give the address that is written on the first desk to the instructor. This is the address of the second desk in the chain.
Return the first desk to the hallway.

Here the analogous steps are

Set firstNode *to the link in the first node.*
Since references to the first node no longer exist, the system automatically recycles its memory.

Figure 7-6 illustrates these steps, and the following Java statement implements them:

```
firstNode = firstNode.next;
```

Figure 7-6   A chain of nodes (a) just prior to removing the first node; (b) just after removing the first node

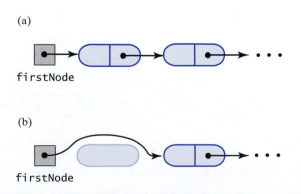

(a)

firstNode

(b)

firstNode

7.8   **Case 2.** In the second case, we remove an entry at a position other than the beginning of the list. Segment 7.4 discussed this case in the context of desks in a room. The necessary steps then were

> *Locate the desk before the one to remove; call it* deskBefore. *The address on* deskBefore *is the address of* deskToRemove.
> *The address on* deskToRemove *is that of the next desk,* deskAfter, *in the chain.*
> *Copy the address on* deskToRemove *to* deskBefore. *(*deskBefore *now references* deskAfter, *which is the desk currently after* deskToRemove.*)*
> *Return* deskToRemove *to the hallway.*

Here the analogous steps are

> *Let* nodeBefore *reference the node before the one to be removed.*
> *Set* nodeToRemove *to* nodeBefore*'s link;* nodeToRemove *now references the node to be removed.*
> *Set* nodeAfter *to* nodeToRemove*'s link;* nodeAfter *now references the node after the one to be removed.*
> *Set* nodeBefore*'s link to* nodeAfter. *(*nodeToRemove *is now disconnected from the chain.)*
> *Set* nodeToRemove *to* null.
> *Since references to the disconnected node no longer exist, the system automatically recycles its memory.*

The following Java statements implement these steps:

```
Node nodeBefore = getNodeAt(givenPosition - 1);
Node nodeToRemove = nodeBefore.next;
Node nodeAfter = nodeToRemove.next;
nodeBefore.next = nodeAfter;
nodeToRemove = null;
```

Figure 7-7a illustrates the chain after the first three statements execute, and Figure 7-7b shows it after the node is removed.

Figure 7-7   A chain of nodes (a) just prior to removing an interior node; (b) just after removing an interior node

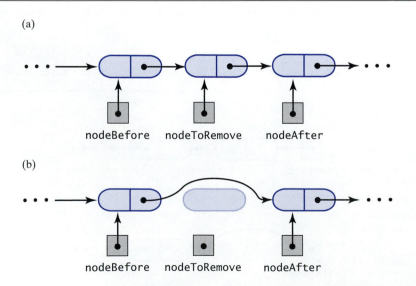

(a)

nodeBefore   nodeToRemove   nodeAfter

(b)

nodeBefore   nodeToRemove   nodeAfter

7.9   **The Java method.** The `remove` method has the following implementation. Recall that the method returns the entry that it deletes from the list. Although the node that contains this entry is recycled, the entry itself is not as long as the client saves the reference to it.

```java
public T remove(int givenPosition)
{
  T result = null;                     // return value

  if ((givenPosition >= 1) && (givenPosition <= length))
  {
    assert !isEmpty();
    if (givenPosition == 1)            // case 1: remove first entry
    {
      result = firstNode.data;         // save entry to be removed
      firstNode = firstNode.next;
    }
    else                               // case 2: givenPosition > 1
    {
      Node nodeBefore = getNodeAt(givenPosition - 1);
      Node nodeToRemove = nodeBefore.next;
      Node nodeAfter = nodeToRemove.next;
      nodeBefore.next = nodeAfter;   // disconnect the node to be removed
      result = nodeToRemove.data;    // save entry to be removed
    } // end if

    length--;
  } // end if

  return result;                         // return removed entry, or
                                         // null if operation fails
} // end remove
```

Notice that we use the private method `getNodeAt`, which we wrote originally for the add methods, to locate the node before the one to be removed. This method is called only when we remove an entry after the first one. Thus, its argument `givenPosition - 1` will always be greater than zero, as its precondition requires.

Also notice that we do not explicitly set `nodeToRemove` to `null` after disconnecting the node. This variable is local to the `remove` method and, as we have mentioned before, local variables do not exist after a method completes executing. So although we could set `nodeToRemove` to `null`, doing so is not necessary.

Question 3   Why is the assertion in the previous method true?

Note: Deallocating memory

After the method `remove` removes a node from a chain, you have no way to reference the removed node, so you cannot use it. As Segment 1.20 noted, the Java run-time environment automatically deallocates and recycles the memory associated with such nodes. No explicit instruction from the programmer is necessary or, in fact, possible to cause deallocation to occur.

The Method `replace`

7.10   Replacing, or revising, a list entry requires us to replace the data portion of a node with other data. We can use the private method `getNodeAt` to locate the node and then simply replace its data portion. Before calling `getNodeAt`, we check that the list is not empty and the given position is valid. The implementation appears as follows:

```java
public boolean replace(int givenPosition, T newEntry)
{
   boolean isSuccessful = true;

   if ((givenPosition >= 1) && (givenPosition <= length))
   {
      assert !isEmpty();
      Node desiredNode = getNodeAt(givenPosition);
      desiredNode.data = newEntry;
   }
   else
      isSuccessful = false;

   return isSuccessful;
} // end replace
```

Note: The method `replace` replaces the data in a node, but not the node itself.

Question 4   Compare the work required in replacing an entry in a list using the previous method `replace` and the method `replace` given in Segment 5.9.

The Method `getEntry`

7.11   Retrieving a list entry is also straightforward:

```java
public T getEntry(int givenPosition)
{
   T result = null; // result to return

   if ((givenPosition >= 1) && (givenPosition <= length))
   {
      assert !isEmpty();
      result = getNodeAt(givenPosition).data;
   } // end if

   return result;
} // end getEntry
```

The method `getNodeAt` returns a reference to the desired node, so

```java
getNodeAt(givenPosition).data
```

is the data portion of that node.

   Although our implementations of `getEntry` and `replace` are easy to write, each does more work than if we had used an array to represent the list. Here, `getNodeAt` starts at the first node in the chain and moves from node to node until it reaches the desired one. In Segment 5.9, you saw that `replace` and `getEntry` can reference the desired array element directly, without involving any other array element.

The Method `contains`

7.12   In this implementation, to discover whether a list contains a given entry, you must look at the entries in the list, one at a time. In Chapter 5, where we used an array to represent the list's entries, we examined each array element—starting at index zero—until we either found the desired entry or discovered that it was not in the array.

We use the same general approach here to search a chain for a particular piece of data. We begin at the first node, and if that does not contain the entry we are seeking, we look at the second node, and so on. When searching an array, we use an index. To search a chain, we use a reference to a node. For example, `currentNode` could reference the node that we want to examine. Initially, `currentNode` must reference the first node in the chain, so we set it to `firstNode`. To make `currentNode` reference the next node, we would execute the statement

```
currentNode = currentNode.next;
```

We used a similar technique in the previous chapter to display a list. Here, our loop iterates until we either find the desired entry or `currentNode` becomes `null`. Thus, the method `contains` has the following implementation:

```
public boolean contains(T anEntry)
{
  boolean found = false;
  Node currentNode = firstNode;

  while (!found && (currentNode != null))
  {
    if (anEntry.equals(currentNode.data))
      found = true;
    else
      currentNode = currentNode.next;
  } // end while

  return found;
} // end contains
```

This method has the same general form as the corresponding method in Segment 5.10.

Question 5   If `currentNode` in the previous method `contains` becomes `null`, what value does the method return when the list is not empty?

Question 6   Trace the execution of the method `contains` when the list is empty. What is the result?

The Remaining Methods

7.13   The method `isFull` should always return false. The only time a list whose implementation is linked could appear full is when the system cannot provide memory to the add method for a new node. In that case, an OutOfMemoryError occurs, which is fatal. A client would not have the opportunity to call isFull.

The implementation of the method getLength is the same as for the array-based implementation that you saw in Chapter 5.

Question 7   What changes to the class LList are necessary to enable a client to serialize instances of the class?

A Class **Node** That Has Set and Get Methods

Since Node is an inner class, the class LList can access Node's private data fields directly by name. Doing so makes the implementation somewhat easier to write, read, and understand, particularly for novice Java programmers. However, some computer scientists feel that you should access a class's data fields only by calling accessor and mutator (set and get) methods. This section adds these methods to Node and explores three ways define this class.

7.14   **As an inner class.** Suppose that we add the methods getData, setData, getNextNode, and setNextNode to the inner class Node, as it appears in Segment 6.18 of the previous chapter. The class would then appear as given in Listing 7-1.

Listing 7-1   The inner class Node with set and get methods

```
private class Node
{
   private T    data; // entry in list
   private Node next; // link to next node

   private Node(T dataPortion)
   {
      data = dataPortion;
      next = null;
   } // end constructor

   private Node(T dataPortion, Node nextNode)
   {
      data = dataPortion;
      next = nextNode;
   } // end constructor

   private T getData()
   {
      return data;
   } // end getData

   private void setData(T newData)
   {
      data = newData;
   } // end setData

   private Node getNextNode()
   {
      return next;
   } // end getNextNode
```

```
        private void setNextNode(Node nextNode)
        {
          next = nextNode;
        } // end setNextNode
} // end Node
```

7.15 With these additions to Node, we could revise the implementation of LList by making changes such as the following:

- Change

      lastNode.next = newNode;

  to

      lastNode.setNextNode(newNode);

- Change

      result = firstNode.data;

  to

      result = firstNode.getData();

- Change

      desiredNode.data = newEntry;

  to

      desiredNode.setData(newEntry);

- Change

      currentNode = currentNode.next;

  to

      currentNode = currentNode.getNextNode();

Project 2 at the end of this chapter asks you to complete these revisions to LList.

Note: Although the next three chapters use our original definition of Node without set and get methods, later chapters will assume that Node does have such methods.

7.16 **As a class within a package.** After we modify Node and LList as just described, Node could remain as a private inner class. Since Node is an implementation detail that we want to hide, making it an inner class is appropriate. But if we ever changed our minds and wanted to define Node outside of LList, we could do so while retaining the modifications to LList made in the previous segment. We could—with a few changes—make Node accessible only within a package, or even make it a public class.

To transform Node, as given in Segment 7.14, into a class accessible only by other classes in its package, you first omit all the access modifiers except the ones on the data fields. You then add <T> after each occurrence of Node within the class definition, except when it is used as a constructor name. The revised class appears in Listing 7-2.

Listing 7-2   The class Node with package access

```
package ListPackage;
class Node<T>
{
  private T        data;
  private Node<T> next;

  Node(T dataPortion) // the constructor's name is Node, not Node<T>
  {
    data = dataPortion;
    next = null;
  } // end constructor

  Node(T dataPortion, Node<T> nextNode)
  {
    data = dataPortion;
    next = nextNode;
  } // end constructor

  T getData()
  {
    return data;
  } // end getData

  void setData(T newData)
  {
    data = newData;
  } // end setData

  Node<T> getNextNode()
  {
    return next;
  } // end getNextNode

  void setNextNode(Node<T> nextNode)
  {
    next = nextNode;
  } // end setNextNode
} // end Node
```

7.17   The class LList can access Node, as just given in Listing 7-2, if both classes are in the same package and we modify LList slightly. Each occurrence of Node within LList must now appear as Node<T>. Thus, we need to make changes to LList, such as those shown in color in Listing 7-3.

Listing 7-3   The class `LList` when `Node` is in the same package

```
package ListPackage;
public class LList<T> implements ListInterface<T>
{
  private Node<T> firstNode;

  . . .

  public boolean add(T newEntry)
  {
    Node<T> newNode = new Node<T>(newEntry);

    if (isEmpty())
      firstNode = newNode;
    else
    {
      Node<T> lastNode = getNodeAt(length);
      lastNode.setNextNode(newNode);
    } // end if

    length++;
    return true;
  } // end add

  . . .
} // end LList
```

Project 3 at the end of this chapter asks you to complete this revision to `LList`.

7.18   **As an inner class with a declared generic type.** The version of `LList` described in the previous segment could define `Node` as an inner class. `Node` would be similar to the class given in Listing 7-2, but would require the following changes:

- Omit the package statement.
- Make the class, constructors, and methods private.
- Replace the generic type `T` with another identifier such as `S`.

Since both `LList` and `Node` declare generic types, they must use different identifiers to represent them.

Project 4 at the end of the chapter asks you to revise `Node` and `LList` as described here.

Tail References

We now consider a variation of our linked implementation that reduces the execution time to add an entry to the end of a list.

7.19   **The problem.** Imagine that we have a collection of data from which we will create a list. That is, our data will be the list's entries. If the data is in the order in which the entries will appear in the list, we create the list by repeatedly adding the next entry to the end of the list.

We could do this by using the list's first add method. However, if you examine the implementation of that method, as given in the previous chapter in Segment 6.23, you will discover that it invokes the private method `getNodeAt` to locate the last node in the chain and hence the last entry in the list. To accomplish this task, `getNodeAt` must begin at the first node and traverse the chain until it locates the last node. Given a reference to the last node, add can insert the new entry at the end of the list. This reference, however, is not retained when the method completes its task. Thus, if we add another entry to the end of the list, add will invoke `getNodeAt` again to traverse the list from its beginning. Since we plan to add entries repeatedly to the end of the list, many repetitious traversals will occur.

7.20   **A solution.** In such cases, maintaining a reference to the end of the chain—as well as a reference to the beginning of the chain—is advantageous. We call such a reference to the end of a chain a **tail reference**. Figure 7-8 illustrates a linked chain with both head and tail references.

Figure 7-8   A linked chain with a head reference and a tail reference

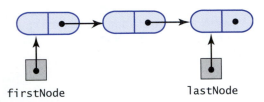

firstNode   lastNode

The tail reference, like the head reference, is a private data field of the class. The private data fields in our revised implementation then would be

```java
private Node firstNode; // head reference to first node
private Node lastNode;  // tail reference to last node
private int  length;    // number of entries in list
```

Question 8   Examine the implementation of the class `LList` given in this chapter and the previous chapter. Which methods would require a new implementation if you used both a head reference and a tail reference?

A Revised Implementation of the List

By examining the class `LList`, as described in the previous chapter and earlier in this chapter, you should find that the two add methods and the methods `remove` and `clear` are the ones that will involve the head and tail references and, thus, need to be revised. We should also revise the assertions in the method `isEmpty`. The rest of the original implementation, including the constructor, remains the same. Let's examine these revisions.

7.21   **The method `clear`.** We begin with the method `clear`, because the constructor calls it. It must initialize both the head and tail references as well as the field `length`:

```java
public final void clear()
{
   firstNode = null;
   lastNode = null;
   length = 0;
} // end clear
```

Here, and in the rest of the revision, changes from the original implementation appear in color.

7.22   **Adding to the end of the list.** The steps required to add an entry to the end of a list depend upon whether the list is empty or not. After an item is added to the end of an empty list, both the head and tail references must reference the new solitary node. Thus, after creating a new node that newNode references, the add method would execute

```
firstNode = newNode;
lastNode = newNode;
```

Adding to the end of a nonempty list no longer requires a traversal to locate the last entry: The tail reference lastNode provides this information. After making the addition, the tail reference must change to refer to the new last entry. The following statements perform these steps, as Figure 7-9 illustrates:

```
lastNode.next = newNode;
lastNode = newNode;
```

Figure 7-9   Adding a node to the end of a nonempty chain that has a tail reference

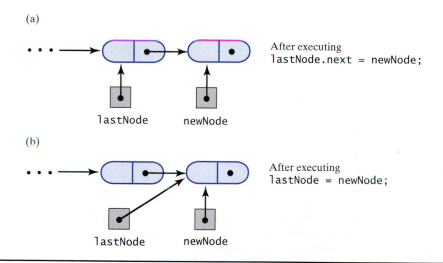

The following revision of the first add method reflects the previous comments:

```
public boolean add(T newEntry)
{
   Node newNode = new Node(newEntry);

   if (isEmpty())
      firstNode = newNode;
   else
      lastNode.next = newNode;

   lastNode = newNode;
   length++;
   return true;
} // end add
```

7.23   **Adding to the list at a given position.** Adding to a list by position affects the tail reference only when we are adding to an empty list or adding to the end of a nonempty list. Other cases do not affect the tail reference, so we treat them as we did in Segment 6.27 when we did not have a tail reference.

Thus, the implementation of the method that adds by position is

```java
public boolean add(int newPosition, T newEntry)
{
  boolean isSuccessful = true;

  if ((newPosition >= 1) && (newPosition <= length+1))
  {
    Node newNode = new Node(newEntry);

    if (isEmpty())
    {
      firstNode = newNode;
      lastNode = newNode;
    }
    else if (newPosition == 1)
    {
      newNode.next = firstNode;
      firstNode = newNode;
    }
    else if (newPosition == length+1)
    {
      lastNode.next = newNode;
      lastNode = newNode;
    }
    else
    {
      Node nodeBefore = getNodeAt(newPosition - 1);
      Node nodeAfter = nodeBefore.next;
      newNode.next = nodeAfter;
      nodeBefore.next = newNode;
    } // end if

    length++;
  }
  else
    isSuccessful = false;

  return isSuccessful;
} // end add
```

7.24   **Removing an entry from a list.** Removing an entry can affect the tail reference in two cases:

- Case 1: If the list contains one entry and we remove it, an empty list results, and we must set both the head and tail references to `null`.
- Case 2: If the list contains several entries and we remove the last one, we must change the tail reference so that it references the new last entry.

Figure 7-10   Removing the last node from a chain that has both head and tail references when the chain
contains (a) one node; (b) more than one node

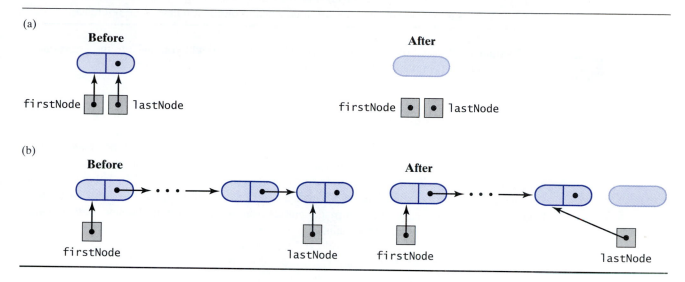

Figure 7-10 illustrates these two cases, and the following method implements them:

```
public T remove(int givenPosition)
{
  T result = null;                        // return value
  if ((givenPosition >= 1) && (givenPosition <= length))
  {
    assert !isEmpty();
    if (givenPosition == 1)
    {
      result = firstNode.data;
      firstNode = firstNode.next;
      if (length == 1)
        lastNode = null;                  // solitary entry was removed
    }
    else
    {
      Node nodeBefore = getNodeAt(givenPosition - 1);
      Node nodeToRemove = nodeBefore.next;
      Node nodeAfter = nodeToRemove.next;
      nodeBefore.next = nodeAfter; // disconnect node to be removed
      result = nodeToRemove.data;  // save entry to be removed

      if (givenPosition == length)
        lastNode = nodeBefore;      // last node was removed
    } // end if

    length--;
  } // end if

  return result;
} // end remove
```

Note: Adding to the end of a chain of linked nodes requires less work when you maintain a tail reference because you avoid a traversal of the chain. Removing the last node from a chain requires a traversal to locate the next-to-last node whether or not you have a tail reference.

Question 9   In light of the tail reference, what changes should you make to the assertions in the method `isEmpty`, as given in Segment 6.31 of the previous chapter?

The Pros and Cons of Using a Chain to Implement the ADT List

7.25   You have seen how to use a chain in the implementation of the ADT list. One of the greatest advantages of this approach is that the chain, and therefore the list, can grow as large as necessary. As long as memory is available, you can add as many nodes to a chain as you wish. Although you can also use dynamic array expansion—as Chapter 5 describes—to allow the list to grow, each time a larger array is necessary, you must copy the entries from the full array to the new array. No such copying is required when you use a chain.

In addition, a chain allows you to add and remove nodes without moving any existing entries that are already in the list. With an array, adding and removing entries usually requires that other entries be moved within the array. However, you must traverse a chain from its beginning to determine where to make the addition or deletion.

Retrieving an existing entry from a chain requires a similar traversal to locate the desired entry. When you use an array instead of a chain, you can access any element directly by position, without searching the array. However, a method such as `contains` that does not have the position of an entry must perform a search regardless of whether an array or a chain represents the list.

Lastly, a chain requires more memory than an array of the same length. Although both data structures contain references to data objects, each node in a chain also contains a reference to another node. However, an array often is larger than necessary, so memory is wasted. A chain uses memory only as needed.

Question 10   When retrieving the entry at a given position in a list, a linked implementation traverses a chain, while an array-based implementation accesses the element directly without a traversal. Suppose that you have an object, and it is in a list, but you do not know its position in the list. Let's add an operation `getPosition` to the ADT list that takes an object as an argument and returns its position within the list. Exercise 2 of Chapter 5 considers such an operation.

a.   Describe how you would implement `getPosition` in `LList` and in `ExpandableArrayList`, as discussed in Segments 5.17 and 5.18 of Chapter 5.
b.   Compare the execution time required by these two versions of `getPosition`.

Java Class Library: The Class `LinkedList`

7.26   Recall from Chapter 4 that the Java Class Library contains the interface `java.util.List`. This interface is like our `ListInterface`, but declares more methods (it does not, however, have a `display` method). Also, some methods have different names or specifications, and the list entries begin at position 0 instead of 1. Segment 4.19 of Chapter 4 summarized these differences.

The same package `java.util` contains the class `LinkedList`. This class implements the interface `List` and contains additional methods that add, remove, and retrieve entries at the beginning or end of a list. These additional methods are as follows:

public void addFirst(T newEntry)
Adds newEntry to the beginning of the list.

public void addLast(T newEntry)
Adds newEntry to the end of the list.

public T removeFirst()
Removes and returns the first entry in the list.

public T removeLast()
Removes and returns the last entry in the list.

public T getFirst()
Returns the first entry in the list.

public T getLast()
Returns the last entry in the list.

As usual, T is the generic type of the list's entries.
Descriptions of other methods in this class are available at

`java.sun.com/j2se/1.5/docs/api/`

CHAPTER SUMMARY

- You can remove any node from a chain of linked nodes by changing at most two references.
- Removing the first node of a chain of linked nodes is a special case; removing the last node is not.
- Adding or removing a node that is last in a chain of linked nodes requires a traversal of the entire chain.
- The class **Node** can be an inner class of **LList** or a class within a package that contains **LList**. In the latter case, **Node** must define set and get methods to provide access to its data fields.
- Maintaining a reference to a chain's last node as well as to its first node eliminates the need for a traversal when adding a node at the end of the chain. A traversal, however, is still necessary when removing the last node. Maintaining the tail reference then makes removing the last node a bit more difficult.

EXERCISES

1. Suppose that you want an operation for the ADT list that removes the first occurrence of a given object from the list. The header of the method could be as follows:

    public boolean remove(T anObject)

    The method returns true if the list contained anObject and the object was removed. Write an implementation of this method for the class LList.

2. Repeat the previous exercise, but remove all occurrences of anObject from the list.

3. Suppose that you want an operation for the ADT list that moves the first item in the list to the end of the list. The header of the method could be as follows:

public void moveToEnd()

Write an implementation of this method for the class LList.

4. Implement a replace method for the class LList that returns the replaced object.

5. Suppose that a list contains Comparable objects. Implement the following methods for the class LList:

public T getMin()
Returns the smallest object in the list.

public T removeMin()
Removes and returns the smallest object in the list.

6. Consider an instance arrayList of ExpandableArrayList, as given in Segments 5.17 and 5.18 of Chapter 5. Let the array have an initial size of 10, and double its size each time it fills. Also, consider an instance of LList called chainList.

a. How large is the array after adding 145 items to arrayList?
b. How large is the array after adding 20 more items to arrayList?
c. How many nodes are in the chain after adding 145 items to chainList?
d. How many nodes are in the chain after adding 20 more items to chainList?
e. Each node in a chain has two references, so a chain of n nodes has $2n$ references. An array of size n, on the other hand, has n references. Count the number of references in each of the situations described in Parts a through d.
f. When will arrayList use fewer references than chainList?
g. When will chainList use fewer references than arrayList?

7. List the steps necessary to remove a node from the doubly linked chain shown in Figure 6-17 of Chapter 6 when the node is

a. First in the chain
b. Last in the chain
c. Between existing nodes in the chain

PROJECTS

1. Write a program that thoroughly tests the class LList.

2. Listing 7-1 in Segment 7.14 shows the inner class Node with set and get methods. Revise the class LList so that it invokes these set and get methods instead of accessing the private data fields data and next directly by name.

3. Listing 7-2 in Segment 7.16 shows Node as a class within a package containing LList. Revise LList to use this version of Node.

4. Revise `Node` and `LList` as described in Segment 7.18.

5. Create a Java interface that contains the six methods described in Segment 7.26 and the method `moveToEnd` described in Exercise 3. Then extend this interface and `ListInterface` to form `DoubleEndedListInterface`. Write a class that implements `DoubleEndedListInterface`. Represent the list's entries by using a chain of nodes that has both a head reference and a tail reference. Write a program that thoroughly tests your class.

6. Repeat Project 5, but do not use a tail reference.

7. Complete the implementation of the ADT bag begun in Project 2 of Chapter 6.

8. Complete the implementation of the ADT set begun in Project 3 of Chapter 6.

9. Adding nodes to or removing nodes from a linked chain requires a special case when the operation is at the beginning of the chain. To eliminate the special case, you can add a **dummy node** at the beginning of the chain. The dummy node is always present but does not contain a list entry. The chain, then, is never empty, and so the head reference is never `null`, even when the list is empty. Modify the class `LList`, as presented in this chapter and the previous one, by adding a dummy node to the chain.

10. In a circularly linked chain, the last node references the first node. Commonly, only one external reference—to the last node—is maintained, since the first node is found easily from the last one.

Modify the class `LList`, as presented in this chapter and the previous one, by using a circular linked chain and a tail reference.

11. Implement as the class `Ring` the ADT ring that Project 6 of Chapter 4 described. Represent the ring as a chain of linked nodes. Consider using a circular linked chain, as described in the previous project.

12. Complete the implementation of the ADT list that you began in either Project 4 or 5 of Chapter 6. The implementation stores the list's entries in a doubly linked chain.

13. You can add a dummy head node, as Project 9 describes, to the beginning of a doubly linked chain. Modify the implementation of the ADT list described in the previous project by adding a dummy head node to the chain.

CHAPTER

8

Iterators

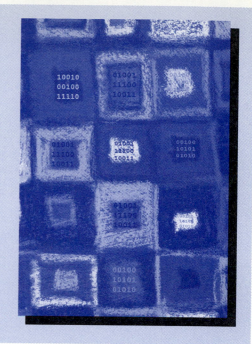

Contents

Prerequisites

Objectives

After studying this chapter, you should be able to

- Describe the concept of an iterator
- Use an iterator to traverse or manipulate a list

- Implement in Java a separate class iterator and an inner class iterator for a list
- Describe the pros and cons of separate class iterators and inner class iterators

An iterator is an object that traverses a collection of data. During the traversal, you can look at the data entries, modify them, add entries, and remove entries. The Java Class Library contains two interfaces, Iterator and ListIterator, that specify methods for an iterator. While you could add these iterator methods to the operations of the ADT list, you should instead implement them as a distinct class that interacts with the ADT list. This iterator class can be outside of the ADT list or hidden within its implementation. We will explore both of these approaches in this chapter.

What Is an Iterator?

8.1   How would you count the number of lines on this page? You could use your finger to point to each line as you counted it. Your finger would keep your place on the page. If you paused at a particular line, your finger would be on the current line, and there would be a previous line and a next line. If you think of this page as a list of lines, you would be traversing the list as you counted the lines.

An **iterator** is a program component that enables you to step through, or **traverse**, a collection of data such as a list, beginning with the first entry. During one complete traversal, or **iteration**, each data item is considered once. You control the progress of the iteration by repeatedly asking the iterator to give you a reference to the next entry in the collection. You also can modify the collection as you traverse it by adding, removing, or simply changing entries.

You are familiar with iteration because you have written loops. For example, if nameList is a list of strings, you can write the following for loop to display the entire list:

```
int listSize = nameList.getLength();
for (int position = 1; position <= listSize; position++)
   System.out.println(nameList.getEntry(position));
```

Here the loop traverses, or **iterates**, through the entries in the list. Instead of simply displaying each entry, we could do other things to or with it.

8.2   Notice that the previous loop is at the client level, since it uses the ADT operation getEntry to access the list. For an array-based implementation of the list, getEntry can retrieve the desired array element directly and quickly. But if a chain of linked nodes represents the list's entries, getEntry must move from node to node until it locates the desired one. For example, to retrieve the nth entry in the list, getEntry would begin at the first node in the chain and then move to the second node, the third node, and so on until it reached the nth node. At the next repetition of the loop, getEntry would retrieve the $n + 1^{st}$ entry in the list by beginning again at the first node in the chain and stepping from node to node until it reached the $n + 1^{st}$ node. This wastes time.

Iteration is such a common operation that we could include it as part of the ADT list. Doing so would enable a more efficient implementation than we were just able to achieve at the client level. Notice that the operation display of the ADT list performs a traversal. It is an example of a traversal controlled by the ADT. A client can invoke display but cannot control it once it begins.

But display only displays the list. What if we want to do something else with the list's entries as we traverse them? We do not want to add another operation to the ADT each time we think of another way to use an iteration. We need a way for a client to step through a collection of data and retrieve or modify the entries. The traversal should keep track of its progress; that is, it should know where it is in the collection and whether it has accessed each entry. An iterator provides such a traversal.

Note: Iterators

An **iterator** is a program component that steps through, or **traverses**, a collection of data. The iterator keeps track of its progress during the traversal, or **iteration**. It can tell you whether a next entry exists and, if so, return a reference to it. During one cycle of the iteration, each data item is considered once.

The Interface `Iterator`

8.3   The package `java.util` in the Java Class Library contains two interfaces—`Iterator` and `ListIterator`—that specify methods appropriate for an iterator. Let's begin by examining the interface `Iterator`, given in Listing 8-1. Like many of the interfaces we have considered, `Iterator` specifies a generic type to represent the data type of the entries involved in the iteration. It specifies only three methods—`hasNext`, `next`, and `remove`—that an iterator can have. These methods enable you to traverse a collection of data from its beginning.

Listing 8-1   Java's interface `java.util.Iterator`

```
package java.util;
public interface Iterator<T>
{
  /** Task: Detects whether the iterator has completed its traversal
   *        and gone beyond the last entry in the collection of data.
   *  @return true if the iterator has another entry to return */
  public boolean hasNext();

  /** Task: Retrieves the next entry in the collection and
   *        advances the iterator by one position.
   *  @return a reference to the next entry in the iteration,
   *          if one exists
   *  @throws NoSuchElementException if the iterator had reached the
   *          end already, that is, if hasNext() is false */
  public T next();

  /** Task: Removes from the collection of data the last entry that
   *        next() returned. A subsequent call to next() will behave
   *        as it would have before the removal.
   *  Precondition: next() has been called, and remove() has not been
   *        called since then. The collection has not been altered
   *        during the iteration except by calls to this method.
   *  @throws IllegalStateException if next() has not been called, or
   *          if remove() was called already after the last call to
   *          next().
   *  @throws UnsupportedOperationException if this iterator does
   *          not permit a remove operation. */
  public void remove(); // Optional method
} // end Iterator
```

8.4   An iterator marks its current position within a collection much as your finger can point to an entry in a list or to a line on this page. However, in Java, the position of an iterator is not *at* an entry. Instead, it is positioned either before the first entry in the collection, between two entries, or after the last entry. The **next entry** in an iteration is the one right after the position of the iterator's **cursor**. The method `hasNext` sees whether a next entry exists and returns true or false accordingly.

As long as `hasNext` returns true, the method `next` moves the iterator's cursor over the next entry and returns a reference to it, as Figure 8-1 illustrates. Repeated calls to `next` traverse through the list. As the iteration progresses, the iterator returns entry after entry. Once `next` has returned the last entry in the collection, a subsequent call to it causes a `NoSuchElementException`.

Figure 8-1   The effect of a call to `next` on a list iterator

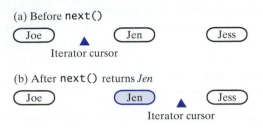

The method `remove` removes the entry that `next` just returned. Contrast this with the ADT list operation `remove`, which removes the entry at a given position within the list. When you implement the `Iterator` interface, you do not have to provide a `remove` operation—it is optional—but you do need to define a method `remove`, because it appears in the interface. Such a method should throw the exception `UnsupportedOperationException` if the client invoked it.

Programming Tip: All of the exceptions mentioned in the interface `Iterator` are run-time exceptions, so no `throws` clause is necessary in any of the methods' headers. In addition, you do not have to write `try` and `catch` blocks when you invoke these methods. However, you will need to import `NoSuchElementException` from the package `java.util`. The other exceptions are in `java.lang`, so no `import` statement is necessary for them.

Using the Interface `Iterator`

8.5   Some details of using an iterator depend on the approach used to implement the iterator methods. A possible, but not optimal, way to provide an ADT with traversal operations is to define them as ADT operations. For example, if `ListInterface` extends `Iterator`, a list object would have iterator methods as well as list methods. Although such an approach provides efficient traversals, it has disadvantages, as you will see.

A better way is to implement the iterator methods within their own class. In one approach, this class is public and separate from the class that implements the ADT in question. The two classes must, of course, interact in some way. We will call an instance of such an iterator class a **separate class iterator**. Alternatively, the iterator class can be a private inner class of the class that implements the ADT. We'll call an instance of this inner class an **inner class iterator**. As you will see, an inner class iterator is usually preferable. This chapter will discuss both approaches.

But first, let's focus on how the methods in the interface `Iterator` behave. A separate class iterator of a list and an inner class iterator of a list are objects distinct from the list. Both of these iterators invoke their methods in the same way. The following examples arbitrarily use a separate class iterator.

8.6   **Example.** Let's look at an example of how the methods `hasNext` and `next` of the interface `Iterator` work with the ADT list. Suppose we create a list of names. We will use strings for the names, but we could instead use instances of the class `Name` that Chapter 1 presented. The following Java statements create such a list:

```
ListInterface<String> nameList = new LList<String>();
nameList.add("Jamie");
nameList.add("Joey");
nameList.add("Rachel");
```

At this point, `nameList` contains the strings

Jamie
Joey
Rachel

Suppose that the public class `SeparateIterator` implements the interface `Iterator`. To create a separate class iterator for `nameList`, we create an instance of `SeparateIterator`, as follows:

```
Iterator<String> nameIterator = new SeparateIterator<String>(nameList);
```

Figure 8-2   The effect of the iterator methods `hasNext` and `next` on a list

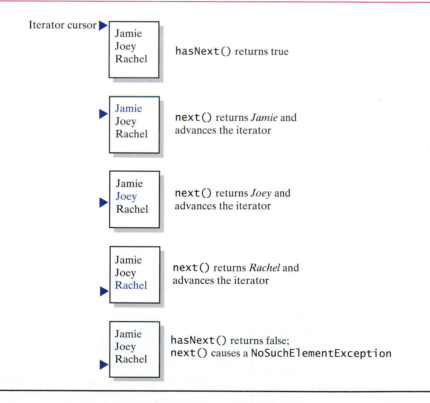

This invocation of `SeparateIterator`'s constructor connects the iterator `nameIterator` to the list `nameList` and positions the iterator just before the first entry in the list. The following sequence of events demonstrates the iterator methods:

- `nameIterator.hasNext()` returns true because a next entry exists.
- `nameIterator.next()` returns the string *Jamie* and advances the iterator.
- `nameIterator.next()` returns the string *Joey* and advances the iterator.
- `nameIterator.next()` returns the string *Rachel* and advances the iterator.
- `nameIterator.hasNext()` returns false because the iterator is beyond the end of the list.
- `nameIterator.next()` causes a `NoSuchElementException`.

Figure 8-2 illustrates these events.

8.7   **Example.** We can use an iterator to display all the entries in a list. The following statements display the strings in the list `nameList`, one per line:

```
Iterator<String> nameIterator = new SeparateIterator<String>(nameList);
while (nameIterator.hasNext())
   System.out.println(nameIterator.next());
```

The iterator `nameIterator` begins just before the first entry in the list. As long as `hasNext` returns true, `next` returns the next entry in the list and advances the iterator. Thus, every entry in the list is retrieved and displayed.

8.8   **Example.** The interface `Iterator` provides an operation to remove an entry from a data collection. This entry is the one returned by the last call to the method `next`. Thus, you must invoke `next` before you can call `remove`.

Figure 8-3   The effect of the iterator methods `next` and `remove` on a list

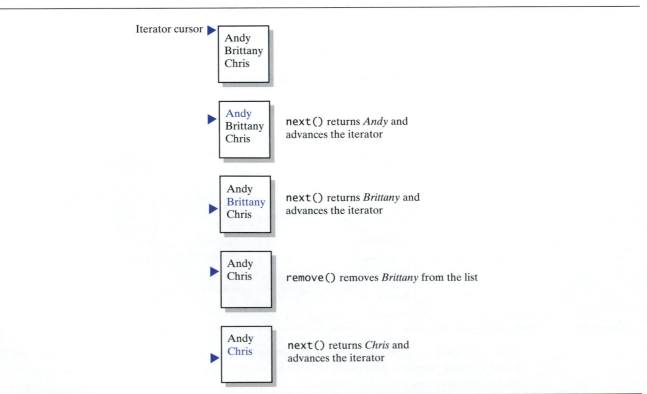

If `nameList` contains the strings *Andy*, *Brittany*, and *Chris*, and `nameIterator` is defined as in the previous example,

- `nameIterator.next()` returns the string *Andy* and advances the iterator.
- `nameIterator.next()` returns the string *Brittany* and advances the iterator.
- `nameIterator.remove()` removes *Brittany* from the list.
- `nameIterator.next()` returns the string *Chris* and advances the iterator.

Figure 8-3 shows the list during the previous iteration.

8.9   **Example.** The requirement that you invoke `next` before you call `remove` results in two situations that cause the exception `IllegalStateException`. If `nameList` is defined as in the previous example, and we write

```
nameIterator = new SeparateIterator<String>(nameList);
nameIterator.hasNext();
nameIterator.remove();
```

an `IllegalStateException` occurs because we did not call `next` before we called `remove`. Similarly, if we write

```
nameIterator.next();
nameIterator.remove();
nameIterator.remove();
```

the second `remove` causes an `IllegalStateException` because `remove` had been called already since the most recent call to `next`.

Question 1   Assume that `nameList` contains the names Jamie, Joey, and Rachel, as it does in Segment 8.6. What output is produced by the following Java statements?

```
Iterator<String> nameIterator = new SeparateIterator<String>(nameList);
nameIterator.next();
nameIterator.next();
nameIterator.remove();
System.out.println(nameIterator.hasNext());
System.out.println(nameIterator.next());
nameList.display();
```

Question 2   Assume that `nameList` is an instance of a class that implements `ListInterface`, and `nameIterator` is defined as in the previous question. If `nameList` contains at least three strings, write Java statements that display the list's third entry.

Question 3   Given `nameList` and `nameIterator` as described in the previous question, write statements that display the even-numbered entries in the list. That is, display the second entry, the fourth entry, and so on.

Question 4   Given `nameList` and `nameIterator` as described in Question 2, write statements that remove all entries from the list.

Note: Java's interface `java.util.Iterator` specifies three methods: `hasNext`, `next`, and `remove`. The method `hasNext` sees whether the iterator has a next entry to return. If so, `next` returns a reference to it. The method `remove` can remove the entry last returned by a call to `next`, or it can simply throw an `UnsupportedOperationException` if you choose to disallow removals by the iterator.

8.10 **Multiple iterators.** Although the previous examples show one iterator traversing a list, we can have several iterations of the same list in progress simultaneously. For example, imagine a printed list of names that are not distinct and are in no particular order. Running one finger down that list to count the names is like having one iteration of a list. Now suppose that you want to count the number of times each name occurs in the printed list. You can use two fingers, as follows. With your left hand, use one finger to point to the first name in the list. With your right hand, use one finger to point to each of the names in the list, starting with the first one. As you traverse the list with your right hand, compare each name to the name that your left hand marks. In this way, you can count the number of times the first name occurs in the list. Now move your left-hand finger to the next name in the list and use your right hand to point to the beginning of the list. Repeat the previous process to count the number of times that the second name appears in the list. Try it with the names in Figure 8-4. (Since your left hand will encounter Jane three times, you will repeat the computation needlessly unless you are careful. We consider this detail a bit later.)

Each of your two fingers can traverse the list independently of the other. They are like two independent iterators that traverse the same list, as you will see in the next example.

Figure 8-4 Counting the number of times that *Jane* appears in a list of names

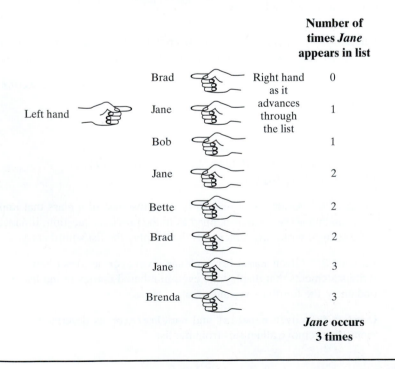

8.11   **Example.** Let's write some code that counts the occurrences of each name in the list in Figure 8-4. Let `nameIterator` correspond to your left hand in the figure. Now we'll define a second iterator, `countingIterator`, that corresponds to your right hand. For each name that your left hand marks, your right hand traverses the entire list to count the occurrences of that name. Thus, we have the following nested loops, assuming that `nameList` is the list:

```java
Iterator<String> nameIterator =
                new SeparateIterator<String>(nameList);
while (nameIterator.hasNext())
{
   String currentName = nameIterator.next();

   int nameCount = 0;

   Iterator<String> countingIterator =
                new SeparateIterator<String>(nameList);
   while (countingIterator.hasNext())
   {
      String nextName = countingIterator.next();
      if (currentName.equals(nextName))
         nameCount++;
   } // end while

   System.out.println(currentName + " occurs " +
                nameCount + " times.");
} // end while
```

To reset `countingIterator` to the list's beginning, we call the constructor again, since `Iterator` does not have a method for this purpose.

With the names given in Figure 8-4, these statements produce the following output:

Brad occurs 2 times.
Jane occurs 3 times.
Bob occurs 1 times.
Jane occurs 3 times.
Bette occurs 1 times.
Brad occurs 2 times.
Jane occurs 3 times.
Brenda occurs 1 times.

As you can see, since `nameIterator` (your left hand) encounters *Brad* twice and *Jane* three times, the computation in the inner loop is repeated needlessly. For example, we compute that *Brad* occurs twice each time `nameIterator` encounters *Brad*.

If `SeparateIterator` supports a remove operation, and if we are allowed to destroy the list, we can remove the duplicate entries—and thereby prevent the repeated computations—by modifying the `if` statement as follows:

```java
if (currentName.equals(nextName))
{
   nameCount++;
   if (nameCount > 1)
      countingIterator.remove();
} // end if
```

When nameCount exceeds 1, nextName must be a name that the iterator countingIterator has already encountered in the list. Thus, we remove that entry. Since countingIterator.next() just retrieved nextName, countingIterator.remove() removes it. The iteration continues with the next entry. Exercise 8 at the end of this chapter considers the case when we cannot destroy the list.

A Separate Class Iterator

We will now examine an implementation of the public class SeparateIterator used in the previous examples. This class implements the interface java.util.Iterator.

8.12   **An outline of the class SeparateIterator.** In the previous examples, we connect an iterator—which is an instance of the class SeparateIterator—with a list by invoking the class's constructor. To accomplish this connection, the class needs a data field that references the list. As you can see in Listing 8-2, the constructor assigns this reference to the field. Also, notice that we make the definition of SeparateIterator independent of a particular implementation of the list, such as AList or LList, by defining the field list as an instance of ListInterface.

In addition to connecting the iterator to the list in question, the constructor initializes it so the iteration will begin at the first entry in the list. To enable this, the class has another data field next-Position that tracks where we are in the iteration. This field is simply the integer position of the entry in the list that the method next last returned. It is convenient to initialize this field to zero.

Listing 8-2   An outline of the class SeparateIterator

```
import java.util.Iterator;
import java.util.NoSuchElementException;
public class SeparateIterator<T> implements Iterator<T>
{
  private ListInterface<T> list;
  private int nextPosition; // position of entry last returned by next()
  private boolean wasNextCalled; // needed by remove

  public SeparateIterator(ListInterface<T> aList)
  {
    list = aList;
    nextPosition = 0;
    wasNextCalled = false;
  } // end constructor

  < Implementations of the methods hasNext, next, and remove go here >
  . . .
} // end SeparateIterator
```

Providing an iterator with a remove operation is optional; however, we shall do so here because the previous examples used one. This desire complicates our class somewhat, because the client must call the method next before each call to remove. This requirement isn't simply a precondition. The remove method must throw an exception if it isn't met. Therefore, we need an additional data field—a boolean flag—that enables remove to check whether next was called. We name this data field wasNextCalled. The constructor initializes this field to false.

8.13   **The method hasNext.** The class `SeparateIterator` has no special access to the private data fields of the class that implements the list. It is a client of the list and so can process the list only by using the list's ADT operations. Figure 8-5 shows a separate class iterator with a reference to a list but with no knowledge of the list's implementation. The implementations of the iterator methods will use methods specified in `ListInterface`. The resulting implementations are rather straightforward but take longer to execute, in general, than the implementation of an inner class iterator. For example, the method `hasNext` calls the list's `getLength` method:

```
public boolean hasNext()
{
   return nextPosition < list.getLength();
} // end hasNext
```

 Question 5   What does the method `hasNext` return when the list is empty? Why?

Figure 8-5   A separate class iterator with a reference to an ADT, an indicator of its position within the iteration, and no knowledge of the ADT's implementation

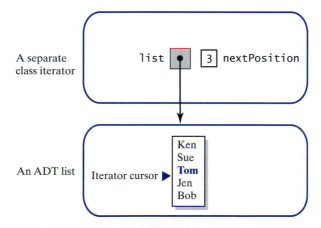

8.14   **The method next.** As long as the iteration has not ended—that is, as long as `hasNext` returns true—the method `next` retrieves the iteration's next entry by calling the list's `getEntry` method. If, however, the iteration has ended, `next` throws an exception.

```
public T next()
{
   if (hasNext())
   {
      wasNextCalled = true;
      nextPosition++;
      return list.getEntry(nextPosition);
   }
   else
      throw new NoSuchElementException("Illegal call to next(); " +
                                       "iterator is after end of list.");
} // end next
```

Since `nextPosition` begins at zero, we must increment it before passing it to `getEntry`. Doing so advances the iterator as required. Notice that we also set the field `wasNextCalled` to true so that the method `remove` can tell that `next` was called.

Question 6   The work performed by the method `next` depends upon the implementation of the ADT list that is ultimately used. For which implementation of the list, array-based or linked, will `next` use the most execution time? Why?

8.15   **The method `remove`.** The iterator's method `remove` removes from the list the entry that the most recent call to `next` returned. If `next` was not called, or if `remove` has been called since the last call to `next`, `remove` throws an `IllegalStateException`. The class's data field `wasNextCalled` helps us to implement this aspect of the method. If the field is true, we know that `next` has been called. Then, by setting the field to false, we enable a subsequent invocation of `remove` to require another call to `next`.

The field `nextPosition` is the position of the entry just returned by `next`, so it is the position of the entry to be removed. Thus, we pass it to the list's `remove` method. Then, since a subsequent call to `next` must behave as it would have before the removal, we must decrement `nextPosition`.

Figure 8-6 shows a list and the field `nextPosition` just before the call to `next`, just after the call to `next` but before the call to `remove`, and just after the call to `remove`. Notice in Part *b* that `next` increments `nextPosition` and then returns a reference to *Chris*, the entry at that position and the next entry in the iteration. A call to `remove` in Part *c* removes the entry—*Chris*—at `nextPosition`. Afterwards, the next entry—*Dan* in the figure—moves to the next lower-numbered position in the list. Thus, `remove` must decrement `nextPosition` so that a subsequent call to `next` will return *Dan*.

Figure 8-6   A list and `nextPosition` (a) just before the call to `next`;
(b) just after the call to `next` but before the call to `remove`; (c) after the call to `remove`

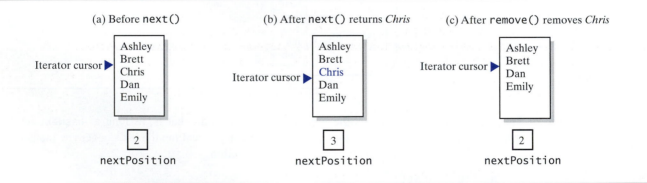

The following implementation of `remove` reflects this discussion.

```java
public void remove()
{
  if (wasNextCalled)
  {
    // nextPosition was incremented by the call to next(), so
    // it is the position number of the entry to be removed
    list.remove(nextPosition);
    nextPosition--;          // a subsequent call to next() must be
                             // unaffected by this removal
```

```
            wasNextCalled = false; // reset flag
      }
      else
         throw new IllegalStateException("Illegal call to remove(); " +
                                         "next() was not called.");
   } // end remove
```

 Note: **Separate class iterators**
A separate class iterator must access an ADT's data by using the public methods of the ADT. However, certain ADTs, such as a stack, do not provide sufficient public access to their data to make such an iterator possible. In addition, the typical separate class iterator takes longer to perform its operations than do other kinds of iterators because of the indirect access to the ADTs data. On the other hand, the implementation of a separate class iterator is usually straightforward. You can also have several independent separate class iterators in existence at the same time for a given ADT.

To provide an iterator for an ADT's implementation that exists and cannot be altered, you might need to define a separate class iterator.

An Inner Class Iterator

8.16   By using separate class iterators, you can have multiple and distinct iterations of a list exist simultaneously. However, separate class iterators belong to a public class, so they can access the list's data fields only indirectly via ADT operations. As a result, the iterations take more time than those performed by other kinds of iterators. For ADTs other than a list, a separate class iterator might have insufficient access to the data fields to perform an iteration.

A desirable alternative is to define the iterator class as an inner class of the ADT. Because the resulting iterator objects are distinct from the ADT, you can have multiple iterations in progress at the same time. Moreover, since the iterator belongs to an inner class, it has direct access to the ADT's data fields. For these reasons, an inner class iterator is usually preferable to a separate class iterator.

In this section, we will implement the interface `Iterator` by adding an inner class to each of two implementations of the ADT list. First, we will use a linked implementation of the list but will provide only the iterator operations `hasNext` and `next`. Then we will use an array-based list and support all three operations of `Iterator`.

A Linked Implementation

8.17   To achieve our goal, we must define the methods specified in `Iterator` within a new inner class of the class that implements the ADT list. We'll name this inner class `IteratorForLinkedList` and name the outer class `LinkedListWithIterator`. The outer class will be much like the class `LList` of Chapters 6 and 7. However, it needs another method that the client can use to create an iterator. This method, `getIterator`, has the following simple implementation:

```
   public Iterator<T> getIterator()
   {
      return new IteratorForLinkedList();
   } // end getIterator
```

We will show you how to use this method shortly.

To accommodate this new method, we create a new interface—shown in Listing 8-3—that extends `ListInterface` instead of changing it. This interface has all the list methods of `ListInterface` and the new method `getIterator`.

Listing 8-3   The interface `ListWithIteratorInterface`

```
import java.util.Iterator;
public interface ListWithIteratorInterface<T> extends ListInterface<T>
{
   public Iterator<T> getIterator();
} // end ListWithIteratorInterface
```

Because a class can implement more than one interface, we could define the class `LinkedListWithIterator` without using our new interface. But having this interface enables us to declare an object of type `ListWithIteratorInterface` and know that the object will have the list methods as well as the method `getIterator`.

8.18   **Example: Using the iterator to display a list.** Once again, let's create a list of strings. Since we've defined the interface `ListWithIteratorInterface` that includes the method `getIterator` and the methods of `ListInterface`, we can use it to create the new list:

```
ListWithIteratorInterface<String> myList =
        new LinkedListWithIterator<String>();
```

We add entries to this list using the list's add methods, as we have done before.

We now can display the list by using an iterator. We first create an iterator object by invoking the new list method `getIterator`:

```
Iterator<String> myIterator = myList.getIterator();
```

The resulting iterator is ready to access the first entry in the list.

We then write a loop like the one you saw in Segment 8.7:

```
while (myIterator.hasNext())
   System.out.println(myIterator.next());
```

8.19   **An outline of the class.** Listing 8-4 outlines the class `LinkedListWithIterator` with its inner classes `IteratorForLinkedList` and `Node`. We will define the methods declared in the interface `Iterator` within the inner class `IteratorForLinkedList`. However, we will not give iterators the ability to remove entries from the data collection.

Listing 8-4   An outline of the class `LinkedListWithIterator`

```
import java.util.Iterator;
import java.util.NoSuchElementException;
public class LinkedListWithIterator<T> implements
                                    ListWithIteratorInterface<T>
{
   private Node firstNode;
   private int  length;
```

```
public LinkedListWithIterator()
{
   clear();
} // end default constructor
```

< Implementations of the methods of the ADT list go here;
   you can see them in Chapters 6 and 7, beginning at Segments 6.23 and 7.9 respectively. >

```
. . .
public Iterator<T> getIterator()
{
   return new IteratorForLinkedList();
} // end getIterator
```

< Segment 8.20 begins a description of the following inner class. >

```
private class IteratorForLinkedList implements Iterator<T>
{
   private Node nextNode;

   private IteratorForLinkedList()
   {
      nextNode = firstNode;
   } // end default constructor
```

< Implementations of the methods in the interface Iterator go here;
   you can see them in Segments 8.21 through 8.23. >

```
   . . .
} // end IteratorForLinkedList
```

< Implementation of the private class Node (Segment 6.18) goes here. >

```
   . . .
} // end LinkedListWithIterator
```

8.20 **The inner class `IteratorForLinkedList`.** As you can see in Listing 8-4, the private inner class `IteratorForLinkedList` has a data field `nextNode` to track an iteration. The constructor initializes this field to `firstNode`, which is a data field of the outer class and references the first node in the chain that contains the list's entries. We cannot position the iterator between nodes, even though we imagine its position to be between entries. Nor can `nextNode` reference the node before the one that `next` will access, because the first node has no node before it. Thus, `nextNode` references the next node in the iteration, that is, the node that the method `next` must access to get the next entry.

 Note: An inner class can refer to its outer class's data fields by name alone, if it does not also use the same names for its own definitions. For example, the constructor of the inner class `IteratorForLinkedList` references the field `firstNode` directly by name since no other `firstNode` exists. But we could have written `LinkedListWithIterator.this.firstNode` instead.

Figure 8-7 illustrates an inner class iterator. The iterator has direct access to the ADT's underlying data structure—a linked chain, in this example. Since the data field `nextNode` maintains the current position of the iteration, the iterator can quickly retrieve the next entry in the iteration without first returning to the beginning of the chain.

We now implement the methods of the interface `Iterator` within the inner class. These methods will be public, even though they appear within a private class, because they are public in `Iterator` and will be used by clients of `LinkedListWithIterator`.

Figure 8-7   An inner class iterator with direct access to the linked chain that implements the ADT

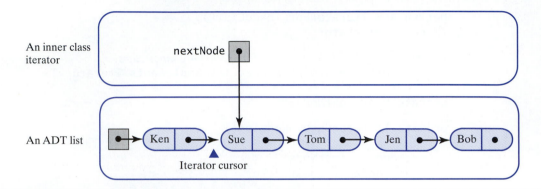

8.21   **The method next.** If the iteration has not ended, `nextNode` references the node containing the next entry in the iteration. Thus, `next` can easily get a reference to this entry. The method then must advance `nextNode` to the next node and return the retrieved list entry. However, `next` must throw an exception if the iteration has already ended.

```
public T next()
{
  if (hasNext())
  {
    Node returnNode = nextNode; // get next node
    nextNode = nextNode.next;   // advance iterator

    return returnNode.data;     // return next entry in iteration
  }
  else
    throw new NoSuchElementException("Illegal call to next();" +
                                     "iterator is after end of list.");
} // end next
```

Note: The definition of the private class `Node` given in Segment 6.18 of Chapter 6 did not include set and get methods for the private data fields `data` and `next`, since we can access them directly by name. As we mentioned in Chapter 7, however, it can be a good idea to include set and get methods when defining a private inner class. If we had done so, as shown in Segment 7.14, we could write `returnNode.getData()` instead of `returnNode.data`, for example. Although we will continue to use the class `Node` in this chapter without set and get methods, we will add set and get methods to the private classes we create subsequently.

8.22   **The method `hasNext`.** After the method `next` returns the last entry in the iteration, `nextNode` will be `null`, since `null` is in the link portion of the last node in the chain. The method `hasNext` can simply compare `nextNode` with `null` to see whether the iteration has ended:

```java
public boolean hasNext()
{
   return nextNode != null;
} // end hasNext
```

Question 7   What does the method `hasNext` return when the list is empty? Why?

8.23   **The method `remove`.** Even though we decided not to support a `remove` operation for this iterator, we must implement the method because it is declared in the interface `Iterator`. If the client invokes `remove`, the method simply throws the run-time exception `UnsupportedOperationException`. Here is an example of how you can define `remove`:

```java
public void remove()
{
   throw new UnsupportedOperationException("remove() is not " +
                                "supported by this iterator");
} // end remove
```

This exception is in the package `java.lang` and so is included automatically in every Java program. Thus, an `import` statement is unnecessary.

Note: The `remove` method
An iterator that does not allow the removal of items during a traversal is not unusual. In such cases, the `remove` method is defined, but it throws an exception if invoked.

Note: Inner class iterators
An inner class iterator has direct access to an ADT's data, so it typically can execute faster than a separate class iterator. Its implementation is usually more involved, however. Both of these iterators have another advantage: Several iterator objects can be in existence at the same time and traverse a list independently of one another.

Question 8   Using the class `LinkedListWithIterator`, what Java statements create the iterators `nameIterator` and `countingIterator` mentioned in Segment 8.11?

Question 9   Implement the method `display` in the class `LinkedListWithIterator` by using iterator methods to display the list. Is there any disadvantage to this implementation as compared to the original one shown in Segment 6.33? Explain.

An Array-Based Implementation

8.24   For the array-based implementation, our iterator will support the `remove` method. Let's begin with an array-based implementation of the ADT list. Chapter 5 presented several classes that implement the ADT list by using an array. `AList` uses a fixed-size array, and `ExpandableArrayList` uses dynamic expansion. Our new class, whose form is shown in Listing 8-5, has the same data fields and methods as the class ExpandableArrayList. But since our new class implements the interface ListWithIteratorInterface, it also includes the method getIterator. Our class also contains the inner class IteratorForArrayList, which implements the interface Iterator.

Listing 8-5 An outline of the class ArrayListWithIterator

```java
import java.util.Iterator;
import java.util.NoSuchElementException;
public class ArrayListWithIterator<T> implements
                                        ListWithIteratorInterface<T>
{
  private T[] list; // array of list entries
  private int length;
  private static final int DEFAULT_INITIAL_CAPACITY = 25;

  public ArrayListWithIterator()
  {
    this(DEFAULT_INITIAL_CAPACITY);
  } // end default constructor

  public ArrayListWithIterator(int initialCapacity)
  {
    length = 0;
    list = (T[]) new Object[initialCapacity];
  } // end constructor

  < Implementations of the methods of the ADT list go here;
    you can see them in Chapter 5, beginning at Segments 5.8 and 5.17. >
  . . .
  public Iterator<T> getIterator()
  {
    return new IteratorForArrayList();
  } // end getIterator

  < Segment 8.25 begins a description of the following inner class. >
  private class IteratorForArrayList implements Iterator<T>
  {
    private int nextIndex;
    private boolean wasNextCalled; // needed by remove

    private IteratorForArrayList()
    {
      nextIndex = 0;
      wasNextCalled = false;
    } // end default constructor

    < Implementations of the methods in the interface Iterator go here;
      you can see them in Segments 8.26 through 8.28. >
    . . .
  } // end IteratorForArrayList
} // end ArrayListWithIterator
```

8.25   **The inner class `IteratorForArrayList`.** Just as you can use your finger to keep track of your place on this page, our iterator implementation uses an index to keep track of the iterator's position within the array of list entries. This index, which we call `nextIndex`, is a data field of the private inner class `IteratorForArrayList`. It will be the index of the next entry in the iteration. The constructor initializes `nextIndex` to zero, as Listing 8-5 shows.

Just as you saw earlier in Segments 8.12 and 8.15, providing an iterator with a remove operation requires an additional data field that the `remove` method can use to see whether `next` was called. Again, we name this data field `wasNextCalled`, but here it is defined within the inner class. The constructor initializes this field to false.

8.26   **The method `hasNext`.** The iterator has a next entry to retrieve if `nextIndex` is less than the length of the list. Thus, `hasNext` has the following straightforward implementation:

```
public boolean hasNext()
{
   return nextIndex < length;
} // end hasNext
```

Notice that `hasNext` returns false when the list is empty, that is, when `length` is zero.

8.27   **The method `next`.** The implementation of the method `next` has the same general form as the version given in Segment 8.14 for the separate class iterator. If `hasNext` returns true, `next` returns the next entry in the iteration. Here, the next entry is `list[nextIndex]`. The method also advances the iteration by incrementing `nextIndex` and sets the flag `wasNextCalled` to true. On the other hand, if `hasNext` returns false, `next` throws an exception.

```
public T next()
{
   if (hasNext())
   {
      wasNextCalled = true;
      T nextEntry = list[nextIndex];
      nextIndex++; // advance iterator

      return nextEntry;
   }
   else
      throw new NoSuchElementException("Illegal call to next();" +
                                "iterator is after end of list.");
} // end next
```

8.28   **The method `remove`.** Removing an entry from the list involves shifting elements within the array `list`. Since we have already developed that code for the list's `remove` method, we will call it instead of accessing the array `list` directly. To do that, we need the position number of the list entry to be removed, rather than its array index. Recall from Segment 4.3 that the position number of an entry in a list begins at 1, so it is 1 larger than the corresponding array index.

Figure 8-8 illustrates how to use `nextIndex` in this implementation. The figure shows the array of list entries and the index `nextIndex` just before the call to `next`, just after the call to `next` but before the call to `remove`, and just after the call to `remove`. Part *b* shows that `next` returns a reference to the next entry, *Chris*, in the iteration and then increments `nextIndex`. The method `remove` must remove this entry from the list. Since `nextIndex` is now 1 larger than the index of *Chris*, it is the position number of the list entry that must be removed. After *Chris* is removed in Part *c*, the next entry—*Deb*—moves to the next lower-numbered position in the array. Thus, `remove` decrements `nextIndex` so that it remains the index of the next entry in the iteration.

Figure 8-8   The array of list entries and `nextIndex` (a) just before the call to `next`; (b) just after the call to `next` but before the call to `remove`; (c) after the call to `remove`

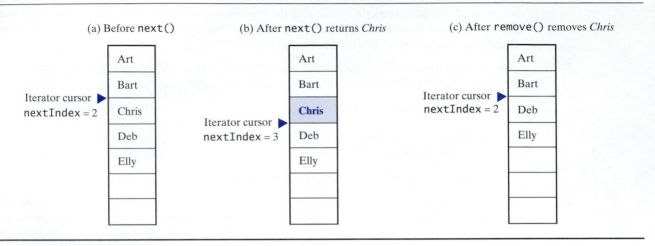

The method `remove` has the following implementation within the inner class `IteratorForArrayList`:

```java
public void remove()
{
  if (wasNextCalled)
  {
    // nextIndex was incremented by the call to next, so it
    // is the position number of the entry to be removed
    ArrayListWithIterator.this.remove(nextIndex);
    nextIndex--;             // index of next entry in iteration
    wasNextCalled = false; // reset flag
  }
  else
    throw new IllegalStateException("Illegal call to remove(); " +
                                    "next() was not called.");
} // end remove
```

To call the list's method `remove`, which is defined in the outer class, from within the iterator's `remove`, we must write the invoking object as `ArrayListWithIterator.this`.

Question 10   Consider the list and the calls to `next` and `remove` in Figure 8-8.

a.   What would a call to `next` return if it occurred after the call to `remove` in Figure 8-8c?
b.   What would a call to `next` return if it occurred after the call to `next` in Figure 8-8b?

Question 11   What changes would be necessary to the methods in the inner class `IteratorForArrayList` if its constructor set `nextIndex` to -1 instead of 0?

Why Are Iterator Methods in Their Own Class?

8.29   Both separate class iterators and inner class iterators enable us to have several distinct iterations of a data collection in progress at the same time. Because inner class iterators have direct access to the structure containing the ADT's data, they can execute faster than separate class iterators, and so are usually preferable.

Why didn't we simply consider the iterator operations as additional ADT operations? To answer this question, let's modify the linked implementation of the list given in the previous two chapters by including the methods specified in Java's interface `Iterator`. To keep this implementation simple, we will not provide the remove operation specified in `Iterator`. The resulting class, outlined in Listing 8-6, is actually quite similar to the class `LinkedListWithIterator`, described in Segment 8.19, which implements an inner class iterator. The differences between these classes appear in color.

The inner class `IteratorForLinkedList` shown in Segment 8.19 does not appear in our new class, but its data field `nextNode` and its iterator methods `hasNext`, `next`, and `remove` do appear unchanged. Instead of the inner class's constructor, we have the public method `resetTraversal`, which sets `nextNode` to `firstNode`. We'll call this method before we begin a traversal.

Listing 8-6   An outline of the class `ListWithTraversal`

```java
import java.util.Iterator;
import java.util.NoSuchElementException;
public class ListWithTraversal<T> implements ListInterface<T>, Iterator<T>
{
  private Node firstNode;
  private int  length;
  private Node nextNode; // node containing next entry in iteration

  public ListWithTraversal()
  {
    clear();
  } // end default constructor

  public final void clear()
  {
    firstNode = null;
    length = 0;
    nextNode = null;
  } // end clear

  < Implementations of the remaining methods of the ADT list go here;
    you can see them in Chapters 6 and 7, beginning at Segments 6.23 and 7.9, respectively. >
  . . .

  < Implementations of the methods in the interface Iterator go here;
    you can see them in Segments 8.21 through 8.23. >
  . . .
  public void resetTraversal()
  {
    nextNode = firstNode;
  } // end resetTraversal

  < Implementation of the private class Node (Segment 6.18) goes here. >
} // end ListWithTraversal
```

8.30   **Example: Traversing a list.** If `myList` is an instance of the previous class `ListWithTraversal`, it has methods of the ADT list as well as the methods in `Iterator`. Thus, if we add strings to `myList` using invocations such as `myList.add("Chris")`, we can display the list as follows:

```
myList.resetTraversal();
while (myList.hasNext())
  System.out.println(myList.next());
```

Invoking `resetTraversal` is essential to set the traversal to the beginning of the list. Notice that the list `myList`, not a separate iterator object, invokes the `Iterator` methods. The reverse was true in Segments 8.7 and 8.18.

> **Question 12**   Implement the method `display` in the class `ListWithTraversal` by using the approach of the previous example to display the list. Is there any disadvantage to this implementation as compared to the original one shown in Segment 6.33? Explain.
>
> **Question 13**   Suppose that you want to omit the method `resetTraversal`.
>
> **a.**   Could the default constructor initialize `nextNode` to `firstNode`? Explain.
> **b.**   Could the add methods initialize `nextNode` to `firstNode`? Explain.

8.31   **What's wrong with this approach?** Although these traversal methods can execute quickly because they have direct access to the underlying data structure of the list, including them as list operations has disadvantages. Only one traversal can be in progress at a time. Moreover, an operation like `resetTraversal`, which is not in the interface `Iterator`, is necessary to initialize the traversal. The resulting ADT has too many operations; it suffers from **interface bloat**.

With a little additional programming effort, you can organize the iterator methods as an inner class. In doing so, you retain the speed of execution and suffer none of the disadvantages.

The Interface `ListIterator`

8.32   The Java Class Library provides a second interface for iterators—`ListIterator`—in the package `java.util`. This type of iterator enables you to traverse a list in either direction and to modify the list during the iteration. In addition to the three methods `hasNext`, `next`, and `remove` that the interface `Iterator` specifies, `ListIterator` contains methods such as `hasPrevious`, `previous`, `add`, and `set`.

We begin by looking at the interface `ListIterator`, which is shown in Listing 8-7.

Listing 8-7   Java's interface `java.util.ListIterator`
_____

```
package java.util;
public interface ListIterator<T> extends Iterator<T>
{
  /** Task: Detects whether the iterator has gone beyond the last
   *        entry in the list.
   *  @return true if the iterator has another entry to return when
   *          traversing the list forward; otherwise returns false */
  public boolean hasNext();

  /** Task: Retrieves the next entry in the list and
   *        advances the iterator by one position.
   *  @return a reference to the next entry in the iteration,
   *          if one exists
```

```
 *   @throws NoSuchElementException if the iterator had reached the
 *          end already, that is, if hasNext() is false */
public T next();


/** Task: Removes from the list the last entry that either next()
 *        or previous() has returned.
 *   Precondition: next() or previous() has been called, but the
 *        iterator's remove() or add() method has not been called
 *        since then. That is, you can call remove only once per
 *        call to next() or previous(). The list has not been altered
 *        during the iteration except by calls to the iterator's
 *        remove(), add(), or set() methods.
 *   @throws IllegalStateException if next() or previous() has not
 *          been called, or if remove() or add() has been called
 *          already after the last call to next() or previous()
 *   @throws UnsupportedOperationException if this iterator does not
 *          permit a remove operation */
public void remove(); // Optional method


// The previous three methods are in the interface Iterator; they are
// duplicated here for reference and to show new behavior for remove.

/** Task: Detects whether the iterator has gone before the first
 *        entry in the list.
 *   @return true if the iterator has another entry to visit when
 *          traversing the list backward; otherwise returns false */
public boolean hasPrevious();


/** Task: Retrieves the previous entry in the list and moves the
 *        iterator back by one position.
 *   @return a reference to the previous entry in the iteration, if
 *          one exists
 *   @throws NoSuchElementException if the iterator has no previous
 *          entry, that is, if hasPrevious() is false */
public T previous();


/** Task: Gets the index of the next entry.
 *   @return the index of the list entry that a subsequent call to
 *          next() would return. If next() would not return an entry
 *          because the iterator is at the end of the list, returns
 *          the size of the list. Note that the iterator numbers
 *          the list entries from 0 instead of 1. */
public int nextIndex();


/** Task: Gets the index of the previous entry.
 *   @return the index of the list entry that a subsequent call to
 *          previous() would return. If previous() would not return
 *          an entry because the iterator is at the beginning of the
 *          list, returns -1. Note that the iterator numbers the
 *          list entries from 0 instead of 1. */
public int previousIndex();
```

```
/** Task: Adds an entry to the list just before the entry, if any,
 *        that next() would have returned before the addition. This
 *        addition is just after the entry, if any, that previous()
 *        would have returned. After the addition, a call to
 *        previous() will return the new entry, but a call to next()
 *        will behave as it would have before the addition.
 *        Further, the addition increases by 1 the values that
 *        nextIndex() and previousIndex() will return.
 *  @param newEntry  an object to be added to the list
 *  @throws ClassCastException if the class of newEntry prevents the
 *          addition to this list
 *  @throws IllegalArgumentException if some other aspect of newEntry
 *          prevents the addition to this list
 *  @throws UnsupportedOperationException if this iterator does not
 *          permit an add operation */
public void add(T newEntry); // Optional method

/** Task: Replaces the last entry in the list that either next()
 *        or previous() has returned.
 *  Precondition: next() or previous() has been called, but the
 *        iterator's remove() or add() method has not been called
 *        since then.
 *  @param newEntry  an object that is the replacement entry
 *  @throws ClassCastException if the class of newEntry prevents the
 *          addition to this list
 *  @throws IllegalArgumentException if some other aspect of newEntry
 *          prevents the addition to this list
 *  @throws IllegalStateException if next() or previous() has not
 *          been called, or if remove() or add() has been called
 *          already after the last call to next() or previous()
 *  @throws UnsupportedOperationException if this iterator does not
 *          permit a set operation */
public void set(T newEntry); // Optional method
} // end ListIterator
```

8.33   **Observations.** Notice that `ListIterator` extends `Iterator`. Thus, `ListIterator` would include the methods `hasNext`, `next`, and `remove` from the interface `Iterator`, even if we did not write them explicitly. We have done so for your reference and to indicate `remove`'s additional behavior.

The methods `remove`, `add`, and `set` are optional in the sense that you can choose not to provide one or more of these operations. In that case, however, each such operation must have an implementation that throws the exception `UnsupportedOperationException` if the client invokes the operation. An iterator of type `ListIterator` that does not support `remove`, `add`, and `set` is still useful, since it enables you to traverse a list in both directions. It is also easier to implement without these operations.

The programming tip given in Segment 8.4 for the interface `Iterator` applies here as well. We repeat it here in terms of `ListInterface`.

Programming Tip: All of the exceptions mentioned in the interface `ListIterator` are run-time exceptions, so no `throws` clause is necessary in any of the methods' headers. In addition, you do not have to write `try` and `catch` blocks when you invoke these methods. However, you will need to import `NoSuchElementException` from the package `java.util`. The other exceptions are in `java.lang`, so no `import` statement is necessary for them.

8.34   **The next entry.** Like `Iterator`, `ListIterator` positions an iterator either before the first entry in a list, between two entries, or after the last entry. Recall that the method `hasNext` sees whether a next entry exists after the iterator's position. If one exists, `next` returns a reference to it and advances the iterator's cursor by one position, as Figure 8-1 illustrated. Repeated calls to `next` step through the list. So far, nothing is different from what you learned about the interface `Iterator` earlier in this chapter.

8.35   **The previous entry.** `ListIterator` also provides access to the entry just before the iterator's position—that is, to the previous entry. The method `hasPrevious` sees whether a previous entry exists. If so, the method `previous` returns a reference to it and moves the iterator's cursor back by one position. Figure 8-9 shows the effect of `previous` on a list. Intermixing calls to `previous` and `next` enables you to move back and forth within the list. If you call `next` and then call `previous`, each method returns the same entry. Like `next`, `previous` throws an exception when called after it has completed its traversal of the list.

Figure 8-9   The effect of a call to `previous` on a list

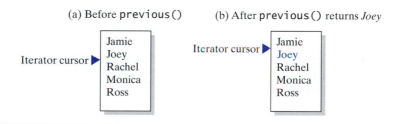

(a) Before `previous()`   (b) After `previous()` returns *Joey*

8.36   **The indices of the current and previous entries.** As Figure 8-10 shows, the methods `nextIndex` and `previousIndex` each return the index of the entry that a subsequent call to `next` or `previous`, respectively, would return. Note that the iterator numbers the list's entries beginning with 0, instead of 1 as the ADT list operations do. If a call to `next` would throw an exception because the iterator is at the end of the list, `nextIndex` returns the size of the list. Similarly, if a call to `previous` would throw an exception because the iterator is at the beginning of the list, `previousIndex` returns -1.

Figure 8-10   The indices returned by the methods `nextIndex` and `previousIndex`

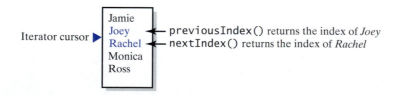

   Note: The interface `ListIterator` specifies nine methods, including the three methods that `Iterator` specifies. They are `hasNext`, `hasPrevious`, `next`, `previous`, `nextIndex`, `previousIndex`, `add`, `remove`, and `set`.

Using the Interface `ListIterator`

8.37   **Example: Traversals.** Let's look at an example of the methods that work with the current and previous entries and then use it to describe the remaining methods in the interface. We make the following assumptions:

- The interface `ListIterator` is implemented as an inner class of the class that implements the ADT list.
- The iterator includes the operations `add`, `remove`, and `set`.
- The method `getIterator` is added to the ADT list.
- The list `nameList` contains the following names:

  Jess
  Jim
  Josh

- The iterator `traverse` is defined as follows:

  ```
  ListIterator<String> traverse = nameList.getIterator();
  ```

Since `traverse` is at the beginning of the list, the Java statements

```
System.out.println("nextIndex     " + traverse.nextIndex());
System.out.println("hasNext       " + traverse.hasNext());
System.out.println("previousIndex " + traverse.previousIndex());
System.out.println("hasPrevious   " + traverse.hasPrevious());
```

produce the output

```
nextIndex      0
hasNext        true
previousIndex -1
hasPrevious    false
```

If we then execute the statements

```
System.out.println("next      " + traverse.next());
System.out.println("nextIndex " + traverse.nextIndex());
System.out.println("hasNext   " + traverse.hasNext());
```

the output is

```
next       Jess
nextIndex 1
hasNext    true
```

Finally, the statements

```
System.out.println("previousIndex " + traverse.previousIndex());
System.out.println("hasPrevious   " + traverse.hasPrevious());
System.out.println("previous      " + traverse.previous());
System.out.println("nextIndex     " + traverse.nextIndex());
System.out.println("hasNext       " + traverse.hasNext());
System.out.println("next          " + traverse.next());
```

produce the output

previousIndex 0
hasPrevious   true
previous   Jess
nextIndex   0
hasNext   true
next   Jess

Question 14 Suppose that `traverse` is an iterator as defined in the previous segment, but the contents of `nameList` are unknown. Write Java statements that display the names in `nameList` in reverse order, beginning at the end of the list.

8.38   **Example: The method set.** The method `set` replaces the entry that either `next` or `previous` just returned. At the end of the preceding segment, `next` had just returned *Jess*, so

```
traverse.set("Jen");
```

replaces *Jess* with *Jen*. Since *Jess* was the first entry in the list, the list now appears as

    Jen
    Jim
    Josh

Note that this replacement operation does not affect the position of the iterator within the list. Thus, calls to `nextIndex` and `previousIndex`, for example, are not affected. In this case, since the iterator is between *Jen* and *Jim*, `nextIndex` returns 1 and `previousIndex` returns 0. Also note that we can call `set` again; doing so here will replace *Jen*.

Question 15 If the iterator's position is between the first two entries of the previous list, write Java statements that replace *Josh* with *Jon*.

8.39   **Example: The method add.** The method `add` inserts an entry into the list just before the iterator's current position. Thus, the insertion is made immediately before the entry, if any, that `next` would have returned before `add` was called and just after the entry, if any, that `previous` would have returned. Note that if the list is empty, `add` inserts a new entry as the only entry in the list.

If the iterator's position is currently between the first two entries of the previous list, the statement

```
traverse.add("Ashley");
```

adds *Ashley* to the list just before *Jim*—that is, at index 1 or, equivalently, at list position 2. After this addition, the list is as follows:

    Jen
    Ashley
    Jim
    Josh

A call to `next` at this point returns *Jim*, since `next` would have returned *Jim* had we not called `add`. If, however, we call `previous` instead of `next`, the new entry *Ashley* will be returned. Furthermore, the addition increases by 1 the values that `nextIndex` and `previousIndex` will return. Thus, immediately after the addition, `nextIndex` will return 2 and `previousIndex` will return 1.

Question 16 If the iterator's position is between *Ashley* and *Jim*, write Java statements that add *Miguel* right after *Jim*.

8.40

Example: The method remove. The behavior of the method remove is similar to that of remove in the interface Iterator, which you saw earlier in this chapter. But in the interface ListIterator, remove is affected by the method previous as well as by next. Thus, remove removes the list entry that the last call to either next or previous returned.

If the list contains

Jen
Ashley
Jim
Josh

and the iterator traverse is positioned between *Ashley* and *Jim*, the statements

```
traverse.previous();
traverse.remove();
```

remove *Ashley* from the list, since previous returns *Ashley*. The iterator's position remains just before *Jim*.

Notice that both set and remove will throw the exception IllegalStateException if neither next nor previous has been called, or if either remove or add has been called already since the last call to next or previous. As you will see in the next section, this behavior complicates the implementation somewhat.

An Array-Based Implementation of the Interface `ListIterator`

8.41

As we did for the interface Iterator earlier in this chapter, we will implement the interface ListIterator as an inner class of a class that uses an array to represent the ADT list. First, we define an interface in Listing 8-8 for the list class that includes the operations of the ADT list and the method getIterator. In this case, the method's return type is ListIterator instead of Iterator.

Listing 8-8   The interface ListWithListIteratorInterface

```
import java.util.ListIterator;
public interface ListWithListIteratorInterface<T> extends
                                             ListInterface<T>
{
  public ListIterator<T> getIterator();
} // end ListWithListIteratorInterface
```

8.42

The class that implements the ADT list. Our class has the same data fields and methods as the class ExpandableArrayList given in Chapter 5, and includes the method getIterator. The class also contains the inner class IteratorForArrayList, which implements the interface ListIterator. Listing 8-9 shows the form of our new class of lists.

Listing 8-9   An outline of the class `ArrayListWithListIterator`

```java
import java.util.ListIterator;
import java.util.NoSuchElementException;
public class ArrayListWithListIterator<T>
            implements ListWithListIteratorInterface<T>
{
  private T[] list;    // array of list entries
  private int length; // current number of entries in list
  private static final int DEFAULT_INITIAL_CAPACITY = 25;

  public ArrayListWithListIterator()
  {
    this(DEFAULT_INITIAL_CAPACITY);
  } // end default constructor

  public ArrayListWithListIterator(int initialCapacity)
  {
    length = 0;
    list = (T[]) new Object[initialCapacity];
  } // end constructor

  < Implementations of the methods of the ADT list go here;
    you can see them in Chapter 5, beginning at Segments 5.8 and 5.17. >
  . . .
  public ListIterator<T> getIterator()
  {
    return new IteratorForArrayList();
  } // end getIterator

  private class IteratorForArrayList implements ListIterator<T>
  {
    < The description of this implementation begins with Segment 8.43. >
    . . .
  } // end IteratorForArrayList
} // end ArrayListWithListIterator
```

The Inner Class

8.43   **The data fields and constructor.** We begin implementing the inner class `IteratorForArrayList` by thinking about how the methods `remove` and `set` will throw the exception `IllegalStateException`. Both of these methods throw this exception for the same reasons, that is, if either

●   `next` or `previous` was not called or
●   `remove` or `add` has been called since the last call to `next` or `previous`

Figure 8-11 shows calls to `remove` in various contexts that cause an `IllegalStateException`.

This aspect of the implementation might be intimidating at first, but it need not be difficult. When we implemented `Iterator`'s remove method in Segment 8.28, we tested the boolean data field `wasNextCalled` to see whether `next` had been called. We could do that here and define analogous

Figure 8-11   Possible contexts in which the method `remove` throws an exception when called by the iterator `traverse`

(a)   ← Neither `next` nor `previous` has been called
`traverse.remove();`   ← Causes an exception

(b) `traverse.next();`

`traverse.remove();`   ← Legal

`traverse.remove();`   ← Causes an exception

(c) `traverse.previous();`

`traverse.remove();`   ← Legal

`traverse.remove();`   ← Causes an exception

(d) `traverse.next();`

`traverse.add(...);`

`traverse.remove();`   ← Causes an exception

(e) `traverse.previous();`

`traverse.add(...);`

`traverse.remove();`   ← Causes an exception

---

fields for the methods `previous` and `add`, but the logic would be more involved than necessary. Instead, let's define a boolean field to indicate whether a call to either `remove` or `set` is legal:

private boolean isRemoveOrSetLegal;

If either `remove` or `set` finds this field to be false, it should throw an `IllegalStateException`. This field should be initialized to false by the constructor. The methods `next` and `previous` should set it to true, and the methods `add` and `remove` should set it to false.

Both `remove` and `set` must know which of `next` or `previous` was called so that they can access the correct list entry. Thus, we define a data field to track the last call to these methods and an enumeration to provide values for the field. The following enumeration will suffice:

private enum Move {NEXT, PREVIOUS}

Since an enumeration is really a class, we define it outside of the inner class `IteratorForArrayList`, but within `ArrayListWithListIterator`. The data field then is simply

private Move lastMove;

In addition to these two data fields, we need a field `nextIndex` to track the index of the next entry in the iteration. This field is just like the one we described earlier in Segment 8.25. Thus, the inner class begins as follows:

```java
private class IteratorForArrayList implements ListIterator<T>
{
  private int nextIndex;
  private boolean isRemoveOrSetLegal;
  private Move lastMove;

  private IteratorForArrayList()
  {
    nextIndex = 0;
    isRemoveOrSetLegal = false;
    lastMove = null;
  } // end default constructor
  . . .
```

8.44 **The method `hasNext`.** The method `hasNext` has the same implementation that it had earlier in Segment 8.26. Recall that it returns true if the iterator has not reached the end of the list.

```java
public boolean hasNext()
{
  return nextIndex < length;
} // end hasNext
```

8.45 **The method `next`.** The implementation of `next` is similar to the one given in Segment 8.27. Here, however, it has different fields to set. We set `lastMove` to `Move.NEXT` and `isRemoveOrSetLegal` to true.

```java
public T next()
{
  if (hasNext())
  {
    lastMove = Move.NEXT;
    isRemoveOrSetLegal = true;

    T nextEntry = list[nextIndex];
    nextIndex++;

    return nextEntry;
  }
  else
    throw new NoSuchElementException("Illegal call to next();" +
                                     "iterator is after end of list.");
} // end next
```

8.46 **The methods `hasPrevious` and `previous`.** The methods `hasPrevious` and `previous` have implementations that are analogous to those of `hasNext` and `next`, respectively.

```java
public boolean hasPrevious()
{
  return (nextIndex > 0) && (nextIndex <= length);
} // end hasPrevious
```

```java
public T previous()
{
  if (hasPrevious())
  {
    lastMove = Move.PREVIOUS;
    isRemoveOrSetLegal = true;

    nextIndex--;
    return list[nextIndex];
  }
  else
    throw new NoSuchElementException("Illegal call to previous();" +
                                "iterator is before beginning of list.");
} // end previous
```

8.47   **The methods `nextIndex` and `previousIndex`.** The method `nextIndex` returns either the index of the entry that the method `next` would return if called or the size of the list if the iterator is after the end of the list.

```java
public int nextIndex()
{
  int result;

  if (hasNext())
    result = nextIndex;
  else
    result = length;

  return result;
} // end nextIndex
```

The method `previousIndex` returns either the index of the entry that the method `previous` would return if called or -1 if the iterator is before the beginning of the list.

```java
public int previousIndex()
{
  int result;

  if (hasPrevious())
    result = nextIndex - 1;
  else
    result = -1;

  return result;
} // end previousIndex
```

8.48   **The method `add`.** The method `add` inserts an entry into the list just before the iterator's current position, that is, immediately before the entry in `list[nextIndex]`, as Figure 8-12 illustrates. To avoid duplicate code and effort, we call the list's add method to add an entry at position `nextIndex` + 1 within the list. Recall that entries after the new entry will be shifted and renumbered. Therefore, we need to increment `nextIndex` so that it will continue to mark the entry that a subsequent call to `next` would return. If we increment `nextIndex` before calling add, we can pass `nextIndex` to add as the position of the insertion. Thus, add has the following implementation:

```
public void add(T newEntry)
{
  isRemoveOrSetLegal = false;
  nextIndex++;
  ArrayListWithListIterator.this.add(nextIndex, newEntry);
} // end add
```

Figure 8-12   The array of list entries and `nextIndex` (a) just before the call to `add`; (b) just after the call to `add`

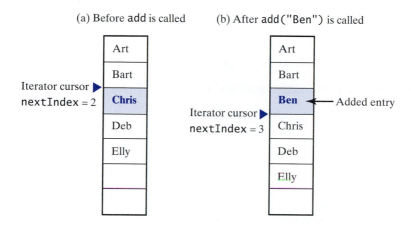

8.49   **The method `remove`.** The logic for the `remove` method when a call to `next` precedes its call is somewhat like the logic for the `remove` method in the interface `Iterator`, which you saw in Segment 8.28.
Recall that Figure 8-8 illustrated the array of list entries and the index `nextIndex` before and after the
calls to `next` and `remove`. Figure 8-13 provides a similar illustration, showing what happens when a
call to `previous` precedes the call to `remove`. In Part *b*, `previous` returns a reference to the previous

Figure 8-13   The array of list entries and `nextIndex` (a) just before the call to `previous`; (b) just after the
call to `previous` but before the call to `remove`; (c) after the call to `remove`

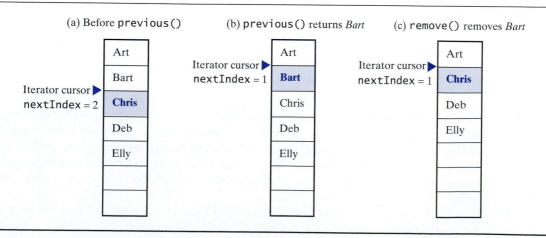

entry—*Bart*—in the iteration and decrements `nextIndex`. The method `remove` must remove this entry from the list. Notice that `nextIndex` is now 1 smaller than the position number of the list entry that must be removed. After the entry *Bart* has been removed in Figure 8-13c, the next entry—*Chris*—moves to the next lower-numbered position in the array. Thus, `nextIndex` remains the index of the next entry in the iteration and so is unchanged.

Remember, `remove` must throw an exception if the field `isRemoveOrSetLegal` is false. If the field is true, the method must set it to false. An implementation of `remove` follows:

```java
public void remove()
{
   if (isRemoveOrSetLegal)
   {
      isRemoveOrSetLegal = false;

      if (lastMove.equals(Move.NEXT))
      {
         // next() called, but neither add() nor remove() has been
         // called since

         // nextIndex is 1 more than the index of the entry returned
         // by next(), so it is the position number of the entry
         // to be removed
         ArrayListWithListIterator.this.remove(nextIndex);
         nextIndex--;
      }
      else
      {
         // previous() called, but neither add() nor remove() has been
         // called since
         assert lastMove.equals(Move.PREVIOUS);

         // nextIndex is the index of the entry returned by previous(),
         // so it is 1 less than the position number of the entry
         // to be removed
         ArrayListWithListIterator.this.remove(nextIndex + 1);
      } // end if
   }
   else
      throw new IllegalStateException("Illegal call to remove(); " +
                        "next() or previous() was not called, OR " +
                        "add() or remove() called since then.");
} // end remove
```

8.50   **The method set.** The method `set` replaces the last entry in the list that either `next` or `previous` has returned. It uses `nextIndex`, as updated by either of the methods `next` or `previous`. Since the method `next` returns `list[nextIndex]` and then increments `nextIndex`, the method `set` would replace the object in `list[nextIndex - 1]` after a call to `next`. Likewise, since `previous` decrements `nextIndex` and then returns `list[nextIndex]`, the method `set` would replace `list[nextIndex]` after a call to `previous`.

The following implementation of `set` reflects these observations and uses the same logic that we used in `remove` to see whether to throw `IllegalStateException`:

```java
public void set(T newEntry)
{
  if (isRemoveOrSetLegal)
  {
    if (lastMove.equals(Move.NEXT))
      list[nextIndex - 1] = newEntry;
    else
    {
      assert lastMove.equals(Move.PREVIOUS);
      list[nextIndex] = newEntry;
    } // end if
  }
  else
    throw new IllegalStateException("Illegal call to set(); " +
                            "next() or previous() was not called, OR " +
                            "add() or remove() called since then.");
} // end set
```

Note: Implementing the entire interface `ListIterator` as an inner class is easier when the associated ADT has an array-based implementation rather than a linked implementation. (See Exercise 17.)

Note: An iterator of type `ListIterator` is simpler to implement when it does not support the operations `add`, `remove`, and `set`. Such an iterator is useful, as it enables you to traverse a list in both directions. We leave this implementation as an exercise.

Java Class Library: The Interface `Iterable`

In a sense, this entire chapter has been about the Java Class Library, since the interfaces `Iterator` and `ListIterator` are components of it. This last section introduces the interface `Iterable` and shows its relation to for-each loops and the interface `java.util.List`.

8.51   The package `java.lang` of the Java Class Library contains the interface `Iterable`. This interface declares only one method, as Listing 8-10 shows.

Listing 8-10   The interface java.lang.Iterable

```java
package java.lang;
public interface Iterable<T>
{
  /** @return an iterator for a collection of objects of type T */
  Iterator<T> iterator()
} // end Iterable
```

The method `iterator` returns an iterator that adheres to the interface `Iterator`. This method has the same purpose as our method `getIterator`, as declared in the interface `ListWithIteratorInterface` in Segment 8.17. Recall that our classes `LinkedListWithIterator` (Segment 8.19) and `ArrayListWithIterator` (Segment 8.24) implement `ListWithIteratorInterface`. These classes could certainly implement the method `iterator` in addition to getIterator. To do so, we could modify the definition of `ListWithIteratorInterface`, as shown in Listing 8-11.

Listing 8-11   The interface `ListWithIteratorInterface` modified to extend `Iterable`

```
import java.util.Iterator;
public interface ListWithIteratorInterface<T> extends ListInterface<T>,
                                                       Iterable<T>
{
   public Iterator<T> getIterator();
} // end ListWithIteratorInterface
```

Declaring the method `iterator` explicitly within the interface is permissible but not necessary, because the interface extends `Iterable`. Since `Iterable` is in `java.lang`, no `import` statement is needed for it.

As both `iterator` and `getIterator` have the same purpose, and since we have already implemented `getIterator`, the implementation of `iterator` should call `getIterator`.

Iterable and for-each loops

8.52   A class that implements the interface `Iterable` has a distinct advantage over classes that do not: You can use a for-each loop to traverse the objects in an instance of such a class. For example, suppose that we have `ListWithIteratorInterface` and `LinkedListWithIterator`, as described in the previous segment. That is, the class `LinkedListWithIterator` implements `Iterable`. You can use a for-each loop to display the items in an instance of this class.

Let's form a list, as follows:

```
ListWithIteratorInterface<String> nameList =
                         new LinkedListWithIterator<String>();
nameList.add("Joe");
nameList.add("Jess");
nameList.add("Josh");
nameList.add("Jen");
```

The statements

```
for (String name : nameList)
   System.out.print(name + " ");
System.out.println();
```

then produce the following output:

Joe Jess Josh Jen

Programming Tip: A class that defines an inner class iterator should implement the interface `Iterable`. A client of the class then can use a for-each loop to traverse the objects in an instance of the class.

The Interface `List` Revisited

8.53 The interface `java.util.List` that we described in Segment 4.19 of Chapter 4 extends the interface `Iterable`, so it has the method `iterator`. Additionally, `List` declares the following methods related to iterators:

```
public ListIterator<T> listIterator(int index);
public ListIterator<T> listIterator();
```

Each of the `listIterator` methods returns an iterator whose methods are specified in the interface `ListIterator`. The iterator returned by the first version of `listIterator` begins at the list element indicated by `index`, where zero indicates the first entry in the list. The second version of this method has the same effect as `listIterator(0)`.

Since the classes `ArrayList`, `LinkedList`, and `Vector` of the package `java.util` implement the interface `List`, they have these two `listIterator` methods as well as the method `iterator`.

CHAPTER SUMMARY

- The interface `Iterator` specifies three methods: `hasNext`, `next`, and `remove`. An iterator that implements this interface need not provide a `remove` operation. Instead, the method `remove` would throw the exception `UnsupportedOperationException`.

- The interface `ListIterator` specifies nine methods, including the three methods that `Iterator` specifies. They are `hasNext`, `next`, `hasPrevious`, `previous`, `nextIndex`, `previousIndex`, `add`, `remove`, and `set`. The methods `add`, `remove`, and `set` are optional in the sense that they can throw the exception `UnsupportedOperationException` instead of affecting the list.

- You can implement each of the interfaces `Iterator` and `ListIterator` as its own class. This class could be an inner class of the class that implements the ADT in question, or it could be public and separate from the ADT's class.

- An inner class iterator enables you to have several independent iterators that traverse an ADT. It also allows the iterator direct access to the underlying data structure, so its implementation can be efficient.

- A separate class iterator also allows multiple and distinct iterations to exist simultaneously. However, since the iterator can access the list's data fields only indirectly via ADT operations, the iteration takes more time than one performed by an inner class iterator. On the other hand, the implementation is usually straightforward.

- Certain ADTs do not provide sufficient public access to their data to make a separate class iterator possible. However, to provide an iterator for an ADT's implementation that exists and cannot be altered, you might need to define a separate class iterator.

PROGRAMMING TIPS

- All of the exceptions mentioned in the interfaces `Iterator` and `ListIterator` are run-time exceptions, so no `throws` clause is necessary in any of the methods' headers. In addition, you do not have to write `try` and `catch` blocks when you invoke these methods. However, you will need to import `NoSuchElementException` from the package `java.util`. The other exceptions are in `java.lang`, so no `import` statement is necessary for them.

- A class that defines an inner class iterator should implement the interface `Iterable`. A client of the class can then use a for-each loop to traverse the objects in an instance of the class.

1. Suppose that `nameList` is a list that contains the following strings: *Kyle, Cathy, Sam, Austin, Sara*. What output is produced by the following sequence of statements?

```
Iterator<String> nameIterator = nameList.getIterator();
System.out.println(nameIterator.next());
nameIterator.next();
System.out.println(nameIterator.next());
nameIterator.remove();
System.out.println(nameIterator.next());
nameList.display();
```

2. Repeat Exercise 1, but instead use the following statements:

```
Iterator<String> nameIterator = nameList.getIterator();
nameIterator.next();
nameIterator.remove();
nameIterator.next();
nameIterator.next();
nameIterator.remove();
System.out.println(nameIterator.next());
nameList.display();
System.out.println(nameIterator.next());
System.out.println(nameIterator.next());
```

3. Suppose that `nameList` is a list of at least one string and that `nameIterator` is defined as follows:

```
Iterator<String> nameIterator = nameList.getIterator();
```

Write Java statements that use `nameIterator` to display only the last string in the list.

4. Given `nameList` and `nameIterator` as described in Exercise 3, write statements that display all strings in the list from last to first.

5. Given `nameList` and `nameIterator` as described in Exercise 3, write statements that use `nameIterator` to remove all the entries from the list.

6. Given `nameList` and `nameIterator` as described in Exercise 3, write statements that remove all occurrences of the string *CANCEL* from the list.

7. Given `nameList` and `nameIterator` as described in Exercise 3, write statements that remove any duplicates in the list.

8. Given `nameList` and `nameIterator` as described in Exercise 3, write statements that count the number of times each string occurs in the list, without altering the list. Assume that you have an implementation of the ADT set, as Project 4 of Chapter 4 describes. The set is an ADT that rejects duplicate entries. It includes the following methods add and `contains`:

```
/** Task: Adds an entry to the set if it is not already present.
 *  @param newEntry  an object to be added as a new entry
 *  @return true if the entry was added */
public boolean add(T newEntry);
```

```
/** Task: Sees whether the set contains a given entry.
 *  @param anEntry  the object that is the desired entry */
 *  @return true if the set contains anEntry */
public boolean contains(T anEntry);
```

9. Suppose that aList and bList are instances of java.util.ArrayList. Use two iterators to find and display all the objects that are common to both lists. Do not alter the contents of either list.

10. Assume that aList and bList are instances of java.util.ArrayList that contain Comparable objects in order from smallest to largest. Use two iterators to move the objects from bList to the appropriate locations in aList. When you are done, the objects in aList should be in order, and bList should be empty.

11. Revise the class SeparateIterator outlined in Segment 8.12 so that it does not support a remove operation. Simplify the class as much as possible.

12. Imagine a class that implements the interface ListWithIteratorInterface, as given in Listing 8-11 of Segment 8.51. Suppose that aList is an instance of this class and contains Comparable objects in no particular order. Using an iterator, implement the following two methods within the class:

   a. getMin returns the smallest object in the list
   b. removeMin removes and returns the smallest object in the list

13. Repeat the previous exercise, but use a for-each loop instead of an iterator.

14. Suppose that nameList is a list that contains the following strings: *Kyle, Cathy, Sam, Austin, Sara*. What output is produced by the following sequence of statements?

```
ListIterator<String> nameIterator = nameList.getIterator();
System.out.println(nameIterator.next());
nameIterator.next();
nameIterator.next();
System.out.println(nameIterator.next());
nameIterator.set("Brittany");
nameIterator.previous();
nameIterator.remove();
System.out.println(nameIterator.next());
nameList.display();
```

15. Repeat the previous exercise, but instead use the following statements:

```
ListIterator<String> nameIterator = nameList.getIterator();
nameIterator.next();
nameIterator.remove();
nameIterator.next();
nameIterator.next();
nameIterator.previous();
nameIterator.remove();
System.out.println(nameIterator.next());
nameIterator.next();
nameIterator.set("Brittany");
System.out.println("Revised list:");
nameList.display();
System.out.println(nameIterator.previous());
System.out.println(nameIterator.next());
```

16. Given a list of strings and an iterator `nameIterator` whose data type is `ListIterator`, write statements that add the string *Bob* after the first occurrence of the string *Sam*.

17. If you wanted to implement the interface `ListIterator` as an inner class iterator by using a linked implementation, what difficulties would you face?

1. Revise the class `LinkedListWithIterator` described in Segment 8.19 so that the inner class `IteratorForLinkedList` provides a `remove` operation. You will need another data field `priorNode` to reference the node before the next one.

2. Implement all of the methods in the interface `ListIterator` as a separate class iterator.

3. Implement the interface `ListIterator` as an inner class, but do not support the operations `add`, `remove`, and `set`.

4. Consider a solitaire matching game in which you have a list of random integer values between 10 and 99. You remove from the list any pair of consecutive integers whose first or second digits match. If all values are removed, then you win.

For example, consider the following sequence of ten integers:

10 82 43 23 89 12 43 84 23 32

The pair 10 and 82 does not match in either digit and so cannot be removed. However, the pair 43 and 23 matches in the second digit and is removed, leaving the following sequence:

10 82 89 12 43 84 23 32

Continue checking for pairs from 89, the value after the removed pair. No other pairs match. Now return to the beginning of the list and check for pairs. The pair 82 and 89 matches in the first digit and can be removed:

10 12 43 84 23 32

No other pairs can be removed, so we lose.

Write a program that simulates this game. It should generate 40 random two-digit integers and place them in an instance of `java.util.ArrayList`, using an instance of `ListIterator`. Then, using this iterator, scan the list and remove matching pairs of values. After each pair is removed, use an iterator to display the values remaining in the list.

5. One statistical operation that is sometimes performed on a set of data values is to remove values that are far from the average. Write a program that reads real values from a text file, one per line. Store the data values as `Double` objects in an instance of the class `java.util.ArrayList`. Then

● Use an iterator to compute the average and standard deviation of the values. Display these results.
● Use a second iterator to remove any value that is more than two standard deviations away from the average.
● Use a for-each loop to display the remaining values and compute the new average. Display the new average.

If the data values are $x_1, x_2, ..., x_n$, their average μ is their sum divided by n, and their standard deviation is

$$\sigma = \sqrt{\frac{1}{n} \sum_{i=1}^{n} (x_i - \mu)^2}$$

6. Consider the following situation. You create a list, and then you add ten items to it. You get an iterator to the list and call `next` twice to advance it. You remove the first five items from the list, using the list's `remove` method. You then call the iterator's `remove` method, expecting to remove the item last returned by the method `next`. However, this entry has already been removed from the list. Changing the state of the list while using the iterator, as you have done here, may result in unpredictable behavior of the iterator.

   Modify the interface `Iterator` so that the methods will throw the exception `StateChangedException` if the state of the list is changed after the iterator was created but before the method is called. Modify the implementation of `LinkedListWithIterator` that Project 1 describes to accommodate the changes to `Iterator`.

7. Revise the class `ArrayListWithIterator` outlined in Segment 8.24 so that it extends the class `ExpandableArrayList`, as discussed in Segments 5.17 and 5.18 of Chapter 5.

9

The Efficiency of Algorithms

CONTENTS

PREREQUISITES

OBJECTIVES

After studying this chapter, you should be able to

- Assess the efficiency of a given algorithm
- Compare the expected execution times of two methods, given the efficiencies of their algorithms

With amazing frequency, manufacturers introduce new computers that are faster and have larger memories than their recent predecessors. Yet we—and likely your computer science professors— ask you to write code that is efficient in its use of time and space (memory). Admittedly, such efficiency is not as pressing an issue as it was fifty years ago, when computers were much slower and their memory size was much smaller than they are now. (Computers had small memories, but they were physically huge, occupying entire rooms.) Even so, efficiency remains an issue—in some circumstances, a critical issue.

This chapter will introduce you to the terminology and methods that computer scientists use to measure the efficiency of an algorithm. With this background, you not only will have an intuitive feel for efficiency, but also will be able to talk about efficiency in a quantitative way.

Motivation

9.1   Perhaps you think that you are not likely to write a program in the near future whose execution time is noticeably long. You might be right, but we are about to show you some simple Java code that does take a long time to perform its computations.

Imagine that we are defining a Java class `Huge` to represent extremely large integers. Of course, we will need to represent the many digits possible in one of these integers, but that is not the subject of this example. We want a method for our class that adds two large integers—that is, two instances of our class—and a method that multiplies two large integers. Suppose that we have implemented the add method successfully and are about to design a `multiply` method.

As you know, multiplication is equivalent to repeated addition. So if we want to compute the product 7562 * 423, for example, we could initialize a variable to zero and add 7562 to it 423 times. Remember that our add method works, so we can readily use it in our implementation of `multiply`.

9.2   Let's write some simple Java code to test our idea. Realize that this code is simply an experiment to verify our approach of repeated addition and does not use anything that we might already have written for our class.

If we use `long` integers in our experiment, we could write the following statements:

```
long firstOperand  = 7562;
long secondOperand =  423;
long product = 0;

for (long counter = secondOperand; counter > 0; counter--)
  product = product + firstOperand;

System.out.println(product);
```

If you execute this code, you will get the right answer of 3198726. Now change the second operand from 423 to 100000000 (that is, a 1 followed by eight zeros), and execute the code again. Once more, you will get the correct answer, which this time is 756200000000 (7562 followed by eight zeros). However, you should notice a delay in seeing this result. Now try 1000000000, which is a 1 followed by nine zeros. Again you will get the correct answer—7562 followed by nine zeros—but you will have to wait even longer for the result. The wait might be long enough for you to suspect that something is broken. If not, try 1 followed by ten zeros!

What's our point? Our class is supposed to deal with really large integers. The integers in our little experiment, while large, are not *really* large. Even so, the previous simple code takes a noticeably long time to execute. Should you use a faster computer? Should you wait for an even faster computer to be invented? We have a better solution.

9.3 The delay in our example is caused by the excessive number of additions that the code must perform. Instead of adding 7562 to an initially zero variable one billion times, we could save time by adding one billion to an initially zero variable 7562 times. This approach won't always be faster, because one operand might not be much smaller than the other. Besides, we can do much better.

Consider again the product 7562 * 423. The second operand, 423, has three digits: A hundreds digit 4, a tens digit 2, and a ones digit 3. That is, 423 is the sum 400 + 20 + 3. Thus,

$$7562 * 423 = 7562 * (400 + 20 + 3)$$
$$= 7562 * 400 + 7562 * 20 + 7562 * 3$$
$$= 756{,}200 * 4 + 75{,}620 * 2 + 7562 * 3$$

Now we can replace the three previous multiplications with additions, so that the desired product is the sum

$$(756{,}200 + 756{,}200 + 756{,}200 + 756{,}200) + (75{,}620 + 75{,}620) + (7562 + 7562 + 7562)$$

There are three parenthesized terms, one for each digit in the second operand. Each of these terms is the sum of d integers, where d is a digit in the second operand. We can conveniently compute this sum from the right—involving first 7562, then 75,620, and finally 756,200—because 75,620 is 10 * 7562, and 756,200 is 10 * 75,620.

9.4 We can use these observations to write pseudocode that will compute this type of sum. Let the operands of the multiplication be `firstOperand` and `secondOperand`. The following pseudocode computes the product of these operands by using addition.

```
secondOperandLength = number of digits in secondOperand
product = 0

for (digitPosition = 1; digitPosition <= secondOperandLength; digitPosition++)
{
  digit = rightmost digit of secondOperand

 for (counter = digit; counter > 0; counter--)
    product = product + firstOperand

 Drop rightmost digit of secondOperand
 Tack 0 onto end of firstOperand
}
// Assertion: product is the result
```

If we use this pseudocode to compute 7562 * 423, `firstOperand` is 7562 and `secondOperand` is 423. The pseudocode computes the sum

$$(7562 + 7562 + 7562) + (75{,}620 + 75{,}620) + (756{,}200 + 756{,}200 + 756{,}200 + 756{,}200)$$

from left to right. The outer loop specifies the number of parenthesized groups as well as their contents, and the inner loop processes the additions within the parentheses.

9.5 Here is some Java code for you to try based on the previous pseudocode. We will implement the last two steps of the pseudocode by dividing by 10 and multiplying by 10. Remember that this is an experiment to verify an approach and is not the implementation of a method in our class of large integers. In the actual implementation of `Huge`, we would have to find another way to implement the pseudocode without multiplying or dividing.

```
long firstOperand = 7562;
long secondOperand = 100000000;

int secondOperandLength = 9;
long product = 0;

for (int digitPosition = 1; digitPosition <= secondOperandLength;
    digitPosition++)
{
  int digit = (int)(secondOperand - (secondOperand / 10) * 10);

  for (int counter = digit; counter > 0; counter--)
    product = product + firstOperand;

  secondOperand = secondOperand / 10; // discard last digit
  firstOperand = 10 * firstOperand;   // tack zero on right
} // end for

System.out.println(product);
```

You should find that this code executes faster than the code in Segment 9.2 after you change second-Operand to 100000000.

Note: As this example shows, even a simple program can be noticeably inefficient.

Measuring an Algorithm's Efficiency

9.6   The previous section should have convinced you that a program's efficiency matters. How can we measure efficiency so that we can compare various approaches to solving a problem? In the previous section, we asked you to run two programs and observe that one was noticeably slower than the other. In general, having to implement several ideas before you can choose one requires too much work to be practical. Besides, a program's execution time depends in part on the particular computer and the programming language used. It would be much better to measure an *algorithm's* efficiency before you implement it.

For example, suppose that you want to go to a store downtown. Your options are to walk, drive your car, ask a friend to take you, or take a bus. What is the best way? First, what is your concept of best? Is it the way that saves money, your time, your friend's time, or the environment? Let's say that the best option for you is the fastest one. After defining your criterion, how do you evaluate your options? You certainly do not want to try all four options so you can discover which is fastest. That would be like writing four different programs that perform the same task so you can measure which one is fastest. Instead you would investigate the "cost" of each option, considering the distance, the speed at which you can travel, the amount of other traffic, the number of stops at traffic lights, the weather, and so on.

9.7   The same considerations apply when deciding what algorithm is best. Again, we need to define what we mean by best. An algorithm has both time and space requirements, called its **complexity**, that we can measure. When we assess an algorithm's complexity, we are not measuring how involved or difficult it is. Instead, we measure an algorithm's **time complexity**—the time it takes to execute—or its **space complexity**—the memory it needs to execute. Typically we analyze these requirements separately. So a "best" algorithm might be the fastest one or the one that uses the least memory.

Note: What's best?
Usually the "best" solution to a problem balances various criteria such as time, space, generality, programming effort, and so on.

The process of measuring the complexity of algorithms is called the **analysis of algorithms**. We will concentrate on the time complexity of algorithms, because it is usually more important than space complexity. You should realize that an inverse relationship often exists between an algorithm's time complexity and its space complexity. If you revise an algorithm to save execution time, you usually will need more space. If you reduce an algorithm's space requirement, it likely will require more time to execute. Sometimes, however, you will be able to save both time and space.

Your measure of the complexity of an algorithm should be easy to compute, certainly easier than implementing the algorithm. You should express this measure in terms of the size of the problem. For example, if you are searching a collection of data, the problem size is the number of items in the collection. Such a measure enables you to compare the relative cost of algorithms as a function of the size of the problem. Typically, we are interested in large problems; a small problem is likely to take little time, even if the algorithm is inefficient.

9.8   Realize that you cannot compute the actual time requirement of an algorithm. After all, you have not implemented the algorithm in Java and you have not chosen the computer. Instead, you find a function of the problem size that behaves like the algorithm's actual time requirement. That is, as the time requirement increases by some factor, the value of the function increases by the same factor, and vice versa. The value of the function is said to be **directly proportional** to the time requirement. Such a function is called a **growth-rate function** because it measures how an algorithm's time requirement grows as the problem size grows. Because they measure time requirements, growth-rate functions have positive values. By comparing the growth-rate functions of two algorithms, you can see whether one algorithm is faster than the other for large-size problems.

You could estimate the maximum time that an algorithm could take—that is, its **worst-case time**. If you can tolerate this worst-case time, your algorithm is acceptable. You also could estimate the minimum or **best-case time**. If the best-case time is still too slow, you need another algorithm. For many algorithms, the worst and best cases rarely occur. A more useful measure is the **average-case time** requirement of an algorithm. This measure, however, is usually harder to find than the best and worst cases. Typically, we will find the worst-case time.

9.9   **Example.** Consider the problem of computing the sum $1 + 2 + \ldots + n$ for any positive integer n. Figure 9-1 contains pseudocode showing three ways to solve this problem. Algorithm A computes the sum $0 + 1 + 2 + \ldots + n$ from left to right. Algorithm B computes $0 + (1) + (1 + 1) + (1 + 1 + 1) + \ldots + (1 + 1 + \ldots + 1)$. Finally, Algorithm C uses an algebraic identity to compute the sum.

Figure 9-1   Three algorithms for computing the sum $1 + 2 + \ldots + n$ for an integer $n > 0$

Algorithm A	Algorithm B	Algorithm C

`sum = 0`
`for i = 1 to n`
`    sum = sum + i`
	`sum = 0`
	`for i = 1 to n`
	`{ for j = 1 to i`
	`    sum = sum + 1`
	`}`
		`sum = n * (n + 1) / 2`

Which algorithm—A, B, or C—is fastest? We can begin to answer this question by considering both the size of the problem and the effort involved. The integer n is a measure of the problem size: As n increases, the sum involves more terms. To measure the effort, or time requirement, of an algorithm, we must find an appropriate growth-rate function. To do so, we begin by counting the number of operations required by the algorithm. Figure 9-2 tabulates the number of assignments, additions, multiplications, and divisions that Algorithms A, B, and C require. These counts do not include the operations that control the loops. We have ignored these operations here to make counting easier, but as you will see later in Segment 9.14, doing so will not affect our final conclusion about algorithm speed.

Figure 9-2   The number of operations required by the algorithms in Figure 9-1

	Algorithm A	Algorithm B	Algorithm C
Assignments	$n + 1$	$1 + n(n+1)/2$	1
Additions	n	$n(n+1)/2$	1
Multiplications			1
Divisions			1
Total operations	$2n + 1$	$n^2 + n + 1$	4

Question 1   For any positive integer n, the identity

$$1 + 2 + \ldots + n = n(n+1)/2$$

is one that you will encounter while analyzing algorithms. Can you derive it? If you can, you will not need to memorize it. *Hint*: Write $1 + 2 + \ldots + n$. Under it write $n + (n - 1) + \ldots + 1$. Then add the terms from left to right.

Question 2   Can you derive the values in Figure 9-2? *Hint*: For Algorithm B, use the identity given in Question 1.

Note: Useful identities

$$1 + 2 + \ldots + n = n(n+1)/2$$
$$1 + 2 + \ldots + (n-1) = n(n-1)/2$$

9.10   The various operations listed in Figure 9-2 probably take different amounts of time to execute. Even so, we will be able to discover which algorithm is fastest. For example, Algorithm A requires $n + 1$ assignments and n additions. If each assignment takes no more than $t_=$ time units and each addition takes no more than t_+ time units, Algorithm A requires no more than $(n + 1) t_= + n t_+$ time units. If we replace $t_=$ and t_+ with the larger of the two values and call it t, Algorithm A requires no more than $(2n + 1) t$ time units. Whether we look at a time estimate such as $(2n + 1) t$ or the total number of operations $2n + 1$, we can draw the same conclusion: Algorithm A requires time directly proportional to $2n + 1$ in the worst case. Thus, Algorithm A's growth-rate function is $2n + 1$.

Using similar reasoning, we can conclude that Algorithm B requires time directly proportional to $n^2 + n + 1$, and Algorithm C requires time that is constant and independent of the value of n. Figure 9-3 plots these time requirements as a function of n. You can see from this figure that as n grows, Algorithm B requires the most time.

9.11   Typical growth-rate functions are algebraically simpler than the ones you have just seen. Why? Recall that since you are not likely to notice the effect of an inefficient algorithm when the problem

Figure 9-3   The number of operations required by the algorithms in Figure 9-1 as a function of n

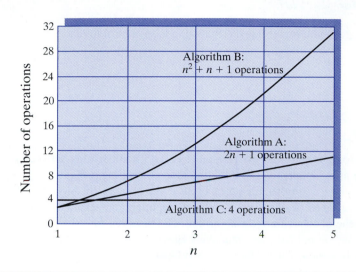

is small, you should focus on large problems. Thus, if we care only about large values of n when comparing the algorithms, we can consider only the dominant term in each growth-rate function.

For example, $n^2 + n + 1$ behaves like n^2 when n is large because n^2 is much larger than $n + 1$ in that case. In other words, the difference between the value of $n^2 + n + 1$ and that of n^2 is relatively small when n is large and can be ignored. So instead of using $n^2 + n + 1$ as Algorithm B's growth-rate function, we can use n^2—the term with the largest exponent—and say that Algorithm B requires time proportional to n^2. Likewise, Algorithm A requires time proportional to n. On the other hand, Algorithm C requires time that is independent of n.

Big Oh Notation

9.12   Computer scientists use a notation to represent an algorithm's complexity. Instead of saying that Algorithm A has a worst-case time requirement proportional to n, we say that A is **O(n)**. We call this notation **Big Oh** since it uses the capital letter O. We read O(n) as either "Big Oh of n" or "order of at most n." Similarly, since Algorithm B has a worst-case time requirement proportional to n^2, we say that B is O(n^2). Algorithm C always requires four operations. Regardless of the problem size n, this algorithm requires the same time, be it worst case, best case, or average case. We say that Algorithm C is O(1). We will discuss Big Oh notation more carefully and introduce other notations in the next section.

9.13   **Example.** Imagine that you are at a wedding reception, seated at a table of n people. In preparation for the toast, the waiter pours champagne into each of n glasses. That task is O(n). Someone makes a toast. It is O(1), even if the toast seems to last forever, because it is independent of the number of guests. If you clink your glass with everyone at your table, you perform an O(n) operation. If everyone at your table does likewise, a total of O(n^2) clinks are performed.

9.14   **Example.** In Segment 9.9, we ignored the operations that control the loops in the algorithms. Obviously this simplification affects the total number of operations, but even if we counted them, we would get the same growth-rate functions that you saw in Segment 9.11. For example, Algorithm A contains the `for` statement

```
for i = 1 to n
```

This statement represents the following loop-control logic:

```
i = 1
while (i <= n)
{
    ...
    i = i + 1
}
```

This logic requires an assignment to i, $n + 1$ comparisons between i and n, n additions to i, and n more assignments to i. In total, the loop-control logic requires $n + 1$ assignments, $n + 1$ comparisons, and n additions, for a total of $3n + 2$ operations. So Algorithm A actually requires $5n + 3$ operations instead of only $2n + 1$. What is important, however, is not the exact count of operations, but the general behavior of the algorithm. The functions $5n + 3$ and $2n + 1$ are each directly proportional to n. We do not have to count every operation to see that Algorithm A requires time that increases linearly with n. Thus, Algorithm A is O(n).

9.15   The growth-rate functions that you are likely to encounter grow in magnitude as follows when $n > 10$:

$$O(1) < O(\log \log n) < O(\log n) < O(\log^2 n) < O(n) < O(n \log n) < O(n^2) < O(n^3) < O(2n) < O(n!)$$

The logarithms given here are base 2. As you will see later in Segment 9.20, the choice of base does not matter.

Figure 9-4 tabulates the magnitudes of these functions for increasing values of the problem size n. From this data you can see that O($\log \log n$), O($\log n$), and O($\log^2 n$) algorithms take much less time than O(n) algorithms. Although O($n \log n$) algorithms take significantly more time than O(n) algorithms, they are markedly better than O(n^2) algorithms.

Figure 9-4   Typical growth-rate functions evaluated at increasing values of n

n	$\log (\log n)$	$\log n$	$\log^2 n$	n	$n \log n$	n^2	n^3	$2n$	$n!$
10	2	3	11	10	33	10^2	10^3	10^3	10^5
10^2	3	7	44	100	664	10^4	10^6	10^{30}	10^{94}
10^3	3	10	99	1000	9966	10^6	10^9	10^{301}	10^{1435}
10^4	4	13	177	10,000	132,877	10^8	10^{12}	10^{3010}	$10^{19,335}$
10^5	4	17	276	100,000	1,660,964	10^{10}	10^{15}	$10^{30,103}$	$10^{243,338}$
10^6	4	20	397	1,000,000	19,931,569	10^{12}	10^{18}	$10^{301,030}$	$10^{2,933,369}$

 Note: When analyzing the time efficiency of an algorithm, consider large problems. For small problems, the difference between the execution times of two solutions to the same problem is usually insignificant.

9.16   **Example.** Segments 9.2 and 9.5 showed you two ways to perform a computation. One way was noticeably slow. You should now be able to predict this behavior without actually running the code. The first way—call it Method 1—used this loop:

```
long product = 0;
for (long counter = secondOperand; counter > 0; counter--)
    product = product + firstOperand;
```

How many times is firstOperand added to product? If secondOperand contains an integer n, then n such additions occur. When n is large, so is the number of additions required to compute the solution. From our discussion in the previous section, we can say that Method 1 is $O(n)$.

The second way—call it Method 2—used the following code, where secondOperandLength is the number of digits in secondOperand:

```
long product = 0;

for (int digitPosition = 1; digitPosition <= secondOperandLength;
        digitPosition++)
{
    int digit = (int)(secondOperand - (secondOperand / 10) * 10);

    for (int counter = digit; counter > 0; counter--)
        product = product + firstOperand;

    secondOperand = secondOperand / 10;
    firstOperand = 10 * firstOperand;
} // end for
```

How many times is firstOperand added to product this time? Each digit of the second operand can be at most 9, so the inner for loop adds firstOperand to product at most nine times. The loop, in fact, executes once for each digit in secondOperand. Since secondOperand contains secondOperandLength digits, the loop adds firstOperand to product at most 9 * secondOperandLength times.

If secondOperand contains an integer n, as it does in Method 1, how does n affect secondOperandLength here? The data in Figure 9-5 can help us answer this question. The figure tabulates $\log_{10} n$ truncated to an integer—which we denote as $\lfloor \log_{10} n \rfloor$—for two-digit, three-digit, and four-digit values of the integer n. (Note that $\lfloor 4.9 \rfloor$, for example, is 4.) You can see that the number of digits in n is $1 + \lfloor \log_{10} n \rfloor$. Therefore, the number of additions that Method 2 requires—at most 9 * secondOperandLength—is at most $9 * (1 + \lfloor \log_{10} n \rfloor)$.

Figure 9-5   The number of digits in an integer n compared with the integer portion of $\log_{10} n$

n	Number of Digits	$\lfloor \log_{10} n \rfloor$
10 – 99	2	1
100 – 999	3	2
1000 – 9999	4	3

Now we need to compare our analyses of Methods 1 and 2. Method 1 requires n additions. Method 2 requires at most $9 * (1 + \lfloor \log_{10} n \rfloor)$ additions. Which approach requires the fewest additions? Let's see if we can answer this question by looking at the data in Figure 9-6.

Figure 9-6   The values of two logarithmic growth-rate functions for various ranges of n

n	$\lfloor \log_{10} n \rfloor$	$9*(1 + \lfloor \log_{10} n \rfloor)$
10 – 99	1	18
100 – 999	2	27
1000 – 9999	3	36
10,000 – 99,999	4	45
100,000 – 999,999	5	54

For values of n greater than 18,

$$n > 9 * (1 + \lfloor \log_{10} n \rfloor)$$

As n increases, n is much larger than $9 * (1 + \lfloor \log_{10} n \rfloor)$. Since Method 1 is O($n$), it requires many more additions than Method 2 when n is large, and so it is much slower. In fact, Method 2 is O(log n) in its worst case. Figure 9-4 shows that an O(n) algorithm is slower than an O(log n) algorithm.

Note: Floors and ceilings
The **floor** of a number x, denoted as $\lfloor x \rfloor$, is the largest integer less than or equal to x. For example, $\lfloor 4.9 \rfloor$ is 4. When you **truncate** a positive real number to an integer, you actually are computing the number's floor by discarding any fractional portion. The **ceiling** of a number x, denoted as $\lceil x \rceil$, is the smallest integer greater than or equal to x. For example, $\lceil 4.1 \rceil$ is 5.

Question 3   When you truncate a negative real number to an integer, are you computing the number's floor or ceiling? Justify your answer with an example.

Formalities

9.17   Big Oh notation has a formal mathematical meaning that can justify some of the sleight-of-hand we used in the previous sections. You saw that an algorithm's actual time requirement is directly proportional to a function f of the problem size n. For example, $f(n)$ might be $n^2 + n + 1$. In this case, we would conclude that the algorithm is of order at most n^2—that is, O(n^2). We essentially have replaced $f(n)$ with a simpler function—let's call it $g(n)$. In this example, $g(n)$ is n^2.

What does it really mean to say that a function $f(n)$ is of order at most $g(n)$—that is, that $f(n) = $ O($g(n)$)? In simple terms, it means that Big Oh provides an **upper bound** on a function's growth rate. More formally, we have the following mathematical definition.

Note: Formal definition of Big Oh
A function $f(n)$ is of order at most $g(n)$—that is, $f(n) = $ O($g(n)$)—if a positive real number c and positive integer N exist such that $f(n) \leq c\, g(n)$ for all $n \geq N$. That is, $c\, g(n)$ is an upper bound on $f(n)$ when n is sufficiently large.

Figure 9-7 illustrates this definition. You can see that when n is large enough—that is, when $n \geq N$—$f(n)$ does not exceed $c\, g(n)$. The opposite is true for smaller values of n. That is unimportant, since we can ignore these values of n.

Figure 9-7   An illustration of the definition of Big Oh

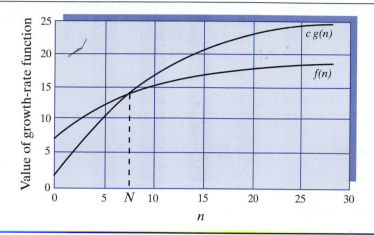

9.18   **Example.** In Segment 9.14, we said that an algorithm that uses $5n + 3$ operations is $O(n)$. We now can show that $5n + 3 = O(n)$ by using the formal definition of Big Oh.

When $n \geq 3$, $5n + 3 \leq 5n + n = 6n$. Thus, if we let $f(n) = 5n + 3$, $g(n) = n$, $c = 6$, and $N = 3$, we have shown that $f(n) \leq 6\, g(n)$ for $n \geq 3$, or $5n + 3 = O(n)$. That is, if an algorithm requires time directly proportional to $5n + 3$, it is $O(n)$.

Other values for the constants c and N will also work. For example, $5n + 3 \leq 5n + 3n = 8n$ when $n \geq 1$. Thus by choosing $c = 8$ and $N = 1$, we have shown that $5n + 3 = O(n)$.

You need to be careful when choosing $g(n)$. For example, we just found that $5n + 3 \leq 8n$ when $n \geq 1$. But $8n < n^2$ when $n \geq 9$. So why wouldn't we let $g(n) = n^2$ and conclude that our algorithm is $O(n^2)$? Although this conclusion is correct, it is not as good—or **tight**—as it could be. You want the upper bound on $f(n)$ to be as small as possible.

Note: The upper bound on an algorithm's time requirement should be as small as possible and should involve simple functions like the ones given in Figure 9-4.

9.19   **Example.** Let's show that $4n^2 + 50n - 10 = O(n^2)$. It is easy to see that

$$4n^2 + 50n - 10 \leq 4n^2 + 50n \text{ for any } n$$

Since $50n \leq 50n^2$ for $n \geq 50$,

$$4n^2 + 50n - 10 \leq 4n^2 + 50n^2 = 54n^2 \text{ for } n \geq 50$$

Thus, with $c = 54$ and $N = 50$, we have shown that $4n^2 + 50n - 10 = O(n^2)$.

Note: To show that $f(n) = O(g(n))$, replace the smaller terms in $f(n)$ with larger terms until only one term is left.

Question 4   Show that $3n^2 + 2n = O(2^n)$. What values of c and N did you use?

9.20 **Example.** Show that $\log_b n = O(\log_2 n)$. Let $L = \log_b n$ and $B = \log_2 b$. From the meaning of a logarithm, we can conclude that $n = b^L$ and $b = 2^B$. Combining these two conclusions, we have

$$n = b^L = (2^B)^L = 2^{BL}$$

Thus, $\log_2 n = BL = B \log_b n$ or, equivalently, $\log_b n = (1/B) \log_2 n$ for any $n \geq 1$. Taking $c = 1/B$ and $N = 1$ in the definition of Big Oh, we reach the desired conclusion.

It follows from this example that the general behavior of a logarithmic function is the same regardless of its base. Often the logarithms used in growth-rate functions are base 2. But since the base really does not matter, we typically omit it.

 Note: The base of a log in a growth-rate function is usually omitted, since $O(\log_a n) = O(\log_b n)$.

9.21 **Identities.** The following identities hold for Big Oh notation:

$$O(k\, g(n)) = O(g(n)) \text{ for a constant } k$$
$$O(g_1(n)) + O(g_2(n)) = O(g_1(n) + g_2(n))$$
$$O(g_1(n))\, O(g_2(n)) = O(g_1(n)\, g_2(n))$$

By using these identities and ignoring smaller terms in a growth-rate function, you can usually ascertain the order of an algorithm's time requirement with little effort. For example, if the growth-rate function is $4n^2 + 50n - 10$,

$$O(4n^2 + 50n - 10) = O(4n^2) \text{ by ignoring the smaller terms}$$
$$= O(n^2) \text{ by ignoring the constant multiplier}$$

9.22 **The complexities of program constructs.** The time complexity of a sequence of statements in an algorithm or program is the sum of the statements' individual complexities. However, it is sufficient to take instead the largest of these complexities. Thus, if $S_1, S_2, \ldots, S_k$ is a sequence of statements, and if g_i is the growth-rate function for statement S_i, the time complexity of the sequence would be $O(\max(g_1, g_2, \ldots, g_k))$.

The time complexity of the **if** statement

```
if (condition)
   S₁
else
   S₂
```

is the sum of the complexity of the condition and the complexity of S_1 or S_2, whichever is largest.

The time complexity of a loop is the complexity of its body times the number of times the body executes. Thus, the complexity of a loop such as

```
for i = 1 to n
   S
```

is $O(n\, g(n))$, where g is the growth-rate function for S.

9.23 **Other notations.** Although we will use Big Oh notation most often in this book, other notations are sometimes useful when describing an algorithm's time requirement $f(n)$. We mention them here primarily to expose you to them. Beginning with the definition of Big Oh that you saw earlier, we define **Big Omega** and **Big Theta**.

- **Big Oh.** $f(n)$ is of order at most $g(n)$—that is, $f(n) = O(g(n))$—if positive constants c and N exist such that $f(n) \leq c\, g(n)$ for all $n \geq N$. The time requirement $f(n)$ is not larger than $c\, g(n)$. That is, $c\, g(n)$ is an upper bound on $f(n)$. Thus, an analysis that uses Big Oh produces a maximum time requirement for an algorithm.
- **Big Omega.** $f(n)$ is of order at least $g(n)$—that is, $f(n) = \Omega(g(n))$—if $g(n) = O(f(n))$. In other words, $f(n) = \Omega(g(n))$ if positive constants c and N exist such that $f(n) \geq c\, g(n)$ for all $n \geq N$. The time requirement $f(n)$ is not smaller than $c\, g(n)$, its **lower bound**. Thus, a Big Omega analysis produces a minimum time requirement for an algorithm.
- **Big Theta.** $f(n)$ is of order $g(n)$—that is, $f(n) = \Theta(g(n))$—if $f(n) = O(g(n))$ and $g(n) = O(f(n))$. Another way to say the same thing is $f(n) = O(g(n))$ and $f(n) = \Omega(g(n))$. The time requirement $f(n)$ is the same as $g(n)$. That is, $c\, g(n)$ is both a lower bound and an upper bound on $f(n)$. A Big Theta analysis assures us that the time estimate is as good as possible. Even so, Big Oh is the more common notation.

Picturing Efficiency

9.24   Much of an algorithm's work occurs during its repetitive phases, that is, during the execution of loops or as a result of recursive calls. In this section, we will illustrate the time efficiency of several examples.

We begin with the loop in Algorithm A of Figure 9-1, which appears in pseudocode as follows:

```
for i = 1 to n
   sum = sum + i
```

The body of this loop requires a constant amount of execution time, and so it is $O(1)$. Figure 9-8 represents that time with one icon, and so a row of n icons represents the loop's total execution time. This algorithm is $O(n)$: Its time requirement grows as n grows.

Figure 9-8   An $O(n)$ algorithm

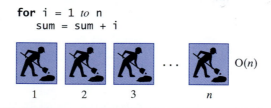

```
for i = 1 to n
   sum = sum + i
```
$O(n)$

   1   2   3 n

9.25   Algorithm B in Figure 9-1 contains nested loops, as follows:

```
for i = 1 to n
{
   for j = 1 to i
      sum = sum + 1
}
```

When loops are nested, you examine the innermost loop first. Here, the body of the inner loop requires a constant amount of execution time, and so it is $O(1)$. If we again represent that time with an icon, a row of i icons represents the time requirement for the inner loop. Since the inner loop is the body of the outer loop, it executes n times. Figure 9-9 illustrates the time requirement for these nested loops, which is proportional to $1 + 2 + \ldots + n$. Question 1 asked you to show that

$$1 + 2 + \ldots + n = n (n + 1) / 2$$

which is $n^2 / 2 + n / 2$. Thus, the computation is $O(n^2)$.

Figure 9-9   An $O(n^2)$ algorithm

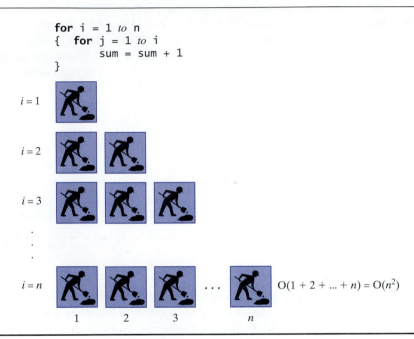

```
for i = 1 to n
{  for j = 1 to i
      sum = sum + 1
}
```

$i = 1$

$i = 2$

$i = 3$

$i = n$ $O(1 + 2 + \ldots + n) = O(n^2)$

1   2   3 n

9.26   The body of the inner loop in the previous segment executes a variable number of times that depends on the outer loop. Suppose we change the inner loop so that it executes the same number of times for each repetition of the outer loop, as follows:

```
for i = 1 to n
{
   for j = 1 to n
      sum = sum + 1
}
```

Figure 9-10 illustrates these nested loops and shows that the computation is $O(n^2)$.

Question 5   Using Big Oh notation, what is the order of the following computation's time requirement?

```
for i = 1 to n
{
   for j = 1 to 5
      sum = sum + 1
}
```

9.27   Let's get a feel for the growth-rate functions in Figure 9-4. As we mentioned, the time requirement for an $O(1)$ algorithm is independent of the problem size n. We can apply such an algorithm

Figure 9-10   Another O(n^2) algorithm

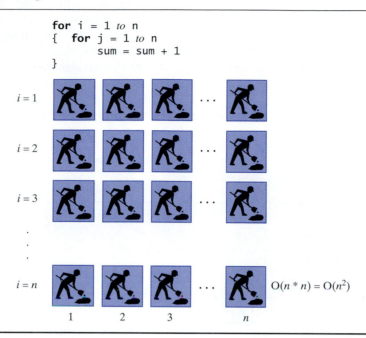

```
for i = 1 to n
{   for j = 1 to n
        sum = sum + 1
}
```

$i = 1$

$i = 2$

$i = 3$

$i = n$ O($n * n$) = O(n^2)

1   2   3 n

to larger and larger problems without affecting the execution time. This situation is ideal, but not typical.

For other orders, what happens if we double the problem size? The time requirement for an O($\log n$) algorithm will change, but not by much. An O(n) algorithm will need twice the time, an O(n^2) algorithm will need four times the time, and an O(n^3) algorithm will need eight times the time. Doubling the problem size for an O(2^n) algorithm squares the time requirement. Figure 9-11 tabulates these observations.

Question 6   Suppose that you can solve a problem of a certain size on a given computer in time t by using an O(n) algorithm. If you double the size of the problem, how fast must your computer be to solve the problem in the same time?

Question 7   Repeat Question 6, but instead use an O(n^2) algorithm.

Figure 9-11   The effect of doubling the problem size on an algorithm's time requirement

Growth-Rate Funtion for Size n Problems	Growth-Rate Funtion for Size $2n$ Problems	Effect on Time Requirement
1	1	None
$\log n$	$1 + \log n$	Negligible
n	$2n$	Doubles
$n \log n$	$2n \log n + 2n$	Doubles and then adds $2n$
n^2	$(2n)^2$	Quadruples
n^3	$(2n)^3$	Multiplies by 8
2^n	2^{2n}	Squares

9.28   Now suppose that your computer can perform one million operations per second. How long will it take an algorithm to solve a problem whose size is one million? We cannot answer this question exactly without knowing the algorithm, but the computations in Figure 9-12 will give you a sense of how the algorithm's Big Oh would affect our answer. An O($\log n$) algorithm would take a fraction of a second, whereas an O(2^n) algorithm would take many trillions of years! Note that these computations estimate the time requirement of an O($g(n)$) algorithm as $g(n)$. Although this approximation is not universally valid, for many algorithms it is reasonable.

Figure 9-12   The time to process one million items by algorithms of various orders at the rate of one million operations per second

Growth-Rate Funtion g	$g(10^6) / 10^6$
$\log n$	0.0000199 seconds
n	1 second
$n \log n$	19.9 seconds
n^2	11.6 days
n^3	31,709.8 years
2^n	$10^{301,016}$ years

Note: You can use O(n^2), O(n^3), or even O(2^n) algorithms as long as your problem size is small. For example, at the rate of one million operations per second, an O(n^2) algorithm would take one second to solve a problem whose size is 1000. An O(n^3) algorithm would take one second to solve a problem whose size is 100. And an O(2^n) algorithm would take about one second to solve a problem whose size is 20.

Question 8   The following algorithm discovers whether an array contains duplicates within its first n items:

```
Algorithm hasDuplicates(array, n)
for (index = 0 to n - 2)
  for (rest = index + 1 to n - 1)
    if (array[index] equals array[rest])
      return true
return false
```

What is the Big Oh of this algorithm in the worst case?

The Efficiency of Implementations of the ADT List

We now consider the time efficiency of two of the implementations of the ADT list that we discussed in previous chapters.

An Array-Based Implementation

One of the implementations of the ADT list given in Chapter 5 used a fixed-size array to represent the list's entries. We can now assess the efficiency of the list operations when implemented in this way.

9.29   **Adding to the end of the list.** Let's begin with the operation that adds a new entry to the end of the list. Segment 5.6 provided the following implementation for this operation:

```
public boolean add(T newEntry)
{
   boolean isSuccessful = true;

   if (!isFull())
   {
      list[length] = newEntry;
      length++;
   }
   else
      isSuccessful = false;

   return isSuccessful;
} // end add
```

Each step in this method—detecting whether the list is full, assigning a new entry to an array element, and incrementing the length—is an O(1) operation. By applying our knowledge of the material presented in Segments 9.21 and 9.22, we can show that this method is O(1). Intuitively, since we know that the new entry belongs at the end of the list, we know what array element should contain the new entry. Thus, we can make this assignment independently of any other entries in the list.

9.30   **Adding to the list at a given position.** The ADT list has another method that adds a new entry to a list, but this one adds the entry at a position that the client specifies:

```
public boolean add(int newPosition, T newEntry)
{
   boolean isSuccessful = true;

   if (!isFull() && (newPosition >= 1) && (newPosition <= length + 1))
   {
      makeRoom(newPosition);
      list[newPosition - 1] = newEntry;
      length++;
   }
   else
      isSuccessful = false;

   return isSuccessful;
} // end add
```

The method's general form is similar to the previous add method in that it sees whether the list is full, assigns the new entry to an array element, and increments the length. Once again, these are all O(1) operations, as are the initial comparisons that check the value of newPosition. What is different here is making room in the array for the new entry. This task is accomplished by the private method makeRoom:

```
private void makeRoom(int newPosition)
{
   int newIndex = newPosition - 1;
   int lastIndex = length - 1;
```

```
      for (int index = lastIndex; index >= newIndex; index--)
         list[index + 1] = list[index];
   } // end makeRoom
```

The worst case occurs when `newPosition` is 1 because the method must shift all of the list elements. If the list contains n entries, the body of the loop is repeated n times in the worst case. Therefore, the method `makeRoom` is $O(n)$ in the worst case. This observation implies that the method `add` is also $O(n)$ in the worst case.

The best case occurs when `newPosition` is `length + 1`, that is, when we add to the end of the list. In this event, `makeRoom`'s loop exits immediately, so `makeRoom` and therefore `add` are $O(1)$ in the best case. This result is consistent with our findings in the previous segment for the first `add` method.

Note: **Adding to an array-based list that has a fixed size**
Adding to the beginning of an array-based list is an $O(n)$ operation. Adding to the end is $O(1)$. Adding to the beginning takes the most time; adding to the end takes the least time. The actual time required to add at other positions depends on the position. As the position number increases, the time needed for an addition decreases.

Note: To simplify our example, we have considered a fixed-size array. Typically, an array-based list dynamically expands the array as needed. Doubling the size of an array is an $O(n)$ operation. As Segment 5.16 noted, the next n additions would share the cost of this doubling.

Question 9   What is the Big Oh of the list method `remove` in the best case and the worst case? (See Segment 5.8.) Assume that a fixed-size array represents the list, and use an argument similar to the one we just made for `add`.

Question 10   What is the Big Oh of the list method `replace` in the best case and the worst case? (See Segment 5.9.) Assume an array-based implementation of the list.

Question 11   Repeat Question 10, but instead analyze the list method `getEntry`. (See Segment 5.9.)

Question 12   Repeat Question 10, but instead analyze the list method `contains`. (See Segment 5.10.)

Question 13   Repeat Question 10, but instead analyze the list method `display`. (See Segment 5.5.)

A Linked Implementation

9.31   **Adding to the end of the list.** Now consider a linked implementation of the ADT list as given in Chapters 6 and 7. Let's begin with the method in Segment 6.23 that adds to the end of the list:

```
public boolean add(T newEntry)
{
   Node newNode = new Node(newEntry);

   if (isEmpty())
      firstNode = newNode;
```

```
    else
    {
      Node lastNode = getNodeAt(length);
      lastNode.next = newNode;
    } // end if

    length++;
    return true;
  } // end add
```

Except for the call to getNodeAt, the statements in this method are all O(1) operations. We need to examine getNodeAt, as described in Segment 6.30:

```
    private Node getNodeAt(int givenPosition)
    {
      Node currentNode = firstNode;
      for (int counter = 1; counter < givenPosition; counter++)
        currentNode = currentNode.next;

      return currentNode;
    } // end getNodeAt
```

Except for the loop, this method contains all O(1) operations. In the worst case, givenPosition is n—the size of the list—and so the loop, and therefore the method, is O(n). When add calls getNodeAt, it passes the size of the list, length, as the argument. This is the worst case. We can conclude that the method add is O(n). This result makes intuitive sense, since to add at the end of the list, the method must traverse the entire chain of linked nodes to locate the last one.

9.32   Adding to the list at a given position. The second add method, given in Segment 6.27 of Chapter 6, adds a new entry at a given position:

```
    public boolean add(int newPosition, T newEntry)
    {
      boolean isSuccessful = true;

      if ((newPosition >= 1) && (newPosition <= length+1))
      {
        Node newNode = new Node(newEntry);

        if (isEmpty() || (newPosition == 1))
        {
          newNode.next = firstNode;
          firstNode = newNode;
        }
        else
        }
          Node nodeBefore = getNodeAt(newPosition - 1);
          Node nodeAfter = nodeBefore.next;
          newNode.next = nodeAfter;
          nodeBefore.next = newNode;
        } // end if

        length++;
      }
      else
        isSuccessful = false;
```

```
      return isSuccessful;
   } // end add
```

The best case occurs when the addition is at the beginning of the list. Since the method has a reference to the chain's first node, no traversal is needed. Thus, the method is O(1) in this case.

To add a new entry at another position, the method must traverse the chain of linked nodes to
determine the point of insertion. It does this by calling getNodeAt. In the worst case, the traversal goes
to the end of the chain. As in the previous segment, getNodeAt and therefore add is O(n) in this case.

Note: **Adding to a list that has a linked implementation**
Adding to the beginning of a chain is an O(1) operation. Adding to the end is O(n). Adding to the
beginning takes the least time; adding to the end takes the most time. The actual time required to
add at other positions depends on the position. As the position number increases, the time
needed for an addition increases.

Question 14   What is the Big Oh of the linked implementation of the method remove in the
best case and the worst case? (See Segment 7.9 of Chapter 7.) Use an argument similar to
the one we just made for add.

9.33   **Retrieving an entry.** Consider the method getEntry, as given in Segment 7.11 of Chapter 7, which
retrieves the item at a given position within a list:

```
public T getEntry(int givenPosition)
{
   T result = null; // result to return

   if ((givenPosition >= 1) && (givenPosition <= length))
      result = getNodeAt(givenPosition).data;

   return result;
} // end getEntry
```

This method uses the method getNodeAt to locate the desired entry in the chain of linked nodes. As
we saw in the previous segment, getNodeAt is O(1) when givenPosition is 1. Hence getEntry is
O(1) in this best case. In the worst case, getNodeAt is O(n), so getEntry is also O(n).

Question 15   What is the Big Oh of the list method replace in the best case and the worst
case? (See Segment 7.10.) Assume a linked implementation of the list.

Question 16   Repeat Question 15, but instead analyze the list method contains. (See
Segment 7.12.)

Question 17   Repeat Question 15, but instead analyze the list method display. (See
Segment 6.33.)

Comparing the Implementations

9.34   Using Big Oh notation, Figure 9-13 summarizes the time complexities of the operations of the ADT
list for the implementations that use a fixed-size array and a chain of linked nodes. For some operations, a Big Oh range is given to indicate the time requirement as the list position increases.

Figure 9-13   The time efficiencies of the ADT list operations for two implementations, expressed in Big
Oh notation

Operation	Fixed-Size Array	Linked
add(new Entry)	O(1)	O(n)
add(newPosition, newEntry)	O(n) to O(1)	O(1) to O(n)
remove(givenPosition)	O(n) to O(1)	O(1) to O(n)
replace(givenPosition, newEntry)	O(1)	O(1) to O(n)
getEntry(givenPosition)	O(1)	O(1) to O(n)
contains(anEntry)	O(1) to O(n)	O(1) to O(n)
display	O(n)	O(n)
clear(), getLength(), isEmpty(), isFull()	O(1)	O(1)

For an array-based implementation of the ADT list, the second `add` method and `remove` require time that ranges from O(n) to O(1). They take less time as the list position increases. The method `contains` takes time that ranges from O(1) to O(n), depending on where or whether the entry is found. The method `display` is always O(n), and the other operations are each O(1).

For a linked implementation, the first `add` method and `display` are O(n). The operations `clear`, `getLength`, `isEmpty`, and `isFull` are each O(1). All the other methods require time that ranges from O(1) to O(n). They take more time as the list position increases.

As you can see, some of the operations have the same Big Oh for both implementations. However, operations that add to the end of a list, replace an entry, or retrieve an entry take less time when you use an array to represent a list than when you use linked nodes. If your application uses these particular operations frequently, an array-based implementation could be attractive. But remember that this particular implementation uses a fixed-size array, which limits the size of the list.

The major operations that add or remove an entry at a given position have time requirements that depend on this position regardless of their implementation. If your application primarily adds and removes entries at or near the beginning of a list, use a linked implementation. If these operations are mostly at or near the end of the list, use an array-based implementation. The operations that you use most in an application should influence your choice of implementation for an ADT.

Adding a tail reference to the linked implementation, as was done in Segments 7.21 through 7.24 of Chapter 7, makes adding to the end of the list an O(1) operation. Exercise 5 at the end of this chapter asks you to analyze this implementation.

Note: Even small changes to an ADT's underlying data structure can increase or decrease the time efficiency of the ADT's operations.

Programming Tip: When choosing an implementation for an ADT, you should consider the operations that your application requires. If you use a particular operation frequently, you want its implementation to be efficient. Conversely, if you rarely use an operation, you can afford to use a class that has an inefficient implementation of that operation.

CHAPTER SUMMARY

- An algorithm's complexity is described in terms of the time and space required to execute it.
- An algorithm's time requirement $f(n)$ is of order at most $g(n)$—that is, $f(n) = O(g(n))$—if positive constants c and N exist such that $f(n) \leq c\, g(n)$ for all $n \geq N$.
- The relationships among typical growth-rate functions are as follows:

$$O(1) < O(\log \log n) < O(\log n) < O(\log^2 n) < O(n) < O(n \log n) < O(n^2) < O(n^3) < O(2^n) < O(n!)$$

- The time complexity of the ADT list operations that add or remove an entry by position depends on the position of the relevant entries. For an array-based implementation, additions and removals at or near the end of the list take less time than those at or near the list's beginning. The opposite is true for a linked implementation.

PROGRAMMING TIP

- When choosing an implementation for an ADT, you should consider the operations that your application requires. If you use a particular operation frequently, you want its implementation to be efficient. Conversely, if you rarely use an operation, you can afford to use a class that has an inefficient implementation of that operation.

EXERCISES

1. Using Big Oh notation, indicate the time requirement of each of the following tasks in the worst case. Describe any assumptions that you make.

   a. After arriving at a party, you shake hands with each person there.
   b. Each person in a room shakes hands with everyone else in the room.
   c. You climb a flight of stairs.
   d. You slide down the banister.
   e. After entering an elevator, you press a button to choose a floor.
   f. You ride the elevator from the ground floor up to the nth floor.
   g. You read a book twice.

2. Describe a way to climb from the bottom of a flight of stairs to the top in time that is no better than $O(n^2)$.

3. Using Big Oh notation, indicate the time requirement of each of the following tasks in the worst case.

   a. Display all the integers in an array of integers.
   b. Display all the integers in a chain of linked nodes.
   c. Display the nth integer in an array of integers.
   d. Compute the sum of the first n even integers in an array of integers.

4. Chapter 5 describes an implementation of the ADT list that uses an array that can expand dynamically. Using Big Oh notation, derive the time complexity of the method doubleArray, as given in Segment 5.18.

5. Suppose that you alter the linked implementation of the ADT list to include a tail reference, as described in Segments 7.21 through 7.24 of Chapter 7. The time efficiencies of what methods, if any, are affected by this change? Use Big Oh notation to describe the efficiencies of any affected methods.

6. By using the definition of Big Oh, show that

    a. $6n^2 + 3$ is $O(n^2)$
    b. $n^2 + 17n + 1$ is $O(n^2)$
    c. $5n^3 + 100 n^2 - n - 10$ is $O(n^3)$
    d. $3n^2 + 2^n$ is $O(2^n)$

7. In the worst case, Algorithm X requires $n^2 + 9n + 5$ operations and Algorithm Y requires $5n^2$ operations. What is the Big Oh of each algorithm?

8. Plot the number of operations required by Algorithms X and Y of Exercise 7 as a function of n. What can you conclude?

9. Show that $O(\log_a n) = O(\log_b n)$ for $a, b > 1$. *Hint*: $\log_a n = \log_b n / \log_b a$.

10. Suppose that your implementation of a particular algorithm appears in Java as follows:

```java
for (int pass = 1; pass <= n; pass++)
{
   for (int index = 0; index < n; index++)
   {
      for (int count = 1; count < 10; count++)
      {
         . . .
      } // end for
   } // end for
} // end for
```

The algorithm involves an array of n items. The previous code shows the only repetition in the algorithm, but it does not show the computations that occur within the loops. These computations, however, are independent of n. What is the order of the algorithm?

11. Repeat Exercise 10, but replace 10 with n in the inner loop.

12. Using Big Oh notation, indicate the time requirement of the methods in Java's interface `Iterator`, as described in Chapter 8, when implemented as a separate class iterator for the ADT list. The implementation begins at Segment 8.12.

13. Using Big Oh notation, indicate the time requirement of the methods in Java's interface `Iterator`, as described in Chapter 8, when implemented as an inner class iterator for the ADT list. The linked implementation begins at Segment 8.19, and the array-based implementation begins at Segment 8.24.

14. Using Big Oh notation, indicate the time requirement of the methods in Java's interface `ListIterator`, as implemented in Chapter 8. The array-based implementation begins at Segment 8.42.

15. If $f(n)$ is $O(g(n))$ and $g(n)$ is $O(h(n))$, use the definition of Big Oh to show that $f(n)$ is $O(h(n))$.

16. Segment 9.15 and the chapter summary showed the relationships among typical growth-rate functions. Indicate where the following growth-rate functions belong in this ordering:

    a. $n^2 \log n$ c. $n^2/\log n$
    b. $\sqrt{n}$ d. 3^n

17. Show that $7n^2 + 5n$ is not $O(n)$.

18. Suppose that you have a dictionary whose words are not sorted in alphabetical order. As a function of the number, n, of words, what is the time complexity of searching for a particular word in this dictionary?

19. Repeat the previous exercise for a dictionary whose words are sorted alphabetically. Compare your results with those for the previous exercise.

20. Consider a football player who runs wind sprints on a football field. He begins at the 0-yard line and runs to the 1-yard line and then back to the 0-yard line. Then he runs to the 2-yard line and back to the 0-yard line, runs to the 3-yard line and back to the 0-yard line, and so on until he has reached the 10-yard line and returned to the 0-yard line.

   a. How many total yards does he run?
   b. How many total yards does he run if he reaches the n-yard line instead of the 10-yard line?
   c. How does his total distance run compare to that of a sprinter who simply starts at the 0-yard line and races to the n-yard line?

21. Exercise 6 in Chapter 4 asked you to write Java statements at the client level that return the position of a given object in a list. Using Big Oh notation, compare the time requirement of these statements with that of the method `getPosition` in Exercise 2 of Chapter 5 and Exercise 4 of Chapter 6.

22. Consider the following definition of a sequence A of positive integers:

$$A_{i+1} = \begin{cases} A_i / 2 \text{ if } A_i \text{ is even} \\ 3A_i - 1 \text{ if } A_i \text{ is odd} \end{cases}$$

If A_0 has some value v, give a Big Oh expression for the

   a. Minimum value
   b. Maximum value

that A_k can have in terms of k and v.

23. Consider two programs, A and B. Program A requires $1000\ n^2$ operations and Program B requires 2^n operations. For which values of n will Program A execute faster than Program B?

24. Consider four programs—A, B, C, and D—that have the following performances:

   A $O(\log n)$
   B $O(n)$
   C $O(n^2)$
   D $O(2^n)$

If each program requires 10 seconds to solve a problem of size 1000, estimate the time required by each program for a problem of size 2000.

PROJECTS

For the following projects, you should know how to time a section of code in Java. One approach is to use the class `java.util.Date`. A `Date` object contains the time at which it was constructed. This time is stored as a `long` integer equal to the number of milliseconds that have passed since 00:00:00.000 GMT on January 1, 1970. By subtracting the starting time in milliseconds from the ending time in milliseconds, you get the run time—in milliseconds—of a section of code.

For example, suppose that `thisMethod` is the name of a method you wish to time. The following statements will compute the number of milliseconds that `thisMethod` requires to execute:

```
Date current = new Date();              // get current time
long startTime = current.getTime();
thisMethod();                           // code to be timed
current = new Date();                   // get current time
long stopTime = current.getTime();
long elapsedTime = stopTime - startTime; // milliseconds
```

1. Write a Java program that implements the three algorithms in Figure 9-1 and times them for various values of *n*. The program should display a table of the run times of each algorithm for various values of *n*.

2. Consider the following two loops:

```
// Loop A
for (i = 1; i <= n; i++)
  for (j = 1; j <= 10000; j++)
    sum = sum + j;

// Loop B
for (i = 1; i <= n; i++)
  for (j = 1; j <= n; j++)
    sum = sum + j;
```

Although Loop A is $O(n)$ and Loop B is $O(n^2)$, Loop B can be faster than Loop A for small values of *n*. Design and implement an experiment to find a value of *n* for which Loop B is faster.

3. Repeat Project 2, but use the following for Loop B:

```
// Loop B
for (i = 1; i <= n; i++)
  for (j = 1; j <= n; j++)
    for (k = 1; k <= n; k++)
      sum = sum + k;
```

4. In mythology, the Hydra was a monster with many heads. Every time the hero chopped off a head, two smaller heads would grow in its place. Fortunately for the hero, if the head was small enough, he could chop it off without two more growing in its place. To kill the Hydra, all our hero needed to do was to chop off all the heads.

Write a program that simulates the Hydra. Instead of heads, we will use strings. A list of strings, then, represents the Hydra. Every time you remove a string from the list, delete the first letter of the string and put two copies of the remaining string back into the list. For example, if you remove *HYDRA*, you add two copies of *YDRA* to the list. If you remove a one-letter word, you add nothing to the list. Exactly where in the list you add or remove strings is up to you. For example, you might always add to the end of the list, or you might add at random positions.

To begin, read a word from the keyboard and place it into an empty list. The Hydra dies when the list has no more strings for you to remove.

Using Big Oh notation, predict the time requirement for this algorithm in terms of the number n of characters in the initial string. Then time the actual execution of the program for various values of n and plot its performance as a function of n. Compare your results when you use the following strategies for removing a string from the list:

a. Always remove the shortest string.
b. Always remove the longest string.

5. Suppose that you have several numbered billiard balls on a pool table. At each step you remove a billiard ball from the table. If the ball removed is numbered n, you replace it with n balls whose number is $n / 2$, where the division is truncated to an integer. For example, if you remove the 5 ball, you replace it with five 2 balls.

Write a program that simulates this process. Use a list of positive integers to represent the balls on the pool table.

Using Big Oh notation, predict the time requirement for this algorithm when the initial list contains only the value n. Then time the actual execution of the program for various values of n and plot its performance as a function of n.

6. Repeat the previous project, but instead replace the n ball with n balls randomly numbered less than n.

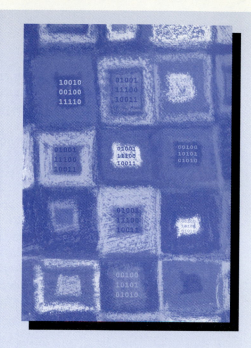

CONTENTS

PREREQUISITES

OBJECTIVES

After studying this chapter, you should be able to

- Decide whether a given recursive method will end successfully in a finite amount of time
- Write a recursive method
- Estimate the time efficiency of a recursive method
- Identify tail recursion and replace it with iteration

Repetition is a major feature of many algorithms. In fact, repeating actions rapidly is a key ability of computers. Two problem-solving processes involve repetition; they are called iteration and recursion. In fact, most programming languages provide two kinds of repetitive constructs, iterative and recursive.

You know about iteration because you know how to write a loop. Regardless of the loop construct you use—`for`, `while`, or `do`—your loop contains the statements that you want to repeat and a mechanism for controlling the number of repetitions. You might have a counted loop that counts repetitions as 1, 2, 3, 4, 5, or 5, 4, 3, 2, 1. Or the loop might execute repeatedly while a boolean variable or expression is true. Iteration often provides a straightforward and efficient way to implement a repetitive process.

At times, however, iterative solutions are elusive or hopelessly complex. For some problems, discovering or verifying such solutions is not a simple task. In these cases, recursion can provide an elegant alternative. Some recursive solutions can be the best choice, some provide insight for finding a better iterative solution, and some should not be used at all because they are grossly inefficient. Recursion, however, remains an important problem-solving strategy.

This chapter will show you how to think recursively.

What Is Recursion?

10.1   You can build a house by hiring a contractor. The contractor in turn hires several subcontractors to complete portions of the house. Each subcontractor might hire other subcontractors to help. You use the same approach when you solve a problem by breaking it into smaller problems. In one special variation of this problem-solving process, the smaller problems are identical except for their size. This special process is called **recursion**.

Suppose that you can solve a problem by solving an identical but smaller problem. How will you solve the smaller problem? If you use recursion again, you will need to solve an even smaller problem that is just like the original problem in every other respect. How will replacing a problem with another one ever lead to a solution? One key to the success of recursion is that eventually you will reach a smaller problem whose solution you know because either it is obvious or it is given. The solution to this smallest problem is probably not the solution to your original problem, but it can help you reach it. Either just before or just after you solve a smaller problem, you usually contribute a portion of the solution. This portion, together with the solutions to the other, smaller problems, provides the solution to the larger problem.

Let's look at an example.

10.2   **Example: The countdown.** It's New Year's Eve and the giant ball is falling in Times Square. The crowd counts down the last ten seconds: "10, 9, 8, . . ." Suppose that I ask you to count down to 1 beginning at some positive integer like 10. You could shout "10" and then ask a friend to count down from 9. Counting down from 9 is a problem that is exactly like counting down from 10, except that there is less to do. It is a smaller problem.

To count down from 9, your friend shouts "9" and asks a friend to count down from 8. This sequence of events continues until eventually someone's friend is asked to count down from 1. That friend simply shouts "1." No other friend is needed. You can see these events in Figure 10-1.

In this example, I've asked you to complete a task. You saw that you could contribute a part of the task and then ask a friend to do the rest. You know that your friend's task is just like the original task, but it is smaller. You also know that when your friend completes this smaller task, your job will be done. What is missing from the process just described is the signal that each friend gives to the previous person at the completion of a task.

Figure 10-1   Counting down from 10

To provide this signal, when you count down from 10, I need you to tell me when you are done. I don't care how—or who—does the job, as long as you tell me when it is done. I can take a nap until I hear from you. Likewise, when you ask a friend to count down from 9, you do not care how your friend finishes the job. You just want to know when it is done so you can tell me that you are done. You can take a nap while you are waiting.

 Note: Recursion is a problem-solving process that breaks a problem into identical but smaller problems.

Ultimately, we have a group of napping people waiting for someone to say "I'm done." The first person to make that claim is the person who shouts "1," as Figure 10-1 illustrates, since that person needs no help in counting down from 1. At this time in this particular example, the problem is solved, but I don't know that because I'm still asleep. The person who shouted "1" says "I'm done" to the person who shouted "2." The person who shouted "2" says "I'm done" to the person who shouted "3," and so on, until you say "I'm done" to me. The job is done; thanks for your help; I have no idea how you did it, and I don't need to know!

10.3   What does any of this have to do with Java? In the previous example, you play the role of a Java method. I, the client, have asked you, the recursive method, to count down from 10. When you ask a friend for help, you are invoking a method to count down from 9. But you do not invoke another method; you invoke yourself!

Note: A method that calls itself is a **recursive method**. The invocation is a **recursive call** or **recursive invocation**.

The following Java method counts down from a given positive integer, displaying one integer per line.

```
/** Task: Counts down from a given positive integer.
 *  @param integer  an integer > 0 */
public static void countDown(int integer)
{
   System.out.println(integer);
   if (integer > 1)
      countDown(integer - 1);
} // end countDown
```

Since the given integer is positive, the method can display it immediately. This step is analogous to you shouting "10" in the previous example. Next the method asks whether it is finished. If the given integer is 1, there is nothing left to do. But if the given integer is larger than 1, we need to count down from integer - 1. We've already noted that this task is smaller but otherwise identical to the original problem. How do we solve this new problem? We invoke a method, but countDown is such a method. It does not matter that we have not finished writing it at this point!

10.4   Will the method countDown actually work? Shortly we will trace the execution of countDown, both to convince you that it works and to show you how it works. But traces of recursive methods are messy, and you usually do not have to trace them. If you follow certain guidelines when writing a recursive method, you can be assured that it will work.

In designing a recursive solution, you need to answer certain questions:

Note: **Questions to answer when designing a recursive solution**

- What part of the solution can you contribute directly?
- What smaller but identical problem has a solution that, when taken with your contribution, provides the solution to the original problem?
- When does the process end? That is, what smaller but identical problem has a known solution, and have you reached this problem, or **base case**?

For the method `countDown`, we have the following answers to these questions:

- The method `countDown` displays the given integer as the part of the solution that it contributes directly. This happens to occur first here, but it need not always occur first.
- The smaller problem is counting down from `integer - 1`. The method solves the smaller problem when it calls itself recursively.
- The `if` statement asks if the process has reached the base case. Here the base case occurs when `integer` is 1. Because the method displays `integer` before checking it, nothing is left to do once the base case is identified.

Note: **Design guidelines for successful recursion**

To write a recursive method that behaves correctly, you generally should adhere to the following design guidelines:

- The method must be given an input value, usually as an argument, but sometimes as a value read.
- The method definition must contain logic that involves this input value and leads to different cases. Typically, such logic includes an `if` statement or a `switch` statement.
- One or more of these cases should provide a solution that does not require recursion. These are the base cases, or **stopping cases**.
- One or more cases must include a recursive invocation of the method. These recursive invocations should in some sense take a step toward a base case by using "smaller" arguments or solving "smaller" versions of the task performed by the method.

Programming Tip: **Infinite recursion**

A recursive method that does not check for a base case, or that misses the base case, will execute "forever." This situation is known as infinite recursion.

10.5   Before we trace the method `countDown`, we should note that we could have written it in other ways. For example, a first draft of this method might have looked like this:

```java
public static void countDown(int integer)
{
  if (integer == 1)
    System.out.println(integer);
  else
  {
    System.out.println(integer);
    countDown(integer - 1);
  } // end if
} // end countDown
```

Here, the programmer considered the base case first. The solution is clear and perfectly acceptable, but you might want to avoid the redundant `println` statement that occurs in both cases.

10.6   Removing the redundancy just mentioned could result in either the version given earlier in Segment 10.3 or the following one:

```java
public static void countDown(int integer)
{
  if (integer >= 1)
  {
    System.out.println(integer);
    countDown(integer - 1);
  } // end if
} // end countDown
```

When `integer` is 1, this method will produce the recursive call `countDown(0)`. This turns out to be the base case for this method, and nothing is displayed.

All three versions of `countDown` produce correct results; there are probably other versions as well. Choose the one that is clearest to you.

10.7   The version of `countDown` just given in Segment 10.6 provides us an opportunity to compare it with the following iterative version:

```java
// Iterative version.
public static void countDown(int integer)
{
  while (integer >= 1)
  {
    System.out.println(integer);
    integer--;
  } // end while
} // end countDown
```

The two methods have a similar appearance. Both compare `integer` with 1, but the recursive version uses an `if`, and the iterative version uses a `while`. Both methods display `integer`. Both compute `integer - 1`.

 Programming Tip: An iterative method contains a loop. A recursive method calls itself. Although some recursive methods contain a loop *and* call themselves, if you have written a `while` statement within a recursive method, be sure that you did not mean to write an `if` statement.

 Question 1   Write a recursive void method that skips *n* lines of output, where *n* is a positive integer. Use `System.out.println()` to skip one line.

Question 2   Describe a recursive algorithm that draws a given number of concentric circles. The innermost circle should have a given diameter. The diameter of each of the other circles should be four-thirds the diameter of the circle just inside it.

Tracing a Recursive Method

10.8   Now let's trace the method `countDown` given in Segment 10.3:

```java
public static void countDown(int integer)
{
   System.out.println(integer);
   if (integer > 1)
      countDown(integer - 1);
} // end countDown
```

For simplicity, suppose that we invoke this method with the statement

```java
countDown(3);
```

from within a `main` method of the class that defines `countDown`. This call behaves like any other call to a nonrecursive method. The argument 3 is copied into the parameter `integer` and the following statements are executed:

```java
System.out.println(3);
if (3 > 1)
   countDown(3 - 1); // first recursive call
```

A line containing 3 is displayed, and the recursive call `countDown(2)` occurs, as Figure 10-2a shows.
      Execution of the method is then suspended until the results of `countDown(2)` are known. In this particular method definition, no statements appear after the recursive call. So although it appears that nothing will happen when execution resumes, it is here that the method returns to the client.

Figure 10-2   The effect of the method call `countDown(3)`

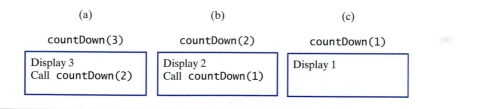

10.9   Continuing our trace, `countDown(2)` causes the following statements to execute:

```java
System.out.println(2);
if (2 > 1)
   countDown(2 - 1); // second recursive call
```

A line containing 2 is displayed, and the recursive call `countDown(1)` occurs, as shown in Figure 10-2b. Execution of the method is then suspended until the results of `countDown(1)` are known.
      The call `countDown(1)` causes the following statements to execute:

```java
System.out.println(1);
if (1 > 1)
```

A line containing 1 is displayed, as Figure 10-2c shows, and no other recursive call occurs.

Figure 10-3 illustrates the sequence of events from the time that `countDown` is first called. The numbered arrows indicate the order of the recursive calls and the returns from the method. The first three arrows trace the steps that we just discussed. After 1 is displayed, the method completes execution and returns to the point (arrow 4) after the call `countDown(2 - 1)`. Execution continues from there, and the method returns to the point (arrow 5) after the call `countDown(3 - 1)`. Ultimately, a return to the point (arrow 6) after the initial recursive call in `main` occurs.

Figure 10-3　Tracing the recursive call `countDown(3)`

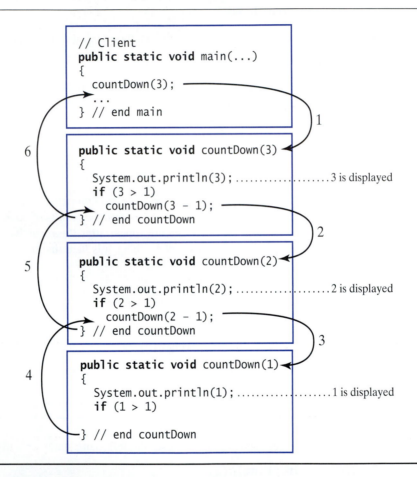

Although tracking these method returns seems like a formality that has gained us nothing, it is an important part of any trace because some recursive methods will do more than simply return to their calling method. You will see an example of such a method shortly.

10.10　Figure 10-3 appears to show multiple copies of the method `countDown`. In reality, however, multiple copies do not exist. Instead, for each call to a method—be it recursive or not—Java records the current state of the method's execution, including the values of its parameters and local variables as well as the location of the current instruction. Each record, called an **activation record**, provides a snapshot of a method's state during its execution. The records are placed into an ADT called a **stack**, much as you would stack photos one on top of the other. The stack organizes the records chronologically, so that the record of the currently executing method is on top. In this way, Java can suspend the execution of a recursive method and invoke it again with new argument values. The

Figure 10-4   The stack of activation records during the execution of the call `countDown(3)`

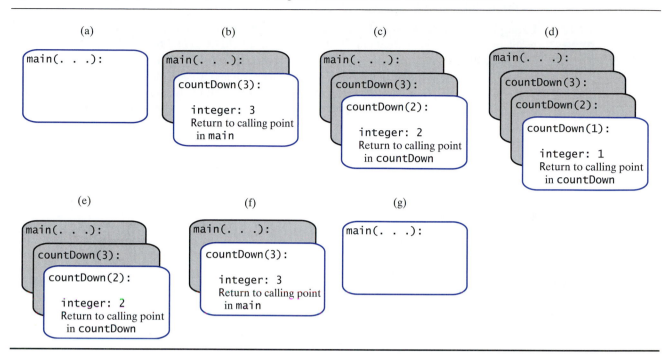

boxes in Figure 10-3 correspond roughly to activation records, although the figure does not show them in the order in which they would appear in a stack. Figure 10-4 illustrates the stack of activation records as a result of the call `countDown(3)` in a main method. Chapter 21 will provide more detail about stacks and the contents of an activation record.

Note: **The stack of activation records**
Each call to a method generates an activation record that captures the state of the method's execution and that is placed into a stack. A recursive method uses more memory than an iterative method, in general, because each recursive call generates an activation record.

Programming Tip: **Stack overflow**
Too many recursive calls can cause the error message "stack overflow." This means that the stack of activation records has become full. In essence, the method has used too much memory. Infinite recursion or large-size problems are the likely causes of this error.

Question 3   Write a recursive void method `countUp(n)` that counts up from 1 to *n*, where *n* is a positive integer. *Hint*: A recursive call will occur before you display anything.

Recursive Methods That Return a Value

10.11   The recursive method `countDown` in the previous sections is a void method. Valued methods can also be recursive. The guidelines for successful recursion given in Segment 10.4 apply to valued methods as well, with an additional note. Recall that a recursive method must contain a statement such as an `if` that chooses among several cases. Some of these cases lead to a recursive call, but at least one case has no recursive call. For a valued method, each of these cases must provide a value for the method to return.

10.12   **Example: Compute the sum 1 + 2 + . . . + *n* for any integer *n* > 0.** The given input value for this problem is the integer *n*. Beginning with this fact will help us to find the smaller problem because its input will also be a single integer. The sum always starts at 1, so that can be assumed.

So suppose that I have given you a positive integer *n* and asked you to compute the sum of the first *n* integers. You need to ask a friend to compute the sum of the first *m* integers for some positive integer *m*. What should *m* be? Well, if your friend computes $1 + . . . + (n - 1)$, you can simply add *n* to that sum to get your sum. Thus, if sumOf(n) is the method call that returns the sum of the first *n* integers, adding *n* to your friend's sum occurs in the expression sumOf(n-1) + n.

What small problem can be the base case? That is, what value of *n* results in a sum that you know immediately? One possible answer is 1. If *n* is 1, the desired sum is 1.

With these thoughts in mind, we can write the following method:

```
/** @param n   an integer > 0
 *  @return the sum 1 + 2 + ... + n */
public static int sumOf(int n)
{
   int sum;
   if (n == 1)
     sum = 1;                 // base case
   else
     sum = sumOf(n - 1) + n; // recursive call

   return sum;
} // end sumOf
```

10.13   The definition of the method sumOf satisfies the design guidelines for successful recursion. Therefore, you should be confident that the method will work correctly without tracing its execution. However, a trace will be instructive here because it will not only show you how a valued recursive method works, but also demonstrate actions that occur after a recursive call is complete.

Suppose that we invoke this method with the statement

```
System.out.println(sumOf(3));
```

The computation occurs as follows:

1. sumOf(3) is sumOf(2) + 3; sumOf(3) suspends execution, and sumOf(2) begins.
2. sumOf(2) is sumOf(1) + 2; sumOf(2) suspends execution, and sumOf(1) begins.
3. sumOf(1) returns 1.

Once the base case is reached, the suspended executions resume, beginning with the most recent. Thus, sumOf(2) returns 1 + 2, or 3; then sumOf(3) returns 3 + 3, or 6. Figure 10-5 illustrates this computation.

Question 4   Write a recursive valued method that computes the product of the integers from 1 to *n*, where *n* > 0.

Note: Should you trace a recursive method?
We have shown you how to trace the execution of a recursive method primarily to show you how recursion works and to give you some insight into how a typical compiler implements recursion. Should you ever trace a recursive method? Usually, no. You certainly should not trace a recursive

method while you are writing it. If the method is incomplete, your trace will be, too, and you are likely to become confused. If a recursive method does not work, follow the suggestions given in the next programming tip. You should trace a recursive method only as a last resort.

Figure 10-5   Tracing the execution of sumOf(3)

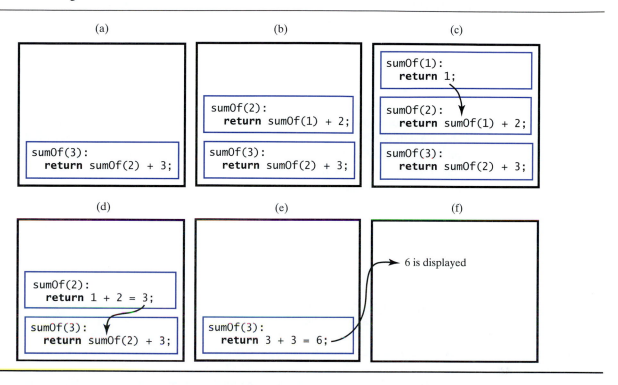

Programming Tip: **Debugging a recursive method**

If a recursive method does not work, answer the following questions. Any "no" answers should guide you to the error.

- Does the method have at least one input value?
- Does the method contain a statement that tests an input value and leads to different cases?
- Did you consider all possible cases?
- Does at least one of these cases cause at least one recursive call?
- Do these recursive calls involve smaller arguments, smaller tasks, or tasks that get closer to the solution?
- If these recursive calls produce or return correct results, will the method produce or return a correct result?
- Is at least one of the cases a base case that has no recursive call?
- Are there enough base cases?
- Does each base case produce a result that is correct for that case?
- If the method returns a value, does each of the cases return a value?

10.14   Our previous examples were simple so that you could study the construction of recursive methods. Since you could have solved these problems iteratively with ease, should you actually use their recursive solutions? Nothing is inherently wrong with these recursive methods. However, given the way that typical present-day systems execute recursive methods, a stack overflow is likely for large values of *n*. Iterative solutions to these simple examples would not have this difficulty and are easy to write. Realize, however, that future computing systems might be able to execute these recursive methods without difficulty.

Recursively Processing an Array

Later in this book we will talk about searching an array for a particular item. We will also look at algorithms that **sort**, or arrange, the items in an array into either ascending or descending order. Some of the more powerful searching and sorting algorithms often are stated recursively. In this section, we will process arrays recursively in ways that will be useful to us later. We have chosen a simple task—displaying the integers in an array—for our examples so that you can focus on the recursion without the distraction of the task. We will consider more-complex tasks later in this book and in the exercises at the end of this chapter.

10.15   Suppose that we have an array of integers and we want a method that displays it. So that we can choose to display all or part of the array, the method will display the array elements whose indices range from `first` through `last`. Thus, we can declare the method as follows:

```
/** Task: Displays the integers in an array.
 *  @param array  an array of integers
 *  @param first  the index of the first element displayed
 *  @param last   the index of the last element displayed,
 *                0 <= first <= last < array.length */
public static void displayArray(int[] array, int first, int last)
```

This task is simple and could readily be implemented using iteration. You might not imagine, however, that we could also implement it recursively in a variety of ways. But we can and will.

10.16   **Starting with** `array[first]`. An iterative solution would certainly start at the first element, `array[first]`, so it is natural to have our first recursive method begin there also. If I ask you to display the array, you could display `array[first]` and then ask a friend to display the rest of the array. Displaying the rest of the array is a smaller problem than displaying the entire array. You wouldn't have to ask a friend for help if you had to display only one element—that is, if `first` and `last` were equal. This is the base case. Thus, we could write the method `displayArray` as follows:

```
public static void displayArray(int array[], int first, int last)
{
   System.out.print(array[first] + " ");
   if (first < last)
      displayArray(array, first + 1, last);
} // end displayArray
```

For simplicity, we assume that the integers will fit on one line. Notice that the client would follow a call to `displayArray` with `System.out.println()` to get to the next line.

10.17   **Starting with `array[last]`.** Strange as it might seem, we can begin with the last element in the array and still display the array from its beginning. Rather than displaying the last element right away, you would ask a friend to display the rest of the array. After the elements `array[first]` through `array[last - 1]` had been displayed, you would display `array[last]`. The resulting output would be the same as in the previous segment.

The method that implements this plan follows:

```
public static void displayArray(int array[], int first, int last)
{
   if (first <= last)
   {
      displayArray(array, first, last - 1);
      System.out.print (array[last] + " ");
   } // end if
} // end displayArray
```

10.18   **Dividing the array in half.** A common way to process an array recursively divides the array into two pieces. You then process each of the pieces separately. Since each of these pieces is an array that is smaller than the original array, each defines the smaller problem necessary for recursion. Our first two examples also divided the array into two pieces, but one of the pieces contained only one element. Here we divide the array into two approximately equal pieces. To divide the array, we find the element at or near the middle of the array. The index of this element is

```
int mid = (first + last)/2;
```

Figure 10-6 shows two arrays and their middle elements. Suppose that we include `array[mid]` in the left "half" of the array, as the figure shows. In Part b, the two pieces of the array are equal in length; in Part a they are not. This slight difference in length doesn't matter.

Figure 10-6   Two arrays with their middle elements within their left halves

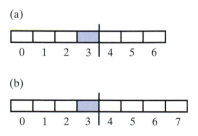

Once again, the base case is an array of one element. You can display it without help. But if the array contains more than one element, you divide it into halves. You then ask a friend to display one half and another friend to display the other half. These two friends, of course, represent the two recursive calls in the following method:

```
public static void displayArray(int array[], int first, int last)
{
   if (first == last)
      System.out.print(array[first] + " ");
   else
   {
      int mid = (first + last)/2;
```

```
      displayArray(array, first, mid);
      displayArray(array, mid + 1, last);
   } // end if
} // end displayArray
```

Question 5   In Segment 10.18, suppose that the array's middle element is not in either half of the array. Instead you can recursively display the left half, display the middle element, and then recursively display the right half. What is the implementation of displayArray if you make these changes?

Note: When you process an array recursively, you can divide it into two pieces. For example, the first or last element could be one piece, and the rest of the array could be the other piece. Or you could divide the array into halves or in some other way.

10.19   **Displaying a list.** In Chapter 5, we used an array to implement the ADT list. We defined the list's display method iteratively, but here we'll use recursion instead. Since display has no parameters and our recursive displayArray methods do, we write displayArray as a private method that display calls. Since the array, list, of list entries is a data field of the class that implements the list, it need not be a parameter of displayArray. The arguments in the call to displayArray would be zero for the first index and length – 1 for the last index, where length is a data field of the list's class. Finally, since display is not a static method, displayArray is not static.

We can use the approach of any version of displayArray given previously. However, we will display objects, one per line, instead of integers on one line. Using the technique shown in Segment 10.16, we revised the methods as follows:

```
public void display()
{
   displayArray(0, length - 1);
} // end display

private void displayArray(int first, int last)
{
   System.out.println(list[first]);
   if (first < last)
      displayArray(first + 1, last);
} // end displayArray
```

Note: A recursive method that is part of an implementation of an ADT often is private, because its use requires knowledge of the underlying data structure. Such a method is unsuitable as an ADT operation.

Recursively Processing a Linked Chain

10.20   We can illustrate the recursive processing of a chain of linked nodes by performing a simple task such as displaying the data in the chain. Once again, we'll implement the method display for the ADT list, but this time let's use the linked implementation introduced in Chapter 6. That implementation defines the field firstNode as a reference to the first node in the chain.

Dividing a linked chain into pieces is not as easy as dividing an array, since we cannot access any particular node without traversing the chain from its beginning. Hence, our first approach displays the data in the first node and then recursively displays the data in the rest of the chain. Thus, as it did in Segment 10.19, `display` will call a private recursive method. We will name that method `displayChain`. As a recursive method, `displayChain` needs an input value. That input should represent the chain, so we give `displayChain` a parameter that references the first node in the chain.

Suppose that we name `displayChain`'s parameter `nodeOne`. Then `nodeOne.data` is the data in the first node, and `nodeOne.next` is a reference to the rest of the chain. What about the base case? Although a one-element array was a fine base case for `displayArray`, using an empty chain as the base case is easier here because we can simply compare `nodeOne` to `null`. Thus, we have the following implementations for the methods `display` and `displayChain`:

```java
public void display()
{
   displayChain(firstNode);
} // end display

private void displayChain(Node nodeOne)
{
   if (nodeOne != null)
   {
      System.out.println(nodeOne.data);  // display data in first node
      displayChain(nodeOne.next);         // display rest of chain
   } // end if
} // end displayChain
```

Note: When you write a method that processes a chain of linked nodes recursively, you use a reference to the chain's first node as the method's parameter. You then can process the first node followed by the rest of the chain.

10.21   **Displaying a chain backwards.** Suppose that you want to traverse a chain of linked nodes in reverse order. In particular, suppose that you want to display the object in the last node, then the one in the next-to-last node, and so on, working your way toward the beginning of the chain. Since each node references the next node but not the previous one, using iteration for this task would be difficult. You could traverse to the last node, display its contents, go back to the beginning and traverse to the next-to-last node, and so on. Clearly, however, this is a tedious and time-consuming approach. Alternatively, you could traverse the chain once and save a reference to each node. You could then use these references to display the objects in the chain's nodes in reverse order. A recursive solution would do this for you.

If a friend could display the nodes in reverse order, beginning with the second node, you could display the first node and complete the task. The following recursive solution implements this idea:

```java
public void displayBackward()
{
   displayChainBackward(firstNode);
} // end displayBackward

private void displayChainBackward(Node nodeOne)
{
```

```
      if (nodeOne != null)
      {
         displayChainBackward(nodeOne.next);
         System.out.println(nodeOne.data);
      } // end if
   } // end displayChainBackward
```

Note: Traversing a chain of linked nodes in reverse order is easier when done recursively than when done iteratively.

Question 6   Trace the previous method `displayBackward` for a chain of three nodes.

The Time Efficiency of Recursive Methods

Chapter 9 showed you how to measure an algorithm's time requirement by using Big Oh notation. We used a count of the algorithm's major operations as a first step in selecting an appropriate growth-rate function. For the iterative examples we examined, that process was straightforward. We will use a more formal technique here to measure the time requirement of a recursive algorithm and thereby choose the right growth-rate function.

The Time Efficiency of `countDown`

10.22   As a first example, consider the `countDown` method given in Segment 10.3. The size of the problem of counting down to 1 from a given integer is directly related to the size of that integer. Since Chapter 9 used n to represent the size of the problem, we will rename the parameter `integer` in `countDown` to n to simplify our discussion. Here is the revised method:

```
      public static void countDown(int n)
      {
         System.out.println(n);
         if (n > 1)
            countDown(n - 1);
      } // end countDown
```

When n is 1, `countDown` displays 1. This is the base case and requires a constant amount of time. When $n > 1$, the method requires a constant amount of time for both the `println` statement and the comparison. In addition, it needs time to solve the smaller problem represented by the recursive call. If we let $t(n)$ represent the time requirement of `countDown(n)`, we can express these observations by writing

$$t(1) = 1$$
$$t(n) = 1 + t(n - 1) \text{ for } n > 1$$

The equation for $t(n)$ is called a **recurrence relation**, since the definition of the function t contains an occurrence of itself—that is, a recurrence. What we need is an expression for $t(n)$ that is not given in terms of itself. One way to find such an expression is to pick a value for n and to write out the equations for $t(n)$, $t(n - 1)$, and so on, until we reach $t(1)$. From these equations, we should be able to guess at an appropriate expression to represent $t(n)$. We then need only to prove that we are right. This is actually easier than it sounds.

10.23 **Solving a recurrence relation.** To solve the previous recurrence relation for $t(n)$, let's begin with $n = 4$. We get the following sequence of equations:

$$t(4) = 1 + t(3)$$
$$t(3) = 1 + t(2)$$
$$t(2) = 1 + t(1) = 1 + 1 = 2$$

Substituting 2 for $t(2)$ in the equation for $t(3)$ results in

$$t(3) = 1 + 2 = 3$$

Substituting 3 for $t(3)$ in the equation for $t(4)$ results in

$$t(4) = 1 + 3 = 4$$

It appears that

$$t(n) = n \text{ for } n \geq 1$$

We can start with a larger value of n, get the same result, and convince ourselves that it is true. But we need to *prove* that this result is true for every $n \geq 1$. This is not hard to do.

10.24 **Proving that $t(n) = n$.** To prove that $t(n) = n$ for $n \geq 1$, we begin with the recurrence relation for $t(n)$, since we know it is true:

$$t(n) = 1 + t(n - 1) \text{ for } n > 1$$

We need to replace $t(n - 1)$ on the right side of the equation. Now, if $t(n - 1) = n - 1$ when $n > 1$, the following would be true for $n > 1$:

$$t(n) = 1 + n - 1 = n$$

Thus, if we can find an integer k that satisfies the equation $t(k) = k$, the next larger integer will also satisfy it. By a similar chain of reasoning, the equation is true for all integers larger than k. Since we are given that $t(1) = 1$, all integers larger than 1 will satisfy the equation. This proof is an example of a **proof by induction**.

To conclude, we now know that `countDown`'s time requirement is given by the function $t(n) = n$. Thus, the method is $O(n)$.

?

Question 7 What is the Big Oh of the method `sumOf` given in Segment 10.12?

Question 8 Computing x^n for some real number x and an integral power $n \geq 0$ has a simple recursive solution:

$$x^n = x\, x^{n-1}$$
$$x^0 = 1$$

a. What recurrence relation describes this algorithm's time requirement?
b. By solving this recurrence relation, find the Big Oh of this algorithm.

The Time Efficiency of Computing x^n

10.25 We can compute x^n for some real number x and an integral power $n \geq 0$ more efficiently than the approach that Question 8 suggests. To reduce the number of recursive calls and therefore the number of multiplications, we can express x^n as follows:

$x^n = (x^{n/2})^2$ when n is even and positive
$x^n = x \, (x^{(n-1)/2})^2$ when n is odd and positive
$x^0 = 1$

This computation could be implemented by a method `power(x, n)` that contains the recursive call `power(x, n/2)`. Since integer division in Java truncates its result, this call is appropriate regardless of whether n is even or odd. Thus, `power(x, n)` would invoke `power(x, n/2)` once, square the result, and, if n is odd, multiply the square by x. These multiplications are O(1) operations. Thus, the execution time for `power(x, n)` is proportional to the number of recursive calls.

The recurrence relation that represents the number of recursive calls and, therefore, the method's time requirement to compute x^n is then

$t(n) = 1 + t(n/2)$ when $n \geq 2$
$t(1) = 1$
$t(0) = 1$

Again, $n/2$ truncates to an integer.

10.26   Since the recurrence relation involves $n/2$, let's choose a power of 2—such as 16—as n's initial value. We then write the following sequence of equations:

$t(16) = 1 + t(8)$
$t(8) = 1 + t(4)$
$t(4) = 1 + t(2)$
$t(2) = 1 + t(1)$

By substituting repeatedly, we get the following:

$t(16) = 1 + t(8) = 1 + (1 + t(4)) = 2 + (1 + t(2)) = 3 + (1 + t(1)) = 4 + t(1)$

Since $16 = 2^4$, $4 = \log_2 16$. This fact, together with the base case $t(1) = 1$, leads us to guess that

$t(n) = 1 + \log_2 n$

10.27   Now we need to prove that this guess is, in fact, true for $n \geq 1$. It is true for $n = 1$, because

$t(1) = 1 + \log_2 1 = 1$

For $n > 1$, we know that the recurrence relation for $t(n)$

$t(n) = 1 + t(n/2)$

is true. Remember that $n/2$ truncates to an integer.

We need to replace $t(n/2)$. If our guess $t(n) = 1 + \log_2 n$ were true for all values of $n < k$, we would have $t(k/2) = 1 + \log_2 (k/2)$, since $k/2 < k$. Thus,

$t(k) = 1 + t(k/2)$
$\quad = 1 + (1 + \log_2 (k/2))$
$\quad = 2 + \log_2 (k/2)$
$\quad = \log_2 4 + \log_2 (k/2)$
$\quad = \log_2 (4k/2)$
$\quad = \log_2 (2k)$
$\quad = \log_2 2 + \log_2 k$
$\quad = 1 + \log_2 k$

To summarize, we assumed that $t(n) = 1 + \log_2 n$ for all values of $n < k$ and showed that $t(k) = 1 + \log_2 k$. Thus, $t(n) = 1 + \log_2 n$ for all $n \geq 1$. Since power's time requirement is given by $t(n)$, the method is O(log n).

A Simple Solution to a Difficult Problem

10.28   The Towers of Hanoi is a classic problem in computer science whose solution is not obvious. Imagine three poles and a number of disks of varying diameters. Each disk has a hole in its center so that it can fit over each of the poles. Suppose that the disks have been placed on the first pole in order from largest to smallest, with the smallest disk on top. Figure 10-7 illustrates this initial configuration for three disks.

Figure 10-7   The initial configuration of the Towers of Hanoi for three disks.

The problem is to move the disks from the first pole to the third pole so that they remain piled in their original order. But you must adhere to the following rules:

1. Move one disk at a time. Each disk you move must be a topmost disk.
2. No disk may rest on top of a disk smaller than itself.
3. You can store disks on the second pole temporarily, as long as you observe the previous two rules.

10.29   The solution is a sequence of moves. For example, if three disks are on pole 1, the following sequence of seven moves will move the disks to pole 3, using pole 2 temporarily:

Move a disk from pole 1 to pole 3
Move a disk from pole 1 to pole 2
Move a disk from pole 3 to pole 2
Move a disk from pole 1 to pole 3
Move a disk from pole 2 to pole 1
Move a disk from pole 2 to pole 3
Move a disk from pole 1 to pole 3

Figure 10-8 illustrates these moves.

Question 9   We discovered the previous solution for three disks by trial and error. Using the same approach, find a sequence of moves that solves the problem for four disks.

With four disks, the problem's solution requires 15 moves, so it is somewhat difficult to find by trial and error. With more than four disks, the solution is much more difficult to discover. What we need is an algorithm that produces a solution for any number of disks. Even though discovering a solution by trial and error is hard, finding a recursive algorithm to produce the solution is fairly easy.

Figure 10-8   The sequence of moves for solving the Towers of Hanoi problem with three disks

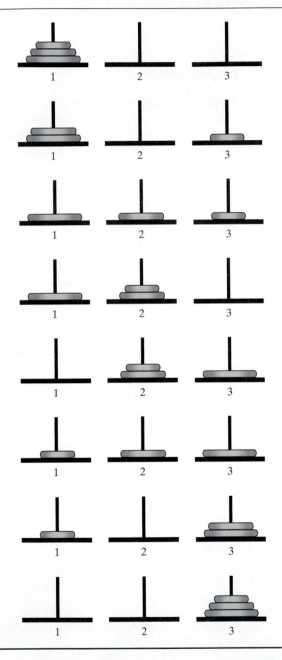

 Note: Invented in the late 1800s, the Towers of Hanoi problem was accompanied by this leg-end. A group of monks was said to have begun moving 64 disks from one tower to another. When they finish, the world will end. When you finish reading this section, you will realize that the monks—or their successors—could not have finished yet. By the time they do, it is quite plausible that the disks, if not the world, will have worn out!

10.30   A recursive algorithm solves a problem by solving one or more smaller problems of the same type. The problem size here is simply the number of disks. So imagine that the first pole has four disks, as in Figure 10-9a, and that I ask you to solve the problem. Eventually, you will need to move the bottom disk, but first you need to move the three disks on top of it. Ask a friend to move these three disks—a smaller problem—according to our rules, but make pole 2 the destination. Allow your friend to use pole 3 as a spare. Figure 10-9b shows the final result of your friend's work.

When your friend tells you that the task is complete, you move the one disk left on pole 1 to pole 3. Moving one disk is a simple task. You don't need help—or recursion—to do it. This disk is the largest one, so it cannot rest on top of any other disk. Thus, pole 3 must be empty before this move. After the move, the largest disk will be first on pole 3. Figure 10-9c shows the result of your work.

Now ask a friend to move the three disks on pole 2 to pole 3, adhering to the rules. Allow your friend to use pole 1 as a spare. When your friend tells you that the task is complete, you can tell me that your task is complete as well. Figure 10-9d shows the final results.

Figure 10-9   The smaller problems in a recursive solution for four disks

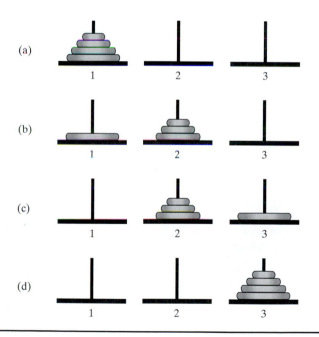

10.31   Before we write some pseudocode to describe the algorithm, we need to identify a base case. If only one disk is on pole 1, we can move it directly to pole 3 without using recursion. With this as the base case, the algorithm is as follows:

> *Algorithm to move* `numberOfDisks` *disks from* `startPole` *to* `endPole` *using* `tempPole`
> *as a spare according to the rules of the Towers of Hanoi problem*
> `if (numberOfDisks == 1)`
>   *Move disk from* `startPole` *to* `endPole`
> `else`
> `{`

> *Move all but the bottom disk from* `startPole` *to* `tempPole`
> *Move disk from* `startPole` *to* `endPole`
> *Move all disks from* `tempPole` *to* `endPole`
> }

At this point, we can develop the algorithm further by writing

Algorithm `solveTowers(numberOfDisks, startPole, tempPole, endPole)`
`if (numberOfDisks == 1)`
  Move disk from `startPole` *to* `endPole`
`else`
`{`
  `solveTowers(numberOfDisks - 1, startPole, endPole, tempPole)`
  Move disk from `startPole` *to* `endPole`
  `solveTowers(numberOfDisks - 1, tempPole, startPole, endPole)`
`}`

If we choose zero disks as the base case instead of one disk, we can simplify the algorithm a bit, as follows:

Algorithm `solveTowers(numberOfDisks, startPole, tempPole, endPole)`
`// Version 2`
`if (numberOfDisks > 0)`
`{`
  `solveTowers(numberOfDisks - 1, startPole, endPole, tempPole)`
  Move disk from `startPole` *to* `endPole`
  `solveTowers(numberOfDisks - 1, tempPole, startPole, endPole)`
`}`

Although somewhat easier to write, the second version of the algorithm executes many more recursive calls. Both versions, however, make the same moves.

Question 10   For two disks, how many recursive calls are made by each version of the algorithm just given?

Your knowledge of recursion should convince you that both forms of the algorithm are correct. Recursion has enabled us to solve a problem that appeared to be difficult. But is this algorithm efficient? Could we do better if we used iteration?

10.32   **Efficiency.** Let's look at the efficiency of our algorithm. How many moves occur when we begin with n disks? Let $m(n)$ denote the number of moves that `solveTowers` needs to solve the problem for n disks. Clearly,

$$m(1) = 1$$

For $n > 1$, the algorithm uses two recursive calls to solve problems that have $n - 1$ disks each. The required number of moves in each case is $m(n - 1)$. Thus, you can see from the algorithm that

$$m(n) = m(n - 1) + 1 + m(n - 1) = 2\,m(n - 1) + 1$$

From this equation, you can see that $m(n) > 2\,m(n - 1)$. That is, solving the problem with n disks requires more than twice as many moves as solving the problem with $n - 1$ disks.

It appears that $m(n)$ is related to a power of 2. Let's evaluate the recurrence for $m(n)$ for a few values of n:

$$m(1) = 1, m(2) = 3, m(3) = 7, m(4) = 15, m(5) = 31, m(6) = 63$$

It seems that

$$m(n) = 2^n - 1$$

We can prove this conjecture by using mathematical induction, as follows.

10.33   **Proof by induction that $m(n) = 2^n - 1$.** We know that $m(1) = 1$ and $2^1 - 1 = 1$, so the conjecture is true for $n = 1$. Now assume that it is true for $n = 1, 2, \ldots, k$, and consider $m(k + 1)$.

$$
\begin{aligned}
m(k + 1) &= 2\,m(k) + 1 &&\text{(use the recurrence relation)}\\
&= 2\,(2^k - 1) + 1 &&\text{(we assumed that } m(k) = 2^k - 1)\\
&= 2^{k+1} - 1
\end{aligned}
$$

Since the conjecture is true for $n = k + 1$, it is true for all $n \geq 1$.

10.34   **Exponential growth.** The number of moves required to solve the Towers of Hanoi problem grows exponentially with the number of disks n. That is, $m(n) = O(2^n)$. This rate of growth is alarming, as you can see from the following values of 2^n:

$$
\begin{aligned}
2^5 &= 32\\
2^{10} &= 1024\\
2^{20} &= 1{,}048{,}576\\
2^{30} &= 1{,}073{,}741{,}824\\
2^{40} &= 1{,}099{,}511{,}627{,}776\\
2^{50} &= 1{,}125{,}899{,}906{,}842{,}624\\
2^{60} &= 1{,}152{,}921{,}504{,}606{,}846{,}976
\end{aligned}
$$

Remember the monks mentioned at the end of Segment 10.29? They are making $2^{64} - 1$ moves. It should be clear that you can use this exponential algorithm only for small values of n, if you want to live to see the results.

Before you condemn recursion and discard our algorithm, you need to know that you cannot do any better. Not you, not the monks, not anyone. We demonstrate this observation next by using mathematical induction.

10.35   **Proof that Towers of Hanoi cannot be solved in fewer than $2^n - 1$ moves.** We have shown that our algorithm for the Towers of Hanoi problem requires $m(n) = 2^n - 1$ moves. Since we know that at least one algorithm exists—we found one—there must be a fastest one. Let $M(n)$ represent the number of moves that this optimal algorithm requires for n disks. We need to show that $M(n) = m(n)$ for $n \geq 1$.

When the problem has one disk, our algorithm solves it in one move. We cannot do better, so we have that $M(1) = m(1) = 1$. If we assume that $M(n - 1) = m(n - 1)$, consider n disks. Looking back at Figure 10-9b, you can see that at one point in our algorithm the largest disk is isolated on one pole and $n - 1$ disks are on another. This configuration would have to be true of an optimal algorithm as well, for there is no other way to move the largest disk. Thus, the optimal algorithm must have moved these $n - 1$ disks from pole 1 to pole 2 in $M(n - 1) = m(n - 1)$ moves.

After moving the largest disk (Figure 10-9c), the optimal algorithm moves $n - 1$ disks from pole 2 to pole 3 in another $M(n - 1) = m(n - 1)$ moves. Altogether, the optimal algorithm makes at least $2\,M(n - 1) + 1$ moves. Thus,

$$M(n) \geq 2\,M(n - 1) + 1$$

Now apply the assumption that $M(n - 1) = m(n - 1)$ and then the recurrence for $m(n)$ given in Segment 10.32 to get

$$M(n) \geq 2\,m(n - 1) + 1 = m(n)$$

We have just shown that $M(n) \geq m(n)$. But since the optimal algorithm cannot require more moves than our algorithm, the expression $M(n) > m(n)$ cannot be true. Thus, we must have $M(n) = m(n)$ for all $n \geq 1$.

10.36 Finding an iterative algorithm to solve the Towers of Hanoi problem is not as easy as finding a recursive algorithm. We now know that any iterative algorithm will require at least as many moves as the recursive algorithm. An iterative algorithm will save the overhead—space and time—of tracking the recursive calls, but it will not really be more efficient than `solveTowers`. An algorithm that uses both iteration and recursion to solve the Towers of Hanoi problem is discussed in the section "Tail Recursion," and an entirely iterative algorithm is the subject of Project 5 at the end of this chapter.

A Poor Solution to a Simple Problem

Some recursive solutions are so inefficient that you should avoid them. The problem that we will look at now is simple, occurs frequently in mathematical computations, and has a recursive solution that is so natural that you are likely to be tempted to use it. Don't!

10.37 **Example: Fibonacci numbers.** Early in the 13th century, the mathematician Leonardo Fibonacci proposed a sequence of integers to model the number of descendants of a pair of rabbits. Later named the **Fibonacci sequence**, these numbers occur in surprisingly many applications.

The first two terms in the Fibonacci sequence are 1 and 1. Each subsequent term is the sum of the preceding two terms. Thus, the sequence begins as $1, 1, 2, 3, 5, 8, 13, \ldots$. Typically, the sequence is defined by the equations

$$F_0 = 1$$
$$F_1 = 1$$
$$F_n = F_{n-1} + F_{n-2} \text{ when } n \geq 2$$

You can see why the following recursive algorithm would be a tempting way to generate the sequence:

```
Algorithm Fibonacci(n)
if (n <= 1)
   return 1
else
   return Fibonacci(n - 1) + Fibonacci(n - 2)
```

10.38 This algorithm makes two recursive calls. That fact in itself is not the difficulty. Earlier, you saw perfectly good algorithms—`displayArray` in Segment 10.18 and `solveTowers` in Segment 10.31—that make several recursive calls. The trouble here is that the same recursive calls are made repeatedly. A call to `Fibonacci(n)` invokes `Fibonacci(n - 1)` and then `Fibonacci(n - 2)`. But the call to `Fibonacci(n - 1)` has to compute `Fibonacci(n - 2)`, so the same Fibonacci number is computed twice.

Things get worse. The call to `Fibonacci(n - 1)` calls `Fibonacci(n - 3)` as well. The two previous calls to `Fibonacci(n - 2)` each invoke `Fibonacci(n - 3)`, so `Fibonacci(n - 3)` is computed three times. Figure 10-10a illustrates the dependency of F_6 on previous Fibonacci numbers and so indicates the number of times a particular number is computed repeatedly by the method `Fibonacci`. In contrast, Figure 10-10b shows that an iterative computation of F_6 computes each prior term once. The recursive solution is clearly less efficient. The next segments will show you just how inefficient it is.

Figure 10-10 The computation of the Fibonacci number F_6 using (a) recursion; (b) iteration

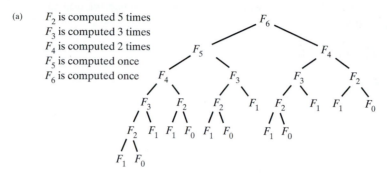

(a) F_2 is computed 5 times
F_3 is computed 3 times
F_4 is computed 2 times
F_5 is computed once
F_6 is computed once

(b) $F_0 = 1$
$F_1 = 1$
$F_2 = F_1 + F_0 = 2$
$F_3 = F_2 + F_1 = 3$
$F_4 = F_3 + F_2 = 5$
$F_5 = F_4 + F_3 = 8$
$F_6 = F_5 + F_4 = 13$

10.39 **The time efficiency of the algorithm Fibonacci.** We can investigate the efficiency of the Fibonacci algorithm by using a recurrence relation, as we did in Segments 10.22 through 10.27. First, notice that F_n requires one add operation plus the operations that F_{n-1} and F_{n-2} require. So if $t(n)$ represents the time requirement of the algorithm in computing F_n, we have

$t(n) = 1 + t(n-1) + t(n-2)$ for $n \geq 2$
$t(1) = 1$
$t(0) = 1$

This recurrence relation looks like the recurrence for the Fibonacci numbers themselves. It should not surprise you, then, that $t(n)$ is related to the Fibonacci numbers. In fact, if you look at Figure 10-10a and count the occurrences of the Fibonacci numbers F_2 through F_6, you will discover a Fibonacci sequence.

To find a relationship between $t(n)$ and F_n, let's expand $t(n)$ for a few values of n:

$t(2) = 1 + t(1) + t(0) = 1 + F_1 + F_0 = 1 + F_2 > F_2$
$t(3) = 1 + t(2) + t(1) > 1 + F_2 + F_1 = 1 + F_3 > F_3$
$t(4) = 1 + t(3) + t(2) > 1 + F_3 + F_2 = 1 + F_4 > F_4$

We guess that $t(n) > F_n$ for $n \geq 2$. Notice that $t(0) = 1 = F_0$ and $t(1) = 1 = F_1$. These do not satisfy the strict inequality of our guess.

We now prove that our guess is indeed fact. (You can skip the proof on your first reading.)

10.40 **Proof by induction that $t(n) > F_n$ for $n \geq 2$.** Since the recurrence relation for $t(n)$ involves two recursive terms, we need two base cases. In the previous segment, we already showed that $t(2) > F_2$ and $t(3) > F_3$. Now if $t(n) > F_n$ for $n = 2, 3, \ldots, k$, we need to show that $t(k+1) > F_{k+1}$. We can do this as follows:

$t(k+1) = 1 + t(k) + t(k-1) > 1 + F_k + F_{k-1} = 1 + F_{k+1} > F_{k+1}$

We can conclude that $t(n) > F_n$ for all $n \geq 2$.

Since we know that $t(n) > F_n$ for all $n \geq 2$, we can say that $t(n) = \Omega(F_n)$. Recall that the Big Omega notation means that $t(n)$ is at least as large as the Fibonacci number F_n. It turns out that we can compute F_n directly without using the recurrence relation given in Segment 10.37. It can be shown that

$$F_n = (a^n - b^n)/\sqrt{5}$$

where $a = (1 + \sqrt{5})/2$ and $b = (1 - \sqrt{5})/2$. Since $|1 - \sqrt{5}| < 2$, we have $|b| < 1$ and $|b^n| < 1$. Therefore, we have

$$F_n > (a^n - 1)/\sqrt{5}$$

Thus, $F_n = \Omega(a^n)$, and since we know that $t(n) = \Omega(F_n)$, we have $t(n) = \Omega(a^n)$. Some arithmetic shows that the previous expression for a equals approximately 1.6. We conclude that $t(n)$ grows exponentially with n. That is, the time required to compute F_n recursively increases exponentially as n increases.

10.41   At the beginning of this section, we observed that each Fibonacci number is the sum of the preceding two Fibonacci numbers in the sequence. This observation should lead us to an iterative solution that is O(n). (See Exercise 9 at the end of this chapter.) Although the clarity and simplicity of the recursive solution makes it a tempting choice, it is much too inefficient to use.

Programming Tip: Do not use a recursive solution that repeatedly solves the same problem in its recursive calls.

Question 11   If you compute the Fibonnaci number F_6 recursively, how many recursive calls are made, and how many additions are performed?

Question 12   If you compute the Fibonnaci number F_6 iteratively, how many additions are performed?

Tail Recursion

10.42   **Tail recursion** occurs when the last action performed by a recursive method is a recursive call. For example, the following method `countDown` from Segment 10.6 is tail recursive:

```
public static void countDown(int integer)
{
   if (integer >= 1)
   {
      System.out.println(integer);
      countDown(integer - 1);
   } // end if
} // end countDown
```

A method that implements the algorithm `Fibonacci` given in Segment 10.37 will not be tail recursive, even though a recursive call *appears* last in the method. A closer look reveals that the last *action* is an addition.

The tail recursion in a method simply repeats the method's logic with changes to parameters and variables. Thus, you can perform the same repetition by using iteration. Converting a tail-recursive method to an iterative one is usually a straightforward process. For example, let's see how to convert the recursive method countDown just given. First we replace the if statement with a while statement. Then, instead of the recursive call, we assign its argument integer - 1 to the method's formal parameter integer. Doing so gives us the following iterative version of the method:

```
public static void countDown(int integer)
{
  while (integer >= 1)
  {
    System.out.println(integer);
    integer = integer - 1;
  } // end while
} // end countDown
```

This method is essentially the same as the iterative method given in Segment 10.7.

Because converting tail recursion to iteration is often uncomplicated, some compilers convert tail-recursive methods to iterative methods to save the overhead involved with recursion. Most of this overhead involves memory, not time. If you need to save space, you should consider replacing tail recursion with iteration.

10.43 **Example.** Let's replace the tail recursion in the second version of the algorithm solveTowers given in Segment 10.31:

```
Algorithm solveTowers(numberOfDisks, startPole, tempPole, endPole)
if (numberOfDisks > 0)
{
  solveTowers(numberOfDisks - 1, startPole, endPole, tempPole)
  Move disk from startPole to endPole
  solveTowers(numberOfDisks - 1, tempPole, startPole, endPole)
}
```

This algorithm contains two recursive calls. The second one is tail recursive, since it is the algorithm's last action. Thus, we could try replacing the second recursive call with appropriate assignment statements and use a loop to repeat the method's logic, including the first recursive call, as follows:

```
Algorithm solveTowers(numberOfDisks, startPole, tempPole, endPole)
while (numberOfDisks > 0)
{
  solveTowers(numberOfDisks - 1, startPole, endPole, tempPole)
  Move disk from startPole to endPole
  numberOfDisks = numberOfDisks - 1
  startPole = tempPole
  tempPole = startPole
  endPole = endPole
}
```

This isn't quite right, however. Obviously, assigning endPole to itself is superfluous. Assigning tempPole to startPole and then assigning startPole to tempPole destroys startPole but leaves tempPole unchanged. What we need to do is exchange tempPole and startPole. Let's look at what is really happening here.

The only instruction that actually moves disks is *Move disk from* startPole *to* endPole. This instruction moves the largest disk that is not already on endPole. The disk to be moved is at the bottom of a pole, so any disks that are on top of it need to be moved first. Those disks are moved by the first recursive call. If we want to omit the second recursive call, what would we need to do instead before repeating the first recursive call? We must make sure that startPole contains the disks that have not been moved to endPole. Those disks are on tempPole as a result of the first recursive call. Thus, we need to exchange the contents of tempPole and startPole.

Making these changes results in the following revised algorithm:

```
Algorithm solveTowers(numberOfDisks, startPole, tempPole, endPole)
while (numberOfDisks > 0)
{
    solveTowers(numberOfDisks - 1, startPole, endPole, tempPole)
    Move disk from startPole to endPole
    numberOfDisks--
    Exchange the contents of tempPole and startPole
}
```

This revised algorithm is unusual in that its loop contains a recursive call. The base case for this recursion occurs when numberOfDisks is zero. Even though the method does not contain an if statement, it does detect the base case, ending the recursive calls.

Note: In a tail-recursive method, the last action is a recursive call. This call performs a repetition that can be done by using iteration. Converting a tail-recursive method to an iterative one is usually a straightforward process.

Mutual Recursion

10.44   Some recursive algorithms make their recursive calls indirectly. For example, we might have the following chain of events: Method A calls Method B, Method B calls Method C, and Method C calls Method A. Such recursion—called **mutual recursion** or **indirect recursion**—is more difficult to understand and trace, but it does arise naturally in certain applications.

For example, the following rules describe strings that are valid algebraic expressions:

- An algebraic expression is either a term or two terms separated by a + or - operator.
- A term is either a factor or two factors separated by a * or / operator.
- A factor is either a variable or an algebraic expression enclosed in parentheses.
- A variable is a single letter.

Suppose that the methods isExpression, isTerm, isFactor, and isVariable detect whether a string is, respectively, an expression, a term, a factor, or a variable. The method isExpression calls isTerm, which in turn calls isFactor, which then calls isVariable and isExpression. Figure 10-11 illustrates these calls.

Project 8 at the end of this chapter describes another example of mutual recursion. For a more detailed discussion of algebraic expressions, see Chapter 21.

Figure 10-11   An example of mutual recursion

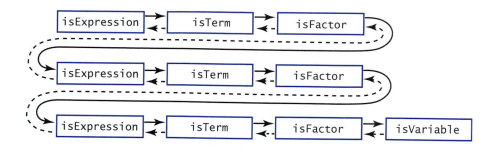

<table>
<tr><td>CHAPTER SUMMARY</td><td>

- Recursion is a problem-solving process that breaks a problem into identical but smaller problems.

- The definition of a recursive method must contain logic that involves an input—often a parameter—to the method and leads to different cases. One or more of these cases are base cases, or stopping cases, because they provide a solution that does not require recursion. One or more cases include a recursive invocation of the method that takes a step toward a base case by solving a "smaller" version of the task performed by the method.

- For each call to a method, Java records the values of the method's parameters and local variables in an activation record. The records are placed into an ADT called a stack that organizes them chronologically. The record most recently added to the stack is of the currently executing method. In this way, Java can suspend the execution of a recursive method and invoke it again with new argument values.

- A recursive method that processes an array often divides the array into portions. Recursive calls to the method work on each of these array portions.

- A recursive method that processes a chain of linked nodes needs a reference to the chain's first node as its parameter.

- A recursive method that is part of an implementation of an ADT often is private, because its use requires knowledge of the underlying data structure. Although such a method is unsuitable as an ADT operation, it can be called by a public method that implements the operation.

- A recurrence relation expresses a function in terms of itself. You can use a recurrence relation to describe the work done by a recursive method.

- Any solution to the Towers of Hanoi problem with n disks requires at least $2^n - 1$ moves. A recursive solution to this problem is clear and as efficient as possible. As an $O(2^n)$ algorithm, however, it is practical only for small values of n.

- Each number in the Fibonacci sequence—after the first two—is the sum of the previous two numbers. Computing a Fibonacci number recursively is quite inefficient, as the required previous numbers are computed several times each.

- Tail recursion occurs when the last action of a recursive method is a recursive call. This recursive call performs a repetition that can be done by using iteration. Converting a tail-recursive method to an iterative one is usually a straightforward process.

- Indirect recursion results when a method calls a method that calls a method, and so on until the first method is called again.

</td></tr>
</table>

PROGRAMMING TIPS

- An iterative method contains a loop. A recursive method calls itself. Although some recursive methods contain a loop *and* call themselves, if you have written a `while` statement within a recursive method, be sure that you did not mean to write an `if` statement.

- A recursive method that does not check for a base case, or that misses the base case, will not terminate normally. This situation is known as infinite recursion.

- Too many recursive calls can cause the error message "stack overflow." This means that the stack of activation records has become full. In essence, the method uses too much memory. Infinite recursion or large-size problems are the likely causes of this error.

- Do not use a recursive solution that repeatedly solves the same problem in its recursive calls.

- If a recursive method does not work, answer the following questions. Any "no" answers should guide you to the error.

    - Does the method have at least one parameter or input value?
    - Does the method contain a statement that tests a parameter or input value, leading to different cases?
    - Did you consider all possible cases?
    - Does at least one of these cases cause at least one recursive call?
    - Do these recursive calls involve smaller arguments, smaller tasks, or tasks that get closer to the solution?
    - If these recursive calls produce or return correct results, will the method produce or return a correct result?
    - Is at least one of the cases a base case that has no recursive call?
    - Are there enough base cases?
    - Does each base case produce a result that is correct for that case?
    - If the method returns a value, does each of the cases return a value?

EXERCISES

1. Consider the method `displayRowOfCharacters` that displays any given character the specified number of times on one line. For example, the call

    ```
    displayRowOfCharacters('*', 5);
    ```

    produces the line

    *****

    Implement this method in Java by using recursion.

2. Describe a recursive algorithm that draws concentric circles, given the diameter of the outermost circle. The diameter of each inner circle should be three-fourths the diameter of the circle that encloses it. The diameter of the innermost circle should exceed 1 inch.

3. Write a method that asks the user for integer input that is between 1 and 10, inclusive. If the input is out of range, the method should recursively ask the user to enter a new input value.

4. The factorial of a positive integer n — which we denote as $n!$ — is the product of n and the factorial of $n - 1$. The factorial of 0 is 1. Write two different recursive methods that each return the factorial of n.

5. Write a recursive method that writes a given array backward. Consider the last element of the array first.

6. Repeat Exercise 5, but instead consider the first element of the array first.

7. Repeat Exercises 5 and 6, but write a string backward instead of an array.

8. A palindrome is a string that reads the same forward and backward. For example *deed* and *level* are palindromes. Write an algorithm in pseudocode that tests whether a string is a palindrome.

9. Segment 10.37 introduced the Fibonacci sequence. Computing this sequence recursively is inefficient and takes too much time. Write two methods that each compute the nth term in the Fibonacci sequence by using iteration instead of recursion. One method should use an array to store the Fibonacci numbers. The other method should use three variables to contain the current term in the sequence and the two terms before it.

   What is the Big Oh for each of your iterative methods? Compare these results with the performance of the recursive algorithm.

10. For three disks, how many recursive calls are made by each of the two `solveTowers` algorithms given in Segment 10.31?

11. Write a recursive method that counts the number of nodes in a chain of linked nodes.

12. If n is a positive integer in Java, n % 10 is its rightmost digit and n / 10 is the integer obtained by dropping the rightmost digit from n. Using these facts, write a recursive method that displays an integer n in decimal. Now observe that you can display n in any base between 2 and 9 by replacing 10 with the new base. Revise your method to accommodate a given base.

13. Consider the method `contains` of the class `AList`, as given in Segment 5.10 of Chapter 5. Write a private recursive method that `contains` can call, and revise the definition of `contains` accordingly.

14. Repeat Exercise 13, but instead use the class `LList` and the method `contains` in Segment 7.12 of Chapter 7.

15. Write four different recursive methods that each compute the sum of integers in an array of integers. Model your methods after the `displayArray` methods given in Segments 10.15 through 10.18 and described in Question 5.

16. Write a recursive method that returns the smallest integer in an array of integers. If you divide the array into two pieces—halves, for example—and find the smallest integer in each of the two pieces, the smallest integer in the entire array will be the smaller of the these two integers. Since you will be searching a portion of the array—for example, the elements `array[first]` through `array[last]`—it will be convenient for your method to have three parameters: the array and two indices, `first` and `last`. You can refer to the method `displayArray` in Segment 10.18 for inspiration.

17. Trace the call `f(16)` to the following method by showing a stack of activation records:

```java
public int f(int n)
{
  int result = 0;
  if (f <= 4)
    result = 1;
```

```
    else
        result = f(n / 2) + f(n / 4);
    return result;
} // end f
```

18. Write a recursive algorithm in pseudocode that finds the second smallest object in a list of `Comparable` objects.

19. Consider the class `AList`, as given in Chapter 5. Implement the method `equals` for `AList` so that it calls a private recursive method.

20. If

$t(1) = 2$
$t(n) = 1 + t(n - 1)$ for $n > 1$

find an expression for $t(n)$ that is not given in terms of itself. Prove that your result is correct by using induction.

21. If

$t(1) = 1$
$t(n) = 2 * t(n - 1)$ for $n > 1$

find an expression for $t(n)$ that is not given in terms of itself. Prove that your result is correct by using induction.

PROJECTS

1. The following algorithm finds the square root of a positive number:

```
Algorithm squareRoot(number, lowGuess, highGuess, tolerance)
newGuess = (lowGuess + highGuess) / 2
if ((highGuess - newGuess) / newGuess < tolerance)
    return newGuess
else if (newGuess * newGuess > number)
    return squareRoot(number, lowGuess, newGuess, tolerance)
else if (newGuess * newGuess < number)
    return squareRoot(number, newGuess, highGuess, tolerance)
else
    return newGuess
```

To begin the computation, you need a value `lowGuess` that is less than the square root of the number and a value `highGuess` that is larger. You can use zero as `lowGuess` and the number itself as `highGuess`. The parameter `tolerance` controls the precision of the result independently of the magnitude of `number`. For example, computing the square root of 250 with `tolerance` equal to 0.00005 results in 15.81. This result has four digits of accuracy.

Implement this algorithm.

2. Implement the two versions of the `solveTower` algorithm given in Segment 10.31. Represent the towers by either single characters or strings. Each method should display directions that indicate the moves that must be made. Insert counters into each method to count the number of times it is called. These counters can be data fields of the class that

contains these methods. Compare the number of recursive calls made by each method for various numbers of disks.

3. Imagine a list of *n* items from which you can choose. You will place the items you choose into a knapsack of size *k*. Each item has a size and a value. Of course, you cannot take more items than you have space for in the knapsack. Your goal is to maximize the total value of the items you take.

   a. Design a recursive algorithm `maxKnapsack` to solve this knapsack problem. The parameters to the algorithm are the knapsack, the list of items, and the position of the next item to consider. The algorithm chooses the items for the knapsack and returns a knapsack containing the chosen items. A knapsack can report its size, its contents, the value of its contents, and the size of its contents.

   Hint: If all items in the list have not been considered, retrieve the next item in the list. You can either put the item in the knapsack, if it fits, or ignore it. Make a recursive call for each of these two cases. Compare the knapsacks returned by these calls to see which one has the most valuable contents. Then return that knapsack.

   b. Write the classes `Knapsack` and `KnapsackItem`. Then write a program that defines the method `maxKnapsack`. The program should read the size of the knapsack and then the size, value, and name of each available item. Here is some sample input data:

   ```
   10
    1   50000    rare coin
    2    7000    small gold coin
    4   10000    packet of stamps
    4   11000    pearl necklace
    5   12000    silver bar
   10   60000    painting
   ```

   After displaying the available items, call `maxKnapsack`. Then display the chosen items, their values, and their total value.

4. Suppose that you are scheduling a room. You are given a list of activities, each of which has a start time and stop time. Two activities are compatible if they do not overlap. For example, in the following list of activities, activity A is compatible with activities B and D, but not with activity C:

Activity	Start Time	Stop Time
A	1	2
B	2	5
C	1	3
D	5	6

   Your goal is to schedule compatible activities that result in a maximum usage of the room.

   a. Design a recursive algorithm to solve this room-scheduling problem. The method whose signature is

   ```
   maxRoomUse(int startTime, int stopTime,
           ListInterface<Activity> activitiesList)
   ```

returns a pair consisting of the maximum usage in hours and the list of activities scheduled. Note that `startTime` is the first time that an activity can be scheduled, `stopTime` is the final time, and `activitiesList` is a list of possible activities.

   b. Write the class `Activity` and a class `Schedule` that represents the pair that `maxRoomUse` returns. Then write a program that defines the method `maxRoomUse`. The program should read the start time and stop time for the room, followed by the start and stop times for each activity (one activity per line). After displaying the given activities, display the maximum usage in hours of the room, along with a list of the scheduled activities.

5. You can get a solution to the Towers of Hanoi problem by using the following iterative algorithm. Beginning with pole 1 and moving from pole to pole in the order pole 1, pole 3, pole 2, pole 1, and so on, make at most one move per pole according to the following rules:

   ● Move the topmost disk from a pole to the next possible pole in the specified order. Remember that you cannot place a disk on top of a smaller one.
   ● If the disk that you are about to move is the smallest of all the disks and you just moved it to the present pole, do not move it. Instead, consider the next pole.

   This algorithm should make the same moves as the recursive algorithms given in Segment 10.31 and pictured in Figure 10-8. Thus, this iterative algorithm is $O(2^n)$ as well. Implement this algorithm.

6. Write an application or applet that animates the solution to the Towers of Hanoi problem. The problem asks you to move n disks from one pole to another, one at a time. You move only the top disk on a pole, and you place a disk only on top of larger disks on a pole. Since each disk has certain characteristics, such as its size, it is natural to define a class of disks.

   Design and implement an ADT tower that includes the following operations:

   ● Add a disk to the top of the disks on the pole
   ● Remove the topmost disk

   Also, design and implement a class that includes a recursive method to solve the problem.

7. Java's class `Graphics` has the following method to draw a line between two given points:

```
/** Task: Draws a line between the points (x1, y1) and (x2, y2).
 */
public void drawLine(int x1, int y1, int x2, int y2)
```

   `Graphics` uses a coordinate system that measures points from the top left corner of a window.

   Write a recursive method that draws a picture of a 12-inch ruler. Mark inches, half inches, quarter inches, and eighth inches. Mark the half inches with marks that are smaller than those that mark the inches. Mark the quarter inches with marks that are smaller than those that mark the half inches, and so on. Your picture need not be full size. *Hint*: Draw a mark in the middle of the ruler and then draw rulers to the left and right of this mark.

8. Imagine a row of *n* lights that can be turned on or off only under certain conditions, as follows. The first light can be turned on or off anytime. Each of the other lights can be turned on or off only when the preceding light is on and all other lights before it are off. If all the lights are on initially, how can you turn them off? For three lights numbered 1 to 3, you can take the following steps, where 1 is a light that is on and 0 is a light that is off:

1 1 1	All on initially
0 1 1	Turn off light 1
0 1 0	Turn off light 3
1 1 0	Turn on light 1
1 0 0	Turn off light 2
0 0 0	Turn off light 1

You can solve this problem in general by using mutual recursion, as follows:

Algorithm `turnOff(n)`
// Turns off n *lights that are initially on.*
```
if (n == 1)
   Turn off light 1
else
{
   if (n > 2)
      turnOff(n - 2)
   Turn off light n
   if (n > 2)
      turnOn(n - 2)
   turnOff(n - 1)
}
```

Algorithm `turnOn(n)`
// Turns on n *lights that are initially off.*
```
if (n == 1)
   Turn on light 1
else
{
   turnOn(n - 1)
   if (n > 2)
      turnOff(n - 2)
   Turn on light n
   if (n > 2)
      turnOn(n - 2)
}
```

a. Implement these algorithms in Java. Use the results in a program to produce a list of directions to turn off *n* lights that initially are on.
b. What recurrence relation expresses the number of times that lights are switched on or off during the course of solving this problem for *n* lights?

CHAPTER

11

An Introduction to Sorting

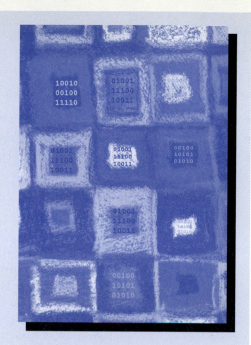

Contents

Prerequisites

OBJECTIVES

After studying this chapter, you should be able to

- Sort an array into ascending order by using the following methods: selection sort, insertion sort, and Shell sort
- Sort a chain of linked nodes into ascending order by using an insertion sort
- Assess the efficiency of a sort and discuss the relative efficiencies of the various methods

We are all familiar with arranging objects in order from smallest to largest or from largest to smallest. Not only do we order numbers this way, but we also can arrange people by height, age, or name; music by title, artist, or album; and so on. Arranging things into either ascending or descending order is called **sorting**. You can sort any collection of items that can be compared with one another. Likewise, in Java you can sort any objects that are `Comparable`—that is, objects of any class that implements the interface `Comparable` and, therefore, defines the method `compareTo`. Exactly how you compare two objects depends on the nature of the objects. For example, you can arrange a row of books on your bookshelf in several ways: by title, by author, by height, by color, and so on. The designer of a class of book objects would choose one of these ways when implementing the method `compareTo`.

Suppose you have a collection of elements that need to be sorted in some way. For example, you might want to arrange a list of numbers from lowest to highest or from highest to lowest, or you might want to create a list of strings in alphabetical order. This chapter discusses and implements a few simple algorithms that sort items into ascending order. That is, our algorithms rearrange the first n entries in a collection so that

entry $1 \leq$ entry $2 \leq \ldots \leq$ entry n

With only small changes to our algorithms, you will be able to sort entries into descending order.

Sorting an array is usually easier than sorting a chain of linked nodes. For this reason, typical sorting algorithms sort an array. In particular, our algorithms will rearrange the first n values in an array a so that

`a[0] ≤ a[1] ≤ a[2] ≤ . . . ≤ a[n - 1]`

However, we also will use one of our algorithms to sort a chain of linked nodes. Thus, we could add a sort method to the ADT list and use one of our algorithms to implement the method.

Sorting is such a common and important task that many sorting algorithms exist. This chapter examines some basic algorithms for sorting data. Although most of our examples will sort integers, the Java implementations given will sort any `Comparable` objects.

The efficiency of a sorting algorithm is significant, particularly when large amounts of data are involved. We will examine the performance of the algorithms in this chapter and find that they are relatively slow. The next chapter will present sorting algorithms that usually are much faster.

Organizing Java Methods That Sort an Array

11.1   One way to organize methods that sort an array is to create a class of static methods that perform the various sorts. The methods define a generic type T for the objects in the array. We use a notation reminiscent of that used for the static method `displayList` in Segment 4.13 of Chapter 4:

public static `<T> void` `displayList(ListInterface<T> list)`

Recall that the list passed to this method can contain objects of any one class.

But we plan to sort an array, not a list, and the objects in that array must be Comparable. Thus, the class that T represents must implement the interface Comparable. To ensure this requirement, we write

<T **extends** Comparable<T>>

instead of simply <T> before the return type in the headers of the sort methods. We then can use T as the data type of the parameters and local variables within the methods. For example, our class could begin as follows:

```
public class SortArray
{
    public static <T extends Comparable<T>> void sort(T[] a, int n)
    { . . .
```

A client could sort an array of 50 objects, for example, by using the statement

SortArray.sort(myArray, 50);

If the objects in myArray are all of type Gadget, the compiler will discover that fact without our help. Gadget, however, must implement Comparable and have a compareTo method.

11.2   **An improvement.** By writing T extends Comparable<T>, we require that Gadget implement the interface Comparable<Gadget>. But insisting that a Gadget object be compared only to another Gadget object is more restrictive than we really need to be. What would happen if we had derived Gadget from Widget, where Widget implements Comparable<Widget>, as Figure 11-1 shows? If gadgets and widgets are similar enough to have the same basis for comparison, Gadget could use the method compareTo it inherits from Widget without defining its own. But then a call to the method sort with an array of gadgets and widgets would not compile.

Figure 11-1   The class Gadget is derived from the class Widget, which implements the interface Comparable

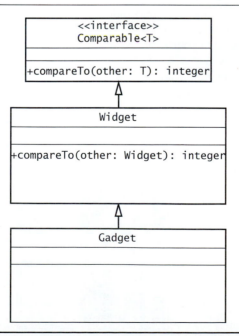

Instead of comparing an object of T only with other objects of T, we can allow comparisons of objects of a superclass of T. So instead of writing T extends Comparable<T>, we write

    T **extends** Comparable<? **super** T>

The **wildcard** ? represents any type, but the notation ? super T means any superclass of T. Thus, the header for the method sort would be

    public static <T **extends** Comparable<? **super** T>> **void** sort(T[] a,
                                      int n)

Programming Tip: To use Comparable with arbitrary types, write Comparable<? super T> instead of Comparable<T>.

Note: Bounded wildcards

When using generic types, the wild card ? represents any class. You can **bound**, or limit, the wildcard in one of two ways. For example, ? super Gizmo means any superclass of Gizmo. We say that Gizmo is the **lower bound** of the wildcard. Analogously, ? extends Gizmo means any subclass of Gizmo. Here, Gizmo is the **upper bound** of the wildcard. Segments 9.17 and 9.23, respectively, provide other meanings for the terms upper bound and lower bound.

We now turn our attention to several ways of sorting an array.

Selection Sort

11.3   Imagine that you want to rearrange the books on your bookshelf by height, with the shortest book on the left. You might begin by tossing all of the books onto the floor. You then could return them to the shelf one by one, in their proper order. If you first return the shortest book to the shelf, and then the next shortest, and so on, you would perform a kind of **selection sort**. But using the floor—or another shelf—to store your books temporarily uses extra space needlessly.

    Instead, approach your intact bookshelf and *select* the shortest book. Since you want it to be first on the shelf, you remove the first book on the shelf and put the shortest book in its place. You still have a book in your hand, so you put it into the space formerly occupied by the shortest book. That is, the shortest book has traded places with the first book, as Figure 11-2 illustrates. You now ignore the shortest book and repeat the process for the rest of the bookshelf.

Figure 11-2   Before and after exchanging the shortest book and the first book

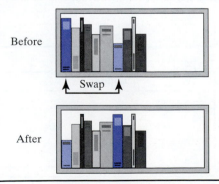

In terms of an array a, the selection sort finds the smallest element in the array and exchanges it with a[0]. Then, ignoring a[0], the sort finds the next smallest element and swaps it with a[1], and so on. Notice that we use only one array. We sort it by making elements trade places with other elements.

We could have copied the array into a second array and then moved the elements back to the original array in their proper order. But that would be like using the floor to store books temporarily. Fortunately, all of that extra space is unnecessary.

11.4   Figure 11-3 shows how a selection sort rearranges an array of integers by interchanging values. Beginning with the original array, the sort locates the smallest value in the array, that is, the 2 in a[3]. The value in a[3] is interchanged with the value in a[0]. After that interchange, the smallest value is in a[0] where it belongs.

The next smallest value is the 5 in a[4]. The sort then interchanges the value in a[4] with the value in a[1]. So far, the values in a[0] and a[1] are the smallest in the array and are in their correct position within the final sorted array. The algorithm then interchanges the next smallest element—the 8—with a[2], and so on until the entire array is sorted.

Figure 11-3   A selection sort of an array of integers into ascending order

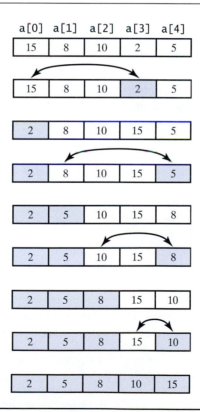

Iterative Selection Sort

11.5   The following pseudocode describes an iterative algorithm for the selection sort:

> *Algorithm* `selectionSort(a, n)`
> *// Sorts the first n elements of an array* `a`*.*
>
> ```
> for (index = 0; index < n - 1; index++)
> {
> ```
>   `indexOfNextSmallest =` *the index of the smallest value among*
>   `a[index], a[index + 1], ..., a[n - 1]`
>   *Interchange the values of* `a[index]` *and* `a[indexOfNextSmallest]`
>   *// Assertion:* $a[0] \le a[1] \le \ldots \le a[index]$*, and these are the smallest*
>   *// of the original array elements. The remaining array elements begin at* `a[index + 1]`*.*
> ```
> }
> ```

Notice that during the last iteration of the `for` loop, the value of `index` is n – 2, even though the last array element is `a[n - 1]`. Once the elements `a[0]` through `a[n - 2]` are in their correct places, only the one element `a[n - 1]` remains to be positioned. But since the other elements are correctly positioned, it must already be in the correct place as well.

Note: **Notation**

In mathematics, one-letter variable names are common. Recognizing this, and seeking to save some space, we use `a` and `n` within the text and pseudocode to represent, respectively, an array and its number of elements. Within Java code elsewhere, we have tried to avoid one-letter identifiers, using them only sparingly. However, the code that you will see in this chapter and the next uses `a` and `n` simply to maintain consistency with the text.

11.6   The class in Listing 11-1 contains the public method `selectionSort` and two private methods that assist in sorting. We can add other sorting methods as we develop them.

It is easy to see that the definition of `selectionSort` is a direct translation of the previous pseudocode into Java code. The method `getIndexOfSmallest` searches the array elements `a[first]` through `a[last]` and returns the index of the smallest among them. The method uses two local variables, `min` and `indexOfMin`. At any point in the search, `min` references the smallest value found so far. That value occurs at `a[indexOfMin]`. At the end of the search, the method returns `indexOfMin`. Notice that for our purposes here, we could have assumed that `last` is always n – 1 and omitted it as a parameter. However, this general version will be useful in other settings.

Since exchanging elements in an array does not involve the method `compareTo`, the method `swap` can simply use `Object` as the type of these elements.

Listing 11-1   A class for sorting an array using selection sort

```
/***********************************************************************
 * Class for sorting an array of Comparable objects from smallest to
 * largest.
 ***********************************************************************/
public class SortArray
{
   /** Task: Sorts the first n objects in an array into ascending order.
    *  @param a  an array of Comparable objects
    *  @param n  an integer > 0 */
   public static <T extends Comparable<? super T>>
         void selectionSort(T[] a, int n)
   {
```

```
      for (int index = 0; index < n - 1; index++)
      {
         int indexOfNextSmallest = getIndexOfSmallest(a, index, n - 1);
         swap(a, index, indexOfNextSmallest);
         // Assertion: a[0] <= a[1] <= . . . <= a[index] <= all other a[i]
      } // end for
   } // end selectionSort

   /** Task: Finds the index of the smallest value in a portion of an
    *        array.
    *   @param a       an array of Comparable objects
    *   @param first   an integer >= 0 and < a.length that is the index of
    *                  the first array element to consider
    *   @param last    an integer >= first and < a.length that is the index
    *                  of the last array element to consider
    *   @return the index of the smallest value among
    *           a[first], a[first + 1], . . . , a[last] */
   private static <T extends Comparable<? super T>>
           int getIndexOfSmallest(T[] a, int first, int last)
   {
      T min = a[first];
      int indexOfMin = first;
      for (int index = first + 1; index <= last; index++)
      {
         if (a[index].compareTo(min) < 0)
         {
            min = a[index];
            indexOfMin = index;
            // Assertion: min is the smallest of a[first] through a[index].
         } // end if
      } // end for

      return indexOfMin;
   } // end getIndexOfSmallest

   /** Task: Swaps the array elements a[i] and a[j].
    *   @param a   an array of objects
    *   @param i   an integer >= 0 and < a.length
    *   @param j   an integer >= 0 and < a.length */
   private static void swap(Object[] a, int i, int j)
   {
      Object temp = a[i];
      a[i] = a[j];
      a[j] = temp;
   } // end swap
} // end SortArray
```

Question 1   Trace the steps that a selection sort takes when sorting the following array into ascending order: 9 6 2 4 8.

Recursive Selection Sort

11.7   Selection sort also has a natural recursive form. Often recursive algorithms that involve arrays operate on a portion of the array. Such algorithms use two parameters, `first` and `last`, to designate the portion of the array composed of the elements `a[first]` through `a[last]`. The method `getIndexOfSmallest` in Listing 11-1 illustrates this technique. The recursive selection sort algorithm uses this notation as well:

> *Algorithm* `selectionSort(a, first, last)`
> *// Sorts the array elements* `a[first]` *through* `a[last]` *recursively.*
>
> ```
> if (first < last)
> {
>    indexOfNextSmallest = the index of the smallest value among
>                          a[first], a[first + 1], . . . , a[last]
>    Interchange the values of a[first] and a[indexOfNextSmallest]
>    // Assertion: a[0] ≤ a[1] ≤ . . . ≤ a[first] and these are the smallest
>    // of the original array elements. The remaining array elements begin at a[first + 1].
>    selectionSort(a, first + 1, last)
> }
> ```

After we place the smallest element into the first position of the array, we ignore it and sort the rest of the array by using a selection sort. If the array has only one element, sorting is unnecessary. In this case, `first` and `last` are equal, so the algorithm leaves the array unchanged.

11.8   When we implement the previous recursive algorithm in Java, the resulting method will have `first` and `last` as parameters. Thus, its header will differ from the header of the iterative method `selectionSort` given in Segment 11.6. We could, however, provide the following method to simply invoke the recursive method:

```
public static <T extends Comparable<? super T>>
       void selectionSort(T[] a, int n)
{
   selectionSort(a, 0, n - 1); // invoke recursive method
} // end selectionSort
```

Whether you make the recursive method `selectionSort` private or public is up to you, but making it public provides the client with a choice of two ways in which to invoke the sort. In a similar fashion, you could revise the iterative selection sort given in Segment 11.6 to use the parameters `first` and `last` (see Exercise 6) and then provide the method just given to invoke it.

With these observations in mind, we will make the subsequent sorting algorithms more general by giving them three parameters—`a`, `first`, and `last`—so that they sort the elements `a[first]` through `a[last]`.

The Efficiency of Selection Sort

11.9   In the iterative method `selectionSort`, the `for` loop executes $n - 1$ times, so it invokes the methods `getIndexOfSmallest` and `swap` $n - 1$ times each. In the $n - 1$ calls to `getIndexOfSmallest`, `last` is $n - 1$ and `first` ranges from 0 to $n - 2$. Each time `getIndexOfSmallest` is invoked, its loop executes `last - first` times. Thus, this loop executes a total of

$$(n - 1) + (n - 2) + \ldots + 1$$

times. This sum is $n(n - 1)/2$. Since the operations in the loop are $O(1)$, the selection sort is $O(n^2)$. Notice that our discussion does not depend on the nature of the data in the array. It could be wildly out of order, nearly sorted, or completely sorted; in any case, selection sort would be $O(n^2)$.

The recursive selection sort performs the same operations as the iterative selection sort, and so it is also O(n^2).

Note: **The time efficiency of selection sort**

Selection sort is O(n^2) regardless of the initial order of the elements in an array.

Insertion Sort

11.10   Another intuitive sorting algorithm is the **insertion sort**. Suppose again that you want to rearrange the books on your bookshelf by height, with the shortest book on the left. If the leftmost book on the shelf were the only book, your shelf would be sorted. But you also have all the other books to sort. Consider the second book. If it is taller than the first book, you now have two sorted books. If not, you remove the second book, slide the first book to the right, and *insert* the book you just removed into the first position on the shelf. The first two books are now sorted.

Now consider the third book. If it is taller than the second book, you now have three sorted books. If not, remove the third book and slide the second book to the right, as Parts *a* through *c* of Figure 11-4 illustrate. Now see whether the book in your hand is taller than the first book. If so, insert the book into the second position on the shelf, as shown in Figure 11-4d. If not, slide the first book to the right, and insert the book in your hand into the first position on the shelf. If you repeat this process for each of the remaining books, your bookshelf will be arranged by the heights of the books.

Figure 11-4   The placement of the third book during an insertion sort

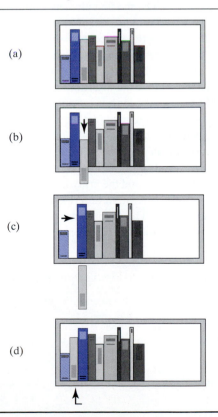

Figure 11-5 shows the bookshelf after several steps of the insertion sort. The books on the left side of the shelf are sorted. You remove the next unsorted book from the shelf and slide sorted books to the right, one at a time, until you find the right place for the book in your hand. You then insert this book into its new sorted location.

Figure 11-5   An insertion sort of books

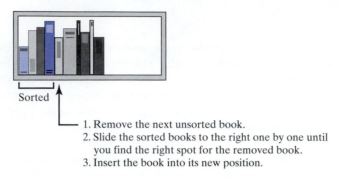

Sorted

1. Remove the next unsorted book.
2. Slide the sorted books to the right one by one until you find the right spot for the removed book.
3. Insert the book into its new position.

Iterative Insertion Sort

11.11   An insertion sort of an array **partitions**—that is, divides—the array into two parts. One part is sorted and initially contains just the first element in the array. The second part contains the remaining elements. The algorithm removes the first element from the unsorted part and inserts it into its proper sorted position within the sorted part. Just as you did with the bookshelf, you choose the proper position by comparing the unsorted element with the sorted elements, beginning at the end of the sorted part and continuing toward its beginning. As you compare, you shift array elements in the sorted part to make room for the insertion.

Figure 11-6 illustrates these steps for a sort that has already positioned the first three elements of the array. The 3 is the next element that must be placed into its proper position within the sorted region. Since 3 is less than 8 and 5 but greater than 2, the 8 and 5 are shifted to make room for the 3.

Figure 11-7 illustrates an entire insertion sort of an array of integers. At each pass of the algorithm, the sorted part expands by one element as the unsorted part shrinks by one element. Eventually, the unsorted part is empty and the array is sorted.

The following iterative algorithm describes an insertion sort of the elements at indices `first` through `last` of the array a. The loop in the algorithm processes the unsorted part and invokes another method—`insertInOrder`—to perform the insertions.

Algorithm **insertionSort(a, first, last)**
// Sorts the array elements a[first] *through* a[last] *iteratively.*

```
for (unsorted = first + 1 through last)
{
    firstUnsorted = a[unsorted]
    insertInOrder(firstUnsorted, a, first, unsorted - 1)
}
```

Algorithm **insertInOrder(element, a, begin, end)**
// Inserts element *into the sorted array elements* a[begin] *through* a[end]*.*

```
index = end
while ( (index >= begin) and (element < a[index]) )
{
  a[index + 1] = a[index] // make room
  index--
}
// Assertion: a[index + 1] is available.
a[index + 1] = element     // insert
```

Figure 11-6   Inserting the next unsorted element into its proper location within the sorted portion of an array during an insertion sort

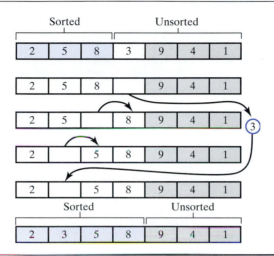

Figure 11-7   An insertion sort of an array of integers into ascending order

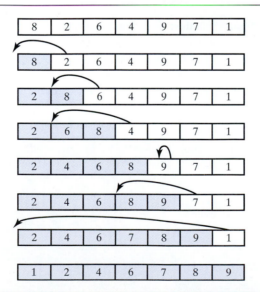

?   **Question 2**   Trace the steps that an insertion sort takes when sorting the following array into ascending order: 9 6 2 4 8.

Recursive Insertion Sort

11.12   You can describe an insertion sort recursively as follows. If you sort all but the last item in the array—a smaller problem than sorting the entire array—you then can insert the last item into its proper position within the rest of the array. The following pseudocode describes a recursive insertion sort:

Algorithm `insertionSort(a, first, last)`
// Sorts the array elements `a[first]` *through* `a[last]` *recursively.*

if *(the array contains more than one element)*
{
   Sort the array elements `a[first]` *through* `a[last - 1]`
   Insert the last element `a[last]` *into its correct sorted position within the rest of*
     the array
}

We can implement this algorithm in Java as follows:

```java
public static <T extends Comparable<? super T>>
        void insertionSort(T[] a, int first, int last)
{
  if (first < last)
  {
    // sort all but the last element
    insertionSort(a, first, last - 1);

    // insert the last element in sorted order
    insertInOrder(a[last], a, first, last - 1);
  } // end if
} // end insertionSort
```

11.13   **The algorithm** `insertInOrder`: **first draft.** The previous method can call the iterative version of `insertInOrder`, given earlier, or the recursive version that we now describe. If the element to insert is greater than or equal to the last item in the sorted portion of the array, the element belongs immediately after this last item, as Figure 11-8a illustrates. Otherwise, we move the last sorted item to the next higher position in the array and insert the element into the remaining portion, as shown in Figure 11-8b.
   We can describe these steps more carefully as follows:

Algorithm `insertInOrder(element, a, begin, end)`
// Inserts `element` *into the sorted array elements* `a[begin]` *through* `a[end]`.
// First draft.

```
if (element >= a[end])
  a[end + 1] = element
else
{
  a[end + 1] = a[end]
  insertInOrder(element, a, begin, end - 1)
}
```

Figure 11-8   Inserting the first unsorted element into the sorted portion of the array. (a) The element is greater than or equal to the last sorted element; (b) the element is smaller than the last sorted element

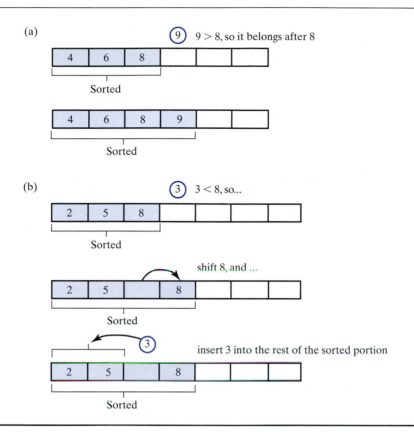

11.14   **The algorithm `insertInOrder`: final draft.** This algorithm is not quite right. The `else` clause will work only if we have more than one element in the remaining portion of the array—that is, if `begin` < `end`. If `begin` and `end` were equal, for example, the recursive call would be equivalent to

```
insertInOrder(element, a, begin, begin - 1);
```

which is incorrect.

Will `end` ever equal `begin`, if they were not equal initially? Yes. When `element` is less than all elements a[begin], ..., a[end], each recursive call decreases `end` by 1 until eventually `end` equals `begin`. What should we do when this happens? Since the sorted portion consists of one element a[end], we will move a[end] to the next higher position and place `element` in a[end].

The following revised algorithm reflects these changes:

Algorithm `insertInOrder(element, a, begin, end)`
// Inserts `element` into the sorted array elements a[begin] through a[end].
// Revised draft.

```
if (element >= a[end])
    a[end + 1] = element
```

```
   else if (begin < end)
   {
      a[end + 1] = a[end]
      insertInOrder(element, a, begin, end - 1)
   }
   else // begin == end and element < a[end]
   {
      a[end + 1] = a[end]
      a[end] = element
   }
```

The Efficiency of Insertion Sort

11.15   Look back at the iterative algorithm `insertionSort` given in Segment 11.11. For an array of n elements, `first` is 0 and `last` is $n - 1$. The for loop then executes $n - 1$ times, and so the method `insertInOrder` is invoked $n - 1$ times. Thus, within `insertInOrder`, `begin` is 0 and `end` ranges from 0 to $n - 2$. The loop within `insertInOrder` executes at most `end - begin + 1` times each time the method is invoked. Thus, this loop executes at most a total of

$$1 + 2 + \ldots + (n - 1)$$

times. This sum is $n (n - 1)/2$, so the insertion sort is $O(n^2)$. The recursive insertion sort performs the same operations as the iterative insertion sort, so it is also $O(n^2)$.

This analysis provides a worst-case scenario. In the best case, the loop in `insertInOrder` would exit immediately. Such is the case if the array is sorted already. In the best case, then, insertion sort is $O(n)$. In general, the more sorted an array is, the less work `insertInOrder` needs to do. This fact and its relatively simple implementation make the insertion sort popular for applications in which the array does not change much. For example, some customer databases add only a small percentage of new customers each day.

The next chapter will use the insertion sort when the array size is small.

Note: The time efficiency of insertion sort

Insertion sort is at best $O(n)$ and at worst $O(n^2)$. The closer an array is to sorted order, the less work an insertion sort does.

Insertion Sort of a Chain of Linked Nodes

11.16   Usually you will sort arrays, but sometimes you might need to sort a chain of linked nodes. When you do, the insertion sort is one that is easy to understand.

Figure 11-9 shows a chain whose nodes contain integers that are sorted into ascending order. To begin to see how we can construct an insertion sort for this chain, imagine that we want to insert a node into this chain so that the integers in the nodes remain in sorted order.

Figure 11-9   A chain of integers sorted into ascending order

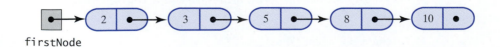

Suppose that the node to be inserted into the chain contains the integer 6. We need to locate where in the chain the new node belongs. If we adapt the algorithm `insertInOrder` given in Segment 11.11, we would begin at the end of the chain and compare 6 with the integer 10. Since 6 belongs before 10, we would then compare 6 with 8. Since 6 belongs before 8, we compare 6 with 5 and discover that 6 belongs between 5 and 8. Can we use the same approach here? We *could*, but we would need to traverse the entire chain to reach the last node. Having a tail reference would not help, because once we've looked at the last node, we then need to look at the next-to-last node. But we cannot locate that node knowing just the last node. We would need to traverse the chain again and stop just before the last node.

A better way is to start at the beginning of the chain and make comparisons as we move toward the end of the chain until we find the correct insertion point. Thus, we would compare 6 with 2, then with 3, with 5, and finally with 8 to see that 6 belongs between 5 and 8. As we saw in Chapter 6, to insert a node into a chain, we need a reference to the node prior to the point of insertion. Thus, during the traversal of the chain, we save a reference to the node before the current one, as Figure 11-10 illustrates. Also remember that inserting at the beginning of the chain differs somewhat from inserting anywhere else in the chain.

Figure 11-10 During the traversal of a chain to locate the insertion point, save a reference to the node before the current one

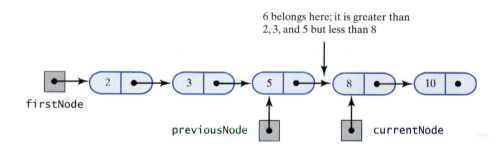

11.17   Imagine that we plan to add a sort method to a class `LinkedChainList` that implements the ADT list. As sorting requires us to compare the objects in the list, they must belong to a class that implements the interface `Comparable`. Thus, the class definition begins as follows:

```
public class LinkedChainList<T extends Comparable<? super T>>
        implements ListInterface<T>
{
   private Node firstNode;
   int length;
   . . .
```

assuming that we add the declaration of the sort method to `ListInterface`.

This class has an inner class `Node` that has set and get methods for its private data fields. The following private method inserts the node that `nodeToInsert` references into the sorted chain that `firstNode` references.

```
private void insertInOrder(Node nodeToInsert)
{
   T item = nodeToInsert.getData();
```

```
            Node currentNode = firstNode;
            Node previousNode = null;

            // locate insertion point
            while ( (currentNode != null) &&
                    (item.compareTo(currentNode.getData()) > 0) )
            {
              previousNode = currentNode;
              currentNode = currentNode.getNextNode();
            } // end while

            // make the insertion
            if (previousNode != null)
            { // insert between previousNode and currentNode
              previousNode.setNextNode(nodeToInsert);
              nodeToInsert.setNextNode(currentNode);
            }
            else // insert at beginning
            {
              nodeToInsert.setNextNode(firstNode);
              firstNode = nodeToInsert;
            } // end if
          } // end insertInOrder
```

The local variable item is the data portion of the node to be inserted. The while loop compares item to the data in each node in the chain until either item is less than or equal to a data value or the end of the chain is reached. The references previousNode and currentNode are then used to insert the given node into its proper position.

11.18   Now that the hard part is done, we can use this method to implement an insertion sort. We can use the same strategy that we used to sort an array: Divide the chain into two parts. The first part is sorted, and it initially contains only the first node. The second part is unsorted and initially is the rest of the chain. Of course, we cannot divide a chain of only one node into two pieces, but such a chain is already sorted!

Figure 11-11 illustrates how to make this division. We first make the variable unsortedPart reference the second node and then set the link portion of the first node to null. To sort the nodes,

Figure 11-11   Breaking a chain of nodes into two pieces as the first step in an insertion sort:
(a) the original chain; (b) the two pieces

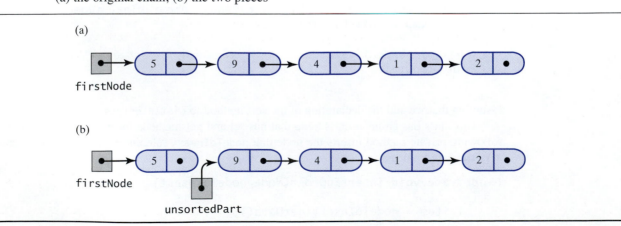

we use the method `insertInOrder` to take each node from the unsorted part and insert it into the sorted part. Notice that our plan relinks existing nodes instead of creating new ones.

The method to perform the insertion sort appears as follows. We assume that `length` is a data field that contains the number of items currently in the list. Thus, `length` is the number of nodes in the chain. The local variable `unsortedPart` starts at the second node and then references each node in the rest of the chain as the loop executes. Each of these nodes is inserted in turn into the sorted part of the chain.

```java
public void insertionSort()
{
  // if zero or one item is in the list, there is nothing to do
  if (length > 1)
  {
    assert firstNode != null;

    // break chain into 2 pieces: sorted and unsorted
    Node unsortedPart = firstNode.getNextNode();
    assert unsortedPart != null;
    firstNode.setNextNode(null);

    while (unsortedPart != null)
    {
      Node nodeToInsert = unsortedPart;
      unsortedPart = unsortedPart.getNextNode();
      insertInOrder(nodeToInsert);
    } // end while
  } // end if
} // end insertionSort
```

Question 3   In the previous method `insertionSort`, if you move the line

```java
unsortedPart = unsortedPart.getNextNode();
```

after the call to `insertInOrder`, will the method still work? Explain.

Question 4   The previous method `insertionSort` is not a static method. Why?

11.19   **The efficiency of an insertion sort of a chain.** For a chain of n nodes, the number of comparisons that the method `insertInOrder` makes is at most the number of nodes in the sorted portion of the chain. The method `insertionSort` calls `insertInOrder` $n - 1$ times. The first time it does so, the sorted portion contains one item, so one comparison is made. The second time, the sorted portion contains two items, so at most two comparisons are made. Continuing in this fashion, you can see that the maximum number of comparisons is

$$1 + 2 + \ldots + (n - 1)$$

This sum is $n(n - 1)/2$, so this insertion sort is $O(n^2)$.

Note: Sorting a chain of linked nodes can be difficult. The insertion sort, however, provides a reasonable way to perform this task.

Shell Sort

11.20   The sorting algorithms that we have discussed so far are simple and often useful, but they are too inefficient to use on large arrays. The Shell sort is a variation of the insertion sort that is faster than O(n^2).

   During an insertion sort, an array element moves to an adjacent location. When an element is far from its correct sorted position, it must make many such moves. So when an array is completely scrambled, an insertion sort takes a good deal of time. But when an array is almost sorted, an insertion sort is more efficient. In fact, Segment 11.15 showed that the more sorted an array is, the less work the method `insertInOrder` needs to do.

   By capitalizing on these observations, Donald Shell devised in 1959 an improved insertion sort, now called the **Shell sort**. Shell wanted elements to move beyond their adjacent locations. To do so, he sorted subarrays of elements at equally spaced indices. Instead of moving to an adjacent location, an element moves several locations away. The result is an array that is almost sorted—one that can be sorted efficiently by using an ordinary insertion sort.

11.21   For example, Figure 11-12 shows an array and the subarrays obtained by considering every sixth element. The first subarray contains the integers 10, 9, and 7; the second subarray contains 16 and 6; and so on. There happen to be six of these subarrays.

   Now we sort each of the six subarrays separately by using an insertion sort. Figure 11-13 shows the sorted subarrays and the state of the original array as a result. Notice that the array is "more sorted" than it was originally.

Figure 11-12   An array and the subarrays formed by grouping elements whose indices are 6 apart

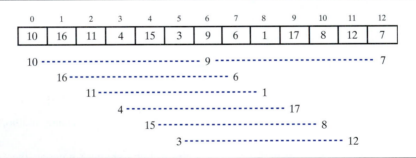

Figure 11-13   The subarrays of Figure 11-12 after each is sorted, and the array that contains them

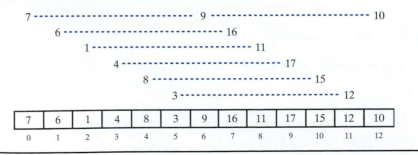

11.22   Now we form new subarrays, but this time we reduce the separation between indices. Shell suggested that the initial separation between indices be *n*/2 and that you halve this value at each pass until it is 1. The array in our example has 13 elements, so we began with a separation of 6. We now reduce the separation to 3. Figure 11-14 shows the resulting subarrays, and Figure 11-15 shows the subarrays after they are sorted.

Figure 11-14   The subarrays of the array in Figure 11-13 formed by grouping elements whose indices are 3 apart

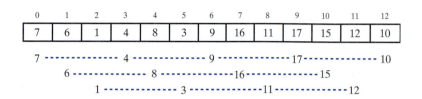

Figure 11-15   The subarrays of Figure 11-14 after each is sorted, and the array that contains them

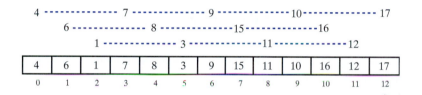

Dividing the current separation, 3, by 2 results in 1. Therefore, the final step is simply an ordinary insertion sort of the entire array. This last step will sort the array regardless of what we have done to it beforehand. Thus, Shell sort will work if you use any sequence of index separations, as long as the last one is 1. But not just any sequence will make the Shell sort efficient, as you will see in Segment 11.24.

Question 5   Apply the Shell sort to the array 9 8 2 7 5 4 6 3 1, with index separations of 4, 2, and 1. What are the intermediate steps?

The Java Code

11.23   The heart of the Shell sort is the adaptation of the insertion sort to work on a subarray of equally spaced elements. By combining and modifying the two algorithms that describe the insertion sort, as given in Segment 11.11, we obtain the following method that sorts array elements whose indices are separated by an increment of space.

```
/** Task: Sorts equally spaced elements of an array into
 *        ascending order.
 *  @param a      an array of Comparable objects
 *  @param first  the integer index of the first array element to
 *                consider; first >= 0 and < a.length
```

```
 *   @param last    the integer index of the last array element to
 *                  consider; last >= first and < a.length
 *   @param space   the difference between the indices of the
 *                  elements to sort */
private static <T extends Comparable<? super T>>
       void incrementalInsertionSort(T[] a, int first, int last,
                                     int space)
{
   int unsorted, index;

   for (unsorted = first + space; unsorted <= last;
        unsorted = unsorted + space)
   {
      T firstUnsorted = a[unsorted];

      for (index = unsorted - space; (index >= first) &&
                   (firstUnsorted.compareTo(a[index]) < 0);
                   index = index - space)
      {
         a[index + space] = a[index];
      } // end for

      a[index + space] = firstUnsorted;
   } // end for
} // end incrementalInsertionSort
```

A method to perform a Shell sort will invoke `incrementalInsertionSort` and supply any sequence of spacing factors. For example, we might write the following method, using the spacing that Segment 11.22 described:

```
public static <T extends Comparable<? super T>>
       void shellSort(T[] a, int first, int last)
{
   int n = last - first + 1; // number of array elements

   for (int space = n / 2; space > 0; space = space / 2)
   {
      for (int begin = first; begin < first + space; begin++)
         incrementalInsertionSort(a, begin, last, space);
   } // end for
} // end shellSort
```

Question 6   Trace the steps that a Shell sort takes when sorting the following array into ascending order: 9 6 2 4 8 7 5 3.

The Efficiency of Shell Sort

11.24   Since the Shell sort uses an insertion sort repeatedly, it certainly seems like much more work than using only one insertion sort. Actually, however, it is not. Although we used an insertion sort several times instead of just once, the initial sorts are of arrays that are much smaller than the original one, the later sorts are on arrays that are partially sorted, and the final sort is on an array that is almost entirely sorted. Intuitively, this seems good. But even though the Shell sort is not very complicated, its analysis is.

Since `incrementalInsertionSort` involves a loop and is called from within nested loops, the Shell sort uses three nested loops. Often such algorithms are $O(n^3)$, but it turns out that the worst-case behavior of the Shell sort is still $O(n^2)$. If n is a power of 2, the average-case behavior is $O(n^{1.5})$. And if you tweak the spacing a bit, you can make the Shell sort even more efficient.

One improvement is to avoid even values of `space`. Figure 11-12 provided an example of the subarrays when `space` was 6. The first subarray contained 10, 9, and 7, for instance. Later, after we halved `space`, the first subarrray contained 7, 4, 9, 17, and 10, as Figure 11-14 shows. Notice that these two subarrays have elements in common, namely the 10, 9, and 7. Thus, the comparisons that you make when `space` is even will be repeated on the next pass when the increment is `space/2`.

To avoid this inefficiency, simply add 1 to `space` whenever it is even. This simple change results in consecutive increments that have no factor in common. The worst-case behavior of the Shell sort is then $O(n^{1.5})$. Other sequences for `space` result in even greater efficiencies, although the proof that this is the case remains elusive. An improved Shell sort can be a reasonable choice for moderately large arrays.

Note: The time efficiency of Shell sort

The Shell sort, as implemented in this chapter, is $O(n^2)$ in the worst case. By adding 1 to `space` anytime that it is even, you can improve the worst-case behavior to $O(n^{1.5})$.

Comparing the Algorithms

11.25   Figure 11-16 summarizes the time efficiencies of the three sorting algorithms presented in this chapter. Generally, the selection sort is the slowest algorithm. The Shell sort, by capitalizing on the best-case behavior of the insertion sort, is the fastest.

Figure 11-16 The time efficiencies of three sorting algorithms, expressed in Big Oh notation

	Best Case	Average Case	Worst Case
Selection sort	$O(n^2)$	$O(n^2)$	$O(n^2)$
Insertion sort	$O(n)$	$O(n^2)$	$O(n^2)$
Shell sort	$O(n)$	$O(n^{1.5})$	$O(n^2)$ or $O(n^{1.5})$

CHAPTER SUMMARY

- A selection sort of an array selects the smallest element and swaps it with the first one. Ignoring the new first element, the sort then finds the smallest element in the rest of the array and swaps it with the second element, and so on.

- Typically, you perform a selection sort iteratively, although a simple recursive form is possible.

- A selection sort is $O(n^2)$ in all cases.

- An insertion sort divides an array into two portions, sorted and unsorted. Initially, the array's first element is in the sorted portion. The sort takes the next unsorted element and compares it with elements in the sorted portion. As the comparisons continue, each sorted element is shifted by one position toward the end of the array until the unsorted element's correct position is located. The sort then inserts the element into its correct position, which has been vacated by the shifts.

- You can perform an insertion sort either iteratively or recursively.

- An insertion sort is $O(n^2)$ in the worst case but is $O(n)$ in the best case. The more sorted an array is, the less work an insertion sort does.

- You can use an insertion sort to sort a chain of linked nodes, a task that typically is difficult.

- The Shell sort is a modification of the insertion sort that sorts subarrays of elements that are equally spaced within the array. The strategy efficiently arranges the array so that it is almost sorted, enabling an ordinary insertion sort to quickly finish the job.

- The worst-case behavior of Shell sort, as implemented in this chapter, is $O(n^2)$. With a simple change, its worst-case behavior can be improved to at least $O(n^{1.5})$.

PROGRAMMING TIP

- To use `Comparable` with arbitrary types, write `Comparable<? super T>` instead of `Comparable<T>`

EXERCISES

1. Sort by hand the array of integers 5 7 4 9 8 5 6 3 into ascending order by using a selection sort. Show the contents of the array each time the sort changes it.

2. Repeat Exercise 1, but use an insertion sort instead.

3. Repeat Exercise 1, but use a Shell sort instead.

4. Revise the selection sort algorithm so that it selects the largest, instead of the smallest, element in the array and sorts the array into descending order.

   a. Using the revised algorithm, repeat Exercise 1.
   b. Revise the iterative method `selectionSort`, as given in Segment 11.6, so that it implements the revised algorithm.

5. Repeat Exercise 4, but this time sort the array into ascending order.

6. Revise the iterative method `selectionSort`, as given in Segment 11.6, so that it has `first` and `last` as parameters instead of n.

7. Consider a revised selection sort algorithm so that on each pass it finds both the largest and smallest values in the unsorted portion of the array. The sort then moves each of these values into its correct location by swapping array elements.

   a. How many comparisons are necessary to sort n values?
   b. Is the answer to Part a greater than, less than, or equal to the number of comparisons required by the original version of selection sort?

8. A **bubble sort** can sort an array of *n* elements into ascending order by making $n - 1$ passes through the array. On each pass, it compares adjacent elements and swaps them if they are out of order. For example, on the first pass, it compares the first and second elements, then the second and third elements, and so on. At the end of the first pass, the largest element is in its proper position at the end of the array. We say that it has bubbled to its correct spot. Each subsequent pass ignores the elements at the end of the array, since they are sorted and are larger than any of the remaining elements. Thus, each pass makes one fewer comparison than the previous pass. Figure 11-17 gives an example of a bubble sort.

   Implement the bubble sort

   a. Iteratively
   b. Recursively

Figure 11-17   A bubble sort of an array (see Exercise 8)

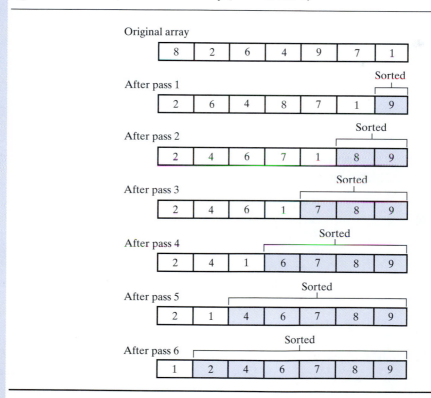

9. How does the efficiency of the bubble sort compare to the other sorting algorithms in this chapter?

10. The bubble sort in Exercise 8 always makes *n* passes. However, it is possible for the array to become sorted before all *n* passes are complete. For example, a bubble sort of the array

   9 2 1 6 4 7 8

is sorted after only two passes:

2 1 6 4 7 8 9 (end of pass 1)
1 2 4 6 7 8 9 (end of pass 2)

But since a swap occurred during the second pass, the sort needs to make one more pass to check that the array is in order. Additional passes, such as the ones that the algorithm in Exercise 8 would make, are unnecessary.

You can skip these unnecessary passes and even do less work by remembering where the last swap occurred. During the first pass, the last swap is of the 9 and 8. The second pass checks up to the 8. But during the second pass, the last swap is of the 6 and 4. You now know that 6, 7, 8, and 9 are sorted. The third pass needs only to check up to the 4, instead of the 7, as an ordinary bubble sort would do. No swaps occur during the third pass, so the index of the last swap during this pass is taken as zero, indicating that no further passes are necessary. Implement this revised bubble sort.

11. Devise an algorithm that detects whether a given array is sorted into ascending order. Write a Java method that implements your algorithm. You can use your method to test whether a sort method has executed correctly.

12. Imagine wanting to perform a selection sort on a list.

   a. What private methods would you need?
   b. Implement a method to perform a selection sort on a list.
   c. Using Big Oh notation, what is the time efficiency of your method?

13. Which recursive algorithms in this chapter are tail recursive?

14. As Segment 11.24 suggests, you can improve the efficiency of the Shell sort by adding 1 to space any time it is even.

   a. By looking at several examples, convince yourself that consecutive increments do not have a common factor.
   b. Subtracting 1 from space any time that it is even does not produce consecutive increments without common factors. Find an example of n that demonstrates this phenomenon.
   c. Revise the implementation of the Shell sort given in Segment 11.23 so that space is not even.

15. Suppose you want to find the largest element in an unsorted array of n elements. Algorithm A searches the entire array sequentially and records the largest element seen so far. Algorithm B sorts the array into descending order and then reports the first element as the largest. Compare the time efficiency of the two approaches.

16. Consider a class `Student` that has private data fields for name, class rank, identification number, and grade point average. Imagine an array of `Student` objects that you want to sort according to any one of the previously listed fields.

   a. What difficulty will you encounter in implementing such a sort?

   b. One solution to this problem defines a new class for each criterion for sorting. Each of these classes encapsulates a `Student` object. In this way, you can use the sorting methods given in this chapter. Provide the details necessary for another programmer to implement this solution.

   c. Another solution to this problem changes the signature and definition of the sorting method. One parameter of the method is an object that can compare two `Student` objects according to a certain criterion. This parameter belongs to one of several new classes that correspond to the sorting criteria. Provide the details necessary for another programmer to implement this solution.

17. Consider a class `Person` that has a string `phoneNumber` as a private data field. Phone numbers have an optional area code, but are written with dashes. For example, two possible phone numbers are 443-555-1232 and 555-0009. Write a method `compareTo` for `Person` that enables an array of `Person` objects to be sorted by phone number.

PROJECTS

1. Graphical demonstrations of various sorting algorithms are instructive, as they provide insight into how an algorithm behaves. Consider a collection of vertical lines of varying lengths, such as the ones in Figure 11-18a. Create a sorting demonstration that sorts the lines by length, as shown in Figure 11-18b. You should draw the configuration of lines after every swap or move that a given sorting algorithm makes. If you delay execution very briefly after each redraw, the result will be an animation of the sort.

   You could begin by drawing 256 lines, each one pixel wide but of different lengths—and perhaps different colors—arranged from shortest to longest so that they appear as a triangle. The user then should exercise an option to scramble the lines. At a user signal, your sorting algorithm should sort the lines.

   You can provide individual demonstrations, perhaps as applets, for each sort algorithm. Or you can include all the algorithms in one program that asks the user to choose an algorithm. Each sort should start with the same scrambled lines so the user can compare methods. You might also choose a sort algorithm at random and see whether the user can guess which one it is.

Figure 11-18   An animated sorting demonstration that sorts vertical lines
(a) before its execution; (b) after its execution

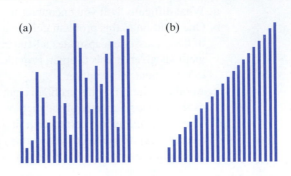

2. Revise the implementations of the insertion sort and the Shell sort so that they count the number of comparisons made during a sort. Use your implementations to compare the two sorts on various arrays of random Integer objects. Also, compare the Shell sort as implemented in Segment 11.23 with a revised Shell sort that adds 1 to space any time it is even.

3. Complete the implementations of the sorting algorithms given in this chapter. Use your implementations to compare the run times of the sorts on various arrays of random Integer objects. See the projects at the end of Chapter 9 for a description of how to time a block of Java code.

4. Consider an *n* by *n* array of integer values.

   a. Write an algorithm to sort the rows of the array by their first value.
   b. Using Big Oh notation, describe the efficiency of your algorithm.
   c. Implement your algorithm.

5. Suppose that you want to perform a Shell sort on a linked chain.

   a. Revise the method incrementalInsertionSort to work with a linked chain instead of an array.
   b. Compare the performance of incrementalInsertionSort on an array with its performance on a linked chain.
   c. Using the revised method, implement a Shell sort for a linked chain.
   d. Find the run time required to sort *n* values in a linked chain for different values of *n*. (See the projects at the end of Chapter 9 for a description of how to time a block of Java code.) Graph the run time versus *n*.
   e. Assuming that the performance of your sort is $O(n^k)$, make an estimate for the value of *k*.

CHAPTER

12

Faster Sorting Methods

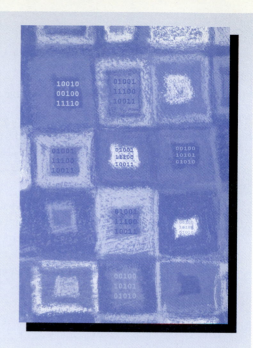

CONTENTS

PREREQUISITES

OBJECTIVES

After studying this chapter, you should be able to

- Sort an array into ascending order by using the following methods: merge sort, quick sort, and radix sort
- Assess the efficiency of a sort and discuss the relative efficiencies of the various methods

The sorting methods that you saw in the previous chapter often are sufficient when you want to sort small arrays. They even can be a reasonable choice if you need to sort a larger array once. Additionally, the insertion sort is a good way to sort a chain of linked nodes. However, when you need to sort very large arrays frequently, those methods take too much time. This chapter presents sorting algorithms that are much faster in general than the methods in Chapter 11.

Merge Sort

12.1 The **merge sort** divides an array into halves, sorts the two halves, and then merges them into one sorted array. The algorithm for merge sort is usually stated recursively. You know that a recursive algorithm expresses the solution to a problem in terms of a smaller version of the same problem. When you divide a problem into two or more smaller but *distinct* problems, solve *each* new problem, and then combine their solutions to solve the original problem, the strategy is said to be a **divide and conquer** algorithm. That is, you divide the problem into pieces and conquer each piece to reach a solution. Although divide and conquer algorithms often are expressed recursively, this is not a requirement.

When expressed recursively, a divide and conquer algorithm contains two or more recursive calls. Most of the recursive solutions that you have seen so far do not use the divide and conquer strategy. For example, Segment 11.7 gave a recursive version of the selection sort. Even though that algorithm considers smaller and smaller arrays, it does not divide the problem into two sorting problems.

The real effort during the execution of a merge sort occurs during the merge step, and this is also the step that involves most of the programming effort, so we will begin there.

Merging Arrays

12.2 Imagine that you have two distinct arrays that are sorted. Merging two sorted arrays is not difficult, but it does require an additional array. Processing both arrays from beginning to end, you compare an element in one array with an element in the other and copy the smaller element to a new third array, as Figure 12-1 shows. After reaching the end of one array, you simply copy the remaining elements from the other array to the new third array.

Figure 12-1   Merging two sorted arrays into one sorted array

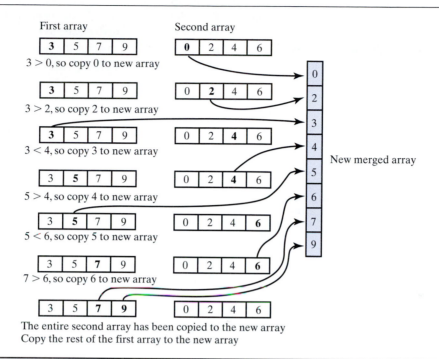

Recursive Merge Sort

12.3   **The algorithm.** In a merge sort, you merge two sorted arrays that are actually halves of the original array. That is, you divide the array into halves, sort each half, and merge the sorted halves into a second temporary array, as Figure 12-2 shows. You then copy the temporary array back to the original array.

Figure 12-2   The major steps in a merge sort

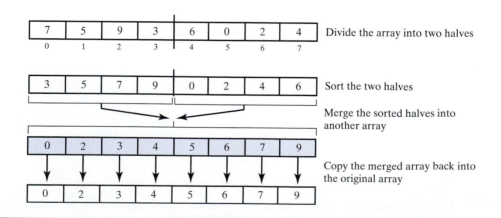

This sounds like a simple plan, but how did we sort the two halves of the array? By using a merge sort, of course! If `mid` is the index of the approximate midpoint of an array of *n* elements, we need to sort the elements indexed by 0 through `mid`, and then the elements indexed by `mid + 1` through n - 1. Since we perform these sorts by making recursive calls to the merge sort algorithm, the algorithm needs two parameters—`first` and `last`—to specify the first and last indices of the subrange of the array to be sorted. We will use the notation `a[first..last]` to mean the array elements `a[first]`, `a[first + 1]`, ..., `a[last]`.

Merge sort has the following recursive formulation:

Algorithm `mergeSort(a, tempArray, first, last)`
// Sorts the array elements `a[first]` *through* `a[last]` *recursively.*

```
if (first < last)
{
   mid = (first + last) / 2
   mergeSort(a, first, mid)
   mergeSort(a, mid + 1, last)
   Merge the sorted halves a[first..mid] and a[mid + 1..last] using the array tempArray
}
```

Notice that the algorithm ignores arrays of one or fewer elements.

The following pseudocode describes the merge step:

Algorithm `merge(a, tempArray, first, mid, last)`
// Merges the adjacent subarrays `a[first..mid]` *and* `a[mid + 1..last]`.

```
beginHalf1 = first
endHalf1 = mid
beginHalf2 = mid + 1
endHalf2 = last
```

// While both subarrays are not empty, compare an element in one subarray with
// an element in the other; then copy the smaller item into the temporary array
```
index = 0 // next available location in tempArray
while ( (beginHalf1 <= endHalf1) and (beginHalf2 <= endHalf2) )
{
   if (a[beginHalf1] < a[beginHalf2])
   {
      tempArray[index] = a[beginHalf1]
      beginHalf1++
   }
   else
   {
      tempArray[index] = a[beginHalf2]
      beginHalf2++
   }
   index++
}
```
// Assertion: One subarray has been completely copied to `tempArray`.

Copy remaining elements from other subarray to `tempArray`
Copy elements from `tempArray` *to array* `a`

12.4   **Tracing the steps in the algorithm.** Let's examine what happens when we invoke `mergeSort` on the array halves. Figure 12-3 shows that `mergeSort` divides an array into two halves and then recursively

Figure 12-3   The effect of the recursive calls and the merges during a merge sort

| 7 | 5 | 9 | 3 | 6 | 0 | 2 | 4 |

```
              1                    11
```

| 7 | 5 | 9 | 3 | | 6 | 0 | 2 | 4 | Effect of
                                               recursive
```
    2    6                    12    16
```
                                               calls to
| 7 | 5 | | 9 | 3 | | 6 | 0 | | 2 | 4 | mergeSort
```
  3    4    7    8      13    14    17    18
```
| 7 | 5 | | 9 | 3 | | 6 | 0 | | 2 | 4 |

```
    5 ▼        9 ▼          15 ▼        19 ▼
```
| 5 | 7 | | 3 | 9 | | 0 | 6 | | 2 | 4 |

```
       ▼ 10                   ▼ 20
```
| 3 | 5 | 7 | 9 | | 0 | 2 | 4 | 6 | Merge steps

```
                  ▼ 21
```
| 0 | 2 | 3 | 4 | 5 | 6 | 7 | 9 |

```
  ▼   ▼   ▼   ▼   ▼   ▼   ▼   ▼
```
| 0 | 2 | 3 | 4 | 5 | 6 | 7 | 9 | Copy to
                                               original array

divides each of those halves into two halves until each half contains only one element. At this point in the algorithm, the merge steps begin. Pairs of one-element subarrays are merged to form a two-element subarray. Pairs of two-element subarrays are merged to form a four-element subarray, and so on.

Numbers on the arrows in the figure indicate the order in which the recursive calls and the merges occur. Notice that the first merge occurs after four recursive calls to mergeSort and before other recursive calls to mergeSort. Thus, the recursive calls to mergeSort are interwoven with calls to merge. The actual sorting takes place during the merge steps and not during the recursive calls.

As you will see, we can use these observations in two ways. First, we can ascertain the algorithm's efficiency. Second, we can formulate the mergeSort algorithm iteratively.

Note: Merge sort rearranges the elements in an array during its merge steps.

Question 1   Trace the steps that a merge sort takes when sorting the following array into ascending order: 9 6 2 4 8 7 5 3.

12.5   **Implementation note.** Although the implementation of the recursive mergesort is straightforward, you should be careful to allocate the temporary array only once. Since the array is an implementation detail, you might be tempted to hide its allocation in the method merge. But since merge is called each time mergesort is called recursively, a temporary array would be allocated and initialized many times. Instead, we can allocate a temporary array in the following public version of mergesort and pass it to a private mergesort that implements the pseudocode given previously:

```
public static <T extends Comparable<? super T>>
        void mergeSort(T[] a, int first, int last)
{
   T[] tempArray = (T[])new Comparable<?>[a.length];
   mergeSort(a, tempArray, first, last);
} // end mergeSort
```

Segment 11.2 in the previous chapter introduced the notation ? super T to mean any superclass of T. When we allocate an array of Comparable objects, we use a wildcard ? to represent any object. We then cast the array to an array of type T objects.

The Efficiency of Merge Sort

12.6   Assume for now that n is a power of 2, so that we can divide n by 2 evenly. The array in Figure 12-3 has $n = 8$ elements. The initial call to mergeSort makes two recursive calls to mergeSort, dividing the array into two subarrays of $n/2$, or 4, elements each. Each of the two recursive calls to merge-Sort makes two recursive calls to mergeSort, dividing the two subarrays into four subarrays of $n/2^2$, or 2, elements each. Finally, recursive calls to mergeSort divide the four subarrays into eight subarrays of $n/2^3$, or 1, element each. It takes three levels of recursive calls to obtain subarrays of one element each. Notice that the original array contained 2^3 elements. The exponent 3 is the number of levels of recursive calls. In general, if n is 2^k, k levels of recursive calls occur.

Now consider the merge steps, because that is where the real work occurs. The merge step makes at most $n - 1$ comparisons among the n elements in the two subarrays. Figure 12-4 provides an example of a merge that requires $n - 1$ comparisons, while Figure 12-1 shows an example where fewer than $n - 1$ comparisons occur. Each merge also requires n moves to a temporary array and n moves back to the original array. In total, each merge requires at most $3n - 1$ operations.

Each call to mergeSort calls merge once. The merge operation as a result of the original call to mergeSort requires at most $3n - 1$ operations. It is O(n). An example of this merge appears as step 21 in Figure 12-3. The two recursive calls to mergeSort result in two calls to merge. Each call merges $n/2$ elements in at most $3n/2 - 1$ operations. The two merges then require at most $3n - 2$ operations. They are O(n). The next level of recursion involves 2^2 calls to mergeSort resulting in four calls to merge. Each call to merge merges $n/2^2$ elements in at most $3n/2^2 - 1$ operations. Together these four merges use at most $3n - 2^2$ operations, so are O(n).

Figure 12-4   A worst-case merge of two sorted arrays

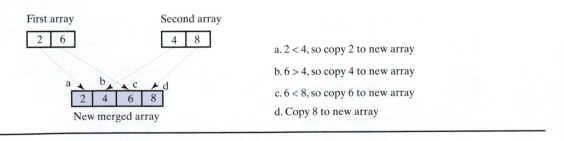

If n is 2^k, the k levels of recursive calls to mergeSort result in k levels of merges. The merges at each level are O(n). Since k is $\log_2 n$, mergeSort is O($n \log n$). When n is not a power of 2, we can find an integer k so that $2^{k-1} < n < 2^k$. For example, when n is 15, k is 4. Thus,

$$k - 1 < \log_2 n < k$$

so if we round $\log_2 n$ up, we will get k. Therefore, the merge sort is O($n \log n$) in this case as well. Notice that the merge steps are O(n) regardless of the initial order of the array. Merge sort is then O($n \log n$) in the worst, best, and average cases.

A disadvantage of merge sort is the need for the temporary array during the merge step. At the beginning of Chapter 11, we spoke of sorting the books on your bookshelf by height. We were able to do so without the extra space that another shelf or the floor would provide. You can see now that the merge sort would require this extra space. Later in this chapter, you will see another algorithm that sorts in O($n \log n$) time without a second array.

Note: **The time efficiency of merge sort**

Merge sort is O($n \log n$) in all cases. Its need for a temporary array is a disadvantage. The time required for copying elements, however, is less in Java than in other programming languages, since references are copied instead of the actual objects.

12.7   **Assessing efficiency another way.** In Chapter 10, we used a recurrence relation to estimate the time efficiency of recursive algorithms. We can use the same technique here. If $t(n)$ represents the time requirement of mergeSort in the worst case, the two recursive calls each require time $t(n/2)$. The merge step is O(n). Thus, we have the following:

$$t(n) = t(n/2) + t(n/2) + n$$
$$= 2\, t(n/2) + n \text{ when } n > 1$$
$$t(1) = 0$$

As a first step in solving this recurrence relation, we evaluate it for a specific value of n. Since $t(n)$ involves $n/2$, choosing n to be a power of 2—8, for example—is convenient. We then have

$$t(8) = 2\, t(4) + 8$$
$$t(4) = 2\, t(2) + 4$$
$$t(2) = 2\, t(1) + 2 = 2$$

By substituting repeatedly, we get the following for $t(8)$:

$$t(8) = 2\, t(4) + 8$$
$$= 2\, [2\, t(2) + 4] + 8$$
$$= 4\, t(2) + 8 + 8$$
$$= 4\, [2\, t(1) + 2] + 8 + 8$$
$$= 8 + 8 + 8$$
$$= 8 * 3$$

Since $8 = 2^3$, $3 = \log_2 8$, so we guess that

$$t(n) = n \log_2 n$$

Just as we did in Chapter 10, we now need to prove that our guess is in fact true. We leave this proof as an exercise.

Iterative Merge Sort

12.8   Once we have the merge algorithm, developing the recursive merge sort is easy. Developing an iterative merge sort is not as simple. We begin by making some observations about the recursive solution.

The recursive calls simply divide the array into *n* one-element subarrays, as you can see in Figure 12-3. Although we do not need recursion to isolate the elements in an array, the recursion controls the merging process. To replace the recursion with iteration, we will need to control the merges. Such an algorithm will be more efficient of both time and space than the recursive algorithm, since it will eliminate the recursive calls and, therefore, the stack of activation records. But an iterative merge sort will be trickier to code without error.

Basically, an iterative merge sort starts at the beginning of the array and merges pairs of individual elements to form two-element subarrays. Then it returns to the beginning of the array and merges pairs of the two-element subarrays to form four-element subarrays, and so on. However, after merging all pairs of subarrays of a particular length, we might have elements left over. Merging these requires some care. Project 2 at the end of this chapter asks you to develop an iterative merge sort. You will see there that you can save much of the time necessary to copy the temporary array back to the original array during the merges.

Merge Sort in the Java Class Library

12.9   The class `Arrays` in the package `java.util` defines several versions of a static method `sort` to sort an array into ascending order. For an array of objects, `sort` uses a merge sort. The method

public static void sort(Object[] a)

sorts an entire array a of objects, while the method

public static void sort(Object[] a, **int** first, **int** last)

sorts the subarray that the indices `first` and `last` define. For both methods, objects in the array must define the `Comparable` interface.

The merge sort used by these methods skips the merge step if none of the elements in the left half of the array are greater than the elements in the right half. Since both halves are sorted already, the merge step is unnecessary in this case.

Question 2   Modify the merge sort algorithm given in Segment 12.3 so that it skips any unnecessary merges, as just described.

Quick Sort

12.10   We now look at another divide and conquer strategy for sorting an array. The **quick sort** divides an array into two pieces, but unlike merge sort, these pieces are not necessarily halves of the array. Instead, quick sort chooses one element in the array—called the **pivot**—and rearranges the array elements so that

● The pivot is in the position that it will occupy in the final sorted array
● Elements in positions before the pivot are less than or equal to the pivot
● Elements in positions after the pivot are greater than or equal to the pivot

This arrangement is called a **partition** of the array.

Creating the partition divides the array into two pieces, which we will call *Smaller* and *Larger*, separated by the pivot, as Figure 12-5 illustrates. Since the elements in *Smaller* are less than or equal to the pivot, and the elements in *Larger* are greater than or equal to the pivot, the pivot is in its correct and final position within the sorted array. If we now sort the two subarrays *Smaller* and *Larger*—by using quick sort, of course—the original array will be sorted. The following algorithm describes our sorting strategy:

```
Algorithm quickSort(a, first, last)
// Sorts the array elements a[first] through a[last] recursively.

if (first < last)
{
   Choose a pivot
   Partition the array about the pivot
   pivotIndex = index of pivot
   quickSort(a, first, pivotIndex - 1) // sort Smaller
   quickSort(a, pivotIndex + 1, last)  // sort Larger
}
```

Figure 12-5 A partition of an array during a quick sort

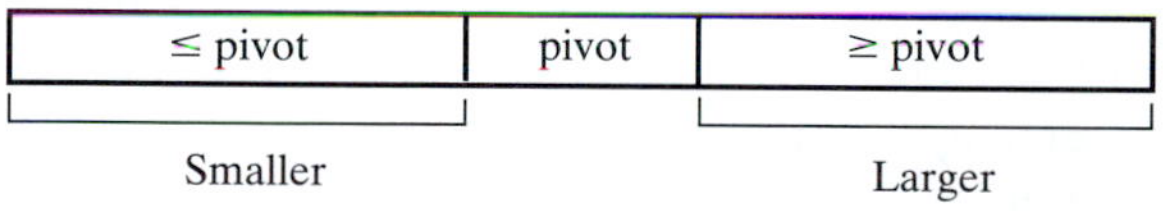

The Efficiency of Quick Sort

12.11   Notice that creating the partition—which accounts for most of quickSort's work—occurs before the recursive calls to quickSort. Contrast this with merge sort, where most of the work occurs during the merge phase *after* the recursive calls to mergeSort. Partitioning will require no more than n comparisons, and so, like merging, it will be an O(n) task. Thus, we can assess the efficiency of quick sort, even though we have not yet developed a partitioning strategy.

The ideal situation occurs when the pivot moves to the center of the array, so the two subarrays that the partition forms are the same size. If every recursive call to quickSort forms a partition with equal-sized subarrays, the quick sort will be like merge sort in that the recursive calls halve the array. Thus, quick sort would be O($n \log n$), and this would be its best case.

This ideal situation might not always occur, however. In the worst case, each partition has one empty subarray. Although one recursive call will have nothing to do, the other call must sort $n - 1$ elements instead of $n/2$. The result is n levels of recursive calls instead of $\log n$. Thus, in the worst case, quick sort is O(n^2).

The choice of pivots, then, affects quick sort's efficiency. Some pivot-selection schemes can lead to worst-case behavior if the array is already sorted or nearly sorted. In practice, nearly sorted arrays can occur more frequently than you might imagine. As you will see later, our pivot-selection scheme will avoid worst-case behavior for sorted arrays.

Although we will not prove it, quick sort is O($n \log n$) in the average case. While merge sort is always O($n \log n$), quick sort can be faster than merge sort in practice and does not require the additional memory that merge sort needs for merging.

Note: **The time efficiency of quick sort**

Quick sort is $O(n \log n)$ in the average case but $O(n^2)$ in the worst case. The choice of pivots affects its behavior.

Creating the Partition

12.12   Various strategies are possible for choosing a pivot and for creating the partition in Figure 12-5. For now, we will assume that you have chosen a pivot, and so we will describe how to create a partition independently of your pivot-selection strategy. Later, our actual pivot-selection scheme will suggest minor changes to this partitioning process.

After choosing a pivot, swap it with the last element in the array so that the pivot is not in your way while you create the partition. Figure 12-6a shows an array after this step. Starting at the beginning of the array and moving toward the end (left to right in the figure), look for the first element that is greater than or equal to the pivot. In Figure 12-6b, that element is 5 and occurs at the index `indexFromLeft`. In a similar fashion, starting at the next-to-last element and moving toward the beginning of the array (right to left in the figure), look for the first element that is less than or equal to the pivot. In Figure 12-6b, that element is 2 and occurs at the index `indexFromRight`. Now, if `indexFromLeft` is less than `indexFromRight`, swap the two elements at those indices. Figure 12-6c shows the result of this step. The 2, which is less than the pivot, has moved toward the beginning of the array while the 5, which is greater than the pivot, has moved in the opposite direction.

Continue the searches from the left and from the right. Figure 12-6d shows that the search from the left stops at 4 and the search from the right stops at 1. Since `indexFromLeft` is less than `indexFromRight`, swap 4 and 1. The array now appears as in Figure 12-6e. Elements equal to the pivot are allowed in either piece of the partition.

Continue the searches again. Figure 12-6f shows that the search from the left stops at 6 while the search from the right goes beyond the 6 to stop at 1. Since `indexFromLeft` is not less than `indexFromRight`, no swap is necessary and the searches end. The only remaining step is to place the pivot between the subarrays *Smaller* and *Larger* by swapping a[`indexFromLeft`] and a[`last`], as Figure 12-6g shows. The completed partition appears in Figure 12-6h.

Note that the previous searches must not go beyond the ends of the array. Soon, in Segment 12.15, you will see a convenient way to implement this requirement.

12.13   **Elements equal to the pivot.** Notice that both of the subarrays *Smaller* and *Larger* can contain elements equal to the pivot. This might seem a bit strange to you. Why not always place any elements that equal the pivot into the same subarray? Such a strategy would tend to make one subarray larger than the other. However, to enhance quick sort's performance, we want the subarrays to be as nearly equal in size as possible.

Notice that both the search from the left and the search from the right stop when they encounter an element that equals the pivot. This means that rather than leaving such elements in place, they are swapped. It also means that such an element has a chance of landing in each of the subarrays.

12.14   **Pivot selection.** Ideally, the pivot should be the median value in the array, so that the subarrays *Smaller* and *Larger* each have the same—or nearly the same—number of elements. One way to find the median value is to sort the array and then get the value in the middle. But sorting the array is the original problem, so this circular logic is doomed. Other ways to find the median are too slow to use.

Since choosing the best pivot takes too much time, we should at least try to avoid a bad pivot. So instead of finding the median of all values in the array, we will take as our pivot the median of

Figure 12-6   A partitioning strategy for quick sort

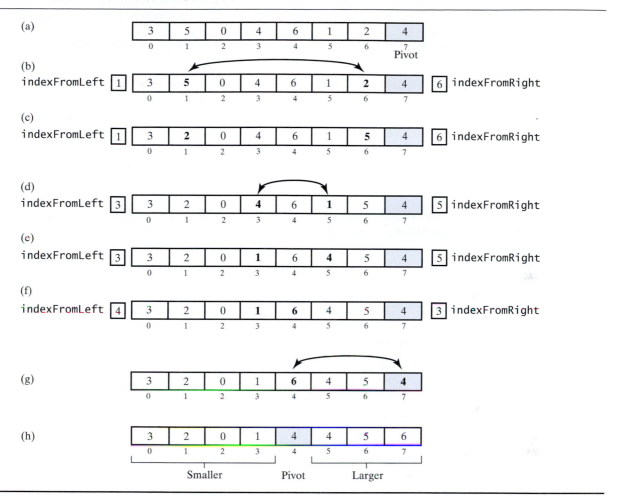

three elements in the array: the first element, the middle element, and the last element. One way to accomplish this task is to sort only those three elements and use the middle element of the three as the pivot. Figure 12-7 shows an array both before and after its first, middle, and last elements are sorted. The pivot is the 5. This pivot selection strategy is called **median-of-three pivot selection**.

Figure 12-7   Median-of-three pivot selection: (a) The original array; (b) the array with its first, middle, and last elements sorted

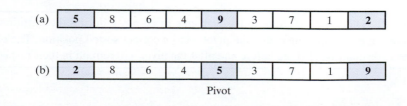

Note: Median-of-three pivot selection avoids worst-case performance by quick sort when the given array is already sorted or nearly sorted. While it theoretically does not avoid worst-case performance for other arrays, such performance is unlikely in practice.

12.15   **Adjusting the partition algorithm.** Median-of-three pivot selection suggests some minor adjustments to our partitioning scheme. Previously, we swapped the pivot with the last element in the array prior to partitioning. But here, the first, middle, and last elements in the array are sorted, so we know that the last element is at least as large as the pivot. Thus, the last element belongs in the subarray *Larger*. We can simply leave the last element in place. To get the pivot out of the way, we can swap it with the next-to-last element, a[last - 1], as Figure 12-8 shows. Thus, the partition algorithm can begin its search from the right at index last - 2.

Figure 12-8   (a) The array with its first, middle, and last elements sorted; (b) the array after positioning the pivot and just before partitioning

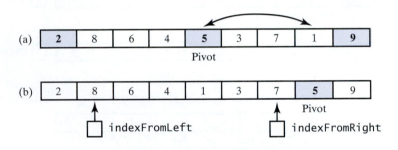

Also notice that the first element is at least as small as the pivot, and so it belongs in the subarray *Smaller*. Thus, we can leave the first element in place and have the partition algorithm begin its search from the left at index first + 1. Figure 12-8b shows the status of the array at this point, just prior to partitioning.

This scheme provides a side benefit that simplifies the loops for the two searches. The search from the left looks for an element that is greater than or equal to the pivot. That search will terminate because, at worst, it will stop at the pivot. The search from the right looks for an element that is less than or equal to the pivot. That search will terminate because, at worst, it will stop at the first element. Thus, the loops need not do anything special to prevent the searches from going beyond the ends of the array.

After the search loops end, we need to position the pivot between the subarrays *Smaller* and *Larger*. We do this by swapping the elements a[indexFromLeft] and a[last - 1].

Note: Quick sort rearranges the elements in an array during the partitioning process. Each partition places one element—the pivot—in its correct sorted position. The elements in each of the two subarrays that are before and after the pivot will remain in their respective subarrays.

Java Code for Quick Sort

12.16 **Pivot selection.** Median-of-three pivot selection requires us to sort three elements. We do this with simple comparisons and swaps, as follows:

```java
/** Task: Sorts the first, middle, and last elements of an
 *        array into ascending order.
 *  @param a       an array of Comparable objects
 *  @param first   the integer index of the first array element;
 *                 first >= 0 and < a.length
 *  @param mid     the integer index of the middle array element
 *  @param last    the integer index of the last array element;
 *                 last - first >= 2, last < a.length */
private static <T extends Comparable<? super T>>
        void sortFirstMiddleLast(T[] a, int first, int mid, int last)
{
  order(a, first, mid); // make a[first] <= a[mid]
  order(a, mid, last);  // make a[mid] <= a[last]
  order(a, first, mid); // make a[first] <= a[mid]
} // end sortFirstMiddleLast

/** Task: Orders two given array elements into ascending order
 *        so that a[i] <= a[j].
 *  @param a  an array of Comparable objects
 *  @param i  an integer >= 0 and < array.length
 *  @param j  an integer >= 0 and < array.length */
private static <T extends Comparable<? super T>>
        void order(T[] a, int i, int j)
{
  if (a[i].compareTo(a[j]) > 0)
    swap(a, i, j);
} // end order

/** Task: Swaps the array elements array[i] and array[j]. */
private static void swap(Object[] array, int i, int j)
{
  Object temp = array[i];
  array[i] = array[j];
  array[j] = temp;
} // end swap
```

After passing the indices of the first, middle, and last elements of the array to the method `sortFirstMiddleLast`, we will have the pivot at the middle index.

12.17 **Partitioning.** Median-of-three pivot selection assumes that the array has at least three elements. If you have only three elements, the pivot selection sorts them, so there is no need for the partition method or for quick sort. Thus, the following partition method assumes that the array contains at least four elements:

```java
/** Task: Partitions an array as part of quick sort into two subarrays
 *        called Smaller and Larger that are separated by a single
 *        element called the pivot.
```

```
 *          Elements in Smaller are <= pivot and appear before the
 *          pivot in the array.
 *          Elements in Larger are >= pivot and appear after the
 *          pivot in the array.
 *  @param a       an array of Comparable objects
 *  @param first   the integer index of the first array element;
 *                 first >= 0 and < a.length
 *  @param last    the integer index of the last array element;
 *                 last - first >= 3; last < a.length
 *  @return the index of the pivot */
private static <T extends Comparable<? super T>>
        int partition(T[] a, int first, int last)
{
  int mid = (first + last)/2;
  sortFirstMiddleLast(a, first, mid, last);

  // Assertion: The pivot is a[mid]; a[first] <= pivot and
  // a[last] >= pivot, so do not compare these two array elements
  // with pivot.

  // move pivot to next-to-last position in array
  swap(a, mid, last - 1);
  int pivotIndex = last - 1;
  T pivot = a[pivotIndex];

  // determine subarrays Smaller = a[first..endSmaller]
  // and                 Larger  = a[endSmaller+1..last-1]
  // such that elements in Smaller are <= pivot and
  // elements in Larger are >= pivot; initially, these subarrays are
    empty

  int indexFromLeft = first + 1;
  int indexFromRight = last - 2;

  boolean done = false;
  while (!done)
  {
    // starting at beginning of array, leave elements that are < pivot;
    // locate first element that is >= pivot; you will find one,
    // since last element is >= pivot
    while (a[indexFromLeft].compareTo(pivot) < 0)
      indexFromLeft++;

    // starting at end of array, leave elements that are > pivot;
    // locate first element that is <= pivot; you will find one,
    // since first element is <= pivot

    while (a[indexFromRight].compareTo(pivot) > 0)
      indexFromRight--;

    assert a[indexFromLeft].compareTo(pivot) >= 0 &&
           a[indexFromRight].compareTo(pivot) <= 0;

    if (indexFromLeft < indexFromRight)
```

```
          {
            swap(a, indexFromLeft, indexFromRight);
            indexFromLeft++;
            indexFromRight--;
          }
          else
            done = true;
      } // end while

      // place pivot between Smaller and Larger subarrays
      swap(a, pivotIndex, indexFromLeft);
      pivotIndex = indexFromLeft;

      // Assertion:
      //    Smaller = a[first..pivotIndex-1]
      //    Pivot = a[pivotIndex]
      //    Larger = a[pivotIndex+1..last]

      return pivotIndex;
   } // end partition
```

12.18   **The quick sort method.** Before completing the Java code for quick sort, we need to think about
small arrays. You have seen that the array should contain at least four elements before you call the
partition method. But simply agreeing to use quick sort only on large arrays is not enough. The
pseudocode given for quick sort in Segment 12.10 shows that partitioning even a very large array
will eventually lead to a recursive call that involves an array as small as two elements. The code for
quick sort needs to screen out these small arrays and use another way to sort them. An insertion sort
is a good choice for small arrays. In fact, using it instead of quick sort on arrays of as many as ten
elements is reasonable. The following method implements quick sort with these observations in
mind. The method assumes a constant MIN_SIZE that specifies the size of the smallest array on
which we will use a quick sort.

```
   /** Task: Sorts an array into ascending order. Uses quick sort with
    *        median-of-three pivot selection for arrays of at least
    *        MIN_SIZE elements, and uses insertion sort for other arrays.
    */
   public static <T extends Comparable<? super T>>
         void quickSort(T[] a, int first, int last)
   {
      if (last - first + 1 < MIN_SIZE)
      {
         insertionSort(a, first, last);
      }
      else
      {
         // create the partition: Smaller | Pivot | Larger
         int pivotIndex = partition(a, first, last);

         // sort subarrays Smaller and Larger
         quickSort(a, first, pivotIndex - 1);
         quickSort(a, pivotIndex + 1, last);
      } // end if
   } // end quickSort
```

?   Question 3   Trace the steps that the method `quickSort` takes when sorting the following array into ascending order: 9 6 2 4 8 7 5 3. Assume that `MIN_SIZE` is 4.

Quick Sort in the Java Class Library

12.19   The class `Arrays` in the package `java.util` uses a quick sort to sort arrays of primitive types into ascending order. The method

public static void sort(*type*[] a)

sorts an entire array a, while the method

public static void sort(*type*[] a, **int** first, **int** last)

sorts the subarray that the indices `first` and `last` define. Note that *type* is either byte, char, double, float, int, long, or short.

Radix Sort

12.20   The sorting algorithms that you have seen so far sort objects that can be compared. The **radix sort** does not compare objects, but to work, it must restrict the data that it sorts. For this restricted data, the radix sort is $O(n)$, and so it is faster than any other sort in this chapter. However, it is not suitable as a general-purpose sorting algorithm, because it treats array elements as if they were strings that have the same length.

Let's look at an example of a radix sort of the following three-digit positive integers:

123 398 210 019 528 003 513 129 220 294

Notice that 19 and 3 are padded with zeros to make them three-digit integers. The radix sort begins by grouping the integers according to their rightmost digits. Since a digit can have one of ten values, we need ten groups, or **buckets**. If bucket d corresponds to the digit d, we place 123 into bucket 3, 398 into bucket 8, and so on. Figure 12-9a shows the result of this process. Notice that each bucket must retain the order in which it receives the integers.

Looking at the buckets sequentially, we see that the integers are now in the following order:

210 220 123 003 513 294 398 528 019 129

We move these integers from the buckets to the original array. We then group the integers by their middle digits, using the now empty buckets. Thus, 210 goes into bucket 1, 220 goes into bucket 2, 123 goes into bucket 2, and so on. Figure 12-9b shows the result of this pass.

The integers in the buckets are now in this order:

003 210 513 019 220 123 528 129 294 398

After moving these integers from the buckets back to the array, we group them by their leftmost digits. Thus, 003 goes into bucket 0, 210 goes into bucket 2, 513 goes into bucket 5, and so on. Figure 12-9c shows the result of this pass.

The integers in the buckets are now in their final sorted order:

003 019 123 129 210 220 294 398 513 528

Figure 12-9   Radix sort: (a) Original array and buckets after first distribution; (b) reordered array and buckets after second distribution; (c) reordered array and buckets after third distribution; (d) sorted array

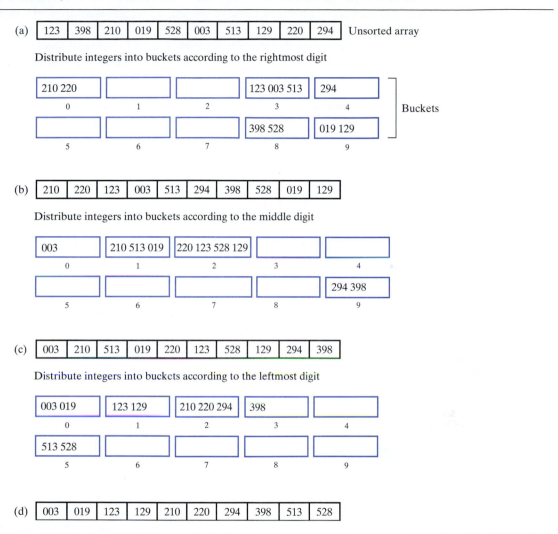

Note: **Origin of the radix sort**
During the early days of computing, data was stored on punched cards. Each card had 80 columns in which to store 80 characters. Each column had 12 rows that were the possible positions for holes. A machine called a card sorter distributed the cards among 12 bins according to the row punched in the column chosen by the machine's operator. These bins are analogous to the buckets in a radix sort. After running a stack of cards through the card sorter, the operator would gather the cards a bin at a time to create a new stack. The cards would be run through the sorter again to sort the next column of holes. By repeating this process, the operator could sort the cards.

Pseudocode for Radix Sort

12.21   Our previous description of radix sort assumed that the integers to be sorted each contain the same number of digits. Actually, this requirement is unnecessary as long as you get 0 when you ask for a digit that does not exist. For example, if you ask for the hundreds digit of a two-digit integer, you should get 0.

The following algorithm describes a radix sort of an array of positive decimal integers. We number the digits in each integer from the right beginning at zero. Thus, the units digit is digit 0, the tens digit is digit 1, and so on.

> *Algorithm* `radixSort(a, first, last, maxDigits)`
> *// Sorts the array of positive decimal integers* `a[first..last]` *into ascending order;*
> *//* `maxDigits` *is the number of digits in the longest integer.*
>
> **for** (i = 0 to maxDigits - 1)
> {
>   *Clear* bucket[0], bucket[1], ..., bucket[9]
>   **for** (index = first *to* last)
>   {
>   digit = *digit* i *of* a[index]
>   *Place* a[index] *at end of* bucket[digit]
>   }
>   *Place contents of* bucket[0], bucket[1], ..., bucket[9] *into the array* a
> }

This algorithm uses an array of buckets. The nature of a bucket is unspecified, but later in this book, you will see that a bucket can be an instance of the ADT queue.

Question 4   Trace the steps that the algorithm `radixSort` takes when sorting the following array into ascending order:

6340 1234 291 3 6325 68 5227 1638

The Efficiency of Radix Sort

12.22   If an array contains n integers, the inner loop in the previous algorithm iterates n times. If each integer contains d digits, the outer loop iterates d times. Thus, the radix sort is $O(d * n)$. The d in this expression tells us that the actual running time for a radix sort depends on the size of the integers. But on a computer, the typical integer is restricted in size to about ten decimal digits, or 32 bits. As long as d is fixed and is much smaller than n, radix sort is simply an $O(n)$ algorithm.

Note: Although radix sort is an $O(n)$ algorithm for certain data, it is not appropriate for all data.

Question 5   One of the difficulties with the radix sort is that the number of buckets depends on the kind of strings you are sorting. You saw that sorting integers requires 10 buckets; sorting words requires at least 26 buckets. If you use radix sort to alphabetize an array of words, what changes would be necessary to the given algorithm?

Comparing the Algorithms

12.23   Figure 12-10 summarizes the efficiencies of the sorting algorithms presented in this chapter and the previous chapter. Although a radix sort is fastest, it is not always applicable. The merge sort and quick sort are generally faster than any of the other algorithms.

Figure 12-10 The time efficiency of various sorting algorithms, expressed in Big Oh notation

	Average Case	Best Case	Worst Case
Radix sort	$O(n)$	$O(n)$	$O(n)$
Merge sort	$O(n \log n)$	$O(n \log n)$	$O(n \log n)$
Quick sort	$O(n \log n)$	$O(n \log n)$	$O(n^2)$
Shell sort	$O(n^{1.5})$	$O(n)$	$O(n^2)$ or $O(n^{1.5})$
Insertion sort	$O(n^2)$	$O(n)$	$O(n^2)$
Selection sort	$O(n^2)$	$O(n^2)$	$O(n^2)$

To give you an idea of how the problem size affects time efficiency, Figure 12-11 tabulates the four growth-rate functions that appear in Figure 12-10 for several values of n. You certainly could use an $O(n^2)$ sort algorithm when n is 10. When n is 100, a Shell sort is almost as fast as a quick sort in the average case. But when n is one million, an average-case quick sort is much faster than a Shell sort and much, much faster than an insertion sort.

If your array has relatively few elements, or if it is nearly sorted, the insertion sort is a good choice. Otherwise, the quick sort is generally preferable. Note that merge sort is useful when the data collection is in an external file because it is too large to reside in main memory all at once.

Figure 12-11 A comparison of growth-rate functions as n increases

n	10	10^2	10^3	10^4	10^5	10^6
$n \log_2 n$	33	664	9966	132,877	1,660,964	19,931,569
$n^{1.5}$	32	10^3	31,623	10^6	31,622,777	10^9
n^2	10^2	10^4	10^6	10^8	10^{10}	10^{12}

CHAPTER SUMMARY

- Merge sort is a divide and conquer algorithm that halves an array, recursively sorts the two halves, and then merges them into one sorted array.
- Merge sort is $O(n \log n)$. However, it does use additional memory to perform the merge step.

- Quick sort is another divide and conquer algorithm that partitions an array into two subarrays that are separated by one element, the pivot. The pivot is in its correct sorted position. The elements in one subarray are less than or equal to the pivot, while the elements in the second subarray are greater than or equal to the pivot. Quick sort recursively sorts the two subarrays.

- Quick sort is $O(n \log n)$ most of the time. Although it is $O(n^2)$ in its worst case, you usually can avoid this case by choosing appropriate pivots.

- Even though merge sort and quick sort are $O(n \log n)$ algorithms, quick sort is usually faster in practice and does not require additional memory.

- Radix sort treats array elements as if they were strings that have the same length. Initially radix sort distributes the elements into buckets according to the character (digit) at one end of the strings. The sort then collects the strings and distributes them again among the buckets according to the character or digit in the next position. The sort continues this process until all character positions are considered.

- Radix sort does not compare array elements. Although it is $O(n)$, it cannot sort all types of data. Thus, it is not appropriate as a general-purpose sorting algorithm.

EXERCISES

1. Suppose that 80 90 70 85 60 40 50 95 represents an array of `Integer` objects. Show the steps that a merge sort takes when sorting this array.

2. Consider the method `quickSort`, as given in Segment 12.18, that sorts an array of objects into ascending order by using a quick sort. Suppose that 80 90 70 85 60 40 50 95 represents an array of `Integer` objects.

   a. What does the array look like after `quickSort` partitions it for the first time? (Show all intermediate results.)
   b. How many comparisons did this partition process require?
   c. The pivot is now between two subarrays called *Smaller* and *Larger*. Will the position of this particular element change during subsequent steps of the sort? Why or why not?
   d. What recursive call to `quickSort` occurs next?

3. Consider the merge step of the merge sort.

   a. What is the minimum number of comparisons needed to merge two subarrays each of size $n/2$?
   b. Give a recurrence relation that counts the number of comparisons made in the best case.
   c. Make an educated guess at the solution to the recurrence relation.

4. How many comparisons does quick sort require in the worst case when median-of-three partitioning is used? What is the Big Oh for the worst case?

5. Show the steps that a radix sort takes when sorting the following array of `Integer` objects:

   783 99 472 182 264 543 356 295 692 491 94

6. Show the steps that a radix sort takes when sorting the following array of strings into alphabetical order:

   joke book back dig desk word fish ward dish wit deed fast dog bend

7. Describe how a card player can use a radix sort to sort a hand of cards.

8. A **counting sort** is a simple way to sort an array of n positive integers that lie between 0 and m, inclusive. You need $m + 1$ counters. Then, making only one pass through the array, you count the number of times each integer occurs in the array. For example, Figure 12-12 shows an array of integers that lie between 0 and 4 and the five counters after a counting sort has made its pass through the array. From the counters, you can see that the array contains one 0, three 1s, two 2s, one 3, and three 4s. These counts enable you to determine that the sorted array should contain 0 1 1 1 2 2 3 4 4 4.

   a. Write a method that performs a counting sort.
   b. How does the efficiency of a counting sort compare to that of an insertion sort or a quick sort?

Figure 12-12 A counting sort of an array (see Exercise 8)

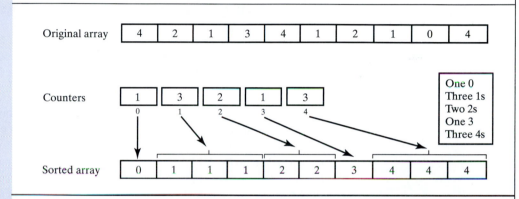

9. Consider a linked implementation LList of the ADT list. Suppose that you want to provide a sort operation for this ADT.

   a. Implement a private method within LList that merges two sorted chains into one new sorted chain.
   b. The method described in Part *a* could be part of a merge sort of a sorted chain. Describe how you could implement such a sort.

10. A sorting algorithm is **stable** if it does not change the relative order of objects that are equal. For example, if object x appears before object y in a collection of data, and x.compareTo(y) is zero, a stable sorting algorithm will leave object x before object y after sorting the data. Stability is important to certain applications. For example, suppose that you sort a group of people, first by name and then by age. A stable sorting algorithm will ensure that people of the same age will remain in alphabetical order.
    What sorting algorithms in Chapters 11 and 12 are stable?

11. Segment 12.7 showed that you can compute the efficiency of merge sort by solving the recurrence relation

    $t(n) = 2\ t(n/2) + n$ when $n > 1$
    $t(1) = 0$

    Prove by induction that $t(n) = n \log_2 n$.

1. Implement the recursive algorithm for merge sort.

2. Segment 12.8 introduced you to an iterative merge sort. This project continues that discussion by providing more details about the merge steps.

a. If n is a power of 2, as it is in Figure 12-3, you would merge pairs of individual elements, starting at the beginning of the array. Then you would return to the beginning of the array and merge pairs of two-element subarrays. Finally, you would merge one pair of four-element subarrays. Notice that the subarrays in each pair of subarrays contain the same number of elements.

In general, n might not be a power of 2. After merging a certain number of pairs of subarrays, you might have too few elements left to make up a complete pair of subarrays. In Figure 12-13a, after merging pairs of single elements, one element is left over. You then merge one pair of two-element subarrays, and merge the leftover two-element subarray with the leftover single element. Parts b and c of Figure 12-13 show two other possibilities.

Implement an iterative merge sort. Use the algorithm `merge` that was given in Segment 12.3. A private method that uses `merge` to merge the pairs of subarrays is useful. After the method completes its task, you can handle the leftovers that we just described.

b. Merging two subarrays requires an additional temporary array. Although you need to use this extra space, you can save much of the time that our earlier merge algorithm spends in copying elements from the temporary array back to the original array. If a is the original array and t is the temporary array, you first merge subarrays of a into the array t. Instead of copying t back to a and continuing the merge, you determine subarrays of t and merge them into a. If you can do this an even number of times, no additional copying is necessary. Make these changes to the iterative merge sort that you wrote in Part a.

3. Consider the following implementation of an iterative merge sort. Scan the array from its beginning and partition it into segments that are each sorted. As you find each segment, represent it as a pair of indices and place the pair at the end of an initially empty list.

Next, remove the first two pairs from the list and merge the array segments they represent. Notice that these segments are adjacent in the array. The merge results in a larger segment that is sorted. Place the pair of indices that represents the resulting segment at the end of the list. Repeat the steps in this paragraph until only one element remains in the list.

Sometimes during the process, the two pairs at the beginning of the list will represent segments that are not adjacent. In this case, move the first pair to the end of the list and continue.

a. What is the best-case performance of this algorithm?
b. What is the worst-case performance of this algorithm?
c. Implement the algorithm.

Figure 12-13 Special cases in an iterative merge sort after merging
one-element subarrays

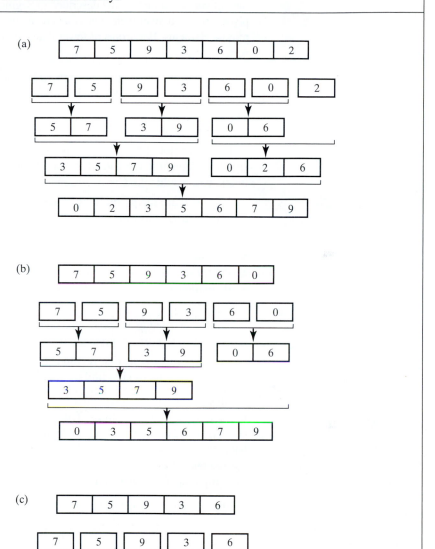

4. Revise the implementation of quick sort as follows. If the array has 7 elements, choose the middle element as the pivot. For arrays of between 8 and 40 elements, use the median-of-three pivot-selection scheme described in Segments 12.14 and 12.16. For larger arrays, the pivot is the median of 9 elements that are about equally spaced, including the first, last, and middle elements. For arrays of fewer than 7 elements, use insertion sort instead of quick sort.

5. Extend Project 1 of Chapter 11 to provide graphical demonstrations of the merge sort and quick sort algorithms introduced in this chapter.

6. The **median** of a collection of data is the middle value. One way to find the median is to sort the data and take the value that is at—or nearly at—the center of the collection. But sorting does more than necessary to find the median. You need to find only the kth smallest element in the collection for an appropriate value of k. To find the median of n items, you would take k as $n/2$ rounded up—that is, $\lceil n/2 \rceil$.

   You can use the partitioning strategy of quick sort to find the kth smallest element in an array. After choosing a pivot and forming the subarrays *Smaller* and *Larger*, as described in Segment 12.10, you can draw one of the following conclusions:

   - If *Smaller* contains k or more elements, it must contain the kth smallest element.
   - If *Smaller* contains $k - 1$ elements, the kth smallest element is the pivot.
   - If *Smaller* contains fewer than $k - 1$ elements, the kth smallest element is in *Larger*.

   You now can develop a recursive solution to finding the kth smallest element. The first and last conclusions correspond to the recursive calls. The remaining one is the base case.

   Implement a recursive method that finds the kth smallest element in an unsorted array. Use your method to find the median in the array.

7. A binary radix sort will sort an array a of n integer values based on their binary bits instead of their decimal digits. This sort will need only two buckets. Represent the buckets as a 2 by n array. You can avoid some work by not copying the contents of the buckets back into the array a at the end of each pass. Instead just add the values from the second bucket to the end of the first bucket.
   Implement this algorithm.

8. Implement a merge sort of the objects in a chain of linked nodes.

9. Implement a radix sort of the strings in a chain of linked nodes.

Sorted Lists

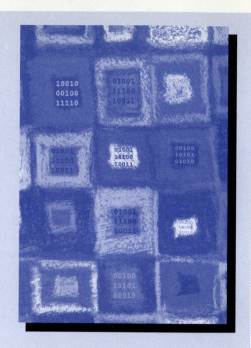

CONTENTS

PREREQUISITES

OBJECTIVES

After studying this chapter, you should be able to

- Use a sorted list in a program
- Describe the differences between the ADT list and the ADT sorted list
- Implement the ADT sorted list by using a chain of linked nodes
- Implement the ADT sorted list by using the operations of the ADT list

Chapter 4 introduced you to the ADT list. The entries in a list are ordered simply by their positions within the list. Thus, a list has a first entry, a second entry, and so on. This ADT enables you to order entries according to any criterion you want—alphabetical or chronological, for instance. In fact, Chapter 4 showed you an example that used a list to organize names in alphabetical order. To do so, the client had to determine where in the list a particular entry belonged.

If your application creates a list and then at some point needs to sort the list's entries into numerical or alphabetical order, for example, you can add a sort operation to the ADT list. You can use one of the algorithms given in Chapters 11 and 12 to implement this operation. But when your application requires only sorted data, having an ADT that orders the data for you would be more convenient than the ADT list. The sorted list is such an ADT.

When you either add an entry to or remove an entry from a sorted list, you provide only the entry. You do not specify where in the list the entry belongs or exists. The ADT determines this for you.

This chapter describes the operations of the ADT sorted list, provides examples of using a sorted list, and presents two possible Java implementations. One of these implementations uses the ADT list, but it is not especially efficient. Chapter 14 addresses the reuse of a class and provides a more efficient implementation of the sorted list as it discusses the use of inheritance.

Specifications for the ADT Sorted List

13.1   The ADT list leaves it up to the client to arrange the objects in a given collection. The client can maintain the objects in any order that meets its needs. Suppose that you want a list of names or other strings that are in alphabetical order. You could certainly use the ADT list for this task, but you would have to determine the position that each string should have within the list. Wouldn't it be more convenient if the list itself alphabetized the entries as you added them? What you need is a different ADT, namely the **sorted list**.

Recall that to use the add operation of the ADT list, you must specify both the new entry and its desired position within the list. Such an operation is not desirable for the ADT sorted list, since the sorted list is responsible for organizing its entries. If you were allowed to specify a new entry's position, you might destroy the order of the sorted list's entries. Instead, the add operation of the ADT sorted list requires only the new entry. The operation compares the new entry to other entries in the sorted list to determine the new entry's position. Thus, the entries in a sorted list must be objects that can be compared with one another.

What, then, can you place in a sorted list? One possibility is strings, since the class String provides a compareTo method for comparing two strings. In general, you can have a sorted list of any objects of a class that has a compareTo method. As you saw in Segment 3.20 of Chapter 3 and again at the beginning of Chapter 11, such classes implement the interface Comparable. Since Java's wrapper classes, such as Integer and Double, implement the Comparable interface, you can place instances of them into a sorted list.

13.2   Let's examine the possible operations for this ADT. For simplicity, we will allow the sorted list to contain duplicate items. Insisting that the sorted list contain only unique items is somewhat more complicated, and we will leave this variation as an exercise.

We've already mentioned that you can add an entry to the sorted list. Since the sorted list determines the position of a new entry, you could ask the ADT for this position. That is, you could ask for the position of an existing entry or for the position in which a proposed entry would occur if you added it to the list. You could also ask the ADT whether it contained a particular entry. And clearly you should be able to remove an entry.

Let's specify these operations more carefully.

```
ABSTRACT DATA TYPE SORTED LIST
```

DATA

- A collection of objects in sorted order and having the same data type
- The number of objects in the collection

OPERATIONS

`add(newEntry)`

Task: Adds `newEntry` to the sorted list so that the list remains sorted.

Input: `newEntry` is the object to be added.

Output: Returns true if the addition is successful, or false if not.

`remove(anEntry)`

Task: Removes the first or only occurrence of `anEntry` from the sorted list.

Input: `anEntry` is the object to be removed.

Output: Returns true if `anEntry` was located and removed, or false if not. In the latter case, the list remains unchanged.

`getPosition(anEntry)`

Task: Gets the position of the first or only occurrence of `anEntry`.

Input: `anEntry` is the object to be found.

Output: Returns the position of `anEntry` if it occurs in the list. Otherwise, returns the position where `anEntry` would occur in the list, but as a negative integer.

The following operations behave as they do for the ADT list and are described in Chapter 4:

```
getEntry(givenPosition)
contains(anEntry)
remove(givenPosition)
clear()
getLength()
isEmpty()
isFull()
display()
```

13.3   The first two methods are straightforward, but `getPosition` deserves some comment. Given an entry in the sorted list, the method `getPosition` returns the entry's position number within the list, as you would expect. We number the entries beginning with 1, just as we do for the ADT list. But what if the given entry is not in the sorted list? In this case, `getPosition` returns the position number where the entry belongs in the list. The returned number is negative, however, to signal that the entry is not in the list. For example, if `missingObject` is not in the sorted list `sList` but belongs at position 3, `sList.getPosition(missingObject)` would return -3.

The sorted list also has some, but not all, of the operations of an ADT list. We have already mentioned that adding an entry at a given position is not possible, because otherwise the client could destroy the order of the sorted list. For the same reason, the list's `replace` method is not available to a sorted list. The other operations of the ADT list, however, are useful for a sorted list as well, including the ones that retrieve or remove the entry at a given position. The methods `getEntry` and `remove` each have a position number as a parameter, but they will not alter the relative order of the entries in the sorted list.

Although the list's `remove` method returns the object removed from the list, it is not necessary for the sorted list's `remove` method to do so. The client already has at least a copy of this entry to enable it to invoke sorted list's `remove`.

13.4   The Java interface in Listing 13-1 specifies these operations in more detail. The notation ? super T, which Segment 11.2 introduced, means any super class of the generic type T.

Listing 13-1   The interface `SortedListInterface`

```
/** An interface for the ADT sorted list.
 *  Entries in the list have positions that begin with 1.
 */
public interface SortedListInterface<T extends Comparable<? super T>>
{
   /** Task: Adds a new entry to the sorted list in its proper order.
    *  @param newEntry  the object to be added as a new entry
    *  @return true if the addition is successful */
   public boolean add(T newEntry);

   /** Task: Removes a specified entry from the sorted list.
    *  @param anEntry  the object to be removed
    *  @return true if anEntry was located and removed */
   public boolean remove(T anEntry);

   /** Task: Gets the position of an entry in the sorted list.
    *  @param anEntry  the object to be found
    *  @return the position of the first or only occurrence of anEntry
    *          if it occurs in the list; otherwise returns the position
    *          where anEntry would occur in the list, but as a negative
    *          integer */
   public int getPosition(T anEntry);

   // The following methods are described in Segment 4.10 of Chapter 4
   // as part of the ADT list:

   public T getEntry(int givenPosition);
   public boolean contains(T anEntry);
   public T remove(int givenPosition);
   public void clear();
   public int getLength();
   public boolean isEmpty();
   public boolean isFull();
   public void display();
} // end SortedListInterface
```

Note: The ADT sorted list can add, remove, or locate an entry, given the entry as an argument. The sorted list has several operations that are the same as ADT list operations, namely `getEntry`, `contains`, `remove` (by position), `clear`, `getLength`, `isEmpty`, `isFull`, and `display`. However, a sorted list will not let you add or replace an entry by position.

Using the ADT Sorted List

13.5   **Example.** To demonstrate the operations of the ADT sorted list that the previous section specifies, we first create a sorted list of strings. We begin by declaring and allocating the list `nameList`, where we assume that `SortedList` is an implementation of the ADT operations specified by the interface `SortedListInterface`:

```
SortedListInterface<String> nameList = new SortedList<String>();
```

Next, we add names in an arbitrary order, realizing that the ADT will organize them alphabetically:

```
nameList.add("Jamie");
nameList.add("Brenda");
nameList.add("Sarah");
nameList.add("Tom");
nameList.add("Carlos");
```

Displaying the sorted list by writing

```
nameList.display();
```

results in the following output:

```
Brenda
Carlos
Jamie
Sarah
Tom
```

13.6   Assuming the list just given, here are some examples of the ADT operations on the sorted list:

```
nameList.getPosition("Jamie") returns 3, the position of Jamie in the list
nameList.contains("Jill") returns false, because Jill is not in the list
nameList.getPosition("Jill") returns –4, because Jill belongs at position 4 in the list
nameList.getEntry(2) returns Carlos, because he is at position 2 in the list
```

Now remove *Tom* and the first name in the list by writing

```
nameList.remove("Tom");
nameList.remove(1);
```

The list now contains

```
Carlos
Jamie
Sarah
```

Removing the last entry, *Tom*, did not change the positions of the other entries in the list, but removing the first entry did. *Carlos* is now at position 1, instead of 2.

Question 1 Suppose that `wordList` is an unsorted list of words. Using the operations of the ADT list and the ADT sorted list, create a sorted list of these words.

Question 2 Assuming that the sorted list you created in the previous question is not empty, write Java statements that

a. Display the last entry in the sorted list.
b. Add the sorted list's first entry to the sorted list again.

A Linked Implementation

As with all ADTs, you have a choice of several ways in which to implement the sorted list. You could store a sorted list's entries in, for example, an array, a chain of linked nodes, an instance of a vector, or an instance of an ADT list. In this chapter, we will consider a chain of linked nodes and an instance of an ADT list. In the next chapter, we will use inheritance to develop a completely different implementation.

13.7 **An outline of the class.** An implementation that uses a chain of linked nodes to store the entries in a sorted list has several details in common with the linked implementation of the ADT list that you studied in Chapters 6 and 7. In particular, it has the same data fields, similar constructors, and the same implementations for several of its methods. Although our implementation also could use the same definition of the inner class `Node`, we will use a definition that includes get and set methods. Thus, we outline in Listing 13-2 a class definition that implements the ADT sorted list.

Listing 13-2 An outline of a linked implementation of the ADT sorted list

```
public class SortedLinkedList<T extends Comparable<? super T>>
            implements SortedListInterface<T>
{
  private Node firstNode; // reference to first node of chain
  private int  length;    // number of entries in sorted list

  public SortedLinkedList()
  {
    firstNode = null;
    length = 0;
  } // end default constructor

  < Implementations of the sorted list operations go here. >
  . . .

  private class Node
  {
    private T    data;
    private Node next;

    < Constructors >
    . . .
```

< *Accessor and mutator methods:* getData, setData, getNextNode, setNextNode >
. . .

```
    } // end Node
} // end SortedLinkedList
```

The Method add

13.8   **Locating the insertion point.** Adding an entry to a sorted list requires that you find where in the list the new entry belongs. Since the entries are sorted, you compare the new entry with the entries in the sorted list until you reach an entry that is not smaller than the new entry. Figure 13-1 depicts a chain of linked nodes, each containing a name, sorted alphabetically. The figure shows where the additional names *Ally, Cathy, Luke, Sue,* and *Tom* would be inserted into the chain and the comparisons that would have to occur to arrive at those locations.

Figure 13-1   Places to insert names into a sorted chain of linked nodes

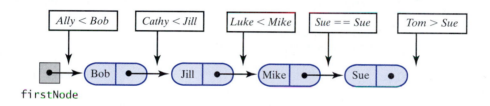

You can see from the figure that, in a string comparison, *Ally* is less than *Bob,* and so it would be inserted at the beginning of the chain. To see where to insert *Luke,* you would find that *Luke* is greater than both *Bob* and *Jill* but less than *Mike.* Thus, *Luke* belongs before *Mike* in the chain. *Sue,* on the other hand, is already in one of the nodes. You would discover that *Sue* is greater than *Bob, Jill,* and *Mike* but not greater than *Sue.* So you would insert the new entry *Sue* just before the existing entry *Sue.* Finally, *Tom* is greater than all the current names in the list, so you would add it to the end of the chain.

Note: Given a sorted list with entries in ascending order, you insert a new entry just before the first entry that is not smaller than the new entry.

13.9   **The algorithm.** Recall from Segment 6.27 of Chapter 6 that you handle the addition of a new node to the beginning of a chain differently from an addition at other points in the chain. Adding to the beginning is easy, since firstNode references the first node in the chain. To add anywhere else, you need a reference to the node that will ultimately occur before the new node. Thus, while you traverse the chain of linked nodes to discover where the new entry belongs, you must retain a reference to the node prior to the one under consideration.

A high-level algorithm that describes our strategy follows:

Algorithm **add(newEntry)**
// Adds a new entry to the sorted list.

Allocate a new node containing newEntry
Search the chain until either you find a node containing newEntry *or you pass the point*
  where it should be
Let nodeBefore *reference the node before the insertion point*
if (*the chain is empty or the new node belongs at the beginning of the chain*)
  Add the new node to the beginning of the chain
else
  Insert the new node after the node referenced by nodeBefore

Increment the length of the sorted list

13.10   **An iterative implementation of add.** A Java implementation of the previous algorithm follows. We use a private method, getNodeBefore, to search the chain for the node before the insertion point.

```java
public boolean add(T newEntry)
{
   Node newNode = new Node(newEntry);
   Node nodeBefore = getNodeBefore(newEntry);

   if (isEmpty() || (nodeBefore == null)) // add at beginning
   {
      newNode.setNextNode(firstNode);
      firstNode = newNode;
   }
   else                                     // add after nodeBefore
   {
      Node nodeAfter = nodeBefore.getNextNode();
      newNode.setNextNode(nodeAfter);
      nodeBefore.setNextNode(newNode);
   } // end if

   length++;
   return true;
} // end add
```

13.11   **The private method getNodeBefore.** We still need to implement the private method getNodeBefore. We will need two references as we traverse the list. Clearly we need a reference to the current node so we can compare its entry to the desired entry. But we also must retain a reference to the previous node, because it is this reference that the method returns. In the following implementation, these references are currentNode and nodeBefore:

```java
/** Task: Finds the node that is before the node that
 *        should or does contain a given entry.
 *  @param anEntry  the object to be located
 *  @return either a reference to the node that is before the node
 *          that contains or should contain anEntry, or null if
 *          no prior node exists (that is, if anEntry belongs at
 *          the beginning of the list) */
private Node getNodeBefore(T anEntry)
{
   Node currentNode = firstNode;
   Node nodeBefore = null;
```

```
while ( (currentNode != null) &&
        (anEntry.compareTo(currentNode.getData()) > 0) )
{
  nodeBefore = currentNode;
  currentNode = currentNode.getNextNode();
} // end while

return nodeBefore;
} // end getNodeBefore
```

Recall that the method `compareTo` returns a negative, zero, or positive integer according to whether the comparison is, respectively, less than, equal to, or greater than.

Question 3   In the `while` statement of the method `getNodeBefore`, how important is the order of the two boolean expressions that the operator `&&` joins? Explain.

Question 4   What does `getNodeBefore` return if the sorted list is empty? How can you use this fact to simplify the implementation of the method `add` given in Segment 13.10?

Question 5   Suppose that you use the previous method `add` to add an entry to a sorted list. If the entry is already in the list, where in the list will `add` insert it? Before the first occurrence of the entry, after the first occurrence of the entry, after the last occurrence of the entry, or somewhere else?

Question 6   What would be the answer to the previous question if you changed `>` to `>=` in the `while` statement of the method `getNodeBefore`?

13.12   **Thinking recursively.** Using recursion to process a chain of linked nodes can be an attractive alternative to an iterative approach. The basic concept is easy, but, as you will see, the implementation is more involved, since Java passes objects to methods as references.

Recall from Segment 10.20 of Chapter 10 that you can process the chain's first node and then process the rest of the chain recursively. Thus, to add a new node to a sorted chain of linked nodes, you use the following logic:

> **if** (*the chain is empty or the new node belongs at the beginning of the chain*)
>   *Add the new node to the beginning of the chain*
> **else**
>   *Ignore the first node and add the new node to the rest of the chain*

Figure 13-2 illustrates the logic needed to recursively add the name *Luke* to a sorted chain of names. Since *Luke* is greater than *Bob,* you recursively consider the subchain that begins at *Jill.* *Luke* is also greater than *Jill,* so you now consider the subchain beginning at *Mike.* Finally, *Luke* is less than *Mike,* so you make the actual addition at the beginning of this subchain—that is, before *Mike.* Adding to the beginning of a chain—or subchain—is the base case of this recursion. Happily, the beginning of a chain is the easiest place to make an addition.

If `currentNode` initially references the chain and later references the rest of the chain, we can add some detail to the previous logic, as follows:

> **if** ((currentNode == null) *or* (newEntry <= currentNode.getData()))
>   currentNode = **new** Node(newEntry, currentNode)
> **else**
>   *Recursively add* newEntry *to the chain beginning at* currentNode.getNextNode()

Figure 13-2   Recursively adding *Luke* to a sorted chain of names

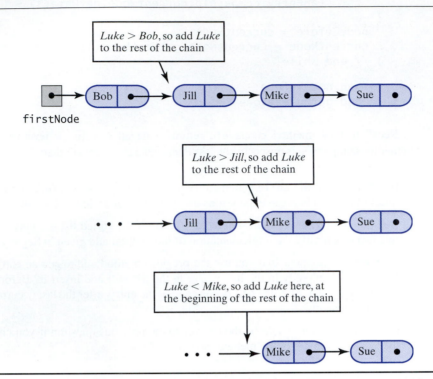

13.13   **A recursive implementation of add.** The example in Segment 10.20 displayed the contents of a chain. Since that operation does not alter the chain, its recursive formulation was straightforward. Obviously, in our present situation, the method add does alter the chain. Getting the recursive method to make these changes is the challenge in Java.

Let's look at the recursive implementation of the method add before we describe why it works. You learned in Segment 10.19 that you write a private method to perform the recursion and you write a public method—typically the one that implements the ADT operation—to invoke this private method. Thus, we have the following method definitions:

```java
public boolean add(T newEntry)
{
    firstNode = add(newEntry, firstNode);
    length++;
    return true;
} // end add

private Node add(T newEntry, Node currentNode)
{
    if ( (currentNode == null) ||
         (newEntry.compareTo(currentNode.getData()) <= 0) )
    {
        currentNode = new Node(newEntry, currentNode);
    }
    else
    {
        Node nodeAfter = add(newEntry, currentNode.getNextNode());
```

```
        currentNode.setNextNode(nodeAfter);
    } // end if

    return currentNode;
} // end add
```

The private method add adds newEntry to the subchain that begins at currentNode. We will trace and explain its logic in a moment.

Question 7   Repeat Question 5, using the method add that was just given.

13.14   **Tracing an addition to the list's beginning.** Suppose that nameList is the sorted list that the chain in Figure 13-3a represents. Let's invoke nameList.add("Ally") to add *Ally* to this list. This addition will occur at the beginning of the chain. The public method add will call the private method add with the invocation add("Ally", firstNode). The reference in the argument firstNode is copied to the parameter currentNode, and so it also references the first node in the chain, as Figure 13-3b illustrates.

Figure 13-3   Recursively adding a node at the beginning of a chain

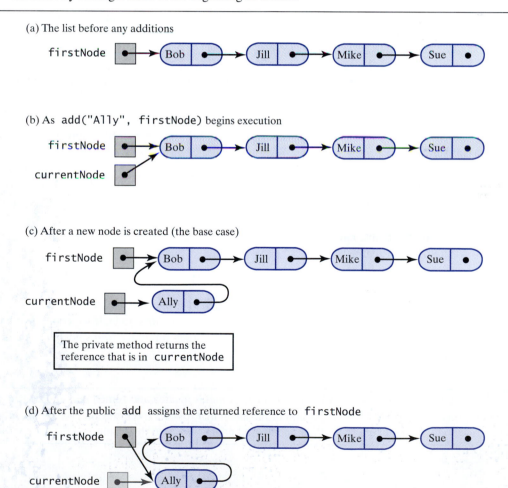

(a) The list before any additions

(b) As add("Ally", firstNode) begins execution

(c) After a new node is created (the base case)

The private method returns the reference that is in currentNode

(d) After the public add assigns the returned reference to firstNode

Since *Ally* will be added to the beginning of the chain, the statement

```
currentNode = new Node("Ally", currentNode);
```

executes and creates a new node for *Ally*. This node is linked to the original chain, as Figure 13-3c shows. Notice that firstNode is unchanged, even though it is the argument that corresponds to the parameter currentNode.

The private method now returns the value of currentNode, and the public method add assigns that value to firstNode. Thus, the chain with the completed addition appears as in Figure 13-3d.

13.15   **Tracing an addition to the list's interior: the recursive calls.** What happens when the addition is not at the beginning of the original chain? Let's trace what happens when we add *Luke* to the chain in Figure 13-4a. The public method add calls the private method add with the invocation add("Luke", firstNode). As in the previous segment, the reference in firstNode is copied to the parameter currentNode, and so it also references the first node in the chain, as Figure 13-4a illustrates.

Since *Luke* comes after *Bob*, another recursive call occurs:

```
add("Luke", currentNode.getNextNode())
```

The second argument is a reference to the chain's second node, the one containing *Jill*. This reference is copied to the parameter currentNode, as Figure 13-4b depicts.

Luke comes after *Jill*, so the recursive process is repeated again, and currentNode references the chain's third node—*Mike*'s node—as shown in Figure 13-4c. *Luke* is less than *Mike*, so no recursive call occurs. We are at the base case. A new node is created that contains *Luke* and references *Mike*'s node, as Figure 13-4d illustrates.

13.16   **Tracing the returns from the recursive method.** Having just created a new node, the private method add returns a reference to it, as Figure 13-4d indicates. The statement that invoked add now resumes execution:

```
nodeAfter = add("Luke", currentNode.getNextNode());
```

Thus, nodeAfter is assigned a reference to the new node containing *Luke*, as Figure 13-4e illustrates.

At this point, currentNode references *Jill*'s node, as it did in Part *b* of the figure. The next statement to execute is

```
currentNode.setNextNode(nodeAfter);
```

Thus, the data field next in *Jill*'s node is changed to reference *Luke*'s node, as shown in Figure 13-4f.

The private method add now returns a reference to *Jill*'s node. If we continue the trace, we will make *Bob*'s node reference *Jill*'s node and firstNode reference *Bob*'s node, even though these references are already in place.

Note: A recursive addition to a chain of nodes locates and remembers the nodes prior to the insertion point. After the portion of the chain that follows the insertion point is linked to the new node, the recursion links the remembered nodes back into the chain.

Figure 13-4   Recursively adding a node between existing nodes in a chain

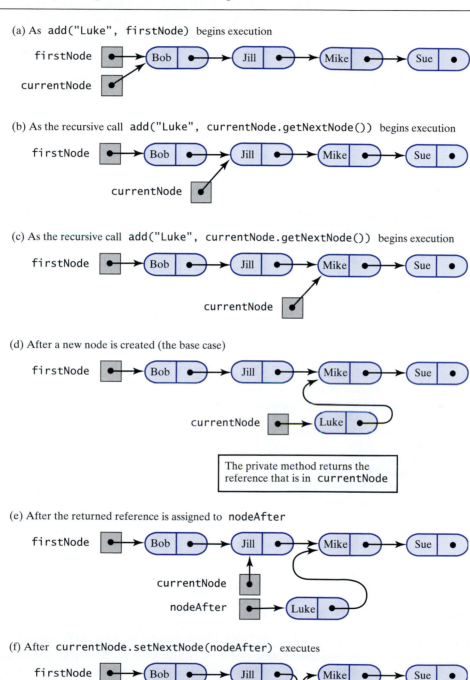

(a) As `add("Luke", firstNode)` begins execution

(b) As the recursive call `add("Luke", currentNode.getNextNode())` begins execution

(c) As the recursive call `add("Luke", currentNode.getNextNode())` begins execution

(d) After a new node is created (the base case)

The private method returns the reference that is in `currentNode`

(e) After the returned reference is assigned to `nodeAfter`

(f) After `currentNode.setNextNode(nodeAfter)` executes

13.17   Projects 1 and 2 at the end of this chapter ask you to complete the iterative and recursive implementations of the sorted list. Notice that many of the sorted list operations are the same as operations of the ADT list and so would have implementations like those you saw in Chapters 6 and 7.

Note: Since the ADTs sorted list and list share many of the same operations, portions of their implementations are identical.

Question 8   What changes to the class `SortedLinkedList` are necessary to enable a client to serialize instances of the class?

The Efficiency of the Linked Implementation

13.18   If you consider the analysis of the linked implementation of the ADT list given in Chapter 9, you will see that the performance of the add method depends on the efficiency of the method get-NodeAt. The latter method locates the insertion point by traversing the chain of nodes. It is an $O(n)$ operation. The add method for the sorted list does its own traversal of the list to locate where to make the addition. This traversal is also $O(n)$, making the addition to a sorted list an $O(n)$ operation.

Figure 13-5 summarizes the performance of the sorted list operations. Deriving these results is left as an exercise. When comparing implementations, you should realize that the worst cases can occur under different circumstances. For example, a worst-case addition to an array-based sorted list occurs at the list's beginning, whereas for a linked implementation, it occurs at the list's end.

Figure 13-5   The worst-case efficiencies of the operations on the ADT sorted list for two implementations

ADT Sorted List Operation	Array	Linked
add(newEntry)	$O(n)$	$O(n)$
remove(anEntry)	$O(n)$	$O(n)$
getPosition(anEntry)	$O(n)$	$O(n)$
getEntry(givenPosition)	$O(1)$	$O(n)$
contains(anEntry)	$O(n)$	$O(n)$
remove(givenPosition)	$O(n)$	$O(n)$
display()	$O(n)$	$O(n)$
clear(), getLength(), isEmpty(), isFull()	$O(1)$	$O(1)$

An Implementation That Uses the ADT List

13.19   As we noted in Segment 13.17, the linked implementation of the ADT sorted list repeats much of the corresponding implementation of the ADT list. Can we avoid this duplication of effort and reuse portions of the list's implementation? The answer to this question is yes, as you will soon see.

You can certainly use the ADT list to create and maintain an alphabetical list of strings. It is natural, then, to consider using the ADT list when implementing the ADT sorted list. Basically, you can do this in one of two ways. Here we will use a list as a data field within the class that implements the sorted list. Figure 13-6 shows an instance of such a sorted list. Recall from Segment 2.1 of Chapter 2 that this approach is called composition and illustrates the *has-a* relationship between

Figure 13-6   An instance of a sorted list that contains a list of its entries

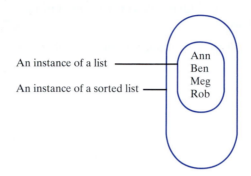

An instance of a list ——————————

An instance of a sorted list ——————

Ann
Ben
Meg
Rob

two classes. The next chapter considers the second approach, using inheritance to derive the sorted list from the list.

13.20   Our class `SortedList` will implement the interface `SortedListInterface`. We begin this class by declaring a list as a data field and defining a default constructor. We assume that the class `LList`, as discussed in Chapters 6 and 7, is an implementation of the interface `ListInterface` for the ADT list. Thus, our class begins as follows:

```java
public class SortedList<T extends Comparable<? super T>>
              implements SortedListInterface<T>
{
    private ListInterface<T> list;

    public SortedList()
    {
        list = new LList<T>();
    } // end default constructor
    . . .
} // end SortedList
```

Note our use of the generic type `T` when we declare the data field `list` and create an instance of `LList`.

13.21   **The method add.** The implementations of the operations of the ADT sorted list are brief, as the list does most of the work. To add a new entry to the sorted list, we first use the method `getPosition`, which is an operation of the sorted list. We assume that it is already implemented, even though we have not written it yet. Recall that `getPosition` finds the position of an existing entry within a sorted list, or the position at which we should insert a new entry that does not occur in the sorted list. The method sets the sign of the integer it returns to indicate whether the entry exists in the list already. When adding an entry to a sorted list that can contain duplicate entries, it does not matter whether the entry exists in the sorted list already. Thus, we can ignore the sign of the integer that `getPosition` returns. Notice that the following implementation uses the method abs of the class `Math` to discard this sign. It also uses the add operation of the ADT list. (In this section, calls to ADT list operations will appear in color.)

```
public boolean add(T newEntry)
{
  int newPosition = Math.abs(getPosition(newEntry));
  return list.add(newPosition, newEntry);
} // end add
```

?

Question 9   Repeat Question 5, using the method add that was just given.

Question 10   Can a client of SortedList invoke the operation add(position, entry) of the ADT list? Explain.

13.22   **The method remove.** We also use getPosition when removing an object from a sorted list. This time, however, we do need to know whether the given entry exists in the sorted list. If it does not exist, we cannot remove it. In such cases, remove returns false. Also notice that the method uses the operation remove of the ADT list to make the deletion. Thus, the method has the following implementation:

```
public boolean remove(T anEntry)
{
  boolean result = false;
  int position = getPosition(anEntry);

  if (position > 0)
  {
    list.remove(position);
    result = true;
  } // end if

  return result;
} // end remove
```

?

Question 11   If a sorted list contains five duplicate objects and you use the previous method remove to remove one of them, what will be removed from the list: the first occurrence of the object, the last occurrence of the object, or all occurrences of the object?

13.23   **The logic for getPosition.** Implementing getPosition is somewhat harder than implementing the previous two methods. To decide where in the list anEntry is or belongs, we need to compare anEntry to the entries already in the list, beginning with the first one. If anEntry is in the list, we obviously compare entries until we find a match. However, if anEntry is not in the list, we want to stop the search at the point where it belongs in the sorted list. We take advantage of the sorted order of the objects by using logic similar to that described in Segment 13.8.

For example, suppose that the sorted list contains the four names *Brenda*, *Carlos*, *Sarah*, and *Tom*. If we want to see where *Jamie* belongs in the sorted list, we discover that, as strings,

Jamie > Brenda
Jamie > Carlos
Jamie < Sarah

Thus, *Jamie* belongs after *Carlos* but before *Sarah*—that is, at position 3 in the sorted list, as Figure 13-7 illustrates.

To compare anEntry to an entry in the sorted list, we first use the list operation getEntry to return the entry at a given position within the sorted list. Then the expression

```
anEntry.compareTo(list.getEntry(position))
```

makes the comparison.

Figure 13-7   A sorted list in which *Jamie* belongs after *Carlos* but before *Sarah*

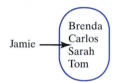

13.24   **The implementation of `getPosition`.** In the following implementation of `getPosition`, the `while` loop finds `anEntry`'s position in the sorted list, and the `if` statement sees whether `anEntry` is in the list.

```
public int getPosition(T anEntry)
{
   int position = 1;
   int length = list.getLength();

   // find position of anEntry
   while ( (position <= length) &&
           (anEntry.compareTo(list.getEntry(position)) > 0) )
   {
      position++;
   } // end while

   // see whether anEntry is in list
   if ( (position > length) ||
        (anEntry.compareTo(list.getEntry(position)) != 0) )
   {
      position = -position; // anEntry is not in list
   } // end if

   return position;
} // end getPosition
```

Question 12   Assume that the sorted list `nameList` contains the four names *Brenda*, *Carlos*, *Sarah*, and *Tom* as strings. By tracing the code for `getPosition`, see what `getPosition` returns when `anEntry` represents

a. *Carlos*   **b.** *Alan*   **c.** *Wendy*   **d.** *Tom*   **e.** *Jamie*

Question 13   Since you can decide whether a given entry is in a particular sorted list by testing the sign of the integer that `getPosition` returns, you can use `getPosition` to implement the method `contains`. Write such an implementation.

13.25   Each of the remaining methods—`contains`, `remove`, `getEntry`, `clear`, `getLength`, `isEmpty`, `isFull`, and `display`—has the same specifications as in the ADT list. Each can simply invoke the corresponding list method. For example, the method `getEntry` has the following implementation in `SortedList`:

```
public T getEntry(int givenPosition)
{
   return list.getEntry(givenPosition);
} // end getEntry
```

Question 14   You can implement the method `contains` by invoking either `getPosition`, as Question 13 suggests, or the ADT list's `contains` method. Which of these implementations will execute faster when the entry sought is not present in the sorted list? Why?

Efficiency Issues

Except perhaps for some subtle logic in `getPosition`, you can write the previous implementation quickly and with few, if any, errors. Saving human time is an attractive feature of using an existing class to build another. But does the implementation use computer time efficiently? In this particular implementation, several methods invoke `getPosition`, so their efficiency depends on `getPosition`'s efficiency.

13.26   **The efficiency of `getPosition`.** As we examine `getPosition`, as given in Segment 13.24, we note that the list method `getLength` is an O(1) operation. Therefore, we need not be concerned with it. On the other hand, a loop examines the entries in the list one at a time by invoking `getEntry` until the desired entry is located. Thus, the efficiency of `getPosition` depends in part on the efficiency of `getEntry`. However, the efficiency of `getEntry` depends upon which implementation of the ADT list you use. We will examine two list implementations that lead to rather different efficiencies for `getPosition`.

Chapter 9 discussed the efficiencies of the ADT list operations. Figure 13-8 recalls the worst-case performance of the list operations that we need to complete our analysis of the sorted list. If you use an array to represent the entries in a list, `getEntry` is always an O(1) operation. The loop in `getPosition` is therefore O(n) in the worst case, and so `getPosition` is O(n) when the list has an array-based implementation.

If you use a chain of linked nodes to contain the entries in a list, the method `getEntry` is O(n). Since `getPosition`'s loop invokes `getEntry`, we see that `getPosition` is O(n²) in the worst case. Each time `getEntry` retrieves the next entry in the list, it starts its search at the beginning of the chain. This fact is the cause of `getPosition`'s inefficiency.

Figure 13-8   The worst-case efficiencies of selected ADT list operations for array-based and linked implementations

ADT List Operation	Array	Linked
`getEntry(givenPosition)`	O(1)	O(n)
`add(newPosition, newEntry)`	O(n)	O(n)
`remove(givenPosition)`	O(n)	O(n)
`contains(anEntry)`	O(n)	O(n)
`display()`	O(n)	O(n)
`clear()`, `getLength()`, `isEmpty()`, `isFull()`	O(1)	O(1)

13.27   **The efficiency of `add`.** The implementation of the sorted list method `add` given in Segment 13.21 contains the following statements:

```
int newPosition = Math.abs(getPosition(newEntry));
return list.add(newPosition, newEntry);
```

For an array-based implementation of the ADT list, both `getPosition` and the list operation `add` are O(n) operations. Thus, the sorted list operation `add` is O(n) in the worst case. For a linked implementation of the list, getPosition's worst-case behavior is $O(n^2)$ and dominates the list operation add, which is only $O(n)$. Thus, the sorted list operation add is $O(n^2)$ in the worst case.

13.28   Figure 13-9 summarizes the efficiencies of the sorted list operations for array-based and linked implementations of the ADT list. Confirmation of these results is left as an exercise. As you can see, the implementation of the sorted list given in this section is easy to write but is not very efficient if the underlying list uses a chain of linked nodes. The next chapter will show you how you can reuse the ADT list in the implementation of the sorted list without sacrificing efficiency.

 Question 15 Give an advantage and a disadvantage of using composition in the implementation of the class SortedList.

Figure 13-9   The worst-case efficiencies of the ADT sorted list operations when implemented using an instance of the ADT list

ADT Sorted List Operation	List Implementation	
	Array	**Linked**
add(new Entry)	$O(n)$	$O(n^2)$
remove(anEntry)	$O(n)$	$O(n^2)$
getPosition(anEntry)	$O(n)$	$O(n^2)$
getEntry(givenPosition)	$O(1)$	$O(n)$
contains(anEntry)	$O(n)$	$O(n)$
remove(givenPosition)	$O(n)$	$O(n)$
display()	$O(n)$	$O(n)$
clear(), getLength(), isEmpty(), isFull()	$O(1)$	$O(1)$

 Note: **Using composition to implement the ADT sorted list**
When you use an instance of an ADT list to represent the entries in the ADT sorted list, you must use the list's operations to access the sorted list's entries, instead of accessing them directly. Such an implementation of the sorted list is easy to write but is inefficient when the underlying list uses a chain of linked nodes to store its entries.

CHAPTER SUMMARY

- The ADT sorted list maintains its entries in sorted order. It, not the client, determines where to place an entry.

- The ADT sorted list can add, remove, or locate an entry, given the entry as an argument.

- The sorted list has several operations that are the same as the corresponding operations of the ADT list. However, a sorted list will not let you add or replace an entry by position.

- A chain of linked nodes provides a reasonably efficient implementation of the sorted list.

- An implementation of the sorted list that uses an ADT list as a data field is easy to write. However, depending upon how the ADT list is implemented, its efficiency can suffer.

1. Suppose that nameList is a sorted list of names. Using the operations of the ADT list and the ADT sorted list, create a list of these names without changing their order.

2. As specified in this chapter, the sorted list can contain duplicate entries. Specify a sorted list of unique items. For example, add could return true if it added an entry to the list but return false if the entry is in the list already.

3. The **mode** of a list of values is the value having the greatest frequency.

   a. Write an algorithm to find the mode of a sorted list using only methods of the ADT sorted list.
   b. What is the Big Oh of the algorithm if the sorted list has an array-based implementation?
   c. What is the Big Oh of the algorithm if the sorted list has a linked implementation?

4. The schedule of activities for a room consists of an **activity list**. Each activity has a description, a start time, and an end time. You can add activities to the list, but they must be compatible with the other activities. Two activities are incompatible if their time intervals overlap. Specify the ADT activity list.

5. Imagine you are working for a geologist who has records for earthquakes that occurred during the past 50 years. Each record includes a date, location, strength, and duration. Design and specify an ADT for this collection of data.

6. Explain how you can use the ADT sorted list in the implementations of the ADTs described in Exercises 4 and 5.

7. Consider an array-based implementation of the sorted list. To implement the method add, you must add an entry to a sorted array so that the array remains sorted.

   a. Describe the steps in this implementation.
   b. On which sort have you based your logic?
   c. Analyze the worst-case efficiency of this implementation of add.

8. Figure 13-5 tabulates the worst-case efficiencies of the sorted list operations for both array-based and linked implementations. Derive these Big Oh expressions.

9. Figure 13-9 tabulates the worst-case efficiencies of the sorted list operations when implemented using an instance of the ADT list. Derive these Big Oh expressions.

10. Consider an array-based implementation of the sorted list. Let the array list be the data field that represents the list's entries. If a constructor is given an array of unsorted list entries, the constructor must place them into list in sorted order. To do so, it could repeatedly use the sorted list's add method to add the entries to the sorted list (and hence to the array list) in their proper order. Or it could copy the entries to list and sort them by using a sort algorithm from Chapters 11 and 12.

    a. If you use the first approach, what sort are you actually using?
    b. Would you ever want to use the second approach? Explain.

11. Consider the implementation of the sorted list that uses an instance of the ADT list. In particular, consider the method contains. One implementation of contains could invoke getPosition (see Question 13 at the end of Segment 13.24). Another

implementation could simply invoke `list.contains`. Compare the efficiencies of these two implementations.

12. Write a linked implementation of the sorted list method `contains`. Your search of the chain should end when it either locates the desired entry or passes the point at which the entry should have occurred.

13. Compare the efficiency of the method `contains` that Exercise 12 describes with that of the list's version of `contains`. Consider the worst case, average case, and best case.

14. Segment 12.2 of Chapter 12 described how to merge two sorted arrays into one sorted array. Add an operation to the ADT sorted list that merges two sorted lists. Implement the merge in three ways, as follows:

   a. Use only sorted list operations.
   b. Assume an array-based implementation.
   c. Assume a linked implementation.

PROJECTS

1. Complete the linked implementation of the ADT sorted list that was begun in this chapter. Use iteration instead of recursion.

2. Repeat Project 1, but use recursion wherever possible.

3. Implement the ADT sorted list by using an array to represent the ADT's entries. Use dynamic array expansion so that the sorted list can grow as large as necessary.

4. Implement the ADT sorted list by using an instance of `Vector` to represent the ADT's entries. Recall that Chapter 5 presented a similar implementation for the ADT list.

5. Exercise 2 asked you to specify an ADT sorted list of unique items. Implement such an ADT using one of the approaches described in this chapter or in the previous projects.

6. Add an iterator to the ADT sorted list by defining an inner class within the class that implements the ADT.

7. A **polynomial** in x is an algebraic expression that involves integer powers of x, as follows:

$$P(x) = a_n x^n + a_{n-1} x^{n-1} + \ldots + a_1 x + a_0$$

The a's are called **coefficients**. The **degree** of the polynomial is n, the highest exponent of x that appears in $P(x)$. Although a_n cannot be zero in a degree n polynomial, any other coefficient can be zero.

Specify an ADT polynomial that includes operations such as `getDegree`, `getCoefficient`, `setCoefficient`, `add`, and `subtract`. Implement this ADT by using a sorted list. The sorted list should not contain any coefficients that are zero.

8. Exercise 3 asked you to create an algorithm to find the mode of a sorted list. Let's add a method to the implementation of a sorted list that finds the list's mode. The header of such a method could be

```
public T mode()
```

Implement this method in three ways, as follows:

a. Use only sorted list operations.
b. Assume an array-based implementation.
c. Assume a linked implementation.

9. You can use a **substitution code** to encode a message. In this scheme, a **key** maps each letter to another letter. Each letter in the **plain-text** message is replaced according to the key to produce the encoded message, or **cipher text**.

Suppose you are given some cipher text, but not the key. One method of breaking such a code is to count the frequency of letters in the cipher text and then make guesses about the mapping based on the frequencies of letters in typical English text. Write a program that reads characters from a file and uses a sorted list to find the frequency of each letter.

14

Inheritance and Lists

CONTENTS

PREREQUISITES

OBJECTIVES

After studying this chapter, you should be able to

- Describe how a class implementation that uses inheritance differs from one that uses composition

- Design a class that contains protected methods to make it suitable for use as a base class

- Write an efficient implementation of a sorted list by using inheritance

Chapter 13 introduced you to the ADT sorted list, which maintains its entries in a sorted order. As with many other ADTs, you can implement the sorted list by using either an array or a chain of linked nodes. The advantage of such implementations is their time efficiency. However, they require you to repeat a portion of the implementation of the ADT list, since the ADTs sorted list and list have several operations in common.

In an attempt to avoid this duplication of effort, Chapter 13 used an instance of the ADT list to contain the entries of the sorted list. This list was a data field of the class implementing the sorted list. The result was an implementation that you could write quickly, because the implementation of the list had done most of the work. But since the sorted list operations used the list in the same way that a client would, these operations were inefficient of time when the ADT list had a linked implementation.

But what if, instead of using composition, as we did in Chapter 13, we use inheritance? This chapter looks at the implications of deriving a sorted list from a list. In doing so we'll find that a subclass (derived class) can be more efficient if it can access the underlying data structures of its superclass (base class). This is possible if the superclass includes methods that enable future subclasses to examine or modify its data fields. A class designer should plan for the future use of a class as well as the present need.

Using Inheritance to Implement a Sorted List

14.1   Recall the implementation of the class SortedList that we developed in Chapter 13 beginning at Segment 13.20. SortedList has an instance of another class, LList in this case, as a data field. SortedList and LList have a *has-a* relationship. Several of SortedList's methods—namely remove (by position), getEntry, contains, clear, getLength, isEmpty, isFull, and display— behave like LList's methods. If SortedList inherited these methods from LList, we would not have to implement them again, as we did in Chapter 13. Thus, we could revise SortedList as follows:

```
public class SortedList<T extends Comparable<? super T>>
              extends LList<T> implements SortedListInterface<T>
{
  public boolean add(T newEntry)
  {
    int newPosition = Math.abs(getPosition(newEntry));
    return super.add(newPosition, newEntry);
  } // end add

  < Implementations of remove(anEntry) and getPosition(anEntry) go here. >
    . . .
} // end SortedList
```

The notation T extends Comparable<? super T>, introduced in Segments 11.1 and 11.2, defines the generic type T. The class that T represents must implement the interface Comparable. Writing ? super T, which means any superclass of T, allows some flexibility when using the method compareTo.

You can see that SortedList is derived from LList. Also notice that we have omitted the data field list and the default constructor that appeared in Segment 13.20. To revise the add method given in Segment 13.21, we simply replaced list with super. That is, we wrote

```
super.add(newPosition, newEntry);
```

to invoke the add operation of the ADT list, instead of

```
list.add(newPosition, newEntry);
```

as we did in Chapter 13. Coincidentally, `SortedList`'s add method overrides and hides the other add method in `LList` that adds to the end of a list.

We would make similar changes to the methods `remove` and `getPosition`. The remaining methods of the sorted list are inherited from `LList`, and so they do not appear explicitly in `SortedList`.

Question 1   Although `SortedList` inherits the method `contains` from `LList`, the method is not as efficient as it could be. Why? Show how you could override `contains` with a more efficient version.

14.2   **A pitfall.** This implementation contains a pitfall that is the direct result of using inheritance. Although `SortedList` conveniently inherits methods such as `isEmpty` from `LList`, it also inherits two methods that a client can use to destroy the order of a sorted list. These two methods appear in `ListInterface` as follows:

```
/** Task: Adds newEntry to the list at position newPosition. */
public boolean add(int newPosition, T newEntry);

/** Task: Replaces the entry at givenPosition with newEntry. */
public boolean replace(int givenPosition, T newEntry);
```

If a client writes

```
SortedList<String> sList = new SortedList<String>();
```

for example, `sList` can invoke any method declared in either `SortedListInterface` or `ListInterface`, including the previous methods `add` and `replace`. Thus, a client could destroy the order of the entries in a sorted list either by adding an entry out of order or by replacing an entry.

14.3   **Possible ways to avoid the pitfall.** What can we do to avoid this pitfall? Here are three possibilities:

● Declare the sorted list as an instance of `SortedListInterface`. For example, if the client contains

```
SortedListInterface<String> sList = new SortedList<String>();
```

`sList` can invoke only methods declared within `SortedListInterface`. Notice that the list operations `add` and `replace` do not appear in `SortedListInterface`. Although this can be a good programming practice, that is all it is. A client need only ignore this practice and define the data type of `sList` as `SortedList` to have all operations of the ADT list available to it. You have already seen how a client can sabotage the sorted list in this case.

● Implement the list's `add` and `replace` methods within the class `SortedList`, but have them return false. For example, `add` could appear as follows:

```
public boolean add(int newPosition, T newEntry)
{
  return false;
} // end add
```

This version of add overrides and hides from the client the version that `LList` implements. If the client invokes this method, the sorted list will remain unchanged. The client can detect that the method was unsuccessful, but not why.

If the list's method were a void method, we could give the overriding version an empty body, but then the client would be unaware that the method did not do anything.

- Implement the list's `add` and `replace` methods within the class `SortedList` and have them throw an exception when invoked. For example, `add` could appear as follows:

```
public boolean add(int newPosition, T newEntry)
{
   throw new UnsupportedOperationException("Illegal attempt to add " +
               "at a specified position within a sorted list.");
} // end add
```

This version of `add` also overrides and hides the version that `LList` implements. If the client invokes this method, an exception occurs. This approach is a common practice, and it is the one we prefer.

The list's `add` method, although overridden, can still be called by `SortedList`'s method `add`, as happens in Segment 14.1. The use of `super` in the call indicates that we are invoking the list's version of the method, not the overriding version in `SortedList`.

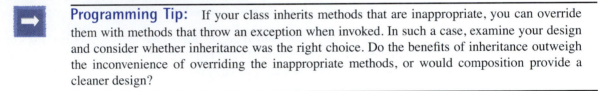

Question 2   As a variation of the second possibility just given, you could implement the ADT list's two `add` methods so that each one calls the `add` method specified in `SortedListInterface`. In this way, the new entry is added in its correct position within the sorted list. Why is this not a good idea?

Programming Tip: If your class inherits methods that are inappropriate, you can override them with methods that throw an exception when invoked. In such a case, examine your design and consider whether inheritance was the right choice. Do the benefits of inheritance outweigh the inconvenience of overriding the inappropriate methods, or would composition provide a cleaner design?

14.4   **Efficiency.** The implementation of `SortedList` given here has the same efficiency—or inefficiency in this case—as the version that uses composition given in the previous chapter. If `LList` had been designed with inheritance in mind, `SortedList` could access `LList`'s underlying data structure and provide faster operations. To this end, we revise the class `LList` in the next section.

Note: The implementation of the sorted list that extends the class `LList` is as inefficient as the implementation that uses composition given in the previous chapter.

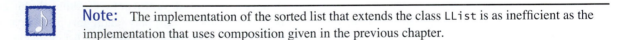

Question 3   Give at least one advantage and one disadvantage of using inheritance in the way shown in this section to implement the class `SortedList`.

Designing a Base Class

14.5   Let's examine the class `LList` that we developed in Chapters 6 and 7 as a linked implementation of the ADT list. Recall that the class places each of the list's entries into its own node. These nodes are linked so that the first entry's node references the node of the second entry, and so on. A data field `firstNode` of the class references the first node, and another data field `length` counts the number of entries in the list.

Like most classes, LList has data fields that are private. The client cannot access these fields directly by name. The class designer must decide whether to provide public methods that give the client indirect access to the data fields. In the case of LList, the public method getLength enables the client to get the length of the list. The client, however, cannot directly change the list's length. Only other member methods, such as add and remove, can alter the length. In addition, LList denies the client access to the field firstNode by not providing public accessor or mutator methods for this field. This design is appropriate, as firstNode is an implementation detail that should be hidden from the client.

14.6 The excerpt of the class LList given in Listing 14-1 shows aspects of the class that are relevant to this discussion. Each node is represented by the private class Node, which is defined within LList and hidden from the client. The method getNodeAt facilitates the implementation of other member methods by returning a reference to the node at a given position. We do not want the client to have access to this node, since it is part of the underlying representation of the list, so we make the method private.

Listing 14-1   Relevant aspects of the class LList

```
public class LList<T> implements ListInterface<T>
{
   private Node firstNode; // reference to first node
   private int  length;    // number of entries in list

   public LList()
   {
      clear();
   } // end default constructor

   public final void clear()
   {
      firstNode = null;
      length = 0;
   } // end clear

   public int getLength()
   {
      return length;
   } // end getLength

   < Implementations of the public methods add, remove, replace, getEntry, contains,
      isEmpty, isFull, and display go here. >
   . . .

   /** Task: Returns a reference to the node at a given position. */
   private Node getNodeAt(int givenPosition)
   {
      . . .
   } // end getNodeAt

   private class Node
   {
      private T data;
      private Node next;
```

```
        . . .
    } // end Node
} // end LList
```

14.7   So far, nothing should be new to you. Now imagine that we want LList to serve as a base class for another class that you are developing. You saw in the previous section of this chapter that a subclass of LList—just like a client of LList—cannot access by name anything declared as private within LList. That is, a subclass cannot access the data field firstNode, the method getNodeAt, or the class Node, as Figure 14-1 illustrates. If we want to extend the capability of LList and do so efficiently, the subclass will need access to these aspects of the class—in other words, to the underlying data structure.

Figure 14-1   A derived class of the class LList cannot access or change anything that is private within LList

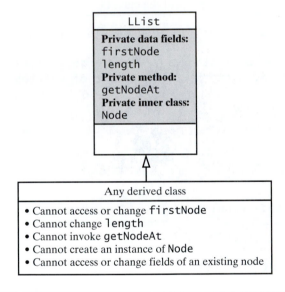

We can revise LList to make it more suitable as a base class by providing its subclasses controlled access to items that are hidden from a client. First, let's recall protected access, which we discussed in Segment 2.17:

Note: Protected access
You can access a protected method or data field by name only within its own class definition C, within a class derived from C, or within any class in the same package as C.

Our goal, then, is to provide a subclass protected but limited access to the underlying chain of nodes. The subclass should be able to traverse or modify the chain efficiently. However, modifications to the chain must be done in a way that helps to maintain its integrity.

14.8 To enable a subclass to access the data fields by name without giving this access to the client, we could declare firstNode and length to be protected. It is more typical, however, to keep them private and to provide protected methods for only the access we desire. The subclass will need to access the head reference firstNode, so we provide a protected get method to do this. Since getLength is public, the subclass can get the value of length.

A subclass likely will need to change firstNode and length, so we could provide protected methods that do so. But while we want an efficient subclass, we also want to keep our data structure intact. So we will not allow a subclass to change these fields directly. Instead, we can provide protected methods that modify our chain of nodes in a way that can satisfy both of our desires. For example, protected methods can add or delete nodes, updating the chain's length in the process. No mutators will be available to directly change either the field length or a node's link. Thus, the subclass can alter the chain efficiently, but we are assured that the nodes will be linked correctly and the chain's length will be accurate.

14.9 As a result of this discussion, we make the following changes to LList:

1. We define a protected method getFirstNode, enabling the subclass to access the head reference firstNode:

```
protected Node getFirstNode()
{
   return firstNode;
} // end getFirstNode
```

2. We define protected methods to add and remove nodes, changing firstNode and length as necessary:

```
/** Task: Adds a node to the beginning of a chain. */
protected void addFirstNode(Node newNode)

/** Task: Adds a node to a chain after a given node. */
protected void addAfterNode(Node nodeBefore, Node newNode)

/** Task: Removes a chain's first node. */
protected T removeFirstNode()

/** Task: Removes the node after a given one. */
protected T removeAfterNode(Node nodeBefore)
```

The implementations of these methods use the techniques presented in Chapters 6 and 7. For example, addFirstNode has the following definition, assuming that the inner class Node has set and get methods:

```
protected void addFirstNode(Node newNode)
{
   assert newNode != null : "null argument in addFirstNode";
   newNode.setNextNode(firstNode);
   firstNode = newNode;
   length++;
} // end addFirstNode
```

To prevent a subclass from overriding these protected methods, you can declare them as final.

3. The public methods of LList and its subclasses can call the previous methods, and thereby reduce the chance of error. For example, we can revise LList's method remove as follows:

```
public T remove(int givenPosition)
{
  T result = null;

  if ((givenPosition >= 1) && (givenPosition <= getLength()))
  {
    assert !isEmpty();

    if (givenPosition == 1)             // case 1: remove first entry
      result = removeFirstNode();
    else                                // case 2: givenPosition > 1
    {
      Node nodeBefore = getNodeAt(givenPosition - 1);
      result = removeAfterNode(nodeBefore);
    } // end if
  } // end if

  return result;
} // end remove
```

4. Next, we make getNodeAt protected instead of private. The client still cannot use this method, but the implementations of the class and any subclass can.

5. We also make the class Node protected instead of private. Node will remain hidden from the client but will be available to any subclass of LList. We could make Node's data fields data and next protected instead of private, but just as we did for LList, we instead make them private and provide protected accessor methods. We also provide a protected set method for a node's data. To ensure the integrity of our chain, we do not allow a subclass to alter the link portion of a node. Thus, Node has the following four methods:

```
protected T getData()
protected void setData(T newData)
protected Node getNextNode()
private void setNextNode(Node nextNode)
```

Finally, we make Node's first constructor protected but leave its second constructor private, since it sets a node's link portion.

Making these changes to the class LList results in a new class, which we will name LListRevised. Figure 14-2 illustrates this class and the access that a derived class has to it. Later in this chapter, we will use LListRevised as the base class for a sorted list.

Programming Tip: Planning for the future

When designing a class, you should plan for its future use as well as the present need. If public accessor methods are not already in your design, provide protected accessor methods. Decide whether you want any future subclass to manipulate your class's data fields. If you do, provide protected methods that enable a subclass to make changes to the data fields both efficiently and safely.

> **Note:** **Serialization**
>
> For completeness, `LListRevised` should implement the interface `java.io.Serializable`, as described in Segment 5.12 of Chapter 5. Recall that serialization allows us to quickly write instances of our list to a file. Notice that the inner class `Node` must also implement `java.io.Serializable`.

Figure 14-2   Access available to a class derived from the class `LListRevised`

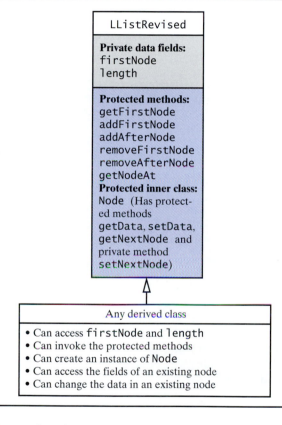

Question 4   Imagine a subclass of the class `LListRevised`.

a.   Implement a method within the subclass that adds an entry to the beginning of the list.

b.   Implement a method within the subclass that adds an entry right after the entry at the midpoint of the list. If the list contains *n* entries, the entry at the midpoint is at position *n* / 2, where the division is truncated to an integer.

Creating an Abstract Base Class

14.10   We can simplify the previous class `LListRevised` by organizing the portion of it that deals with the chain of linked nodes into an abstract base class. Listing 14-2 outlines such a class, `LinkedChain-Base`. Note that this class is abstract by virtue of the keyword `abstract`. All of its methods are implemented, but we do not allow instances of this class.

Listing 14-2   The abstract base class `LinkedChainBase`

```java
public abstract class LinkedChainBase<T> implements java.io.Serializable
{
  private Node firstNode; // reference to first node
  private int  length;    // number of nodes in chain

  public LinkedChainBase()
  {
    clear();
  } // end default constructor
```

  < *Implementations of the public methods* `clear`, `getLength`, `isEmpty`, `isFull`, *and* `display` *go here.* >
  . . .

  < *Implementations of the protected methods* `getNodeAt`, `getFirstNode`, `addFirstNode`, `addAfterNode`, `removeFirstNode`, *and* `removeAfterNode` *go here.* >
  . . .

```java
  protected class Node implements java.io.Serializable
  {
    private T data;    // data portion
    private Node next; // next to next node

    protected Node(T dataPortion)
    {
      data = dataPortion;
      next = null;
    } // end constructor

    private Node(T dataPortion, Node nextNode)
    {
      data = dataPortion;
      next = nextNode;
    } // end constructor
```

    < *Implementations of the protected methods* `getData`, `setData`, *and* `getNextNode` *go here.* >
    . . .

    < *Implementation of the private method* `setNextNode` *goes here.* >
    . . .

```java
  } // end Node
} // end LinkedChainBase
```

14.11   We can now revise the class `LListRevised`, as shown in Listing 14-3.

Listing 14-3   A revision of `LListRevised` that extends `LinkedChainBase`

```java
public class LListRevised<T> extends LinkedChainBase<T>
            implements ListInterface<T>, java.io.Serializable
```

```
{
  public LListRevised()
  {
    super();
  } // end default constructor
```

  < Implementations of the public methods add, remove, replace, getEntry, *and* contains
    go here. >
  . . .

```
} // end LListRevised
```

The base class `LinkedChainBase` can be useful in other contexts as well. You can use it or `LListRevised` to define an efficient implementation of the ADT sorted list, as you will see next.

An Efficient Implementation of a Sorted List

14.12   Instead of calling ADT list operations to perform operations on an ADT sorted list, our implementation will execute faster if it can be similar to the linked implementation that we wrote in the previous chapter, beginning at Segment 13.7. The protected methods defined in the class `LinkedChainBase` will enable us to manipulate the list's underlying data structure faster than if we had to rely solely on the operations of the ADT list to do so. Thus, we want our class to extend `LinkedChainBase`. We begin it by writing

```
public class SortedLinkedList<T extends Comparable<? super T>>
             extends LinkedChainBase<T>
             implements SortedListInterface<T>, java.io.Serializable
```

As before, we will implement a sorted list of `Comparable` objects.

The Method add

14.13   The add operation in our new class is quite similar to the one given in Segment 13.10 for the class `SortedLinkedList`. However, the details of the addition that appear in Segment 13.10 are hidden within the protected methods `addFirstNode` and `addAfterNode` of `LinkedChainBase`. Thus, our revised method appears as follows (changes to the add method of Segment 13.10 appear in color):

```
public boolean add(T newEntry)
{
  Node newNode = new Node(newEntry);
  Node nodeBefore = getNodeBefore(newEntry);

  if (nodeBefore == null) // no need to call isEmpty
    addFirstNode(newNode);
  else
    addAfterNode(nodeBefore, newNode);

  return true;
} // end add
```

Preceding each of the protected methods with super is optional, since no other methods have their names.

Question 4 in Segment 13.11 of Chapter 13 suggested the simplification for empty lists that we made here. When a list is empty, getNodeBefore returns null. Thus, we can omit a call to isEmpty in the if statement.

14.14   **The private method getNodeBefore.** We still need to implement the private method getNodeBefore. The implementation is like the one given in Segment 13.11, but it uses getFirstNode() instead of firstNode:

```
private Node getNodeBefore(T anEntry)
{
   Node currentNode = getFirstNode();
   Node nodeBefore = null;

   while ( (currentNode != null) &&
           (anEntry.compareTo(currentNode.getData()) > 0) )
   {
      nodeBefore = currentNode;
      currentNode = currentNode.getNextNode();
   } // end while

   return nodeBefore;
} // end getNodeBefore
```

14.15   **Efficiency.** This version of the method add executes faster than the versions given in Segments 14.1 and 13.21. Those earlier versions can use only the operations of the ADT list—that is, the public methods of the class LList. Recall that those add methods first invoke getPosition to find where in the list the new entry belongs, and then they invoke the list's add method. The implementation of getPosition given in Segment 13.24 traverses the sorted list to determine the position for the new entry. Within the O(n) loop that performs this traversal is an invocation of the method getEntry. When getEntry has a linked implementation, it also traverses the sorted list, and so it is O(n). Thus, getPosition is O(n^2). It follows that the add methods in Segment 14.1 and Segment 13.21 are each O(n^2).

Our improved add method in Segment 14.13 adds a new node in its proper location by traversing the chain of nodes at most once. Even though the method must use the protected methods to alter the chain of linked nodes, it can add the new node as soon as it finds its proper location, without traversing the chain repeatedly. Thus, it is an O(n) operation.

14.16   **The rest of the class.** To implement remove and getPosition, we would make similar changes to their linked implementations. Recall that Chapter 13 left these implementations as an exercise. Finally, we need to implement the remaining operations of the ADT list that are common to the ADT sorted list.

Note: You can use inheritance *and* maintain efficiency if your base class provides protected access to its underlying data structure.

Note: More than one implementation of an ADT is often possible. When choosing a particular implementation for a given application, you should consider all of the factors relevant to your situation. Execution time, memory use, and extensibility are just some of the issues that you should weigh. These same variables should also be examined when you implement an ADT.

CHAPTER SUMMARY

- This chapter demonstrated the difference between implementations that use composition and those that use inheritance. The basic ideas are the same as those described in Chapter 2. With composition, a class has an object as a data field. The class's methods must act as clients of the object, so they use only the object's public methods. With inheritance, a class inherits all the public methods of its base class. Its implementation, as well as its client, can use these public methods.

- A base class can provide protected methods that enable its subclasses to manipulate its data fields in ways that its client cannot. In this way, a subclass's methods can be more efficient than if they had to use only public methods, as the client must.

- You can derive the sorted list from a base class that has appropriate protected methods and still have an efficient implementation.

PROGRAMMING TIPS

- If your class inherits methods that are inappropriate, you can override them with methods that throw an exception when invoked. In such a case, examine your design and consider whether inheritance was the right choice. Do the benefits of inheritance outweigh the inconvenience of overriding the inappropriate methods, or would composition provide a cleaner design?

- When designing a class, you should plan for its future use as well as the present need. If public accessor methods are not already in your design, provide protected accessor methods. Decide whether you want any future subclass to manipulate your class's data fields. If you do, provide protected methods that enable a subclass to make changes to the data fields both efficiently and safely.

EXERCISES

1. Implement the method `contains` for the class `SortedLinkedList`, as described in Segment 14.12. Take advantage of the list's sorted nature.

2. Write a constructor for the class `SortedLinkedList`, as described in Segment 14.12, that has as a parameter an instance of a class that implements `ListInterface`. The new sorted list should contain all the elements of the list, but in sorted order.

3. Write an `equals` method for the class `SortedLinkedList`, as described in Segment 14.12, that overrides the method `equals` inherited from the class `Object`. Assuming that objects in the list have an appropriate implementation of `equals`, your new method should return true if each entry in one list equals the corresponding entry in a second list.

4. Repeat Exercise 3 for the class `LListRevised`, as described in Segment 14.11, instead of the class `SortedLinkedList`.

5. If the class `LinkedChainBase` had the method `getIterator`, as described in Segment 8.17 of Chapter 8, what would you need to do to define an iterator for the class `SortedLinkedList`?

6. Compare the time efficiency of the sorted list method

public boolean add(T newEntry)

as given in Segment 14.13, with that of the list method

public boolean add(**int** newPosition, T newEntry)

7. Exercise 5 in Chapter 13 asked you to design an ADT for a list of earthquake records. Can you implement this ADT by using inheritance, with LinkedChainBase as the base class? Which methods would you need to override? Is containment more appropriate?

8. Repeat Exercise 7, but consider the class SortedLinkedList, as described in Segment 14.12, instead of LinkedChainBase.

9. Suppose that the class LinkedChainBase, as described in Segment 14.10, implements the interface java.util.ListIterator, as given in Segment 8.32. If LinkedChainBase is a base class of SortedLinkedList, which of the iterator methods are appropriate for a sorted list?

PROJECTS

1. Complete the implementation of the class SortedLinkedList that Segment 14.12 began.

2. Derive the class SortedLinkedList from the class LListRevised, as described in Segment 14.11. What is the disadvantage of this approach?

3. Exercise 4 in Chapter 13 asked you to design the ADT activity list. Show how you would implement such a class by using inheritance, with LListRevised as the base class.

4. Project 8 in Chapter 13 asked you to implement the method mode. Show how you would implement this method for the class SortedLinkedList, as described in Segment 14.12.

5. Using inheritance, derive the class LinkedListWithIterator, as described in Segment 8.19, from the class LListRevised.

Mutable, Immutable, and Cloneable Objects

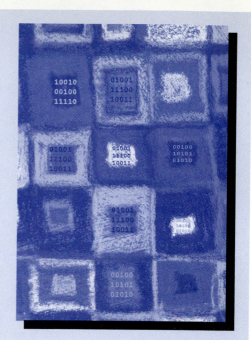

CONTENTS

PREREQUISITES

OBJECTIVES

After studying this chapter, you should be able to

- Distinguish among mutable and immutable objects
- Define a class of immutable objects
- Define companion classes, one of immutable objects and the other of mutable objects
- Define a method `clone` for a given class
- Clone an array or chain of objects
- Implement an ADT such as a sorted list that clones the objects added to it

When a class has public mutator, or set, methods, a client can use these methods to alter objects of that class. Although this ability seems reasonable, it is unreasonable if another class organizes those objects in a particular way. For example, a sorted list of names maintains the names in alphabetical order. If a client can alter a name in the list, it can destroy the order of the list.

This chapter looks at two strategies that prevent this problem. The first one simply requires a client to place into the ADT only objects that cannot be altered. The second strategy requires the ADT to make a copy, or **clone**, of any object that a client adds to it. With this technique, the client has no reference to the copy and so cannot change it. In describing this approach, we discuss how to write methods that make clones of objects.

Mutable and Immutable Objects

15.1   Many of the classes you have studied so far have private data fields and public methods that either look at or change these fields. As you know, such methods are called accessor methods and mutator methods—or, alternatively, get and set methods. An object that belongs to a class that has public mutator methods is said to be **mutable** because the client can use the set methods to change the values of the object's data fields. For example, you saw the class Name of two-part names in Segment 1.16 of Chapter 1. It has the following two data fields:

```
private String first; // first name
private String last;  // last name
```

To change these fields, the class has the mutator methods setFirst and setLast. To look at the fields, it has the accessor methods getFirst and getLast.

Note: A mutable object belongs to a class that has mutator (set) methods for its data fields.

15.2   Let's use this class to create an object for *Chris Coffee* by writing the following Java statement:

```
Name chris = new Name("Chris", "Coffee");
```

Figure 15-1 illustrates this object and the reference variable chris.

Figure 15-1   An object and its reference variable chris

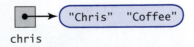

chris

Now suppose we create a list and then add chris to the list by writing

```
ListInterface<Name> nameList = new LList<Name>();
nameList.add(1, chris);
```

Since chris is a mutable object, we can change its data fields by writing, for example,

```
chris.setLast("Smith");
```

After this change, the object chris represents the name *Chris Smith*. Nothing is surprising here. What might be surprising, however, is that the list has changed! That's right: If we retrieve the first item in the list by writing, for instance,

```
System.out.println(nameList.getEntry(1));
```

we will get *Chris Smith* instead of *Chris Coffee*.

15.3   How can it be that the list, which we created before changing the name, contains the changed name? Remember that in Java, the list contains references to the actual objects that the client places in it. So the list has a reference to its first item, but so does the client, since it has the variable chris, as Figure 15-2a shows.

Figure 15-2   An object in the list nameList (a) initially; (b) after the reference variable chris is used to change it

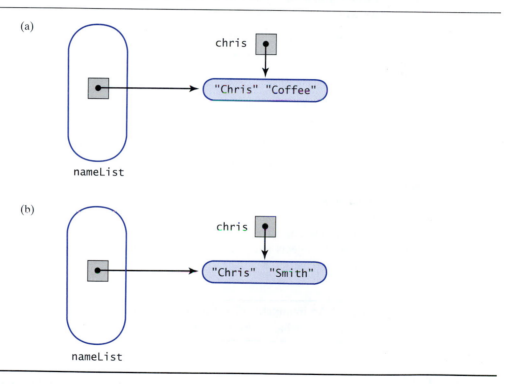

When we altered the object by executing

```
chris.setLast("Smith");
```

we changed the one and only copy of the object, as Figure 15-2b shows. Since the list still references that object, nameList.getEntry(1) returns a reference to the object. This aspect of Java can be a convenient way for the client to alter the objects it has placed in a list.

Note: When a client creates a mutable object and adds it to an ADT list, only one copy of the object ordinarily exists. Thus, if the client alters the object, the list changes. Ideally, the client will use the replace operation to revise an entry in the list, but we cannot force the client to do so.

15.4   The ability to alter mutable objects in an ADT can permit a client to destroy the ADT's integrity. For example, suppose that we create a sorted list of names instead of a list of names. If we write

```
Name jesse = new Name("Jesse", "Java");
Name rob = new Name("Rob", "Bean");
SortedListInterface<Name> alphaList = new SortedList<Name>();
alphaList.add(jesse);
alphaList.add(rob);
alphaList.display();
```

we would get the sorted list

> Rob Bean
> Jesse Java

assuming that `Name` implements the interface `Comparable`. (See Question 9 of Chapter 3.) Now if we write

```
rob.setLast("Smith");
alphaList.display();
```

the list changes to

> Rob Smith
> Jesse Java

This sorted list is no longer alphabetical. One solution to this problem is to require the client to use immutable objects, as the next segment describes.

15.5   An **immutable** object is one whose data fields cannot be altered by a client. The class to which an immutable object belongs has no public mutator (set) methods, so once you create the object, you cannot change its data fields. If you need to change them, you will have to discard the object and create a new one with the revised fields. Such a class is said to be **read only**. A client that places immutable objects into a sorted list cannot alter those objects and thus cannot destroy the sorted order of the list.

Note: An immutable object belongs to a read-only class. Such a class prevents a client from changing the values of its data fields.

Note: When an ADT—such as a sorted list—organizes objects in a certain way, a client should not destroy this organization by altering the objects directly. Yet if the client retains references to the objects, that is exactly what a client could do. You can prevent this problem by adding only immutable objects to the ADT.

15.6   **Mutable or immutable?** Most classes have set methods, so their instances are mutable. Being able to change an object's data is convenient and efficient, particularly when an object's state must change often during the course of a program's execution. For example, a bank must regularly update the object that represents your checking account. If that object were immutable, it would be discarded and a new object representing the updated data would be created each time there was a change. But revising an object takes less time than replacing it.

On the other hand, sharing a mutable object can be dangerous. Suppose that you have two references, a and b, to the same object. If you use a to modify the object, you might get confused when you use b to reference it. But sharing immutable objects is safe, since no matter how you reference them, they remain unchanged.

> **Programming Tip:** Use an immutable object if it will be shared or added to an ADT that can be corrupted by changes to the object. Use a mutable object if its data will change frequently.

Creating a Read-Only Class

15.7   To convert the previous class Name into a read-only class, we can change the access modifiers of the methods setFirst, setLast, and setName from public to private to prevent a client from invoking them. (We could instead omit these methods altogether, modifying the other methods that invoke them.) We also omit Name's method giveLastNameTo.

Let's call the resulting class ImmutableName. If we place instances of ImmutableName in a list or a sorted list, we will not be able to change these objects by using any references that we might have retained to them. Of course, we can use the replace operation of the ADT list to replace a particular item in a list, but no such operation exists for a sorted list. To change an entry in a sorted list, we would remove the entry and add a new one. In this way, the sorted list maintains its sorted order.

Suppose that ImmutableName had protected mutator methods such as setFirst and setLast. A programmer could use inheritance to alter the behavior of the class. Imagine deriving a class of mutable objects from ImmutableName. You then could add instances of this new class to a sorted list of ImmutableName objects. Since these entries are mutable, you could change them and destroy the order of the sorted list. To prevent this from happening, we can make the class final, as described in Segment 2.23 of Chapter 2.

15.8   Listing 15-1 defines ImmutableName as a final class. Since the class has no set methods, we did not define a default constructor. You could define one, even though its use is unnecessary.

Listing 15-1   The read-only class ImmutableName

```
public final class ImmutableName
{
   private String first; // first name
   private String last;  // last name

   public ImmutableName(String firstName, String lastName)
   {
      first = firstName;
      last = lastName;
   } // end constructor

   public String getFirst()
   {
      return first;
   } // end getFirst

   public String getLast()
   {
      return last;
   } // end getLast
```

```
public String getName()
{
  return toString();
} // end getName

public String toString()
{
  return first + " " + last;
} // end toString
} // end ImmutableName
```

15.9   We have one more concern. Imagine a class that has a Name object as a data field. The class has accessor methods, including one that returns the Name field, but has no mutator methods. However, a client of this class can access the Name field and then use Name's set methods to alter the field's value. In other words, the class is not read only. To make it read only, we can define the field as final. Note that the fields of ImmutableName are strings, which are immutable, so we need not make them final.

Note: **Design guidelines for a read-only class**

- The class should be final.
- Data fields should be private.
- The class should not have public set methods.
- Data fields that are mutable objects should be final.

Question 1   Define a constructor for ImmutableName that has a Name object as a parameter.

Companion Classes

15.10   Although immutable objects are desirable for certain applications, mutable objects have their place. Sometimes we will want to represent an object in both immutable and mutable forms. In such cases, a pair of **companion classes** can be convenient. The classes ImmutableName and Name are examples of two such companion classes. The objects in both classes represent names, but one type of object cannot be altered, while the other can be.

    To make the classes even more convenient, you could include constructors and/or methods that convert an object from one type to the other. For example, we might add the following constructor and method to the class ImmutableName:

```
// add to the class ImmutableName:
public ImmutableName(Name aName)
{
  first = aName.getFirst();
  last  = aName.getLast();
} // end constructor

public Name getMutable()
{
  return new Name(first, last);
} // end getMutable
```

Similarly, we could add the following constructor and method to the class `Name`:

```
// add to the class Name
public Name(ImmutableName aName)
{
  first = aName.getFirst();
  last  = aName.getLast();
} // end constructor

public ImmutableName getImmutable()
{
  return new ImmutableName(first, last);
} // end getMutable
```

Figure 15-3 illustrates the two classes `Name` and `ImmutableName`.

Figure 15-3   The classes `Name` and `ImmutableName`

Name
first last
getFirst() getLast() getName() setFirst(firstName) setLast(lastName) setName(firstName, lastName) giveLastNameTo(aName) toString() getImmutable()

ImmutableName
first last
getFirst() getLast() getName() toString() getMutable()

15.11   **Example.** Let's see how we can use the previous additions to our companion classes. If we have a `Name` object such as `flexibleName` in the statement

```
Name flexibleName = new Name("Maria", "Mocha");
```

and we no longer need the capability to change it, we can use `ImmutableName`'s constructor, as follows:

```
ImmutableName fixedName = new ImmutableName(flexibleName);
```

The new object `fixedName` has the same data fields as `flexibleName`, but it is immutable. Alternatively, we could have invoked `Name`'s method `getImmutable`, as follows:

```
ImmutableName fixedName = flexibleName.getImmutable();
```

Similarly, if we have another instance of `ImmutableName`, such as

```
ImmutableName persistent = new ImmutableName("Jesse", "Java");
```

and we find that we need to alter it, we can define a new mutable object as either

```
Name transient = new Name(persistent);
```

or

```
Name transient = persistent.getMutable();
```

The new object `transient` has the same data fields as `persistent`, but it also has set methods to change them.

Question 2   Write Java statements that take the following steps:

- Create an object of the class `Name`.
- Convert the object to an immutable object without changing its data fields.
- Add the object to the sorted list `nameList`.

Question 3   Write Java statements that take the following steps:

- Create an object of the class `Immutable Name`.
- Convert the object to a mutable object without changing its data fields.
- Change the last name of the new object.
- Convert the revised mutable object to an immutable object.

Note: Java's class `String` is a read-only class. That is, instances of `String` are immutable. Once you create a string, you cannot change it. Frequently, however, string applications require that you either remove a portion of a string or join two strings together. For such applications, Java provides the class `StringBuilder` of mutable strings. `StringBuilder` provides several methods that modify a string by adding, removing, or replacing substrings. Appendix A describes some of the methods that belong to these two classes.

String and `StringBuilder` are a pair of companion classes. `String` has a constructor that takes an instance of `StringBuilder` as an argument and produces an immutable string with the same value. `StringBuilder` has an analogous constructor that creates mutable strings from immutable ones. `StringBuilder` also has the methods `substring` and `toString` that return instances of `String`.

Cloneable Objects

15.12   In Segment 15.4, we created a sorted list of mutable objects. Unfortunately, the client of this list can modify the objects so that they are no longer sorted. As you saw then, one solution is to always place immutable objects in a sorted list.

A more involved solution has the ADT copy the client's objects. The ADT then can control what the client can and cannot do to the copies. This section examines how to make a copy of an object.

15.13   In Java, a **clone** is a copy of an object. Typically, we clone only mutable objects. Since sharing an immutable object is safe, cloning it is usually unnecessary.

The class `Object` contains a protected method `clone` that returns a copy of an object. The method has the following header:

protected Object clone() **throws** CloneNotSupportedException

Since `clone` is protected, and since `Object` is the superclass of all other classes, the implementation of any method can contain the invocation

super.`clone()`

But clients of a class cannot invoke `clone` unless the class overrides it and declares it public. Making copies of objects can be expensive, so it might be something you do not want a class to do. By making `clone` a protected method, the designers of Java force you to think twice about cloning.

Programming Tip: Not all classes should have a public `clone` method. In fact, most classes, including read-only classes, do not have one.

15.14   If you want your class to contain a public method `clone`, the class needs to state this fact by implementing the Java interface `Cloneable`, which is in the package `java.lang` of the Java Class Library. Such a class would begin as follows:

public class MyClass **implements** Cloneable
{ . . .

The interface `Cloneable` is simply

public interface Cloneable
{
}

As you can see, the interface is empty. It declares no methods and serves only as a way for a class to indicate that it implements `clone`. If you forget to write `implements Cloneable` in your class definition, instances of your class that invoke `clone` will cause the exception `CloneNotSupportedException`. This result can be confusing at first, particularly if you did implement `clone`.

Programming Tip: If your program produces the exception `CloneNotSupportedException` even though you implemented a method `clone` in your class, you probably forgot to write `implements Cloneable` in your class definition.

Note: **The `Cloneable` interface**
The empty `Cloneable` interface is not a typical interface. A class implements it to indicate that it will provide a public `clone` method. Since the designers of Java wanted to provide a default implementation of the method `clone`, they included it in the class `Object` and not in the interface `Cloneable`. But because the designers did not want every class to automatically have a public `clone` method, they made `clone` a protected method.

Note: **Cloning**
Cloning is not an operation that every class should be able to do. If you want your class to have this ability, you must

- Declare that your class implements the `Cloneable` interface
- Override the protected method `clone` that your class inherits from the class `Object` with a public version

15.15   **Example: Cloning a `Name` object.** Let's add a method `clone` to the class `Name` of Segment 15.10. Before we begin, we should add `implements Cloneable` to the first line of the class definition, as follows:

public class Name **implements** Cloneable

The public method `clone` within `Name` must invoke the method `clone` of its superclass by executing `super.clone()`. Because `Name`'s base class is `Object`, `super.clone()` invokes `Object`'s protected method `clone`. `Object`'s version of `clone` can throw an exception, so we must enclose each call to it in a `try` block and write a `catch` block to handle the exception. The method's final action should return the cloned object.

Thus, `Name`'s method `clone` could appear as follows:

```
public Object clone()
{
   Name theCopy = null;

   try
   {
      theCopy = (Name)super.clone();
   }
   catch (CloneNotSupportedException e)
   {
      System.err.println("Name cannot clone: " + e.toString());
   }

   return theCopy;
} // end clone
```

Since `super.clone()` returns an instance of `Object`, we must cast this instance to `Name`. After all, we are creating a `Name` object as the clone. The `return` statement will implicitly cast `theCopy` to `Object`, as required.

The exception that `Object`'s method `clone` can throw is `CloneNotSupportedException`. Since we are writing a `clone` method for our class `Name`, this exception will never occur. Even so, we still must use `try` and `catch` blocks when invoking `Object`'s `clone` method. Instead of the `println` statement in the `catch` block, we could write the simpler statement

throw new Error(e.toString());

Programming Tip: Every public `clone` method must invoke the method `clone` of the base class by executing `super.clone`. Ultimately, `Object`'s protected `clone` method will be invoked. That invocation must appear in a `try` block, even though a `CloneNotSupportedException` will never occur.

15.16   **Two ways to copy.** What does this method `clone` actually do? You want it to make copies of the data fields associated with the invoking object. When a data field is an object, you can copy it in one of two ways:

● You can copy the reference to the object and share the object with the clone, as illustrated in Figure 15-4a. This copy is called a **shallow copy**; the clone is a **shallow clone**.
● You can copy the object itself, as illustrated in Figure 15-4b. This copy is called a **deep copy**; the clone is a **deep clone**.

Note: `Object`'s `clone` method returns a shallow clone.

Figure 15-4   (a) A shallow clone; (b) a deep clone

(a)

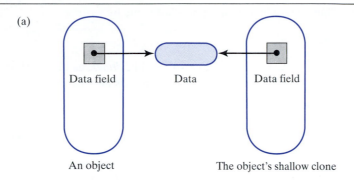

An object   The object's shallow clone

(b)

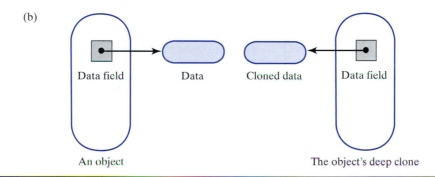

An object   The object's deep clone

15.17   **Name's clone is shallow.** The class Name has the data fields first and last, which are instances of String. Each field contains a reference to a string. It is these references that are copied when clone invokes super.clone(). For example, Figure 15-5 illustrates the objects that the following statements create:

```
Name april = new Name("April", "Jones");
Name twin = (Name)april.clone();
```

The clone twin is a shallow clone because the strings that are the first and last names are not copied.

Figure 15-5   An instance of Name and its shallow clone

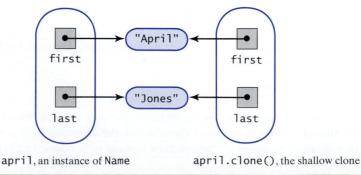

april, an instance of Name   april.clone(), the shallow clone

A shallow clone is good enough for the class Name. Recall that instances of String are immutable. Having an instance of Name and its clone share the same strings is not a problem because no one can change the strings. This is good news since, like many classes that Java provides, String has no method clone. Thus, if we change the clone's last name by writing

```
twin.setLast("Smith");
```

twin's last name will be *Smith*, but april's will still be *Jones*, as Figure 15-6 shows. That is, setLast changes twin's data field last so that it references another string *Smith*. It does not change april's last, so it still references *Jones*.

Figure 15-6   The clone twin, after the statement twin.setLast("Smith") changes one of its data fields

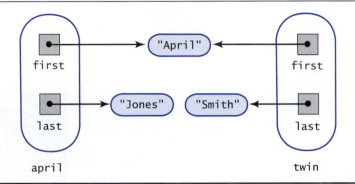

 Programming Tip: Shallow copies of data fields that reference immutable objects are typically sufficient for a clone. Sharing an immutable object is usually safe.

15.18   **Example: Creating a deep clone of a single field.** Sometimes a shallow clone is unsuitable. If a class has mutable objects as data fields, you must clone the objects and not simply copy their references. For example, let's add a method clone to the class Student that we encountered in Segment 2.2 of Chapter 2. Recall that the class has the following form:

```
public class Student
{
   private Name   fullName;
   private String id;

   < Constructors and the methods setStudent, setName, setId, getName, getId, and
      toString >
   . . .
} // end Student
```

Since the class Name has set methods, the data field fullName is a mutable object. Therefore, we should be sure to clone fullName within the definition of Student's clone method. We can do that because we added a clone method to Name in Segment 15.15. Since String is read only, id is immutable, and so cloning it is unnecessary. Thus, we can define a `clone` method for the class `Student` as follows:

```java
public Object clone()
{
   Student theCopy = null;

   try
   {
      theCopy = (Student)super.clone();
   }
   catch (CloneNotSupportedException e)
   {
      throw new Error(e.toString());
   }

   theCopy.fullName = (Name)fullName.clone();
   return theCopy;
} // end clone
```

After invoking `super.clone()`, we clone the mutable data field `fullName` by calling `Name`'s public `clone` method. This latter invocation need not be within a `try` block. Only `Object`'s `clone` method contains a `throws` clause.

Figure 15-7 illustrates an instance of `Student` and the clone that this method returns. As you can see, the `Name` object that represents the student's full name is copied, but the strings that represent the first and last names, as well as the ID number, are not.

Figure 15-7   An instance of `Student` and its clone, including a deep copy of `fullName`

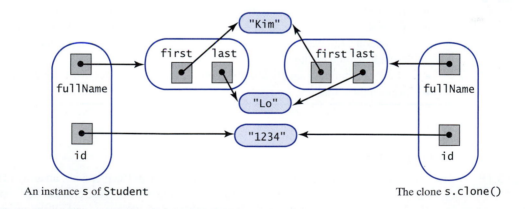

An instance s of **Student**   The clone s.clone()

Had we failed to clone the data field `fullName`—that is, had we omitted the statement

```java
theCopy.fullName = (Name)fullName.clone();
```

the student's full name would be shared by the original instance and its clone. Figure 15-8 illustrates this situation.

Figure 15-8   An instance of `Student` and its clone, including a shallow copy of `fullName`

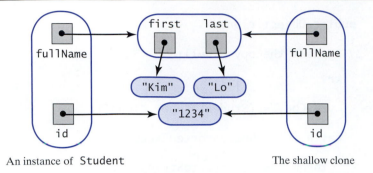

An instance of `Student`   The shallow clone

Question 4   Suppose that x is an instance of `Student` and y is its clone; that is,

```
Student y = (Student)x.clone();
```

a.   If you change x's last name by executing

```
Name xName = x.getName();
xName.setLast("Smith");
```

does y's last name change? Explain.

b.   If you fail to clone `fullName` within `Student`'s `clone` method, will changing x's last name change y's last name as well? Explain.

Note: Within each public `clone` method, you typically perform the following tasks:

- Invoke the `clone` method of the superclass by writing `super.clone()`.
- Enclose this call to `clone` in a `try` block, and write a `catch` block to handle the possible exception `CloneNotSupportedException`. You can skip this step if `super.clone()` invokes a public `clone` method.
- Clone the mutable data fields of the object that `super.clone()` returned, when possible.
- Return the clone.

Cloning an Array

15.19   The classes `AList` and `ExpandableArrayList` that you saw in Chapter 5 use an array to implement the ADT list. Suppose that we want to add a `clone` method to each of these classes. Let's consider `AList`.

While making a copy of the list, `clone` needs to copy the array and all the objects in it. Thus, the objects in the list must have a `clone` method as well. Recall that `AList` defines a generic type T for the objects it contains. Beginning `AList` as

```
public class AList<T extends Cloneable> . . . // incorrect
```

will not work correctly, since the interface `Cloneable` is empty.

Instead, we define a new interface that declares a public method `clone` to override `Object`'s protected method:

```
public interface Copyable extends Cloneable
{
  public Object clone();
} // end Copyable
```

We then can begin AList with any of the following statements:

- **public class** AList<T **extends** Copyable> **implements** ListInterface<T>, Cloneable
- **public class** AList<T **extends** Copyable> **implements** ListInterface<T>, Copyable
- **public class** AList<T **extends** Copyable> **implements** CloneableListInterface<T>

where CloneableListInterface is defined as follows:

```
public interface CloneableListInterface<T>
                 extends ListInterface<T>, Copyable // or Cloneable
{
} // end CloneableListInterface
```

The notation

```
AList<T extends Copyable>
```

requires the objects in the list to belong to a class that implements our interface Copyable.

Note that CloneableListInterface extends two interfaces, ListInterface and either Copyable or Cloneable. As noted in Segment 3.25 of Chapter 3, an interface can extend more than one interface, even though a class can extend only one other class.

Programming Tip: When bounding generic types, use an interface that declares a public method clone instead of using Cloneable. The new interface must extend Cloneable, however.

15.20   Using Copyable as a bound for T requires us to change the implementation of AList's constructor. Recall from Segment 5.5 that one field of AList is an array of list entries:

```
private T[] list;
```

Writing

```
list = (T[]) new Object[maxSize];
```

in the constructor causes a ClassCastException. Instead, we write

```
list = (T[]) new Copyable[maxSize];
```

15.21   Now we can implement clone. We will invoke super.clone() within a try block but perform the rest of the tasks after the catch block. Thus, we have the following outline for AList's method clone:

```
public Object clone()
{
  AList<T> theCopy = null;

  try
  {
    theCopy = (AList<T>)super.clone(); // not enough by itself
  }
```

```
catch (CloneNotSupportedException e)
{
   throw new Error(e.toString());
}
```

< For a deep copy, we need to do more here, as you will see. >

```
. . .
   return theCopy;
} // end clone
```

The method first invokes `super.clone` and casts the returned object to `AList<T>`. To perform a deep copy, we need to clone the data fields that are or could be mutable objects. Thus, we need to clone the array `list`.

15.22   Arrays in Java have a `clone` method; in other words, they implement `Cloneable`. So we can add the following statement to the list's `clone` method:

```
theCopy.list = (T[])list.clone();
```

No `try` and `catch` blocks are necessary here.

An array's `clone` method creates a shallow copy of each object in the array. For our deep copy, we need to clone each array element. Since we insisted that the list's entries have a public `clone` method, we can write a loop whose body contains the following statement:

```
theCopy.list[index] = (T)list[index].clone();
```

We can control the loop by using `AList`'s data field `length`, which records the number of entries in the list.

Thus, we have the following definition of `clone` for the class `AList`:

```
public Object clone()
{
   AList<T> theCopy = null;

   try
   {
      theCopy = (AList<T>)super.clone();
   }
   catch (CloneNotSupportedException e)
   {
      throw new Error(e.toString());
   }

   theCopy.list = (T[])list.clone();

   for (int index = 0; index < length; index++)
      theCopy.list[index] = (T)list[index].clone();

   return theCopy;
} // end clone
```

The definition of `clone` for `ExpandableArrayList` is similar.

> **Note:** To make a deep clone of an array a of cloneable objects, you invoke `a.clone()` and then clone each object in the array. For example, if `myArray` is an array of `Thing` objects, and `Thing` implements `Cloneable`, you would write
>
> ```
> Thing[] clonedArray = (Thing[])myArray.clone();
>
> for (int index = 0; index < myArray.length; index++)
>    clonedArray[index] = (Thing)myArray[index].clone();
> ```

Cloning a Chain

15.23   Now suppose that we want to add a `clone` method to a linked implementation of the ADT list, such as the class `LList` of Chapters 6 and 7 or the class `LinkedChainBase` of Chapter 14. (The `clone` methods for these classes are virtually identical.) Given the interface `Copyable`, we can begin the class in one of the ways given in Segment 15.19. Ultimately, the class and the objects in the list must implement the interface `Cloneable`. Thus, `LList`, for example, could begin as follows:

```
public class LList<T extends Copyable>
             implements CloneableListInterface<T>
{
  private Node firstNode; // reference to first node
  private int  length;    // number of entries in list
  . . .
```

The first part of the `clone` method would be like the code that you saw in Segment 15.21, except that we would replace `AList` with `LList`. If we invoked only `super.clone()`, our method would produce a shallow copy of the list, as Figure 15-9 illustrates. In other words, both the original list and its clone would reference the same chain of nodes, and these nodes would reference one set of data.

As before, `clone` needs to do more to perform a deep copy. It needs to clone the chain of nodes as well as the data that the nodes reference. Figure 15-10 shows a list with its deep clone.

15.24   **Cloning a node.** To clone the nodes in the chain, we need to add a method `clone` to the inner class `Node`. First, we add `implements Cloneable` to the declaration of the class `Node`. Note that `Node` is private in `LList` but protected in `LinkedChainBase`. `Node`'s `clone` method begins like other `clone` methods, but then it goes on to clone the data portion of the node. We do not bother cloning the link, since the list's `clone` method will set it. With these changes, the revised class `Node` appears in `LList` as follows (changes are indicated in color):

```
private class Node implements Cloneable
{
  private T    data;
  private Node next;

  < Constructors >
  . . .

  < Accessor and mutator methods getData, setData, getNextNode, and setNextNode >
  . . .
```

Figure 15-9   A list and its shallow clone: linked implementation

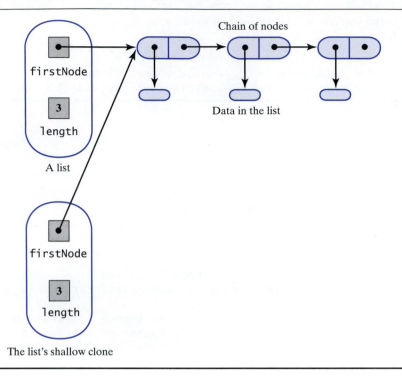

Figure 15-10   A list and its deep clone: linked implementation

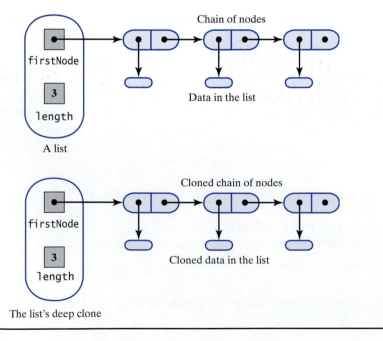

```
    protected Object clone()
    {
      Node theCopy = null;
      try
      {
        theCopy = (Node)super.clone();
      }
      catch (CloneNotSupportedException e)
      {
        throw new Error(e.toString());
      }

      theCopy.data = (T)data.clone();
      theCopy.next = null; // don't clone link; it's set later

      return theCopy;
    } // end clone
} // end Node
```

Remember that data invokes a public method clone that does not throw an exception, and so data.clone() can appear outside of a try block.

15.25   **Cloning the chain.** LList's clone method invokes super.clone() in a statement such as

```
    LList<T> theCopy = (LList<T>)super.clone();
```

The method then must clone the chain of nodes that stores the list's data. To do so, the method needs to traverse the chain, clone each node, and link the cloned nodes appropriately. We begin by cloning the first node so that we can set the data field firstNode correctly:

```
    // make a copy of the first node
    theCopy.firstNode = (Node)firstNode.clone();
```

Next, we traverse the rest of the chain. A reference newRef references the last node that we have added to the new chain, while the reference oldRef keeps track of where we are in the traversal of the original chain. The statement

```
    newRef.setNextNode((Node)oldRef.clone()); // attach cloned node
```

clones the current node in the original chain, along with its data, and then links the clone to the end of the new chain. Recall that Node's clone method also clones the data that a node references.

The following statements incorporate the previous ideas and clone the rest of the chain:

```
    Node newRef = theCopy.firstNode;        // last node in new chain
    Node oldRef = firstNode.getNextNode(); // next node in old chain

    for (int count = 2; count <= length; count++)
    {
      newRef.setNextNode((Node)oldRef.clone()); // attach cloned node
      newRef = newRef.getNextNode();            // update references
      oldRef = oldRef.getNextNode();
    } // end for
```

15.26   The code in the previous segment assumes a nonempty chain of nodes. The complete clone method that follows checks for an empty chain.

```java
public Object clone()
{
    LList<T> theCopy = null;

    try
    {
        theCopy = (LList<T>) super.clone();
    }
    catch (CloneNotSupportedException e)
    {
        throw new Error(e.toString());
    }

    // copy underlying chain of nodes
    if (firstNode == null) // if chain is empty
    {
        theCopy.firstNode = null;
    }
    else
    {
        // make a copy of the first node
        theCopy.firstNode = (Node)firstNode.clone();

        // make a copy of the rest of chain
        Node newRef = theCopy.firstNode;
        Node oldRef = firstNode.getNextNode();

        for (int count = 2; count <= length; count++)
        {
            // clone node and its data; link clone to new chain
            newRef.setNextNode((Node)oldRef.clone());
            newRef = newRef.getNextNode();
            oldRef = oldRef.getNextNode();
        } // end for
    } // end if

    return theCopy;
} // end clone
```

 Note: To make a deep clone of a chain of linked nodes that reference cloneable objects, you must clone the nodes as well as the objects.

 Question 5 The for statement in Segment 15.26 is controlled by the number of nodes in the chain. Revise this statement and its associated loop so that it is controlled by oldRef.

A Sorted List of Clones

15.27   Segment 15.4 talked about the danger of placing mutable objects in an ADT such as a sorted list. If the client retains a reference to any of the objects, it could alter those objects and destroy the integrity of the ADT. In the case of a sorted list, the client could destroy the sorted order of the objects.

Segment 15.5 offered one solution to this problem, namely to place only immutable objects in the ADT. This section offers another solution that enables you to place mutable objects in the ADT.

Suppose that a client adds an object to an ADT. Imagine that the ADT clones the object before adding it to its data. The client then would be able to access or change the ADT's data only by using ADT operations. It would not have a reference to the clone that it could use to alter the clone. Of course, this scenario requires that the added object be `Cloneable`. Let's examine the details of such an implementation of the ADT sorted list.

15.28   Segment 13.1 noted that objects in a sorted list must be `Comparable`—that is, they must have a `compareTo` method. In this case, we also want the objects to be `Cloneable`. Segment 15.19 defined an interface `Copyable` that declares a public method `clone`. Using that interface, let's create another one:

```
public interface ComparableAndCopyable<T>
                 extends Comparable<T>, Copyable
{
} // end ComparableAndCopyable
```

This interface will enable us to bound the generic type of the objects we place into the sorted list, as the next segment will show.

A class that implements `ComparableAndCopyable` must define the methods `compareTo` and `clone`. For example, the class `Name` mentioned in Segment 15.15 could begin as follows:

```
public class Name implements ComparableAndCopyable<Name>
```

`Name`'s method `clone` is given in Segment 15.15, and you wrote `compareTo` when you answered Question 9 in Chapter 3 (see Appendix E for this method).

15.29   Since we want the sorted list to contain only objects that are both `Comparable` and `Copyable`, we can begin the definition of a class `SortedList` as follows:

```
public class SortedList<T extends ComparableAndCopyable<? super T>>
```

We introduced this notation in Segments 11.1 and 11.2 of Chapter 11. The class that `T` represents must implement the interface `ComparableAndCopyable`. The notation `? super T`, which means any superclass of `T`, affects the interface `Comparable`—as you can see by looking at `ComparableAndCopyable`—and hence the method `compareTo`.

We can revise our interface for a sorted list as follows:

```
public interface SortedListInterface
                 <T extends ComparableAndCopyable<? super T>>
```

and then use it in the definition of `SortedList`:

```
public class SortedList<T extends ComparableAndCopyable<? super T>>
             implements SortedListInterface<T>
```

15.30   With these logistics out of the way, we propose the following changes to the implementation of the ADT sorted list. You can apply these changes to the implementations discussed in Chapters 13 and 14:

● In `add`, place a clone of the desired entry into the sorted list instead of the entry itself. That is, place `newEntry.clone()` into the list instead of `newEntry`. Thus, the body of the method could begin with

```
Node newNode = new Node((T)newEntry.clone());
```

Since clone returns an `Object`, the cast to the generic type `T` is necessary.

- In getEntry, return a clone of the desired entry instead of the entry itself. For example, you could return (T)result.clone() instead of result.

Let's examine these changes more closely. Suppose that a client has a reference, newEntry, to an object, and it adds the object to an ADT. The ADT clones the object and adds the clone instead of the original object, as Figure 15-11 illustrates. The client has no reference to the ADT's data. If the client modifies the object that newEntry references, the ADT is not changed.

What if getEntry did not return a clone of the desired entry but instead returned a reference to the desired entry in the ADT? As Figure 15-12 illustrates, the client would be able to change the entry within the ADT. So even though the ADT contains a clone of the client's original object, getEntry would give the client access to the clone. Thus, it is necessary for getEntry to return a clone of the desired entry. This is a clone of the clone of the client's original object, as Figure 15-13 shows.

Figure 15-11 An ADT and its client after the clone of an object is added to the ADT

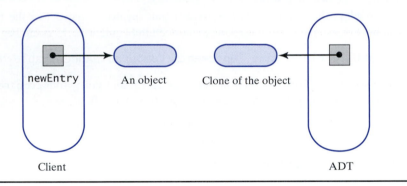

Figure 15-12 The effect of getEntry if it did not return a clone

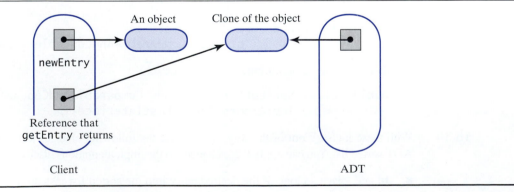

Figure 15-13 The effect of `getEntry` when it returns a clone

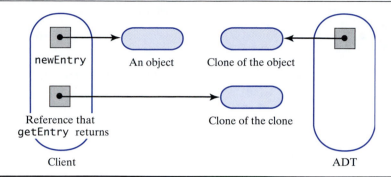

 Note: An ADT can clone the objects that a client adds to it, but you will have duplicates of each entry in the ADT. For complex objects, the time and memory needed to make each copy can be substantial.

15.31 Realize that some devious programming could defeat the purpose of our sorted list of clones. You could write a `clone` method that retains a reference to the clone. Then, knowing when an ADT calls `clone`, you could get and retain the reference to the clone. Restricting the contents of an ADT to immutable objects is a safer way to maintain its integrity.

CHAPTER SUMMARY

- An object that belongs to a class having public mutator (set) methods is mutable because the client can use the methods to change the values of the object's data fields. If a client cannot change the values of an object's data fields, the object's class is read only, and the object is immutable.

- A read-only class is final, has private data fields that, if mutable, are final, and has no public set methods.

- Companion classes represent the same data in both immutable and mutable forms.

- The class `Object` includes a protected method `clone` that makes an identical copy of an object. A class can override `clone` and declare it public, thus making it available to a client of the class. Such a class must implement the Java interface `Cloneable`. If a class does not override `clone`, it has no `clone` method, since `clone` is protected in `Object`.

- A `clone` method should invoke `super.clone()` to ensure that all aspects of an object are copied.

- Every array has a `clone` method that copies the array but not the objects in it. A separate step is necessary to clone these objects.

- To create a deep clone of a chain of linked nodes, you must clone the nodes, including their data objects.

EXERCISES

1. Is the class `Student` that is mentioned in Segment 15.18 mutable or immutable? Describe what you would do to create a companion class for `Student`.

2. **a.** Using the method `getEntry` of the ADT list, describe a client-level method that modifies the entry at a given position within a list.
   b. What must you know about the entries in the list for your method to work?
   c. Does the method `replace` of the ADT list have any advantage over your method?

3. Implement the method `compareTo` for the class `ImmutableName`.

4. Consider the following class definition:

```
public class Friend
{
   private Name    friendsName;
   private String friendsAddress;

   public Friend(Name aName, String anAddress)
   {
      friendsName = aName;
      friendsAddress = anAddress;
   } // end constructor

   public Name getName()
   {
      return friendsName;
   } // end getName

   public String getAddress()
   {
      return friendsAddress;
   } // end getAddress
} // end Friend
```

Is this class read only? Why?

5. Given the class `Name`, define a companion class `ImmutableName` by using composition. That is, `ImmutableName` should contain an instance of `Name` as a data field. What are the advantages and disadvantages of using composition to define companion classes?

6. Given the class `ImmutableName`, define a companion class `Name` by using inheritance. What are the advantages and disadvantages of using inheritance to define companion classes?

7. Define an interface, `ImmutableNameInterface`, that declares the methods in the class `ImmutableName`. Define another interface, `MutableNameInterface`, that extends `ImmutableNameInterface` and declares the methods in the class `Name`. Then modify the classes `ImmutableName` and `Name` so that they implement `ImmutableNameInterface` and `MutableNameInterface`, respectively.

8. A variable of type `ImmutableNameInterface` can reference objects of what type?

9. A variable of type `MutableNameInterface` can reference objects of what type?

10. A variable of type `Name` can reference objects of what type?

11. A variable of type `ImmutableName` can reference objects of what type?

12. The class `NickName` given in Segment 2.7 has a data field that is an instance of the class `Name` and two methods, `setNickName` and `getNickName`. Implement a method `clone` for `NickName`, assuming that `Name` implements the interface `Cloneable`.

13. Consider a class that implements `ListInterface` but does not make clones of objects added to the list. Suggest two ways that we can make a list of clones.

14. Consider a class that implements `ListInterface` and makes clones of objects added to the list. Suggest two ways that we can make a list of the original objects.

15. Consider the following class definition:

```
public class FamilyMember implements Cloneable
{
  private Name myName;
  private FamilyMember mySpouse;

  public FamilyMember(Name aName)
  {
    myName = aName;
  } // end constructor

  public Name getName()
  {
    return myName;
  } // end getName

  public FamilyMember getSpouse()
  {
    return mySpouse;
  } // end getSpouse
```

```java
   public void setSpouse(FamilyMember spouse)
   {
     mySpouse = spouse;
   } // end setSpouse

   public Object clone()
   {
     FamilyMember theCopy = null;
     try
     {
       theCopy = (FamilyMember)super.clone();
     }
     catch(CloneNotSupportedException e)
     {
       System.err.println("FamilyMember cannot clone:" +
                          e.toString());
     }
     return theCopy;
   } // end clone
} // end FamilyMember
```

Draw a diagram showing the state of the objects after the following code executes.

```java
FamilyMember jack = new FamilyMember(new Name("Jack", "Buck"));
FamilyMember jane = new FamilyMember(new Name("Jane", "Doe"));
jack.setSpouse(jane);
jane.setSpouse(jack);
FamilyMember copy = (FamilyMember)jane.clone();
```

PROJECTS

1. Define a pair of companion classes modeled after the class Student, as given in Segment 2.2.

2. Project 3 in Chapter 10 asked you to write a class KnapsackItem of items that would be placed in a list. Design and implement a pair of companion classes for such knapsack items.

3. Project 4 in Chapter 10 asked you to write a class Activity of activities that would be placed in a list. Design and implement a pair of companion classes for such activities.

4. Chapter 5 describes an implementation of the ADT list that uses an instance of the class Vector to represent the entries in the list. Write a clone method for this implementation and demonstrate that it works. Note that Vector implements the interface Cloneable.

5. Revise the linked implementation of the ADT sorted list, as given in Chapter 13, according to the suggestions about cloning given in Segment 15.30. That is, the method add should place a clone of the desired entry, instead of the entry itself, into the sorted list. Additionally, the method getEntry should return a clone of the desired entry, instead of returning the entry itself.

6. Suppose that you wanted to implement a deep copy for the class FamilyMember defined in Exercise 15 in this chapter.

   a. What difficulty will arise?
   b. Implement a clone method for FamilyMember that makes a deep copy.

16
Searching

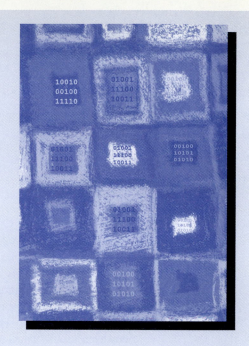

CONTENTS

PREREQUISITES

417

OBJECTIVES

After studying this chapter, you should be able to

- Search an array by using a sequential search
- Search an array by using a binary search
- Search a chain of linked nodes sequentially
- Describe the time efficiency of a search

People are always looking for something, be it a date, a mate, or a lost sock. In fact, searching is one of the most common tasks done for us by computers. Just think of how many times you search the World Wide Web. This chapter looks at two simple search strategies, the sequential search and the binary search. You can use these strategies when implementing the method `contains` for either the ADT list or the ADT sorted list. A binary search is usually much faster than a sequential search when the data is in an array rather than a chain of linked nodes and when the data is sorted. Sorting data, however, usually takes much more time than searching it. This fact should influence your choice of search method in a given situation.

The Problem

16.1   Like the people in Figure 16-1, you can search your desk for a pen, your closet for your favorite sweater, or a list of names to see whether you are on it. Searching for a particular item—sometimes called the **target**—among a collection of many items is a common task.

Figure 16-1   Searching is an everyday occurrence

Let's find your name on that list. If `nameList` is an instance of an ADT list whose entries are names, we can search it by using the list operation `contains`. Recall that this method is boolean-valued and returns true if a given item is in the list.

The implementation of `contains` depends upon how we store the list entries. Among the implementations of the ADT list given in Chapters 5, 6, and 7 is one that stores the list's entries in an array and another that uses a chain of linked nodes. Let's look at the array first.

Searching an Unsorted Array

16.2   As Segment 5.10 mentioned, a **sequential search** of a list compares the desired item—the target—with the first entry in the list, the second entry in the list, and so on until it either locates the desired entry or looks at all the entries without success. In an array-based implementation of the list, we search the array that contains the list's entries. We can implement this search either iteratively or recursively. This section looks at both approaches and examines their efficiencies.

Recall that two data fields of our list implementation in Chapter 5 are the array `list`, which contains the list's entries, and the integer `length`, which is the number of entries.

An Iterative Sequential Search of an Unsorted Array

16.3   The following implementation of `contains` was given in Segment 5.10. It uses a loop to search the array `list` containing `length` objects having the generic type `T` for a particular object `anEntry`:

```java
public boolean contains(T anEntry)
{
  boolean found = false;

  for (int index = 0; !found && (index < length); index++)
  {
    if (anEntry.equals(list[index]))
      found = true;
  } // end for

  return found;
} // end contains
```

The loop exits as soon as it locates the first entry in the array that matches the desired item. In this case, `found` is true. On the other hand, if the loop examines all the entries in the list without finding one that matches `anEntry`, `found` remains false. Figure 16-2 provides an example of these two outcomes. For simplicity, our illustrations use integers.

Figure 16-2   An iterative sequential search of an array that (a) finds its target; (b) does not find its target

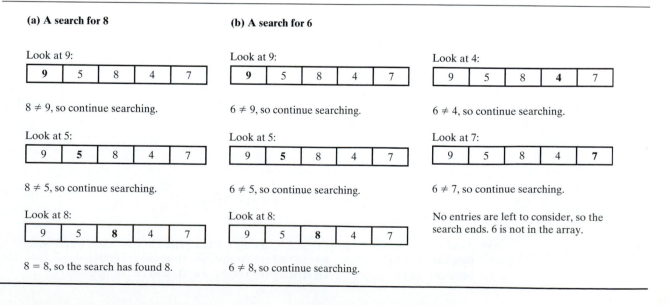

(a) A search for 8

Look at 9:

| 9 | 5 | 8 | 4 | 7 |

8 ≠ 9, so continue searching.

Look at 5:

| 9 | 5 | 8 | 4 | 7 |

8 ≠ 5, so continue searching.

Look at 8:

| 9 | 5 | 8 | 4 | 7 |

8 = 8, so the search has found 8.

(b) A search for 6

Look at 9:

| 9 | 5 | 8 | 4 | 7 |

6 ≠ 9, so continue searching.

Look at 5:

| 9 | 5 | 8 | 4 | 7 |

6 ≠ 5, so continue searching.

Look at 8:

| 9 | 5 | 8 | 4 | 7 |

6 ≠ 8, so continue searching.

Look at 4:

| 9 | 5 | 8 | 4 | 7 |

6 ≠ 4, so continue searching.

Look at 7:

| 9 | 5 | 8 | 4 | 7 |

6 ≠ 7, so continue searching.

No entries are left to consider, so the search ends. 6 is not in the array.

Question 1   Write a method `contains` that returns the index of the first array element that equals `anEntry`. If the array does not contain such an element, return -1.

Question 2   Write a method `contains` that performs an iterative sequential search of a list by using only operations of the ADT list. The method should return true if a given item is in a given list.

A Recursive Sequential Search of an Unsorted Array

16.4   We begin a sequential search of an array by looking at the first entry in the array. If that entry is the desired one, we end the search. Otherwise we search the rest of the array. Since this new search is also sequential and since the rest of the array is smaller than the original array, we have a recursive description of a solution to our problem. Well, almost. We need a base case. An empty array could be the base case because it never contains the desired item.

For the array a, we search the n elements a[0] through a[n - 1] by beginning with the first element, a[0]. If it is not the one we seek, we need to search the rest of the array—that is, we search array elements a[1] through a[n - 1]. In general, we search the array elements a[first] through a[n - 1]. To be even more general, we can search array elements a[first] through a[last], where first ≤ last.

16.5   The following pseudocode describes the logic of our recursive algorithm:

> *Algorithm to search* a[first] *through* a[last] *for* desiredItem
> **if** (*there are no elements to search*)
>   **return false**
> **else if** (desiredItem *equals* a[first])
>   **return true**
> **else**
>   **return** *the result of searching* a[first + 1] *through* a[last]

Figure 16-3 illustrates a recursive search of an array.

16.6   The method that implements this algorithm will need parameters `first` and `last`. To spare the client the detail of providing values for these parameters, and to allow the method `contains` to have the same header as it did in Segment 16.3, we implement the algorithm as a private method `search` that `contains` invokes. Since we again assume the array-based list implementation from Chapter 5, the array `list` takes the place of the array a in the previous algorithm, and `length` is the number of elements to search. Because `list` and `length` are data fields of the class that implements the list, they are not parameters of the methods that follow.

```
/** Task: Searches the list for anEntry. */
public boolean contains(T anEntry)
{
  return search(0, length - 1, anEntry);
} // end contains

/** Task: Searches list[first] through list[last] for desiredItem.
 *  @param first        an integer index >= 0 and < length
 *  @param last         an integer index >= 0 and < length
```

```
    *  @param desiredItem  the object to be found
    *  @return true if desiredItem is found */
   private boolean search(int first, int last, T desiredItem)
   {
      boolean found;

      if (first > last)
         found = false; // no elements to search
      else if (desiredItem.equals(list[first]))
         found = true;
      else
         found = search(first + 1, last, desiredItem);

      return found;
   } // end search
```

Figure 16-3   A recursive sequential search of an array that (a) finds its target; (b) does not find its target

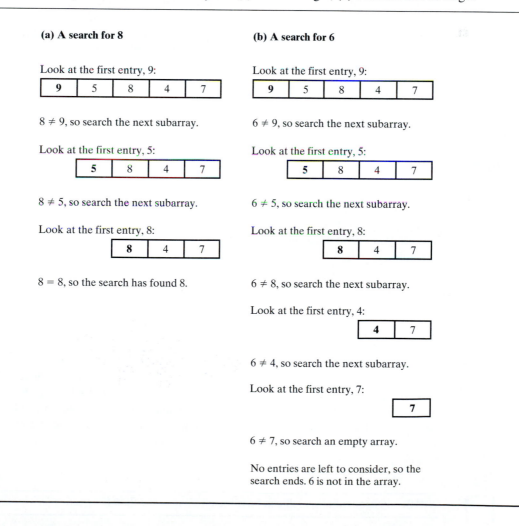

(a) A search for 8

Look at the first entry, 9:

| 9 | 5 | 8 | 4 | 7 |

8 ≠ 9, so search the next subarray.

Look at the first entry, 5:

| 5 | 8 | 4 | 7 |

8 ≠ 5, so search the next subarray.

Look at the first entry, 8:

| 8 | 4 | 7 |

8 = 8, so the search has found 8.

(b) A search for 6

Look at the first entry, 9:

| 9 | 5 | 8 | 4 | 7 |

6 ≠ 9, so search the next subarray.

Look at the first entry, 5:

| 5 | 8 | 4 | 7 |

6 ≠ 5, so search the next subarray.

Look at the first entry, 8:

| 8 | 4 | 7 |

6 ≠ 8, so search the next subarray.

Look at the first entry, 4:

| 4 | 7 |

6 ≠ 4, so search the next subarray.

Look at the first entry, 7:

| 7 |

6 ≠ 7, so search an empty array.

No entries are left to consider, so the search ends. 6 is not in the array.

Question 3   List the comparisons that the previous method `search` makes while searching for the object o in the array of objects

o1 o2 o3 o4 o5

Question 4   Implement at the client level a recursive method `search` by using only operations of the ADT list. The method should return true if a given item is in a given list.

The Efficiency of a Sequential Search of an Array

16.7   Whether you implement a sequential search iteratively or recursively, the number of comparisons will be the same. In the best case, you will locate the desired item first in the array. You will have made only one comparison, and so the search will be O(1). In the worst case, you will search the entire array. Either you will find the desired item at the end of the array or you will not find it at all. In either event, you will have made n comparisons for an array of n elements. The sequential search in the worst case is therefore O(n). Typically, you will look at about one-half of the elements in the array. Thus, the average case is O($n/2$), which is just O(n).

Note: **The time efficiency of a sequential search of an array**

Best case:	O(1)
Worst case:	O(n)
Average case:	O(n)

Searching a Sorted Array

A sequential search of an unsorted array is rather easy to understand and to implement. When the array contains relatively few elements, the search is efficient enough to be practical. However, when the array contains many elements, a sequential search can be time-consuming. For example, imagine that you are looking through a jar of coins for one minted during the year of your birth. A sequential search of 10 coins is not a problem. With 1000 coins, the search could be lengthy; with 1 million coins, it is overwhelming. A faster search method would be welcome. Fortunately, faster searches are possible.

A Sequential Search of a Sorted Array

16.8   Suppose that before you begin searching your coins, someone arranges them in sorted order by their dates. If you search the sorted coins in Figure 16-4 sequentially for the date 1989, you would look at the coins dated 1982, 1985, and 1987 before arriving at 1989. If, instead, you look for the date 1990, you would look at the first five coins without finding it. Should you keep looking? If the coins are sorted into ascending order and you have reached the one dated 1998, you will not find 1990 beyond it. If the coins were not sorted, you would have to examine all of them to see that 1990 was not present.

Note: A sequential search can be more efficient if the data is sorted.

Figure 16-4   Coins sorted by their mint dates

If our array is sorted into either ascending or descending order, we can use the previous ideas to revise the sequential search. This modified search can tell whether an item does not occur in an array faster than a sequential search of an unsorted array. The latter search always examines the entire array in this case. With a sorted array, however, the modified sequential search often makes far fewer comparisons to make the same determination. Exercise 2 at the end of this chapter asks you to implement a sequential search of a sorted array.

After expending the effort to sort an array, you often can search it even faster by using the method that we discuss next.

A Binary Search of a Sorted Array

16.9   Think of a number between 1 and 1 million. When I guess at your number, tell me whether my guess is correct, too high, or too low. At most, how many attempts will I need before I guess correctly? You should be able to answer this question by the time you reach the end of this section!

If you had to find a new friend's telephone number in a printed directory, what would you do? Typically you would open the book to a page near its middle, glance at the entries, and quickly see whether you were on the correct page. If you were not, you would decide whether you had to look at earlier pages—those in the left "half" of the book—or later pages—those in the right "half." What aspect of a telephone directory enables you to make this decision? The alphabetical order of the names.

If you decided to look in the left half, you could ignore the entire right half. In fact, you could tear off the right half and discard it, as Figure 16-5 illustrates. You have reduced the size of the search problem dramatically, as you have only half of the book left to search. You then would repeat the process on this half. Eventually you would either find the telephone number or discover that it is not there. This approach—called a **binary search**—sounds suspiciously recursive.

16.10   Let's adapt these ideas to searching an array a of n integers that are sorted into ascending order. (Descending order would also work with a simple change in our algorithm.) We know that

$$a[0] \le a[1] \le a[2] \le \ldots \le a[n-1]$$

Because the array is sorted, we can rule out whole sections of the array that could not possibly contain the number we are looking for—just as you ruled out an entire half of the telephone directory.

For example, if we are looking for the number 7 and we know that a[5] is equal to 9, then, of course, we know that 7 is less than a[5]. But we also know that 7 cannot appear after a[5] in the array, because the array is sorted. That is,

$$7 < a[5] \le a[6] \le \ldots \le a[n-1]$$

Figure 16-5 Ignoring one half of the data when the data is sorted

We know this without looking at the elements beyond a[5]. We therefore can ignore these elements as well as a[5]. Similarly, if the sought-after number were greater than a[5] (for example, if we were looking for 10), we could ignore a[5] and all the elements before it.

Replacing the index 5 in the preceding example with whatever index is in the middle of the array leads to a first draft of an algorithm for a binary search of an array:

> *Algorithm to search* a[0] *through* a[n - 1] *for* desiredItem
> mid = *approximate midpoint between* 0 *and* n - 1
> **if** (desiredItem *equals* a[mid])
>   **return true**
> **else if** (desiredItem < a[mid])
>   **return** *the result of searching* a[0] *through* a[mid - 1]
> **else if** (desiredItem > a[mid])
>   **return** *the result of searching* a[mid + 1] *through* a[n - 1]

Notice that to

> *Search* a[0] *through* a[n - 1]

you have to either

> *Search* a[0] *through* a[mid - 1]

or

> *Search* a[mid + 1] *through* a[n - 1]

These two searches of a portion of the array are smaller versions of the very task we are solving, and so can be accomplished by calling the algorithm itself recursively.

16.11 One complication arises, however, when we write the recursive calls in the previous pseudocode. Each call searches a subrange of the array. In the first case, it is the elements indexed by 0 through `mid - 1`. In the second case, it is the elements indexed by `mid + 1` through `n - 1`. Thus, we need two extra parameters—`first` and `last`—to specify the first and last indices of the subrange of the array that is to be searched. That is, we search `a[first]` through `a[last]` for `desiredItem`.

Using these parameters and making the recursive calls look more like Java, we can express the pseudocode as follows:

```
Algorithm binarySearch(a, first, last, desiredItem)
mid = approximate midpoint between first and last
if (desiredItem equals a[mid])
  return true
else if (desiredItem < a[mid])
  return binarySearch(a, first, mid - 1, desiredItem)
else if (desiredItem > a[mid])
  return binarySearch(a, mid + 1, last, desiredItem)
```

To search the entire array, we initially set `first` to 0 and `last` to n - 1. Each recursive call will then use some other values for `first` and `last`. For example, the recursive call that appears first would set `first` to 0 and `last` to `mid - 1`.

When you write any recursive algorithm, you should always check that the recursion is not infinite. Let's check whether every possible invocation of the algorithm will lead to a base case. Consider the three cases in the nested `if` statement in the previous pseudocode. In the first case, the sought-after item is found in the array, so there is no recursive call, and the process terminates. In each of the other two cases, a smaller portion of the array is searched by a recursive call. If the sought-after item is in the array, the algorithm uses smaller and smaller portions of the array until it finds the item. But what if the item is not anywhere in the array? Will the resulting series of recursive calls eventually lead to a base case? Unfortunately not, but that is not hard to fix.

16.12 Note that in each recursive call, either the value of `first` is increased or the value of `last` is decreased. If they ever pass each other and `first` actually becomes larger than `last`, we will have run out of array elements to check. In that case, `desiredItem` is not in the array. If we add this test to our pseudocode and refine the logic a bit, we get the following more complete algorithm:

```
Algorithm binarySearch(a, first, last, desiredItem)
mid = (first + last)/2 // approximate midpoint
if (first > last)
  return false
else if (desiredItem equals a[mid])
  return true
else if (desiredItem < a[mid])
  return binarySearch(a, first, mid - 1, desiredItem)
else // desiredItem > a[mid]
  return binarySearch(a, mid + 1, last, desiredItem)
```

Figure 16-6 provides an example of a binary search.

Question 5   When the previous binary search algorithm searches the array in Figure 16-6 for 8 and for 16, how many comparisons to an array element are necessary in each case?

Figure 16-6　A recursive binary search of a sorted array that (a) finds its target; (b) does not find its target

(a) A search for 8

Look at the middle entry, 10:

2	4	5	7	8	**10**	12	15	18	21	24	26
0	1	2	3	4	5	6	7	8	9	10	11

$8 < 10$, so search the left half of the array.

Look at the middle entry, 5:

2	4	**5**	7	8
0	1	2	3	4

$8 > 5$, so search the right half of the array.

Look at the middle entry, 7:

7	8
3	4

$8 > 7$, so search the right half of the array.

Look at the middle entry, 8:

8
4

$8 = 8$, so the search ends. 8 is in the array.

(b) A search for 16

Look at the middle entry, 10:

2	4	5	7	8	**10**	12	15	18	21	24	26
0	1	2	3	4	5	6	7	8	9	10	11

$16 > 10$, so search the right half of the array.

Look at the middle entry, 18:

12	15	**18**	21	24	26
6	7	8	9	10	11

$16 < 18$, so search the left half of the array.

Look at the middle entry, 12:

12	15
6	7

$16 > 12$, so search the right half of the array.

Look at the middle entry, 15:

15
7

$16 > 15$, so search the right half of the array.

The next subarray is empty, so the search ends. 16 is not in the array.

16.13   Imagine an array-based implementation of the ADT sorted list. An array `list`—which is a private data field—holds the list's entries in sorted order. Another field `length` records the number of entries. When implementing the ADT's method `contains`, the algorithm `binarySearch` becomes a private method that `contains` invokes. The array `list` takes the place of the array a in the algorithm, and `length` takes the place of n. As before in Segment 16.6, since `list` and `length` are data fields, they are not parameters of `contains` and `binarySearch`.

Although the implementations of the sequential search that were given in Segments 16.3 and 16.6 use the method `equals` to make the necessary comparisons, the binary search requires more than a test for equality. To make the necessary comparisons, we need the method `compareTo`. Since all classes inherit `equals` from the class `Object` and can override it, all objects can invoke `equals`. But for an object to invoke `compareTo`, it must belong to a class that implements the interface `Comparable`. Such is the case for objects in a sorted list, as Segment 13.1 indicated.

Like the class `SortedLinkedList` in Segment 13.7, our implementation of a sorted list could begin, as follows:

```
public class SortedArrayList<T extends Comparable<? super T>>
            implements SortedListInterface<T>
```

Thus, the method `binarySearch` can have the following implementation:

```
private boolean binarySearch(int first, int last, T desiredItem)
{
  boolean found;
  int mid = (first + last) / 2;

  if (first > last)
    found = false;
  else if (desiredItem.equals(list[mid]))
    found = true;
  else if (desiredItem.compareTo(list[mid]) < 0)
    found = binarySearch(first, mid - 1, desiredItem);
  else
    found = binarySearch(mid + 1, last, desiredItem);

  return found;
} // end binarySearch
```

Now `contains` appears as follows:

```
public boolean contains(T anEntry)
{
  return binarySearch(0, length - 1, anEntry);
} // end contains
```

Programming Tip: Classes that implement the `Comparable` interface must define a compareTo method. Such classes should also define an `equals` method that overrides the `equals` method inherited from `Object`. Both `compareTo` and `equals` should use the same test for equality. The previous method `binarySearch` calls both the method `equals` and the method `compareTo`. If the objects in the array did not have an appropriate `equals` method, `binarySearch` would not execute correctly. Note, however, that you could use `compareTo` instead of `equals` to test for equality.

> **?**

Question 6   During a binary search, which elements in the array

4 8 12 14 20 24

are compared to the target when the target is **a.** 2; **b.** 8; **c.** 15.

Question 7   Modify the previous method `contains` so that it returns the index of the first array element that equals `anEntry`. If the array does not contain such an element, return –1. You will have to modify `binarySearch` also.

Question 8   What changes to the binary search algorithm are necessary when the array is sorted in descending order (from largest down to smallest) instead of ascending order, as we have assumed during our discussion?

Java Class Library: The Method `binarySearch`

16.14   The class `Arrays` in the package `java.util` defines several versions of a static method `binary-Search` with the following specification:

```
/** Task: Searches an entire array for a given item.
 *    @param array        an array sorted in ascending order
 *    @param desiredItem  the item to be found in the array
 *    @return index of the array element that equals desiredItem;
 *            otherwise returns -belongsAt - 1, where belongsAt is
 *            the index of the array element that should contain
 *            desiredItem */
public static int binarySearch(type[] array, type desiredItem);
```

Here, both occurrences of *type* must be the same; *type* can be `Object` or any of the primitive types `byte`, `char`, `double`, `float`, `int`, `long`, or `short`.

The Efficiency of a Binary Search of an Array

16.15   The binary search algorithm eliminates about half of the array from consideration after examining only one element. It then eliminates another quarter of the array, and then another eighth, and so on. Thus, most of the array is not searched at all, saving much time. Intuitively, the binary search algorithm is very fast.

But just how fast is it? Counting the comparisons that occur will provide a measure of the algorithm's efficiency. To see the algorithm's worst-case behavior, you count the maximum number of comparisons that can occur when searching an array of n items. Comparisons are made each time the algorithm divides the array in half. After each division, half of the items are left to search. That is, beginning with n items, we would be left with $n/2$ items, then $n/4$ items, and so on. In the worst case, the search would continue until only one item was left. That is, $n/2^k$ would equal 1 for some value of k. This value of k gives us the number of times the array is divided in half, or the number of recursive calls to `binarySearch`.

If n is a power of 2, $n = 2^k$ for some positive k. By the definition of a logarithm, $k = \log_2 n$. If n is not a power of 2, you can find a positive integer k so that n lies between 2^{k-1} and 2^k. For example, if n is 14, $2^3 < 14 < 2^4$. Thus, we have for some $k \geq 1$,

$$2^{k-1} < n < 2^k$$
$$k - 1 < \log_2 n < k$$

$k = 1 + \log_2 n$ rounded down
    $= \log_2 n$ rounded up

To summarize,

$k = \log_2 n$ when n is a power of 2
$k = \lceil \log_2 n \rceil$ when n is not a power of 2

In general, k—the number of recursive calls to `binarySearch`—is $\lceil \log_2 n \rceil$.

Each call to `binarySearch`, with the possible exception of the last one, makes two comparisons between the target and the middle element in the array: One tests for equality and one for less than or greater than. Thus, the binary search performs at most $2\lceil \log_2 n \rceil$ comparisons, and so in the worst case is O(log n).

To search an array of 1000 elements, the binary search will compare the target to about 10 array elements in the worst case. In contrast, a simple sequential search could compare the target to as many as all 1000 array elements, and on average will compare it to about 500 array elements.

Note: **The time efficiency of a binary search of an array**

Best case: O(1)
Worst case: O(log n)
Average case: O(log n)

Question 9 Think of a number between 1 and 1 million. When I guess at your number, tell me whether my guess is correct, too high, or too low. At most, how many attempts will I need before I guess correctly? *Hint*: You are counting guesses, not comparisons.

16.16 **Another approach.** The binary search makes comparisons each time it locates the midpoint of the array. Thus, to search n items, the binary search looks at the middle item and then searches $n/2$ items. If we let $t(n)$ represent the time requirement for searching n items, we find that at worst

$t(n) = 1 + t(n/2)$ for $n > 1$
$t(1) = 1$

We encountered this recurrence relation in Segment 10.25 of Chapter 10. There, we showed that

$t(n) = 1 + \log_2 n$

Thus, the binary search is O(log n) in the worst case.

Searching an Unsorted Chain

16.17 Within a linked implementation of either the ADT list or the ADT sorted list, the method `contains` would search a chain of linked nodes for the target. As you will see, a sequential search is really the only practical choice. We begin with a chain whose data is unsorted, as typically would be the case for the ADT list.

Regardless of a list's implementation, a sequential search of the list looks at consecutive entries in the list, beginning with the first one, until either it finds the desired entry or it looks at all entries without success. When the implementation is linked, however, moving from node to node is not as simple as moving from one array location to another. Despite this fact, you can implement a sequential search of a chain of linked nodes either iteratively or recursively and with the same efficiency as that of a sequential search of an array.

An Iterative Sequential Search of an Unsorted Chain

16.18   Figure 16-7 illustrates a chain of linked nodes that contain the list's entries. Recall from Segment 6.19 of Chapter 6 that `firstNode` is a data field of the class that implements the list. While it is clear that a method can access the first node in this chain by using the reference `firstNode`, how can it access the subsequent nodes? Since `firstNode` is a data field that always references the first node in the chain, we would not want our search to alter it or any other aspect of the list. Thus, an iterative method `contains` should use a local reference variable `currentNode` that initially contains the same reference as `firstNode`. To make `currentNode` reference the next node, we would execute the statement

```
currentNode = currentNode.getNextNode();
```

Figure 16-7   A chain of linked nodes that contain the entries in a list

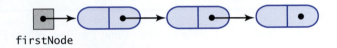

firstNode

The iterative sequential search has the following straightforward implementation:

```
public boolean contains(T anEntry)
{
    boolean found = false;
    Node currentNode = firstNode;

    while (!found && (currentNode != null))
    {
        if (anEntry.equals(currentNode.getData()))
            found = true;
        else
            currentNode = currentNode.getNextNode();
    } // end while

    return found;
} // end contains
```

This implementation is like the one given in Segment 7.12 of Chapter 7, but here `Node` has accessor methods `getData` and `getNextNode`.

A Recursive Sequential Search of an Unsorted Chain

16.19   When done recursively, a sequential search looks at the first entry in the list and, if it is not the desired entry, searches the rest of the list. This recursive approach is the same regardless of whether you implement the search at the client level by using only the list's ADT operations—as you did in Question 4—or as a public method of an array-based implementation of the list—as we did in Segment 16.6. We use the same approach for a linked implementation of the list, as follows.

How would you implement the step *search the rest of the list* when the list's entries are in a chain of linked nodes? The iterative method contains that you saw in the previous segment uses a local variable currentNode to move from node to node. A recursive method could not have currentNode as a local variable, since currentNode would get reset to an initial value at each recursive call. Instead, such a method needs currentNode as a formal parameter. But then we would have a method whose parameter depends on the list's implementation, making it unsuitable as a public method. Just as we did earlier in Segments 16.6 and 16.13, we would make this search method private and call it from the public method contains.

16.20   The private recursive method search examines the list entry in the node that its parameter currentNode references. If the entry is not the desired one, the method recursively calls itself with an argument that references the next node in the chain. Thus, the method search has the following implementation:

```
/** Task: Recursively searches a chain of nodes for desiredItem,
 *          beginning with the node that currentNode references. */
private boolean search(Node currentNode, T desiredItem)
{
  boolean found;

  if (currentNode == null)
    found = false;
  else if (desiredItem.equals(currentNode.getData()))
    found = true;
  else
    found = search(currentNode.getNextNode(), desiredItem);

  return found;
} // end search
```

Now we write the public method contains as follows:

```
public boolean contains(T anEntry)
{
  return search(firstNode, anEntry);
} // end contains
```

Notice that the call to the method search initializes the parameter currentNode to firstNode, much as an iterative method initializes its local variable currentNode to firstNode.

The Efficiency of a Sequential Search of a Chain

16.21   The efficiency of a sequential search of a chain is really the same as that of a sequential search of an array. In the best case, the desired item will be first in the chain. Thus, at best the search will be O(1), since you will have made only one comparison. In the worst case, you will search the entire chain, making n comparisons for a chain of n nodes. Therefore, the sequential search in the worst case is O(n). Typically, you will look at about half of the elements in the chain. Thus, the average-case search is O($n/2$), which is just O(n).

Note: **The time efficiency of a sequential search of a chain of linked nodes**

Best case: O(1)
Worst case: O(n)
Average case: O(n)

Searching a Sorted Chain

We now search a chain whose data is sorted. Such a chain would occur in a linked implementation of the ADT sorted list.

A Sequential Search of a Sorted Chain

16.22   Searching a chain of linked nodes whose data is sorted is similar to sequentially searching a sorted array, as described in Segment 16.8. Here, we incorporate that logic into the following implementation of `contains`:

```
public boolean contains(T anEntry)
{
   Node currentNode = firstNode;

   while ( (currentNode != null) &&
          (anEntry.compareTo(currentNode.getData()) > 0) )
   {
      currentNode = currentNode.getNextNode();
   } // end while

   return (currentNode != null) &&
          anEntry.equals(currentNode.getData());
} // end contains
```

The method traverses the chain until it either reaches a node that could contain the desired object or examines all nodes without success. Following the traversal, a final test is necessary to draw a conclusion.

A Binary Search of a Sorted Chain

16.23   A binary search of an array looks first at the element that is at or near the middle of the array. It is easy to determine the index `mid` of this element by computing `(first + last)/2`, where `first` and `last` are the indices of the first and last elements, respectively, in the array. Accessing this middle element is also easy: For an array `a`, it is simply `a[mid]`.

Now consider searching a chain of linked nodes, such as the one you saw earlier in Figure 16-7, whose nodes are sorted. How would you access the entry in the middle node? Since this chain has only three nodes, you can get to the middle node quickly, but what if the chain contained 1000 nodes? In general, you need to traverse the chain, beginning at the first node, until you reach the middle node. How will you know when you get there? If you know the length of the chain, you can divide the length in half and count nodes as you traverse. The details are not as important as a real-ization that it takes a bit of work to access the middle node.

After looking at the entry in the middle node, you probably need to ignore half of the chain and search the other half. Do not change the chain when ignoring part of it. Remember that you want to search the chain, not destroy it. Once you know which half to search, you must find its middle node, again by traversing the chain. It should be clear to you that a binary search of a linked chain of nodes would be challenging to implement and less efficient than a sequential search.

 Note: A binary search of a chain of linked nodes is impractical.

Choosing a Search Method

16.24   **Choosing between a sequential search and a binary search.** You just saw that you should use a sequential search to search a chain of linked nodes. But if you want to search an array of objects, you need to know which algorithms are applicable. To use a sequential search, the objects must have a method `equals` that ascertains whether two distinct objects are equal in some sense. Since all objects inherit `equals` from the class `Object`, you must ensure that the objects you search have overridden `equals` with an appropriate version. To perform a binary search on an array of objects, on the other hand, the objects must have a `compareTo` method and the array must be sorted. If these conditions are not met, you must use a sequential search.

If both search algorithms are applicable to your array, what search should you use? If the array is small, you can simply use a sequential search. If the array is large and already sorted, a binary search is typically much faster than a sequential search. But if the array is not sorted, should you sort it and then use a binary search? The answer depends on how often you plan to search the array. Sorting takes time, typically more time than a sequential search would. If you plan to search an unsorted array only a few times, sorting the array so that you can use a binary search likely will not save you time; use a sequential search instead.

Figure 16-8 summarizes the time efficiencies of the sequential search and the binary search. Only the sequential search is applicable to unsorted data. The efficiencies given for the binary search are for an array-based list. For a large, sorted list, the binary search is typically much faster than a sequential search.

Figure 16-8   The time efficiency of searching, expressed in Big Oh notation

	Best Case	Average Case	Worst Case
Sequential search (unsorted data)	O(1)	O(n)	O(n)
Sequential search (sorted data)	O(1)	O(n)	O(n)
Binary search (sorted array)	O(1)	O(log n)	O(log n)

16.25   **Choosing between an iterative search and a recursive search.** Since the recursive sequential search is tail recursive, you can save some time and space by using the iterative version of the search. The binary search is fast, so using recursion will not require much additional space for the recursive calls. Also, coding the binary search recursively is somewhat easier than coding it iteratively. To convince yourself of this, try to code an iterative version of the binary search. (See Exercise 6 at the end of this chapter.)

CHAPTER SUMMARY

- A sequential search of either a list, an array, or a chain looks at the first item, the second item, and so on until it either finds a particular item or discovers that the item does not occur in the group.

- The average-case performance of a sequential search is O(n).

- Typically, you perform a sequential search iteratively, although a simple recursive approach is also possible.

- A binary search of an array requires that the array be sorted. It looks first to see whether the desired item is at the middle of the array. If it is not, the search decides in which half of the array the item can occur and repeats this strategy on only this half.

- A binary search is O(log n) in the worst case.

- Typically, you perform a binary search recursively, although an iterative approach is also possible.

- A binary search of a linked chain of nodes is impractical.

PROGRAMMING TIP

- Classes that implement the `Comparable` interface must define a `compareTo` method. Such classes should also define an `equals` method that overrides the `equals` method inherited from `Object`. Both `compareTo` and `equals` should use the same test for equality. The method `binarySearch` in Segment 16.13 calls both the method `equals` and the method `compareTo`. If the objects in the array did not have an appropriate `equals` method, `binarySearch` would not execute correctly. Note, however, that you could use `compareTo` instead of `equals` to test for equality.

EXERCISES

1. Revise the recursive method `search`, as given in Segment 16.6, so that it looks at the last entry in the array instead of the first one.

2. When searching a sorted array sequentially, you can ascertain that a given item does not appear in the array without searching the entire array. For example, if you search the array

    2 5 7 9

    for 6, you can use the approach described in Segment 16.8. That is, you compare 6 to 2, then to 5, and finally to 7. Since you did not find 6 after comparing it to 7, you do not have to look further, because the other elements in the array are greater than 7 and therefore cannot equal 6. Thus, you do not simply ask whether 6 equals an array element, you also ask whether it is greater than the element. Since 6 is greater than 2, you continue the search. Likewise for 5. Since 6 is less than 7, you have passed the point in the array where 6 would have had to occur, so 6 is not in the array.

   a. Write an iterative method `contains` to take advantage of these observations when searching a sorted array sequentially.
   b. Write a recursive method `search` that a method `contains` can call to take advantage of these observations when searching a sorted array sequentially.

3. How many comparisons are made by the recursive method `search` described in Part *b* of the previous exercise when searching the array in Figure 16-6 for 8 and for 16?

4. Trace the method `binarySearch`, as given in Segment 16.13, when searching for 4 in the following array of values:

     5 8 10 13 15 20 22 26 30 31 34 40

Repeat the trace when searching for 34.

5. Modify the method `binarySearch` in Segment 16.13 so that it returns the index of the first array element that equals `desiredItem`. If the array does not contain such an element, return `-(belongsAt + 1)`, where `belongsAt` is the index of the array location that should contain `desiredItem`. At the end of Segment 16.13, Question 7 asked you to return –1 in this case. Notice that both versions of the method return a negative integer if and only if `desiredItem` is not found.

6. Implement a binary search of an array iteratively. Model your methods after the ones given in Segment 16.13.

7. Write a recursive method to find the largest object in an array-based list of `Comparable` objects. Like the binary search, your method should divide the array into halves. Unlike the binary search, your method should search both halves for the largest object. The largest object in the array will then be the larger of these two largest objects.

8. Suppose that you are searching an unsorted array of objects that might contain duplicates. Devise an algorithm that returns a list of the indices of all objects in the array that match a given object. If the desired object is not in the list, return an empty list.

9. Repeat the previous exercise for a sorted array. Your algorithm should be recursive and efficient.

10. In Segment 16.13, the method `contains` calls a private method that performs a binary search of an array. Assuming a linked implementation of the ADT sorted list, revise this private method to perform a binary search of a chain of nodes. Do not alter the chain.

11. a. Write a recurrence relation for the number $f(n)$ of comparisons that a sequential search makes in the worst case.
   b. Prove by induction on n that $f(n) = n$.

12. At the end of Segment 16.3, Question 2 asked you to write a method that performs an iterative sequential search of a list by using only operations of the ADT list. Compare the time efficiency of this method with the ADT operation `contains`.

13. In Segment 16.7, we said that a sequential search of an array will examine on average about half of the *n* entries. Let's look a little more carefully at this computation.

A sequential search is either successful or not. Let α be the probability that we will find the desired value in the array and 1 - α be the probability that we will not. We further assume that the value, if found, is equally likely to be in each of the locations of the array. We need to consider each possibility.

For each case, we count the comparisons and determine its probability of occurrence. To find the average number of comparisons made by the search, we first multiply each probability by the number of comparisons in each case. The following table summarizes these results:

	Probability	Number of Comparisons	Product
Found at index 0	α / n	1	α / n
Found at index 1	α / n	2	$2\alpha / n$
Found at index 2	α / n	3	$3\alpha / n$
...	...	...	...
Found at index $n - 2$	α / n	$n - 1$	$(n - 1)\alpha / n$
Found at index $n - 1$	α / n	n	α
Not found	$1 - \alpha$	n	$(1 - \alpha) n$

   a. Compute the average number of comparisons by adding all the products in the last column of the table.

   b. What is the average number of comparisons if the search is guaranteed to be successful ($\alpha = 1$)?

   c. What is the average number of comparisons if the search is guaranteed not to be successful ($\alpha = 0$)?

   d. What is the average number of comparisons if the search is successful half of the time ($\alpha = 0.5$)?

14. Repeat Part *a* of the previous exercise, but now assume that we are not equally likely to search for each value in the array. We could arrange the *n* items in the array such that the ones we are more likely to search for occur first. Suppose that we search for the first item one half of the time, the second item one quarter of the time, the third item one eighth of the time, and so on. We will search for the last two items $1/2^{n-1}$ of the time. Revise the table in the previous exercise accordingly.

PROJECTS

1. When an object does not occur in an array, a sequential search for it must examine the entire array. If the array is sorted, you can improve the search by using the approach described in Exercise 2. A **jump search** is an attempt to reduce the number of comparisons even further.

Instead of examining the *n* objects in the array *a* sequentially, you look at the elements $a[j]$, $a[2j]$, $a[3j]$, and so on, for some positive $j < n$. If the target *t* is less than one of these objects, you need to search only the portion of the array between the current object and the previous object. For example, if *t* is less than $a[3j]$ but is greater than

$a[2j]$, you search the elements $a[2j + 1]$, $a[2j + 2]$, ..., $a[3j - 1]$ by using the method in Exercise 2. What should you do when $t > a[k * j]$, but $(k + 1) * j > n$?

    Devise an algorithm for performing a jump search. Then, using $\lceil \sqrt{n} \rceil$ as the value of j, implement the jump search.

2. An **interpolation search** assumes that the data in an array is sorted and uniformly distributed. Whereas a binary search always looks at the middle item in an array, an interpolation search looks where the sought-for item is more likely to occur. For example, if you searched your telephone book for Victoria Appleseed, you probably would look near its beginning rather than its middle. And if you discovered many Appleseeds, you would look near the last Appleseed.

    Instead of looking at the element a[mid] of an array a, as the binary search would, an interpolation search examines a[index], where

```
p = (desiredElement - a[first])/(a[last] - a[first])
index = first + ⌈(last - first)·p⌉
```

Implement an interpolation search of an array. For particular arrays, compare the outcomes of an interpolation search and of a binary search. Consider arrays that have uniformly distributed elements and arrays that do not.

3. Suppose that you have numerical data stored in a two-dimensional array, such as the one in Figure 16-9. The data in each row and in each column is sorted in increasing order.

    a. Devise an efficient search algorithm for an array of this type.
    b. If the array has m rows and n columns, what is the Big Oh performance of your algorithm?
    c. Implement and test your algorithm.

Figure 16-9   A two-dimensional array for Project 3

1	4	55	88
7	15	61	91
14	89	90	99

4. Consider an array data of n numerical values in sorted order and a list of numerical target values. Your goal is to compute the smallest range of array indices that contains all of the target values. If a target value is smaller than data[0], the range should start with -1. If a target value is larger than data[n - 1], the range should end with n.

    For example, given the array in Figure 16-10 and the target values (8, 2, 9, 17), the range is -1 to 5.

a. Devise an efficient algorithm that solves this problem.
b. If you have n data values in the array and m target values in the list, what is the Big Oh performance of your algorithm?
c. Implement and test your algorithm.

Figure 16-10 An array for Project 4

5	8	10	13	15	20	22	26
0	1	2	3	4	5	6	7

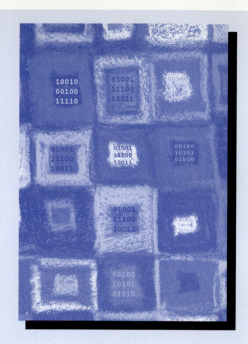

CONTENTS

PREREQUISITES

OBJECTIVES

After studying this chapter, you should be able to

- Describe the operations of the ADT dictionary
- Distinguish between a dictionary and a list
- Use a dictionary in a program

If you need to check the meaning of a word, you look it up in a dictionary. If you need a friend's address, you consult your address book. If you need someone's telephone number, you use a telephone directory—or call 411 to ask someone to look it up for you.

Each of these examples is actually a kind of dictionary. Each uses the concept of a two-part entry that consists of

- A keyword such as an English word or a person's name
- Other data such as a definition, an address, or a telephone number

The keyword enables you to locate the desired entry.

This chapter describes and uses an abstract data type that generalizes our everyday notion of a dictionary. Subsequent chapters will examine implementations of this ADT.

The previous examples—finding a word's definition, a friend's address, or someone's telephone number—are all examples of searching a dictionary. Chapter 16 examined how to search a list. You will see that a dictionary provides a more powerful way to organize data that will be searched.

Specifications for the ADT Dictionary

17.1   The ADT **dictionary**—also called a **map**, **table**, or **associative array**—contains entries that each have two parts: a keyword, usually called a **search key**, and a value associated with that key. Figure 17-1 illustrates an everyday English dictionary. Each entry has a word as the search key and the word's definition as the value associated with the key. In general, the search keys and values in an ADT dictionary are objects, as shown in Figure 17-2. Each search key is paired with a corresponding value.

The ADT dictionary organizes and identifies its entries by their search keys, rather than by another criterion such as position. Thus, you can retrieve or remove an entry from a dictionary given only the entry's search key. The fact that every entry in a dictionary has a search key distinguishes the dictionary from other ADTs such as a list. Although you certainly could put an entry that has a search key in a list, a list's data is organized by position, not by search key.

Figure 17-1   An English dictionary

computer A device for the processing and storage of information.

Figure 17-2   An instance of an ADT dictionary has pairs of search keys and corresponding values

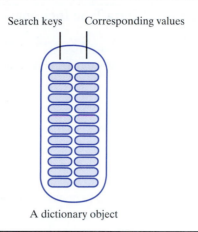

Search keys   Corresponding values

A dictionary object

Some dictionaries have distinct search keys, but others allow two or more entries to have the same search key. For example, a dictionary of student records organized by student identification numbers has distinct search keys, since those numbers are unique. On the other hand, an English-language dictionary has duplicate search keys, since it often has several meanings for a word. For example, my dictionary has three entries for the word "book": One is a noun, one is a verb, and one is an adjective.

Printed versions of a natural-language dictionary, a telephone directory, a library catalog, and a thesaurus all have entries sorted by their search keys. These databases are dictionaries, but the ADT dictionary does not require sorted entries. Some dictionaries do sort their entries by search key, while other dictionaries have unsorted entries. Why do our examples of printed dictionaries sort their entries? To make it easier for the reader to find a particular entry. In contrast, if you searched a computerized thesaurus for a word, you would not be aware of the order of its entries. Nor would you care, as long as you could retrieve a particular entry. Thus, whether a dictionary has sorted or unsorted search keys is more of an implementation detail than a necessary characteristic of the dictionary. But remember that the details of any implementation affect the efficiencies of the ADT operations in various ways.

17.2   The ADT dictionary has the same major operations—insert, delete, retrieve, search, and traverse— that are common to most databases, even if a particular implementation sorts its entries or allows duplicate search keys. In particular, these operations are

- Add a new entry to the dictionary, given a search key and associated value
- Remove an entry, given its associated search key
- Retrieve the value associated with a given search key
- See whether the dictionary contains a given search key
- Traverse all the search keys in the dictionary
- Traverse all the values in the dictionary

In addition, the ADT dictionary has the following basic operations that are often included in an ADT:

- Detect whether a dictionary is empty or full
- Get the number of entries in the dictionary
- Remove all entries from the dictionary

The following specifications define a set of operations for the ADT dictionary:

Abstract Data Type Dictionary

DATA

- A collection of pairs (k, v) of objects k and v, where k is the search key and v is the corresponding value
- The number of pairs in the collection

OPERATIONS

`add(key, value)`

Task: Adds the pair (`key`, `value`) to the dictionary.
Input: `key` is an object search key, `value` is an associated object.
Output: None.

`remove(key)`

Task: Removes from the dictionary the entry that corresponds to a given search key.
Input: `key` is an object search key.
Output: Returns either the value that was associated with the search key or `null` if no such object exists.

`getValue(key)`

Task: Retrieves the value that corresponds to a given search key.
Input: `key` is an object search key.
Output: Returns either the value associated with the search key or `null` if no such object exists.

`contains(key)`

Task: Sees whether any entry in the dictionary has a given search key.
Input: `key` is an object search key.
Output: Returns true if an entry in the dictionary has `key` as its search key.

`getKeyIterator()`

Task: Creates an iterator that traverses all search keys in the dictionary.
Input: None.
Output: Returns an iterator that provides sequential access to the search keys in the dictionary.

`getValueIterator()`

Task: Creates an iterator that traverses all values in the dictionary.
Input: None.
Output: Returns an iterator that provides sequential access to the values in the dictionary.

`isEmpty()`

Task: Sees whether the dictionary is empty.
Input: None.
Output: Returns true if the dictionary is empty.

`isFull()`	Task: Sees whether the dictionary is full. Input: None. Output: Returns true if the dictionary is full.
`getSize()`	Task: Gets the size of the dictionary. Input: None. Output: Returns the number of entries (key-value pairs) currently in the dictionary.
`clear()`	Task: Removes all entries from the dictionary. Input: None. Output: None.

 Note: The ADT dictionary contains entries that are key-value pairs organized by their search keys. You can add a new entry, and you can locate, retrieve, or remove an entry, given its search key. In addition, you can traverse a dictionary's search keys or values.

17.3   **Refining the specifications.** Even though all dictionaries can have this common set of operations, you do need to refine some of the specifications according to whether a dictionary's search keys are distinct:

- **Distinct search keys.** The method add can ensure that the search keys in a dictionary are distinct. If key is already in the dictionary, the operation add(key, value) could either refuse to add another key-value entry or change the existing value associated with key to value. In the latter case, the method could return the old replaced value instead of not having an output, as indicated earlier.

    Regardless of how add guarantees distinct search keys, the remaining methods can have simpler implementations than if duplicate search keys are allowed. For example, the methods remove and getValue will either find the one value associated with a given search key or discover that no such entry exists.

- **Duplicate search keys.** If the method add adds every given key-value entry to a dictionary, the methods remove and getValue must deal with multiple entries that have the same search key. Which entry should be removed or returned? The method remove could either remove the first value it finds or remove all values associated with the given search key. If getValue returns an object, it could return the first value it finds. Or you could modify getValue to return a list of values, for example.

    Another possibility is to have a secondary search key that is used only when several entries have the same primary search key. For example, if you call directory assistance for a common name like John Smith, you most certainly will be asked for John's address.

For simplicity, we will assume distinct search keys and consider duplicate search keys in the exercises and projects at the end of this chapter.

A Java Interface

17.4   Listing 17-1 contains a Java interface for the ADT dictionary that specifies distinct search keys. The add method replaces the value associated with any search key that is already in the dictionary.

Like the interfaces for the ADTs list and sorted list, this interface specifies the data type of its entries generically. Since the search keys can have a data type that differs from the type of the associated values, we use two formal type parameters, K and V. K represents the data type of the search keys, and V is the type of the associated values.

Listing 17-1   An interface for the ADT dictionary

```
/** A dictionary with distinct search keys. */
import java.util.Iterator;
public interface DictionaryInterface<K, V>
{
  /** Task: Adds a new entry to the dictionary. If the given search
   *        key already exists in the dictionary, replaces the
   *        corresponding value.
   *  @param key    an object search key of the new entry
   *  @param value  an object associated with the search key
   *  @return either null if the new entry was added to the dictionary
   *          or the value that was associated with key if that value
   *          was replaced */
  public V add(K key, V value);

  /** Task: Removes a specific entry from the dictionary.
   *  @param key  an object search key of the entry to be removed
   *  @return either the value that was associated with the search key
   *          or null if no such object exists */
  public V remove(K key);

  /** Task: Retrieves the value associated with a given search key.
   *  @param key  an object search key of the entry to be retrieved
   *  @return either the value that is associated with the search key
   *          or null if no such object exists */
  public V getValue(K key);

  /** Task: Sees whether a specific entry is in the dictionary.
   *  @param key  an object search key of the desired entry
   *  @return true if key is associated with an entry in the
   *          dictionary */
  public boolean contains(K key);

  /** Task: Creates an iterator that traverses all search keys in the
   *        dictionary.
   *  @return an iterator that provides sequential access to the search
   *          keys in the dictionary */
  public Iterator<K> getKeyIterator();

  /** Task: Creates an iterator that traverses all values in the
   *        dictionary.
   *  @return an iterator that provides sequential access to the values
   *          in the dictionary */
  public Iterator<V> getValueIterator();
```

```
/** Task: Sees whether the dictionary is empty.
 *  @return true if the dictionary is empty */
public boolean isEmpty();

/** Task: Sees whether the dictionary is full.
 *  @return true if the dictionary is full */
public boolean isFull();

/** Task: Gets the size of the dictionary.
 *  @return the number of entries (key-value pairs) currently
 *          in the dictionary */
public int getSize();

/** Task: Removes all entries from the dictionary. */
public void clear();
} // end DictionaryInterface
```

17.5   Let's see how to create an instance of a class `Dictionary` that implements `DictionaryInterface`. This dictionary will contain data about the students at your school. Assume that student numbers are the search keys and that we have the class `Student` to represent the student data. The following statement creates the instance `dataBase`:

```
DictionaryInterface<String, Student> dataBase =
    new Dictionary<String, Student>();
```

`String` corresponds to the parameter `K` in `DictionaryInterface`, so each occurrence of `K` in the interface is replaced by `String`. Similarly, `Student` replaces every occurrence of `V` in the interface. The same correspondence occurs between these actual types and the generic types of the class `Dictionary`.

We will examine several examples of dictionaries in more detail later in this chapter.

Iterators

17.6   The methods `getKeyIterator` and `getValueIterator` each return an iterator that conforms to the interface `java.util.Iterator` that we discussed in Chapter 8. You can create iterators for the dictionary `dataBase` that we instantiated in the previous segment by writing

```
Iterator<String> keyIterator = dataBase.getKeyIterator();
Iterator<Student> valueIterator = dataBase.getValueIterator();
```

Recall that `Iterator` specifies a generic type in its definition. Here we have defined an iterator for the `String` search keys and another for the `Student` values.

You can use each of these iterators either separately or together. That is, you can traverse

- All of the search keys in a dictionary without traversing the values
- All of the values without traversing the search keys
- All the search keys and all the values in parallel

In the last case, the ith search key returned by `keyIterator` corresponds to the ith dictionary value returned by `valueIterator`, as Figure 17-3 illustrates. Clearly, the two iterations have the same length, since the number of search keys in a dictionary must be the same as the number of values.

Figure 17-3 Two iterators that traverse a dictionary's keys and values in parallel

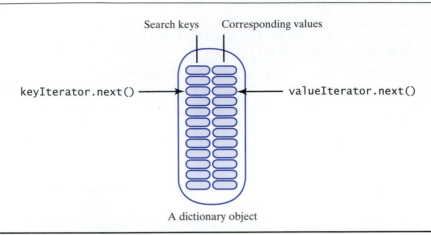

A dictionary object

The following loop displays each entry in the dictionary as a key-value pair:

```java
while (keyIterator.hasNext())
    System.out.println(keyIterator.next() + ", " + valueIterator.next());
```

For a sorted dictionary, `keyIterator` traverses the search keys in sorted order. For an unsorted dictionary, this traversal order is not specified. The examples in the next section demonstrate these iterators in several contexts.

Note: An iteration of a dictionary's values corresponds to an iteration of its search keys. That is, the ith value in one iteration is associated in the dictionary with the ith search key in the second iteration.

Question 1 If the class `Dictionary` implements `DictionaryInterface`, write a Java statement that creates an empty dictionary `myDictionary`. This dictionary will contain the names and telephone numbers of your friends. Assume that the names are the search keys, and you have the class `Name` to represent them. Let each telephone number be a string.

Question 2 Write a Java statement that adds your name and telephone number to the dictionary that you created in Question 1.

Question 3 Write Java statements that display either Britney Spheres' telephone number, if she is in the dictionary described in Question 1, or an error message if she is not.

Using the ADT Dictionary

The three examples in this section demonstrate how to use the ADT dictionary in a program. We begin by creating a telephone directory.

A Directory of Telephone Numbers

17.7   A telephone directory contains the names and telephone numbers of the people who live in a given geographical region. The most frequent operation performed on a telephone directory is the retrieval of a telephone number, given a person's name. Thus, using the ADT dictionary to represent a telephone directory is a good choice. Clearly, the name should be the search key, and the telephone number should be the corresponding value. Often, but not always, retrieval is more efficient when the dictionary is sorted. Additionally, a sorted dictionary would make it easier to create a printed directory with entries alphabetized by name. To simplify this example, we assume that the directory will contain distinct names with no duplicates.

A major task, at least initially, is to create the directory from the available names and telephone numbers. Having this data in a text file will make this task convenient. After the telephone directory is created, operations on the directory, such as adding an entry, removing an entry, or changing a telephone number, will be used less often than searching for a given name. Traversing the directory is important to create either a hard copy or a text file of the data, but this operation too is not done frequently. As we noted in Chapter 9, you should choose an implementation of an ADT based on the efficiency of its expected use.

17.8   **Design and use of the class `TelephoneDirectory`.** Our next step is to design a class to represent the telephone directory. A sorted dictionary will represent the data, which consists of name-number pairs. Each person's name can be an instance of the class `Name` that we first encountered in Chapter 1, and the telephone number can be a string without embedded blanks. Figure 17-4 shows a class diagram for our design. The class `TelephoneDirectory` contains an instance `phoneBook` of a dictionary. The class has the method `readFile`, which reads the data from the file and adds it to `phoneBook`. It also has the method `getPhoneNumber` to retrieve a telephone number, given a name. For simplicity, we are ignoring any other operations mentioned in the previous segment.

Figure 17-4   A class diagram for a telephone directory

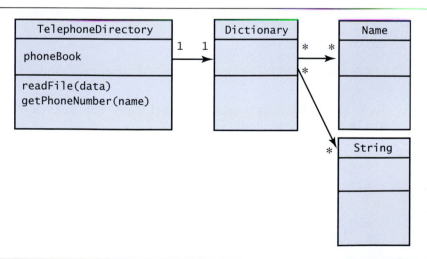

Before we implement the class `TelephoneDirectory`, let's consider its use. A client would create an instance of `TelephoneDirectory` and read the data file by invoking the method `readFile`.

The first two highlighted lines in the main method of Listing 17-2 perform these steps. Given the name data.txt of the text file, main creates a scanner for the file and passes it to readFile. Note the exceptions that might occur in creating the scanner. If you need more information about either exceptions or files, consult Appendices B and C, respectively.

After the file is read, main interacts with the user via the private method getName. Each name read from the user is passed to the method getPhoneNumber, where it will be the key in a search of the telephone directory. Notice how getName uses Scanner to both read the user's input and then process it.

Listing 17-2   A client of the class TelephoneDirectory

```java
import java.util.Scanner;
import java.io.File;
import java.io.FileNotFoundException;
import java.io.IOException;
public class Driver
{
   private static final Name INPUT_ERROR = new Name("error", "error");
   private static final Name QUIT = new Name("quit", "quit");

   public static void main(String[] args)
   {
      TelephoneDirectory directory = new TelephoneDirectory();
      String fileName = "data.txt"; // or file name could be read

      try
      {
         Scanner data = new Scanner(new File(fileName));
         directory.readFile(data);
      }
      catch (FileNotFoundException e)
      {
         System.out.println("File not found: " + e.getMessage());
      }
      catch (IOException e)
      {
         System.out.println("I/O error " + e.getMessage());
      }

      Name nextName = getName(); // get name for search from user
      while (!nextName.equals(QUIT))
      {
         if (nextName.equals(INPUT_ERROR))
            System.out.println("Error in entering name. Try again.");
         else
         {
            String phoneNumber = directory.getPhoneNumber(nextName);
            if (phoneNumber == null)
               System.out.println(nextName + " is not in the directory.");
            else
               System.out.println("The phone number for " + nextName +
                                  " is " + phoneNumber);
         } // end if

         nextName = getName();
      } // end while
```

```
      System.out.println("Bye!");
    } // end main

    /** @return either the name read from user, INPUT_ERROR, or QUIT */
    private static Name getName()
    {
      Name result = null;
      Scanner keyboard = new Scanner(System.in);

      System.out.print("Enter first name and last name, or quit to end: ");
      String line = keyboard.nextLine();

      if (line.trim().toLowerCase().equals("quit"))
        result = QUIT;
      else
      {
        String firstName = null;
        String lastName = null;
        Scanner scan = new Scanner(line);

        if (scan.hasNext())
        {
          firstName = scan.next();

          if (scan.hasNext())
            lastName = scan.next();
          else
            result = INPUT_ERROR;
        }
        else
          result = INPUT_ERROR;

        if (result == null)
          result = new Name(firstName, lastName);
      } // end if

      return result;
    } // end getName
} // end Driver
```

OUTPUT

> Enter first name and last name or quit to end: **Maria Lopez**
> The phone number for Maria Lopez is 401-555-1234
> Enter first name and last name or quit to end: **Hunter**
> Error in entering name. Try again.
> Enter first name and last name or quit to end: **Hunter Smith**
> Hunter Smith is not in the directory.
> Enter first name and last name or quit to end: **quit**
> Bye!

17.9   **Beginning the implementation.** The class TelephoneDirectory begins as shown in Listing 17-3. We assume that the class SortedDictionary implements a sorted version of the ADT dictionary having distinct search keys. A sorted dictionary requires its search keys to belong to a class that implements the interface Comparable. We assume that Name does so.

Listing 17-3   An outline of the class TelephoneDirectory

```java
import java.util.Scanner;

public class TelephoneDirectory
{
  private DictionaryInterface<Name, String> phoneBook;

  public TelephoneDirectory()
  {
    phoneBook = new SortedDictionary<Name, String>();
  } // end default constructor

  /** Task: Reads a text file of names and telephone numbers.
   *  @param data  a text scanner for the text file of data */
  public void readFile(Scanner data)
  {
    . . . < See Segment 17.10. >
  } // end readFile

  /** Task: Gets the phone number of a given person. */
  public String getPhoneNumber(Name personName)
  {
    . . . < See Segment 17.11. >
  } // end getPhoneNumber
} // end TelephoneDirectory
```

17.10   To implement the method readFile, you need to know what the data file looks like. Suppose that each line in the file contains three strings—a first name, a last name, and a telephone number—separated by blanks. Thus, a typical line might appear as

Suzanne Nouveaux   401-555-1234

The method readFile must read each of these strings. Recall that the main method in Listing 17-2 in Segment 17.8 creates a scanner for the file and passes it to readFile. Using Scanner's method next, readFile can read each string in a line of data and assign them, respectively, to the variables firstName, lastName, and phoneNumber. The following Java statements, then, will add the desired entry to the dictionary phoneBook:

```java
Name fullName = new Name(firstName, lastName);
phoneBook.add(fullName, phoneNumber);
```

We assume that the text file contains distinct names.
Here is the definition of readFile:

```java
/** Task: Reads a text file of names and telephone numbers.
 *  @param data  a text scanner for the text file of data */
public void readFile(Scanner data)
{
  while (data.hasNext())
  {
```

```
            String firstName   = data.next();
            String lastName    = data.next();
            String phoneNumber = data.next();

            Name fullName = new Name(firstName, lastName);
            phoneBook.add(fullName, phoneNumber);
        } // end while

        data.close();
    } // end readFile
```

Using Scanner's methods hasNext and next, we extract each name and telephone number as strings from the text file. Then, using the two statements we examined earlier, we create a Name object and add it and the telephone number to the dictionary.

Programming Tip: `java.util.Scanner`

The class Scanner enables you to break a string into substrings, or **tokens**, that are separated by characters called **delimiters**. By default, white-space characters are the delimiters. You pass to Scanner's constructor either the string to be **parsed** or a text file represented as an instance of the class java.io.File.

The following methods in the class Scanner enable you to extract the tokens from any string:

```
public String next();
public boolean hasNext();
```

Appendix A discusses Scanner in more detail, beginning at Segment A.80.

Question 4   Although the statement

```
directory.readFile(data);
```

is inside a try block near the beginning of the method main in Listing 17-2, it need not be. Explain its present location, why it can appear outside of a try block, and what you can do to move it.

17.11   **A method that searches.** The class TelephoneDirectory has a method to find a person's telephone number. This method needs the person's name, and the user must supply it. If we assume that the client will interact with the user and provide the desired name to the method—as does the client in Listing 17-2—we could define the method as follows:

```
public String getPhoneNumber(Name personName)
{
    return phoneBook.getValue(personName);
} // end getPhoneNumber
```

The method either returns a string that contains the desired telephone number or returns null if the number is not found.

We could define a similar method instead of or in addition to the previous method, as follows:

```
public String getPhoneNumber(String firstName, String lastName)
{
    Name fullName = new Name(firstName, lastName);
    return phoneBook.getValue(fullName);
} // end getPhoneNumber
```

Additional methods to add or remove a person or to change a person's telephone number are straightforward and are left as exercises.

Question 5   Implement a method for the class `TelephoneDirectory` that removes an entry from the directory. Given the person's name, the method should return either the person's telephone number or `null` if the person is not in the directory.

Question 6   Implement a method for the class `TelephoneDirectory` that changes a person's telephone number. Given the person's name, the method should return either the person's old telephone number or `null` if the person was not in the directory but has been added to it.

The Frequency of Words

17.12   Some word processors provide a count of the number of times each word occurs in a document. In this example, we will create a class `FrequencyCounter` that provides this capability. This class is somewhat like the one in the previous example, so we will omit some of the design details.

Basically, the class needs to count each occurrence of a word as it reads the document from a text file. It then needs to display the results. For example, if the text file contains

row, row, row your boat

the desired output would be

boat   1
row   3
your   1

The class will have a constructor and the methods `readFile` and `display`. As in the previous example, `readFile` will read the input text from a file. Then `display` will write the output. Listing 17-4 shows a client of `FrequencyCounter`. It is similar to the beginning of the client in the previous example.

Listing 17-4   A client of the class `FrequencyCounter`

```java
import java.util.Scanner;
import java.io.File;
import java.io.FileNotFoundException;
import java.io.IOException;

public class Driver
{
    public static void main(String[] args)
    {
        FrequencyCounter wordCounter = new FrequencyCounter();

        String fileName = "Data.txt"; // or file name could be read

        try
        {
            Scanner data = new Scanner(new File(fileName));
            wordCounter.readFile(data);
        }
        catch (FileNotFoundException e)
        {
```

```
                System.out.println("File not found: " + e.getMessage());
             }
             catch (IOException e)
             {
                System.out.println("I/O error " + e.getMessage());
             }

             wordCounter.display();
             System.out.println("Bye!");
       } // end main
    } // end Driver
```

OUTPUT

boat 1
row 3
your 1

17.13   Is the ADT dictionary the right one to use for this problem? A word and its frequency of occurrence in the document form a pair that is suitable as an entry in a dictionary. If we want to know a given word's frequency, the word should be the search key. Also, the words in the dictionary must be distinct, and if they are sorted, we can display them in alphabetical order. Thus, a sorted dictionary with distinct search keys is an appropriate choice for this problem. As in the previous example, we assume `SortedDictionary` is such an implementation.

The dictionary will be a data field of a new class `FrequencyCounter`, which will begin much like the class `TelephoneDirectory` in the previous example. Let's call the dictionary for this example `wordTable`. Since the value portion of any dictionary entry is an object, we use the wrapper class `Integer` to represent each frequency. Thus, our class can begin as shown in Listing 17-5.

Listing 17-5   An outline of the class `FrequencyCounter`

```
import java.util.Iterator;
import java.util.Scanner;

public class FrequencyCounter
{
    private DictionaryInterface<String, Integer> wordTable;

    public FrequencyCounter()
    {
        wordTable = new SortedDictionary<String, Integer>();
    } // end default constructor

    /** Task: Reads a text file of words and counts their frequencies
     *         of occurrence.
     *  @param data   a text scanner for the text file of data */
    public void readFile(Scanner data)
    {
        . . . < See Segment 17.16. >
    } // end readFile
```

```
/** Task: Displays words and their frequencies of occurrence. */
public void display()
{
    . . . < See Segment 17.17. >
} // end display
} // end FrequencyCounter
```

17.14   **Creating the dictionary.** Now let's look at the method `readFile`, which creates the dictionary from the text file. We invoke this method like we did earlier in Listing 17-4 of Segment 17.12. That is, the client passes to `readFile` a `Scanner` object associated with the text file. The method then can process the text file by using the `Scanner` methods `hasNext` and `next`, in the same way that `readFile` processed the file in Segment 17.10.

After extracting the next word from the file, `readFile` checks whether the word is in the dictionary. If it is not, we add it with an associated value of 1. That is, this word has occurred once so far. However, if the word is in the dictionary already, we retrieve its associated value—its count—increment it, and store it back into the dictionary. To avoid issues of case, `readFile` can change all the words it reads to lowercase.

17.15   **Delimiters.** The programming tip at the end of Segment 17.10 mentioned that, by default, `Scanner` uses white-space characters as delimiters. But as in the example given in Segment 17.12, our data can contain punctuation, so those characters must also be delimiters. You can use the `Scanner` method `useDelimiter` to specify the delimiters. You represent them by using the notation shown in Figure A-6 of Appendix A. (See Segment A.82.) You then pass a string of the delimiters to `useDelimiter`.

The simplest way to specify white space and punctuation as delimiters is to use the notation `\W`, since it represents any character other than a letter, digit, or underscore. We then write `useDelimiter`'s argument as `"\\W+"`. Remember that we must duplicate the backslash to distinguish the notation from an escape character. The plus sign means *one or more occurrences of*. Thus, the statement

```
dataFile.useDelimiter("\\W+");
```

sets the delimiters to one or more occurrences of punctuation, white-space characters, and some other characters that will not occur in our data.

Programming Tip: When using a `Scanner` object to process text, any character can be a delimiter if it does not occur in any desired token. You create a string of these delimiters using a special notation and give it to the `Scanner` method `useDelimiter`. Consult Segment A.81 of Appendix A for more details.

17.16   The following implementation of the method `readFile` reflects the previous discussion:

```
/** Task: Reads a text file of words and counts their frequencies
 *           of occurrence.
 * @param data  a text scanner for the text file of data */
public void readFile(Scanner data)
{
    data.useDelimiter("\\W+");
    while (data.hasNext())
    {
```

```
        String nextWord = data.next();
        nextWord = nextWord.toLowerCase();
        Integer frequency = wordTable.getValue(nextWord);

        if (frequency == null)
        { // add new word to table
          wordTable.add(nextWord, new Integer(1));
        }
        else
        { // increment count of existing word; replace wordTable entry
          frequency++;
          wordTable.add(nextWord, frequency);
        } // end if
      } // end while

      data.close();
    } // end readFile
```

Question 7   The previous method readFile does not call contains to see whether a word is already in the dictionary, but instead calls getValue. Why did we do this?

17.17   **Displaying the dictionary.** Now that we have created the dictionary, we need to display the results. An iteration of the search keys will produce the words in alphabetical order. A parallel iteration of the values provides the corresponding frequencies. The following method is a possible solution for this task:

```
public void display()
{
    Iterator<String> keyIterator = wordTable.getKeyIterator();
    Iterator<Integer> valueIterator = wordTable.getValueIterator();

    while (keyIterator.hasNext())
    {
      System.out.println(keyIterator.next() + " " +
                            valueIterator.next());
    } // end while
} // end display
```

Question 8   Implement a second method display for the class FrequencyCounter that displays only words that occur with a frequency given as the method's sole parameter.

A Concordance of Words

17.18   An index provides a way to locate the occurrence of certain words within a larger document. For example, the index to this book is an alphabetical listing of words paired with the page numbers on which the words occur. The example in this section will create a simpler kind of index—called a **concordance**—to all the words in a text file. Instead of page numbers, a concordance provides the line numbers that contain a particular word.

For example, suppose that a text file contains only these lines:

Learning without thought is labor lost;
thought without learning is perilous.

The following concordance of all the words in the file indicates the line numbers in which the words occur:

is 1 2
labor 1
learning 1 2
lost 1
perilous 2
thought 1 2
without 1 2

Although a word can appear in several lines of the file, it appears only once in the concordance. Like the previous word-frequency example, this feature of the concordance suggests that we use a dictionary whose search keys are the words in the concordance. But unlike the word-frequency example, the value associated with each of these words is a list of line numbers. Since the line numbers are sorted, we could use the ADT sorted list. However, by processing the lines in the file in order, we can add the line numbers to the end of an ordinary unsorted list and achieve a sorted order.

17.19   A class Concordance to represent the concordance and the class FrequencyCounter from the previous example are quite similar in their design and implementation. In fact, the use of these classes is virtually identical. By replacing FrequencyCounter with Concordance in Listing 17-4 of Segment 17.12, you will have a client for Concordance.

Listing 17-6 contains an outline of the class Concordance. Note the similarities to the outline of FrequencyCounter given in Listing 17-5 of Segment 17.13. The major difference, other than the implementations of the methods, is the data type of the value of each dictionary entry. Since the value is a list of Integer objects, and since we will want to traverse each list to display the line numbers, we give the value a data type of ListWithIteratorInterface<Integer>. Segment 8.17 of Chapter 8 defined this interface as having the method getIterator as well as the methods of ListInterface.

Listing 17-6   An outline of the class Concordance

```java
import java.util.Iterator;
import java.util.Scanner;
public class Concordance
{
  private DictionaryInterface<String, ListWithIteratorInterface<Integer>>
          wordTable;

  public Concordance()
  {
    wordTable =
      new SortedDictionary<String, ListWithIteratorInterface<Integer>>();
  } // end default constructor

  /** Task: Reads a text file of words and creates a concordance.
   * @param data  a text scanner for the text file of data */
  public void readFile(Scanner data)
  {
    . . . < See Segment 17.20. >
  } // end readFile
```

```
/** Task: Displays words and the lines in which they occur. */
public void display()
{
    . . . < See Segment 17.21. >
} // end display
} // end Concordance
```

17.20   **The method `readFile`.** The method `readFile` reads the text file and uses the dictionary `wordTable` to create the concordance. Since we must record the line number of each word, we read the file a line at a time. We process all the words in a line before moving on to the next line. Thus, the following definition of `readFile` contains two loops that are nested. The outer loop uses the scanner passed to the method as an argument to read lines from the file. The inner loop uses another scanner to extract the words from a line as soon as it is read. The class `LinkedListWithIterator` from Segment 8.19 of Chapter 8 is used to form each list of line numbers.

```
public void readFile(Scanner data)
{
    int lineNumber = 1;

    while (data.hasNext())
    {
        String line = data.nextLine();
        line = line.toLowerCase();

        Scanner lineProcessor = new Scanner(line);
        lineProcessor.useDelimiter("\\W+");
        while (lineProcessor.hasNext())
        {
            String nextWord = lineProcessor.next();
            ListWithIteratorInterface<Integer> lineList =
                                    wordTable.getValue(nextWord);

            if (lineList == null)
            { // create new list for new word; add list and word to index
                lineList = new LinkedListWithIterator<Integer>();
                wordTable.add(nextWord, lineList);
            } // end if

            // add line number to end of list so list is sorted
            lineList.add(lineNumber);
        } // end while

        lineNumber++;
    } // end while

    data.close();
} // end readFile
```

The most interesting part of this method is the list of line numbers as the value associated with a search key. Since we have chosen a linked implementation of the list, we need to be concerned with the efficiency of adding to the end of the list. If the underlying chain of nodes has only a reference to the first node—as is true of `LinkedListWithIterator`—each such addition requires a traversal to reach the end of the chain. Choosing a list implementation that maintains a reference to the last node in the chain would make the addition to the end of the list quite efficient. We discussed such tail references in Chapter 7. We should make this adjustment to our class of lists for this application.

17.21   **The method display.** Earlier, we chose a list implementation that included an iterator so that the following method `display` could display the line numbers in the concordance efficiently. Notice that we use the dictionary iterators, just as we did in the analogous method `display` given in Segment 17.17 for the previous example. But here each value is a list with its own iterator, which we use to traverse the list's line numbers.

```java
public void display()
{
   Iterator<String> keyIterator = wordTable.getKeyIterator();
   Iterator<ListWithIteratorInterface<Integer>> valueIterator =
                                    wordTable.getValueIterator();

   while (keyIterator.hasNext())
   {
      // display the word
      System.out.print(keyIterator.next() + " ");

      // get line numbers and iterator
      ListWithIteratorInterface<Integer> lineList =
                                    valueIterator.next();
      Iterator<Integer> listIterator = lineList.getIterator();

      // display line numbers
      while (listIterator.hasNext())
      {
         System.out.print(listIterator.next() + " ");
      } // end while

      System.out.println();
   } // end while
} // end display
```

Question 9   Write a method `getLineNumbers` for the class `Concordance` that returns a list of the numbers of the lines that contain a given word.

Java Class Library: The Interface Map

17.22   The standard package `java.util` contains the interface `Map<K, V>` that is similar to our interface for the ADT dictionary. The following method headers are for a selection of methods in `Map` that are like the ones you have seen in this chapter. We have used blue to indicate where they differ from our methods.

```java
public V put(K key, V value);
public V remove(Object key);
public V get(Object key);
public boolean containsKey(Object key);
public boolean containsValue(Object value);
```

```
public Set<K> keySet();
public Collection<V> values();
public boolean isEmpty();
public int size();
public void clear();
```

Notice the differences in the names of the methods. Map uses the method names put, get, containsKey, and size instead of our names add, getValue, contains, and getSize. Map also has the additional method containsValue that finds out whether a dictionary contains a given value.

Instead of our methods getKeyIterator and getValueIterator that return iterators to a dictionary's keys and values, respectively, Map specifies the methods keySet, which returns a set of keys, and values, which returns a collection of values. The Java Class Library contains the interfaces Set and Collection, and each of these interfaces has a method iterator that returns an iterator to the values in the corresponding ADT.

Duplicate search keys are not permitted in a dictionary that conforms to the Map interface. Each key must correspond to only one value. Also, some of Map's methods use Object as the data type of the search key, whereas we use the more specific type K.

CHAPTER SUMMARY

- The entries in the ADT dictionary each contain two parts: a search key and a value associated with that key. The dictionary identifies its entries by their search keys.

- Dictionaries can organize their search keys in either sorted or unsorted order. The search keys can be either distinct or duplicate.

- You can add an entry to a dictionary given its search key and value. You can retrieve or remove an entry given only its search key. By using an iterator, you can traverse all the keys or all the values in a dictionary.

- An English dictionary, a directory of telephone numbers, an address book, and a library catalog are common examples of dictionaries.

- The Java Class Library contains the interface Map, which is similar to our DictionaryInterface.

PROGRAMMING TIPS

- The class Scanner enables you to break a string into substrings, or tokens, that are separated by characters called delimiters. By default, white-space characters are the delimiters. You pass to Scanner's constructor either the string to be parsed or a text file represented as an instance of the class java.io.File.

- The following methods in the class Scanner enable you to extract the tokens from any string:

```
public String next();
public boolean hasNext();
```

Appendix A discusses Scanner in more detail beginning at Segment A.80.

- When using a Scanner object to process text, any character can be a delimiter, if it does not occur in any desired token. You create a string of these delimiters using a special notation and give it to the Scanner method useDelimiter. Consult Segment A.81 of Appendix A for more details.

1. How does a dictionary differ from a sorted list?

2. Implement a method for the class `TelephoneDirectory`—described in Segment 17.9—that adds an entry to the directory, given the person's name and telephone number. The method should return true if the entry was added. If the person is already in the directory, the method should replace the person's telephone number and return false.

3. Implement a method for the telephone directory example of Segment 17.9 to display everyone's name and telephone number.

4. In the telephone directory example of Segment 17.9, the case of the letters in a name affects the name's order in the dictionary. What steps can you take so that case variations in the input file do not affect this order?

5. In the telephone directory example of Segment 17.9, suppose that the text file of names and telephone numbers is sorted by name.

   a. What impact would this aspect of the file have on the efficiency of the method `read-File` for various implementations of the dictionary?
   b. Would it matter whether the file was in reverse alphabetical order?

6. A **reverse directory** allows one to search for the name corresponding to a given telephone number. Modify the class `TelephoneDirectory` of Segment 17.9 to give it this capability. Use a second dictionary as the reverse directory. Add a query method and modify the method `readFile` accordingly.

7. Draw a class diagram for the class `FrequencyCounter`, as outlined in Segment 17.13, that is analogous to the diagram in Figure 17-4 of Segment 17.8.

8. The word-frequency example of Segment 17.12 finds the frequency with which each distinct word occurs within some given text. Describe the changes that you could make to the class `FrequencyCounter` if you wanted to list the words that occur for each frequency.

9. Repeat Exercise 7 for the class `Concordance`, as outlined in Segment 17.19.

10. In the concordance example of Segment 17.18, if a word occurs more than once in a single line, the number of that line appears more than once in the concordance. Revise the Java code given in Segment 17.20 so that the line numbers associated with a given word are distinct.

11. Design an ADT that stores the side effects of various drugs. Each drug should have a list of associated side effects. Provide a method that returns the side effects of a given drug. Then use a dictionary to implement the class `DrugSideEffects`.

12. Consider a look-up service for the television shows on a given date. A file contains information about these shows. Each show's data appears on two lines. The first line gives the name of the station, the channel, the start time, the stop time, the name of the show, and a rating. These entries are separated by tildes (~), and the times are in 24-hour notation (for example, 1 p. m. is 13:00). The second line briefly describes the show.
    Implement a method with the header

public void readFile(Scanner data)

to read the file into a dictionary that will be searched. Decide what data should be the search key and what should be the associated value. Design any classes needed for the key and the value.

13. The ADT dictionary that we discussed in this chapter assumes distinct search keys. Revise the specifications of the dictionary to remove this restriction. Consider each of the following possibilities:

a. The method `add` adds an entry whose search key is already in the dictionary but whose value is not. The `remove` method deletes all entries with a given search key. The method `getValue` retrieves all values associated with a given search key.

b. The methods behave as Part *a* describes, but a secondary search key enables `remove` and `getValue` to delete or retrieve a single entry.

PROJECTS

1. To simplify the telephone directory example of Segment 17.7, we assumed that the text file contained distinct names. Remove this assumption, with and without a secondary search key. (See Exercise 13.)

2. Discovering the authorship of certain famous pieces of literature is an interesting problem. Comparisons are made between pieces whose authorship is disputed and those of known authorship. One approach is to compare the frequency of pairs of letters. There are 26 * 26 different pairs of letters. Not all of them will appear in a piece of writing. For example, "qz" is unlikely to appear, while "th" is likely to appear often. Design a program, similar to the frequency counter of Segments 17.12 through 17.17, that counts all the pairs of letters that appear in a given piece of text.

3. A compiler must examine tokens in a program and decide whether or not they are reserved words or identifiers defined by the user. Design a program that reads a Java program and makes a list of all the identifiers. To do this, you should make use of two dictionaries. The first dictionary should hold all the Java reserved words. The second dictionary should hold all the identifiers that you find. Whenever you encounter a token, you first should search the dictionary of reserved words. If the token is not a reserved word, you then should search the dictionary of identifiers. If the token is not in either dictionary, you should add it to the dictionary of identifiers.

4. Suppose that we want to implement the ADT set. Recall from Project 4 of Chapter 4 that a set is an unordered collection of objects where duplicates are not allowed. The operations that a set should support are

- Add a given object to the set
- Remove a given object from the set
- See whether the set contains a given object
- Clear all objects from the set
- Get the number of objects in the set
- Return an iterator to the set
- Return a set that combines the items in two sets (the union)
- Return a set of those items that occur in both of two sets (the intersection)

Define a class `Set` that uses a dictionary internally to implement these operations.

5. Suppose that we want to help physicians to diagnose illnesses. A physician observes a patient's symptoms and considers the illnesses that could be associated with those symptoms. Design and implement a class `PhysiciansHelper` that provides a list of those illnesses.

   `PhysiciansHelper` should contain a dictionary of illnesses and symptoms. A method should read a file of illnesses with their symptoms into the dictionary. Each line in the file will contain the name of an illness followed by a colon and a comma-separated list of symptoms. For example, one line could be

   head cold: nasal stuffiness, sneezing, runny nose

   `PhysiciansHelper` should maintain a list of symptoms for the current patient. A method should add a symptom to this list and return a list of illnesses that is associated with those symptoms. Another method should remove a given symptom from the list, and a method should clear the patient symptom list.

6. Write a program that plays the game tic-tac-toe. Represent the game board by an array of nine values. Each location in the array contains either an X, an O, or a blank. The total number of possible board configurations is 3^9, or approximately 20,000. Associated with every possible configuration is a best move.

   Generate all possible board configurations, and let them be search keys in a dictionary. Let the best moves be their associated values. Once you have created the dictionary, use it to decide the moves for a computer-based player in a game of tic-tac-toe.

Dictionary Implementations

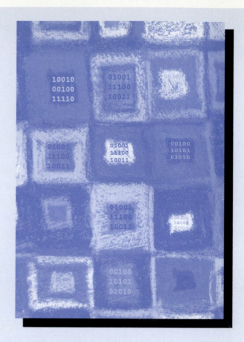

CONTENTS

PREREQUISITES

OBJECTIVES

After studying this chapter, you should be able to

● Implement the ADT dictionary by using either an array, a vector, or a chain of linked nodes

The implementations of the ADT dictionary that we present in this chapter employ techniques like the ones we used to implement the ADT list. We will store the dictionary's entries in either an expandable array, an instance of Vector, or a chain of linked nodes. In doing so, we will consider both sorted and unsorted dictionaries with distinct search keys. Later chapters will present more-sophisticated implementations of the ADT dictionary.

Array-Based Implementations

18.1　The ability to expand an array dynamically, as introduced in Segment 5.14 of Chapter 5, means that an array can provide as much storage as necessary for the entries in a dictionary. Remember that each entry consists of two parts—a search key and a value. You can encapsulate the two parts into an object, as Figure 18-1a illustrates. With this approach, you define a class Entry to represent the entries. A second, less attractive approach uses two arrays, as shown in Figure 18-1b. One array represents the search keys and a second, **parallel array** represents the corresponding values. We will discuss the first approach and leave the exploration of the second as an exercise. At that time, you will see that parallel arrays can be awkward to manage.

Figure 18-1　Two possible ways to use arrays to represent the entries in a dictionary:
(a) an array of objects that encapsulate each search key and corresponding value;
(b) parallel arrays of search keys and values

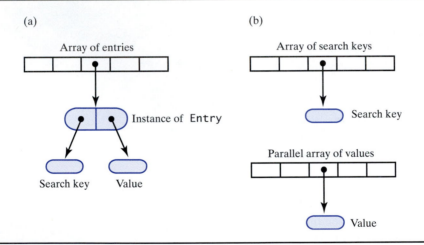

Question 1　Figure 18-1 shows two ways to represent an array-based dictionary. How do the memory requirements for the two representations compare?

An Unsorted Array-Based Dictionary

18.2　**Beginning the implementation.** Our implementation uses one array, as pictured in Figure 18-1a, to represent the dictionary. Each element in the dictionary, and therefore the array, is an instance of a class Entry that we must define. We can make this class either public, part of a package, or private and internal to the dictionary class. We chose the latter approach in defining the private class Entry shown in Listing 18-1.

The outer class ArrayDictionary begins with its data fields and constructors stated in terms of type parameters K and V. These parameters represent the data types of the search keys and their associated values, respectively.

Listing 18-1   The class `ArrayDictionary` and its private inner class `Entry`

```java
import java.util.Iterator;
import java.util.NoSuchElementException;
import java.io.Serializable;

public class ArrayDictionary<K, V> implements DictionaryInterface<K, V>,
                                               Serializable
{
  private Entry<K, V>[] dictionary; // array of unsorted entries
  private int currentSize;          // number of entries
  private final static int DEFAULT_CAPACITY = 25;

  public ArrayDictionary()
  {
    this(DEFAULT_CAPACITY); // call next constructor
  } // end default constructor

  public ArrayDictionary(int initialCapacity)
  {
    dictionary = new Entry[initialCapacity];
    currentSize = 0;
  } // end constructor

  < Implementations of methods in DictionaryInterface >
  . . .

  private class Entry<S, T> implements Serializable
  {
    private S key;
    private T value;

    private Entry(S searchKey, T dataValue)
    {
      key = searchKey;
      value = dataValue;
    } // end constructor

    private S getKey()
    {
      return key;
    } // end getKey

    private T getValue()
    {
      return value;
    } // end getValue

    private void setValue(T newValue)
    {
      value = newValue;
    } // end setValue
  } // end Entry
} // end ArrayDictionary
```

Notice that the inner class `Entry` has no method `setKey` to set or change the search key. Even though `setValue` can be useful in the implementation of add, you never need to change the search key. Without `setKey`, a default constructor would be useless, so none is defined.

Both the outer class `ArrayDictionary` and the inner class `Entry` implement the interface `Serializable`. This aspect is necessary if we want to serialize instances of `ArrayDictionary`. Recall that serialization is discussed in Segment 5.12 and Appendix C.

Note: **Compiler warning**

The constructor for `ArrayDictionary`, as shown in Listing 18-1, allocates memory for the array dictionary as follows:

```
dictionary = new Entry[initialCapacity];
```

The compiler sees an array whose elements have type `Entry` assigned to an array whose elements are of type `Entry<K, V>`. It therefore warns us of an unchecked conversion. An attempt to cast the new array to `Entry<K, V>[]` results in a similar warning. In either event, all should be well despite the compiler's concern.

18.3   **Some private methods.** One problem with array-based implementations of an ADT is the finite size of the array. To avoid a full dictionary, we double the array's size as necessary, just as we did in Chapter 5. We will use private methods as we did then. Their specifications are as follows:

```
/** Task: Detects whether the array of entries is full. */
private boolean isArrayFull()

/** Task: Doubles the size of the array of entries. */
private void doubleArray()
```

Adding, removing, or retrieving an entry requires a sequential search, since the search keys are not sorted. A sequential search must look at all the search keys in the array to conclude that an entry is not present in the dictionary. Implementing this search as the following private method will simplify the definitions of these three dictionary operations:

```
/** Task: Returns either the index of the entry that contains key or
 *        currentSize if no such entry exists. */
private int locateIndex(K key)
```

18.4   **Adding an entry.** Another potential problem with array-based implementations is the shifting of array elements that often occurs. When a dictionary's search keys are unsorted, however, we can add or remove an entry without shifting other entries. When adding a new key-value entry, we can insert it after the last entry in the array and not move any other entry, as Figure 18-2 shows. In this case, add returns `null`. However, if the search key was in the dictionary already, we replace its corresponding value with the new value and return the original value. The following algorithm performs these steps:

Algorithm add(key, value)
// Adds a new key-value entry to the dictionary and returns `null`. *If* key *already exists*
// in the dictionary, returns the corresponding value and replaces it with value.

result = **null**
Search the array for an entry containing key

```
if (an entry containing key is found in the array)
{
    result = value currently associated with key
    Replace key's associated value with value
}
else // insert new entry
{
    if (array is full)
        Double size of array

    Insert a new entry containing key and value after the last entry in the array
    Increment the size of the dictionary
}
return result
```

Figure 18-2   Adding a new entry to an unsorted array-based dictionary

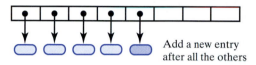

Add a new entry
after all the others

18.5   **The method add.** The following implementation of the method add invokes the private methods specified in Segment 18.3:

```java
public V add(K key, V value)
{
    V result = null;

    int keyIndex = locateIndex(key);

    if (keyIndex < currentSize)
    {
        // key found; return and replace old value
        result = dictionary[keyIndex].getValue();
        dictionary[keyIndex].setValue(value);
    }
    else
    {
        if (isArrayFull())
            doubleArray(); // expand array

        dictionary[currentSize] = new Entry<K, V>(key, value);
        currentSize++;
    } // end if

    return result;
} // end add
```

To search an unsorted array, locateIndex has the following definition:

```java
private int locateIndex(K key)
{
    int index = 0;
```

```
      while ( (index < currentSize) &&
              !key.equals(dictionary[index].getKey()) )
         index++;

      return index;
   } // end locateIndex
```

18.6   **Removing an entry.** To remove an entry from an unsorted array-based dictionary, we first locate the entry and then replace it with the last entry in the dictionary, as Figure 18-3 illustrates. Thus, we can fill the "hole" in the array without shifting the other entries. Since the size of the dictionary is reduced by 1, the extra reference remaining after the current entries will be ignored.

Figure 18-3   Removing an entry from an unsorted array-based dictionary

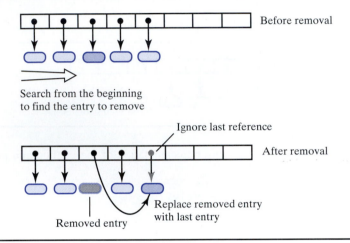

The following algorithm describes the remove operation:

Algorithm `remove(key)`
// Removes an entry from the dictionary, given its search key, and returns its value.
// If no such entry exists in the dictionary, returns `null`.

result = `null`
Search the array for an entry containing `key`

`if` *(an entry containing* `key` *is found in the array)*
{
    `result` = *value currently associated with* `key`
    Replace the entry with the last entry in the array
    Decrement the size of the dictionary
}
// else `result` *is* `null`

`return result`

This logic can be implemented as follows:

```
public V remove(K key)
{
   V result = null;
   int keyIndex = locateIndex(key);
```

```
    if (keyIndex < currentSize)
    {
      result = dictionary[keyIndex].getValue();
      dictionary[keyIndex] = dictionary[currentSize - 1];
      currentSize--;
    } // end if

    return result;
  } // end remove
```

18.7   **The remaining methods.** We leave the rest of the dictionary implementation to you as an exercise, since it is not difficult once you have reached this point. Note that an iteration, or traversal, of the dictionary entries simply moves from location to location within the array. Since the search keys are not sorted, the order of the iteration is not specified. Whatever order is easy to implement is fine. Typically, you start with the first element in the array and move sequentially through the remaining elements.

18.8   **Efficiency.** For this implementation, the worst-case efficiencies of the operations are as follows:

Addition   O(n)
Removal   O(n)
Retrieval   O(n)
Traversal   O(n)

Even though additions occur after the last entry in the array dictionary without shifting any data, the search necessary to prevent duplicate search keys in the dictionary makes the overall operation O(n). Deletions and retrievals use a similar search of the array, making them O(n) as well. Finally, traversing an array is an O(n) operation.

Realize that if you fill the array of dictionary entries, you must allocate a new, larger array and copy elements from the original array to the new array. This requirement adds overhead to any array-based implementation that the previous analysis does not reflect. In Java, the array elements are references to objects, so copying the array is fast. But for languages whose arrays contain objects instead of references, copying can be quite time-consuming. Ideally, you want to choose a sufficiently large array, but not one that wastes space because it is overly large.

A Sorted Array-Based Dictionary

18.9   Some of the implementation for an unsorted dictionary, as shown in Segment 18.2, is independent of the order of the dictionary's entries, and so can be used for a sorted dictionary. However, the search keys must belong to a class that implements the interface Comparable so that we can order them. An outline for an implementation of a sorted dictionary appears in Listing 18-2. The notation K extends Comparable<? super K>, which was first introduced in Segment 11.2 of Chapter 11, defines the generic type K. It allows us to compare objects of type K with either objects of type K or objects of any superclass of K.

Listing 18-2   An outline of the class SortedArrayDictionary

```
import java.util.Iterator;
import java.util.NoSuchElementException;
import java.io.Serializable;
```

```
public class SortedArrayDictionary<K extends Comparable<? super K>, V>
             implements DictionaryInterface<K, V>, Serializable
{
    < Data fields as shown in Listing 18-1 of Segment 18.2 >
    . . .

    < Constructors analogous to those in Listing 18-1 >
    . . .

    public V add(K key, V value)
    {
        . . . < See Segment 18.10. >
    } // end add

    < Implementations of other methods in DictionaryInterface >
    . . .

    < The private class Entry, as shown in Listing 18-1. >
} // end SortedArrayDictionary
```

18.10   **Adding an entry.** When the dictionary's key-value entries are sorted by their search keys, adding a new entry requires a search of the array of entries to see where the new entry belongs. After you determine the correct position for the new entry, you must make room for it in the array. You do this by shifting subsequent array elements up by one position, beginning at the last entry, as Figure 18-4 shows. You then insert the new entry into the array so it is in its proper order by search key.

The following algorithm for adding an entry has similarities to the one given in Segment 18.4 for an unsorted dictionary:

> *Algorithm* add(key, value)
> // *Adds a new key-value entry to the dictionary and returns* null. *If* key *already exists*
> // *in the dictionary, returns the corresponding value and replaces it with* value.
>
> *result =* null
> *Search the array until you either find an entry containing* key *or locate the point where it*
>   *should be*
> if (*an entry containing* key *is found in the array*)
> {
>   result = *value currently associated with* key
>   *Replace* key's *associated value with* value
> }
> else // *insert new entry*
> {
>   if (*array is full*)
>   *Double size of array*
>
>   *Make room in the array for a new entry at the index determined by the previous search*
>   *Insert a new entry containing* key *and* value *into the vacated location of the array*
>   *Increment the size of the dictionary*
> }
> return result

Question 2   Describe how the previous algorithm differs from the one given in Segment 18.4 for an unsorted dictionary.

Figure 18-4   Adding an entry to a sorted array-based dictionary: (a) search; (b) make room; (c) insert

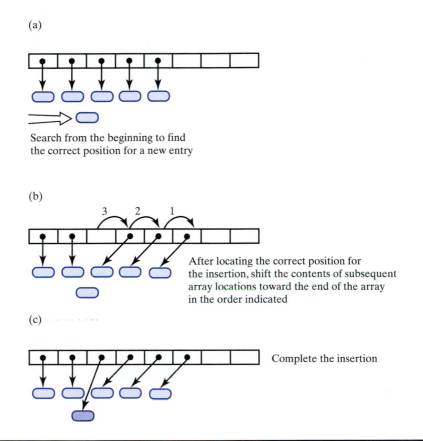

18.11   **The method add.** We can implement this algorithm by using the private methods described in Segment 18.3, but we need to use a different implementation for `locateIndex`. When the dictionary is unsorted, `locateIndex` simply detects whether the dictionary contains a given search key. But here, `locateIndex` must also determine where in the array to make the insertion. Thus, we revise the method's specification as follows:

```
/** Task: Returns either the index of the entry that contains key or
 *        the location that should contain key, if no such entry
 *        exists. */
private int locateIndex(K key)
```

The following additional method will also be helpful in the implementation:

```
/** Task: Makes room for a new entry at a given index by shifting
 *        array elements towards the end of the array. */
private void makeRoom(int keyIndex)
```

Using these methods, we can implement the method add as follows:

```java
public V add(K key, V value)
{
  V result = null;

  int keyIndex = locateIndex(key);

  if ( (keyIndex < currentSize) &&
          key.equals(dictionary[keyIndex].getKey()) )
  {
    // key found; return and replace old value
    result = dictionary[keyIndex].getValue();
    dictionary[keyIndex].setValue(value);
  }
  else
  {
    if (isArrayFull())
      doubleArray(); // expand array

    makeRoom(keyIndex);
    dictionary[keyIndex] = new Entry<K, V>(key, value);
    currentSize++;
  } // end if

  return result;
} // end add
```

18.12   **The method `locateIndex`.** Since the array is sorted, `locateIndex` can generally search it in less time than it could search an unsorted array. Recall from Segment 16.8 of Chapter 16 that a sequential search can detect when an entry is not in a sorted array without searching the entire array. Using that technique, we define the private method `locateIndex` as follows:

```java
private int locateIndex(K key)
{
  // search until you either find an entry containing key or
  // pass the point where it should be
  int index = 0;
  while ( (index < currentSize) &&
            key.compareTo(dictionary[index].getKey()) > 0 )
    index++;

  return index;
} // end locateIndex
```

The difference between this method and the one given in Segment 18.5 for an unsorted dictionary appears in color.

Question 3   A binary search would be faster, in general, than the modified sequential search just given—particularly when the dictionary is large. Implement the private method `locateIndex` for a sorted dictionary using a binary search.

18.13   **Removing an entry.** To remove an entry from a sorted array-based dictionary, we first locate the entry by calling the method `locateIndex` that we used in the previous segment for the add method. Since the entries are sorted, we must maintain their order. Thus, any entries after the one to be removed must shift to the next lower position in the array. Figure 18-5 illustrates these two steps.

Figure 18-5   Removing an entry from a sorted array-based dictionary: (a) search; (b) shift entries

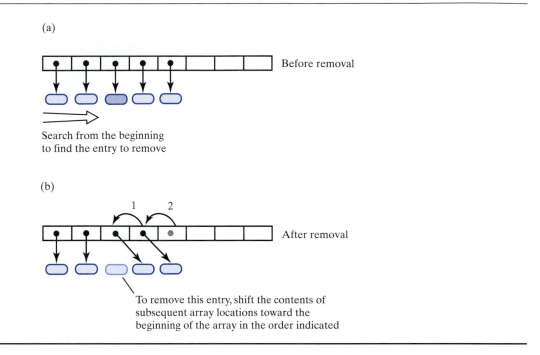

The following algorithm describes the remove operation:

Algorithm `remove(key)`
// Removes an entry from the dictionary, given its search key, and returns its value.
// If no such entry exists in the dictionary, returns `null`*.*

result = `null`
Search the array for an entry containing key

`if` *(an entry containing* key *is found in the array)*
{
   result = value currently associated with key
   Shift any entries that are after the located one to the next lower position in the array
   Decrement the size of the dictionary
}
`return` `result`

We leave the implementation of this algorithm as an exercise. Defining the following private method will be helpful:

```
/** Task: Removes an entry at a given index by shifting array
 *        elements toward the entry to be removed. */
private void removeArrayElement(int keyIndex)
```

18.14   **The remaining methods.** At the heart of the method `getValue`, which retrieves the value in an existing entry given its search key, is the method `locateIndex`, as described earlier. Since the array of entries is sorted, `locateIndex` can use a binary search, as Question 3 indicated.

An iteration, or traversal, of the entries in the dictionary starts with the first element in the array and moves sequentially through the remaining elements. This part of the implementation can be the same as for an unsorted dictionary. But here, since the array is sorted, the iteration will traverse the dictionary in sorted search-key order.

We leave the completion of this implementation to you as an exercise.

18.15   **Efficiency.** When `locateIndex` uses a binary search in the sorted array-based implementation, the worst-case efficiencies of the dictionary operations are as follows:

Addition	O(n)
Removal	O(n)
Retrieval	O(log n)
Traversal	O(n)

This implementation is suitable for an application that creates a dictionary and then makes many retrievals. This tip from Chapter 9 bears repeating here:

Programming Tip: When choosing an implementation for an ADT, you should consider the operations that your application requires. If you use a particular ADT operation frequently, you want its implementation to be efficient. Conversely, if you rarely use an operation, you can afford to use a class that has an inefficient implementation of that operation.

Programming Tip: Include comments in a class's implementation that advertise the efficiencies of its methods.

Question 4   When the sorted array-based implementation of a dictionary uses a binary search, its retrieval operation is O(log n). Since `add` and `remove` use a similar search, why are they not O(log n) as well?

Vector-Based Implementations

18.16   An implementation that uses an instance of Java's class `Vector` is similar in spirit to an array-based implementation. You can use one or two vectors, much like the one or two arrays pictured in Parts *a* and *b* of Figure 18-1. Since the underlying implementation of the class `Vector` is array based, the algorithms for the dictionary operations and their efficiencies are essentially the same whether you use an array or a vector.

With a vector, you do not need the private methods `doubleArray`, `isArrayFull`, `makeRoom`, and `removeArrayElement` that are in the array-based implementations. A vector accommodates the addition of a new entry—expanding as necessary—without any extra effort by us. A vector also shifts its entries if necessary when you either add or remove an entry. Lastly, a vector counts its entries, so you do not have to.

18.17   As an example of how to use a vector to implement a dictionary, consider the sorted implementation outlined in Listing 18-3. The type parameters K and V of `SortedVectorDictionary` are like those for `SortedArrayDictionary` shown in Listing 18-2 of Segment 18.9. The inner class `Entry` uses these type parameters, whereas the definition of `Entry` within `SortedArrayDictionary` (see Listing 18-1 of Segment 18.2) defines its own type parameters. Although we could use either definition here, this simpler one is fine because we are not allocating an array of `Entry` objects.

Listing 18-3   An outline of the class `SortedVectorDictionary`

```java
import java.util.Vector;
import java.util.Iterator;
import java.util.NoSuchElementException;
import java.io.Serializable;

public class SortedVectorDictionary<K extends Comparable<? super K>, V>
             implements DictionaryInterface<K, V>, Serializable
{
  private Vector<Entry> dictionary;

  public SortedVectorDictionary()
  {
    dictionary = new Vector<Entry>(); // doubles in size, as necessary
  } // end default constructor

  public SortedVectorDictionary(int initialCapacity)
  {
    dictionary = new Vector<Entry>(initialCapacity);
  } // end constructor

  < Implementations of methods in DictionaryInterface >

  < Private classes KeyIterator and ValueIterator (See Segment 18.20) >

  private class Entry implements Serializable
  {
    private K key;
    private V value;

    private Entry(K searchKey, V dataValue)
    {
      key = searchKey;
      value = dataValue;
    } // end constructor

    private K getKey()
    {
      return key;
    } // end getKey

    private V getValue()
    {
      return value;
    } // end getValue

    private void setValue(V newValue)
    {
      value = newValue;
    } // end setValue
  } // end Entry
} // end SortedVectorDictionary
```

18.18   **The method add.** The implementation of the method add is similar to the one given earlier in Segment 18.11 for the sorted array-based implementation. This version is shorter, since much of the busy work is handled for us by Vector. You should compare this code with the code given earlier.

Assuming that we have already revised locateIndex, as given in Segment 18.12, to work with vectors, we call it with the statement

```
int keyIndex = locateIndex(key);
```

where key is the search key of the new entry. To see whether an entry having key as its search key is already in the dictionary, we check whether key is the same as the search key of the entry at key-Index. Using Vector's method get, we reference this entry by writing

```
dictionary.get(keyIndex)
```

To get this entry's search key, we write

```
(dictionary.get(keyIndex)).getKey()
```

The pair of blue parentheses is optional. This expression is now the argument of the method equals that is invoked by key, the new entry's search key:

```
key.equals((dictionary.get(keyIndex)).getKey())
```

Ordinarily, we could simplify this expression by first assigning the argument of equals to a local variable, as follows:

```
Entry currentEntry = dictionary.get(keyIndex);
```

We then could write the expression as

```
key.equals(currentEntry.getKey())
```

But in our case, we also need to check the value of keyIndex. Thus, we are left with the choice of one long if clause or several awkwardly nested but shorter if statements. We settle for the following implementation of add:

```
public V add(K key, V value)
{
  V result = null;
  int keyIndex = locateIndex(key);

  if ( (keyIndex < dictionary.size()) &&
        key.equals( (dictionary.get(keyIndex)).getKey() ) )
  {
    // key found; return and replace old value
    Entry currentEntry = dictionary.get(keyIndex);
    result = currentEntry.getValue();
    currentEntry.setValue(value);
  }
  else // add new entry
  {
    Entry newEntry = new Entry(key, value);
    dictionary.add(keyIndex, newEntry);
  } // end if

  return result;
} // end add
```

18.19   **The private method `locateIndex`.** To revise `locateIndex`, as given in Segment 18.12, to work with a vector instead of an array, we modify the boolean expression in the `while` statement. The resulting expression is similar to the boolean expression in the previous segment, but it invokes `compareTo` instead of `equals`. Thus, the revised method appears as follows:

```
private int locateIndex(K key)
{
  // search until you either find an entry containing key or
  // pass the point where it should be
  int currentSize = dictionary.size();
  int index = 0;
  while ( (index < currentSize) &&
            key.compareTo( (dictionary.get(index)).getKey() ) > 0 )
    index++;

  return index;
} // end locateIndex
```

The differences between this method and the array version appear in color. In `SortedArrayDictionary`, `currentSize` is a data field. Here it is a local variable set to `dictionary.size()`, the vector's size

Implementations for the methods `remove` and `getValue` are similar to the implementation for `add`, and we leave them as exercises.

18.20   **An iterator for search keys.** Our goal in providing iterators for the dictionary is to give the client an easy way to traverse the search keys and their corresponding values. The interface for the dictionary given in Segment 17.4 of the previous chapter specifies two iterators, one for search keys and one for values. That chapter showed you how to use these iterators, and here we implement an iterator for the search keys.

Recall that the interface `java.util.Iterator` specifies the methods `hasNext`, `next`, and `remove`. We can define a private class `KeyIterator` that implements this interface and is internal to the class `SortedVectorDictionary`. We then implement the public method `getKeyIterator` within `SortedVectorDictionary` as follows:

```
public Iterator<K> getKeyIterator()
{
  return new KeyIterator();
} // end getKeyIterator
```

The implementation of the class `KeyIterator` is shown in Listing 18-4. Vector's iterator `dictionary.iterator` traverses the entries in the vector `dictionary` and is the basis of this implementation. Each entry in the vector is an instance of `Entry`, so we use `Entry`'s method `getKey` to get each search key.

`Iterator`'s method `remove` is not relevant to the traversal of the search keys, so we do not support it. Instead we make `remove` throw an exception if it is invoked.

Listing 18-4   `SortedVectorDictionary`'s private inner class `KeyIterator`

```
private class KeyIterator implements Iterator<K>
{
  private Iterator<Entry> traverser;
```

```
    private KeyIterator()
    {
      traverser = dictionary.iterator();
    } // end default constructor

    public boolean hasNext()
    {
      return traverser.hasNext();
    } // end hasNext

    public K next()
    {
      Entry nextEntry = traverser.next();
      return nextEntry.getKey();
    } // end next

    public void remove()
    {
      throw new UnsupportedOperationException();
    } // end remove
  } // end KeyIterator
```

The method `getValueIterator` has an analogous implementation: You define another inner class similar to `KeyIterator`. We leave the details an exercise.

18.21   **Using `ArrayList` instead of `Vector`.** Since `ArrayList` and `Vector` each implement the interface `java.util.List`, and since we were careful to use only methods in this interface, you could replace `Vector` with `ArrayList` in the implementation of `SortedVectorDictionary`.

Linked Implementations

18.22   The last implementations of the ADT dictionary that we will consider in this chapter store the dictionary's entries in a chain of linked nodes. As presented in Chapters 6 and 7, a chain can provide as much storage as necessary for the entries. You can encapsulate the two parts of an entry into an object, as Figure 18-6a illustrates, just as you did for an array or vector. If you choose this option, your dictionary class can use the classes `Node` from Segment 7.14 and `Entry` from Segment 18.17.

Another option does not use the class `Entry`. You could use two chains, as in Figure 18-6b, but a simpler approach is to revise the definition of a node to include both parts of the entry, as Figure 18-6c illustrates. The private inner class `Node`, defined within the dictionary class, would then contain the data fields

```
    private K key;
    private V value;
    private Node next;
```

The generic types K and V are defined by the outer class. In addition to constructors, the class `Node` would contain the methods `getKey`, `getValue`, `setValue`, `getNextNode`, and `setNextNode`. Since changing the search key is not necessary and, in fact, could destroy the order of a sorted dictionary, no `setKey` method is provided.

Figure 18-6   Three possible ways to use linked nodes to represent the entries in a dictionary:
(a) a chain of nodes that each reference an entry object; (b) parallel chains of search keys
and values; (c) a chain of nodes that each reference a search key and a value

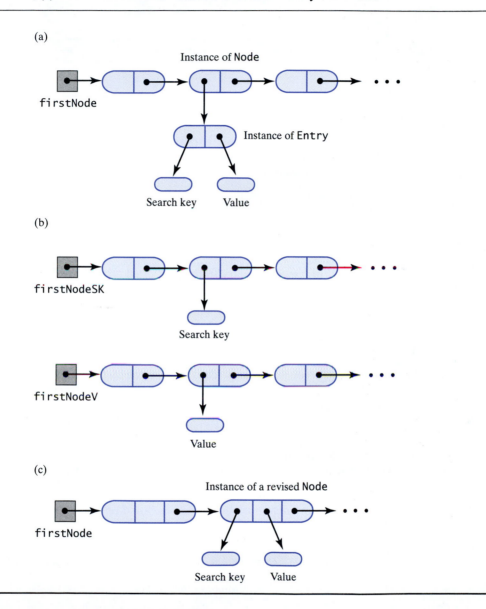

An Unsorted Linked Dictionary

18.23   Since the entries in an unsorted dictionary are in no particular order, you add a new entry in the
most efficient manner. When the entries are in a linked chain, the fastest addition is at the beginning
of the chain, as Figure 18-7 shows. (If the class also maintains a tail reference to the last node of the
chain, adding an entry after the last node would be equally fast.) While this aspect of an addition is
O(1), preventing duplicate search keys requires a sequential search from the beginning of the chain.

Figure 18-7   Adding to an unsorted linked dictionary

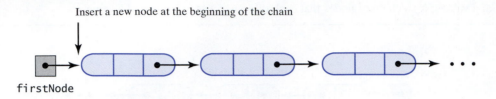

Just as you would for an array, you would have to look at all the search keys in the chain to learn that a particular entry was not present. Removing or retrieving an entry uses a similar search. A traversal of either the search keys or the values involves the entire chain. Thus, for this implementation, the worst-case efficiencies of the operations are as follows:

Addition $O(n)$
Removal $O(n)$
Retrieval $O(n)$
Traversal $O(n)$

Question 5   To remove an entry from an unsorted array-based dictionary, we replaced the removed entry with the last entry in the array (see Segment 18.6). Should we use the same strategy to remove an entry from an unsorted linked dictionary? Explain.

A Sorted Linked Dictionary

18.24   **Adding an entry.** When the nodes in a chain are sorted by their search keys, adding a new entry to the dictionary requires a sequential search of the chain from its beginning to determine the correct location for the new node. Since the search keys are sorted, you can detect that a desired search key does not exist in the chain as soon as you pass the node that should have contained it. That is, you do not have to look at the entire chain, as you would if the search keys were unsorted. Segments 16.8 and 16.22 describe this variation of a sequential search.

The following algorithm adds a new entry to a sorted linked dictionary:

Algorithm add(key, value)
// Adds a new key-value entry to the dictionary and returns null. *If key already exists*
// in the dictionary, returns the corresponding value and replaces it with value.

result = null
Search the chain until either you find a node containing key or you pass the point where
    it should be
if *(a node containing key is found in the chain)*
{
    result = *value currently associated with* key
    Replace key's associated value with value
}
else if *(the chain is empty or the new entry belongs at the beginning of the chain)*
{
    Allocate a new node containing key *and* value
    Add the new node to the beginning of the chain
    Increment the size of the dictionary
}

```
      else
      {
         Insert the new node before the last node that was examined during the search
         Increment the size of the dictionary
      }
      return result
```

18.25   Listing 18-5 shows the beginning of the class SortedLinkedDictionary and the implementation of the method add. Implementations for the methods remove and getValue are similar to the implementation for add, but are a bit simpler. We leave them as exercises.

Listing 18-5   The class SortedLinkedDictionary

```java
import java.util.Iterator;
import java.util.NoSuchElementException;
import java.io.Serializable;

public class SortedLinkedDictionary<K extends Comparable<? super K>, V>
            implements DictionaryInterface<K, V>, Serializable
{
  private Node firstNode;    // reference to first node of chain
  private int  currentSize; // number of entries

  public SortedLinkedDictionary()
  {
    firstNode = null;
    currentSize = 0;
  } // end default constructor

  public V add(K key, V value)
  {
    V result = null;

    // search chain until you either find a node containing key
    // or pass the point where it should be
    Node currentNode = firstNode;
    Node nodeBefore = null;
    while ( (currentNode != null) &&
            key.compareTo(currentNode.getKey()) > 0 )
    {
      nodeBefore = currentNode;
      currentNode = currentNode.getNextNode();
    } // end while

    if ( (currentNode != null) && key.equals(currentNode.getKey()) )
    {
      result = currentNode.getValue();
      currentNode.setValue(value); // replace value
    }
    else
    {
      Node newNode = new Node(key, value); // create new node
      currentSize++; // increase length for both cases
```

```
            if (nodeBefore == null)
            { // add at beginning (includes empty chain)
              newNode.setNextNode(firstNode);
              firstNode = newNode;
            }
            else // add elsewhere in non-empty chain
            {
              newNode.setNextNode(currentNode);// currentNode is after new node
              nodeBefore.setNextNode(newNode); // nodeBefore is before new node
            } // end if
          } // end if

          return result;
        } // end add

        < Implementations of the other methods in DictionaryInterface >
        . . .

        < Private classes KeyIterator and ValueIterator (See Segment 18.26) >
        . . .

        < The private class Node >
        . . .

} // end SortedLinkedDictionary
```

18.26   Iterators. As we mentioned in Segment 18.20, iterators provide the client with an easy way to traverse a dictionary's search keys and their corresponding values. The public methods getKeyIterator and getValueIterator have the same implementations here as they do in SortedVectorDictionary. The private inner classes KeyIterator and ValueIterator, however, differ. Each has a data field nextNode to mark an iteration's place in the chain as the traversal progresses. Listing 18-6 shows the private class KeyIterator. ValueIterator has a similar definition. Both of these classes are like the inner class IteratorForLinkedList that appears in Segments 8.19 through 8.23 of Chapter 8.

Listing 18-6   SortedLinkedDictionary's private inner class KeyIterator

```
private class KeyIterator implements Iterator<K>
{
  private Node nextNode; // node containing next entry in iteration

  private KeyIterator()
  {
    nextNode = firstNode;
  } // end default constructor

  public boolean hasNext()
  {
    return nextNode != null;
  } // end hasNext

  public K next()
  {
    K result;
```

```
        if (hasNext())
        {
          result = nextNode.getKey();
          nextNode = nextNode.getNextNode();
        }
        else
          throw new NoSuchElementException();

        return result;
      } // end next

      public void remove()
      {
        throw new UnsupportedOperationException();
      } // end remove
    } // end KeyIterator
```

18.27   **Efficiency.** Like adding an entry, removing or retrieving an entry requires a sequential search of the chain. Traversal of a sorted chain proceeds just as it would for an unsorted chain. Thus, the worst-case efficiencies of the dictionary operations for a sorted linked implementation are as follows:

Addition	$O(n)$
Removal	$O(n)$
Retrieval	$O(n)$
Traversal	$O(n)$

The addition or removal of an entry is an $O(n)$ operation regardless of whether you use an array, a vector, or a chain to implement a dictionary. Realize, however, that an array requires you to shift its elements, whereas a linked chain does not. Also, the preceding linked implementation does not require a good estimate of the dictionary's ultimate size. When you use an array that is too small, you can expand it by copying its elements to a new, larger array, but this takes time. If you use an array that is larger than necessary, you waste space. The same is true if you use a vector, but neither of these situations occur with a linked implementation.

CHAPTER SUMMARY

- You can implement a dictionary by using either an array that you expand dynamically, a vector, or a chain of linked nodes. A linked implementation does not require a good estimate of the dictionary's ultimate size. When you use an array that is too small, you need to copy its elements to a new, larger array. If you use an array that is larger than necessary, you waste space. The same is true if you use a vector, but neither of these situations occur with a linked implementation.

- The worst-case efficiencies of the dictionary operations for array-based and linked implementations are as follows:

	Array-Based		Linked	
	Unsorted	**Sorted**	**Unsorted**	**Sorted**
Addition	$O(n)$	$O(n)$	$O(n)$	$O(n)$
Removal	$O(n)$	$O(n)$	$O(n)$	$O(n)$
Retrieval	$O(n)$	$O(\log n)$	$O(n)$	$O(n)$
Traversal	$O(n)$	$O(n)$	$O(n)$	$O(n)$

- For a sorted or unsorted dictionary, the addition or removal of an entry is an O(n) operation regardless of whether you use an array, a vector, or a chain to implement it. Realize, however, that an array or vector requires the shifting of its elements, whereas a linked chain does not.

- Using either an array or a vector to implement a sorted dictionary allows for an efficient retrieval operation because you can use a binary search.

- To implement the method `getKeyIterator` or `getValueIterator`, define a private inner class for the dictionary class. This private class should implement the interface `java.util.Iterator`.

PROGRAMMING TIP

- When choosing an implementation for an ADT, you should consider the operations that your application requires. If you use a particular ADT operation frequently, you want its implementation to be efficient. Conversely, if you rarely use an operation, you can afford to use a class that has an inefficient implementation of that operation.

- Include comments in a class's implementation that advertise the efficiencies of its methods.

EXERCISES

1. Begin an array-based implementation of the ADT dictionary according to the data structure illustrated in Figure 18-1b. Declare the data fields, define the constructors, and define the method add for unsorted data. Use arrays that you can expand during execution.

2. Begin two linked implementations of the ADT dictionary according to the two data structures illustrated in Parts *a* and *b* of Figure 18-6. Declare the data fields, define the constructors, and define the method add for unsorted data.

3. In the sorted, vector-based implementation of a dictionary, replace the sequential search performed by the method `locateIndex` with a binary search. (See Segment 18.19.)

4. For a sorted linked implementation of a dictionary, write iterative versions of the methods `remove` and `getValue`.

5. For a sorted linked implementation of a dictionary, write recursive versions of the methods `add`, `remove`, and `getValue`.

6. Segment 18.26 defines the class `KeyIterator`. An instance of this class is an iterator that traverses the search keys in the dictionary. In a similar fashion, define a class `ValueIterator` to provide a way to traverse the dictionary's values.

7. Define an iterator for the ADT dictionary that returns entries containing both a search key and a value. Describe the class of these entries. Implement a method `getEntryIterator` that returns such an iterator.

8. Consider adding operations to the ADT dictionary to form the union and intersection of two given dictionaries. Each operation returns a new dictionary. The union should combine the entries in both dictionaries into a third dictionary. The intersection should be a dictionary of the entries common to both of the two dictionaries.

    Within each given dictionary, search keys are not repeated. However, an entry in one dictionary could have the same search key as an entry in the second dictionary. Propose and discuss ways to specify these two operations for this case.

9. Implement the union and intersection operations that Exercise 8 describes for an unsorted array-based dictionary.

10. Repeat Exercise 9 for a sorted array-based dictionary.

11. Repeat Exercise 9 for a sorted linked dictionary.

PROJECTS

1. Implement an unsorted array-based dictionary. Allow the array to expand as necessary during execution.

2. Repeat the previous project, but maintain the search keys in sorted order.

3. Implement a dictionary by using an instance of `Vector` or `ArrayList`. Do not maintain the search keys in sorted order, and do not shift the entries during additions and removals.

4. Repeat the previous project, but maintain the search keys in sorted order.

5. Implement an unsorted dictionary by using a chain of linked nodes.

6. Implement a sorted dictionary by using a chain of linked nodes.

7. In this chapter, the ADT dictionary has distinct search keys. Implement a dictionary that removes this restriction. Choose one of the following possibilities:

   ● The method `add` adds an entry whose search key is already in the dictionary but whose value is not. The method `remove` deletes all occurrences of the search key. The method `getValue` retrieves all values associated with a search key.
   ● The methods behave as just described, but a secondary search key enables `remove` and `getValue` to delete or retrieve a single entry.

8. Segment 17.7 of the previous chapter began a discussion of a telephone directory. Use your dictionary implementation from Project 7 in a revision of the telephone directory that allows duplicate names.

9. Figure 18-1b illustrates how you can use parallel arrays to represent the entries in a dictionary. Implement the ADT dictionary by using this approach.

10. Revise the class `Entry` given in Listing 18-1 of Segment 18.2 as a top-level class that implements the interface `Comparable`. You compare two `Entry` objects by comparing their search keys. Using this class and an implementation of the ADT sorted list, write an implementation for a sorted dictionary. The classes, including `Entry`, should belong to the same package.

11. Revise the class `Pair`, which is in Segment 2.6 of Chapter 2, to give it accessor methods for its data fields `first` and `second`. Implement a sorted dictionary by using an array of `Pair` objects.

12. Repeat the previous project, but instead use a chain of linked nodes that each reference an instance of `Pair`.

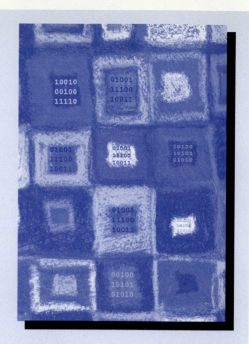

CONTENTS

PREREQUISITES

OBJECTIVES

After studying this chapter, you should be able to

- Describe the basic idea of hashing
- Describe the purpose of a hash table, a hash function, and a perfect hash function
- Explain why you should override the method `hashCode` for objects used as search keys
- Describe how a hash function compresses a hash code into an index to the hash table
- Describe collisions and explain why they occur
- Describe open addressing as a method to resolve collisions
- Describe linear probing, quadratic probing, and double hashing as particular open addressing schemes
- Describe algorithms for the dictionary operations `getValue`, `add`, and `remove` when open addressing resolves collisions

- Describe separate chaining as a method to resolve collisions
- Describe algorithms for the dictionary operations `getValue`, `add`, and `remove` when separate chaining resolves collisions
- Describe clustering and the problems it causes

Because searching databases is such a widespread application of computers, the dictionary is an important abstract data type. The implementations that we discussed in the previous chapter are fine for certain applications, but for others they are inadequate. For example, if locating data is critical, even an O(log *n*) search can be too slow. Such is the case for the emergency telephone (911) system. If you call 911, your telephone number is the key in a search of a dictionary of street addresses. Obviously, you want this search to find your address immediately!

This chapter introduces a technique called hashing that ideally can result in O(1) search times. We will complete our exploration of this topic in the next chapter. Hashing can be an excellent choice for implementing a dictionary when searching is the primary task. But as good as hashing can be, it is not always appropriate. For example, hashing cannot provide a traversal of the search keys in sorted order. Later in this book we will consider other implementations of the ADT dictionary.

What Is Hashing?

19.1   **A place for everything; everything in its place.** Do you spend time looking for your keys in the morning? Or do you know exactly where they are? Some of us spend too much time sequentially searching our unsorted possessions. Others have a special place for things and know just where to find each one.

An array can provide a place for a dictionary's entries. Admittedly, arrays have their disadvantages, but you can access any element in an array directly if you know its index. No other array element need be involved. **Hashing** is a technique that determines this index using only an entry's search key, without searching. The array itself is called a **hash table**.

A **hash function** takes a search key and produces the integer index of an element in the hash table. This array element is where you would either store or look for the search key's associated value. For example, the 911 emergency system can take your telephone number, convert it to a suitable integer *i*, and store a reference to your street address in the array element `a[i]`. We say that the telephone number—that is, the search key—**maps**, or **hashes**, to the index `i`. This index is called a **hash index.** Sometimes we will say that the search key maps, or hashes, into the table location at the index `i`.

19.2   **Ideal hashing.** Consider an emergency system for a small town where everyone's telephone number begins with 555. Let the hash function *h* convert a telephone number to its last four digits. For example,

$$h(555\text{-}1214) = 1214$$

If `hashTable` is the hash table, we would place a reference to the street address associated with this telephone number in `hashTable[1214]`, as Figure 19-1 illustrates. If the cost of evaluating the hash function is low, adding an entry to the array `hashTable` is an O(1) operation.

Figure 19-1   A hash function indexes its hash table

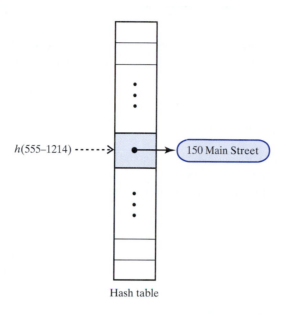

Hash table

To later find the street address associated with the number 555-1214, we once again com-pute h(555-1214) and use the result to index `hashTable`. Thus, from `hashTable[1214]`, we get the desired street address. This operation also is O(1). Notice that we did not search the array `hashTable`.

Let's summarize what we know so far by writing simple algorithms for the dictionary opera-tions that add or retrieve entries:

```
Algorithm add(key, value)
index = h(key)
hashTable[index] = value


Algorithm getValue(key)
index = h(key)
return hashTable[index]
```

Will these algorithms always work? We can make them work if we know all the possible search keys. In this example, the search keys range from 555-0000 to 555-9999, so the hash func-tion will produce indices from 0 to 9999. If the array `hashTable` has 10,000 elements, each tele-phone number will correspond to one unique element in `hashTable`. That element references the appropriate street address. This scenario describes the ideal case for hashing, and the hash function here is a **perfect hash function**.

Note: A perfect hash function maps each search key into a different integer that is suitable as an index to the hash table.

19.3   **Typical hashing.** Because we need a database of all street addresses in the previous example, we must have one entry in the hash table for each telephone number. Our perfect hash function needs a hash table this large because it produces 10,000 different indices between 0 and 9999 from the 10,000 possible search keys. This hash table is always full if every telephone number in the 555 exchange is assigned. Although a full hash table is quite reasonable for this application, most hash tables are not full and can even be **sparse**—that is, have only a few of their elements actually in use.

For example, if our small town required only 700 telephone numbers, most of the 10,000-location hash table would be unused. We would waste most of the space allocated to the hash table. If the 700 numbers were not sequential, we would need a different hash function if we wanted to use a smaller hash table.

We might develop this hash function as follows. Given a nonnegative integer i and a hash table with n locations, the value of i modulo n ranges from 0 to $n-1$. Since i is nonnegative, i modulo n is the integer remainder after dividing i by n. This value is a valid index for the hash table. So a hash function h for a telephone number could have the following algorithm:

Algorithm `getHashIndex(phoneNumber)`
// Returns an index to an array of `tableSize` *locations.*

i = *last four digits of* `phoneNumber`
`return` i `% tableSize`

This hash function—like typical hash functions—performs two steps:

1. Convert the search key to an integer called the **hash code**.
2. **Compress** the hash code into the range of indices for the hash table.

Often the search key is not an integer, and frequently it is a string. So a hash function first converts the key to an integer hash code. Next, it transforms that integer into one that is suitable as an index to the particular hash table.

The hash function that the algorithm `getHashIndex` describes is not a perfect hash function when `tableSize` is less than 10,000. Since 10,000 telephone numbers map into `tableSize` indices, some telephone numbers will map into the same index. We call such an occurrence a **collision**. For example, if `tableSize` is 101, `getHashIndex("555-1214")` and `getHashIndex("555-8132")` each map into 52. If we have already stored the street address for 555-1214 in `hashTable[52]`, as Figure 19-2 shows, what will we do with the address for 555-8132? Handling such collisions is called **collision resolution**. Before we look at collision resolution, we explore hash functions a bit further.

Note: Typical hash functions are not perfect, because they can allow more than one search key to map into a single index, causing a collision in the hash table.

Figure 19-2   A collision caused by the hash function *h*

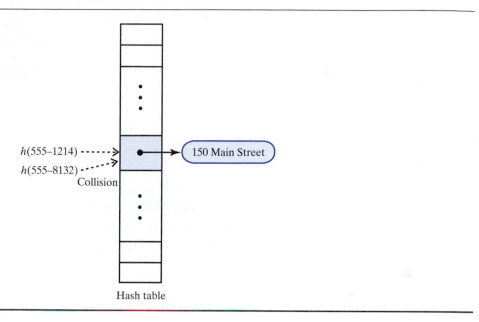

Hash table

Hash Functions

19.4   **General characteristics.** Any function can be a hash function if it produces an integer that is suitable as an array index. But not every such function is a *good* hash function. Our previous discussions suggest that a good hash function should

- Minimize collisions
- Be fast to compute

Recall that a typical hash function first converts a search key to an integer hash code. The hash function then compresses the hash code into an integer that is suitable as an index to the particular hash table.

Note: To reduce the chance of a collision, choose a hash function that distributes entries uniformly throughout the hash table.

First, consider how to convert a search key to an `int`. Realize that a search key can be either a primitive type or an instance of a class.

Computing Hash Codes

19.5   **The hash code for a class type.** Java's base class `Object` has a method `hashCode` that returns an integer hash code. Since every class is a subclass of `Object`, all classes inherit this method. But unless a class overrides `hashCode`, the method will return an `int` value based on the invoking object's memory address. This default hash code usually is not appropriate for hashing, because equal but distinct objects will have different hash codes. To be useful as a dictionary implementation, hashing must map equal objects into the same location in a hash table. Thus, a class should define its own version of `hashCode` that adheres to the following guidelines.

Note: **Guidelines for the method hashCode**

- If a class overrides the method equals, it should override hashCode.
- If the method equals considers two objects equal, hashCode must return the same value for both objects.
- If an object invokes hashCode more than once during the execution of a program, and if the object's data remains the same during this time, hashCode must return the same hash code.
- An object's hash code during one execution of a program can differ from its hash code during another execution of the same program.

A perfect hash function would require that unequal objects have distinct hash codes. In general, however, unequal objects might have the same hash codes. Since duplicate hash codes lead to collisions, you want to avoid this situation when possible.

19.6   **A hash code for a string.** Search keys are often strings, so generating a good hash code from a string is important. Typically, you begin by assigning an integer to each character in the string. For example, you could assign the integers 1 through 26 to the letters "A" through "Z" and the integers 27 through 52 to the letters "a" through "z." However, using a character's Unicode integer is more common and actually easier to do.

Suppose that the search keys for a telephone directory are names such as *Brett*, *Carol*, *Gail*, and *Josh*. You can compute hash codes for these names in several ways. For example, you could take the Unicode value of the first letter in each name and get distinct hash codes. But if several names begin with the same letter, their hash codes will be the same if you use this scheme. Since the letters that occur in any one position of a name do not occur with equal probability, a hash function that uses any particular letter will not distribute the names uniformly throughout the hash table.

Suppose that you sum the Unicode values for each letter in the search key. In an application where two different search keys never contain the same letters, this approach can work. But if your search keys are airport codes, for example, *DUB* and *BUD* would have the same hash code. This approach also can restrict the range of the hash codes, since the Unicode values for letters lie between 65 and 122. Thus, three-letter words would map into values between 195 and 366 under this plan.

Note: Real-world data is not uniformly distributed.

19.7   **A better hash code for a string.** A better approach to generating a hash code for a string involves multiplying the Unicode value of each character by a factor based on the character's position within the string. The hash code is then the sum of these products. Specifically, if the string s has n characters, let u_i be the Unicode value for the ith character in s (i is zero for the first character). Then the hash code can have the form

$$u_0 \, g^{n-1} + u_1 \, g^{n-2} + \ldots + u_{n-2} \, g + u_{n-1}$$

for some positive constant g. This expression is a polynomial in g. To minimize the number of arithmetic operations, write the polynomial in the following algebraically equivalent form:

$$(\ldots((u_0 \, g + u_1) \, g + u_2) \, g + \ldots + u_{n-2}) \, g + u_{n-1}$$

This way of evaluating a polynomial is called **Horner's method**.

The following Java statements perform this computation for the string s and the int constant g:

```
int hash = 0;
int n = s.length();
for (int i = 0; i < n; i++)
   hash = g * hash + s.charAt(i);
```

The ith character of the string is s.charAt(i). Adding this character to the product g * hash actually adds the character's Unicode value. An explicit cast of s.charAt(i) to int is not necessary and would not affect the result.

This computation can cause an overflow, particularly for long strings. Java ignores these overflows and, for an appropriate choice of g, the result will be a reasonable hash code. Current implementations of the method hashCode in Java's class String use this computation with 31 as the value of g. Realize, however, that the overflows can produce a negative result. You can deal with that when you compress the hash code into an appropriate index for the hash table.

Question 1 Calculate the hash code for the string *Java* when *g* is 31. Compare your result with the value of the expression "Java".hashCode().

19.8 **The hash code for a primitive type.** This segment contains Java operations that might be unfamiliar to you. However, they are not essential to the rest of this chapter.

If the search key's data type is int, you can use the key itself as the hash code. If the search key is an instance of either byte, short, or char, you can cast it to an int to get a hash code. Thus, casting to an int is one way to generate a hash code.

For other primitive types, you manipulate their internal binary representations. If the search key is an integer of type long, it contains 64 bits. An int has 32 bits. Simply casting the 64-bit search key to an int—or performing a modulo 2^{32}—would lose its first 32 bits. As a result, all keys that differ in only their first 32 bits will have the same hash code and collide. For this reason, ignoring part of a search key can be a problem.

Note: Derive the hash code from the *entire* search key. Do not ignore part of it.

Instead of ignoring a part of a long search key, divide it into several pieces. Then combine the pieces by using either addition or a bit-wise boolean operation such as **exclusive or**. This process is called **folding**.

For example, let's divide a long search key into two 32-bit halves. To get the left half, we can **shift** the search key to the right by a certain number of bits, or places. For example, if we shift the 8-bit binary number 10101100 to the right by 4 bits, we will get 00001010. We have isolated the number's left half and discarded its right half. If we now combine 00001010 with the original value and ignore the left half of the result, we will effectively have combined the left and right halves of the original key.

Now let's see how to do this in Java. The expression key >> 32 shifts the 64-bit key to the right by 32 bits, in effect eliminating its right half. Java's exclusive-or operator is ∧ and has the following effect on 1-bit quantities:

0 ∧ 0 is 0
1 ∧ 1 is 0
0 ∧ 1 is 1
1 ∧ 0 is 1

For two multibit quantities, the operator combines pairs of corresponding bits. So

1100 ∧ 1010 is 0110

Thus, the expression key ∧ (key >> 32) uses an exclusive-or operation to combine the halves of a 64-bit key. Although the result has 64 bits, the rightmost 32 bits contain the combined halves of key. We discard the leftmost 32 bits by casting the result to an int. Thus, the necessary computation is

```
(int)(key ∧ (key >> 32))
```

We can perform a similar computation for a search key of type double. Since key is a real value, we cannot use it in the previous expression. Instead, we must get key's bit pattern by calling Double.doubleToLongBits(key). Thus, the following statements produce the desired hash code:

```
long bits = Double.doubleToLongBits(key);
int hashCode = (int)(bits ∧ (bits >> 32));
```

Why not simply cast the search key from double to int? Since the search key is a real value, casting it to an int will simply give us the integral portion of the value. For example, if the key's value is 32.98, casting it to int results in the integer 32. While we could use 32 as the hash code, all search keys that have 32 as their integer portion also would have a hash code of 32. Unless you know that your real values have distinct integral portions, casting them to int values can cause many collisions.

The hash code of a search key of type float can be simply its 32 bits. You get these by calling Float.floatToIntBits(key).

These computations of hash codes for the primitives types are actually used by the corresponding wrapper classes in their implementations of the method hashCode.

Compressing a Hash Code into an Index for the Hash Table

19.9   The most common way to scale an integer so that it lies within a given range of values is to use Java's % operator. For a positive hash code c and a positive integer n, c % n divides c by n and takes the remainder as the result. This remainder lies between 0 and n - 1. Thus, c % n is ideal for the index of a hash table that has n locations.

So n should equal the size of the hash table, but not any n will do. For example, if n is even, c % n has the same **parity** as c—that is, if c is even, c % n is even; if c is odd, c % n is odd. If the hash codes are biased toward either even or odd values (and note that hash codes based on memory addresses are typically even), the indices to the hash table will have the same bias. Instead of a uniform distribution of indices, you will leave out the indices of many table locations if n is even. Thus, n—the size of the hash table—always should be an odd number.

When n is a **prime** number—one that is divisible only by 1 and itself—c % n provides values that are distributed throughout the index range 0 through n - 1. Prime numbers—with the exception of 2—are odd.

Note: The size of a hash table should be a prime number n greater than 2. Then, if you compress a positive hash code c into an index for the table by using c % n, the indices will be distributed uniformly between 0 and n - 1.

One final detail remains. You saw earlier that the method hashCode might return a negative integer, so you need to be a bit careful. If *c* is negative, *c* % *n* lies between 1 - *n* and 0. A zero result is fine, but if *c* % *n* is negative, add *n* to it so that it lies between 1 and *n* - 1.

19.10   We now can implement a hash function for the ADT dictionary. The following method computes the hash index for a given search key whose data type is the generic object type K. The data field hashTable is the array that serves as the hash table. Realize that hashTable.length is the size of the array, not the number of current entries in the hash table. We assume that this size is a prime number and that the method hashCode returns a hash code consistent with the previous discussion.

```
private int getHashIndex(K key)
{
  int hashIndex = key.hashCode() % hashTable.length;
  if (hashIndex < 0)
    hashIndex = hashIndex + hashTable.length;

  return hashIndex;
} // end getHashIndex
```

Question 2   Question 1 in Segment 19.7 asked you to compute the hash code for the string *Java*. Use that value to calculate what getHashIndex("Java") returns when the length of the hash table is 101.

Question 3   What one-character string, when passed to getHashIndex, will cause the method to return the same value as in the previous question?

Resolving Collisions

19.11   When adding to a dictionary, if your hash function maps a search key into a location in the hash table that is already in use, you need to find another spot for the search key's value. You have two fundamental choices:

- Use another location in the hash table
- Change the structure of the hash table so that each array location can represent more than one value

Finding an unused, or open, location in the hash table is called **open addressing**. This choice sounds simple, but it can lead to several complications. Changing the structure of the hash table is not as difficult as it might sound and can be a better choice for resolving collisions than using an open addressing scheme. We will examine both approaches, beginning with several variations of open addressing.

Open Addressing with Linear Probing

19.12   When a collision occurs during the addition of an entry to a hash table, an open addressing scheme locates an alternate location in the hash table that is available, or open. You then use this location to reference the new entry.

Locating an open location in the hash table is called **probing**, and various probing techniques are possible. With **linear probing**, if a collision occurs at hashTable[k], we see whether hashTable[k + 1] is available. If not, we look at hashTable[k + 2], and so on. The table locations that we consider in this search make up the **probe sequence**. If a probe sequence reaches the end of the hash table, it continues at the beginning of the table. Thus, we treat the hash table as if it were circular: The first location in the table comes immediately after the last location.

 Note: **Linear probing** resolves a collision during hashing by examining consecutive locations in the hash table—beginning at the original hash index—to find the next available one.

19.13 **Additions that collide.** Recall the example illustrated in Figure 19-2. The search keys 555-1214 and 555-8132 both mapped into the index 52. Suppose that 555-4294 and 555-2072 also map into that same index, and we make the following additions to an empty dictionary addressBook:

```
addressBook.add("555-1214", "150 Main Street");
addressBook.add("555-8132", "75 Center Court");
addressBook.add("555-4294", "205 Ocean Road");
addressBook.add("555-2072", "82 Campus Way");
```

The first addition would use hashTable[52]. The second addition would find hashTable[52] occupied, and so it would probe ahead and use hashTable[53]. The third addition would find both hashTable[52] and hashTable[53] occupied, and so it would probe ahead and use hashTable[54]. Finally, the fourth addition would probe the locations at indices 52, 53, and 54 before using hashTable[55] for the addition. Figure 19-3 shows the result of these additions to the hash table.

Figure 19-3 The effect of linear probing after adding four entries whose search keys hash to the same index

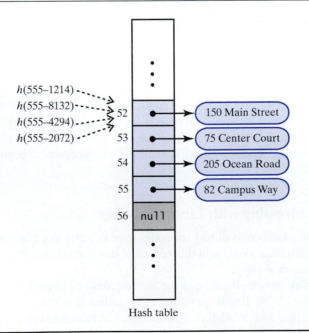

Hash table

Note: Linear probing can examine every location in a hash table. As a result, this type of probing ensures the success of the add operation as long as the hash table is not full.

19.14   **Retrievals.** Now that we've used linear probing to resolve collisions while adding our four entries, how do we retrieve the street address associated with the last search key we added, 555-2072? That is, if the statement

    String streetAddress = addressBook.getValue("555-2072");

is executed, what will getValue do? Since getHashIndex("555-2072") is 52, getValue will search consecutive locations in the array beginning at hashTable[52] until it finds the street address associated with the search key 555-2072. But wait! How can we tell which street address is the right one? We can't, unless we package a search key with its value. Segment 18.2 of Chapter 18 provided a class Entry that we could use for this purpose. Figure 19-4 shows the hash table given in Figure 19-3 after we make this revision.

Figure 19-4   A revision of the hash table shown in Figure 19-3 when linear probing resolves collisions; each entry contains a search key and its associated value

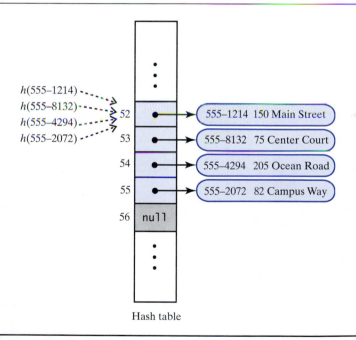

Hash table

Now the search for 555-2072 can follow the same probe sequence that was used to add this search key and its value to the hash table. This fact will be useful later when we assess the efficiency of hashing.

Note: A successful search for an entry that corresponds to a given search key follows the same probe sequence used to add the entry to the hash table.

What happens if the search key is not in the hash table? The search of the probe sequence would encounter a `null` location, indicating an unsuccessful search. But before we can reach this conclusion, we need to know what the `remove` method does, because it has the potential to adversely affect subsequent retrievals.

19.15   **Removals.** Suppose that after the four additions illustrated in Figure 19-4, we removed two entries by executing

```
addressBook.remove("555-8132");
addressBook.remove("555-4294");
```

The simplest way to remove an entry from an array location is to place `null` in the location. Figure 19-5 shows the hash table after `remove` places `null` into `hashTable[53]` and `hashTable[54]`. But now an attempt to find the search key 555-2072 will terminate unsuccessfully at `hashTable[53]`. Although a location in the hash table that was never used should end a search, a location that had been used and is now available again for use should not.

Figure 19-5   A hash table if `remove` used `null` to remove entries

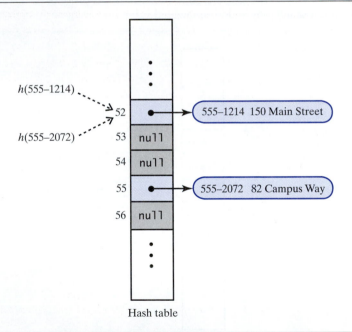

Thus, we need to distinguish among three kinds of locations in the hash table:

- Occupied—the location references an entry in the dictionary
- Empty—the location contains `null` and always has
- Available—the location's entry was removed from the dictionary

Accordingly, the method `remove` should not place `null` into the hash table, but instead should encode the location as available. The search during a retrieval should then continue if it encounters an available location and should stop only if it is successful or reaches a `null` location. A search during a removal behaves in the same way.

Question 4   Suggest ways to implement the three states of a location in a hash table. Should this state be a responsibility of the location or of the dictionary entry that it references?

19.16   **Reusing locations in the hash table during an addition.** Recall the hash table pictured in Figure 19-4. The entry whose search key is 555-2072 mapped into `hashTable[52]` but was added to the hash table at `hashTable[55]` due to collisions. Figure 19-6a shows this hash table again, but in a simpler form. The four occupied locations constitute a probe sequence; the other locations contain `null`. Since the search key 555-2072 maps into the first location of the probe sequence but actually occurs in the fourth location, a brief sequential search will find it.

Now let's try removing the middle two entries of the probe sequence, as Figure 19-6b shows. A search for 555-2072 starts at the beginning of the probe sequence, must continue beyond the removed entries, and stops successfully at the last location in the probe sequence. If 555-2072 does not occur in this last location, the search will end unsuccessfully at the next location, since it contains `null`. Figure 19-6c illustrates these searches.

Finally, consider what happens when we add an entry that maps into this probe sequence. For example, the search key 555-1062 maps into `hashTable[52]`. The add operation first must see whether this search key is in the hash table already. To do so, it searches the probe sequence. It has to search the entire probe sequence and reach a `null` location to discover that 555-1062 is not in the table. Figure 19-6d shows that this search ends at `hashTable[56]`. Should add place the new entry in this location? It could, but that would fill the hash table faster than if add reused a location that is presently in the available state. Two such locations are at the indices 53 and 54. We should place the new entry at `hashTable[53]`—that is, closest to the beginning of the probe sequence—so we can find it more quickly later. Figure 19-6e illustrates the hash table after this addition.

Note: Searches that dictionary operations require when open addressing resolves collisions

- To retrieve an entry, `getValue(key)` searches the probe sequence for `key`. It examines entries that are present and ignores locations that are in the available state. The search stops when either `key` is found or `null` is reached.
- The operation `remove(key)` searches the probe sequence using the same logic as a retrieval. If it finds `key`, it marks the location as available.
- The operation `add(key, value)` searches the probe sequence using logic like that of a retrieval, but it also notes the index of the first location encountered that is either in the available state or contains `null`. The operation uses this location for a new entry if `key` is not found.

19.17   **Clustering.** Collisions that are resolved with linear probing cause groups of consecutive locations in the hash table to be occupied. Each group is called a **cluster**, and the phenomenon is known as **primary clustering**. Each cluster is actually a probe sequence that you must search when adding, removing, or retrieving a table entry. When few collisions occur, probe sequences remain short and can be searched rapidly. But during an addition, any collision within a cluster increases the size of the cluster. Bigger clusters mean longer search times following a collision. As the clusters grow in size, they can merge into even larger clusters, compounding the problem. This occurrence can place many entries in one part of the hash table while another part is relatively empty.

Figure 19-6   A linear probe sequence (a) after adding an entry; (b) after removing two entries; (c) after a search; (d) during the search while adding an entry; (e) after an addition to a formerly occupied location

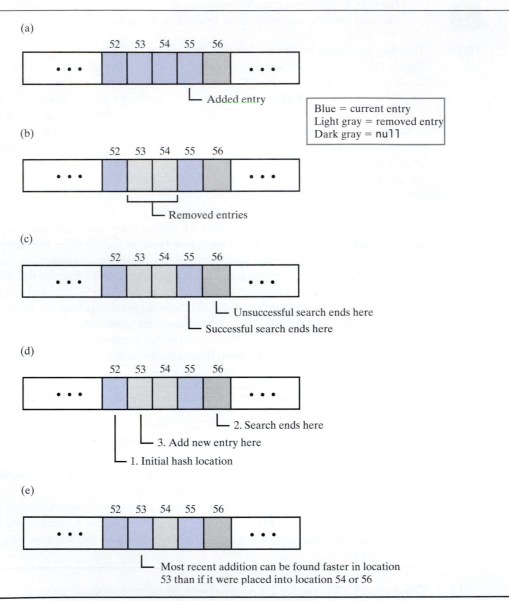

 Note: Linear probing is apt to cause primary clustering. Each cluster is a group of consecutive and occupied locations in the hash table. During an addition, any collision with any location within a cluster causes the cluster to get larger.

Open Addressing with Quadratic Probing

19.18   You can avoid primary clustering by changing the probe sequence that you use to resolve a collision. As we discussed in the previous section, if a given search key hashes to index k, linear probing looks at the consecutive locations beginning at index k. **Quadratic probing**, on the other hand, considers the locations at indices $k + j^2$ for $j \geq 0$—that is, it uses the indices $k, k + 1, k + 4, k + 9$, and so on. As before, if the probe sequence reaches the end of the hash table, it wraps around to the beginning of the table. This open addressing scheme separates the entries in the probe sequence, after the first two. In fact, this separation increases as the sequence grows in length. Figure 19-7 highlights the locations in a hash table that form one such probe sequence of five entries.

Figure 19-7   A probe sequence of length five using quadratic probing

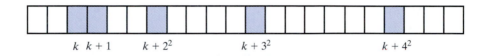

$$k \quad k + 1 \qquad k + 2^2 \qquad\qquad k + 3^2 \qquad\qquad\qquad k + 4^2$$

Except for the change in probe sequence, quadratic probing is like linear probing. It uses the three states that Segment 19.15 describes: occupied, empty, and available. Additionally, it reuses table locations in the available state, as described in Segment 19.16.

Although quadratic probing avoids primary clustering, entries that collide with an existing table entry use the same probe sequence. This phenomenon—called **secondary clustering**—is usually not a serious problem.

An advantage of linear probing is that it can reach every location in the hash table. As we mentioned earlier, this property is important since it guarantees the success of the add operation when the hash table is not full. Quadratic probing can also guarantee a successful add operation, as long as the hash table is at most half full and its size is a prime number. (See Exercise 8 at the end of this chapter.)

Quadratic probing requires more effort to compute the indices for the probe sequence than does linear probing. Exercise 2 at the end of this chapter shows how to compute these indices without multiplications or divisions.

Note: **Quadratic probing**

- Resolves a collision during hashing by examining locations in the hash table at the original hash index plus j^2, for $j \geq 0$
- Reaches half of the locations in the hash table if the size of the table is a prime number
- Avoids primary clustering but can lead to secondary clustering

Open Addressing with Double Hashing

19.19   Beginning at the original hash index k, both linear probing and quadratic probing add increments to k to define a probe sequence. These increments—1 for linear probing and j^2 for quadratic probing—are independent of the search key. **Double hashing** uses a second hash function to compute these increments in a key-dependent way. Thus, double hashing avoids both primary and secondary clustering.

Double hashing, like other open addressing schemes, should produce a probe sequence that reaches the entire table. Such will be the case if the size of the hash table is a prime number. (See Exercise 9 at the end of this chapter.) The second hash function must be different from the original hash function and must never have a zero value, since zero is not an appropriate increment.

19.20   **Example.** For example, consider the following pair of hash functions for a hash table whose size is 7:

$h_1(key) = key$ modulo 7
$h_2(key) = 5 - key$ modulo 5

This hash table is unusually small, but it allows us to study the behavior of the probe sequence. For a search key of 16, we have

$h_1(16) = 2$
$h_2(16) = 4$

The probe sequence begins at 2 and probes locations at increments of 4, as Figure 19-8 illustrates. Remember that when probing reaches the end of the table, it continues at the table's beginning. The table locations in the probe sequence then have the following indices: 2, 6, 3, 0, 4, 1, 5, 2, ... This sequence reaches all locations in the table and then repeats itself. Notice that the table size, 7, is a prime number.

Figure 19-8   The first three locations in a probe sequence generated by double hashing for the search key 16

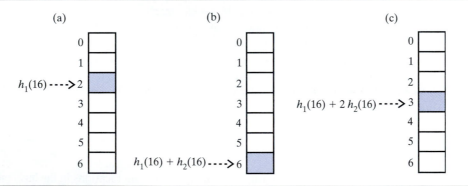

What happens if we change the size of the table to 6 and use the hash functions

$h_1(key) = key$ modulo 6
$h_2(key) = 5 - key$ modulo 5

For a search key of 16, we have

$h_1(16) = 4$
$h_2(16) = 4$

The probe sequence begins at 4 and probes locations at increments of 4. The sequence's indices are then 4, 2, 0, 4, 2, 0, ... The probe sequence does not reach all table locations before it begins to repeat. Notice that the table size, 6, is not prime.

Note: **Double hashing**

- Resolves a collision during hashing by examining locations in the hash table at the original hash index plus an increment defined by a second hash function. The second hash function should
    - Differ from the first hash function
    - Depend on the search key
    - Have a nonzero value
- Reaches every location in the hash table, if the size of the table is a prime number
- Avoids both primary clustering and secondary clustering

Question 5   What probe sequence does double hashing use when the search key is 16 and the hash functions are

$h_1(key) = key$ modulo 13
$h_2(key) = 7 - key$ modulo 7

Question 6   What size hash table should you use with the hash functions given in the previous question? Why?

A Potential Problem with Open Addressing

19.21   The previous three open addressing schemes for collision resolution assume that each table location is in one of three states: occupied, empty, or available. Recall that only empty locations contain null. Frequent additions and removals can cause every location in the hash table to reference either a current entry or a former entry. That is, a hash table might have no location that contains null, regardless of how many or how few entries are actually in the dictionary. If this happens, our approach to searching a probe sequence will not work. Instead, every unsuccessful search can end only after considering every location in the hash table. Also, detecting the end of the search will be somewhat more involved and costly than simply looking for null.

You should safeguard your implementation against this failure. Increasing the size of the hash table (see Segment 20.7 in Chapter 20) can correct the problem, if you act in time. Separate chaining—which we consider next—does not have this problem.

Note: Open addressing can be simplified when an application does not require removals. Such is the case, for example, when a compiler builds a symbol table. It can use a dictionary that does not permit removals. Locations in the hash table will either reference a dictionary entry or contain null. Defining the three states given in Segment 19.15 is not needed. Project 1 at the end of this chapter asks you to develop this implementation.

Separate Chaining

19.22   A second general approach to collision resolution alters the structure of the hash table so that each location can represent more than one value. Such a location is called a **bucket**. Anytime a new search key maps into a particular location, you simply place the key and its associated value in the bucket, much as we did with open addressing. To find a value, you hash the search key, locate the bucket, and look through the key-value pairs in it. In all likelihood, the bucket contains few values, so this mini-search will be fast. When you remove an entry, you find it in its bucket and delete it. Thus, the entry no longer exists in the hash table.

What can you use to represent a bucket? A list, a sorted list, a chain of linked nodes, an array, or a vector are some possibilities with which you are familiar. Anything that involves an array or vector will cause a substantial memory overhead, since each location in the hash table will have a fixed amount of memory allocated to it. Much of this memory will be unused. Either a linked implementation of a list or a chain of linked nodes is a reasonable choice for a bucket, since memory is allocated to the bucket only as needed. Figure 19-9 illustrates a hash table with linked chains as buckets. In this arrangement, each location in the hash table is a head reference to a chain of linked nodes that make up the bucket. Each node contains references to a search key, to the key's associated value, and to the next node in the chain. Notice that a node must reference the search key so that you can locate it later when you search the chain. Resolving collisions by using buckets that are linked chains is called **separate chaining**.

Figure 19-9   A hash table for use with separate chaining; each bucket is a chain of linked nodes

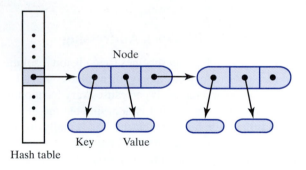

19.23   If your dictionary allows duplicate search keys, adding a new entry to the beginning of the appropriate chain is fastest, as Figure 19-10a indicates. However, if you want distinct search keys, adding a new entry requires you to search a chain for the search key. If you do not find it, you will be at the end of the chain, where you can add the new entry. Figure 19-10b illustrates this case. But since you have to search the chain anyway, you could maintain the chain in sorted order by search key, as Figure 19-10c shows. Subsequent searches would then be a little faster. As you will see, however, typical chains are short, so this refinement might not be worth the effort.

Question 7   Consider search keys that are distinct integers. If the hash function is

$h(key) = key$ modulo 5

and separate chaining resolves collisions, where in the hash table do the following search keys appear after being added? 4, 6, 20, 14, 31, 29

Figure 19-10 Where to insert a new entry into a linked bucket when the integer search keys are
(a) duplicate and unsorted; (b) distinct and unsorted; (c) distinct and sorted

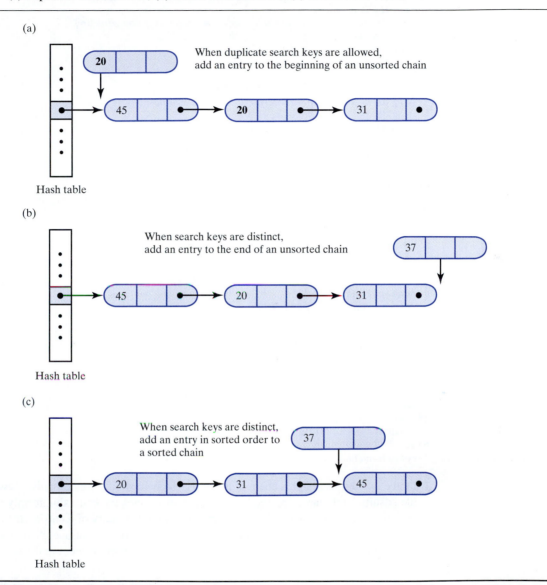

(a)

When duplicate search keys are allowed,
add an entry to the beginning of an unsorted chain

Hash table

(b)

When search keys are distinct,
add an entry to the end of an unsorted chain

Hash table

(c)

When search keys are distinct,
add an entry in sorted order to
a sorted chain

Hash table

19.24   With distinct search keys and unsorted chains, the algorithms for the dictionary's add, remove, and
getValue methods are as follows:

```
Algorithm add(key, value)
index = getHashIndex(key)
if (hashTable[index] == null)
{
   hashTable[index] = new Node(key, value)
   numberOfEntries++
   return null
}
```

```
    else
    {
        Search the chain that begins at hashTable[index] for a node that contains key
        if (key is found)
        { // assume currentNode references the node that contains key
            oldValue = currentNode.getValue()
            currentNode.setValue(value)
            return oldValue
        }
        else // add new node to end of chain
        { // assume nodeBefore references the last node
            newNode = new Node(key, value)
            nodeBefore.setNextNode(newNode)
            numberOfEntries++
            return null
        }
    }
```

Algorithm `remove(key)`
`index = getHashIndex(key)`
Search the chain that begins at `hashTable[index]` *for a node that contains* key
`if` (key *is found*)
`{`

   Remove the node that contains key *from the chain*
   `numberOfEntries--`
   return *value in removed node*
`}`
`else`
   return null

Algorithm `getValue(key)`
`index = getHashIndex(key)`
Search the chain that begins at `hashTable[index]` *for a node that contains* key
`if` (key *is found*)
   return *value in found node*
`else`
   return null

All three operations search a chain of nodes. Each chain should contain only a few entries, if the hash table is sufficiently large and the hash function distributes the entries uniformly throughout the table. Thus, these operations should be time efficient. For a dictionary of n entries, the operations certainly are faster than $O(n)$. In the worst case, however, all entries are in one chain, so the efficiency degenerates to $O(n)$. We will discuss the efficiency of hashing in more detail in the next chapter.

Note: **Separate chaining** provides an efficient and simple way to resolve collisions. Because the structure of the hash table is altered, however, separate chaining requires more memory than open addressing.

Question 8   With distinct search keys and separate chaining with sorted chains, write an algorithm for the dictionary's add method.

Question 9   Can you define an iteration of a dictionary's search keys in sorted order when you use hashing in its implementation? Explain.

CHAPTER SUMMARY

- Hashing is a dictionary implementation that stores entries into an array called the hash table. A hash function transforms an entry's search key into the index of the array location that will contain the entry.

- All classes have a method **hashCode** that returns an integer hash code. If a class's instances are to be search keys, you should override **hashCode** to produce suitable hash codes. A hash code should depend on the entire search key.

- A hash function uses **hashCode** to compute a hash code from a search key and then compresses that hash code into an index to the hash table. A typical way to compress the hash code c is to compute c modulo n, where n is a prime number and the size of the hash table. This computation produces an index whose magnitude lies between 0 and $n - 1$.

- A perfect hash function maps each search key into a distinct location in the hash table. You can find such a function if you know all possible search keys. Using a perfect hash function makes possible $O(1)$ implementations of the dictionary operations.

- With a typical hash function, more than one search key can map into the same location in the hash table. This occurrence is called a collision.

- Various methods are available to deal with collisions. Among them are open addressing and separate chaining.

- With open addressing, all entries that map into the same location are ultimately stored within the hash table. These entries are in a sequence of locations called the probe sequence. Several different versions of open addressing are common. Linear probing uses consecutive locations. Quadratic probing spaces the locations in a probe sequence at increasing increments. These increments are 1, 4, 9, and so on—that is, the squares of the integers 1, 2, 3, ... Double hashing uses a fixed increment that depends on the search key. A second hash function provides this increment.

- With open addressing, you remove an entry by placing it into a removed state. You do not set its table location to **null**, because that would terminate subsequent searches prematurely. You retrieve an entry by searching its probe sequence, ignoring removed entries, until you either find the desired entry or encounter **null**. You perform the same search when you add a new entry, but while searching, you note the first location—if any—that references a removed entry. You use this location for the added entry. If no such location exists, the addition extends the probe sequence by using the **null** location encountered after searching the entire sequence.

- A disadvantage of linear probing and quadratic probing is clustering. Clustering lengthens a probe sequence and so increases the time to search it. Double hashing avoids this problem.

- With separate chaining, the hash table is an array of buckets. All entries that map into the same array location are stored in the bucket that the location references. Each bucket can be a chain of linked nodes, for example. That is, each location in the hash table can reference the beginning of a chain.

- You can add new entries to a chain in sorted search-key order. Although sorted chains can improve search time somewhat, they usually are unnecessary, as typical chains are short. You add new entries to an unsorted chain either at the beginning, if duplicates are allowed, or at the end if not.

- With separate chaining, you retrieve or remove an entry by mapping its search key into a table location. You then search the bucket that the location references.

- An iteration of the entire hash table will not be in sorted order even if separate chaining with sorted buckets is used to resolve collisions.

1. Define a hashCode method for the class Name, as given in Segment 1.16 of Chapter 1.

2. Quadratic probing uses the following indices to define a probe sequence:

$$(k + j^2) \text{ modulo } n \text{ for } j \geq 0$$

where k is the hash index and n is the size of the hash table.

   a. If the hash table contains 17 locations and the hash index is 3, what are the first six indices of the array locations in the probe sequence that quadratic probing defines?
   b. You can compute the indices for the probe sequence more efficiently by using the recurrence relation

$$k_{i+1} = (k_i + 2i + 1) \text{ modulo } n \text{ for } i \geq 0 \text{ and } k_0 = k$$

   Derive this recurrence relation.
   c. Demonstrate that you can replace the modulo operation in Part b with one comparison and an occasional subtraction.

3. Project 11 in Chapter 18 revised the class Pair, which is in Segment 2.6 of Chapter 2, to give it accessor methods, and then used it in an implementation of a dictionary. Consider a hash table of Pair objects. Without further changes to the definition of Pair, how could you indicate a removed entry?

4. Suppose that the size of your hash table is 31, that you use the hash code described in Segment 19.7, and that you use separate chaining to resolve collisions. List five different names that would hash to the same location in the table.

5. Assume the hash table and hash function described in Exercise 4, but use open addressing with linear probing to resolve collisions. List five different names that do not all hash to the same location in the table yet would nonetheless result in collisions and clustering.

6. Repeat Exercise 5, but instead use open addressing with quadratic probing to resolve collisions.

7. Give an example of a probe sequence produced by quadratic probing that does not reach the entire hash table, even if the size of the table is a prime number.

8. Demonstrate that quadratic probing will guarantee a successful addition, if the hash table is at most half full and its size is a prime number.

9. Demonstrate that double hashing will produce a probe sequence that reaches the entire table, if the size of the hash table is a prime number. *Hint*: Show that this is true if the increment and the table size are relatively prime. Then, if the table size is prime, all increments will be relatively prime to it.

10. Imagine that you alter the linear probing scheme of Segment 19.12 as follows. When a collision occurs at hashTable[k], you check hashTable[k + c], hashTable[k + 2 * c], hashTable[k + 3 * c], and so on, where c is a constant. Does this scheme eliminate primary clustering?

11. Consider data whose search key consists of three floating-point values (longitude, latitude, and altitude, for example). Suggest at least two possible hash functions for this data.

12. You have approximately 1000 thumbnail images that you want to store in a dictionary that uses hashing in its implementation. Each image is 20 pixels wide by 20 pixels high, and each pixel is one of 256 colors. Suggest some possible hash functions that you could use.

PROJECTS

1. The note at the end of Segment 19.21 describes a dictionary that does not support a remove operation. Implement this dictionary by using open addressing with linear probing to resolve collisions.

2. Consider records for patients at a medical facility. Each record contains an integer identification for a patient and strings for the date, the reason for the visit, and the treatment prescribed. Design and implement the class `PatientRecord` so that it overrides the method `hashCode`. Write a main program that tests your new class.

3. Design a class `PatientDataBase` that stores instances of `PatientRecord`, as described in the previous project. The class should provide at least three query operations, as follows. Given a patient identification and date, the first operation should return the reason for the visit, and the second operation should return the treatment. The third query operation should return a list of dates, given a patient identification.

4. The following experiment compares the performance of linear probing and quadratic probing. You will need a list of 500 names or user names that can be obtained from your instructor or from a system administrator. Implement a hash table of size 1000, and use the hash code described in Segment 19.7. Count the number of collisions that occur for both linear probing and quadratic probing when 500 names are added to the table. Repeat the experiment for tables of size 950, 900, 850, 800, 750, 700, 650, and 600.

5. Design an experiment similar to the one in Project 4, but instead of comparing linear probing and quadratic probing, compare two different hash functions.

20

Hashing as a Dictionary Implementation

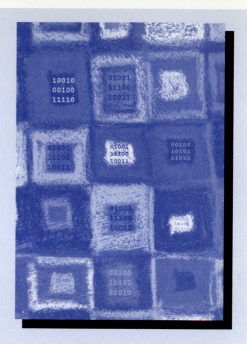

CONTENTS

PREREQUISITES

OBJECTIVES

After studying this chapter, you should be able to

- Describe the relative efficiencies of the various collision resolution techniques
- Describe a hash table's load factor

- Describe rehashing and why it is necessary
- Use hashing to implement the ADT dictionary

The previous chapter described hashing as a technique for implementing a dictionary when searching is the primary task. We now study hashing's performance and examine the details of its implementation in Java.

The Efficiency of Hashing

20.1   As you saw in the previous chapter, implementations of the ADT dictionary depend on whether the dictionary requires distinct search keys. In this section, we consider only dictionaries with distinct search keys. Recall that the add method for such a dictionary must ensure that duplicate search keys do not occur.

Each of the dictionary operations getValue, remove, and add searches the hash table for a given search key. The success or failure of a search for a given key directly affects the success or failure of the retrieval and removal operations. The successful addition of a new entry occurs after a search for a given key fails. An unsuccessful addition replaces the value of an existing entry instead of adding a new entry. This operation occurs after a successful search for a given key. Thus, we have the following observations about the time efficiency of these operations:

- A successful retrieval or removal has the same efficiency as a successful search
- An unsuccessful retrieval or removal has the same efficiency as an unsuccessful search
- A successful addition has the same efficiency as an unsuccessful search
- An unsuccessful addition has the same efficiency as a successful search

So it is sufficient to analyze the time efficiency of searching the hash table for a given search key.

Note: The successful retrieval of an entry searches the same chain or probe sequence that was searched when the entry was first added to the hash table. Thus, the cost of a successful retrieval of an entry is the same as the cost of inserting that entry.

The Load Factor

20.2   We began our discussion of hashing in the previous chapter with a perfect hash function that caused no collisions. If you can find a perfect hash function for your particular set of search keys, using it to implement the ADT dictionary will provide operations that are each O(1). Such an implementation is ideal. The good news is that finding a perfect hash function is quite feasible in certain situations. Unfortunately, using a perfect hash function is not always possible or practical. In those situations, collisions are likely to occur.

Resolving a collision takes time and thus causes the dictionary operations to be slower than an O(1) operation. As a hash table fills, collisions occur more often, decreasing performance even further. Since collision resolution takes considerably more time than evaluating the hash function, it is the prime contributor to the cost of hashing.

To help us express this cost, we define a measure of how full a hash table is. This measure—the **load factor** λ—is the ratio of the size of the dictionary to the size of the hash table. That is,

$$\lambda = \frac{Number\ of\ entries\ in\ the\ dictionary}{Number\ of\ locations\ in\ the\ hash\ table}$$

Notice that λ is zero when the dictionary—and hence the hash table—is empty. The maximum value of λ depends on the type of collision resolution you use. For open addressing schemes, λ's maximum value is 1 when the hash table is full. In that case, each entry in the dictionary uses one location in the hash table. Notice that the number of locations in the available state does not affect λ. For separate chaining, the number of entries in the dictionary can exceed the size of the hash table, so λ has no maximum value.

Note: **The load factor**

The load factor λ is a measure of the cost of collision resolution. It is the ratio of the number of entries in the dictionary to the size of the hash table. λ is never negative. For open addressing, λ does not exceed 1. For separate chaining, λ has no maximum value. As you will see, restricting the size of λ improves the performance of hashing.

Question 1   When λ is 0.5 with open addressing, how many locations in the hash table contain dictionary entries?

Question 2   With separate chaining, does λ indicate how many buckets in the hash table are not empty? Explain.

The Cost of Open Addressing

20.3 Recall that all open addressing schemes use one location in the hash table per entry in the dictionary. The dictionary operations `getValue`, `remove`, and `add` each require a search of the probe sequence indicated by both the search key and the collision resolution scheme in effect. Analyzing the efficiency of these searches is sufficient.

For each open addressing scheme that we considered earlier, we will state the number of comparisons necessary to locate a search key in the hash table. We will express these numbers in terms of the load factor λ. The derivations of these numbers are messy at best and in some cases difficult, so we omit them. Interpreting the results, however, is straightforward. Recall that for open addressing, λ ranges from 0, when the table is empty, to 1 when it is full.

20.4 **Linear probing.** When you use linear probing, more collisions will likely occur as the hash table fills. After a collision, you search a probe sequence that forms a cluster. If you add a new entry, the cluster grows in size. So you would expect the probe sequences to grow and, therefore, require longer search times. In fact, the average number of comparisons needed to search the probe sequence for a given search key is about

$$\frac{1}{2}\left\{1 + \frac{1}{(1-\lambda)^2}\right\} \text{ for an unsuccessful search and}$$

$$\frac{1}{2}\left\{1 + \frac{1}{(1-\lambda)}\right\} \text{ for a successful search}$$

After evaluating these expressions for a few values of λ, we get the results in Figure 20-1. As λ increases—that is, as the hash table fills—the number of comparisons for these searches increases. This result satisfies our initial intuition. For example, when the hash table is half full—that is, when λ is 0.5—an average unsuccessful search requires about 2.5 comparisons and an average successful search requires about 1.5 comparisons. As λ increases beyond 0.5, the number of comparisons for an unsuccessful search increases much more rapidly than for a successful search. Thus, performance degrades rapidly when the hash table is more than half full. Should this happen, you'd need to define a larger hash table, as we describe a bit later in this chapter in the section "Rehashing."

 Note: The performance of hashing with linear probing degrades significantly as the load factor λ increases. To maintain reasonable efficiency, the hash table should be less than half full. That is, keep $\lambda < 0.5$.

Figure 20-1   The average number of comparisons required by a search of the hash table for given values of the load factor λ when using linear probing

λ	Unsuccessful Search	Successful Search
0.1	1.1	1.1
0.3	1.5	1.2
0.5	2.5	1.5
0.7	6.1	2.2
0.9	50.5	5.5

20.5   **Quadratic probing and double hashing.** Secondary clustering as a result of quadratic probing is not as serious as the primary clustering that occurs when you use linear probing. Here, the average number of comparisons needed to search the probe sequence for a given search key is about

$$\frac{1}{(1-\lambda)} \text{ for an unsuccessful search and}$$

$$\frac{1}{\lambda} \log\left(\frac{1}{1-\lambda}\right) \text{ for a successful search}$$

Figure 20-2 evaluates these expressions for the same values of λ that we used for linear probing. Notice that the number of comparisons for an unsuccessful search grows with λ more rapidly than for a successful search. Although, the degradation in performance as λ increases is not as severe as with linear probing, you still want $\lambda < 0.5$ to maintain efficiency.

Even though double hashing avoids the clustering of linear probing and quadratic probing, the estimate of its efficiency is the same as for quadratic probing.

 Note: If you use quadratic probing or double hashing, the hash table should be less than half full. That is, λ should be less than 0.5.

Figure 20-2   The average number of comparisons required by a search of the hash table for given values of the load factor λ when using either quadratic probing or double hashing

λ	Unsuccessful Search	Successful Search
0.1	1.1	1.1
0.3	1.4	1.2
0.5	2.0	1.4
0.7	3.3	1.7
0.9	10.0	2.6

The Cost of Separate Chaining

20.6   With separate chaining as the collision resolution strategy, each entry in the hash table can reference a chain of linked nodes. The number of such chains, including empty ones, is then the size of the hash table. Thus, the load factor λ is the number of dictionary entries divided by the number of chains. That is, λ is the average number of dictionary entries per chain. Since this number is an average, we expect some chains to contain fewer than λ entries—or even none—and some to have more. We assume that the chains are not sorted and that the search keys in the dictionary are distinct.

The dictionary operations getValue, remove, and add each require a search of the chain indicated by the search key. As was the case for open addressing, analyzing the efficiency of these searches is sufficient. Again, we will state the number of comparisons necessary to locate a search key in the hash table in terms of the load factor λ.

An unsuccessful search of a hash table sometimes will encounter an empty chain, and so that operation is O(1) and would be the best case. But for the average case when the chains are not sorted, searching for an entry in the hash table without success examines λ nodes. In contrast, a successful search always inspects a chain that is not empty. In addition to seeing that the table location at the hash index is not null, an average successful search considers a chain of λ nodes and locates the desired entry after looking at λ/2 of them. Thus, the average number of comparisons during a search when separate chaining is used is about

$$\lambda \qquad \text{for an unsuccessful search}$$
$$1 + \lambda/2 \qquad \text{for a successful search}$$

After evaluating these expressions for a few values of λ, we get the results in Figure 20-3. The number of comparisons for these searches increases only slightly as λ increases—that is, as the hash table fills. A typical upper bound for λ is 1, as smaller values do not provide significantly better performance. Notice the unusual result: Successful searches take more time than unsuccessful searches when λ < 2.

Remember that these results are for the average case. In the worst case, all search keys map into the same table location. Thus, all entries occur in the same chain of nodes. The worst-case search time, then, is O(n), where n is the number of entries.

 Note: The average performance of hashing with separate chaining does not degrade significantly as the load factor λ increases. To maintain reasonable efficiency, you should keep λ < 1.

Figure 20-3   The average number of comparisons required by a search of the hash table for given values of the load factor λ when using separate chaining

λ	Unsuccessful Search	Successful Search
0.1	0.1	1.1
0.3	0.3	1.2
0.5	0.5	1.3
0.7	0.7	1.4
0.9	0.9	1.5
1.1	1.1	1.6
1.3	1.3	1.7
1.5	1.5	1.8
1.7	1.7	1.9
1.9	1.9	2.0
2.0	2.0	2.0

Note: **Maintaining the performance of hashing**

Collisions and their resolution typically cause the load factor λ to increase and the efficiency of the dictionary operations to decrease. To maintain efficiency, you should restrict the size of λ as follows:

$\lambda < 0.5$ for open addressing
$\lambda < 1.0$ for separate chaining

Should the load factor exceed these bounds, you must increase the size of the hash table, as the next section describes.

Rehashing

20.7   The previous section discussed the efficiency of hashing as a dictionary implementation when using various ways of resolving collisions. As you saw, to ensure an efficient implementation, you must not let the load factor λ get too large. You can readily compute λ and see whether it exceeds the upper limit for the particular collision resolution scheme, as given in the previous note.

So what do you do when λ reaches its limit? First, you can expand the array that serves as the hash table, as described in Chapter 5. Typically, you double the size of an ordinary array, but here you need to ensure that the array's size is a prime number. Expanding the array's size to a prime number that is at least twice its previous size is not too difficult.

Ordinarily, when you expand an array, the next step is to copy the contents of the original array into corresponding locations of the new array. This is not the case for a hash table, however. Since you have changed the size n of the hash table, the compression function $c \% n$ will compute different indices than it did for the original hash table. For example, if the hash table originally contained 101 locations, the function $c \% 101$ compresses the hash code 505 to the index 0. The new hash table will contain 211 locations, since 211 is the smallest prime number greater than 2 times 101. But now $c \% 211$ compresses 505 to the index 83. You cannot simply copy the location at index 0 from the original table to the location at index 0 in the new table. And you cannot copy it to the location at index 83 in the new table, because you also need to consider collisions.

After creating a new, larger hash table of an appropriate size, you use the dictionary method add to add each item in the original hash table to the new table. The method computes the hash index using the size of the new table and handles any collisions. This process of enlarging a hash table and computing new hash indices for its contents is called **rehashing**. You can see that increasing the size of a hash table requires considerably more work than increasing the size of an ordinary array. Rehashing is a task that you should not do often.

Note: Rehashing

When the load factor λ becomes too large, expand the hash table. To compute the table's new size, first double its present size and then increase the result to the next prime number. Use the method add to add the current entries in the dictionary to the new hash table.

Question 3   Consider a hash table of size 5. The function $c \% 5$ places the hash codes 20, 6, 18, and 14 into locations at indices 0, 1, 3, and 4, respectively. Show the effects of rehashing on this hash table when linear probing resolves collisions.

Note: Dynamic hashing allows a hash table to grow or shrink in size without the expense of rehashing. This technique, which we will not cover, is particularly useful in database management environments when the database is stored in external files.

Comparing Schemes for Collision Resolution

20.8   In previous segments, you saw how the load factor λ affects the average number of comparisons required by a search of a hash table for various ways to resolve collisions. The graphs in Figure 20-4 illustrate this effect for various collision resolution schemes. When λ is less than 0.5, the average number of comparisons for a successful search is about the same regardless of the process used to resolve collisions. For unsuccessful searches, the three open addressing schemes have about the same efficiency when λ is less than 0.5. However, separate chaining is somewhat more efficient in this case.

As λ exceeds 0.5, the efficiency of open addressing degrades rapidly, with linear probing the least efficient. Separate chaining, on the other hand, remains efficient for values of λ up to 1. In fact, the tabulated data in Figure 20-3 shows that its efficiency degrades only slightly for λ between 1 and 2.

Separate chaining certainly appears to be the fastest approach. But separate chaining can require more memory than open addressing, since each location in the hash table can reference a chain of linked nodes. On the other hand, the hash table itself can be smaller than when you use an open addressing scheme, since λ can be larger. Thus, space need not be a deciding factor in how you resolve collisions.

If all of these collision resolution schemes used hash tables of equal size, open addressing would be more likely to lead to rehashing than separate chaining would. To reduce the likelihood of rehashing, an open addressing strategy could use a large hash table. Remember that in Java, the table contains references that do not require much memory. So even though at least half of the table must remain unused, the actual space allocation would not be excessive.

Among open addressing schemes, double hashing is a good choice. It uses fewer comparisons than linear probing. Additionally, its probe sequence can reach the entire table, whereas quadratic probing cannot.

Figure 20-4   The average number of comparisons required by a search of the hash table versus the load factor λ for four collision resolution techniques when the search is (a) successful; (b) unsuccessful

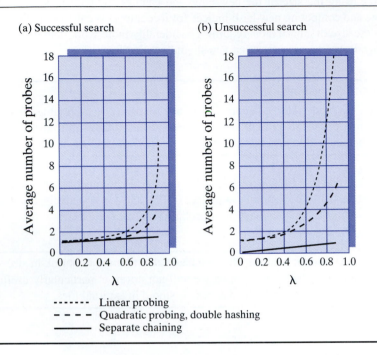

A Dictionary Implementation That Uses Hashing

The efficiency of separate chaining makes it a desirable method for resolving collisions that occur during hashing. Because its implementation is relatively straightforward, we leave it to you to implement. Instead, we will implement the linear probing method of open addressing. Most of this dictionary implementation is independent of the particular open addressing technique that you use. Adapting it to use quadratic probing or double hashing involves few changes.

Entries in the Hash Table

20.9   Our hash table will be like the array in Figure 18-1a of Chapter 18 that we used to implement the dictionary. Each array location can reference an object that contains a search key and an associated value. The class `TableEntry` of these objects is similar to the class `Entry` that you saw in Segment 18.2.

However, with open addressing, each location in the hash table is in one of three states: occupied, empty, or available. (See Segment 19.15 of the previous chapter.) An empty location contains `null`. Rather than altering the structure of the hash table to indicate the other states, we make the entry objects indicate whether they are currently in the table or have been removed from it. Hence, we add another data field to the class of entry objects. This field is a boolean flag; it is true if the entry is in the dictionary or false if it has been removed. Figure 20-5 illustrates the hash table and one dictionary entry.

Figure 20-5   A hash table and one of its entry objects

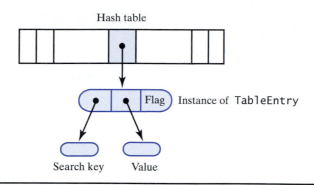

Thus, we create the private class `TableEntry` and make it internal to the dictionary class. `TableEntry` begins as follows:

```
private class TableEntry<S, T> implements Serializable
{
  private S key;
  private T value;
  private boolean inTable; // true if entry is in hash table

  private TableEntry(S searchKey, T dataValue)
  {
    key = searchKey;
    value = dataValue;
    inTable = true;
  } // end constructor
  . . .
```

In addition to the methods `getKey`, `getValue`, and `setValue`, this class has the methods `isIn`, `isRemoved`, `setToIn`, and `setToRemoved` to either interrogate or set the value of the boolean flag `inTable`.

Note: A location in the hash table in the available state contains an entry in the removed state.

Data Fields and Constructors

20.10   If you do not use a perfect hash function, you must expect collisions. All open addressing methods for resolving collisions become less efficient as the hash table fills, so you need to increase the size of the table. As Segment 19.21 mentioned, increasing the size of the table can also ensure that it will contain a `null` entry—a necessity for ending the search of a probe sequence. Since our hash table is an array, we expand it and rehash the dictionary entries, as described in Segment 20.7. However, we modify the definition of the load factor λ by replacing the number of dictionary entries with the number of table locations in either the occupied or available state. This change increases λ so that rehashing occurs before the table loses its last `null` entry. Thus, the class begins as shown in Listing 20-1.

Listing 20-1 An outline of the class `HashedDictionary`

```java
import java.util.Iterator;
import java.util.NoSuchElementException;
import java.io.Serializable;

public class HashedDictionary<K, V>
            implements DictionaryInterface<K, V>, Serializable
{
  private TableEntry<K, V>[] hashTable; // dictionary entries
  private int numberOfEntries;
  private int locationsUsed; // number of table locations not null
  private static final int DEFAULT_SIZE = 101;        // must be prime
  private static final double MAX_LOAD_FACTOR = 0.5; // fraction of hash
                                                     // table that can be filled

  public HashedDictionary()
  {
    this(DEFAULT_SIZE); // call next constructor
  } // end default constructor

  public HashedDictionary(int tableSize)
  {
    int primeSize = getNextPrime(tableSize);

    hashTable = new TableEntry[primeSize];
    numberOfEntries = 0;
    locationsUsed = 0;
  } // end constructor

  < Implementations of methods in DictionaryInterface >
  . . .

  < Implementations of private methods >
  . . .

  private class TableEntry<S, T> implements Serializable
  {
    < See Segment 20.9 >
  } // end TableEntry
} // end HashedDictionary
```

The field `locationsUsed` counts the number of locations in the hash table that are in either the occupied or available state and is incremented each time an entry is added to the dictionary. In contrast, the field `numberOfEntries` counts the number of entries currently in the dictionary. Thus, it is incremented when an entry is added to the dictionary but decremented when an entry is removed.

Each constructor allocates an array for the hash table. The second constructor lets the client specify a minimum size for the hash table. To ensure that the table's size is prime and at least as big as the client wants, this constructor calls the private method `getNextPrime` to find the first prime number that is greater than or equal to a given integer. The default constructor invokes the second constructor, giving it a predetermined size.

Note: To implement getNextPrime(anInteger), first see whether anInteger is even. If it is, it cannot be prime, so add 1 to make it odd. Then use a private method isPrime to find the first prime number among the parameter anInteger and subsequent odd integers.

To implement isPrime, note that 2 and 3 are prime but 1 and even integers are not. An odd integer 5 or greater is prime if it is not divisible by every odd integer up to its square root.

The Methods getValue, remove, and add

We now consider next the major operations of the dictionary: getValue, remove, and add. The note at the end of Segment 19.16 in the previous chapter summarized just what these operations need to do.

20.11 **The method getValue.** We begin with an algorithm for the retrieval method getValue:

Algorithm getValue(key)
// Returns the value associated with the given search key, if it is in the dictionary.
// Otherwise, returns null.

index = getHashIndex(key)
Search the probe sequence that begins at hashTable[index] *for* key
if (key *is found*)
  return *value in found entry*
else
  return null

In addition to the private method getHashIndex, which you saw in Segment 19.10, this algorithm suggests another private method that searches the probe sequence. We name this method locate and specify it informally as follows:

locate(index, key)
Follows the probe sequence that begins at index (key's hash index) and returns either the index of the entry containing key or –1, if no such entry exists.

We'll implement locate in Segment 20.13.

The method getValue then has the following implementation:

```
public V getValue(K key)
{
  V result = null;

  int index = getHashIndex(key);
  index = locate(index, key);

  if (index != -1)
    result = hashTable[index].getValue(); // key found; get value

  // else key not found; return null

  return result;
} // end getValue
```

20.12   **The method remove.** Removing an entry from the hash table, like retrieving an entry, involves locating the search key. If found, the entry is flagged as removed. The following pseudocode describes the necessary steps for this operation:

Algorithm remove(key)
// Removes a specific entry from the dictionary, given its search key.
// Returns either the value that was associated with the search key or null *if no such object*
// exists.

index = getHashIndex(key)
Search the probe sequence that begins at hashTable[index] *for* key
if (key *is found*)
{
    Flag entry as removed
    numberOfEntries--
    return *value in removed entry*
}
else
    return null

As the following implementation shows, you call the private method locate to locate the desired entry. If you find it, you change its state to removed and return its value. Otherwise, you return null.

```java
public V remove(K key)
{
    V removedValue = null;

    int index = getHashIndex(key);
    index = locate(index, key);

    if (index != -1)
    { // key found; flag entry as removed and return its value
        removedValue = hashTable[index].getValue();
        hashTable[index].setToRemoved();
        numberOfEntries--;
    } // end if

    // else key not found; return null

    return removedValue;
} // end remove
```

20.13   **The private method locate.** Before we look at add, let's implement the method locate that both getValue and remove invoke. The method looks for the given search key along the probe sequence that begins at hashTable[index], where index is the key's hash index. Recall that the search must ignore entries that are in the removed state. The search continues until it locates either key or null.

To follow the probe sequence, locate must implement a particular open addressing scheme to resolve collisions. For simplicity, we will implement linear probing. The following algorithm summarizes our approach:

Algorithm locate(index, key)
// Returns either the index of the entry containing key or –1 if no such entry is found.

while (key *is not found and* hashTable[index] *is not* null)

```
{
   if (hashTable[index] references an entry that is in the dictionary and contains key)
      Exit loop
   else
      index = next probe index
}

if (key is found)
   return index
else
   return -1
```

The implementation of `locate` now follows from this pseudocode:

```
private int locate(int index, K key)
{
   boolean found = false;

   while ( !found && (hashTable[index] != null) )
   {
      if ( hashTable[index].isIn() &&
           key.equals(hashTable[index].getKey()) )
         found = true; // key found
      else // follow probe sequence
         index = (index + 1) % hashTable.length; // linear probing
   } // end while
   // Assertion: either key or null is found at hashTable[index]

   int result = -1;
   if (found)
      result = index;

   return result;
} // end locate
```

You can change from linear probing to another open addressing scheme for collision resolution by replacing the highlighted assignment statement in the previous method.

20.14   **The method add.** We begin with the algorithm for adding a new entry:

Algorithm add(key, value)
// Adds a new key-value entry to the dictionary. If key is already in the dictionary,
// returns its corresponding value and replaces it in the dictionary with value.

if (hash table is too full)
   rehash()

index = getHashIndex(key)
Check for collision and resolve it (this step can alter index)
if (key is not found)
{ // add entry to hash table
   hashTable[index] = new TableEntry(key, value)
   numberOfEntries++
   locationsUsed++
   return null
}
else // search key is in table; return and replace entry's value

```
{
  oldValue = hashTable[index].getValue()
  hashTable[index].setValue(value)
  return oldValue
}
```

This algorithm suggests that you write several more private methods. We specify them informally as follows:

`isHashTableTooFull()`
Returns true if the hash table's load factor is ≥ `MAX_LOAD_FACTOR`. Here we define the load factor as the ratio `locationsUsed/hashTable.length`.

`rehash()`
Expands the hash table to a size that is both prime and at least double its current size, and then adds the current entries in the dictionary to the new hash table.

`probe(index, key)`
Detects whether key collides with `hashTable[index]` and resolves it by following a probe sequence. Returns the index of either an available location along the probe sequence or the entry containing key. This index is always legal, since the probe sequence stays within the hash table.

Using these private methods, we implement the method add as follows:

```
public V add(K key, V value)
{
  V oldValue; // value to return

  if (isHashTableTooFull())
    rehash();

  int index = getHashIndex(key);
  index = probe(index, key); // check for and resolve collision

  // Assertion: index is within legal range for hashTable
  assert (index >= 0) && (index < hashTable.length);

  if ( (hashTable[index] == null) || hashTable[index].isRemoved())
  { // key not found, so insert new entry
    hashTable[index] = new TableEntry<K,V>(key, value);
    numberOfEntries++;
    locationsUsed++;
    oldValue = null;
  }
  else
  { // key found; get old value for return and then replace it
    oldValue = hashTable[index].getValue();
    hashTable[index].setValue(value);
  } // end if

  return oldValue;
} // end add
```

20.15   **The private method probe.** The method `probe(key, index)` is similar to the method `locate` in that it looks for key along the probe sequence that begins at `hashTable[index]`. The search ignores entries that are in the removed state and continues until it locates either key or `null`. During this search, the method records the index of the first location, if any, that references an entry that has been removed from the table. This additional task is what distinguishes `probe` from `locate`. Thus, `probe` returns the index of a table location that either references an entry containing key or is available for an addition to the table.

Notice that `probe` returns the index of the removed entry that it *first* encounters along the probe sequence. Since add will insert a new entry into this location, a subsequent search for this entry will encounter it sooner than if add had inserted it in a location further along the probe sequence.

The following pseudocode summarizes the logic of `probe`:

Algorithm `probe(index, key)`
// Searches the probe sequence that begins at `index`. *Returns either the index of the entry*
// containing key *or the index of an available location in the hash table.*

while (key *is not found and* `hashTable[index]` *is not* `null`)
{
  if (`hashTable[index]` *references an entry in the dictionary*)
  {
    if (*the entry in* `hashTable[index]` *contains* key)
      Exit loop
    else
      `index` = *next probe index*
  }
  else // `hashTable[index]` *references a removed entry*
  {
    if (*this is the first removed entry encountered*)
      `removedStateIndex` = `index`

    `index` = *next probe index*
  }
}
if (key *is found or a removed entry was not encountered*)
  return `index`
else
  return `removedStateIndex` // *index of first entry removed*

The following method implements this algorithm:

```java
private int probe(int index, K key)
{
  boolean found = false;
  int removedStateIndex = -1; // index of first location in
                              // removed state
  while ( !found && (hashTable[index] != null) )
  {
    if (hashTable[index].isIn())
    {
      if (key.equals(hashTable[index].getKey()))
        found = true; // key found
      else // follow probe sequence
        index = (index + 1) % hashTable.length; // linear probing
    }
    else // skip entries that were removed
```

```
      {
         // save index of first location in removed state
         if (removedStateIndex == -1)
            removedStateIndex = index;

         index = (index + 1) % hashTable.length; // linear probing
      } // end if
   } // end while
   // Assertion: either key or null is found at hashTable[index]

   if (found || (removedStateIndex == -1) )
      return index;                    // index of either key or null
   else
      return removedStateIndex; // index of an available location
} // end probe
```

The methods probe and locate are so similar that you can omit locate and use probe instead. To do so, you must change the implementations of remove and getValue slightly. The following question asks you to make this change.

Question 4   What changes to the methods remove and getValue are necessary so they can call probe instead of locate?

20.16   **The private method rehash.** Recall that the method rehash expands the hash table to a size that is both prime and at least double its current size. Since the hash function depends on the size of the table, you cannot copy elements from the old array and put them into the same positions in the new array. You need to apply the revised hash function to each entry to determine its proper position in the new table. But doing so can lead to collisions that need to be resolved. Thus, you should use the method add to add the existing entries to the new and larger hash table. Since add increments the data field numberOfEntries, you must remember to set this field to zero before adding the entries.

The method has the following implementation:

```
private void rehash()
{
   TableEntry<K, V>[] oldTable = hashTable;
   int oldSize = hashTable.length;
   int newSize = getNextPrime(oldSize + oldSize);
   hashTable = new TableEntry[newSize]; // increase size of array

   numberOfEntries = 0; // reset number of dictionary entries, since
                        // it will be incremented by add during rehash
   locationsUsed = 0;

   // rehash dictionary entries from old array to the new and bigger
   // array; skip both null locations and removed entries
   for (int index = 0; index < oldSize; index++)
   {
      if ( (oldTable[index] != null) && oldTable[index].isIn() )
         add(oldTable[index].getKey(), oldTable[index].getValue());
   } // end for
} // end rehash
```

As we traverse the old hash table, notice that we skip both the null locations and the entries that have been removed from the dictionary but are still in the hash table.

This method does not retain the instances of TableEntry that were in the old hash table. Instead, it uses an entry's key and value to create a new entry. You can avoid this reallocation of entries; Exercise 4 at the end of this chapter asks you to investigate this possibility.

Question 5   When the method add calls rehash, rehash calls add. But when rehash calls add, does add call rehash? Explain.

Iterators

20.17   Finally, we provide iterators for the dictionary, much as we did in Chapter 18. For example, we can implement an internal class KeyIterator to define an iteration of the search keys. The iteration must traverse the hash table, ignoring cells that either contain null or reference removed entries. Figure 20-6 shows a sample hash table. Cells in blue reference the dictionary entries, light gray cells reference removed entries, and dark gray cells contain null. As we traverse this table, we skip cells that are gray. The only real concern in this implementation is detecting when the iteration ends—that is, when the method hasNext should return false. The occurrence of a gray cell and the size of the hash table are not the proper criteria for this determination. Instead, you simply count backward from currentSize each time the method next returns the next search key.

Figure 20-6   A hash table containing dictionary entries, removed entries, and null values

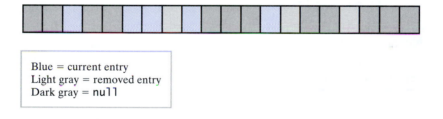

Blue = current entry
Light gray = removed entry
Dark gray = null

The implementation of KeyIterator follows. A class that defines an iteration of values would have a similar implementation.

```
private class KeyIterator implements Iterator<K>
{
  private int currentIndex; // current position in hash table
  private int numberLeft;   // number of entries left in iteration

  private KeyIterator()
  {
    currentIndex = 0;
    numberLeft = numberOfEntries;
  } // end default constructor

  public boolean hasNext()
  {
    return numberLeft > 0;
  } // end hasNext
```

```java
    public K next()
    {
      K result = null;

      if (hasNext())
      {
        // find index of next entry
        while ( (hashTable[currentIndex] == null) ||
                   hashTable[currentIndex].isRemoved() )
        {
          currentIndex++;
        } // end while

        result = hashTable[currentIndex].getKey();
        numberLeft--;
        currentIndex++;
      }
      else
        throw new NoSuchElementException();

      return result;
    } // end next

    public void remove()
    {
      throw new UnsupportedOperationException();
    } // end remove
  } // end KeyIterator
```

 Note: Hashing as an implementation of the ADT dictionary does not provide the ability to sort its entries. Such an implementation is not suitable for any application that requires a sorted iteration of the entries.

Java Class Library: The Class **HashMap**

20.18   The standard package `java.util` contains the class `HashMap<K, V>`. This class implements the interface `java.util.Map` that we mentioned in Segment 17.22. Recall that this interface is similar to our `DictionaryInterface`. `HashMap` assumes that the search-key objects belong to a class that overrides the methods `hashCode` and `equals`.

   The hash table is a collection of buckets, where each bucket can contain several entries. As you know, a hash table's load factor λ is a measure of how full the table is. The constructors for `HashMap` enable you to specify the initial number of buckets and the maximum load factor λ_{max}. These constructors are as follows:

public HashMap()
Creates an empty hash table with a default initial size of 16 and a default maximum load factor of 0.75.

public HashMap(**int** initialSize)
Creates an empty hash table with a given initial size and a default maximum load factor of 0.75.

public HashMap(**int** initialSize, **float** maxLoadFactor)
Creates an empty hash table with a given initial size and a given maximum load factor.

`public HashMap(Map<? extends K,? extends V> table)`
Creates a hash table with the same entries as `table`.

The authors of `HashMap` chose a default maximum load factor of 0.75 to provide a balance between time and memory requirements. Even though higher values of the load factor permit smaller hash tables, they cause higher search times, which in turn reduce the efficiency of the `get`, `put`, and `remove` methods.

When the number of entries in the hash table exceeds λ_{max} times the number of buckets, the size of the hash table is increased by using rehashing. But rehashing takes time. You can avoid rehashing if you choose

$$Number\ of\ buckets > \frac{Maximum\ number\ of\ entries\ in\ the\ dictionary}{\lambda_{max}}$$

Of course, too large a hash table wastes space.

CHAPTER SUMMARY

- Hashing is efficient as long as the ratio of dictionary size to hash-table size remains small. This ratio is called the load factor. The load factor should be less than 1 for separate chaining and less than 0.5 for open addressing. If the load factor exceeds these bounds, you must rehash the table.

- Rehashing is the process that increases the size of a hash table to a prime number that is greater than twice the table's current size. Since the hash function depends on the table size, you cannot simply copy entries from the old table to the new one. Instead, you use the method **add** to add all current entries to the new table.

- Separate chaining, as compared to open addressing, provides faster dictionary operations on average, can use a smaller hash table, and needs rehashing less frequently. If both approaches have the same size array for a hash table, separate chaining uses more memory due to its linked chains.

- Hashing as a dictionary implementation does not support operations that involve sorted search keys. For example, you cannot easily traverse the keys in sorted order, find keys that lie within a given range, or identify the largest or smallest search key.

- The package `java.util` contains the class `HashMap<K, V>`, which implements the interface `Map<K, V>`.

EXERCISES

1. Suppose that you use open addressing to resolve collisions. Now imagine that your hash table is getting full. To avoid the bad performance that results from a nearly full hash table, you should create a new, larger hash table.

   a. What steps should you take to move all of your entries to this new table?
   b. What happens to the hash function?

2. To guarantee that the average number of probes is less than or equal to 4, what is the maximum load factor that a hash table can have if it uses

   a. Linear probing
   b. Double hashing
   c. Separate chaining

3. Revise the method add given in Segment 20.14 when duplicate search keys are allowed in the dictionary.

4. The method rehash does not retain the instances of TableEntry that were in the old hash table. It could if the method add had an entry as its parameter instead of the search key and value. Write such a method as an additional but private add method, and then revise rehash so it retains the instances of TableEntry that were in the old hash table.

5. Imagine a collection of names that are instances of the class Name, as modified in Exercise 1 of Chapter 19. For each name, imagine a string that represents a nickname. Suppose that each nickname is a search key, and you plan to add nickname-name pairs to a dictionary that is an instance of the class HashMap, as described in Segment 20.18.

   a. Suppose that you plan to add 1000 entries to this dictionary. Create an instance of the class HashMap that can accommodate the 1000 entries without rehashing.
   b. Write statements that add four nickname-name pairs to your dictionary. Then write statements that retrieve and display the name that corresponds to a nickname of your choice.

PROJECTS

1. Implement the ADT dictionary by using hashing and separate chaining. Use a chain of linked nodes as each bucket. The dictionary's entries should have distinct search keys.

2. Repeat Project 1, but use the ADT list for each bucket instead of a chain of linked nodes. What implementation of the list would be reasonable?

3. Implement the class PatientDataBase, that you designed in Project 3 of the previous chapter. Use a hash table to store the patient records. Write a main program that demonstrates and tests this class.

4. Even though two implementations of a hash table may require the same average number of comparisons, their distributions may be different. The following experiment will examine this possibility for linear probing and double hashing. You will need two disjoint lists of names: one with at least 1000 names and the other with at least 10,000 names.

   a. For both of the collision resolution schemes linear probing and double hashing, determine the load factor that results in an average of 1.5 comparisons for an unsuccessful search of a hash table holding 100 objects. From the load factor, determine the size of the table required.
   b. Create two hash tables of the appropriate size and two corresponding empty lists, which will hold counts. Use linear probing for one table and double hashing for the other. Inside a loop that iterates 1000 times, do the following:

      - Clear the hash tables.
      - Randomly choose 100 names from the list of 1000 and insert them into the tables.
      - Randomly choose 100 names from the list of 10,000 and search the tables for each name. (Each search will be unsuccessful because the two lists have no names in common.)
      - Count the number of comparisons made in each table for the 100 searches and record the count in the list corresponding to the table.

After the iteration is complete, each list should contain 1000 values. Each of these values is the total number of comparisons required to search for 100 names. Compute and display the average and standard deviation of each list. We expect the average number of comparisons for both hash tables to be equal to 150 (1.5 times 100).

5. Modify the previous project as follows:

- Let the user enter the desired average number of comparisons.
- Display a histogram of the results. A histogram shows the frequency of data values in given intervals of the same length. Use the floor of the average number of comparisons as the interval length.

21

Stacks

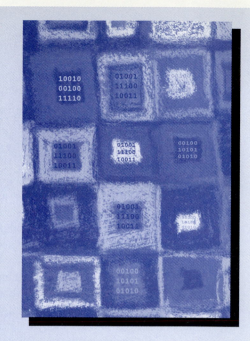

CONTENTS

PREREQUISITES

OBJECTIVES

After studying this chapter, you should be able to

- Describe the operations of the ADT stack
- Use a stack to decide whether the parentheses, brackets, and braces in an algebraic expression are paired correctly
- Use a stack to convert an infix expression to a postfix expression
- Use a stack to evaluate a postfix expression
- Use a stack to evaluate an infix expression

- Use a stack in a program
- Describe how the Java run-time environment uses a stack to track the execution of methods
- Use a stack to implement a recursive algorithm iteratively

In everyday life, a stack is a familiar thing. You might see a stack of books on your desk, a stack of dishes in the cafeteria, a stack of towels in the linen closet, or a stack of boxes in the attic. When you add an item to a stack, you place it on top of the stack. When you remove an item, you take the topmost one. This topmost item is the last one that was added to the stack. So when you remove an item, you remove the item added most recently. That is, the last item added to the stack is the first one removed.

In spite of our examples of a stack, everyday life usually does not follow this **last-in**, **first-out**, or **LIFO**, behavior. Although the employee hired most recently is often the first one fired during a layoff, we live in a first-come, first-served society. In the computer science world, however, last-in, first-out is exactly the behavior required by many important algorithms. These algorithms often use the abstract data type stack, which is an ADT that exhibits a last-in, first-out behavior. For example, a compiler uses a stack to interpret the meaning of an algebraic expression, and a run-time environment uses a stack when executing a recursive method.

This chapter describes the ADT stack and provides several examples of its use.

Specifications of the ADT Stack

21.1   The ADT **stack** organizes its entries according to the order in which they were added. All additions are to one end of the stack called the **top**. The **top entry**—that is, the entry at the top—is thus the newest item among the items currently in a stack. Figure 21-1 shows some stacks that should be familiar to you.

Figure 21-1   Some familiar stacks

   Note: Among the items currently in a stack, the one added most recently is at the top of the stack. (Other items might have been added to the stack more recently and then removed.)

The stack is the first ADT we've seen that restricts access to its entries. A client can look at or remove only the top entry. The only way to look at an entry that is not at the top of the stack is to repeatedly remove items from the stack until the desired item reaches the top. If you were to remove all of a stack's entries, one by one, you would get them in reverse chronological order, beginning with the most recent and ending with the first item added to the stack.

21.2   Typically, a stack has no search operation.[1] An entry can have a search key, but the key is not relevant to the stack or to the entry's position within the stack. The operation that adds an entry to a stack is traditionally called push. The remove operation is pop. The operation that retrieves the top entry without removing it is named peek. The following specifications define a set of operations for the ADT stack.

ABSTRACT DATA TYPE STACK

DATA

- A collection of objects in reverse chronological order and having the same data type

OPERATIONS

push(newEntry)	Task: Adds a new entry to the top of the stack. Input: newEntry is the new entry. Output: None.
pop()	Task: Removes and returns the stack's top entry. Input: None. Output: Returns either the stack's top entry or, if the stack is empty before the operation, null.
peek()	Task: Retrieves the stack's top entry without changing the stack in any way. Input: None. Output: Returns either the stack's top entry or, if the stack is empty, null.
isEmpty()	Task: Detects whether the stack is empty. Input: None. Output: Returns true if the stack is empty.
clear()	Task: Removes all entries from the stack. Input: None. Output: None.

---

1. However, the stack within the Java Class Library does have a search method, as you will see later in this chapter.

Note: **Alternate names for methods**

It is not unusual for a class designer to include aliases for certain methods. For example, you could include the additional methods add and `remove` (or `insert` and `delete`) in the ADT stack to mean push and pop. Moreover, `pull` is sometimes used to mean pop, and getTop can mean peek, so including them as aliases is reasonable.

21.3   The Java interface in Listing 21-1 specifies a stack of objects. The generic type T—which can be any class type—represents the data type of the items in the stack.

Listing 21-1   An interface for the ADT stack

```java
public interface StackInterface<T>
{
   /** Task: Adds a new entry to the top of the stack.
    *  @param newEntry  an object to be added to the stack */
   public void push(T newEntry);

   /** Task: Removes and returns the stack's top entry.
    *  @return either the object at the top of the stack or, if the
    *          stack is empty before the operation, null */
   public T pop();

   /** Task: Retrieves the stack's top entry.
    *  @return either the object at the top of the stack or null if
    *          the stack is empty */
   public T peek();

   /** Task: Detects whether the stack is empty.
    *  @return true if the stack is empty */
   public boolean isEmpty();

   /** Task: Removes all entries from the stack */
   public void clear();
} // end StackInterface
```

21.4   **Example: Demonstrating the stack methods.** The following statements add, retrieve, and remove strings from a stack. We assume that the class LinkedStack implements StackInterface and is available for our use.

```java
StackInterface<String> myStack = new LinkedStack<String>();
myStack.push("Jim");
myStack.push("Jess");
myStack.push("Jill");
myStack.push("Jane");
myStack.push("Joe");

String top = myStack.peek(); // returns "Joe"
System.out.println(top + " is at the top of the stack.");
```

```
top = myStack.pop();           // removes and returns "Joe"
System.out.println(top + " is removed from the stack.");

top = myStack.peek();          // returns "Jane"
System.out.println(top + " is at the top of the stack.");

top = myStack.pop();           // removes and returns "Jane"
System.out.println(top + " is removed from the stack.");
```

Parts *a* through *e* of Figure 21-2 show five additions to the stack. At this point, the stack contains—from top to bottom—the strings *Joe*, *Jane*, *Jill*, *Jess*, and *Jim*. The string at the top of the stack is *Joe*; peek retrieves it. The method pop retrieves *Joe* again and then removes it (Figure 21-2f). A subsequent call to peek retrieves *Jane*. Then pop retrieves *Jane* and removes it (Figure 21-2g).

Three more calls to pop would remove *Jill*, *Jess*, and *Jim*, leaving the stack empty. A subsequent call to either pop or peek would return null.

Figure 21-2   A stack of strings after (a) push adds *Jim*; (b) push adds *Jess*; (c) push adds *Jill*; (d) push adds *Jane*; (e) push adds *Joe*; (f) pop retrieves and removes *Joe*; (g) pop retrieves and removes *Jane*

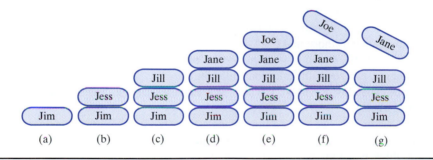

Question 1   After the following statements execute, what string is at the top of the stack and what string is at the bottom?

```
StackInterface<String> myStack = new LinkedStack<String>();
myStack.push("Jim");
myStack.push("Jess");
myStack.pop();
myStack.push("Jill");
myStack.push("Jane");
myStack.pop();
```

Question 2   Consider the stack that was created in Question 1, and define a new empty stack yourStack.

a.   Write a loop that pops the strings from myStack and pushes them onto yourStack.
b.   Describe the contents of the stacks myStack and yourStack when the loop that you just wrote completes its execution.

Programming Tip: Methods such as peek and pop must behave reasonably when the stack is empty. Here, we specify that they return null. Another possibility is to have them throw an exception.

Using a Stack to Process Algebraic Expressions

21.5   In mathematics, an algebraic expression is composed of operands that are variables or constants and operators, such as + and *. We will use the Java notation +, -, *, and / to indicate addition, subtraction, multiplication, and division. We will use ^ to indicate exponentiation, with the warning that Java has no operator for exponentiation; in Java ^ is the exclusive-or operator.[2]

Operators generally have two operands, and so are called **binary operators**. For example, the + in $a + b$ is a binary operator. The operators + and - can also be **unary operators** when they have one operand. For example, the minus sign in –5 is a unary operator.

When an algebraic expression has no parentheses, operations occur in a certain order. Exponentiations occur first; they take **precedence** over the other operations. Next, multiplications and divisions occur, and then additions and subtractions. For example, the expression

20 - 2 * 2 ^ 3

evaluates as 20 - 2 * 8, then as 20 - 16, and finally as 4.

But what happens when two or more adjacent operators have the same precedence? Exponentiations, such as those in $a \wedge b \wedge c$, occur right to left. Thus, 2 ^ 2 ^ 3 means 2 ^ (2 ^ 3), or 2^8, instead of (2 ^ 2) ^ 3, which is 4^3. Other operations occur left to right, such as the multiplication and division in $a * b / c$ or the addition and subtraction in $a - b + c$. Therefore, 8 - 4 + 2 means (8 - 4) + 2, or 6, instead of 8 - (4 + 2), which is 2. Parentheses in an expression override the normal operator precedence.

Ordinarily, we place a binary operator between its operands, as in $a + b$. An expression in this familiar notation is called an **infix expression**. Other notations are possible. For example, you could write a binary operator before its two operands. Thus, $a + b$ becomes $+ a b$. This expression is called a **prefix expression**. Or you could write a binary operator after its two operands, so $a + b$ becomes $a b +$. This expression is a **postfix expression**. Although infix expressions are more familiar to us, both prefix and postfix expressions are simpler to process because they do not use precedence rules or parentheses. The precedence of an operator in either a prefix expression or a postfix expression is implied by the order in which the operators and operands occur in the expression. We will learn more about these types of expressions later in this chapter.

Our first example looks at ordinary infix expressions.

Note: **Algebraic expressions**
In an infix expression, each binary operator appears between its operands, as in $a + b$.
In a prefix expression, each binary operator appears before its operands, as in $+ a b$.
In a postfix expression, each binary operator appears after its operands, as in $a b +$.

---

2. Chapter 19 used the Java operator ^ in a hash function, in Segment 19.8.

Note: The notation in a prefix expression is sometimes called **Polish notation**, because it was invented by the Polish mathematician Jan Lukasiewicz in the 1920s. The notation in a postfix expression is sometimes called **reverse Polish notation**.

Checking for Balanced Parentheses, Brackets, and Braces in an Infix Algebraic Expression

21.6   Although programmers use parentheses when writing an arithmetic expression in Java, mathematicians use parentheses, square brackets, and braces for the same purpose. These delimiters must be paired correctly. For example, an open parenthesis must correspond to a close parenthesis. In addition, pairs of delimiters must not intersect. Thus, an expression can contain a sequence of delimiters such as

   { [( ) ( )] ( ) }

but not

   [( ])

For convenience, we will say that a **balanced expression** contains delimiters that are paired correctly, or are **balanced**.

   We want an algorithm that detects whether an infix expression is balanced.

21.7   **Example: A balanced expression.** Let's see whether the expression

   $a \, \{b \, [c \, (d + e)/2 - f] + 1\}$

is balanced. We scan the expression from left to right, looking for delimiters and ignoring any characters that are not delimiters. When we encounter an open delimiter, we must save it. When we find a close delimiter, we must see whether it corresponds to the most recently encountered open delimiter. If it does, we discard the open delimiter and continue scanning the expression. If we are able to scan the entire expression without a mismatch, the delimiters in the expression are balanced.

   The ADT that enables us to store objects and then retrieve or remove the most recent one is a stack. Figure 21-3 shows the contents of a stack as we scan the previous expression. Since we ignore all characters that are not delimiters, it is sufficient for us to represent the expression as

   { [( )] }

   After pushing the first three open delimiters onto the stack, the open parenthesis is at the top of the stack. The next delimiter, the close parenthesis, pairs with the open parenthesis at the top of the stack. We pop the stack and continue by comparing the close bracket with the delimiter now at the top of the stack. They correspond, so we pop the stack again and continue by comparing the close brace with the top entry of the stack. These delimiters correspond, so we pop the stack. We have reached the end of the expression, and the stack is empty. Each open delimiter correctly corresponds to a close delimiter, so the delimiters are balanced.

Figure 21-3   The contents of a stack during the scan of an expression that contains the balanced
delimiters { [( )] }

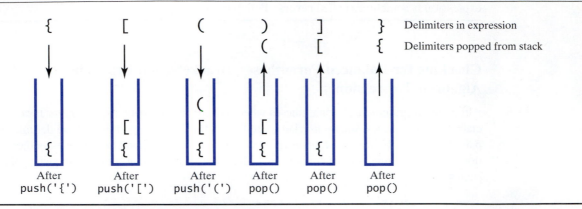

21.8   **Example: Unbalanced expressions.** Let's examine some expressions that contain unbalanced
delimiters. Figure 21-4 shows a stack during the scan of an expression that contains the delimiters
{ [( ]) }. This is an example of intersecting pairs of delimiters. After we push the first three open
delimiters onto the stack, the open parenthesis at the top of the stack does not correspond to the
close bracket that comes next in the expression.

Figure 21-4   The contents of a stack during the scan of an expression that contains the unbalanced
delimiters { [( ]) }

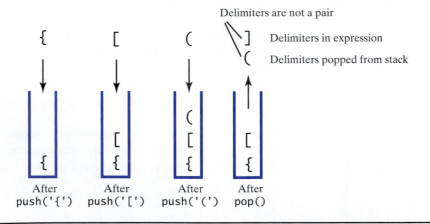

Figure 21-5 shows a stack during the scan of an expression that contains the unbalanced delimiters [( )] }. The close brace does not have a corresponding open brace. When we finally reach the
close brace, the stack is empty. Since the stack does not contain an open brace, the delimiters are
unbalanced.

Figure 21-5   The contents of a stack during the scan of an expression that contains the unbalanced delimiters [( )] }

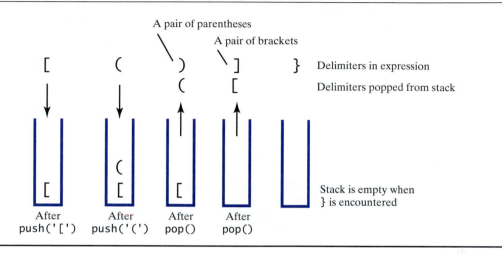

Figure 21-6 shows a stack during the scan of an expression that contains the unbalanced delimiters { [( )]. The open brace does not have a corresponding close brace. When you reach the end of the expression, having processed the brackets and parentheses, the stack still contains the open brace. Since this delimiter is left over, the expression contains unbalanced delimiters.

Figure 21-6   The contents of a stack during the scan of an expression that contains the unbalanced delimiters { [( )]

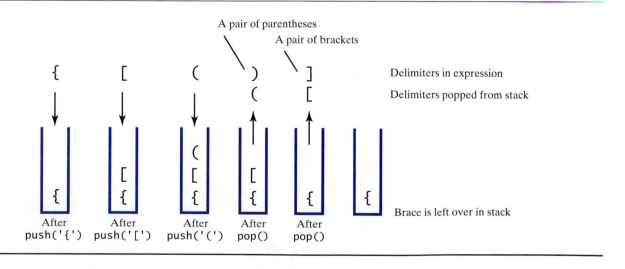

21.9   **The algorithm.** The previous discussion and figures reveal the paths that our algorithm must take. We formalize these observations in the following pseudocode:

Algorithm `checkBalance(expression)`
// Returns true if the parentheses, brackets, and braces in an expression are paired correctly.

```
isBalanced = true
while ( (isBalanced == true) and not at end of expression)
{
   nextCharacter = next character in expression
   switch (nextCharacter)
   {
      case '(': case '[': case '{':
         Push nextCharacter onto stack
         break

      case ')': case ']': case '}':
         if (stack is empty)
            isBalanced = false
         else
         {
            openDelimiter = top entry of stack
            Pop stack
            isBalanced = true or false according to whether openDelimiter and
                              nextCharacter are a pair of delimiters
         }
         break
   }
}

if (stack is not empty)
   isBalanced = false

return isBalanced
```

21.10   Let's examine this algorithm for each of the examples given in the previous figures. For the balanced expression in Figure 21-3, the `while` loop ends with an empty stack and `isBalanced` set to `true`. For the expression in Figure 21-4, the loop ends when it finds that the close bracket does not correspond to the open parenthesis. The flag `isBalanced` is `false`; the fact that the stack is not empty does not affect the outcome of the algorithm.

With the expression in Figure 21-5, the loop ends at the close brace because the stack is empty at that point. Retrieving or popping the top entry of the empty stack results in `null`, so the flag `isBalanced` is set to false. Finally, with the expression in Figure 21-6, the loop ends at the end of the expression with `isBalanced` set to true. But the stack is not empty—it contains an open brace—so after the loop, `isBalanced` becomes false.

Question 3   Show the contents of the stack as you trace the algorithm `checkBalance`, as given in Segment 21.9, for each of the following expressions. What does `checkBalance` return in each case?

a.   [a {b / (c − d) + e / (f + g)} − h]
b.   {a [b + (c + 2)/d] + e) + f }
c.   [a {b + [c (d + e) − f] + g }

21.11   **Java implementation.** The class `BalanceChecker`, shown in Listing 21-2, implements our algorithm as the static method `checkBalance`. The method has one parameter, the expression as a string. We assume that the class `LinkedStack` implements `StackInterface` and is available. Since `StackInterface` specifies a stack of objects, but the previous algorithm uses a stack of characters, `checkBalance` uses the wrapper class `Character` to create objects suitable for the stack.

Listing 21-2   The class `BalanceChecker`

```java
public class BalanceChecker
{
   /** Task: Decides whether the parentheses, brackets, and braces
    *        in a string occur in left/right pairs.
    *  @param expression  a string to be checked
    *  @return true if the delimiters are paired correctly */
   public static boolean checkBalance(String expression)
   {
      StackInterface<Character> openDelimiterStack =
                                        new LinkedStack<Character>();

      int characterCount = expression.length();
      boolean isBalanced = true;
      int index = 0;
      char nextCharacter = ' ';

      for (; isBalanced && (index < characterCount); index++)
      {
         nextCharacter = expression.charAt(index);
         switch (nextCharacter)
         {
            case '(': case '[': case '{':
               openDelimiterStack.push(nextCharacter);
               break;

            case ')': case ']': case '}':
               if (openDelimiterStack.isEmpty())
                  isBalanced = false;
               else
               {
                  char openDelimiter = openDelimiterStack.pop();
                  isBalanced = isPaired(openDelimiter, nextCharacter);
               } // end if
               break;

            default: break;
         } // end switch
      } // end for

      if (!openDelimiterStack.isEmpty())
         isBalanced = false;

      return isBalanced;
   } // end checkBalance
```

```
/** Task: Detects whether two delimiters are a pair of
 *          parentheses, brackets, or braces.
 *   @param open    a character
 *   @param close   a character
 *   @return true if open/close form a pair of parentheses, brackets,
 *                  or braces */
private static boolean isPaired(char open, char close)
{
   return (open == '(' && close == ')') ||
          (open == '[' && close == ']') ||
          (open == '{' && close == '}');
} // end isPaired
} // end BalanceChecker
```

The following statements provide an example of how you might use this class:

```
String expression = "a {b [c (d + e)/2 - f] + 1}";
boolean isBalanced = BalanceChecker.checkBalance(expression);
if (isBalanced)
   System.out.println(expression + " is balanced");
else
   System.out.println(expression + " is not balanced");
```

Transforming an Infix Expression to a Postfix Expression

21.12   Our ultimate goal is to show you how to evaluate infix algebraic expressions, but postfix expressions are easier to evaluate. So we first look at how to represent an infix expression by using postfix notation.

   Recall that in a postfix expression, a binary operator follows its two operands. Here are a few examples of infix expressions and their corresponding postfix forms:

Infix	**Postfix**
$a + b$	$a\ b +$
$(a + b) * c$	$a\ b + c *$
$a + b * c$	$a\ b\ c * +$

Notice that the order of the operands a, b, and c in an infix expression is the same in the corresponding postfix expression. However, the order of the operators might change. This order depends on the precedence of the operators and the existence of parentheses. As we mentioned, parentheses do not appear in a postfix expression.

21.13   **A pencil and paper scheme.** One way to determine where the operators should appear in a postfix expression begins with a fully parenthesized infix expression. For example, we write the infix expression $(a + b) * c$ as $((a + b) * c)$. By adding parentheses, we remove the expression's dependence on the rules of operator precedence. Each operator is now associated with a pair of parentheses. We now move each operator to the right so that it appears immediately before its associated close parenthesis to get $((a\ b +)\ c\ *)$. Finally, we remove the parentheses to obtain the postfix expression $a\ b + c *$.

   This scheme should give you some understanding of the order of the operators in a postfix expression. It also can be useful when checking the results of a conversion algorithm. However, the algorithm that we will develop next is not based on this approach.

Question 4   Using the previous scheme, convert each of the following infix expressions to postfix expressions:

a. $a + b * c$
b. $a * b / (c - d)$
c. $a / b + (c - d)$
d. $a / b + c - d$

21.14   **The basics of a conversion algorithm.** To convert an infix expression to postfix form, we scan the infix expression from left to right. When we encounter an operand, we place it at the end of the new expression that we are creating. Recall that operands in an infix expression remain in the same order in the corresponding postfix expression. When we encounter an operator, we must save it until we determine where in the output expression it belongs. For example, to convert the infix expression $a + b$, we append a to the initially empty output expression, save +, and append b to the output expression. We now need to retrieve the + and put it at the end of the output expression to get the postfix expression $a\ b\ +$. Retrieving the operator saved most recently is easy if we have saved it in a stack.

In this example, we saved the operator until we processed its second operand. In general, we hold the operator in a stack at least until we compare its precedence with that of the next operator. For example, to convert the expression $a + b * c$, we append a to the output expression, push + onto a stack, and then append b to the output. What we do now depends on the relative precedences of the next operator, *, and the + at the top of the stack. Since * has a greater precedence than +, b is not the addition's second operand. Instead, the addition waits for the result of the multiplication. Thus, we push * onto the stack and append c to the output expression. Having reached the end of the input expression, we now pop each operator from the stack and append it to the end of the output expression, getting the postfix expression $a\ b\ c\ *\ +$. Figure 21-7 illustrates these steps. The stack is shown horizontally; the leftmost element is at the bottom of the stack.

Figure 21-7   Converting the infix expression $a + b * c$ to postfix form

Next Character	Postfix	Operator Stack (bottom to top)
a	a	
+	a	+
b	$a\ b$	+
*	$a\ b$	+ *
c	$a\ b\ c$	+ *
	$a\ b\ c\ *$	+
	$a\ b\ c\ *\ +$	

21.15   **Successive operators with the same precedence.** What if two successive operators have the same precedence? We need to distinguish between operators that have a left-to-right association—namely +, -, *, and /—and exponentiation, which has a right-to-left association. For example, consider the expression $a - b + c$. When we encounter the +, the stack will contain the operator - and the incomplete postfix expression will be ab. The subtraction operator belongs to the operands a and b, so we pop the stack and append - to the end of the expression ab. Since the stack is empty, we push the + onto the stack. We then append c to the result, and finally we pop the stack and append the +. The result is a b - c +. Figure 21-8a illustrates these steps.

Now consider the expression $a \wedge b \wedge c$. By the time we encounter the second exponentiation operator, the stack contains $\wedge$, and the result so far is ab. As before, the current operator has the same precedence as the top entry of the stack. But since $a \wedge b \wedge c$ means $a \wedge (b \wedge c)$, we must push the second $\wedge$ onto the stack, as Figure 21-8b shows.

Figure 21–8   Converting an infix expression to postfix form: (a) $a - b + c$; (b) $a \wedge b \wedge c$

(a)

Next Character	Postfix	Operator Stack (bottom to top)
a	a	
$-$	a	
b	$a\ b$	$-$
$+$	$a\ b -$	$-$
	$a\ b -$	$+$
c	$a\ b - c$	$+$
	$a\ b - c +$	

(b)

Next Character	Postfix	Operator Stack (bottom to top)
a	a	
$\wedge$	a	$\wedge$
b	$a\ b$	$\wedge$
$\wedge$	$a\ b$	$\wedge\ \wedge$
c	$a\ b\ c$	$\wedge\ \wedge$
	$a\ b\ c \wedge$	$\wedge$
	$a\ b\ c \wedge\wedge$	

Question 5   In general, when should you push an exponentiation operator $\wedge$ onto the stack?

Note:

- If an operator other than $\wedge$ has the same precedence as the operator at the top of the stack, you pop the stack.
- If an operator is $\wedge$, you push it onto the stack regardless of what is at the top of the stack.

21.16   **Parentheses.** Parentheses override the rules of operator precedence. We always push an open parenthesis onto the stack. Once it is in the stack, we treat an open parenthesis as an operator with the lowest precedence. That is, any subsequent operator will get pushed onto the stack. When we encounter a close parenthesis, we pop operators from the stack and append them to the forming postfix expression until we pop an open parenthesis. The algorithm continues with no parentheses added to the postfix expression.

21.17   **The infix-to-postfix algorithm.** To summarize, we take the following actions, according to the symbols we encounter, as we process the infix expression from left to right:

- Operand   Append each operand to the end of the output expression.

- Operator ^   Push ^ onto the stack.

- Operator +, -, *, or /   Pop operators from the stack, appending them to the output expression, until the stack is empty or its top entry has a lower precedence than the new operator. Then push the new operator onto the stack.

- Open parenthesis   Push (onto the stack.

- Close parenthesis   Pop operators from the stack and append them to the output expression until an open parenthesis is popped. Discard both parentheses.

The following algorithm encompasses these observations. For simplicity, all operands in our expression are single-letter variables.

Algorithm `convertToPostfix(infix)`
// Converts an infix expression to an equivalent postfix expression.

```
operatorStack = a new empty stack
postfix = a new empty string
while (infix has characters left to parse)
{
   nextCharacter = next nonblank character of infix
   switch (nextCharacter)
   {
      case variable:
         Append nextCharacter to postfix
         break

      case '^' :
         operatorStack.push(nextCharacter)
         break

      case '+' : case '-' : case '*' : case '/' :
         while (!operatorStack.isEmpty() and
                  precedence of nextCharacter <= precedence of operatorStack.peek())
         {
            Append operatorStack.peek() to postfix
            operatorStack.pop()
         }

         operatorStack.push(nextCharacter)
         break
```

```
      case '(' :
         operatorStack.push(nextCharacter)
         break

      case ')' : // stack is not empty if infix expression is valid
         topOperator = operatorStack.pop()
         while (topOperator != '(')
         {
            Append topOperator to postfix
            topOperator = operatorStack.pop()
         }
         break

      default: break
   }
}

while (!operatorStack.isEmpty())
{
   topOperator = operatorStack.pop()
   Append topOperator to postfix
}
return postfix
```

Figure 21-9 traces this algorithm for the infix expression $a\ /\ b\ *\ (c + (d - e))$. The resulting postfix expression is $a\ b\ /\ c\ d\ e\ -\ +\ *$.

Figure 21-9   The steps in converting the infix expression $a\ /\ b\ *\ (c + (d - e))$ to postfix form

Next Character	Postfix	Operator Stack (bottom to top)
a	a	
/	a	/
b	a b	/
*	a b /	
	a b /	*
(	a b /	* (
c	a b / c	* (
+	a b / c	* (+
(	a b / c	* (+ (
d	a b / c d	* (+ (
−	a b / c d	* (+ (−
e	a b / c d e	* (+ (−
)	a b / c d e −	* (+ (
	a b / c d e −	* (+
)	a b / c d e − +	* (
	a b / c d e − +	*
	a b / c d e − + *	

Question 6   Using the previous algorithm, represent each of the following infix expressions as a postfix expression.

   a. $(a + b) / (c - d)$
   b. $a / (b - c) * d$
   c. $a - (b / (c - d) * e + f) \wedge g$
   d. $(a - b * c) / (d * e \wedge f * g + h)$

21.18   **The Java implementation.** The class `Postfix`, shown in Listing 21-3, implements this algorithm as the static method `convertToPostfix`. The method has one parameter, the expression as a string. Note the use of the class `java.lang.StringBuilder` in forming the postfix expression. `StringBuilder` is like `String`, but its instances are mutable—that is, they can change in value. (See Segment A.78 in Appendix A.)

Listing 21-3   The class `Postfix`

```java
public class Postfix
{
  /** Task: Creates a postfix expression that represents a given infix
   *        expression.
   *  @param infix  a string that is a valid infix expression
   *  @return a string that is the postfix expression equivalent to
   *          infix */
  public static String convertToPostfix(String infix)
  {
    StringBuilder postfix = new StringBuilder();
    StackInterface<Character> operatorStack =
                                        new LinkedStack<Character>();
    int characterCount = infix.length();
    char topOperator;

    for (int index = 0; index < characterCount; index++)
    {
      boolean done = false;
      char nextCharacter = infix.charAt(index);

      if (isVariable(nextCharacter))
        postfix = postfix.append(nextCharacter);
      else
      {
        switch (nextCharacter)
        {
          case '^':
            operatorStack.push(nextCharacter);
            break;

          case '+': case '-': case '*': case '/':
            while (!done && !operatorStack.isEmpty())
            {
              topOperator = operatorStack.peek();
```

```java
            if (getPrecedence(nextCharacter) <=
                getPrecedence(topOperator))
            {
              postfix = postfix.append(topOperator);
              operatorStack.pop();
            }
            else
              done = true;
          } // end while

          operatorStack.push(nextCharacter);
          break;

        case '(':
          operatorStack.push(nextCharacter);
          break;

        case ')': // stack is not empty if infix expression is valid
          topOperator = operatorStack.pop();
          while (topOperator != '(')
          {
            postfix = postfix.append(topOperator);
            topOperator = operatorStack.pop();
          } // end while
          break;

        default: break;
      } // end switch
    } // end if
  } // end for

  while (!operatorStack.isEmpty())
  {
    topOperator = operatorStack.pop();
    postfix = postfix.append(topOperator);
  } // end while

  return postfix.toString();
} // end convertToPostfix

/** Task: Indicates the precedence of a given operator.
 *  @param operator  a character that is (, ), +, -, *, /, or ^
 *  @return an integer that indicates the precedence of operator:
 *          0 if ( or ), 1 if + or -, 2 if * or /, 3 if ^, -1 if
 *          anything else */
private static int getPrecedence(char operator)
{
  switch (operator)
  {
    case '(': case ')': return 0;
    case '+': case '-': return 1;
    case '*': case '/': return 2;
    case '^':           return 3;
  } // end switch

  return -1;
} // end getPrecedence
```

```
    private static boolean isVariable(char character)
    {
      return Character.isLetter(character);
    } // end isVariable
} // end Postfix
```

Evaluating Postfix Expressions

21.19   Evaluating a postfix expression requires no rules of operator precedence, since the order of its operators and operands dictates the order of the operations. Additionally, a postfix expression contains no parentheses to complicate the evaluation.

As we scan the postfix expression, we must save operands until we find the operators that apply to them. For example, to evaluate the postfix expression $a\ b\ /$, we locate the variables a and b and save their values.[3] When we identify the operator $/$, its second operand is the most recently saved value—that is, b's value. The value saved before that—a's value—is the operator's first operand. Storing values in a stack enables us to access the necessary operands for an operator. Figure 21-10 traces the evaluation of $a\ b\ /$ when a is 2 and b is 4. The result of 0 assumes integer division.

Figure 21-10   The stack during the evaluation of the postfix expression $a\ b\ /$ when a is 2 and b is 4

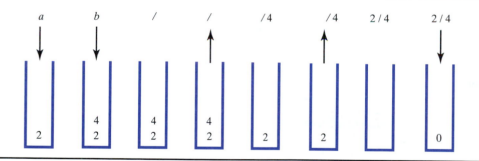

Now consider the postfix expression $a\ b + c\ /$, where a is 2, b is 4, and c is 3. The expression corresponds to the infix expression $(a + b) / c$, so its value should be 2. After finding the variable a, we push its value 2 onto a stack. Likewise, we push b's value 4 onto the stack. The + operator is next, so we pop two values from the stack, add them, and push their sum 6 onto the stack. Notice that this sum will be the first operand of the $/$ operator. The variable c is next in the postfix expression, so we push its value 3 onto the stack. Finally, we encounter the operator $/$, so we pop two values from the stack and form their quotient, 6/3. We push this result onto the stack. We are at the end of the expression, and one value, 2, is in the stack. This value is the value of the expression. Figure 21-11 traces the evaluation of this postfix expression.

---

3. Finding the value of a variable is not an easy task, but we will not explore this detail in this book.

Figure 21-11   The stack during the evaluation of the postfix expression *a b* + *c* / when *a* is 2, *b* is 4, and *c* is 3

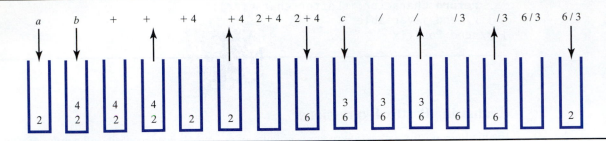

21.20   The evaluation algorithm follows directly from these examples:

> *Algorithm* `evaluatePostfix(postfix)`
> *// Evaluates a postfix expression.*
>
> `valueStack` = *a new empty stack*
> **while** (`postfix` *has characters left to parse*)
> {
>   `nextCharacter` = *next nonblank character of* `postfix`
>   **switch** (`nextCharacter`)
>   {
>   **case** *variable*:
>   `valueStack.push`(*value of the variable* `nextCharacter`)
>   **break**
>
>   **case** `'+'`: **case** `'-'`: **case** `'*'`: **case** `'/'`: **case** `'^'`:
>   `operandTwo` = `valueStack.pop()`
>   `operandOne` = `valueStack.pop()`
>   `result` = *the result of the operation in* `nextCharacter` *and its operands*
>   `operandOne` *and* `operandTwo`
>   `valueStack.push(result)`
>   **break**
>   **default: break**
>   }
> }
>
> **return** `valueStack.peek()`

We can implement this algorithm as a static method of the class `Postfix` that was given in Segment 21.18. The implemenftation is left as an exercise.

Question 7   Using the previous algorithm, evaluate each of the following postfix expressions. Assume that *a* = 2, *b* = 3, *c* = 4, *d* = 5, and *e* = 6.

a.   *a e* + *b d* - /
b.   *a b c* * *d* * -
c.   *a b c* - / *d* *
d.   *e b c a* ^ * + *d* -

Evaluating Infix Expressions

Using the two algorithms in Segments 21.17 and 21.20, we could evaluate an infix expression by converting it to an equivalent postfix expression and then evaluating it. We can save some intermediate work, however, by combining the two algorithms into one that evaluates an infix expression directly by using two stacks. This combined algorithm maintains a stack of operators according to the algorithm that converts an infix expression to postfix form. But instead of appending operands to the end of an expression, the new algorithm pushes the value of an operand onto a second stack according to the algorithm that evaluates a postfix expression.

21.21

Example. Consider the infix expression $a + b * c$. When a is 2, b is 3, and c is 4, the expression's value is 14. To compute this result, we push the value of the variable a onto a stack of values, push the + onto a stack of operators, and push the value of b onto the stack of values. Since * has a higher precedence than the + at the top of the operator stack, we push it onto the stack. Finally, we push the value of c onto the stack of values. Figure 21-12a shows the state of the two stacks at this point.

Figure 21-12 Two stacks during the evaluation of $a + b * c$ when a is 2, b is 3, and c is 4:
(a) after reaching the end of the expression; (b) while performing the multiplication;
(c) while performing the addition

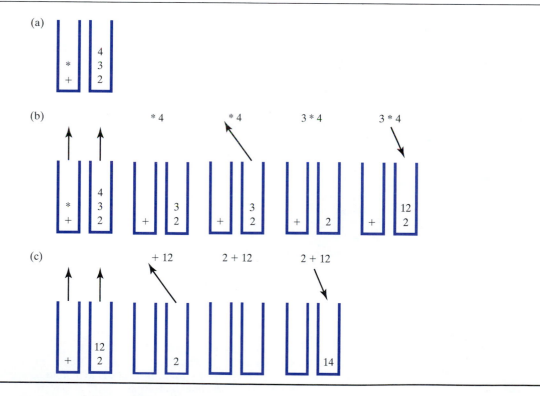

We now pop the operator stack and get the *. We get this operator's second and first operands, respectively, by popping the stack of values twice. After computing the product 3 * 4, we push the result 12 onto the stack of values, as Figure 21-12b shows. In a similar fashion, we pop the operator stack once and the value stack twice, compute 2 + 12, and push the result, 14, onto the stack of values. Since the operator stack is now empty, the value of the expression—14—is at the top of the stack of values. Figure 21-12c shows these final steps.

21.22   **The algorithm.** The algorithm to evaluate an infix expression follows. You should recognize aspects of its logic from the previous algorithms.

```
Algorithm evaluateInfix(infix)
// Evaluates an infix expression.

operatorStack = a new empty stack
valueStack = a new empty stack
while (infix has characters left to process)
{
   nextCharacter = next nonblank character of infix
   switch (nextCharacter)
   {
      case variable:
         valueStack.push(value of the variable nextCharacter)
         break

      case '^' :
         operatorStack.push(nextCharacter)
         break

      case '+' : case '-' : case '*' : case '/' :
         while (!operatorStack.isEmpty() and
                precedence of nextCharacter <= precedence of operatorStack.peek())
         {
            // Execute operator at top of operatorStack
            topOperator = operatorStack.pop()
            operandTwo = valueStack.pop()
            operandOne = valueStack.pop()
            result = the result of the operation in topOperator and its operands
                     operandOne and operandTwo
            valueStack.push(result)
         }

         operatorStack.push(nextCharacter)
         break

      case '(' :
         operatorStack.push(nextCharacter)
         break

      case ')' : // stack is not empty if infix expression is valid
         topOperator = operatorStack.pop()
         while (topOperator != '(')
         {
            operandTwo = valueStack.pop()
            operandOne = valueStack.pop()
            result = the result of the operation in topOperator and its operands
                     operandOne and operandTwo
            valueStack.push(result)
            topOperator = operatorStack.pop()
         }
         break

      default: break
   }
}
```

```
while (!operatorStack.isEmpty())
{
   topOperator = operatorStack.pop()
   operandTwo = valueStack.pop()
   operandOne = valueStack.pop()
   result = the result of the operation in topOperator and its operands
           operandOne and operandTwo
   valueStack.push(result)
}

return valueStack.peek()
```

Question 8   Using the previous algorithm, evaluate each of the following infix expressions. Assume that $a = 2$, $b = 3$, $c = 4$, $d = 5$, and $e = 6$.

a. $a + b * c - 9$
b. $(a + e) / (b - d)$
c. $a + (b + c * d) - e / 2$
d. $e - b * c \wedge a + d$

The Program Stack

21.23   When a program executes, a special location called the **program counter** references the current instruction. The program counter might be part of an actual computer or, in the case of Java, part of a virtual computer.[4]

When a method is called, the program's run-time environment creates an object called an **activation record**, or **frame**, for the method. The activation record shows the method's state during its execution. In particular, the activation record contains the method's arguments, local variables, and a reference to the current instruction—that is, a copy of the program counter. At the time the method is called, the activation record is pushed onto a stack called the **program stack** or, in Java, the **Java stack**. Since one method can call another, the program stack often contains more than one activation record. The record at the top of the stack belongs to the method that is currently executing. The record just beneath the top record belongs to the method that called the current method, and so on.

Figure 21-13 illustrates a program stack for a main method that calls methodA, which then calls methodB. When main begins execution, its activation record is at the top of the program stack (Figure 21-13a). When main calls methodA, a new record is pushed onto the stack. The program counter is 50 at that time. Figure 21-13b shows the updated record for main and the new record for methodA just as the method begins execution. When methodA calls methodB, the program counter is 120. A new activation record is pushed onto the stack. Figure 21-13c shows the unchanged record for main, the updated record for methodA, and the new record for methodB just as it begins execution.

As methodB executes, its activation record is updated, but the records for main and methodA remain unchanged. The record for methodA, for example, represents the method's state at the time it called methodB. When methodB completes its execution, its record is popped from the stack. The program counter is reset to 120 and then advanced to the next instruction. Thus, methodA resumes execution with the values of its argument and local variable as given in its activation

---

4.   To maintain computer independence, Java runs on a virtual computer called the **Java Virtual Machine (JVM)**.

record. Ultimately, methodA completes its execution, its activation record is popped from the program stack, and main continues its execution to completion.

Figure 21-13 The program stack at three points in time: (a) when main begins execution; (b) when methodA begins execution; (c) when methodB begins execution

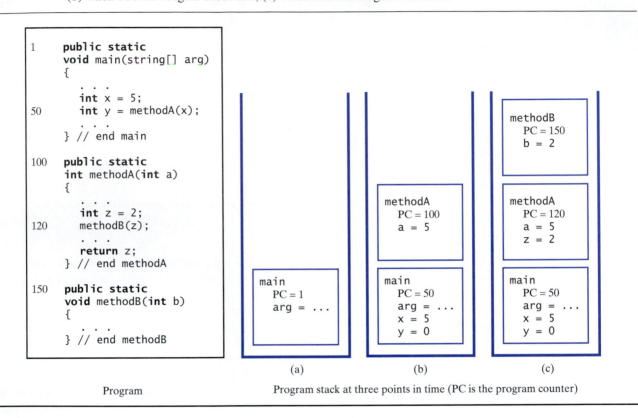

Program   Program stack at three points in time (PC is the program counter)

Recursive Methods

21.24   Figure 21-13 illustrates an example in which methodA and methodB are distinct methods. However, they need not be. That is, the program stack enables a run-time environment to execute recursive methods. Each invocation of a method produces an activation record that is pushed onto the program stack. The activation record of a recursive method is not special in any way.

Figures 10-4 and 10-5 in Chapter 10 traced the execution of two recursive methods. The activation records in those figures show less detail than the records illustrated in Figure 21-13. Exercise 12 at the end of this chapter asks you to provide such detail.

A recursive method that makes many recursive calls will place many activation records in the program stack. You now should see why a recursive method can use more memory than an iterative method. You also should appreciate that too many recursive calls can use all the memory available for the program stack and cause an error message.

One way to replace recursion with iteration is to simulate the program stack. In fact, we can implement a recursive algorithm by using a stack instead of recursion. The next section provides an example of such an implementation.

Using a Stack Instead of Recursion

21.25   Chapter 13 introduced the ADT sorted list. Like the ADT list, the sorted list has a search operation `contains`. When the implementation of the sorted list is array based, we can perform a binary search of the array of list items to implement `contains`. The array is a data field of the class that implements the sorted list. Since we are searching for a particular item in the list, the list items must be `Comparable`.

To hide the detail of array indices, `contains` invokes a private method `binarySearch` that actually does the binary search. The methods `contains` and a recursive version of `binarySearch` appear here as they did in Segment 16.13 of Chapter 16. Recall that the generic type `T` represents the data type of the entries in the sorted list.

```java
public boolean contains(T anEntry)
{
   return binarySearch(0, length - 1, anEntry);
} // end contains

/** Task: Searches list[first] through list[last] for desiredItem,
 *        where the array list is a data field.
 *  @param first   an integer index >= 0 and < length of sorted list
 *  @param last    an integer index >= 0 and < length of sorted list
 *  @param anEntry  the object to be found in the array
 *  @return true if anEntry is found */
private boolean binarySearch(int first, int last, T desiredItem)
{
   boolean found;
   int mid = (first + last)/2;

   if (first > last)
      found = false;
   else if (desiredItem.equals(list[mid]))
      found = true;
   else if (desiredItem.compareTo(list[mid]) < 0)
      found = binarySearch(first, mid - 1, desiredItem);
   else
      found = binarySearch(mid + 1, last, desiredItem);

   return found;
} // end binarySearch
```

An Iterative Binary Search

21.26   We can replace the recursive method `binarySearch` given in the previous segment with an iterative version by using a stack that mimics the program stack. To do so, we create a stack that is local to the method. We push objects onto this stack that are like the activation records described in Segment 21.23. An activation record in a Java stack contains the method's arguments, local variables, and a reference to the current instruction. Our objects need not contain all of this. In `binary-Search`, for example, only the first two arguments change, and so only they must be saved in a record. The third argument stays the same in each recursive call, so we can omit it. Since both recursive calls to `binarySearch` occur right before the method's `return` statement, there is no need to distinguish between them by storing a representation of the program counter in the record. This simplification is not true in general, however.

To represent a record, we define a class that, in this case, has data fields for the method's arguments `first` and `last`. The following simple class is sufficient if we make it internal to the sorted list class:

```java
private class Record
{
  private int first, last;

  private Record(int firstIndex, int lastIndex)
  {
    first = firstIndex;
    last = lastIndex;
  } // end constructor
} // end Record
```

21.27   In general, when a method begins execution, it pushes an activation record onto a program stack. At its return, a record is popped from this stack. We want an iterative `binarySearch` to maintain its own stack. When the method begins execution, it should push a record onto this stack. Each recursive call should do likewise. As long as the stack is not empty, the method should remove a record from the stack and act according to the contents of the record. The method ends its execution when the stack becomes empty.

Here is an iterative version of `binarySearch` that uses a stack as we just described:

```java
private boolean binarySearch(int first, int last, T desiredItem)
{
  StackInterface<Record> programStack = new LinkedStack<Record>();
  boolean found = false;
  boolean done = false;

  programStack.push(new Record(first, last));

  while (!done && !programStack.isEmpty())
  {
    Record topRecord = programStack.pop();
    first = topRecord.first;
    last = topRecord.last;
    int mid = (first + last)/2;

    if (first > last)
    {
      found = false;
      done = true;
    }
    else if (desiredItem.equals(list[mid]))
    {
      found = true;
      done = true;
    }
    else
    {
      if (desiredItem.compareTo(list[mid]) < 0)
        programStack.push(new Record(first, mid - 1));
      else
        programStack.push(new Record(mid + 1, last));
```

```
    } // end if
  } // end while

  return found;
} // end binarySearch
```

This approach does not always produce an elegant solution. We certainly could write an iterative version of `binarySearch` that was easier to understand than this version and did not require a stack. But sometimes a simple iterative solution is not apparent; the stack approach offers a possible solution. You will see a more useful example of a stack-based iteration in Segment 26.14 of Chapter 26.

Java Class Library: The Class `Stack`

21.28 The package `java.util` contains the class `Stack<T>`. `Stack` has only one constructor—a default constructor that creates an empty stack. In addition, the following four methods in this class are similar to methods in our `StackInterface`. We have used blue to indicate where they differ from our methods.

```
public T push(T item);
public T pop();
public T peek();
public boolean empty();
```

`Stack` also has the following methods that enable you to either search or traverse the stack:

```
/** Task: Searches for a given object in the stack.
 *  @param desiredItem  the object to be found
 *  @return either the position of desiredItem if it is in the stack
 *          or -1 if it is not; the top of the stack is at position 1 */
public int search(Object desiredItem);

/** @return an iterator for the stack that conforms to Java's
 *          interface Iterator */
public Iterator<T> iterator();

/** @return an iterator for the stack that conforms to Java's
 *          interface ListIterator */
public ListIterator<T> listIterator();
```

Finally, `Stack` has methods from the class `Vector`, since `Stack` extends `Vector`. Such methods are not supported by a traditional stack ADT.

CHAPTER SUMMARY

- The ADT stack organizes its entries on a last-in, first-out basis. The entry at the top of the stack is the one added most recently.

- A stack's major operations—**push**, **pop**, and **peek**—deal only with the top of the stack. The method **push** adds an entry to the top of the stack; **pop** removes and returns the top entry, and **peek** just returns it.

- Arithmetic operators that have two operands are binary operators. When an operator such as + or − has one operand, it is a unary operator.

- An algebraic expression often contains parentheses, square brackets, and braces. You can use a stack to discover whether these delimiters are paired correctly.

- Ordinary algebraic expressions are called infix expressions, because each binary operator appears between its two operands. An infix expression requires rules of operator precedence and can use parentheses to override these rules.

- In a postfix expression, each binary operator appears after its two operands. In a prefix expression, each binary operator appears before its two operands. Postfix and prefix expressions use no parentheses and have no rules of operator precedence.

- You can use a stack of operators when forming a postfix expression that is equivalent to a given infix expression.

- You can use a stack of values to evaluate a postfix expression.

- You can use two stacks—one for operators and one for values—to evaluate an infix expression.

- When a method is called, the Java run-time environment creates an activation record, or frame, to record the status of the method. The record contains the method's arguments and local variables, along with the address of the current instruction. The record is placed in a stack called the program stack.

- You can use a stack instead of recursion to implement a recursive algorithm. This stack mimics the behavior of the program stack.

PROGRAMMING TIP

- Methods such as **peek** and **pop** must behave reasonably when the stack is empty. For example, they could return **null** or throw an exception.

EXERCISES

1. If you push the objects x, y, and z onto an initially empty stack, in what order will three pop operations remove them from the stack?

2. Suppose that s and t are empty stacks and a, b, c, and d are objects. What do the stacks contain after the following sequence of operations executes?

```
s.push(a);
s.push(b);
s.push(c);
t.push(d);
t.push(s.pop());
t.push(s.peek());
s.push(t.pop());
t.pop();
```

3. Consider the following Java statements:

```
int n = 4;
StackInterface<Integer> myStack = new LinkedStack<Integer>();
```

```
while (n > 0)
{
   myStack.push(n);
   n--;
} // end while
int result = 1;
while (!myStack.isEmpty())
{
   int integer = myStack.pop();
   result = result * integer;
} // end while
System.out.println("result = " + result);
```

a. What value is displayed when this code executes?
b. What mathematical function does the code evaluate?

4. Show the contents of the stack as you trace the algorithm checkBalance, given in Segment 21.9, for each of the following expressions:

   a. $a\ \{b\ [c\ *\ (d\ +\ e)]\ -f\}$
   b. $\{a\ (\ b\ *\ c\ )\ /\ [d+e]\ /f)-\ g\}$
   c. $a\ \{b\ [c\ -\ d]\ e])\ f$

5. Using the algorithm convertToPostfix, given in Segment 21.17, convert each of the following infix expressions to postfix expressions:

   a. $a\ *\ b\ /\ (c\ -\ d)$
   b. $(a\ -\ b\ *\ c)\ /\ (d\ *\ e\ *f+g)$
   c. $a\ /\ b\ *\ (c\ +\ (d\ -\ e))$
   d. $(a\wedge b\ *\ c\ -\ d)\wedge e+f\wedge g\wedge h$

6. Using the algorithm evaluatePostfix, given in Segment 21.20, evaluate each of the following postfix expressions. Assume that $a = 2, b = 3, c = 4, d = 5$, and $e = 6$.

   a. $a\ b\ +\ c\ *\ d\ -$
   b. $a\ b\ *\ c\ a\ -\ /\ d\ e\ *\ +$
   c. $a\ c\ -\ b\wedge d\ +$

7. Implement the algorithm evaluatePostfix, given in Segment 21.20, as a static method of the class Postfix.

8. Show the contents of the two stacks as you trace the algorithm evaluateInfix, given in Segment 21.22, to evaluate each of the following infix expressions. Assume that $a = 2$, $b = 3, c = 4, d = 5, e = 6$, and $f = 7$.

   a. $(a + b)\ /\ (c - d) - 5$
   b. $(d\ *f+\ 1)*\ e\ /\ (a\wedge b-b\ *\ c+1) - 72$
   c. $(a\wedge c-f)\wedge a-a\wedge b\wedge a$

9. A **palindrome** is a string of characters (a word, phrase, or sentence) that is the same regardless of whether you read it forward or backward—assuming that you ignore spaces, punctuation, and case. For example, *Race car* is a palindrome. So is *A man, a plan, a canal: Panama*. Describe how you could use a stack to test whether a string is a palindrome.

```
while (n > 0)
{
   myStack.push(n);
   n--;
} // end while

int result = 1;
while (!myStack.isEmpty())
{
   int integer = myStack.pop();
   result = result * integer;
} // end while
System.out.println("result = " + result);
```

   a. What value is displayed when this code executes?
   b. What mathematical function does the code evaluate?

4. Show the contents of the stack as you trace the algorithm checkBalance, given in Segment 21.9, for each of the following expressions:

   a. $a \{b [c * (d + e)] - f\}$
   b. $\{a (b * c) / [d + e] / f)- g\}$
   c. $a \{b [c - d] e]) f$

5. Using the algorithm convertToPostfix, given in Segment 21.17, convert each of the following infix expressions to postfix expressions:

   a. $a * b / (c - d)$
   b. $(a - b * c) / (d * e * f + g)$
   c. $a / b * (c + (d - e))$
   d. $(a \wedge b * c - d) \wedge e + f \wedge g \wedge h$

6. Using the algorithm evaluatePostfix, given in Segment 21.20, evaluate each of the following postfix expressions. Assume that $a = 2, b = 3, c = 4, d = 5$, and $e = 6$.

   a. $a\ b + c * d -$
   b. $a\ b * c\ a - / d\ e * +$
   c. $a\ c - b \wedge d +$

7. Implement the algorithm evaluatePostfix, given in Segment 21.20, as a static method of the class Postfix.

8. Show the contents of the two stacks as you trace the algorithm evaluateInfix, given in Segment 21.22, to evaluate each of the following infix expressions. Assume that $a = 2$, $b = 3, c = 4, d = 5, e = 6$, and $f = 7$.

   a. $(a + b) / (c - d) - 5$
   b. $(d * f + 1) * e / (a \wedge b - b * c + 1) - 72$
   c. $(a \wedge c - f) \wedge a - a \wedge b \wedge a$

9. A **palindrome** is a string of characters (a word, phrase, or sentence) that is the same regardless of whether you read it forward or backward—assuming that you ignore spaces, punctuation, and case. For example, *Race car* is a palindrome. So is *A man, a plan, a canal: Panama*. Describe how you could use a stack to test whether a string is a palindrome.

10. Suppose that you read a binary string—that is, a string of 0s and 1s—one character at a time. Describe how you could use a stack but no arithmetic to see whether the number of 0s is equal to the number of 1s. When these counts are not equal, state how you could tell which character—0 or 1—occurs most frequently and by how much its count exceeds the other's.

11. Write Java code that displays all the objects in a stack *s* in the order in which they were pushed onto the stack. After all the objects are displayed, *s* should have the same contents as when you started.

12. Chapter 10 traced the execution of two recursive methods in Figures 10-4 and 10-5. Revise those figures to provide the detail in the activation records that Figure 21-13 provides.

13. Consider a checkerboard that has a dollar amount printed on each of its squares. You can place a checker on the board anywhere you want and then move it across the board with standard diagonal moves. Once you reach the other side, you are finished. You will collect an amount of money equal to the sum of the values written on the squares that your checker traveled over.

    a. Give a recursive algorithm that will compute the maximum amount you can collect.
    b. Give an iterative algorithm that uses a stack that will compute the maximum amount.

PROJECTS

1. Consider the following algorithm to sort the entries in a stack S_1. First create two empty stacks, S_2 and S_3. At any given time, stack S_2 will hold the entries in sorted order, with the smallest at the top of the stack. Move the top entry of S_1 to S_2. Pop and consider the top entry *t* of S_1. Pop entries of stack S_2 and push them onto stack S_3 until you reach the correct place to put *t*. Then push *t* onto S_2. Next move all the entries from S_3 to S_2.

    a. Implement this algorithm both recursively and iteratively.
    b. Consider the following revision of this algorithm. After moving the top entry of S_1 to S_2, compare the new top entry *t* of S_1 with the top entry of S_2 and the top entry of S_3. Then either move entries from S_2 to S_3 or from S_3 to S_2 until you locate the correct position for *t*. Push *t* onto S_2. Continue until S_1 is empty. Finally, move any entries remaining in S_3 to S_2. Implement this revised algorithm.

2. In the language Lisp, each of the four basic arithmetic operators appears before an arbitrary number of operands, which are separated by spaces. The resulting expression is enclosed in parentheses. The operators behave as follows:

    - (+ a b c ...) returns the sum of all the operands, and (+) returns 0.
    - (- a b c ...) returns a - b - c - ..., and (- a) returns -a. The minus operator must have at least one operand.
    - (* a b c ...) returns the product of all the operands, and (*) returns 1.
    - (/ a b c ...) returns a / b / c / ..., and (/ a) returns 1 / a. The divide operator must have at least one operand.

You can form larger arithmetic expressions by combining these basic expressions using a fully parenthesized prefix notation. For example, the following is a valid Lisp expression:

```
(+ (- 6) (* 2 3 4) (/ (+ 3) (*) (- 2 3 1)))
```

This expression is evaluated successively as follows:

```
(+ (- 6) (* 2 3 4) (/ 3 1 -2))
(+ -6 24 -1.5)
16.5
```

Design and implement a recursive algorithm that uses a stack to evaluate a legal Lisp expression composed of the four basic operators and integer values. Write a program that reads such expressions and demonstrates your algorithm.

3. Consider arithmetic expressions like the ones described in the previous project. Allow operands to be either integer values or variable names that are strings of letters. Design and implement an iterative algorithm that uses a stack to test whether an expression is legal in Lisp. Write a program that reads potential expressions and demonstrates your algorithm.

Each expression that your program reads can be split across several lines, which is the style used by typical Lisp programmers. For example, the following expression is legal in Lisp:

```
(+ (- height)
   (* 3 3 4)
   (/ 3 width length)
   (* radius radius)
)
```

In contrast, the following expressions are illegal in Lisp:

<pre>(+ (-)
   (* 3 3 4)
   (/ 3 width length)
   (* radius radius)
)</pre>
	<pre>(+ (- height)
	   (* 3 3 4))
	(* (/ 3 width length)
	   (* radius radius)
	)</pre>

<pre>(+ (- height)
   (* 3 3 4)
   (/ 3 width length))
   (* radius radius)
)</pre>
	<pre>(+ (- height)
	   (* 3 3 4)
	   ((/ 3 width length))
	   (* radius radius)
	)</pre>

22

Stack Implementations

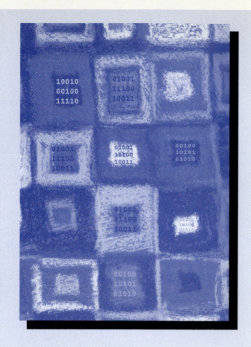

CONTENTS

PREREQUISITES

OBJECTIVES

After studying this chapter, you should be able to

- Implement the ADT stack by using either a linked chain, an array, or a vector
- Compare and contrast the various implementations and their performance

The implementations of the ADT stack described in this chapter use techniques like the ones we used to implement the ADT list. We will use, in turn, a chain of linked nodes, an array, and an instance of Vector to store the stack's entries. You should be pleasantly surprised by the simplicity and efficiency of these implementations.

A Linked Implementation

22.1   Each of the operations push, pop, and peek of the ADT stack involve the top of the stack. If we use a chain of linked nodes to implement a stack, where in the chain should we place the stack's top entry? Recall that when a chain has only a head reference, we can add, remove, or retrieve its first node faster than any other node. Thus, the stack operations will execute fastest if the first node in the chain references the top entry in the stack, as Figure 22-1 illustrates.

Also note in the figure that each node in the chain references one entry in the stack. Nodes are allocated—that is, created—only when needed for a new entry. They are deallocated when an entry is removed. Recall from the note in Segment 7.9 of Chapter 7 that the Java run-time environment automatically reclaims, or deallocates, memory that a program no longer references, without explicit instruction from the programmer.

   Note: If you use a chain of linked nodes to implement a stack, the first node should reference the stack's top entry.

Figure 22-1   A chain of linked nodes that implements a stack

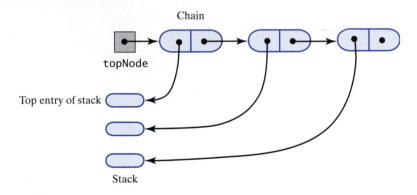

22.2   **An outline of the class.** The linked implementation of the stack has a data field topNode, which is the head reference of the chain of nodes. The default constructor sets this field to null. An outline of our class appears in Listing 22-1.

Each node in the chain is an instance of the private class Node that is defined within the class LinkedStack. This class has set and get methods and is like the one you saw in Segment 7.14 of Chapter 7, but it implements the interface java.io.Serializable.

Listing 22-1   An outline of a linked implementation of the ADT stack

```
public class LinkedStack<T> implements StackInterface<T>,
                                        java.io.Serializable
{
    private Node topNode; // references the first node in the chain
```

```java
public LinkedStack()
{
    topNode = null;
} // end default constructor
```

< Implementations of the stack operations go here. >

. . .

```java
private class Node implements java.io.Serializable
{
    private T     data; // entry in stack
    private Node next; // link to next node
```

< Constructors and the methods `getData`, `setData`, `getNextNode`, *and* `setNextNode`
are here. >

```java
} // end Node
} // end LinkedStack
```

22.3 **Adding to the top.** We push an entry onto the stack by first allocating a new node that references the stack's existing chain, as Figure 22-2a illustrates. This reference is in `topNode`, the head reference to the chain. We then set `topNode` to reference the new node, as in Figure 22-2b. Thus, the method `push` has the following definition:

```java
public void push(T newEntry)
{
    Node newNode = new Node(newEntry, topNode);
    topNode = newNode;
} // end push
```

This operation requires no search and is independent of the other entries in the stack. Its performance is thus O(1).

Figure 22-2   (a) A new node that references the node at the top of the stack; (b) the new node is now at the top of the stack

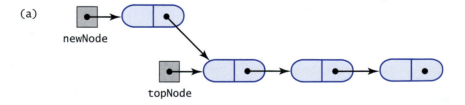

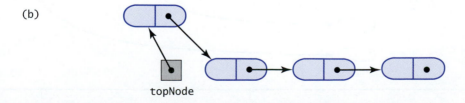

22.4   **Retrieving the top.** We get the top entry in the stack by accessing the data portion of the first node in the chain. Thus, peek, like push, is an O(1) operation. Note that if the stack is empty, peek returns null.

```java
public T peek()
{
    T top = null;

    if (topNode != null)
        top = topNode.getData();

    return top;
} // end peek
```

22.5   **Removing the top.** We pop, or remove, the top entry in the stack by setting topNode to the reference in the first node. Thus, topNode will reference what was the second node in the chain, as Figure 22-3 shows. Since we also want the operation to return the stack's top entry before it is

Figure 22-3   The stack (a) before and (b) after the first node in the chain is deleted

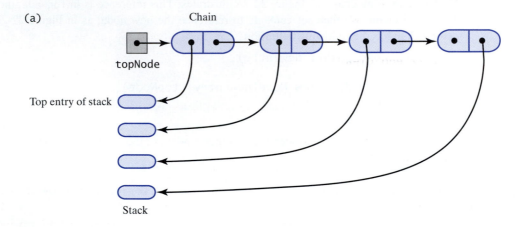

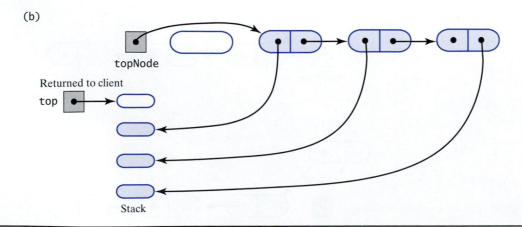

removed, the method pop has the following implementation:

```java
public T pop()
{
   T top = peek();

   if (topNode != null)
      topNode = topNode.getNextNode();

   return top;
} // end pop
```

This operation also is O(1).

Question 1   Revise the previous implementation of pop so that it does not call peek.

22.6   **The rest of the class.** The remaining public methods isEmpty and clear involve only topNode:

```java
public boolean isEmpty()
{
   return topNode == null;
} // end isEmpty
public void clear()
{
   topNode = null;
} // end clear
```

Question 2   Is an implementation of the ADT stack reasonable if the top of the stack is at the end of a chain of linked nodes instead of its beginning? Explain.

An Array-Based Implementation

22.7   If we use an array to implement the stack, where should we place the stack's top entry? If the first location of the array references the top entry, as shown in Figure 22-4a, we must move all the elements in the array any time we add or remove a stack entry. We can have more efficient stack operations if the first array location references the bottom entry of the stack. The top entry of the stack is then referenced by the last occupied location in the array, as Figure 22-4b shows. This configuration allows us to add or remove stack entries without moving other array elements. Thus, one disadvantage of a typical array-based implementation does not apply here. The exercises at the end of this chapter consider other ways to place a stack's entries in an array.

Using dynamic array expansion avoids a stack that is too full to accept another entry. However, unlike the linked chain in the previous section, the array in Figure 22-4 contains locations that are unused. If we eventually fill the array with additional stack entries, we can expand the size of the array—but then we will have more unused locations. The chain has its downside as well, in that it uses additional memory for the link portions of its nodes.

Note: If you use an array to implement a stack, the array's first location is the bottom of the stack. The last occupied location in the array, then, references the stack's top entry.

Figure 22-4   An array that implements a stack; its first location references (a) the top entry in the stack; (b) the bottom entry in the stack

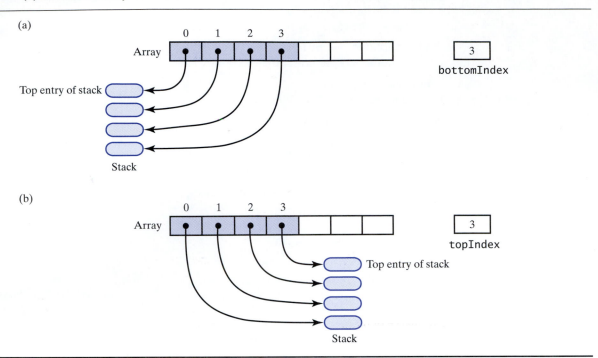

22.8   **An outline of the class.** The array-based implementation of the stack has as data fields an array of stack entries and an index to the top entry. The default constructor allocates an array with a default size; another constructor lets the client choose the array size. Listing 22-2 outlines our class in this case.

Listing 22-2   An outline of an array-based implementation of the ADT stack

```java
public class ArrayStack<T> implements StackInterface<T>,
                                      java.io.Serializable
{
  private T[] stack;    // array of stack entries
  private int topIndex; // index of top entry
  private static final int DEFAULT_INITIAL_CAPACITY = 50;

  public ArrayStack()
  {
    this(DEFAULT_INITIAL_CAPACITY);
  } // end default constructor

  public ArrayStack(int initialCapacity)
  {
    stack = (T[]) new Object[initialCapacity];
    topIndex = -1;
  } // end constructor
```

> *< Implementations of the stack operations go here. >*

```
    . . .
} // end ArrayStack
```

To indicate an empty stack, we have assigned -1 to `topIndex` as its initial value. This choice allows `push` to simply increment `topIndex` before using it when placing a new entry in the array.

22.9   **Adding to the top.** The `push` operation first checks whether the array has room for a new entry. If it does not, `push` doubles the size of the array. It then places the new entry immediately after the last occupied location in the array:

```
public void push(T newEntry)
{
   topIndex++;

   if (topIndex >= stack.length) // if array is full,
      doubleArray();             // expand array

   stack[topIndex] = newEntry;
} // end push
```

When `push` does not invoke `doubleArray`, it is an $O(1)$ operation, since its performance is independent of the size of the stack. However, `doubleArray` is an $O(n)$ operation, so when the array is full, the performance of `push` degrades to $O(n)$. If this happens, however, the very next `push` is $O(1)$ again. To be fair, all `push` operations should share the cost of the occasional execution of `doubleArray`. That is, we **amortize** the cost of doubling the array over all additions to the stack. Unless we must double the array many times, each `push` is almost $O(1)$.

22.10   **Retrieving the top.** The operation `peek` returns either the array element at `topIndex` or `null` if the stack is empty:

```
public T peek()
{
   T top = null;

   if (!isEmpty())
      top = stack[topIndex];

   return top;
} // end peek
```

This operation is $O(1)$.

22.11   **Removing the top.** The `pop` operation, like `peek`, retrieves the top entry in the stack, but then removes it. To remove the stack's top entry in Figure 22-4b, we could simply decrement `topIndex`, as Figure 22-5a illustrates. This simple step would be sufficient, since the other methods would behave correctly. For example, given the stack pictured in Figure 22-5a, `peek` would return the item that `stack[2]` references. However, the object that previously was the top entry and has now been returned to the client would still be referenced by the array. No harm will come from this situation if our implementation is correct. To be safe, `pop` can set `stack[topIndex]` to `null` before decrementing `topIndex`. Figure 22-5b illustrates the stack in this case.

Figure 22-5   An array-based stack after its top entry is removed by (a) decrementing `topIndex`;
(b) setting `stack[topIndex]` to `null` and then decrementing `topIndex`

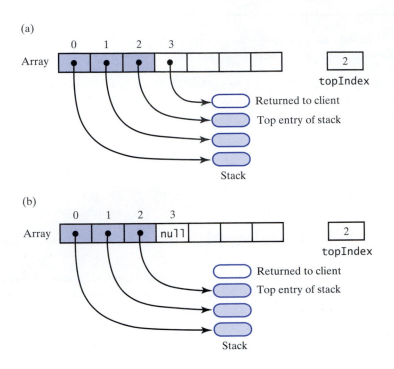

The following implementation of pop reflects these comments:

```java
public T pop()
{
  T top = null;

  if (!isEmpty())
  {
    top = stack[topIndex];
    stack[topIndex] = null;
    topIndex--;
  } // end if

  return top;
} // end pop
```

Like peek, pop is an O(1) operation.

Question 3   Revise the previous implementation of pop so that it calls peek.

Question 4   If we were to implement a stack of primitives instead of a stack of objects, what changes should we make to the method pop?

22.12   **The rest of the class.** The method `isEmpty` involves only `topIndex`:

```
public boolean isEmpty()
{
    return topIndex < 0;
} // end isEmpty
```

If the method `clear` simply set `topIndex` to -1, the stack methods would behave correctly as though the stack were empty. However, the objects that were in the stack would remain allocated. Just as pop sets `stack[topIndex]` to `null`, `clear` should set to `null` each array location that was used for the stack. Alternatively, `clear` could call pop repeatedly until the stack is empty. We leave the implementation of `clear` as an exercise.

The private method `doubleArray` is like `doubleArray` in Segment 5.18 of Chapter 5, except for the names of the arrays.

Question 5   If `stack` is an array that contains the entries in a stack, what is a disadvantage of maintaining the top entry of the stack in `stack[0]`?

Question 6   If you use the locations at the end of an array `stack` for a stack's entries before you use the array's first locations, should the stack's top entry or its bottom entry be in `stack[stack.length - 1]`? Why?

Question 7   Write an implementation of `clear` that sets to `null` each array location that was used for the stack.

Question 8   Write an implementation of `clear` that repeatedly calls pop until the stack is empty.

A Vector-Based Implementation

22.13   Using a vector is like using an array to implement the stack, but easier. We let the first element of the vector be the bottom entry of the stack. Thus, the vector looks like the array in Figure 22-4b. We do not need to maintain an index to the top entry of the stack, however, as we can infer this index from the vector's size, which is readily available. Also, the vector expands as necessary, so we do not have to worry about this detail.

Since the implementation of `Vector` is based on an array that can be expanded dynamically, the performance of this implementation of the stack is like that of the array-based implementation given in the previous section.

> **Note:**   If you use a vector to implement a stack, the vector's first element should be the stack's bottom entry. Then the last occupied location in the vector references the stack's top entry.

22.14   **An outline of the class.** The class that implements the stack begins by declaring a vector as a data field and allocating the vector in its constructors. Listing 22-3 outlines our class.

Listing 22-3   An outline of a vector-based implementation of the ADT stack

```java
import java.util.Vector;
public class VectorStack<T> implements StackInterface<T>,
                                        java.io.Serializable
{
  private Vector<T> stack;    // last element is the top entry in stack

  public VectorStack()
  {
    stack = new Vector<T>(); // vector doubles in size if necessary
  } // end default constructor

  public VectorStack(int initialCapacity)
  {
    stack = new Vector<T>(initialCapacity);
  } // end constructor

  < Implementations of the stack operations go here. >
  . . .
} // end VectorStack
```

22.15   **Adding to the top.** We use Vector's method add to add an entry to the end of the vector, that is, to the top of the stack.

```java
public void push(T newEntry)
{
  stack.add(newEntry);
} // end push
```

22.16   **Retrieving the top.** We retrieve the stack's top entry by using Vector's method lastElement.

```java
public T peek()
{
  T top = null;

  if (!isEmpty())
    top = stack.lastElement();

  return top;
} // end peek
```

22.17   **Removing the top.** We can remove the stack's top entry by using Vector's method remove. The argument to this method is the index of the last entry in the vector, since that entry is at the top of the stack. This index is 1 less than the vector's current size stack.size().

```java
public T pop()
{
  T top = null;

  if (!isEmpty())
  {
```

```
        top = stack.lastElement();
        stack.remove(stack.size() - 1);
    } // end if
    return top;
} // end pop
```

22.18   **The rest of the class.** The remaining public methods isEmpty and clear invoke analogous Vector methods:

```
public boolean isEmpty()
{
    return stack.isEmpty();
} // end isEmpty

public void clear()
{
    stack.clear();
} // end clear
```

We also can use an instance of the ADT list to represent a stack. Such an implementation is similar to the vector implementation, and we leave it to you as a programming project.

Question 9   If a vector contains the entries in a stack, is it reasonable to maintain the stack's top entry in the vector's first element?

Note: **Should VectorStack extend Vector?**

The previous implementation of VectorStack contains an instance of Vector. Suppose that we instead used inheritance to derive VectorStack from Vector. The resulting class would have all the methods of Vector in addition to those in StackInterface. These Vector methods would allow a client to add or remove entries anywhere within the stack, however, thus violating the premise of the ADT stack. Instead of a stack, we would have an enhanced vector. But a stack is not a vector. Since we do not have an *is-a* relationship between stacks and vectors, we should not use inheritance to define VectorStack.

As we mentioned in Segment 21.28 of the previous chapter, the class java.util.Stack in the Java Class Library extends Vector. Thus, an instance of Stack is not really a stack.

CHAPTER SUMMARY

- You can implement a stack by using a chain of linked nodes that has only a head reference. The stack operations execute fastest if the first node in the chain references the stack's top entry. This is true because you can add, remove, or access a chain's first node faster than any other node.

- The stack operations are O(1) for a linked implementation.

- You can implement a stack by using an array. If the first location in the array contains the stack's bottom entry, no array elements will be moved when you add or remove stack entries.

- Using dynamic array expansion avoids a stack that is too full to accept another entry. However, the array generally contains locations that are unused.

- The stack operations are O(1) for an array-based implementation. However, when the array is full, **push** doubles the size of the array. In that case, **push** is O(n). If you spread this extra cost over all other pushes, and if doubling the array is not frequent, **push** is almost O(1).

- You can implement a stack by using a vector. You maintain the stack's bottom entry at the beginning of the vector.

- Since the implementation of `Vector` is based on an array that can be expanded dynamically, the performance of a vector-based implementation is like that of the array-based implementation.

EXERCISES

1. Discuss the advantages and disadvantages of an array-based implementation of the ADT stack as compared to a linked implementation.

2. Imagine a linked implementation of the ADT stack that places the top entry of the stack at the end of a chain of linked nodes. Describe how you can define the stack operations push, pop, and peek so that they do not traverse the chain.

3. Consider adding an iterator to the ADT stack. Should a stack iterator support the remove operation?

4. Implement an iterator for the linked implementation of a stack using an inner class.

5. Implement an iterator for the array-based implementation of a stack using an inner class.

6. Segment 22.9 noted that an array-based push method is normally $O(1)$, but when a stack needs to be doubled in size, push is $O(n)$. This observation is not as bad as it seems, however. Suppose that you double the size of a stack from n elements to $2n$ elements.

   a. How many calls to push can you make before the stack must double in size again?
   b. Remembering that each of these calls to push is $O(1)$, what is the average cost of all the push operations? (The average cost is the total cost of all calls to push divided by the number of calls to push.)

7. Suppose that instead of doubling the size of an array-based stack when it becomes full, you just increase the size of the array by some positive constant k.

   a. If you have an empty stack that uses an array whose initial size is k, and you perform n pushes, how many resize operations will be performed? Assume that $n > k$.
   b. What is the average cost of the n push operations?

8. Suppose that instead of doubling the size of an array-based stack when it becomes full, you increase the size of the array by the following sequence $3k, 5k, 7k, 9k, ...$ for some positive constant k.

   a. If you have an empty stack that uses an array whose initial size is k, and you perform n pushes, how many resize operations will be performed? Assume that $n > k$.
   b. What is the average cost of the n push operations?

9. When an array becomes full, you can double its size or use one of the schemes described in Exercises 7 and 8. What are the advantages and disadvantages of each of these three schemes?

10. After doubling the size of an array-based stack, suppose that later fewer than half of the array's locations are actually used by the stack. Describe an implementation that halves the size of the array in this case. What are the advantages and disadvantages of such an implementation?

PROJECTS

1. Implement the ADT stack by using an array `stack` to contain its entries. Expand the array dynamically, as necessary. Choose one of the following possibilities and defend your choice:

- Maintain the stack's bottom entry in `stack[stack.length - 1]`.
- Maintain the stack's top entry in `stack[stack.length - 1]`.

2. Write the implementation of the ADT stack that Exercise 2 describes.

3. Implement the ADT stack by using an instance of either `ExpandableArrayList`, as given in Chapter 5, or `LList`, as given in Chapters 6 and 7, to contain its entries. Discuss the efficiency of your implementation as it relates to the implementation of the list.

4. Write a Java program that uses a stack to test whether an input string is a palindrome. Exercise 9 in Chapter 21 defines "palindrome" and asks you to describe a solution to this problem.

5. The ADT stack lets you peek at its top element without removing it. For some applications of stacks, you also need to peek at the element beneath the top element without removing it. We will call such an operation `peek2`. If the stack has more than one element, `peek2` returns the second element from the top without altering the stack. If the stack has fewer than two elements, `peek2` returns `null`. Write a linked implementation of a stack that includes a method `peek2`.

6. When the client attempts to either retrieve or remove an item from an empty stack, our stacks return `null`. An alternative action is to throw an exception.

a. Modify the interface `StackInterface` so that an `EmptyStackException` is thrown in these cases. (This exception is defined in the package `java.util`.)
b. Modify the array-based implementation of the stack to conform to your changes to `StackInterface`. Write a program that demonstrates the modifications.

7. Suppose that we wish to implement the resizing schemes from Exercises 7 and 8 in addition to the doubling scheme from this chapter.

a. Write a new version of the array-based stack that lets the client specify the resizing scheme and the associated constant when a stack is created.
b. Write a program that demonstrates the modifications.
c. Discuss the advantages and disadvantages of adding methods that allow the client to change the resize scheme and constant after the stack has been created.

23

Queues, Deques, and Priority Queues

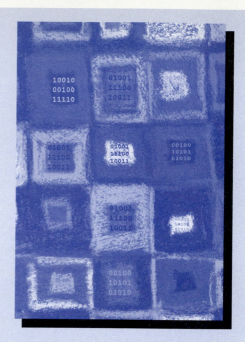

CONTENTS

PREREQUISITES

OBJECTIVES

After studying this chapter, you should be able to

- Describe the operations of the ADT queue
- Use a queue to simulate a waiting line
- Use a queue in a program that organizes data in a first-in, first-out manner
- Describe the operations of the ADT deque
- Use a deque in a program that organizes data chronologically and can operate on both the oldest and newest entries
- Describe the operations of the ADT priority queue
- Use a priority queue in a program that organizes data objects according to their priorities

Waiting for your turn is a fact of life. Most people have spent much time standing in lines at stores, banks, or movie theaters. You have probably waited on the telephone for an airline representative or a technical support person, and you may have waited for your printed output to finally reach the printer in the computer lab. In each of these examples, people wait with the expectation that they will be served before everyone who has come after them. That is, first come, first served.

A **queue** is another name for a waiting line, and it is the name of one of the ADTs that we will investigate in this chapter. Queues are used within operating systems and to simulate real-world events—that is, they come into play whenever processes or events must wait.

Sometimes you need more flexibility than a queue permits. A **double-ended queue**, or **deque**, organizes data like a queue but enables you to operate on both its oldest and newest entries. And when the importance of an object depends on criteria other than its arrival time, you can assign it a priority. You can organize such objects within a **priority queue** according to their priorities instead of chronologically.

The queue, deque, and priority queue are three ADTs that this chapter will explore.

Specifications of the ADT Queue

23.1   Like a stack, the ADT **queue** organizes its entries according to the order in which they were added. But while a stack has a last-in, first-out behavior, a queue exhibits a **first-in**, **first-out**, or **FIFO**, behavior. To achieve this behavior, all additions to a queue are at its **back**. The item added most recently, then, is at the back of a queue. The item that was added earliest is at the **front** of a queue. Figure 23-1 provides examples of some common queues.

Figure 23-1   Some everyday queues

 Note: Among the items in a queue, the one added first, or earliest, is at the **front** of the queue, and the one added most recently is at the **back** of the queue.

A queue, like a stack, restricts access to its entries. Although someone might cut into a line of people, additions to a software queue must occur at its back. A client can look at or remove only the entry at the front of the queue. The only way to look at an entry that is not at the front of a queue is to repeatedly remove items from the queue until the desired item reaches the front. If you were to remove all of a queue's entries one by one, you would get them in chronological order, beginning with the first item added to the queue.

The queue has no search operation. An entry can have a search key, but the key is not relevant to the queue or to the entry's position within the queue.

23.2 The operation that adds an entry to a queue is traditionally called enqueue (pronounced "N-Q"). The operation to remove an entry is dequeue (pronounced "D-Q"). The operation that retrieves the queue's front entry is called getFront. The following specifications define a set of operations for the ADT queue:

Abstract Data Type Queue

DATA

- A collection of objects in chronological order and having the same data type

OPERATIONS

enqueue(newEntry)

Task: Adds a new entry to the back of the queue.
Input: newEntry is the new entry.
Output: None.

dequeue()

Task: Removes and returns the entry at the front of the queue.
Input: None.
Output: Returns either the queue's front entry or, if the queue is empty before the operation, null.

getFront()

Task: Retrieves the queue's front entry without changing the queue in any way.
Input: None.
Output: Returns either the queue's front entry or, if the queue is empty, null.

isEmpty()

Task: Detects whether the queue is empty.
Input: None.
Output: Returns true if the queue is empty.

clear()

Task: Removes all entries from the queue.
Input: None.
Output: None.

> **Note:**   **Alternate names for methods**
> As we mentioned in Chapter 21, class designers often include aliases for certain methods. For a queue, you could include the additional methods `put` and `get` to mean `enqueue` and `dequeue`. The names `add`, `insert`, `remove`, and `delete` are also reasonable aliases. Likewise, you could provide a method `peek` to mean `getFront`.

23.3   The Java interface in Listing 23-1 specifies a queue of objects. The generic type T—which can be any class type—represents the data type of the items in the queue.

Listing 23-1   An interface for the ADT queue

```java
public interface QueueInterface<T>
{
   /** Task: Adds a new entry to the back of the queue.
    *  @param newEntry  an object to be added */
   public void enqueue(T newEntry);

   /** Task: Removes and returns the entry at the front of the queue.
    *  @return either the object at the front of the queue or, if the
    *          queue is empty before the operation, null */
   public T dequeue();

   /** Task: Retrieves the entry at the front of the queue.
    *  @return either the object at the front of the queue or, if the
    *          queue is empty, null */
   public T getFront();

   /** Task: Detects whether the queue is empty.
    *  @return true if the queue is empty, or false otherwise */
   public boolean isEmpty();

   /** Task: Removes all entries from the queue. */
   public void clear();
} // end QueueInterface
```

23.4   **Example: Demonstrating the queue methods.** The following statements add, retrieve, and remove strings from a queue. We assume that the class `LinkedQueue` implements `QueueInterface` and is available.

```java
QueueInterface<String> myQueue = new LinkedQueue<String>();
myQueue.enqueue("Jim");
myQueue.enqueue("Jess");
myQueue.enqueue("Jill");
myQueue.enqueue("Jane");
myQueue.enqueue("Joe");

String front = myQueue.getFront(); // returns "Jim"
System.out.println(front + " is at the front of the queue.");

front = myQueue.dequeue();          // removes and returns "Jim"
System.out.println(front + " is removed from the queue.");

myQueue.enqueue("Jerry");
```

```
front = myQueue.getFront();          // returns "Jess"
System.out.println(front + " is at the front of the queue.");

front = myQueue.dequeue();           // removes and returns "Jess"
System.out.println(front + " is removed from the queue.");
```

Parts *a* through *e* of Figure 23-2 illustrate the five additions to the queue. Following these additions, the queue contains—from front to back—the strings *Jim, Jess, Jill, Jane*, and *Joe*. The string at the front of the queue is *Jim*; getFront retrieves it. The method dequeue retrieves *Jim* again and then removes it from the queue (Figure 23-2f). A subsequent call to enqueue adds *Jerry* to the back of the queue but does not affect the front (Figure 23-2g). Thus, getFront retrieves *Jess*, and dequeue retrieves *Jess* and then removes it (Figure 23-2h).

If we now were to execute dequeue repeatedly until the queue was empty, an additional call to either dequeue or getFront would return null.

Figure 23-2   A queue of strings after (a) enqueue adds *Jim*; (b) enqueue adds *Jess*; (c) enqueue adds *Jill*; (d) enqueue adds *Jane*; (e) enqueue adds *Joe*; (f) dequeue retrieves and removes *Jim*; (g) enqueue adds *Jerry*; (h) dequeue retrieves and removes *Jess*

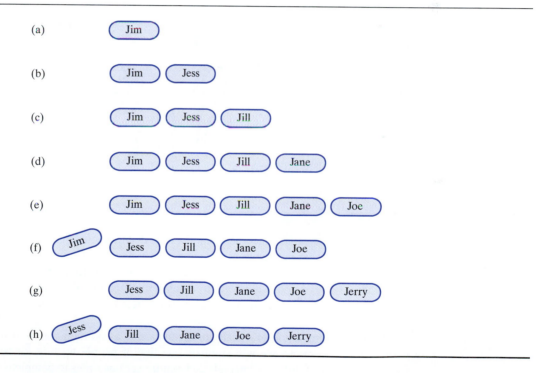

Question 1   After the following nine statements execute, what string is at the front of the queue and what string is at the back?

```
QueueInterface<String> myQueue = new LinkedQueue<String>();
myQueue.enqueue("Jim");
myQueue.enqueue("Jess");
myQueue.enqueue("Jill");
myQueue.enqueue("Jane");
String name = myQueue.dequeue();
```

```
myQueue.enqueue(name);
myQueue.enqueue(myQueue.getFront());
name = myQueue.dequeue();
```

 Programming Tip: Methods such as getFront and dequeue must behave reasonably when the queue is empty. Here, we specify that they return null. Another possibility is to have them throw an exception.

Using a Queue to Simulate a Waiting Line

23.5   In many everyday situations, you will wait in a line. Whether the line is at a store, a ticket window, or a car wash, a line behaves like the ADT queue. The person at the front of the line is served first; newcomers go to the back of the line, as Figure 23-3 shows.

Figure 23-3   A line, or queue, of people

Most businesses are concerned with the time that their customers must wait for service. A short wait time enables an organization to increase customer satisfaction, serve more people, and make more money. If two agents serve one line, you will wait less time than if only one agent is on duty. A business, however, does not want to employ more people than necessary. And a car wash certainly would not build an additional service bay to test its effect on the time its customer's wait in a single line.

Computer simulation of a real-world situation is a common way to test various business scenarios. In this example, we will simulate one line of people waiting for service from one agent. Customers arrive at different intervals and require various times to complete their transactions. One way to achieve this variety is to assume that the events are random.

In a **time-driven simulation**, a counter enumerates simulated units of time—minutes, for example. Customers arrive at random times during the simulation and enter the queue. Each customer is assigned a random transaction time—that is, the amount of time required for the customer's transaction—that does not exceed some arbitrary upper bound. During the simulation, the time that each customer waits in the queue is recorded. At the conclusion of the simulation, summary statistics are generated, including the number of customers served and the average time that each waited.

The Classes `WaitLine` and `Customer`

23.6   **Design.** Two kinds of objects occur in the description of this problem: the waiting line and the customers. We can design a class for each of these.

The class `WaitLine` simulates the waiting line for a given period of time. During this time, customers enter the line at random intervals and leave it after being served. At the conclusion of the simulation, the class computes the summary statistics. Figure 23-4 shows a CRC card for this class.

The class `Customer` records and makes available the customer's arrival time, transaction time, and customer number. Figure 23-5 contains a class diagram for `WaitLine` and `Customer`.

Figure 23-4   A CRC card for the class `WaitLine`

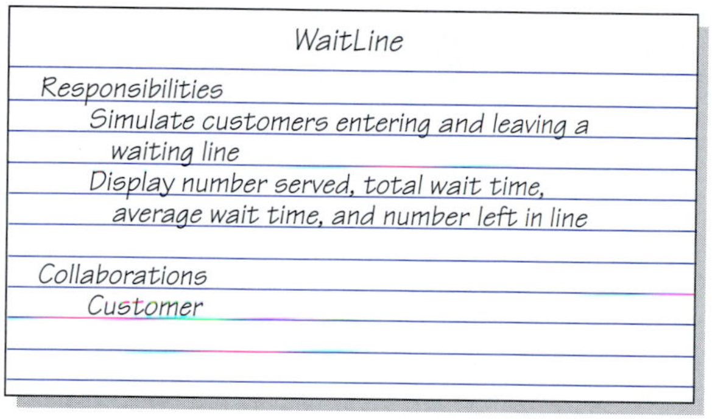

Figure 23-5   A diagram of the classes `WaitLine` and `Customer`

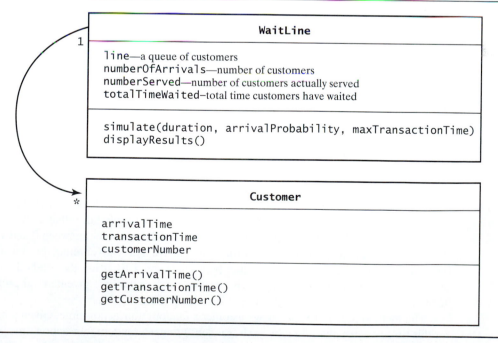

23.7   **The method `simulate`.** The method `simulate` is the heart of this example and of the class `WaitLine`. To maintain the clock for this time-driven simulation, `simulate` contains a loop that counts up to a given duration. For example, the clock could simulate one hour by counting minutes, beginning at 0 and continuing until 60.

At each value of the clock, the method sees whether the current customer is still being served and whether a new customer has arrived. If a new customer arrives, the method creates a new customer object, assigns it a random transaction time, and places the customer into the queue. If a customer is still being served, the clock advances; if not, a customer leaves the front of the queue and begins service. At this point, the time the customer waited is noted. Figure 23-6 provides an example of the queue for a portion of the simulation.

The following pseudocode describes the method `simulate`. It assumes that the class `WaitLine` has initialized its data fields as follows: `line` is an empty queue, and `numberOfArrivals`, `number-Served`, and `totalTimeWaited` are each zero.

```
Algorithm simulate(duration, arrivalProbability, maxTransactionTime)
transactionTimeLeft = 0
for (clock = 0; clock < duration; clock++)
{
  if (a new customer arrives)
  {
    numberOfArrivals++
    transactionTime = a random time that does not exceed maxTransactionTime
    nextArrival = a new customer containing clock, transactionTime, and
                     a customer number that is numberOfArrivals
    line.enqueue(nextArrival)
  }

  if (transactionTimeLeft > 0)  // if present customer is still being served
    transactionTimeLeft--
  else if (!line.isEmpty())
  {
    nextCustomer = line.dequeue()
    transactionTimeLeft = nextCustomer.getTransactionTime() - 1
    timeWaited = clock - nextCustomer.getArrivalTime()
    totalTimeWaited = totalTimeWaited + timeWaited
    numberServed++
  }
}
```

Question 2　Consider the simulation begun in Figure 23-6.

　a.　At what time does Customer 4 finish and depart?
　b.　How long does Customer 5 wait before beginning the transaction?

23.8　**Implementation details for `simulate`.** At each value of the clock, `simulate` must determine whether a new customer has arrived. To do so, it needs the probability that a customer will arrive. This arrival probability is a parameter of the method and has a value between 0 and 1. For example, if there is a 65 percent chance that a customer will arrive at any given time, the arrival probability is 0.65. We then generate a random number between 0 and 1 by using the method `random` in Java's class `Math`. If the value returned by `Math.random()` is less than the given arrival probability, `simulate` creates a new customer and places it into the queue.

The method assigns to each new customer a random transaction time. Given a maximum value for this time, we can multiply it by `Math.random()` to get a random transaction time. Adding 1 to the result ensures that the transaction time is never 0 but allows a small chance that the transaction time will exceed the given maximum value by 1. For simplicity, we will tolerate this small imprecision.

Figure 23-6   A simulated waiting line

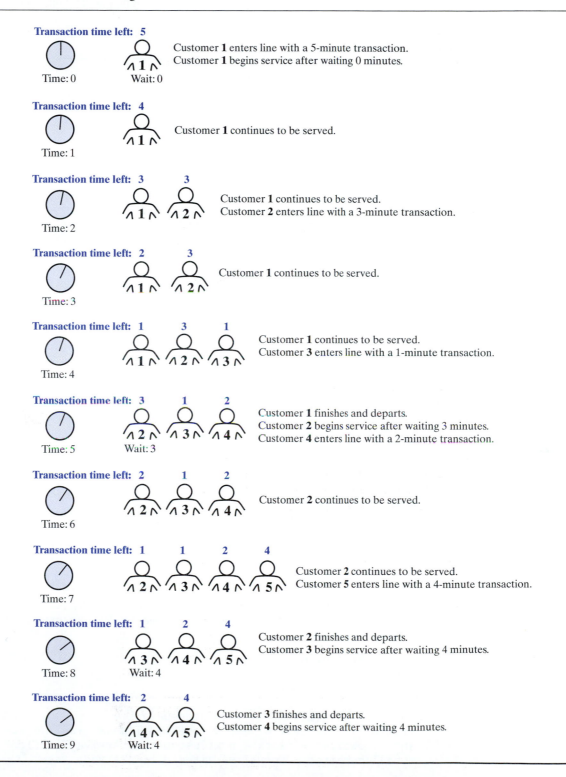

An implementation of the class `WaitList` appears in Listing 23-2. The definition of the method `simulate` contains print statements to help you follow the simulation. The other methods in the class are straightforward.

Listing 23-2   The class `WaitLine`

```java
/** Simulates a waiting line. */
public class WaitLine
{
  private QueueInterface<Customer> line;
  private int numberOfArrivals;
  private int numberServed;
  private int totalTimeWaited;

  public WaitLine()
  {
    line = new LinkedQueue<Customer>();
    reset();
  } // end default constructor

  /** Task: Simulates a waiting line with one serving agent.
   *  @param duration   the number of simulated minutes
   *  @param arrivalProbability   a real number between 0 and 1, and the
   *                              probability that a customer arrives at
   *                              a given time
   *  @param maxTransactionTime   the longest transaction time for a
   *                              customer */
  public void simulate(int duration, double arrivalProbability,
                       int maxTransactionTime)
  {
    int transactionTimeLeft = 0;

    for (int clock = 0; clock < duration; clock++)
    {
      if (Math.random() < arrivalProbability)
      {
        numberOfArrivals++;
        int transactionTime = (int)(Math.random() * maxTransactionTime +
                                    1);
        Customer nextArrival = new Customer(clock, transactionTime,
                                            numberOfArrivals);

        line.enqueue(nextArrival);
        System.out.println("Customer " + numberOfArrivals
                        + " enters line at time " + clock
                        + ". Transaction time is " + transactionTime);
      } // end if

      if (transactionTimeLeft > 0)
        transactionTimeLeft--;
      else if (!line.isEmpty())
      {
        Customer nextCustomer = line.dequeue();
        transactionTimeLeft = nextCustomer.getTransactionTime() - 1;
        int timeWaited = clock - nextCustomer.getArrivalTime();
        totalTimeWaited = totalTimeWaited + timeWaited;
```

```
            numberServed++;
            System.out.println("Customer " + nextCustomer.getCustomerNumber()
                            + " begins service at time " + clock
                            + ". Time waited is " + timeWaited);
        } // end if
      } // end for
   } // end simulate

   /** Task: Displays summary results of the simulation. */
   public void displayResults()
   {
      System.out.println();
      System.out.println("Number served = " + numberServed);
      System.out.println("Total time waited = " + totalTimeWaited);
      double averageTimeWaited = ((double)totalTimeWaited) / numberServed;
      System.out.println("Average time waited = " + averageTimeWaited);
      int leftInLine = numberOfArrivals - numberServed;
      System.out.println("Number left in line = " + leftInLine);
   } // end displayResults

   /** Task: Initializes the simulation. */
   public final void reset()
   {
      line.clear();
      numberOfArrivals = 0;
      numberServed = 0;
      totalTimeWaited = 0;
   } // end reset
} // end WaitLine
```

23.9   **Sample output.** The Java statements

```
      WaitLine customerLine = new WaitLine();
      customerLine.simulate(20, 0.5, 5);
      customerLine.displayResults();
```

simulate the line for 20 minutes with a 50 percent arrival probability and a 5-minute maximum transaction time. They produce the following results:

Customer 1 enters line at time 0. Transaction time is 4
Customer 1 begins service at time 0. Time waited is 0
Customer 2 enters line at time 2. Transaction time is 2
Customer 3 enters line at time 4. Transaction time is 1
Customer 2 begins service at time 4. Time waited is 2
Customer 4 enters line at time 6. Transaction time is 4
Customer 3 begins service at time 6. Time waited is 2
Customer 4 begins service at time 7. Time waited is 1
Customer 5 enters line at time 9. Transaction time is 1
Customer 6 enters line at time 10. Transaction time is 3
Customer 5 begins service at time 11. Time waited is 2
Customer 7 enters line at time 12. Transaction time is 4
Customer 6 begins service at time 12. Time waited is 2

Customer 8 enters line at time 15. Transaction time is 3
Customer 7 begins service at time 15. Time waited is 3
Customer 9 enters line at time 16. Transaction time is 3
Customer 10 enters line at time 19. Transaction time is 5
Customer 8 begins service at time 19. Time waited is 4

Number served = 8
Total time waited = 16
Average time waited = 2.0
Number left in line = 2

Since this example uses random numbers, another execution of the Java statements likely will have different results.

> **Note: Pseudo-random numbers**
> Java's method `Math.random` generates numbers that are uniformly distributed over the interval from 0 to 1. Actual times for processing customer transactions, however, are not uniformly distributed. They are close together, and few times are far from the average transaction time. One such distribution is called a **Poisson distribution**. Ideally, this simulation should use a different pseudo-random number generator. Since our maximum transaction time is small, however, using `Math.random` probably has little effect on the average wait time.

Using a Queue to Compute the Capital Gain in a Sale of Stock

23.10   Suppose that you buy n shares of a stock or mutual fund for d dollars each. Later you sell some of these shares. If the sale price exceeds the purchase price, you have made a profit—a **capital gain**. On the other hand, if the sale price is lower than the purchase price, you experience a loss. We will designate a loss as a negative capital gain.

Typically, investors buy shares in a particular company or fund over a period of time. For example, suppose that last year you bought 20 shares of Presto Pizza at $45 per share. Last month, you bought 20 additional shares at $75 per share, and today you sold 30 shares at $65 per share. What is your capital gain? Well, which of your 40 shares did you actually sell? Unfortunately, you cannot pick and choose. When computing capital gains, you must assume that you sell shares in the order in which you purchased them (meaning that stock sales are a first-in, first-out application). So in our example, you sold the 20 shares that you bought at $45 each and 10 of the shares that you bought at $75 each. Your cost for the 30 shares is $1650. You sold them for $1950, a profit of $300.

The Classes StockLedger and StockPurchase

23.11   **Design.** Let's design a way to record our investment transactions chronologically and to compute the capital gain of any stock sale. To simplify the example, we assume that all transactions are for stocks of a single company and that there is no commission charge for the transactions. The class `StockPurchase` records the cost of a single share of stock.

Figure 23-7 shows a CRC card for the class `StockLedger`. The class enables us to record stock purchases in chronological order. At the time of sale, the class computes the capital gain and updates the record of stocks owned. These last two steps are related, so we combine them into one method. Thus, the class has two methods, `buy` and `sell`, as Figure 23-8 illustrates.

Figure 23-7   A CRC card for the class `StockLedger`

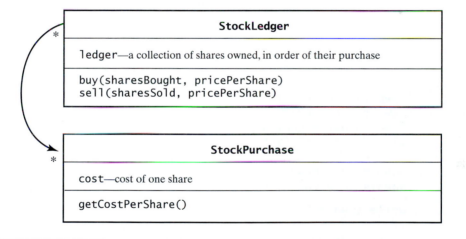

The following statements demonstrate how we could use `StockLedger` to record the transactions given in Segment 23.10:

```
StockLedger myStocks = new StockLedger();
myStocks.buy(20, 45);                  // buy  20 shares at $45
myStocks.buy(20, 75);                  // buy  20 shares at $75
double capGain = myStocks.sell(30, 65); // sell 30 shares at $65
```

23.12   **Implementation.** In this example, `StockLedger` records instances of `StockPurchase`—which represent the shares we own—in a queue. A queue orders the shares chronologically, so we can sell them in the order in which we purchased them. The method buy then just enqueues each share that is bought.

The method `sell` removes from the queue as many shares as are sold. As it does this, it computes the total capital gain from the sale and returns it. The class `StockLedger` is given in Listing 23-3.

Listing 23-3   The class `StockLedger`

```
/** Records the purchase and sale of stocks, and provides the capital
    gain or loss. */
public class StockLedger
{
  private QueueInterface<StockPurchase> ledger;

  public StockLedger()
  {
    ledger = new LinkedQueue<StockPurchase>();
  } // end default constructor

  /** Task: Records a stock purchase in the ledger.
   *  @param sharesBought   the number of shares purchased
   *  @param pricePerShare  the price per share */
  public void buy(int sharesBought, double pricePerShare)
  {
    for (; sharesBought > 0; sharesBought--)
    {
      StockPurchase purchase = new StockPurchase(pricePerShare);
      ledger.enqueue(purchase);
    } // end for
  } // end buy

  /** Task: Removes from the ledger any shares that were sold
   *         and computes the capital gain or loss.
   *  @param sharesSold     the number of shares sold
   *  @param pricePerShare  the price per share
   *  @return the capital gain (loss) */
  public double sell(int sharesSold, double pricePerShare)
  {
    double saleAmount = sharesSold * pricePerShare;
    double totalCost = 0;

    while (sharesSold > 0)
    {
      StockPurchase share = ledger.dequeue();
      double shareCost = share.getCostPerShare();
      totalCost = totalCost + shareCost;
      sharesSold--;
    } // end while

    return saleAmount - totalCost; // gain or loss
  } // end sell
} // end StockLedger
```

23.13   **An observation about this solution.** A typical stock transaction involves multiple shares, and the methods buy and `sell` reflect this reality in their parameters. For example, the invocation `myStocks.buy(30, 45)` indicates a purchase of 30 shares at $45 per share. However, notice that the implementation of buy adds each of the 30 shares to a queue. Figure 23-9a shows such a queue. The advantage of this approach is that `sell` can remove as many or as few shares as necessary.

Suppose that we instead encapsulate the purchase of 30 shares into one object and add it to the queue, as Figure 23-9b illustrates. If we then sell 20 of those shares, we would remove the object from the queue and learn the shares' purchase price. But we would have 10 shares that must remain in the queue. Since these are the oldest shares, we could not simply add them to the back of the queue; they must remain at the front. The ADT queue has no operation that modifies its front entry, nor does it have one to add an object to its front. If each entry is mutable, however, Java will allow the client to modify the one at the front by using the reference that getFront returns. In this case, you would not remove the front entry until you have sold all of the shares it represents. Exercise 10 at the end of this chapter asks you to explore this approach.

On the other hand, if each entry in the queue is immutable, you would not be able to modify it. The queue would not be the right ADT to use when each entry represents more than one share of stock. Segment 23.15 explores another ADT that you can use instead.

Figure 23-9   A queue of (a) individual shares of stock; (b) grouped shares

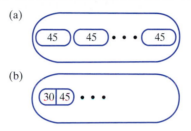

Java Class Library: The Interface Queue

23.14   The standard package java.util in the Java Class Library contains an interface Queue that is similar to our QueueInterface but specifies more methods. We list here a selection of method headers similar to the ones you have seen in this chapter. We have used blue to indicate where they differ from our methods. Once again, T is the generic type.

public boolean add(T newEntry)
Adds a new entry to the back of the queue, returning true if successful and throwing an exception if not.

public boolean offer(T newEntry)
Adds a new entry to the back of the queue, returning true or false according to the success of the operation.

public T remove()
Retrieves and removes the entry at the front of the queue, but throws NoSuchElementException if the queue is empty prior to the operation.

public T poll()
Retrieves and removes the entry at the front of the queue, but returns null if the queue is empty prior to the operation.

public T element()
Retrieves the entry at the front of the queue, but throws NoSuchElementException if the queue is empty.

public T peek()
Retrieves the entry at the front of the queue, but returns null if the queue is empty.

public boolean isEmpty()
Detects whether the queue is empty.

public void clear()
Removes all entries from the queue.

public int size()
Gets the number of elements currently in the queue.

public Iterator<T> iterator()
Returns an iterator for the elements in the queue.

Some of these methods occur in pairs. Both add and offer add a new entry to the queue. If the operation is unsuccessful, add throws an exception but offer returns false. Likewise, each of the methods remove and poll removes and returns the entry at the front of the queue. If the queue is empty before the operation, remove throws an exception but poll returns null. Finally, peek and element each retrieve the entry at the front of the queue. If the queue is empty, element throws an exception but peek returns null.

You can learn more about Queue and the other components of the Java Class Library at java.sun.com/j2se/1.5/docs/api/.

Specifications of the ADT Deque

23.15   Imagine that you are in a line at the post office. When it is finally your turn, the postal agent asks you to fill out a form. You step aside to do so and let the agent serve the next person in the line. After you complete the form, the agent will serve you next. Essentially, you go to the front of the line, rather than waiting in line twice.

Similarly, suppose that you join a line at its end but then immediately decide it is too long, so you leave it. To simulate both of these examples, you want an ADT whose operations enable you to add, remove, or retrieve entries at both the front and back of a queue. Such an ADT is called a **double-ended queue**, or **deque** (pronounced "deck").

A deque has both queuelike operations and stacklike operations. For example, the deque operations addToBack and removeFront resemble the queue operations enqueue and dequeue, respectively. And addToFront and removeFront are like the stack operations push and pop, respectively. In addition, a deque has the operations getFront, getBack, and removeBack. Figure 23-10 illustrates a deque and these methods.

 Note: Although the ADT deque is called a double-ended queue, it actually behaves like a double-ended stack. As Figure 23-10 shows, you can push, pop, or get items at either of its ends.

Figure 23-10 An instance d of a deque

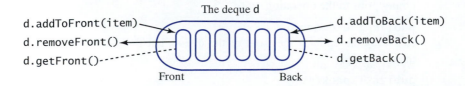

Since the specifications for the deque operations are like those you have already seen for a queue and a stack, we provide the brief Java interface in Listing 23-4 without comments.

Listing 23-4   An interface for the ADT deque

```java
public interface DequeInterface<T>
{
   public void addToFront(T newEntry);
   public void addToBack(T newEntry);
   public T removeFront();
   public T removeBack();
   public T getFront();
   public T getBack();
   public boolean isEmpty();
   public void clear();
} // end DequeInterface
```

A comparison of the operations that add, remove, and retrieve the entries of a stack, queue, and deque is provided in Figure 23-11.

Figure 23-11   A comparison of operations for a stack s, a queue q, and a deque d: (a) add; (b) remove; (c) retrieve

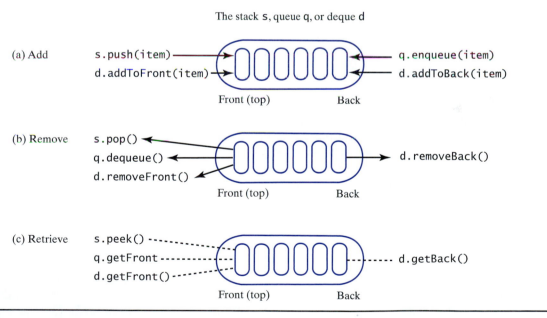

Question 3   After the following nine statements execute, what string is at the front of the deque and what string is at the back?

```java
DequeInterface<String> myDeque = new LinkedDeque<String>();
myDeque.addToFront("Jim");
myDeque.addToBack("Jess");
myDeque.addToFront("Jill");
myDeque.addToBack("Jane");
```

```
String name = myDeque.getFront();
myDeque.addToBack(name);
myDeque.removeFront();
myDeque.addToFront(myDeque.removeBack());
```

23.16   **Example.** When typing at your keyboard, you might make a mistake. If you backspace to correct your mistake, what logic is used to decipher your intention? For example, if the symbol ← represents a backspace, and you type

cm←ompte←←utr←er

the result should be

computer

Each backspace erases the previous character entered.

To replicate this process, as characters are entered, we retain them in an ADT. We want this ADT to be stacklike so we can access the most recently entered character. But since we ultimately want the corrected characters to be in the order in which they were entered, we want the ADT to also behave like a queue. The ADT deque can satisfy these requirements.

The following pseudocode uses a deque to read and display a line of keyboard input:

```
// read a line
d = a new empty dequeue
while (not end of line)
{
    character = next character read
    if (character == ←)
        d.removeBack()
    else
        d.addToBack(character)
}

// display the corrected line
while (!d.isEmpty())
    System.out.print(d.removeFront())
System.out.println()
```

Using a Deque to Compute the Capital Gain in a Sale of Stock

23.17   When we concluded the capital gain example, Segment 23.13 noted that our queue contained individual shares of stock. Since a typical stock transaction involves more than one share, representing a transaction as one object is more natural. But you saw that the transaction object must be mutable if we use a queue. If we use a deque instead, these objects can be either mutable or immutable.

In this section, we revise the implementation, but not the design, of the class StockLedger that was introduced in Segment 23.11. We also revise the class StockPurchase so that it represents the purchase of *n* shares of stock at *d* dollars per share, as Segment 23.13 suggests. The revised class has the data fields shares and cost, a constructor, and the accessor methods getNumberOfShares and getCostPerShare.

We can revise the implementation of the class StockLedger given in Segment 23.12 as follows. The data field ledger is now an instance of a deque instead of a queue. The method buy creates an instance of StockPurchase and places it at the back of the deque, as follows:

```
public void buy(int sharesBought, double pricePerShare)
{
```

```
    StockPurchase purchase = new StockPurchase(sharesBought, pricePerShare);
    ledger.addToBack(purchase);
} // end buy
```

The method `sell` is more involved. It must remove a `StockPurchase` object from the front of the deque and decide whether that object represents more shares than the number sold. If it does, the method creates a new instance of `StockPurchase` to represent the shares that remain in the portfolio. It then adds that instance to the front of the deque, since it is these shares that would be sold next.

```
public double sell(int sharesSold, double pricePerShare)
{
    double saleAmount = sharesSold * pricePerShare;
    double totalCost = 0;

    while (sharesSold > 0)
    {
        StockPurchase transaction = ledger.removeFront();
        double shareCost = transaction.getCostPerShare();
        int numberOfShares = transaction.getNumberOfShares();

        if (numberOfShares > sharesSold)
        {
            totalCost = totalCost + sharesSold * shareCost;
            int numberToPutBack = numberOfShares - sharesSold;
            StockPurchase leftOver = new StockPurchase(numberToPutBack,
                                                       shareCost);
            ledger.addToFront(leftOver); // return leftover shares
            // Note: loop will exit since sharesSold will be <= 0 later
        }
        else
            totalCost = totalCost + numberOfShares * shareCost;

        sharesSold = sharesSold - numberOfShares;
    } // end while

    return saleAmount - totalCost; // gain or loss
} // end sell
```

Specifications of the ADT Priority Queue

23.18   Although a bank serves its customers in the order in which they arrive, an emergency room treats patients according to the urgency of their malady. The bank organizes its customers into chronological order by using a queue. A hospital assigns a **priority** to each patient that overrides the time at which the patient arrived.

The ADT **priority queue** organizes objects according to their priorities. Exactly what form a priority takes depends on the nature of the object. Priorities can be integers, for example. A priority of 1 can be the highest priority, or it can be the lowest. By making the objects `Comparable`, we can hide this detail in the objects' method `compareTo`. The priority queue then can use `compareTo` to compare objects by their priorities. Thus, the priority queue can have the Java interface given in Listing 23-5. We use the notation ? `super` T, which Segment 11.2 of Chapter 11 introduced, to mean any super class of the generic type T.

Listing 23-5   An interface for the ADT priority queue

```java
public interface PriorityQueueInterface<T extends Comparable<? super T>>
{
   /** Task: Adds a new entry to the priority queue.
    *  @param newEntry  an object */
   public void add(T newEntry);

   /** Task: Removes and returns the item with the highest priority.
    *  @return either the object with the highest priority or, if the
    *          priority queue is empty before the operation, null */
   public T remove();

   /** Task: Retrieves the item with the highest priority.
    *  @return either the object with the highest priority or, if the
    *          priority queue is empty, null */
   public T peek();

   /** Task: Detects whether the priority queue is empty.
    *  @return true if the priority queue is empty, or false otherwise */
   public boolean isEmpty();

   /** Task: Gets the size of the priority queue.
    *  @return the number of entries currently in the priority queue */
   public int getSize();

   /** Task: Removes all entries from the priority queue */
   public void clear();
} // end PriorityQueueInterface
```

Question 4   After the following statements execute, what string is at the front of the priority queue and what string is at the back?

```java
PriorityQueueInterface<String> myPriorityQueue =
                        new LinkedPriorityQueue<String>();
myPriorityQueue.add("Jane");
myPriorityQueue.add("Jim");
myPriorityQueue.add("Jill");
String name = myPriorityQueue.remove();
myPriorityQueue.add(name);
myPriorityQueue.add("Jess");
```

Using a Priority Queue to Track Your Assignments

23.19   Professors and bosses like to assign tasks for us to do by certain dates. Let's organize those tasks in the order in which we should complete them. To keep our example simple, we will order them only by their due dates. A task with the earliest due date will have the highest priority.

We can define a class `Assignment` of tasks that includes a data field date representing a task's due date. Figure 23-12 shows a diagram of such a class. We assume that date is an instance of a Comparable class such as java.sql.Date in the Java Class Library. Thus, date.compareTo(otherDate) is negative, for example, if date occurs before otherDate. The compareTo method for Assignment is then

```
public int compareTo(Assignment other)
{
  return -date.compareTo(other.date);
} // end compareTo
```

A more sophisticated version of `Assignment` could include other criteria in `compareTo` to assess priority.

Figure 23-12   A diagram of the class `Assignment`

Assignment
course—the course code task—a description of the assignment date—the due date
getCourseCode() getTask() getDueDate() compareTo()

Note: **The class `java.sql.Date`**

The class `Date` in the package `java.sql` of the Java Class Library has a constructor whose parameter specifies the date as the number of milliseconds since midnight GMT on January 1, 1970. A more convenient way for us to construct a `Date` object is to use the following static method `valueOf`:

public static Date valueOf(String s)
Returns a `Date` object whose value is given by a string s in the form *yyyy-mm-dd*.

For example, the expression `Date.valueOf("2008-02-29")` returns a `Date` object representing February 29, 2008.

`Date` implements the interface `Comparable<Date>` and overrides `toString`.

23.20   We can either add instances of `Assignment` directly to a priority queue or write a simple wrapper class `AssignmentLog` to organize our assignments. As Figure 23-13 shows, `AssignmentLog` has a data field `log`, which is an instance of a priority queue that contains the assignments in priority order. The methods `addProject`, `getNextProject`, and `removeNextProject` manipulate the priority queue indirectly.

An implementation of `AssignmentLog` appears in Listing 23-6.

Listing 23-6   The class `AssignmentLog`

```
import java.sql.Date;
public class AssignmentLog
{
  private PriorityQueueInterface<Assignment> log;
```

Figure 23-13 A diagram of the class `AssignmentLog`

AssignmentLog
log—a priority queue of assignments
addProject(newAssignment) addProject(courseCode, task, dueDate) getNextProject() removeNextProject()

```java
public AssignmentLog()
{
   log = new PriorityQueue<Assignment>();
} // end constructor

public void addProject(Assignment newAssignment)
{
   log.add(newAssignment);
} // end addProject

public void addProject(String courseCode, String task, Date dueDate)
{
   Assignment newAssignment = new Assignment(courseCode, task, dueDate);
   addProject(newAssignment);
} // end addProject

public Assignment getNextProject()
{
   return log.peek();
} // end getNextProject

public Assignment removeNextProject()
{
   return log.remove();
} // end removeNextProject
} // end AssignmentLog
```

23.21   The following statements could appear in a client of `AssignmentLog`:

```java
AssignmentLog myHomework = new AssignmentLog();
myHomework.addProject("CSC211", "Pg 50, Ex 2",
                      Date.valueOf("2007-10-21"));
Assignment pg75Ex8 = new Assignment("CSC215", "Pg 75, Ex 8",
                                    Date.valueOf("2007-10-14"));
myHomework.addProject(pg75Ex8);
. . .
System.out.println("The following assignment is due next:");
System.out.println(myHomework.getNextProject());
```

The assignment with the earliest due date is displayed but is not removed from the assignment log.

CHAPTER SUMMARY

- The ADT queue organizes its entries on a first-in, first-out basis. Among its items, the one added first, or earliest, is at the front of the queue, and the one added most recently is at the back of the queue.

- A queue's major operations—`enqueue`, `dequeue`, and `getFront`—deal only with the ends of the queue. The method `enqueue` adds an entry to the back of the queue; `dequeue` removes and returns the entry at the front of the queue, and `getFront` just returns it.

- You can use a queue to simulate a waiting line. A time-driven simulation counts simulated units of time. Customers arrive at random times, are assigned a random transaction time, and enter a queue.

- When computing the capital gain from a sale of stock, you must sell shares in the order in which you purchased them. If you record your purchases of individual shares in a queue, they will be in the order in which they must be sold.

- A double-ended queue, or deque, has operations that add, remove, or retrieve entries at both its front and back. As such, it combines and expands the operations of a queue and a stack. The deque's major operations are `addToFront`, `removeFront`, `getFront`, `addToBack`, `removeBack`, and `getBack`.

- A priority queue organizes its entries according to their priorities, as determined by the entries' `compareTo` method. Besides adding entries to a priority queue, you can retrieve and remove the entry with the highest priority.

PROGRAMMING TIP

- Methods such as `getFront` and `dequeue` must behave reasonably when a queue is empty. Here, we specify that they return `null`. Another possibility is to have them throw an exception.

EXERCISES

1. If you add the objects x, y, and z to an initially empty queue, in what order will three dequeue operations remove them from the queue?

2. If you add the objects x, y, and z to an initially empty deque, in what order will three `removeBack` operations remove them from the deque?

3. After the following statements execute, what are the contents of the queue?

```
QueueInterface<String> myQueue = new LinkedQueue<String>();
myQueue.enqueue("Jane");
myQueue.enqueue("Jess");
myQueue.enqueue("Jill");
myQueue.enqueue(myQueue.dequeue());
myQueue.enqueue(myQueue.getFront());
myQueue.enqueue("Jim");
String name = myQueue.dequeue();
myQueue.enqueue(myQueue.getFront());
```

4. After the following statements execute, what are the contents of the deque?

```
DequeInterface<String> myDeque = new LinkedDeque<String>();
myDeque.addToFront("Jim");
myDeque.addToFront("Jess");
myDeque.addToBack("Jill");
myDeque.addToBack("Jane");
String name = myDeque.removeFront();
```

```
myDeque.addToBack(name);
myDeque.addToBack(myDeque.getFront());
myDeque.addToFront(myDeque.removeBack());
myDeque.addToFront(myDeque.getBack());
```

5. After the following statements execute, what are the contents of the priority queue?

```
PriorityQueueInterface<String> myPriorityQueue =
                                new LinkedPriorityQueue<String>();
myPriorityQueue.add("Jim");
myPriorityQueue.add("Jess");
myPriorityQueue.add("Jill");
myPriorityQueue.add("Jane");
String name = myPriorityQueue.remove();
myPriorityQueue.add(name);
myPriorityQueue.add(myPriorityQueue.peek());
myPriorityQueue.add("Jim");
myPriorityQueue.remove();
```

6. Consider strings that can be split so that their first half is the same as their second half (ignoring blanks, punctuation, and case). For example, the string "booboo" can be split into "boo" and "boo". Another example is "hello, hello". After ignoring blanks and the comma, the two halves of the string are the same. However, the string "rattan" has unequal halves, as does the string "abcab". Describe how you could use a queue to test whether a string has this property.

7. Complete the simulation begun in Figure 23-6. Let Customer 6 enter the line at time 10 with a transaction time of 2.

8. Assume that customerLine is an instance of the class WaitLine given in Segment 23.8. The call customerLine.simulate(15, 0.5, 5) produces the following random events:

> Customer 1 enters the line at time 6 with a transaction time of 3.
> Customer 2 enters the line at time 8 with a transaction time of 3.
> Customer 3 enters the line at time 10 with a transaction time of 1.
> Customer 4 enters the line at time 11 with a transaction time of 5.

During the simulation, how many customers are served, and what is their average waiting time?

9. Repeat Exercise 8, but instead use the following random events:

> Customer 1 enters the line at time 0 with a transaction time of 4.
> Customer 2 enters the line at time 1 with a transaction time of 4.
> Customer 3 enters the line at time 3 with a transaction time of 1.
> Customer 4 enters the line at time 4 with a transaction time of 4.
> Customer 5 enters the line at time 9 with a transaction time of 3.
> Customer 6 enters the line at time 12 with a transaction time of 2.
> Customer 7 enters the line at time 13 with a transaction time of 1.

10. When using a queue to compute capital gains, we observed in Segment 23.13 that the queue's entries could not both represent more than one share of stock and be immutable. Revise the class `StockPurchase` so that each of its instances is mutable and represents the purchase of multiple shares of one company's stock. Then revise the class `StockLedger`, using a queue to contain the `StockPurchase` objects.

11. Stacks, queues, and deques are similar in operation in many ways. Suppose that we wanted to create an abstract base class `QueueBase` and then use it and inheritance to implement each of the three ADTs. (We used an abstract base class to implement `LListRevised` in Chapter 14.) Design the class `QueueBase`. Indicate whether each field and method should be public, protected, or private, and explain why.

12. Segment 12.21 in Chapter 12 provided the pseudocode for a radix sort of an array. Each bucket in that algorithm is actually a queue. Describe why you can use a queue but not a stack for a radix sort.

13. Exercise 9 of Chapter 21 describes a palindrome. Can you use one of the ADTs described in this chapter instead of a stack to see whether a string is a palindrome? If so, develop an algorithm to do so for each applicable ADT.

14. Consider a special kind of stack that has a finite size but allows an unlimited number of push operations. If the stack is full when a push occurs, the stack makes room for the new entry by deleting the entry at its bottom. A browser that maintains a limited history could use this kind of stack. Implement this stack by using a deque.

PROJECTS

1. Project 3 of Chapter 12 used a list in the implementation of an iterative merge sort. In that project, the list was used as if it were a queue. Repeat the project, but use a queue instead of a list.

2. Implement the radix sort, as given in Segment 12.21 of Chapter 12, by using a queue for each bucket.

3. Expand the capital gains example described in this chapter to allow more than one type of stock in the portfolio. Identify different stocks by using a string for the stock's symbol. Record the shares of each company in a separate queue, deque, or priority queue. Maintain the collection of these ADTs in a list or dictionary.

4. Simulate a small airport with one runway. Airplanes waiting to take off join a queue on the ground. Planes waiting to land join a queue in the air. Only one plane can use the runway at any given time. All planes in the air must land before any plane can take off.

5. Repeat Project 4, but use a priority queue for the planes waiting to land. Develop a priority schedule for situations such as low fuel or mechanical problems.

6. When each object in a collection has a priority, how should you organize several objects that have the same priority? One way is to order the objects with the same priority in chronological order. Thus, you can create a priority queue of queues. Design such an ADT.

7. Write a program to simulate a train route. A train route consists of a number of stations, starting and ending with a terminal station. The time that the train needs to travel between a pair of consecutive stations on the route is given. Associated with each station is a queue of passengers. Passengers are generated at random times, assigned to entry stations randomly, and given random destination stations. Trains leave a terminal at regular intervals and visit the stations on the route. When a train stops at a station, all passengers for that station exit first. Then any passengers waiting in the queue at the station board the train until either the queue is empty or the train is full.

8. Write a program to simulate job scheduling in an operating system. Jobs are generated at random times. Each job is given both a random priority from 1 to 4—where 1 is the highest priority—and a random amount of time to complete its execution.

   Jobs do not begin execution and run to completion, but instead share the processor. The operating system executes a job for a fixed unit of time called a **time slice**. At the end of the time slice, the current job's execution is suspended. The job is then placed on a priority queue, where it waits for its next share of processor time. The job having the highest priority is then removed from the priority queue and executed for a time slice.

   When a job is first generated, it will begin executing immediately if the processor is free. Otherwise it will be placed on the priority queue.

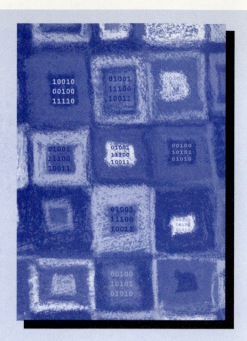

CHAPTER

24

Queue, Deque, and Priority Queue Implementations

OBJECTIVES

After studying this chapter, you should be able to

- Implement the ADT queue by using either a chain of linked nodes, an array, or a vector
- Add nodes to or delete nodes from a chain of doubly linked nodes
- Implement the ADT deque by using a chain of doubly linked nodes
- Implement the ADT priority queue by using either an array or a chain of linked nodes

The implementations of the ADT queue that are in this chapter use techniques like the ones we used to implement the ADT list and the ADT stack. We will use either a chain of linked nodes, an array, or an instance of Vector to store the queue's entries. Although the stack implementations we saw in Chapter 22 were quite simple, the implementations of a queue are a bit more involved.

We also present a linked implementation of the double-ended queue, or deque. Since the deque allows access to both its front and its back, an ordinary chain of linked nodes is not sufficient. For example, deleting the last node in a chain is not possible without a reference to the preceding node. Thus, we use a new kind of chain, one that links its nodes in both directions. That is, a node in this chain references both the next node and the one that precedes it. Such a chain provides an efficient implementation of the deque.

Finally, we suggest some implementations of the ADT priority queue. We note, however, that a more efficient implementation will be possible when we encounter the ADT heap in Chapter 25.

A Linked Implementation of a Queue

24.1   If we use a chain of linked nodes to implement a queue, the two ends of the queue will be at opposite ends of the chain. If we have only a head reference to the chain, accessing the chain's last node will be inefficient. Using a tail reference, as described in Chapter 7, is one approach to this problem and is the one we will take here.

With both head and tail references, which node should be the front of the queue and which node should be the back? We must be able to remove the entry at the front of the queue. If it is at the beginning of the chain, we will be able to remove it easily. If it is at the end of the chain, removing it requires a reference to the preceding node. To get such a reference, we must traverse the chain.

Placing the front of the queue at the beginning of the chain obviously forces the back of the queue to the chain's end. Since we add entries only to the back of the queue, and since we have a tail reference for the chain, this arrangement will work.

Figure 24-1 illustrates a chain of linked nodes with both head and tail references. The chain contains one node for each entry in the queue. Nodes are allocated only when needed for a new entry and are deallocated when an entry is removed.

Figure 24-1   A chain of linked nodes that implements a queue

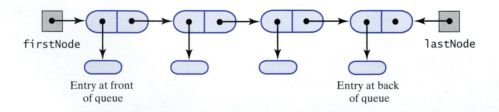

Entry at front
of queue

Entry at back
of queue

24.2   **An outline of the class.** The linked implementation of the queue has two data fields. The field firstNode references the chain's first node, which contains the queue's front entry. And lastNode references the chain's last node, which contains the entry at the back of the queue. Since both of these fields are null when the queue is empty, the default constructor sets them to null. An outline of our class appears in Listing 24-1.

The class also contains the private class Node, like the one you saw in Segment 7.14 of Chapter 7. We also used this class in Chapter 22 for an implementation of the ADT stack.

Listing 24-1   An outline of a linked implementation of the ADT queue

```java
public class LinkedQueue<T> implements QueueInterface<T>,
                                       java.io.Serializable
{
  private Node firstNode; // references node at front of queue
  private Node lastNode;  // references node at back of queue

  public LinkedQueue()
  {
    firstNode = null;
    lastNode = null;
  } // end default constructor
```

< *Implementations of the queue operations go here.* >
. . .

```java
  private class Node implements java.io.Serializable
  {
    private T    data; // entry in queue
    private Node next; // link to next node
```

< *Constructors and the methods* getData, setData, getNextNode, *and* setNextNode
  are here. >
. . .

```java
  } // end Node
} // end LinkedQueue
```

24.3 **Adding to the back.** To add an entry to the back of the queue, we allocate a new node and add it to the end of the chain. If the queue—and therefore the chain—is empty, we make both data fields, firstNode and lastNode, reference the new node, as Figure 24-2 illustrates. Otherwise, both the last node in the chain and the data field lastNode must reference the new node, as shown in Figure 24-3. Thus, the definition of enqueue appears as follows:

```java
public void enqueue(T newEntry)
{
  Node newNode = new Node(newEntry, null);

  if (isEmpty())
    firstNode = newNode;
  else
    lastNode.setNextNode(newNode);

  lastNode = newNode;
} // end enqueue
```

This operation requires no search and is independent of the other entries in the queue. Its performance is thus O(1).

Figure 24-2   (a) Before adding a new node to an empty chain; (b) after adding it

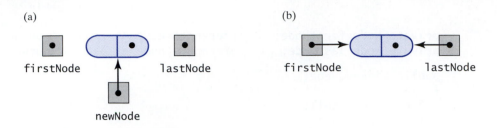

Figure 24-3   (a) Before adding a new node to the end of a chain; (b) after adding it

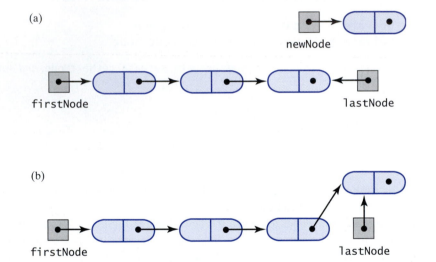

24.4 **Retrieving the front entry.** We get the entry at the front of the queue by accessing the data portion of the first node in the chain. Like enqueue, getFront is an O(1) operation.

```
public T getFront()
{
   T front = null;

   if (!isEmpty())
      front = firstNode.getData();

   return front;
} // end getFront
```

24.5 **Removing the front entry.** The method dequeue retrieves the entry at the front of the queue and then removes the chain's first node by making firstNode reference the second node in the chain, as shown in Figure 24-4. If the chain had only one node, dequeue would make the chain empty by setting both firstNode and lastNode to null, as Figure 24-5 illustrates.

```java
public T dequeue()
{
    T front = null;

    if (!isEmpty())
    {
        front = firstNode.getData();
        firstNode = firstNode.getNextNode();

        if (firstNode == null)
            lastNode = null;
    } // end if

    return front;
} // end dequeue
```

Like enqueue, dequeue requires no search and is independent of the other entries in the queue. Its performance is thus O(1).

Figure 24-4   (a) A queue of more than one entry; (b) after removing the entry at the front of the queue

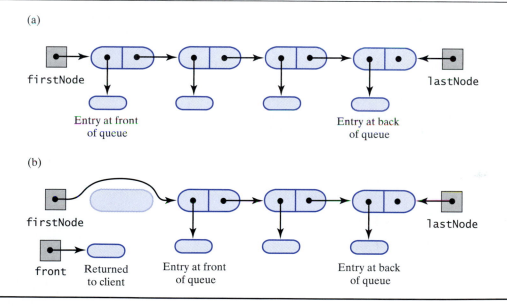

Figure 24-5   (a) A queue of one entry; (b) after removing the entry at the front of the queue

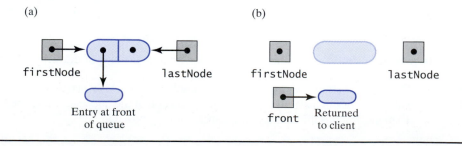

24.6   **The rest of the class.** The remaining public methods `isEmpty` and `clear` are straightforward:

```
public boolean isEmpty()
{
   return (firstNode == null) && (lastNode == null);
} // end isEmpty

public void clear()
{
   firstNode = null;
   lastNode = null;
} // end clear
```

?   **Question 1**   Why is a tail reference desirable when you use a chain of linked nodes to implement a queue?

An Array-Based Implementation of a Queue

24.7   If we use an array `queue` to contain the entries in a queue, we could let `queue[0]` be the queue's front, as Figure 24-6a shows. Here, `frontIndex` and `backIndex` are the indices of the entries at the queue's front and back, respectively. But what happens when we remove the front entry? If we insist that the new front entry be in `queue[0]`, we would need to shift each array element by one position toward the beginning of the array. This arrangement would make the operation `dequeue` inefficient.

Instead, we can leave other array entries in their current positions when we remove the queue's front entry. For example, if we begin with the array in Figure 24-6a and execute `dequeue` twice, the array will be as shown in Figure 24-6b. Not moving array elements is attractive, but after several additions and removals, the array can look like the one pictured in Figure 24-6c. The queue entries have migrated to the end of the array. The last available array location is allocated to the last entry added to the queue. We could expand the array, but the queue has only three entries. Since most of the array is unoccupied, why not use this space for future additions? In fact, that is just what we will do next.

A Circular Array

24.8   Once the queue reaches the end of the array, as in Figure 24-6c, we can add subsequent entries to the beginning of the array. Figure 24-6d shows the array after two such additions to the queue. We make the array behave as though it were **circular**, so that its first location follows its last one. To do this, we use modulo arithmetic on the indices. Specifically, when we add an entry to the queue, we first increment `backIndex` modulo the size of the array. For example, if `queue` is the name of the array, we increment `backIndex` with the statement

```
backIndex = (backIndex + 1) % queue.length;
```

To remove an entry, we increment `frontIndex` modulo the size of the array in a similar fashion.

?   **Question 2**   When we used an array to implement the ADT list, as we did in Chapter 5, we shifted entries in the array. Yet the implementation of the queue just described does not do so. Explain why this difference in implementations is possible.

Figure 24-6   An array that represents a queue without shifting its entries: (a) initially; (b) after removing the entry at the front twice; (c) after several more additions and removals; (d) after two additions that wrap around to the beginning of the array

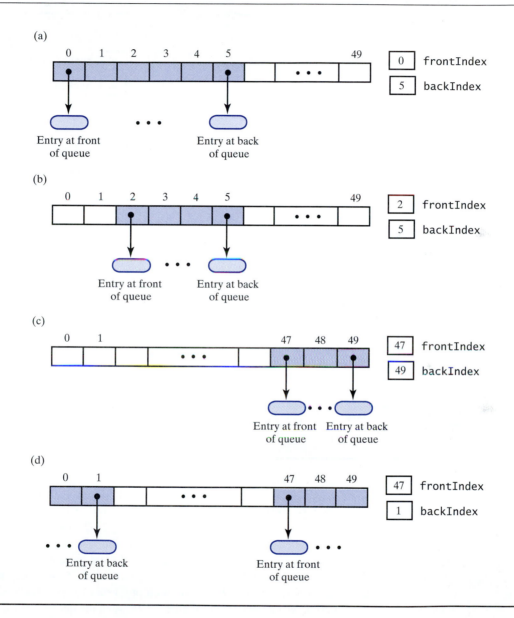

24.9   **Complications.** Using a circular array complicates the implementation somewhat. For example, how can we detect when the array is full? Clearly the array in Figure 24-7a is full. This array is the result of several additions to the queue pictured in Figure 24-6d. So it appears that the queue is full when `frontIndex` is `backIndex + 1`.

Figure 24-7   A circular array that represents a queue: (a) when full; (b) after removing two entries; (c) after removing three more entries; (d) after removing all but one entry; (e) after removing the remaining entry

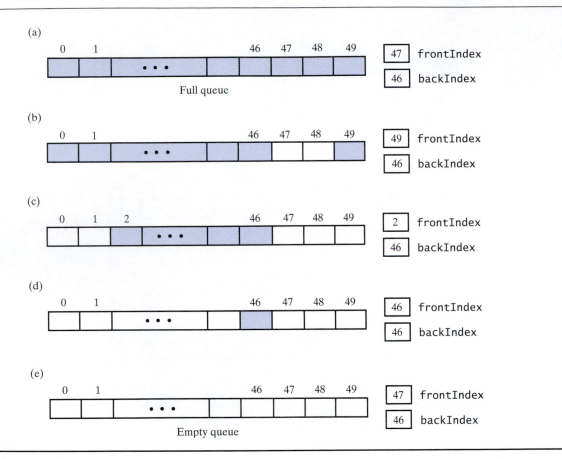

Now remove some entries from the queue. Figure 24-7b shows the array after executing dequeue twice. Notice that frontIndex advances to 49. If we continue to remove items from the queue, frontIndex will wrap around to zero and beyond. Figure 24-7c shows the array after three more items are removed. As we remove more items from the queue, frontIndex advances. Figure 24-7d shows the array after all but one item is removed from the queue. Now let's remove that one item. In Figure 24-7e, we see that this last removal has caused frontIndex to advance so that it is 1 more than backIndex. Although the queue is empty, frontIndex is backIndex + 1. This is exactly the same condition we encountered in Figure 24-7a when the queue was full.

Note: With a circular array, frontIndex equals backIndex + 1 both when the queue is empty and when it is full.

As you can see, we cannot test whether the queue is empty or full by using `frontIndex` and `backIndex`. One solution is to maintain a count of queue items. If the count is zero, the queue is empty; if the count equals the array's capacity, the queue is full. When the queue is full, the next enqueue operation can double the array's size before adding a new entry.

Having a counter as a data field leads to a reasonable implementation, but each enqueue and dequeue must update the count. We can avoid this extra work by leaving one array location unused. We develop this approach next.

A Circular Array with One Unused Location

24.10 Not using one array location allows us to distinguish between an empty queue and a full queue by examining only `frontIndex` and `backIndex`. In Java, each array location contains only a reference, so we waste little memory by having an unused location. Here we will leave unused the array location that follows the back of the queue. Project 2 at the end of this chapter considers a different location.

Figure 24-8 illustrates a seven-element circular array that represents a queue of at most six entries. As we add and remove entries, you should observe the effect on the indices `frontIndex` and `backIndex`. Part *a* of the figure shows the array initially, when the queue is empty. Notice that `frontIndex` is zero and `backIndex` contains the index of the array's last location. Adding an entry to this queue increments the initial value of `backIndex` so that it becomes zero, as shown in Part *b*. Part *c* illustrates the queue after five more additions, making it full. Now remove the front entry and add an entry to the back, as Parts *d* and *e* show. The queue is full once again. Repeating this pair of operations leads to the queues shown in Parts *f* and *g*. Now repeatedly remove the entry at the front until the queue is empty. Part *h* shows the queue after the first of these `dequeue` operations, Part *i* shows it after all but one entry is removed, and Part *j* shows the empty queue.

To summarize, the queue is full in Parts *c*, *e*, and *g* of this figure. In each of these examples, the index of the unused location is 1 more than `backIndex` and 1 less than `frontIndex`, if we treat the array as circular. That is, `frontIndex` is 2 more than `backIndex`. Thus, the queue is full when

```
frontIndex equals (backIndex + 2) % queue.length
```

The queue is empty in Parts *a* and *j*. In those cases, `frontIndex` is 1 more than `backIndex`. Thus, the queue is empty when

```
frontIndex equals (backIndex + 1) % queue.length
```

Admittedly, these criteria are more involved than checking a counter of the number of entries in the queue. However, once we have them, the rest of the implementation is simpler and more efficient because there is no counter to maintain.

24.11 **An outline of the class.** This array-based implementation of a queue begins with four data fields and two constructors. The fields are the array of queue entries, indices to the front and back of the queue, and an initial capacity for the queue that the default constructor creates. Another constructor lets the client choose the initial queue capacity. The initial size of the array is one more than the queue's initial capacity. Listing 24-2 outlines the class.

Listing 24-2 An outline of an array-based implementation of the ADT queue

```java
public class ArrayQueue<T> implements QueueInterface<T>,
                                       java.io.Serializable
{
  private T[] queue; // circular array of queue entries and one unused
                     // location
  private int frontIndex;
  private int backIndex;
  private static final int DEFAULT_INITIAL_CAPACITY = 50;

  public ArrayQueue()
  {
    this(DEFAULT_INITIAL_CAPACITY);
  } // end default constructor

  public ArrayQueue(int initialCapacity)
  {
    queue = (T[]) new Object[initialCapacity + 1];
    frontIndex = 0;
    backIndex = initialCapacity;
  } // end constructor

  < Implementations of the queue operations go here. >
  . . .
} // end ArrayQueue
```

24.12 **Adding to the back.** The method enqueue doubles the size of the array if it is full and places the new entry immediately after the last occupied location in the array. To determine the index of this location, we increment backIndex. But since the array is circular, we use the operator % to make backIndex zero after reaching its maximum value.

```java
public void enqueue(T newEntry)
{
  if (isArrayFull()) // isArrayFull and
    doubleArray();   // doubleArray are private

  backIndex = (backIndex + 1) % queue.length;
  queue[backIndex] = newEntry;
} // end enqueue
```

The methods isArrayFull and doubleArray are private. Their implementations differ from the ones given in Chapter 5 because the array here is circular. We will see how to implement them shortly.

The performance of enqueue when it does not invoke doubleArray is independent of the size of the queue. Thus, it is O(1) in this case. However, its performance degrades to O(n) when the array is full, because doubleArray is an O(n) operation. If this happens, however, the very next enqueue is O(1) again. As we mentioned in Segment 22.9, we could amortize the cost of doubling the array over all additions to the queue. That is, we let all enqueue operations share the cost of executing doubleArray. Unless the array is doubled many times, each enqueue is almost O(1).

Figure 24-8   A seven-location circular array that contains at most six entries of a queue

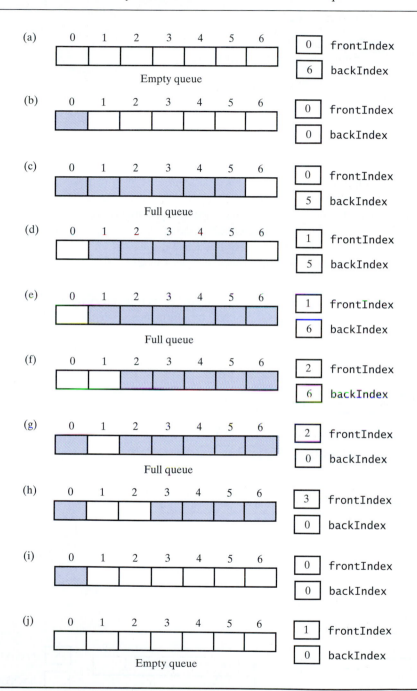

24.13   **Retrieving the front entry.** The method getFront returns either the array element at frontIndex or null if the queue is empty:

```
public T getFront()
{
  T front = null;

  if (!isEmpty())
    front = queue[frontIndex];

  return front;
} // end getFront
```

This operation is O(1).

24.14   **Removing the front entry.** The method dequeue, like getFront, retrieves the entry at the front of the queue, but then it removes it. To remove the front entry of the queue shown in Figure 24-9a, we could simply increment frontIndex, as Figure 24-9b illustrates. This step would suffice because the other methods would behave correctly. For example, getFront would return the item that queue[6] references. However, the object that previously was the front of the queue and is returned to the client would still be referenced by the array. This fact is of no real concern if our implementation is correct. To be safe, dequeue can set queue[frontIndex] to null before incrementing frontIndex. Figure 24-9c illustrates the queue in this case.

Figure 24-9   An array-based queue: (a) initially; (b) after removing its front entry by incrementing frontIndex; (c) after removing its front entry by setting queue[frontIndex] to null and then incrementing frontIndex

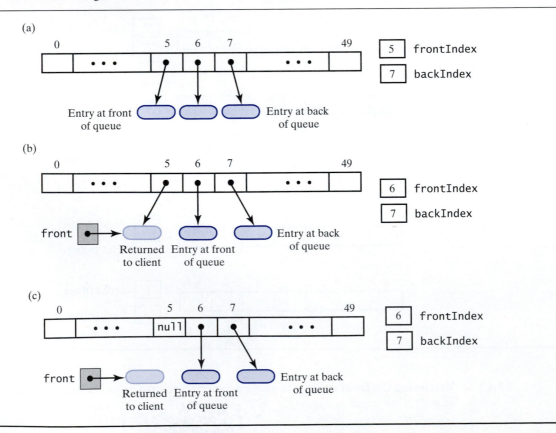

The following implementation of dequeue reflects these comments:

```java
public T dequeue()
{
   T front = null;

   if (!isEmpty())
   {
      front = queue[frontIndex];
      queue[frontIndex] = null;
      frontIndex = (frontIndex + 1) % queue.length;
   } // end if

   return front;
} // end dequeue
```

Like getFront, dequeue is an O(1) operation.

24.15   **The private method doubleArray.** As you saw in Segment 5.15 of Chapter 5, when we increase the size of an array, we must copy its entries into the newly allocated space. We need to be careful, though, because here the array is circular. We must copy entries in the order in which they appear in the queue.

For example, the seven-element array in Figure 24-8g is full. Call this array oldQueue. After allocating a new array queue of 14 locations, we copy the front of the queue from oldQueue[frontIndex] to queue[0]. We continue copying elements from the old array to the new array, proceeding to the end of the old array and wrapping around to its beginning, as Figure 24-10 shows. In addition, doubleArray must set frontIndex and backIndex to reflect the reorganized array.

Figure 24-10 Doubling the size of an array-based queue

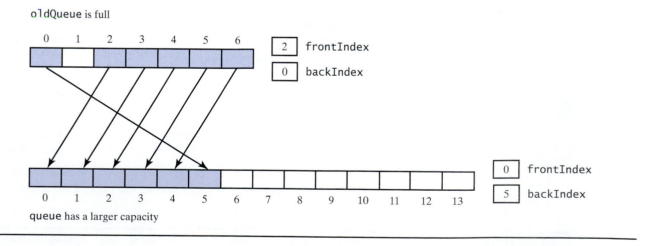

The substantive differences between this method and the analogous method in Chapter 5 appear in color:

```java
private void doubleArray()
{
   T[] oldQueue = queue;
   int oldSize = oldQueue.length;

   queue = (T[]) new Object[2 * oldSize];

   for (int index = 0; index < oldSize - 1; index++)
   {
      queue[index] = oldQueue[frontIndex];
      frontIndex = (frontIndex + 1) % oldSize;
   } // end for

   frontIndex = 0;
   backIndex = oldSize - 2;
} // end doubleArray
```

You can use the method System.arraycopy, as mentioned in Chapter 5, to copy the array. However, since the array is circular, you will need two calls to this method. Exercise 1 at the end of this chapter asks you to revise doubleArray in this way.

24.16   **The rest of the class.** The public method isEmpty and the private method isArrayFull have the following implementations, based on our comments at the end of Segment 24.10:

```java
public boolean isEmpty()
{
   return frontIndex == ((backIndex + 1) % queue.length);
} // end isEmpty

private boolean isArrayFull()
{
   return frontIndex == ((backIndex + 2) % queue.length);
} // end isArrayFull
```

The method clear could simply set frontIndex to 0 and backIndex to queue.length - 1. The other queue methods would behave as expected for an empty queue. However, the objects that were in the queue would then remain allocated. To deallocate them, clear should set to null each array location that was used for the queue. Alternatively, clear could call dequeue repeatedly until the queue is empty, if dequeue sets queue[frontIndex] to null. We leave the implementation of clear as an exercise.

Question 3   Write an implementation of clear that sets to null each array location that was used for the queue.

Question 4   Write an implementation of clear that repeatedly calls dequeue until the queue is empty. How does this implementation compare to the one you wrote for Question 3?

Question 5   If queue is an array that contains the entries in a queue, and queue is not treated as a circular array, what is a disadvantage of maintaining the back of the queue at queue[0]?

Note: In some languages other than Java, leaving an array location empty wastes memory because the location contains an object instead of a reference to an object. Project 3 at the end of this chapter considers an array-based implementation of a queue that does not have an unused location and does not maintain a counter.

A Vector-Based Implementation of a Queue

24.17   Using a vector to represent a queue's entries is relatively easy. We maintain the front of the queue at the beginning of the vector, as Figure 24-11 illustrates. We can use Vector's method add to add an entry to the back of the queue. When we remove the queue's front entry from the vector, the vector's elements move so that the new front entry in the queue will be at the beginning of the vector. Thus, we do not need to maintain indices to the front and back of the queue. Also, the vector expands as necessary, so we do not have to worry about this detail.

Figure 24-11   A vector that represents a queue

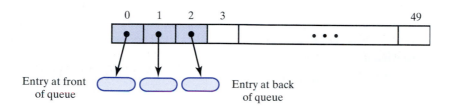

24.18   **An outline of the class.** The class that implements the queue begins by declaring a vector as a data field and allocating the vector in its constructors, as Listing 24-3 shows.

Listing 24-3   An outline of a vector-based implementation of the ADT queue

```java
import java.util.Vector;
public class VectorQueue<T> implements QueueInterface<T>,
                                        java.io.Serializable
{
   private Vector<T> queue; // queue's front entry is first in the vector

   public VectorQueue()
   {
      queue = new Vector<T>(); // vector doubles in size if necessary
   } // end default constructor

   public VectorQueue(int initialCapacity)
   {
      queue = new Vector<T>(initialCapacity);
   } // end constructor

   < Implementations of the queue operations go here. >
   . . .
} // end VectorQueue
```

24.19   **Adding to the back.** We use Vector's method add to add an entry to the end of the vector—that is, to the back of the queue.

```java
   public void enqueue(T newEntry)
   {
      queue.add(newEntry);
   } // end enqueue
```

24.20   **Retrieving the front entry.** We retrieve the entry at the front of the queue by using Vector's method get with an argument of zero:

```java
public T getFront()
{
  T front = null;

  if (!isEmpty())
    front = queue.get(0);

  return front;
} // end getFront
```

24.21   **Removing the front entry.** We can retrieve and remove the entry at the front of the queue by using Vector's method remove with an argument of zero. This method returns the removed entry, which is just what dequeue needs to do:

```java
public T dequeue()
{
  T front = null;

  if (!isEmpty())
    front = queue.remove(0);

  return front;
} // end dequeue
```

24.22   **The rest of the class.** The remaining public methods isEmpty and clear invoke analogous Vector methods:

```java
public boolean isEmpty()
{
  return queue.isEmpty();
} // end isEmpty

public void clear()
{
  queue.clear();
} // end clear
```

24.23   **Efficiency.** The implementation of Vector is based on an array that expands dynamically, but not one that is circular. Since we add entries to one end of a queue and remove them from the other end, the vector implementation inherently moves its entries after each removal. Thus, dequeue is O(n), while the other operations are O(1). However, expanding the vector degrades the performance of enqueue. The efficiency of this implementation is not as good as that of the one that uses a circular array.

24.24   We can also use an instance of the ADT list—such as Java's ArrayList or our ExpandableArray-List—to represent a queue. Such an implementation is similar to the vector implementation, and we leave it to you as an exercise.

Circular Linked Implementations of a Queue

24.25   Figure 24-1 in Segment 24.1 shows a chain of linked nodes that implements the ADT queue. This chain has two external references—one to the first node and one to the last node in the chain. Recall that these references are particularly useful for a queue implementation, since a queue's operations affect both of its ends. Like the chains you have seen before, the last node in this chain contains null. Such chains are sometimes called **linear linked chains**, regardless of whether they have a tail reference in addition to a head reference.

In a **circular linked chain**, the last node references the first node, so no node contains null in its next field. Despite the fact that each node references the next node, a circular linked chain has a beginning and an end. We could have an external reference to the chain's first node, but then a traversal of the chain would be necessary to locate the last node. Having both a reference to the first node and a reference to the last node is usually more than is necessary. Since the chain's last node references its first node, we can have a solitary reference to the last node and still locate the first node quickly. Figure 24-12 illustrates such a chain.

When a class uses a circular linked chain to represent a queue, its only data field is the reference lastNode to the chain's last node. The implementation therefore does not have the overhead of maintaining a data field that references the first node. Any time such a reference is needed, the expression lastNode.getNextNode() provides it. Despite this simplification, this approach is not necessarily better than the one used in the first section of this chapter. It is mostly just different, as you will see if you complete Project 4 at the end of this chapter.

We now investigate another way to use a circular linked chain to represent a queue.

Figure 24-12 A circular linked chain with an external reference to its last node that (a) has more than one node; (b) has one node; (c) is empty

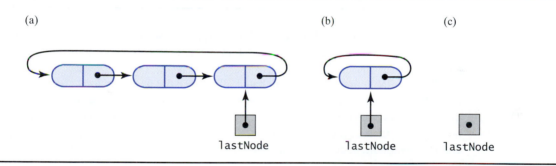

(a)

(b)

(c)

lastNode   lastNode   lastNode

A Two-Part Circular Linked Chain

24.26   When a linked chain—whether it is linear or circular—represents a queue, it has one node for each entry in the queue. When we add an entry to the queue, we allocate a new node for the chain. When we remove an entry from the queue, a node is deallocated.

In the circular array implementation, the queue uses a subset of the fixed number of array locations available. When we add an entry to the queue, we use the next unoccupied location in the array. When we remove an entry from the queue, we make its array location available for the queue's later use. Since additions and removals are at the ends of a queue, the queue occupies contiguous locations in the circular array. The available locations also are contiguous, again because the array is circular. Thus, the circular array has two parts: One part contains the queue and the other part is available for the queue.

Suppose that we had two parts in a circular linked chain. The linked nodes that form the queue are followed by linked nodes that are available for use in the queue, as Figure 24-13 illustrates. Here queueNode references the node assigned to the front of the queue; freeNode references the

Figure 24-13 A two-part circular linked chain that represents both a queue and the nodes available to the queue

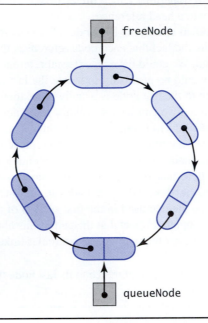

first available node that follows the end of the queue. You could think of this configuration as two chains—one for the queue and one for the available nodes—that are joined at their ends to form a circle.

The available nodes are not allocated all at once the way locations are allocated for an array. Initially there are no available nodes; we allocate a node each time we add a new entry to the queue. However, when we remove an entry from the queue, we keep its node in the circle of nodes rather than deallocating it. Thus, a subsequent addition to the queue uses a node from the chain of available nodes. But if no such node is available, we allocate a new one and link it into the chain.

24.27 Detecting an empty queue or an absence of available nodes is easier if one node in the circular linked chain is unused. The situation is analogous to the circular array that we used in Segment 24.10. Figure 24-14a shows the queue when it is empty. Both queueNode and freeNode reference the same unused node. Notice that the node references itself. We can tell that the queue is empty because queueNode equals freeNode.

To add an entry to this empty queue, we allocate a new node and link it into the circular chain. Figure 24-14b shows the resulting chain for a queue of one entry. To simplify the figure, we have not illustrated the actual object in the queue. Although a node in the chain references an object in the queue, we will sometimes say that the node is in the queue.

While queueNode references the node assigned to the queue, freeNode still references the unused node. After three more additions to the queue, three more nodes are allocated and linked into the chain. Segment 24.29 will describe exactly how to accomplish this. The chain now appears as in Figure 24-14c. Again, freeNode references the unused node. Since queueNode references the node at the front of the queue, retrieving the front entry is easy.

Figure 24-14 A two-part circular linked chain that represents a queue: (a) when it is empty; (b) after adding one entry; (c) after adding three more entries; (d) after removing the front entry; (e) after adding one more entry

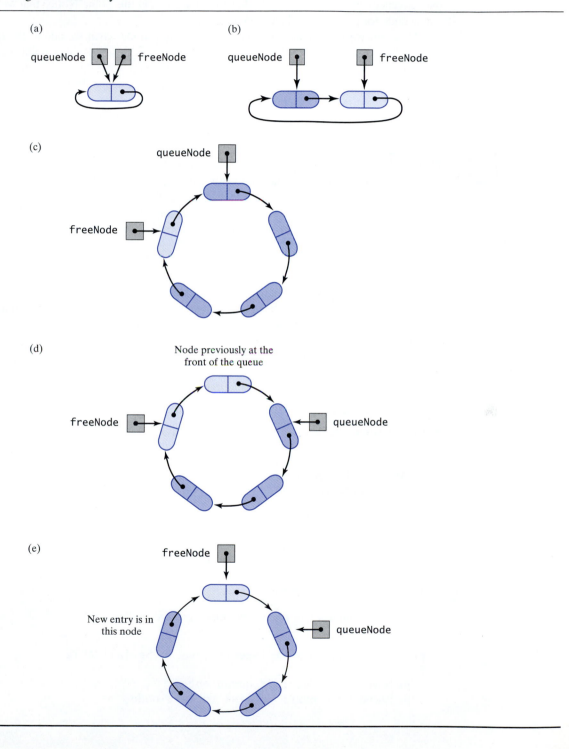

Now if we remove the entry at the front of the queue, we advance queueNode so the chain is as pictured in Figure 24-14d. The node that was at the front of the queue is not deallocated. A subsequent addition—since it is at the back of the queue—uses the node that freeNode references. We then advance freeNode. Figure 24-14e shows the chain at this point. Notice that we did not allocate a new node for the additional entry in this case.

How can we tell whether we must allocate a new node when we add to the queue? We must do so if we want to add to the queue shown in Figure 24-14e. At this point, queueNode equals freeNode.getNextNode(). That was not the case when we added an entry to the queue in Figure 24-14d; a node was available without allocating a new one. But notice in Figure 24-14a that queueNode also equals freeNode.getNextNode() when the queue is empty. This makes sense, because to add to an empty queue, we need to allocate a new node.

Note: In a two-part circular linked implementation of a queue, one node is unused. Two external references partition the chain into two parts: queueNode references the front node of the queue and freeNode references the node that follows the queue. The queue is empty if queueNode equals freeNode. You use the node at freeNode for a new entry. This node is either the first available node or the unused node. You must allocate a new unused node if queueNode equals freeNode.getNextNode().

24.28   **An outline of the class.** The class that implements the queue by using a two-part circular linked chain has the references queueNode and freeNode as data fields. Since the chain must always contain at least one node, the default constructor allocates a node, makes the node reference itself, and sets queueNode and freeNode to reference this new node. Thus, the class appears as outlined in Listing 24-4.

Listing 24-4   An outline of a two-part circular linked implementation of the ADT queue

```
public class TwoPartCircularLinkedQueue<T> implements QueueInterface<T>,
                                                       java.io.Serializable
{
  private Node queueNode; // references first node in queue
  private Node freeNode;  // references node after back of queue

  public TwoPartCircularLinkedQueue()
  {
    freeNode = new Node(null, null);
    freeNode.setNextNode(freeNode);
    queueNode = freeNode;
  } // end default constructor

  < Implementations of the queue operations go here. >
  . . .

  private class Node implements java.io.Serializable
  {
    private T    data; // queue entry
    private Node next; // link to next node
```

> < *Constructors and the methods* getData, setData, getNextNode, *and* setNextNode
> *are here.* >
>   . . .
>   } // end Node
> } // end TwoPartCircularLinkedQueue

Programming Tip: When a circular linked chain has one node, the node must reference itself. Forgetting this step is easy to do and leads to an error during execution.

24.29 **Adding to the back.** Before adding an entry to the queue, we see whether a node is available in the chain. If one is not, we must allocate a new one and link it into the chain. We insert a new node into the chain *after* the node that freeNode references, as we are about to do in Figure 24-15a. We do not insert it before this node, because we would need a reference to the previous node to do so. Getting such a reference would take time. The node that freeNode references joins the queue and will contain the new entry. The new node becomes the unused node, and we make freeNode reference it, as Figure 24-15b shows.

Figure 24-15 A chain that requires a new node for an addition to a queue: (a) before the addition; (b) after the addition

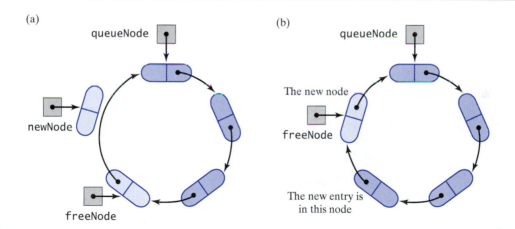

If a node is available in the chain, we use the node that freeNode references for the new entry. Figure 24-16 shows the chain before and after two existing nodes become part of the queue. After each addition, freeNode references the node that follows the back of the queue. In Figure 24-16b, this node is available for another addition, but in Figure 24-16c, it is unused.

The method enqueue is easier to write and to understand if we hide the detail of seeing whether to allocate a new node within the private method isChainFull. It returns true if the chain has no nodes available for use in the queue. The implementation of isChainFull is not difficult and appears later in Segment 24.32.

Figure 24-16 (a) A chain with nodes available for additions to a queue; (b) the chain after one addition; (c) the chain after another addition

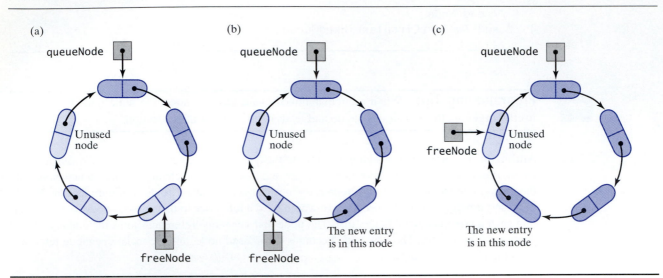

The following implementation of enqueue is an O(1) operation:

```
public void enqueue(T newEntry)
{
    freeNode.setData(newEntry);

    if (isChainFull())
    {
        // allocate a new node and insert it after the node that
        // freeNode references
        Node newNode = new Node(null, freeNode.getNextNode());
        freeNode.setNextNode(newNode);
    } // end if

    freeNode = freeNode.getNextNode();
} // end enqueue
```

Question 6   Adding an entry to the queue pictured in Figure 24-16c requires the creation of a new node. Where in the chain would you insert the new node? Which node would contain the new entry?

24.30   **Retrieving the front.** If the queue is not empty, queueNode references its front node. The method getFront is therefore straightforward:

```
public T getFront()
{
    T front = null;

    if (!isEmpty())
        front = queueNode.getData();
```

```
      return front;
   } // end getFront
```

This method is O(1).

24.31   **Removing the front.** The method `dequeue` returns the entry at the front of the queue. It then moves the node at the front from the queue's part of the chain to the available part simply by advancing `queueNode`. Parts *c* and *d* of Figure 24-14 show a chain before and after this step. Since the node that contained the removed entry is not deallocated, it still references the removed entry. Thus, we set the node's data portion to `null`.

Like `getFront`, `dequeue` is an O(1) operation:

```
public T dequeue()
{
   T front = null;

   if (!isEmpty())
   {
      front = queueNode.getData();
      queueNode.setData(null);
      queueNode = queueNode.getNextNode();
   } // end if

   return front;
} // end dequeue
```

24.32   **The rest of the class.** The methods `isEmpty` and `isChainFull` follow from the discussion in Segment 24.27:

```
public boolean isEmpty()
{
   return queueNode == freeNode;
} // end isEmpty

private boolean isChainFull()
{
   return queueNode == freeNode.getNextNode();
} // end isChainFull
```

The method `clear` sets `queueNode` equal to `freeNode` to make the queue appear empty. It retains all nodes currently in the chain. However, unless you set the data portions of these nodes to `null`, the objects in the queue are not deallocated. We leave the implementation of `clear` as an exercise.

Question 7   Describe two different ways in which you could implement the method `clear`.

24.33   **Choosing a linked implementation.** So far, we have discussed several possible linked implementations of the ADT queue. You can use a linear chain with both head and tail references, as shown in Figure 24-1, or an equivalent circular chain with one external reference, as shown in Figure 24-12. In both of these implementations, removing an entry from the queue disconnects and deallocates a node in the chain. If, after removing entries from the queue, you seldom add entries, these implementations are fine. But if you frequently add an entry after removing one, the two-part circular chain saves the time of deallocating and reallocating nodes.

Java Class Library: The Class AbstractQueue

24.34   The standard package `java.util` in the Java Class Library contains the abstract class `Abstract-Queue`. This class implements the interface `java.util.Queue` and does not allow `null` entries in the queue. Recall from Segment 23.14 of the previous chapter the following methods in this interface:

```
public boolean add(T newEntry)
public boolean offer(T newEntry)
public T remove()
public T poll()
public T element()
public T peek()
public boolean isEmpty()
public void clear()
public int size()
public Iterator<T> iterator()
```

AbstractQueue provides implementations of the methods `add`, `remove`, and `element` that invoke `offer`, `poll`, and `peek`, respectively.

You can define a class of queues by using inheritance to extend `AbstractQueue`. Your class must override at least the following methods: `offer`, `poll`, `peek`, `size`, and `iterator`.

To learn more about `AbstractQueue`, consult the Web site at `java.sun.com/j2se/1.5/docs/api/`.

A Doubly Linked Implementation of a Deque

24.35   Earlier, in Segment 24.1, we planned the linked implementation of the queue and noticed that the front of the queue should not be at the tail of the chain of linked nodes. If it were, we would have to traverse the chain to get a reference to the preceding node so that we could remove the queue's front entry.

Although placing the front of the queue at the head of the chain solved our problem, such is not the case for a deque. We must be able to remove both the front *and* the back of a deque. So even if the deque's front is at the head of the chain, the deque's back will be at the chain's tail—and therein lies the problem.

Each node in a chain references only the next node. Thus, a chain, with its head reference, permits us to begin at the first node and move ahead from node to node. Having a tail reference lets us access the last node in the chain, but not the next-to-last node. That is, we cannot move backward from a node, and this is just what we need to do to remove the back of a deque.

24.36   What we need is a node that can reference the previous node as well as the next node in a chain. We call a chain of such nodes a **doubly linked chain**. We sometimes will call an ordinary chain a **singly linked chain** when a distinction is necessary. Figure 24-17 illustrates a doubly linked chain with its head and tail references. While an interior node references both the next node and the previous node, the first and last nodes each contain one `null` reference. Thus, when traversing the chain from the first node to the last, we will encounter `null` when we reach the last node. Likewise, when traversing the chain from the last node to the first, we will encounter `null` when we reach the first node.

Figure 24-17 A doubly linked chain with head and tail references

firstNode   lastNode

The node in a doubly linked chain is an instance of an inner class similar to the class Node. We will call this inner class DLNode and give it three data fields: next and previous are references to two other nodes, and data is a reference to the node's data. DLNode also has the methods getData, setData, getNextNode, setNextNode, getPreviousNode, and setPreviousNode.

24.37   **An outline of the class.** The doubly linked implementation of the deque begins much like the linked implementation of the queue given in Segment 24.2. The class has two data fields— firstNode and lastNode—that the default constructor sets to null, as you can see in Listing 24-5.

Listing 24-5   An outline of a linked implementation of the ADT deque

```java
public class LinkedDeque<T> implements DequeInterface<T>,
                                       java.io.Serializable
{
  private DLNode firstNode; // references node for front of deque
  private DLNode lastNode;  // references node for back of deque

  public LinkedDeque()
  {
    firstNode = null;
    lastNode = null;
  } // end default constructor

  < Implementations of the deque operations go here. >
  . . .

  private class DLNode implements java.io.Serializable
  {
    private T     data;     // deque entry
    private DLNode next;     // link to next node
    private DLNode previous; // link to previous node

    < Constructors and the methods getData, setData, getNextNode, setNextNode,
      getPreviousNode, and setPreviousNode are here. >
    . . .
  } // end DLNode
} // end LinkedDeque
```

24.38   **Adding an entry.** The implementation of the method addToBack is like the implementation of enqueue given in Segment 24.3. Both methods add a node to the end of a chain so that the chain's current last node references the new node. Here, we also make the new node reference the current last node by passing the deque's data field lastNode to the node's constructor. The addition to the back of a chain that is not empty is illustrated in Figure 24-18. An implementation of the method follows:

```java
public void addToBack(T newEntry)
{
    DLNode newNode = new DLNode(lastNode, newEntry, null);

    if (isEmpty())
        firstNode = newNode;
    else
        lastNode.setNextNode(newNode);

    lastNode = newNode;
} // end addToBack
```

Aside from its name, this method differs from `enqueue` only in the statement that allocates a new node.

Figure 24-18 Adding to the back of a nonempty deque: (a) after the new node is allocated; (b) after the addition is complete

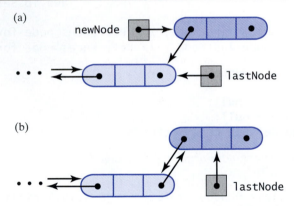

The method `addToFront` has an analogous implementation. When adding a node to the beginning of a doubly linked chain, we must make the chain's current first node reference the new node by passing the deque's data field `firstNode` to the node's constructor. Compare the following definition for `addToFront` with the one just given for `addToBack`:

```java
public void addToFront(T newEntry)
{
    DLNode newNode = new DLNode(null, newEntry, firstNode);

    if (isEmpty())
        lastNode = newNode;
    else
        firstNode.setPreviousNode(newNode);

    firstNode = newNode;
} // end addToFront
```

As given here, both `addToFront` and `addToBack` are O(1) operations.

24.39 **Removing an entry.** The method removeFront has an implementation much like that of dequeue given in Segment 24.5, but it has one other concern. After detaching the first node, if the deque is not empty, removeFront must set the field previous in the new first node to null. This step occurs in the else clause of the following definition:

```java
public T removeFront()
{
  T front = null;

  if (!isEmpty())
  {
    front = firstNode.getData();
    firstNode = firstNode.getNextNode();

    if (firstNode == null)
      lastNode = null;
    else
      firstNode.setPreviousNode(null);
  } // end if

  return front;
} // end removeFront
```

Aside from its name, this method differs from dequeue only in the addition of the else clause. Figure 24-19 illustrates the effect of removeFront for a deque of at least two entries.

The method removeBack has an analogous definition:

```java
public T removeBack()
{
  T back = null;

  if (!isEmpty())
  {
    back = lastNode.getData();
    lastNode = lastNode.getPreviousNode();

    if (lastNode == null)
      firstNode = null;
    else
      lastNode.setNextNode(null);
  } // end if

  return back;
} // end removeBack
```

The implementations of removeFront and removeBack are each O(1).

24.40 **Retrieving an entry.** The method getFront has the same implementation as given in Segment 24.4 for a queue. The method getBack is analogous to getFront and is left as an exercise. Both getFront and getBack are O(1) operations.

Question 8   Implement the method getBack for the ADT deque when a doubly linked chain contains the deque's entries.

Figure 24-19   (a) A deque containing at least two entries; (b) after removing the first node and obtaining a
reference to the deque's new first entry

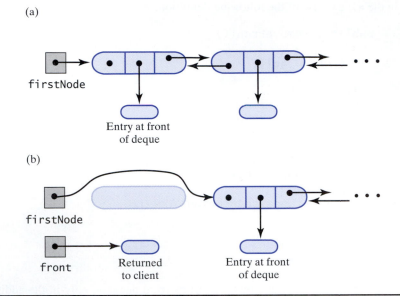

(a)

firstNode

Entry at front
of deque

(b)

firstNode

front

Returned
to client

Entry at front
of deque

24.41   **Reusing this implementation.** Once you have implemented the ADT deque, you can use it to implement other ADTs such as the queue and the stack. These implementations are straightforward and are left as exercises.

Note: In a doubly linked chain, the first and last nodes each contain one `null` reference, since the first node has no previous node and the last node has no node after it. In a **circular doubly linked chain**, the first node references the last node, and the last node references the first. Only one external reference is necessary—a reference to the first node—since you can quickly get to the last node from the first node. You can use a circular doubly linked chain in an implementation of the ADT deque. Project 8 asks you to do this.

Possible Implementations of a Priority Queue

24.42   We can use an array, a linked chain, or a sorted list to implement the ADT priority queue. In each of these cases, we would maintain the entries in sorted order by their priorities. With an array, the entry with the highest priority should occur at the end of the array, so removing it would leave the other entries in their present places. Figure 24-20a illustrates this implementation.

If a linked chain contains the entries in a priority queue, the entry with the highest priority should occur at the beginning of the chain, where it is easy to remove. Figure 24-20b shows such a chain.

A sorted list can maintain a priority queue's entries in priority order, doing much of the work for us. Project 13 at the end of this chapter asks you to complete such an implementation.

The next chapter describes a more efficient implementation of a priority queue that uses an ADT called a **heap**.

Figure 24-20 Two possible implementations of a priority queue using (a) an array; (b) a chain of linked nodes

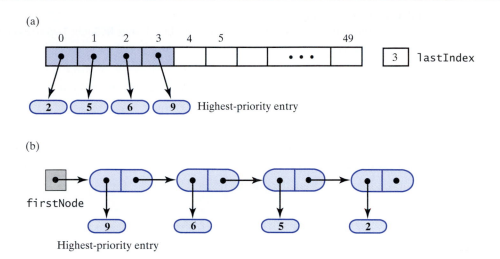

(a)

(b)

firstNode

Highest-priority entry

Highest-priority entry

lastIndex

Java Class Library: The Class `PriorityQueue`

24.43   The class `PriorityQueue`, which is in the package `java.util`, extends `java.util.AbstractQueue` and implements the methods declared in the interface `java.util.Queue`. However, the behaviors of these methods adhere to the specifications of the ADT priority queue instead of the ADT queue.

The class provides several constructors. The following two constructors create priority queues whose elements must implement the `Comparable` interface. These priority queues order their elements by using the method `compareTo` such that the element with the smallest value has the highest priority.

```
PriorityQueue()
```
Creates a priority queue with an initial capacity of 11 elements.

```
PriorityQueue(int initialCapacity)
```
Creates a priority queue with a given initial capacity.

The following methods are specified as follows within the class `PriorityQueue`:

```
public boolean add(T newEntry)
```
Adds a new entry to the priority queue, returning true if successful or throwing an exception if not.

```
public boolean offer(T newEntry)
```
Adds a new entry to the priority queue, returning true or false according to the success of the operation.

```
public T remove()
```
Retrieves and removes the entry having the highest priority, but throws `NoSuchElement Exception` if the priority queue is empty before the operation.

public T poll()
Retrieves and removes the entry having the highest priority, but returns null if the priority queue is empty before the operation.

public T element()
Retrieves the entry having the highest priority, but throws NoSuchElementException if the priority queue is empty.

public T peek()
Retrieves the entry having the highest priority, but returns null if the priority queue is empty.

public boolean isEmpty()
Detects whether the priority queue is empty.

public void clear()
Removes all entries from the priority queue.

public int size()
Gets the number of objects in the priority queue.

public Iterator<T> iterator()
Returns an iterator of the objects in the priority queue, but the order of traversal is unspecified.

The Web site at java.sun.com/j2se/1.5/docs/api/ describes the class PriorityQueue in more detail.

CHAPTER SUMMARY

- You can implement a queue by using a chain of linked nodes that has both a head reference and a tail reference. The first node in the chain represents the front of the queue, because you can remove or access a chain's first node faster than any other node. The tail reference allows you to quickly add a node to the end of the chain, which is the queue's back.

- The queue operations are O(1) for a linked implementation.

- You can implement a queue by using an array. Once a queue entry is added to the array, it does not move. After many additions, the last array location will be used. Removals, however, will free locations at the beginning of the array. Thus, the array can appear full even when it is not. To solve this problem, you treat the array as if it were circular.

- The queue operations are O(1) for an array-based implementation. However, when the array is full, **enqueue** doubles the size of the array. In that case, **enqueue** is O(n). Typically, we amortize the cost of doubling the array over all additions to the queue. If the array is doubled occasionally, each **enqueue** is almost O(1).

- You can implement a queue by using a vector. Since the entry at the front of the queue is always first in the vector, and since the implementation of **Vector** is based on an array that is expanded as necessary, entries in the vector move. Thus, the vector-based implementation is less efficient than our array-based implementation. However, it is easier to write.

- In a circular linked chain, every node references the next node in the chain. No node contains **null** in its **next** field. A circular linked chain can have a beginning and an end. Since the last node references the first node in the chain, one external reference to the last node provides convenient access to both the chain's last node and its first node.

- You can use a circular linked chain to implement a queue in much the same way that you use a linear linked chain that has both head and tail references. With both kinds of chain, **dequeue** removes a node and deallocates it.

- Another implementation of a queue uses a circular linked chain that has two parts. One part is used for the queue and the other part contains one unused node and any nodes that are available for use. In this implementation, **dequeue** removes an entry from the queue but does not remove a node from the chain. Instead, the node joins the available part of the chain.

- Since a deque has operations that add and remove entries at both ends, you can use a doubly linked chain whose nodes reference both the next node and the previous node. A doubly linked chain with head and tail references provides O(1) implementations of the deque operations.

- In a circular doubly linked chain, every node references the next node as well as the previous node in the chain. No node contains **null** in its **next** and **previous** fields. One external reference to the first node provides fast access to both the chain's last node and its first node. You can use a circular doubly linked chain in the implementation of a deque.

- You can use an array, a chain, or a sorted list to implement a priority queue, but a more efficient implementation is possible by using a heap.

PROGRAMMING TIP

- When a circular linked chain has one node, the node must reference itself. Forgetting this step is easy to do and leads to an error during execution.

EXERCISES

1. Segment 24.15 defines the private method `doubleArray` for an array-based implementation of the ADT queue. Revise that method to use the method `System.arraycopy` to copy the old array to a new expanded array.

2. Segment 24.32 describes an implementation of the queue's method `clear` when a two-part circular linked chain represents the queue. Write two different implementations of `clear`. One version should repeatedly invoke `dequeue`. The other version should set the data portion of each node in the queue to `null`.

3. Suppose that we want to add a method to a class of queues that will splice two queues together. This method adds to the end of a queue all items that are in a second queue. The header of the method could be as follows:

   public void splice(QueueInterface<T> anotherQueue)

   Write this method in such a way that it will work in any class that implements `QueueInterface<T>`.

4. Consider the method `splice` that Exercise 3 describes. Implement this method specifically for the class `ArrayQueue`. Take advantage of your ability to manipulate the array representation of the queue.

5. Consider the method `splice` that Exercise 3 describes. Implement this method specifically for the class `LinkedQueue`. Take advantage of your ability to manipulate the chain that represents the queue.

6. Implement the ADT queue by using an ADT list to contain its entries.

7. Implement the ADT queue by using an ADT deque to contain its entries.

8. Implement the ADT stack by using an ADT deque to contain its entries.

9. Describe an implementation of a queue that uses two stacks, and comment on its efficiency.

10. Implement the ADT deque by using a vector to contain its entries.

11. Can you use a hash table to implement a priority queue? Explain.

12. Consider an application that uses a priority queue. You have two implementations available. One implementation uses an array to maintain the entries in the priority queue, while the other uses a linked chain. Compare the performances of these implementations for each of the following sequences of operations on a priority queue.

   a. Insert 100 objects having the priorities 1, 2, 3,..., 99, 100.
   b. Insert 100 objects having priorities 100, 99, 98,...., 2, 1.
   c. Add 100 objects having random priorities within the range 1 to 100.
   d. Starting with 100 objects in the priority queue having priorities 1 through 100, remove them all.
   e. Starting with 100 objects in the priority queue having priorities 1 through 100, repeat the following pair of operations 1000 times:

   • Add an item having a random priority within the range 1 to 100.
   • Remove an item.

PROJECTS

1. Use a circular array, as described in Segments 24.8 and 24.9, to implement the queue. Count entries to ascertain whether the queue is empty or full.

2. The implementation of the ADT queue that was introduced in Segment 24.10 uses a circular array with one unused location. Revise that implementation so that the unused location is always before the front of the queue, with frontIndex as the index of this unused location. Let backIndex be the index of the entry at the back of the queue. Initially, both frontIndex and backIndex are set to the maximum size of the queue (the array will be 1 larger than this number). You can distinguish an empty queue from a full queue by examining these indices. What tests should you perform to do so?

3. The array-based implementations of the ADT queue in this chapter used a circular array. One implementation counted the entries in the queue, while the other left one location in the array unused. We used these strategies to tell when the queue was empty and when it was full.

   A third strategy is possible. It does not count and does not have an unused location in the circular array. After initializing frontIndex to 0 and backIndex to -1, you do not use modulo arithmetic when you increment these fields. Instead, you use modulo arithmetic when you index the array, but without changing `frontIndex` and `backIndex`. Thus, if queue is the array, `queue[frontIndex % queue.length]` is the front entry, and the entry at the back of the queue is `queue[backIndex % queue.length]`.

Now if `backIndex` is less than `frontIndex`, the queue is empty. The number of entries in the queue is `backIndex - frontIndex + 1`. You can compare this number with the size of the array to see whether the array is full.

Since `frontIndex` and `backIndex` can continue to grow, they might become too large to represent. To reduce the chance of this happening, set `frontIndex` to 0 and `backIndex` to -1 whenever the implementation detects an empty queue. Note that adding to a full queue invokes `doubleArray`, which sets `frontIndex` to 0 and `backIndex` to the index of the entry at the back of the queue.

Complete this array-based implementation of the ADT queue.

4. Implement the ADT queue by using a circular linked chain, as shown in Figure 24-12. Recall that this chain has only an external reference to its last node.

5. Consider a new kind of queue that allows only a single copy of an object in the queue. If an object is added to the queue, but it is already there, leave the queue unchanged. This queue has another operation `moveToBack` that takes an object in the queue and moves it to the back. If an object is not in the queue, the operation adds it at the back of the queue.

   Create an interface `NoDuplicatesQueueInterface` that extends `QueueInterface`. Then write an array-based implementation of `NoDuplicatesQueueInterface`. Finally, write a program that adequately demonstrates your new class.

6. Implement the ADT deque by using an array to contain its entries. Expand the array dynamically when necessary.

7. One difficulty with implementing the doubly linked chain described in Segment 24.36 is the number of special cases that occur at the beginning and end of the chain. You can eliminate these cases if the chain is never empty. Thus, you begin each chain with a **dummy node** that you do not use for data.

   Revise the implementation of the deque given in this chapter by using a dummy node.

8. Use a circular doubly linked chain (see the note at the end of Segment 24.41) to implement the ADT deque.

9. Repeat the previous project, but add a dummy node to the chain, as Project 7 describes.

10. In Project 5 you created a queue that does not allow duplicates. In this project you will create a deque that does not allow duplicates. The function of the deque's operations `addToBack` and `addToFront` should be analogous to the changed enqueue method in Project 5. Add two operations, `moveToBack` and `moveToFront`.

    Create an interface `NoDuplicatesDequeInterface` that extends `DequeInterface`. Then write a linked implementation of `NoDuplicatesDequeInterface`. Finally, write a program that adequately demonstrates your new class.

11. Implement the ADT priority queue by using an array, as pictured in Figure 24-20a.

12. Implement the ADT priority queue by using a chain of linked nodes, as pictured in Figure 24-20b.

13. Implement the ADT priority queue by using an instance of a sorted list.

14. Revise the interface for the ADT priority queue, as given in Segment 23.18 of the previous chapter, by replacing the method add with the following method:

```
public void add(T newEntry, Comparable<? super T> priorityValue)
```

The client provides an entry and its priority value to this method. The priority queue does not use newEntry's compareTo method to assess its priority. Implement this version of the priority queue.

15. In Project 5 you created a queue that does not allow duplicates. In this project you will create a priority queue that does not allow duplicates. The function of the add operation should be analogous to the changed enqueue method in Project 5. In this case, the test for equals should not include the priority, so the header of the add method should be changed to the one given in the previous project. A new operation move will change the priority of a given item, if it is already in the priority queue. If the item is not in the priority queue, move will add it with the given priority.

    Create an interface for a priority queue that does not allow duplicates. Then write a class that implements this interface. Finally, write a program that adequately demonstrates your new class.

16. Implement a priority queue of queues, as described in Project 6 of the previous chapter.

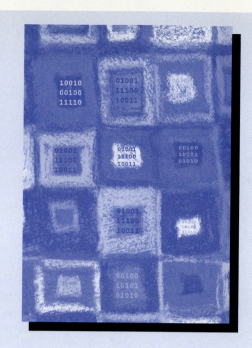

CONTENTS

PREREQUISITES

OBJECTIVES

After studying this chapter, you should be able to

- Describe binary trees and general trees, using standard terminology
- Traverse a tree in one of four ways: preorder, postorder, inorder, or level order
- Give examples of binary trees, including expression trees, decision trees, binary search trees, and heaps
- Give examples of general trees, including parse trees and game trees

As a plant, a tree is well known. As a way to organize data, the tree is more familiar than you might think. A family tree or a chart of players in a tournament are two common examples of a tree. A tree provides a hierarchical organization in which data items have ancestors and descendants. The organization is richer and more varied than any you have seen previously.

This chapter explores the ADT tree in its two forms—binary and general—and provides several examples of how such trees are used.

Tree Concepts

25.1   The data organizations that you have seen so far have placed data in a linear order. Objects in a list, dictionary, stack, or queue appear one after the other. As useful as these organizations are, you often must categorize data into groups and subgroups. Such a classification is **hierarchical**, or **nonlinear**, since the data items appear at various levels within the organization.

We begin by looking at several familiar examples of hierarchical data. Each example will be illustrated by a diagram that represents a tree.

Hierarchical Organizations

25.2   **Example: Family trees.** Your relatives can be arranged hierarchically in more than one way. Figure 25-1 shows Carole's children and grandchildren. Her son Brett has one daughter, Susan. Carole's daughter, Jennifer, has two children—Jared and Jamie.

Using a different arrangement, Figure 25-2 shows Jared's parents and grandparents. Jared's father is John and his mother is Jennifer. John's father and mother are James and Mary; Jennifer's parents are Robert and Carole.

Figure 25-1   Carole's children and grandchildren

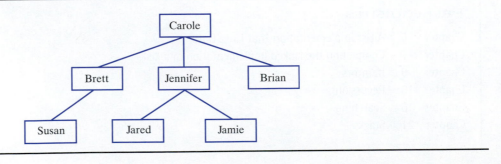

Figure 25-2   Jared's parents and grandparents

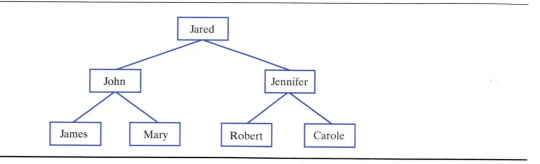

25.3 **Example: A university's organization.** Corporations, schools, churches, and governments all organize their staff hierarchically. For example, Figure 25-3 shows a portion of the administrative structure of a typical university. All offices ultimately report to the president. Immediately beneath the president are three vice presidents. The Vice President for Academic Affairs, for example, oversees the deans of the colleges. The deans in turn supervise the chairs of the various academic departments, such as computer science and accounting.

Figure 25-3   A portion of a university's administrative structure

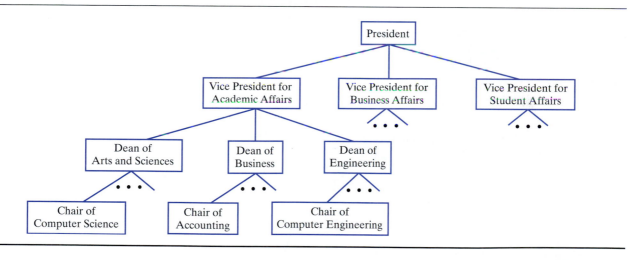

25.4 **Example: File directories.** Typically, you organize the files on your computer into **folders**, or **directories**. Each folder contains several other folders and/or files. Figure 25-4 shows the organization of the folders and files on Paul's computer. This organization is hierarchical. That is, all of Paul's files are organized within folders that are ultimately within the folder myStuff. For example, to look at his budget, Paul would start with the folder myStuff, find the folder home, and finally locate the file budget.txt.

Figure 25-4   Computer files organized into folders

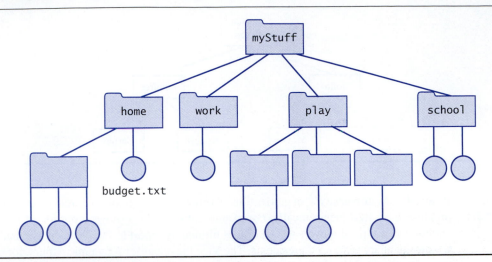

Tree Terminology

25.5   Each of the previous figures is an example of a tree. A **tree** is a set of **nodes** connected by **edges** that indicate the relationships among the nodes. The nodes are arranged in **levels** that indicate the nodes' hierarchy. At the top level is a single node called the **root**. Figure 25-5 shows a tree that, except for the names of the nodes, is identical to the tree in Figure 25-4. In Figure 25-4, the root of the tree is the folder myStuff; in Figure 25-5, the root is node A.

Figure 25-5   A tree equivalent to the tree in Figure 25-4

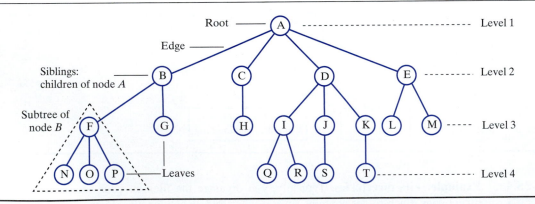

The nodes at each successive level of a tree are the **children** of the nodes at the previous level. A node that has children is the **parent** of those children. In Figure 25-5, node A is the parent of nodes B, C, D, and E. Since these children have the same parent, they are called **siblings**. They also are the **descendants** of node A, and node A is their **ancestor**. Furthermore, node P is a descendant of A, and A is an ancestor of P. Notice that node P has no children. Such a node is called a **leaf**. A node that is not a leaf—that is, one that has children—is called either an **interior node** or a **non-leaf**. Such a node is also a parent.

Note: Trees

While the roots of most plants are firmly in the ground, the root of an ADT tree is at the tree's top; it is the origin of a hierarchical organization. Each node can have children. A node with children is a parent; a node without children is a leaf. The root is the only node that has no parent; all other nodes have one parent each.

Question 1   Consider the tree in Figure 25-5.

a. Which nodes are the leaves?
b. Which nodes are the siblings of node *K*?
c. Which nodes are the children of node *B*?
d. Which nodes are the descendants of node *B*?
e. Which nodes are the ancestors of node *N*?
f. Which nodes are parents?

25.6 In general, each node in a tree can have an arbitrary number of children. We sometimes call such a tree a **general tree**. If each node has no more than *n* children, the tree is called an ***n*-ary tree**. Realize that not every general tree is an *n*-ary tree. If each node has at most two children, the tree is called a **binary tree**. The tree in Figure 25-2 is a binary tree, but the trees in the other previous figures are general trees.

Note: Can a tree be empty?

We allow any of our trees to be empty. Some people allow empty binary trees but require that general trees contain at least one node. While the reasons for doing so are quite valid, we will avoid confusion here by not making this subtle distinction between binary and general trees.

Any node and its descendants form a **subtree** of the original tree. A **subtree of a node** is a tree rooted at a child of that node. For example, one subtree of node *B* in Figure 25-5 is the tree rooted at *F*. A **subtree of a tree** is a subtree of the tree's root.

Question 2   This book has a hierarchical organization that you can represent by using a tree. Sketch a portion of this tree and indicate whether it is a general tree or a binary tree.

25.7 The **height** of a tree is the number of levels in the tree. We number the levels in a tree beginning with the root at level 1. The tree in Figure 25-5 has four levels, and so its height is 4. The height of a one-node tree is 1, and the height of an empty tree is 0.

We can express the height of a nonempty tree recursively by considering its subtrees:

Height of tree *T* = 1 + height of the tallest subtree of *T*

The root of the tree in Figure 25-5 has four subtrees of heights 3, 2, 3, and 2. Since the tallest of these subtrees has height 3, the tree has height 4.

We can reach any node in a tree by following a **path** that begins at the root and goes from node to node along the edges that join them. The path between the root and any other node is unique. The **length of a path** is the number of edges that compose it. For example, in Figure 25-5, the path that passes through the nodes *A*, *B*, *F*, and *N* has length 3. No other path from the root to a leaf is longer than this particular path. This tree has height 4, which is 1 more than the length of this longest path.

In general, the height of a tree is 1 more than the length of the longest of the paths between its root and its leaves. Alternatively, the height of a tree is the number of nodes along the longest path between the root and a leaf.

Note: The path between a tree's root and any other node is unique.

Note: The **height of a tree** is the number of levels in the tree. The height also equals the number of nodes along the longest path between the root and a leaf.

Note: **Alternate definitions of height and level**
Some people define both the height of a tree and its levels to be 1 less than those we will use in this book. For example, a one-node tree would have height 0 instead of 1. Also, the root of a tree would be at level 0 instead of 1.

Question 3   What are the heights of the trees in Figures 25-4, 25-1, and 25-2?

25.8   **Binary trees.** As we mentioned earlier, each node in a binary tree has at most two children. They are called the **left child** and the **right child**. For example, each tree in Figure 25-6 is a binary tree. In Figure 25-6a, nodes B, D, and F are left children, and nodes C, E, and G are right children. The root of this binary tree has two subtrees. The **left subtree** is rooted at B and the **right subtree** is rooted at C. Thus, the left subtree of a binary tree is the left subtree of its root; likewise for the right subtree.

Figure 25-6   Three binary trees

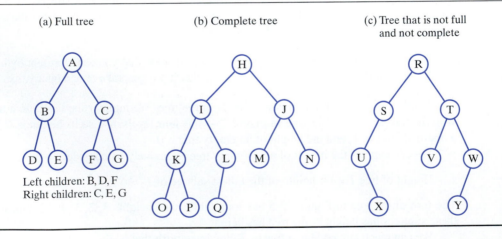

Every subtree in a binary tree is also a binary tree. In fact, we can think of a binary tree recursively, as follows:

Note: A binary tree is either empty or has the following form:

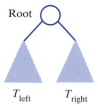

where T_{left} and T_{right} are binary trees.

When a binary tree of height h has all of its leaves at level h and every nonleaf (parent) has exactly two children, the tree is said to be **full**. Figure 25-6a shows a full binary tree. If all levels of a binary tree but the last contain as many nodes as possible, and the nodes on the last level are filled in from left to right—as in Figure 25-6b—the tree is **complete**. The binary tree in Figure 25-6c is neither full nor complete. In this case, a node can have a left child but no right child (for example, node S), or a right child but no left child (for example, node U).

Note: All leaves in a **full binary tree** are on the same level and every nonleaf has exactly two children. A **complete binary tree** is full to its next-to-last level, and its leaves on the last level are filled from left to right. Binary trees are used extensively, and these special trees will be important to our later discussions.

25.9   **The height of full or complete trees.** In later chapters, the height of trees that are either full or complete will be important in our discussions of efficiency. Figure 25-7 shows some full trees that get progressively taller. We can compute the number of nodes that each tree contains as a function of its height. Beginning at the root of the tallest tree in the figure, we can see that the number of nodes at each level doubles as we move toward the leaves. The total number of nodes in this tallest tree is $1 + 2 + 4 + 8 + 16$, or, 31. In general, the number of nodes in a full binary tree is

$$\sum_{i=0}^{h-1} 2^i$$

where h is the tree's height. This sum is equal to $2^h - 1$. You can convince yourself that this result is true by examining Figure 25-7, and you can prove it as an exercise by using mathematical induction.

Figure 25-7   The number of nodes in a full binary tree as a function of the tree's height

Full Tree	Height	Number of Nodes
○	1	$1 = 2^1 - 1$
	2	$3 = 2^2 - 1$
	3	$7 = 2^3 - 1$
	4	$15 = 2^4 - 1$
	5	$31 = 2^5 - 1$

Number of
nodes per level

1
2
4
8
16

Now, if n is the number of nodes in a full tree, we have the following results:

$$n = 2^h - 1$$
$$2^h = n + 1$$
$$h = \log_2 (n + 1)$$

That is, the height of a full tree that has n nodes is $\log_2 (n + 1)$.

We leave it to you as an exercise to prove that the height of a complete tree having n nodes is $\log_2 (n + 1)$ rounded up.

Note: The height of a binary tree with n nodes that is either complete or full is $\log_2 (n + 1)$ rounded up.

Programming Tip: To compute $\log_2 x$ in Java, first observe that $\log_a x = \log_b x/\log_b a$. In Java, `Math.log(x)` returns the natural logarithm of x. So `Math.log(x)/Math.log(2.0)` computes the base 2 logarithm of x.

 Question 4   Show that the relationship between a tree's height and its number of nodes is true for the binary trees in Parts *a* and *b* of Figure 25-6.

Question 5   How many nodes are in a full binary tree of height 6?

Question 6   What is the height of a complete tree that contains 14 nodes?

Traversals of a Tree

25.10   Until now, we treated the contents of the nodes in a tree simply as labels for identification. Because the tree is an ADT, however, its nodes contain data that we process. We now consider the nodes in this way.

Traversing the items in a data collection is a common operation that we have seen in previous chapters. In those cases, data was arranged linearly, so the sequence of the items in the traversal was clear. Such is not the case for a tree.

In defining a traversal, or iteration, of a tree, we must **visit**, or process, each data item exactly once. However, the order in which we visit items is not unique. We can choose an order suitable to our application. Because traversals of a binary tree are somewhat easier to understand than traversals of a general tree, we begin there. To simplify our discussion, we will use the phrase "visit a node" to mean "process the data within a node."

 Note: "Visiting a node" means "processing the data within a node." It is an action that we perform during a traversal of a tree. A traversal can pass through a node without visiting it at that moment.

Traversals of a Binary Tree

25.11   We know that the subtrees of the root of a binary tree are themselves binary trees. Using this recursive nature of a binary tree in the definition of its traversal is natural. To visit all the nodes in a binary tree, we must

> Visit the root
> Visit all the nodes in the root's left subtree
> Visit all the nodes in the root's right subtree

Visiting the nodes in the left subtree before visiting those in the right subtree is simply a convention. Whether we visit the root before, between, or after visiting these two subtrees, however, defines three common orders for a traversal.

In a **preorder traversal**, we visit the root *before* we visit the root's subtrees. We then visit all the nodes in the root's left subtree before we visit the nodes in the right subtree. Figure 25-8 numbers the nodes in a binary tree in the order in which a preorder traversal visits them. After first visiting the root, we visit the nodes in the root's left subtree. Since this subtree is a binary tree, visiting its nodes

Figure 25-8   The visitation order of a preorder traversal

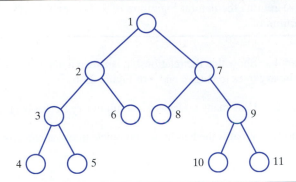

in preorder means that we visit its root before visiting its left subtree. The traversal continues in this recursive manner until all nodes are visited.

25.12   An **inorder traversal** visits the root of a binary tree *between* visiting the nodes in the root's subtrees. In particular, it visits nodes in the following order:

> Visit all the nodes in the root's left subtree
> Visit the root
> Visit all the nodes in the root's right subtree

Figure 25-9 numbers the nodes in a binary tree in the order in which an inorder traversal visits them. Recursively visiting the nodes in the left subtree results in visiting the leftmost leaf first. We visit that leaf's parent next and then the parent's right child. We visit the tree's root after we have visited all of the nodes in the root's left subtree. Finally, we visit the nodes in the root's right subtree in this recursive manner.

Figure 25-9   The visitation order of an inorder traversal

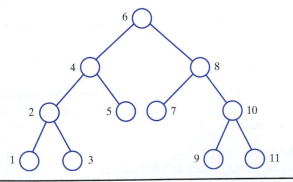

25.13   A **postorder traversal** visits the root of a binary tree *after* visiting the nodes in the root's subtrees. In particular, it visits nodes in the following order:

> Visit all the nodes in the root's left subtree
> Visit all the nodes in the root's right subtree
> Visit the root

Figure 25-10 numbers the nodes in a binary tree in the order in which a postorder traversal visits them. Recursively visiting the nodes in the left subtree results in visiting the leftmost leaf first.

We then visit that leaf's sibling and then their parent. After visiting all the nodes in the root's left subtree, we visit the nodes in the root's right subtree in this recursive manner. Finally we visit the root.

Figure 25-10 The visitation order of a postorder traversal

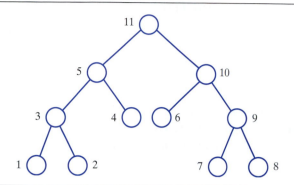

25.14   We will consider only one more traversal order. A **level-order traversal** begins at the root and visits nodes one level at a time. Within a level, it visits nodes from left to right. Figure 25-11 numbers the nodes in a binary tree in the order in which a level-order traversal visits them.

Figure 25-11 The visitation order of a level-order traversal

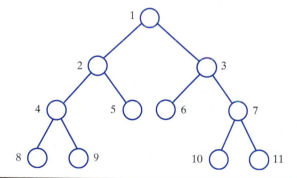

The level-order traversal is an example of a **breadth-first traversal**. It follows a path that explores an entire level before moving to the next level. The preorder traversal is an example of a **depth-first traversal**. This kind of traversal fully explores one subtree before exploring another. That is, the traversal follows a path that descends the levels of a tree as deeply as possible until it reaches a leaf.

Note: **Traversals of a binary tree**
A preorder traversal visits the root of a binary tree before visiting the nodes in its two subtrees.
An inorder traversal visits the root between visiting the nodes in its two subtrees.
A postorder traversal visits the root after visiting the nodes in its two subtrees.
A level-order traversal visits nodes from left to right within each level of the tree, beginning with the root.

Question 7   Suppose that visiting a node means simply displaying the data in the node. What are the results of each of the following traversals of the binary tree in Figure 25-2? Preorder, postorder, inorder, and level order.

Traversals of a General Tree

25.15   A general tree has traversals that are in level order, preorder, and postorder. An inorder traversal is not well defined for a general tree.

A level-order traversal visits nodes level by level, beginning at the root. This traversal is just like a level-order traversal of a binary tree, except that nodes in a general tree can have more than two children each.

A preorder traversal visits the root and then visits the nodes in each of the root's subtrees. A postorder traversal first visits the nodes in each of the root's subtrees and then visits the root last. Figure 25-12 gives an example of a preorder traversal and a postorder traversal for a general tree.

Figure 25-12   The visitation order of two traversals of a general tree: (a) preorder; (b) postorder

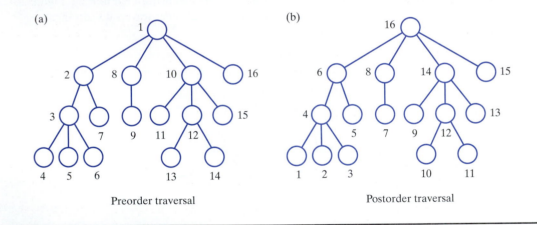

Question 8   In what order will a level-order traversal visit the nodes of the tree in Figure 25-12?

Java Interfaces for Trees

Trees come in many shapes and have varied applications. Writing one Java interface for an ADT tree that satisfies every use would be an unwieldy task. Instead we will write several interfaces that we can combine as needed for a particular application. We will include these interfaces in a package that also will contain the classes that implement them. In this way, the package can contain implementation details, such as a class of nodes, that we want to hide from the trees' clients. The next chapter will examine these implementations.

Interfaces for All Trees

25.16 **Fundamental operations.** We begin with an interface that specifies operations common to all trees. The interface in Listing 25-1 uses the generic type T as the type of data in the nodes of the tree.

Listing 25-1   An interface of methods common to all trees

```
package TreePackage;
public interface TreeInterface<T>
{
   public T getRootData();
   public int getHeight();
   public int getNumberOfNodes();
   public boolean isEmpty();
   public void clear();
} // end TreeInterface
```

This interface is quite basic. It does not include operations to add or remove nodes, as even the specification of these operations depends on the kind of tree. We also did not include traversal operations in this interface, since not every application uses them. Instead we will provide a separate interface for traversals.

25.17 **Traversals.** One way to traverse a tree is to use an iterator that has the methods hasNext and next, as given in the interface java.util.Iterator. As in previous chapters, we can define a method that returns such an iterator. Since we can have several kinds of traversals, a tree class could have several methods that each return a different kind of iterator. Listing 25-2 defines an interface for these methods. A tree class can implement this interface and define as many of the methods as are needed.

Listing 25-2   An interface of traversal methods for a tree

```
package TreePackage;
import java.util.Iterator;
public interface TreeIteratorInterface<T>
{
   public Iterator<T> getPreorderIterator();
   public Iterator<T> getPostorderIterator();
   public Iterator<T> getInorderIterator();
   public Iterator<T> getLevelOrderIterator();
} // end TreeIteratorInterface
```

An Interface for Binary Trees

25.18 Many applications of trees in fact use binary trees. We could use a Java class of general trees for such an application, but using a special class of binary trees is more convenient and efficient. Because binary trees occur so frequently, developing special Java classes for them is worthwhile.

We can define an interface for a basic binary tree by adding methods to those already in the interfaces TreeInterface and TreeIteratorInterface. Since a Java interface can extend more than one interface, we can write the interface shown in Listing 25-3 for a class of binary trees.

Listing 25-3   An interface for a binary tree

```
package TreePackage;
public interface BinaryTreeInterface<T> extends TreeInterface<T>,
                                                 TreeIteratorInterface<T>
{
   /** Task: Sets an existing binary tree to a new one-node binary tree.
    *  @param rootData   an object that is the data in the new tree's root
    */
   public void setTree(T rootData);

   /** Task: Sets an existing binary tree to a new binary tree.
    *  @param rootData   an object that is the data in the new tree's root
    *  @param leftTree   the left subtree of the new tree
    *  @param rightTree  the right subtree of the new tree */
   public void setTree(T rootData, BinaryTreeInterface<T> leftTree,
                                   BinaryTreeInterface<T> rightTree);

} // end BinaryTreeInterface
```

The two `setTree` methods transform an existing binary tree object into a new tree composed of given arguments. The first method forms a one-node tree from a given data object. The second method forms a tree whose root node contains a given data object and has as its subtrees the two given binary trees. A class that implements this interface certainly could have constructors that perform the same tasks as these two methods. However, since an interface cannot contain constructors, we have no way to force an implementor to provide them.

25.19 **Example.** Suppose that the class `BinaryTree` implements the interface `BinaryTreeInterface`. To construct the binary tree in Figure 25-13, we first represent each of its leaves as a one-node tree. Notice that each node in this tree contains a one-letter string. Moving up the tree from its leaves, we use `setTree` to form larger and larger subtrees until we have the desired tree. Here are some Java statements that build the tree and then display some of its characteristics:

```
// represent each leaf as a one-node tree
BinaryTreeInterface<String> dTree = new BinaryTree<String>();
dTree.setTree("D");
BinaryTreeInterface<String> fTree = new BinaryTree<String>();
fTree.setTree("F");
BinaryTreeInterface<String> gTree = new BinaryTree<String>();
gTree.setTree("G");
BinaryTreeInterface<String> hTree = new BinaryTree<String>();
hTree.setTree("H");
BinaryTreeInterface<String> emptyTree = new BinaryTree<String>();

// form larger subtrees
BinaryTreeInterface<String> eTree = new BinaryTree<String>();
eTree.setTree("E", fTree, gTree); // subtree rooted at E

BinaryTreeInterface<String> bTree = new BinaryTree<String>();
bTree.setTree("B", dTree, eTree); // subtree rooted at B

BinaryTreeInterface<String> cTree = new BinaryTree<String>();
cTree.setTree("C", emptyTree, hTree); // subtree rooted at C
```

```
BinaryTreeInterface<String> aTree = new BinaryTree<String>();
aTree.setTree("A", bTree, cTree); // desired tree rooted at A

// display root, height, number of nodes
System.out.println("Root of tree contains " + aTree.getRootData());
System.out.println("Height of tree is " + aTree.getHeight());
System.out.println("Tree has " + aTree.getNumberOfNodes() +
                   " nodes");

// display nodes in preorder
System.out.println("A preorder traversal visits nodes in this " +
                   "order:");
Iterator<String> preorder = aTree.getPreorderIterator();
while (preorder.hasNext())
   System.out.print(preorder.next() + " ");
System.out.println();
```

Figure 25-13 A binary tree whose nodes contain one-letter strings

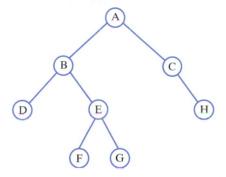

Examples of Binary Trees

We now look at some examples that use trees to organize data, leaving details of the implementations for the next chapter. Our first example includes a demonstration of some of the traversals introduced earlier in this chapter.

Expression Trees

25.20   We can use a binary tree to represent an algebraic expression whose operators are binary. Recall from Segment 21.5 in Chapter 21 that a binary operator has two operands. For example, we can represent the expression a / b as the binary tree in Figure 25-14a. The root of the tree contains the operator / and the root's children contain the operands for the operator. Notice that the order of the children matches the order of the operands. Such a binary tree is called an **expression tree.** Figure 25-14 also contains other examples of expression trees. Notice that any parentheses in an expression do not appear in its tree. The tree in fact captures the order of the expression's operations without the need for parentheses.

Figure 25-14 Expression trees for four algebraic expressions

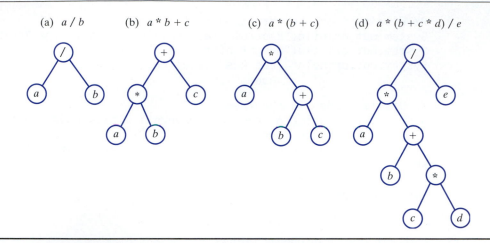

(a) a / b (b) $a * b + c$ (c) $a * (b + c)$ (d) $a * (b + c * d) / e$

25.21   Segment 21.5 mentioned that we can write an algebraic expression in several ways. The expressions that we normally write, in which each binary operator appears between its two operands, are called infix expressions. A prefix expression places each operator before its two operands, and a postfix expression places each operator after its two operands. Various traversals of an expression tree are related to these forms of an expression.

   An inorder traversal of an expression tree visits the variables and operators in the tree in the order in which they appear in the original infix expression. If we were to write each node's contents when we visited it, we would get the infix expression, but without any parentheses.

   A preorder traversal produces a prefix expression that is equivalent to the original infix expression. For example, a preorder traversal of the tree in Figure 25-14b visits nodes in this order: $+ * a\ b\ c$. This result is the prefix form of the infix expression $a * b + c$. Recall that, like an expression tree, a prefix expression never contains parentheses.

   A postorder traversal produces a postfix expression that is equivalent to the original expression. A postfix expression also has no parentheses, so the traversal produces the correct result. For example, a postorder traversal of the tree in Figure 25-14b visits nodes in the following order: $a\ b * c\ +$. This result is the postfix form of the infix expression $a * b + c$.

Question 9   Write an expression tree for each of these algebraic expressions.

a. $a + b * c$
b. $(a + b) * c$

Question 10   In what order are nodes visited by a preorder, inorder, and postorder traversal of the trees in Parts $a, c,$ and d of Figure 25-14?

Question 11   Which trees, if any, in Figure 25-14 are full? Which are complete?

25.22   **Evaluating an algebraic expression.** Since an expression tree represents the order of an expression's operations, we can use it to evaluate the expression. The root of an expression tree is always an operator whose operands are represented by the root's left and right subtrees. If we can evaluate the subexpressions that these subtrees represent, we can evaluate the entire expression. Notice that such is the case for each expression tree in Figure 25-14, if we know the values of the variables.

A postorder traversal of an expression tree visits the root's left subtree, then the root's right subtree, and finally the root. If during the visits to the subtrees we evaluate their expressions, we can combine the results with the operator in the root and get the value of the original expression. Thus, the value of an expression tree is given by the following recursive algorithm:

Algorithm `evaluate(expressionTree)`
`if` (`expressionTree` *is empty*)
  `return` 0
`else`
`{`
  `firstOperand` = `evaluate`(*left subtree of* `expressionTree`)
  `secondOperand` = `evaluate`(*right subtree of* `expressionTree`)
  `operator` = *the root of* `expressionTree`
  `return` *the result of the operation* `operator` *and its operands*
       `firstOperand` *and* `secondOperand`
`}`

We will implement an expression tree in the next chapter.

Question 12 What value does the previous algorithm return for the expression tree in Figure 25-14b? Assume that *a* is 3, *b* is 4, and *c* is 5.

Decision Trees

25.23   **Example: Expert systems.** An **expert system** helps its users solve problems or make decisions. Such a program might help you pick a major or apply for financial aid. It reaches a conclusion based upon your answers to a series of questions.

A **decision tree** can be the basis of an expert system. Each parent (nonleaf) in a decision tree is a question that has a finite number of responses. For example, we might use questions whose answers are true or false, yes or no, or multiple choice. Each possible answer to the question corresponds to a child of that node. Each child might be an additional question or a conclusion. Nodes that are conclusions would have no children, and so they would be leaves.

In general, a decision tree is an *n*-ary tree so that it can accommodate multiple-choice questions. Often, however, a decision tree is a binary tree. For example, the decision tree in Figure 25-15 shows part of a binary tree of yes-or-no questions that diagnose a problem with a television. To use this decision tree, we first would display the question in the root. According to the user's answer, we would move to the appropriate child and display its contents. Thus, we move along a path in a decision tree from the root to a leaf according to responses made by the user. At each nonleaf, we display a question. When we reach a leaf, we provide a conclusion. Notice that each node in a binary decision tree either has two children or is a leaf.

A decision tree provides operations that move us along a path through the tree and access the current node. Listing 25-4 contains a possible Java interface for a binary decision tree.

Listing 25-4   An interface for a binary decision tree

```
package TreePackage;
public interface DecisionTreeInterface<T> extends BinaryTreeInterface<T>
{
   /** Task: Gets the data in the current node.
    *  @return the data object in the current node, or
    *          null if the current node is null */
   public T getCurrentData();
```

```
/** Task: Sets the data in the current node.
 *   Precondition: The current node is not null.
 *   @param newData   the new data object */
public void setCurrentData(T newData);

/** Task: Sets the data in the children of the current node,
 *           creating them if they do not exist.
 *   Precondition: The current node is not null.
 *   @param answerForNo    the new data object for the left child
 *   @param answerForYes   the new data object for the right child */
public void setAnswers(T answerForNo, T answerForYes);

/** Task: Sees whether the current node contains an answer.
 *   @return true if the current node is a leaf, or
 *           false if it is a nonleaf */
public boolean isAnswer();

/** Task: Sets the current node to its left child.
 *           If the child does not exist, sets the current node to null.
 *   Precondition: The current node is not null. */
public void advanceToNo();

/** Task: Sets the current node to its right child.
 *           If the child does not exist, sets the current node to null.
 *   Precondition: The current node is not null. */
public void advanceToYes();

/** Task: Makes the root of the tree the current node.*/
public void reset();
} // end DecisionTreeInterface
```

Figure 25-15 A portion of a binary decision tree

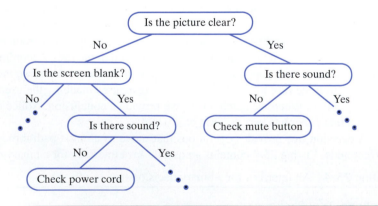

25.24   **Example: Guessing game.** In a guessing game, you think of something and I have to guess what
it is by asking you questions that have a yes or no answer. Suppose that a program asks the questions for me. This program uses a binary decision tree that grows as the game progresses. Instead
of creating the tree before it is used, the program acquires facts from the user and adds them to

the decision tree. Thus, the program learns by playing the game and becomes more proficient over time.

To simplify the problem, let's restrict your choice of things. For example, suppose that you think of a country. The program could begin with the simple three-node tree pictured in Figure 25-16. With this tree, the program asks the question in the root and makes one of two guesses. Depending on the answer to the question. Here is one possible exchange between the program and the user (user replies are bold):

> Is it in North America?
> **Yes**
> My guess is U. S. A. Am I right?
> **Yes**
> I win.
> Play again?

The program has guessed correctly; the tree remains unchanged.

Figure 25-16 An initial decision tree for a guessing game

25.25   **Augmenting the tree in the guessing game.** Suppose the user is thinking of something else. The exchange might go like this:

> Is it in North America?
> **No**
> My guess is Brazil. Am I right?
> **No**
> I give up; what are you thinking of?
> **England**
> Give me a question whose answer is yes for England and no for Brazil.
> **Is it in Europe?**
> Play again?

With this new information, we augment the tree, as in Figure 25-17. We replace the contents of the leaf that contained the wrong answer—Brazil in this case—with the new question provided by the user. We then give the leaf two children. One child contains the guess that was in the former leaf (Brazil), and the other contains the user's answer (England) as a new guess. The program now can distinguish between Brazil and England.

25.26   **A class for the guessing game.** We demonstrate some of the methods declared in the interface DecisionTreeInterface by implementing part of a class GuessingGame. This class, as shown in Listing 25-5, begins with a decision tree as a data field and a constructor that creates an initial tree. The tree has one yes-or-no question as its root and two guesses as children, one guess for each possible answer to the question. We assume that DecisionTree will have the constructors that we used here.

Figure 25-17 The decision tree for a guessing game after acquiring another fact

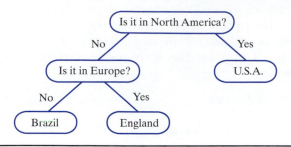

Listing 25-5   The class GuessingGame

```java
import TreePackage.DecisionTreeInterface;
import TreePackage.DecisionTree;

public class GuessingGame
{
  private DecisionTreeInterface<String> tree;

  public GuessingGame(String question, String noAnswer, String yesAnswer)
  {
    DecisionTree<String> no = new DecisionTree<String>(noAnswer);
    DecisionTree<String> yes = new DecisionTree<String>(yesAnswer);
    tree = new DecisionTree<String>(question, no, yes);
  } // end default constructor

  public void play()
  {
    tree.reset();

    while (!tree.isAnswer())
    {
      // ask current question
      System.out.println(tree.getCurrentData());

      if (Client.isUserResponseYes())
        tree.advanceToYes();

      else
        tree.advanceToNo();
    } // end while

    assert tree.isAnswer(); // Assertion: leaf is reached

    // make guess
    System.out.println("My guess is " + tree.getCurrentData() +
                       ". Am I right?");

    if (Client.isUserResponseYes())
      System.out.println("I win.");

    else
```

```
        learn();
    } // end play

    private void learn()
    {
        < Implementation left as a project in the next chapter. >
        . . .
    } // end learn
} // end GuessingGame
```

The public method `play` uses methods of `DecisionTree` to maintain the tree. Since the game requires user interaction, we assume that the client of `GuessingGame` provides methods that communicate with the user. In particular, we assume that a class `Client` has a static method `isUser-ResponseYes` that returns true if the user responds "yes" to a question.

The private method `learn` asks the user for a question that distinguishes between two guesses. Using this information, the method adds nodes to the decision tree, as described earlier in Segment 25.25. The next chapter will give you the tools to implement this method.

Question 13   Why should the method `learn` be private within the class `GuessingGame`?

Binary Search Trees

25.27   Earlier chapters have already discussed the importance of searching for data. Since we can traverse the nodes in any tree, searching a tree for a specific piece of data is certainly feasible. Doing so, however, can be as inefficient as performing a sequential search of an array. A **search tree**, on the other hand, organizes its data so that a search can be more efficient. In this chapter, we present the simplest kind of search tree, the binary search tree. Chapter 29 will look at other search trees.

A **binary search tree** is a binary tree whose nodes contain `Comparable` objects and are organized as follows:

Note: For each node in a binary search tree,

- The node's data is greater than all the data in the node's left subtree
- The node's data is less than all the data in the node's right subtree

For example, Figure 25-18 shows a binary search tree of names. As a string, *Jared* is greater than all the names in *Jared*'s left subtree but less than all names in *Jared*'s right subtree. These characteristics are true for every node in the tree, not only for the root. Notice that each of *Jared*'s subtrees is itself a binary search tree.

Note: Every node in a binary search tree is the root of a binary search tree.

The previous definition of a binary search tree implies that the tree's entries are distinct. We have imposed this restriction to make our discussion simpler, but we could revise our definition to allow duplicate entries. Chapter 27 considers this possibility.

Figure 25-18 A binary search tree of names

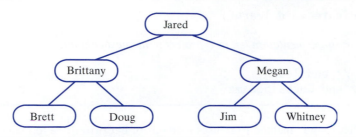

25.28   The configuration of a binary search tree is not unique. That is, we can form several different binary search trees from the same set of data. For example, Figure 25-19 shows two binary search trees containing the same names that are in Figure 25-18; other binary search trees are possible.

Question 14   How many different binary search trees can you form from the strings a, b, and c?

Question 15   What are the heights of the shortest and tallest trees that you formed in Question 14?

Figure 25-19 Two binary search trees containing the same data as the tree in Figure 25-18

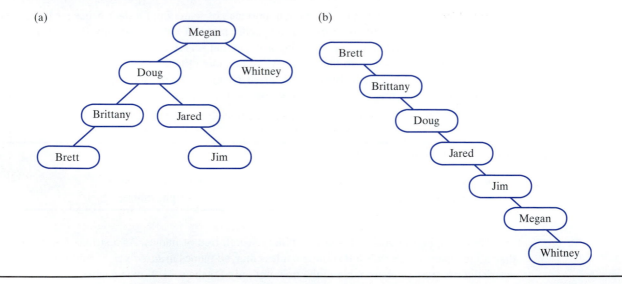

25.29   **Searching a binary search tree.** The organization of the nodes in a binary search tree enables us to search the tree for a particular data object, given its search key. For example, suppose that we search the tree in Figure 25-18 for the string *Jim*. Beginning at the root of the tree, we compare *Jim* with *Jared*. Since the string *Jim* is greater than the string *Jared*, we search the right subtree of the root. Comparing *Jim* to *Megan*, we find that *Jim* is less than *Megan*. We search *Megan*'s left subtree next and find *Jim*.

To search for *Laura*, we would compare *Laura* with *Jared*, then with *Megan*, and then with *Jim*. Since *Laura* is greater than *Jim*, we would search *Jim*'s right subtree. But this subtree is empty, so we conclude that *Laura* does not occur in the tree.

We can express our search algorithm recursively: To search a binary search tree, we search one of its two subtrees. The search ends when either we find the item we seek or we encounter an empty subtree. We can formalize this search by writing the following pseudocode:

Algorithm `bstSearch(binarySearchTree, desiredObject)`
// Searches a binary search tree for a given object.
// Returns true if the object is found.

`if` (binarySearchTree *is empty*)
  `return false`
`else if` (desiredObject `==` *object in the root of* binarySearchTree)
  `return true`
`else if` (desiredObject `<` *object in the root of* binarySearchTree)
  `return` bstSearch(*left subtree of* binarySearchTree, desiredObject)
`else`
  `return` bstSearch(*right subtree of* binarySearchTree, desiredObject)

This algorithm is somewhat like a binary search of an array. Here we search one of two subtrees; a binary search searches one half of an array. You will see how to implement this algorithm in Chapter 27.

If you think that you could implement the ADT dictionary by using a binary search tree, you would be right. Chapter 27 will show you how.

25.30   **The efficiency of a search.** The algorithm `bstSearch` examines nodes along a path through a binary search tree, beginning at the tree's root. The path ends at either the node that contains the desired object or some other node that is a leaf. In the previous segment, the search for *Jim* in Figure 25-18 examined the three nodes containing *Jared*, *Megan*, and *Jim*. In general, the number of comparisons that a successful search requires is the number of nodes along the path from the root to the node that contains the desired item.

Searching for *Jim* in Figure 25-19a requires four comparisons; searching Figure 25-19b for *Jim* requires five comparisons. Both trees in Figure 25-19 are taller than the tree in Figure 25-18. As you can see, the height of a tree directly affects the length of the longest path from the root to a leaf and hence affects the efficiency of a worst-case search. Thus, searching a binary search tree of height h is O(h).

Note that the tree in Figure 25-19b is as tall as a tree containing seven nodes can be. A search of this tree has the performance of a sequential search of either a sorted array or a sorted linked chain. Each of these searches has an efficiency of O(n).

To make searching a binary search tree as efficient as possible, the tree must be as short as possible. The tree in Figure 25-18 is full and is the shortest possible binary search tree that we can form with this data. As you will see in Chapter 27, inserting or deleting nodes can change the shape of a binary search tree. Thus, such operations can decrease the time efficiency of a search. Chapter 29 will show you strategies for maintaining the search's efficiency.

Heaps

25.31   **Definitions.** A **heap** is a complete binary tree whose nodes contain `Comparable` objects and are organized as follows. Each node contains an object that is no smaller (or no larger) than the objects in its descendants. In a **maxheap**, the object in a node is greater than or equal to its descendant objects. In a **minheap**, the relation is less than or equal to. Figure 25-20 gives an example of a maxheap and a minheap. For simplicity, we use integers instead of objects in our illustrations.

Figure 25-20 (a) A maxheap and (b) a minheap that contain the same values

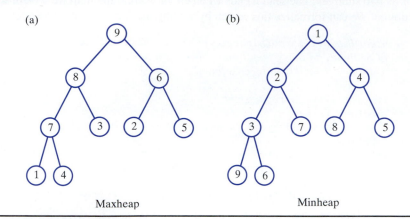

(a)   (b)

Maxheap   Minheap

The root of a maxheap contains the largest object in the heap. Notice that the subtrees of any node in a maxheap are also maxheaps. Although we will focus on maxheaps, minheaps behave in an analogous fashion.

Note: A maxheap is a complete binary tree such that each node in the tree contains a `Compa-rable` object that is greater than or equal to the objects in the node's descendants.

25.32   **Operations.** In addition to typical ADT operations such as `add`, `isEmpty`, `getSize`, and `clear`, a heap has operations that retrieve and remove the object in its root. This object is either the largest or the smallest object in the heap, depending on whether we have a maxheap or a minheap. This characteristic enables us to use a heap to implement the ADT priority queue, as you will see in the next segment.

The Java interface in Listing 25-6 specifies operations for a maxheap.

Listing 25-6   An interface for a maxheap

```java
public interface MaxHeapInterface<T extends Comparable<? super T>>
{
   /** Task: Adds a new entry to the heap.
    *  @param newEntry  an object to be added */
   public void add(T newEntry);

   /** Task: Removes and returns the largest item in the heap.
    *  @return either the largest object in the heap or,
    *          if the heap is empty before the operation, null */
   public T removeMax();

   /** Task: Retrieves the largest item in the heap.
    *  @return either the largest object in the heap or,
    *          if the heap is empty, null */
   public T getMax();

   /** Task: Detects whether the heap is empty.
    * @return true if the heap is empty, else returns false */
   public boolean isEmpty();
```

```
/** Task: Gets the size of the heap.
 *  @return the number of entries currently in the heap */
public int getSize();

/** Task: Removes all entries from the heap. */
public void clear();
} // end MaxHeapInterface
```

If you place items into a maxheap and then remove them, you will get the items in descending order. Thus, we can use a heap to sort an array, as you will see in Chapter 28.

Question 16 Does a maxheap that contains a given set of objects have a unique root? Justify your answer by using the maxheap in Figure 25-20a as an example.

Question 17 Is a maxheap that contains a given set of objects unique? Justify your answer by using the maxheap in Figure 25-20a as an example.

25.33   **Priority queues.** We can use a heap to implement the ADT priority queue. Assuming that the class MaxHeap implements MaxHeapInterface, a class that implements the priority queue as an adapter class begins as given in Listing 25-7. Recall that we defined PriorityQueueInterface in Segment 23.18 of Chapter 23.

Listing 25-7   The beginning of the class PriorityQueue

```
public class PriorityQueue<T extends Comparable<? super T>>
            implements PriorityQueueInterface<T>, java.io.Serializable
{
   private MaxHeapInterface<T> pq;
   public PriorityQueue()
   {
      pq = new MaxHeap<T>();
   } // end default constructor
   public void add(T newEntry)
   {
      pq.add(newEntry);
   } // end add
   < Implementations of remove, peek, isEmpty, getSize, and clear are here. >
   . . .
} // end PriorityQueue
```

Alternatively, the class MaxHeap could implement PriorityQueueInterface. We then could define a priority queue of strings, as follows:

```
PriorityQueueInterface<String> pq = new MaxHeap<String>();
```

Examples of General Trees

We conclude this chapter with two examples of general trees. A parse tree is useful in the construction of a compiler; a game tree is a generalization of the decision tree that Segment 25.23 described.

Parse Trees

25.34   Segment 10.44 in Chapter 10 gave the following rules to describe strings that are valid algebraic expressions:

- An algebraic expression is either a term or two terms separated by a + or - operator.
- A term is either a factor or two factors separated by a * or / operator.
- A factor is either a variable or an algebraic expression enclosed in parentheses.
- A variable is a single letter.

These rules form a **grammar** for algebraic expressions, much like the grammar that describes the English language. In fact, every programming language has a grammar.

Typically, computer scientists use a notation to write the rules of a grammar. For example, the rules just given for algebraic expressions could appear as follows, where the symbol | means "or":

<expression> ::= <term> | <term> + <term> | <term> - <term>
<term> ::= <factor> | <factor> * <factor> | <factor> / <factor>
<factor> ::= <variable> | (<expression>)
<variable> ::= a | b | ... | z | A | B ... | Z

To see whether a string is a valid algebraic expression—that is, to check its syntax—we must see whether we can derive the string from *<expression>* by applying these rules. If we can, the derivation can be given as a **parse tree** with *<expression>* as its root and the variables and operators of the algebraic expression as its leaves. A parse tree for the expression *a * (b + c)* is shown in Figure 25-21. Beginning at the tree's root, we see that an expression is a term. A term is the product of two factors. The first factor is a variable, in particular, *a*. The second factor is an expression enclosed in parentheses. That expression is the sum of two terms. Each of those terms is a factor; each of those factors is a variable. The first variable is *b*; the second is *c*. Since we are able to form this parse tree, the string *a * (b + c)* is a valid algebraic expression.

A parse tree must be a general tree so that it can accommodate any expression. In fact, we are not restricted to algebraic expressions. We can use a parse tree to check the validity of any string according to any grammar. Since programming languages have grammars, compilers use parse trees both to check the syntax of a program and to produce executable code.

Question 18   Draw a parse tree for the algebraic expression *a * b + c*.

Game Trees

25.35   For a two-person game such as tic-tac-toe, we can use a general decision tree to represent the possible moves in any situation. Such a decision tree is called a **game tree**. If a given node in the tree represents the state of the game after one player has made a move, the node's children represent the states possible after the second player makes a move. Figure 25-22 shows a portion of a game tree for tic-tac-toe.

We can use a game tree like the one shown in the figure in a program that plays tic-tac-toe. We could create the tree ahead of time or have the program build the tree as it plays. In either case, the program could ensure that poor moves do not remain in the tree. In this way, the program could use a game tree to improve its play.

Figure 25-21 A parse tree for the algebraic expression *a* * (*b* + *c*)

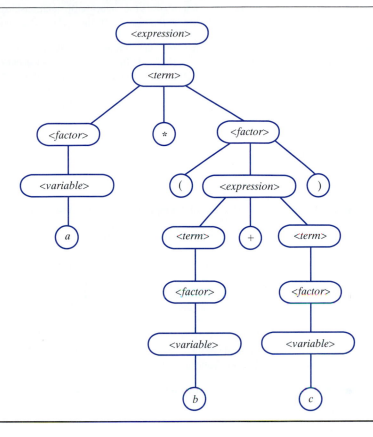

Figure 25-22 A portion of a game tree for tic-tac-toe

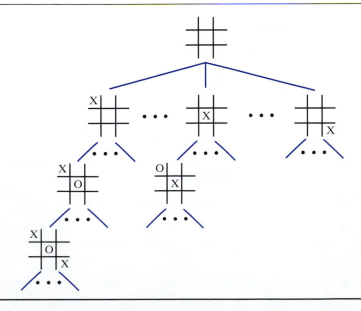

- A tree is a set of nodes connected by edges that indicate the relationships among the nodes. The nodes are arranged in levels that denote their hierarchy. At the top level is a single node called the root.

- At each successive level of a tree are nodes that are the children of the nodes at the previous level. A node with no children is called a leaf. A node that has children is the parent of those children. The root is the only node with no parent. All other nodes have one parent each.

- A node in a binary tree has at most two children. In an *n*-ary tree, a node can have up to *n* children. In a general tree, a node can have any number of children.

- The height of a tree is the number of levels in the tree. The height also equals the number of nodes along the longest path between the root and a leaf.

- All leaves in a full binary tree are on the same level, and every nonleaf has exactly two children.

- A full tree of height h has $2^h - 1$ nodes, which is as many as it can contain

- A complete binary tree is full to its next-to-last level. Its leaves on the last level are filled from left to right.

- The height of a binary tree with n nodes that is either complete or full is $\log_2 (n + 1)$ rounded up.

- You can traverse the nodes in a tree by visiting each node exactly once. Several traversal orders are possible. A level-order traversal begins at the root and visits nodes from left to right, one level at a time. In a preorder traversal, you visit the root before you visit nodes in the root's subtrees. In a postorder traversal, you visit the root after you visit the root's subtrees. For a binary tree, an inorder traversal visits the nodes in the left subtree, then the root, and finally the nodes in the right subtree. For a general tree, an inorder traversal is not well defined.

- An expression tree is a binary tree that represents an algebraic expression whose operators are binary. The operands of the expression appear in the tree's leaves. Any parentheses in an expression do not appear in the tree. You can use an expression tree to evaluate an algebraic expression.

- A decision tree contains a question in each nonleaf. Each child of the nonleaf corresponds to one possible response to the question. Within each of these children is either an additional question or a conclusion. Nodes that are conclusions have no children, and so they are leaves. You can use a decision tree to create an expert system.

- A binary search tree is a binary tree whose nodes contain `Comparable` objects that are organized as follows:

    The data in a node is greater than the data in the node's left subtree.
    The data in a node is less than the data in the node's right subtree.

- A search of a binary search tree can be as fast as O(log *n*) or as slow as O(*n*). The performance of the search depends on the shape of the tree.

- A heap is a complete binary tree whose nodes contain `Comparable` objects. The data in each node is no smaller (or no larger) than the data in the node's descendants.

- You can use a heap to implement a priority queue.

- Certain rules form a grammar that describes an algebraic expression. A parse tree is a general tree that pictures how these rules apply to a specific expression. You can use a parse tree to check the syntax of a given expression.

- A game tree is a general decision tree that contains the possible moves for a game such as tic-tac-toe.

1. In Chapter 10, Figure 10-10a shows the recursive computation of the term F_6 in the Fibonacci sequence. Recall that this sequence is defined as follows:

$$F_0 = 1, F_1 = 1, F_n = F_{n-1} + F_{n-2} \text{ when } n \geq 2$$

The root of the tree is the value for F_6. The children of F_6 are F_5 and F_4, the two values necessary to compute F_6. Notice that the leaves of the tree contain the base-case values F_0 and F_1.

Using Figure 10-10a as an example, draw a binary tree that represents the recursive calls in the algorithm mergeSort, as given in Segment 12.3 of Chapter 12. Assume an array of 20 elements.

2. What is the height of the shortest binary tree that contains 21 nodes? Is this tree full?

3. Consider a binary tree that has three levels.

   a. What is the maximum number of nodes in this tree?
   b. What is the maximum number of leaves in this tree?
   c. Answer the previous two questions for a binary tree that has ten levels.

4. Write a recursive algorithm that counts the nodes in a binary tree.

5. Suppose that you draw a binary tree so that no two nodes align vertically. Demonstrate that a vertical line moving from left to right across the tree crosses the nodes in the same order in which an inorder traversal visits nodes.

6. Consider a traversal of a binary tree. Suppose that visiting a node means to simply display the data in the node. What are the results of each of the following traversals of the tree in Figure 25-23a?

   a. Preorder
   b. Postorder
   c. Inorder
   d. Level order

Figure 25-23 Two trees for Exercises 6, 7, and 8

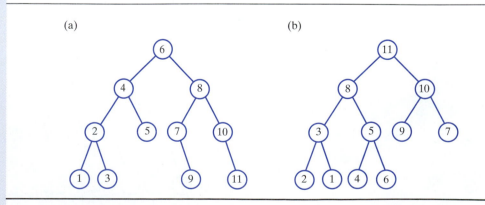

(a)

(b)

7. Repeat Exercise 6, but instead traverse the tree in Figure 25-23b.

8. The two trees in Figure 25-23 contain integer data.

   a. Is the tree in Part *a* a binary search tree? Why or why not?
   b. Is the tree in Part *b* a maxheap? Why or why not?

9. Draw the shortest possible binary search tree from the following strings: *Ann, Ben, Chad, Drew, Ella, Jenn, Jess, Kip, Luis, Pat, Rico, Scott, Tracy, Zak.* Is your tree unique?

10. Suppose we know that the preorder traversal of a binary search tree is

    6 2 1 4 3 7 10 9 11

    What is the postorder traversal of the tree?

11. Draw a maxheap from the strings given in Exercise 9. Is your maxheap unique?

12. Can a binary search tree ever be a maxheap? Explain.

13. Prove that the sum

    $$\sum_{i=0}^{h-1} 2^i$$

    is equal to $2^h - 1$. Use mathematical induction.

14. At most, how many nodes can a binary tree have at level *n*? Use induction to prove your answer.

15. Prove that the height of a complete tree having *n* nodes is $\log_2 (n + 1)$ rounded up.

16. Suppose that you number the nodes of a complete binary tree in the order in which a level-order traversal would visit them. The tree's root would then be node 1. Figure 25-24 shows an example of such a tree. What number is node *i*'s

   a. Sibling, if any
   b. Left child, if any
   c. Right child, if any
   d. Parent, if any

Figure 25-24   A complete binary tree with its nodes numbered in level order (Exercise 16)

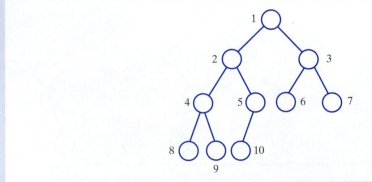

17. Consider a full *n*-ary tree of height *h*. Its leaves are all on the last level. During the traversal of such a tree,

    a. What fraction of the time would be spent at a leaf node?

    b. What fraction of the time would be spent at nodes in the top half of the tree (nodes at levels 1 through *h*/2)?

    c. Compare the fractions in Parts *a* and *b* for *n* = 2, 10, and 100.

18. Suppose that you have *n* values to put into an empty binary search tree.

    a. In how many different orders can you add the *n* values to the tree? This is not the same as the number of possible binary search trees for *n* values. Explain why.

    b. Figure 25-19b shows a binary search tree that effectively acts like a sorted list. In how many different orders can you add the *n* values to the tree such that every parent has only one child? Such a tree has worst-case performance.

    c. What is the probability that a randomly constructed binary search tree has worst-case performance? *Hint*: Compute the fraction of the total number of possible orders that results in the worst case.

19. Draw an expression tree for the algebraic expression $(a + b) * (c - d)$.

20. What value does the algorithm given in Segment 25.22 return for the expression tree in Figure 25-14c? Assume that *a* is 3, *b* is 4, and *c* is 5.

21. Draw a parse tree for each of the following algebraic expressions:

    a. $a + b * c$

    b. $(a + b) * (c - d)$

PROJECTS

1. Draw a class diagram for the guessing game described in Segments 25.24 through 25.26.

For each of the following projects, assume that you have a class that implements `BinaryTreeInterface`, *given in Segment 25.18. The next chapter will discuss such implementations.*

2. Write Java code like the code in Segment 25.19 that creates a binary tree whose nodes contain the strings *A, B, . . ., H*, such that the inorder traversal of the tree visits the nodes in alphabetical order. Write one version that creates a full tree and one version that creates a tree of maximum height. The inorder traversals of both trees should produce the same result.

3. Given an array `wordList` of 15 strings in any order, write Java code that creates a full binary tree whose inorder traversal returns the strings in alphabetical order. *Hint*: Sort the list of strings and then use the eighth string as the root.

4. Write a program that takes a postfix expression and produces a binary expression tree. You can assume that the postfix expression is a string that has only binary operators and one-letter operands.

5. Develop an interface `GeneralTreeInterface` for a general tree.

6. Given a class `GeneralTree` that implements the `GeneralTreeInterface` from Project 5, implement a program that will read a fully parenthesized Lisp expression, as described in Projects 2 and 3 of Chapter 21, and create an expression tree. For example, the expression

```
(+ (- height)
   (* 3 3 4)
   (/ 3 width length)
   (* radius radius)
)
```

has the expression tree shown in Figure 25-25.

Figure 25-25 An expression tree for Project 6

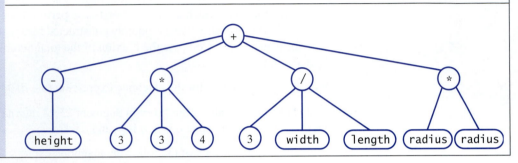

26

Tree Implementations

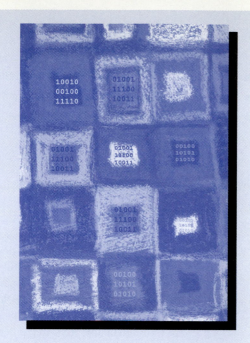

OBJECTIVES

After studying this chapter, you should be able to

- Describe the necessary operations on a node within a binary tree
- Implement a class of nodes for a binary tree
- Implement a class of binary trees

- Implement an expression tree by extending the class of binary trees
- Describe the necessary operations on a node within a general tree
- Use a binary tree to represent a general tree

The most common implementation of a tree uses a linked structure. Nodes, analogous to the nodes we used in a linked chain, represent each element in the tree. Each node can reference its children, which are other nodes in the tree. This chapter emphasizes binary trees, although it concludes with a brief discussion of general trees. We do not cover binary search trees here, as the entire next chapter is devoted to them.

Although we could use either an array or a vector to implement a tree, we will not do so in this chapter. These implementations are attractive only when the tree is complete. In such cases, the link between a parent and child is not stored explicitly, so the data structure is simpler than if the tree is not complete. In Chapter 28, we will encounter a use for a complete tree, so we will postpone until then any other implementation of the tree.

The Nodes in a Binary Tree

26.1   The elements in a tree are called nodes, as are the Java objects in a linked chain. We will use similar objects to represent a tree's nodes and call them nodes as well. The distinction between a node in a tree that you draw and the Java node that represents it usually is not essential.

A node object that represents a node in a tree references both data and the node's children. We could define one class of nodes for all trees, regardless of how many children a node has. But such a class would not be convenient or efficient for a node in a binary tree, since it has at most two children. Figure 26-1 illustrates a node for a binary tree. It contains a reference to a data object and references to its left child and right child, which are other nodes in the tree. Either reference to a child could be null. If both of them are null, the node is a leaf node.

Figure 26-1   A node in a binary tree

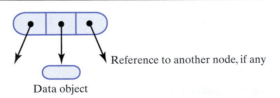

Reference to another node, if any

Data object

Although the nodes in a linked chain belong to a private class Node that is internal to classes such as LList and LinkedStack, our class of tree nodes will not be internal to the class of binary trees. Since any class that extends our fundamental class of binary trees might need to manipulate nodes, we will define our class of tree nodes outside of our binary tree class. But we will not make this class of nodes public. Instead, we will give it package access within a package that contains the classes of the various trees and their interfaces. In this way the node remains an implementation detail that is not available to any of the tree's clients.

Note: A node object in a linked chain references another node in the chain. Although we can process the chain recursively, a node does not reference a chain. Likewise, a node object in a binary tree references other nodes in the tree. Although we often think of a binary tree recursively, as Segment 25.8 describes, a tree node does not reference another tree.

An Interface for a Node

26.2   Listing 26-1 contains a Java interface for a class of nodes suitable for a binary tree. We place the interface in the package `TreePackage` and omit its access modifier. Without this modifier, the interface is accessible only by classes within `TreePackage`.

Listing 26-1   An interface for the nodes in a binary tree

```java
package TreePackage;
interface BinaryNodeInterface<T>
{
   /** Task: Retrieves the data portion of the node.
    *  @return the object in the data portion of the node */
   public T getData();

   /** Task: Sets the data portion of the node.
    *  @param newData  the data object */
   public void setData(T newData);

   /** Task: Retrieves the left child of the node.
    *  @return the node that is this node's left child */
   public BinaryNodeInterface<T> getLeftChild();

   /** Task: Retrieves the right child of the node.
    *  @return the node that is this node's right child */
   public BinaryNodeInterface<T> getRightChild();

   /** Task: Sets the node's left child to a given node.
    *  @param leftChild  a node that will be the left child */
   public void setLeftChild(BinaryNodeInterface<T> leftChild);

   /** Task: Sets the node's right child to a given node.
    *  @param rightChild  a node that will be the right child */
   public void setRightChild(BinaryNodeInterface<T> rightChild);

   /** Task: Detects whether the node has a left child.
    *  @return true if the node has a left child */
   public boolean hasLeftChild();

   /** Task: Detects whether the node has a right child.
    *  @return true if the node has a right child */
   public boolean hasRightChild();

   /** Task: Detects whether the node is a leaf.
    *  @return true if the node is a leaf */
   public boolean isLeaf();
```

```
    /** Task: Counts the nodes in the subtree rooted at this node.
     *  @return the number of nodes in the subtree rooted at this node */
    public int getNumberOfNodes();

    /** Task: Computes the height of the subtree rooted at this node.
     *  @return the height of the subtree rooted at this node */
    public int getHeight();

    /** Task: Copies the subtree rooted at this node.
     *  @return the root of a copy of the subtree rooted at this node */
    public BinaryNodeInterface<T> copy();
} // end BinaryNodeInterface
```

These nodes have more responsibilities than the nodes in a linked chain. Soon you will see how the last three methods in this interface simplify the implementation of the binary tree. But first we will implement this interface as the class `BinaryNode`.

An Implementation of BinaryNode

26.3   Since we want to hide the node from clients of the binary tree, we place `BinaryNode` within `TreePackage`, along with `BinaryNodeInterface`, and omit its access modifier. We present a portion of the implementation of `BinaryNode` in Listing 26-2.

Listing 26-2   The class `BinaryNode`

```
package TreePackage;
class BinaryNode<T> implements BinaryNodeInterface<T>,
                               java.io.Serializable
{
  private T data;
  private BinaryNode<T> left;
  private BinaryNode<T> right;

  public BinaryNode()
  {
    this(null); // call next constructor
  } // end default constructor

  public BinaryNode(T dataPortion)
  {
    this(dataPortion, null, null); // call next constructor
  } // end constructor

  public BinaryNode(T dataPortion, BinaryNode<T> leftChild,
                                   BinaryNode<T> rightChild)
  {
    data = dataPortion;
    left = leftChild;
    right = rightChild;
  } // end constructor

  public T getData()
  {
```

```
      return data;
   } // end getData

   public void setData(T newData)
   {
      data = newData;
   } // end setData

   public BinaryNodeInterface<T> getLeftChild()
   {
      return left;
   } // end getLeftChild

   public void setLeftChild(BinaryNodeInterface<T> leftChild)
   {
      left = (BinaryNode<T>)leftChild;
   } // end setLeftChild

   public boolean hasLeftChild()
   {
      return left != null;
   } // end hasLeftChild

   public boolean isLeaf()
   {
      return (left == null) && (right == null);
   } // end isLeaf
```

< *Implementations of* getRightChild, setRightChild, *and* hasRightChild *are analogous to their left-child counterparts.* >

< *Implementation of* copy *appears in Segment 26.6.* >

< *Implementations of* getHeight *and* getNumberOfNodes *appear in Segment 26.11.* >

. . .

```
} // end BinaryNode
```

Note: Typically, the class that represents a node in a tree is a detail that you hide from the client. Omitting its access modifier and placing it within a package of classes that implement trees makes it available only to other classes in the package.

An Implementation of the ADT Binary Tree

The previous chapter described several variations of a binary tree. The expression tree and decision tree, for example, each include operations that augment the basic operations of a binary tree. We will define a class of binary trees that can be the superclass of other classes like the class of expression trees.

Creating a Basic Binary Tree

26.4 Recall from Segment 25.18 of the previous chapter the following interface for a class of binary trees:

```
public interface BinaryTreeInterface<T>
        extends TreeInterface<T>, TreeIteratorInterface<T>
{
  public void setTree(T rootData);

  public void setTree(T rootData, BinaryTreeInterface<T> leftTree,
                                  BinaryTreeInterface<T> rightTree);

} // end BinaryTreeInterface
```

Recall that `TreeInterface` in Segment 25.16 specifies basic operations—`getRootData`, `getHeight`, `getNumberOfNodes`, `isEmpty`, and `clear`—common to all trees, and `TreeIteratorInterface` in Segment 25.17 specifies operations for traversals of a tree. These three interfaces are in our package `TreePackage`.

We begin our implementation of a binary tree with constructors and the `setTree` methods, as given in Listing 26-3. The private method `privateSetTree` has parameters of type `BinaryTree`, whereas the public `setTree` that the interface specifies has parameters of type `BinaryTreeInterface`. We use this private method in the implementation of `setTree` to simplify the casts from `BinaryTreeInterface` to `BinaryTree`.

The third constructor—which has parameters of type `BinaryTree`—also calls `privateSetTree`. If it called `setTree`, we would declare `setTree` as a final method so that no subclass could override it and thereby change the effect of the constructor. Note as well that we could have named the private method `setTree` instead of `privateSetTree`.

Listing 26-3 A first draft of the class `BinaryTree`

```
package TreePackage;
import java.util.Iterator;
import java.util.NoSuchElementException;
import StackAndQueuePackage.*; // needed by tree iterators

public class BinaryTree<T> implements BinaryTreeInterface<T>,
                                      java.io.Serializable
{
  private BinaryNodeInterface<T> root;

  public BinaryTree()
  {
    root = null;
  } // end default constructor

  public BinaryTree(T rootData)
  {
    root = new BinaryNode<T>(rootData);
  } // end constructor

  public BinaryTree(T rootData, BinaryTree<T> leftTree,
                                BinaryTree<T> rightTree)
  {
```

```
        privateSetTree(rootData, leftTree, rightTree);
    } // end constructor

    public void setTree(T rootData)
    {
        root = new BinaryNode<T>(rootData);
    } // end setTree

    public void setTree(T rootData, BinaryTreeInterface<T> leftTree,
                                   BinaryTreeInterface<T> rightTree)
    {
        privateSetTree(rootData, (BinaryTree<T>)leftTree,
                                 (BinaryTree<T>)rightTree);
    } // end setTree

    private void privateSetTree(T rootData, BinaryTree<T> leftTree,
                                            BinaryTree<T> rightTree)
    {
        < FIRST DRAFT - See Segments 26.5 - 26.8 for improvements. >
        root = new BinaryNode<T>(rootData);

        if (leftTree != null)
          root.setLeftChild(leftTree.root);

        if (rightTree != null)
          root.setRightChild(rightTree.root);
    } // end privateSetTree

    < Implementations of getRootData, getHeight, getNumberOfNodes, isEmpty, clear, and the
      methods specified in TreeIteratorInterface are here. >
    . . .
} // end BinaryTree
```

Programming Tip: No cast is needed when you pass an instance of `BinaryTree` to a method whose parameter has the type `BinaryTreeInterface`. The converse, however, requires a cast.

The Method `privateSetTree`

26.5   **A problem.** The implementation of `privateSetTree` just given is really not sufficient to handle all possible uses of the method. Suppose that the client defines three distinct instances of `Binary-Tree`—`treeA`, `treeB`, and `treeC`—and executes the statement

```
    treeA.setTree(a, treeB, treeC);
```

Since `setTree` calls `privateSetTree`, `treeA` shares nodes with `treeB` and `treeC`, as Figure 26-2 illustrates. If the client now changes `treeB`, for example, `treeA` also changes. This result generally is undesirable.

26.6   **One solution.** One solution is for `privateSetTree` to copy the nodes in `treeB` and `treeC`. Then `treeA` will be separate and distinct from `treeB` and `treeC`. Any subsequent changes to either `treeB` or `treeC` will not affect `treeA`. Let's explore this approach.

Figure 26-2   The binary tree `treeA` shares nodes with `treeB` and `treeC`

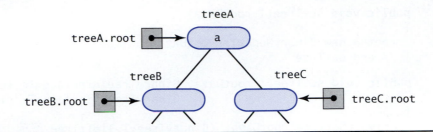

Since we are copying nodes, we use the method copy as specified in the interface `BinaryNode-Interface`. To copy a node, we actually must copy the subtree rooted at the node. Beginning with the node, we copy it and then copy the nodes in its left and right subtrees. Thus, we perform a preorder traversal of the subtree. For simplicity, we will not copy the data in the nodes.

The method copy appears in the class `BinaryNode` as follows:

```java
public BinaryNodeInterface<T> copy()
{
   BinaryNode<T> newRoot = new BinaryNode<T>(data);

   if (left != null)
     newRoot.left = (BinaryNode<T>)left.copy();

   if (right != null)
     newRoot.right = (BinaryNode<T>)right.copy();

   return newRoot;
} // end copy
```

Now `privateSetTree` can invoke copy to copy the nodes from the two given subtrees:

```java
private void privateSetTree(T rootData, BinaryTree<T> leftTree,
                                        BinaryTree<T> rightTree)
{
   root = new BinaryNode<T>(rootData);

   if ((leftTree != null) && !leftTree.isEmpty())
     root.setLeftChild(leftTree.root.copy());

   if ((rightTree != null) && !rightTree.isEmpty())
     root.setRightChild(rightTree.root.copy());
} // end privateSetTree
```

Since copying nodes is expensive, we could consider other implementations of `private-SetTree`. As you will see next, we must copy at least some nodes in certain situations.

Question 1   In the previous method copy, are the casts to `BinaryNode<T>` necessary? Explain.

26.7   **Another approach, more problems.** Instead of always copying nodes, `privateSetTree` could behave as follows. Returning to our earlier example,

```java
treeA.setTree(a, treeB, treeC);
```

privateSetTree first could link the root node of `treeA` to the root nodes of `treeB` and `treeC`. It then could set `treeB.root` and `treeC.root` to `null`. This approach solves the problem of a node appearing in more than one tree, but it makes the trees that the client passed as arguments empty. As a result, two other difficulties can occur.

Suppose that the client executes

```
treeA.setTree(a, treeA, treeB);
```

If `privateSetTree` makes the subtrees empty, `setTree` will destroy the new `treeA`!

Another problem occurs if the client executes

```
treeA.setTree(a, treeB, treeB);
```

In this case, the left and right subtrees of `treeA`'s root will be identical, as Figure 26-3 illustrates. The solution to this dilemma is to copy the nodes of `treeB` so that the subtrees are distinct. Thus, the general case cannot avoid copying nodes, but such copying will be infrequent.

We now implement a solution to these difficulties.

Figure 26-3   treeA has identical subtrees

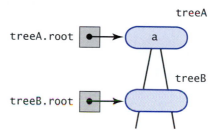

26.8   **The second solution.** To summarize, `privateSetTree` should take the following steps:

1. Create a root node *r* containing the given data.
2. If the left subtree exists and is not empty, attach its root node to *r* as a left child.
3. If the right subtree exists, is not empty, and is distinct from the left subtree, attach its root node to *r* as a right child. But if the right and left subtrees are the same, attach a copy of the right subtree to *r* instead.
4. If the left subtree exists and differs from the invoking tree object, set its data field `root` to `null`.
5. If the right subtree exists and differs from the invoking tree object, set its data field `root` to `null`.

An implementation of `privateSetTree` follows:

```
private void privateSetTree(T rootData, BinaryTree<T> leftTree,
                                        BinaryTree<T> rightTree)
{
   root = new BinaryNode<T>(rootData);

   if ((leftTree != null) && !leftTree.isEmpty())
      root.setLeftChild(leftTree.root);
```

```
    if ((rightTree != null) && !rightTree.isEmpty())
    {
      if (rightTree != leftTree)
        root.setRightChild(rightTree.root);
      else
        root.setRightChild(rightTree.root.copy());
    } // end if

    if ((leftTree != null) && (leftTree != this))
      leftTree.clear();

    if ((rightTree != null) && (rightTree != this))
      rightTree.clear();
  } // end privateSetTree
```

Question 2   At the end of the implementation of privateSetTree, can you set rightTree to null instead of invoking clear? Explain.

Accessor and Mutator Methods

26.9   The public methods getRootData, isEmpty, and clear are easy to implement. In addition to these methods, we define several protected methods—setRootData, setRootNode, and getRootNode—that will be useful in the implementation of a subclass. The implementations of these methods follow:

```
public T getRootData()
{
  T rootData = null;

  if (root != null)
    rootData = root.getData();

  return rootData;
} // end getRootData

public boolean isEmpty()
{
  return root == null;
} // end isEmpty

public void clear()
{
  root = null;
} // end clear

protected void setRootData(T rootData)
{
  root.setData(rootData);
} // end setRootData

protected void setRootNode(BinaryNodeInterface<T> rootNode)
{
  root = rootNode;
} // end setRootNode

protected BinaryNodeInterface<T> getRootNode()
{
```

```
   return root;
} // end getRootNode
```

Computing the Height and Counting Nodes

26.10 **Methods within BinaryTree.** The methods getHeight and getNumberOfNodes are more interesting than the methods given in the previous segment. Although we could perform the necessary computations within the class BinaryTree, performing them within the class BinaryNode is easier. Thus, the following methods of BinaryTree invoke analogous methods of BinaryNode:

```
public int getHeight()
{
   return root.getHeight();
} // end getHeight

public int getNumberOfNodes()
{
   return root.getNumberOfNodes();
} // end getNumberOfNodes
```

We now complete the methods getHeight and getNumberOfNodes within BinaryNode.

26.11 **Methods within BinaryNode.** Within BinaryNode, the method getHeight returns the height of the subtree rooted at the node that invokes the method. Likewise, getNumberOfNodes returns the number of nodes within that same subtree.

The public method getHeight can call a private recursive method getHeight that has a node as its parameter. The height of the tree rooted at a node is 1—for the node itself—plus the height of the node's tallest subtree. Thus, we have the following implementation:

```
public int getHeight()
{
   return getHeight(this); // call private getHeight
} // end getHeight

private int getHeight(BinaryNode<T> node)
{
   int height = 0;

   if (node != null)
      height = 1 + Math.max(getHeight(node.left),
                            getHeight(node.right));

   return height;
} // end getHeight
```

We could implement getNumberOfNodes by using the same approach, but instead we will show you another way. The number of nodes in a tree rooted at a given node is 1—for the node itself—plus the number of nodes in both the left and right subtrees. Thus, we have the following recursive implementation:

```
public int getNumberOfNodes()
{
   int leftNumber = 0;
   int rightNumber = 0;
```

```
    if (left != null)
       leftNumber = left.getNumberOfNodes();

    if (right != null)
       rightNumber = right.getNumberOfNodes();

    return 1 + leftNumber + rightNumber;
} // end getNumberOfNodes
```

Traversals

26.12   **Traversing a binary tree recursively.** The previous chapter described four orders in which we could traverse all the nodes in a binary tree: inorder, preorder, postorder, and level order. An inorder traversal, for example, visits all nodes in the root's left subtree, then visits the root, and finally visits all nodes in the root's right subtree. Since an inorder traversal visits the nodes in the subtrees by using an inorder traversal, its description is recursive.

We could add a recursive method to the class `BinaryTree` to perform an inorder traversal. Such a method, however, must do something specific to or with the data in each node that it visits. For simplicity, we will display the data, even though a class that implements an ADT generally should not perform input or output.

For the method to process the subtrees recursively, it needs the root of a subtree as a parameter. To hide this detail from the client, we make the recursive method private and call it from a public method that has no parameters. Thus, we have the following result:

```
public void inorderTraverse()
{
   inorderTraverse(root);
} // end inorderTraverse

private void inorderTraverse(BinaryNodeInterface<T> node)
{
   if (node != null)
   {
      inorderTraverse(node.getLeftChild());
      System.out.println(node.getData());
      inorderTraverse(node.getRightChild());
   } // end if
} // end inorderTraverse
```

We could implement similar methods for preorder and postorder traversals.

Question 3   Trace the method `inorderTraverse` with the binary tree in Figure 26-4. What data is displayed?

Question 4   Implement a recursive method `preorderTraverse` that displays the data in a binary tree in preorder.

Note: Generally, the methods in a class that implements an ADT should not perform input and output. We are doing so here to simplify the discussion that follows. However, instead of actually displaying the data in the tree, a method like `inorderTraverse` could return a string composed of the data. The client that uses the tree could display this string by using a statement such as

```
System.out.println(myTree.inorderTraverse());
```

Figure 26-4   A binary tree

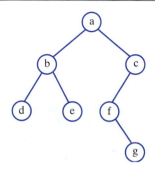

26.13   **Traversals that use an iterator.** A method such as `inorderTraverse` is not hard to implement, but this method only displays the data during the traversal. In addition, the entire traversal takes place once the method is invoked. To provide the client with more flexibility, we should define the traversals as iterators. In this way, the client can do more than simply display data during a visit and can control when each visit takes place.

Recall that Java's interface `Iterator` declares the methods `hasNext` and `next`. These methods enable a client to retrieve the data from the current node in the traversal at any time. That is, the client can retrieve a node's data, do something with it, perhaps do something else, and then retrieve the data in the next node in the iteration.

If we look at `BinaryTreeInterface` in Segment 26.4, we see that the class `BinaryTree` must implement the methods in the interface `TreeIteratorInterface`. For example, the method `getInorderIterator` can be implemented within `BinaryTree` as follows:

```
public Iterator<T> getInorderIterator()
{
   return new InorderIterator();
} // end getInorderIterator
```

As we did in earlier chapters, we define the class `InorderIterator` as a private inner class of `BinaryTree`.

An iterator must be able to pause during a traversal. This suggests that we not use recursion in its implementation. Chapter 21 showed how to use a stack instead of recursion. That is what we will do here.

26.14   **An iterative version of `inorderTraverse`.** Before we define an iterator, let's consider an iterative version of the method `inorderTraverse`. This method will be a little easier to construct than the iterator, yet it will take similar steps.

Figure 26-5 shows the tree in Figure 26-4 and the result of using a stack to perform its inorder traversal. We begin by pushing the root, a, onto the stack. We then traverse to the left as far as possible, pushing each node onto the stack. We then pop the d from the stack and display it. Since d has no children, we pop the stack again and display b. Now b has a right child, e, which we push onto the

Figure 26-5   Using a stack to perform an inorder traversal of a binary tree

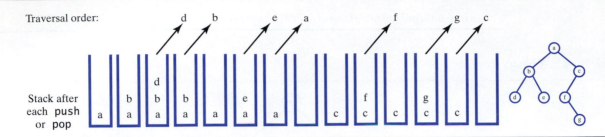

stack. Since *e* has no children, we pop it from the stack and display it. The process continues until we have visited all the nodes—that is, until both the stack is empty and the current node is `null`.

Here is an iterative implementation of `inorderTraverse`:

```java
public void inorderTraverse()
{
  StackInterface<BinaryNodeInterface<T>> nodeStack =
                    new LinkedStack<BinaryNodeInterface<T>>();
  BinaryNodeInterface<T> currentNode = root;

  while (!nodeStack.isEmpty() || (currentNode != null))
  {
    // find leftmost node with no left child
    while (currentNode != null)
    {
      nodeStack.push(currentNode);
      currentNode = currentNode.getLeftChild();
    } // end while

    // visit leftmost node, then traverse its right subtree
    if (!nodeStack.isEmpty())
    {
      BinaryNodeInterface<T> nextNode = nodeStack.pop();
      assert nextNode != null; // since nodeStack was not empty
                               // before the pop
      System.out.println(nextNode.getData());
      currentNode = nextNode.getRightChild();
    } // end if
  } // end while
} // end inorderTraverse
```

Question 5   In the previous method, if you replace each occurrence of `BinaryNodeInter-face` with `BinaryNode`, what other changes, if any, must you make?

26.15   **The private class `InorderIterator`.** Now let's implement an inorder traversal as an iterator. We distribute the logic of the previous method `inorderTraverse` among the iterator's constructor and the methods `hasNext` and `next`. The stack and the variable `currentNode` are data fields in the iterator class. The method `next` advances `currentNode`, adds to the stack as necessary, and eventually pops the stack to return the data in the node that is next in the iteration. Thus, the implementation of the private inner class `InorderIterator` appears as given in Listing 26-4.

Listing 26-4 The private inner class `InorderIterator`

```java
private class InorderIterator implements Iterator<T>
{
  private StackInterface<BinaryNodeInterface<T>> nodeStack;
  private BinaryNodeInterface<T> currentNode;

  public InorderIterator()
  {
    nodeStack = new LinkedStack<BinaryNodeInterface<T>>();
    currentNode = root;
  } // end default constructor

  public boolean hasNext()
  {
    return !nodeStack.isEmpty() || (currentNode != null);
  } // end hasNext

  public T next()
  {
    BinaryNodeInterface<T> nextNode = null;

    // find leftmost node with no left child
    while (currentNode != null)
    {
      nodeStack.push(currentNode);
      currentNode = currentNode.getLeftChild();
    } // end while

    // get leftmost node, then move to its right subtree
    if (!nodeStack.isEmpty())
    {
      nextNode = nodeStack.pop();
      assert nextNode != null; // since nodeStack was not empty
                               // before the pop
      currentNode = nextNode.getRightChild();
    }
    else
      throw new NoSuchElementException();

    return nextNode.getData();
  } // end next

  public void remove()
  {
    throw new UnsupportedOperationException();
  } // end remove
} // end InorderIterator
```

26.16   **Preorder, postorder, and level-order traversals.** Figure 26-6 shows the result of using a stack to perform a preorder traversal and a postorder traversal of the tree in Figure 26-4. A level-order traversal has logic similar to that of a preorder traversal, but we use a queue instead of a stack.

Figure 26-6   Using a stack to traverse a binary tree in (a) preorder; (b) postorder

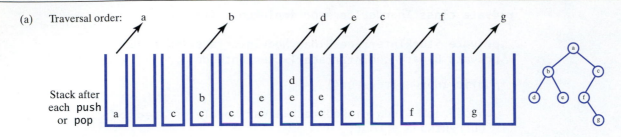

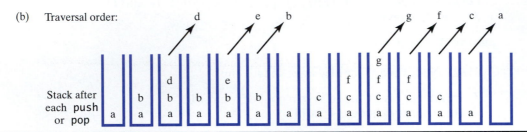

Figure 26-7 shows the result of using a queue to perform a level-order traversal of the same tree. We leave the implementation of the necessary iterator classes for you as an exercise.

Figure 26-7   Using a queue to traverse a binary tree in level order

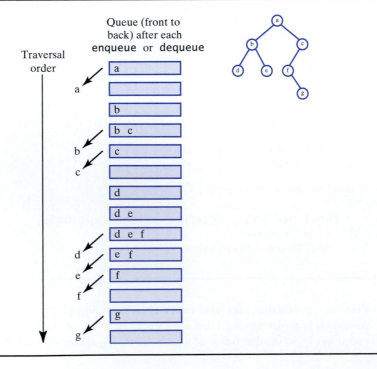

Programming Tip: An iterator object that has not traversed the entire binary tree can be adversely affected by changes to the tree.

 Note: A complete traversal of an *n*-node binary tree is an O(*n*) operation, if visiting a node is O(1), for both recursive and iterative implementations.

An Implementation of an Expression Tree

26.17   In the previous chapter, you saw that an expression tree is a binary tree that represents an algebraic expression. Figure 25-14 provided some examples of these trees. By using the algorithm given in Segment 25.22, we can evaluate the expression in this type of tree.

We can define an interface for an expression tree by extending the interface for a binary tree and adding a declaration for the method `evaluate`, as shown in Listing 26-5. Since you can treat the components of an expression as strings, we assume that an expression tree contains strings as its data.

Listing 26-5   An interface for an expression tree

```
package TreePackage;
public interface ExpressionTreeInterface
                extends BinaryTreeInterface<String>
{
  /** Task: Computes the value of the expression in the tree.
   *  @return the value of the expression */
  public double evaluate();
} // end ExpressionTreeInterface
```

26.18   An expression tree is a binary tree, so we can derive a class of expression trees from `BinaryTree`. We implement the method `evaluate` as a part of the derived class. A portion of the class `ExpressionTree` appears in Listing 26-6.

Listing 26-6   The class `ExpressionTree`

```
package TreePackage;
public class ExpressionTree extends BinaryTree<String>
                            implements ExpressionTreeInterface
{
  public ExpressionTree()
  {
  } // end default constructor
```

```java
public double evaluate()
{
  return evaluate(getRootNode());
} // end evaluate

private double evaluate(BinaryNodeInterface<String> rootNode)
{
  double result;

  if (rootNode == null)
    result = 0;
  else if (rootNode.isLeaf())
  {
    String variable = rootNode.getData();
    result = getValueOf(variable);
  }
  else
  {
    double firstOperand = evaluate(rootNode.getLeftChild());
    double secondOperand = evaluate(rootNode.getRightChild());
    String operator = rootNode.getData();
    result = compute(operator, firstOperand, secondOperand);
  } // end if

  return result;
} // end evaluate

private double getValueOf(String variable)
{
  . . .
} // end getValueOf

private double compute(String operator, double firstOperand,
                                        double secondOperand)
{
  . . .
} // end compute
} // end ExpressionTree
```

The public method `evaluate` calls a private method `evaluate` that is recursive. This private method calls the private methods `getValueOf` and `compute` as well as methods declared in `BinaryNodeInterface`. The method `getValueOf` returns the numeric value of a given variable in the expression, and `compute` returns the result of a given arithmetic operation and two given operands.

Notice how important the methods of the class `BinaryNode` are to the implementation of `evaluate`. For this reason, we do not want `BinaryNode` to be hidden within `BinaryTree`. Rather, it should be part of a package.

Note: The class ExpressionTree is serializable because its base class BinaryTree is serializable.

Question 6   Trace the method evaluate for the expression tree in Figure 25-14c. What value is returned? Assume that *a* is 3, *b* is 4, and *c* is 5.

General Trees

To wrap up our discussion of tree implementations, we will consider one way to represent a node for a general tree. Rather than developing an implementation of a general tree that uses this node, we will see that we can use a binary tree to represent a general tree.

A Node for a General Tree

26.19   Since a node in a binary tree can have only two children, it is reasonable for each node to contain two references to these children. In addition, the number of node operations that test for, set, or get each child is reasonable. But dealing with more children per node in this way quickly becomes unwieldy.

We can define a node for a general tree that accommodates any number of children by referencing an object, such as a list or a vector, that contains the children. For example, the node in Figure 26-8 contains two references. One reference is to the data object, and the other is to a list of child nodes. An iterator for the list enables us to access these children.

Figure 26-8   A node for a general tree

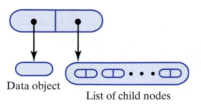

Data object   List of child nodes

In the interface for a general node given in Listing 26-7, getChildrenIterator returns an iterator to the node's children. A separate operation adds a child to the node, assuming that the children are in no particular order. If the order of the children is important, the iterator could provide an operation to insert a new child at the current position within the iteration.

Listing 26-7   An interface for a node in a general tree

```java
package TreePackage;
import java.util.Iterator;
interface GeneralNodeInterface<T>
{
   public T getData();
   public void setData(T newData);
   public boolean isLeaf();
   public Iterator<T> getChildrenIterator();
   public void addChild(GeneralNodeInterface<T> newChild);
} // end GeneralNodeInterface
```

Using a Binary Tree to Represent a General Tree

26.20   Instead of the implementation just suggested, we can use a binary tree to represent any general tree. For example, let's represent the general tree in Figure 26-9a as a binary tree. As an intermediate step, we connect the nodes with new edges, as follows. We give the root *A* one of its original children—*B* in this case—as a left child. We then draw an edge from *B* to its sibling *C* and from *C* to another sibling *D*, as Figure 26-9b shows. Likewise, we give each parent in the general tree one of its original children as a left child in the binary tree, and link these children by edges.

If we consider each node in Figure 26-9b that is to the right of its sibling as the right child of that sibling, we will have a binary tree that has an unorthodox form. We can move the nodes in the drawing without disconnecting them to get the familiar look of a binary tree, as Figure 26-9c shows.

26.21   **Traversals.** Let's examine the various traversals of the general tree in Figure 26-9a and compare them with traversals of the equivalent binary tree pictured in Figure 26-9c. The general tree has the following traversals:

Preorder:	A B E F C G H I D J
Postorder:	E F B G H I C J D A
Level order:	A B C D E F G H I J

The traversals of the binary tree are as follows:

Preorder:	A B E F C G H I D J
Postorder:	F E I H G J D C B A
Level order:	A B E C F G D H J I
Inorder:	E F B G H I C J D A

The preorder traversals of the two trees are the same. The postorder traversal of the general tree is the same as the inorder traversal of the binary tree. We must invent a new kind of traversal of the binary tree to get the same results as a level-order traversal of the general tree. We leave that task to you as an exercise.

Question 7   What binary tree can represent the general tree in Figure 25-1 of the previous chapter?

Figure 26-9   (a) A general tree; (b) an equivalent binary tree; (c) a more conventional view of the same binary tree

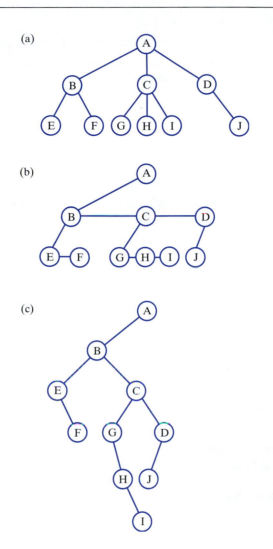

CHAPTER SUMMARY

- A node in a binary tree is an object that references a data object and two child nodes in the tree.

- A basic class of binary trees contains methods common to all trees: `getRootData`, `getHeight`, `get-NumberOfNodes`, `isEmpty`, `clear`, and various traversals. The basic class also has a method that sets the root and subtrees of an existing binary tree to given values.

- The implementation of `getHeight` and `getNumberOfNodes` is easier if the class of nodes has similar methods.

- Preorder, postorder, and inorder traversals have simple recursive implementations. But to implement a traversal as an iterator, you must use an iterative approach, since an iterator needs to be able to pause during the traversal. You use a stack for preorder, postorder, and inorder traversals; you use a queue for a level-order traversal.

- You can derive a particular binary tree, such as an expression tree, from the class of basic binary trees.

- A node in a general tree is an object that references its children and a data object. To accommodate any number of children, the node can reference a list or a vector, for example. An iterator can provide access to the children. In this way, the node contains only two references.

- Instead of creating a general node for a general tree, you can use a binary tree to represent a general tree.

PROGRAMMING TIPS

- No cast is needed when you pass an instance of `BinaryTree` to a method whose parameter has the type `BinaryTreeInterface`. The converse, however, requires a cast.

- An iterator object that has not traversed the entire binary tree can be adversely affected by changes to the tree.

EXERCISES

1. Implement `getHeight` in the class `BinaryNode`, using the approach that Segment 26.11 uses for `getNumberOfNodes`.

2. Implement `getNumberOfNodes` in the class `BinaryNode`, using the approach that Segment 26.11 uses for `getHeight`.

3. Implement a recursive method `postorderTraverse` that displays the data in a binary tree in postorder.

4. Trace the iterative method `inorderTraverse` given in Segment 26.14 with the binary tree in Figure 26-10. Show the contents of the stack after each push and pop.

Figure 26-10   A binary tree for Exercises 4, 5, 6, and 17

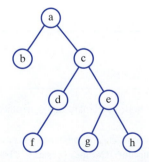

5. Show the contents of the stack after each push and pop during a preorder traversal of the binary tree in Figure 26-10. Repeat for a postorder traversal.

6. Show the contents of the queue after each `enqueue` and `dequeue` during a level-order traversal of the binary tree in Figure 26-10.

7. Suppose we want to create a method for the class `BinaryTree` that counts the number of times an object occurs in the tree. The header of the method could be as follows:

    public int count(T anObject)

    a. Write this method using a private recursive method of the same name.
    b. Write the method using one of the iterators of the binary tree.
    c. Compare the efficiencies of the previous two versions of the method.

8. Trace the method `evaluate` given in Segment 26.18 for the expression tree in Figure 25-14d of the previous chapter. What value is returned? Assume that a is 2, b is 4, c is 5, d is 6, and e is 4.

9. Replace the method `copy`, as discussed in Segment 26.6, with a method `clone`. That is, make `BinaryNode` implement the interface `Cloneable`. Cloning a node should also clone the node's data object.

10. What binary tree represents the general tree in each of the following figures from the previous chapter?

    a. Figure 25-5
    b. Figure 25-21

11. Given a general tree, consider an equivalent binary tree. Define a traversal of this binary tree that is equivalent to a level-order traversal of the general tree.

12. Knowing the preorder and inorder traversals of a binary tree will enable you to uniquely define the tree. The same is true for the postorder and inorder traversals.

    a. Draw the unique binary tree that has the following preorder and inorder traversals:

       Preorder: A, B, D, E, C, F, G, H
       Inorder: E, D, B, A, G, F, H, C

    b. Draw the unique binary tree that has the following postorder and inorder traversals:

       Postorder: B, D, F, G, E, C, A
       Inorder: B, A, D, C, F, E, G

13. Although you can uniquely construct a binary tree from either its preorder and inorder traversals or its postorder and inorder traversals, more than one binary tree can have the same preorder traversal and the same postorder traversal. Give an example of two different binary trees with the same preorder and postorder traversals.

14. Suppose we want to create a method for the class `BinaryTree` that decides whether two trees have the same structure. The header of the method could be as follows:

    public boolean isIsomorphic(BinaryTreeInterface<T> otherTree)

    Write this method, using a private recursive method of the same name.

15. Consider two binary trees that have the same structure. A node in one tree can contain different data than the corresponding node in the other tree. Write code that uses a dictionary to map the objects in the first tree to the corresponding objects in the second tree.

16. Sometimes you need to move from a tree node to its parent. To do this, a binary tree node would need a reference to its parent. You then would be able to traverse a path from a leaf to the root. Redesign the node used in a binary tree so that each one has a reference to its parent as well as to its left child and right child. What methods will need to be changed?

17. Another way of representing a binary tree is to use an array. The items in the tree are assigned to locations in the array in a level-order fashion. For example, Figure 26-11 shows an array that represents the binary tree in Figure 26-10. Notice that gaps in the array correspond to missing nodes in the tree. The array is sufficiently large to represent any binary tree up to height 4.

    a. What are the indices of the children of the node stored at index *i*?
    b. What is the parent of the node stored at index *i*?
    c. What are the advantages and disadvantages of this representation?

Figure 26-11   An array for Exercise 17 that represents the binary tree in Figure 26-10

a	b	c			d	e					f		g	h
0	1	2	3	4	5	6	7	8	9	10	11	12	13	14

PROJECTS

1. Using the examples in Figures 26-6 and 26-7 to suggest algorithms, implement iterator classes for preorder, postorder, and level-order traversals of a binary tree.

2. Write a Java program that distinguishes among ten different animals. The program should play a guessing game similar to the one described in Segment 25.24. The user thinks of one of the ten animals, and the program asks a sequence of questions until it can guess the animal.

    Your program should learn from the user. If the program makes an incorrect guess, it asks the user to enter a new question that can distinguish between the correct animal and the program's incorrect guess. The decision tree should be updated with this new question.

3. Complete the implementation of an expression tree that was begun in Segment 26.18. To simplify the method `getValueOf`, you can restrict the choice of variables and give them specific values.

4. Consider the redesigned node for a binary tree that Exercise 16 describes. Add an additional data field to the node to record the height of the subtree tree rooted at the node. Modify all the methods in the implementation of the binary tree so that the height field is updated anytime the structure of the tree changes.

5. Project 5 of Chapter 25 asked you to develop an interface `GeneralTreeInterface` for a general tree. Using that interface as a base, develop an interface `GeneralSearchTreeInterface` for a general search tree. Then write the class `GeneralSearchTree` that implements `GeneralSearchTreeInterface`. Use a binary tree to represent the general tree, as described in Segment 26.20. Implement iterators for the preorder and postorder traversals. As an extra challenge, implement an iterator for the level-order traversal.

6. Some implementations of a binary tree do not use `null` to indicate the absence of a child. Instead, they use references to a single dummy node. The reference to an empty tree is to this same dummy node. Modify the implementation of `BinaryTree` in this way.

7. Implement the class `ArrayBinaryTree` that uses an array representation of the tree, as described in Exercise 17.

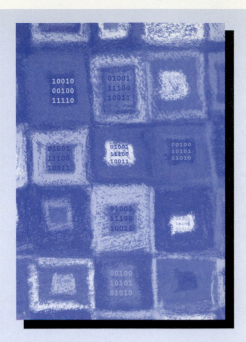

OBJECTIVES

After studying this chapter, you should be able to

- Decide whether a binary tree is a binary search tree
- Locate a given entry in a binary search tree using the fewest comparisons
- Traverse the entries in a binary search tree in sorted order
- Add a new entry to a binary search tree
- Remove an entry from a binary search tree
- Describe the efficiency of operations on a binary search tree
- Use a binary search tree to implement the ADT dictionary

Recall from Chapter 25 that a search tree stores data in a way that facilitates searching. In particular, we saw the binary search tree, which is both a binary tree and a search tree. The nature of a binary search tree enables us to search it by using a simple recursive algorithm. This algorithm is similar in spirit to a binary search of an array and can be just as efficient. However, the shape of a binary search tree affects the efficiency of this algorithm. Since we can create several different binary search trees from the same data, we want to pick the tree whose shape provides the most efficient search.

For a database that remains stable, a binary search tree provides a relatively simple way to achieve an efficient search. Most databases, however, change to remain current. Thus, we must add nodes to and remove nodes from the binary search tree. Unfortunately, these operations change the shape of the tree, often making a search less efficient.

This chapter implements the binary search tree and, in doing so, describes the algorithms for adding and removing entries. Chapter 29 looks at ways that a search tree can provide an efficient search despite additions and removals.

Getting Started

27.1   A **binary search tree** is a binary tree whose nodes contain `Comparable` objects and are organized as follows. For each node in the tree,

- The data in a node is greater than the data in the node's left subtree
- The data in a node is less than the data in the node's right subtree

Figure 27-1 shows the binary search tree that you saw in Chapter 25.

Figure 27-1   A binary search tree of names

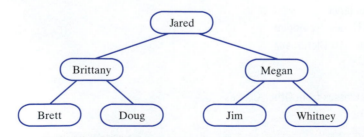

Recall that a `Comparable` object belongs to a class that implements the interface `Comparable`. We use the class's method `compareTo` to compare such objects. The basis for this comparison varies from class to class, depending on the data fields `compareTo` examines.

An Interface for the Binary Search Tree

27.2   **The operations.** In addition to the common operations of a tree, as given in the interface `Tree-Interface`, a binary search tree has basic database operations that search, retrieve, add, remove, and traverse its entries. We can design an interface for a binary search tree, as well as for other search trees that you will see in Chapter 29. Listing 27-1 provides such an interface.

Listing 27-1   An interface for a search tree

```
package TreePackage;
import java.util.Iterator;
public interface SearchTreeInterface<T extends Comparable<? super T>>
        extends TreeInterface<T>
{
  /** Task: Searches for a specific entry in the tree.
   *  @param entry  an object to be found
   *  @return true if the object was found in the tree */
  public boolean contains(T entry);

  /** Task: Retrieves a specific entry in the tree.
   *  @param entry  an object to be found
   *  @return either the object that was found in the tree or
   *          null if no such object exists */
  public T getEntry(T entry);

  /** Task: Adds a new entry to the tree.
   *          If the entry matches an object that exists in the tree
   *          already, replaces the object with the new entry.
   *  @param newEntry  an object to be added to the tree
   *  @return either null if newEntry was not in the tree already, or
   *          an existing entry that matched the parameter newEntry
   *          and has been replaced in the tree */
  public T add(T newEntry);

  /** Task: Removes a specific entry from the tree.
   *  @param entry  an object to be removed
   *  @return either the object that was removed from the tree or
   *          null if no such object exists */
  public T remove(T entry);

  /** Task: Creates an iterator that traverses all entries in the tree.
   *  @return an iterator that provides sequential and ordered access to
   *          the entries in the tree */
  public Iterator<T> getInorderIterator();
} // end SearchTreeInterface
```

27.3   **Understanding the specifications.** These specifications allow us to use a binary search tree in the implementation of the ADT dictionary, as you will see later in this chapter. The methods use return values instead of exceptions to indicate whether an operation has failed. The return value for a successful retrieve, add, or remove operation, however, might seem strange at first. For example, it appears that the retrieve operation, `getEntry`, returns the same entry it is given to find. In fact, `getEntry` returns an object that is in the tree and that matches the given entry according to the entry's `compareTo` method. Let's look at an example that adds entries and then retrieves them.

Imagine a class `Person` that has two strings as data fields representing the person's name and identification number. The class implements the `Comparable` interface, and so has a `compareTo` method. Suppose that `compareTo` bases its comparison only on the name field. Consider the following statements that create and add to a binary search tree:

```
SearchTreeInterface<Person> myTree = new BinarySearchTree<Person>();
Person whitney = new Person("Whitney", "111223333");
Person returnValue = myTree.add(whitney);
```

Following the add operation, `returnValue` is `null`, since `whitney` was not in the tree already. Now suppose we try to add another *Whitney*, who has a different identification number:

```
Person whitney2 = new Person("Whitney", "444556666");
returnValue = myTree.add(whitney2);
```

Since `whitney` and `whitney2` have the same names, they are equal. That is, the expression `whitney.compareTo(whitney2)` is zero. Therefore, the add method will not add `whitney2` to the tree. Instead it replaces `whitney` with `whitney2` and returns `whitney`, the original object in the tree, as Figure 27-2 illustrates. We can think of this as a way to change the identification number of a person named *Whitney*.

Figure 27-2   Adding an entry that matches an entry already in a binary search tree

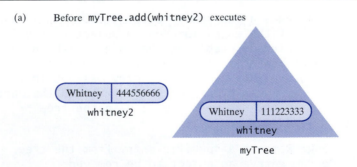

(a)   Before `myTree.add(whitney2)` executes

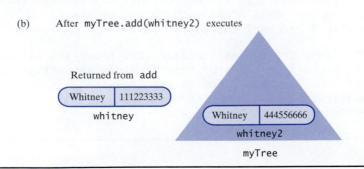

(b)   After `myTree.add(whitney2)` executes

Now the statement

```
returnValue = myTree.getEntry(whitney);
```

sets `returnValue` to `whitney2`, since it is in the tree and matches `whitney`. Similarly,

```
returnValue = myTree.remove(whitney);
```

returns and removes `whitney2`.

Now imagine that the method `compareTo` uses both the name and identification fields of a `Person` object to make a comparison. Since `whitney` and `whitney2` would not be equal according to this `compareTo`, we could add both objects to the tree. Then `getEntry(whitney)` would return `whitney`, and `remove(whitney)` would remove and return `whitney`.

Duplicate Entries

27.4   To make our discussion a bit simpler, we insist that a binary search tree contain distinct entries. Notice that the `add` method in `SearchTreeInterface` ensures that duplicates are never added to the tree. In practice, this restriction can be desirable for many applications, but sometimes it is not. By making a small change to our definition of a binary search tree, we can allow duplicate entries, that is, multiple entries that are equal according to `compareTo`.

Figure 27-3 shows a binary search tree in which *Jared* occurs twice. If we are at the root of this tree and want to know whether *Jared* occurs again, it would help to know in which subtree we should look. Thus, if any entry *e* has a duplicate entry *d*, we arbitrarily require that *d* occur in the right subtree of *e*'s node. Accordingly, we modify our definition as follows:

For each node in a binary search tree,

- The data in a node is greater than the data in the node's left subtree
- The data in a node is less than *or equal to* the data in the node's right subtree

Notice that an inorder traversal of the tree in Figure 27-3 visits the duplicate entry *Jared* immediately after visiting the original *Jared*.

Figure 27-3   A binary search tree with duplicate entries

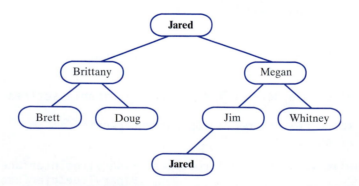

With duplicate entries permitted, the `add` method has less to do. But which entry will `getEntry` retrieve? Will the method `remove` delete the first occurrence of an entry or all occurrences? Exactly

what happens is up to the class designer, but these questions should indicate the complications that duplicate entries cause. We will not consider duplicate entries any further, and will leave this issue to you as a programming project.

Note: Duplicate entries
If you permit duplicate entries in a binary search tree, you can arbitrarily place the duplicate of an entry in the entry's right subtree. Once you choose the right subtree, you must be consistent. Programming Project 2 suggests another strategy for handling duplicates.

Question 1   If you add a duplicate entry *Megan* to the binary search tree in Figure 27-3 as a leaf, where should you place the new node?

Beginning the Class Definition

27.5   **An outline of the class.** Let's begin the definition of a class of binary search trees. Since a binary search tree is a binary tree, we derive our new class from the class BinaryTree that we defined in the previous chapter. Thus, we begin our class as indicated in Listing 27-2. Note the call by the constructor to the protected method setRootNode, which the class inherits from BinaryTree. Segment 26.9 of the previous chapter contains a definition of setRootNode.

Listing 27-2   An outline of the class BinarySearchTree

```java
package TreePackage;
import java.util.Iterator;
public class BinarySearchTree<T extends Comparable<? super T>>
            extends BinaryTree<T>
            implements SearchTreeInterface<T>, java.io.Serializable
{
  public BinarySearchTree()
  {
    super();
  } // end default constructor

  public BinarySearchTree(T rootEntry)
  {
    super();
    setRootNode(new BinaryNode<T>(rootEntry));
  } // end constructor

  public void setTree(T rootData) // disable setTree (see Segment 27.6)
  {
    throw new UnsupportedOperationException();
  } // end setTree

  public void setTree(T rootData, BinaryTreeInterface<T> leftTree,
                                  BinaryTreeInterface<T> rightTree)
  {
    throw new UnsupportedOperationException();
  } // end setTree
```

< Implementations of contains, getEntry, add, *and* remove *are here. Their definitions appear in subsequent sections of this chapter. Other methods in* SearchTreeInterface *are inherited from* BinaryTree. *>*

. . .

```
} // end BinarySearchTree
```

27.6   **Disable** setTree. Before we go any further, consider the two setTree methods that our class inherits from BinaryTree. The client could use these methods to create a tree that, unfortunately, is not a binary search tree. This outcome would be impossible if the client used SearchTreeInterface to declare an instance of the tree. For example, if we wrote

```
SearchTreeInterface<String> dataSet = new BinarySearchTree<String>();
```

dataSet would not have either of the setTree methods, since they are not in SearchTreeInterface. But if we wrote

```
BinarySearchTree<String> dataSet = new BinarySearchTree<String>();
```

dataSet would have the setTree methods.

To prevent a client from using either version of setTree, we should override these two methods so that they throw an exception if called. Listing 27-2 shows definitions for these methods that do just that.

Question 2   Is it necessary to define the methods isEmpty and clear within the class BinarySearchTree? Explain.

Searching and Retrieving

27.7   **The search algorithm.** Segment 25.29 presented the following recursive algorithm to search a binary search tree:

Algorithm bstSearch(binarySearchTree, desiredObject)
// Searches a binary search tree for a given object.
// Returns true if the object is found.

if (binarySearchTree *is empty*)
   return false
else if (desiredObject == *object in the root of* binarySearchTree)
   return true
else if (desiredObject < *object in the root of* binarySearchTree)
   return bstSearch(*left subtree of* binarySearchTree, desiredObject)
else
   return bstSearch(*right subtree of* binarySearchTree, desiredObject)

This algorithm is the basis of the method getEntry.

Note: Searching a binary search tree is like performing a binary search of an array: You search one of two subtrees of the binary search tree instead of searching one of two halves of an array.

27.8   While it is convenient to express our recursive algorithm in terms of trees and subtrees, our implementation of a binary tree in the previous chapter suggests that we use root nodes instead. The root node of a tree or subtree provides a way for us to search or manipulate its descendant nodes.

The following algorithm is equivalent to the one just given, but describes our actual implementation more closely:

Algorithm **bstSearch(binarySearchTreeRoot, desiredObject)**
// Searches a binary search tree for a given object.
// Returns true if the object is found.

if (binarySearchTreeRoot *is* **null**)
  return false
else if (desiredObject **==** *object in* binarySearchTreeRoot)
  return true
else if (desiredObject **<** *object in* binarySearchTreeRoot)
  return bstSearch(*left child of* binarySearchTreeRoot, desiredObject)
else
  return bstSearch(*right child of* binarySearchTreeRoot, desiredObject)

We will continue to express subsequent algorithms in terms of trees and subtrees, but will use root nodes in our implementations without explicitly mentioning it.

27.9   **The method getEntry.** As is often the case with recursive algorithms, we implement the actual search as a private method findEntry that the public method getEntry invokes. Although the algorithm returns a boolean value, our implementation will return the located data object. Thus, we have the following methods:

```java
public T getEntry(T entry)
{
  return findEntry(getRootNode(), entry);
} // end getEntry

private T findEntry(BinaryNodeInterface<T> rootNode, T entry)
{
  T result = null;

  if (rootNode != null)
  {
    T rootEntry = rootNode.getData();

    if (entry.equals(rootEntry))
      result = rootEntry;
    else if (entry.compareTo(rootEntry) < 0)
      result = findEntry(rootNode.getLeftChild(), entry);
    else
      result = findEntry(rootNode.getRightChild(), entry);
  } // end if

  return result;
} // end findEntry
```

We use the methods compareTo and equals to compare the given entry with the existing entries in the tree. Also, notice our use of methods from the class BinaryNode. We assume that we have at least package access to this class.

You can implement getEntry iteratively as well, with or without the use of a private method such as findEntry. We leave this implementation as an exercise.

Question 3   When getEntry calls findEntry, it passes getRootNode() as the first argument. This argument's data type is BinaryNodeInterface<T>, which corresponds to the type of the parameter rootNode. If you change rootNode's type to BinaryNode<T>, what other changes, if any, must you make?

27.10   **The method contains.** The method contains can simply call getEntry to see whether a given entry is in the tree:

```
public boolean contains(T entry)
{
   return getEntry(entry) != null;
} // end contains
```

Traversing

27.11   SearchTreeInterface provides the method getInorderIterator, which returns an inorder iterator. Since our class is a subclass of BinaryTree, it inherits getInorderIterator. For a binary search tree, this iterator traverses the entries in ascending order, as defined by the entries' method compareTo.

Question 4   Under what circumstance will a client of BinarySearchTree be able to call the other methods in TreeIteratorInterface? Under what circumstance will such a client be unable to call these methods?

Adding an Entry

27.12   Adding entries to a binary search tree is an essential operation, since that is how we build one initially. So suppose that we have a binary search tree and we want to add a new entry to it. We cannot add it just anywhere in the tree, because we must retain the relationships among the nodes. That is, the tree must still be a binary search tree after the addition. Also, the method getEntry must be able to locate the new entry. For example, if we want to add the entry *Chad* to the tree in Figure 27-4a, we could not add the new node to *Jared*'s right subtree. Since *Chad* comes before *Jared*, *Chad* must be in *Jared*'s left subtree. Since *Brittany* is the root of this left subtree, we compare *Chad* with *Brittany* and find that *Chad* is larger. Thus, *Chad* belongs in *Brittany*'s right subtree. Continuing, we compare *Chad* with *Doug* and find that *Chad* belongs in *Doug*'s left subtree. But this subtree is empty. That is, *Doug* has no left child.

If we make *Chad* the left child of *Doug*, we will get the binary search tree in Figure 27-4b. Now getEntry will be able to locate *Chad* by making the same comparisons we just described. That is, getEntry will compare *Chad* with *Jared*, *Brittany*, and *Doug* before locating *Chad*. Notice that the new node is a leaf.

Note: Every addition to a binary search tree adds a new leaf to the tree.

Figure 27-4   (a) A binary search tree; (b) the same tree after adding *Chad*

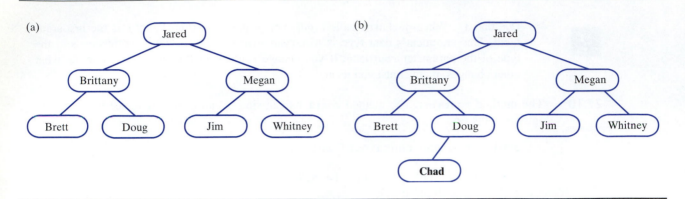

Question 5   Add the names *Chris*, *Jason*, and *Kelley* to the binary search tree in Figure 27-4b.

Question 6   Add the name *Miguel* to the binary search tree in Figure 27-4a, and then add *Nancy*. Now go back to the original tree and add *Nancy* and then add *Miguel*. Does the order in which you add the two names affect the tree that results?

A Recursive Implementation

27.13   The method add has an elegant recursive implementation. Consider again the example given in the previous segment. If we want to add *Chad* to the binary search tree in Figure 27-4a, we take the following steps:

- To add *Chad* to the binary search tree whose root is *Jared*:

    Observe that *Chad* is less than *Jared*.
    Add *Chad* to *Jared*'s left subtree, whose root is *Brittany*.

- To add *Chad* to the binary search tree whose root is *Brittany*:

    Observe that *Chad* is greater than *Brittany*.
    Add *Chad* to *Brittany*'s right subtree, whose root is *Doug*.

- To add *Chad* to the binary search tree whose root is *Doug*:

    Observe that *Chad* is less than *Doug*.
    Since *Doug* has no left subtree, make *Chad* the left child of *Doug*.

We can see that adding an entry to the tree rooted at *Jared* depends upon adding to progressively smaller subtrees, as Figure 27-5 shows.

Figure 27-5   Recursively adding *Chad* to smaller subtrees of a binary search tree

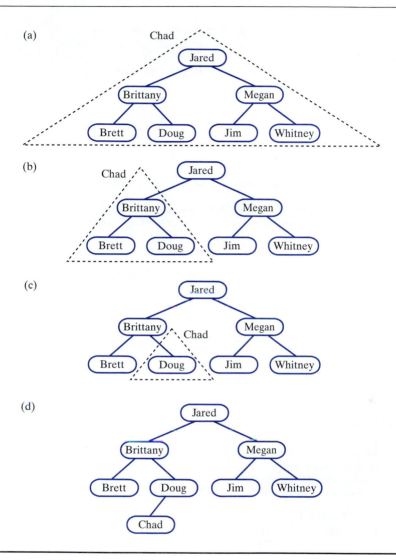

27.14   **A recursive algorithm for adding a new entry.** The following recursive algorithm formalizes this approach, in accordance with the specifications of the method add in SearchTreeInterface. Recall that we decided to have only distinct entries in the binary search tree. If we try to add an entry to a tree that matches an entry already in the tree, we replace that entry with the new entry and return the old entry.

To simplify our algorithm, let's assume for the moment that the binary search tree is not empty:

> *Algorithm* `addEntry(binarySearchTree, newEntry)`
> *// Adds a new entry to a binary search tree that is not empty.*
> *// Returns* `null` *if* `newEntry` *did not exist already in the tree. Otherwise, returns the*
> *// tree entry that matched and was replaced by* `newEntry`.
>
> `result = ` **`null`**
> **`if`** `(newEntry` *matches the entry in the root of* `binarySearchTree)`
> `{`
>   `result = ` *entry in the root*
>   *Replace entry in the root with* `newEntry`
> `}`
> **`else if`** `(newEntry <` *entry in the root of* `binarySearchTree)`
> `{`
>   **`if`** `(`*the root of* `binarySearchTree` *has a left child*`)`
>   `result = addEntry(`*left subtree of* `binarySearchTree, newEntry)`
>   **`else`**
>   *Give the root a left child containing* `newEntry`
> `}`
> **`else`** `// newEntry >` *entry in the root of* `binarySearchTree`
> `{`
>   **`if`** `(`*the root of* `binarySearchTree` *has a right child*`)`
>   `result = addEntry(`*right subtree of* `binarySearchTree, newEntry)`
>   **`else`**
>   *Give the root a right child containing* `newEntry`
> `}`
> **`return`** `result`

We can handle the addition to an empty binary search tree as a special case within another algorithm that invokes `addEntry`, as follows:

> *Algorithm* `add(binarySearchTree, newEntry)`
> *// Adds a new entry to a binary search tree.*
> *// Returns* `null` *if* `newEntry` *did not exist already in the tree. Otherwise, returns the*
> *// tree entry that matched and was replaced by* `newEntry`.
>
> `result = ` **`null`**
> **`if`** `(binarySearchTree` *is empty*`)`
>   *Create a node containing* `newEntry` *and make it the root of* `binarySearchTree`
> **`else`**
>   `result = addEntry(binarySearchTree, newEntry)`
>
> **`return`** `result;`

27.15   **The private recursive method `addEntry`.** Recall the recursive search algorithm given in Segment 27.7. The public method `getEntry` in Segment 27.9 invokes a private recursive method `findEntry` that implements the search algorithm. We have a similar organization here. The public method add calls a private recursive method `addEntry`, if the tree is not empty. Like `findEntry`, `addEntry` has a node as a parameter that is initially the root node of the tree. When `addEntry` is called recursively, this parameter is either the left child or the right child of the current root.

Remember where we place a new node into a binary search tree. As Figures 27-4 and 27-5 illustrate, a new node always becomes a leaf in the tree. Now imagine the recursive calls to `addEntry` when adding *Chad* to the tree in Figure 27-5a. Eventually, the node containing *Doug* is passed to `addEntry` as its argument (Figure 27-5c). Since *Chad* is less than *Doug*, and *Doug*'s node has no left child, `addEntry` creates one containing *Chad* (Figure 27-5d).

The following implementation of `addEntry` closely follows the pseudocode given in Segment 27.14:

```java
/** Task: Adds newEntry to the nonempty subtree rooted at rootNode.*/
private T addEntry(BinaryNodeInterface<T> rootNode, T newEntry)
{
   assert rootNode != null;
   T result = null;
   int comparison = newEntry.compareTo(rootNode.getData());

   if (comparison == 0)
   {
      result = rootNode.getData();
      rootNode.setData(newEntry);
   }
   else if (comparison < 0)
   {
      if (rootNode.hasLeftChild())
         result = addEntry(rootNode.getLeftChild(), newEntry);
      else
         rootNode.setLeftChild(new BinaryNode<T>(newEntry));
   }
   else
   {
      assert comparison > 0;

      if (rootNode.hasRightChild())
         result = addEntry(rootNode.getRightChild(), newEntry);
      else
         rootNode.setRightChild(new BinaryNode<T>(newEntry));
   } // end if

   return result;
} // end addEntry
```

We begin by comparing the new entry with the entry in the root. If the entries match, we replace and return the original entry in the root. If the comparison is "less than," and the root has a left child, we pass that child to `addEntry`. Remember that when we are coding a recursive method such as `addEntry`, we assume that it works when we write the recursive call. Thus, `addEntry` places a new node containing `newEntry` into the root's left subtree. If the root has no left child, we give it one containing the new entry. Analogous code handles the case when the new entry is greater than the entry in the root.

27.16   **The public method add.** The public method add not only invokes the recursive `addEntry`, it ensures that the tree it passes to `addEntry` is not empty. Accordingly, add deals with empty trees itself. The following implementation of add adheres to the algorithm given in Segment 27.14. Note the use of the protected methods `setRootNode` and `getRootNode` that are inherited from `BinaryTree`.

```java
public T add(T newEntry)
{
  T result = null;

  if (isEmpty())
    setRootNode(new BinaryNode<T>(newEntry));
  else
    result = addEntry(getRootNode(), newEntry);

  return result;
} // end add
```

An Iterative Implementation

You can implement the method addEntry iteratively. We will mimic the logic of the recursive version of addEntry given earlier, so you can compare the two approaches. Exercise 12 at the end of this chapter suggests another iterative algorithm.

27.17   **An iterative algorithm for adding a new entry.** The following iterative algorithm adds a new entry to a binary search tree that is not empty:

```
Algorithm addEntry(binarySearchTree, newEntry)
// Adds a new entry to a binary search tree that is not empty.
// Returns null if newEntry did not exist already in the tree. Otherwise, returns the
// tree entry that matched and was replaced by newEntry.

result = null
currentNode = root node of binarySearchTree
found = false

while (found is false)
{
  if (newEntry matches the entry in currentNode)
  {
    found = true
    result = entry in currentNode
    Replace entry in currentNode with newEntry
  }
  else if (newEntry < entry in currentNode)
  {
    if (currentNode has a left child)
      currentNode = left child of currentNode
    else
    {
      found = true
      Give currentNode a left child containing newEntry
    }
  }
  else // newEntry > entry in currentNode
  {
    if (currentNode has a right child)
      currentNode = right child of currentNode
    else
    {
      found = true
      Give currentNode a right child containing newEntry
    }
  }
}
return result
```

The while loop tries to match the new entry with an existing entry in the tree. If the new entry is not in the tree already, the search for it ends at a node's null child reference. This is where a new node belongs. But if the new entry matches an entry in the tree, we return the existing entry and replace it in the tree with the new entry.

27.18   **An iterative implementation of the method addEntry.** The Java implementation of the previous algorithm closely follows the algorithm's logic. Note the use of the protected method getRootNode that is inherited from BinaryTree.

```java
private T addEntry(T newEntry)
{
  BinaryNodeInterface<T> currentNode = getRootNode();
  assert currentNode != null;
  T result = null;
  boolean found = false;

  while (!found)
  {
    T currentEntry = currentNode.getData();
    int comparison = newEntry.compareTo(currentEntry);

    if (comparison == 0)
    { // newEntry matches currentEntry;
      // return and replace currentEntry
      found = true;
      result = currentEntry;
      currentNode.setData(newEntry);
    }
    else if (comparison < 0)
    {
      if (currentNode.hasLeftChild())
        currentNode = currentNode.getLeftChild();
      else
      {
        found = true;
        currentNode.setLeftChild(new BinaryNode<T>(newEntry));
      } // end if
    }
    else
    {
      assert comparison > 0;

      if (currentNode.hasRightChild())
        currentNode = currentNode.getRightChild();
      else
      {
        found = true;
        currentNode.setRightChild(new BinaryNode<T>(newEntry));
      } // end if
    } // end if
  } // end while

  return result;
} // end addEntry
```

The method add that calls this iterative addEntry is like the one given in segment 27.16, except for the actual invocation of addEntry. Since the iterative addEntry has one parameter instead of two, the invocation is addEntry(newEntry) instead of addEntry(getRootNode(), newEntry).

Whether you use this iterative addEntry method, the one suggested in Exercise 12, or the recursive version given earlier depends in part on which approach is clearest to you. You'll spend less time debugging if you really understand your algorithm.

Removing an Entry

27.19   To remove an entry from a binary search tree, we pass a matching entry to the method remove. The desired entry is then removed from the tree and returned to the client. If no such entry exists, the method returns null and the tree remains unchanged.

Removing an entry is somewhat more involved than adding an entry, as the required logic depends upon the number of children that belong to the node containing the entry. We have three possibilities:

- The node has no children—it is a leaf
- The node has one child
- The node has two children

We now consider these three cases.

Removing an Entry Whose Node Is a Leaf

27.20   The simplest case in removing an entry is when the node is a leaf, that is, has no children. For example, suppose that node N contains the entry to be removed from the binary search tree. Figure 27-6a shows two possibilities for node N: It could be either the left child or the right child of its parent node P. Since N is a leaf, we can delete it by setting the appropriate child reference in node P to null. Figure 27-6b shows the result of this operation.

Figure 27-6   (a) Two possible configurations of a leaf node N; (b) the resulting two possible configurations after removing node N

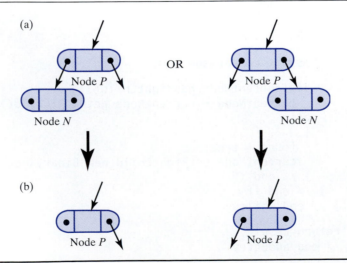

Removing an Entry Whose Node Has One Child

27.21   Now imagine that the entry to be removed is in a node N that has exactly one child C. Figure 27-7a shows the four possibilities for node N and its parent P. To remove the entry in N, we remove N from the tree. We do this by making C a child of P instead of N. As Figure 27-7b shows, if N was a left child of P, we make C be the left child of P. Likewise, if N was a right child of P, we make C be the right child of P.

Figure 27-7   (a) Four possible configurations of a node N that has one child; (b) the resulting two possible configurations after removing node N

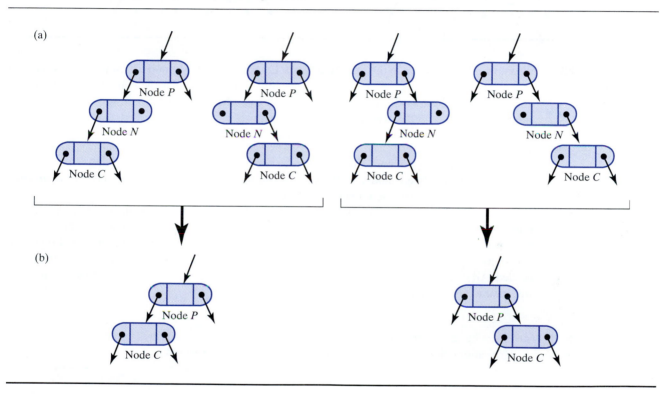

Removing an Entry Whose Node Has Two Children

27.22   The previous two cases are really not too difficult, conceptually or in practice. But this last case is a bit involved. Once again, suppose that the entry to be removed is in a node N, but now N has two children. Figure 27-8 shows two possible configurations for N. If we try to remove node N, we will leave its two children without a parent. Although node P could reference one of them, it hasn't room for both. Thus, removing node N is not an option.

We do not actually have to remove node N to remove its entry. Let's find a node A that is easy to remove—it would have no more than one child—and replace N's entry with the entry now in A. We then can remove node A and still have the correct entries in the tree. But will the tree still be a binary search tree? Clearly, node A cannot be just any node; it must contain an entry in the tree that legally can be in node N.

Figure 27-8   Two possible configurations of a node N that has two children

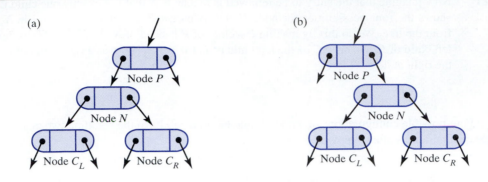

27.23   We know that the entries in the tree are distinct. Let e be the entry in node N. Since node N has two children, e is larger than the entry in N's left child and smaller than the entry in N's right child. Thus, e cannot be the smallest entry in the tree, nor can it be the largest. So, if we imagine the tree's entries in ascending order, we can write

... $a < e < b$ ...

Here, a is the entry that is immediately before e, and b is the one that is immediately after. An inorder traversal of the tree would visit these entries in this same order. Thus, a is called the **inorder predecessor** of e, and b is the **inorder successor** of e.

The entry a must occur in a node in N's left subtree; b is in a node in N's right subtree, as Figure 27-9a illustrates. Moreover, a is the largest entry in N's left subtree, since a is the entry that is immediately before e. Suppose that we are able to delete the node that contains a and replace e with a, as Figure 27-9b shows. Now all of the remaining entries in N's left subtree are less than a, as needed. All of the entries in N's right subtree are greater than e and so are greater than a. Thus, we still have a binary search tree.

Figure 27-9   Node N and its subtrees: (a) the entry a is immediately before the entry e, and b is immediately after e; (b) after deleting the node that contained a and replacing e with a

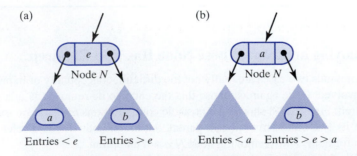

27.24   **Locating the entry a.** The previous segment assumed that we could find the appropriate entry a and delete its node. So let's locate the node that contains a and verify that it does not have two children. Consider again the original tree in Figure 27-9a. We already know that a must be in N's left subtree, and that *a* is the largest entry in that subtree. To find an entry larger than the one in any given node, we look at the node's right child. Thus, *a* occurs in the subtree's rightmost node *R*, as Figure 27-10 illustrates. Node *R* cannot have a right child, because if it did, the child's entry would be greater than *a*. Therefore, node *R* has no more than one child and so can be removed from the tree easily.

Figure 27-10 The largest entry *a* in node *N*'s left subtree occurs in the subtree's rightmost node *R*

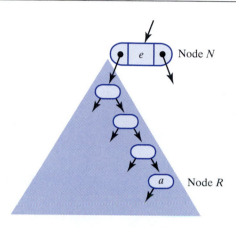

27.25   The following pseudocode summarizes this discussion:

Algorithm Delete the entry e from a node N that has two children
Find the rightmost node R in N's left subtree
Replace the entry in node N with the entry that is in node R
Delete node R

An alternate approach involves *b*, the entry that is immediately after *e* in sorted order. We have already noted that *b* occurs in *N*'s right subtree. It would have to be the smallest entry in that subtree, so it would occur in the leftmost node in the subtree. Thus, we have the following alternate pseudocode:

Algorithm Delete the entry e from a node N that has two children
Find the leftmost node L in N's right subtree
Replace the entry in node N with the entry that is in node L
Delete node L

Both approaches work equally well.

 Note: To remove an entry whose node has two children, you first replace the entry with another whose node has no more than one child. You then remove the second node from the binary search tree.

27.26   **Example.** Figure 27-11 shows several consecutive removals from a binary search tree of names. The first algorithm given in the previous segment is used. To remove *Chad* from the tree in Figure 27-11a, we replace it with its inorder predecessor *Brittany*. We then remove the node that contained *Brittany* to get the tree in Figure 27-11b. To remove *Sean* from this new tree, we replace it with its inorder predecessor *Reba* and remove *Reba*'s original node. This gives us the tree in Figure 27-11c. Finally, to remove *Kathy* from this tree, we replace it with its inorder predecessor *Doug* and remove *Doug*'s original node, to get the tree in Figure 27-11d.

Figure 27-11   (a) A binary search tree; (b) after removing *Chad*; (c) after removing *Sean*; (d) after removing *Kathy*

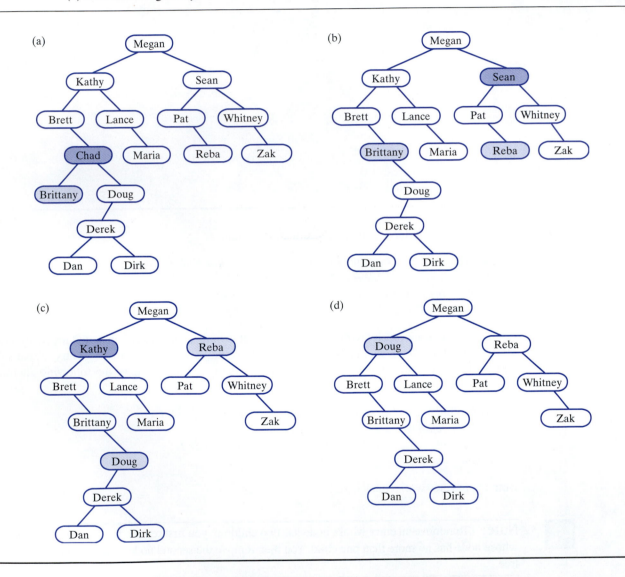

 Question 7   The second algorithm described in Segment 27.25 involves the inorder successor. Using this algorithm, remove *Sean* and *Chad* from the tree in Figure 27-11a.

Question 8   Remove *Megan* from the tree in Figure 27-11a in two different ways.

Removing an Entry in the Root

27.27   Removing an entry that is in the root of the tree is a special case only if we actually remove the root node. That will occur when the root has at most one child. If the root has two children, the previous segment shows that we would replace the root's entry and delete a different node.

   If the root is a leaf, the tree has only one node. Deleting it results in an empty tree. If the root has one child, as Figure 27-12 illustrates, the child is either a right child or a left child. In either case, we simply delete the root node by making the child node *C* the root of the tree.

Figure 27-12   (a) Two possible configurations of a root that has one child; (b) after removing the root

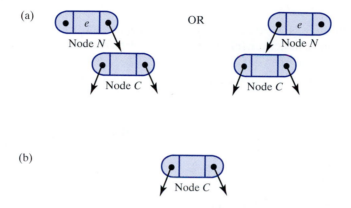

A Recursive Implementation

27.28   **The algorithm.** The entry to be removed from the tree is the one that matches the object passed to the method `remove` as its argument. The method returns the removed entry. The following recursive algorithm describes the method's logic at a high level:

```
Algorithm remove(binarySearchTree, entry)
oldEntry = null
if (binarySearchTree is not empty)
{
    if (entry matches the entry in the root of binarySearchTree)
    {
        oldEntry = entry in root
        removeFromRoot(root of binarySearchTree)
    }
    else if (entry < entry in root)
        oldEntry = remove(left subtree of binarySearchTree, entry)
    else   // entry > entry in root
        oldEntry = remove(right subtree of binarySearchTree, entry)
}
return oldEntry
```

The method `removeFromRoot` will remove the entry in the root of a given subtree based on how many children belong to the root.

27.29   **The public method remove.** We have several details to consider before implementing the previous algorithm. The public method `remove` should have only one parameter—`entry`—so just as the method `add` calls the private recursive method `addEntry`, `remove` will call a private recursive method `removeEntry`.

As we mentioned in Segment 27.8, we will pass the root of the tree, instead of the tree itself, to `removeEntry`. Since the method might remove the root node from the tree, we must be careful to always retain a reference to the tree's root. As a result, we make `removeEntry` return a reference to the root of the revised tree, which `remove` can save. But `removeEntry` must also give to `remove` the entry it removes. A solution is to pass another parameter—`oldEntry`—to `removeEntry` and have the method change its value to the removed entry. Thus, the header for `removeEntry` will be

```
private BinaryNodeInterface<T> removeEntry(BinaryNodeInterface<T>
                             rootNode, T entry, ReturnObject oldEntry)
```

`ReturnObject` is an inner class that has a single data field and simple methods `set` and `get` to manipulate it. Initially, `oldEntry`'s data field is `null`, since `remove` returns `null` when the entry is not found in the tree.

Thus, the public `remove` has the following implementation:

```
public T remove(T entry)
{
   ReturnObject oldEntry = new ReturnObject(null);
   BinaryNodeInterface<T> newRoot = removeEntry(getRootNode(), entry,
                                         oldEntry);

   setRootNode(newRoot);

   return oldEntry.get();
} // end remove
```

27.30   **The private method `removeEntry`.** Since `remove` handles the communication with `removeEntry`, most of the algorithm of Segment 27.28 is left for `removeEntry`. If the entry to be removed is in the root, `removeEntry` calls the yet-to-be-written method `removeFromRoot` to remove it. If the entry is in either of the root's subtrees, `removeEntry` calls itself recursively. The implementation of `removeEntry` follows:

```
/** Task: Removes an entry from the tree rooted at a given node.
 *  @param rootNode  a reference to the root of a tree
 *  @param entry     the object to be removed
 *  @param oldEntry  an object whose data field is null
 *  @return the root node of the resulting tree; if entry matches
 *          an entry in the tree, oldEntry's data field is the entry
 *          that was removed from the tree; otherwise it is null */
private BinaryNodeInterface<T> removeEntry(BinaryNodeInterface<T>
                             rootNode, T entry, ReturnObject oldEntry)
{
  if (rootNode != null)
  {
    T rootData = rootNode.getData();
    int comparison = entry.compareTo(rootData);

    if (comparison == 0)       // entry == root entry
    {
      oldEntry.set(rootData);
```

```
      rootNode = removeFromRoot(rootNode);
    }
    else if (comparison < 0)    // entry < root entry
    {
      BinaryNodeInterface<T> leftChild = rootNode.getLeftChild();
      BinaryNodeInterface<T> subtreeRoot = removeEntry(leftChild,
                                            entry, oldEntry);
      rootNode.setLeftChild(subtreeRoot);
    }
    else                        // entry > root entry
    {
      BinaryNodeInterface<T> rightChild = rootNode.getRightChild();
      rootNode.setRightChild(removeEntry(rightChild, entry,
                                    oldEntry));
    } // end if
  } // end if

  return rootNode;
} // end removeEntry
```

27.31 **The algorithm removeFromRoot.** The previous method removeEntry removes the entry in the root of a given subtree by calling the method removeFromRoot. In that method, we see whether the root node has zero, one, or two children and then proceed according to the discussion in Segments 27.20 through 27.27. If the given node has at most one child, we delete the node and its entry. To remove the entry in a node having two children, we must find the largest entry in the node's left subtree. We remove the node containing this largest entry. The largest entry then replaces the entry to be removed.

The following algorithm summarizes these steps:

Algorithm removeFromRoot(rootNode)
// *Removes the entry in a given root node of a subtree.*

if (rootNode *has two children*)
{
  largestNode = *node with the largest entry in the left subtree of* rootNode
  Replace the entry in rootNode *with the entry in* largestNode
  Remove largestNode *from the tree*
}
else if (rootNode *has a right child*)
  rootNode = rootNode's *right child*
else
  rootNode = rootNode's *left child* // *possibly* null
// *Assertion: if* rootNode *was a leaf, it is now* null

return rootNode

27.32 **The private method removeFromRoot.** The implementation of the previous algorithm calls the private methods findLargest and removeLargest, which we will write shortly. Although remove-FromRoot is not recursive, both findLargest and removeLargest are.

Given the root of a subtree, removeFromRoot returns the root of the subtree after a node is removed.

```
/** Task: Removes the entry in a given root node of a subtree.
 *  @param rootNode  the root node of the subtree
 *  @return the root node of the revised subtree */
private BinaryNodeInterface<T> removeFromRoot(BinaryNodeInterface<T>
                                                   rootNode)
{
  // Case 1: rootNode has two children
  if (rootNode.hasLeftChild() && rootNode.hasRightChild())
  {
    // find node with largest entry in left subtree
    BinaryNodeInterface<T> leftSubtreeRoot = rootNode.getLeftChild();
    BinaryNodeInterface<T> largestNode = findLargest(leftSubtreeRoot);

    // replace entry in root
    rootNode.setData(largestNode.getData());

    // remove node with largest entry in left subtree
    rootNode.setLeftChild(removeLargest(leftSubtreeRoot));
  } // end if

  // Case 2: rootNode has at most one child
  else if (rootNode.hasRightChild())
    rootNode = rootNode.getRightChild();
  else
    rootNode = rootNode.getLeftChild();

  // Assertion: if rootNode was a leaf, it is now null

  return rootNode;
} // end removeEntry
```

27.33   **The private method `findLargest`.** The node with the largest entry will occur in the rightmost node of a binary search tree. Thus, as long as a node has a right child, we search the subtree rooted at that child. The following recursive method performs this search, given the tree:

```
/** Task: Finds the node containing the largest entry in a
 *        given tree.
 *  @param rootNode  the root node of the tree
 *  @return the node containing the largest entry in the tree */
private BinaryNodeInterface<T> findLargest(BinaryNodeInterface<T>
                                                   rootNode)
{
  if (rootNode.hasRightChild())
    rootNode = findLargest(rootNode.getRightChild());

  return rootNode;
} // end findLargest
```

27.34   **The private method `removeLargest`.** To remove the node with the largest entry, we cannot simply call `findLargest` and then remove the returned node. We cannot remove a node from a tree knowing only its reference. We must have a reference to its parent as well. The following recursive method removes the node with the largest entry—that is, the rightmost node—but unfortunately it must repeat the search that findLargest just performed.

```
/** Task: Removes the node containing the largest entry in a
 *          given tree.
 *   @param rootNode  the root node of the tree
 *   @return the root node of the revised tree */
private BinaryNodeInterface<T> removeLargest(BinaryNodeInterface<T>
                                              rootNode)
{
  if (rootNode.hasRightChild())
  {
    BinaryNodeInterface<T> rightChild = rootNode.getRightChild();
    BinaryNodeInterface<T> root = removeLargest(rightChild);
    rootNode.setRightChild(root);
  }
  else
    rootNode = rootNode.getLeftChild();

  return rootNode;
} // end removeLargest
```

The method begins much like findLargest. To remove the rightmost node from the given tree, we remove the rightmost node from tree's right subtree. The recursive call returns the root of the revised subtree. This root must become the right child of the original tree's root.

When a tree's root has no right child, the left child is returned, effectively deleting the root. Notice that this recursive method does not explicitly keep track of the parent of the current right child. Rather, a reference to this parent is retained in the implicit stack of the recursion.

27.35　The previous recursive approach to removing an entry from a binary search tree is typical. A language, such as Java, that uses only call-by-value to pass arguments tends to complicate this recursive implementation by forcing methods to return references to root nodes. You might find the following iterative approach somewhat easier to understand. Since it deletes the node containing the inorder predecessor without repeating the search for it, the iterative remove is more efficient than the recursive version.

An Iterative Implementation

27.36　**The algorithm.** Recall that the method remove is given an entry that matches the entry to be removed from the tree. So remove's first step is to search the tree. We locate the node whose data matches the given entry, and we note the node's parent, if any. Whether we delete the node we've found or another one depends on how many children it has. Although Segment 27.19 listed three possibilities, we can collapse them into two cases:

1. The node has two children
2. The node has at most one child

In the second case, we delete the node itself. But if the node has two children, we delete another node that has at most one child. That is, we transform Case 1 into Case 2.

The following pseudocode describes what remove must do:

Algorithm remove(entry)
result = **null**
currentNode = *node that contains a match for* entry
parentNode = currentNode's *parent*

if (currentNode != **null**) // *that is, if entry is found*
{
  result = currentNode's *data (the entry to be removed from the tree)*

  // *Case 1*
  if (currentNode *has two children*)
  {
    // *get node to remove and its parent*
    nodeToRemove = *node containing* entry's *inorder predecessor; it has at most one child*
    parentNode = nodeToRemove's *parent*

    Copy entry from nodeToRemove *to* currentNode
    currentNode = nodeToRemove
    // *Assertion:* currentNode *is the node to be removed; it has at most one child*
    // *Assertion: Case 1 has been transformed to Case 2*
  }
  // *Case 2:* currentNode *has at most one child*
  Delete currentNode *from the tree*
}
return result

27.37 **The public method remove.** We will implement the major steps of the previous algorithm as private methods that remove can call. The private method findNode locates the node that contains a match for the given entry. Since we need a reference to that node as well as one to its parent, we make findNode return a pair of nodes. To that end, we design a private class NodePair that has constructors and the accessor methods getFirst and getSecond. NodePair will be an inner class of our class BinarySearchTree.

The private method getNodeToRemove finds the node containing the inorder predecessor of the the entry in a given node. Since we also need that node's parent, the method returns a pair of nodes as an instance of the class NodePair.

Finally, the private method removeNode deletes a node that has at most one child. We give the method references to the node and its parent, if any.

Using these private methods, we can implement remove, as follows:

```
public T remove(T entry)
{
  T result = null;

  // locate node (and its parent) that contains a match for entry
  NodePair pair = findNode(entry);
  BinaryNodeInterface<T> currentNode = pair.getFirst();
  BinaryNodeInterface<T> parentNode = pair.getSecond();

  if (currentNode != null) // entry is found
  {
    result = currentNode.getData(); // get entry to be removed
```

```
    // Case 1: currentNode has two children
    if (currentNode.hasLeftChild() && currentNode.hasRightChild())
    {
      // replace entry in currentNode with the entry in another node
      // that has at most one child; that node can be deleted

      // get node to remove (contains inorder predecessor; has at
      // most one child) and its parent
      pair = getNodeToRemove(currentNode);
      BinaryNodeInterface<T> nodeToRemove = pair.getFirst();
      parentNode = pair.getSecond();

      // copy entry from nodeToRemove to currentNode
      currentNode.setData(nodeToRemove.getData());

      currentNode = nodeToRemove;
      // Assertion: currentNode is the node to be removed; it has at
      // most one child
      // Assertion: Case 1 has been transformed to Case 2
    } // end if

    // Case 2: currentNode has at most one child; delete it
    removeNode(currentNode, parentNode);
  } // end if

  return result;
} // end remove
```

27.38   **The private method `findNode`.** To find the node that contains a match for a given entry, we use the compareTo method within a loop to compare the given entry with the other entries in the tree. The method returns a pair of references to the desired node and its parent as an instance of the class NodePair. Thus, findNode has the following form:

```
private NodePair findNode(T entry)
{
  NodePair result = new NodePair();
  boolean found = false;
  . . .

  if (found)
    result = new NodePair(currentNode, parentNode);
    // found entry is currentNode.getData()

  return result;
} // end findNode
```

The details of the implementation of findNode are left as an exercise.

Question 9   Complete the implementation of the method findNode.

27.39   **The private method `getNodeToRemove`.** After remove locates the node that contains the entry to be removed from the tree, it proceeds according the number of the node's children. If the node has two children, remove must remove another node that has no more than one child. The private method getNodeToRemove finds this node. In particular, the method implements the first step of the pseudocode given in Segment 27.25:

Find the rightmost node R in N's left subtree

Here, node *N* is currentNode and node *R* is rightChild.

The details of this step are described by the following pseudocode:

```
// find the inorder predecessor by searching the left subtree; it will be the largest
// entry in the subtree, occurring in the node as far right as possible
leftSubtreeRoot = left child of currentNode
rightChild = leftSubtreeRoot
priorNode = currentNode

while (rightChild has a right child )
{
  priorNode = rightChild
  rightChild = right child of rightChild
}
// Assertion: rightChild is the node to be removed and has no more than one child
```

The following Java code implements getNodeToRemove:

```
private NodePair getNodeToRemove(BinaryNodeInterface<T> currentNode)
{
  // find node with largest entry in left subtree by
  // moving as far right in the subtree as possible
  BinaryNodeInterface<T> leftSubtreeRoot = currentNode.getLeftChild();
  BinaryNodeInterface<T> rightChild = leftSubtreeRoot;
  BinaryNodeInterface<T> priorNode = currentNode;

  while (rightChild.hasRightChild())
  {
    priorNode = rightChild;
    rightChild = rightChild.getRightChild();
  } // end while

  // rightChild contains the inorder predecessor and is the node to
  // remove; priorNode is its parent

  return new NodePair(rightChild, priorNode);
} // end getNodeToRemove
```

27.40   **The private method removeNode.** Our last method assumes that the node to remove—call it nodeToRemove—has at most one child. If nodeToRemove is not the root, parentNode is its parent.

The method begins by setting childNode to the child, if any, of nodeToRemove. If nodeToRemove is a leaf, childNode is set to null. Then the method removes nodeToRemove, accounting for the case when the node is the root as follows:

```
if (nodeToRemove is the root of the tree)
  Set the root of the tree to childNode
else
  Link parentNode to childNode, thereby deleting nodeToRemove
```

If we set the root of the tree to childNode, realize that we will correctly set the root to null if nodeToRemove is a leaf.

The implementation of removeNode follows:

```
private void removeNode(BinaryNodeInterface<T> nodeToRemove,
                        BinaryNodeInterface<T> parentNode)
{
  BinaryNodeInterface<T> childNode;

  if (nodeToRemove.hasLeftChild())
    childNode = nodeToRemove.getLeftChild();
  else
    childNode = nodeToRemove.getRightChild();

  // Assertion: if nodeToRemove is a leaf, childNode is null
  assert (nodeToRemove.isLeaf() && childNode == null) ||
         !nodeToRemove.isLeaf();

  if (nodeToRemove == getRootNode())
    setRootNode(childNode);
  else if (parentNode.getLeftChild() == nodeToRemove)
    parentNode.setLeftChild(childNode);
  else
    parentNode.setRightChild(childNode);
} // end removeNode
```

The Efficiency of Operations

27.41 Each of the operations add, remove, and getEntry requires a search that begins at the root of the tree. When adding an entry, the search ends at a leaf if the entry is not already in the tree; otherwise, the search can end sooner. When removing or retrieving an entry, the search ends at a leaf if it is unsuccessful; a successful search can end sooner. So in the worst case, these searches begin at the root and examine each node on a path that ends at a leaf. The longest path from the root to a leaf has a length that equals the height of the tree. Thus, the maximum number of comparisons that each operation requires is directly proportional to the height h of the tree. That is, the operations add, remove, and getEntry are $O(h)$.

Recall that several different binary search trees can contain the same data. Figure 27-13 contains two such trees. Figure 27-13a is the shortest binary search tree that we can form from this data; Figure 27-13b is the tallest such tree.

The tallest tree has height n if it contains n nodes. In fact, this tree looks like a linked chain, and searching it is like searching a linked chain. It is an $O(n)$ operation. Thus, add, remove, and getEntry for this tree are also $O(n)$ operations.

In contrast, the shortest tree is full. Searching this tree will be as efficient as possible. In Chapter 25, we saw that the height of a full tree containing n nodes is $\log_2 (n + 1)$. Thus, in the worst case, searching a full binary search tree is an $O(\log n)$ operation. So add, remove, and getEntry are $O(\log n)$ operations in this case.

Question 10 What is the worst-case efficiency of the method contains?

Question 11 What is the worst-case efficiency of the method isEmpty?

Figure 27-13 Two binary search trees that contain the same data

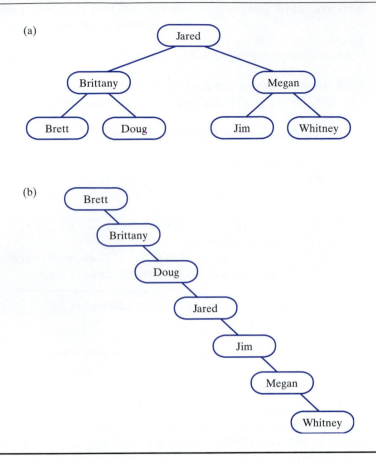

The Importance of Balance

27.42   We do not need a full binary search tree to get O(log *n*) performance from the addition, removal, and retrieval operations. For example, if we remove some of the leaves from a full tree, we will not change the performance of these operations. In particular, a complete tree will also give us O(log *n*) performance.

   The notion of *balance* affects the performance of a particular search tree. In a **completely balanced** tree, the subtrees of each node have exactly the same height. The only completely balanced binary trees are full. Other trees are said to be **height balanced**, or simply **balanced**, if the subtrees of each node in the tree differ in height by no more than 1. A complete binary tree is height balanced, for example, but so are some trees that are not complete, as Figure 27-14 shows. Moreover, the concept of balance applies to all trees, not just binary trees or binary search trees.

   It happens that the addition, removal, and retrieval operations of a binary search tree will have O(log *n*) performance if the tree is height balanced. Certainly when we create a binary search tree, we want it to be height balanced. Unfortunately, we can disturb the balance of a binary search tree by adding or removing entries, since these operations affect the shape of the tree.

Figure 27-14 Some binary trees that are height balanced

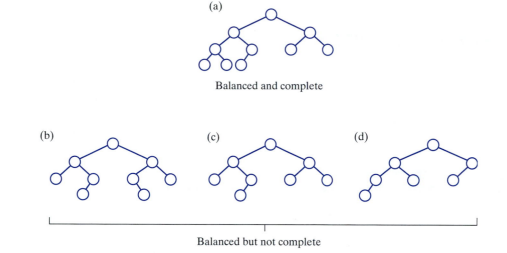

(a)

Balanced and complete

(b) (c) (d)

Balanced but not complete

The Order in Which Nodes Are Added

27.43   If you answered Question 6 in Segment 27.12 correctly, you realized that the order in which you add entries to a binary search tree affects the shape of the tree. This observation is most important when you create a binary search tree by making additions to an initially empty tree.

For example, suppose that we want to create the full binary search tree in Figure 27-13a from a given set of data. Often such data sets are sorted, so it is reasonable to assume that we have the names in alphabetical order. Now imagine that we define an empty binary search tree and then add the names to it in the following order: *Brett, Brittany, Doug, Jared, Jim, Megan, Whitney.* Figure 27-13b shows the tree that results from these additions. It is as tall as possible and has the least efficient operations among the trees that we could build.

 Note: If you add entries into an initially empty binary search tree, do not add them in sorted order.

27.44   In what order should we add the entries? *Jared* is the root of the tree in Figure 27-13a, so let's add *Jared* first. Next add *Brittany* and then *Brett* and *Doug.* Finally, add *Megan, Jim,* and *Whitney.* While it should be clear that by using this order we get the tree in Figure 27-13a, how do we determine the order ahead of time? Looking at our alphabetical set of names, notice that *Jared* is exactly in the middle. We add *Jared* first. *Brittany* is in the middle of the left half of the data set, so we add *Brittany* next. The halves that *Brittany* defines each contain only one name, so we add them next. We repeat this process with the names that occur after *Jared*—that is, the right half of the data set.

We shouldn't have to do this much work! In fact, if we add data to a binary search tree in random order, we can expect a tree whose operations are O(log *n*). It probably will not be the shortest tree we could create, but it will be close.

The operations of a binary search tree ensure that the tree remains a binary search tree. Unfortunately, they do not ensure that the tree remains balanced. Chapter 29 looks at search trees that are responsible for maintaining their balance, and hence their efficiency.

An Implementation of the ADT Dictionary

27.45 We can use the ideas developed thus far in this chapter to implement the ADT dictionary. Recall from Chapter 17 that a dictionary stores search keys and their associated values. For example, suppose that you want a dictionary of names and telephone numbers. In terms of the ADT dictionary, the name could be the search key and the telephone number could be the corresponding value. To retrieve a telephone number, we would provide a name, and the dictionary would return its value.

Here is the interface for a dictionary as given in Segment 17.4, but without the comments:

```java
import java.util.Iterator;
public interface DictionaryInterface<K, V>
{
   public V add(K key, V value);
   public V remove(K key);
   public V getValue(K key);
   public boolean contains(K key);
   public Iterator<K> getKeyIterator();
   public Iterator<V> getValueIterator();
   public boolean isEmpty();
   public boolean isFull();
   public int getSize();
   public void clear();
} // end DictionaryInterface
```

Earlier in this book we saw several implementations of the ADT dictionary. A dictionary implementation that uses a balanced search tree to store its entries can be an attractive alternative to these implementations. As an example of such an implementation, we will use a binary search tree here, even though it might not remain balanced after additions or removals. Chapter 29 presents search trees that are always balanced and could be used instead to implement the dictionary.

27.46 **The data entries.** We need a class of data objects that will contain both a search key and an associated value. A class Entry—similar to the class we used in the array-based implementation of the ADT dictionary in Chapter 18—is suitable for our purpose. Here, we make the class Comparable by defining the method compareTo. This method compares two instances of Entry by comparing their search keys. Thus, the search keys of this dictionary must belong to a Comparable class.

The class Entry can be private and internal to the class Dictionary, as Listing 27-3 shows. This listing also shows Dictionary's data field—a binary search tree—as well as the constructor that allocates the tree. Notice how Entry is used in both the declaration and allocation of the tree.

Listing 27-3 An outline of an implementation of the ADT dictionary that uses a binary search tree

```java
import TreePackage.SearchTreeInterface;
import TreePackage.BinarySearchTree;
import java.util.Iterator;
public class Dictionary<K extends Comparable<? super K>, V>
        implements DictionaryInterface<K, V>, java.io.Serializable
```

```
{
  private SearchTreeInterface<Entry<K, V>> bst;

  public Dictionary()
  {
    bst = new BinarySearchTree<Entry<K, V>>();
  } // end default constructor
```

< *Methods that implement dictionary operations are here.* >
. . .

```
  private class Entry<S extends Comparable<? super S>, T>
          implements Comparable<Entry<S, T>>, java.io.Serializable
  {
    private S key;
    private T value;

    private Entry(S searchKey, T dataValue)
    {
      key = searchKey;
      value = dataValue;
    } // end constructor

    public int compareTo(Entry<S, T> other)
    {
      return key.compareTo(other.key);
    } // end compareTo
```

< *The class* Entry *also defines the methods* equals, getKey, getValue, *and* setValue;
  no setKey *method is provided.* >
. . .

```
  } // end Entry
} // end Dictionary
```

27.47   **The `Dictionary` methods.** The method add encapsulates the given search key and value into an instance of Entry that it passes to BinarySearchTree's add method. It then uses the entry that this method returns to form its own return value. Dictionary's add method has the following implementation:

```
    public V add(K key, V value)
    {
      Entry<K, V> newEntry = new Entry<K, V>(key, value);
      Entry<K, V> returnedEntry = bst.add(newEntry);

      V result = null;
      if (returnedEntry != null)
        result = returnedEntry.getValue();

      return result;
    } // end add
```

Both `remove` and `getValue` have implementations that are similar to `add`'s. Since these methods have only a search key as a parameter, the instances of `Entry` that they form encapsulate the key and a `null` value. For example, `remove` begins as

```java
public V remove(K key)
{
   Entry<K, V> findEntry = new Entry<K, V>(key, null);
   Entry<K, V> returnedEntry = bst.remove(findEntry);
```

and ends just like the method `add`. The implementation of the method `getValue` is identical to that of `remove`, except that it calls `getEntry` from `BinarySearchTree` instead of `remove`.

We can implement the methods `getSize`, `isEmpty`, `contains`, and `clear` by calling appropriate methods of `BinarySearchTree`. We leave these to you as exercises.

Question 12 Implement each of the `Dictionary` methods `getSize`, `isEmpty`, `contains`, and `clear` by calling methods of `BinarySearchTree`.

Question 13 Write another implementation of the method `contains` by invoking `Dictionary`'s method `getValue`.

27.48   **The iterators.** `DictionaryInterface` specifies two methods that return iterators. The method `getKeyIterator` returns an iterator that accesses the search keys in sorted order; `getValueIterator` returns an iterator that provides the values belonging to these search keys.

For example, `getKeyIterator` has the following implementation:

```java
public Iterator<K> getKeyIterator()
{
   return new KeyIterator();
} // end getKeyIterator
```

The class `KeyIterator` is internal to `Dictionary` and uses the method `getInorderIterator` from `BinarySearchTree`. It has the following implementation:

```java
private class KeyIterator implements Iterator<K>
{
   Iterator<Entry<K, V>> localIterator;

   public KeyIterator()
   {
      localIterator = bst.getInorderIterator();
   } // end default constructor

   public boolean hasNext()
   {
      return localIterator.hasNext();
   } // end hasNext

   public K next()
   {
      Entry<K, V> nextEntry = localIterator.next();
      return nextEntry.getKey();
   } // end next
```

```
public void remove()
{
    throw new UnsupportedOperationException();
} // end remove
} // end KeyIterator
```

You implement `getValueIterator` in a similar manner.

27.49 **Comments.** This implementation of the ADT dictionary is as time efficient as the underlying search tree. When the binary search tree is balanced, the operations are O(log n). But a binary search tree can lose its balance, and so the efficiency of the dictionary operations can degrade to O(n) as entries are added or removed. A search tree that stays balanced, such as those you will see in Chapter 29, would provide a better implementation of the dictionary than the one shown here.

Also notice that a binary search tree maintains the dictionary entries in sorted order by their search keys. As a result, `getKeyIterator` enables us to traverse the search keys in sorted order. In contrast, other dictionary implementations—hashing, for example—traverse the search keys in unsorted order.

CHAPTER SUMMARY

- A binary search tree is a binary tree whose nodes contain `Comparable` objects. For each node in the tree,
  - The data in a node is greater than the data in the node's left subtree
  - The data in a node is less than (or equal to) the data in the node's right subtree

- A search tree has the operations `contains`, `getEntry`, `add`, `remove`, and `getInorderIterator`, in addition to the operations common to all trees.

- The class `BinarySearchTree` can be a subclass of `BinaryTree`, but it must disallow `setTree`. A client must create a binary search tree by using only the `add` method, to avoid changing the order of the nodes in the tree.

- The search algorithm to locate an entry in a binary search tree forms the basis of the methods `getEntry`, `add`, and `remove`. These methods each have reasonable iterative and recursive implementations.

- Each addition of an entry to a binary search tree adds a leaf to the tree. The new entry is placed where the search algorithm will find it.

- Removing an entry from a binary search tree depends on the number of children that belong to the node containing the entry. When the node is a leaf or has one child, you remove the node itself. The node's parent can adopt a solitary child when it exists. However, when the node N has two children, you replace the node's entry with another one r whose node is easy to remove. To maintain the order of the binary search tree, this entry r can be either the largest entry in N's left subtree or the smallest entry in N's right subtree. It follows that r's node is either a leaf or a node with one child.

- In a completely balanced binary tree, the subtrees of each node have exactly the same height. Such trees must be full. Other binary trees are said to be height balanced if the subtrees of each node in the tree differ in height by no more than 1.

- The retrieve, add, and remove operations on a binary search tree can be as fast as O(log n) or as slow as O(n). The performance of the search depends on the shape of the tree. When the tree is height balanced, the operations on a binary search tree are O(log n).

- The order in which you add entries to a binary search tree affects the tree's shape and hence its balance. Random additions, as opposed to sorted ones, tend to result in a balanced tree.

- You can implement the ADT dictionary by using a binary search tree. Although the implementation is not difficult to write, its efficiency can suffer if additions and removals destroy the balance of the tree.

1. Show the results of adding the following search keys to an initially empty binary search tree: $10, 5, 6, 13, 15, 8, 14, 7, 12, 4$.

2. What ordering of the search keys $10, 5, 6, 13, 15, 8, 14, 7, 12, 4$ would result in the most balanced tree if they were added to an initially empty binary search tree?

3. Give four different orderings of the search keys $10, 5, 6, 13, 15, 8, 14, 7, 12, 4$ that would result in the least balanced tree if they were added to an initially empty binary search tree.

4. In Chapter 10, Figure 10-10a shows the recursive computation of the term F_6 in the Fibonacci sequence. Is this tree height balanced?

5. Implement the method getEntry iteratively.

6. Remove *Doug* from the binary search tree pictured in Figure 27-11a. Then remove *Chad* in two different ways.

7. Remove *Doug* from the binary search tree pictured in Figure 27-11d in two different ways.

8. Suppose that a node with two children contains an entry e, as Figure 27-9a illustrates. Show that you will have a binary search tree if you replace e with its inorder successor b and remove the node that contains b.

9. Why does an inorder traversal of a binary search tree visit the nodes in sorted search-key order? Use the definition of a binary search tree given in Segment 27.1.

10. Consider the full binary search tree pictured in Figure 27-13a. Now imagine that you traverse the tree and save its data in a file. If you then read the file and add the data to an initially empty binary search tree, what tree will you get if the traversal was

    a. Preorder   **b.** Inorder   **c.** Level order   **d.** Postorder

11. Imagine that you traverse a binary search tree and save its data in a file. If you then read the file and add the data to an initially empty binary search tree, what traversal should you use when writing the file so that the new tree is

    a. As tall as possible
    b. Identical to the original binary search tree

12. Segment 27.17 gave an iterative algorithm for the method addEntry. Implement the following alternate algorithm for this method:

    Algorithm **addEntry(binarySearchTree, newEntry)**

    ```
    result = null
    currentNode = root node of binarySearchTree
    parentNode = null

    while (newEntry is not found and currentNode is not null)
    {
        if (newEntry matches entry in currentNode)
        {
            result = entry in currentNode
    ```

```
        Replace entry in currentNode with newEntry
    }
    else if (newEntry < entry in currentNode)
    {
        parentNode = currentNode
        currentNode = the left child of currentNode
    }
    else // newEntry > entry in currentNode
    {
        parentNode = currentNode
        currentNode = the right child of currentNode
    }
}

if (newEntry is not found in the tree)
{
    Create a new node and place newEntry into it

    if (newEntry < entry in parentNode)
        Make the new node the left child of parentNode
    else
        Make the new node the right child of parentNode
}

return result
```

13. The methods `remove` and the recursive `removeEntry`, as described in Segments 27.28 through 27.30, use the inner class `ReturnObject`. In this way, `removeEntry` can convey to `remove` both the root of the revised tree and the entry it removed. Revise these methods to instead use a class `Pair<T1, T2>`, like the one given in Segment 2.6 of Chapter 2. `Pair` will need accessor methods for its fields. The method `removeEntry` can then return the root and the removed entry as a `Pair` object.

14. Segment 27.44 builds a balanced binary search tree from one particular set of search keys. Generalize this approach, and write a recursive algorithm that creates a balanced binary search tree from a sorted collection of *n* items.

15. Write an algorithm that returns the smallest search key in a binary search tree.

16. Beginning with Segment 27.23, you saw how to find the inorder predecessor or the inorder successor of a node with two children. Unfortunately, this approach will not work for a leaf node. For a node with one child, the technique will find either the predecessor or the successor, but not both. Discuss how the structure of a node might be modified so that the inorder predecessor or the inorder successor can be found for any node.

17. Write an algorithm that returns the second largest value in a binary search tree containing at least two nodes.

18. Why might a binary search tree work poorly as an implementation of a priority queue?

19. Consider a method for a binary search tree that decides whether the tree is height balanced, as Segment 27.42 describes. The header of the method could be as follows:

```
public boolean isBalanced()
```

Write this method for the class `BinarySearchTree`. It should call a private recursive method of the same name.

20. Consider two empty binary search trees that allow duplicate entries with the same search key. To one of the trees, add *m* unique entries, each with a different search key. To the other, add each of these *m* entries *k* times for a total of *m k* entries. Assuming that each entry is stored in a single node, compare the heights of the two trees. Discuss how the order in which entries are added to the second tree affects its height. Give the addition orders that lead to the tallest tree and the shortest tree.

21. Segment 27.4 describes a binary search tree that allows duplicates. You place the duplicate of an entry in the entry's right subtree.

a. What is an advantage and a disadvantage of this scheme?
b. Suppose that we change the definition of a binary search tree so that the duplicate of an entry can be in either the entry's right subtree or its left subtree. If we choose the subtree randomly, what is an advantage and a disadvantage of this scheme?

PROJECTS

1. Specify and implement a class of binary search trees in which duplicate entries are allowed. Place the duplicate of an entry in the entry's right subtree, as suggested in Segment 27.4. Provide a method that searches the tree for a given entry and returns the first one it finds. Also, provide a similar method that returns a list of all entries that match the given one.

2. Repeat the previous project, but instead randomly place the duplicate of an entry in the entry's left or right subtree. Thus, we modify the definition of a binary search tree as follows.

For each node in a binary search tree,

- The data in a node is greater than *or equal to* the data in the node's left subtree
- The data in a node is less than *or equal to* the data in the node's right subtree

Searching for a duplicate must allow a search of both subtrees.

3. Implement the ADT sorted list by using a binary search tree.

4. Devise an algorithm that uses a binary search tree to sort an array of objects. Such a sort is called **treesort**. Implement and test your algorithm. Discuss the time efficiency of your treesort in both the average and worst cases.

5. Implement a binary search tree that includes the following methods based on Exercises 15 and 16:

```
/** @return the entry with the smallest search key */
public T getMin();

/** @return the entry with the largest search key */
public T getMax();

/** @return either the inorder predecessor of entry, or
 *          entry if it's the smallest element in the tree, or
 *          null if entry is not in the tree */
public T getPredecessor(T entry);
```

```
/** @return either the inorder successor of entry, or
 *             entry if it's the largest element in the tree, or
 *             null if entry is not in the tree */
public T getSuccessor(T entry);
```

6. Implement the class `ArrayBinarySearchTree` that extends `ArrayBinaryTree`, described in Project 7 of Chapter 26.

7. Write Java code that creates a binary search tree from n random integer values and returns the height of the search tree. Run the code for $n = 2^h-1$, where h ranges from 4 to 12. Compare the height of the randomly built search tree with h, the height of the shortest binary search tree.

8. Repeat Project 3 of Chapter 17, but use binary search trees to implement the two dictionaries. Write Java code that will create within the first dictionary a balanced binary search tree of the reserved words in the Java language. Why is it important that the search tree containing Java reserved words be balanced? Can you guarantee that the search tree of user-defined identifiers is also balanced?

9. This project compares the performance of two binary search trees as more objects are added to them. Initially, one tree is balanced and the other is not.

   First modify `BinarySearchTreeInterface` and `BinarySearchTree` so that the add method returns the number of comparisons used. Then write a program that uses the new version of `BinarySearchTree`, as follows.

   Create two empty binary search trees. Associate two variables with each tree. One variable sums the number of comparisons used in adding values to a tree, and the other sums the heights of a tree at certain times following the insertion of several values. Name these variables `comparisonSum1`, `comparisonSum2`, `heightSum1`, and `heightSum2`.

   In a loop that executes 100 times, do the following:

   - Add the values 1000, 2000, 3000, 4000, 5000, 6000, and 7000 to both trees. In the first tree, add them in increasing order. In the second, add them in an order that forms a complete tree. Your first tree will be unbalanced, while the second tree will be balanced.
   - Generate ten random values between 0 and 8000. Add these values to each tree in the same order. After each of these additions, update each tree's `comparisonSum` variable by the number of comparisons performed for the insertion.
   - Add each tree's height to its `heightSum` variable.
   - Clear the two trees.

   After the loop ends, compute the average number of comparisons needed to insert values into each tree. (For each tree, divide its `comparisonSum` by 1000. Note that 1000 is 100—the number of iterations—multiplied by 10—the number of values inserted in one iteration.) Also compute the average height of each tree after the insertions. (Divide each `heightSum` variable by 100.) Display and record your results.

   Run the program a second time, but instead add 100 random values between 0 and 8000 during each iteration of the loop. Run it a third time, but instead add 1000 random values. Discuss your results and draw a conclusion.

28

A Heap Implementation

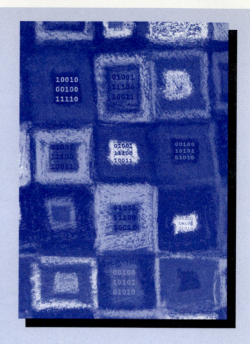

CONTENTS

PREREQUISITES

OBJECTIVES

After studying this chapter, you should be able to

- Use an array to represent a heap
- Add an entry to an array-based heap
- Remove the root of an array-based heap
- Create a heap from given entries
- Sort an array by using a heap sort

Recall from Chapter 25 that a heap is a complete binary tree whose nodes are ordered in a certain manner. When a binary tree is complete, you can use an array to represent it in an efficient and elegant way. The most common implementation of a heap uses an array, and that is the one we will describe in this chapter.

As you saw in Chapter 25, you can use a heap as an efficient implementation of the ADT priority queue. Later, this chapter will show you how to sort an array by using a heap.

Reprise: The ADT Heap

28.1   A heap is a complete binary tree whose nodes contain `Comparable` objects. In a maxheap, the object in each node is greater than or equal to the objects in the node's descendants. Segment 25.32 provided the following interface for the maxheap:

```java
public interface MaxHeapInterface<T extends Comparable<? super T>>
{
    public void add(T newEntry);
    public T removeMax();
    public T getMax();
    public boolean isEmpty();
    public int getSize();
    public void clear();
} // end MaxHeapInterface
```

We will use this interface in our implementation of a maxheap.

Note: You may also have heard the word "heap" used to refer to the collection of memory cells that are available for allocation to your program when the `new` operator executes. But that heap is not an instance of the ADT heap that we will discuss in this chapter. It would be considered, however, in a book about programming languages.

Using an Array to Represent a Heap

28.2   **Representing a complete binary tree.** We begin by using an array to represent a complete binary tree. A complete tree is full to its next-to-last level, and its leaves on the last level are filled in from left to right. Thus, until we get to the last leaf, a complete tree has no holes.

Suppose that we number the nodes in a complete binary tree in the order in which a level-order traversal would visit them, beginning with 1. Figure 28-1a shows such a tree numbered in this way. Now suppose that we place the result of this tree's level-order traversal into consecutive array locations beginning at index 1, as Figure 28-1b shows. This representation of the data in the tree enables us to implement any needed tree operations. By beginning at index 1 instead of 0, we can simplify the implementation somewhat, as you will see.

28.3   Since the tree is complete, we can locate either the children or the parent of any node by performing a simple computation on the node's number. This number is the same as the node's corresponding array index. Thus, the children of the node i—if they exist—are stored in the array at indices $2i$ and $2i + 1$. The parent of this node is at array index $i/2$, unless of course the node is the root. In that case, $i/2$ is 0, since the root is at index 1. To detect the root, we can watch for either this index or a special value—called a **sentinel**—that we place at index 0.

Figure 28-1   (a) A complete binary tree with its nodes numbered in level order; (b) its representation as an array

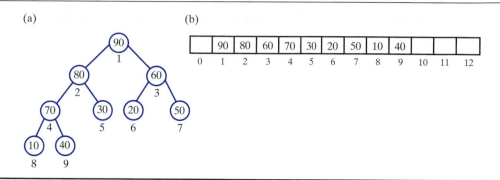

Note: When a binary tree is complete, using an array instead of linked nodes is desirable. You can use a level-order traversal to store the tree's data into consecutive locations of an array. This representation enables you to quickly locate the data in a node's parent or children. If you begin storing the tree at index 1 of the array—that is, if you skip the array's first element—the node at array index i

- Has a parent at index $i/2$, unless the node is the root (i is 1)
- Has any children at indices $2i$ and $2i + 1$

The complete binary tree in Figure 28-1 is actually a maxheap. We will now use the previous array representation of a complete tree in our implementation of a maxheap.

Question 1   If an array contains the entries of a heap in level order beginning at index 0, what array entries represent a node's parent, left child, and right child?

28.4   **Beginning the class MaxHeap.** As Listing 28-1 shows, our class begins with the following data fields: an array of `Comparable` heap entries, the index of the last entry in the array, and a constant for the default initial capacity of the heap. If `lastIndex` is less than 1, the heap is empty, since we begin the heap at index 1. Two simple constructors are similar to constructors we have seen before in array-based implementations. We allocate one extra array location, since we will not use the first one. The methods `getMax`, `isEmpty`, `getSize`, and `clear` have simple implementations that are shown in this listing. We consider the methods `add` and `removeMax` next.

Listing 28-1   The class `MaxHeap`, partially completed

```
public class MaxHeap<T extends Comparable<? super T>>
        implements MaxHeapInterface<T>, java.io.Serializable
{
   private T[] heap;        // array of heap entries
   private int lastIndex;   // index of last entry
```

```java
        private static final int DEFAULT_INITIAL_CAPACITY = 25;
        public MaxHeap()
        {
          this(DEFAULT_INITIAL_CAPACITY); // call next constructor
        } // end default constructor
        public MaxHeap(int initialCapacity)
        {
          heap = (T[]) new Comparable[initialCapacity + 1];
          lastIndex = 0;
        } // end constructor
        public void add(T newEntry)
        {
          < See Segment 28.8. >
        } // end add
        public T removeMax()
        {
          < See Segment 28.12. >
        } // end removeMax
        public T getMax()
        {
          T root = null;
          if (!isEmpty())
            root = heap[1];
          return root;
        } // end getMax
        public boolean isEmpty()
        {
          return lastIndex < 1;
        } // end isEmpty
        public int getSize()
        {
          return lastIndex;
        } // end getSize
        public void clear()
        {
          for (; lastIndex > -1; lastIndex--)
            heap[lastIndex] = null;
          lastIndex = 0;
        } // end clear
        < Private methods >
        . . .

} // end MaxHeap
```

Adding an Entry

28.5   **The basic algorithm.** The algorithm to add an entry to a heap is not difficult. Recall that in a max-heap, the object in a node is greater than or equal to its descendant objects. Suppose that we want to add 85 to the maxheap in Figure 28-1. We first would place the new entry as the next leaf in the tree. Figure 28-2a shows that we add 85 as a left child of the 30. Notice that we actually would place 85 at index 10 of the array in Figure 28-1b.

Figure 28-2a is no longer a heap, since 85 is out of place. To transform the tree into a heap, we let 85 *float up* to its correct location. Since 85 is larger than its parent, 30, we swap it with the parent, as Figure 28-2b shows. The 85 is still larger than its new parent, 80, so we swap again (Figure 28-2c). Now 85 is less than its parent, so we have transformed the tree in Figure 28-2a into a maxheap.

Figure 28-2   The steps in adding 85 to the maxheap in Figure 28-1a

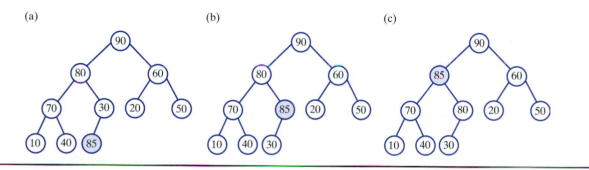

Question 2   What steps are necessary to add 100 to the heap in Figure 28-2c?

28.6   **Avoiding swaps.** Although the swaps mentioned in the previous segment make the algorithm easier to understand and to describe, they require more work than is actually necessary. Instead of placing the new entry in the next available position within the tree, as we did in Figure 28-2a, we need only reserve space for it. In an array-based implementation, we simply check that the array is not full. Figure 28-3a shows the new child as an empty circle.

We then compare the new entry—the 85 in this example—with the parent of the new child. Since 85 is larger than 30, we move the 30 to the new child, as Figure 28-3b shows. We treat the node that originally contained 30 as if it were empty. We now compare 85 with the parent, 80, of the empty node. Since 85 is larger than 80, we move the 80 to the empty node, as Figure 28-3c shows. Since 85 is not larger than the next parent, 90, we place the new entry into the empty node, as Figure 28-3d shows.

Note: To add a new entry to a heap, you begin at the next available position for a leaf. You follow a path from this leaf toward the root until you find the correct position for the new entry. As you do, you move entries from parent to child to ultimately make room for the new entry.

Figure 28-3   A revision of the steps shown in Figure 28-2, to avoid swaps

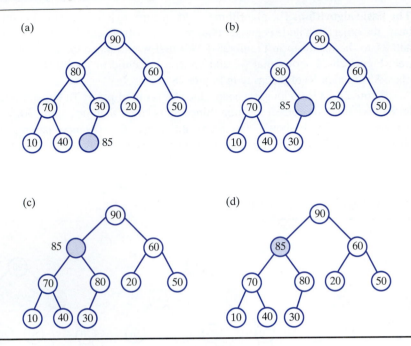

Figure 28-4 shows these same steps from the viewpoint of the array that represents the heap. In Part *a*, which is analogous to Figure 28-3a, we note that we have room for a new entry at index 10. The parent of this location is at location 10/2, or 5. We thus compare the new entry 85 to 30, the contents of the location at index 5. Since 85 > 30, we move 30 to the location at index 10 (Figures 28-4b and 28-3b.) The remaining steps proceed in a similar fashion. Note that Figure 28-4d corresponds to Figure 28-3c, and Figure 28-4f corresponds to Figure 28-3d.

28.7   **The refined algorithm.** The following algorithm summarizes the steps that add a new entry to a heap. Notice that the array is expanded dynamically as necessary.

Algorithm **add(newEntry)**
if (*the array* heap *is full*)
  Double the size of the array

newIndex = index of next available array location
`parentIndex = newIndex/2`   // *index of parent of available location*
while (`parentIndex > 0` *and* `newEntry > heap[parentIndex]`)
`{`
  `heap[newIndex] = heap[parentIndex]`   // *move parent to available location*

  // *update indices*
  `newIndex = parentIndex`
  `parentIndex = newIndex/2`
`}`

`heap[newIndex] = newEntry`   // *place new entry in correct location*

Figure 28-4   An array representation of the steps in Figure 28-3

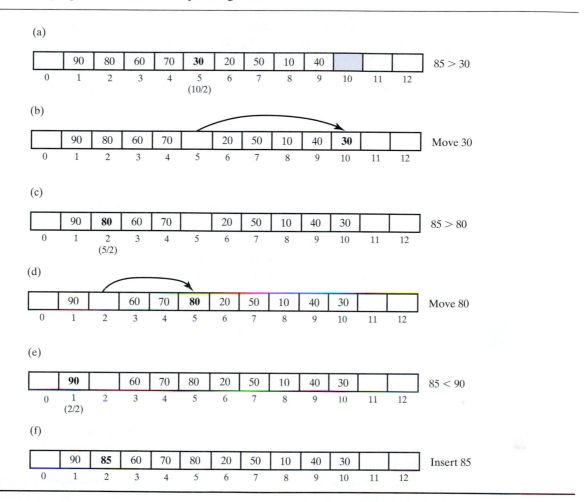

To ignore the first location of the array, we simply ensure that `parentIndex` is greater than 0.

> **Question 3**   Repeat Question 2 using the previous algorithm without swaps. Show the heap at each step as a tree and as an array.

28.8   **The method add.** We now implement the previous algorithm. The add method begins by incrementing the index `lastIndex` of the last array entry and then checks that the array is large enough to hold a new entry. If it is not, we double the size of the array, as we have done in previous chapters. (See Segment 5.15 of Chapter 5, for example.) The rest of the implementation closely follows the pseudocode.

```
public void add(T newEntry)
{
    lastIndex++;

    if (lastIndex >= heap.length)
```

```
            doubleArray(); // expand array

      int newIndex = lastIndex;
      int parentIndex = newIndex / 2;
      while ( (parentIndex > 0) &&
              newEntry.compareTo(heap[parentIndex]) > 0)
      {
        heap[newIndex] = heap[parentIndex];

        newIndex = parentIndex;
        parentIndex = newIndex / 2;
      } // end while

      heap[newIndex] = newEntry;
   } // end add
```

We can omit the test of `parentIndex` in the `while` statement if we place a sentinel value in the unused array location at index 0. We can use `newEntry` as this sentinel. You should answer Question 4 and convince yourself that this change will work.

In the worst case, this method follows a path from a leaf to the root. In Segment 25.9 of Chapter 25, we saw that the height of a complete tree having n nodes is $\log_2 (n + 1)$ rounded up. Thus, the add method is an O($\log n$) operation in the worst case.

 Question 4   Revise the previous method add by placing `newEntry` as a sentinel value in the unused array location at index 0. You then can omit the test of `parentIndex` in the `while` statement.

Removing the Root

28.9   **The basic algorithm.** The `removeMax` method for a maxheap removes and returns the heap's largest object. This object is in the root of the maxheap. Let's remove the entry in the root of the heap in Figure 28-3d. Figure 28-5a shows this heap as if its root was empty.

We do not want to rip the root node out of the heap, as this will leave two disjoint subtrees. Instead we remove a leaf, namely the last one in the heap. To do so, we copy the leaf's data—30—to the root and then remove the leaf from the tree, as Figure 28-5b illustrates. Of course, in the array-based implementation, removing this leaf simply means adjusting `lastIndex`.

The 30 is out of place, so we no longer have a heap. We let the 30 *sink down* to its correct location. As long as 30 is less than its children, we swap it with its larger child. Thus, in Figure 28-5c, we have swapped 30 and 85. Continuing, we swap 30 and 80, as Figure 28-5d shows. In this case the 30 has settled at a leaf. In general, the out-of-place entry will settle at a node whose children are not greater than the entry.

 Question 5   What steps are necessary to remove the root from the heap in Figure 28-5d?

28.10   **Transforming a semiheap into a heap.** The tree in Figure 28-5b is called a **semiheap**. Except for the root, the objects in a semiheap are ordered as they are in a heap. In removing the root of the heap, we formed a semiheap and then transformed it back into a heap. As in the method add, we can save time by not swapping entries. Figure 28-6 shows the semiheap from Figure 28-5b and the steps that transform it into a heap without the swaps.

Figure 28-5 The steps to remove the entry in the root of the maxheap in Figure 28-3d

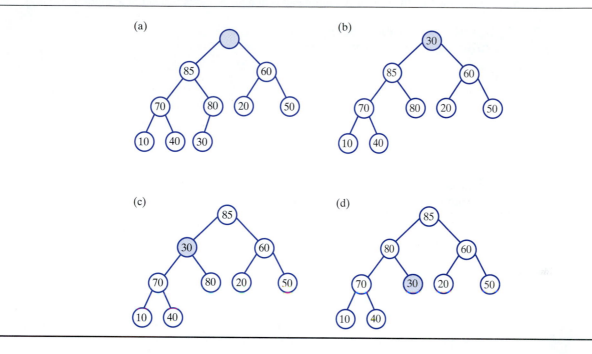

Figure 28-6 The steps that transform a semiheap into a heap without swaps

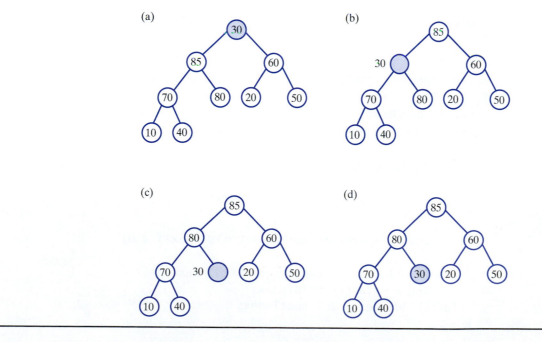

The following algorithm transforms a semiheap to a heap. To make the algorithm more general, we assume that the root of the semiheap is at a given index instead of at index 1.

```
Algorithm reheap(rootIndex)
// Transforms the semiheap rooted at rootIndex into a heap

done = false
orphan = heap[rootIndex]

while (!done and heap[rootIndex] has a child)
{
  largerChildIndex = index of the larger child of heap[rootIndex]
  if (orphan < heap[largerChildIndex])
  {
    heap[rootIndex] = heap[largerChildIndex]
    rootIndex = largerChildIndex
  }
  else
    done = true
}

heap[rootIndex] = orphan
```

As you will see, this algorithm has several uses.

Question 6   Show the contents of the array heap as you trace the steps of the algorithm reheap that correspond to those pictured in Figure 28-6.

28.11   **The method reheap.** The implementation of the reheap algorithm as a private method follows:

```
private void reheap(int rootIndex)
{
  boolean done = false;
  T orphan = heap[rootIndex];
  int leftChildIndex = 2 * rootIndex;

  while (!done && (leftChildIndex <= lastIndex) )
  {
    int largerChildIndex = leftChildIndex; // assume larger
    int rightChildIndex = leftChildIndex + 1;
    if ( (rightChildIndex <= lastIndex) &&
          heap[rightChildIndex].compareTo(heap[largerChildIndex]) > 0)
    {
      largerChildIndex = rightChildIndex;
    } // end if

    if (orphan.compareTo(heap[largerChildIndex]) < 0)
    {
      heap[rootIndex] = heap[largerChildIndex];
      rootIndex = largerChildIndex;
      leftChildIndex = 2 * rootIndex;
    }
```

```
    else
        done = true;
    } // end while

    heap[rootIndex] = orphan;
} // end reheap
```

In the worst case, the method `reheap` follows a path from the root to a leaf. The number of nodes along this path is less than or equal to the height h of the heap. Thus, `reheap` is O(h). Recall that the height of a complete n-node tree is $\log_2 (n + 1)$ rounded up, so `reheap` is an O($\log n$) operation.

28.12   **The method `removeMax`.** The method `removeMax` replaces the heap's root with its last leaf to form a semiheap like the one in Figure 28-6a. The method then calls `reheap` to transform the semiheap back into a heap. Thus, `removeMax` has the following implementation:

```
public T removeMax()
{
    T root = null;

    if (!isEmpty())
    {
        root = heap[1];                  // return value
        heap[1] = heap[lastIndex]; // form a semiheap
        lastIndex--;                     // decrease size
        reheap(1);                       // transform to a heap
    } // end if

    return root;
} // end removeMax
```

Since `reheap` is an O($\log n$) operation in the worst case, so is `removeMax`.

> **Note:** To remove a heap's root, you first replace the root with the heap's last leaf. This step forms a semiheap, so you use the method `reheap` to transform the semiheap to a heap.

Creating a Heap

28.13   **Using add.** We could create a heap from a collection of objects by using the `add` method to add each object to an initially empty heap. Figure 28-7 shows the steps that this approach would take to add 20, 40, 30, 10, 90, and 70 to a heap. Since `add` is an O($\log n$) operation, creating the heap in this manner would be O($n \log n$).

Notice that we have a heap after each addition. This process does more than we really need. With less work, we can create one heap from a collection of objects without maintaining a heap at each intermediate step, as the next segment shows.

Figure 28-7   The steps in adding 20, 40, 30, 10, 90, and 70 to an initially empty heap

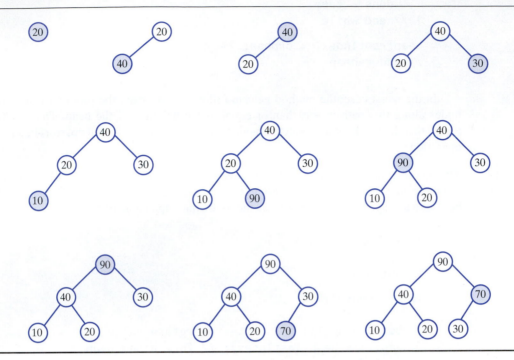

28.14   **Using reheap.** A more efficient way to create a heap uses the method reheap. We begin by placing the entries for the heap into an array beginning at index 1. Figure 28-8a provides an example of one such array. This array can represent the complete tree shown in Figure 28-8b. Does this tree contain any semiheaps that we can transform into heaps? The leaves are semiheaps, but they are also heaps. Thus, we can ignore the entries 70, 90, and 10. These entries are at the end of the array.

Moving toward the beginning of the array, we encounter 30, which is the root of a semiheap within the tree pictured in Figure 28-8b. If we apply reheap to this semiheap, we get the tree in Figure 28-8c. Continuing in this manner, we apply reheap to the semiheap rooted at 40 and then to the one rooted at 20. Parts *d*, *e*, and *f* of Figure 28-8 show the results of these steps. Figure 28-8f is the desired heap.

The following Java statements transform the array heap—whose entries are at the indices 1 through lastIndex—into a heap:

```
for (int rootIndex = lastIndex/2; rootIndex > 0; rootIndex--)
    reheap(rootIndex);
```

In applying reheap, we begin at the first nonleaf closest to the end of the array. This nonleaf is at index lastIndex/2, since it is the parent of the last leaf in the tree. We then work toward heap[1].

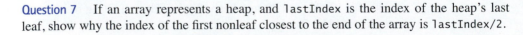

Question 7   If an array represents a heap, and lastIndex is the index of the heap's last leaf, show why the index of the first nonleaf closest to the end of the array is lastIndex/2.

28.15   Using reheap to transform an array of entries into a heap takes less work than if we used add to add the entries to the heap. In fact, building a heap in this manner is O(*n*), as we will now demonstrate.

Figure 28-8   The steps in creating a heap of the entries 20, 40, 30, 10, 90, and 70 by using `reheap`

(a) An array of entries

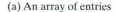

(b) The complete tree that
the array represents

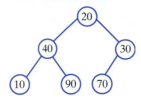

(c) After `reheap(3)`

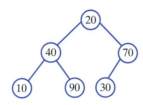

(d) After `reheap(2)`

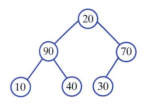

(e) During `reheap(1)`

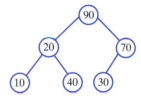

(f) After `reheap(1)`

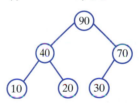

By the observation at the end of Segment 28.11, `reheap` is $O(h_i)$, where h_i is the height of the subtree rooted at index i. In the worst case, the heap would be a full tree of height h. Each node in level $l < h$ is the root of a subtree whose height is $h - l + 1$. Moreover, level l contains 2^{l-1} nodes. Thus, the sum of the heights of the subtrees rooted at level l of a full heap is $(h - l + 1) \cdot 2^{l-1}$.

Since the loop in the previous segment ignores the nodes in the last level—level h—of the heap, its complexity is

$$O\left(\sum_{l=1}^{h-1} (h - l + 1) \cdot 2^{l-1} \right)$$

Exercise 6 at the end of this chapter asks you to show that this expression is equivalent to $O(2^h)$, which is $O(n)$.

Note: You can create a heap more efficiently by using the method `reheap` instead of the method add.

28.16   **Another constructor.** We can use the technique described in Segment 28.14 to implement another constructor for the class MaxHeap. Suppose that *n* entries for our heap are given in an array of exactly *n* locations. The following constructor takes this array, copies it into the data field heap, and uses reheap to create a heap. Remember that although the entries in the given array begin at index 0, we place them into the array heap beginning at index 1.

```
public MaxHeap(T[] entries)
{
  heap = (T[]) new Comparable[entries.length + 1];
  lastIndex = entries.length;

  // copy given array to data field
  for (int index = 0; index < entries.length; index++)
    heap[index + 1] = entries[index];

  // create heap
  for (int rootIndex = lastIndex/2; rootIndex > 0; rootIndex--)
    reheap(rootIndex);
} // end constructor
```

Heap Sort

28.17   We can use a heap to sort an array. If we place the array items into a maxheap and then remove them one at a time, we will get the items in descending order. We saw in Segments 28.13 and 28.14 that using reheap instead of add is a more efficient way to create a heap from an array of items. In fact, we wrote a constructor in the previous segment that invoked reheap for this purpose. So if a is the array of items—strings, for example—we could use this constructor to create the heap, as follows:

```
MaxHeapInterface<String> myHeap = new MaxHeap<String>(a);
```

As we remove the items from myHeap, we could place them in order back into the array a. The problem with this approach is the additional memory required, since the heap uses an array besides the given array. However, by mimicking the heap's array-based implementation, we can make this approach more efficient without using the class MaxHeap. The resulting algorithm is called a **heap sort**.

28.18   To create an initial heap from the given array, we call reheap repeatedly, as we did in the constructor given in Segment 28.16. Parts *a* and *b* of Figure 28-9 show an array and the heap that results after this step. Since the array to be sorted begins at index 0, but in the constructor the heap begins at index 1, we must adjust reheap, as you will see.

The largest item in the array of Figure 28-9b is now first in the array, so we swap it with the last item in the array, as Figure 28-9c shows. The array is now partitioned into a tree region and a sorted region.

Following this swap, we call reheap on the tree portion—transforming it into a heap—and perform another swap, as Figures 28-9d and 28-9e illustrate. We repeat these operations until the tree region consists of one item (Figure 28-9k). The array is now sorted into ascending order. Notice that the array actually is sorted in Figure 28-9g, but the algorithm does not detect this fact.

Figure 28-9   A trace of heap sort

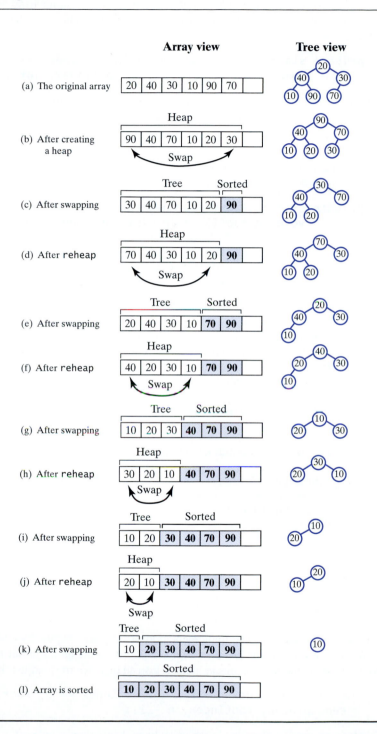

28.19   **Adjusting reheap.** We must revise the method reheap so that it is suitable for our sorting algorithm. The original method in Segment 28.11 uses the data fields heap and lastIndex of the class MaxHeap. Here, we make them parameters of the method. Thus, we change the method's header, as follows:

```
private static <T extends Comparable<? super T>>
        void reheap(T[] heap, int rootIndex, int lastIndex)
```

The portion of the array heap that represents the heap ranges from the index 0 to the index lastIndex. The semiheap is rooted at the index rootIndex.

Since the heap begins at index 0 instead of 1, as it did in Segment 28.11, the left child of the node at index i is at index $2i + 1$ instead of $2i$. Recall that Question 1 asked you to find this index. This change affects the two statements within reheap that determine leftChildIndex.

The revised reheap appears as follows:

```
private static <T extends Comparable<? super T>>
        void reheap(T[] heap, int rootIndex, int lastIndex)
{
   boolean done = false;
   T orphan = heap[rootIndex];
   int leftChildIndex = 2 * rootIndex + 1;

   while (!done && (leftChildIndex <= lastIndex))
   {
      int largerChildIndex = leftChildIndex;
      int rightChildIndex = leftChildIndex + 1;
      if ( (rightChildIndex <= lastIndex) &&
            heap[rightChildIndex].compareTo(heap[largerChildIndex]) > 0)
      {
         largerChildIndex = rightChildIndex;
      } // end if

      if (orphan.compareTo(heap[largerChildIndex]) < 0)
      {
         heap[rootIndex] = heap[largerChildIndex];
         rootIndex = largerChildIndex;
         leftChildIndex = 2 * rootIndex + 1;
      }
      else
         done = true;
   } // end while

   heap[rootIndex] = orphan;
} // end reheap
```

28.20   **The method heapSort.** The implementation of heap sort begins by calling reheap repeatedly, as we did in the constructor given in Segment 28.16, to create an initial heap from the given array. However, since the heap begins at index 0 instead of 1, we must adjust the loop somewhat:

```
for (int rootIndex = n/2 - 1; rootIndex >= 0; rootIndex--)
   reheap(heap, rootIndex, n - 1);
```

This loop assumes n elements in the array heap, beginning at index 0. Exercise 3 at the end of this chapter asks you to verify the starting value of rootIndex.

The complete method appears as follows:

```
public static <T extends Comparable<? super T>>
        void heapSort(T[] array, int n)
{
  // create first heap
  for (int rootIndex = n/2 - 1; rootIndex >= 0; rootIndex--)
    reheap(array, rootIndex, n - 1);

  swap(array, 0, n - 1);

  for (int lastIndex = n - 2; lastIndex > 0; lastIndex--)
  {
    reheap(array, 0, lastIndex);
    swap(array, 0, lastIndex);
  } // end for
} // end heapSort
```

Like merge sort and quick sort, heap sort is an O($n \log n$) algorithm. As implemented here, heap sort does not require a second array, but merge sort does. Recall from Chapter 12 that quick sort is O($n \log n$) most of the time, but is O(n^2) in its worst case. Since we usually can avoid quick sort's worst case by choosing appropriate pivots, it generally is the preferred sorting method.

Note: **The time efficiency of heap sort**
Although heap sort is O($n \log n$) in the average case, quick sort usually is the sorting method of choice.

Question 8   Trace the steps that the method `heapSort` takes when sorting the following array into ascending order: 9 6 2 4 8 7 5 3.

CHAPTER SUMMARY

- Since a heap is a complete binary tree, it has an efficient array-based implementation.

- You add a new entry to a heap as the next leaf in a complete binary tree. You then make the entry float up to its proper location within the heap.

- You begin to remove the root entry of a heap by replacing it with the entry in the last leaf and then removing the leaf. The result is a semiheap. You transform the semiheap into a heap by making the new root entry sink down to its proper location within the heap.

- You could create a heap from a given array of entries by adding each entry to the heap. A more efficient approach considers the complete tree that the array represents and treats each nonleaf as a semiheap. You transform each such semiheap into a heap by using the same technique that you use when removing the root of the heap.

- A heap sort uses a heap to sort the entries in a given array.

1. Trace the formation of a maxheap by the constructor given in Segment 28.16 for each of the following arrays:

   a. 10 20 30 40 50
   b. 10 20 30 40 50 60 70 80 90 100

2. Trace the addition of each of the following values to an initially empty maxheap:

   10 20 30 40 50

   Compare your trace with the results of Exercise 1a.

3. The method `heapSort` given in Segment 28.20 contains a loop that creates an initial heap from an array of n values. The loop variable `rootIndex` begins at n/2 - 1. Derive this starting value and show that the loop executes the same number of times as the corresponding loop in the constructor given in Segment 28.16.

4. Trace the steps of a heap sort on each of the following arrays:

   a. 10 20 30 40 50 60
   b. 60 50 40 30 20 10
   c. 20 50 40 10 60 30

5. Consider an array that represents a heap. Suppose that you replace the value at index i with a new value. It is likely that you will no longer have a heap. Write an algorithm that will give you a heap again.

6. Segment 28.15 showed that the complexity of creating a heap by using `reheap` is

$$O\left(\sum_{l=1}^{h-1} (h - l + 1) \cdot 2^{l-1} \right)$$

   Show that this expression is equivalent to $O(2^h)$, which is $O(n)$. *Hint*: First, change the summation variable from l to j, where $j = h - l + 1$. Then show by induction that

$$\sum_{j=2}^{h} j/2^j = 3/2 - \frac{h+2}{2^h}$$

7. Consider the loop in a heap sort that creates the initial heap from an array of n values (see Segment 28.20):

```
// create first heap
for (int rootIndex = n/2 - 1; rootIndex >= 0; rootIndex--)
   reheap(array, rootIndex, n - 1);
```

   Show that the actual number of calls to the method `compareTo` during the execution of this loop is no less than $n - 1$.

8. Consider again the loop mentioned in the previous exercise. Show that the actual number of calls to the method `compareTo` during the execution of this loop is no greater than $n \log_2 n$.

9. Heap sort is not the only way to sort an array using a heap. In this exercise you will explore a less efficient algorithm. After building an initial heap, as you would in the first step of a heap sort, the largest value will be in the first position of the array. If you leave this value in place and then build a new heap using the remaining values, you will get the next largest value in the entire array. By continuing in this manner, you can sort the array into descending order. If you use a minheap instead of a maxheap, you will sort the array into ascending order.

a. Implement one of these sorts as the method `newSortUsingAHeap`.
b. What is the Big Oh performance of this method?

PROJECTS

1. Recall from Segment 25.31 of Chapter 25 that in a minheap, the object in each node is less than or equal to the objects in the node's descendants. While a maxheap has the method `getMax`, a minheap has the method `getMin` instead. Use an array to implement a minheap.

2. Compare the execution times of heap sort, merge sort, and quick sort on various arrays chosen at random. The "Projects" section of Chapter 9 described one way to time the execution of code.

3. Use a binary search tree in the implementation of `MaxHeapInterface`.
   Where in the tree will the largest entry occur? How efficient is this implementation?

4. Consider the problem of combining two heaps together into a single heap.

   a. Write an efficient algorithm for combining two heaps, one with size n and the other with size 1. What is the Big Oh performance of your algorithm?
   b. Write an efficient algorithm for combining two heaps of equal size n. What is the Big Oh performance of your algorithm?
   c. Write an efficient algorithm for combining two arbitrary sized heaps into one heap. What is the Big Oh performance of your algorithm?
   d. Implement the algorithm that you wrote in Part c.

5. You can study the average performance of the first step in a heap sort—building the initial heap—by taking the following steps:

   - Modify the method `reheap` so that it returns the number of calls made to `compareTo`.
   - Write a program that will iterate 1000 times. During each iteration, generate n random values and place them into an array. Count the number of comparisons needed by the code given in Exercise 7 to convert the array into a heap. Add the number of comparisons in each iteration into a total. After the loop has ended, compute the average number of comparisons needed to build the heap by dividing the number of comparisons by 1000.
   - In the previous step, let $n = 10, 20, 30, 40, 50, 60, 70, 80, 90, 100, 200, 400$, and 800. For each n, see whether the average number of calls to `compareTo` is greater than or equal to the lower bound $n - 1$ (see Exercise 7) and less than or equal to the upper bound $n \log_2 n$ (see Exercise 8).

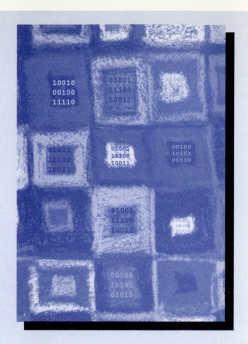

CONTENTS

PREREQUISITES

OBJECTIVES

After studying this chapter, you should be able to

- Perform a rotation to restore the balance of an AVL tree after an addition

- Search for or add an entry to a 2-3 tree

- Search for or add an entry to a 2-4 tree
- Form a red-black tree from a given 2-4 tree
- Search for or add an entry to a red-black tree
- Describe the purpose of a B-tree

In Chapter 27, you saw that the operations on a binary search tree are O(log n) if the tree is balanced. Unfortunately, the add and remove operations do not ensure that a binary search tree remains balanced. This chapter will consider search trees that maintain their balance, and hence their efficiency.

Our goal is to introduce you to several types of balanced search trees and compare them. We will discuss the algorithms that add entries to a search tree while retaining its balance. We also will show you how to search the trees. We will not, however, cover the algorithms that remove entries, leaving this topic for a future course.

The entries in a tree are usually objects, but to make the pictures of trees clear and concise, we will show the entries as integers.

AVL Trees

29.1   Segment 25.28 in Chapter 25 showed that you can form several differently shaped binary search trees from the same collection of data. Some of these trees will be balanced and some will not. You could take an unbalanced binary search tree and rearrange its nodes to get a balanced binary search tree. Recall that every node in a balanced binary tree has subtrees whose heights differ by no more than 1.

This idea of rearranging nodes to balance a tree was first developed in 1962 by two mathematicians, Adel'son-Vel'skii and Landis. Named after them, the **AVL tree** is a binary search tree that rearranges its nodes whenever it becomes unbalanced. The balance of a binary search tree is upset only when you add or remove a node. Thus, during these operations, the AVL tree rearranges nodes as necessary to maintain its balance.

For example, Parts a, b, and c of Figure 29-1 show a binary search tree as we add 60, 50, and 20 to it. After the third addition, the tree is not balanced. An AVL tree would rearrange its nodes to restore balance, as shown in Figure 29-1d. This particular reorganization is called a **right rotation**, since you can imagine the nodes rotating about 50. If we now add 80 to the tree, it remains balanced, as Figure 29-2a shows. Adding 90 disrupts the balance (Figure 29-2b), but a **left rotation** restores it (Figure 29-2c). Here the rotation is about 80. Notice that after each rotation, the tree is still a binary search tree.

In discussing balance, we sometimes will mention a **balanced node**. A node is balanced if it is the root of a balanced tree, that is, if its two subtrees differ in height by no more than 1.

Single Rotations

29.2   **Right rotations.** Let's examine the previous rotations in more detail. Figure 29-3a shows a subtree of an AVL tree that is balanced. The heights of the subtrees T_1, T_2, and T_3 are the same. An addition that occurs in the left subtree T_1 of node C will add a leaf to T_1. Suppose that such an addition increases the

Figure 29-1   After inserting (a) 60; (b) 50; and (c) 20 into an initially empty binary search tree, the tree is not balanced; (d) a corresponding AVL tree rotates its nodes to restore balance

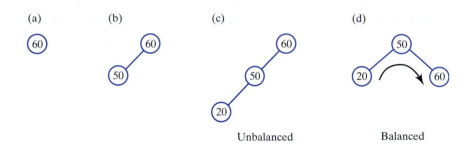

Figure 29-2   (a) Adding 80 to the tree in Figure 29-1d does not change the balance of the tree; (b) a subsequent addition of 90 makes the tree unbalanced; (c) a left rotation restores its balance

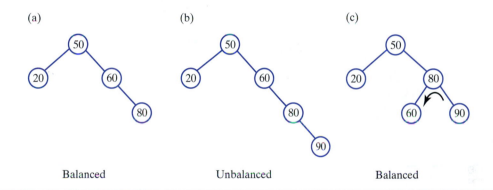

height of T_1 by 1, as Figure 29-3b shows. The subtree rooted at node N is now unbalanced. N is the first node that is unbalanced along the path between the inserted leaf and N. A right rotation about node C restores the balance of the tree, as Figure 29-3c shows. After the rotation, C is above N, and the tree has the same height as it did before the addition of a node.

Since we had a binary search tree before the rotation (Figure 29-3b), the value in node N is greater than the value in node C and all the values in T_2. Moreover, all values in T_2 are greater than the value in node C. These relationships are maintained after the rotation (Figure 29-3c), since node N is a right child of node C, and T_2 is a left subtree of node N. Finally, the subtrees T_1 and T_3 have their original parents in the new tree. Thus, the resulting tree is still a binary search tree.

Figure 29-4 provides a specific instance of the right rotation depicted in Figure 29-3. Part *a* of the figure shows an imbalance at node N after 4 was added to the tree. A right rotation restores the tree's balance, as Part *b* illustrates. To simplify the figure, we have labeled only the roots of the subtrees $T_1, T_2,$ and T_3.

If node N had a parent before the rotation, we would make node C a child of that parent after the rotation. However, if node N was the root of the AVL tree, node C would become the root. Figure 29-4 is an example of this latter case.

Figure 29-3   Before and after an addition to an AVL subtree that requires a right rotation to maintain its balance

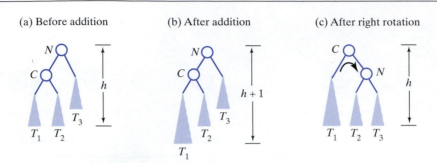

(a) Before addition   (b) After addition   (c) After right rotation

Figure 29-4   Before and after a right rotation restores balance to an AVL tree

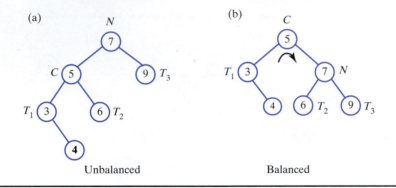

(a)   (b)

Unbalanced   Balanced

The following algorithm performs the right rotation illustrated in Figures 29-3 and 29-4:

Algorithm `rotateRight(nodeN)`
// Corrects an imbalance at a given node `nodeN` *due to an addition*
// in the left subtree of `nodeN`*'s left child.*

`nodeC =` *left child of* `nodeN`
Set `nodeN`*'s left child to* `nodeC`*'s right child*
Set `nodeC`*'s right child to* `nodeN`
return `nodeC`

Question 1   Using the notation of Figure 29-3, label nodes N and C, and subtrees T_1, T_2, and T_3, in Parts c and d of Figure 29-1.

29.3   **Left rotations.** Figure 29-5 shows a left rotation in a mirror image of Figure 29-3. The following algorithm performs this left rotation:

Algorithm `rotateLeft(nodeN)`
// Corrects an imbalance at a given node `nodeN` *due to an addition*
// in the right subtree of `nodeN`*'s right child.*

> nodeC = *right child of* nodeN
> *Set* nodeN*'s right child to* nodeC*'s left child*
> *Set* nodeC*'s left child to* nodeN
> **return** nodeC

Figure 29-5   Before and after an addition to an AVL subtree that requires a left rotation to maintain its balance

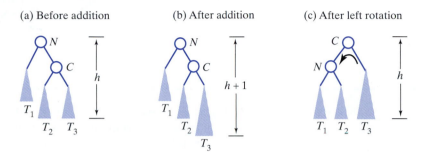

(a) Before addition   (b) After addition   (c) After left rotation

Question 2   Why is the tree in Figure 29-5c a binary search tree?

Question 3   Using the notation of Figure 29-5, label nodes N and C, and subtrees T_1, T_2, and T_3, in Parts b and c of Figure 29-2.

Question 4   Just as Figure 29-4 gave an example of a right rotation, provide a specific example of the left rotation illustrated in Figure 29-5.

Note: An imbalance at node N of an AVL tree due to an addition to the tree can be corrected by a single rotation if

- The addition occurred in the left subtree of N's left child C (right rotation), or
- The addition occurred in the right subtree of N's right child C (left rotation)

In both cases, we can imagine node C rotating above node N.

Double Rotations

29.4   **Right-left double rotations.** Now we add 70 to the AVL tree in Figure 29-2c. An imbalance occurs at the node containing 50, as Figure 29-6a shows. A right rotation about the node containing 60 results in the tree in Figure 29-6b. The mechanics of this rotation are the same as the one in Figure 29-3, where the rotation is about node C. The subtree heights differ in these two figures, however.

Unfortunately, this rotation does not balance the tree. A subsequent left rotation about the node containing 60—corresponding to node C in Figure 29-5b—is necessary to restore the balance (Figure 29-6c). Together, these two rotations are called a **right-left double rotation**. First, 60 rotates above 80 and then it rotates above 50. Again, notice that after each rotation, the tree is still a binary search tree.

Figure 29-6   (a) Adding 70 to the tree in Figure 29-2c destroys its balance; to restore the balance, perform both (b) a right rotation and (c) a left rotation

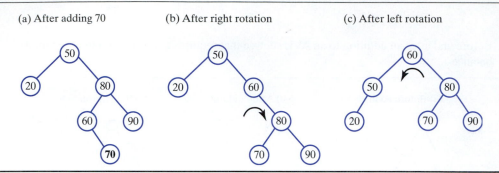

    (a) After adding 70   (b) After right rotation   (c) After left rotation

       Let's look at the general case. Figure 29-7a shows a subtree of an AVL tree that is height balanced. Node N has a child C and a grandchild G. An addition that occurs in the right subtree T_3 of node G adds a leaf to T_3. When such an addition increases the height of T_3, as Figure 29-7b shows, the subtree rooted at N becomes unbalanced. Notice that nodes N, C, and G correspond to the nodes in Figure 29-6a that contain 50, 80, and 60, respectively.

       Node N is the first node that is unbalanced along the path between the inserted leaf and N. After a right rotation about node G, the subtree rooted at G is unbalanced, as Figure 29-7c shows. A left rotation about G restores the balance of the tree, as you can see in Figure 29-7d. Note that G first rotates above C and then above N.

Figure 29-7   Before and after an addition to an AVL subtree that requires both a right rotation and a left rotation to maintain its balance

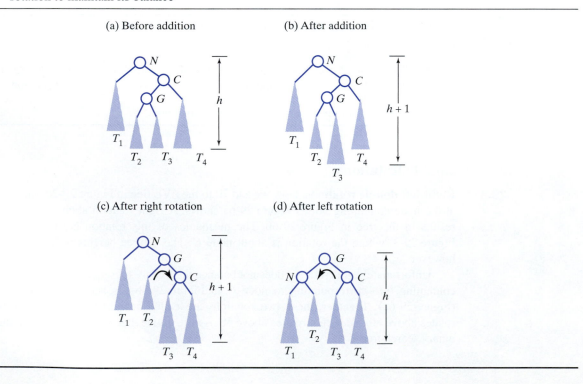

    (a) Before addition   (b) After addition

    (c) After right rotation   (d) After left rotation

The following algorithm performs the right-left double rotation illustrated in Figure 29-7:

Algorithm `rotateRightLeft(nodeN)`
// Corrects an imbalance at a given node `nodeN` *due to an addition*
// in the left subtree of `nodeN`*'s right child.*

`nodeC` = *right child of* `nodeN`
Set `nodeN`*'s right child to the node returned by* `rotateRight(nodeC)`
`return rotateLeft(nodeN)`

The right rotation transforms the tree in Figure 29-7b into the one in Figure 29-7c. The left rotation then transforms Figure 29-7c to Figure 29-7d.

Question 5   Using the notation of Figure 29-7, label nodes N, C, and G, and subtrees T_1, T_2, T_3, and T_4 in Figure 29-6.

29.5   **Left-right double rotations.** Now we add 55, 10, and 40 to the tree in Figure 29-6c to get the tree in Figure 29-8a. As long as we add 55 first, these additions maintain the tree's balance without rotations. After we add 35, as Figure 29-8b shows, the tree is unbalanced at the node containing 50. To restore the balance, we perform a left rotation about the node containing 40—so 40 rotates above 20—to get the tree in Figure 29-8c. Then we perform a right rotation about the node containing 40—so 40 rotates above 50—to get the balanced tree in Figure 29-8d.

Figure 29-8   (a) The AVL tree in Figure 29-6c after additions that maintain its balance; (b) after an addition that destroys the balance; (c) after a left rotation; (d) after a right rotation

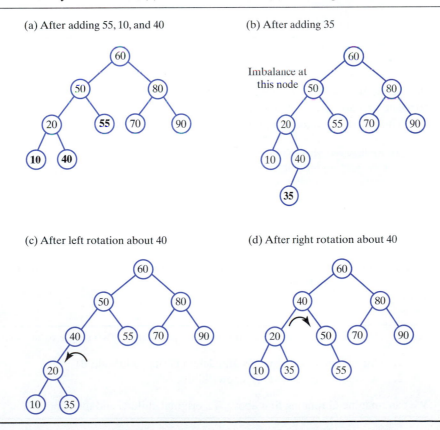

(a) After adding 55, 10, and 40

(b) After adding 35

(c) After left rotation about 40

(d) After right rotation about 40

Figure 29-9 Before and after an addition to an AVL subtree that requires both a left rotation and a right rotation to maintain its balance

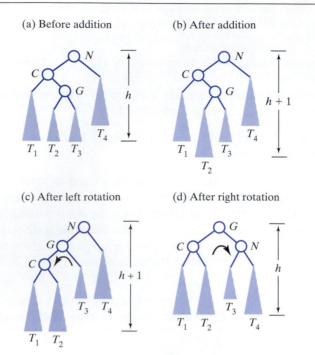

(a) Before addition   (b) After addition

(c) After left rotation   (d) After right rotation

Figure 29-9 shows a left-right double rotation in general. It is a mirror image of the right-left double rotation pictured in Figure 29-7. Both left-right and right-left double rotations cause node G to rotate first above node C and then above node N.

The following algorithm performs the left-right double rotation illustrated in Figure 29-9:

Algorithm `rotateLeftRight(nodeN)`
// Corrects an imbalance at a given node `nodeN` *due to an addition*
// in the right subtree of `nodeN`*'s left child.*

`nodeC` = *left child of* `nodeN`
Set `nodeN`*'s left child to the node returned by* `rotateLeft(nodeC)`
return `rotateRight(nodeN)`

Question 6   Using the notation of Figure 29-9, label nodes N, C, and G, and subtrees T_1, T_2, T_3, and T_4 in Figure 29-8.

Note: A double rotation is accomplished by performing two single rotations:

1. A rotation about node N's grandchild G (its child's child)
2. A rotation about node N's new child

We can imagine G rotating first above N's original child C and then above N.

Note: An imbalance at node *N* of an AVL tree can be corrected by a double rotation if

- The addition occurred in the left subtree of *N*'s right child (right-left rotation), or
- The addition occurred in the right subtree of *N*'s left child (left-right rotation)

29.6 **Summary comments about rotation after an addition.** Following an addition to an AVL tree, a temporary imbalance might occur. Let *N* be an unbalanced node that is closest to the new leaf. Either a single or double rotation will restore the tree's balance. No other rotations are necessary. To see this, remember that before the addition, the tree was balanced; after all, it is an AVL tree. After an addition that causes a rotation, the tree has the same height as it did before the addition. Therefore, no node above *N* can be unbalanced now if it was balanced before the addition. Moreover, the four rotations cover the only four possibilities for the cause of the imbalance at node *N*:

- The addition occurred in the left subtree of *N*'s left child (right rotation)
- The addition occurred in the right subtree of *N*'s left child (left-right rotation)
- The addition occurred in the left subtree of *N*'s right child (right-left rotation)
- The addition occurred in the right subtree of *N*'s right child (left rotation)

Removing an entry from a binary search tree results in the removal of a node, but not necessarily the node that contained the entry. Thus, removing an entry from an AVL tree can lead to a temporary imbalance. We restore the tree's balance by using one single or double rotation as described previously for addition, where node *N* is the node at which the imbalance occurs and that is closest to the removed node. We leave the details for you to develop in Project 1.

 Note: One single or double rotation during the addition or removal of an entry will restore the balance of an AVL tree.

 Question 7   What AVL tree results when you make the following additions to an initially empty AVL tree? 70, 80, 90, 20, 10, 50, 60, 40, 30

Question 8   What tree results when you make the same additions given in the previous question to an initially empty binary search tree? How does this tree compare to the AVL tree you created in the previous question?

Question 9   Why is the tree shown in Figure 29-7d a binary search tree?

Question 10   Why is the tree shown in Figure 29-9d a binary search tree?

29.7 **An AVL tree versus a binary search tree.** We created the AVL tree in Figure 29-8d by adding 60, 50, 20, 80, 90, 70, 55, 10, 40, and 35 to an initially empty AVL tree. Figure 29-10a shows that tree again. If we make the same additions to an initially empty binary search tree, we get the tree in Figure 29-10b. This tree is unbalanced and is taller than the AVL tree.

Implementation Details

29.8 **An outline of the class.** Listing 29-1 outlines our class of AVL trees. Since an AVL tree is also a binary search tree, we will derive the class `AVLTree` from the class `BinarySearchTree`, which we discussed in Chapter 27. The methods `add` and `remove` are like those in `BinarySearchTree` but require logic to detect and correct any imbalance that might occur. Thus, we need to override these methods. The other methods specified in `SearchTreeInterface` are inherited from `BinarySearchTree`.

Figure 29-10   The result of adding 60, 50, 20, 80, 90, 70, 55, 10, 40, and 35 to an initially empty (a) AVL
tree; (b) binary search tree

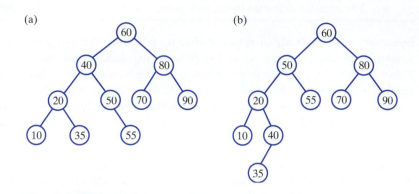

Listing 29-1   An outline of the class AVLTree

```
package TreePackage;
public class AVLTree<T extends Comparable<? super T>>
               extends BinarySearchTree<T>
               implements SearchTreeInterface<T>, java.io.Serializable
{
  public AVLTree()
  {
    super();
  } // end default constructor

  public AVLTree(T rootEntry)
  {
    super(rootEntry);
  } // end constructor
```

< Implementations of add *and* remove *are here. A definition of* add *appears in Segment 29.12 of
this chapter. Other methods in* SearchTreeInterface *are inherited. >*
```
    . . .
```
< Implementations of private methods to rebalance the tree using rotations are here. >
```
    . . .

} // end AVLTree
```

29.9   **Rotations.** As we discussed earlier, an AVL tree uses rotations to maintain its balance following the
addition or removal of a node. The methods that perform these rotations closely follow the pseudocode
given in the previous segments.

For example, consider the algorithm for a single right rotation, as given in Segment 29.2:

Algorithm rotateRight(nodeN)
// Corrects an imbalance at a given node nodeN *due to an addition*
// in the left subtree of nodeN*'s left child.*

```
nodeC  = left child of nodeN
Set nodeN's left child to nodeC's right child
Set nodeC's right child to nodeN
return nodeC
```

The following method implements this pseudocode as a private method of the class `AVLTree`:

```
/** Task: Corrects an imbalance at the node closest to a structural
 *       change in the left subtree of the node's left child.
 *  @param nodeN  a node, closest to the newly added leaf, at which
 *                an imbalance occurs and that has a left child. */
private BinaryNodeInterface<T> rotateRight(BinaryNodeInterface<T>
                                                  nodeN)
{
   BinaryNodeInterface<T> nodeC = nodeN.getLeftChild();
   nodeN.setLeftChild(nodeC.getRightChild());
   nodeC.setRightChild(nodeN);
   return nodeC;
} // end rotateRight
```

The method `rotateLeft` has a similar implementation and is left as an exercise.

Since a double rotation is equivalent to two single rotations, the methods that perform double rotations each call the methods that perform single rotations. For example, the algorithm for a right-left double rotation, as it appeared in Segment 29.4, is

Algorithm `rotateRightLeft(nodeN)`
// Corrects an imbalance at a given node `nodeN` *due to an addition*
// in the left subtree of `nodeN`*'s right child.*

```
nodeC = right child of nodeN
Set nodeN's right child to the node returned by rotateRight(nodeC)
return rotateLeft(nodeN)
```

An implementation of this pseudocode follows:

```
/** Task: Corrects an imbalance at the node closest to a structural
 *       change in the left subtree of the node's right child.
 *  @param nodeN  a node, closest to the newly added leaf, at which
 *                an imbalance occurs and that has a right child. */
private BinaryNodeInterface<T> rotateRightLeft(BinaryNodeInterface<T>
                                                  nodeN)
{
   BinaryNodeInterface<T> nodeC = nodeN.getRightChild();
   nodeN.setRightChild(rotateRight(nodeC));
   return rotateLeft(nodeN);
} // end rotateRightLeft
```

The method `rotateLeftRight` has a similar implementation and is left as an exercise.

Question 11 Implement the algorithm given in Segment 29.3 for a single left rotation.

29.10   **Rebalancing.** As you saw previously, you can correct an imbalance at node *N* of an AVL tree caused by the addition of a node by performing only one of the following rotations, according to where in the tree the change to its structure occurred:

- Right rotation if the addition occurred in the left subtree of *N*'s left child
- Left-right rotation if the addition occurred in the right subtree of *N*'s left child
- Left rotation if the addition occurred in the right subtree of *N*'s right child
- Right-left rotation if the addition occurred in the left subtree of *N*'s right child

The following pseudocode uses these criteria and the rotation methods to rebalance the tree:

> *Algorithm* `rebalance(nodeN)`
> `if` (*nodeN's left subtree is taller than its right subtree by more than 1*)
> { // *addition was in* `nodeN`*'s left subtree*
>   `if` (*the left child of* `nodeN` *has a left subtree that is taller than its right subtree*)
>   `rotateRight(nodeN)`   // *addition was in left subtree of left child*
>   `else`
>   `rotateLeftRight(nodeN)` // *addition was in right subtree of left child*
> }
> `else if` (*nodeN's right subtree is taller than its left subtree by more than 1*)
> { // *addition was in* `nodeN`*'s right subtree*
>   `if` (*the right child of* `nodeN` *has a right subtree that is taller than its left subtree*)
>   `rotateLeft(nodeN)`   // *addition was in right subtree of right child*
>   `else`
>   `rotateRightLeft(nodeN)` // *addition was in left subtree of right child*
> }

No rebalancing is needed if the heights of node *N*'s two subtrees either are the same or differ by 1.

29.11   **The method `rebalance`.** A method `getHeightDifference` that returns the difference in the heights of a node's left and right subtrees would help us to implement the previous algorithm. By giving a sign to the height difference it returns, `getHeightDifference` can indicate which subtree is taller. This method can be defined within either the class `AVLTree` or the class `BinaryNode`. The latter choice would be more efficient if each node maintained height information as one or more data fields instead of recomputing it each time the method is called. (See Project 4.)

A node is unbalanced if its two subtrees differ in height by more than 1, that is, if `getHeight-Difference` returns a value either greater than 1 or less than –1. If this return value is greater than 1, the left subtree is taller; if it is less than –1, the right subtree is taller.

Using the method `getHeightDifference`, we can implement the previous pseudocode for `rebalance` within the class `AVLTree` as follows:

```
private BinaryNodeInterface<T> rebalance(BinaryNodeInterface<T>
                                              nodeN)
{
  int heightDifference = getHeightDifference(nodeN);

  if (heightDifference > 1)
  { // left subtree is taller by more than 1,
    // so addition was in left subtree
    if (getHeightDifference(nodeN.getLeftChild()) > 0)
      // addition was in left subtree of left child
      nodeN = rotateRight(nodeN);
    else
```

```
        // addition was in right subtree of left child
        nodeN = rotateLeftRight(nodeN);
   }
   else if (heightDifference < -1)
   { // right subtree is taller by more than 1,
     // so addition was in right subtree
     if (getHeightDifference(nodeN.getRightChild()) < 0)
        // addition was in right subtree of right child
        nodeN = rotateLeft(nodeN);
     else
        // addition was in left subtree of right child
        nodeN = rotateRightLeft(nodeN);
   } // end if
   // else nodeN is balanced

   return nodeN;
} // end rebalance
```

29.12   **The method add.** Adding to an AVL tree is just like adding to a binary search tree, but with a rebalancing step. For example, we can begin with the recursive implementations of the methods add and addEntry of BinarySearchTree (Segments 27.15 and 27.16 in Chapter 27) and insert calls to rebalance. The resulting methods in AVLTree are as follows:

```
public T add(T newEntry)
{
   T result = null;

   if (isEmpty())
      setRootNode(new BinaryNode<T>(newEntry));
   else
   {
      BinaryNodeInterface<T> rootNode = getRootNode();
      result = addEntry(rootNode, newEntry);
      setRootNode(rebalance(rootNode));
   } // end if

   return result;
} // end add

private T addEntry(BinaryNodeInterface<T> rootNode, T newEntry)
{
   assert rootNode != null;
   T result = null;
   int comparison = newEntry.compareTo(rootNode.getData());

   if (comparison == 0)
   {
      result = rootNode.getData();
      rootNode.setData(newEntry);
   }
   else if (comparison < 0)
   {
      if (rootNode.hasLeftChild())
      {
```

```
         BinaryNodeInterface<T> leftChild = rootNode.getLeftChild();
         result = addEntry(leftChild, newEntry);
         rootNode.setLeftChild(rebalance(leftChild));
      }
      else
         rootNode.setLeftChild(new BinaryNode<T>(newEntry));
   }
   else
   {
      assert comparison > 0;

      if (rootNode.hasRightChild())
      {
         BinaryNodeInterface<T> rightChild = rootNode.getRightChild();
         result = addEntry(rightChild, newEntry);
         rootNode.setRightChild(rebalance(rightChild));
      }
      else
         rootNode.setRightChild(new BinaryNode<T>(newEntry));
   } // end if

   return result;
} // end addEntry
```

Although `rebalance` is called several times during the course of executing these methods, a rebalancing of the tree occurs at most once. Most calls to `rebalance` simply check whether a rebalancing is needed.

As attractive as an AVL tree might seem, better search trees have been developed, as you will now see.

2–3 Trees

29.13   A **2-3 tree** is a general search tree whose interior nodes must have either two or three children. A **2-node** contains one data item s and has two children, like the nodes in a binary search tree. This data s is greater than any data in the node's left subtree and less than any data in the right subtree. That is, the data in the node's left subtree is less than s, and any data in the right subtree is greater than s, as Figure 29-11a shows.

A **3-node** contains two data items, s and l, and has three children. Data that is less than the smaller data item s occurs in the node's left subtree. Data that is greater than the larger data item l occurs in the node's right subtree. Data that is between s and l occurs in the node's middle subtree. Figure 29-11b shows a typical 3-node.

Because it can contain 3-nodes, a 2-3 tree tends to be shorter than a binary search tree. To make the 2-3 tree balanced, we require that all leaves occur on the same level. Thus, a 2-3 tree is completely balanced.

Note: A 2-3 tree is a general search tree whose interior nodes must have either two or three children and whose leaves occur on the same level. A 2-3 tree is completely balanced.

Figure 29-11 (a) A 2-node; (b) a 3-node

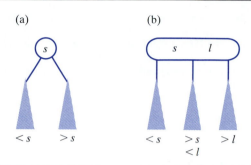

Searching a 2-3 Tree

29.14   If we had a 2-3 tree, such as the one in Figure 29-12, how would we search it? Notice that each 2-node adheres to the ordering of a binary search tree. The 3-node leaf <35 40> contains values that are between the values in its parent. Knowing this, we can search for the 40, for example, by first comparing 40 with the root value 60. We then move to 60's left subtree and compare 40 with the values in the root of this subtree. Since 40 lies between 20 and 50, it would occur in the middle subtree, if it appears at all. While searching the middle subtree, we compare 40 with 35 and then finally with 40.

Figure 29-12 A 2-3 tree

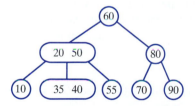

The search algorithm is an extension of the search algorithm for a binary search tree:

Algorithm `search23Tree(23Tree, desiredObject)`
// Searches a 2-3 tree for a given object.
// Returns true if the object is found.

if (23Tree *is empty*)
    return false
else if (desiredObject *is in the root of* 23Tree)
    return true
else if (*the root of* 23Tree *contains two entries*)
{
    if (desiredObject < *smaller object in the root*)
        return search23Tree(*left subtree of* 23Tree, desiredObject)
    else if (desiredObject > *larger object in the root*)
        return search23Tree(*right subtree of* 23Tree, desiredObject)
    else

```
        return search23Tree(middle subtree of 23Tree, desiredObject)
    }
    else if (desiredObject < object in the root)
        return search23Tree(left subtree of 23Tree, desiredObject)
    else
        return search23Tree(right subtree of 23Tree, desiredObject)
```

Question 12 What comparisons are made while searching the 2-3 tree in Figure 29-12 for each of the following values?

a. 5   **b.** 55   **c.** 41   **d.** 30

Adding Entries to a 2-3 Tree

29.15   Using an example, we will describe how to add an entry to a 2-3 tree. So that we can compare our results with an AVL tree, we will make the same sequence of additions to an initially empty 2-3 tree that we made when forming the AVL tree in Figure 29-10a.

As we did when adding to a binary search tree, we add an entry to a 2-3 tree at a leaf. We locate this leaf by using the search algorithm that we described in the previous segment. Thus, once we make the addition, the search algorithm will be able to locate the new entry.

We will now add the following entries: 60, 50, 20, 80, 90, 70, 55, 10, 40, and 35.

29.16   **Adding 60, 50, and 20.** After we add 60, the 2-3 tree consists of a single 2-node. After we add 50, the tree is a single 3-node. Figures 29-13a and 29-13b show the tree after each of these additions.

Now we add 20. To facilitate our description of this addition, we show the 20 in Figure 29-13c within the only node in the tree. This is an imaginary placement, since a 3-node can contain only two data items. We would not actually place more data in this node. Since the node cannot accommodate the 20, we **split** it into three nodes, moving the middle value 50 up one level. In this case, we are splitting a leaf that is also the tree's root. Moving the 50 up requires that we create a new node that becomes the new root of the tree. This step increases the height of the tree by 1, as Figure 29-13d shows.

Figure 29-13 An initially empty 2-3 tree after adding (a) 60 and (b) 50; (c), (d) adding 20 causes the 3-node to split

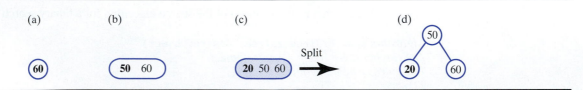

29.17   **Adding 80, 90, and 70.** To add 80, we note that the search algorithm would look for 80 in the tree's rightmost leaf. Since this leaf has room for another data entry, that is where we should add 80. Figure 29-14a shows the result of this addition.

The search algorithm would look for 90 in the leaf to which we just added 80. Although the leaf has no room for another entry, we imagine that we have added 90 there. We then move the middle value—the 80—up a level and split the leaf into two nodes for the 60 and 90, as Figure 29-14b shows. Since the root can accept the 80, the addition is complete.

The entry 70 belongs in the root's middle subtree, and since this leaf can accept another entry, we add 70 there. Figure 29-14c shows the tree after this addition.

Figure 29-14   The 2-3 tree after adding (a) 80; (b) 90; (c) 70

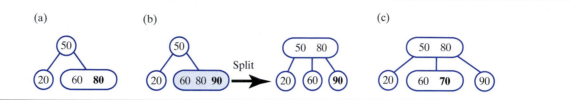

29.18   **Adding 55.** When we add 55 to the tree in Figure 29-14c, the search algorithm terminates at the root's middle subtree—a leaf—as Figure 29-15a indicates. Since this leaf cannot accommodate another entry, we split the leaf and move 60 up a level to the root, as shown in Figure 29-15b. Moving the 60 causes the root to split, and 60 moves up another level to a new node that becomes the new root. Figure 29-15c shows the result of this addition.

Figure 29-15   Adding 55 to the 2-3 tree causes a leaf and then the root to split

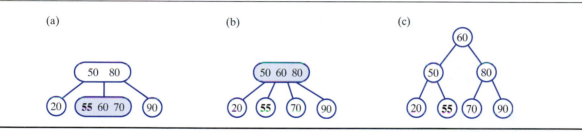

29.19   **Adding 10, 40, and 35.** The leaf that contains 20 has room for 10 as an additional entry, as Figure 29-16a shows. An additional entry, 40, belongs in the same leaf. Since the leaf already contains two entries, we split it and move 20 up a level to the node that contains 50. Figures 29-16b and 29-16c show this result. Finally, Figure 29-17 shows the result of adding 35 to the tree. The leaf that contains 40 accommodates this new entry.

Figure 29-16   The 2-3 tree after adding (a) 10; (b), (c) 40

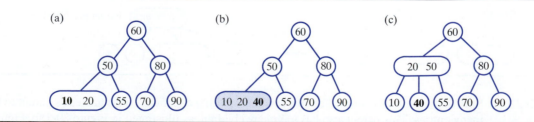

Figure 29-17 The 2-3 tree after adding 35

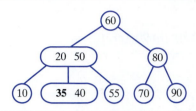

Compare the final 2-3 tree in Figure 29-17 with the AVL tree in Figure 29-10a. We used the same sequence of additions to form both trees. The 2-3 tree is completely balanced and shorter than the balanced AVL tree. Later, we will compare these trees with the 2-4 tree in the next section and draw some conclusions.

Splitting Nodes During Addition

29.20 **Splitting a leaf.** During the addition of a new entry to a 2-3 tree, the first node that splits is a leaf that already contains two entries. Figure 29-18a shows a leaf that would need to accommodate three entries. These entries are shown in ascending order as s, m, and l: s is the smallest entry in the node, m is the middle entry, and l is the largest. The node splits into two nodes that contain s and l, respectively, and the middle entry m moves up a level. If the parent of the leaf has room for m, no further action is necessary. This is the case in Figure 29-18a. But in Figure 29-18b, the parent already contains two entries, so we must split it as well. We consider that case next.

Although Figure 29-18 shows the leaf as a right child of its parent, other analogous configurations are possible.

Figure 29-18 Splitting a leaf to accommodate a new entry when the leaf's parent contains (a) one entry; (b) two entries

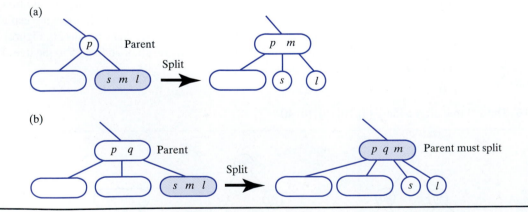

29.21 **Splitting an internal node.** You just saw that splitting a leaf can cause the leaf's parent to have too many entries. This parent also has too many children, as illustrated in Figure 29-18b. Figure 29-19 shows such an internal node in general. This node must accommodate three entries s, m, and l, given in ascending order, and four children that are the roots of the subtrees T_1 through T_4. Thus, we split the node, move the middle entry m up to the node's parent, place s and l into their own nodes, and distribute the original node's subtrees between s and l. If the parent has room for m, no further splitting is necessary. If not, we split the parent as just described.

Other analogous configurations for an internal node are possible.

Figure 29-19 Splitting an internal node to accommodate a new entry

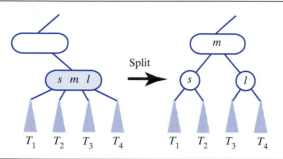

29.22   **Splitting the root.** Splitting a root proceeds just like the previous cases, except that when we move an entry up a level, we allocate a new node for the entry. This new node becomes the root of the tree, as Figure 29-20 illustrates. Notice that only this case increases the height of a 2-3 tree.

Figure 29-20 Splitting the root to accommodate a new entry

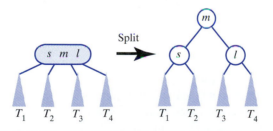

Question 13 What tree results when you add 30 to the 2-3 tree in Figure 29-17?

Question 14 What 2-3 tree results when you make the following additions to an initially empty 2-3 tree? 70, 80, 90, 20, 10, 50, 60, 40, 30

Question 15 How does the tree that you created in the previous question compare to the AVL tree you created in Question 7?

2–4 Trees

29.23   A **2-4 tree**, sometimes called a **2-3-4 tree**, is a general search tree whose interior nodes must have either two, three, or four children and whose leaves occur on the same level. In addition to 2-nodes and 3-nodes, as we described in the previous section, this tree also contains 4-nodes. A **4-node** contains three data items s, m, and l and has four children. Data that is less than the smallest data item s occurs in the node's left subtree. Data that is greater than the largest data item l occurs in the node's right subtree. Data that is between s and the middle data item m or between m and l occurs in the node's middle subtrees. Figure 29-21 illustrates a typical 4-node.

Searching a 2-4 tree is like searching a 2-3 tree, but with additional logic to handle the 4-nodes. This search forms the basis of an algorithm to add entries to a 2-4 tree.

Figure 29-21   A 4-node

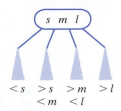

Note: A 2-4 tree is a general search tree whose interior nodes must have two, three, or four children and whose leaves occur on the same level. A 2-4 tree is completely balanced.

Adding Entries to a 2-4 Tree

29.24   Recall how we add a new entry to a 2-3 tree. We make comparisons along a path that begins at the root and ends at a leaf. At this point, if the leaf is a 3-node, it already contains two data entries, and so we must split it. Since an entry would now move up a level, this split could require splits in nodes above the leaf. Thus, adding to a 2-3 tree can require us to retrace the path from the leaf back to the root.

In a 2-4 tree, we avoid this retrace by splitting each 4-node as soon as we first consider it during the search from root to leaf. After a split, the next node along the comparison path is the result of the split, and so is not a 4-node. If this node has a 4-node child that we consider next, it has room for the entry that moves up from this child. No other splits occur, as would happen in a 2-3 tree. You will see an example of this shortly.

As in the previous section, we will use an example to demonstrate how to add entries to a 2-4 tree. So that we can compare our results with previous trees, we will use the same sequence of additions—namely, 60, 50, 20, 80, 90, 70, 55, 10, 40, and 35—that we used earlier.

29.25   **Adding 60, 50, and 20.** Figure 29-22 shows the effect of adding 60, 50, and 20 to an initially empty 2-4 tree. The resulting tree consists of a single 4-node.

Figure 29-22   An initially empty 2-4 tree after adding (a) 60; (b) 50; (c) 20

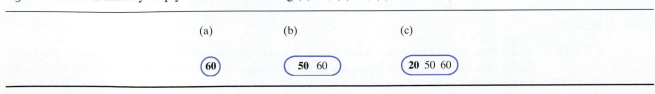

29.26   **Adding 80 and 90.** To add an entry to the 2-4 tree in Figure 29-22c, we find that the root is a 4-node. We split it by moving the middle entry, 50, up. Since we are at a root, we create a new node for the 50. That node becomes the new root of the tree, as shown in Figure 29-23a. We now can add 80 and 90 to the root's right leaf, as Figures 29-23b and 29-23c illustrate.

Figure 29-23   The 2-4 tree after (a) splitting the root; (b) adding 80; (c) adding 90

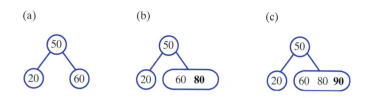

29.27   **Adding 70.** While searching the 2-4 tree in Figure 29-23c for a place to add 70, we encounter the 4-node that is the root's right child. We split this node into two nodes and move the middle entry 80 up to the root. The result of this split is shown in Figure 29-24a. We now have room to add 70 to the root's middle child, as Figure 29-24b shows.

Figure 29-24   The 2-4 tree after (a) splitting a 4-node; (b) adding 70

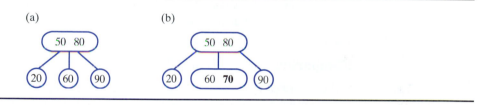

29.28   **Adding 55, 10, and 40.** The 2-4 tree in Figure 29-24b can accommodate the addition of 55, 10, and 40 without splitting nodes. Figure 29-25 shows the results of these additions.

Figure 29-25   The 2-4 tree after adding (a) 55; (b) 10; (c) 40

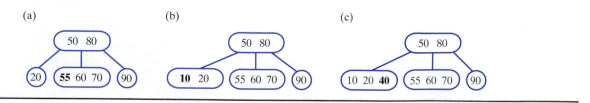

29.29   **Adding 35.** While adding 35 to the 2-4 tree in Figure 29-25c, our search encounters the root's left child, which is a 4-node. We split this node into two nodes and move the middle entry, 20, up to the root, as shown in Figure 29-26a. We now can add 35 to the root's middle left child, as Figure 29-26b shows. This is the final addition that we will make.

Figure 29-26 The 2-4 tree after (a) splitting the leftmost 4-node; (b) adding 35

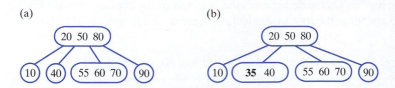

> **Note:**   When adding a new entry to a 2-4 tree, you split any 4-node as soon as you encounter it during the search for the new entry's position in the tree. The addition is complete right after this search ends. Thus, adding to a 2-4 tree is more efficient than adding to a 2-3 tree.

Question 16   What comparisons are made while searching the 2-4 tree in Figure 29-26b for each of the following values?

a. 5   **b.** 56   **c.** 41   **d.** 30

Question 17   What tree results when you add 30 to the 2-4 tree in Figure 29-26b?

Question 18   What 2-4 tree results when you make the following additions to an initially empty 2-4 tree? 70, 80, 90, 20, 10, 50, 60, 40, 30

Question 19   How does the tree that you created in the previous question compare to the 2-3 tree you created in Question 14?

Comparing AVL, 2-3, and 2-4 Trees

29.30   Earlier we asked you to compare the final 2-3 tree in Figure 29-17 with the AVL tree in Figure 29-10a. We also want to compare those results with the 2-4 tree that we just constructed. Figure 29-27 shows these trees again. The AVL tree is a balanced binary search tree of height 4. The other trees are completely balanced general search trees. The height of the 2-3 tree is 3; the height of the 2-4 tree is 2. In general, 2-4 trees are shorter than 2-3 trees, which are shorter than AVL trees.

Figure 29-27 Three balanced search trees obtained by adding 60, 50, 20, 80, 90, 70, 55, 10, 40, and 35:
(a) AVL tree; (b) 2-3 tree; (c) 2-4 tree

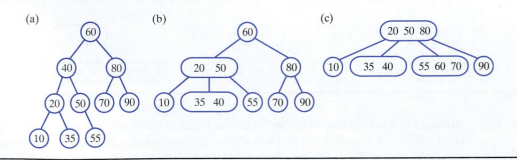

You saw in Segment 27.42 of Chapter 27 that searching a balanced binary search tree, such as an AVL tree, is an O(log n) operation. Since 2-3 and 2-4 trees are no taller than a corresponding

AVL tree, we usually can search them by examining fewer nodes. However, 3-nodes and 4-nodes contain more entries than 2-nodes, and so they require a longer search time. In general, searching an AVL, 2-3, or 2-4 tree is an O(log n) operation.

A 2-3 tree is appealing because maintaining its balance is easier than for an AVL tree. Maintaining the balance of a 2-4 tree is even easier. But defining search trees whose nodes contain more than three data items is usually counterproductive, because the number of comparisons per node increases. As you will see later in this chapter, such a search tree is attractive when it is maintained in external storage, such as a disk, instead of internal memory.

Red–Black Trees

29.31   You just saw that maintaining the balance of a 2-4 tree is easier than maintaining either an AVL tree or a 2-3 tree. While a 2-4 tree is a general tree, a **red-black tree** is a binary tree that is equivalent to a 2-4 tree. Adding an entry to a red-black tree is like adding an entry to a 2-4 tree, in that only one pass from root to leaf is necessary. But a red-black tree is a binary tree, so it uses simpler operations to maintain its balance than does a 2-4 tree. Additionally, the implementation of a red-black tree uses only 2-nodes, whereas a 2-4 tree requires 2-nodes, 3-nodes, and 4-nodes. This added requirement of a 2-4 tree makes it less desirable than a red-black tree.

> **Note:**   A red-black tree is a binary tree that is equivalent to a 2-4 tree. Conceptually, a red-black tree is more involved than a 2-4 tree, but its implementation uses only 2-nodes and so is more efficient.

29.32   When designing a node for the 2-4 tree, you need to decide how to represent the entries that are in the node. Since you must order these entries, you could use an ADT such as the sorted list for the entries. You might also use a binary search tree. For example, consider the 2-4 tree in Figure 29-27c. The entries in the root of this tree are 20, 50, and 80. We can represent these entries as a binary search tree whose root is 50 and whose subtrees are 20 and 80. Likewise, the entries in the 3-node leaf of this 2-4 tree are 35 and 40. We can represent these entries as one of two binary search trees: One has 35 as its root and 40 as its right subtree; the other has 40 as its root and 35 as its left subtree. Thus, we can convert all 3-nodes and 4-nodes to 2-nodes. The result is a binary search tree instead of a 2-4 tree.

Each time we convert a 3-node or a 4-node to a 2-node, we increase the height of the tree. We use color to highlight the new nodes that cause this increase in height. We use black for all the nodes in the original 2-4 tree. Since we do not change the 2-nodes, they remain black in the new tree.

Figure 29-28a shows how to represent a 4-node by using 2-nodes. The root of the resulting subtree remains black, but we color its children. The traditional color is red. Our figures use blue since that is our book's second color. Similarly, Figure 29-28b shows how to represent a 3-node by using one of two different subtrees, each having a black root and a red child.

With this notation, we can draw the 2-4 tree in Figure 29-27c as the balanced binary search tree in Figure 29-29. This binary search tree is called a red-black tree.

Question 20   What comparisons are made while searching the 2-4 tree in Figure 29-27c and the equivalent red-black tree in Figure 29-29 for

a. 60   **b.** 55

Figure 29-28   Using 2-nodes to represent (a) a 4-node; (b) a 3-node

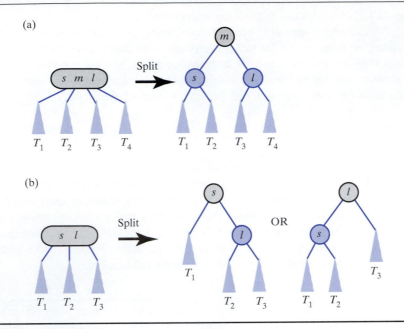

(a)

(b)

Figure 29-29   A red-black tree that is equivalent to the 2-4 tree in Figure 29-27c

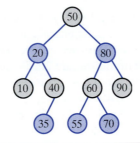

Properties of a Red-Black Tree

29.33   The root of every red-black tree is black. If the original 2-4 tree had a 2-node as its root, the 2-node would be black. And if its root was either a 3-node or a 4-node, we would replace it with a subtree whose root is black, as shown in Figure 29-28.

Since we create red nodes only when we convert 3-nodes and 4-nodes to 2-nodes, every red node has a black parent, as you can see in Figure 29-29. It follows that a red node cannot have red children. If it did, the red child would have a red parent, and this contradicts our previous conclusion that every red node has a black parent.

When we formed a red-black tree equivalent to a 2-4 tree, 2-nodes stayed black and the representation of any other node contained one black node. Thus, every node in a 2-4 tree produced exactly one black node in the equivalent red-black tree. Since a 2-4 tree is completely balanced, all paths from its root to a leaf connect the same number of nodes. So every path from the root to a leaf in a red-black tree must contain the same number of black nodes.

Note: **Properties of a red-black tree**

1. The root is black.
2. Every red node has a black parent.
3. Any children of a red node are black; that is, a red node cannot have red children.
4. Every path from the root to a leaf contains the same number of black nodes.

Question 21 Show that the red-black tree in Figure 29-29 satisfies the four properties just given.

Question 22 What red-black tree is equivalent to the 2-4 tree in Figure 29-25c?

Question 23 Show that the red-black tree that answers Question 22 satisfies the four properties given previously.

Note: **Creating a red-black tree**
In practice, you do not convert 2-4 trees into red-black trees. You create a red-black tree by adding entries to an initially empty tree according to the steps described in the following section. These steps consider both the balance of the tree and the color of its nodes.

Note: **Searching a red-black tree**
A red-black tree is really a binary search tree whose nodes are either red or black. If you ignore these colors, you can search a red-black tree by using the same algorithm you use to search a binary search tree.

Adding Entries to a Red-Black Tree

29.34   **Adding a leaf.** What color should we assign to a new node that we add to the tree? An addition to a binary search tree always occurs at a leaf, so the same is true for a red-black tree. If we use black for a new leaf, we will increase the number of black nodes on the paths to that leaf. This increase violates the fourth property of a red-black tree. Thus, any new node must be red. However, do not assume that all the leaves in a red-black tree are red. Adding or removing entries can change the color of various nodes, including that of leaves added earlier.

Note: **The color of nodes added to a red-black tree**
Adding an entry to a red-black tree results in a new red leaf. The color of this leaf can change later when other entries are added or removed.

Consider some simple cases of adding to a red-black tree. A one-node red-black tree has one black node, its root. Figure 29-30 shows two possibilities when we add a new entry *e* to this tree. In each case, the new red node maintains the properties of a red-black tree, so it is legal.

Figure 29-30 The result of adding a new entry *e* to a one-node red-black tree

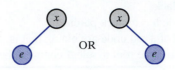

Now suppose that the red-black tree had two nodes before we added the new entry *e*. Figure 29-31a shows this original tree when it consists of a root *x* and right child *y*. Also pictured is the 2-4 tree that is equivalent to the original red-black tree. The rest of the figure shows the possible outcomes of the addition, depending on how *e* compares with *x* and *y*. In Part *b*, *e* is the left child of the root, and we are done. In Part *c*, a red node has a red child. These two consecutive red nodes are illegal in a red-black tree (properties 2 and 3). To understand what further action is necessary, consider the equivalent 2-4 tree. The original 2-node red-black tree is equivalent to the 2-4 tree that contains the one node <*x y*> (Figure 29-31a). If we add an entry *e* that is larger than *y*, the 2-4 tree becomes the single node <*x y e*> (Figure 29-31c). Notice the red-black tree that is equivalent to this 3-node. This tree is the one we need as the result of adding *e*. We can get it from the first red-black

Figure 29-31 The possible results of adding a new entry *e* to a two-node red-black tree

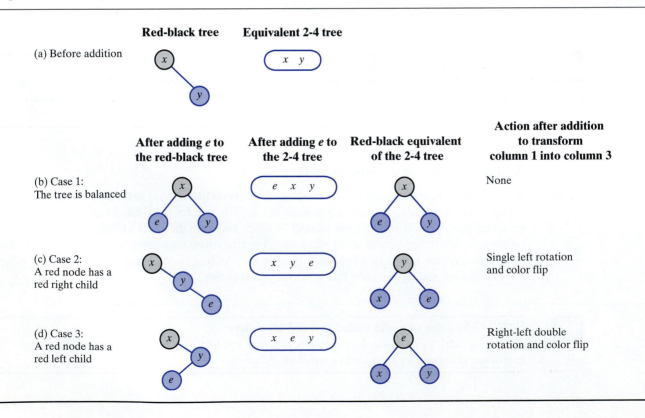

tree shown in Part *c* by first performing a single left rotation about the node containing *y*. You have seen this rotation before in Figures 29-5b and 29-5c when we talked about AVL trees. After the rotation, we need to reverse the colors of the nodes containing *x* and *y*—that is, the original parent and grandparent of the new node. We call this step a **color flip**.

Figure 29-31d shows the last possible result of adding *e* to the two-node red-black tree. Here, a right-left double rotation followed by a color flip of the new node and its original grandparent are necessary to avoid two consecutive red nodes. Figures 29-7b, 29-7c, and 29-7d show the rotation in general in the context of an AVL tree.

Figure 29-32 shows mirror images of the cases in Figure 29-31.

Figure 29-32   The possible results of adding a new entry *e* to a two-node red-black tree: mirror images of Figure 29-31

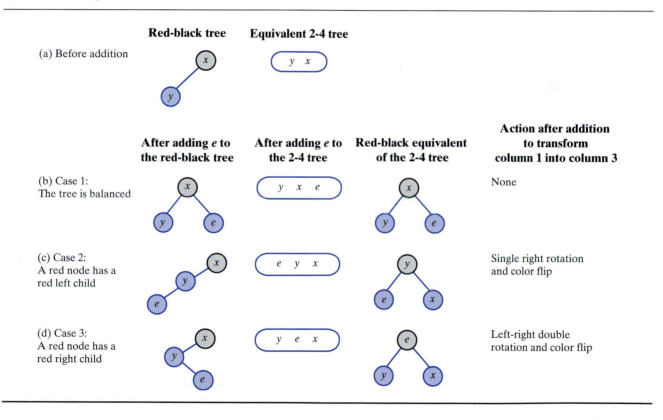

29.35   **Splitting a 4-node whose parent is black.** During an addition to a 2-4 tree, we split any 4-nodes that we encounter as we move along the path from the root to the eventual insertion point. We must perform an equivalent action during an addition to a red-black tree. Figure 29-28a shows that when a black node has two red children, we have encountered the red-black representation of a 4-node. We will call this configuration a red-black 4-node, or simply a 4-node.

Note: A red-black 4-node
A red-black 4-node consists of a black node and two red children.

Figure 29-33a recalls how to split a 4-node when its parent in the 2-4 tree is a 2-node. The middle entry m moves up to the node's parent, and the other entries s and l are given their own nodes as replacement children of the parent. Figure 29-33b shows the corresponding red-black trees. Notice that the three nodes in the subtree rooted at m reverse colors. Thus, we split the red-black representation of a 4-node by performing a color flip.

A color flip is all that is necessary when a red-black 4-node has a black parent. As you can see from Figure 29-33, a black parent corresponds to a 2-node in the 2-4 tree. If a 4-node in a 2-4 tree has a 3-node as its parent, the red-black 4-node will have a red parent. We examine this situation in the next segment.

Figure 29-33 Splitting a 4-node whose parent is a 2-node in (a) a 2-4 tree; (b) a red-black tree

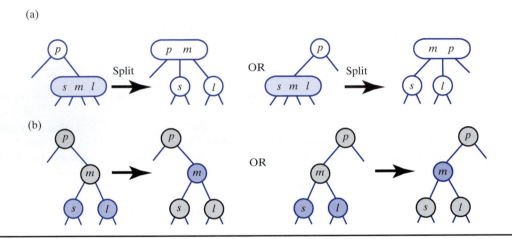

29.36   **Splitting a 4-node whose parent is red: Case 1.** Figure 29-34a shows the splitting of a 4-node that has a 3-node parent within a 2-4 tree. Here, the 4-node is the right child of its parent. Figure 29-34b shows the red-black representations of the two trees in Part a. How can we transform the first red-black tree into the second? Figure 29-35 shows the necessary steps. In Part a, we detect a 4-node at m, since this black node has two red children. A color flip results in two adjacent red nodes, as shown in Figure 29-35b. Earlier, in Figure 29-31c, we saw this configuration of a black node and two consecutive right descendants that are red. As we did then, we perform a left rotation about p, as Figure 29-35c shows, and then we reverse the colors of the nodes containing p and g. This color flip, together with the rotation, resolves the illegal red nodes. The result in Figure 29-35d is the desired red-black tree that we saw in Figure 29-34b.

Since a 3-node has two different red-black representations, we can replace Figure 29-35a with a different red-black tree. We leave it to you to show that the final result will be the same, but with less work. (See Exercise 13.)

29.37   **Splitting a 4-node whose parent is red: Case 2.** The 4-node in Figure 29-34a is a right child of its parent. If it were a left child, the red-black representation would be as in Figure 29-36a. The rest of this figure shows that both color flips and a right rotation are necessary to split the 4-node.

As before, we can replace Figure 29-36a with a different red-black tree and get the same final result. Again we leave the details to you as an exercise. (See Exercise 14.)

Figure 29-34 Splitting a 4-node that has a 3-node parent within (a) a 2-4 tree; (b) a red-black tree

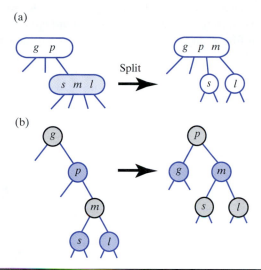

Figure 29-35 Splitting a 4-node that has a red parent within a red-black tree: Case 1

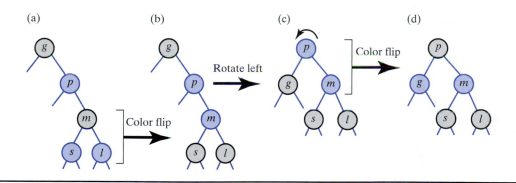

Figure 29-36 Splitting a 4-node that has a red parent within a red-black tree: Case 2

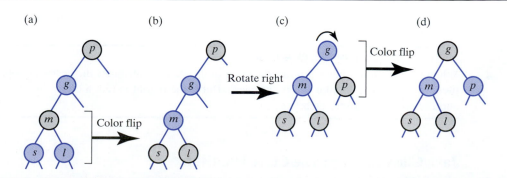

29.38   **Splitting a 4-node whose parent is red: Cases 3 and 4.** Now consider the case in which the 4-node is the middle child of its 3-node parent. This time, we look at both red-black representations that the 3-node parent produces. Figure 29-37a shows one possible red-black tree. After the color flip in Part *b*, we resolve the consecutive red nodes as we did in Figure 29-31d. A right-left double rotation followed by a color flip produces the desired results, as you can see in the rest of Figure 29-37.

Figure 29-38a shows the second possible red-black tree. After the color flip in Part *b*, we resolve the consecutive red nodes as we did in Figure 29-32d. A left-right double rotation followed by a color flip is necessary, as the rest of Figure 29-38 shows. Notice that the tree in Figure 29-38e is the same as the one in Figure 29-37e.

Figure 29-37   Splitting a 4-node that has a red parent within a red-black tree: Case 3

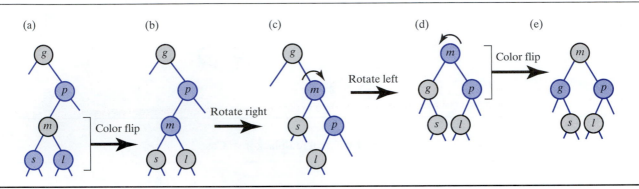

Figure 29-38   Splitting a 4-node that has a red parent within a red-black tree: Case 4

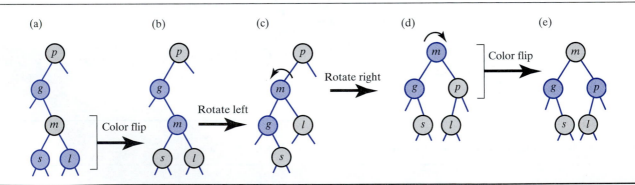

 Note: Splitting a red-black 4-node
When splitting a red-black 4-node, the color of its parent determines the necessary operations. If the parent is black, a color flip is sufficient. But if the parent is red, a color flip, a rotation, and another color flip are necessary.

Java Class Library: The Class TreeMap

29.39   The package `java.util` contains the class `TreeMap<K, V>`. This class uses a red-black tree to implement the methods in the interface `SortedMap<K, V>` in the same package. SortedMap extends the interface Map<K, V>, which we described in Segment 17.22 of Chapter 17. Recall that the interface Map is similar to our interface for the ADT dictionary. SortedMap specifies a sorted dictionary in which the search keys are maintained in ascending order. Because TreeMap uses a red-black tree, methods such as get, put, remove, and containsKey are each an O(log *n*) operation.

B–Trees

29.40   A **multiway search tree of order** *m*—or sometimes an ***m*-way search tree**—is a general tree whose nodes have up to *m* children each. A node that has *k* - 1 data items and *k* children is called a ***k*-node**. An order *m* multiway search tree can contain *k*-nodes for values of *k* ranging from 2 to *m*.

A binary search tree is a multiway search tree of order 2. You know that not all binary search trees are balanced; likewise, not all multiway search trees are balanced. However, 2-3 trees and 2-4 trees are balanced multiway search trees of orders 3 and 4, respectively. We maintained the balance of a 2-3 tree, for example, by insisting that every interior node have two or three children and that all leaves occur on the same level.

A **B-tree of order** *m* is a balanced multiway search tree of order *m* that has the following additional properties to maintain its balance:

- The root has either no children or between 2 and *m* children.
- Other interior nodes (nonleaves) have between $\lceil m/2 \rceil$ and *m* children each.
- All leaves are on the same level.

2-3 and 2-4 trees satisfy these constraints, and so are examples of B-trees.

29.41   The search trees that you have seen so far maintain their data within the main memory of a computer. At some point, we probably will save this data in external memory, such as a disk. As long as we can read the data back into internal memory, we can use any of the previous search trees. But what happens when your database becomes too large to be retained entirely within internal memory? Typically, you use a B-tree.

Accessing data in external memory is much slower than accessing data in main memory. When reading external data, the major cost is locating it on the storage device. Data on a disk, for example, is organized sequentially into **blocks**, whose size depends on the physical characteristics of the disk. When you read data from a disk, an entire block is read. Locating the block takes much more time than reading the data. If each block contains the data for at least one node, you can reduce the access time by placing numerous data items in each node. Although many comparisons per node could be necessary, their cost is much less than the cost of accessing external data.

Since increasing the number of data items per node decreases the tree's height, you decrease the number of nodes that you must search and hence the number of disk accesses. A high-order B-tree fits these requirements. You would choose the order *m* so that *m* - 1 data items fit into a block on the disk.

 Note: Although a high-order B-tree is usually counterproductive for an internal database because the number of comparisons per node increases, it is attractive when it is maintained in external storage such as a disk.

CHAPTER SUMMARY

- An AVL tree is a balanced binary search tree that rearranges its nodes whenever it becomes unbalanced. If adding or deleting a node causes an imbalance, one single or double rotation restores the tree's balance.

- A 2-node is a node that has two children and one data item. A 3-node has three children and two data items.

- A 2-3 tree is a balanced search tree that contains 2-nodes and 3-nodes. When an addition to the tree would cause a leaf to have three data items, the leaf splits into two 2-nodes. These nodes contain the smallest and largest of the three data items and become the children of the former leaf's parent. The middle data item moves up to this parent node, possibly causing the node to split.

- A disadvantage of the 2-3 tree is that the addition algorithm follows a path from the root to a leaf and then returns along that path as nodes split.

- A 4-node has four children and three data items.

- A 2-4 (or 2-3-4) tree is a balanced search tree that contains 2-nodes, 3-nodes, and 4-nodes. During an addition to the tree, each 4-node is split as it is considered during the search from root to leaf. Thus, returning along the path to the root is unnecessary.

- A red-black tree is a binary search tree that is logically equivalent to a 2-4 tree. Conceptually, a red-black tree is more involved than a 2-4 tree, but its implementation is more efficient because it uses only 2-nodes.

- Additions to a red-black tree maintain the tree's balance and status as a red-black tree by using color flips as well as rotations like those used for an AVL tree.

- A k-node is a node that has k children and $k-1$ data items.

- A multiway search tree of order m is a general tree that contains k-nodes for values of k ranging from 2 to m. A B-tree of order m is a balanced multiway search tree of order m. To maintain its balance, a B-tree requires every interior node to have a certain number of children and has all its leaves on the same level.

- A 2-3 tree is a B-tree of order 3; a 2-4 tree is a B-tree of order 4.

- A B-tree is useful when data is maintained in external storage, such as a disk.

EXERCISES

1. Implement the algorithm for a left-right double rotation, as given in Segment 29.5.

2. Add 62 and 65 to the AVL tree in Figure 29-27a.

3. Add 62 and 65 to the 2-3 tree in Figure 29-27b.

4. Add 62 and 65 to the 2-4 tree in Figure 29-27c.

5. Add 62 and 65 to the red-black tree in Figure 29-29.

6. Each of the trees in Figures 29-27 and 29-29 contains the same values. Exercises 2 through 5 asked you to add 62 and 65 to each of them. Describe the effect that these additions had on each tree.

7. What red-black tree is equivalent to the 2-4 tree in Figure 29-25b?

8. What tree results when you add the values 10, 20, 30, 40, 50, 60, 70, 80, 90, and 100 to each of the following initially empty trees?

   a. An AVL tree   **b.** A 2-3 tree   **c.** A 2-4 tree   **d.** A red-black tree

9. Add the values given in Exercise 8 to an initially empty binary search tree. Compare the resulting tree with the trees you created in Exercise 8. Which tree could you search most efficiently?

10. Draw the shortest possible tree that contains 20 values for each of the following kinds of trees:

    a. An AVL tree   **b.** A 2-3 tree   **c.** A 2-4 tree   **d.** A red-black tree

11. Draw the tallest possible tree that contains 20 values for each of the following kinds of trees:

    a. An AVL tree   **b.** A 2-3 tree   **c.** A 2-4 tree   **d.** A red-black tree

12. Using pseudocode, describe an inorder traversal of

    a. A 2-3 tree   **b.** A 2-4 tree

13. Figure 29-34a shows a 4-node within a 2-4 tree that is the right child of a 3-node parent containing data items *g* and *p*. When converting these nodes to red-black notation, make *p* be the parent of *g*. Revise Figure 29-35 to show that a color flip is all that is necessary to get the desired red-black tree.

14. Repeat Exercise 13, but this time assume that the 4-node is a left child.

15. Color the nodes in each tree in Figure 29-39 so that it is a red-black tree.

Figure 29-39 Three binary trees for Exercise 15

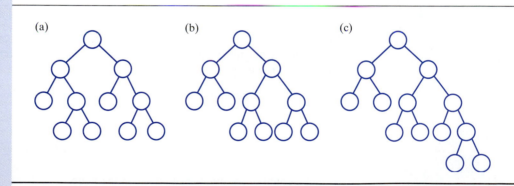

(a)   (b)   (c)

16. Which of the trees that you studied in this chapter could be used to implement a priority queue? Recall that we discussed the priority queue in Chapter 23.

17. How efficiently could a red-black tree or an AVL tree implement the add and remove methods of a priority queue?

18. Consider a B-tree of order 1000 whose height is 3. What is the smallest number of values that this tree can contain? What is the largest number of values? Generalize your results to a B-tree of order 1000 and height *h*.

1. You remove an entry from an AVL tree in the same way that you remove an entry from a binary search tree. However, after you remove the appropriate node from the tree, an imbalance can occur that you must correct by performing a single or double rotation. Develop an algorithm that removes a node from an AVL tree.

2. Implement a class of AVL trees.

3. Consider the implementation of the method `rebalance` for an AVL tree, as given in Segment 29.11. The performance of this method depends on the cost of a rotation and the cost of the method `getHeightDifference`.

   a. Assume that the tree has height h and that `nodeN` is at height k. What is the cost, using Big O notation, of each of the following tasks?

      ● A rotation
      ● Executing the method `getHeightDifference`
      ● Executing the method `rebalance`

   b. Suppose that a node is added at the bottom of the tree by the method `add`. How many times will `rebalance` be called? Give a Big Oh expression for the cost of adding a node.

4. Design and implement a class of nodes that you can use in the implementation of an AVL tree. You can derive this class from `BinaryNode`. Each node, as the root of a subtree, should contain the height of this subtree. Implement a class of AVL trees using your new class of nodes.

5. Design a class of nodes that you can use in the implementation of a 2-4 tree. Is one class enough, or will you need several?

6. Implement a class of 2-4 trees in which only additions and retrievals are permitted.

7. Implement a class of red-black trees that permit only additions and retrievals.

8. Design and carry out an experiment to compare the heights of ordinary binary search trees with the heights of either AVL trees or red-black trees. You first will need to complete either Project 2 or Project 7.

9. Design a class `BTreeNode` of nodes for a B-tree of order m. Consider operations that allow you to

   ● Get a particular value from the node
   ● Insert a value into the node while maintaining the links to subtrees (remember that the B-tree is a search tree)
   ● Get a count of the number of values in the node
   ● Replace a value in the node, if the search tree is maintained
   ● Replace a subtree
   ● Split a node into two nodes, each containing half the values

   Give an algorithm for adding a new value to a B-tree whose implementation uses your definition of `BTreeNode`.

10. Implement a priority queue by using one of the balanced search trees in this chapter.

30

Graphs

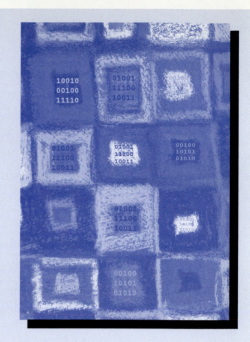

CONTENTS

PREREQUISITES

OBJECTIVES

After studying this chapter, you should be able to

- Describe the characteristics of a graph, including its vertices, edges, and paths
- Give examples of graphs, including those that are undirected, directed, unweighted, and weighted
- Give examples of vertices that are adjacent and that are not adjacent for both directed and undirected graphs

- Give examples of paths, simple paths, cycles, and simple cycles
- Give examples of connected graphs, disconnected graphs, and complete graphs
- Perform a depth-first traversal and a breadth-first traversal on a given graph
- List a topological order for the vertices of a directed graph without cycles
- Detect whether a path exists between two given vertices of a graph
- Find the path with the fewest edges that joins one vertex to another
- Find the path with the lowest cost that joins one vertex to another in a weighted graph
- Describe the operations for the ADT graph

The news media often use line graphs, pie charts, and bar graphs to help us visualize certain statistics. But these common graphs are *not* examples of the kind of graph that we will study in this chapter. The graphs that computer scientists and mathematicians use include the trees that you saw in Chapter 25. In fact, a tree is a special kind of graph. These graphs represent the relationships among data elements. This chapter will present the terminology we use when discussing graphs, the operations on them, and some typical applications.

Some Examples and Terminology

Although the graphs you have drawn in the past likely are not the kind of graph we will discuss here, the examples in this section will be familiar. But you probably have never called them graphs!

Road Maps

30.1   Figure 30-1 contains a portion of a road map for Cape Cod, Massachusetts. Small circles represent the towns, and the lines that join them represent the roads. A road map is a graph. In a graph, the

Figure 30-1   A portion of a road map

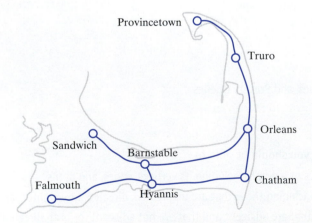

circles are called **vertices**, or **nodes**, and the lines are called **edges**. A **graph**, then, is a collection of distinct vertices and distinct edges. A **subgraph** is a portion of a graph that is itself a graph, just as the road map in Figure 30-1 actually is a part of a larger map.

Since you can travel in both directions along the roads in Figure 30-1, the corresponding graph and its edges are said to be **undirected**. But cities often have one-way streets. The graph in Figure 30-2 has a vertex for each intersection in a city's street map. The edges each have a direction and are called **directed edges**. A graph with directed edges is called a **directed graph**, or **digraph**. You can transform an undirected graph into a directed graph by replacing each undirected edge with two directed edges that have opposite directions.

Figure 30-2   A directed graph representing a portion of a city's street map

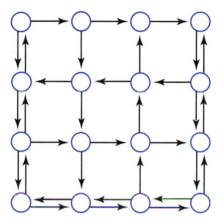

30.2   **Paths.** A **path** between two vertices in a graph is a sequence of edges. A path in a directed graph must consider the direction of the edges, and is called a **directed path**. The **length** of a path is the number of edges that it comprises. If the path does not pass through any vertex more than once, it is a **simple path**. Figure 30-1 contains a simple path from Provincetown to Orleans of length 2.

A **cycle** is a path that begins and ends at the same vertex. A **simple cycle** passes through other vertices only once each. In Figure 30-1, the cycle Chatham-Hyannis-Barnstable-Orleans-Chatham is a simple cycle. A graph that has no cycles is **acyclic**.

You use a road or street map to see how to get from point A to point B. The path you choose between these points will usually be a simple path. In doing so, you avoid retracing your steps or going around in circles. People who take a ride to view the autumn leaves, however, would follow a cycle that begins and ends at home.

30.3   **Weights.** You might be happy just to get from one place to another, but you often have a choice of several paths. You could choose the shortest, the fastest, or the cheapest path, for example. To do so, you use a **weighted graph**, which has values on its edges. These values are called either **weights** or **costs**. For example, Figure 30-3 shows the road map from Figure 30-1 as a weighted graph. In this version, each weight represents the distance in miles between two towns. Other types of weights you might use could represent the driving time or the cost of traveling by taxi.

A path in a weighted graph also has a weight, or cost, that is the sum of its edge weights. For example, the weight of the path from Provincetown to Orleans in Figure 30-3 is 27.

Figure 30-3   A weighted graph

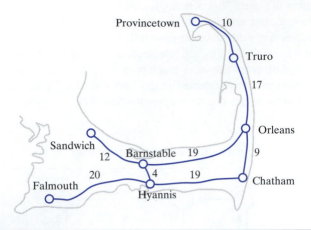

Question 1   Consider the graph in Figure 30-3.

a.   What is the length of the path that begins in Provincetown, passes through Truro and Orleans, and ends in Chatham?

b.   What is the weight of the path just described?

c.   Consider all paths from Truro to Sandwich that do not have cycles. Which path has the shortest length?

d.   Of the paths you considered in Part *c*, which one has the smallest weight?

30.4   **Connected graphs.** The towns on a road map are connected by roads in a way that enables you to go from any town to any other town. That is, you can get from here to there. A graph that has a path between every pair of distinct vertices is **connected**. A **complete graph** goes even further; it has an edge between every pair of distinct vertices. Figure 30-4 provides examples of undirected graphs that are connected, complete, or **disconnected**—that is, not connected. Notice the simple path in Part *a* and the simple cycle in Part *c*.

Figure 30-4   Undirected graphs

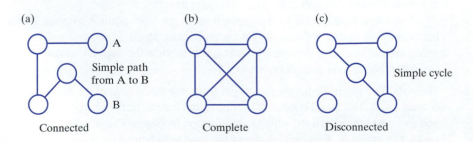

30.5   **Adjacent vertices.** Two vertices are **adjacent** in an undirected graph if they are joined by an edge. In Figure 30-3, Orleans and Chatham are adjacent, but Orleans and Sandwich are not. Adjacent vertices are called **neighbors**. In a directed graph, vertex i is adjacent to vertex j if a directed edge begins at j and ends at i. In Figure 30-5, vertex A is adjacent to vertex B, but vertex B is not adjacent to vertex A. That is, vertex A is vertex B's neighbor, but the converse is not true.

When convenient, we will place vertex labels within the circles that represent the vertices, as in Figure 30-5. But sometimes, the vertex labels will appear next to the circles, as in Figure 30-3.

Figure 30-5   Vertex A is adjacent to vertex B, but B is not adjacent to A

30.6   **The number of edges.** If a directed graph has n vertices, how many edges can it have? If the graph is complete, each vertex is a neighbor of all the other vertices. Thus, each vertex ends $n - 1$ directed edges. Consequently, the graph has $n(n-1)$ edges. A complete undirected graph has half that number of edges. For example, the graph in Figure 30-4b has 4 vertices and $4 \cdot 3 / 2$, or 6, edges. To make the graph directed and complete, we would replace each edge with two directed edges, which results in a graph having 12 edges.

Note: If a graph has n vertices, it can have at most

- $n(n-1)$ edges if the graph is directed
- $n(n-1)/2$ edges if the graph is undirected

A graph is **sparse** if it has relatively few edges. It is **dense** if it has many edges. While these terms have no precise definition, we will say that a sparse graph has $O(n)$ edges, and a dense graph has $O(n^2)$ edges. The graph in Figure 30-1 has eight vertices and eight edges. It is sparse.

Note: Typical graphs are sparse.

Airline Routes

30.7   A graph that represents the routes that an airline flies is similar to one that represents a road map. They are different, however, because not every city has an airport, and not every airline flies to or from every airport. For example, the graph in Figure 30-6 shows the flights for a small airline on the East Coast of the United States. The graph is undirected and consists of two **subgraphs** that are each connected. The entire graph, however, is disconnected.

Notice that you can fly from Boston to Provincetown, but not from Boston to Key West. Algorithms exist that see whether a flight between given cities is possible.

Note: Figure 30-6 contains one graph that consists of two distinct subgraphs. Although each subgraph is connected, the entire graph is disconnected.

Figure 30-6   Airline routes

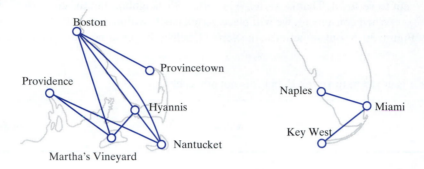

Mazes

30.8   Mazes have been constructed in Victorian English gardens and modern-day cornfields. A typical maze, like the one in Figure 30-7a, has a path from its entrance to its exit. Other paths begin at the entrance, but some lead to dead ends, rather than to the exit. Can you find your way through the maze?

We can represent this maze as a graph by placing a vertex at the entrance and exit, at each turn in the path, and at each dead end, as Figure 30-7b shows. This graph, like the road map in Figure 30-1, is connected. For such graphs, we can find a path between any two vertices, as you will see later in this chapter.

Figure 30-7   (a) A maze; (b) its representation as a graph

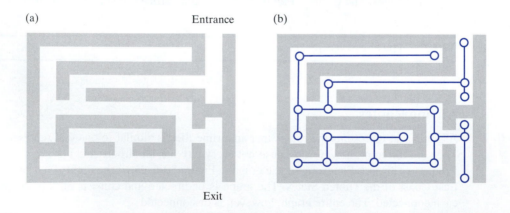

Course Prerequisites

30.9   As a college student, you must take a sequence of courses in your major. Each course has certain prerequisite courses that you must complete first. In what order can you take the required courses and satisfy the prerequisites?

To answer this question, we first create a directed graph to represent the courses and their prerequisites. Figure 30-8 is an example of such a graph. Each vertex represents a course, and each directed edge begins at a course that is a prerequisite to another. Notice, for example, that you must complete cs1, cs2, cs4, cs7, cs9, *and* cs5 before you can take cs10.

This graph has no cycles. In a directed graph without cycles, we can arrange the vertices so that vertex *a* precedes vertex *b* whenever a directed edge exists from *a* to *b*. The order of the vertices in this arrangement is called a **topological order**. Later in this chapter, you will see how to find this order and, therefore, the order in which you should complete your course requirements.

Figure 30-8   The prerequisite structure for a selection of courses as a directed graph without cycles

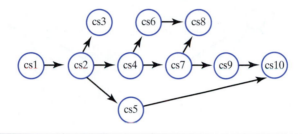

Trees

30.10   The ADT tree is a kind of graph that uses parent-child relationships to organize its nodes in a hierarchical fashion. One particular node, the root, is the ancestor of all other nodes in the tree. But not all graphs have a hierarchical organization, and so not all graphs are trees.

Note: All trees are graphs, but not all graphs are trees. A tree is a connected graph without cycles.

Question 2   What physical systems in a typical house could you represent as a graph?

Question 3   Is the graph in Figure 30-1 connected? Is it complete?

Question 4   Is the graph in Figure 30-8 a tree? Explain.

Question 5   For the graph in Figure 30-8,

a. Is cs1 adjacent to cs2?   **c.** Is cs1 adjacent to cs4?
b. Is cs2 adjacent to cs1?   **d.** Is cs4 adjacent to cs1?

Traversals

30.11   As you learned in earlier chapters, you usually search a tree for a node that contains a particular value. Graph applications, however, focus on the connections between vertices, rather than the contents of vertices. These applications often are based on a traversal of the graph's vertices.

In Chapter 25, we examined several orders in which we could visit the nodes of a tree. The preorder, inorder, and postorder traversals are examples of a **depth-first traversal**. This kind of traversal follows a path that descends the levels of a tree as deeply as possible until it reaches a leaf, as Figure 30-9a shows. More generally, a depth-first traversal of a graph follows a path that goes as deeply into the graph as possible before following other paths. After visiting a vertex, this traversal visits the vertex's neighbor, the neighbor's neighbor, and so on.

The level-order traversal of a tree is an example of a **breadth-first traversal**. It follows a path that explores an entire level before moving to the next level, as Figure 30-9b shows. In a graph, a breadth-first traversal visits all neighbors of a node before visiting the neighbors' neighbors.

Figure 30-9   The visitation order of two traversals: (a) depth first; (b) breadth first

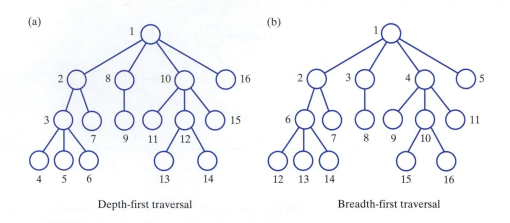

Depth-first traversal   Breadth-first traversal

Note: Visiting a node in either a tree or a graph is an action that we perform during a traversal. In a tree, "visit a node" means to "process the node's data." In a graph, "visit a node" means simply to "mark the node as visited."

A traversal of a tree visits all of the tree's nodes beginning with the root. However, a graph traversal begins at any vertex—called the **origin vertex**—and visits only the vertices that it can reach. Only when a graph is connected can such a traversal visit all the vertices.

Breadth-First Traversal

30.12   Given an origin vertex, a breadth-first traversal visits the origin and the origin's neighbors. It then considers each of these neighbors and visits their neighbors. The traversal uses a queue to hold the visited vertices. When we remove a vertex from this queue, we visit and enqueue the vertex's unvisited neighbors. The traversal order is then the order in which vertices are added to the queue. We can maintain this traversal order in a second queue.

The following algorithm performs a breadth-first traversal of a nonempty graph beginning at a given vertex.

Algorithm `getBreadthFirstTraversal(originVertex)`
`traversalOrder` = *a new queue for the resulting traversal order*
`vertexQueue` = *a new queue to hold vertices as they are visited*

```
        Mark originVertex as visited
        traversalOrder.enqueue(originVertex)
        vertexQueue.enqueue(originVertex)

        while (!vertexQueue.isEmpty())
        {
          frontVertex = vertexQueue.dequeue()
          while (frontVertex has a neighbor)
          {
            nextNeighbor = next neighbor of frontVertex
            if (nextNeighbor is not visited)
            {
              Mark nextNeighbor as visited
              traversalOrder.enqueue(nextNeighbor)
              vertexQueue.enqueue(nextNeighbor)
            }
          }
        }
        return traversalOrder
```

Figure 30-10 traces this algorithm for a directed graph.

Note: **Breadth-first traversal**
A breadth-first traversal visits a vertex and then each of the vertex's neighbors before advancing. The order in which these neighbors are visited is not specified and can depend on the graph's implementation.

Question 6   In what order does a breadth-first traversal visit the vertices in the graph shown in Figure 30-10 when you begin at vertex *E* and visit neighbors in alphabetic order?

Figure 30-10 A trace of a breadth-first traversal beginning at vertex *A* of a directed graph

frontVertex	nextNeighbor	Visited vertex	vertexQueue (front to back)	traversalOrder (front to back)
		A	A	A
A			*empty*	
	B	B	B	AB
	D	D	BD	ABD
	E	E	BDE	ABDE
B			DE	
D			E	
	G	G	EG	ABDEG
E			G	
	F	F	GF	ABDEGF
	H	H	GFH	ABDEGFH
G			FH	
F			H	
	C	C	HC	ABDEGFHC
H			C	
	I	I	CI	ABDEGFHCI
C			I	
I			*empty*	

Depth-First Traversal

30.13   Given an origin vertex, a depth-first traversal visits the origin, then a neighbor of the origin, and a neighbor of the neighbor. It continues in this fashion until it finds no unvisited neighbor. Backing up by one vertex, it considers another neighbor. This traversal has a recursive feel, since traversing from the origin leads to a traversal from the origin's neighbor. It should not surprise you, then, that we use a stack in the iterative description of this traversal.

We begin by pushing the origin vertex into the stack. When the vertex at the top of the stack has an unvisited neighbor, we visit and push that neighbor onto the stack. If no such neighbor exists, we pop the stack. The traversal order is the order in which vertices are added to the stack. We can maintain this traversal order in a queue.

The following algorithm performs a depth-first traversal of a nonempty graph, beginning at a given vertex:

Algorithm `getDepthFirstTraversal(originVertex)`
`traversalOrder` = *a new queue for the resulting traversal order*
`vertexStack` = *a new stack to hold vertices as they are visited*

Mark `originVertex` *as visited*
`traversalOrder.enqueue(originVertex)`
`vertexStack.push(originVertex)`

`while` `(!vertexStack.isEmpty())`
`{`
  `topVertex = vertexStack.peek()`
  `if` `(topVertex` *has an unvisited neighbor*`)`
  `{`
    `nextNeighbor =` *next unvisited neighbor of* `topVertex`
    Mark `nextNeighbor` *as visited*
    `traversalOrder.enqueue(nextNeighbor)`
    `vertexStack.push(nextNeighbor)`
  `}`
  `else` *// all neighbors are visited*
    `vertexStack.pop()`
`}`
`return traversalOrder`

Figure 30-11 traces this algorithm for the same directed graph as in Figure 30-10.

Note: Depth-first traversal
A depth-first traversal visits a vertex, then a neighbor of the vertex, a neighbor of the neighbor, and so on, advancing as far as possible from the original vertex. It then backs up by one vertex and considers another neighbor. The order in which these neighbors are visited is not specified and can depend on the graph's implementation.

Question 7   In what order does a depth-first traversal visit the vertices in the graph shown in Figure 30-11 when you begin at vertex *E* and visit neighbors in alphabetic order?

Figure 30-11   A trace of a depth-first traversal beginning at vertex *A* of a directed graph

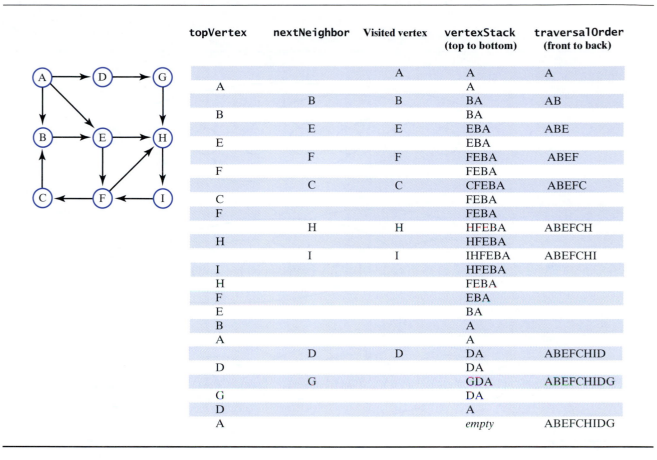

topVertex	nextNeighbor	Visited vertex	vertexStack (top to bottom)	traversalOrder (front to back)
		A	A	A
A			A	
	B	B	BA	AB
B			BA	
	E	E	EBA	ABE
E			EBA	
	F	F	FEBA	ABEF
F			FEBA	
	C	C	CFEBA	ABEFC
C			FEBA	
F			FEBA	
	H	H	HFEBA	ABEFCH
H			HFEBA	
	I	I	IHFEBA	ABEFCHI
I			HFEBA	
H			FEBA	
F			EBA	
E			BA	
B			A	
A			A	
	D	D	DA	ABEFCHID
D			DA	
	G	G	GDA	ABEFCHIDG
G			DA	
D			A	
A			*empty*	ABEFCHIDG

Topological Order

30.14   Figure 30-8 shows a graph that represents the prerequisite structure of a group of computer science courses. This graph is a directed graph without cycles. Recall that you can place the vertices of such a graph in a topological order.

Note: In a topological order of the vertices in a directed graph without cycles, vertex *a* precedes vertex *b* whenever a directed edge exists from *a* to *b*.

The vertices in a graph can have several different topological orders. For example, one such order for the graph in Figure 30-8 is cs1, cs2, cs5, cs4, cs7, cs9, cs10, cs6, cs8, cs3. That is, if you complete the courses in this order, you will satisfy all prerequisites. Suppose that you can move the vertices in the graph so that they align in this order, stretching the edges as needed. The result will be like the graph in Figure 30-12a. Each edge points toward a node that comes after the edge's origin node. You will be able to find at least one such arrangement for every directed graph, if the graph has no cycles. Figure 30-12 shows two other topological orders for the graph in Figure 30-8 as well. As is true for this example, any one topological order is usually sufficient to solve a given problem.

Figure 30-12   Three topological orders for the graph in Figure 30-8

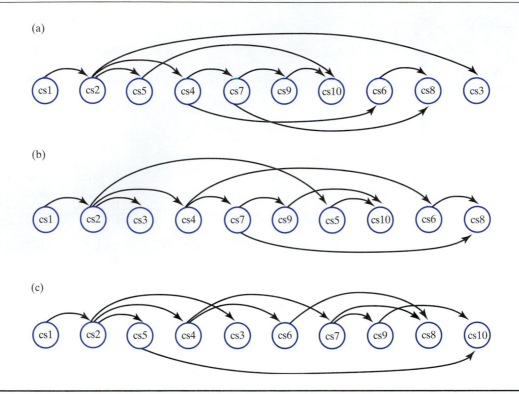

(a)

(b)

(c)

A topological order is not possible for a graph that has a cycle. If vertices *a* and *b* are on the cycle, a path exists from *a* to *b* and from *b* to *a*. One of these paths will contradict any order that we choose for *a* and *b*. For example, the graph in Figure 30-13 contains a cycle. You need to complete cs15 and cs20 before taking cs30. But you need to complete cs30 before taking cs20. This circular logic is caused by the cycle and creates an impossible situation.

Figure 30-13   An impossible prerequisite structure for three courses, as a directed graph with a cycle

Question 8   What is another topological order of the vertices in the graph in Figure 30-8?

30.15   The process that discovers a topological order for the vertices in a graph is called a **topological sort**. Several algorithms for this process are possible. We can begin a topological sort by locating a vertex that has no successor, that is, no adjacent vertex. Finding this vertex is possible because the graph has no cycles. We mark the vertex as visited and push it onto a stack. We continue by finding another vertex *u* that is unvisited and whose neighbors, if any, are visited. We mark *u* as visited and push it onto the stack. We proceed in this way until we have visited all the vertices. At that time, the stack contains the vertices in topological order, beginning at the top of the stack.

The following algorithm describes this topological sort:

```
Algorithm getTopologicalOrder()
vertexStack = a new stack to hold vertices as they are visited
numberOfVertices = number of vertices in the graph
for (counter = 1 to numberOfVertices)
{
    nextVertex = an unvisited vertex whose neighbors, if any, are all visited
    Mark nextVertex as visited
    vertexStack.push(nextVertex)
}
return vertexStack
```

Figure 30-14 traces this algorithm for the graph in Figure 30-8. At each iteration of the algorithm's loop, nextVertex becomes shaded in the figure as it is visited. The topological order is the opposite of the order in which this shading occurs. In this example, the topological order is the one pictured in Figure 30-12a.

Paths

Learning whether a particular airline flies between two given cities is important to the average traveler. We can obtain this information by using a graph—such as the one in Figure 30-6—to represent the airline's routes and testing whether a path exists from vertex *a* to vertex *b*. If a path exists, we can also find out what it is. If not any path will do, we can find the one that is shortest or cheapest.

Finding a Path

30.16   For the moment we are content to find any path, not necessarily the best one. A depth-first traversal—discussed in Segment 30.13—stays on a path through the graph as it visits as many vertices as possible. We can easily modify this traversal to locate a path between two vertices. We begin at the origin vertex. Each time we visit another vertex, we see whether that vertex is the desired destination. If so, we are done and the resulting stack contains the path. Otherwise, we continue the traversal until either we are successful or the traversal ends. We leave the development of this algorithm as an exercise.

The Shortest Path in an Unweighted Graph

30.17   **Example.** A graph can have several different paths between the same two vertices. In an unweighted graph, we can find the path with the shortest length, that is, the path that has the fewest edges. For example, consider the unweighted graph in Figure 30-15a. Suppose that we want to know the shortest path from vertex *A* to vertex *H*. By inspecting the graph, we can see that several simple paths—shown in Part *b* of the figure—are possible between these two vertices. The path from *A* to *E* to *H* has length 2 and is the shortest.

Figure 30-14   Finding a topological order for the graph in Figure 30-8

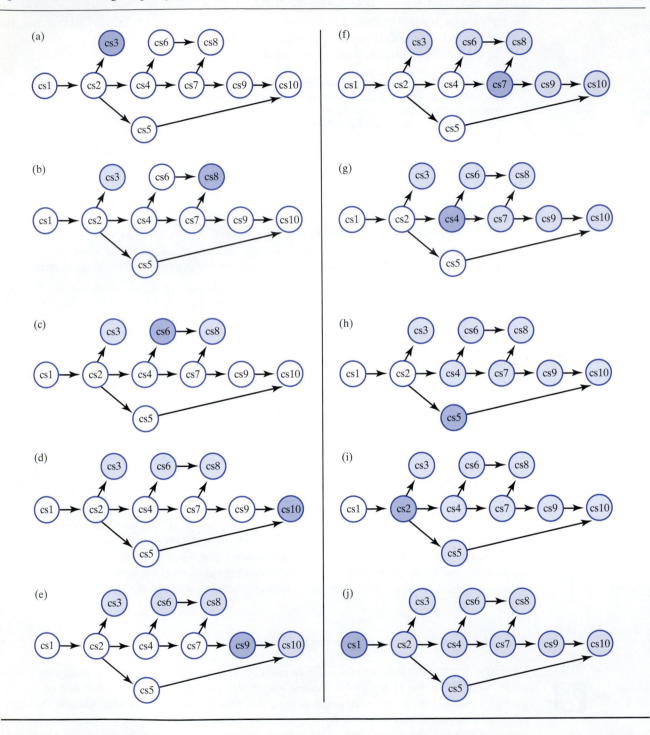

Figure 30-15   (a) An unweighted graph and (b) the possible paths from vertex *A* to vertex *H*

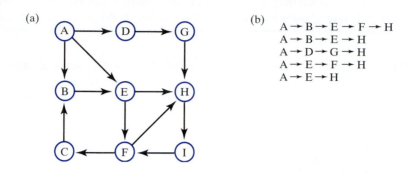

(a)

(b)

$A \rightarrow B \rightarrow E \rightarrow F \rightarrow H$
$A \rightarrow B \rightarrow E \rightarrow H$
$A \rightarrow D \rightarrow G \rightarrow H$
$A \rightarrow E \rightarrow F \rightarrow H$
$A \rightarrow E \rightarrow H$

30.18   **Developing the algorithm.** The algorithm to find the shortest path between two given vertices in an unweighted graph is based on a breadth-first traversal. Recall that this traversal visits the origin vertex, then the origin's neighbors, the neighbors of each of these neighbors, and so on. Each vertex is placed into a queue as it is visited.

To find the shortest path, we enhance the breadth-first traversal as follows. When we visit a vertex v and mark it as visited, we note the vertex p that we just left to reach v. That is, p precedes v in the graph. We also note the length of the path that the traversal followed to reach v. This length is 1 more than the length of the path to vertex p. We place both the length of the path to v and a reference to p into vertex v. At the end of the traversal, we will use this data in the vertices to construct the shortest path. Let's jump ahead to that part of the algorithm.

Figure 30-16a shows the state of the graph in Figure 30-15a after the algorithm has traversed from vertex A to vertex H. Each vertex contains its label, the length of the path to it, and the vertex that precedes it on this path, as shown in Figure 30-16b. Although a vertex also contains other data fields, we have ignored them in this figure.

Figure 30-16   (a) The graph in Figure 30-15a after the shortest-path algorithm has traversed from vertex *A* to vertex *H*; (b) the data in a vertex

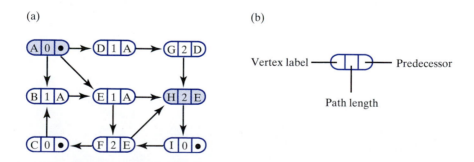

(a)

(b)

Vertex label —— —— Predecessor

Path length

Now, by examining the destination vertex—H—we find that the length of the shortest path from A to H is 2. We also find that H's predecessor along this shortest path is vertex E. From vertex E we see that its predecessor is vertex A. Thus, the desired shortest path from vertex A to vertex H is $A \rightarrow E \rightarrow H$. Our algorithm has discovered what we of course knew to be true by inspecting this simple graph.

Note: In an unweighted graph, the shortest path between two given vertices has the shortest length—that is, it has the fewest edges. The algorithm to find this path is based on a breadth-first traversal. If several paths have the same shortest length, the algorithm will find only one of them.

30.19 **The algorithm.** The following algorithm finds the shortest path in an unweighted graph between the vertices `originVertex` and `endVertex`. Like the breath-first traversal in Segment 30.12, the algorithm uses a queue to hold the vertices as they are visited. It then uses the given, initially empty stack `path` to construct the shortest path.

```
Algorithm getShortestPath(originVertex, endVertex, path)
done = false
vertexQueue = a new queue to hold vertices as they are visited
Mark originVertex as visited
vertexQueue.enqueue(originVertex)

while (!done && !vertexQueue.isEmpty())
{
   frontVertex = vertexQueue.dequeue()

   while (!done && frontVertex has a neighbor)
   {
      nextNeighbor = next neighbor of frontVertex
      if (nextNeighbor is not visited)
      {
         Mark nextNeighbor as visited
         Set the length of the path to nextNeighbor to 1 + length of path to frontVertex
         Set the predecessor of nextNeighbor to frontVertex
         vertexQueue.enqueue(nextNeighbor)
      }

      if (nextNeighbor equals endVertex)
         done = true
   }
}

// traversal ends - construct shortest path
pathLength = length of path to endVertex
path.push(endVertex)

vertex = endVertex
while (vertex has a predecessor)
{
   vertex = predecessor of vertex
   path.push(vertex)
}
return pathLength
```

When the algorithm ends, the stack `path` contains the vertices along the shortest path, with the origin at the top of the stack. The value returned is the length of this shortest path.

30.20 **Tracing the algorithm.** Figure 30-17 traces the steps that the algorithm takes to produce the path information shown in Figure 30-16a for the unweighted graph in Figure 30-15a. After adding the origin—vertex A—to the queue, we visit the origin's three neighbors—B, D, and E—and

Figure 30-17 A trace of the traversal in the algorithm to find the shortest path from vertex A to vertex H in an unweighted graph

	frontVertex	nextNeighbor	Visited vertex	vertexQueue (front to back)
			A	(A|0|•)
	(A|0|•)			empty
		B	B	(B|1|A)
		D	D	(B|1|A) (D|1|A)
		E	E	(B|1|A) (D|1|A) (E|1|A)
	(B|1|A)			(D|1|A) (E|1|A)
	(D|1|A)			(E|1|A)
		G	G	(E|1|A) (G|2|D)
	(E|1|A)			(G|2|D)
		F	F	(G|2|D) (F|2|E)
		H	H	(G|2|D) (F|2|E) (H|2|E)

enqueue them. The length of each path from A to these neighbors is 1. Since vertex A has no more neighbors, we remove vertex B from the queue. This vertex has vertex E as a neighbor, but E has been visited already. This implies that we can get to E from A without first going through B. That is, B is not on any shortest path that begins at A and goes through E. Indeed, the path $A \rightarrow B \rightarrow E$ is longer than the path $A \rightarrow E$. We do not know whether our final path involves E, but if it does, it will not pass through B.

The algorithm now removes vertex D from the queue. Its neighbor G is unvisited, so we set G's path-length field to 2 and its predecessor to D. We then enqueue G. The algorithm continues in this manner and eventually encounters the destination vertex, H. After H is updated, the outer loop ends. We then construct the path by working back from H, as we did earlier in Segment 30.18.

Question 9   Continue the trace begun in Figure 30-17 to find the shortest path from vertex A to vertex C.

The Shortest Path in a Weighted Graph

30.21   **Example.** In a weighted graph, the shortest path is not necessarily the one with the fewest edges. Rather, it is the one with the smallest edge-weight sum. Figure 30-18a shows a weighted graph obtained by adding weights to the graph in Figure 30-15a. The possible paths from vertex A to vertex H are the same as you saw in Figure 30-15b. This time, however, we list each path with its weight—that is, the sum of the weights of its edges—in Figure 30-18b.

We can see that the smallest path weight is 8, so the shortest path is $A \rightarrow D \rightarrow G \rightarrow H$. When the weights are distances, the term "shortest" is appropriate. When the weights represent costs, we might think of this path as the "cheapest" path.

Figure 30-18   (a) A weighted graph and (b) the possible paths from vertex *A* to vertex *H*, with their weights

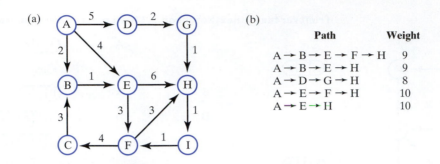

30.22   **Developing the algorithm.** The algorithm to find the shortest, or cheapest, path between two given vertices in a weighted graph is based on a breadth-first traversal. It is similar to the algorithm we developed for an unweighted graph. In that algorithm, we noted the number of edges in the path that led to the vertex under consideration. Here, we compute the sum of the edge weights in the path leading to a vertex. In addition, we must record the cheapest of the possible paths. Whereas before we used a queue to order vertices, this algorithm uses a priority queue.

 Note: In a weighted graph, the shortest path between two given vertices has the smallest edge-weight sum. The algorithm to find this path is based on a breadth-first traversal. Several paths in a weighted graph might share the same minimum edge-weight sum. Our algorithm will find only one of these paths.

Each entry in the priority queue is an object that contains a vertex, the cost of the path to that vertex from the origin vertex, and the previous vertex on that path. The priority value is the cost of the path, with the smallest value having the highest priority. Thus, the cheapest path is at the front of the priority queue, and it is thus the first one removed. Note that several entries in the priority queue might contain the same vertex but different costs.

At the conclusion of the algorithm, the vertices in the graph contain predecessors and costs that enable us to construct the cheapest path, much as we constructed the path with the fewest edges from the graph in Figure 30-16a.

30.23   **Tracing the algorithm.** Figure 30-19 traces the traversal portion of the algorithm for the weighted graph in Figure 30-18a when vertex *A* is the origin. Initially, an object containing *A*, zero, and `null` is placed in the priority queue. We begin a loop by removing the front entry from the priority queue. We use the contents of this entry to change the state of the indicated vertex—*A* in this case—in the graph. Thus, we store a path length of zero and a `null` predecessor into *A*. We also mark *A* as visited.

Vertex *A* has three unvisited neighbors, *B*, *D*, and *E*. The costs of the paths from *A* to each of these neighbors is 2, 5, and 4, respectively. These costs, along with *A* as the previous vertex, are used to create objects that are placed into the priority queue. The priority queue orders these objects so that the cheapest path is first.

We remove the front entry from the priority queue. The entry contains vertex *B*, so we visit *B*. We also store within vertex *B* the path cost 2 and its predecessor *A*. Now *B* has vertex *E* as its sole unvisited neighbor. The cost of the path $A \rightarrow B \rightarrow E$ is the cost of the path $A \rightarrow B$ plus the weight of

Figure 30-19 A trace of the traversal in the algorithm to find the cheapest path from vertex *A* to vertex *H* in a weighted graph

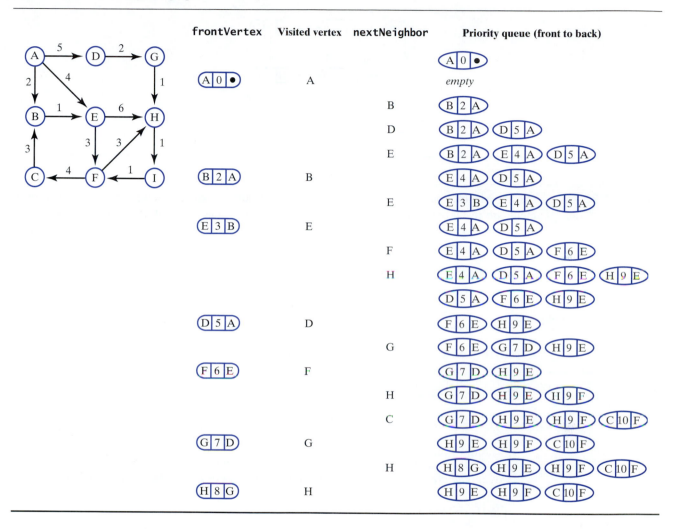

the edge from *B* to *E*. This total cost is 3. We encapsulate *E*, the cost 3, and the predecessor *B* into an object that we add to the priority queue. Notice that two objects in the priority queue involve vertex *E*, but the most recent one has the cheapest path.

We again remove the front entry from the priority queue. The entry contains vertex *E*, so we visit it and store into *E* the path cost 3 and *E*'s predecessor *B*. Vertex *E* has two unvisited neighbors, *F* and *H*. The cost of each path to a neighbor is the cost of the path to *E* plus the weight of the edge to the neighbor. Two new objects are added to the priority queue.

The next object removed from the priority queue contains the vertex *E*, but since *E* has been visited, we ignore it. We then remove the next object from the priority queue. The algorithm continues until the destination vertex *H* is visited.

Figure 30-20 shows the state of the graph at the conclusion of the trace given in Figure 30-19. By looking at the destination vertex *H*, we can see that the weight of the cheapest path from *A* to *H* is 8. Tracing back from *H* to *A*, we see that this path is *A* → *D* → *G* → *H*, as we noted in Segment 30.21.

Figure 30-20 The graph in Figure 30-18a after finding the cheapest path from vertex *A* to vertex *H*

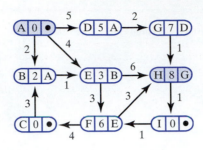

30.24   **The algorithm.** The pseudocode for the algorithm we just described follows. Objects in the priority queue are instances of a private class `EntryPQ`. Following the traversal, the algorithm pushes the vertices that occur along the cheapest path from `originVertex` to `endVertex` into a given, initially empty stack `path`.

```
Algorithm getCheapestPath(originVertex, endVertex, path)
done = false
priorityQueue = a new priority queue

priorityQueue.add(new EntryPQ(originVertex, 0, null))

while (!done && !priorityQueue.isEmpty())
{
  frontEntry = priorityQueue.remove()
  frontVertex = vertex in frontEntry

  if (frontVertex is not visited)
  {
    Mark frontVertex as visited
    Set the cost of the path to frontVertex to the cost recorded in frontEntry
    Set the predecessor of frontVertex to the predecessor recorded in frontEntry

    if (frontVertex equals endVertex)
      done = true
    else
    {
      while (frontVertex has a neighbor)
      {
        nextNeighbor = next neighbor of frontVertex
        weightOfEdgeToNeighbor = weight of edge to nextNeighbor

        if (nextNeighbor is not visited)
        {
          nextCost = weightOfEdgeToNeighbor + cost of path to frontVertex
          priorityQueue.add(new EntryPQ(nextNeighbor, nextCost, frontVertex))
        }
      }
    }
  }
}
```

```
// traversal ends; construct cheapest path
pathCost = cost of path to endVertex
path.push(endVertex)

vertex = endVertex
while (vertex has a predecessor)
{
   vertex = predecessor of vertex
   path.push(vertex)
}
return pathCost
```

The origin of the cheapest path will be at the top of the stack path. At the bottom of the stack is the destination vertex. The cost of the path is returned by the algorithm.

This algorithm is based on Dijkstra's algorithm, which finds the shortest paths from an origin to all other vertices.

Question 10 Continue the trace begun in Figure 30-19 to find the shortest (cheapest) path from vertex *A* to vertex *C*.

Question 11 Why do we place instances of EntryPQ into the priority queue, instead of placing vertices?

Java Interfaces for the ADT Graph

30.25 The ADT graph is a bit different from other ADTs in that, once you create it, you do not add, remove, or retrieve components. Instead, you use a graph to answer questions based on the relationships among its vertices.

We will divide the graph operations into two Java interfaces. You use the operations in the first interface to create the graph and to obtain basic information such as the number of vertices. The second interface specifies operations such as the traversals and path searches that we discussed earlier in this chapter. For convenience, we define a third interface, GraphInterface, that combines the first two interfaces.

To make these interfaces as general as possible, we have them specify graphs that are either directed or undirected, and weighted or unweighted. The first interface appears in Listing 30-1. The generic type T represents the data type of the objects that label the graph's vertices.

Listing 30-1 An interface of basic graph operations

```
/** An interface of methods providing basic operations for directed
 *  and undirected graphs that are either weighted or unweighted. */
package GraphPackage;
public interface BasicGraphInterface<T>
{
   /** Task: Adds a given vertex to the graph.
    *  @param vertexLabel  an object that labels the new vertex and
    *                           is distinct from the labels of current vertices
    *  @return true if the vertex is added, or false if not */
   public boolean addVertex(T vertexLabel);
```

```
/** Task: Adds a weighted edge between two given distinct vertices that
 *         are currently in the graph. The desired edge must not already
 *         be in the graph. In a directed graph, the edge points
 *         toward the second vertex given.
 *  @param begin  an object that labels the origin vertex of the edge
 *  @param end    an object, distinct from begin, that labels the end
 *                vertex of the edge
 *  @param edgeWeight  the real value of the edge's weight
 *  @return true if the edge is added, or false if not */
public boolean addEdge(T begin, T end, double edgeWeight);

/** Task: Adds an unweighted edge between two given distinct vertices
 *         that are currently in the graph. The desired edge must not
 *         already be in the graph. In a directed graph, the edge points
 *         toward the second vertex given.
 *  @param begin  an object that labels the origin vertex of the edge
 *  @param end    an object, distinct from begin, that labels the end
 *                vertex of the edge
 *  @return true if the edge is added, or false if not */
public boolean addEdge(T begin, T end);

/** Task: Sees whether an edge exists between two given vertices.
 *  @param begin  an object that labels the origin vertex of the edge
 *  @param end    an object that labels the end vertex of the edge
 *  @return true if an edge exists */
public boolean hasEdge(T begin, T end);

/** Task: Sees whether the graph is empty.
 *  @return true if the graph is empty */
public boolean isEmpty();

/** Task: Gets the number of vertices in the graph.
 *  @return the number of vertices in the graph */
public int getNumberOfVertices();

/** Task: Gets the number of edges in the graph.
 *  @return the number of edges in the graph */
public int getNumberOfEdges();

/** Task: Removes all vertices and edges from the graph. */
public void clear();
} // end BasicGraphInterface
```

30.26 **Example.** The following statements create the graph shown in Figure 30-21, which is a portion of the graph in Figure 30-6:

```
BasicGraphInterface<String> airMap = new UndirectedGraph<String>();
airMap.addVertex("Boston");
airMap.addVertex("Provincetown");
airMap.addVertex("Nantucket");
airMap.addEdge("Boston", "Provincetown");
airMap.addEdge("Boston", "Nantucket");
```

At this point,

        airMap.getNumberOfVertices()

returns 3, and

        airMap.getNumberOfEdges()

returns 2.

Question 12   What revisions to the previous Java statements are necessary to make `airMap` a weighted graph?

Figure 30-21   A portion of the flight map in Figure 30-6

30.27   The algorithms discussed earlier in this chapter use graph operations that are not specified in the previous interface. Although we could add these operations to the interface so the client could implement various algorithms, such as the topological sort, we choose not to do so. Instead, methods that implement the graph algorithms will be a part of the graph class. The interface in Listing 30-2 specifies these methods. Again, the data type of the objects that label the graph's vertices are represented by the generic type T.

Listing 30-2   An interface of operations on an existing graph

```
/** An interface of methods that process an existing graph. */
package GraphPackage;
import ADTPackage.*; // classes that implement various ADTs
public interface GraphAlgorithmsInterface<T>
{
  /** Task: Performs a breadth-first traversal of a graph.
   *  @param origin  an object that labels the origin vertex of the
   *                    traversal
   *  @return a queue of labels of the vertices in the traversal, with
   *           the label of the origin vertex at the queue's front */
  public QueueInterface<T> getBreadthFirstTraversal(T origin);

  /** Task: Performs a depth-first traversal of a graph.
   *  @param origin  an object that labels the origin vertex of the
   *                    traversal
   *  @return a queue of labels of the vertices in the traversal, with
```

```
 *              the label of the origin vertex at the queue's front */
public QueueInterface<T> getDepthFirstTraversal(T origin);

/** Task: Performs a topological sort of the vertices in a graph
 *        without cycles.
 *  @return a stack of vertex labels in topological order, beginning
 *          with the stack's top */
public StackInterface<T> getTopologicalOrder();

/** Task: Finds the path between two given vertices that has the
 *        shortest length.
 *  @param begin  an object that labels the path's origin vertex
 *  @param end    an object that labels the path's destination vertex
 *  @param path   a stack of labels that is empty initially;
 *                at the completion of the method, this stack contains
 *                the labels of the vertices along the shortest path;
 *                the label of the origin vertex is at the top, and
 *                the label of the destination vertex is at the bottom
 *  @return the length of the shortest path */
public int getShortestPath(T begin, T end, StackInterface<T> path);

/** Task: Finds the least-cost path between two given vertices.
 *  @param begin  an object that labels the path's origin vertex
 *  @param end    an object that labels the path's destination vertex
 *  @param path   a stack of labels that is empty initially;
 *                at the completion of the method, this stack contains
 *                the labels of the vertices along the cheapest path;
 *                the label of the origin vertex is at the top, and
 *                the label of the destination vertex is at the bottom
 *  @return the cost of the cheapest path */
public double getCheapestPath(T begin, T end, StackInterface<T> path);
} // end GraphAlgorithmsInterface
```

The interface in Listing 30-3 combines BasicGraphInterface and GraphAlgorithmsInterface.

Listing 30-3   An interface for the ADT graph

```
package GraphPackage;
public interface GraphInterface<T> extends BasicGraphInterface<T>,
                                           GraphAlgorithmsInterface<T>
{
} // end GraphInterface
```

30.28   **Example.** Imagine that we want to find the shortest route between the towns of Truro and Falmouth. By "shortest route" we mean the route with the least number of miles, not the path with the fewest edges. We first could create the graph in Figure 30-3, using statements much like those in Segment 30.26. We then could use the method getCheapestPath to answer our question. The following statements indicate how to perform these steps and to display the names of the cities along the shortest route:

```
GraphInterface<String> roadMap = new UndirectedGraph<String>();
roadMap.addVertex("Provincetown");
roadMap.addVertex("Truro");
. . .
roadMap.addVertex("Falmouth");

roadMap.addEdge("Provincetown", "Truro", 10);
. . .
roadMap.addEdge("Hyannis", "Falmouth", 20);

StackInterface<String> bestRoute = new LinkedStack<String>();
double distance = roadMap.getCheapestPath("Truro", "Falmouth",
                                            bestRoute);
System.out.println("The shortest route from Truro to Falmouth is " +
                    distance + " miles long and " +
                    "passes through the following towns:");
while (!bestRoute.isEmpty())
  System.out.println(bestRoute.pop());
```

 Note: The operations of the ADT graph enable you to create a graph and answer questions about the relationships among its vertices.

 Question 13 The previous example finds the shortest route between two towns. Why did we invoke the method `getCheapestPath` instead of `getShortestPath`?

CHAPTER SUMMARY

- A graph is a collection of distinct vertices and distinct edges. Each edge joins two vertices. A subgraph is a portion of a graph that is itself a graph.
- A tree is a special graph that has a hierarchical order and a root that is the ancestor of all other nodes—that is, vertices—in the tree.
- Each edge in a directed graph has a direction from one vertex to another. The edges in an undirected graph are bidirectional.
- A path from one vertex to another is a sequence of edges. The length of the path is the number of these edges. A simple path passes through each of its vertices once. A cycle is a path that begins and ends at the same vertex. A simple cycle passes through its other vertices once.
- The edges in a weighted graph have values called weights or costs. A path in a weighted graph has a weight, or cost, that is the sum of its edge weights.
- A graph that has a path between every pair of distinct vertices is connected. A complete graph has an edge between every pair of distinct vertices.
- Two vertices in an undirected graph are adjacent if they are joined by an edge. In a directed graph, vertex i is adjacent to vertex j if a directed edge begins at j and ends at i. Adjacent vertices are called neighbors.

- You can traverse the vertices in a graph by using either a depth-first traversal or a breadth-first traversal. A depth-first traversal follows a path that goes as deeply into the graph as possible before following other paths. A breadth-first traversal visits all neighbors of a vertex before visiting the neighbors' neighbors.

- A directed graph without cycles imposes an order on its vertices called a topological order. This order is not unique. You use a topological sort to discover these orders.

- You can use a depth-first traversal of a graph to see whether a path exists between two given vertices.

- You can modify the breadth-first traversal of a graph to find the path between two given vertices that has the fewest edges.

- You can modify the breadth-first traversal of a weighted graph to find the path between two given vertices that has the lowest cost.

EXERCISES

1. Suppose that five vertices are arranged at the corners of an imaginary pentagon. Draw a connected graph that contains these vertices.

2. Describe each graph in Figure 30-22, using the terms introduced in Segments 30.1 through 30.4.

Figure 30-22 Graphs for Exercise 2

(a)   (b)   (c)

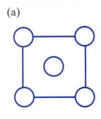   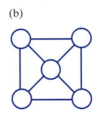   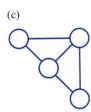

3. Consider a graph that represents acquaintances among people. Each vertex represents a person. Each edge represents an acquaintance between two people.

   a. Is this graph directed or undirected ?
   b. Consider all vertices adjacent to a given vertex x. What does this set of vertices represent?
   c. What does a path in this graph represent?
   d. In what circumstance might one want to know the shortest path between two vertices in this graph?
   e. Is the graph associated with all the people alive on January 1, 1979, connected? Justify your answer.

4. In what order does a breadth-first traversal visit the vertices in the graph in Figure 30-10 when you begin at

   a. Vertex G
   b. Vertex F

5. Repeat the previous exercise, but perform a depth-first traversal instead.

6. Consider the directed graph that appears in Figure 30-10, and remove the edge between vertices *E* and *F*, and the edge between vertices *F* and *H*.

   a. In what order will a breadth-first traversal visit the vertices when you begin at vertex *A*?

   b. Repeat Part *a*, but perform a depth-first traversal instead.

7. Draw a directed graph that depicts the prerequisite structure of the courses required for your major. Find a topological order for these courses.

8. Construct the topological ordering for the weighted, directed, acyclic graph in Figure 30-23.

Figure 30-23 A graph for Exercises 8 and 21

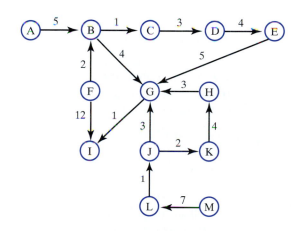

9. A computer network such as the World Wide Web or a local area network can be represented as a graph. Each computer is a vertex in the graph. An edge between two vertices represents a direct connection between two computers. Explain when and why you would be interested in each of the following tasks:

   a. Finding a path in this graph

   b. Finding multiple paths from one particular vertex to another

   c. Finding the shortest path from one particular vertex to another

   d. Seeing whether the graph is connected

10. Write an algorithm that finds a path from vertex *a* to vertex *b* in a directed graph by using a slightly modified depth-first traversal. Segment 30.16 outlines an approach to this problem.

11. A tree is a connected graph without cycles.

    a. What is the smallest number of edges that could be removed from the graph in Figure 30-1 to make it a tree?

    b. Give one example of such a set of edges.

12. Figure 30-7b shows a graph that represents a maze. Label the vertices of this graph, with the uppermost vertex labeled S (the entrance to the maze) and the lowest vertex labeled T (the exit from the maze).

    a. Is this graph a tree?

    b. What is the shortest path from S to T?

    c. What is the longest simple path in this graph?

13. Revise the unweighted, directed graph in Figure 30-15a by adding a directed edge from D to H. The resulting graph has two paths from A to H that are shortest among all paths between these two vertices. Which of these two paths will the algorithm `getShortestPath` in Segment 30.19 find?

14. Repeat the previous exercise, but remove the directed edge from E to H instead of adding a directed edge from D to H.

15. Revise the weighted, directed graph in Figure 30-18a by adding a directed edge from D to H. Let the weight of this new edge be 3. The resulting graph has two paths from A to H that are cheapest among all paths between these two vertices. Which of these two paths will the algorithm `getCheapestPath` in Segment 30.24 find?

16. Find a map of the routes of a major U. S. airline. Such maps are usually printed at the back of in-flight magazines. You could also search the Internet for one. The map is a graph like the one in Figure 30-6. Consider the following pairs of cities:

       Providence (RI) and San Diego (CA)
       Albany (NY) and Phoenix (AZ)
       Boston (MA) and Baltimore (MD)
       Dallas (TX) and Detroit (MI)
       Charlotte (NC) and Chicago (IL)
       Portland (ME) and Portland (OR)

    a. Which pairs of cities in this list have edges (nonstop flights) between them?

    b. Which pairs are not connected by any path?

    c. For each of the remaining pairs, find the path with the fewest edges.

17. Find the trail map of a cross-country ski area. Represent the trail map as an undirected graph, where each intersection of trails is a vertex, and each section of trail between intersections is an edge. Consider a cross-country skier who wishes to take the longest tour possible, but does not want to ski on any trail more than once. What is the longest path that starts and ends at the ski lodge and does not traverse any section of trail more than once? (Intersections may be passed through more than once, and some sections of trail may be left unskied.)

18. Find the trail map of a downhill ski area. Represent the trail map as a graph, where each intersection of trails is a vertex, and each section of trail between intersections is an edge.

   a. Is the graph directed or undirected?
   b. Does the graph have cycles?
   c. Find the longest path possible that begins at the top of the mountain and ends at the ski lodge.

19. Write statements appropriate for the client of the class `UndirectedGraph` that create the graph in Figure 30-3. Assume that `UndirectedGraph` implements `GraphInterface`.

20. Write statements appropriate for the client of the class `DirectedGraph` that create the graph in Figure 30-8. Assume that `DirectedGraph` implements `GraphInterface`. Then write statements to find and display a topological order for this graph.

21. A **critical path** in a weighted, directed, acyclic graph is the path with the greatest weight. Let's assume that all edge weights are positive. Give each vertex a value equal to the weight of a path to that vertex. Initially, each vertex's value is zero.

   We can find the critical path by considering the vertices one at a time in topological order. For each vertex, consider all the edges that leave the vertex. For each of these edges, add the weight of the edge and the value of the edge's source vertex. Compare the sum with the value of the edge's destination vertex. Make the larger of these values the value of the destination vertex. After all vertices have been visited, the largest value stored in a vertex will be the weight of the critical path.

   Find the critical path for the graph in Figure 30-23.

PROJECTS

1. In a search tree, it is easy to search for any value. For other trees in which the children of a node are not ordered in any particular way, you can use a breadth-first search, as described for graphs, to find a path from the root to some other node (vertex) *v*. Implement such a method for a general tree.

2. Write Java code that creates the graph given in Figure 30-1. Find the shortest path from Sandwich to Falmouth. Do the same for the weighted graph in Figure 30-3. (See Exercise 19.)

3. Write Java code that creates the graph in Figure 30-10. Perform a breadth-first traversal of the graph, beginning at the node labeled *A*.

4. In the game of Nim, an arbitrary number of chips are divided into an arbitrary number of piles. Each player can remove as many chips as desired from any single pile. The last player to remove a chip wins.

   Consider a limited version of this game, in which three piles contain 3, 5, and 8 chips, respectively. You can represent this game as a directed graph. Each vertex in this graph is a possible configuration of the piles (chips in each pile). The initial configuration, for example, is (3, 5, 8). Each edge in the graph represents a legal move in the game.

   a. Write Java statements that will construct this directed graph.
   b. Discuss how a computer program might use this graph to play Nim.

5. The **diameter** of an unweighted graph is the maximum of all the shortest distances between pairs of vertices in the graph.

   a. Give an algorithm for computing the diameter of a graph.
   b. What is the Big Oh performance of your algorithm in terms of the number of vertices and edges in the graph?
   c. Implement your algorithm.
   d. Discuss possible ways that you can improve the performance of the algorithm.

6. Exercise 21 described how to find the critical path in a weighted, directed, acyclic graph. Write a method that will find the critical path. You may assume the existence of a method that tests whether a graph is acyclic.

31

Graph Implementations

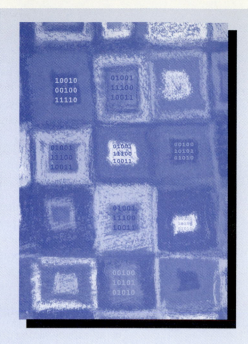

CONTENTS

PREREQUISITES

OBJECTIVES

After studying this chapter, you should be able to

- Describe an adjacency matrix
- Describe an adjacency list
- Specify and implement the classes that represent the vertices and edges of a graph
- Implement the ADT graph by using adjacency lists

Like the ADTs you have seen previously, graphs have several implementations. Each implementation must represent the vertices in the graph and the edges between the vertices. In general, you use either a list or a dictionary to hold the vertices, and an array or a list to represent the edges. Each representation of the edges has its own advantages, but the list representation is most typical.

An Overview of Two Implementations

Two common implementations of the ADT graph use either an array or a list to represent the graph's edges. The array is typically a two-dimensional array called an **adjacency matrix**. The list is called an **adjacency list**. Each of these constructs represents the connections—that is, the edges—among the vertices in the graph.

The Adjacency Matrix

31.1   The adjacency matrix for a graph of n vertices has n rows and n columns. Each row and each column corresponds to a vertex in the graph. You number the vertices from 0 through $n - 1$ to match the row indices and the column indices. If a_{ij} is the element in row i and column j of the matrix, a_{ij} indicates whether an edge exists between vertex i and vertex j. For an unweighted graph, you can use boolean values in the matrix. For a weighted graph, you can use edge weights when edges exist and a representation of infinity otherwise.

Figure 31-1 provides an example of an unweighted, directed graph and its adjacency matrix. Let's consider vertex A of the graph, which we have numbered as vertex 0. Since directed edges exist from vertex A to each of the vertices B, D, and E, the matrix elements a_{01}, a_{03}, and a_{04} are true. We have used a "T" in the figure to represent true. The other entries in the first row are false (blank in the figure).

Although a directed edge exists from vertex A to vertex B, the converse is not true. Therefore, a_{10} is false, even though a_{01} is true. The adjacency matrix for an undirected graph, however, is **symmetric**; that is, a_{ij} and a_{ji} have the same value. When an undirected graph has an edge from vertex i to vertex j, it also has an edge from vertex j to vertex i.

Figure 31-1   (a) An unweighted, directed graph and (b) its adjacency matrix

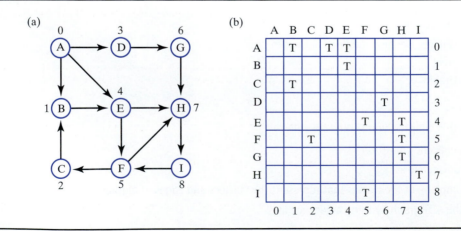

31.2   From an adjacency matrix, you quickly can see whether an edge exists between any two given vertices. This operation is O(1). But if you want to know all the neighbors of a particular vertex, you need to scan an entire row of the matrix, an O(n) task. Additionally, the matrix occupies a considerable, fixed amount of space that depends on the number of vertices but not on the number of edges. In fact, an adjacency matrix represents every possible edge in a graph, regardless of whether the edges actually exist. However, most graphs have relatively few of the many edges possible—that is, they are sparse. For such graphs, an adjacency list uses less space, as you will now see.

 Note: An adjacency matrix uses a fixed amount of space that depends on the number of vertices, but not the number of edges, in a graph. The adjacency matrix for a sparse graph wastes space, because the graph has relatively few edges.

 Note: Seeing whether an edge exists between any two given vertices of a graph can be done quickly when you use an adjacency matrix. But you need to scan an entire row of the matrix if you want to know all the neighbors of a particular vertex.

 Question 1   Consider the graph in Figure 30-4b of the previous chapter. Number the vertices from 0 through 3, starting at the vertex in the upper left corner and moving in a clockwise direction. What adjacency matrix represents this graph?

The Adjacency List

31.3   An adjacency list for a given vertex represents only those edges that originate from the vertex. In Figure 31-2, each vertex of the graph in Figure 31-1a references a list of adjacent vertices. Space is not reserved for edges that do not exist. Thus, the adjacency lists, taken together, use less memory than the corresponding adjacency matrix in Figure 31-1b. For this reason, implementations of sparse graphs use adjacency lists. The implementation that we present in this chapter will do so also, since typical graphs are sparse.

   Although the adjacency lists in our diagram contain vertices, they will actually contain edges in our implementation. Each of these edges, however, will contain the illustrated vertex as its terminal vertex.

 Note: An adjacency list for a given vertex represents only those edges that originate from the vertex. For a sparse graph, an adjacency list uses less memory than an adjacency matrix. For a dense graph, an adjacency matrix can be the better choice.

 Note: Using adjacency lists, you can find all the neighbors of a particular vertex by traversing a list. If you want to know whether an edge exists between any two given vertices, you need to search a list. If the graph contains n vertices, each of these operations is O(n) at worst, but is faster on average.

Figure 31-2   Adjacency lists for the directed graph in Figure 31-1a

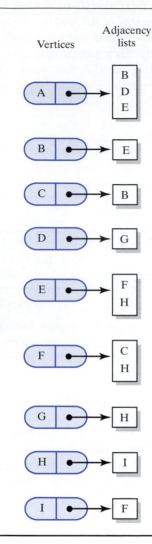

Question 2   What adjacency lists represent the graph described in Question 1?

Vertices and Edges

31.4   While designing a class that implements the ADT graph, we encounter two other types of objects, the vertex and the edge. These objects are interrelated: A vertex has edges that leave it, and an edge is defined by the vertices at its ends.

A vertex in a graph is somewhat like a node in a tree. Both vertices and nodes are implementation details that we hide from the client. In the implementation of a binary tree, we used a package-friendly class BinaryNode. (See Segment 26.3 of Chapter 26.) Here, a graph will have package access to the class Vertex. Previously, we simplified the implementation of a binary tree by giving BinaryNode more than simple accessor and mutator operations. The same is true now for the implementation of the ADT graph. In fact, the specifications of the ADT graph that you saw in the previous chapter (Segment 30.25) omit the operations necessary to implement various graph algorithms. We assign these operations to the vertices.

The structure of a vertex is more like the structure of a node in a general tree than the structure of a node in a binary tree. Both the general node in Figure 26-8 and a vertex reference a list that you use to address other nodes or vertices.

Specifying the Class `Vertex`

31.5   **Identifying vertices.** First, we need a way to identify the vertices in a graph. One simple way is to use either integers or strings. A more general approach—the one we will use—labels each vertex with an object. This label will be a data field of the class `Vertex`. One operation of `Vertex`, then, is to retrieve a vertex's label. We'll use the constructor to set the label, omitting a mutator method for this field.

31.6   **Visiting vertices.** The algorithms that we discussed in the previous chapter required us to mark certain vertices when they were visited. We therefore give operations to `Vertex` that mark a vertex as visited, test whether a vertex has been visited, and remove the mark.

31.7   **The adjacency list.** As we mentioned earlier in this chapter, a vertex's adjacency list indicates its neighbors. Rather than placing this list within the class of graphs, it is more convenient to make it a part of the class `Vertex`. Soon we will define a simple class `Edge` whose instances we will place in these adjacency lists. Thus, a particular vertex's adjacency list contains the edges that leave the vertex. Each edge indicates its weight, if any, and references the vertex that ends the edge. `Vertex` then needs methods to add edges to the adjacency list. These methods essentially connect a vertex to its neighbors.

In addition, we must provide access to the adjacency list for a given vertex. Thus, we define an iterator that returns a vertex's neighbors, as well as an iterator that returns the weights of the edges to those neighbors. For convenience, we also include a method to test whether a vertex has at least one neighbor.

As you will see, the adjacency list is the only place where we need instances of `Edge`. Thus, `Edge` is an implementation detail that we can hide within `Vertex` as an inner class.

31.8   **Path operations.** While finding a path through a graph, we must be able to locate the vertex that comes before a given vertex on the path—in other words, the vertex's predecessor. Thus, we need set, get, and test operations for a vertex's predecessor. Certain algorithms find the path with the shortest length or the path that has the smallest weight, or cost. A vertex can record either the length or the weight of the path from the origin to itself. Thus, we have operations that set and get this recorded value.

31.9   **The Java interface.** The interface in Listing 31-1 specifies the vertex operations that we have just introduced. Recall from the previous chapter that the generic type `T` represents the data type of the object that labels a vertex.

Listing 31-1   An interface for the vertices in a graph

```java
package GraphPackage;
import java.util.Iterator;
public interface VertexInterface<T>
{
```

```
/** Task: Gets the vertex's label.
 *  @return the object that labels the vertex */
public T getLabel();

/** Task: Marks the vertex as visited. */
public void visit();

/** Task: Removes the vertex's visited mark. */
public void unvisit();

/** Task: Sees whether the vertex is marked as visited.
 *  @return true if the vertex is visited */
public boolean isVisited();

/** Task: Connects this vertex and a given vertex with a weighted edge.
 *         The two vertices cannot be the same, and must not already
 *         have this edge between them. In a directed graph, the edge
 *         points toward the given vertex.
 *  @param endVertex   a vertex in the graph that ends the edge
 *  @param edgeWeight  a real-valued edge weight, if any
 *  @return true if the edge is added, or false if not */
public boolean connect(VertexInterface<T> endVertex,
                       double edgeWeight);

/** Task: Connects this vertex and a given vertex with an unweighted
 *         edge. The two vertices cannot be the same, and must not
 *         already have this edge between them. In a directed graph,
 *         the edge points toward the given vertex.
 *  @param endVertex   a vertex in the graph that ends the edge
 *  @return true if the edge is added, or false if not */
public boolean connect(VertexInterface<T> endVertex);

/** Task: Creates an iterator of this vertex's neighbors by following
 *         all edges that begin at this vertex.
 *  @return an iterator of the neighboring vertices of this vertex */
public Iterator<VertexInterface<T>> getNeighborIterator();

/** Task: Creates an iterator of the weights of the edges to this
 *         vertex's neighbors.
 *  @return an iterator of edge weights for edges to neighbors of this
 *          vertex */
public Iterator<Double> getWeightIterator();

/** Task: Sees whether this vertex has at least one neighbor.
 *  @return true if the vertex has a neighbor */
public boolean hasNeighbor();

/** Task: Gets an unvisited neighbor, if any, of this vertex.
 *  @return either a vertex that is an unvisited neighbor or null
 *          if no such neighbor exists */
public VertexInterface<T> getUnvisitedNeighbor();

/** Task: Records the previous vertex on a path to this vertex.
 *  @param predecessor  the vertex previous to this one along a path */
public void setPredecessor(VertexInterface<T> predecessor);
```

```
/** Task: Gets the recorded predecessor of this vertex.
 *  @return either this vertex's predecessor or null if no predecessor
 *              was recorded */
public VertexInterface<T> getPredecessor();

/** Task: Sees whether a predecessor was recorded.
 *  @return true if a predecessor was recorded for this vertex */
public boolean hasPredecessor();

/** Task: Records the cost of a path to this vertex.
 *  @param newCost  the cost of the path */
public void setCost(double newCost);

/** Task: Gets the recorded cost of the path to this vertex.
 *  @return the cost of the path */
public double getCost();
} // end VertexInterface
```

The Inner Class Edge

31.10   As we mentioned, we will place instances of the class Edge in a vertex's adjacency list to indicate the edges that originate at the vertex. Thus, each edge must record both the vertex that ends it and the edge's weight, if any. Recording an edge weight is the only reason we need a class of edges. For unweighted graphs, we could simply place vertices in the adjacency list. Using edge objects, however, allows us to use one class of vertices for both weighted and unweighted graphs.

Since Vertex is the only class that uses Edge, we make Edge an inner class of Vertex. Listing 31-2 shows an implementation of Edge. We provide a data field for an edge's weight, if any. For unweighted graphs, we will set this field to zero rather than creating a class of unweighted edges.

Listing 31-2   The protected class Edge, as an inner class of Vertex

```
protected class Edge implements java.io.Serializable
{
  private VertexInterface<T> vertex; // end vertex
  private double weight;

  protected Edge(VertexInterface<T> endVertex, double edgeWeight)
  {
    vertex = endVertex;
    weight = edgeWeight;
  } // end constructor

  protected VertexInterface<T> getEndVertex()
  {
    return vertex;
  } // end getEndVertex
```

```
    protected double getWeight()
    {
      return weight;
    } // end getWeight
} // end Edge
```

 Note: An instance of the inner class `Edge` contains both the vertex that ends it and the edge's weight, if any. Although not necessary for unweighted graphs, `Edge` allows us to use one class of vertices for both weighted and unweighted graphs.

Implementing the Class Vertex

31.11   **An outline of the class.** To hide `Vertex` from the clients of the graph, we place it within the package `GraphPackage` that we introduced in the previous chapter. Listing 31-3 outlines the class and shows its data fields and constructor. An ADT list that has an iterator serves as the adjacency list `edgeList`. We have chosen the linked implementation `LinkedListWithIterator` discussed in Segment 8.19 of Chapter 8.

Listing 31-3   An outline of the class `Vertex`

```
package GraphPackage;
import java.util.Iterator;
import java.util.NoSuchElementException;
import ADTPackage.*; // classes that implement various ADTs
class Vertex<T> implements VertexInterface<T>, java.io.Serializable
{
  private T label;
  private ListWithIteratorInterface<Edge> edgeList; // edges to neighbors
  private boolean visited;                          // true if visited
  private VertexInterface<T> previousVertex; // on path to this vertex
  private double cost;                       // of path to this vertex

  public Vertex(T vertexLabel)
  {
    label = vertexLabel;
    edgeList = new LinkedListWithIterator<Edge>();
    visited = false;
    previousVertex = null;
    cost = 0;
  } // end constructor

  < Implementations of the vertex operations go here. >
  . . .

  protected class Edge implements java.io.Serializable
  {
```

< See Listing 31-2. >
```
    } // end Edge
} // end Vertex
```

Note: The data fields of the class `Vertex` facilitate the implementation of the algorithms presented in the previous chapter. For example, the fields `previousVertex` and `cost` are useful in a breadth-first search for the cheapest path from one vertex to another.

31.12   **The connect methods.** Each method `connect` places an edge into a vertex's adjacency list. We first implement the method for weighted graphs and then use it to implement the method for unweighted graphs. Preventing the addition of an edge that either exists in the graph already or connects a vertex with itself consumes most of the method's effort. Once those details are complete, `connect` simply calls the ADT list's add method to add the edge.

```java
public boolean connect(VertexInterface<T> endVertex,
                       double edgeWeight)
{
  boolean result = false;

  if (!this.equals(endVertex))
  { // vertices are distinct
    Iterator<VertexInterface<T>> neighbors =
                                 this.getNeighborIterator();
    boolean duplicateEdge = false;

    while (!duplicateEdge && neighbors.hasNext())
    {
      VertexInterface<T> nextNeighbor = neighbors.next();
      if (endVertex.equals(nextNeighbor))
        duplicateEdge = true;
    } // end while

    if (!duplicateEdge)
    {
      edgeList.add(new Edge(endVertex, edgeWeight));
      result = true;
    } // end if
  } // end if

  return result;
} // end connect

public boolean connect(VertexInterface<T> endVertex)
{
  return connect(endVertex, 0);
} // end connect
```

Although adding to a list can be done in O(1) time, scanning the list to prevent duplicate edges takes more time. Since each vertex in a graph of *n* vertices can be the origin of at most *n* - 1 edges, connect is an O(*n*) operation. For a sparse graph, however, the number of edges originating at any vertex is much less than *n*. In this case, connect is significantly faster than O(*n*).

31.13   **The iterators.** The method getNeighborIterator returns an iterator to a vertex's adjacent vertices, that is, its neighbors. We define a private inner class—neighborIterator—within Vertex that implements Java's interface Iterator. Thus, getNeighborIterator has the following implementation:

```
public Iterator<VertexInterface<T>> getNeighborIterator()
{
   return new neighborIterator();
} // end getNeighborIterator
```

The class neighborIterator appears in Listing 31-4. The constructor establishes an instance of the iterator defined in LinkedListWithIterator. The method next uses this iterator to traverse the edges in the vertex's adjacency list. Then, using Edge's method getEndVertex, next accesses the neighboring vertex and returns it.

Listing 31-4   The private class neighborIterator, as an inner class of Vertex

```
private class neighborIterator implements Iterator<VertexInterface<T>>
{
   private Iterator<Edge> edges;

   private neighborIterator()
   {
      edges = edgeList.getIterator();
   } // end default constructor

   public boolean hasNext()
   {
      return edges.hasNext();
   } // end hasNext

   public VertexInterface<T> next()
   {
      VertexInterface<T> nextNeighbor = null;

      if (edges.hasNext())
      {
         Edge edgeToNextNeighbor = edges.next();
         nextNeighbor = edgeToNextNeighbor.getEndVertex();
      }
      else
         throw new NoSuchElementException();

      return nextNeighbor;
   } // end next

   public void remove()
   {
```

```
    throw new UnsupportedOperationException();
  } // end remove
} // end neighborIterator
```

In a similar manner, the method `getWeightIterator` returns an instance of a private inner class `weightIterator`. This class is similar to the class `neighborIterator`.

31.14 **The methods `hasNeighbor` and `getUnvisitedNeighbor`.** The method `hasNeighbor` uses the method `isEmpty` of `LinkedListWithIterator` to test whether `edgeList` is empty:

```
public boolean hasNeighbor()
{
  return !edgeList.isEmpty();
} // end hasNeighbor
```

Using the iterator returned by `getNeighborIterator`, the method `getUnvisitedNeighbor` returns an adjacent vertex that is unvisited. This task is necessary in a topological sort.

```
public VertexInterface<T> getUnvisitedNeighbor()
{
  VertexInterface<T> result = null;

  Iterator<VertexInterface<T>> neighbors = getNeighborIterator();
  while (neighbors.hasNext() && (result == null) )
  {
    VertexInterface<T> nextNeighbor = neighbors.next();
    if (!nextNeighbor.isVisited())
      result = nextNeighbor;
  } // end while

  return result;
} // end getUnvisitedNeighbor
```

31.15 **The remaining methods.** `Vertex` should override the method `equals`. Two vertices are equal if their labels are equal.

```
public boolean equals(Object other)
{
  boolean result;

  if ((other == null) || (getClass() != other.getClass()))
    result = false;
  else
  {
    Vertex<T> otherVertex = (Vertex<T>)other;
    result = label.equals(otherVertex.label);
  } // end if

  return result;
} // end equals
```

The remaining methods of `Vertex` have uncomplicated implementations and are left as exercises.

Question 3   Given the interface `VertexInterface` and the class `Vertex`, write Java statements that create the vertices and edges for the following directed, weighted graph. This graph contains three vertices—A, B, and C—and four edges, as follows: $A \rightarrow B$, $B \rightarrow C$, $C \rightarrow A$, $A \rightarrow C$. These edges have the weights 2, 3, 4, and 5, respectively.

An Implementation of the ADT Graph

We now consider how to use `Vertex` in an implementation of a directed graph that can be either weighted or unweighted.

Basic Operations

31.16   **Beginning the class.** Whether our implementation uses an adjacency list—as it will here—or an adjacency matrix, it must have a container for the graph's vertices. If we use integers to identify the vertices, a list would be a natural choice for this container, since each integer could correspond to a position within the list. If we use an object such as a string to identify them, a dictionary is a better choice. That is what we will do here.

Note: Regardless of the kind of graph or how you implement it, you need a container such as a dictionary for the graph's vertices.

Figure 31-3 illustrates a dictionary of vertices for a small directed graph. Each of the vertices A and D has an adjacency list of the edges that originate at that vertex. The letters within these edges represent references to corresponding vertices within the dictionary. Since the ADT dictionary consists of key-value pairs, we can use the vertex labels as the search keys and the vertices themselves as the corresponding values. This organization allows us to quickly locate a particular vertex, given its label.

Figure 31-3   (a) A directed graph and (b) its implementation using adjacency lists

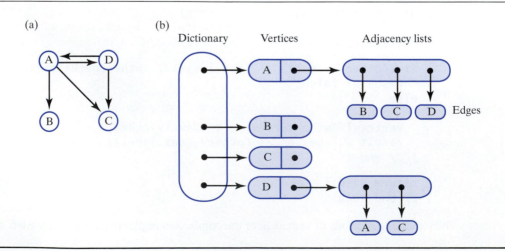

Our class begins as shown in Listing 31-5. Recall that the generic type T represents the data type of the objects that label the graph's vertices. The class's first data field is a dictionary of vertices. A count of vertices is not necessary, since the dictionary will count the vertices for us.

Since each vertex maintains its own adjacency list, the edges in the graph are not easily counted. Thus, we should maintain an edge count as a data field within the graph class.

Listing 31-5   An outline of the class `DirectedGraph`

```
package GraphPackage;
import java.util.Iterator;
import ADTPackage.*; // classes that implement various ADTs
public class DirectedGraph<T> implements GraphInterface<T>,
                                    java.io.Serializable
{
  private DictionaryInterface<T, VertexInterface<T>> vertices;
  private int edgeCount;

  public DirectedGraph()
  {
    vertices = new LinkedDictionary<T, VertexInterface<T>>();
    edgeCount = 0;
  } // end default constructor

  < Implementations of the graph operations go here. >
  . . .

} // end DirectedGraph
```

31.17   **Adding vertices.** The method `addVertex` uses `Vertex`'s constructor to create a new vertex. It then adds the vertex to the dictionary by invoking the dictionary's method `add`:

```
  public boolean addVertex(T vertexLabel)
  {
    VertexInterface<T> isDuplicate =
                vertices.add(vertexLabel, new Vertex(vertexLabel));
    return isDuplicate == null; // was add to dictionary successful?
  } // end addVertex
```

Notice that `vertexLabel` is the search key for the dictionary entry, and the new vertex is the associated value. Recall from the listing in Segment 17.4 of Chapter 17 that `add` returns `null` if the addition to the dictionary is successful. We use this fact to determine the return value for `addVertex`.

31.18   **Adding edges.** Methods such as `addEdge` that identify an existing vertex by its label must locate the vertex within the dictionary `vertices`. To do this, they invoke the dictionary method `getValue`, using the vertex label as the search key. Having located the two vertices that delineate the edge to be added, `addEdge` adds an edge to the adjacency list of the origin vertex. It does this by invoking `Vertex`'s `connect` method. If the edge is added successfully, `edgeCount` is incremented. Thus, our graph's `addEdge` methods have the following definitions, one for weighted graphs and one for unweighted graphs:

```
      public boolean addEdge(T begin, T end, double edgeWeight)
      {
        boolean result = false;

        VertexInterface<T> beginVertex = vertices.getValue(begin);
        VertexInterface<T> endVertex = vertices.getValue(end);

        if ( (beginVertex != null) && (endVertex != null) )
          result = beginVertex.connect(endVertex, edgeWeight);

        if (result)
          edgeCount++;

        return result;
      } // end addEdge

      public boolean addEdge(T begin, T end)
      {
        return addEdge(begin, end, 0);
      } // end addEdge
```

31.19   **Testing for an edge.** The method hasEdge begins like addEdge, by locating the two vertices that define the desired edge. With the origin vertex in hand, hasEdge invokes Vertex's method getNeighborIterator and searches the origin's adjacency list for the desired edge. In the following implementation, you can see why defining the equals method in Vertex is important.

```
      public boolean hasEdge(T begin, T end)
      {
        boolean found = false;

        VertexInterface<T> beginVertex = vertices.getValue(begin);
        VertexInterface<T> endVertex = vertices.getValue(end);

        if ( (beginVertex != null) && (endVertex != null) )
        {
          Iterator<VertexInterface<T>> neighbors =
                                    beginVertex.getNeighborIterator();
          while (!found && neighbors.hasNext())
          {
            VertexInterface<T> nextNeighbor = neighbors.next();
            if (endVertex.equals(nextNeighbor))
              found = true;
          } // end while
        } // end if

        return found;
      } // end hasEdge
```

31.20   **Miscellaneous methods.** The methods isEmpty, clear, getNumberOfVertices, and getNumber-OfEdges have the following simple implementations:

```
      public boolean isEmpty()
      {
        return vertices.isEmpty();
      } // end isEmpty

      public void clear()
      {
```

```
      vertices.clear();
      edgeCount = 0;
  } // end clear

  public int getNumberOfVertices()
  {
      return vertices.getSize();
  } // end getNumberOfVertices

  public int getNumberOfEdges()
  {
      return edgeCount;
  } // end getNumberOfEdges
```

31.21   **Resetting vertices.** You saw in Segment 31.11 that the class `Vertex` has the data fields `visited`, `previousVertex`, and `cost`. These fields are necessary for the implementation of the graph algorithms that we introduced in the previous chapter. Once you have searched a graph for a shortest path, for example, many of the vertices will have been visited and marked accordingly. Before you could perform a topological sort on the same graph, you would have to reset the field `visited` for each vertex in the graph.

The following method `resetVertices` sets the fields `visited`, `previousVertex`, and `cost` to their initial values. To do so, the method uses one of the iterators declared in the interface `DictionaryInterface`. The method is not public, as we will call it only from methods declared in `GraphAlgorithmsInterface`.

```
      protected void resetVertices()
      {
        Iterator<VertexInterface<T>> vertexIterator =
                                 vertices.getValueIterator();
        while (vertexIterator.hasNext())
        {
          VertexInterface<T> nextVertex = VertexIterator.next();
          nextVertex.unvisit();
          nextVertex.setCost(0);
          nextVertex.setPredecessor(null);
        } // end while
      } // end resetVertices
```

?   **Question 4**   Create an instance of the class `DirectedGraph` for the graph described in Question 3.

31.22   **Efficiency.** Adding a vertex to a graph is an $O(n)$ operation, since the vertex is added to a linked dictionary. Adding an edge involves retrieving two vertices from the dictionary and then calling `Vertex`'s method `connect`. Thus, the method `addEdge` is also $O(n)$. Likewise, `hasEdge` is $O(n)$, as it first retrieves two vertices from the dictionary. It then iterates through the edges that leave the first vertex to see whether one of them ends at the second vertex. As you can see, the performance of these three graph operations depends on the number of vertices in the graph. The remaining methods in `BasicGraphInterface` are each $O(1)$. Figure 31-4 summarizes these observations.

Figure 31-4   The performance of basic operations of the ADT graph when implemented by using adjacency lists

addVertex	O(n)
addEdge	O(n)
hasEdge	O(n)
isEmpty	O(1)
getNumberOfVertices	O(1)
getNumberOfEdges	O(1)
clear	O(1)

Graph Algorithms

31.23   **Breadth-first traversal.** Segment 30.12 of the previous chapter presented an algorithm for a breadth-first traversal of a nonempty graph, beginning at a given origin vertex. Recall that the traversal first visits the origin and the origin's neighbors. It then visits each neighbor of the origin's neighbors. The traversal uses a queue to hold the vertices as they are visited. The traversal order is the order in which vertices are added to this queue. But since the algorithm must remove vertices from this queue, we maintain the traversal order in a second queue. Since this second queue is returned to the client, we enqueue vertex labels instead of vertices. Remember that the class Vertex is unavailable to the client.

The following implementation of the method getBreadthFirstTraversal closely follows the pseudocode given in the previous chapter. The parameter origin is an object that labels the origin vertex of the traversal.

```java
public QueueInterface<T> getBreadthFirstTraversal(T origin)
{
  resetVertices();
  QueueInterface<T> traversalOrder = new LinkedQueue<T>();
  QueueInterface<VertexInterface<T>> vertexQueue =
                          new LinkedQueue<VertexInterface<T>>();

  VertexInterface<T> originVertex = vertices.getValue(origin);
  originVertex.visit();
  traversalOrder.enqueue(origin);    // enqueue vertex label
  vertexQueue.enqueue(originVertex); // enqueue vertex

  while (!vertexQueue.isEmpty())
  {
    VertexInterface<T> frontVertex = vertexQueue.dequeue();

    Iterator<VertexInterface<T>> neighbors =
                          frontVertex.getNeighborIterator();
    while (neighbors.hasNext())
    {
      VertexInterface<T> nextNeighbor = neighbors.next();
      if (!nextNeighbor.isVisited())
      {
```

```
        nextNeighbor.visit();
        traversalOrder.enqueue(nextNeighbor.getLabel());
        vertexQueue.enqueue(nextNeighbor);
      } // end if
    } // end while
  } // end while

  return traversalOrder;
} // end getBreadthFirstTraversal
```

The implementation of a similar method to perform a depth-first traversal is left as an exercise.

 Question 5   Write Java statements that display the vertices in a breadth-first traversal of the graph that you created in Question 4, beginning with vertex *A*.

31.24   **Shortest path.** The shortest path of all paths from one vertex to another in an unweighted graph is the path that has the fewest edges. The algorithm that finds this path—as you saw in Segment 30.19 of the previous chapter—is based on a breadth-first traversal. When we visit a vertex *v*, we mark it as visited, note the vertex *p* that precedes *v* in the graph, and note the length of the path that the traversal followed to reach *v*. We place both this path length and a reference to *p* into the vertex *v*. When the traversal reaches the desired destination, we can construct the shortest path from this data in the vertices.

The implementation of the method getShortestPath closely follows the pseudocode given in the previous chapter. The parameters begin and end are objects that label the origin and destination vertices of the path. The third parameter path is an initially empty stack. At the conclusion of the method, this stack contains the labels of the vertices along the shortest path. The method returns the length of this path.

```
public int getShortestPath(T begin, T end, StackInterface<T> path)
{
  resetVertices();
  boolean done = false;
  QueueInterface<VertexInterface<T>> vertexQueue =
                        new LinkedQueue<VertexInterface<T>>();

  VertexInterface<T> originVertex = vertices.getValue(begin);
  VertexInterface<T> endVertex = vertices.getValue(end);

  originVertex.visit();
  // Assertion: resetVertices() has executed setCost(0)
  // and setPredecessor(null) for originVertex

  vertexQueue.enqueue(originVertex);

  while (!done && !vertexQueue.isEmpty())
  {
    VertexInterface<T> frontVertex = vertexQueue.dequeue();

    Iterator<VertexInterface<T>> neighbors =
                        frontVertex.getNeighborIterator();
    while (!done && neighbors.hasNext())
    {
      VertexInterface<T> nextNeighbor = neighbors.next();
```

```
      if (!nextNeighbor.isVisited())
      {
        nextNeighbor.visit();
        nextNeighbor.setCost(1 + frontVertex.getCost());
        nextNeighbor.setPredecessor(frontVertex);
        vertexQueue.enqueue(nextNeighbor);
      } // end if

      if (nextNeighbor.equals(endVertex))
        done = true;
    } // end while
  } // end while

  // traversal ends; construct shortest path
  int pathLength = (int)endVertex.getCost();
  path.push(endVertex.getLabel());

  VertexInterface<T> vertex = endVertex;
  while (vertex.hasPredecessor())
  {
    vertex = vertex.getPredecessor();
    path.push(vertex.getLabel());
  } // end while

  return pathLength;
} // end getShortestPath
```

The implementation of the method `getCheapestPath` for a weighted graph is left as an exercise.

 Question 6   Write statements that display the vertices in the shortest path from vertex *A* to vertex *C* for the graph that you created in Question 4. Also, display the length of this path.

CHAPTER SUMMARY

- An adjacency list for a given vertex contains references to the vertex's neighbors.

- Using an adjacency list, you can quickly find all the neighbors of a particular vertex. But if you want to know whether an edge exists between any two given vertices, you need to search a list.

- An adjacency matrix is a two-dimensional array that represents the edges in a graph. If you number the vertices from 0 through $n - 1$, the element in row i and column j of the matrix indicates whether an edge exists between vertex i and vertex j. For an unweighted graph, you can use boolean values in the matrix. For a weighted graph, you can use edge weights when edges exist and a representation of infinity otherwise

- Using an adjacency matrix, you can quickly discover whether an edge exists between any two given vertices. But if you want to know all the neighbors of a particular vertex, you need to scan an entire row of the matrix.

- Each adjacency list represents only those edges that originate from a vertex, but an adjacency matrix reserves space for every possible edge in a graph. Thus, when a graph is sparse, adjacency lists use less memory than a corresponding adjacency matrix. For this reason, typical graph implementations use adjacency lists.

- One way to implement an adjacency list is to make it a data field of a class **Vertex**. So that you can represent weighted graphs as well as unweighted graphs, you place instances of a class **Edge** in the adjacency list. **Edge**'s data fields include the terminal vertex of an edge and the edge weight. **Vertex** is accessed from within a package instead of publicly. **Edge** is an inner class of **Vertex**. Thus, both **Vertex** and **Edge** are hidden from the graph's client.

- To facilitate the implementation of various graph algorithms, an instance of the class **Vertex** can indicate whether it has been visited. It also can record data about a path to it, such as the previous vertex and the path's cost.

EXERCISES

1. What adjacency matrix represents the graph in Figure 30-15a of the previous chapter?

2. What adjacency matrix represents the graph in Figure 30-18a of the previous chapter?

3. What adjacency lists represent the graph in Figure 30-15a of the previous chapter?

4. What adjacency lists represent the graph in Figure 30-18a of the previous chapter?

5. When is an adjacency matrix just as space-efficient as adjacency lists?

6. Suppose that you want only to test whether an edge exists between two particular vertices. Does an adjacency matrix or an adjacency list provide a more efficient way of doing this?

7. Suppose that you want only to find all vertices that are adjacent to some particular vertex. Does an adjacency matrix or an adjacency list provide a more efficient way of doing this?

8. Complete the implementation of the class **Vertex** that was begun in Segment 31.11.

9. What is the Big Oh of the methods `getBreadthFirstTraversal` and `getShortestPath`, as given in Segments 31.23 and 31.24?

10. Implement the method `getDepthFirstTraversal`. Segment 30.13 of the previous chapter presents the pseudocode for this method. What is its Big Oh?

11. Implement the method `getCheapestPath` for a weighted graph. The pseudocode for this method appears in Segment 30.24 of the previous chapter. What is its Big Oh?

12. Draw a class diagram that shows the relationships among the classes `DirectedGraph`, `Vertex`, and any other supporting classes such as `LinkedDictionary`.

13. The **out degree** of a vertex is the number of edges that originate at the vertex. The **in degree** of a vertex is the number of edges that terminate at the vertex. Modify the class `DirectedGraph` so that it can compute the in degree and out degree of any of its vertices.

14. Suppose that you have a weighted, directed graph in which the out degree and in degree of every vertex is at most 4. (See the previous exercise.) If the graph has n vertices, you could represent it by using an array that has n rows and 4 columns. Each of the n rows is associated with a different vertex in the graph. The entries in a row associated with vertex v are the vertices at the ends of the edges that begin at v. Since the out degree of a vertex can be less than 4, some entries in a row might be null.

What is the Big Oh of each of the following operations?

a. Testing whether two given vertices are adjacent

b. Finding all vertices adjacent to a given vertex

15. A graph is said to be **bipartite** if the vertices can be divided into two groups such that every edge goes from a vertex in one group to a vertex in the other group. Figure 30-1 of the previous chapter contains a bipartite graph. We could put Sandwich, Hyannis, Orleans, and Provincetown in group *A*, and Barnstable, Falmouth, Chatham, and Truro in group *B*. Every edge goes from a vertex of group *A* to a vertex of group *B*.

a. Which of the graphs in Figure 30-4, 30-6, and 30-7b are bipartite?

b. How might the implementation of a bipartite graph differ from that of a regular graph to take advantage of its bipartite nature?

16. A graph is said to be **biconnected** if two paths that do not share edges or vertices exist between every pair of vertices.

a. Which graphs in Figure 30-1 and 30-4 are biconnected?

b. What are some applications that would use a biconnected graph?

17. A **loop** is an edge that starts and ends at the same vertex. Figure 31-5 shows an example of a loop in a directed, weighted graph.

a. Give an example of a problem where allowing loops would be useful.

b. Can the adjacency matrix and adjacency list representations of a graph support loops?

Figure 31-5   A graph for Exercise 17

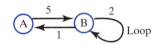

18. A **multiple edge** occurs when two vertices are joined by two or more edges in the same direction. Figure 31-6 shows a directed, weighted graph that has a multiple edge from *D* to *B*.

a. Give an example of a problem in which allowing multiple edges would be useful.

b. Can an adjacency matrix represent an unweighted graph that has multiple edges?

c. Can an adjacency matrix represent a weighted graph that has multiple edges?

d. Can adjacency lists represent an unweighted graph that has multiple edges?

e. Can adjacency lists represent a weighted graph that has multiple edges?

Figure 31-6   A graph for Exercise 18

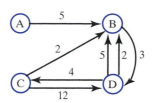

1. Complete the implementation of the class `DirectedGraph` that was begun in Segment 31.16 of this chapter.

2. Implement a class of undirected graphs by extending the class `DirectedGraph`. What methods should you override? What methods, if any, in `DirectedGraph` do not apply to an undirected graph? If such methods exist, what should you do in your new class? Note that the method `getNumberOfEdges` is the only accessor method to a data field of `DirectedGraph`.

3. Revise the class `DirectedGraph` by defining protected mutator methods for the data fields `vertices` and `edgeCount`. Also, define a protected accessor method for `vertices`. Then repeat Project 2, using your revised `DirectedGraph`. Compare the performance of the `addEdge` methods in this implementation of an undirected graph versus the implementation possible under the assumptions of Project 2.

4. Implement the classes `Vertex` and `DirectedGraph` by using an adjacency matrix.

5. Assuming an implementation of a class of undirected graphs, implement a method that detects whether an undirected graph is acyclic. You can look for cycles during either a breadth-first traversal or a depth-first traversal by discovering an edge to a vertex that is not the predecessor and has already been visited. To simplify the problem initially, you can assume that the graph is connected. Then remove this assumption.

6. Implement a method that detects whether a graph is connected.

7. Create the classes `LimitedVertex` and `LimitedDirectedGraph` that use the representation described in Exercise 14.

8. A **graph coloring** assigns a color to every vertex in a graph, with the restriction that two vertices of the same color cannot be adjacent. A graph is said to be **k-colorable** if it can be colored in k or fewer colors.

   a. Give an algorithm that will return true if a graph is 2-colorable and false otherwise.
   b. Exercise 15 defined a bipartite graph. Show that a graph is bipartite if and only if it is 2-colorable. Then, using this fact, implement a method that detects whether a graph is bipartite.

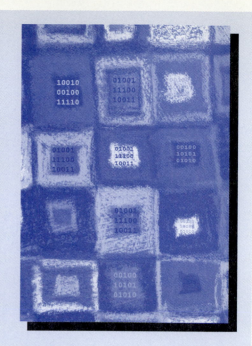

CONTENTS

PREREQUISITE

Knowledge of a programming language

This book assumes that you know how to write programs in Java. If you know some other programming language, this appendix will help you to learn Java by reviewing the essential elements of the language. Chapters 1 and 2 supplement the coverage of Java that is presented here by discussing methods, classes, and inheritance. Appendices B, C, and D cover exceptions, file I/O, and comments.

If you already know Java, note that this book uses applications, not applets. If you know only about applets, you should read at least the first few pages of this appendix.

Introduction

Applications and Applets

A.1   There are two kinds of Java programs, applications and applets. An **application** is simply a program that runs on your computer like any other program. It is a **stand-alone** program. In contrast, an **applet** is a program that cannot run without the support of a browser or a viewer. Typically, an applet is sent to another location on the Internet and is run there. The term "applet" is meant to suggest a little application.

Applets and applications are almost identical. Once you know how to design and write one, it is easy to learn to write the other. This book uses applications rather than applets.

Objects and Classes

A.2   An **object** is a program construct that contains data and can perform certain actions. When a Java program is run, the objects interact with one another to accomplish a particular task. The actions performed by objects are defined by **methods** in the program. When you ask an object to perform an action, you **invoke**, or **call**, a method. Java has two kinds of methods. A **valued method** uses a `return` statement to return a result, but a **void method** does not.

All objects of the same kind are said to be in the same class. So a **class** is a category or kind or type of object. All objects in the same class have the same types of data and the same methods.

You will see some objects and methods in the next section and again when we discuss the classes `Math`, `Scanner`, and `String` later in this appendix. Chapter 1 reviews classes, objects, and methods in more detail. If you are not familiar with these concepts, you should read at least Segment 1.1 in Chapter 1 now and the rest of Chapter 1 and Chapter 2 later.

A First Java Application Program

A.3   To give you a feel for the Java language, let's take a brief, informal look at the following sample Java application program:

```java
import java.util.Scanner;
public class FirstProgram
{
  public static void main(String[] args)
  {
    Scanner keyboard = new Scanner(System.in);
    System.out.println("Hello out there.");
    System.out.println("Want to talk some more?");
    System.out.println("Answer yes or no.");

    String answer = keyboard.next();
    if (answer.equals("yes"))
      System.out.println("Nice weather we are having.");
    System.out.println("Good-bye.");
  } // end main
} // end FirstProgram
```

The program is stored in the file `FirstProgram.java`.

Figure A-1 shows two screen displays that might be produced when a user runs and interacts with this program. The text typed by the user is shown in boldface.

Figure A-1   Two possible results when running the sample program

```
Hello out there.
Want to talk some more?
Answer yes or no.
yes
Nice weather we are having.
Good-bye.
```

```
Hello out there.
Want to talk some more?
Answer yes or no.
no
Good-bye.
```

A.4   This program uses the class `Scanner`, which is a part of the **Java Class Library**. This library contains many standard classes that you can use in your Java programs. The classes in the library are organized into groups called **packages**. The `import` statement indicates that this program uses the class `Scanner` from the package `java.util`.

The program contains the definition of a class that begins with the lines

```
public class FirstProgram
{
```

and ends with

```
} // end FirstProgram
```

Within the class definition is a method called `main` that begins with the statements

```
public static void main(String[] args)
{
```

and ends with

```
} // end main
```

Statements within this pair of braces are the **body** of the method `main`. Generally, a class contains several methods, each defining a specific task and each having a name of our choosing. An application program, however, must contain a method that is called `main`.

A.5   The line

```
Scanner keyboard = new Scanner(System.in);
```

gets us ready to read data from the keyboard using Java's class `Scanner`. It defines the `Scanner` object `keyboard` and associates it with the object `System.in`. This latter object represents the computer's keyboard. `System.in` is in the class `System`, which is in the package `java.lang` of the Java Class Library.

Programming Tip: No `import` statement is necessary when you use a class from the package `java.lang` of the Java Class Library.

A.6   The next three lines display text for the user of the program:

```
System.out.println("Hello out there.");
System.out.println("Want to talk some more?");
System.out.println("Answer yes or no.");
```

Each of these lines causes the quoted characters, or **string**, given within the parentheses to be displayed on the screen. `System.out` is an object within the class `System` that can send output to the screen via its method `println`. You invoke an object's method by writing the object name followed by a period, or **dot**, followed by the method name and some parentheses that may or may not have something inside them. The text inside the parentheses is called an **argument** and provides the information the method needs to carry out its action. In each of these three lines, the method `println` writes the value of its argument—here, the characters inside the quotes—to the screen.

The method `println` is an example of a void method. It performs an action, but does not return a value.

A.7   The next line of the program reads the characters that are typed at the keyboard and stores them in the variable `answer` as a string:

```
String answer = keyboard.next();
```

The `Scanner` object `keyboard` invokes its method `next` to read the word that the user types at the keyboard. The user presses the Enter key (also called the Return key) after typing the word. Although the method `next` has no arguments, the parentheses are required. You will learn more about the class `Scanner` later in this appendix.

The method `next` is an example of a valued method. It returns the value read. Its **invocation**, `keyboard.next()`, represents this value.

A.8   The next two lines of the program make a decision to do or not do something based on the value of the variable `answer`. The first line asks whether the string stored in `answer` is the string *yes*. If it is, a message is displayed on the screen. Otherwise, the message is not displayed.

Notice that the first sample dialogue in Figure A-1 displays the string *Nice weather we are having,* and the second one does not. That is because, in the first run of the program, the string *yes* is stored in the variable `answer`, and in the second run of the program, the string *no* is stored in `answer`.

A.9   Of course, precise rules govern how you write each part of a Java program. For example, a final semicolon ends each Java statement. These rules form the **grammar** for the Java language, just as there are rules for the grammar of the English language. The grammar rules for a programming language (or any language) are called the **syntax** of the language. We now look at the elements of Java in more detail.

Java Basics

In this section, we examine how to use Java to perform arithmetic computations.

Identifiers

A.10   You use **identifiers** to name certain parts of a program. An identifier in Java consists entirely of letters, digits, the underscore character _, and the dollar sign $. An identifier cannot start with a digit and must not contain a space or any other special character such as a period or an asterisk. There is no official limit to the length of a name, though in practice, there is always a limit. Although Java allows identifiers to contain a dollar sign, it is reserved for special purposes, and so you should not use $ in a Java identifier.

Java is **case sensitive**. This means that it treats uppercase letters and lowercase letters as different characters. For example, `mystuff`, `myStuff`, and `MyStuff` are three different identifiers. Having these identifiers in the same program could be confusing to human readers, and therefore doing so is a poor programming practice. But the Java compiler would be happy with them.

Java uses a character set, called **Unicode**, that includes characters from languages other than English. Java allows you to use these extra characters in identifiers, but you are not likely to find them on most keyboards. Segment A.67 discusses Unicode further.

A.11   Although it is not required by the Java language, the common practice, and the one followed in this book, is to start the names of classes with uppercase letters and to start the names of objects, methods, and variables (which you are about to see) with lowercase letters. These names are usually spelled using only letters and digits. We separate multiword names by using uppercase letters, since we cannot use spaces. For example, the following are all legal identifiers that follow this well-established convention:

```
inputStream    YourClass    CarWash    hotCar    theTimeOfDay
```

Some people use an underscore to separate the words in an identifier, but typically we will not.

The following are all illegal identifiers in Java, and the compiler will complain if you use any of them:

```
.MyClass    goTeam-    7eleven
```

The first two contain an illegal character, either a dot or a dash. The last name is illegal because it starts with a digit.

Reserved Words

A.12   Some words, such as the word **if**, have a special predefined meaning in the Java language. You cannot use these words, called **reserved words** or **keywords**, for anything other than their intended meaning. A full list of reserved words for Java is given on the inside cover of this book. Within a programming environment, the names of reserved words are often highlighted in some way. In this book, they will appear in boldface.

Some other words, such as String, name classes that are supplied with Java. They have a predefined meaning but are not reserved words. This means that you can change their meaning, but doing so could easily confuse you or somebody else reading your program.

Variables

A.13   A **variable** in a program represents a memory location that stores data such as numbers and letters. The number, letter, or other data item in a variable is called its **value**. This value can be changed, so that at one time the variable contains, say, 6, and at another time after the program has run for a while, the variable contains a different value, such as 4.

You use an identifier to name a variable. Besides following the rules and conventions for identifiers, you should choose variable names that suggest their use or the kind of data they will hold. For example, if a variable is used to count something, you might name the variable count. If the variable is used to hold the speed of an automobile, you might call the variable speed. You should almost never use single-letter variable names like x and y.

A.14   A variable's **data type**—or simply **type**—determines what kind of value the variable can hold. If the type is int, the variable can hold integers. If the type is double, the variable can hold numbers with a decimal point and a fractional part after the decimal point. If the type is char, the variable can hold any one character from the computer keyboard.

Java has two kinds of types, reference types and primitive types. A **reference type**—also called a **class type**—is a type that represents a class, that is, a type for objects of a class. For example, String is a class type. A **primitive type** is a simpler type. Values of a primitive type are not complex items but simple, indecomposable values, such as a single number or a single letter. The types int, double, and char are primitive types. The names of primitive types begin with a lowercase letter. By convention, the names of class types begin with an uppercase letter. Also by convention, variable names of either class types or primitive types begin with a lowercase letter.

Note: Naming conventions help you to distinguish among identifiers when reading a program.

A.15   A **variable declaration** indicates the type of data the variable will hold. Different types of data are stored in the computer's memory in different ways. Variable declarations are necessary so that the value of a variable can be correctly stored in or retrieved from the computer's memory. Even though the mechanisms for storing values in the variables of class types differ from the mechanisms used for primitive types, you declare variables for class types and primitive types in the same way.

You declare a variable by writing a type name followed by a list of variable names separated by commas and ending with a semicolon. All the variables named in the list will have the type given at the start of the declaration. For example,

```
int numberOfBaskets, eggsPerBasket, totalEggs;
String myName;
```

The first line declares that the three variables `numberOfBaskets`, `eggsPerBasket`, and `totalEggs` will contain values of type `int`. The second line declares that `myName` will store a `String` object.

You must declare a variable in a Java program before you use it. Normally, you declare a variable either just before it is used or at the start of a method definition.

Primitive Types

A.16   A whole number without a decimal point, such as 0, 1, or –2, is called an **integer**. A number with a decimal point, such as 3.14159, –8.63, or 5.0, is called a **floating-point number**. Notice that 5.0 is a floating-point number, not an integer. If a number has a fractional part, even if the fractional part is zero, it is a floating-point number.

All the Java primitive types appear inside the cover of this book. Notice that there are four types for integers—namely `byte`, `short`, `int`, and `long`. The only difference among the various integer types is the range of integers they can store and the amount of computer memory they use. If you cannot decide which integer type to use, use the type `int`. It has a large enough range for most purposes and does not use as much memory as the type `long`.

Java has two types for floating-point numbers, `float` and `double`. If you cannot decide between the types `float` and `double`, use `double`. It allows a wider range of values and is used as a default type for floating-point numbers.

You use the primitive type `char` for single characters, such as letters, digits, or punctuation. For example, the following declares the variable `symbol` to be of type `char`, stores the character for uppercase *A* in `symbol`, and then displays that value—the *A*—on the screen:

```
char symbol;
symbol = 'A';
System.out.println(symbol);
```

Notice that we enclose the character *A* in single quotes. Again note that uppercase letters and lowercase letters are different characters. For example, `'a'` and `'A'` represent two different characters.

Finally, the primitive type `boolean` has two values, true and false. You can use a variable of type `boolean` to store the answer to a true/false question such as "Is `myTime` less than `yourTime`?"

Constants

A.17   A variable can have its value changed; its value *varies*. A literal number like 2 cannot change. It is always 2. It is never 3. Values like 2 or 4.8 are called **constants**, or **literals**, because their values do not change.

You write constants of integer types with an optional plus sign or minus sign, but without commas or decimal points. Floating-point constants have an optional plus sign or a minus sign and no commas. You can write a floating-point constant in one of two ways. One way looks like the everyday way of writing numbers. For example, 9.8, -3.14, and 5.0 are floating-point constants, because they contain a decimal point. The second way is to include a multiplier that is a power of 10. You use the letter e to represent both the multiplication sign and the 10. For example, you would write 8.65×10^8 in Java as 8.65e8 (or in the less convenient form 865000000.0). The two forms, 8.65e8 and 865000000.0, are equivalent in a Java program. Similarly, the number 4.83×10^{-4}, which is equal to 0.000483, can be written as 4.83e-4 in Java.

The e stands for "exponent," since it is followed by a number that is thought of as an exponent of 10. The number before the e can be a number with or without a decimal point. The number after the e cannot contain a decimal point.

Other types of literal expressions are also called constants. You write constants of type char by placing the character in single quotes. For example, 'Y' is a constant of type char. A string constant is a sequence of characters enclosed in double quotes, as in "Java".

Assignment Statements

A.18   You can use an **assignment statement** to give a value to a variable. For example, if answer is a variable of type int and we want to give it the value 42, we could use the following assignment statement:

```
answer = 42;
```

An assignment statement always consists of a single variable on the left-hand side of an equal sign and an expression on the right-hand side followed by a semicolon. The expression can be another variable, a constant, or a more complicated expression made up by combining **operators**, such as + and *, with variables and constants. The value of the expression is assigned to the variable on the left of the equal sign.

For example, the following are all examples of assignment statements:

```
amount = 3.99;
firstInitial = 'B';
score = numberOfCards + handicap;
```

Here we assume that amount is a variable of type double, firstInitial is of type char, and the rest of the variables are of type int. If the variable numberOfCards has the value 7 and handicap has the value 2, the value of the variable score is 9.

The equal sign, =, which is called the **assignment operator**, does not mean equality. You can think of the assignment operator as saying, "Make the value of the variable equal to what follows." For example, in the statement

```
eggsPerBasket = eggsPerBasket - 2;
```

the variable eggsPerBasket occurs on both sides of the assignment operator. This statement subtracts 2 from the present value of eggsPerBasket and assigns the new value to eggsPerBasket. In effect, the statement decreases the value of eggsPerBasket by 2.

A.19   A variable that has been declared but that has not yet been given a value by the program is **uninitialized**. If the variable has a class type, it literally has no value. If the variable has a primitive type, it may have some default value. However, your program will be clearer if you explicitly give the variable a value, even if you are simply reassigning it the default value. (The exact details on default values have been known to change and should not be counted on.)

One easy way to ensure that you do not have an uninitialized variable is to initialize it within the declaration. Simply combine the declaration and an assignment statement, as in the following examples:

```
int count = 0;
double taxRate = 0.075;
char grade = 'A';
int balance = 1000, newBalance;
```

Note that a single declaration, such as the last statement above, can initialize some variables and not others.

Sometimes the compiler may complain that you have failed to initialize a variable. In most cases, this is indeed true. Occasionally, the compiler is mistaken about this. However, the compiler will not compile your program until you convince it that the variable in question is initialized. To make the compiler happy, initialize the variable when it is declared, even if the variable will be given a different value before you use it for anything. In such cases, you cannot argue with the compiler.

Assignment Compatibilities

A.20   You cannot put a square peg in a round hole, and similarly you cannot put a value of one type in a variable of another type. You cannot put an `int` value like 42 in a variable of type `char`. You cannot put a `double` value like 3.5 in a variable of type `int`. You cannot even put the `double` value 3.0 in a variable of type `int`. You cannot store a value of one type in a variable of another type unless the value is somehow converted to match the type of the variable.

When dealing with numbers, however, this conversion will sometimes—but not always—be performed for you automatically. For example, you can always assign a value of an integer type to a variable of a floating-point type, such as when you write either

```
double interestRate = 7;
```

or

```
int wholeRate = 7;
double interestRate = wholeRate;
```

More generally, you can assign a value of any type on the following list to a variable of any type that appears further down on the list:

```
byte → short → int → long → float → double
```

For example, you can assign a value of type `long` to a variable whose type is either `long`, `float`, or `double`. Notice that you can assign a value of any integer type to a variable of any floating-point type. This is not an arbitrary ordering of the types. As you move down the list from left to right, the types become more complex, or **wider**, either because they allow larger values or because they allow decimal points in the numbers. Thus, you can assign a value of one type to a variable of either the same type or a wider type.

In addition, you can assign a value of type char to a variable of type int or to any of the numeric types that follow int in the previous list of types. However, we do not advise doing so, because the result could be confusing.[1]

If you want to assign a value of type double to a variable of type int, you must change the type of the value explicitly by using a type cast, as we explain next.

Type Casting

A.21   A **type cast** is the changing of the type of a value to some other type, such as changing the type of 2.0 from double to int. The previous segment described when a change in type is done for you automatically. In all other cases, if you want to assign a value of one type to a variable of another type, you must perform a type cast. For example, you cannot simply assign a value of type double to a variable of type int, even if the value of type double happens to have all zeros after the decimal point and so is conceptually a whole number. Thus, the second of the following statements is illegal:

```
double distance = 9.0;
int points = distance; // ILLEGAL
```

To cast the type of distance to int, you enclose int within parentheses and place it in front of distance. For example, we would replace the preceding illegal assignment with

```
int points = (int)distance; // casting from double to int
```

Note that when you type-cast from any floating-point type to any integer type, the value is not rounded. The part after the decimal point is simply discarded, or **truncated**. For example, if the variable distance contains 25.86, (int)distance has an int value of 25. A type cast does not really change the value of a variable; distance is still 25.86, but points is 25.

Recall that when you assign an integer value to a variable of a floating-point type, the type cast is done automatically for you.

Note: When casting, some programmers place a space before the variable, as in (int) sum. We prefer to treat casting much like a minus sign. Just as we write minus five as -5, we cast sum to an integer by writing (int)sum.

Arithmetic Operators and Expressions

A.22   In Java, you perform arithmetic by using the **arithmetic operators** +, -, *, /, and %. You combine variables and constants with these operators and parentheses to form an **arithmetic expression**. The variables and constants in an expression are called **operands**. Spaces around the operators, operands, and parentheses within an expression are ignored.

---

1. Readers who have used certain other languages, such as C or C++, may be surprised to learn that we cannot assign a value of type char to a variable of type byte. This is because Java uses the Unicode character set rather than the ASCII character set, and so Java reserves two bytes of memory for each value of type char, but naturally reserves only one byte of memory for values of type byte. This is one of the few cases where we might notice that Java uses the Unicode character set. Indeed, if we convert from an int to a char or vice versa, we can expect to get the usual correspondence of ASCII numbers and characters.

A **unary operator** is one that has only one operand, like the operator - in the assignment statement

```
bankBalance = -cost;
```

A **binary operator** has two operands, like the operators + and * in

```
total = cost + (tax * discount);
```

Note that the operators - and + can be used as both unary and binary operators.

The meaning of an expression is basically what you expect it to be, but there are some subtleties about the type of the result and occasionally even about the value of the result. The type of the value produced when an expression is evaluated depends on the types of the values being combined. Consider an expression with only two operands, such as

```
amount - adjustment
```

If both `amount` and `adjustment` are of type `int`, the result of the subtraction has type `int`. If either `amount` or `adjustment`, or both, is of type `double`, the result is of type `double`. If we replace the operator - with any of the operators +, *, /, or %, the type of the result is determined in the same way. However, the operator % is typically used with integers, as you will see soon.

Larger expressions using more than two operands are viewed as a series of steps, each of which involves only two operands. For example, to evaluate the expression

```
balance + (balance * rate)
```

we evaluate `balance * rate` and obtain a number, and then we add that number to `balance`. Thus, if `balance` is `int` and `rate` is `double`, `balance * rate` is `double` and so is the entire expression.

Note: If all the items in an arithmetic expression have the same type, the result has that type. If at least one of the items has a floating-point type, the result has a floating-point type.

Knowing whether the value produced has an integer type or a floating-point type is typically all that you need. However, if you need to know the exact type of the value produced by an arithmetic expression, you can use the following rule:

Note: The data type of an arithmetic expression's value matches the most complex, or widest, data type among the operands in the expression. In other words, the data type matches the type that appears rightmost in the following list:

```
byte → short → int → long → float → double
```

For example, if `sum` is `float` and `more` is `int`, `sum + more` is `float`.

A.23   The division operator / deserves special attention, because the type of its operands can affect the value produced in a dramatic way. When you combine two numbers with the division operator / and at least one of the numbers has a floating-point type, the result has a floating-point type. For example, `9.0 / 2` has one operand of type `double`, namely `9.0`. Hence, the result is the type `double` number 4.5. However, when both operands have an integer type, the result can be surprising. For example 9 / 2 has two operands of type int, and so it yields the result 4 of type int, not 4.5. The fraction after the decimal point is simply lost. When you divide two integers, the result is truncated, *not* rounded. The part after the decimal point is discarded no matter how large it is. So, 11 / 3 is 3, not 3.6666 . . . . If nothing but a zero is after the decimal point, that decimal point and zero are still lost. Even this seemingly trivial difference can be of some significance. For example, 8.0 / 2 has the value 4.0 of type double, which technically is only an approximate quantity. However, 8 / 2 has the int value 4, which is an exact quantity. The approximate nature of 4.0 can affect the accuracy of any further calculation that is performed with this result.

Often, the % operator has operands only of integer types. You use it to recover the equivalent of the fraction after the decimal point. When you divide one integer by another, you get a result (which some call a quotient) and a remainder. For example, 14 divided by 4 yields 3 with a remainder of 2 (or with 2 left over). The % operation gives the remainder—that is, the amount left over after doing the division. So 14 / 4 is 3 and 14 % 4 is 2, because 14 divided by 4 is 3 with 2 left over. The % operator is called the **remainder operator**.

The % operator has more applications than you might at first suspect. It allows your program to count by 2s, 3s, or any other number. For example, if you want to do something to every other integer, you need to know whether the integer is even or odd. An integer n is even if n % 2 is zero, and it is odd if n % 2 is not zero. Similarly, if you want your program to do something to every third integer, you test whether the integer n is divisible by 3. It will be if n % 3 is zero.

 Programming Tip: To make your arithmetic expressions more readable, place a space on both sides of each binary operator.

Parentheses and Precedence Rules

A.24   You can use parentheses to group portions of an arithmetic expression in the same way that you use parentheses in algebra and arithmetic. With the aid of parentheses, you can indicate which operations are performed first, second, and so forth. For example, consider the following two expressions that differ only in the positioning of their parentheses:

```
(cost + tax) * discount
cost + (tax * discount)
```

To evaluate the first expression, the computer first adds cost and tax and then multiplies the result by discount. To evaluate the second expression, it multiplies tax by discount and then adds the result to cost. If you use some numbers for the values of the variables and carry out the two evaluations, you will see that they produce different results.

If you omit parentheses, as in the assignment statement

```
total = cost + tax * discount;
```

multiplication occurs before addition. Thus, the previous statement is equivalent to

```
total = cost + (tax * discount);
```

More generally, when the order of operations is not determined by parentheses, the operations occur in an order determined by the following **precedence rules**:

Note: Precedence of arithmetic operators
Arithmetic operators in an expression execute in the following order:
The unary operators +, −
The binary operators *, /, %
The binary operators +, −

Operators that are listed higher on the list are said to have **higher precedence**. Operators of higher precedence execute before operators of lower precedence, unless parentheses override this order. Operators at the same level have the same precedence. When two operators have equal precedence, the operations are performed using this convention:

Note: Binary operators of equal precedence in an expression are performed in left-to-right order.

Increment and Decrement Operators

A.25   The increment and decrement operators increase or decrease the value of a variable by 1. The **increment operator** is written as two plus signs, ++. For example, the following Java statement will increase the value of the variable `count` by 1:

```
count++;
```

If the variable `count` has the value 5 before this statement is executed, it will have the value 6 after the statement is executed. Thus, this statement is equivalent to

```
count = count + 1;
```

You can use the increment operator with variables of any numeric type, but it is used most often with variables of an integer type such as `int`.

The **decrement operator** is similar, except that it subtracts 1 rather than adds 1 to the value of the variable. The decrement operator is written as two minus signs, −−. For example, the following will decrease the value of the variable `count` by 1:

```
count--;
```

If the variable `count` has the value 5 before this statement is executed, it will have the value 4 after the statement is executed. This statement is equivalent to

```
count = count - 1;
```

A.26   You can use the increment and decrement operators within expressions, but when you do, the increment operator or the decrement operator changes the value of the variable it is applied to and returns a value. Although we do not recommend using the increment and decrement operators in expressions, you should be familiar with them used in this way, because you might see this use in other people's code.

In expressions, you can place the ++ or −− either before or after a variable, but your choice affects the result. For example, consider the code

```
int n = 3;
int m = 4;
int result = n * (++m);
```

After this code executes, the value of n is unchanged at 3, the value of m is 5, and the value of result is 15. Thus, ++m changes the value of m and returns that changed value to the multiply operator.

In the previous example, we placed the increment operator before the variable m. If we place it after the variable m, something slightly different happens. Consider the code

```java
int n = 3;
int m = 4;
int result = n * (m++);
```

Now, after the code executes, the value of n is 3 and the value of m is 5, just as in the previous example. However, the value of result is 12, not 15. What happened?

The two expressions n * (++m) and n * (m++) both increase the value of m by 1, but the first expression increases the value of m *before* it does the multiplication, whereas the second expression increases the value of m *after* it does the multiplication. Both ++m and m++ have the same effect on the final value of m, but when we use them as part of an arithmetic expression, they give a different value to the expression.

Similarly, both --m and m-- have the same effect on the final value of m, but when we use them as part of an arithmetic expression, they give a different value to the expression. If the -- is *before* the m, the value of m is decreased *before* its value is used in the expression. If the -- is *after* the m, the value of m is decreased *after* its value is used in the expression.

The increment and decrement operators can be applied only to variables. They cannot be applied to constants or to entire, more complicated arithmetic expressions.

Programming Tip: To avoid errors and confusing code, use the operator ++ or -- only in a statement that involves one variable and no other operators.

Special Assignment Operators

A.27   You can combine the simple assignment operator (=) with an arithmetic operator, such as +, to produce a kind of special-purpose assignment operator. For example, the following will increase the value of the variable amount by 5:

```java
amount += 5;
```

This is really just a shorthand for

```java
amount = amount + 5;
```

You can do the same thing with any of the other arithmetic operators -, *, /, and %. For example, the statement

```java
amount *= 25;
```

is equivalent to

```java
amount = amount * 25;
```

Named Constants

A.28   You probably recognize the number 3.14159 as the approximate value of *pi*, the number that is used in many circle calculations and that is often written as π. However, when you see 3.14159, you might not be sure that it is π and not some other number; somebody other than you might have no idea of where the number 3.14159 came from. To avoid such confusion, you should always give a name to constants, such as 3.14159, and use the name instead of writing out the number. For example, we might give the number 3.14159 the name `PI`. Then the assignment statement

```
area = 3.14159 * radius * radius;
```

could be written more clearly as

```
area = PI * radius * radius;
```

How do you give a number, or other constant, a name like `PI`? You could use a variable named `PI` and initialize it to the desired value 3.14159. But then you might inadvertently change the value of this variable. However, Java provides a mechanism that allows you to define and initialize a variable and moreover fix the variable's value so it cannot be changed. The syntax is

```
public static final type name = constant;
```

For example, the statement

```
public static final double PI = 3.14159;
```

gives the name `PI` to the constant 3.14159. The part

```
double PI = 3.14159;
```

simply declares `PI` as a variable and initializes it to 3.14159. The word `public` says that there are no restrictions on where we can use the name `PI`. The word `static` defines one copy of `PI` that every object of the class can access instead of having its own copy of `PI`. The word `final` means that the value 3.14159 is the *final* value assigned to `PI` or, to phrase it another way, it means that the program cannot change the value of `PI`. Chapter 1 provides more details about `static` and `final`.

It is a good practice to place named constants near the beginning of a class and outside of any method definitions. That way, your named constants are handy in case you need to modify them. You might, for example, want to change the number of digits you provide for a constant.

Note: The class `Math` in the Java Class Library defines a static named constant `PI` just as we did in this segment, but with more decimal places. The following segment describes this class and shows how to access `PI`. You should use `Math`'s `PI` instead of defining your own.

Programming Tip: Programmers typically use all uppercase letters when naming constants to distinguish constants from ordinary variables. They use an underscore as a separator in multi-word names. For example, `FEET_PER_MILE` follows this convention.

The Class `Math`

A.29   The class `Math` in the package `java.lang` of the Java Class Library provides a number of standard mathematical methods. These methods are **static methods**. (Segment 1.28 of Chapter 1 discusses static methods in more detail.) When you invoke a static method, you write the class name—`Math`, in this case—a dot, the name of the method, and a pair of parentheses. Using the name of a class to invoke a method is not typical. Ordinarily, you use the name of an object to invoke a method.

     Most `Math` methods require that you specify items within the pair of parentheses. As we noted earlier in this appendix, these items are called arguments to the method. Thus, a typical invocation of a method in this class has the form `Math.`*method_name*`(`*arguments*`)`.

     You can invoke the method in an assignment statement, such as

> *variable* `= Math.`*method_name*`(`*arguments*`);`

or embed it within an arithmetic expression. That is, you can use `Math.`*method_name*`(`*arguments*`)` anyplace that you can use a variable of a primitive data type. Figure A-2 describes some of the available methods in this class.

     The class `Math` also has two predefined named constants. `E` is the base of the natural logarithm system—often written e in mathematical formulas—and is approximately 2.72. `PI` is used in calculations involving circular geometric figures—often written π in mathematical formulas—and is approximately 3.14159. Because these constants are defined in the class `Math`, you use them by writing `Math.E` and `Math.PI`.

Simple Input and Output Using the Keyboard and Screen

The input and output of data is usually referred to as **I/O**. A Java program can perform I/O in many different ways. In this section, we present some ways to handle simple text input that we type at the keyboard and simple text output displayed on the screen.

Screen Output

A.30   Statements like

```
System.out.println("Enter a whole number from 1 to 99.");
```

and

```
System.out.println(quarters + " quarters");
```

send output to the display screen. As we mentioned near the beginning of this appendix, `System.out` is an object within the class `System`, which is a class in the Java Class Library. This object has `println` as one of its methods. So the preceding output statements are calls to the method `println` of the object `System.out`. You simply follow `System.out.println` with a pair of parentheses that contain what you want to display. You end the statement with a semicolon.

     Within the parentheses can be strings of text in double quotes, like `"Enter a whole number from 1 to 99."`, variables like `quarters`, numbers like 5 or 7.3, and almost any other object or value. To display more than one thing, simply place a plus sign between them. For example,

```
System.out.println("Lucky number = " + 13 +
                   "Secret number = " + number);
```

Figure A-2   Some methods in the class `Math`

In each of the following methods, the argument and the return value are `double`:

`Math.cbrt(x)`	Returns the cube root of x.
`Math.ceil(x)`	Returns the nearest whole number that is $\geq x$.
`Math.cos(x)`	Returns the trigonometric cosine of the angle x in radians.
`Math.exp(x)`	Returns e^x.
`Math.floor(x)`	Returns the nearest whole number that is $\leq x$.
`Math.hypot(x, y)`	Returns the square root of the sum $x^2 + y^2$.
`Math.log(x)`	Returns the natural (base e) logarithm of x.
`Math.log10(x)`	Returns the base 10 logarithm of x.
`Math.pow(x, y)`	Returns x^y.
`Math.random()`	Returns a random number that is ≥ 0 but < 1.
`Math.sin(x)`	Returns the trigonometric sine of the angle x in radians.
`Math.sqrt(x)`	Returns the square root of x, assuming that $x \geq 0$.
`Math.tan(x)`	Returns the trigonometric tangent of the angle x in radians.
`Math.toDegrees(x)`	Returns an angle in degrees equivalent to the angle x in radians.
`Math.toRadians(x)`	Returns an angle in radians equivalent to the angle x in degrees.

In each of the following methods, the argument and the return value have the same type—either `int`, `long`, `float`, or `double`:

`Math.abs(x)`	Returns the absolute value of x.
`Math.max(x, y)`	Returns the larger of x and y.
`Math.min(x, y)`	Returns the smaller of x and y.
`Math.round(x)`	Returns the nearest whole number to x. If x is `float`, returns an `int`; if x is `double`, returns a `long`.

If the value of number is 7, the output will be

Lucky number = 13Secret number = 7

Notice also that no spaces are added. If we want a space between the 13 and the word "Secret" in the preceding output—and we probably do—we should add a space to the beginning of the string "Secret number = " so that it becomes " Secret number = ".

Notice that you use double quotes, not single quotes, and that the opening and closing quotes are the same symbol. Finally, notice that you can place the statement on two lines if it is too long. However, you should break the line before or after a + sign, not in the middle of a quoted string or a variable name. You also should indent the second line to make the entire statement easier to read.

Later, in the section about the class String, you will see that the + operator joins, or **concatenates**, two strings. In the preceding System.out.println statement, Java converts the number 13 to the string "13". Likewise, it converts the integer 7 in the variable number to the string "7". Then the + operator joins the strings and the System.out.println statement displays the result. You do need to be a bit careful, however. If you write a + between two numeric values or variables, they will be added rather than concatenated.

You can also use the println method to display the value of a String variable, as illustrated by the following:

```
String greeting = "Hello Programmers!";
System.out.println(greeting);
```

This will cause the following to be written on the screen.

Hello Programmers!

A.31   Every invocation of println ends a line of output. If you want the output from two or more output statements to appear on a single line, use print instead of println. For example,

```
System.out.print("One, two,");
System.out.print(" buckle my shoe.");
System.out.println(" Three, four,");
System.out.println("shut the door.");
```

will produce the following output:

One, two, buckle my shoe. Three, four,
shut the door.

Notice that a new line is not started until you use println, rather than print. Also notice that the new line starts *after* displaying the items specified in the println statement. This is the only difference between print and println.

Keyboard Input Using the Class Scanner

A.32   A Java program can read data from either the keyboard or another source such as a disk, and place it into memory. The Java Class Library provides the class Scanner for this purpose. Here, we will use the methods in Scanner to read data typed at the keyboard and place it into variables that we specify.

As we noted earlier, the class `Scanner` is in the package `java.util`. To use `Scanner` in your program, you must **import** it from this package by writing the following `import` statement before the rest of your program:

```
import java.util.Scanner;
```

Before you can use any of the methods in `Scanner`, you must create a `Scanner` object by writing a statement such as

```
Scanner keyboard = new Scanner(System.in);
```

The variable `keyboard`—which could be any variable of your choosing—is assigned a `Scanner` object that is associated with the input device that `System.in` represents. This device by convention is the keyboard. The variable `keyboard` has a class type.

A.33 `Scanner` provides several methods that read input data. You can use any of these methods by writing a statement that has the following form, where `keyboard` is the `Scanner` object that we defined previously:

variable = `keyboard.`*method_name*`();`

The named method reads a value from the keyboard and returns it. That is, the expression `keyboard.`*method_name*`()` represents the value that was read. The previous statement then assigns this value to the indicated variable.

You can read integers and real numbers by using the following expressions:

```
keyboard.nextInt()
```
Returns the next integer encountered in the input data.

```
keyboard.nextDouble()
```
Returns the next real number encountered in the input data.

Each of these expressions ignores any **white space** that might precede or follow the number typed at the keyboard. Whitespace characters are the characters that appear as spaces when printed on paper or displayed on the screen. The blank-space character is likely the only white space character that will concern us at first, but the start of a new line and the tab symbol are also white space characters.

A.34   **Example.** To read an integer from the keyboard, you can write a statement such as

```
size = keyboard.nextInt();
```

where `size` has been declared previously as an `int` variable. The user of your program would type an integer and press the Enter, or Return, key. The value is read by the method `nextInt`, returned, and assigned to the variable `size`.

Typically, you should display a message, or **prompt**, for the user to enter data. For example, your program might contain the following statements:

```
System.out.println("What is your age?");
int age = keyboard.nextInt();
```

Whatever the user types appears in the same window as the prompt. Here, the prompt would appear on one line and the user would type his or her age on the next.

A.35

Example. To read a real number from the keyboard, you can write statements such as

```
System.out.print("Enter the area of your room in square feet: ");
double area = keyboard.nextDouble();
```

After the user types a real number at the keyboard and presses the Enter key, the value of the number is assigned to the variable `area`. Since we have used `print` instead of `println`, both the prompt and the input data appear on the same line on the display.

A.36

Example. You can read more than one value per line of input. For example,

```
System.out.println("Please enter your height in feet and inches:");
int feet = keyboard.nextInt();
int inches = keyboard.nextInt();
```

The user could type either

```
6    2
```

on one line or

```
6
2
```

on two lines. In either case, `feet` is 6 and `inches` is 2.

Note: **Streams**

The characters that a user types at the keyboard are directed into the memory assigned to your program by an object known as an **input stream**. The name of the input stream associated with the keyboard is `System.in`. Likewise, an **output stream** is an object that directs data from your program to an output device. `System.out` is such an object, directing characters to a display.

A.37

More input methods. The class `Scanner` includes the following method to read a string:

```
nextLine()
```
Returns the string that appears next in the input data.

For example, if `keyboard` is defined as shown earlier, the statement

```
String message = keyboard.nextLine();
```

reads the entire string that the user types before pressing the Enter key—including any spaces—and assigns it to the variable `message`.

The method `next` in the class `Scanner` reads the next group of contiguous characters that are not white space and returns it as a string. For example, you can use this method to read the next word that appears in the input data, as follows:

```
String word = keyboard.next();
```

We used `next` in Segment A.3 to read the user's yes or no response.

The `Scanner` methods we've looked at—`nextInt`, `nextDouble`, `nextLine`, and `next`—often are invoked in simple assignment statements, although that is not necessary. Since each method returns a value, you can call it within an arithmetic expression, for example.

The if-else Statement

A.38   In programs, as in everyday life, things can sometimes go in one of two different ways. If you have money in your checking account, some banks will pay you a little interest. On the other hand, if you have overdrawn your checking account, you will be charged a penalty. This might be reflected in the bank's accounting program by the following Java statement, known as an **if-else statement**:

```
if (balance >= 0)
   balance = balance + (INTEREST_RATE * balance) / 12;
else
   balance = balance - OVERDRAWN_PENALTY;
```

The two-symbol operator >= means "greater than or equal to" in Java. We use two symbols because the one-character symbol ≥ is not on the keyboard.

The meaning of an if-else statement is really just the meaning it would have if read as an English sentence. When your program executes an if-else statement, it first checks the expression in parentheses after the if. This expression must evaluate to either true or false. If it is true, the statement after the if is executed. If the expression is false, the statement after the else is executed. In the preceding example, if balance is positive or zero, the following action occurs:

```
balance = balance + (INTEREST_RATE * balance) / 12;
```

(We divide by 12 because the interest is for only 1 of 12 months.) On the other hand, if the value of balance is negative, the following is executed instead:

```
balance = balance - OVERDRAWN_PENALTY;
```

The indentation in the if-else statement is conventional as an aid in reading the statement; it does not affect the statement's meaning.

A.39   If you want to include more than one statement in either of the two portions of the if-else statement, you simply enclose the statements in braces, as in the following example:

```
if (balance >= 0)
{
   System.out.println("Good for you. You earned interest.");
   balance = balance + (INTEREST_RATE * balance) / 12;
}
else
{
   System.out.println("You will be charged a penalty.");
   balance = balance - OVERDRAWN_PENALTY;
} // end if
```

When you enclose several statements within braces, you get one larger statement called a **compound statement**. Compound statements are seldom used by themselves but often are used as substatements of a larger statement such as an if-else statement.

Programming Tip: Some programmers always use compound statements within other statements such as if-else, even when only a single statement appears between the braces. Doing so makes it easier to add another statement to the compound statement, but more importantly, it avoids the error that would occur if you forgot to add the braces. We encourage you to follow this convention, even though we do not do so in this book to save space.

A.40   You can omit the `else` part. If you do, nothing happens when the tested expression is false. For example, if your bank does not charge an overdraft penalty, the statement would be the following, instead of the previous one:

```
if (balance >= 0)
{
  System.out.println("Good for you. You earned interest.");
  balance = balance + (INTEREST_RATE * balance) / 12;
} // end if
```

If `balance` is negative, the statement after the closing brace executes next.

Boolean Expressions

A.41   A **boolean expression** is an expression that is either true or false. The expression

```
balance >= 0
```

that we used in the previous `if-else` statement is an example of a simple boolean expression. Such expressions compare two things, like numbers, variables, or other expressions. Figure A-3 shows the various Java **comparison operators** you can use to compare two expressions.

Figure A-3   Java comparison operators

Math Notation	Name	Java Operator	Java Examples
≥	Greater than or equal to	`>=`	`points >= 60`
≤	Less than or equal to	`<=`	`expenses <= income`
>	Greater than	`>`	`expenses > income`
<	Less than	`<`	`pressure < max`
=	Equal to	`==`	`balance == 0` `answer == 'y'`
≠	Not equal to	`!=`	`income != tax` `answer != 'y'`

A.42   **Logical operators.** Often, when you write an `if-else` statement, you will want to use a boolean expression that is more complicated than a simple comparison. You can form more-complicated boolean expressions from simpler ones by joining expressions with either the Java version of "and," which is &&, or the Java version of "or," which is ||. For example, consider the following:

```
if ((pressure > min) && (pressure < max))
  System.out.println("Pressure is OK.");
else
  System.out.println("Warning: Pressure is out of range.");
```

If the value of `pressure` is greater than `min`, *and* the value of `pressure` is less than `max`, the output will be

> Pressure is OK.

Otherwise, the output is

> Warning: Pressure is out of range.

Note that you *cannot* use a string of inequalities in Java, like the following:

> `min < pressure < max` ◀———Illegal!

Instead, you must express each inequality separately and connect them with `&&`, as follows:

> `(pressure > min) && (pressure < max)`

The parentheses in the previous expression are not necessary, but we typically include them. The parentheses that surround the entire expression in an `if-else` statement are required, however.

The binary operators `&&` and `||` together with the unary operator `!` are **logical operators**. We look at each of them next.

A.43 **The operator `&&`.** When you form a larger boolean expression by connecting two smaller expressions with `&&`, the entire larger expression is true provided that both of the smaller expressions are true. Thus, if at least one of `pressure > min` and `pressure < max` is false, the larger expression is false. Moreover, if the first part of the larger expression is false, the second part is ignored, since the larger expression must be false regardless of the value of the second part. For example, if `pressure` is less than `min`, we know that

> `(pressure > min) && (pressure < max)`

is false without looking at `pressure < max`.

A.44 **The operator `||`.** You also can use `||` to form a larger boolean expression from smaller ones in the same way that you use `&&`, but with different results. The meaning is essentially the same as the English word "or." For example, consider

```
if ((salary > expenses) || (salary + savings > expenses))
   System.out.println("Solvent");
else
   System.out.println("Bankrupt");
```

If the value of `salary` is greater than the value of `expenses` *or* the value of `salary + savings` is greater than the value of `expenses`—or both—the output will be

> Solvent

Otherwise, the output will be

> Bankrupt

The entire larger expression is true if either of the smaller expressions is true. Moreover, if the first part of the larger expression is true, the second part is ignored, since the larger expression must be true regardless of the value of the second part. For example, if `salary` is greater than `expenses`, we know that

> `(salary > expenses) || (salary + savings > expenses)`

is true without looking at `salary + savings > expenses`.

You use parentheses in expressions containing the || operator in the same way that you use them with &&.

Note: Short-circuit evaluation

When two boolean expressions are joined by either && or ||, the second expression is not evaluated if the value of the first expression implies the value of the entire expression. Such is the case if the first expression is false when the operator is && or true when the operator is ||. This behavior is known as the **short-circuit evaluation** of a boolean expression.

Besides saving execution time, short-circuit evaluation can prevent execution errors. For example, the following statement prevents a division by zero:

```
if ((count != 0) && (sum / count > minimum))
```

If count is zero, the expression count != 0 is false. Thus, the expression sum / count > minimum is not evaluated, thereby avoiding the erroneous division.

A.45   **The operator !.** You can negate a boolean expression by preceding it with the operator !. For example, the expression

```
!(number >= min)
```

has the same meaning as the expression

```
number < min
```

In this case, you can and should avoid using !.

Sometimes, however, the use of ! makes perfect sense. For example, if you have two strings that should be the same for normal processing to continue, you would compare them and issue a warning if they are not equal. Later, in the section about the class String, you will see that you use the equals method to compare two strings. For example,

```
stringOne.equals(stringTwo)
```

is true if the strings stringOne and stringTwo are equal. But if we want to know whether these strings are not equal, we could write

```
if (!stringOne.equals(stringTwo))
    System.out.println("Warning: The strings are not the same.");
```

The precedence of the boolean operators in relation to each other and to the arithmetic operators follows:

Note: Precedence of a selection of Java operators

Operators in the same expression execute in the following order:
The unary operators +, -, !
The binary arithmetic operators *, /, %
The binary arithmetic operators +, -
The comparison operators <, >, <=, >=
The comparison operators ==, !=
The logical operator &&
The logical operator ||

Nested Statements

A.46   Notice that an if-else statement contains smaller statements within it. These smaller statements can be any sort of Java statements. In particular, you can use one if-else statement within another if-else statement to get **nested** if-else statements, as illustrated by the following:

```java
if (balance >= 0)
  if (INTEREST_RATE >= 0)
    balance = balance + (INTEREST_RATE * balance) / 12;
  else
    System.out.println("Cannot have a negative interest.");
else
  balance = balance - OVERDRAWN_PENALTY;
```

If the value of balance is greater than or equal to zero, the entire following if-else statement is executed:

```java
if (INTEREST_RATE >= 0)
  balance = balance + (INTEREST_RATE * balance) / 12;
else
  System.out.println("Cannot have a negative interest.");
```

When writing nested if-else statements, you may sometimes become confused about which if goes with which else. To eliminate this confusion, you can add braces as follows:

```java
if (balance >= 0)
{
  if (INTEREST_RATE >= 0)
    balance = balance + (INTEREST_RATE * balance) / 12;
  else
    System.out.println("Cannot have a negative interest.");
}
else
  balance = balance - OVERDRAWN_PENALTY;
```

Here, the braces are an aid to clarity but are not, strictly speaking, needed. In other cases, they are needed. While you should use indentation to indicate your intentions, remember that it is ignored by the compiler.

A.47   If you omit an else, things get a bit trickier. The following two if-else statements differ only in that one has a pair of braces, but they do not have the same meaning:

```java
// First Version
if (balance >= 0)
{
  if (INTEREST_RATE >= 0)
    balance = balance + (INTEREST_RATE * balance) / 12;
}
else
  balance = balance - OVERDRAWN_PENALTY;

// Second Version
if (balance >= 0)
  if (INTEREST_RATE >= 0)
    balance = balance + (INTEREST_RATE * balance) / 12;
else
  balance = balance - OVERDRAWN_PENALTY;
```

In the second version, without braces, the `else` is paired with the second `if`, not the first one, as the indentation leads us to believe. Thus, the meaning is

```
// Equivalent to Second Version
if (balance >= 0)
{
  if (INTEREST_RATE >= 0)
    balance = balance + (INTEREST_RATE * balance) / 12;
  else
    balance = balance - OVERDRAWN_PENALTY;
}
```

To clarify the difference a bit more, consider what happens when `balance` is less than zero. The first version causes the following action:

```
balance = balance - OVERDRAWN_PENALTY;
```

However, the second version takes no action.

Note: In an `if-else` statement, each `else` is paired with the nearest previous unmatched `if`.

Programming Tip: Indentation within an `if-else` statement does not affect the action of the statement. For clarity, you should use indentation that matches the logic of the statement.

Multiway `if-else` Statements

A.48   Since an `if-else` statement has two outcomes, and each of these two outcomes can have an `if-else` statement with two outcomes, you can use nested `if-else` statements to produce any number of possible effects. Convention provides a standard way of doing this. Let's start with an example.

Suppose `balance` is a variable that holds your checking account balance and you want to know whether your balance is positive, negative (overdrawn), or zero. To avoid any questions about accuracy, let's assume that `balance` is of type `int`—that is, `balance` is the number of dollars in your account, with the cents ignored. To find out if your balance is positive, negative, or zero, you could use the following nested `if-else` statement:

```
if (balance > 0)
  System.out.println("Positive balance");
else if (balance < 0)
  System.out.println("Negative balance");
else if (balance == 0)
  System.out.println("Zero balance");
```

This is really an ordinary nested `if-else` statement, but it is indented differently than before. The indentation reflects the logic more clearly and is preferred. Although this is not a separate kind of `if-else` statement, we call this nested construction a **multiway `if-else` statement**.

When a multiway `if-else` statement is executed, the computer tests the boolean expressions one after the other, starting from the top. When it finds the first true boolean expression, it executes the statement after the expression. The rest of the if-else statement is ignored. For example, if balance is greater than zero, the preceding statements will display

Positive balance

Exactly one of the three possible messages will be displayed, depending on the value of the variable balance.

A.49   The previous example has three possibilities, but you can have any number of possibilities by adding more else-if parts. In this example, the possibilities are **mutually exclusive**. That is, only one of the three possibilities can actually occur for any given value of balance. However, you can use any boolean expressions, even if they are not mutually exclusive. If more than one boolean expression is true, only the action associated with the first true boolean expression is executed. A multiway if-else statement never performs more than one action.

If none of the boolean expressions is true, nothing happens. However, it is a good practice to add an else clause—without any if—at the end, to be executed in case none of the boolean expressions is true. In fact, we can rewrite our previous example in this way. We know that if balance is neither positive nor negative, it must be zero. So we do not need the test

```
if (balance == 0)
```

Thus, we can and should write the previous if-else statement as

```
if (balance > 0)
    System.out.println("Positive balance");
else if (balance < 0)
    System.out.println("Negative balance");
else
    System.out.println("Zero balance");
```

The Conditional Operator *(Optional)*

A.50   To allow compatibility with older programming styles, Java includes an operator that is a notational variant on certain forms of the if-else statement. A **conditional operator expression** consists of a boolean expression followed by a question mark and two expressions separated by a colon. For example, the expression on the right side of the assignment operator in the following statement is a conditional operator expression:

```
max = (n1 > n2) ? n1 : n2;
```

The ? and : together form a **ternary operator** that has three operands and is known as the **conditional operator**. If the boolean expression is true, the value of the first of the two expressions is returned; otherwise, the value of the second of the two expression is returned. Thus, the logic of this example is equivalent to

```
if (n1 > n2)
    max = n1;
else
    max = n2;
```

This book will not use conditional operator expressions, as they are less clear than equivalent `if-else` statements. If you decide to use them in your program, realize that not everyone will know their meaning.

The `switch` Statement

A.51   Multiway `if-else` statements can become unwieldy when you must choose from among many possible courses of action. If the choice is based on the value of an integer or character expression, the **switch statement** can make your code easier to read.

The `switch` statement begins with the word `switch` followed by an expression in parentheses. This expression is called the **controlling expression**. Its value must be of type `int`, `char`, `byte`, or `short`. The `switch` statement in the following example determines the price of a ticket according to the location of the seat in a theater. An integer code that indicates the seat location is the controlling expression:

```java
int seatLocationCode;
double price;
< Code here assigns a value to seatLocationCode >
. . .
switch (seatLocationCode)
{
  case 1:
    System.out.println("Balcony.");
    price = 15.00;
    break;
  case 2:
    System.out.println("Mezzanine.");
    price = 30.00;
    break;
  case 3:
    System.out.println("Orchestra.");
    price = 40.00;
    break;
  default:
    System.out.println("Unknown ticket code.");
    break;
} // end switch
```

The `switch` statement contains a list of cases, each consisting of the reserved word `case`, a constant, a colon, and a list of statements that are the actions for the case. The constant after the word `case` is called a **case label**. When the `switch` statement executes, the controlling expression — in this example, `seatLocationCode` — is evaluated. The list of alternative cases is searched until a case label that matches the current value of the controlling expression is found. Then the action associated with that label is executed. You are not allowed to have duplicate case labels, as that would be ambiguous.

If no match is found, the case labeled `default` is executed. The `default` case is optional. If there is no `default` case, and no match is found to any of the cases, no action takes place. Although the `default` case is optional, we encourage you to always use it. If you think your cases cover all the possibilities without a `default` case, you can insert an error message or an assertion as the `default` case. You never know when you might have missed some obscure case.

Notice that the action for each case in the previous example ends with a **break statement**. If you omit the break statement, the action just continues with the statements in the next case until it reaches either a break statement or the end of the switch statement. Sometimes this feature is desirable, but sometimes omitting the break statement causes unwanted results.

Note: The controlling expression in a switch statement provides an entry point to a case within the statement. Execution continues from this point until it reaches either a break statement or the end of the switch.

A.52   At times, you will want to take the same action in more than one case. You can list cases one after the other so that they all apply to the same action. In the following example, we have changed the seat location code to a character instead of an integer. A code of *B* or *b*, for example, indicates a balcony seat:

```
char seatLocationCode;
double price;
< Code here assigns a value to seatLocationCode >
. . .
switch (seatLocationCode)
{
  case 'B':
  case 'b':
    System.out.println("Balcony.");
    price = 15.00;
    break;
  case 'M': case 'm':
    System.out.println("Mezzanine.");
    price = 30.00;
    break;
  case 'O': case 'o':
    System.out.println("Orchestra.");
    price = 40.00;
    break;
  default:
    System.out.println("Unknown ticket code.");
    break;
} // end switch
```

The first case, *B*, has no break statement; in fact, the case has no action statements at all. Execution continues with the case for *b*, as desired. Note that we have written the cases in two ways to show two common programming styles.

The controlling expression in a switch statement need not be a single variable. It can be a more complicated expression, but it must evaluate to a single value. The expression cannot indicate a range of values. That is, the expression cannot be a boolean expression like the ones you use in an if-else statement. Thus, if you want to take one action when the controlling expression has values from 1 to 10 and a second action for values from 11 to 20, you would need a case label for each value. In situations like this, a switch statement would be harder to write than an if-else statement.

Programming Tip: **Omitting a break statement**

If you test a program that contains a `switch` statement and it executes two cases when you expect it to execute only one case, you probably have forgotten to include a `break` statement where one is needed.

Enumerations

A.53   To compute a student's quality-point average—also known as a grade-point average—a program could assign the number of quality points for a given letter grade to the `double` variable `quality-Points`. You could use a `char` variable `grade` for the letter grade, but then it could contain any character, not just the letters A, B, C, D, and F. Instead, to restrict the contents of `grade` to the values you specify, you could declare it as an **enumerated data type**, or **enumeration**. An enumeration itemizes the values that a variable can have.

For example, the following statement defines `LetterGrade` as an enumeration:

```
enum LetterGrade {A, B, C, D, F}
```

`LetterGrade` behaves as a class type, so we can declare `grade` to have this type, as follows:

```
LetterGrade grade;
```

The items listed between the braces in the definition of `LetterGrade` are objects that `grade` can reference. For example, you can write

```
grade = LetterGrade.A;
```

to assign `A` to `grade`. Assigning a value other than `A, B, C, D,` or `F` to `grade` will cause a syntax error. These values behave as static constants. You qualify each of them with the name of the enumeration just as you qualify the constant `PI` with the name of its class `Math`.

Note: An enumeration is actually a class. Therefore, you cannot define an enumeration within a method. Instead, define enumerations outside of any method definitions, preferably near the beginning of your class. Also, note that no semicolon follows an enumeration's definition. Writing one, however, will not cause a syntax error; the semicolon will simply be ignored.

A.54   **Example.** You can use a `switch` statement with a variable whose data type is an enumeration. For example, if we define `LetterGrade` and `grade` as in the previous segment, the following `switch` statement assigns the correct number of quality points to the `double` variable `qualityPoints`:

```
switch (grade)
{
    case A:
        qualityPoints = 4.0;
        break;
    case B:
        qualityPoints = 3.0;
        break;
```

```
        case C:
            qualityPoints = 2.0;
            break;
        case D:
            qualityPoints = 1.0;
            break;
        case F:
            qualityPoints = 0.0;
            break;
        default:
            qualityPoints = -9.0;
    } // end switch
```

Since the data type of the expression in the `switch` statement is an enumeration, the case labels are assumed to belong to that enumeration without qualification. In fact, writing `case LetterGrade.A`, for example, is a syntax error. However, if you need to reference one of the enumerated values elsewhere within the `switch` statement, you must qualify it.

Since we know that `grade` cannot have values other than those in the enumeration, a default case is unnecessary. However, if you choose to omit the default case, you must assign a value to `qualityPoints` prior to the `switch` statement to avoid a syntax error. Without this initialization, the compiler would think it possible for `qualityPoints` to remain uninitialized after the `switch` statement.

A.55 When the compiler encounters an enumeration, it creates a class that has several methods. Among them is the method `ordinal`, which you can use to access the **ordinal value** of an object within an enumeration. These values begin at zero. Thus, in `LetterGrade`, the ordinal values of A and F are 0 and 4, respectively. For example, if you have the following assignment:

```
    LetterGrade yourGrade = LetterGrade.A;
```

the expression

```
    yourGrade.ordinal()
```

returns 0. Likewise, the expression

```
    LetterGrade.B.ordinal()
```

returns 1.

The method `equals` tests whether `yourGrade` is equal to a given object within the enumeration. For example, you might write

```
    if (yourGrade.equals(LetterGrade.A))
        System.out.println("Congratulations, your grade is A!");
```

Finally, the static method `valueOf` takes a string and returns a matching object in a given enumeration. For example, the expression

```
    LetterGrade.valueOf("A")
```

returns `LetterGrade.A`. The string passed to `valueOf` must match the name of the constant exactly.

Chapter 1 discusses enumerations further, beginning at Segment 1.30.

Scope

A.56   The **scope** of a variable (or a named constant) is the portion of a program in which the variable is available. That is, a variable does not exist outside of its scope. A variable's scope begins at its declaration and ends at the closing brace of the pair of braces that enclose the variable's declaration.

For example, consider the following statements that involve two variables, `counter` and `greeting`:

```
{
   // counter and greeting are not available here
   . . .
   int counter = 1;
   // counter is available here
   . . .
   {
      String greeting = "Hello!";
      // both greeting and counter are available here
      . . .
   } // end scope of greeting
   . . .
   // only counter is available here
   . . .
} // end scope of counter
```

The variable `counter` is available anywhere after its declaration. The variable `greeting` is available only within the inner pair of braces.

The concept of scope applies to every pair of braces within a Java program, regardless of whether they delineate the definition of a class or a method, appear within an `if-else` statement or `switch` statement, or appear within the loops described in the next section.

Loops

A.57   Programs often need to repeat some action. For example, a grading program would contain some code that assigns a letter grade to a student based on the student's scores on assignments and exams. To assign grades to the entire class, the program would repeat this action for each student in the class. A portion of a program that repeats a statement or group of statements is called a **loop**. The statement (or group of statements) to be repeated in a loop is called the **body** of the loop. Each repetition of the loop body is called an **iteration** of the loop.

When you design a loop, you need to decide what action the body of the loop should take and when the loop should stop repeating this action. Once you have made these choices, you can pick one of three Java statements to implement the loop: the `while` statement, the `for` statement, or the do-`while` statement.

The `while` Statement

A.58   One way to construct a loop in Java is with a **`while` statement**, which is also known as a **`while` loop**. A `while` statement repeats its action again and again until a controlling boolean expression becomes false. That is, the loop is repeated *while* the controlling boolean expression is true. The general form of a `while` statement is

while (*expression*)
  statement;

The `while` loop starts with the reserved word `while` followed by a boolean expression in parentheses. The loop body is a statement, typically a compound statement enclosed in braces {}. The loop body is repeated while the boolean expression is true. The loop body normally contains some action that can change the value of the boolean expression from true to false and so end the loop.

For example, the following `while` statement displays the integers from 1 to a given integer `number`:

```
int number;
. . . // assign a value to number here
int count = 1;
while (count <= number)
{
   System.out.println(count);
   count++;
} // end while
```

Let's suppose that `number` is 2. The variable `count` begins at 1. Since the boolean expression `count <= number` is true at this point, the body of the loop executes. Thus, 1 is displayed and then `count` becomes 2. The expression `count <= number` is still true, so the loop's body executes a second time, displaying 2 and incrementing `count` to 3. Now `count <= number` is false, so the `while` loop ends. Execution continues with the statement, if any, that follows the loop.

Notice that if `number` is zero or negative in the previous example, nothing is displayed. The body of the loop would not execute at all, since `count`, which is 1, would be greater than `number`.

Programming Tip: A `while` loop can perform zero iterations
The body of a `while` loop can execute zero times. When a `while` loop executes, its first action is to check the value of the boolean expression. If the boolean expression is false, the loop body is not executed even one time. Perhaps the loop adds up the sum of all your expenses for the day. If you did not go shopping on a given day, you do not want the loop body to execute at all.

A.59   **Infinite loops.** A common program bug is a loop that does not end but simply repeats its loop body again and again. A loop that iterates its body repeatedly without ever ending is called an **infinite loop**. Normally, a statement in the body of the loop will change some variables so that the controlling boolean expression becomes false. If this variable does not change in the right way, you can get an infinite loop.

For instance, let's consider a slight variation to the previous example of a `while` loop. If we forget to increment `count`, the boolean expression will never change and the loop will be infinite:

```
int count = 1;
while (count <= number)
{
   System.out.println(count);
} // end while
```

Some infinite loops will not really run forever but will instead end your program abnormally when a system resource is exhausted. However, some infinite loops will run forever if left alone. To end a program that is in an infinite loop, you should learn how to force a program to stop running. The way to do this depends on your particular operating system. For example, in a Unix operating system, you would press Ctrl-C.

Sometimes a programmer might intentionally write an infinite loop. For example, an ATM machine would typically be controlled by a program with an infinite loop that handles deposits and withdrawals indefinitely. However, at this point in your programming, an infinite loop is likely to be an error.

The for Statement

A.60   When a counter controls the number of iterations in a `while` loop, you can replace the `while` statement with a **for statement**, or **for loop**. The `for` statement has the following general form:

> **for** (*initialize*; *test*; *update*)
>   *statement*;

Here *initialize* is an optional assignment of a value to a variable, *test* is a boolean expression, and *update* is an optional assignment that can change the value of *test*.

For example, the following `for` statement is exactly equivalent to the `while` statement in Segment A.58:

```
int count, number;
. . . // assign a value to number here
for (count = 1; count <= number; count++)
   System.out.println(count);
```

The first of the three expressions in parentheses, `count = 1`, initializes the counter before the loop body is executed for the first time. The second expression, `count <= number`, is a boolean expression that determines whether the loop should continue execution. This boolean expression is tested immediately after the first expression executes and again after each execution of the third expression. The third expression, `count++`, executes after each iteration of the loop body. Thus, the loop body is executed while `count <= number` is true.

In the previous example, we declared `count` before the `for` statement. After the loop completes its execution, `count` is still available as a variable. We could instead declare `count` within the `for` statement, as follows:

```
int number;
. . . // assign a value to number here
for (int count = 1; count <= number; count++)
   System.out.println(count);
```

In this case, `count` is defined only within the `for` loop and is not available after the loop completes its execution.

Programming Tip: Although declaring a variable within a `for` statement is convenient, realize that the variable's scope is then the `for` loop. The variable is not available after the loop completes its execution.

The counter in a `for` statement is not restricted to an integer type. It can have any primitive type. You can omit any of the expressions *initialize*, *test*, and *update* from a `for` statement, but you cannot omit their semic lons. Sometimes it is more convenient to write the *initialize* part before the for statement or to place the *update* part within the body of the loop. This is especially true when these parts are lengthy. Although you technically can omit the *test* from a for loop, you will get an infinite loop if you do.

Some Java programmers tend to favor the for statement over the while statement because in the for statement the initialization, testing, and incrementing of the counter all appear at the beginning of the loop.

Note: A for statement is basically another notation for a kind of while loop. Thus, like a while loop, a for statement might not execute its loop body at all.

A.61   **The comma in for statements.** A for loop can perform more than one initialization. To use a list of initialization actions, separate the actions with commas, as in the following example:

```
int n, product;
for (n = 1, product = 1; n <= 10; n++)
    product = product * n;
```

This for loop initializes n to 1 and product to 1. Note that you use a comma, not a semicolon, to separate the initialization actions.

You can have multiple update actions that are separated by commas. This can sometimes lead to a situation in which the for statement has an empty body and still does something useful. For example, we can rewrite the previous for statement in the following equivalent way:

```
for (n = 1, product = 1; n <= 10; product = product * n, n++);
```

In effect, we have made the loop body part of the update action. Notice the semicolon at the end of the statement. Since a semicolon at the end of a for statement is often the result of a programming error, a clearer way to write this loop makes the empty body explicit:

```
for (n = 1, product = 1; n <= 10; product = product * n, n++)
{
}
```

However, the most readable style uses the update action only for variables that control the loop, as in the original version of this for loop.

Finally, you cannot have multiple boolean expressions to test for ending a for loop. However, you can string together multiple tests by using the && and || operators to form one larger boolean expression.

Programming Tip: If you have used other programming languages that have a general-purpose comma operator, be warned that the comma operator in Java can appear only in for statements.

A.62   **Using an enumeration with a for statement.** The for statement has another form when you want to repeat statements for each object in an enumeration. For example, if you define

```
enum Suit {CLUBS, DIAMONDS, HEARTS, SPADES}
```

the for loop

```
for (Suit nextSuit : Suit.values())
    System.out.println(nextSuit);
```

displays

CLUBS
DIAMONDS
HEARTS
SPADES

You declare a variable to the left of a colon in the `for` statement. To the right of the colon, you represent the values that the variable will have. For the enumeration `Suit`, the expression `Suit.values()` represents the four possible values CLUBS, DIAMONDS, HEARTS, and SPADES. As the loop executes, `nextSuit` takes on each of these values.

This kind of loop—called a **for-each loop**—can be used with other collections of data, as you will see.

The do-while Statement

A.63   The **do-while statement**, or **do-while loop**, is similar to the `while` statement, but the body of a do-while statement always executes at least once. As you saw earlier, the body of a `while` loop might not execute at all.

The general form of a do-while statement is

do
    statement;
while (*expression*);

The do-while loop starts with the reserved word `do`. The loop body is a statement, typically a compound statement enclosed in braces {}. The loop ends with the reserved word `while` followed by a boolean expression in parentheses and a semicolon.

 Programming Tip: Be sure to include a semicolon at the end of a do-while statement.

The loop body executes and is repeated while the boolean expression is true. The loop body normally contains some action that can change the value of the boolean expression from true to false and so end the loop. The boolean expression is tested at the end of the loop, not at its beginning, as it is in a `while` statement. Thus, the loop body executes at least once even if the boolean expression starts out false.

The following do-while statement displays the integers from 1 to a given integer `number`:

```
int number;
. . . // assign a value to number here
int count = 1;
do
{
  System.out.println(count);
  count++;
} while (count <= number);
```

Again, let's suppose that `number` is 2. The variable `count` begins at 1 and is displayed. Next, `count` is incremented to 2. Since the expression `count <= number` is true at this point, the body of the loop executes again. The value of `count` (2) is displayed, and then `count` becomes 3. The expression `count <= number` is now false, so the do-while loop ends. Execution continues with the statement that follows the loop.

If `number` is zero or negative in the previous example, 1 is displayed, since the body of the loop executes at least once. If `number` can possibly be zero or negative, we should use either a `while` loop or a `for` loop here instead of a do-while loop.

Notice that we placed the ending brace and the `while` on the same line. Some programmers prefer to place them on different lines. Either form is fine, but be consistent.

To better understand a do-while loop, let's rewrite the previous example in the following way:

```
int number;
. . . // assign a value to number here
int count = 1;
{
   System.out.println(count);
   count++;
}
while (count <= number)
{
   System.out.println(count);
   count++;
}
```

When you compare the two versions, it is obvious that a do-while loop differs from a while loop in only one detail. With a do-while loop, the loop body is always executed at least once. With a while loop, the loop body might not execute at all.

Additional Loop Information

A.64   **Choosing a loop statement.** Suppose you decide that your program needs a loop. How do you decide whether to use a `while` statement, a `for` statement, or a `do-while` statement? You *cannot* use a `do-while` statement unless you are certain that the loop body should execute at least one time. If you are certain of this, a `do-while` statement is likely to be a good choice. However, more often than you might think, a loop requires the possibility that the body will not execute at all. In those cases, you must use either a `while` statement or a `for` statement. If it is a computation that changes some numeric quantity by some equal amount on each iteration, consider a `for` statement. If the `for` statement does not work well, use a `while` statement. The `while` statement is always a safe choice, since you can use it for any sort of loop. But sometimes one of the other alternatives is easier or clearer.

 Programming Tip: A `while` loop can do anything that another loop can do.

A.65   **The break and continue statements in loops.** You can use the `break` statement in a `switch` statement or in any kind of loop statement. When the `break` statement executes in a loop, the immediately enclosing loop ends, and the remainder of the loop body is not executed. Execution continues with the statement after the loop.

Adding a `break` statement to a loop can make the loop more difficult to understand. Without a `break` statement, a loop has a simple, easy-to-understand structure. There is a test for ending the loop at the top (or bottom) of the loop, and every iteration will go to the end of the loop body. When you add a `break` statement, the loop might end because either the condition given at the top (or bottom) of the loop is false or the `break` statement has executed. Some loop iterations may go to the end of the loop body, but one loop iteration might end prematurely. Because of the complications they introduce, you should avoid `break` statements in loops. Some authorities contend that a `break` statement should never be used to end a loop, but virtually all programming authorities agree that they should be used at most sparingly.

The `continue` statement ends the current iteration of a loop. The loop continues with the next iteration. Using a `continue` statement in this way has the same problems as using a `break` statement. However, replacing an empty loop body with a `continue` statement is acceptable. For example, you can revise the loop at the end of Segment A.61, as follows:

```
for (n = 1, product = 1; n <= 10; product = product*n, n++)
   continue;
```

Programming Tip: In general, do not use `break` or `continue` statements within the body of a loop.

The Class **String**

A.66 Strings of characters, such as `"Enter the amount:"`, do not have a primitive type in Java. However, Java does provide a class, called `String`, that you use to create and process strings of characters. The string constant `"Enter the amount:"`, in fact, is a value of type `String`. The class `String` is part of the package `java.lang` in the Java Class Library.

A variable of type `String` can name one of these string values. The statement

```
String greeting;
```

declares `greeting` to be the name of a `String` variable, and the following statement sets the value of `greeting` to the `String` value `"Hello!"`:

```
greeting = "Hello!";
```

These two statements are often combined into one, as follows:

```
String greeting = "Hello!";
```

We now can display `greeting` on the screen by writing

```
System.out.println(greeting);
```

The screen will show

    Hello!

Characters Within Strings

A.67 Most programming languages use the **ASCII** character set, which assigns a standard number to each of the characters normally used on an English-language keyboard. Java, however, uses the Unicode character set instead. The Unicode character set includes all the ASCII characters plus many of the characters used in languages that have an alphabet different from English. As it turns out, this is not likely to be a big issue if you are using an English-language keyboard. Normally, you can just program as if Java were using the ASCII character set, since the codes for the ASCII characters are the same in Unicode. The advantage of the Unicode character set is that it allows you to easily handle languages other than English. The disadvantage of the Unicode character set is that it requires two bytes to store each character, whereas the ASCII character set requires one.

A.68   **Escape characters.** Suppose we want to display the following line on the screen:

The word "Java" names a language and a drink!

This string contains quotes, so the statement

```
System.out.println("The word "Java" names a language and a drink!");
```

will not work: It produces a compiler error message. The problem is that the compiler sees

```
"The word "
```

as a perfectly valid quoted string. Then the compiler sees

```
Java"
```

which is not valid in the Java language. The compiler does not know that we mean to include the quote character as part of the string unless we tell it that we want to do so. We tell the compiler this by placing a backslash \ before the troublesome character, like so:

```
System.out.println("The word \"Java\" names a language and a drink!");
```

Some other special characters also need a backslash in order to be included in strings. They are listed in Figure A-4. These are often called **escape characters** because they escape from the usual meaning of a character in Java, such as the usual meaning of the double-quote character.

It is important to note that each escape sequence is a single character, even though it is spelled with two symbols. So the string "Say \"Hi\"!" contains 9 characters, not 11.

To include a backslash in a string, you must write two backslashes. Displaying the string "abc\\def" on the screen would produce

abc\def

Figure A-4   Escape characters

\"	Double quote.
\'	Single quote (apostrophe).
\\	Backslash.
\n	New line. (Go to the beginning of the next line.)
\r	Carriage return. (Go to the beginning of the current line.)
\t	Tab. (Insert whitespace up to the next tab stop.)

Writing the string with only one backslash, as in `"abc\def"`, is likely to produce the error message "Invalid escape character," because `\d` is invalid.

The escape sequence `\n` indicates that the string starts a new line at the `\n`. For example, the statement

```
System.out.println("The motto is\nGo for it!");
```

will write the following to the screen

The motto is
Go for it!

You can include a single quote (apostrophe) inside a quoted string, such as `"How's this?"`, but you cannot write a single quote within single quotes. Thus, to define a single-quote character, you use the escape sequence `\'`, as follows:

```
char singleQuote = '\'';
```

Concatenation of Strings

A.69   You can join two strings by using the + operator. Joining two strings together, end to end, to obtain a larger string is called **concatenation**. When + is used with strings, it is sometimes called the **concatenation operator**. For example, the statements

```
String greeting = "Hello";
String sentence = greeting + "my friend.";
System.out.println(sentence);
```

set the variable `sentence` to `"Hellomy friend."` and will write the following on the screen:

Hellomy friend.

No space separates the first two words, because no spaces are added when you concatenate two strings. If we want `sentence` to contain `"Hello my friend."`, we could change the assignment statement to

```
sentence = greeting + " my friend.";
```

Notice the space before the word "my."

You can concatenate any number of `String` objects by using the + operator. You can even concatenate a `String` object to any other type of object and get a `String` object as a result. Java can express any object as a string when you concatenate it to a string. For primitives like numbers, Java does the obvious thing. For example,

```
String solution = "The answer is " + 42;
```

will set the `String` variable `solution` to `"The answer is 42"`. This is so natural that it may seem as though nothing special is happening, but it does require a real conversion from one type to another. The Java literal 42 is an integer, whereas `"42"` is a string consisting of the two characters 4 and 2. Java converts the integer constant 42 to the string constant `"42"` and then concatenates the two strings `"The answer is "` and `"42"` to obtain the longer string `"The answer is 42"`.

> **Note:** Every class has a method `toString` that Java uses to get a string representation of any object. If you do not define `toString` for a class that you write, the default `toString` will return a representation of an object's location in memory. Thus, you generally should provide your own `toString` method when you define a class. Chapters 1 and 2 discuss this method in more detail.

You can also concatenate a single character to a string by using +. For example,

```
String label = "mile";
String pluralLabel = label + 's';
```

sets `pluralLabel` to the string `"miles"`.

Segment A.72 will show you another way to concatenate strings.

String Methods

Readers who need to review methods should consult Chapter 1 before reading this section.

A.70 A `String` object has methods as well as a value. You use these methods to manipulate string values. A few of these `String` methods are described here. You invoke, or call, a method for a `String` object by writing the object name, a dot, and the name of the method, followed by a pair of parentheses. Some methods require nothing within the parentheses, while others require that you specify arguments. Let's look at some examples.

A.71 **The method `length`.** The method `length` gets the number of characters in a string. For example, suppose we declare two `String` variables as follows:

```
String command = "Sit Fido!";  // 9 characters
String answer = "bow-wow";     // 7 characters
```

Now `command.length()` has the value 9 (it returns 9), and `answer.length()` returns 7. Notice that you must include a pair of parentheses, even though there are no arguments to the method `length`. Also notice that spaces, special symbols, and repeated characters are all counted in computing the length of a string. All characters except the double quotes that enclose the string are counted.

You can use a call to the method `length` anywhere that you can use a value of type `int`. For example, all of the following are legal Java statements:

```
int count = command.length();
System.out.println("Length is " + command.length());
count = answer.length() + 3;
```

A.72 **The method `concat`.** You can use the method `concat` instead of the + operator to concatenate two strings. For example, if we declare the `String` variables

```
String one = "sail";
String two = "boat";
```

the expressions

```
one + two
```

and

```
one.concat(two);
```

are the same string, *sailboat*.

A.73 **Indices.** Some of the methods in the class `String` refer to the **positions** of the characters in the string. Positions in a string start with 0, not with 1. Thus, in the string `"Hi Mom"`, *H* is in position 0, *i* is in position 1, the blank character is in position 2, and so forth. A position is usually referred to as an **index**. So it would be more normal to say that *H* is at index 0, *i* is at index 1, and so on. Figure A-5 illustrates how index positions are numbered in a string.

Figure A-5   Indices 0 through 11 for the string `"Java is fun."`

0	1	2	3	4	5	6	7	8	9	10	11
J	a	v	a		i	s		f	u	n	.

A.74 **The methods `charAt` and `indexOf`.** The method `charAt` returns the character at the index given as its one argument. For example, the statements

```
String phrase = "Time flies like an arrow.";
char sixthCharacter = phrase.charAt(5);
```

assign the character *f* to the variable `sixthCharacter`, since the *f* in *flies* is at index 5. (Remember, the first index is 0, not 1.)

The method `indexOf` tests whether a string contains a given substring and, if it does, returns the index at which the substring begins. Thus, `phrase.indexOf("flies")` will return 5 because the substring *flies* begins at index 5 within `phrase`.

Note: Out-of-bounds index

`String` methods such as `charAt` that take an index as an argument will cause an error during execution if the index is negative or too large. Such an index is said to be **out of bounds**. The error causes a `StringIndexOutOfBoundsException`. Appendix B discusses exceptions.

A.75 **Changing case.** The method `toLowerCase` returns a string obtained from its argument string by replacing any uppercase letters with their lowercase counterparts. Thus, if `greeting` is defined by

```
String greeting = "Hi Mary!";
```

the expression

```
greeting.toLowerCase()
```

returns the string `"hi mary!"`. An analogous method, `toUpperCase`, converts any lowercase letters in a string to uppercase.

A.76 **The method `trim`.** The method `trim` trims off any leading and trailing white space, such as blanks. So the statements

```
String command = "   Sit Fido!   ";
String trimmedCommand = command.trim();
```

set `trimmedCommand` to the string `"Sit Fido!"`. The blanks between words are not affected.

A.77   **Comparing strings.** You use the method `compareTo` to compare two strings. Strings are ordered according to the Unicode values of their characters. This ordering—called **lexicographic ordering**—is analogous to alphabetic ordering. The expression

   `stringOne.compareTo(stringTwo)`

returns a negative integer or a positive integer, depending on whether `stringOne` occurs before or after `stringTwo`. The expression returns zero if the two strings are equal.

   The method `compareToIgnoreCase` behaves similarly to `compareTo`, except that the uppercase and lowercase versions of the same letter are considered to be equal. For example, the method `compareTo` places the string `"Hello"` before the string `"hello"`, but the method `compareToIgnoreCase` finds these strings to be equal.

Programming Tip: Do not use the operators ==, !=, <, <=, >, or >= to compare the contents of two strings.

   If you want only to see whether two strings are equal—that is, contain the same values—you can use the method `equals`. Thus,

   `stringOne.equals(stringTwo)`

is true if `stringOne` equals `stringTwo` and is false if they are not equal. The method `equalsIgnoreCase` behaves similarly to `equals`, except that the uppercase and lowercase versions of the same letter are equal. For example, the method `equals` finds the strings `"Hello"` and `"hello"` unequal, but the method `equalsIgnoreCase` finds them equal.

Programming Tip: When applied to two strings (or to any two objects), the operator == tests whether they are stored in the same memory location. Sometimes that is sufficient, but if you want to know whether two strings that are in different memory locations contain the same sequence of characters, use the method `equals`.

The Class `StringBuilder`

A.78   Once you create a string object of the class `String`, you cannot alter it. But sometimes you would like to. For example, we might define the string

   `String name = "rover";`

and then decide that we want to capitalize its first letter. We cannot. We could, of course, write

   `name = "Rover";`

but this statement creates a new string *Rover* and discards *rover*.

   The class `String` has no method that modifies a `String` object. However, the class `StringBuilder` in the package `java.lang` has methods such as the following:

   public `StringBuilder append(String s)`
   Concatenates the string `s` to the end of this string and returns a reference to the result.

public StringBuilder delete(**int** start, **int** end)
Removes the substring of this string beginning at the index start and ending at either the index end - 1 or the end of the string, whichever occurs first, and returns a reference to the result. Throws StringIndexOutOfBoundsException if start is invalid.

public StringBuilder insert(**int** index, String s)
Inserts the string s into this string at the given index and returns a reference to the result. Throws StringIndexOutOfBoundsException if the index is invalid.

public StringBuilder replace(**int** start, **int** end, String s)
Replaces a substring of this string with the string s. The substring to be replaced begins at the index start and ends at either the index end - 1 or the end of the string, whichever occurs first. Returns a reference to the result. Throws StringIndexOutOfBoundsException if start is invalid.

public void setCharAt(**int** index, **char** character)
Sets the character at the given index of this string to a given character. Throws IndexOutOf-BoundsException if the index is invalid.

If you are not familiar with exceptions, think of them as error messages for now. The next appendix will explain them to you.

StringBuilder has other versions of the methods append and insert that take data of any type as arguments. While the classes StringBuilder and String have some methods in common, several methods in String are not in StringBuilder.

A.79   **Examples.** If we have the following instance of StringBuilder

```
StringBuilder message = new StringBuilder("rover");
```

we can capitalize its first letter by writing

```
message.setCharAt(0, 'R');
```

Now the statement

```
message.append(", roll over!");
```

changes message to the string *Rover, roll over!*, and

```
message.insert(7, "Rover, ");
```

changes it to *Rover, Rover, roll over!* Next,

```
message.delete(0, 7);
```

changes message to *Rover, roll over!*, and

```
message.replace(7, 16, "come here");
```

changes message to *Rover, come here!*
Each of the previous methods except setCharAt returns the result of the operation. So, for example, if we write

```
newMessage = message.append(", roll over!");
```

both newMessage and message reference the same sequence of characters.

Using Scanner to Extract Pieces of a String

A.80   Segments A.32 through A.37 show how the class Scanner is used to read data that a user types at the keyboard. Methods in Scanner—such as nextInt, nextDouble, and next—read a group of contiguous characters, or **token**, as an integer, a real number, or a string, respectively. When more than one token appears in the input data, they are separated by one or more characters known as **delimiters**. By default, Scanner uses white space as the delimiter.

In addition to reading data from the keyboard, you can use Scanner to process a string that you define within your program. You simply use the string instead of System.in when creating a Scanner object.

For example, the statements

```
String phrase = "one potato        two     potato three potato four";
Scanner scan = new Scanner(phrase);
System.out.println(scan.next());
System.out.println(scan.next());
System.out.println(scan.next());
System.out.println(scan.next());
```

display the words

```
one
potato
two
potato
```

We essentially have read tokens from a string instead of from the keyboard. The tokens here are separated by white space, the default delimiter.

A.81   **Specifying delimiters.** Whether you read characters from an input device such as a keyboard or from a string defined in your program, you can specify the delimiters that Scanner will use. The Scanner method useDelimiter sets the delimiters to those indicated in its string argument. For example, to use a comma as a delimiter, you would write

```
scan.useDelimiter(",");
```

where scan is a Scanner object. Thus, the statements

```
String data = "one,potato,two,potato";
Scanner scan = new Scanner(data);
scan.useDelimiter(",");
System.out.println(scan.next());
System.out.println(scan.next());
System.out.println(scan.next());
System.out.println(scan.next());
```

display the words

```
one
potato
two
potato
```

A.82   **Example.** To extract the words *one*, *two*, *three*, and *four* from the string phrase that we defined in Segment A.80, you would describe the delimiter as one or more blanks, the word *potato*, and one or more blanks. You use the notation in Figure A-6 to describe the delimiters. For example, \s+ denotes one or more white-space characters. You must duplicate each backslash character in this notation when it appears between the quotes of a string literal to distinguish it from escape characters such as \n.

Figure A-6   Some notation used to define the delimiters that Scanner uses

\d	Any digit 0 through 9
\D	Any character other than a digit
\s	Any white-space character
\S	Any character other than white space
\w	Any letter, digit, or underscore
\W	Any character other than a letter, digit, or underscore
-	Any character
X	One occurrence of *X*
X?	Zero or one occurrence of *X*
X*	Zero or more occurrences of *X*
X+	One or more occurrences of *X*
X{*n*}	Exactly *n* occurrences of *X*
X{*n*,}	At least *n* occurrences of *X*

The following statement sets the delimiter of the Scanner object scan to the word *potato* with leading and trailing white-space characters:

```
scan.useDelimiter("\\s+potato\\s+");
```

Thus, the statements

```
String phrase = "one potato two potato three potato four";
Scanner scan = new Scanner(phrase);
scan.useDelimiter("\\s+potato\\s+");
System.out.println(scan.next());
System.out.println(scan.next());
System.out.println(scan.next());
System.out.println(scan.next());
```

display the words

one
two
three
four

A.83

Example. The statements

```
String phrase = "5 potato         6potato 7 potato more";
Scanner scan = new Scanner(phrase);
scan.useDelimiter("\\s*\\d\\s*");
System.out.println(scan.next());
System.out.println(scan.next());
System.out.println(scan.next());
```

display the words

    potato
    potato
    potato more

The delimiter is a digit with optional leading and trailing white space.
If you now write

```
scan = new Scanner(phrase);
scan.useDelimiter("\\s*potato\\s*");
System.out.println(scan.nextInt());
System.out.println(scan.nextInt());
System.out.println(scan.next());
System.out.println(scan.next());
```

you will get the following output

    5
    6
    7
    more

Here the delimiter is the word *potato* with optional leading and trailing white space.

A.84

Example. The statements

```
String phrase = "one - two     -     three four";
Scanner scan = new Scanner(phrase);
scan.useDelimiter("\\s+-?\\s*");
System.out.println(scan.next());
System.out.println(scan.next());
System.out.println(scan.next());
System.out.println(scan.next());
```

display the words

    one
    two

three
four

The delimiter is at least one white space character optionally followed by a dash and more white space.

Arrays

A.85   In Java, an array is a special kind of object that stores a finite collection of elements having the same data type. For example, you can create an array of seven elements of type `double` as follows:

```
double[] temperature = new double[7];
```

The left side of the assignment operator declares `temperature` as an array whose elements are of type `double`. The right side uses the `new` operator to request seven memory locations for the array. This is like declaring the following strangely named variables to have type `double`:

```
temperature[0], temperature[1], temperature[2], temperature[3],
temperature[4], temperature[5], temperature[6]
```

Note that the numbering starts with 0, not 1. Each of these seven variables can be used just like any other variable of type `double`. For example, we can write

```
temperature[3] = 32;
temperature[6] = temperature[3] + 5;
System.out.println(temperature[6]);
```

But these seven variables are more than just seven plain old variables of type `double`. The number in square brackets—called an **index**, or **subscript**—can be any arithmetic expression whose value is an integer. In this example, the index value must be between 0 and 6, because we declared that the array `temperature` should have seven elements. A variable such as `temperature[3]` is called either an **indexed variable**, a **subscripted variable**, or simply an **element** of the array.

For example, the following statements read seven temperatures into an array and compare them with their average:

```
public static final int DAYS_PER_WEEK = 7;
Scanner keyboard = new Scanner(System.in);
. . .

double[] temperature = new double[DAYS_PER_WEEK];

System.out.println("Enter " + DAYS_PER_WEEK + " temperatures:");
double sum = 0;
for (int index = 0; index < DAYS_PER_WEEK; index++)
{
  temperature[index] = keyboard.nextDouble();
  sum = sum + temperature[index];
} // end for

double average = sum / DAYS_PER_WEEK;

System.out.println("The average temperature is " + average);
System.out.println("The temperatures are");
```

```
for (int index = 0; index < DAYS_PER_WEEK; index++)
{
  if (temperature[index] < average)
    System.out.println(temperature[index] + " below average.");
  else if (temperature[index] > average)
    System.out.println(temperature[index] + " above average.");
  else // temperature[index] == average
    System.out.println(temperature[index] + " average.");
} // end for
```

Figure A-7 illustrates the array `temperature` after seven values have been read into it.

Figure A-7   An array of seven temperatures

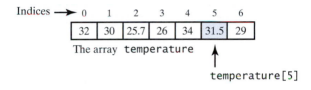

Each location in the array `temperature` contains a temperature. That is, the array is full. But arrays are not always full. You need to distinguish between the number of locations in an array—its **length**—and the number of items currently stored in the array.

An array has a data field `length` that contains the declared maximum number of elements in the array. For example, if we create an array by writing

```
int[] age = new int[50];
```

then `age.length` is 50. Notice that `length` is not a method, so no parentheses follow it. If we place only 10 values into the first 10 locations of this array, `age.length` is still 50. If we need to know how many values we place into an array, we will need to keep track of that ourselves.

Array Parameters and Returned Values

Readers who need to review methods should consult Chapter 1 before reading this section.

A.86   **Array parameters.** You can pass an indexed variable as an argument to a method anyplace that you can pass an ordinary variable of the array's base type. For example, if a method has the header

```
public double compute(double value)
```

and `temperature` is the array of `double` values that we defined earlier, we can invoke the method by writing

```
double result = compute(temperature[3])
```

An entire array can also be a single argument to a method. For example, the following method

```
public static void incrementArrayBy2(double[] array)
{
  for (int index = 0; index < array.length; index++)
```

```
        array[index] = array[index] + 2;
} // end incrementArrayBy2
```

will accept any array of double values as its single argument. We declare the parameter array in the method's header just as we would declare any other array: by specifying the type of the array elements followed by square brackets. We do not specify the length of the array.

The following statement is an example of how we would invoke this method:

```
incrementArrayBy2(temperature);
```

You use no square brackets when you pass an entire array as an argument to a method. Notice that the method can take any length array as an argument. The method incrementArrayBy2 adds 2 to each element in the argument array temperature. That is, the method actually changes the values in the argument array.

Note: A method can change the values in an argument array.

A.87   **Arrays as return values.** In Java, a method can return an array. For example, rather than modifying its array argument, the previous method incrementArrayBy2 could return an array whose values are 2 more than the corresponding values in the array argument. You specify the method's return type in the same way that you specify a type for an array parameter. The method would then look like this:

```
public static double[] incrementArrayBy2(double[] array)
{
  double[] result = new double[array.length];
  for (int index = 0; index < array.length; index++)
    result[index] = array[index] + 2;
  return result;
} // end incrementArrayBy2
```

The following statements invoke this method:

```
double[] originalArray = new double[10];
< Statements that place values into originalArray >
  . . .
double[] revisedArray = incrementArrayBy2(originalArray);
< At this point, originalArray is unchanged. >
```

Programming Tip: When a method returns an array that you want to assign to an array variable, you should declare the variable but not allocate memory for an array. For example, to invoke the method in the previous example, you do not write

```
double[] revisedArray = new double[10]; // WRONG!
revisedArray = incrementArrayBy2(originalArray);
```

The first statement allocates ten locations for a new array, but these locations are discarded when the second statement executes.

Initializing Arrays

A.88   You can provide initial values for the elements in an array when you declare it. To do this, you enclose the values for the array in braces and place them after the assignment operator, as in the following example:

```
double[] reading = {3.3, 15.8, 9.7};
```

You do not explicitly state the array's length. Instead the length is the minimum number of locations that will hold the given values. This initializing declaration is equivalent to the following statements:

```
double[] reading = new double[3];
reading[0] = 3.3;
reading[1] = 15.8;
reading[2] = 9.7;
```

If you do not initialize the elements of an array, they are given initial default values according to their type. For example, if you do not initialize an array of integers, each element of the array will be initialized to zero. In an array of objects, each element is initialized to null. However, it is usually clearer to do your own explicit initialization, either when you declare the array or later by using a loop and assignment statements.

Array Index Out of Bounds

A.89   When programming with arrays, making a mistake with an index is easy. This is especially true if that index is an expression. If the array temperature has seven elements, but an index is some integer other than 0 through 6, the index is said to be **out of bounds**. An out-of-bounds index expression will compile without any error message, but will cause an error when you run your program. In particular, you will get an IndexOutOfBoundsException. As we mentioned in Segment A.74, a similar situation can occur when you work with strings. (See Appendix B for a discussion of exceptions.)

Use of = and == with Arrays

A.90   **The operator =.** Recall that a variable for an object really contains the memory address of the object. The same is true of arrays. All array locations are together in one section of memory so that one memory address can specify the location of the entire array. The assignment operator copies this memory address. For example, if a and b are arrays of the same size, the assignment b = a gives the array variable b the same memory address as the array variable a. In other words, a and b are two different names for the same array. These variables are **aliases**. Thus, when you change the value of a[2], you are also changing the value of b[2]. Chapter 1 talks more about aliases and references.

   If you want the array b to have the same values as the array a, but in separate memory locations, then instead of one assignment statement you must use something like the following:

```
for (int index = 0; index < a.length; index++)
  b[index] = a[index];
```

A.91   **The operator ==.** The equality operator == tests two arrays to see if they are stored in the same place in the computer's memory. It does not test whether the arrays contain the same values. To do so, you must compare the two arrays element by element. For example, if the arrays a and b contain primitive values and have the same length, the following code could be used:

```
boolean match = true;
int index = 0;
while (match && (index < a.length))
{
  if (a[index] != b[index])
    match = false;
  else
    index++;
} // end while

if (match)
  System.out.println("Arrays have the same contents");
else
  System.out.println("Arrays have different contents");
```

If the arrays contained objects instead of primitive values, we would use the boolean expression `!a[index].equals(b[index])` instead of `a[index] != b[index]`.

Note: **Are arrays really objects?**
Arrays behave very much like objects. On the other hand, arrays do not belong to any class. Because arrays were used by programmers for many years before classes and objects (as we have used them) were invented, arrays use a special notation of their own. Other features of objects do not apply to arrays, such as inheritance (which we discuss in Chapter 2). So whether or not arrays should be considered objects is primarily an academic debate. Whenever Java documentation says that something applies to all objects, it also applies to arrays.

Note: **Array types are reference types**
A variable of an array type holds only the address where the array is stored in memory. This memory address is often called a **reference** to the array object in memory. For this reason, an array type is a reference type. A reference type is any type whose variables hold references—that is, memory addresses—as opposed to the actual item named by the variable. Array types and class types are both reference types. Primitive types are not reference types.

Arrays and the For-Each Loop

A.92   Earlier we used a for-each loop to process all the values in an enumeration. We can use a similar for-each loop to process all the values in an array. For example, the following statements compute the sum of the integers in an array:

```
int[] anArray = {1, 2, 3, 4, 5};
int sum = 0;
```

```
for (int element : anArray)
  sum = sum + element;
System.out.println(sum);
```

Similarly, the following statements display all the strings in an array:

```
String[] friends = {"Gavin", "Gail", "Jared", "Jessie"};
for (String name : friends)
  System.out.println(name);
```

Multidimensional Arrays

A.93 You can have an array with more than one index. For example, suppose we wanted to store the dollar amounts shown in Figure A-8 in some sort of array. The bold items are just labeling. There are 60 entries. If we use an array with one index, the array will have a length of 60, and keeping track of which entry goes with which index would be almost impossible. On the other hand, if we allow ourselves two indices, we can use one index for the row and one index for the column. This arrangement is illustrated in Figure A-9.

Figure A-8   A table of values

The effect of various interest rates on $1000 when compounded annually (rounded to whole dollars)						
Year	5.00%	5.50%	6.00%	6.50%	7.00%	7.50%
1	$1050	$1055	$1060	$1065	$1070	$1075
2	$1103	$1113	$1124	$1134	$1145	$1156
3	$1158	$1174	$1191	$1208	$1225	$1242
4	$1216	$1239	$1262	$1286	$1311	$1335
5	$1276	$1307	$1338	$1370	$1403	$1436
6	$1340	$1379	$1419	$1459	$1501	$1543
7	$1407	$1455	$1504	$1554	$1606	$1659
8	$1477	$1535	$1594	$1655	$1718	$1783
9	$1551	$1619	$1689	$1763	$1838	$1917
10	$1629	$1708	$1791	$1877	$1967	$2061

Note that, as was true for the simple arrays you have already seen, you begin numbering indices with 0 rather than 1. If the array is named `table` and it has two indices, the Java notation `table[3][2]` specifies the entry in the fourth row and third column. By convention, we think of the first index as denoting the row and the second as denoting the column. Arrays that have exactly two indices can be displayed on paper as a two-dimensional table and are called **two-dimensional**

arrays. More generally, an array is said to be an *n*-dimensional array if it has *n* indices. Thus, the ordinary one-index arrays that we have used up to now are **one-dimensional arrays**.

Figure A–9   Row and column indices for an array named `table`; `table[3][2]` is the element in the fourth row and third column

Row index 3   `table[3][2]`   Column index 2

Indices	0	1	2	3	4	5
0	1050	1055	1060	1065	1070	1075
1	1103	1113	1124	1134	1145	1156
2	1158	1174	1191	1208	1225	1242
3	1216	1239	1262	1286	1311	1335
4	1276	1307	1338	1370	1403	1436
5	1340	1379	1419	1459	1501	1543
6	1407	1455	1504	1554	1606	1659
7	1477	1535	1594	1655	1718	1783
8	1551	1619	1689	1763	1838	1917
9	1629	1708	1791	1877	1967	2061

A.94   Arrays with multiple indices are handled much like arrays with one index. To declare and create the array `table` with 10 rows and 6 columns, we write

```java
int[][] table = new int[10][6];
```

You can have arrays with any number of indices. To get more indices, you just use more square brackets in the declaration.

Indexed variables for multidimensional arrays are just like indexed variables for one-dimensional arrays, except that they have multiple indices, each enclosed in a pair of square brackets. For example, the following statements set all the elements in `table` to zero:

```java
for (int row = 0; row < 10; row++)
  for (int column = 0; column < 6; column++)
    table[row][column] = 0;
```

Note that we used two `for` loops, one nested within the other. This is a common way of stepping through the indexed variables in a two-dimensional array. If we had three indices, we would use three nested `for` loops, and so forth for higher numbers of indices.

As was true of the indexed variables for one-dimensional arrays, indexed variables for multidimensional arrays are variables of the array's base type and can be used anywhere that a variable of the base type is allowed. For example, for the two-dimensional array `table`, an indexed variable such as `table[3][2]` is a variable of type `int` and can be used anyplace that an ordinary `int` variable can be used.

A multidimensional array can be a parameter of a method. For example, the following method header has a two-dimensional array as a parameter:

```java
public static void clearArray(double[][] array)
```

A.95   Java implements multidimensional arrays as one-dimensional arrays. For example, consider the array

```
int[][] table = new int[10][6];
```

The array `table` is in fact a one-dimensional array of length 10, and its base type is `int[]`. Thus, each entry in the array `table` is a one-dimensional array of length 6. In other words, a multidimensional array is an array of arrays.

Normally, you do not need to be concerned with this fact, since this detail is handled automatically by the compiler. However, sometimes you can profit from this knowledge. For example, consider the previous nested `for` loops that filled the two-dimensional array `table` with zeros. We used the constants 6 and 10 to control the `for` loops, but it would be better style to use the data field `length` instead. To do so, we need to think in terms of an array of arrays. For example, the following is a rewrite of the nested `for` loops:

```
for (int row = 0; row < table.length; row++)
    for (int column = 0; column < table[row].length; column++)
        table[row][column] = 0;
```

Here, `table.length` is the number of rows in `table`, and `table[row].length` is the number of columns.

Wrapper Classes

A.96   Java makes a distinction between the primitive types, such as `int`, `double`, and `char`, and the class types, such as `String` and the classes that you write. Java sometimes treats primitive types and class types differently. For example, an argument to a method and the assignment operator = behave differently for primitive types and class types. To make things uniform, Java provides a **wrapper class** for each of the primitive types that enables us to convert a value of a primitive type to an object of a corresponding class type.

For example, the wrapper class for the primitive type `int` is the predefined class `Integer`. If we want to convert an `int` value, such as 10, to an object of type `Integer`, we can do so in one of three ways, as the following statements demonstrate:

```
Integer ten = new Integer(10);
Integer fiftyTwo = new Integer("52");
Integer eighty = 80;
```

In the first way, you supply an `int` value as a literal, a variable, or an expression. In the second, you provide a string that contains an `int` value. The third way allows you to simply assign an `int` value without using the `new` operator.

A.97   Once you have defined `Integer` objects, you can compare them by using the methods `compareTo` and `equals`, much as you compare strings or the other objects we have discussed in this appendix. Do not use operators such as ==. Just as for strings and other objects, operators like == compare the memory addresses of objects, not their values.

If you need the value of an `Integer` object as a primitive, you can use methods such as `intValue` or `doubleValue`. For example, if `ten` is defined as in the previous segment, the expression

```
ten.intValue()
```

returns the `int` value 10, whereas

```
ten.doubleValue()
```

returns the double value 10.0. You also can simply assign the Integer object to an int variable, as in

```
int primitive10 = ten;
```

No type cast is necessary; however, using one is not an error.

A.98   **Boxing and unboxing.** When performing arithmetic with Integer objects, you can use the same operators that you use for arithmetic with primitives. You can also intermix primitive integers with Integer objects. Thus, you can write statements such as the following:

```
Scanner keyboard = new Scanner(System.in);
System.out.print("What is his age? ");
int hisAge = keyboard.nextInt();
System.out.print("What is her age? ");
Integer herAge = keyboard.nextInt();

Integer ageDifference = Math.abs(hisAge - herAge);
System.out.println("He is " + hisAge + ", she is " + herAge +
                   ": a difference of " + ageDifference + ".");
```

Java converts between int and Integer as necessary. The process of converting from a primitive type to a corresponding wrapper class is called **boxing**. **Unboxing** is the process used to convert in the other direction. Since these conversions happen automatically, they are often called **auto-boxing** and **auto-unboxing**. Realize that the previous statements are just a demonstration of what is possible. Using only primitive integers for this simple computation is certainly adequate.

A.99   The wrapper classes for the primitive types double, float, long, and char are Double, Float, Long, and Character, respectively. You create objects of these classes in a way analogous to how you create Integer objects. Except for Character, each wrapper class has methods that return a value in a variety of types. Integer has the methods doubleValue, floatValue, intValue, and longValue. Double, Float, and Long also have these same methods. The class Character has only the analogous method charValue.

Many of the classes that we study in this book represent collections of objects. If your data has a primitive type, an appropriate wrapper class enables you to represent the data as objects so that you can use these classes.

A.100   Wrapper classes also contain some useful static constants. For example, you can find the largest and smallest values of any of the primitive number types by using the associated wrapper class. The largest and smallest values of type int are

```
Integer.MAX_VALUE and Integer.MIN_VALUE
```

The largest and smallest values of type double are

```
Double.MAX_VALUE and Double.MIN_VALUE
```

A.101   Wrapper classes have static methods that can be used to convert a string to the corresponding number of type int, double, long, or float. For example, suppose your program needs to convert the string "199.98" to a double value (which will turn out to be 199.98, of course). The static method parseDouble of the wrapper class Double will convert a string to a value of type double. So if theString is a variable of type String whose value is "199.98",

```
Double.parseDouble(theString)
```

returns the double value 199.98. The other wrapper classes Integer, Long, and Float have the analogous methods parseInt, parseLong, and parseFloat.

If there is any possibility that the string named by `theString` has extra leading or trailing blanks, you should instead use

```
Double.parseDouble(theString.trim())
```

As we discussed in Segment A.76, the method `trim`, included in the class `String`, trims off leading or trailing white space, such as blanks. If the string is not a correctly formed number, the invocation of `Double.parseDouble` will crash your program. The use of `trim` helps some in avoiding this problem.

A.102   Each of the numeric wrapper classes also has a static method called `toString` that will convert in the other direction—that is, it will convert from a primitive numeric value to a string representation of the numeric value. For example,

```
Integer.toString(42)
```

returns the string value `"42"`, and

```
Double.toString(199.98)
```

returns the string value `"199.98"`. Additionally, each wrapper class, like all other classes, has a non-static version of `toString`. For example, if we define `n` as follows:

```
Integer n = new Integer(198);
```

then `n.toString()` returns the string `"198"`.

Note: Wrapper classes
Every primitive type has a wrapper class. Wrapper classes allow you to represent values of a primitive type as a class type. They also contain a number of useful predefined constants and methods.

A.103   `Character` is the wrapper class for the primitive type `char`. The following piece of code illustrates some of the basic methods for this class:

```
Character c1 = new Character('a');
Character c2 = new Character('A');
if (c1.equals(c2))
  System.out.println(c1.charValue() + " is the same as " +
                        c2.charValue());
else
  System.out.println(c1.charValue() + " is not the same as " +
                        c2.charValue());
```

This displays

a is not the same as A

The `equals` method checks for equality of characters, so uppercase and lowercase letters are considered different.

Some of the static methods in the class `Character` follow:

`public static char` `toLowerCase(`**`char`** `ch)`
Returns the lowercase equivalent of ch, if ch is a letter; otherwise returns ch.

Examples:

```
Character.toLowerCase('a') returns 'a'
Character.toLowerCase('A') returns 'a'
Character.toLowerCase('5') returns '5'
```

`public static char` `toUpperCase(`**`char`** `ch)`
Returns the uppercase equivalent of ch, if ch is a letter; otherwise returns ch.

Examples:

```
Character.toUpperCase('a') returns 'A'
Character.toUpperCase('A') returns 'A'
Character.toUpperCase('5') returns '5'
```

`public static boolean` `isLowerCase(`**`char`** `ch)`
Returns true if ch is a lowercase letter.

Examples:

```
Character.isLowerCase('a') returns true
Character.isLowerCase('A') returns false
Character.isLowerCase('5') returns false
```

`public static boolean` `isUpperCase(`**`char`** `ch)`
Returns true if ch is an uppercase letter.

Examples:

```
Character.isUpperCase('a') returns false
Character.isUpperCase('A') returns true
Character.isUpperCase('5') returns false
```

`public static boolean` `isLetter(`**`char`** `ch)`
Returns true if ch is a letter.

Examples:

```
Character.isLetter('a') returns true
Character.isLetter('A') returns true
Character.isLetter('5') returns false
```

`public static boolean` `isDigit(`**`char`** `ch)`
Returns true if ch is a digit.

Examples:

```
Character.isDigit('a') returns false
Character.isDigit('A') returns false
Character.isDigit('5') returns true
```

public static boolean isLetterOrDigit(**char** ch)
Returns true if ch is either a letter or a digit.

Examples:

```
Character.isLetterOrDigit('a') returns true
Character.isLetterOrDigit('A') returns true
Character.isLetterOrDigit('5') returns true
Character.isLetterOrDigit('%') returns false
```

public static boolean isWhitespace(**char** ch)
Returns true if ch is a white-space character.

Examples:

```
Character.isWhitespace('a') returns false
Character.isWhitespace(' ') returns true
```

A.104   Java also has a wrapper class Boolean. This class has the two constants Boolean.TRUE and Boolean.FALSE. However, the Java reserved words true and false are much easier to use for these constants. So the constants in the class Boolean will not be of much help to us. The methods of the class Boolean are also not used very often. Although the class Boolean is not useless, it will be of little use to us in this text and we will discuss it no further.

PROGRAMMING TIPS

- No import statement is necessary when you use a class from the package java.lang of the Java Class Library.

- To make your arithmetic expressions more readable, place a space on both sides of each binary operator.

- To avoid errors and confusing code, use the operator ++ or -- only in a statement that involves one variable and no other operators.

- Programmers typically use all uppercase letters when naming constants to distinguish constants from ordinary variables. They use an underscore as a separator in multiword names. For example, FEET_PER_MILE follows this convention.

- Some programmers always use compound statements within other statements such as if-else, even when only a single statement appears between the braces. Doing so makes it easier to add another statement to the compound statement, but more importantly, it avoids the error that would occur if you forgot to add the braces. We encourage you to follow this convention, even though we do not do so in this book to save space.

- Indentation within an if-else statement does not affect the action of the statement. For clarity, you should use indentation that matches the logic of the statement.

- If you test a program that contains a switch statement and it executes two cases when you expect it to execute only one case, you probably have forgotten to include a break statement where one is needed.

- The body of a while loop can execute zero times. When a while loop executes, its first action is to check the value of the boolean expression. If the boolean expression is false, the loop body is not executed even one time. Perhaps the loop adds up the sum of all your expenses for the day. If you did not go shopping on a given day, you do not want the loop body to execute at all.

- Although declaring a variable within a for statement is convenient, realize that the variable's scope is then the for loop. The variable is not available after the loop completes its execution.

- If you have used other programming languages that have a general-purpose comma operator, be warned that the comma operator in Java can appear only in **for** statements.

- Be sure to include a semicolon at the end of a **do-while** statement.

- A **while** loop can do anything that another loop can do.

- In general, do not use **break** or **continue** statements within the body of a loop.

- Do not use the operators ==, !=, <, <=, >, or >= to compare the contents of two strings.

- When applied to two strings (or any two objects), the operator == tests whether they are stored in the same memory location. Sometimes that is sufficient, but if you want to know whether two strings in different memory locations contain the same sequence of characters, use the method **equals**.

- When a method returns an array that you want to assign to an array variable, you should declare the variable but not allocate memory for an array. For example, you should write

```
double[] revisedArray = myMethod(originalArray);
```

instead of

```
double[] revisedArray = new double[10]; // WRONG!
revisedArray = myMethod(originalArray);
```

The 10 locations that are allocated for the new array are discarded when the last statement executes.

Exception Handling

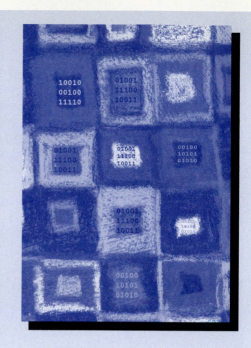

CONTENTS

PREREQUISITES

Java provides a way to handle certain kinds of special conditions in your program. This facility enables you to divide a program or method definition into separate sections for the normal case and for the exceptional case. This appendix will show you how to handle an exceptional case within a method or to tell another method that an exceptional case has occurred.

Basic Exception Handling

B.1   An **exception** is an object that is created as a signal that an unusual event has occurred during the execution of a program. The process of creating an exception is called

throwing an exception. You place the code that deals with the exceptional case at another place in your program—perhaps in a separate class or method. The code that detects and deals with the exception is said to **handle the exception**.

Using exceptions is most important when a method has a special case that some programs will treat in one way and that others will treat in another way. As you will see, such a method can throw an exception if the special case occurs. In this way, the special case can be handled outside of the method in a way that is appropriate to the situation.

B.2

Example. Let's begin with a simple example that does not use exceptions. Here, an `if-else` statement avoids a division by zero—which is an error—if you have no milk:

```java
Scanner keyboard = new Scanner(System.in);

System.out.println("Enter number of donuts:");
int donutCount = keyboard.nextInt();

System.out.println("Enter number of glasses of milk:");
int milkCount = keyboard.nextInt();

if (milkCount < 1)
{
  System.out.println("No Milk!");
  System.out.println("Go buy some milk.");
}
else
{
  double donutsPerGlass = donutCount / (double)milkCount;
  System.out.println(donutCount + " donuts.");
  System.out.println(milkCount + " glasses of milk.");
  System.out.println("You have " + donutsPerGlass +
                      " donuts for each glass of milk.");
} // end if
```

Now let's see how we can rewrite this code so that it uses Java's exception-handling facilities:

```java
Scanner keyboard = new Scanner(System.in);

System.out.println("Enter number of donuts:");
int donutCount = keyboard.nextInt();

System.out.println("Enter number of glasses of milk:");
int milkCount = keyboard.nextInt();

try
{
  if (milkCount < 1)
    throw new Exception("Exception: No Milk!");
  else
  {
    double donutsPerGlass = donutCount / (double)milkCount;
    System.out.println(donutCount + " donuts.");
    System.out.println(milkCount + " glasses of milk.");
    System.out.println("You have " + donutsPerGlass +
                        " donuts for each glass of milk.");
```

```
    } // end if
  } // end try
  catch (Exception e)
  {
    System.out.println(e.getMessage());
    System.out.println("Go buy some milk.");
  } // end catch
```

This code is basically the same as the previous version, except that it is divided into sections—called **blocks**—by the words try and catch. Additionally, the new if statement

```
if (milkCount < 1)
  throw new Exception("Exception: No Milk!");
```

does something exceptional, that is, it throws an exception if we have no milk. When it does so, the code after the word catch executes next. In other words, the normal situation is dealt with by the code in the **try block**, and the code in the **catch block** executes only in exceptional circumstances. We have separated the normal case from the exceptional case. In this simple example, that separation does not really buy us much, but in other situations, it will prove to be very helpful. Let's look at the details.

B.3   **The try block.** A try block contains the code for the basic algorithm. It is called a try block because we are not completely sure that all will go smoothly, but we want to give it a try. An invoked method might detect that something is wrong and throw an exception. Or we might make that determination ourselves and throw an exception, as we did in the previous example. The try block has the syntax

```
try
{
  < Some code >
  < Code that might throw an exception >
  < More code >
}
```

B.4   **The throw statement.** In Segment B.2, the throw statement

```
throw new Exception("Exception: No Milk!");
```

creates a new object of the class Exception and throws it. Exception is a predefined class that is supplied with Java. You can use Exception, but using another predefined class of exceptions or your own class is preferable, as you will see later. The string "Exception: No Milk!" is an argument for the constructor of the class Exception. The Exception object contains that string in a data field. This object—and this string—is available to the catch block.

B.5   **The catch block.** When an exception is thrown, execution of the code in the try block ends and another portion of code, known as a catch block, begins execution. Executing the catch block is called **catching the exception**. When an exception is thrown, it should ultimately be caught by some catch block. The catch block or blocks immediately follow the try block.

A catch block looks a little like a method definition that has a parameter. *It is not a method definition*, but in some ways, a catch block is like a method that the throw statement calls. The identifier e in

```
catch (Exception e)
```

is the **catch block parameter**. It represents the object thrown by the `throw` statement. Its type— `Exception` in this example—is the name of a class of exceptions. This class indicates the kind of exception the `catch` block can handle. Since all exception classes are derived from `Exception`, this `catch` block will handle any exception. You can have several `catch` blocks, one for each kind of exception you want to handle. For now, we'll consider only one `catch` block.

Every exception has a method called `getMessage` that retrieves the string given to the exception object by its constructor when the exception was thrown. So in the `catch` block

```
catch (Exception e)
{
  System.out.println(e.getMessage());
  System.out.println("Go buy some milk.");
}
```

`e.getMessage()` returns the string *Exception: No Milk!*. Thus, when the `catch` block executes, the following is displayed on the screen:

Exception: No Milk!
Go buy some milk.

B.6   To summarize, a `try` block contains some code that includes either a `throw` statement or a call to a method that contains a `throw` statement. The `throw` statement is normally executed only in exceptional circumstances, but when it is executed, it throws an exception of some exception class. (So far, `Exception` is the only exception class we know of, but there are others as well.) When an exception is thrown, an exception object is created. All the rest of the code in the `try` block is ignored and control passes to a suitable `catch` block. The exception object is represented by the `catch` block parameter, and the statements in the `catch` block are executed.

A `catch` block applies only to the nearest preceding `try` block. For now, we will assume that every `try` block is followed by an appropriate `catch` block. Later, we will discuss what happens when there is no appropriate `catch` block.

If no exception is thrown in the `try` block—that is, if a `throw` statement does not execute—the `try` block completes its execution. Program execution then continues with the code after the `catch` block(s). In other words, any `catch` blocks that follow the `try` block are ignored if no exception is thrown. Most of the time, the `throw` statement will not execute, and so in most cases, the code in the `try` block will run to completion and the code in the `catch` block(s) will be ignored completely.

Programming Tip: A method should throw an exception only in unusual or unexpected situations. If you can write code that actually deals with such an occurrence, do not throw an exception.

Programming Tip: If an exception can occur within a loop, place the loop within a `try` block, rather than the converse.

Exception Classes in the Java Class Library

B.7   When you learn about the methods of existing classes, you will sometimes be told that they might throw certain types of exceptions. Usually, these are predefined exception classes. If you use one of these methods, you can put the method invocation in a `try` block and follow it with a `catch` block to catch the exception. The names of exceptions in the Java Class Library are designed to be self-explanatory. Some of these classes are

```
ClassNotFoundException
FileNotFoundException
IOException
NoSuchMethodException
WriteAbortedException
```

When you catch an exception of one of these predefined exception classes, the string returned by the `getMessage` method will usually provide you with enough information to identify the source of the exception. Thus, if you have a class called `SampleClass` and it has a method called `doStuff` that throws exceptions of the class `IOException`, you might use the following code:

```
SampleClass object = new SampleClass();
try
{
  < Possibly some code >
  object.doStuff(); // can throw IOException
  < Possibly some more code >
}
catch (IOException e)
{
  < Code to handle the exception, probably including the following: >
  System.out.println(e.getMessage());
}
```

If the cause of the exception makes it unwise to continue program execution, you can end execution by calling `System.exit(0)` within the `catch` block.

Note: Sometimes your program can encounter a situation that makes continuing with the program pointless. In these cases, you can end your program by calling the `exit` method, as follows:

```
System.exit(0);
```

The number 0 given as the argument to `System.exit` is returned to the operating system. Most operating systems use zero to indicate a normal termination of the program and nonzero to indicate an abnormal termination of the program. In this case, "normal" means that the program did not violate any system or other important constraints. It does not mean that the program did what you wanted it to do.

Programming Tip: Every exception class is a descendant of the class `Exception`. Although you can use the class `Exception` itself, as we did earlier in this appendix, catching specific exceptions is preferable, since it enables you to provide more accurate messages.

Defining Your Own Exception Classes

B.8   You can define your own exception classes, but they must be derived from an existing exception class. You can derive an exception class from any predefined exception class or from any exception

class that you have already successfully defined. Our examples will be derived classes of the class
`Exception`, but you can use any existing exception class.

When you define an exception class, the constructors are the most important and often the only
methods, other than those inherited from the base class. For example, consider the following exception class called `DivideByZeroException`:

```
public class DivideByZeroException extends Exception
{
  public DivideByZeroException()
  {
    super("Dividing by Zero!");
  } // end default constructor

  public DivideByZeroException(String message)
  {
    super(message);
  } // end constructor
} // end DivideByZeroException
```

The only methods are a default constructor and a constructor that has one `String` parameter.
For our purposes, that is all we need to define. However, the class does inherit all the methods of the
class `Exception`.[1] In particular, the class `DivideByZeroException` inherits the method `getMessage`,
which returns a string message. In the default constructor, for example, this string message is set by
the statement `super("Dividing by Zero!")`. This is a call to a constructor of the base class
`Exception`. As we have already noted, passing a string to the constructor for the class `Exception`
sets the value of a `String` data field that later can be recovered by a call to `getMessage`. The class
`DivideByZeroException` inherits this `String` data field as well as the method `getMessage`.

For example, if we throw an exception by executing

throw new DivideByZeroException();

and the corresponding `catch` block contains the statement

System.out.println(e.getMessage());

the following line will appear on the screen:

Dividing by Zero!

The class `DivideByZeroException` defines a second constructor that has one parameter of type
`String`. This constructor allows us to choose any message when we throw an exception. If the
`throw` statement is

throw new DivideByZeroException("Oops. Didn't mean to use zero.");

and the corresponding `catch` block contains

System.out.println(e.getMessage());

the following line will appear on the screen:

Oops. Didn't mean to use zero.

---

1. Some programmers would prefer to derive the class `DivideByZeroException` from the class `ArithmeticException`, but that would make it a kind of exception that we are not required to catch in our code, and so we would lose the help of the compiler in keeping track of uncaught exceptions. For more details, see the section "Exceptions That Do Not Need to Be Caught," later in this appendix.

Note: **Guidelines for programmer-defined exception classes:**

- Derive each exception class from an already existing exception class.
- If you have no compelling reason to use a particular base class, derive your class from the class Exception.
- Define a default constructor and at least one other constructor that has a String argument.
- Begin each constructor definition with a call to the constructor of the base class by using super. The default constructor should call super with a String argument that indicates the kind of exception. The second constructor should call super with the string that was passed to the constructor as its argument. This string can then be recovered later by calling the method getMessage from within a catch block.
- Your exception class inherits the method getMessage. Normally, you do not need to add any other methods, but it is legal to do so.

Programming Tip: As a general rule, if you insert a throw statement in your code, it is probably best to define your own exception class. In that way, when your code catches an exception, your catch blocks can tell the difference between your exceptions and exceptions thrown by methods in predefined classes.

Multiple catch Blocks

B.9   A try block potentially can throw one of any number of exceptions, and these exceptions can have different types. Each catch block can catch exceptions of only one type. You can, however, place several catch blocks after a try block to catch exceptions of different types.

   The order in which you place the catch blocks can be important. When an exception is thrown in a try block, the catch blocks are considered in their order of appearance. The first catch block that matches the type of the exception thrown is the one that is executed. Thus, the following sequence of catch blocks would not be good:

```
catch (Exception e)
{
    . . .
}
catch (DivideByZeroException e)
{
    . . .
}
```

With this ordering, the catch block for DivideByZeroException will never be used, because all exceptions will be caught by the first catch block. Recall that all exceptions ultimately are derived from Exception. Fortunately, the compiler will probably warn you about this. The correct ordering is to reverse the catch blocks so that the more specific exception comes before its base exception class, as follows:

```
catch (DivideByZeroException e)
{
    . . .
```

```
    }
    catch (Exception e)
    {
        . . .
    }
```

Programming Tip: Catch the most specific exception first.

Programming Tip: Despite our previous examples, avoid using `Exception` in a `catch` block. Catch as specific an exception as you can.

The `finally` Block

B.10   If you have code that must execute regardless of whether an exception occurs, you could place it at the end of the `try` block and at the end of each `catch` block. An easier way to accomplish this, however, is to place one copy of the code in question within a `finally` block that follows the last `catch` block. Code within a `finally` block executes after the `try` block ends. Although optional, the `finally` block is a good way to provide clean-up services, such as closing a file or releasing system resources.

The following code shows the placement of the `finally` block:

```
    try
    {
        < Code that might throw an exception either by executing a throw statement
          or by calling a method that throws an exception >
    }
    catch (AnException e)
    {
        < Code that handles exceptions of type AnException or a derived class of anException >
    }

    < Possibly other catch blocks to handle other types of exceptions >
    . . .
    finally
    {
        < Code that executes after the try block ends >
    }
```

Note: Statements within a `finally` block execute after its corresponding `try` block completes its execution, even if a `return` executes. However, if an exception occurs, and it is caught by one of the `catch` blocks, the `finally` block executes after that `catch` block. A `finally` block does not execute if either the `try` block or a `catch` block calls `System.exit`.

B.11   **Example.** Imagine that you open the refrigerator door and reach for the milk. Whether you find milk or not, you should close the door. In the following code, the method `takeOutMilk` will throw an exception if no milk is found. Whether an exception occurs or not, `closeRefrigerator` is called within the `finally` block.

```
try
{
   openRefrigerator();
   takeOutMilk();
   pourMilk();
   putBackMilk();
}
catch (NoMilkException e)
{
   System.out.println(e.getMessage());
   System.out.println("Go buy some milk.");
}
finally
{
   closeRefrigerator();
}
```

Methods That Throw but Do Not Catch Exceptions

B.12   Sometimes it makes sense to delay handling an exception. For example, you might have a method with code that throws an exception if there is an attempt to divide by zero, but you might not want to catch the exception in that method. Perhaps some programs that use that method should simply end if the exception is thrown, while others should do something else, so you would want to leave the handling of the exception to the invoking program. In these cases, it makes sense not to catch the exception in the method definition. Instead, any program (or other code) that uses the method would place the method invocation in a `try` block and catch the exception in a subsequent `catch` block.

   When a method does not handle an exception, it must warn programmers that any invocation of the method might possibly throw an exception. This warning is called a **throws clause.** For example, a method that might possibly throw a `DivideByZeroException` but does not catch the exception would have a header similar to the following:

   public void sampleMethod() **throws** DivideByZeroException

The part `throws DivideByZeroException` is a `throws` clause. It says that an invocation of the method `sampleMethod` might throw a `DivideByZeroException`.

   The `throws` clause absolves `sampleMethod` of the responsibility to catch any exceptions of type `DivideByZeroException` that might occur during its execution. If, however, some `methodB` calls `sampleMethod`, then `methodB` must deal with the exception. It can do so either by handling the exception with `try` and `catch` blocks or by passing the exception on to whoever calls `methodB` by including the same `throws` clause in its header. In a well-written program, every exception that is thrown should eventually be caught somewhere by a `catch` block.

912 APPENDIX B   Exception Handling

A `throws` clause can contain more than one exception type. In such cases, commas separate the exception types, as in the following example:

public int myMethod() **throws** IOException, DivideByZeroException

Note: Most exceptions that can occur during the execution of a method should be accounted for in one of two ways:

- Catch the possible exception in a `catch` block that is within the method definition.
- Declare the possible exception in a `throws` clause in the method's header. Then whoever uses the method must either catch the exception or declare it in another `throws` clause.

In any one method, you can catch some exceptions and declare other exceptions in a `throws` clause.

Programming Tip: Avoid using `Exception` in a `throws` clause. Instead, use as specific an exception as you can.

Note: **A throws clause in a derived class**

If you override (redefine) a method in a derived class, you cannot add exceptions to its `throws` clause. This, of course, means that you cannot throw any exceptions that are not either caught in a `catch` block or already listed in the `throws` clause of the method in the base class. You can, however, declare fewer exceptions in the `throws` clause of the redefined method.

Exceptions That Do Not Need to Be Caught

B.13   Exceptions in Java are said to be either checked or unchecked. A **checked exception** must either be caught in a `catch` block or declared in a `throws` clause. Such exceptions indicate serious problems that likely should lead to program termination. The exceptions listed at the beginning of Segment B.7 are all checked exceptions in the Java Class Library.

An **unchecked** or **runtime exception** need not be caught in a `catch` block or declared in a `throws` clause. These exceptions usually indicate that something is wrong with your code and that you should fix it. Normally, you would not have written a `throw` statement for these exceptions. For example, if your program attempts to use an array index that is out of bounds, an `ArrayIndexOutOfBoundsException` occurs. A `NoSuchMethodException` occurs when you use a method but you have not provided a definition for that method name. For such exceptions, you should repair your code, not add a `catch` block. Note that an uncaught runtime exception terminates program execution.

How do you know if an exception is checked or unchecked? You can consult the documentation for the Java Class Library at `java.sun.com/j2se/1.5/docs/api/`. It will indicate whether an exception is derived from `RuntimeException`, in which case it is unchecked.

Note: **Unchecked exceptions in the Java Class Library**

The following classes in the Java Class Library represent unchecked (runtime) exceptions that you are likely to encounter.

```
ArithmeticException
ArrayIndexOutOfBoundsException
ClassCastException
IllegalStateException
IndexOutOfBoundsException
NoSuchElementException
NullPointerException
UnsupportedOperationException
```

 Note: Unchecked exceptions are descendants of the class `RuntimeException` or any of its descendants. They do not need to be caught. All other exceptions are checked. Checked exceptions are descendants of the class `Exception`. Both `RuntimeException` and `Exception` are in the package `java.lang` of the Java Class Library.

 Note: If you fail to catch a checked exception, the compiler will tell you. You then can either catch it or add it to a `throws` clause. If an unchecked exception is thrown but never caught, program execution ends.

 Programming Tip: When designing a method that throws an exception, you need to decide whether to make the exception checked or unchecked. If the client can reasonably recover from the exception, use a checked exception. If the client can do no more than note the exception, use an unchecked one.

B.14   **The class `Error`.** The class `Error` and its descendant classes are not considered to be exception classes, as they are not descendants of the class `Exception`. However, objects of the class `Error` are similar to unchecked exceptions in that you need not catch or declare them, even though you could. Errors are more or less beyond your control. For example, an `OutOfMemoryError` occurs if your program has run out of memory. This means that you must either revise your program to make it more efficient in its use of memory, change a setting to let Java access more memory, or buy more memory for your computer. Adding a `catch` block will not help in this case.

PROGRAMMING TIPS
- A method should throw an exception only in unusual or unexpected situations. If you can write code that actually deals with such a situation, do not throw an exception.

- If an exception can occur within a loop, place the loop within a **try** block, rather than the converse.

- Every exception class is a descendant of the class `Exception`. Although you can use the class `Exception` itself, as we did earlier in this appendix, catching specific exceptions is preferable, since it enables you to provide more accurate messages.

- As a general rule, if you insert a `throw` statement in your code, it is probably best to define your own exception class. In that way, when your code catches an exception, your `catch` blocks can tell the difference between your exceptions and exceptions thrown by methods in predefined classes.

- Catch the most specific exception first.

- Avoid using `Exception` in a `catch` block. Catch as specific an exception as you can.

- Avoid using `Exception` in a `throws` clause. Instead, use as specific an exception as you can.

- When designing a method that throws an exception, you need to decide whether to make the exception checked or unchecked. If the client can reasonably recover from the exception, use a checked exception. If the client can do no more than note the exception, use an unchecked one.

APPENDIX

C

File Input and Output

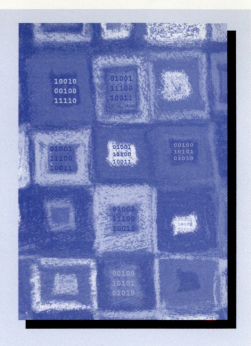

CONTENTS

PREREQUISITES

Program input and output is also known as **I/O**. Input can be taken from the keyboard or from a file. Similarly, output can be sent to the screen or to a file. In this appendix, we explain how you can read input from a file and send output to another file. One advantage of files is that their contents exist after your program completes its execution.

Overview

A **file** is a collection of data that is in a particular storage medium such as a disk. You already use files to store your Java classes and programs. You also can use files to store input for a program or to hold output from a program. Before you learn how to write and read files, you need to know more about them, including some terminology.

Streams

C.1   In Java, all I/O is handled by **streams**. A stream is an object that either

- Delivers data to a destination, such as a file or the screen, or
- Takes data from a source, such as a file or the keyboard, and delivers it to your program

Thus, a stream is a flow of data. The data might be characters, numbers, or bytes consisting of binary digits. If the data flows into your program, the stream is called an **input stream**. If the data flows out of your program, the stream is called an **output stream**.

For example, if an input stream is connected to the keyboard, the data flows from the keyboard into your program. The object System.in is such an input stream. If an input stream is connected to a file, data flows from the file into your program. Likewise, if an output stream is connected to a display, data flows from your program to the display. The object System.out is such an output stream. If an output stream is connected to a file, data flows from your program to the file. Figure C-1 illustrates these actions.

Note: Input and output are done from the perspective of the program. Thus, "input" means that data moves *into your program* from a file or the keyboard. The word "output" means that data moves *out of your program* to a file or the screen.

Figure C-1   Input and output streams

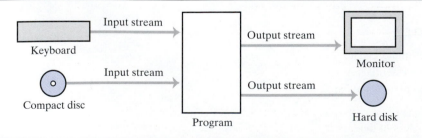

The Advantage of Files

C.2   When a program ends, the data typed at the keyboard and the data left on the screen go away. In other words, the data is temporary. In contrast, data in a file exists after the program has finished running. The contents of a file remain until either a person or a program changes the file.

Ê   An input file can be read over and over again by different programs without the need to type in the data separately for each program. Files also provide us with a convenient way to deal with large quantities of data.

Kinds of Files

C.3   All of the data in any file is stored as binary digits, or bits, that is, as a sequence of zeros and ones. However, we can think of the contents of some files as sequences of characters. Such files are called **text files** and can be created and read by using a text editor. For example, when you write a Java program, you use a text editor to store the program in a text file.

Ê   Files whose contents are not sequences of characters are called **binary files**. You cannot conveniently read a binary file by using a text editor, even though some editors might be able to read some of the information in some binary files. Binary files represent data in a compact way that can be read or written by your programs. Thus, a binary file is a good place to store data that a program reads or writes.

Note: Your Java programs can create or read both text files and binary files. Writing a text file and writing a binary file require similar steps. Likewise, reading a text file is similar to reading a binary file. The kind of file, however, determines which classes we use to perform the I/O.

Programming Tip: Use a text file if you want a text editor to either create a file that a program will read or read a file that a program created. In other cases, consider a binary file, as it occupies less space.

Note: **Character sets**

Java uses the **Unicode** character set, which includes many letters in natural languages very different from English. The Unicode representation of each character requires two bytes. Most text editors and operating systems use the **ASCII** character set, which is the character set normally used for English and for typical Java programs. The ASCII character set is a subset of the Unicode character set. The representation of each character in ASCII requires one byte.

Note: **The contents of a text file**

A text file contains a sequence of characters in which each character is represented as one or two bytes, depending on the system's default encoding. When a program writes a value to a text file, the number of characters written is the same as if you had written the value to a display using `System.out.println`. For example, writing the `int` value 12345 to a text file places five characters in the file. In general, writing an integer places between 1 and 11 characters in a text file.

> **Note:** **The contents of a binary file**
>
> Values of the same primitive type are represented by the same number of bytes in a binary file. For example, all `int` values occupy four bytes each in a binary file, and all `double` values require eight bytes each. A `String` value is represented as a sequence of characters of indeterminate length.

File Names

C.4 You name files according to the rules of your operating system; Java does not have its own rules for file names. Most common operating systems allow you to use letters, digits, and the dot symbol when creating file names. Typically, file names have a suffix, such as `.txt` or `.bin`. This suffix has no special meaning to a Java program. Using a suffix is simply a convention, not a rule. In this book, we use the suffix `.txt` to indicate a text file and the suffix `.bin` to mean a binary file.

The Package `java.io`

C.5 All Java streams are instances of various stream classes in the Java Class Library. In particular, these classes are in the package (library) `java.io`. Thus, every program or class that does file I/O using any of the techniques given in this appendix must begin with the following statement:

```
import java.io.*;
```

This statement tells the Java compiler and linker that our program uses the `java.io` package. Note that the class `Scanner` is not in this package. As you saw in Appendix A, `Scanner` is in the package `java.util`. Thus, any program that uses `Scanner` must include the statement

```
import java.util.Scanner;
```

Writing to a Text File Using `PrintWriter`

C.6 When you write a program to send output to a text file, you use a method named `println` that behaves like `System.out.println`, but that is a method in the class `PrintWriter`. The class `PrintWriter` is the preferred stream class for writing to a text file. The following simple example reads four lines from the keyboard and writes them to a text file.

```java
String fileName = "data.txt";
PrintWriter toFile = null;

try
{
   toFile = new PrintWriter(fileName); // can throw
                                       // FileNotFoundException
}
catch (FileNotFoundException e)
{
   System.out.println("PrintWriter error opening the file " +
                      fileName);
   System.exit(0);
} // end try/catch

System.out.println("Enter four lines of text:");
```

```
Scanner keyboard = new Scanner(System.in);

for (int count = 1; count <= 4; count++)
{
  String line = keyboard.nextLine();
  toFile.println(count + " " + line);
} // end for

System.out.println("Four lines were written to " + fileName);

toFile.close();
```

These statements create a text file named *data.txt* that either a text editor or another Java program can read.

C.7   **Opening the file.** Before you can write to a text file you must **open** it by writing

```
toFile = new PrintWriter(fileName);
```

These statements connect a stream to the file named by the string in `fileName`, that is, *data.txt*. The variable `toFile` references the stream associated with the actual file. The file has a name like *data.txt* that the operating system uses. But after you connect the file to the stream, your program always refers to the file by using the stream variable.

When you connect a file to an output stream in this way, your program always starts with an empty file. If the file *data.txt* already exists, its old contents will be lost. If the file *data.txt* does not exist, a new, empty file named *data.txt* will be created.

C.8   **Exceptions.** Because the `PrintWriter` constructor might throw a `FileNotFoundException` while attempting to open the file, its invocation must appear within a `try` block. Any exception is caught in a `catch` block. Notice that the `try` block need not contain the calls to `println` and `close`, as they do not throw checked exceptions.

If the constructor throws an exception, it does not necessarily mean that the file was not found. After all, if you are creating a new file, it doesn't already exist. In that case, an exception is thrown if the file could not be created because, for example, the file name is already used for a directory (folder) name.

C.9   **Writing the file.** The method `println` of the class `PrintWriter` works the same for writing to a text file as the method `System.out.println` works for writing to the screen. The class `Print-Writer` also has the method `print`, which behaves just like `System.out.print`, except that the output goes to a text file. Notice that the variable `toFile` is declared outside of the `try` block so that `toFile` is available outside of the `try` block. Remember, anything declared in a block—even a `try` block—is local to the block.

Instead of sending output to a file immediately, `PrintWriter` waits to send a larger packet of data. Thus, the output from a `println`, for example, is not sent to the output file right away. Instead, it is saved and placed into memory called a **buffer**, along with the output from other invocations of `println`. When the buffer is too full to accept more output, its contents are written to the file. Thus, the output from several `println` statements is written at the same time, instead of each time a `println` executes. This technique is called **buffering**.

C.10   **Closing the file.** When your program is finished writing to a file, it should **close** the stream connected to that file. In our previous example, the statement

```
toFile.close();
```

closes the stream connected to the file *data.txt*. When you close a stream, the system releases any resources used to connect the stream to the file and does some other housekeeping. If you do not close a stream, Java will close it for you when the program ends. However, it is safest to close the stream with an explicit call to close. All stream classes include a method named close.

When you write data to a file, the data may not immediately reach its destination. Closing an output stream forces any pending output to be written to the file. If you do not close the stream and your program terminates abnormally, Java might not be able to close it for you, and data can be lost. The sooner you close a stream, the less likely it is that this will happen. If your program writes to a file and later reads from the same file, it must close the stream after it is through writing to the file and then reopen the file for reading. (Java does have a class that allows a file to be open for both reading and writing, but we will not cover that class in this book.)

Programming Tip: To avoid losing data, close an output stream when you are finished writing to it.

C.11   **Flushing an output file.** You can force any pending output that is currently in a buffer to be written to its destination file by calling PrintWriter's method flush, as follows:

```
toFile.flush();
```

The method close automatically calls the method flush, so for most simple applications, you do not need to call flush explicitly. However, if you continue to program, you will eventually encounter situations where you will have to use flush.

Note: The PrintWriter constructor that we used in Segment C.6 is new to Java 5. If we were to use an earlier version of Java, we would be left without a PrintWriter constructor that takes a file name as its argument. In that case, we would use the class FileWriter, which does have such a constructor, in addition to the class PrintWriter. Details for this approach appear in the note at the end of the next segment.

Appending to a Text File

C.12   In our previous example, if the file *data.txt* had already existed, its old contents would be lost and replaced with new output. Sometimes that is not what you want. Sometimes you want to add a program's output to the end of the file. This is called **appending to a file**. If you want to append program output to the file *data.txt*, you would revise the example given in Segment C.6 as follows:

```
String fileName = "data.txt";

FileWriter fw = null;
PrintWriter toFile = null;

try
{
   fw = new FileWriter(fileName, true); // can throw IOException
   toFile = new PrintWriter(fw);    // can throw FileNotFoundException
}
catch (FileNotFoundException e)
{
   System.out.println("PrintWriter error opening the file " +
                      fileName);
```

```
        System.exit(0);
    }
    catch (IOException e)
    {
        System.out.println("FileWriter error opening the file " +
                                fileName);
        System.exit(0);
    } // end try/catch

    System.out.println("Enter four lines of text:");
```
< The remaining statements are as in Segment C.6. >
. . .

The class `FileWriter` has a constructor whose first parameter is the name of a text file and whose second parameter is a boolean value that indicates whether to append data to the file. In this example, if the file *data.txt* already exists, the old file contents will remain, and the program's output will be placed after the old contents of the file. If the file *data.txt* does not already exist, Java will create an empty file of that name and write the output to this empty file.

However, `FileWriter` provides only basic support for text files, whereas the class `Print-Writer` has useful methods such as `println`. Using both classes provides an appropriate constructor and convenient methods. To do so, we pass the instance of `FileWriter` to a constructor of `PrintWriter`.

Note: You can use the previous approach to create a new text file instead of appending data to one. To do so, simply omit the second argument of `FileWriter`'s constructor. Thus, in the previous example, you would open the file by writing

```
fw = new FileWriter(fileName);
toFile = new PrintWriter(fw);
```

You would use this technique if your compiler does not support Java 5.

Note: **Reading a File Name from the Keyboard**
We have used the `String` variable `fileName` to represent the name of a file. Although we assigned it a literal value, we could read the name a user types and assign it to `fileName`. For example, you might write the following:

```
Scanner keyboard = new Scanner(System.in);
System.out.println("Enter file name:");
String fileName = keyboard.nextLine();
```

You can use a `String` variable when you open text files and binary files, regardless of whether you open them for input or output.

Reading a Text File

Suppose that the text file *data.txt* was created by either a text editor or a Java program containing statements like those in Segment C.6. You can read such a text file by using either of the classes `Scanner` or `BufferedReader`. The following segments will show you how.

Using Scanner to Read a Text File

C.13

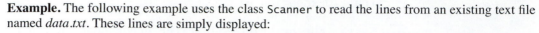

Example. The following example uses the class Scanner to read the lines from an existing text file named *data.txt*. These lines are simply displayed:

```java
String fileName = "data.txt";
Scanner fromFile = null;
System.out.println("The file " + fileName +
                   " contains the following lines:");
try
{
  fromFile = new Scanner(new File(fileName));
}
catch (FileNotFoundException e)
{
  System.out.println("Error opening the file " + fileName);
  System.exit(0);
} // end try/catch

while (fromFile.hasNextLine())
{
  String line = fromFile.nextLine();
  System.out.println(line);
} // end while

fromFile.close();
```

Figure C-2 shows the file *data.txt* and the output when these statements read the file.

Figure C-2   (a) The text file *data.txt* and (b) the output of the code in Segment C.13 after reading the file

(a)
```
1 2
buckle my shoe.
3 4
shut the door.
```

(b)
```
The file data.txt contains the following lines:
1 2
buckle my shoe.
3 4
shut the door.
```

C.14   We open the file by writing

```java
fromFile = new Scanner(new File(fileName));
```

Unlike PrintWriter, Scanner has no constructor that takes a file name as its argument. However, Scanner does accept a File object as an argument. File is a class that represents a file in a system-independent way. Its constructor can have a string that is a file name as its argument. We will discuss File in more detail later in this appendix, in Segment C.31. Since Scanner's constructor can throw a FileNotFoundException, we invoke it within a try block.

The while loop uses the Scanner methods hasNextLine and nextLine to read the lines in the text file. In this example, the lines are simply displayed. When the end of the file is reached, has-NextLine returns false and the loop ends. At that time, we close the file. Notice that the methods hasNextLine, nextLine, and close do not throw checked exceptions, and so they need not appear within a try block.

Note: We use the method hasNextLine to prevent nextLine from reading beyond the end of the file. If nextLine were to read beyond the end of a file, it would throw a NoSuchElementException, which is a runtime (unchecked) exception.

Note: **Other methods in Scanner**

The previous example simply reads and displays entire lines of a text file. However, Scanner has other convenient methods that read data in various formats. Segment A.33 of Appendix A mentioned nextInt and nextDouble in conjunction with reading from the keyboard. You can use these and other similar methods to read data from a text file as well.

Using BufferedReader to Read a Text File

C.15

Example. As in the previous example, we assume that we have created the text file *data.txt* by using either a text editor or a Java program containing statements like those in Segment C.6. The following example reads the lines from a text file and displays them on the screen:

```java
String fileName = "data.txt";
BufferedReader fromFile = null;
try
{
  FileReader fr = new FileReader(fileName); // can throw
                                            // FileNotFoundException
  fromFile = new BufferedReader(fr);

  System.out.println("The file " + fileName +
                   " contains the following lines:");
  String line = fromFile.readLine();        // can throw IOException

  while (line != null)
  {
    System.out.println(line);
    line = fromFile.readLine();             // can throw IOException
  } // end while
}
catch (FileNotFoundException e)
{
  System.out.println("Error opening the file " + fileName);
  System.exit(0);
}
catch (IOException e)
{
  System.out.println("Error reading the file " + fileName);
} // end try/catch
finally
{
```

```
        try
        {
          if (fromFile != null)
            fromFile.close();                        // can throw IOException
        }
        catch (IOException e)
        {
          System.out.println("Error closing the file " + fileName);
          System.exit(0);
        } // end try/catch
      } // end finally
```

C.16 We open the file *data.txt* by writing

```
        FileReader fr = new FileReader(fileName);
        fromFile = new BufferedReader(fr);
```

where `fromFile` is declared earlier as a `BufferedReader`. If desired, you can combine these statements, as follows:

```
        fromFile = new BufferedReader(new FileReader(fileName));
```

As was true of the class `Scanner`, the class `BufferedReader` has no constructor that takes a file name as its argument, so we need to use another class—`FileReader` in this case—to help with opening the file. `FileReader`'s constructor will accept a file name as its argument and produce a stream that can be the argument for `BufferedReader`'s constructor. Like `FileWriter`, `FileReader` provides only basic support for text files. However, the class `BufferedReader` has methods such as `readLine`. We use both classes to provide an appropriate constructor and convenient methods.

BufferedReader's method `readLine` reads the next line of input from the input stream and returns that line. If the read goes beyond the end of the file, `null` is returned. In contrast, `Scanner`'s method `nextLine` throws a runtime exception if it attempts to read beyond the end of the file.

Notice that we catch two kinds of exceptions, `FileNotFoundException` and `IOException`. Opening the file might throw a `FileNotFoundException`, and any invocation of `readLine` might throw an `IOException`. Because a `FileNotFoundException` is a kind of `IOException`, we could choose to catch only `IOException`. However, if we do this, we would not know the reason for the exception. Was it caused by opening the file or by reading from the file after it was opened?

After we are finished reading the text file, we close it by invoking the method `close`, much as we did when we were finished writing a file. This time, however, we call `close` from within a `try` block because `BufferedReader`'s `close` can throw an `IOException`. Since `readLine` can also throw this exception, we give `close` its own `try` and `catch` blocks so we can tell why an `IOException` occurred. We place the `try` block and its corresponding `catch` block within a `finally` block that is associated with the first `try` block in the example. In this way, we will close the file even if an exception occurs while reading the file.

Note: If you pass stream A to the constructor of stream B, closing stream B also closes stream A. Thus, in our example in Segment C.15, closing the stream `fromFile` also closes the underlying stream `fr`.

C.17 The class `BufferedReader` does not have any methods—such as `nextInt` in `Scanner`—that can read a number. The only way that you can read a number from a text file using the class `BufferedReader` is to read it as a string and then convert the string to a number. Some techniques for converting strings to numbers are discussed in Segment A.101 of Appendix A.

The class `BufferedReader` does, however, have a method `read` that reads a single character. This method returns a positive integer of type `int` that corresponds to the character read; it does not return the character itself. Thus, to get the character, you must use a type cast, as in

```
char nextChar = (char)(fromFile.read());
```

If the read goes beyond the end of the file, `read` returns –1. You would check for this condition before casting the returned integer to a character.

Although `Scanner` does not have an analogous read method, you could use `Scanner`'s method `findInLine` with the pattern `"."` to return a one-character string.

Note: **Testing for the End of a Text File**

What happens if your program tries to read beyond the end of a text file? If you use the class `Scanner` to read the file, you can call the method `hasNextLine`. It returns false if the end of the file is encountered. Segment C.13 showed how we used this method in a loop to read all the lines in a file. If you use the class `BufferedReader`, the methods `readLine` and `read` return `null` and –1, respectively, at the end of the file. The example in Segment C.15 checked the return value of `readLine` to detect this condition.

Note: **Scanner versus BufferedReader**

Reading a text file is easier if you use the class `Scanner` instead of the class `BufferedReader`. In addition, `Scanner` has more methods than `BufferedReader`, so reading data in various formats is more convenient. If your compiler does not support Java 5, however, `Scanner` will be unavailable to you.

Defining a Method to Open a Stream

C.18   Imagine that we want to write a method that opens a file. We will use a text file here and open it for output, but the idea is applicable to any kind of file. Our method has a `String` parameter that represents the file name. The client of this method could either read the file name from the user, as shown earlier, or use a literal for the file name. The method that follows creates an output stream, connects it to the given file, and returns the stream to the client.

```
public static PrintWriter openOutputTextFile(String fileName)
                            throws FileNotFoundException, IOException
{
    PrintWriter toFile = new PrintWriter(fileName);
    return toFile;
} // end openOutputTextFile
```

We could invoke this method as follows:

```
      PrintWriter toFile = null;
      try
      {
        PrintWriter toFile = openOutputTextFile("data.txt");
      }
      < appropriate catch blocks are here >
```

and go on to use `toFile` to write to the file.

What if we had written the method as a void method, so that instead of returning an output stream, it had the stream as a parameter? The following method looks reasonable, but it has a problem:

```
      // This method does not do what we want it to do.
      public static void openFile(String fileName, PrintWriter stream)
                       throws FileNotFoundException, IOException
      {
        stream = new PrintWriter(fileName);
      } // end openFile
```

Let's consider, for example, the following statements that invoke the method:

```
      PrintWriter toFile = null;
      try
      {
        openFile("data.txt", toFile);
      }
```

After this code is executed, the value of `toFile` is still `null`. The file that was opened in the method `openFile` went away when the method ended. The problem has to do with how Java handles arguments of a class type. These arguments are passed to the method as a memory address that cannot be changed. The object at the memory address normally can be changed, but the memory address itself cannot be changed. Thus, you cannot change `toFile`.

This applies only to arguments of methods. If the stream variable is either a data field or declared locally within the body of the method, you can open a file and connect it to the stream and this problem will not occur. Once a stream is connected to a file, however, you can pass the stream variable as an argument to a method, and the method can change the file.

I/O with Binary Files

C.19   Binary files store primitive data in the same format used in the computer's main memory. This fact is the reason why a program can process numeric data in binary files so efficiently. Values of the same primitive type are represented by the same number of bytes in a binary file. For example, all `int` values occupy four bytes each in a binary file, and all `double` values require eight bytes each.

You can use a Java program to create a binary file on one computer and have it read by a Java program on another computer. Normally, you cannot use a text editor to read binary files.

The most commonly used stream classes for processing binary files are `DataInputStream` and `DataOutputStream`. Each class has methods to read or write data one byte at a time. These streams can also convert numbers and characters to bytes that can be stored in a binary file. They allow your program to write data to or read data from a binary file as if the data were not just bytes but strings or items of any of Java's primitive data types. If you do not need to access your files via an editor, the easiest and most efficient way to read and write data to files is to use `DataInputStream` and `DataOutputStream` with a binary file.

Writing to a Binary File Using `DataOutputStream`

C.20   If you want to create a binary file to store either `String` values or values of any of the primitive data types, you can use the stream class `DataOutputStream`. The following example uses the method `writeInt` of this class to write an `int` value to the file *integers.bin*:

```java
String fileName = "integers.bin";
Scanner keyboard = new Scanner(System.in);
System.out.println("Creating a file of integers that you enter.");

try
{
    FileOutputStream fos = new FileOutputStream(fileName); // can throw
                                                // FileNotFoundException
    DataOutputStream toFile = new DataOutputStream(fos);

    System.out.println("Enter nonnegative integers, one per line.");
    System.out.println("Enter a negative number at the end.");

    int number = keyboard.nextInt();
    while (number >= 0)
    {
        toFile.writeInt(number);                    // can throw IOException
        number = keyboard.nextInt();
    } // end while
}
catch (FileNotFoundException e)
{
    System.out.println("Error opening the file " + fileName);
    System.exit(0);
}
catch (IOException e)
{
    System.out.println("Error writing the file " + fileName);
    System.exit(0);
} // end try/catch
finally
{
    try
    {
        if (toFile != null)
            toFile.close();                         // can throw IOException
    }
    catch (IOException e)
    {
        System.out.println("Error closing the file " + fileName);
        System.exit(0);
    } // end try/catch
} // end finally
```

C.21   **Opening the file.** The output stream for writing to the file *integers.bin* is created and named when we open the file:

```java
FileOutputStream fos = new FileOutputStream(fileName);
DataOutputStream toFile = new DataOutputStream(fos);
```

The class DataOutputStream has no constructor whose argument can be a file name. Thus, as we have done earlier, we use an intermediate class—in this case, FileOutputStream—whose constructor does take a file name to create a stream that we pass to the constructor of DataOutputStream. We do not use FileOutputStream by itself, because its methods are not as convenient as those in DataOutputStream.

If the file *integers.bin* does not exist, these statements will create an empty file named *integers.bin*. If the file *integers.bin* exists already, these statements effectively will erase its contents so that the file starts out empty.

C.22   **Writing the file.** The stream toFile, which is an object of the class DataOutputStream, has some similarity to the stream System.out. While both objects have methods for handling program output, these methods have different names and somewhat different behaviors. Instead of a method named println, DataOutputStream has the method writeInt, for example. This method writes a single int value to a file. In particular, the statement

```
toFile.writeInt(number);
```

writes the value of the int variable number to the file *integers.bin*.

The numbers in a binary file are not written in a human-readable form. Instead, they are encoded as a sequence of bytes in the same way that the numbers would be encoded in the computer's main memory. These coded int values cannot be read with a text editor. Realistically, they can be read only by another Java program. The numbers are written in the file, one immediately after the other. No lines or other separators are between them.

Notice that our example sends output to two different places by using two different output streams. The stream toFile is connected to the binary file *integers.bin* and sends its output to that file. The other output stream is System.out. You may have used System.out so often that you don't think of it in this way, but it is an output stream that is connected to your computer's display. So statements that use System.out.println send their output to the screen.

When you are finished writing the file, you should close it by using a statement such as

```
toFile.close();
```

Closing a binary file flushes the buffer, as you saw in Segment C.11 for text files. You can flush the buffer at any time by calling the method flush.

C.23   **Exceptions.** Since the constructor of FileOutputStream and the methods writeInt and close each can throw an exception, much of the code shown in Segment C.20 is within try blocks. A problem that occurs when opening a file causes a FileNotFoundException, while writing to or closing the file can cause an IOException. We catch each of these exceptions in its own catch block, so that if an exception occurs, we get an appropriate error message. Notice that we call close from within its own try block, as we did in Segment C.15. This try block and its catch block are within a finally block. If a FileNotFoundException or an IOException occurs while writing to the file, the program terminates because the catch blocks for these exceptions call System.exit. In these cases, the finally block does not execute. But if an exception not derived from IOException occurs—for example, if an unchecked exception such as InputMismatchException occurs while reading from the keyboard—the finally block will execute and the file will be closed.

C.24   **Other methods in DataOutputStream.** You can use a stream from the class DataOutputStream to write values of any primitive type and also to write data of the type String. The class DataOutputStream has the methods writeLong, writeDouble, and writeFloat, which are analogous to writeInt. Each of these methods can throw an IOException. The method writeChar writes a single character, but writeChar expects its argument to be of type int. If you start with a value of type char, the char value must be type-cast to an int before it is passed to the method writeChar. Java will automatically convert a char value to an int value for you, so you do not need to write the type cast explicitly. Thus, if toFile is a stream of type DataOutputStream, you could write, for example,

    toFile.writeChar('A');

and have it mean

    toFile.writeChar((**int**)'A');

The method writeBoolean writes a single boolean value:

    toFile.writeBoolean(**false**);

To write a string to a binary file, you use the method writeUTF. For example, the following will write the string *Hi Mom* to the file connected to the stream toFile:

    toFile.writeUTF("Hi Mom");

Of course, with writeUTF or any of the write methods, you can use a variable of the appropriate type (in this case, the type String) as an argument to the method.

Note: The **Unicode Text Format**, or **UTF**, coding scheme is an alternative coding scheme that uses one byte for each ASCII character but two bytes for other Unicode characters. Recall that Java uses the Unicode character set, which includes characters for many languages other than English. Each character has a two-byte Unicode representation. The ASCII character set is a subset of the Unicode character set and is often used for English and typical Java programs. Each ASCII character occupies one byte.

Like PrintWriter, DataOutputStream has a method flush that you can use to empty the output buffer at any time.

C.25   When the method writeInt writes an integer to a binary file, it stores four bytes for each value of type int. Likewise, when writeDouble writes a real value, it stores eight bytes for each value of type double. Each write method except for writeUTF writes a fixed number of bytes every time it writes a value.

The method writeUTF uses differing numbers of bytes to store different strings in a file. Longer strings require more bytes than shorter strings. This can present a problem, because data items in a binary file have no separators between them. Thus, writeUTF precedes each string with its length in bytes. This length value allows a subsequent read operation to know how many bytes to read from the file.

Note: **Multiple data types in one binary file**
You can write output of different types to the same binary file. For example, you can write a combination of int, double, and String values. However, mixing types in a file does require special care so that you can read them from the file later. To read a file of mixed types, you need to know the order in which the various types appear in the file because, as you will see, a program that reads from the file uses a different method to read data of each different type.

C.26   **Appending to a binary file.** To add a program's output to the end of the data already in a binary file—that is, to append data to the file—you would revise the invocation of `FileOutputStream`'s constructor in Segment C.20, as follows:

```
FileOutputStream fos = new FileOutputStream(fileName, true);
```

The second parameter of the constructor is a boolean value that indicates whether to append data to an existing file. If *integers.bin* does not exist already, Java will create an empty file of that name and write the output to this empty file. However, if *integers.bin* does exist, the program's output will be placed after the old contents of the file.

Reading from a Binary File Using `DataInputStream`

C.27   If you use `DataOutputStream` to write data to a binary file, you can read that file by using the stream class `DataInputStream`. Each output method in `DataOutputStream` corresponds to an input method in `DataInputStream`. For example, if you use the method `writeInt` to write an integer to a binary file, you can read that integer back by using the method `readInt`. If you write a number to a file using the method `writeDouble`, you can read that number back by using the method `readDouble`, and so forth.

The following statements demonstrate how to read the binary file of integers that we created in Segment C.20:

```java
String fileName = "integers.bin";
DataInputStream fromFile = null;

try
{
   FileInputStream fis = new FileInputStream(fileName); // can throw
                                               // FileNotFoundException
   fromFile = new DataInputStream(fis);
   System.out.println("Reading all the integers in the file " +
                     fileName);

   while (true)
   {
      int nextNumber = fromFile.readInt(); // can throw EOFException,
                                     //               IOException
      System.out.println(nextNumber);
   } // end while
}
catch (FileNotFoundException e)
{
   System.out.println("Cannot open file " + fileName);
   System.exit(0);
}
catch (EOFException e)
{
   System.out.println("End of the file " + fileName + " reached.");
}
catch (IOException e)
{
   System.out.println("Error reading the file " + fileName);
   System.exit(0);
} // end try/catch
```

```
        finally
        {
          try
          {
            if (toFile != null)
              fromFile.close();                    // can throw IOException
          }
          catch (IOException e)
          {
            System.out.println("Error closing the file " + fileName);
            System.exit(0);
          } // end try/catch
        } // end finally
```

C.28   **Opening the file.** You open a binary file for input in a manner similar to opening it for output, as described in Segment C.21. You use the class `DataInputStream` instead of `DataOutputStream`, and you use the class `FileInputStream` instead of `FileOutputStream`. Since `FileInputStream` can throw a `FileNotFoundException`, we invoke the constructors within a `try` block. This `try` block is followed by a `catch` block for the `FileNotFoundException`, other `catch` blocks, and a `finally` block to close the file.

C.29   **Reading the file.** Since we know that the binary file contains integers, we use the method `readInt` in `DataInputStream` to read them. This method can throw either an `IOException`—if an error occurs—or an `EOFException` when the end of the file is reached. Thus, the loop that reads and displays the file is within the `try` block mentioned in the previous segment.

The loop uses a `while` statement whose boolean expression is the constant `true`. We depend on the `EOFException` to interrupt the execution of the loop. At that time, we catch the exception and display a message. Whereas we treat an `IOException` as a fatal error, we consider an `EOFException` as a normal and expected occurrence. Following the `catch` blocks is a `finally` block that closes the input stream and handles any `IOException` that might occur as a result.

C.30   **More about reading a binary file.** You can use a stream from the class `DataInputStream` to read values of any primitive type and also to read data of the type `String`. In addition to `readInt`, `DataInputStream` has the methods `readLong`, `readDouble`, and `readFloat`, which are analogous to `readInt`.

The method `readChar` reads a single character that was written using `writeChar`. Likewise, `readBoolean` reads a single boolean value that was written using `writeBoolean`. To read a string from a binary file that was written using `writeUTF`, you use the method `readUTF`. All of these methods can throw either an `IOException` or an `EOFException`.

A binary file can contain data of differing types, and you can use `DataInputStream` to read such a file. You must be careful, however, to match read methods with data of the appropriate type. If a data item in the file is not of the type expected by the reading method, the result is likely to be wrong. For example, if your program writes an integer using `writeInt`, any program that reads that integer should read it using `readInt`. If you instead use `readDouble`, for example, your program will misbehave. This and subsequent read operations will most likely not match the file and will be incorrect.

Programming Tip: Binary files and text files encode their data in different ways. A stream that expects to read a binary file, such as a stream in the class `DataInputStream`, will have problems reading a text file. If you attempt to read a text file with a stream in the class `DataInputStream`, your program either will read "garbage values" or will encounter some other error condition.

Programming Tip: Check for the end of a file

When reading from a file, your program should check for the end of the file and do something appropriate when it reaches it. If your program tries to read beyond the end of a file, it may enter an infinite loop or end abnormally. Even if you think your program will not read past the end of the file, you should provide for this eventuality just in case things do not go exactly as you planned.

Programming Tip: Ways to check for the end of a file

Here are some possible ways to test for the end of a file:

- End the file with a special value to serve as a **sentinel value**. Then your program can stop reading when it reads the sentinel value. For example, a file of nonnegative integers could use a negative integer at the end as a sentinel value. Using a sentinel value, however, restricts your data to values other than the sentinel.
- Catch an EOFException, if the read method that you use throws one. When reading from a binary file, the methods in DataInputStream throw an EOFException when they try to read beyond the end of a file.
- Test for a special value, such as null, if the read method that you use returns one. When reading from a text file, the methods in BufferedReader return either null or -1 when they try to read beyond the end of a file. (See the Note at the end of Segment C.17.)

The Class File

C.31   Java provides a class named File that is like a wrapper class for file names. A string such as *data.txt* might be a file name, but it has only string properties. It has no file-name properties. A File object, on the other hand, knows that it is supposed to name a file. You can use File to check certain properties of files. For example, you can check whether a file with a specified name exists and whether a file is readable.

You usually—but not always—can pass an object of type File to a stream constructor as an argument whenever you can use a string as the argument. In particular, the classes FileInputStream, FileOutputStream, FileReader, FileWriter, PrintWriter, and Scanner each have a constructor that accepts a File object as an argument.

C.32   You can create a File object by writing a statement such as the following one:

```
File fileObject = new File("data.txt");
```

You then can use the method exists of the class File to test whether any file with the name *data.txt* exists, as in this example:

```
if (!fileObject.exists())
  System.out.println("No file named " + fileObject.getName() +
                     " exists.");
```

The method `getName` simply returns the file's name.

Most operating systems let you designate some files as not readable or as readable only by certain applications. So if you know that a file has a certain name, you can see whether the file exists *and* whether the operating system will let you read it by using the method `canRead`, as follows:

```
if (!fileObject.canRead())
   System.out.println("Not allowed to read the file " +
                          fileObject.getName() + ".");
```

C.33   Here is a selection of methods in the class `File`, including those that you have just seen:

public boolean canRead()
Tests whether the file exists and can be read.

public boolean canWrite()
Tests whether the file exists and can be written.

public boolean delete()
Deletes the file and signals whether deletion was possible.

public boolean exists()
Tests whether the file exists.

public String getName()
Returns the name of the file.

public String getPath()
Returns the path name of the file.

public long length()
Returns the length of the file in bytes.

Note: Path names
When passing a file name as an argument to a constructor of classes like `File` and `FileReader`, you can use a simple file name. Java assumes that the file is in the same directory (folder) as the one that contains the program. You also can use a full or relative path name. A **path name** gives not only the name of the file, but also tells what directory (folder) the file is in. A **full path name**, as the name suggests, gives a complete path name. A **relative path name** gives the path to the file starting in the directory that contains your program. Path names depend on your operating system rather than the Java language.

Object Serialization

C.34   You have seen how to write primitive values and strings to a file, and how to read them again. How would you write and read objects other than strings? You could, of course, write an object's data fields to a file and invent some way to reconstruct the object when you read the file. When you consider that a data field could be another object that itself could have an object as a data field, completing this task sounds formidable.

Fortunately, Java provides a simple way—called **object serialization**—to represent an object as a sequence of bytes that can be written to a binary file. This process will occur automatically for any object that belongs to a class that implements the interface `Serializable`. This interface, which is in the package `java.io`, is empty, so you have no additional methods to implement. Adding only the words `implements Serializable` to the class's definition is enough.

For example, we could begin a class `Student` as follows:

```
import java.io.Serializable;
public class Student implements Serializable
{
    . . .
```

The `Serializable` interface tells the compiler that `Student` objects can be serialized. Since `Serializable` appears only once in the definition of the class `Student`, you could conveniently omit the `import` statement and begin the class as follows:

```
public class Student implements java.io.Serializable
```

To serialize an object and write it to a binary file, you use the method `writeObject` from the class `ObjectOutputStream`. To read a serialized object from a binary file, you use the method `readObject` from the class `ObjectInputStream`.

C.35

Example. To serialize the `Student` object `aStudent` and write it to a binary file, we would write the following statements within one or more `try` blocks:

```
FileOutputStream fos = new FileOutputStream(fileName);
ObjectOutputStream toFile = new ObjectOutputStream(fos);
. . .
toFile.writeObject(aStudent);
```

Any objects that are data fields of `aStudent` must also belong to a class that implements `Serializable`. Such objects are serialized when `aStudent` is serialized. Many classes in the Java Class Library—including `String`—implement `Serializable`.

To read the `Student` object from the binary file, we would write

```
FileInputStream fis = new FileInputStream(fileName);
ObjectInputStream fromFile = new ObjectInputStream(fis);
. . .
Student joe = (Student)fromFile.readObject();
```

within one or more `try` blocks.

C.36   We will call a class **serializable** if all of the following are true:

- The class implements the interface `Serializable`
- Any of its object data fields are instances of a serializable class
- Its direct super class, if any, is either serializable or defines a default constructor

---

Note: Any subclass of a serializable class is serializable.

C.37   **Arrays.** Since Java treats arrays as objects, you can use `writeObject` to write an array to a binary file, and you can use `readObject` to read it from the file. For example, suppose that `group` is an array of `Student` objects. If `toFile` is an instance of `ObjectOutputStream` that is associated with a binary file, we can write the array to that file by executing the statement

```
toFile.writeObject(group);
```

After creating the file, we can read the array by using the statement

```
Student[] myArray = (Student[])fromFile.readObject();
```

where `fromFile` is an instance of `ObjectInputStream` that is associated with the file that we just created.

Note: **Checked exceptions thrown by a selection of classes and methods in `java.io`**

Class and Methods	Exceptions[1]

`BufferedReader`
Constructor
`close, read,`
  `readLine`
	
	None
	IOException

`BufferedWriter`
Constructor
`close`
	
	None
	IOException

`DataInputStream`
Constructor
`close`
`readInt`, other read
  methods
	
	None
	IOException
	`EOFException, IOException`

`DataOutputStream`
Constructor
`close, flush,`
  `writeInt`, other write
  methods
	
	None
	IOException

`File`
Constructor,
  `canRead, canWrite,`
  `delete, exists,`
  `getName, getPath,`
  `length`
	
	None

`FileInputStream`
Constructor
`close`
	
	`FileNotFoundException`
	IOException

`FileOutputStream`
Constructor
`close`
	
	`FileNotFoundException`
	IOException

`FileReader`
Constructor
`close`
	
	`FileNotFoundException`
	IOException

---

1. Unless otherwise noted, all exceptions are in the package `java.io`.

FileWriter
Constructor, close   IOException

ObjectInputStream
Constructor   IOException, StreamCorruptedException
close   IOException
readObject   java.lang.ClassNotFoundException, InvalidClassException,
                               OptionalDataException, StreamCorruptedException,
                               IOException

ObjectOutputStream
Constructor, close   IOException
writeObject   InvalidClassException, IOException, NotSerializableException

PrintWriter
Constructor   FileNotFoundException
close, flush   IOException
print, println   None

Scanner
Constructor   FileNotFoundException
Other methods   None

PROGRAMMING TIPS

● Use a text file if you want a text editor to either create a file that a program will read or read a file that a program created. In other cases, consider a binary file, as it occupies less space.

● To avoid losing data, close an output stream when you are finished writing to it.

● Binary files and text files encode their data in different ways. A stream that expects to read a binary file, such as a stream in the class `DataInputStream`, will have problems reading a text file. If you attempt to read a text file with a stream in the class `DataInputStream`, your program either will read "garbage values" or will encounter some other error condition.

● When reading from a file, your program should check for the end of the file and do something appropriate when it reaches it. If your program tries to read beyond the end of a file, it may enter an infinite loop or end abnormally. Even if you think your program will not read past the end of the file, you should provide for this eventuality just in case things do not go exactly as you planned.

● Here are some possible ways to test for the end of a file:

  ■ End the file with a special value to serve as a sentinel value. Then your program can stop reading when it reads the sentinel value. For example, a file of nonnegative integers could use a negative integer at the end as a sentinel value. Using a sentinel value, however, restricts the values that you can place in the file.

  ■ Catch an `EOFException`, if the read method that you use throws one. When reading from a binary file, the methods in `DataInputStream` throw an `EOFException` when they try to read beyond the end of a file.

  ■ Test for a special value, such as `null`, if the read method that you use returns one. When reading from a text file, the methods in `BufferedReader` return either `null` or –1 when they try to read beyond the end of a file.

D

Documentation and Programming Style

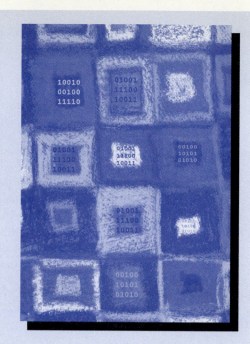

Most programs are used many times and are changed either to fix bugs or to accommodate new demands by the user. If the program is not easy to read and to understand, it will not be easy to change. It might even be impossible to change without heroic efforts. Even if you use your program only once, you should pay some attention to its readability. After all, you will have to read the program to debug it.

In this appendix, we discuss three techniques that can help make your program more readable: meaningful names, indenting, and comments.

Naming Variables and Classes

D.1 Names like x and y are almost never good variable names. The name you give to a variable should suggest what the variable is used for. If the variable holds a count of something, you might name it count. If the variable holds a tax rate, you might name it taxRate.

In addition to choosing names that are meaningful and legal in Java, you should follow the normal practice of other programmers. That way it will be easier for them to read your code and to combine your code with their code, should you work on a project with more than one person. By convention, each variable name begins with a lowercase letter, and each class name begins with an uppercase letter. If the name consists of more than one word, use capital letters at the word boundaries, as in the variable numberOfTries and the class StringBuffer.

Use all uppercase letters for named constants to distinguish them from other variables. Use the underscore character to separate words, if necessary, as in INCHES_PER_FOOT.

Indenting

D.2 A program has a structure: Smaller parts are within larger parts. You use indentation to indicate this structure and thereby make your program easier to read. Although Java ignores any indentation you use, indenting consistently is essential to good programming style.

Each class begins at the left margin and uses braces to enclose its definition. For example, you might write

```java
public class CircleCalculation
{
    . . .
} // end CircleCalculation
```

The data fields and methods appear indented within these braces, as illustrated in the following simple program:

```java
public class CircleCalculation
{
    public static final double PI = Math.PI;

    public static void main(String[] args)
    {
        double radius; // in inches
        double area;   // in square inches
        . . .
    } // end main
} // end CircleCalculation
```

Within each method, you indent the statements that form the method's body. These statements in turn might contain compound statements that are indented further. Thus, the program has statements nested within statements.

Each level of nesting should be indented from the previous level to show the nesting more clearly. The outermost structure is not indented at all. The next level of nested structure is indented. The nested structure within that is double indented, and so on. Typically, you should indent two or three spaces at each level of indentation. You want to see indentation clearly, but you want to use most of the line for the Java statement.

If a statement does not fit on one line, you can write it on two or more lines. However, when you write a single statement on more than one line, indent the successive lines more than the first line, as in the following example:

```
System.out.println("The volume of a sphere whose radius is " + radius +
                   " inches is " + volume + " cubic inches.");
```

Ultimately, you need to follow the rules for indenting—and for programming style in general—given by your instructor or project manager. In any event, you should indent consistently within any one program.

Comments

D.3   The documentation for a program describes what the program does and how it does it. The best programs are **self-documenting**. That is, their clean style and well-chosen names make the program's purpose and logic clear to any programmer who reads the program. Although you should strive for such self-documenting programs, your programs will also need a bit of explanation to make them completely clear. This explanation can be given in the form of **comments**.

Comments are notations in your program that help a person understand the program, but that are ignored by the compiler. Many text editors automatically highlight comments in some way, such as showing them in color. In Java, there are several ways of forming comments.

Single-Line Comments

D.4   To write a comment on a single line, begin the comment with two slashes //. Everything after the slashes until the end of the line is treated as a comment and is ignored by the compiler. This form is handy for short comments, such as

```
String sentence; // Spanish version
```

If you want a comment of this kind to span several lines, each line must contain the symbols //.

Comment Blocks

D.5   Anything written between the matching pairs of symbols /* and */ is a comment and is ignored by the compiler. This form usually is not used to document a program. Instead, the pair /* and */ is handy during debugging to temporarily disable a group of Java statements. However, Java programmers do use the pair /** and */ to delimit comments written in a certain form, as you will see in Segment D.7.

When to Write Comments

D.6   It is difficult to explain just when you should write a comment. Too many comments can be as bad as too few. Too many comments can hide the really important ones. Too few comments can leave a reader baffled by things that were obvious to you. Just remember that you also will read your program. If you read it next week, will you remember what you did just now?

Every program file should begin with an explanatory comment. This comment should give all the important information about the file: what the program does, the name of the author, how to contact the author, the date that the file was last changed, and in a course, what the assignment is. Every method should begin with a comment that explains the method.

Within methods, you need comments to explain any nonobvious details. Notice the poor comments on the following declarations of the variables radius and area:

```
double radius; // the radius
double area;   // the area
```

Because we chose descriptive variable names, these comments are obvious. But rather than simply omitting these comments, can we write something that is not obvious? What units are used for the radius? Inches? Feet? Meters? Centimeters? We will add a comment that gives this information, as follows:

```
double radius; // in inches
double area;   // in square inches
```

Java Documentation Comments

D.7   The Java language comes with a utility program named **javadoc** that will generate HTML documents that describe your classes. These documents tell people who use your program or class how to use it, but omit all the implementation details.

The program javadoc extracts the header for your class, the headers for all public methods, and comments that are written in a certain form. No method bodies and no private items are extracted.

For javadoc to extract a comment, the comment must satisfy three conditions:

- The comment must occur immediately before a public class definition or the header of a public method.
- The comment must begin with /** and end with */.
- Each line of the comment must begin with *.

Segment D.12 contains an example of a comment in this style.

Placing extra asterisks is both allowed and common. You can insert HTML commands in your comments so that you gain more control over javadoc, but that is not necessary and we will not do so in this book.

D.8   **Tags.** Comments written for javadoc usually contain special **tags** that identify such things as the programmer and a method's parameters and return value. Tags begin with the symbol @. We will describe only four tags in this appendix.

The tag @author identifies the programmer's name and is required of all classes and interfaces. (To save space, we will ignore this requirement in this book.) The other tags of interest to us are used with methods. They must appear in the following order within a comment that precedes a method's header:

```
@param
@return
@throws
```

We will describe each of these tags next.

D.9   **The @param tag.** You must write a @param tag for every parameter in a method. You should list these tags in the order in which the parameters appear in the method's header. After the @param tag, you give the name and description of the parameter. Typically, you use a phrase instead of a sentence to describe the parameter, and you mention the parameter's data type first. Do not use punctuation between the parameter name and its description, as javadoc inserts one dash when creating its documentation.

For example, the comments

```
* @param code      the character code of the ticket category
* @param customer  the string that names the customer
```

will produce the following lines in the documentation:

```
code - the character code of the ticket category
customer - the string that names the customer
```

D.10 **The @return tag.** You must write a @return tag for every method that returns a value, even if you have already described the value in the method's description. Try to say something more specific about this value here. This tag must come after any @param tags in the comment. Do not use this tag for void methods and constructors.

D.11 **The @throws tag.** If a method throws a checked exception, you name it next by using a @throws tag. Recall that any checked exceptions that a method throws will also appear in a throws clause in the method's header. You also should list any unchecked exceptions—other than NullPointerException—that a client might catch.

Include a @throws tag for each exception, and list them alphabetically by name.

D.12 **Example.** Here is a sample javadoc comment for a method. We usually begin such comments with a brief description of the method's purpose. Often, we will precede that description with the word "Task." This is our convention, as javadoc has no tag for this purpose.

```
/** Task: Adds a new entry to a roster.
 *  @param newEntry     the object to be added to the roster
 *  @param newPosition  the position of newEntry within the roster
 *  @return true if the addition is successful
 *  @throws RosterException if newPosition < 1 or newPosition >
 *                          1 + the length of the list */
public boolean add(Object newEntry, int newPosition)
        throws RosterException
```

The documentation that javadoc prepares from the previous comment appears as follows:

add

```
public boolean add(java.lang.Object newEntry,
                   int newPosition)
        throws RosterException
```

Task: Adds a new entry to a roster.

Parameters:
    newEntry - the object to be added to the roster
    newPosition - the position of newEntry within the roster
Returns:
    true if the addition is successful
Throws:
    RosterException - if newPosition < 1 or newPosition > 1 + the length of the roster

To save space in this book, we sometimes omit portions of a comment that we would include in our actual programs. For example, some methods might have only a description of their purpose, and some might have only a @return tag.

Running javadoc

D.13   You run javadoc on an entire package. However, if you want to run it on a single class, you can make the class into a package simply by inserting the following at the start of the file for the class:

package *package_name*;

Remember that the package name should describe a relative path name for the directory or folder containing the files in the package.

To run javadoc, you must be in the folder that contains the package's folder, but not in the package folder itself. Then you execute the following command:

javadoc -d *document_folder* *package_name*

Replace *document_folder* with the name of the folder in which you want javadoc to place the HTML documents it produces. The folder must already exist; javadoc will not create it for you.

For example, suppose you want to use javadoc to generate documentation for the class MyClass. Create a folder to hold a package; for instance, you might call the folder—and the package— MyStuff. Place the file MyClass.java in the folder MyStuff, and place the following at the start of the file MyClass.java:

package MyStuff;

The package MyStuff now contains the class MyClass.

Next, create a folder to receive the HTML documents. For example, you might call this folder MyDocs. Place MyDocs in the folder containing MyStuff. Do not place it within MyStuff.

Finally, use the command cd to change to the directory that contains both MyStuff and MyDocs, and give the following command:

javadoc -d MyDocs MyStuff

If you then look in the folder MyDocs, you will see a number of HTML documents whose names end in .html. You can view these files by using your browser. The HTML documents will describe the package MyStuff, including the class MyClass.

If you wish, you can use the folder MyStuff in place of MyDocs, so that both the source file MyClass.java and the HTML documents end up in the same folder.

Further details about javadoc are available at java.sun.com/j2se/javadoc/index.jsp.

Answers to Self-Test Questions

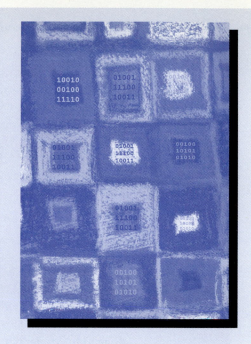

Chapter 1

1. `Name myName = new Name();`
   `myName.setFirst("Joseph");`
   `myName.setLast("Brown");`

2. `System.out.println(myName.getLast() + ", " + myName.getFirst());`

3. Valued: `getFuelLevel`, `getSpeed`, `getMileage`.
   Void: `goForward`, `goBackward`, `accelerate`, `decelerate`.

4. Mutator.

5. Valued.

6. Void.

7. A client could set the data field to an illegal value.

8. `number` is 5 and `aName` references `jamie`.

9. Yes, by using `Name`'s set methods.

10. No.

11. A default constructor is a constructor that has no parameters.

12. You invoke a constructor by using the `new` operator.

13. If you do not define a constructor, the compiler defines a default constructor.

14. The compiler does not define additional constructors. Thus, the class will not have a default constructor.

15. An object that is not referenced is marked for garbage collection. Eventually, the Java run-time environment deallocates the object by returning its memory locations to the operating system so that they can be used again.

16. ```
    public Name(Name aName)
    {
       this(aName.getFirst(), aName.getLast());
    } // end constructor
    ```
    ```

17. Each instance (object) of a class will have a copy of a constant data field that is not static.

18. Yes, as long as the methods also have different parameters. Return type alone is not sufficient to distinguish the methods.

19. **a.** 2
    b. false
    c. `LetterGrade.A_MINUS`

20. A-, because the method `toString` is called implicitly.

Chapter 2

1. Some possibilities are `roomNumber` and `dorm`, or `street`, `city`, `state`, `zip`.

2. `private Address residence;`
   Add the methods `setAddress` and `getAddress`.

3. The constructors, `setStudent`, and `toString`.

4. ```
   public Student()
   {
      this(new Name(), "");
   } // end default constructor
   ```

5. `toString`

6. No. The class defines only one generic type.

7. Yes. You can write the same data type twice to correspond to both S and T.

8. ```
   Name kristen = new Name("Kristen", "Doe");
   Student kris = new Student(kristen, "8000041");
   Name luci = new Name("Luci", "Lei");
   Student lu = new Student(luci, "7705263");
   OrderedPair<Student> labPartners = new OrderedPair<Student>();
   labPartners.setPair(kris, lu);
   ```

9. ```
   Name kristen = new Name("Kristen", "Doe");
   Student kris = new Student(kristen, "8000041");
   Name dean = new Name("Dean", "Brown");
   Pair<Student, Name> aPair = new Pair<Student, Name>(kris, dean);
   ```

10. ```
    NickName bob = new NickName();
    bob.setNickName("Bob");
    System.out.println(bob.getNickName());
    ```

11. The `Vehicle` class has two subclasses, `WheeledVehicle` and `WheellessVehicle`. The subclasses of `WheeledVehicle` are `Automobile` and `Wagon`. `Boat` is a subclass of `WheellessVehicle`. The remaining subclasses are the same as given in the figure.

12. No. Since `getNickName` returns a string, the first statement implicitly calls the method `toString` defined in the class `String`. Thus, *Bob* is displayed. Since the class `NickName` does not define its own version of `toString`, the second statement invokes `Object`'s `toString`. The output involves the memory address of the object referenced by bob.

13. Overloading. The constructors have the same name but different signatures.

14. Overriding. The revised version of `setStudent` in `CollegeStudent` has the same signature and return type as the version in the base class `Student`.

15. Yes. You can assign an object of a class to a variable of any ancestor type. An object of type `HighSchoolStudent` can do anything that an object of type `Student` can do.

16. No. The `Student` object does not have all the behaviors expected of a `HighSchoolStudent` object.

17. `if (sue.equals(susan))`

18. The statements given in Segment 2.5, for example, would begin with

```
OrderedPair fruit = new OrderedPair();
fruit.setPair("apples", "oranges");
```

The disadvantage to this version of `OrderedPair` is that the compiler cannot warn you if you pair objects of different types. Thus, you could write

```
Name joe = new Name("Joe", "Java");
String joePhone = "(401) 555-1234";
OrderedPair joeEntry = new OrderedPair();
joeEntry.setPair(joe, joePhone);
```

19. Overload. The two methods have the same name but different signatures: One has a parameter, one does not.

20. Overriding. The methods have the same signatures and return types.

21. At one time, overloading was an example of polymorphism. Today, polymorphism describes a situation in which an object determines at execution time which action of a method it will use for a method name that is overridden either directly or indirectly.

22. No. Each call to `displayAt` will invoke the correct version of `display`. The first invocation calls `display` in `UndergradStudent`; the second invocation calls `display` in `GradStudent`.

Chapter 3

1. A client interface describes how to use the class. It contains the headers for the class's public methods, the comments that tell you how to use these methods, and any publicly defined constants of the class. The implementation consists of all data fields and the definitions of all methods, including those that are public, private, and protected.

2. A television is one example. The remote control and the controls on the TV form the client interface. The implementation is inside the TV itself.

3. Here are three possibilities:

```
/** Task: Sets the side of the square to a new value.
 *  @param newSide  a real number >= 0 */
public void setSide(double newSide)

/** Task: Sets the side of the square to a new value.
 *  @param newSide  a real number
 *  @return true if the side is set, or
 *          false if newSide is < 0 */
public boolean setSide(double newSide)

/** Task: Sets the side of the square to a new value.
 *  @param newSide  a real number
 *  @throws IllegalArgumentException if newSide is < 0 */
public void setSide(double newSide)
```

4. `// Assertion: max is the largest of array[0],..., array[index]`

5.
```
public interface StudentInterface
{
   public void setStudent(Name studentName, String studentId);
   public void setName(Name studentName);
   public Name getName();
   public void setId(String studentId);
   public String getId();
   public String toString();
} // end StudentInterface
```

6. `public class Student implements StudentInterface`

7. Replace `Name` with `NameInterface` in the methods `setStudent`, `setName`, and `getName`.

8.
```
public boolean equals(Object other)
{
   boolean result;
   if ((other == null) || (getClass() != other.getClass()))
     result = false;
   else
   {
     Circle otherCircle = (Circle)other;
     result = (radius == otherCircle.radius);
   } // end if
   return result;
} // end equals
```

9.
```
public class Name implements Comparable<Name>
{
   . . .
   public int compareTo(Name other)
   {
     int result = last.compareTo(other.last);

     // if last names are equal, check first names
     if (result == 0)
       result = first.compareTo(other.first);

     return result;
   } // end compareTo
   . . .
```

10. No. The class `Pet` must state that it implements `Nameable` in an `implements` clause.

11.

Student
Responsibilities
Set name and ID
Set name
Set ID
Get name
Get ID
Get a string that represents a student
Collaborations
String
Name

12.

Name
-first: String
-last: String
+setName(firstName: String, lastName: String): void
+getName(): String
+setFirst(firstName: String): void
+getFirst(): String
+setLast(lastName: String): void
+getLast(): String
+giveLastNameTo(aName: Name): void
+toString(): String

13. Add a unidirectional association (arrow) from AllCourses to Course with a cardinality of 1 on its tail and * on its head.

Chapter 4

1.
```
myList.add(c)
myList.add(1, a)
myList.add(2, b)
myList.add(4, d)
```

2.
```
seven = myList.remove(7)
three = myList.remove(3)
myList.add(3, seven)
myList.add(7, three)
```

Another solution:
```
seven = myList.getEntry(7)
three = myList.getEntry(3)
myList.replace(3, seven)
myList.replace(7, three)
```

3.
```
ListInterface<Integer> rList = new AList<Integer>();
rList.add(16);
rList.add(4);
rList.add(33);
rList.add(27);
rList.display();
```

4.
```
bob = alphaList.remove(3);
ellen = alphaList.remove(2);
alphaList.add(2, bob);
alphaList.add(3, ellen);
drew = alphaList.remove(4);
ellen = alphaList.remove(3);
alphaList.add(3, drew);
alphaList.add(4, ellen);
```

Another solution uses getEntry and replace, much like the second solution to Question 2.

5. The change to `getEntry` would affect its use by requiring a cast to the type of entry retrieved. Thus, you would write

```
Name secondName = (Name)nameList.getEntry(2);
```

A similar statement without the type cast would be incorrect. A reference to `Object` cannot be assigned to a `Name` variable without a cast.

Chapter 5

1. When the name comes after the name of the student in the last occupied desk; the new student then sits at the desk after the last one that is currently occupied.

2. The students remain in consecutively numbered positions. You do not have to keep track of the locations of the empty desks.

3. Time is saved by not moving the students.

4. The method `clear` could take one of the following actions to deallocate the objects currently in a list: (1) Set elements of the array `list` to `null`; (2) repeatedly remove the last entry by repeatedly calling `remove(length)`; (3) reallocate the array `list`.

5. Advantage: It is easier to implement this add method. Your code will more likely be correct if the other add method is correct.
   Disadvantage: Invoking another method uses more execution time. Additionally, the second add method invokes `makeRoom` needlessly.

6. **a.** a b c d w e
   b. a b c d e w
   c. The operation in Part *a*

7. `myList.add(newEntry)`. The other add method validates the position 6 and then needlessly invokes `makeRoom`.

8. If the list is empty, `length` is zero, so `(givenPosition >= 1) && (givenPosition <= 0)` is always false. Thus, the only way that the previous expression can be true is if the list is not empty.

9. By the reasoning given in the previous answer, if the list is empty, the initial value of `result` is returned.

10. We could, but it is not necessary. After `remove` decrements `length`, `list[length]` is the array location that Haley originally occupied. So `list[length]` and `list[length - 1]` both reference Haley. Since we are not deallocating Haley, we do not have to set `list[length]` to `null`. We can simply ignore its contents.

11. Advantage: You can access any array location directly if you know its index.
    Disadvantages: The array has a fixed size, so you will either waste space or run out of room. When you add or remove an entry, you likely will need to move the other entries within the array.

12.
```java
public boolean add(int newPosition, T newEntry)
{
   boolean isSuccessful = true;

   if ((newPosition >= 1) && (newPosition <= length + 1))
   {
      if (isArrayFull())
         doubleArray();
```

```
        makeRoom(newPosition);
        list[newPosition - 1] = newEntry;
        length++;
      }
    else
      isSuccessful = false;

    return isSuccessful;
  } // end add
```

13. `System.arraycopy(oldList, 0, list, 0, oldSize);`

Chapter 6

1. **a.** First.
   b. The student who arrived last (most recently).
2. At the beginning.
3. **a.** First.
   b. The student who arrived first.
4. At the end.
5. Advantage: You use only as much memory as you need; moving data is unnecessary. Disadvantage: You must traverse the chain to access items that are not first.
6. The student whose name is alphabetically first is in the first desk. You know the address of that desk. The student whose name is alphabetically last is in the last desk. You must traverse the chain to locate it.
7. No. The statements given in Segment 6.22 do not assign a new value to `firstNode`. Also, when the list is empty, `length` is zero. The precondition of `getNodeAt` given in Listing 6-1 requires a positive argument. Even if you redesign `getNodeAt`, the empty list will remain a special case.
8. When the chain is empty, `firstNode` is null. Setting `newNode.next` to `firstNode` sets it to null. Since `newNode.next` already is null as necessary, no harm is done by the additional assignment.
9. **a.** `assert !isEmpty() && (newPosition > 1);`
   b. `getNodeAt(newPosition)`
   c. No. Calling `getNodeAt` to get a reference to the node after the one that `nodeBefore` references results in another traversal of the chain from its beginning. The expression `nodeBefore.next` provides a much faster way to get the required reference.
10. No. If the list is empty, the data field `length` is zero. Thus, the first `if` statement will ensure that `newPosition` is 1 when the second `if` statement executes. If the list is not empty, `newPosition` could have any legal value at this point. In both cases, the decision can be based solely on the value of `newPosition`.
11. The first method add invokes `getNodeAt` only if the list is not empty. Thus, the argument `length` passed to `getNodeAt` is ≥ 1 and ≤ itself. The second method add checks the validity of `newPosition` and then calls `getNodeAt` only if the list is not empty and `newPosition > 1`. It is possible for `newPosition` to equal `length + 1`, but since `getNodeAt`'s argument is `newPosition -1`, the argument's value is ≤ `length` as required.
12. The loop in `getNodeAt` can iterate no more than `length - 1` times. After the first iteration, `currentNode` references the second node. After the second iteration, it references the third node. If the loop were to iterate `length - 1` times, `currentNode` would reference the last node.

13. When the method add calls the method isEmpty, isEmpty returns false because length incorrectly is not zero. Thus, the method getNodeAt is invoked. The second assert statement in getNodeAt causes an AssertionError, because currentNode is null.

14. **a.** The for statement iterates once for each entry in the list, so it is clear that the entire list is displayed.
    b. The while statement ensures that currentNode is not null, so that currentNode.data and currentNode.next are legal.

15. The version of display that calls getNodeAt performs much more work than the original version. Each call to getNodeAt results in a traversal of the chain of nodes from its first node to the desired node. The original version of display traverses the chain only once.

Chapter 7

1. By asking the instructor, get the address of the first desk.
   By looking at the address written on the first desk, get the address of the second desk. This desk is deskBefore.
   By looking at the address written on the second desk, get the address of the third desk. This desk is deskToRemove.
   Copy the address on deskToRemove to deskBefore.
   Return deskToRemove to the hallway.

2. By asking the instructor, locate the first desk.
   Give the address that is written on the first desk to the instructor.
   Return the first desk to the hallway.

3. If the list is empty, length is zero. Thus, (givenPosition >= 1) && (givenPosition <= 0) is always false, and the method would then return null. The only way the body of the first if statement can execute is if the list is not empty.

4. The method replace given in this chapter performs more work than an array-based replace because it must traverse the chain to locate the entry to replace. An array-based replace can locate the desired entry directly, given its array index.

5. The method returns false. If currentNode becomes null, the entire list has been searched without success.

6. Since the list is empty, firstNode—and hence currentNode—is null. The while loop ends immediately and the method returns false.

7. Add java.io.Serializable to the implements clause in the first line of the definition of LList. Add implements java.io.Serializable to the definition of Node.

8. The methods add, remove, and clear. We also should revise the assertions in isEmpty.

9. The first assertion should be

   assert (firstNode == **null**) && (lastNode == **null**);

   The second assertion should be

   assert (firstNode != **null**) && (lastNode != **null**);

10. **a.** To locate the position of an entry in a chain, you traverse the chain from its beginning. You count nodes as you move from node to node until you find the desired entry. To locate the position of an entry in an array, you traverse the array from its beginning, counting locations

as you advance. In both implementations of the list, the definition of `getPosition` contains a loop similar to the one in the method `contains`, but with a counter.

b. The two versions of `getPosition` require about the same time.

Chapter 8

1. The output is

   true
   Rachel
   Jamie
   Rachel

2. ```
   nameIterator.next();
   nameIterator.next();
   System.out.println(nameIterator.next());
   ```

3. ```
   nameIterator.next(); // skip first entry; list has > 1 entry
   while (nameIterator.hasNext())
   {
     System.out.println(nameIterator.next()); // display even-numbered entry
     if (nameIterator.hasNext())
       nameIterator.next();                    // skip odd-numbered entry
   } // end while
   ```

4. ```
   while (nameIterator.hasNext())
   {
     nameIterator.next();
     nameIterator.remove();
   } // end while
   ```

5. False. When the list is empty, both `nextPosition` and `list.getLength()` are zero.

6. Linked. The particular implementation of the list affects the amount of work that the method `getEntry` must perform. For an array-based implementation, `getEntry` accesses the required entry directly and immediately. For a linked implementation, `getEntry` must traverse a chain of nodes to find the desired entry. This takes more time to accomplish than accessing an array element.

7. False. When the list is empty, `firstNode`, and therefore `nextNode`, is `null`.

8. Create the iterators by writing

   ```
   Iterator<String> nameIterator = nameList.getIterator();
   Iterator<String> countingIterator = nameList.getIterator();
   ```

9. ```
   public void display()
   {
     Iterator<T> traverser = getIterator();
     while (traverser.hasNext())
       System.out.println(traverser.next());
   } // end display
   ```

   Other than the overhead of calling methods, this version of `display` has no other disadvantages. In fact, it is easier to write.

10. **a.** Deb.
    b. Deb.

11. Originally, `nextIndex` is the index of the next element that `next` will return. The change makes `nextIndex` the index of the last element that `next` returned. Thus, the following changes are needed:

   - `hasNext` should compare `nextIndex` to `length - 1` instead of `length`
   - `next` should increment `nextIndex` before accessing `list[nextIndex]`
   - `remove` should remove the entry at `nextIndex + 1`

12.
```
public void display()
{
  resetIterator();
  while (hasNext())
    System.out.println(next());
} // end display
```

A disadvantage is that if you have an iteration in progress, and you pause it to call `display`, you will not be able to resume your iteration.

13. **a.** No. The default constructor creates an empty list. If it set `nextNode` to `firstNode`, `nextNode` would be set to `null`.
   b. Yes, but with a disadvantage. Each addition to the list would set `nextNode` to `firstNode`. After creating a list, you could traverse it. However, the only way you could reset the traversal to the list's beginning would be to add another entry to the list.

14.
```
while (traverse.hasNext())
  traverse.next();

while (traverse.hasPrevious())
  System.out.println(traverse.previous());
```

15.
```
traverse.next();      // return Jim
traverse.next();      // return Josh
traverse.set("Jon");  // replace Josh
```

16.
```
traverse.next();        // return Jim
traverse.add("Miguel"); // add Miguel after Jim
```

Chapter 9

1. If you follow the hint given in the question, you will get the sum of n occurrences of $n + 1$, which is $(n + 1) + (n + 1) + \ldots + (n + 1)$. This sum is simply the product $n * (n + 1)$. To get this sum, we added $1 + 2 + \ldots + n$ to itself. Thus, $n * (n + 1)$ is $2 * (1 + 2 + \ldots + n)$. The desired conclusion follows immediately from this fact.

2. Algorithm A: The loop iterates n times, so there are n additions and a total of $n + 1$ assignments. Algorithm B: For each value of i, the inner loop iterates i times, and so performs i additions and i assignments. The outer loop iterates n times. Together, the loops perform $1 + 2 + \ldots + n$ additions and the same number of assignments. Using the identity given in Question 1, the number of additions is $n (n + 1) / 2$. The additional assignment to set `sum` to zero makes the total number of assignments equal to $1 + n (n + 1) / 2$.

3. Ceiling. For example, $\lfloor -4.9 \rfloor$ is -5, but $\lceil -4.9 \rceil$ is -4, which is the integer you get when you truncate -4.9.

4. $3n^2 + 2^n < 2^n + 2^n = 2 * 2^n$ when $n \geq 8$. So $3n^2 + 2^n = O(2^n)$, using $c = 2$ and $N = 8$.

5. The inner loop requires a constant amount of time, and so it is $O(1)$. The outer loop is $O(n)$, and so the entire computation is $O(n)$.

6. Twice as fast.

7. Four times as fast.

8. Let's tabulate the maximum number of times the inner loop executes for various values of index:

index	Inner Loop Iterations
0	$n - 1$
1	$n - 2$
2	$n - 3$
. . .	. . .
$n - 2$	1

As you can see, the maximum number of times the inner loop executes is $1 + 2 + \ldots + n - 1$, which is $n (n - 1) / 2$. Thus, the algorithm is $O(n^2)$ in the worst case.

9. $O(1)$; $O(n)$.

10. $O(1)$ in both cases.

11. $O(1)$ in both cases.

12. $O(1)$ when the entry is found immediately in position 1. $O(n)$ when the entry is found in the last position or is not found at all.

13. $O(n)$ in both cases.

14. $O(1)$; $O(n)$.

15. $O(1)$; $O(n)$.

16. $O(1)$; $O(n)$.

17. $O(n)$ in both cases.

Chapter 10

1.
```java
public static void skipLines(int givenNumber)
{
  if (givenNumber >= 1)
  {
    System.out.println();
    skipLines(givenNumber - 1);
  } // end if
} // end skipLines
```

2. *Algorithm* drawConcentricCircles(givenNumber, givenDiameter, givenPoint)
```
if (givenNumber >= 1)
{
    Draw a circle whose diameter is givenDiameter and whose center is at givenPoint
    givenDiameter = 4 * givenDiameter / 3
    drawConcentricCircles(givenNumber - 1, givenDiameter, givenPoint)
}
```

3. ```java
public static void countUp(int n)
{
   if (n >= 1)
   {
      countUp(n - 1);
      System.out.println(n);
   } // end if
} // end countUp
```

4. ```java
public static int productOf(int n)
{
   int result = 1;
   if (n > 1)
      result = n * productOf(n - 1);
   return result;
} // end productOf
```

5. ```java
public static void displayArray(int[] array, int first, int last)
{
   if (first == last)
      System.out.print(array[first] + " ");
   else
   {
      int mid = (first + last)/2;
      displayArray(array, first, mid - 1);
      System.out.print(array[mid] + " ");
      displayArray(array, mid + 1, last);
   } // end if
} // end displayArray
```

6. The order of events is as follows:

displayBackward()
displayChainBackward(firstNode)
displayChainBackward(*a reference to the second node*)
displayChainBackward(*a reference to the third node*)
displayChainBackward(null)
*Print the data in the third node*
*Print the data in the second node*
*Print the data in the first node*

Activation records for the calls to displayChainBackward appear in a stack, as follows (dCB is an abbreviation for displayChainBackward; the stack is shown top to bottom):

dCB(firstNode)
dCB(*reference to second node*) dCB(firstNode)
dCB(*reference to third node*) dCB(*reference to second node*) dCB(firstNode)
dCB(null) dCB(*reference to third node*) dCB(*reference to second node*) dCB(firstNode)
dCB(*reference to third node*) dCB(*reference to second node*) dCB(firstNode)
*Print the data in the third node*
dCB(*reference to second node*) dCB(firstNode)
*Print the data in the second node*
dCB(firstNode)
*Print the data in the first node*

7. O(n). You can use the same recurrence relation that was shown in Segments 10.22 and 10.23 for the method countDown.
```

8. a. $t(n) = 1 + t(n - 1)$ for $n > 0$, $t(0) = 1$.
   b. Since $t(n) = n + 1$, the algorithm is O(n).

9. Move a disk from pole 1 to pole 2
Move a disk from pole 1 to pole 3
Move a disk from pole 2 to pole 3
Move a disk from pole 1 to pole 2
Move a disk from pole 3 to pole 1
Move a disk from pole 3 to pole 2
Move a disk from pole 1 to pole 2
Move a disk from pole 1 to pole 3
Move a disk from pole 2 to pole 3
Move a disk from pole 2 to pole 1
Move a disk from pole 3 to pole 1
Move a disk from pole 2 to pole 3
Move a disk from pole 1 to pole 2
Move a disk from pole 1 to pole 3
Move a disk from pole 2 to pole 3

10. 2 and 6, respectively.

11. 24 recursive calls and 12 additions.

12. 5 additions.

Chapter 11

1. 9 6 2 4 8
2 6 9 4 8
2 4 9 6 8
2 4 6 9 8
2 4 6 8 9

2. 9 6 2 4 8
6 9 2 4 8
2 6 9 4 8
2 4 6 9 8
2 4 6 8 9

3. No; `insertInOrder` links the node to be inserted into the sorted part of the chain so that the node no longer references the rest of the unsorted part. Since `unsortedPart` still references the inserted node, executing the line in question next would make `unsortedPart` either reference a node in the sorted part or be `null`.

4. The public method `insertionSort` implements an operation that we have added to the ADT list. Therefore, a list object will invoke it.

5. First, you consider the subarray of equally spaced integers at the indices 0, 4, and 8 (they appear in bold):

9 8 2 7 **5** 4 6 3 **1**

Now sort them to get

1 8 2 7 **5** 4 6 3 **9**

The indices 0, 4, and 8 have a separation of 4. Next, consider the integers at indices 1 and 5:

1 **8** 2 7 5 **4** 6 3 9

Sort them to get

1 **4** 2 7 5 **8** 6 3 9

Then sort the integers at indices 2 and 6; they already are in order:

1 4 **2** 7 5 8 **6** 3 9

Next, consider the integers at indices 3 and 7. Sort them to get

1 4 2 **3** 5 8 6 **7** 9

Now decrease the separation between indices to 2. You consider the integers at the indices 0, 2, 4, 6, and 8:

1 4 **2** 3 **5** 8 **6** 7 **9**

You find that they are sorted. Then consider the integers at indices 1, 3, 5, and 7:

1 **4** 2 **3** 5 **8** 6 **7** 9

Sort them to get

1 **3** 2 **4** 5 **7** 6 **8** 9

Decreasing the separation to 1 results in an ordinary insertion sort of an array that is almost sorted.

6. **9** 6 2 4 **8** 7 5 3
   8 6 2 4 **9** 7 5 3
   8 **6** 2 4 9 **7** 5 3
   8 6 **2** 4 9 7 **5** 3
   8 6 2 **4** 9 7 5 **3**
   8 6 2 **3** 9 7 5 **4**
   8 6 2 3 **9** 7 5 4
   2 6 5 3 8 7 **9** 4
   2 **6** 5 3 8 7 9 **4**
   2 **3** 5 4 8 **6** 9 **7**
   Now apply a regular insertion sort.

Chapter 12

1.   9 6 2 4 8 7 5 3
      9 6 2 4   8 7 5 3
      9 6   2 4   8 7   5 3
      9 6   2 4   8 7   5 3
      6 9   2 4   7 8   3 5
      2 4 6 9   3 5 7 8
         2 3 4 5 6 7 8 9

2. *Algorithm* `mergeSort(a, tempArray, first, last)`
```
if (first < last)
{
   mid = (first + last) / 2
```

```
    mergeSort(a, first, mid)
    mergeSort(a, mid + 1, last)
    if (array[mid] > array[mid + 1]))
        Merge the sorted halves a[first..mid] and a[mid+1..last] using the array tempArray
}
```

3. quickSort(array, 0, 7)
   partition(array, 0, 7)
    9 6 2 4 8 7 5 3
    3 6 2 4 8 7 5 9
    3 6 2 5 8 7 4 9
    3 2 6 5 8 7 4 9
    3 2 4 5 8 7 6 9
   quickSort(array, 0, 1)
   insertionSort(array, 0, 1)
    2 3 4 5 8 7 6 9
   quickSort(array, 3, 7)
   partition(array, 3, 7)
    2 3 4 5 8 7 6 9
    2 3 4 5 8 6 7 9
    2 3 4 5 6 8 7 9
    2 3 4 5 6 7 8 9
   quickSort(array, 3, 4)
   insertionSort(array, 3, 4)
    2 3 4 5 6 7 8 9
   quickSort(array, 6, 7)
   insertionSort(array, 6, 7)
    2 3 4 5 6 7 8 9

4. 6340 1234 0291 0003 6325 0068 5227 1638
   6340 0291 0003 1234 6325 5227 0068 1638
   0003 6325 5227 1234 1638 6340 0068 0291
   0003 0068 5227 1234 0291 6325 6340 1638
   0003 0068 0291 1234 1638 5227 6325 6340
   0003 0068 0291 1234 1638 5227 6325 6340

5. *Algorithm* radixSort(a, first, last, wordLength)
   // Sorts the array of lowercase words a[first..last] *into ascending order;*
   // treats each word as if it was padded on the right with blanks to make all words have
   // the same length, wordLength.

   for (i = 1 *to* wordlength)
   {
     Clear bucket['a'], bucket['b'], . . . , bucket['z'], bucket[' ']
     for (index = first *to* last)
     {
       letter = i^{th} *letter from the right of* a[index]
       Place a[index] *at end of* bucket[letter]
     }
     Place contents of bucket['a'], bucket['b'], . . . , bucket['z'], bucket[' ']
       into the array a
   }

Chapter 13

1. ```
SortedListInterface<String> sortedWordList = new SortedList<String>();
int numberOfWords = wordList.getLength();
for (int position = 1; position <= numberOfWords; position++)
   sortedWordList.add(wordList.getEntry(position));
```

2. **a.** ```
int length = sortedWordList.getLength();
String lastEntry = sortedWordList.getEntry(length);
System.out.println(lastEntry);
```
   b. `sortedList.add(sortedList.getEntry(1));`

3. The order is critical. When currentNode is null, currentNode != null is false. Thus, the entire expression in the while statement is false without executing the call currentNode.get-Data(). If the latter call were to execute first when currentNode was null, an exception would occur. Thus, the while statement should remain as written.

4. When the sorted list is empty, getNodeBefore returns null. Thus, in the definition of add, you can omit the call to isEmpty in the if statement.

5. Before the first occurrence of the entry.

6. After the last occurrence of the entry.

7. Before the first occurrence of the entry.

8. The class SortedLinkedList, the private inner class Node, and the class of objects in the sorted list must all implement the interface java.io.Serializable. Thus, SortedLinkedList begins as
   ```
public class SortedLinkedList<T extends Comparable<? super T>>
            implements SortedListInterface<T>, java.io.Serializable
```
   and the class Node begins as
   ```
private class Node implements java.io.Serializable
```

9. Before the first occurrence of the entry. Note that getPosition returns the position of the first occurrence of the entry within the list.

10. No. The field list is private so its methods are unavailable to a client of SortedList.

11. The first occurrence of the object. Note that getPosition returns the position of the first occurrence of the entry within the list.

12. **a.** 2; **b.** -1; **c.** -5; **d.** 4; **e.** -3.

13. ```
public boolean contains(T anEntry)
{
   return getPosition(anEntry) > 0;
} // end contains
```

14. The implementation that invokes getPosition will execute faster. Because the list is sorted, the method getPosition does not always search the entire list when the entry is not present. However, the list's method contains always searches the entire list in this case.

15. Advantage: The implementation is easy to write.

   Disadvantage: The implementation is not efficient when the implementation of the underlying list is linked.
```

Chapter 14

1. The list's method `contains` searches the entire list when the desired entry is not present. By calling `getPosition`, `contains` can take advantage of the sorted order of the entries. The answer to Question 13 of Chapter 13 gives such a method. By adding this method to `SortedList`, you can override `LList`'s `contains`.

2. The client will be unaware of what has happened and will not know where in the sorted list the addition was made.

3. Advantages: The implementation is easy to write. You inherit methods such as `isEmpty` that you do not have to implement.
   Disadvantages: The implementation is not efficient, especially when the implementation of the underlying list is linked. Using inheritance in this way is as inefficient as using composition. You inherit methods (add and replace by position) that you do not want. Moreover, since inheritance implies an *is a* relationship between the sorted list and the list, type compatibility dictates that the sorted list be able to behave like a list. This clearly is not the case, since you cannot insert or replace entries at any given position. Thus, a sorted list is not really a list.

4. **a.**
```
public void addToBeginning(T newEntry)
{
   addFirstNode(new Node(newEntry));
} // end addToBeginning
```

   b.
```
public void addAfterMidpoint(T newEntry)
{
   Node nodeBefore = getNodeAt(getLength() / 2);
   addNodeAfter(nodeBefore, new Node(newEntry));
} // end addAfterMidpoint
```

Chapter 15

1.
```
public ImmutableName(Name aName)
{
   first = aName.getFirst();
   last  = aName.getLast();
} // end constructor
```

2.
```
// Create an object of the class Name
Name derek = new Name("Derek", "Greene");
// Convert the object to an immutable object; don't change its data fields
ImmutableName derekI = derek.getImmutable();
// Add the object to the sorted list nameList
SortedListInterface<ImmutableName> nameList =
                                    new SortedList<ImmutableName>();
nameList.add(derekI);
```

3.
```
// Create an object of the class ImmutableName
ImmutableName lila = new ImmutableName("Lila", "Bleu");
// Convert the object to a mutable object; don't change its data fields
Name changer = lila.getMutable();
// Change the last name of the new object
changer.setLast("Greene");
// Convert the revised mutable object to an immutable object
ImmutableName unchanger = changer.getImmutable();
```

4. **a.** No. The clone y has a name object that is distinct from x's name object, because a deep copy was made. (See Figure 15-7.)

   b. Yes. Both objects share one name object. (See Figure 15-8.)

5.
```java
Node newRef = theCopy.firstNode;
for (Node oldRef = firstNode.getNextNode(); oldRef != null;
        oldRef = oldRef.getNextNode())
{
  newRef.setNextNode((Node)oldRef.clone());
  newRef = newRef.getNextNode();
} // end for
```

Chapter 16

1.
```java
public int contains(T anEntry)
{
  boolean found = false;
  int result = -1;
  for (int index = 0; !found && (index < length); index++)
  {
    if (anEntry.equals(list[index]))
    {
      found = true;
      result = index;
    } // end if
  } // end for

  return result;
} // end contains
```

2.
```java
public static <T> boolean contains(AList<T> theList, T anEntry)
{
  boolean found = false;
  int length = theList.getLength();
  for (int position = 1; !found && (position <= length); position++)
  {
    if (anEntry.equals(theList.getEntry(position)))
      found = true;
  } // end for

  return found;
} // end contains
```

3. The object o is compared with o1, then o2, o3, o4, and o5.

4.
```java
public static <T> boolean contains(AList<T> theList, T anEntry)
{
  return search(theList, 1, theList.getLength(), anEntry);
} // end contains

private static <T> boolean search(AList<T> theList, int first, int last,
                                  T desiredItem)
{
  boolean found;

  if (first > last)
    found = false;
  else if (desiredItem.equals(theList.getEntry(first)))
    found = true;
  else
    found = search(theList, first + 1, last, desiredItem);
```

```
        return found;
    } // end search
```

5. Searching for 8 requires seven comparisons, as follows:

   8 == 10?
   8 < 10?
   8 == 5?
   8 < 5?
   8 == 7?
   8 < 7?
   8 == 8?

   Searching for 16 requires eight comparisons, as follows:

   16 == 10?
   16 < 10?
   16 == 18?
   16 < 18?
   16 == 12?
   16 < 12?
   16 == 15?
   16 < 15?

6. **a.** 12 and 4.
   b. 12, 4, and 8.
   c. 12, 20, and 14.

7.
```
public int contains(T anEntry)
{
    return binarySearch(0, length - 1, anEntry);
} // end contains

private int binarySearch(int first, int last, T desiredItem)
{
    int result;
    int mid = (first + last)/2;

    if (first > last)
        result = -1;
    else if (desiredItem.equals(list[mid]))
        result = mid;
    else if (desiredItem.compareTo(list[mid]) < 0)
        result = binarySearch(first, mid - 1, desiredItem);
    else
        result = binarySearch(mid + 1, last, desiredItem);

    return result;
} // end binarySearch
```

8. In the second else if, change < to >.

9. 20 (log 1,000,000 rounded up).

Chapter 17

1.
```
DictionaryInterface<Name, String> myDictionary =
        new Dictionary<Name, String>();
```

2.
```
myDictionary.add(new Name("Joe", "Java"), "555-1234");
```

3.
```
if (myDictionary.contains(new Name("Britney", "Spheres")))
   System.out.println("Britney's phone number is "
                              + myDictionary.getValue(new Name("Britney", "Spheres")));
else
   System.out.println("Britney is not in the dictionary");
```

   or

```
String phoneNumber = myDictionary.getValue(new Name("Britney", "Spheres"));
if (phoneNumber == null)
   System.out.println("Britney is not in the dictionary");
else
   System.out.println("Britney's phone number is " + phoneNumber);
```

4. The Scanner methods hasNext and next that readFile calls throw only runtime exceptions, which need not be caught. So although the call to readFile can be outside of a try block, it is inside the try block because its argument—the Scanner object data—is local to the try block. By declaring data outside of the try block, you could move the call to readFile after the last catch block.

5.
```
public String remove(Name personName)
{
   return phoneBook.remove(personName);
} // end remove
```

6.
```
public String changePhoneNumber(Name personName, String newPhoneNumber)
{
   return phoneBook.add(personName, newPhoneNumber);
} // end changePhoneNumber
```

7. To simplify the logic. If we called contains and found that the current word was already in the dictionary, we would need to call getValue to get its frequency. But we can use the result of getValue to see whether the word is in the dictionary.

8.
```
/** Task: Displays only the words that occur with a given frequency.
 * @param frequency  an integer count of the desired frequency. */
public void display(int frequency)
{
   Iterator<String> keyIterator = wordTable.getKeyIterator();
   Iterator<Integer> valueIterator = wordTable.getValueIterator();

   System.out.println("Words that occur " + frequency + " times:");
   boolean atLeastOneWord = false;
   while (keyIterator.hasNext())
   {
      String word = keyIterator.next();
      Integer count = valueIterator.next();

      if (count.equals(frequency))
      {
         atLeastOneWord = true;
         System.out.println(word);
      } // end if
   } // end while

   if (atLeastOneWord == false)
      System.out.println("(There are none.)");
} // end display
```

9.
```java
public ListWithIteratorInterface<Integer> getLineNumbers(String word)
{
    return wordTable.getValue(word);
} // end getLineNumbers
```

Chapter 18

1. The memory requirements for the search keys and the values are the same for each representation, so let's ignore them. The memory requirement for the representation shown in Figure 18-1a uses three references for each entry in the dictionary: one in the array and two in the `Entry` object. The parallel arrays in Figure 18-1b require only two references for each dictionary entry. Thus, the representation in Part *a* uses 50 percent more memory than the representation in Part *b*.

2. The initial search determines the insertion point when the dictionary is sorted, whereas the insertion point for an unsorted dictionary is always right after the last entry in the array. Insertion into a sorted dictionary generally requires shifting other entries in the array. No shifting is necessary for an unsorted dictionary.

3.
```java
private int locateIndex(K key)
{
    return binarySearch(0, currentSize - 1, key);
} // end locateIndex

private int binarySearch(int first, int last, K key)
{
    int result;

    if (first > last)
        result = first;
    else
    {
        int mid = (first + last)/2;
        K midKey = dictionary[mid].getKey();

        if (key.equals(midKey))
            result = mid;
        else if (key.compareTo(midKey) < 0)
            result = binarySearch(first, mid - 1, key);
        else
            result = binarySearch(mid + 1, last, key);
    } // end if

    return result;
} // end binarySearch
```

4. Typically, add must shift array entries to make room for a new entry, and `remove` must shift array entries to avoid a vacancy within the array. These shifts of data are $O(n)$ operations in the worst case. The best case occurs when the addition or removal is at the end of the array. These operations are $O(1)$.

5. No. Replacing the entry to be removed with the last entry in a chain would require a traversal of the chain. We would need references to both the last node and the next-to-last node so that we could delete the last node. Although we can ignore the last entry in an array, we should shorten the chain by setting the link portion of the next-to-last node to `null`. Note that having a tail reference does not eliminate the need for a traversal, since we need but do not have a

reference to the next-to-last node. The strategy for an unsorted array-based dictionary avoids shifting any of the other entries. No shifting is needed in a linked implementation. After locating the node to delete, you simply adjust either the head reference or the reference in the preceding node.

Chapter 19

1. 2301506. `"Java".hashCode()` has the same value.

2. 19

3. `"x"`

4. Since the implementation defines both the hash table and the dictionary entry, you have a choice as to where to add a field to indicate the state of a location in a hash table. You could add a field having three states to each table location, but you really need only a boolean field, since a `null` location is empty. If the field is true, the location is occupied; if it is false, it is available.

   Adding a similar data field to the dictionary entry instead of to the hash table leads to a cleaner implementation. As before, if the table location is `null`, it is empty. If the entry's field is true, the location is occupied; if it is false, it is available. Note that the implementation that appears in Chapter 20 uses this scheme.

5. 3, 8, 0, 5, 10, 2, 7, 12, 4, 9, 1, 6, 11, 3, ...

6. 13. Since 13 is both prime and the modulo base in h_1, the probe sequence can reach all locations in the table before it repeats.

7. `hashTable[0]` $\rightarrow$ 20
   `hashTable[1]` $\rightarrow$ 6 $\rightarrow$ 31
   `hashTable[2]` is `null`
   `hashTable[3]` is `null`
   `hashTable[4]` $\rightarrow$ 4 $\rightarrow$ 14 $\rightarrow$ 29

8. The add algorithm is the same as the one given in Segment 19.24, but it uses a different search of a chain. Regardless of whether the chain is sorted, you stop the search as soon as you find the desired search key. However, if the key is not in the chain, you have to search an entire unsorted chain to learn this. If the chain is sorted, you can stop the search when you reach the point where the key should have occurred if it were present.

9. No. Suppose that a, b, c, and d are search keys in sorted order in the hash table. With separate chaining, b and d might appear in one chain while the other keys appear in another. Traversing the chains in order will not visit the keys in sorted order. The same is true of open addressing when traversing the occupied array locations.

Chapter 20

1. Half of them.

2. No. Even when λ is large, all entries could be in one bucket.

3. After expanding the table to 11 locations (11 is the prime number larger than twice the current table size of 5), the function $c \% 11$ places 20 at index 9, 6 at index 6, and 14 at index 3. 18 causes a collision at index 9, so we probe ahead and place it at index 10.

4. In each method, replace the statements

```
index = locate(index, key);
if (index != -1)
```

with

```
index = probe(index, key);
if ((hashTable[index] != null) && (hashTable[index].isIn()))
```

5. No. The table size has increased, so rehashing is not necessary.

Chapter 21

1. *Jill* is at the top, and *Jim* is at the bottom.

2. **a.** `StackInterface<String> yourStack = new LinkedStack<String>();`
   `while (!myStack.isEmpty())`
   `   yourStack.push(myStack.pop());`
   b. myStack is empty, and yourStack contains the strings that were in myStack but in reverse order (*Jim* is at the top, and *Jill* is at the bottom).

3. The following stacks are shown bottom to top when read from left to right.

a.	**b.**	**c.**
[	{	[
[{	{ [	[{
[{ (	{ [(	[{ [
[{	{ [	[{ [(
{ { (	{	[{ [
[{		[{
[		[
empty		

The algorithm checkBalance returns true for the expression in Part *a* and false for the other two.

4. **a.** *a b c* * +
   b. *a b* * *c d* - /
   c. *a b* / *c d* - +
   d. *a b* / *c* + *d* -

5. Always. Segment 21.15 showed that you push ∧ onto the stack if another ∧ is already at the top of the stack. But if a different operator is at the top, ∧ has a higher precedence, so you push it onto the stack in that situation as well.

6. **a.** *a b* + *c d* - /
   b. *a b c* - / *d* *
   c. *a b c d* - / *e* * *f* + *g* ∧ -
   d. *a b c* * - *d e f* ∧ * *g* * *h* + /

7. **a.** -4.
   b. -58.
   c. -10.
   d. 49.

8. **a.** 5.
   b. -4.
   c. 22.
   d. -37.

Chapter 22

1.
```
public T pop()
{
   T top = null;

   if (topNode != null)
   {
      top = topNode.getData();
      topNode = topNode.getNextNode();
   } // end if

   return top;
} // end pop
```

2. No. Although a tail reference would enable you to either access the stack's top entry or push a new entry onto the stack efficiently, it is not enough to pop the stack. You need a reference to the next-to-last node to remove the chain's last node. To get that reference, you could either traverse the chain or maintain a reference to the next-to-last node in addition to the tail reference. Thus, placing the stack's top entry at the end of the chain is not as efficient or easy to implement as placing it at the beginning.

3.
```
public T pop()
{
   T top = peek();

   if (!isEmpty()) // or (top != null)
   {
      stack[topIndex] = null;
      topIndex--;
   } // end if

   return top;
} // end pop
```

4. Change T to the primitive type and do not assign null to stack[topIndex].

5. Each push or pop would need to move all of the entries currently in the stack.

6. The bottom entry. You can then push entries onto the stack without moving the other elements already in the array.

7.
```
public void clear()
{
   for (; topIndex > -1; topIndex--)
      stack[topIndex] = null;
} // end clear
```

8. ```
public void clear()
{
  while (!isEmpty())
    pop();
} // end pop
```

9. No. Since `Vector` uses an array and dynamic expansion, each `push` would need to move all of the entries in the vector to vacate its first location.

# Chapter 23

1. *Jill* is at the front, *Jess* is at the back.
2. **a.** 11.
   **b.** 4.
3. *Jill* is at the front, *Jane* is at the back.
4. *Jim* is at the front, *Jane* is at the back.

# Chapter 24

1. The back of the queue is at the end of the chain. Since you add to the back of a queue, you need to add a node to the end of the chain. A tail reference allows you to do this without first traversing the chain to locate its last node. Thus, a tail reference enables an efficient `enqueue` operation.

2. Entries in a list have a particular position within the list and, thus, the array. Queue entries have positions that are relative to one another, but not to the queue and not to the array.

3. ```
public void clear()
{
  if (!isEmpty())
  {
    for (int index = frontIndex; index != backIndex;
         index = (index + 1) % queue.length)
    {
      queue[index] = null;
    } // end for

    queue[backIndex] = null;
  } // end if

  frontIndex = 0;
  backIndex = queue.length - 1;
} // end clear
```

4. ```
public void clear()
{
  while (!isEmpty())
    dequeue();
} // end clear
```

   This version of `clear` is easier to write than the version given in Question 3.

5. Each enqueue operation needs to move all of the entries in the queue to vacate `queue[0]` before it adds a new entry.
```

6. You place the new entry into the node that `freeNode` currently references. You then insert a new node after that node and make `freeNode` reference the new node. The new node is now the unused node.

7. You can repeatedly call `dequeue` until the queue is empty, as in the answer to Question 4. Or you can set the data fields of each node in the queue to `null` and then set `queueNode` equal to `freeNode`.

8.
```
public T getBack()
{
  T back = null;

  if (!isEmpty())
    back = lastNode.getData();

  return back;
} // end getBack
```

Chapter 25

1. **a.** N, O, P, G, H, Q, R, S, T, L, M.
    b. I, J.
    c. F, G.
    d. F, G, N, O, P.
    e. F, B, A.
    f. A, B, C, D, E, F, I, J, K

2. A tree that represents the organization of this book is a general tree, such as the following:

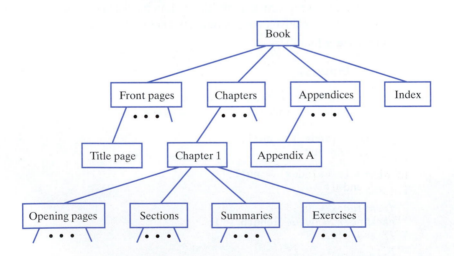

3. 4, 3, and 3, respectively.

4. **a.** For the tree in Figure 24-6a, n is 7 and h is 3. Since the tree is full and $7 = 2^3 - 1$, the relationship $n = 2^h - 1$ is true. Also, $3 = \log_2 (7 + 1)$, so the relationship $h = \log_2 (n + 1)$ is true.
    b. For the tree in Figure 24-6b, n is 10 and h is 4. The tree is complete, and $\log_2 (10 + 1)$ is approximately 3.5, which rounded up is 4. Thus, the relationship $h = \log_2 (n + 1)$ rounded up is true.

5. $2^6 - 1$, or 63.

6. $\log_2 (14 + 1)$ is approximately 3.9. When rounded up, we get 4

7. Preorder: Jared, John, James, Mary, Jennifer, Robert, Carole
Postorder: James, Mary, John, Robert, Carole, Jennifer, Jared
Inorder: James, John, Mary, Jared, Robert, Jennifer, Carole
Level order: Jared, John, Jennifer, James, Mary, Robert, Carole

8.

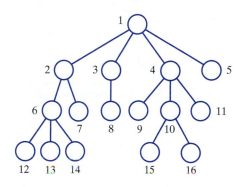

9.

(a) $a + b * c$ (b) $(a + b) * c$

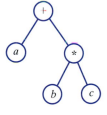 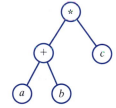

10. Figure 25-14a
Preorder: $/\ a\ b$
Inorder: $a\ /\ b$
Postorder: $a\ b\ /$

Figure 25-14c
Preorder: $*\ a + b\ c$
Inorder: $a * b + c$
Postorder: $a\ b\ c + *$

Figure 25-14d
Preorder: $/\ *\ a + b\ *\ c\ d\ e$
Inorder: $a * b + c * d / e$
Postorder: $a\ b\ c\ d\ * + *\ e\ /$

11. The tree in Figure 25-14a is full; the tree in Figure 25-14b is complete.

12. 17.

13. The method `learn` augments the tree under conditions that the class `GuessingGame` must control. It would be inappropriate for a client to invoke this method.

14. 5.

15. The shortest tree has height 2; the tallest tree has height 3.

16. The root of a maxheap contains the object with the largest value. If this object is unique in the set of objects, the root is unique. If another object has the same value, it would be a child of the root. In Figure 25-20a, only 9 can be the root.

17. No. The order of siblings is not specified in a heap, so several different heaps can contain the same data. For example, in Figure 25-20a, you could exchange 2 and 5, or you could exchange the root's two subtrees, and still have a maxheap.

18.

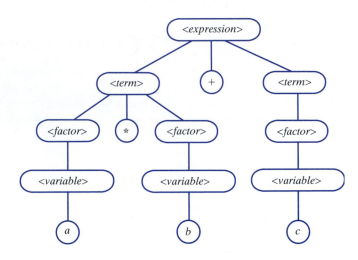

Chapter 26

1. Yes. The fields `left` and `right` of `BinaryNode` (see Segment 26.3) have `BinaryNode<T>` as their data type, but the return type of the method `copy` is `BinaryNodeInterface<T>`.

2. No. Setting `rightTree` to `null` affects only the local copy of the reference argument `rightTree`. An analogous comment applies to `leftTree`.

3. The data in the objects d, b, e, a, f, g, and c is displayed on separate lines.

4.
```java
public void preorderTraverse()
{
   preorderTraverse(root);
} // end preorderTraverse

private void preorderTraverse(BinaryNodeInterface<T> node)
{
   if (node != null)
   {
      System.out.println(node.getData());
      preorderTraverse(node.getLeftChild());
      preorderTraverse(node.getRightChild());
   } // end if
} // end preorderTraverse
```

5. You must cast to `BinaryNode<T>` three times, as follows:

- `BinaryNode<T> currentNode = (BinaryNode<T>)root;`
- `currentNode = (BinaryNode<T>)currentNode.getLeftChild();`
- `currentNode = (BinaryNode<T>)nextNode.getRightChild();`

6. 27.

7.

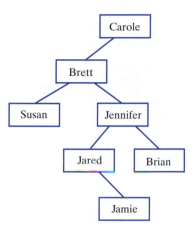

Chapter 27

1. As the left child of the node that contains *Whitney*.

2. No; `BinarySearchTree` inherits these methods from `BinaryTree`.

3. In `getEntry`'s call to `findEntry`, you would cast `getRootNode()` to `BinaryNode<T>`, as follows:

   `findEntry((BinaryNode<T>)getRootNode(), entry)`

   Within `findEntry`, the first recursive call to `findEntry` must be

   `findEntry((BinaryNode<T>)rootNode.getLeftChild(), entry)`

   since the return type of `getLeftChild` is `BinaryNodeInterface<T>`. Analogous comments apply to the second recursive call and `getRightChild`.

4. The situation is like that described for `setTree` in Segment 27.6. `BinarySearchTree` inherits the methods declared in `TreeIteratorInterface` from `BinaryTree`. An object whose static type is `BinarySearchTree` can invoke these methods, but an object whose static type is `SearchTreeInterface` cannot.

5. *Chris* is the right child of *Chad*. *Jason* is the left child of *Jim*. *Kelley* is the right child of *Jim*.

6. When you add *Miguel* first, *Miguel* is the left child of *Whitney*, and *Nancy* is the right child of *Miguel*.
   When you add *Nancy* first, *Nancy* is the left child of *Whitney*, and *Miguel* is the left child of *Nancy*. Thus, the order of the additions does affect the tree that results.

7.

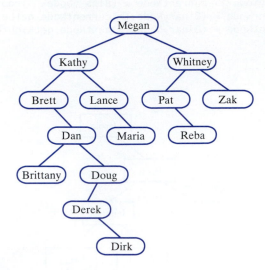

8.

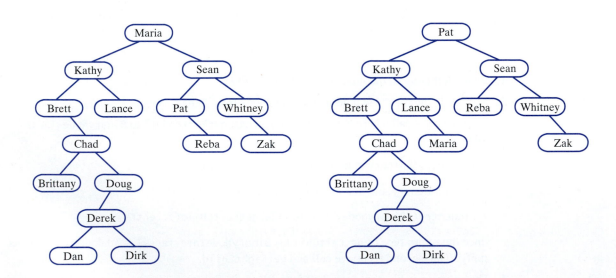

9. ```
   private NodePair findNode(T entry)
   {
      NodePair result = new NodePair();
      boolean found = false;

      BinaryNodeInterface<T> currentNode = getRootNode();
      BinaryNodeInterface<T> parentNode = null;
   ```
   ```

```
    while (!found && (currentNode != null) )
    {
      T currentEntry = currentNode.getData();
      int comparison = entry.compareTo(currentEntry);

      if (comparison < 0)
      {
        parentNode = currentNode;
        currentNode = currentNode.getLeftChild();
      }
      else if (comparison > 0)
      {
        parentNode = currentNode;
        currentNode = currentNode.getRightChild();
      }
      else // comparison == 0
        found = true;
    } // end while

    if (found)
      result = new NodePair(currentNode, parentNode);
      // found entry is currentNode.getData()

    return result;
  } // end findNode
```

10. Since the method `contains` invokes `getEntry`, the efficiency of these methods is the same. So if the tree's height is as small as possible, the efficiency is $O(\log n)$. If the tree's height is as large as possible, the efficiency is $O(n)$.

11. $O(1)$.

12.
```
public int getSize()
{
  return bst.getNumberOfNodes();
} // end getSize

public boolean isEmpty()
{
  return bst.isEmpty();
} // end isEmpty

public boolean contains(K key)
{
  Entry<K, V> findEntry = new Entry<K, V>(key, null);

  return bst.contains(findEntry);
} // end contains

public void clear()
{
  bst.clear();
} // end clear
```

13.
```
public boolean contains(K key)
{
  return getValue(key) != null;
} // end contains
```

Chapter 28

1. The node at array index i

   ● Has a parent at index $(i - 1)/2$, unless the node is the root (i is 0).
   ● Has any children at indices $2i + 1$ and $2i + 2$.

2. Place 100 as a right child of 80. Then swap 100 with 80, swap 100 with 85, and finally swap 100 with 90.

3.

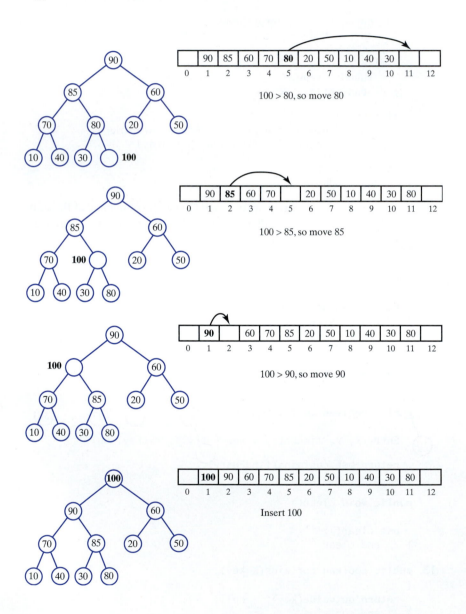

100 > 80, so move 80

100 > 85, so move 85

100 > 90, so move 90

Insert 100

4.
```
public void add(T newEntry)
{
  lastIndex++;

  if (lastIndex >= heap.length)
    doubleArray          // expand array

  heap[0] = newEntry; // sentinel
  int newIndex = lastIndex;
  int parentIndex = newIndex / 2;

  while (newEntry.compareTo(heap[parentIndex]) > 0)
  {
    heap[newIndex] = heap[parentIndex];

    newIndex = parentIndex;
    parentIndex = newIndex / 2;
  } // end while

  heap[newIndex] = newEntry;
} // end add
```

5.

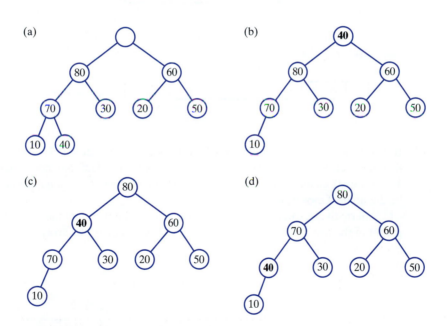

(a)

(b)

(c)

(d)

6.

(a)

85 is larger child of 30; 30 < 85, so move 85

	30	**85**	60	70	80	20	50	10	40	
0	1	2	3	4	5	6	7	8	9	10

(b)

80 is larger child of vacated node; 30 < 80, so move 80

	85		60	70	**80**	20	50	10	40	
0	1	2	3	4	5	6	7	8	9	10

(c)

Reached leaf

	85	80	60	70		20	50	10	40	
0	1	2	3	4	5	6	7	8	9	10

(d)

Insert 30

	85	80	60	70	**30**	20	50	10	40	
0	1	2	3	4	5	6	7	8	9	10

7. If a node at index i has children, they are at indices $2i$ and $2i + 1$. The node at `lastIndex/2` then has a child at `lastIndex`. Since this child is the last leaf, any nodes beyond the one at `lastIndex/2` cannot have children and so must be leaves. Thus, the node at `lastIndex/2` must be the nonleaf closest to the end of the array.

Alternatively, examine some complete trees and notice that the desired nonleaf is the parent of the last child. This child is at index `lastIndex` of the array representation, so its parent has index `lastIndex/2`.

8.

9 6 2 4 8 7 5 3	Original array
9 8 7 4 6 2 5 3	After repeated calls to `reheap`
3 8 7 4 6 2 5 **9**	After swap
8 6 7 4 3 2 5 **9**	After reheap
5 6 7 4 3 2 **8 9**	After swap
7 6 5 4 3 2 **8 9**	After reheap
2 6 5 4 3 **7 8 9**	After swap
6 4 5 2 3 **7 8 9**	After reheap
3 4 5 2 **6 7 8 9**	After swap
5 4 3 2 **6 7 8 9**	After reheap
2 4 3 **5 6 7 8 9**	After swap
4 2 3 **5 6 7 8 9**	After reheap
3 2 **4 5 6 7 8 9**	After swap

```
3 2 4 5 6 7 8 9      After reheap
2 3 4 5 6 7 8 9      After swap
2 3 4 5 6 7 8 9      Done
```

Chapter 29

1. Node N contains 60, and node C contains 50. T_1 is the one-node subtree containing 20. T_2 and T_3 are empty.

2. Since we had a binary search tree before the rotation, the value in node N is less than the value in node C and all the values in T_2. Moreover, all values in T_2 are less than the value in node C. These relationships are maintained after the rotation, since node N is a left child of node C, and T_2 is a right subtree of node N. Also, the subtrees T_1 and T_3 have their original parents in the new tree. Thus, the resulting tree is a binary search tree.

3. Node N contains 60, and node C contains 80. T_3 is the one-node subtree containing 90. T_1 and T_2 are empty.

4. Part a of the following figure shows an imbalance at node N after 10 was added to the tree. A left rotation restores the tree's balance, as Part b illustrates.

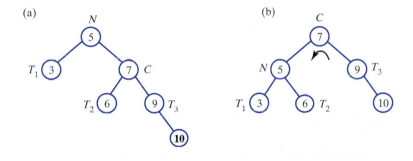

5. Node N contains 50, node C contains 80, and node G contains 60. T_1, T_3, and T_4 are one-node subtrees: T_1 contains 20, T_3 contains 70, and T_4 contains 90. T_2 is empty. In Parts a and b, T_2 is the left subtree of 60. In Part c, it is the right subtree of 50.

6. Node N contains 50, node C contains 20, and node G contains 40. T_1, T_2, and T_4 are one-node subtrees: T_1 contains 10, T_2 contains 35, and T_4 contains 55. T_3 is empty. In Parts a, b and c, T_3 is the right subtree of 40. In Part d, it is the left subtree of 50.

7.

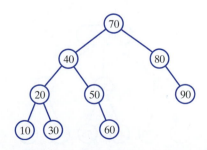

8. The following binary search tree is taller than the previous AVL tree, and it is not balanced:

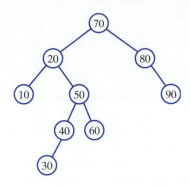

9. Since we had a binary search tree before the rotation, the value in node N is less than the values in nodes C and G and all the values in T_2 and T_3. The value in node C is greater than the value in node G, and each of these two values is greater than all values in T_2. Moreover, all values in T_3 are less than the value in node C but greater than the value in node G. These relationships are maintained after the rotation: Node G has node N as its left child and node C as its right child; T_2 is a right subtree of node N, and T_3 is a left subtree of node C. The subtrees T_1 and T_4 have their original parents in the new tree. Thus, the resulting tree is a binary search tree.

10. Since we had a binary search tree before the rotation, the value in node N is greater than the values in nodes C and G and all the values in T_2 and T_3. The value in node C is less than the value in node G, and each of these two values is less than all values in T_3. Moreover, all values in T_2 are less than the value in node G but greater than the value in node C. These relationships are maintained after the rotation: Node G has node C as its left child and node N as its right child; T_2 is a right subtree of node C, and T_3 is a left subtree of node N. The subtrees T_1 and T_4 have their original parents in the new tree. Thus, the resulting tree is a binary search tree.

11.
```
private BinaryNodeInterface<T> rotateLeft(BinaryNodeInterface<T> nodeN)
{
   BinaryNodeInterface<T> nodeC = nodeN.getRightChild();
   nodeN.setRightChild(nodeC.getLeftChild());
   nodeC.setLeftChild(nodeN);
   return nodeC;
} // end rotateLeft
```

12. **a.** $60, 20, 10.$
    b. $60, 20, 50, 55.$
    c. $60, 20, 50, 35, 40.$
    d. $60, 20, 50, 35.$

13.

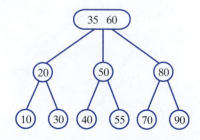

14.

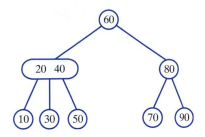

15. It is shorter and balanced.

16. **a.** 20, 10.
 b. 20, 50, 80, 55, 60.
 c. 20, 50, 35, 40.
 d. 20, 50, 35.

17.

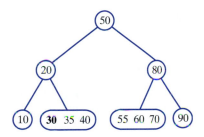

18.

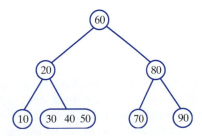

19. Both trees are completely balanced, and they have the same height. The 2-4 tree has fewer nodes.

20. **a.** 2-4: 20, 50, 80, 55, 60; Red-black: 50, 80, 60.
 b. 2-4: 20, 50, 80, 55; Red-black: 50, 80, 60, 55.

21. The first three properties follow immediately by observing the tree. Every path from the root to a leaf contains two black nodes.

22.

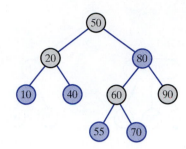

If you tried to form a red-black tree whose root is 80, you would find that the tree was not balanced and so could not be a red-black tree. (You normally do not convert 2-4 trees into red-black trees, but doing so as an exercise should give you some insight into the rationale of red-black trees.)

23. The first three properties follow immediately by observing the tree. Every path from the root to a leaf contains two black nodes.

Chapter 30

1. a. 3.
   b. 36.
   c. Truro-Orleans-Barnstable-Sandwich, with a length of 3.
   d. Truro-Orleans-Barnstable-Sandwich, with a weight of 48.

2. Electrical (or telephone or TV) wires, plumbing, hallways or other connections between rooms.

3. The graph is connected but not complete.

4. No; cs8 and cs10 each would have 2 parents.

5. a. No; **b.** Yes; **c.** No; **d.** No.

6. E, F, H, C, I, B.

7. E, F, C, B, H, I.

8. cs1, cs2, cs4, cs7, cs9, cs5, cs10, cs6, cs8, cs3; or cs1, cs2, cs3, cs4, cs5, cs6, cs7, cs8, cs9, cs10.

9. Remove vertex G from the queue. G's neighbor H has been visited already. Now remove F from the queue. F's neighbor C is unvisited. Set C's predecessor to F and its path-length field to 3 (1 + the length recorded in F). Add C to the queue. Since C is the destination, construct the path by working backward from C, as we did in Segment 30.18. The shortest path is $A \rightarrow E \rightarrow F \rightarrow C$, with a length of 3.

10. Vertex H has one unvisited neighbor, I. The cost of the path to I is the cost of the path to H plus the weight of the edge from H to I. This total cost is 9. Encapsulate vertex I, the cost 9, and the predecessor H into an object and add it to the priority queue.

   Now remove the front entry from the priority queue. The entry contains H, and since H is visited already, ignore the entry. Remove the next entry. This entry also contains H, which is visited, so ignore it and remove the next entry. This entry contains I, which is unvisited. Visit *I*. *I*'s neighbor *F* is visited, so remove the next entry from the priority queue. This entry contains *C*, so visit *C*.

Since *C* is the destination, construct the path by working backward from *C*, as we did in Segment 30.18. The shortest (cheapest) path is $A \rightarrow B \rightarrow E \rightarrow F \rightarrow C$, with a weight (cost) of 10.

11. Two or more entries in the priority queue can record data about the same vertex. For example, consider the trace in Figure 30-19. After we visit vertex *B*, the first two entries in the priority queue record data about vertex *E*. The first entry involves the path from *B* to *E*, while the second entry involves the path from *A* to *E*. While vertex *E* can record similar data for one path, it cannot do so for multiple paths.

12. In the two calls to addEdge, you would add an edge weight as a third argument.

13. The method getCheapestPath finds the path with the smallest weight sum, which gives us the shortest route when measured in miles; getShortestPath finds the path that contains the fewest number of edges.

Chapter 31

1.

	0	1	2	3
0		T	T	T
1	T		T	T
2	T	T		T
3	T	T	T	

2. Vertex 0 references the list 1, 2, 3.
   Vertex 1 references the list 0, 2, 3.
   Vertex 2 references the list 0, 1, 3.
   Vertex 3 references the list 0, 1, 2.

3.
```
VertexInterface<String> vertexA = new Vertex<String>("A");
VertexInterface<String> vertexB = new Vertex<String>("B");
VertexInterface<String> vertexC = new Vertex<String>("C");
vertexA.addEdge(vertexB, 2.0);
vertexB.addEdge(vertexC, 3.0);
vertexC.addEdge(vertexA, 4.0);
vertexA.addEdge(vertexC, 5.0);
```

4.
```
DirectedGraph<String> myGraph = new DirectedGraph<String>();
myGraph.addVertex("A");
myGraph.addVertex("B");
myGraph.addVertex("C");
myGraph.addEdge("A", "B", 2.0);
myGraph.addEdge("B", "C", 3.0);
myGraph.addEdge("C", "A", 4.0);
myGraph.addEdge("A", "C", 5.0);
```

5.
```java
QueueInterface<String> bfs = myGraph.getBreadthFirstTraversal("A");
while (!bfs.isEmpty())
  System.out.print(bfs.dequeue() + " ");
System.out.println();
```

6.
```java
StackInterface<String> path = new LinkedStack<String>();
int pathLength = myGraph.getShortestPath("A", "C", path);
System.out.println("The shortest path from A to C has length " + pathLength +
                   " and passes through the following vertices:");
while (!path.isEmpty())
  System.out.print(path.pop() + " ");
System.out.println();
```

Index

Operator Precedence

In the following list, operators on the same line are of equal precedence. As you move down the list, each line is of lower precedence. When the order of operations is not dictated by parentheses, the operator of higher precedence executes before an operator of lower precedence. When operators have equal precedence, binary operators execute in left-to-right order, and unary operators execute in right-to-left order.

Highest Precedence

The unary operators +, -, ++, - -, !, ~
The unary operators new and (*type*)
The binary operators *, /, %
The binary operators +, -
The binary (shift) operators <<, >>, >>>
The binary operators <, >, <=, >=
The binary operators ==, !=
The binary operator &
The binary operator ^
The binary operator |
The binary operator &&
The binary operator | |
The ternary (conditional) operator ? :
Assignment operators =, *=, /=, %=, +=, -=, <<=, >>=, >>>=, &=, ^=, |=

Lowest Precedence